T0220788

Lecture Notes in Computer Science 11065

More information about this series at http://www.springer.com/series/7409

Xingming Sun · Zhaoqing Pan
Elisa Bertino (Eds.)

Cloud Computing and Security

4th International Conference, ICCCS 2018
Haikou, China, June 8–10, 2018
Revised Selected Papers, Part III

Editors
Xingming Sun
Nanjing University of Information Science and Technology
Nanjing
China

Zhaoqing Pan
Nanjing University of Information Science and Technology
Nanjing
China

Elisa Bertino
Department of Computer Science
Purdue University
West Lafayette, IN
USA

ISSN 0302-9743 ISSN 1611-3349 (electronic)
Lecture Notes in Computer Science
ISBN 978-3-030-00011-0 ISBN 978-3-030-00012-7 (eBook)
https://doi.org/10.1007/978-3-030-00012-7

Library of Congress Control Number: 2018952646

LNCS Sublibrary: SL3 – Information Systems and Applications, incl. Internet/Web, and HCI

This Springer imprint is published by the registered company Springer Nature Switzerland AG
The registered company address is: Gewerbestrasse 11, 6330 Cham, Switzerland

Preface

The 4th International Conference on Cloud Computing and Security (ICCCS 2018) was held in Haikou, China, during June 8–10, 2018, and hosted by the School of Computer and Software at the Nanjing University of Information Science and Technology. ICCCS is a leading conference for researchers and engineers to share their latest results of research, development, and applications in the field of cloud computing and information security.

We made use of the excellent Tech Science Press (TSP) submission and reviewing software. ICCCS 2018 received 1743 submissions from 20 countries and regions, including USA, Canada, UK, Italy, Ireland, Japan, Russia, France, Australia, South Korea, South Africa, India, Iraq, Kazakhstan, Indonesia, Vietnam, Ghana, China, Taiwan, and Macao. The submissions covered the areas of cloud computing, cloud security, information hiding, IOT security, multimedia forensics, and encryption, etc. We thank our Technical Program Committee members and external reviewers for their efforts in reviewing papers and providing valuable comments to the authors. From the total of 1743 submissions, and based on at least two reviews per submission, the Program Chairs decided to accept 386 papers, yielding an acceptance rate of 22.15%. The volume of the conference proceedings contains all the regular, poster, and workshop papers.

The conference program was enriched by six keynote presentations, and the keynote speakers were Mauro Barni, University of Siena, Italy; Charles Ling, University of Western Ontario, Canada; Yunbiao Guo, Beijing Institute of Electronics Technology and Application, China; Yunhao Liu, Michigan State University, USA; Nei Kato, Tokyo University, Japan; and Jianfeng Ma, Xidian University, China. We thank them very much for their wonderful talks.

There were 42 workshops organized in conjunction with ICCCS 2018, covering all the hot topics in cloud computing and security. We would like to take this moment to express our sincere appreciation for the contribution of all the workshop chairs and their participants. In addition, we would like to extend our sincere thanks to all authors who submitted papers to ICCCS 2018 and to all PC members. It was a truly great experience to work with such talented and hard working researchers. We also appreciate the work of the external reviewers, who assisted the PC members in their particular areas of expertise. Moreover, we would like to thank our sponsors: Nanjing University of Information Science and Technology, Springer, Hainan University, IEEE Nanjing Chapter, ACM China, Michigan State University, Taiwan Cheng Kung University, Taiwan Dong Hwa University, Providence University, Nanjing University of Aeronautics and Astronautics, State Key Laboratory of Integrated Services Networks, Tech Science Press, and the National Nature Science Foundation of China. Finally, we would like to thank all attendees for their active participation and the organizing team, who nicely managed this conference. Next year, ICCCS will be renamed as the International Conference on Artificial Intelligence and Security (ICAIS). We look forward to seeing you again at the ICAIS.

July 2018

Xingming Sun
Zhaoqing Pan
Elisa Bertino

Organization

General Chairs

Xingming Sun	Nanjing University of Information Science and Technology, China
Han-Chieh Chao	Taiwan Dong Hwa University, Taiwan, China
Xingang You	China Information Technology Security Evaluation Center, China
Elisa Bertino	Purdue University, USA

Technical Program Committee Chairs

Aniello Castiglione	University of Salerno, Italy
Yunbiao Guo	China Information Technology Security Evaluation Center, China
Zhangjie Fu	Nanjing University of Information Science and Technology, China
Xinpeng Zhang	Fudan University, China
Jian Weng	Jinan University, China
Mengxing Huang	Hainan University, China
Alex Liu	Michigan State University, USA

Workshop Chair

Baowei Wang	Nanjing University of Information Science and Technology, China

Publication Chair

Zhaoqing Pan	Nanjing University of Information Science and Technology, China

Publicity Chair

Chuanyou Ju	Nanjing University of Information Science and Technology, China

Local Arrangement Chair

Jieren Cheng	Hainan University, China

Website Chair

Wei Gu	Nanjing University of Information Science and Technology, China

Technical Program Committee Members

Saeed Arif	University of Algeria, Algeria
Zhifeng Bao	Royal Melbourne Institute of Technology University, Australia
Lianhua Chi	IBM Research Center, Australia
Bing Chen	Nanjing University of Aeronautics and Astronautics, China
Hanhua Chen	Huazhong University of Science and Technology, China
Jie Chen	East China Normal University, China
Xiaofeng Chen	Xidian University, China
Ilyong Chung	Chosun University, South Korea
Jieren Cheng	Hainan University, China
Kim-Kwang Raymond Choo	University of Texas at San Antonio, USA
Chin-chen Chang	Feng Chia University, Taiwan, China
Robert H. Deng	Singapore Management University, Singapore
Jintai Ding	University of Cincinnati, USA
Shaojing Fu	National University of Defense Technology, China
Xinwen Fu	University of Central Florida, USA
Song Guo	Hong Kong Polytechnic University, Hong Kong, China
Ruili Geng	Spectral MD, USA
Russell Higgs	University College Dublin, Ireland
Dinh Thai Hoang	University of Technology Sydney, Australia
Robert Hsu	Chung Hua University, Taiwan, China
Chih-Hsien Hsia	Chinese Culture University, Taiwan, China
Jinguang Han	Nanjing University of Finance & Economics, China
Debiao He	Wuhan University, China
Wien Hong	Nanfang College of Sun Yat-Sen University, China
Qiong Huang	South China Agricultural University, China
Xinyi Huang	Fujian Normal University, China
Yongfeng Huang	Tsinghua University, China
Zhiqiu Huang	Nanjing University of Aeronautics and Astronautics, China
Mohammad Mehedi Hassan	King Saud University, Saudi Arabia
Farookh Hussain	University of Technology Sydney, Australia
Hai Jin	Huazhong University of Science and Technology, China
Sam Tak Wu Kwong	City University of Hong Kong, China
Patrick C. K. Hung	University of Ontario Institute of Technology, Canada

Krzysztof Szczypiorski	Warsaw University of Technology, Poland
Frank Y. Shih	New Jersey Institute of Technology, USA
Arun Kumar Sangaiah	VIT University, India
Jing Tian	National University of Singapore, Singapore
Cezhong Tong	Washington University in St. Louis, USA
Shanyu Tang	University of West London, UK
Tsuyoshi Takagi	Kyushu University, Japan
Xianping Tao	Nanjing University, China
Yoshito Tobe	Aoyang University, Japan
Cai-Zhuang Wang	Ames Laboratory, USA
Xiaokang Wang	St. Francis Xavier University, Canada
Jie Wang	University of Massachusetts Lowell, USA
Guiling Wang	New Jersey Institute of Technology, USA
Ruili Wang	Massey University, New Zealand
Sheng Wen	Swinburne University of Technology, Australia
Jinwei Wang	Nanjing University of Information Science and Technology, China
Ding Wang	Peking University, China
Eric Wong	University of Texas at Dallas, USA
Pengjun Wan	Illinois Institute of Technology, USA
Jian Wang	Nanjing University of Aeronautics and Astronautics, China
Honggang Wang	University of Massachusetts-Dartmouth, USA
Liangmin Wang	Jiangsu University, China
Xiaojun Wang	Dublin City University, Ireland
Q. M. Jonathan Wu	University of Windsor, Canada
Shaoen Wu	Ball State University, USA
Yang Xiao	The University of Alabama, USA
Haoran Xie	The Education University of Hong Kong, China
Zhihua Xia	Nanjing University of Information Science and Technology, China
Yang Xiang	Deakin University, Australia
Naixue Xiong	Northeastern State University, USA
Shuangkui Xia	Beijing Institute of Electronics Technology and Application, China
Fan Yang	University of Maryland, USA
Kun-Ming Yu	Chung Hua University, Taiwan, China
Xiaoli Yue	Donghua University, China
Ming Yin	Harvard University, USA
Aimin Yang	Guangdong University of Foreign Studies, China
Qing Yang	University of North Texas, USA
Ching-Nung Yang	Taiwan Dong Hwa University, Taiwan, China
Ming Yang	Southeast University, China
Qing Yang	Montana State University, USA
Xinchun Yin	Yangzhou University, China

Yong Yu	University of Electronic Science and Technology of China, China
Guomin Yang	University of Wollongong, Australia
Wei Qi Yan	Auckland University of Technology, New Zealand
Shaodi You	Australian National University, Australia
Yanchun Zhang	Victoria University, Australia
Mingwu Zhang	Hubei University of Technology, China
Wei Zhang	Nanjing University of Posts and Telecommunications, China
Weiming Zhang	University of Science and Technology of China, China
Yan Zhang	Simula Research Laboratory, Norway
Yao Zhao	Beijing Jiaotong University, China
Linna Zhou	University of International Relations, China

Organization Committee Members

Xianyi Chen	Nanjing University of Information Science and Technology, China
Yadang Chen	Nanjing University of Information Science and Technology, China
Beijing Chen	Nanjing University of Information Science and Technology, China
Chunjie Cao	Hainan University, China
Xianyi Chen	Hainan University, China
Xianmei Chen	Hainan University, China
Fa Fu	Hainan University, China
Xiangdang Huang	Hainan University, China
Zhuhua Hu	Hainan University, China
Jielin Jiang	Nanjing University of Information Science and Technology, China
Zilong Jin	Nanjing University of Information Science and Technology, China
Yan Kong	Nanjing University of Information Science and Technology, China
Jingbing Li	Hainan University, China
Jinlian Peng	Hainan University, China
Zhiguo Qu	Nanjing University of Information Science and Technology, China
Le Sun	Nanjing University of Information Science and Technology, China
Jian Su	Nanjing University of Information Science and Technology, China
Qing Tian	Nanjing University of Information Science and Technology, China
Tao Wen	Hainan University, China
Xianpeng Wang	Hainan University, China

Lizhi Xiong	Nanjing University of Information Science and Technology, China
Chunyang Ye	Hainan University, China
Jiangyuan Yao	Hainan University, China
Leiming Yan	Nanjing University of Information Science and Technology, China
Yu Zhang	Hainan University, China
Zhili Zhou	Nanjing University of Information Science and Technology, China

Contents – Part III

Cloud Security

Encryption

Cloud Security

Digital Continuity Guarantee Based on Data Consistency in Cloud Storage

Yongjun Ren[1,2(✉)], Yepeng Liu[1,2], and Chengshan Qian[1,2]

[1] School of Computer and Software, Nanjing University of Information Science and Technology, Nanjing 210044, China
renyj100@126.com

[2] Jiangsu Collaborative Innovation Center of Atmospheric Environment and Equipment Technology (CICAEET), Nanjing University of Information Science and Technology, Nanjing 210044, China

Abstract. Since the British National Archives put forward the concept of the digital continuity in 2007, Some developed countries have developed a digital continuity plan of action. At the same time, digital continuity has become a hot topic in electronic document research. However, there is still a lack of technologies and measures to protect digital continuity.

Data usability is the foundation of digital continuity, and its focus is on making digital information readable and operational. Data consistency is the essential requirement of data usability. If there is no data consistency, then there is no data availability. Therefore, ensuring digital consistency of electronic records is the basis for digital continuity. This paper proposes a framework for verifying the consistency of electronic record data based on functional dependency theory. Moreover, an example of verifying the data consistency based on functional dependency theory is given to check the data consistency of electronic record periodically.

Keywords: Electronic record · Digital continuity · Data usability
Data consistency · Function dependency

1 Introduction

The explosive development of information technology has enabled the continuous expansion of cloud storage systems. However, as the number of storage media increases, storage cell failure has become the norm [1]. Therefore, ensuring the availability of data in cloud storage systems has become an important research direction.

Digital continuity refers to the ability to preserve the creator's digital information. When digital technology changes, data can still be used when needed [2]. It focuses on ensuring that the information is complete and available. Digital continuity includes information management, information risk assessment and management technology environment and file format conversion. It plays a significant role in the evolution of cloud storage systems.

X. Sun et al. (Eds.): ICCCS 2018, LNCS 11065, pp. 3–11, 2018.
https://doi.org/10.1007/978-3-030-00012-7_1

Some survey shows that the lack of digital continuity poses a significant challenge to digital information readability [3–9]. To solve this problem, countries around the world have put forward solutions to ensure digital continuity, such as UK's Digital Continuity Project, New Zealand's Digital Continuity Action Plan, and Australia's Digital Continuity 2020 Policy [10–12]. When it comes to the cloud storage, many cloud service companies use multiple copy and erasure code mechanisms to ensure data readability.

This article is written as follows: Sect. 2 introduces the related works. Section 3 analyzes the digital continuity based on data consistency for the electronic record. Moreover, in Sect. 4, the functional dependency theory is utilized to construct a digital continuity guarantee scheme based on data consistency. Finally, Sect. 5 concludes this paper.

2 Related Work

2.1 Cloud Storage Expansion

The exponential growth of data volume is the driving force for building large-scale cloud storage systems. In other words, the storage system deployed in the first half of the year will most likely not be able to provide enough capacity for existing data. The expansion of the storage system is to increase I/O performance while expanding the space capacity. For systems that use erasure codes to enhance data continuity, cluster expansion faces some new challenges. For example, the data distribution strategy of erasure code clusters is very flexible. It is necessary to design a capacity expansion scheme in combination with the access mode and data locality.

2.2 Cold Data Archiving

Cold data archiving is another application scenario of digital continuity. In distributed storage systems, the reliability of hot data is often improved through multiple copies of storage. For example, GFS, HDFS, and Amazon S3 all guarantee data durability through three-part redundancy. Over time, most data are accessed less and less frequently during the life cycle, so archiving raw data with erasure codes can reduce the operating costs of the storage system. Due to the inherent characteristics of erasure codes, traditional archiving methods are susceptible to single-node bottlenecks, resulting in low archiving efficiency. After improvements, scholars have introduced pipeline technology to storage archiving. In other words, the computing operations involved in filing cannot be divided into multiple nodes, which also poses a challenge to digital continuity.

2.3 Digital Continuity Content

The digital continuity mainly solves the problem that the records are lost or unreadable due to IT technology changes during the long-term preservation of digital resources [13]. It is a theory of long-term preservation of digital information [14]. In the final analysis, Digital continuity is necessarily a continuous process but not a simple result of long-term conservation.

Digital continuity also needs to tackle ordinal regression problems. If the message is forwarded through an agent, the security of the agent needs to be considered. Scholars construct an identity-based conditional proxy re-encryption scheme with excellent grain policy, which allows semi-trusted agents to convert ciphertext that satisfies a condition [15, 16].

Digital continuity strategy consists of the principle of digital continuity, digital continuity plans, guidelines and practical results, and other digital continuity of the constitution.

3 Digital Continuity Based on Data Consistency

Ensuring digital continuity requires an understanding of the way the agent manages information. Digital continuity plans recommend reviewing agency information. In other words, it is necessary to record the data information created, captured and used in the business management process, and clarify the responsibilities, obligations, conditions, costs, benefits, and risks of digital information management. Data consistency is the fundamental property of digital continuity and requirements.

Data consistency refers to the validity and integrity of data representing real-world entities. Its aim is detecting errors (inconsistencies and conflicts) in the data, typically identifying as violations of data dependencies. Typically, data consistency mainly evaluates the consistency of data records, format, and content within a single data set or among plurality data sets. Typically, data consistency evaluates mostly the condition of consistency of data records, the format, and content and so on within a single data set or a plurality of data. Some researchers have shown that: the consistent representation, consistency, and synchronization these two properties are included in the study of constant, the relationship can be expressed as follows:

$$D_{Cons1} = D_{ConsR} \tag{1}$$

$$D_{cons1} = D_{ConsR} + D_{cons} \tag{2}$$

$$D_{Cons2} = D_{cons,syn} \tag{3}$$

$$D_{cons2} = D_{cons,syn} + D_{cons} \tag{4}$$

According to the joint problems [17], the data consistency issues specifically are divided into the following five kinds (see Table 1). If any violated data consistency in Table 1, it will violate the requirements of data consistency. In the table, the format consistency, content consistency, and accuracy of data have specific relevance; while time consistency and data timeliness properties are related.

Definition 1. The violation of consistency pattern: assuming that there are two specific relations patterns $R(A_1 : d_1, \cdots A_n : d_n)$ and $R'(A'_1 : d'_1, \cdots A'_n : d'_n)$. It exists n attributes A_i $(i = 1, \cdots n)$ in $R(A_1 : d_1, \cdots A_n : d_n)$, the corresponding domain is d_i and D is an

Table 1. Category of data consistency

Category	Function description
Concept consistency	*The matching degree of the information system and physical structure of data set*
Format consistency	*The matching degree of data structure, attribute and relation of multi-source data set;* *The unified degree of field value format from the single source dataset*
Consistency of value	*The matching degree of meeting the requirements of the value range*
Content consistency	*The accuracy of the specific field values of the same attribute on the single source dataset*
Time consistency	*The correctness of ordered data*

instance of R. The similar domain is d_i' and D' is an instance of R'. There is existing a consistent rule set, which includes l rules φ_l. φ_l is accurate. For any $FD\alpha = (R_{std} : X \rightarrow A, t_p)$, data inconsistency occurs if any of the following conditions are satisfied.

a. $\forall t_i \in R$, assume that $t_p[A]$ is a constant. $t[X] = t_p[X]$, but $t[A] \neq t_p[A]$.
b. Assume $t_p[A]$ is a variety, t and t' are two tuples in R. $t[X] = t_p[X]$, $t[A] \neq t_p[A]$, $t'[X] = t_p[X]$; $t[A] \neq t_p[A]$ and $t[X] = t'[X]$, but $t[A] \neq t'[A]$.
c. Assume $t_p[A]$ is a variety, t is a tuple in R, t' is a tuple in R'. $t[X] = t_p[X]$ and $t[A] = t_p[A]$, $t'[X] = t_p[X]$, $t[X] = t'[X]$, but $t[A] \neq t'[A]$.

Where (a) is called data consistency violation of single-source and single-tuple, (b) is called data consistency violation of single-source and multi-tuples, (c) is known as data consistency violation of multi-source and single-tuple. If meet the condition (a), t_i will be included in the set of violating data consistency, that is $t_i \in \sum Vio(D_{cons})$ in the pattern R. If the condition (b) is met and t_i' will be included in the set of breaking data consistency, that is $t_i, t_i' \in \sum Vio(D_{cons})$ in the pattern R. If the condition (c) is met and t_i' will be included in the sets of violating data consistency, that is $t_i \in \sum Vio(D_{cons})$ and $t_i' \in \sum Vio(D_{cons})$ respectively in the pattern R and R'.

Definition 2. The definition of widespread consistency pattern violation: in the information system, for two specific relation patterns. For the attributes $A_i(i = 1, \cdots n)$ in two particular patterns of relations $R(A_1 : d_1, \cdots A_n : d_n)$, corresponding domain is Data collection instance R of d_i, D. There are n' attributes $A_i'(i = 1, \cdots n')$ in $R'(A_1' : d_1', \cdots A_n' : d_n')$; corresponding domain is the data collection instance R' of d_i', D'.

Given a set of consistent set of rules, which has l rules φ_l. φ_l is accurate. When meeting any of the following conditions, data inconsistency is said to occur.

d. $\forall t_i \in R$, assume that $t_p[A]$ is a constant, $t[X] = t_p[X]$, but $t[A] \neq t_p[A]$ and $Q_{cons1} = F(\sum (n_{ti} - n_{tiVio})/n_{ti}) < q_{cons1}$, where Q_{cons1} represents the results of data conformity assessment 1; q_{cons1} is the data consistency requirements of the standard coefficient 1 which is given according to digital business continuity, n_{t_i} means the number of the attributes of unit group, $n_{t_{iviolate}}$ means the amount of the attributes which violate the consistency.

e. Assume $t_p[A]$ is a variety, t and t' are two tuples in R, $t[X] = t_p[X]$, $t'[X] = t_p[X]$; and $t[A] \neq t_p[A]$, $t[X] = t'[X]$, but $t[A] \neq t'[A]$ and $Q_{cons2} = F(\sum (n_{ti} - n_{tiVio})/n_{ti}) < q_{cons2}$, where Q_{cons2} represents the results of data conformity assessment 2; q_{cons2} is the data consistency requirements of the standard coefficient two which is given according to digital business continuity. Means the total number of tuples, $n_{t_{iviolate}}$ means the number of the tuples which violate the data consistency.

f. Assume $t_p[A]$ is a variety, t and t' are a tuple in R and R' respectively, $t[X] = t_p[X]$ and $t[A] \neq t_p[A]$, $t'[X] = t[X]$; $t[A] = t_p[A]$, $t[X] = t'[X]$, but $t[A] \neq t''[A]$, $Q_{cons3} = F(\sum (n_{ti} - n_{tiVio})/n_{ti}) < q_{cons}$, where Q_{cons3} represents the results of data conformity assessment 3, q_{cons3} is the data consistency requirements of the standard coefficient three which is given according to digital business continuity. Means the total pairs of the calculated tuple (t_i, t_i'), n_{tiVio} means the total pairs of the tuples (t_i, t_i') which violate the data consistency.

Where (d) is called single-source unit group data consistency violation, (e) is called single-source tuples violate data consistency (f) is known as multi-source data unit group violate data consistency. We called that the data consistency is low when meet $Q_{consi} < q_{consi}$, the degree of the violation of data consistency is defined as follows: $Vio_{com}(R, R_{stad})$. In the case of meet (d): aid t_i into the set of violating data consistency, that is $t_i \in \sum Vio(D_{cons})$ in the pattern R. In the case of meet (e): aid t_i and t_i' into the set of violating data consistency, that is $t_i, t_i' \in \sum Vio(D_{cons})$ in the pattern R. In the case of meet (f): aid t_i and t_i' into the set of violating data consistency, that is $t_i, t_i' \in \sum Vio(D_{cons})$ in the pattern R and R'.

4 Digital Continuity Based on Functional Dependency Theory

In relational data systems, function dependency theory defines the relationship between attributes, which is an abstract reflection of the real-world data built-in links. Over time, researchers apply functional dependency theory to data cleaning, assign semantic relationships among data, and detect inconsistent data. This section uses functional dependencies to check data consistency.

4.1 Functional Dependency Theory

Functional dependency theory can model the consistency of the data's semantics. Functional dependency can define semantic constraints of the attributes of a relational database; it is the abstraction reaction in a database of the built-in link between the real-world. Since Codd proposed functional dependency, researchers have suggested the data dependency including inclusion dependency, multivalued dependency and joined dependency. A consolidated one order statement can describe the data dependency of the classic relations theory:

$$\forall x_1 \cdots \forall x_n[\varphi(x_1,\cdots,x_n) \rightarrow \exists z_1 \cdots \exists z_k \psi(y_1,\cdots,y_n)] \tag{5}$$

$(x_1,\cdots,x_n), (y_1,\cdots,y_m), (z_1,\cdots,z_k)$ are the collection of attribute variables. And $(z_1,\cdots,z_k) = (y_1,\cdots,y_m) - (x_1,\cdots,x_n)$. φ is the precondition of the first-order logic statements, it is the conjunction of an empty set or relational predicates and atomic equality formula, ψ is the conclusion of first-order logic statements, it is the conjunction of co-relational predicates or equality atomic formula. The form of the relational predicates is $R(w_1,\cdots,w_l)$, the form of the atomic equality formula is $w = w'$, where R is a relational model, $w, w', w_1,\cdots,w_l$ is a property variable. We can convert the precise formula to several common dependencies, such as full dependency, tuple-generating dependency, and equality-generating dependency.

Functional dependency involves only the equation atomic formulas which are used to judge whether the relational predicates are equal to the attribute values, we cannot express the constraints of the value of the property, but in fact, there are many such constraints. For example, we need to decide the level of the enterprises according to the number of the people which were hired by the enterprises. These functional dependencies cannot express this type of semantic constraints; therefore, we need the functional dependence which has stronger expression ability to express such semantic constraints.

Denial constraints enhance the inconsistent data which are used to describe the semantic conflicts by inequality. That is:

$$\forall \bar{x}_1,\cdots,\bar{x}_m \neg[P_1(\bar{x}_1) \wedge \cdots \wedge P_m(\bar{x}_m) \wedge \varphi(\bar{x}_1,\cdots,\bar{x}_m)] \tag{6}$$

$\bar{x}_1,\cdots,\bar{x}_m$ represents the attribute variable sequence, $P_1,\cdots P_m$ represents the relational predicates and φ is the built-in predicates conjunctive formula.

Constraints-generating dependency is the extension of dependence on equivalence, describe the property value constraints by the conjunctions of built-in predicates atomic formula, its format is as follows:

$$\forall \bar{x}(R_1(\bar{x}) \wedge \cdots \wedge R_k(\bar{x}) \wedge \xi(\bar{x}) \rightarrow \xi'(\bar{x})) \tag{7}$$

R_i is the relational predicates, ξ and ξ' are the properties variable constraints Built-in predicates.

Universal constraints are the extension of the full dependency and allow using the inequality disjunction to appoint semantic constraints. The form of it is $\forall x_1,\cdots \forall x_n[\varphi(x_1,\cdots x_n) \rightarrow \phi(x_1,\cdots x_n)]$, where φ is the conjunction of the relational predicates, ϕ is the conjunction of the relational predicates and built-in predicates, in which the form of the built-in Predicate atomic formula is $x\theta y$; x, y are the variable of properties or the constant of the whole region, built-in predicates holds $\theta \in \{\leq, <, =, \neq, >, \geq\}$.

Improving the expressing ability has been the focus of research in functional dependency. Function dependencies use a set of dependency constraints as a precondition for establishing a definition. Function dependencies are given only on subsets of data that satisfy the constraint. Moreover, ensure that the specified function dependencies are only established on the subset of data that satisfies the constraint. Its concrete form is $\xi \rightarrow (Z \rightarrow W)$, where ξ is the disjunction of attribute variable constraints with built-in predicates. Functional dependencies $Z \leftarrow W$ just apply to the subset of the data which satisfy the condition ξ.

Constrained functional dependencies can only express the conditions of the establishments of the functional dependencies. To further enhance the ability of the expression, researchers further proposed the constrained tuple-generating dependencies, express the constraints which depend on any attributes they have by atomic inequality formula. The form of it is the following formulation:

$$\forall \bar{x}(R_1(\bar{x}) \wedge \cdots \wedge R_k(\bar{x}) \wedge \xi(\bar{x}) \longrightarrow \exists \bar{y}(R'_1(\bar{x},\bar{y}) \wedge \cdots \wedge R'_k(\bar{x},\bar{y}) \wedge \xi'(\bar{x},\bar{y})) \quad (8)$$

$R_i, R'_j(i,j \in [1,k])$ are relational predicates. ξ and ξ' are the attribute variable constraints which have built-in predicates.

4.2 Digital Continuity Based on Functional Dependency Theory

Definition 3. Assuming a relationship Schema R, $attr(R)$ means the attribute set defined in R. For each attribute, it has $A \subset attr(R)$, the domain of A can be expressed as $dom(A)$. A conditional functional dependency φ, defined on R, can be expressed as $R : X \rightarrow Y, T_p$. In which: (1) X and Y are two attribute sets defined on $attr(R)$. (2) $\{R : X \rightarrow Y\}$ is a standard functional dependency. (3) T_p is a schema tuple related to X and Y, which defines the constraint of the attribute value. The value can be a constant or '–' ('–' is not equal to null, which means that the value of the corresponding attribute may be any value in the field, but it should be consistent with the constraint).

From the above definition, it can be concluded that in some cases, the standard function dependency can be expressed as a conditional function dependency (CFD).

Definition 4. When the relationship instance I of relation schema R meet the conditional functional dependency φ, it is called $I \models \varphi$. There exist any two tuples t_1 and t_2 in *I*. And each tuple t_p of schema tuple T_p has the following match relationship:

If $t_1[X] = t_2[X] \approx t_p[X]$, then $t_1[Y] = t_2[Y] \approx t_p[Y]$; where wildcard includes the following matching rules: (1) a and b are constants, and $a = b$. (2) if a or b is '–,' it holds that $a \approx b$. The rules can be applied to the tuples. It assumes that the corresponding tuple of t_i is $(a, \_)$, and that of t_2 is $(\_, b)$. Then it holds that $(a, b) \approx (\_, b) = (a, \_)$ and $t_1 \approx t_2$.

Because CFDs achieve the constraints which are more precise and specific semantically, the detection of inconsistent data is more accurate and efficient. Moreover, the SQL query can be directly used to detect the consistency of the data. As a result, it reduces the complexity of the related operations. At First, we consider the case of only one CFD.A typical detection method based on SQL is present; a condition functional dependency $\varphi : \{R : B \rightarrow A, T_p\}$ is taken as an example. B and A are both single attributes; detection statements are as follows:

Q^C_φ Select t from R_t, T_p, where ($t[B] = t_p[B]$ or $t_p[B] = '\_'$) and ($t[A] \neq t_p[A]$ and $t_p[A] \neq '\_'$); Q^V_φ Select distinct t from R_t, T_p, where $t[B] = t_p[B]$ and $t_p[B] = '\_'$. Group by t having count (distinct A) >1.

Data consistency testing is divided into two steps. First query statement Q^C_φ detects a single tuple. To match the attribute B as a precondition, try to find a tuple that does not match the attribute A. This step mainly checks whether the attribute A matches.

The query Q^C_φ detects multiple tuples. First, the 'where' statement is used to filter the data and identify tuples T_p that match attribute B before performing grouping and sorting. The 'distinct' statement is used to query whether the A attribute has duplicate instances. If there is more than one instance A, the query returns the value of attribute B. Simply put, the query only returns the value of tuple attribute B, not the entire tuple. More specifically, for any two tuples t_1 and t_2, it holds that $t_1[B] = t_2[B] \approx t_p[B]$, that is, the attribute B is matching the mode tuples T_p. When $t_1[A] \neq t_2[A]$, the inquiring result of A is more than one instance, and the value of attribute B for t_1 is achieved, which equals t_2. Obviously, when it holds $t_p[A] = '\_'$, Q^V_φ can be rerun to filter tuples, which can't be detected by Q^C_φ. For φ_1, the corresponding attribute has the value '–' in T_p. Moreover, Q^C_φ is unable to finish the whole detection, Q^V_φ is needed to detect the inconsistency thoroughly. Moreover, all the values of T_p and φ_2 are constant. Thus, all the violation tuple can be detected in the queries.

In fact, each electronic record may have multiple functional dependencies. Therefore, each function dependency can be detected in the above manner, that is, each FD corresponds to one query pair. Naturally, as the number of function dependencies increases, retrieval operations will become more and more complicated. Therefore, the conditions for various CFDs are integrated, and new constraints are formed. At the same time, it must be taken into account that different CFD attribute sets have different problems and how to construct new compatible mode tuples.

5 Conclusion

Digital continuity has penetrated into many aspects of cloud storage today. Maintaining data consistency is the basis of digital continuity. This paper theoretically describes the application of functional dependency theory in data consistency and proposes a data consistency assurance framework based on functional dependency theory. The framework periodically detects the consistency of archived data and provides digital continuity protection.

Acknowledgment. This work is supported by the NSFC (NO. 61772280 and 61702236), Jiangsu Province Natural Science Research Program (NO. BK20130809, BK2012461), the six talent peaks project in Jiangsu Province (2013-WLW-012, XYDXXJS-040), the industrial Strategic Technology Development Program (10041740) funded by the Ministry of Trade, Industry and Energy (MOTIE) Korea, the research fund from Jiangsu Technology & Engineering Center of Meteorological Sensor Network in NUIST under Grant (No. KDXG1301), the PAPD fund and the national training programs of innovation and entrepreneurship for undergraduates (NO. N1885014041, N1885012119). Prof. Chengshan Qian is the corresponding author.

References

1. Schroeder, B., Gibson, G.: A large-scale study of failures in high-performance computing systems. IEEE Trans. Dependable Secure Comput. **7**(4), 337–350 (2010)
2. MacLean, M., Davis, B.H.: Time & Bits: Managing Digital Continuity. Getty Publications, Los Angeles (1998)
3. Turnbaugh, R.C.: What is an electronic record? In: Dearstyne, B.W. (ed.) Effective Approaches for Managing Electronic Records and Archives, pp. 23–34. The Scarecrow Press, Lanham (2006). HTML Standard (2015). http://www.whatwg.org/
4. UK National Archives: Digital continuity marketing brochure: if you don't protect your digital assets, they can't protect you [EB/OL]. http://www.Nationalarchives.gov.uk/documents/tna-digital-continuity.pdf. Accessed 10 July 2016
5. Hong, K.D., Son, Y.: A study on the smart virtual machine for executing virtual machine codes on smart platforms, pp. 93–106. Oxford University Press (2012)
6. Ren, Y., Xu, X., Ji, S., Wang, J., Jin, Y.: Digital continuity guarantee based on data consistency (2017)
7. Wang, J., Yin, Y., Zhang, J., Lee, S., Sherratt, R.S.: Mobility based energy efficient and multi-sink algorithms for consumer home networks. IEEE Trans. Consum. Electron. **59**(1), 77–84 (2013)
8. Shen, J., Tan, H.W., Wang, J., Wang, J.W., Lee, S.Y.: A novel routing protocol providing good transmission reliability in underwater sensor networks. J. Internet Technol. **16**(1), 171–178 (2015)
9. Cochrane, E.: Digital continuity action plan: collaborative long-term information and data management across the New Zealand public sector (2016). http://www.statisphere.govt.nz//media/Statistics/about-us/statisphere/Files/os-forum-2010/1-1300-euan-cochrane.pdf. Accessed 17 Nov 2015
10. Waller, M., Sharpe, R.: Mind the gap: assessing digital preservation needs in the UK, digital preservation coalition, York (2006)
11. The National Archives: Understanding digital continuity version 1.2 [EB/OL]. http://www.Nationalarchives.gov.uk/documents/information-management/understanding-digit-al-continuity.pdf. Accessed 20 Mar 2017
12. Xia, Z., Wang, X., Sun, X., Wang, Q.: A secure and dynamic multi-keyword ranked search scheme over encrypted cloud data. IEEE Trans. Parallel Distrib. Syst. **27**(2), 340–352 (2016)
13. Ren, Y., Shen, J., Liu, D., Wang, J., Kim, J.U.: Evidential quality preserving of electronic record in cloud storage. J. Internet Technol. **17**(6), 1125–1132 (2016)
14. Tao, S.L., Xue, S.X., Tian, L., Zhang, G.G., Li, C.. Research on electronic archives evidence protection in the heterogeneous systems. Arch. Sci. Study **2012**(5), 50–54 (2012)
15. Ge, C., Susilo, W., Wang, J., Fang, L.: Identity-based conditional proxy re-encryption with fine grain policy. Comput. Stand. Interfaces **52**, 1–9 (2017)
16. Ge, C., Susilo, W., Fang, L., Wang, J., Shi, Y.: A CCA-secure key-policy attribute-based proxy re-encryption in the adaptive corruption model for dropbox data sharing system. Des. Codes Crypt. **86**, 1–17 (2018)
17. Ding, X.O., Wang, H.Z., Zhang, X.Y., Li, J.Z., Gao, H.: Association relationships study of multi-dimensional data quality. J. Softw. **27**(7), 1626–1644 (2016)

Dynamic Risk Access Control Model for Cloud Platform

Lixia Xie(✉), Ruixin Wei, Yuguang Ning, and Hongyu Yang

School of Computer Science and Technology,
Civil Aviation University of China, Tianjin 300300, China
lxxie@126.com, ruixinwei@outlook.com,
nyxlxxg@outlook.com, yhyxlx@hotmail.com

Abstract. In cloud environment, the traditional risk access control model cannot match rules dynamically and the risk values are insensitive for access requests. This paper proposed a cloud platform dynamic risk access control model (CPDAC) to solve the above problems. Firstly, the attribute-based access control model was improved by introducing the event calculus mechanism, and then the dynamic rule-matching module was constructed in the CPDAC. Secondly, based on programming regression (PR), the risk-evaluation-index weight distribution module was designed, and the risk assessment module with high sensitive value to access requests was constructed. Experimental results show that CPDAC is effective and feasible; in addition, the model is better in real-time and dynamic than other existing models.

Keywords: Risk assessment · Access control · Index weight · Cloud platform

1 Introduction

In cloud environment, as the traditional access control model, defined by static access control policy, has the problems that cannot dynamically match the rules, efficiently make use of massive data of user's historical behavior, evaluate the current security system level, researchers improved the adaptability of existing access control model by introducing the risk factors in traditional model [1].

In the last decade, there has been substantial research in the area of access control model of cloud platform [2–11], and those studies have been mainly divided into two types. One of them was models focused on assessing the system risks, e.g. graph-based risk assessment model [6], access control model based on fuzzy multi-criteria decision technology [7], the other focused on current access request risks, such as: multi-risk indicators access control model [8]. However, both the former two types of models faced the challenges of effectively make use of system security state and user's historical behavior information while assessing the system risks. In [9], Bouchami et al. proposed to quantify the user's historical behavior information and system security states as risk evaluation index to assess the current access request risks, but unfortunately without giving a specific risk access control model. Afterwards, Chen [10] presented a dynamic risk-based access control (DRAC) model with data flow method to quantify user's historical behavior information and constructed a risk evaluation

X. Sun et al. (Eds.): ICCCS 2018, LNCS 11065, pp. 12–22, 2018.
https://doi.org/10.1007/978-3-030-00012-7_2

index combined with the system security state, but regretfully, this attribute-based access control (ABAC) policy cannot dynamically match the rules or adjust the weight which leads to complexity increase and less flexibility of this static-ABAC policy. According to [9, 10], some widely adopted methods used to dynamically assign weight, such as normalized method, principal component analysis method and entropy method have the disadvantages of low accuracy or bad real-time.

To further tackle the above problems, in this paper, we put forward a cloud platform dynamic risk access control model (CPDAC). Firstly, the event calculus (EC) mechanism is chosen to enhance the dynamicity and the flexibility of rule matching module. Secondly, according to system security state and the user's historical behavior information, we construct the risk evaluation index, then propose a mathematical model to calculate the risk-evaluation-index weight and design programming regression (PR) algorithm [12] to derive the corresponding weight, which allows for improving the sensitivity of risk value to access requests. Our work is geared towards putting forward a novel dynamic threshold calculation method to increase the risk assessment accuracy.

2 Risk Access Control Model for Cloud Platform (CPDAC)

2.1 Research Goals

As the existing model with static ABAC policy cannot dynamically match the rules and lack the feasibility while allocating the risk-evaluation-index weight, hence we adopt the following strategies to solve the problems above:

1. Event-Calculus-based Rule Matching Module (ECRM). To address the general weakness and largely enhance the dynamicity of static ABAC policy in cloud environment, we use EC mechanism to improve static ABAC policy and then design a rule-matching module, which includes both rule assessment phase and trust computation phase. Dynamic access control is achieved by assessing the trust degree under the circumstance when the attributes of subjects or guests change.
2. Risk assessment module based on programming regression (PRRA). In terms of the disadvantage of constant weight, we present this module to improve the sensitive value to access control request through considering both of user's historical behavior information and system security state.

2.2 Dynamic Risk Access Control Model

In this text, we propose a risk access control Model (CPDAC) on cloud platform by implementing policies mentioned above. The model structure is shown in Fig. 1.

The CPDAC model consists of ECRM module, PRRA module, dynamic threshold calculation module and final decision module. The core function of each module is designed as follows:

1. ECRM module is used to match the rules according to the user requests and the rule matching module, and generate the matching results P through EC mechanism.

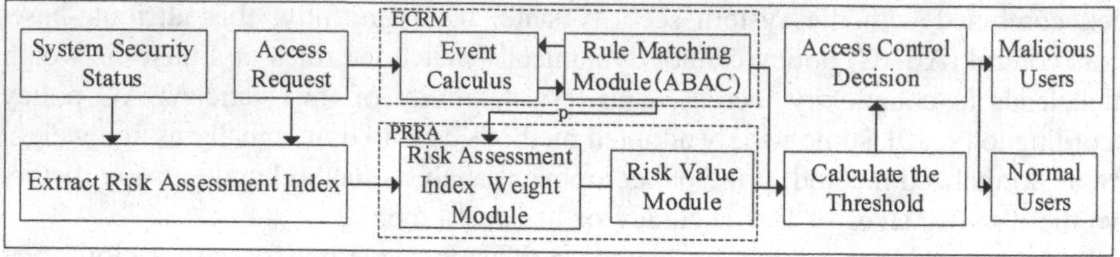

Fig. 1. Framework of CPDAC model

2. PRRA module calculates the weight of each index based on the extracted risk evaluation index and *P*, then assigns the corresponding weight to calculate the risk value *R* of current access request.
3. The dynamic threshold calculation module calculates the risk threshold value based on *P* and *R*.
4. The final decision module determines the final access control decisions according to the system requirements threshold value, the rule matching result *P* and the risk value *R*.

3 Event-Calculus-Based Rule Matching Module (ECRM)

3.1 Problem Analysis

As a static access control model policy, ABAC is inadequate to apply in some situations:

1. When the attributes of subject or guest change, ABAC cannot dynamically adjust the access rules.
2. When the visitor's background (time, location, etc.) changes, ABAC is lack of adaptability while there is a need to adjust the corresponding rules.

When the access request needs to match the corresponding rule in the rule base, time cost will increase while searching in a largescale database.

3.2 Formal Definitions

In order to clearly illustrate the ECRM module, we introduce following definitions:

Definition 1. For each access request, we regard it as an event which is denoted as E_k ($k = 1, 2, 3$). For different value of *k*, we define the following events: E_1: Rule-matching phase occurs (*MR*) or not (*MMR*); E_2: access request trust evaluation success (*TES*) or fail (*TEF*); E_3: Accept rule accepted (*AR*), Deny the rule (*DR*) or Rule is unavailable (*RDA*).

Definition 2. For each result processed by the EC mechanism for event E_k, we denote it as a flow F_k ($k = 1, 2, 3$), where different *k* value means different results: F_1: Rule target holds (*RTHs*); F_2: Trust holds (*THs*); F_3: Rule is permitted (*RIP*), rule is denied (*RID*), or rule is not available (*RINA*).

Definition 3. (Req_i, *Happens*) is defined as the binary group of the ith (i = 1, 2…) access request to store event already occurred.

3.3 Framework of ECRM and Execution Flow

In this part, we will first depict the structure of ECRM module which is shown in Fig. 2, subsequently, we will explain the execution flow of ECRM

1. Request generation module generates a series of requests (Req_i (i = 1, 2…)).
2. Input (Req_i, *Happens*) into the rule matching module for matching the rules; if the rule is successfully matched, then event *MR* will be added in Happens, flow *RTHs* = 1. otherwise, add event *MMR*, flow *RTHs* = 0.
3. Input (Req_i *Happens*) into trust degree computing module to evaluate the request; if the subject's trust value ≥ average value of subject, activity and average background trust value, add event *TES*, flow *THs* = 1 to the Happens; Otherwise, add event *TEF*, flow *THs* = 0.
4. Input (Req_i, *Happens*) to the rule evaluation module for evaluation; if Req_i successfully match a rule, then evaluate the condition and effect of the rule and add event *AR*/*DR*/*RDA*, flow *RIP*/*RID*/*RINA* in Happens.
5. Derive results of Happens and *flow*1, *flow*2, *flow*3.

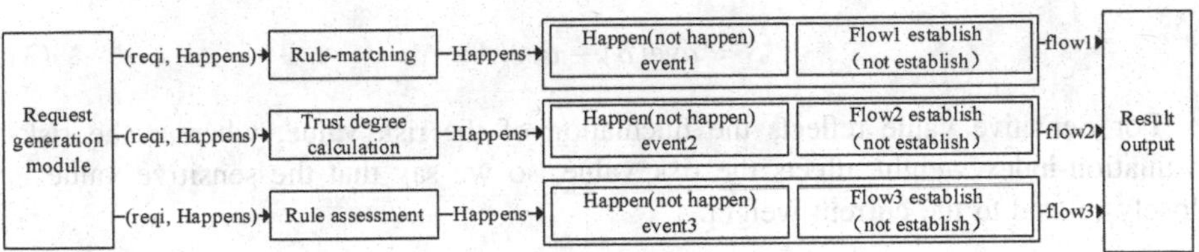

Fig. 2. Structure of ECRM

4 PR-Based Risk Evaluation Module

4.1 Problem Analysis

Calculation method of risk value can be summarized as follows:

$$R(req_i) = a_1 \times index1_i + a_2 \times index2_i + \cdots + a_n \times indexn_i \tag{1}$$

Where $a_1 + a_2 + a_3 = 1$, index j_i (j = 1, 2...) represents the jth quantified evaluation value of the risk evaluation index in the ith access request req_i, and a_j (j = 1, 2...) is the weight of jth risk evaluation index. During the phase of risk assessment, the value of *indexj*$_i$ should be determined by the actual situation, thus a_j is one of the main factors affecting the risk value. However, this method has the following two problems:

1. The weight of risk evaluation index is a constant.
2. The risk value is insufficiently sensitive to access requests.

To improve the sensitive value of risk value to the access request, in PRRA module, we propose to dynamically change the weight of the risk evaluation index according to the user's historical behavior information and the system security state, based on this, we define the following model.

4.2 Formal Definitions

Definition 4. Risk-threshold value *Th* is defined by following formula:

$$Th = \frac{1}{2} \times (avg(A) + avg(B)) \tag{2}$$

where function *avg* () is used to compute the average risk value of access request for the set. The number of access request, which is decided by users and used to compute *Th* value, is divided into set *A*, and set B respectively, where set *A* is a set of access request risk values for acceptance (P = 1) while set *B* is a set of risk values for refuse (P = 0).

Definition 5. The sensitive value *S* is defined as the difference between the average risk of the access request when P = 0 and P = 1:

$$S = avg(B) - avg(A) \tag{3}$$

For Sensitive value reflects the fluctuation of the risk value, whereas the risk-evaluation-index weight affects the risk value, so we say that the sensitive value is closely related to the current weight.

4.3 Risk-Evaluation-Index Weight Distribution Mathematical Module

In this context, we use (*I*, *T*, *V*) as the risk evaluation index, wherein *I* represents the frequency recorded in history documentary of current activities accepted (P = 0) by ECRM module [8]; *T* is decided by the subject's attribute of the access request, the higher the subject's attribute is, the smaller the *T* is. The risk value can be calculated below by:

$$R^{+/-} = a_1 I + a_2 T + a_3 V \tag{4}$$

In this formula, $a1 + a2 + a3 = 1$. If $a1$, $a2$, $a3$ are artificially set and cannot be changed dynamically, the situation that risk value of the normal access will higher than malicious access may frequently occurs, which results in obtaining an unreasonable threshold and the accuracy rate decrease. However, while $R^+ \to 0$ and $R^- \to 1$, then

$R^{-} - R^{+} \to 1$, we could see that the sensitive value, range of threshold and the risk evaluation accuracy increase based on formula (2). Nevertheless, for most of normal access requests ($P = 0$) and malicious access requests ($P = 1$) in ECRM, if $R^{+/-} \to P$, we can use risk evaluation index to dynamically set the corresponding weight. Therefore, the mathematical model of risk allocation index is defined as follows:

objective function:

$$P = a_1 I + a_2 T + a_3 V + \varepsilon \tag{5}$$

constraint condition:

$$\begin{cases} a_1 + a_2 + a_3 = 1 \\ a_1 > 0, a_2 > 0, a_3 > 0 \end{cases} \tag{6}$$

5 Experiment and Result

5.1 Experimental Environment and Data

To validate the performance of the ECRM module, PRRA module and CPDAC model, we worked our experiment on PC (experimental environment is shown in Table 1 and tested by the data set with 1550 randomly selected access requests, from which each access request information contains four main attributes: subject, guest, access activity and access time, for those four attributes, each one contains layered sub-attributes (e.g. subject = {manager, member, non-member}, manager = {manager1, manager2, manager3,…}).

Table 1. Experimental environment

Hardware configuration	Software environment
Inter Core i3-2350 M CPU @ 2.30 GHz	Windows7 64-bit operating system
4.0 GB RAM	MATLAB R2010b

We assess those 1500 requests by ECRM to get the assessment *P*, then quantify the risk evaluation index (*I*, *T*, *V*) for each request.

In our experiment, the training set contains 1500 (*I*, *T*, *V*) risk evaluation indexes and ECRM module evaluation results P_{train}, Meanwhile, the testing set is composed of 50 (*I*, *T*, *V*) data and ECRM module evaluation results P_{test}.

5.2 ECRM Module Evaluation and Performance Analysis

To evaluate the performance of ECRM module when the attributes change, we generated a normal access request for user1 (non-member) and evaluated it. After a period

Table 2. Result of changed subject attributes

Time	User	Rule	Event 1	Event 2	Event 3	Flow1	Flow2	Flow3
09/27/2017, 09:13	user1	1	MR	TEF	DR	RTHs	THs	RINA
11/16/2017, 15:24	user1	1	MR	TES	AR	RTHs	THs	RIP

of time, we changed the attribute of user1 from non-member to member, still evaluated the new generated access request by ECRM. The result is shown in Table 2.

As can be seen from Table 2, when user1 has a low-level attribute, even if the rule is successfully matched, trust evaluation still eventually fails (TEF). Only when the level of attributes improved can trust degree evaluation be successful (TES). In this sense, we could draw the conclusion that ECRM successfully achieved the dynamic adjustment evaluation policy based on ever changing attributes.

To evaluate the performance when changed the access background, we first generated a normal access request for user5 with high-level subject attribute and evaluated it with ECRM. After adjusting the time attribute of the access request to abnormal time (0:00–9:00, 17:00–0:00), we then evaluated with ECRM and obtained the results shown in Table 3.

Table 3. ECRM evaluation results after changing subject's access background

Time	User	Rule	Event 1	Event 2	Event 3	Flow1	Flow2	Flow3
08/2017 16:40	user5	25	MR	TES	AR	RTHs	THs	RIP
08/2017, 20:30	user5	25	MR	TES	RDA	RTHs	THs	RINA

The above table demonstrates that, although the subject has a higher authority, ECRM can still dynamically adjust the access control policy since the access background (time, place etc.) of subject is illegal.

5.3 PRRA Module Evaluation and Performance Analysis

Our experiment is composed with the following steps:

Step 1. Randomly select 1000, 500, 250, 100 pieces of risk evaluation indexes (*I*, *T*, *V*) of access requests and the corresponding ECRM module risk evaluation value *P*, construct 4 groups of training sets.

Step 2. Derive the result of corresponding weight b^* and minimum error Q_{min} by PR Algorithm.

Step 3. Compute the corresponding weight of the former risk evaluation index by formula (4).

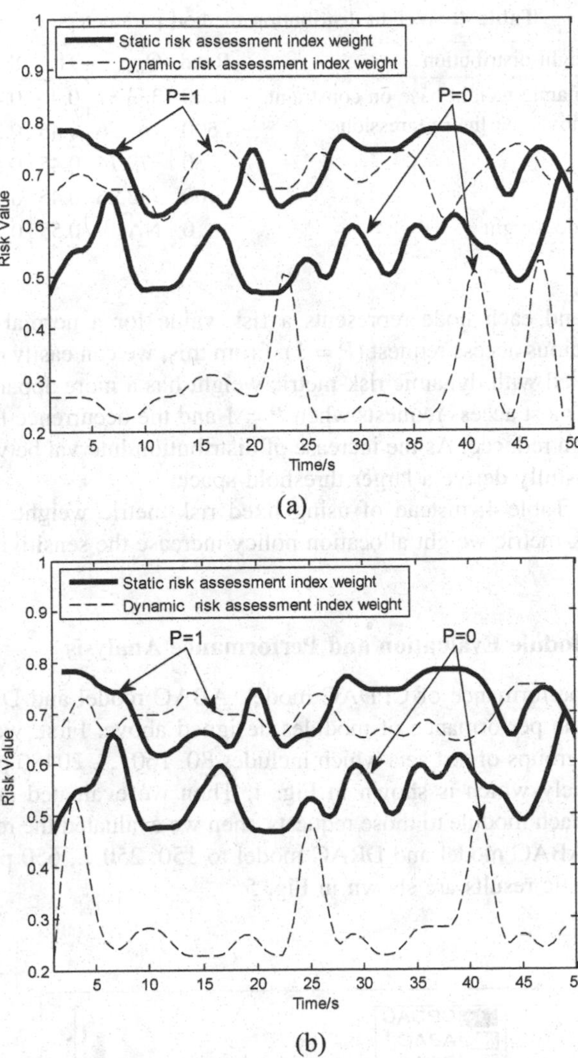

Fig. 3. Risk value distribution of different numbers of access requests when Rand = 1000, b^* = (0.01, 0.13, 0.86) and Rand = 250, b^* = (0.01, 0.14, 0.85)

Step 4. Every 1 s, calculate risk value of each access request in training set in succession through risk calculation formula, which is shown in Fig. 3 by solid line.
Step 5. Calculate risk value of test set with fixed risk value (1/3, 1/3, 1/3) [8–10], the result is depicted in Fig. 3 by dotted line.
Step 6. Calculate the corresponding risk threshold *Th* and sensitive value *S* then we derive Table 4.

In Fig. 3, the dotted line and solid line indicate the trend of risk value calculated with dynamic risk-metric weight and fixed risk-metric weight respectively over a

Table 4. Weight distribution method parameters

Weight distribution	Rand	Q_{min}	Th	S
Dynamic weight base on constraint multivariate liner regression	1000	333.87	0.40	0.40
	500	161.26	0.45	0.30
	250	79.74	0.45	0.50
	100	32.26	0.45	0.30
Static weight	0	NA	0.55	0.10

period of time, and each node represents a risk value for a normal access request ($P = 0$) or a malicious access request ($P = 1$). From this, we can easily observe that the risk value computed with dynamic risk-metric weight has a more apparent fluctuation. The risk value of most access requests when $P = 1$ and the occurrence frequency when $R^{+} > R^{-}$ have been reduced. As the increase of distribution interval between $P = 0$ and $P = 1$, we successfully derive a larger threshold space.

According to Table 4, instead of using fixed risk-metric weight, PRRA module with dynamic risk-metric weight allocation policy increase the sensitivity of risk value to access request.

5.4 CPDAC Module Evaluation and Performance Analysis

To compare the performance of CPDAC model, ABAC model and DRAC model as well as analysis the performance of modules designed above. First, we design 9 randomly generated groups of test sets which includes 80, 160, … 20480 pieces of access requests respectively which is shown in Fig. 4. Then we evaluated and denoted the response time of each module to those requests, then we evaluated the response time of CPDAC model, ABAC model and DRAC model to 150, 250…, 650 pieces of access requests, the statistic results are shown in Fig. 5.

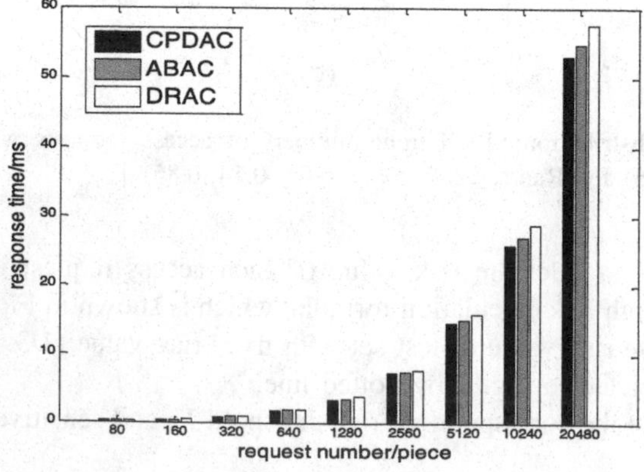

Fig. 4. Response time of 3 models for 850–24800 requests

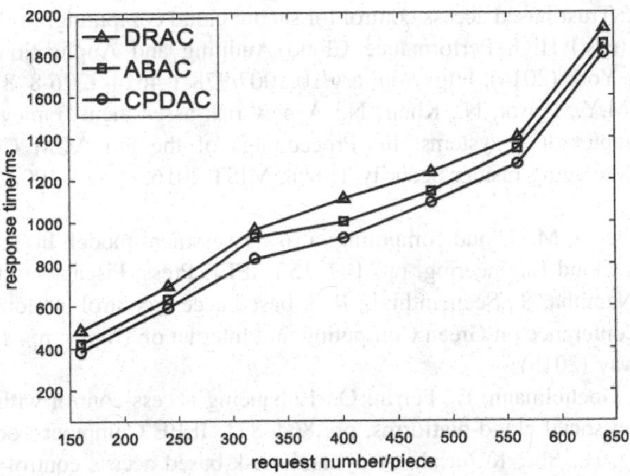

Fig. 5. Response time of 3 models for 150–650 requests

In Fig. 4, through the response time of CPDAC model, ABAC model and DRAC model increase as the number of requests increase, for PRRA module applying inheritance mechanism largely shrink the time while matching the rules, CPDAC model perform the best owning the least response time. That also shows the promising advantage of CPDAC model to applying to the large-scale data. From Fig. 5, we could see that there is a limit response time difference between CPDAC and DRAC (100 ms) or ABAC (150 ms) while evaluating a small amount of data, however, the performance of CPDAC model is still superior to the other two models.

6 Conclusion

In order to overcome the disadvantages of most risk access control models that cannot dynamically match the rules and adjust weight adaptively, we proposed a cloud platform dynamic risk access control model (CPDAC), improved the ABAC policy by introducing Event Calculus and constructed the dynamic rule matching module to better adapt the rule assessment under the cloud platform. Also, we enhanced the sensitive value of risk to the access request by introducing the Programming Regression (PR) in risk evaluation index distribution model. The experiment shows that CPDAC is feasible and risk value calculated by this model is sensitive to access requests.

References

1. Li, H., Min, Z., Feng, D., et al.: Research on access control of big data. Chin. J. Comput. (2017)
2. Wang, Y., Yang, J., Xu, C.: Survey on access control technologies for cloud computing. J. Softw. **26**(5), 1129–1150 (2015)

3. Ray, I., Ray, I.: Trust-based access control for secure cloud computing. In: Han, K., Choi, B. Y., Song, S. (eds.) High Performance Cloud Auditing and Applications, pp. 189–213. Springer, New York (2014). https://doi.org/10.1007/978-1-4614-3296-8_8
4. Naghmouchi, M.Y., Perrot, N., Kheir, N.: A new risk assessment framework using graph theory for complex ICT systems. In: Proceedings of the 8th ACM CCS International Workshop on Managing Insider Security Threat, MIST 2016, pp. 97–100. ACM Press, New York (2016)
5. Sendi, A.S., Cheriet, M.: Cloud computing: a risk assessment model. In: IEEE International Conference on Cloud Engineering, pp. 147–152. IEEE Press, Piscataway (2014)
6. Lakshmi, H., Namitha, S., Seemanthini.: Risk based access control in cloud computing. In: International Conference on Green Computing and Internet of Things, pp. 1502–1505. IEEE Press, Piscataway (2015)
7. Bouchami, A., Goettelmann, E., Perrin, O.: Enhancing access-control with risk-metrics for collaboration on social cloud-platforms, pp. 864–871. IEEE Computer Society (2015)
8. Chen, A., Xing, H., She, K., et al.: A dynamic risk-based access control model for cloud computing. In: IEEE International Conferences on Big Data and Cloud Computing, pp. 579–584. IEEE Press, Piscataway (2016)
9. Zhou, L.: Research on Information Security Risk Assessment Model Based on Fuzzy Grey Relational Analysis. Southwest University, Chongqing (2013)
10. Xiong, J., Qin, H., Li, J., et al.: Method of determining index weight in security risk evaluation based on information entropy. J. Syst. Sci. 82–84 (2013)
11. Zahoor, E., Perrin, O., Bouchami, A.: CATT: a cloud based authorization framework with trust and temporal aspects. In: International Conference on Collaborative Computing: Networking, Applications and Worksharing, pp. 285–294. IEEE Press, Piscataway (2014)
12. Fang, K., Wang, D., Wu, G.: A class of constrained regression—programming regression. Mathematica Numerica Sinica 57–69 (1982)

Efficient Multiparty Quantum Secret Sharing Scheme in High-Dimensional System

Ming-Ming Wang[1,2(✉)], Lu-Ting Tian[1], and Zhi-Guo Qu[3]

[1] Shaanxi Key Laboratory of Clothing Intelligence, School of Computer Science, Xi'an Polytechnic University, Xi'an 710048, China
bluess1982@126.com

[2] State and Local Joint Engineering Research Center for Advanced Networking and Intelligent Information Services, School of Computer Science, Xi'an Polytechnic University, Xi'an 710048, China

[3] Jiangsu Engineering Center of Network Monitoring, Nanjing University of Information Science and Technology, Nanjing 210044, China

Abstract. Quantum secret sharing (QSS) is an important component of quantum cryptograph. The original QSS scheme was proposed based on entangled GHZ states. But a drawback of the scheme is that only half of the quantum resource is effective, and the other half has to be discarded. To enhance the efficiency of the scheme, we propose an efficient multiparty QSS scheme and generalized it in high-dimensional system. By using a measurement-delay strategy on the dealer's side, the efficiency of the improved QSS schemes can be raised to 100%, rather than 50% or $\frac{1}{d}$ in previous schemes.

Keywords: Quantum secret sharing · Multiparty
High-dimensional system · Efficiency

1 Introduction

Quantum computation [1,2] and quantum communications [3,4] have become increasingly hot topics in scientific community in last decades. With the development of quantum information processing technology, quantum physics has also been introduced in the field of modern cryptography, which leads the research direction of quantum cryptography [5]. Since its first appearance, many branches of quantum cryptograph have been developed during the last decades. Applications such as quantum key distribution (QKD) [3,4,6,7], quantum secure direct communication (QSDC) [8–10], quantum signature [11,12], quantum data hiding [13,14] have been studied extensively.

As a primitive of modern cryptography, secret sharing plays a fundamental role in secure multiparty computation. In 1979, Blakley [15] and Shamir [16] firstly introduced the idea of secret sharing into cryptography for protecting

X. Sun et al. (Eds.): ICCCS 2018, LNCS 11065, pp. 23–31, 2018.
https://doi.org/10.1007/978-3-030-00012-7_3

highly sensitive information. In their secret sharing scheme, a dealer can split a secret into several pieces and send these pieces to different participants in such a way that any qualified participants set can reconstruct the secret cooperatively, but any unqualified participants set cannot get any information about the secret. As an important area of quantum cryptograph, quantum secret sharing (QSS) [17–19] has also been developed to achieve high-level security than their classical counterparts [15,16].

The first QSS scheme was proposed by Hillary et al. in 1999 based on entangled Greenberger-Horne-Zeilinger (GHZ) state [17], which will be called as the HBB-QSS protocol hereafter. In the well-known HBB-QSS scheme, the dealer Alice can create a secret for two players Bob and Charlie in such a way that the secret can only be recovered if Bob and Charlie work together, but one of them cannot get anything useful about the secret. A GHZ triplet is shared among three participants as quantum resource. Each of them measures their own qubit either in the Pauli X or Y basis, randomly. In half of the chance, their measurement results will be correlated, which means their measurement results could be used for secret generating or eavesdropping detection. The quantum resource efficiency of the HBB-QSS scheme is only 50% and half of the entangled GHZ states have to be discarded.

Besides of entanglement-based QSS protocols, QSS protocols without entanglement have also been developed [20,21]. According to the secret information shared among players, QSS can be divided into two types, i.e., QSS protocols for sharing classical information and QSS protocols for sharing quantum states [22,23], which is also known as quantum state sharing (QSTS) [24]. It should be mentioned that a QSTS protocol has also been proposed in Ref. [17]

Since the appearance of the HBB-QSS scheme, multiparty QSS has been developed based on entangled GHZ states. In Ref. [25], Xiao et al. generalized the HBB-QSS scheme into arbitrary multiparties. To improve the efficiency of the HBB-QSS scheme, they also proposed two methods, i.e., the favored-measuring-basis and the measuring-basis-encrypted, respectively. However, some per-shared keys [25] or different probability parameters are required in these methods. Furthermore, Yu et al. further extended [26] the HBB-QSS scheme in high-dimensional system. By using mutually unbiased or biased bases, their scheme is secure against the intercept-resend attack. The efficiency of the scheme in high-dimensional system is $\frac{1}{d}$, where d is the dimension of the quantum system, which is similar to HBB-QSS scheme.

In this paper, we study the problem of how to improve the efficiency of HBB-QSS scheme for sharing classical information. By using a simple measurement-delay strategy, we present two improved versions of QSS schemes based GHZ states, i.e. multiparty QSS and high-dimensional QSS. The quantum resource efficiency of these two proposed schemes can be increased to 100% rather than 50% in [17], asymptotically 100% in [25], or $\frac{1}{d}$ in [26]. The organization of the paper is as follows. In Sect. 2, we propose the improved multiparty QSS scheme. Then we extend the idea to high-dimension situation in Sect. 3. The paper is discussed and concluded in Sect. 4.

2 Improved Multiparty QSS Scheme

In this section, we are going to present our improved multiparty QSS scheme. The quantum resource used in the multiparty QSS scheme is the n-partite GHZ state which has the following form

$$|\Phi_n\rangle = \frac{1}{\sqrt{2}}(|0\rangle^{\otimes n} + |1\rangle^{\otimes n})_{12\ldots n}. \tag{1}$$

In our multiparty QSS scheme, the dealer Alice wants to distribute her secret to $n-1$ participants, named Bob_2, Bob_3, ..., Bob_n where only if all participants work together can they recover the secret. Our improved multiparty QSS scheme can be described as follows.

Step 1. Resources preparation and distribution

(a) Alice prepares a sequence of n-qubit GHZ states in Eq. (1) with length $m+l$. The sequence can be represented as

$$S = \{P_1(1,2,\ldots,n), P_2(1,2,\ldots,n), \ldots, P_{m+l}(1,2,\ldots,n)\}, \tag{2}$$

where the subscript denotes the order of entangled state in the sequence.

(b) Alice divides the sequence into n subgroups

$$S_i = \{P_1(i), P_2(i), \ldots, P_{m+l}(i)\}, \tag{3}$$

with $i = 1, 2, \ldots, n$. Then Alice keeps S_1 in her hand, while sends other S_i to Bob_i respectively.

Step 2. Eavesdropping detection

(a) After receiving the sequence, each Bob_i returns the number of received qubits to Alice. If the number is $m+l$, Alice goes to the next step; or else, she terminates the scheme.

(b) Alice randomly chooses a subset with length l in S_1 for eavesdropping detection. She publishes the positions of these chosen sampling qubits. Then each Bob_i measures the corresponding qubits in S_i in the X basis or the Y basis randomly. After that, Bob_i declares his measurement outcomes to Alice (the measurement bases are not included). When all participants finish their declarations, they declare their measurement bases in a reverse order. For example, Bob_2 declares his measurement outcome at first while he declares his measurement basis at last, and so on. According to all of Bob_i's measurement bases, Alice chooses the right bases to measure the sample qubits in S_1. That is, if the number of all of Bob_i's selections for the Y basis is even in one position, Alice then chooses the X basis; otherwise, she chooses the Y basis. Here, Alice can evaluate whether the error rate is normal. If the error exceeds a certain threshold, she aborts the scheme; otherwise, continues.

Step3. Secret splitting

(a) Each Bob$_i$ deletes the sampling qubits in S_i and measures the rest of the m qubits in the X or the Y basis randomly. The measurement results will be in $\{|x_+\rangle, |x_-\rangle, |y_+\rangle, |y_-\rangle\}$, where $|x_+\rangle$ and $|y_+\rangle$ are denoted as 0 while $|x_-\rangle$ and $|y_-\rangle$ are denoted as 1. Bob records his measurement outcomes as $b_j^{(i)}$, where $b_j^{(i)} \in \{0, 1\}$ with $i \in \{2, 3, \ldots, n\}, j \in \{1, 2, \ldots, m\}$.

(b) Bob$_i$ announces his measurement bases to Alice and the declaring order is random for every player. Then, Alice measures qubits in S_1 and the measurement basis is chosen according to all of Bob$_i$'s measurement bases. Suppose the number of Bob$_i$ for selecting the Y basis is B_y, then Alice chooses the X basis if B_y is even, while she chooses Y if B_y is odd. Besides, if B_y is divisible by 4 ($B_y \mod 4 \equiv 0$), Alice encodes the two sets of measurement results $\{|x_+\rangle, |y_+\rangle\}$ and $\{|x_-\rangle, |y_-\rangle\}$ into 0 and 1, respectively. Otherwise, she encodes $\{|x_+\rangle, |y_+\rangle\}$ and $\{|x_-\rangle, |y_-\rangle\}$ into 1 and 0. Alice records her measurement outcomes as a where $a_j \in \{0, 1\}$ with $j \in \{1, 2, \ldots, m\}$.

Step 4. Secret recovery

(a) After the execution of the above processing, an m-bit string a created by Alice has been shared among all of participants Bob$_i$ in such a way that

$$a = \bigoplus_{i=2}^{n} b^{(i)}, \tag{4}$$

where $a = \{a_1, a_2, \ldots a_m\}$, and $b^{(i)} = \{b_1^{(i)}, b_2^{(i)}, \ldots b_m^{(i)}\}$ denotes Bob$_i$'s m-bit share, with $i \in \{2, \ldots, n\}$. For each of Alice's secret bit, it has the following expression

$$a_j = \bigoplus_{i=2}^{n} b_j^{(i)}, \tag{5}$$

which is the summation module 2 of all of Bob$_i$'s share in related position. In this phase, all participant Bob$_i$ can cooperate to recover Alice's secret a, while any participants group less than $n - 1$ cannot get any useful information about a.

3 Improved High-Dimensional Multiparty QSS Scheme

In the section, we are going to extend our improved multiparty QSS scheme from two-dimensional system to high-dimensional quantum system, which is an improved version of the protocol in Ref. [26].

3.1 Preliminaries

In d-dimensional system, an n-qudit GHZ state can be written as

$$|\Phi(u_1, u_2, \ldots, u_n)\rangle = \frac{1}{\sqrt{d}} \sum_{j=0}^{d-1} \omega^{ju_1} |j, j + u_2, \ldots, j + u_n\rangle, \tag{6}$$

where $\omega = e^{2\pi i/d}$, $u_t \in \{0, 1, \ldots, d-1\}$ with $t \in \{1, 2, \ldots, n\}$, symbols "+" and "−" represent the adder and the subtractor modulo d, respectively.

As is noted in [26], one can construct d mutually biased bases (MBBs) in d-dimensional system. The d sets of MBBs have the form

$$|\Theta(H,h)\rangle = \frac{1}{\sqrt{d}}\sum_{j=0}^{d-1}\omega^{hj}|j\rangle + \frac{1}{\sqrt{d}}(\omega^{H}-1)|0\rangle, \tag{7}$$

where $H \in \{0, \ldots, d-1\}$ denotes the basis and $h \in \{0, \ldots, d-1\}$ indicates the vector in a given basis.

Suppose an n-qudit GHZ state in $|\Phi(0, 0, \ldots, 0)\rangle$ is shared among Alice and Bob_2, Bob_3, ..., Bob_n. If each participant Bob_i performs a single-qudit measurement in the basis labeled by B_i and obtains the outcome $|\Theta(B_i, b_i)\rangle$, then Alice's qudit will be

$$|\Theta(A,a)\rangle = (\langle\Theta(B_2,b_2)|\langle\Theta(B_3,b_3)|\cdots\langle\Theta(B_n,b_n)|)|\Phi(0,0,\ldots,0)\rangle, \tag{8}$$

which yields the following consistency conditions

$$A + B_2 + B_3 + \cdots + B_n \equiv 0 \pmod{d}, \tag{9}$$

$$a + b_2 + b_3 + \cdots + b_n \equiv 0 \pmod{d}. \tag{10}$$

The above conditions can be used for eavesdropping detection and secret splitting in d-dimensional system. That is, after receiving the measurement outcomes from every Bob_i, Alice selects the right basis $|\Theta(A, h)\rangle$ to measure her qudit according to (9). Certainly, she will get the outcome a because of (10).

To increase the detection rate, another $d+1$ high-dimensional mutually unbiased bases (MUBs) [27,28] can be constructed if d is either an odd prime or any power of an odd prime. One of the bases is the computational basis $\{|j\rangle; j = 0, \ldots, d-1\}$ and the other d sets of MUBs are

$$|\Psi(H,h)\rangle = \frac{1}{\sqrt{d}}\sum_{j=0}^{d-1}\omega^{Hj^2+hj}|j\rangle, \tag{11}$$

where $H \in \{1, \ldots, d\}$ and $h \in \{0, \ldots, d-1\}$. These bases are mutually unbiased since $|\langle\Psi(H,h)|\Psi(H',h')\rangle| = \frac{1}{\sqrt{d}}$, for $H \neq H'$. Similarly, if Bob_i measures his qudit and gets the outcome $|\Psi(B_i, b_i)\rangle$, we obtain

$$|\Psi(A,a)\rangle = (\langle\Psi(B_2,b_2)|\langle\Psi(B_3,b_3)|\cdots\langle\Psi(B_n,b_n)|)|\Phi(0,0,\ldots,0)\rangle. \tag{12}$$

This then yields the same consistency conditions (9) and (10) for a valid measurement as for MUBs, and they can also be used for eavesdropping detection and secret splitting.

3.2 The Scheme

Our improved multiparty QSS scheme in high-dimensional system can be described as follows.

Step 1. Resources preparation and distribution

(a) Alice prepares a sequence of n-qudit high-dimensional GHZ state in

$$|\Phi(0,0,\ldots,0)\rangle = \frac{1}{\sqrt{d}}\sum_{j=0}^{d-1}|j,j,\ldots,j\rangle, \tag{13}$$

with length $m+l$. The sequence is denoted as

$$S = \{P_1(1,2,\ldots,n), P_2(1,2,\ldots,n),\ldots,P_{m+l}(1,2,\ldots,n)\}, \tag{14}$$

where the subscript labels the order of entangled state in the sequence.

(b) Alice divides the sequence into n subgroups

$$S_i = \{P_1(i), P_2(i),\ldots,P_{m+l}(i)\}, \tag{15}$$

with $i = 1,2,\ldots,n$. Then Alice sends S_i to Bob$_i$ for $i > 1$, while she keeps S_1.

Step 2. Eavesdropping detection

(a) Each Bob$_i$ returns the number of received qubits to Alice after receiving the sequence. Alice goes to the next step if the number is $m+l$; or else, she terminates the scheme.

(b) Alice randomly chooses a subset with length l in S_1 for eavesdropping detection. she publishes the positions of these chosen sampling qubits. Then Bob$_i$ measures the corresponding qubits in S_i in d MBBs (or $d+1$ MUBs for specific d) randomly and his measurement basis is denoted as B_i. After that, Bob$_i$ declares his measurement outcomes b_i to Alice. When all participants finish their announcements, they declare their measurement bases B_i in a reverse order. According to all of Bob$_i$'s measurement bases, Alice chooses the right bases to measure the sample qubits in S_1. That is, Alice's basis A should satisfy $A+\sum B_i \equiv 0 \pmod d$ in each position. She will get the outcome a because of (10). Here Alice can determine whether to abort the scheme based on the error rate.

Step 3. Secret splitting

(a) Each Bob$_i$ gets rid of the sampling qubits in S_i. Then he measures the rest of the m qubits in d MBBs (or $d+1$ MUBs) randomly and his measurement basis is denoted as B_i. Bob$_i$ records his measurement outcome as $b_j^{(i)}$, where $b_j^{(i)} \in \{0,1,\ldots,d-1\}$ with $i \in \{2,3,\ldots,n\}, j \in \{1,2,\ldots,m\}$.

(b) Bob$_i$ announces his measurement bases B_i to Alice and the declaring order is random for every position. Then, Alice measures qubits in S_1 and the measurement basis A is chosen according to all of Bob$_i$'s measurement bases such that $A + B_2 + B_3 + \cdots + B_n \equiv 0 \pmod d$. Alice records her measurement outcomes as a_j where $a_j \in \{0,1,\ldots,d-1\}$ with $j \in \{1,2,\ldots,m\}$.

Step 4. Secret recovery

(a) After the above processing, an m-dit string a has been shared among all of Bob_i such that

$$a \equiv (\sum_{i=2}^{n} b^{(i)}) \mod d, \tag{16}$$

where $a = \{a_1, a_2, \ldots a_m\}$, $b^{(i)} = \{b_1^{(i)}, b_2^{(i)}, \ldots b_m^{(i)}\}$ with $i \in \{2, \ldots, n\}$ denotes the participant Bob_i's m-dit share. For each dit, we have $a_j \equiv (\sum_{i=2}^{n} b_j^{(i)}) \mod d$. Still, all participant Bob_i can cooperate to recover Alice's secret a, while any participants group less than $n-1$ cannot get any useful information about a.

4 Discussions and Conclusions

Our improved QSS schemes are secure against both the outside attacker and dishonest participants. These schemes are the improved version of Refs. [25,26], respectively. The security issues of GHZ based QSS schemes have also been discussed extensively in Refs. [17,25,26,29,30]. And the security of these schemes are guaranteed by the entanglement correlations of the GHZ states. Neither the outside attacker nor the dishonest participants can break the security requirements of the QSS schemes.

The comparisons of the proposed schemes and existing schemes are shown in Table 1. In Ref. [25], two methods were proposed to increase the efficiency of multiparty QSS scheme. Their first method, the favored-measuring-basis (FMB), uses a higher probability to choose Y basis than X basis. Since each participant chooses the X basis with a large probability than the Y basis, the security detection efficiency of the scheme will be affected. While the second method, the measuring-basis-encrypted (MBE), uses a shared key among participants to decide which measurement basis each participant will choose. Additional n-control keys are needed to control the valid choices of measuring bases for the n participants.

Table 1. Comparisons of existing schemes to ours.

	Ref. [17]	Ref. [25]	Ref. [26]	Ours
Dimension	2	2	d	$2, d$
Players	Three-party	Multiparty	Multiparty	Multiparty
Efficiency	50%	≈100%	$\frac{1}{d}$	100%
Methods	-	FMB/MBE	-	Measurement-delay

To improve the efficiency of GHZ based QSS scheme, we have introduced a measurement-delay strategy in the dealer Alice's side. In eavesdropping detection and secret splitting procedures of each improved scheme, instead of performs measurement independently, the dealer Alice measures her participles until she has received all of the participants' measurement bases, which means she can always select the right basis. But each participant's measurement bases is independent of each other, so their secret share is still independent. Compared with Ref. [25], our method is simpler and more effective. It will not affect the security detection efficiency, while no pre-shared control key is required.

In summary, we have proposed a series of efficient QSS schemes in multiparty circumstance and high-dimensional system. Our schemes have the following features. For one thing, compared with some previous QSS schemes such as HBB-QSS [17], the proposed scheme has 100% efficiency since the dealer Alice can always select the right measurement bases and every GHZ state can be used for security detection and secret distribution. For another, our schemes are simpler since no per-shared key [25] or different probability parameter is required. With the development of current technologies [31–34], these schemes can be experimentally implemented in the near future.

Acknowledgments. This project was supported by NSFC (Grant Nos. 61601358, 61373131).

References

1. Shor, P.W.: Polynomial-time algorithms for prime factorization and discrete logarithms on a quantum computer. SIAM J. Comput. **26**(5), 1484–1509 (1997)
2. Grover, L.K.: Quantum mechanics helps in searching for a needle in a haystack. Phys. Rev. Lett. **79**(2), 325 (1997)
3. Bennett, C.H., Brassard, G.: Quantum cryptography: public key distribution and coin tossing. In: Proceedings of IEEE International Conference on Computers Systems and Signal Processing, pp. 175–179. IEEE, New York (1984)
4. Bennett, C.H., Brassard, G., Crepeau, C., Jozsa, R., Peres, A., Wootters, W.K.: Teleporting an unknown quantum state via dual classical and einstein-podolsky-rosen channels. Phys. Rev. Lett. **70**(13), 1895–1899 (1993)
5. Gisin, N., Ribordy, G., Tittel, W., Zbinden, H.: Quantum cryptography. Rev. Mod. Phys. **74**, 145–195 (2002)
6. Ekert, A.K.: Quantum cryptography based on Bell's theorem. Phys. Rev. Lett. **67**(6), 661–663 (1991)
7. Scarani, V., Acin, A., Ribordy, G., Gisin, N.: Quantum cryptography protocols robust against photon number splitting attacks for weak laser pulse implementations. Phys. Rev. Lett. **92**(5) (2004). https://doi.org/10.1103/PhysRevLett.92.057901
8. Boström, K., Felbinger, T.: Deterministic secure direct communication using entanglement. Phys. Rev. Lett. **89**(18) (2002). https://doi.org/10.1103/PhysRevLett.89.187902
9. Deng, F.G., Long, G.L., Liu, X.S.: Two-step quantum direct communication protocol using the Einstein-Podolsky-Rosen pair block. Phys. Rev. A **68**(4) (2003). https://doi.org/10.1103/PhysRevA.68.042317
10. Gong, L.H., Liu, Y., Zhou, N.R.: Novel quantum virtual private network scheme for PON via quantum secure direct communication. Int. J. Theor. Phys. **52**(9), 3260–3268 (2013)
11. Gottesman, D., Chuang, I.: Quantum digital signatures, arXiv (2001). arXiv:quant-ph/0105032

12. Wang, M.M., Chen, X.B., Yang, Y.X.: A blind quantum signature protocol using the GHZ states. Sci. China Phys. Mech. Astron. **56**(9), 1636 (2013)
13. Terhal, B.M., DiVincenzo, D.P., Leung, D.W.: Hiding bits in Bell states. Phys. Rev. Lett. **86**(25), 5807 (2001)
14. Qu, Z.G., Chen, X.B., Zhou, X.J., Niu, X.X., Yang, Y.X.: Novel quantum steganography with large payload. Opt. Commun. **283**(23), 4782–4786 (2010)
15. Blakley, G.R.: Safeguarding cryptographic key. In: Proceedings of the 1979 AFIPS National Computer Conference, pp. 313–317, AFIPS Press, Montvale (1979)
16. Shamir, A.: How to share a secret. Commun. ACM **22**(11), 612 (1979)
17. Hillery, M., Bužek, V., Berthiaume, A.: Quantum secret sharing. Phys. Rev. A **59**(3), 1829 (1999)
18. Wang, M.M., Chen, X.B., Chen, J.G., Yang, Y.X.: Quantum state sharing of arbitrary known multi-qubit and multi-qudit states. Int. J. Quantum Inf. **12**(03) (2014). https://doi.org/10.1142/S0219749914500142
19. Wang, M.M., Chen, X.B., Yang, Y.X.: Comment on "high-dimensional deterministic multiparty quantum secret sharing without unitary operations.". Quantum Inf. Process. **12**(2), 785–792 (2013)
20. Guo, G.P., Guo, G.C.: Quantum secret sharing without entanglement. Phys. Lett. A **310**(4), 247–251 (2003)
21. Zhang, Z.J., Li, Y., Man, Z.X.: Multiparty quantum secret sharing. Phys. Rev. A **71**(4) (2005). https://doi.org/10.1103/PhysRevA.71.044301
22. Cleve, R., Gottesman, D., Lo, H.K.: How to share a quantum secret. Phys. Rev. Lett. **83**(3), 648–651 (1999)
23. Gottesman, D.: Theory of quantum secret sharing. Phys. Rev. A **61**(4) (2000). https://doi.org/10.1103/PhysRevA.61.042311
24. Lance, A.M., Symul, T., Bowen, W.P., Sanders, B.C., Lam, P.K.: Tripartite quantum state sharing. Phys. Rev. Lett. **92**(17) (2004). https://doi.org/10.1103/PhysRevLett.92.177903
25. Xiao, L., Long, G.L., Deng, F.G., Pan, J.W.: Efficient multiparty quantum-secret-sharing schemes. Phys. Rev. A **69**(5) (2004). https://doi.org/10.1103/PhysRevA.69.052307
26. Yu, I.C., Lin, F.L., Huang, C.Y.: Quantum secret sharing with multilevel mutually (un) biased bases. Phys. Rev. A **78**, 12344–12348 (2008)
27. Wootters, W.K., Fields, B.D.: Optimal state-determination by mutually unbiased measurements. Ann. Phys. **191**(2), 363–381 (1989)
28. Pittenger, A.O., Rubin, M.H.: Mutually unbiased bases, generalized spin matrices and separability. Linear Algebra Appl. **390**, 255–278 (2004)
29. Karlsson, A., Koashi, M., Imoto, N.: Quantum entanglement for secret sharing and secret splitting. Phys. Rev. A **59**(1), 162–168 (1999)
30. Qin, S.J., Gao, F., Wen, Q.Y., Zhu, F.C.: Cryptanalysis of the Hillery-Buzcaronek-Berthiaume quantum secret-sharing protocol. Phys. Rev. A **76**(6) (2007). https://doi.org/10.1103/PhysRevA.76.062324
31. Tittel, W., Zbinden, H., Gisin, N.: Experimental demonstration of quantum secret sharing. Phys. Rev. A **63**(4) (2001). https://doi.org/10.1103/PhysRevA.63.042301
32. Chen, Y.A., et al.: Experimental quantum secret sharing and third-man quantum cryptography. Phys. Rev. Lett. **95**(20) (2005). https://doi.org/10.1103/PhysRevLett.95.200502
33. Lvovsky, A.I., Sanders, B.C., Tittel, W.: Optical quantum memory. Nature Photonics **3**(12), 706–714 (2009)
34. Dai, H.N., et al.: Holographic storage of biphoton entanglement. Phys. Rev. Lett. **108**(21) (2012). https://doi.org/10.1103/PhysRevLett.108.210501

EkCRNN: A kNN Privacy Preserving Query Algorithm Based on Circular Region Extension

Honghao Zhou[1], Tinghuai Ma[1,2(✉)], Jing Jia[1], Yuan Tian[3], and Mznah Al-Rodhaan[3]

[1] School of Computer Software, Nanjing University of Information Science and Technology, Nanjing 210-044, Jiangsu, China
thma@nuist.edu.cn

[2] CICAEET, Jiangsu Engineering Centre of Network Monitoring, Nanjing University of Information Science and Technology, Nanjing 210-044, Jiangsu, China

[3] Computer Science Department, College of Computer and Information Sciences, KingSaud University, Riyadh 11362, Saudi Arabia

Abstract. In location based services, users can request interesting services around them at any time and anywhere through mobile devices. They need to send their locations to get the service, which may cause the disclosure of their location privacy. In order to protect the location privacy, a typical way is to convert the specific location into a location area. After finding the interest points around the region, the server needs to refine the result set to get the exact result of the query. In this article, we extended the existing kNN query algorithm based on the circular region, and proposed an algorithm called EkCRNN. This algorithm used an anonymous server to exchange information between the user and the LBS server. We compared two algorithms through experiments, and the experimental results show that our algorithm has higher accuracy.

Keywords: Location privacy protection · LBS · Circular region

1 Introduction

With the rapid development of the mobile Internet technology, mobile users are paying more and more attention to location-based service (LBS) [2,5,7,19]. By providing their own location to the server, the users can query their surroundings such as restaurants in the vicinity, gas stations, etc. However, LBS brings us benefits as well as troubles. It is argued that the leakage of position information may cause the path leakage, which leads to the release of sensitive information. Privacy leakage has restrained the development of LBS to a certain extent. Therefore, how to protect location privacy of mobile users while using LBS is a current research hot spot [11–13,15,20].

Location Cloaking technology [1,14,17,18] is a typical way to protect user location privacy. It can transform real user location into a location region, which

X. Sun et al. (Eds.): ICCCS 2018, LNCS 11065, pp. 32–43, 2018.
https://doi.org/10.1007/978-3-030-00012-7_4

will be sent to the server. The LBS server then figures out the users in this region and returns a result set to the user. Finally, the user can find the nearest one from the result set according to his real location. Figure 1 describes an example of a one nearest neighbor query. The user a sends the confusion area R to the server, and the server returns the target set b,c,d to the user. The user a finds the closest point c to him according to his real position. In this process, the server only knows the area R where the user is located.

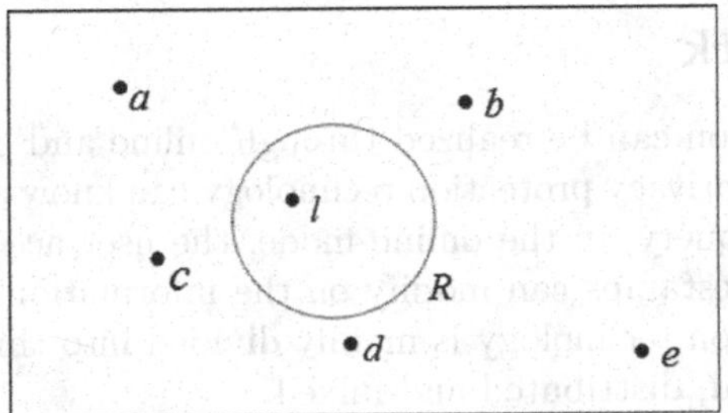

Fig. 1. Location Cloaking

In order to reduce the client bandwidth, researchers proposed a centralized structure on privacy protection. As is shown in Fig. 2, centralized structure consists of mobile terminals, trusted anonymous server and LBS server. The user can send the query request through the mobile terminals and receive the final query result. The trusted anonymous server contains two modules, namely, anonymous processing module and query result refining module. The anonymous processing module processes the precise location sent by mobile terminal, then forwards to the LBS server; the query result refining module is capable of receiving the query candidate result set returned from LBS and refining the result set. After that the refined results are returned to the mobile terminal.

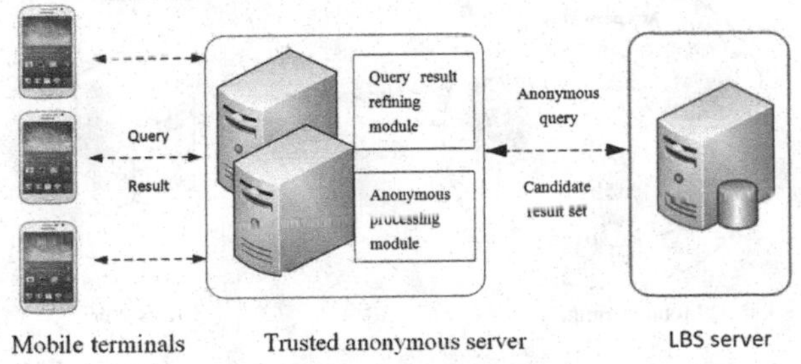

Fig. 2. Centralized structure

Researchers have proposed many algorithms for query request processing [3,6,9,25], while query results refining algorithms are relatively few. Therefore, a query refinement algorithm EkCRNN (the extended circular-region-based kNN) is proposed in this paper, which is an extension to the existing kNN query algorithm based on circular region. In general, the main contributions of the paper the EkCRNN algorithm which proposed to extend the existing kCRNN algorithm. These two algorithms are compared through experiments.

The first section introduces the research contents of the paper; the second section summarizes the related work; the third section introduces our algorithm and gives the experiment.

2 Related Work

LBS privacy protection can be realized through online and offline architectures [22]: in offline mode, privacy protection technology can know all spatial-temporal information of LBS query; in the online mode, the user accessing to new locations in different timestamps can modify on the information of LBS query [21]. LBS privacy protection technology is mainly divided into three kinds of system structures: centralized, distributed and mixed.

The centralized structure knows the overall information of users. The effect of privacy protection is better, and the communication cost between the mobile terminal and the anonymous server is also relatively small. But there are also some disadvantages: anonymous server will become the key point of attack and the system performance bottleneck. In reality, a trusted anonymous server with large number of user information is hard to deploy.

The distributed structure consists of mobile terminals and LBS server, such as Fig. 3. The advantage of the distributed structure is that it removes the bottleneck of the system, and shows better effects on privacy protection. But there are also some disadvantages: greatly increased the computational cost and communication cost of the mobile terminal may be the first. In addition, when the number of users are no enough, it will be difficult to complete the process of anonymous.

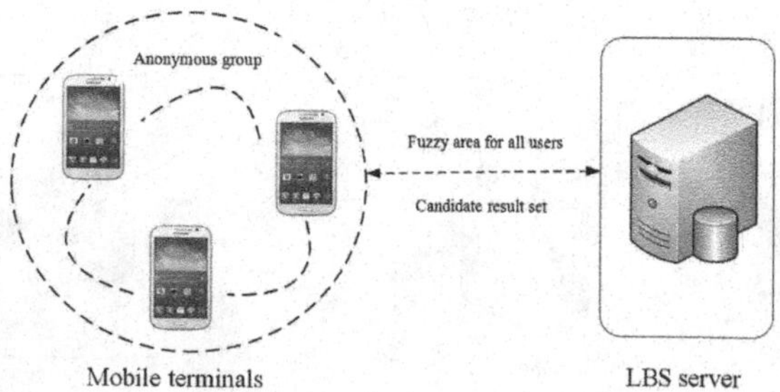

Fig. 3. Distributed structure

A hybrid structure is also made up of mobile terminals, trusted anonymous servers, and LBS servers, as Fig. 4. The anonymous server knows all the information of the users' locations, identities, service requests. The advantages of hybrid structure with centralized and distributed structure is that it can better balance the load between the client and the anonymous server. The server can reduce the anonymous side load caused by the large number of mobile terminal location update. In the case of sparse distribution of users, it can still ensure the availability of services. But the shortcoming is that the system parameters are much more, so the setting and adjustment are very complex, which seriously affects the practicability of the system.

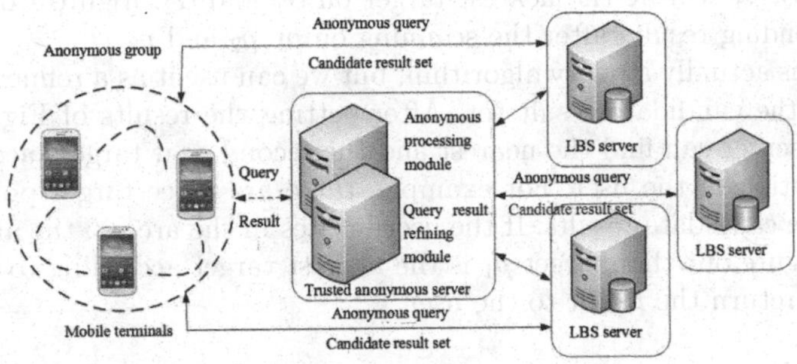

Fig. 4. Hybrid structure

For all of these structures, while received the confusing area of the request, the LBS server side needs to execute an kNN query algorithm to find the interest points. In this section, we will introduce some existing algorithms for querying interest points: the Voronois, the segmentation based method, the extension based method, the Hilbert curve.

Um et al. [23] proposed a kNN query algorithm based on the Voronois, which is used for rectangular area. This method divides the candidate set into several Voronois, and considers the set of Voronois that overlap the query rectangle as the result set (the interest area). On the other side, Panos et al. [8] proposed a circular kNN query algorithm (CkNN), which is used to calculate the interest points of the nearest neighbor in a circle. CkNN divides the circumference into intersecting arcs and finds the nearest k point targets for each segment of the arcs. Mokbel et al. [16] put forward a server side query processing algorithm called New Casper, which is a query algorithm for rectangular area. The algorithm extended the original rectangular area to a larger one as the candidate set. Khoshgozaran and Shahabi [10] proposed a method of NN query using Hilbert curve. Its main idea is to map all dynamic and static targets into another space by using a transformation, and then query in the converted space. Xu et al. [25] also proposed a circular kNN query algorithm (kCRNN). This algorithm can find out the closest, the second nearest target around the circular area. The main idea is to scan target points one by one. During every scan process, they kept the set of arcs for each target, which are the closest or second nearest target of the arc. Figure 5(a) provides an example for the 2CRNN query.

Assuming there are three target points p_1, p_2 and p_3 after the first scan on p_1, p_1 is the 1NN result of all points in the circle Ω. After scanning on p_2, the midnormal of p_1 and p_2 is divided Ω into two arcs α and β. Therefore, p_2 will replace p_1 to be the nearest target of all points on arc β, and p_1 will become the second near target on β and the nearest target on α. p_2 is the nearest target on β and the second near target on α. After scanning on p_3, the midnormals between p_1, p_2 and p_3 will divide α and β into $\alpha_1, \alpha_2, \alpha_3$ and $\beta_1, \beta_2, \beta_3$, respectively. At that time, p_3 will be the nearest target on α_3 and β_1, and the second near target on α_2 and β_2. p_1 will be the nearest target on α_1 and α_2. Figure 5(b) describe the corresponding results after the scanning on p_1, p_2 and p_3.

kCRNN is actually a query algorithm, but we can use it as a refine algorithm for refining the candidate result set. After getting the results of Fig. 5(b), the anonymous server can find the nearest and the second near targets according to the real location of the user. For example, there are three target points p_1, p_2 and p_3 in the candidate results. If the user locates in the arc α_1, the anonymous server can figure out that target p_1 is the nearest target according to the user's request and return the result to the user.

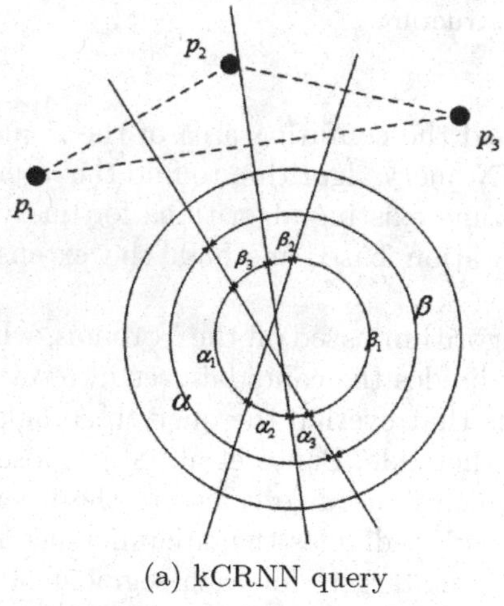

(a) kCRNN query

After scanning p1

	1NN	2NN
p1	Ω	

After scanning p2

	1NN	2NN
p1	α	β
p2	β	α

After scanning p3

	1NN	2NN
p1	α1,α2	α3,β3
p2	β2,β3	α1,β1
p3	α3,β1	α2,β2

(b) Query results

Fig. 5. kCRNN

3 Extended kCRNN Algorithm (EkCRNN)

The kCRNN only consider about the obtuse triangle which formed by three target points. In this section, we will extend it to adapt to acute triangle, quadrangle and even polygon with more targets. The procedures of EkCRNN for different targets are actually similar to the one on three targets.

3.1 Three Target Points

As is shown in Fig. 6, there are three target points p_1, p_2 and p_3 around the circular area Ω, and the three target points form a acute triangle. Finding out the midnormals of p_1, p_2 and p_3, these three lines will divide the circle Ω into six arcs $\alpha_1, \alpha_2, \alpha_3$ and β_1, β_2, β_3, respectively. At this point, to the corresponding area of arc α_1, the distances between the three target points can be represented as $p_1 < p_2 < p_3$. To the corresponding area of arc α_2, the distances between the three target points should be $p_1 < p_3 < p_2$. To the corresponding area of arc α_3, that is $p_3 < p_1 < p_2$. For arc β_1, β_2 and β_3, the distances between them seem to be $p_2 < p_1 < p_3, p_2 < p_3 < p_1$ and $p_3 < p_2 < p_1$, respectively.

The anonymous server gets these results through EkCRNN algorithm, and then finds the corresponding results according to the real user locations and the number of targets the user requested, and finally returns the results to the user. For example, the user is located in the area corresponding to arc α_2. He wants to find the two nearest neighbour target points around. The anonymous server can find the corresponding result set according to the result of EkCRNN algorithm, and then return the result set to the user.

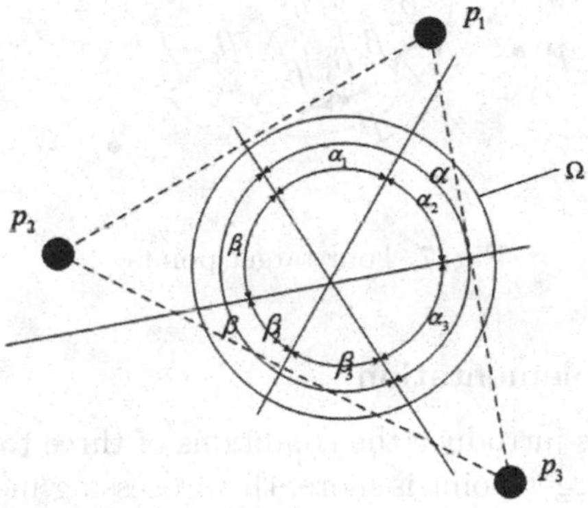

Fig. 6. Three target points

3.2 More Target Points

When the circular area Ω has four targets around, as shown in Fig. 7, the first midnormal divides the circle into two parts α and β. Subsequently, the four point scanning on p_3 and p_4 bring 12 arcs divided by the midnormals of these four points, respectively α_1 to α_5 and β_1 to β_7. For each section of the arc, we can compare the distance between each target point. For the area corresponding to the arc $\alpha_1, p_1 < p_2 < p_4 < p_3$. For the area corresponding to the arc $\beta_1, p_2 < p_1 < p_4 < p_3$. For the area corresponding to the arc $\beta_7, p_4 < p_3 < p_2 < p_1$. The anonymous server can find the target that meets the user's requirements according to the results of the algorithm and the real location of the user, and return it to the user. If the user is in the area corresponding to β_3 and wants for the nearest three target points around it, the anonymous server will return p_2, p_3 and p_1.

When there are multiple target points around the circular area Ω, similar to the above two kinds of circumstances, we first find all the midnormals formed by these targets. These lines then divide the circle into several arcs, which have their own nearest and second near target points. The anonymous server decides which arc the user belongs to according to the real location of the user, then gets the nearest k neighbor target point corresponding to the arcs, and finally finds the corresponding target point to return to the user according to the user's query request.

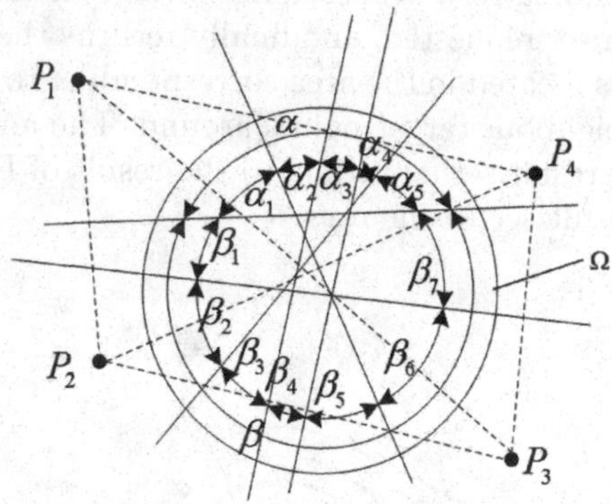

Fig. 7. Four target points

3.3 Algorithm Implementation

The above two sections introduce the conditions of three target points and four target points. If the target point is more, the processing method is actually the same as the three target points. In general, when a target point p_i is scanned, we assume that p_i is even further away from the arc than all the results in the candidate set. The (p_i, p_j) pair is checked, in which p_j is from the candidate result set. For a point p_j, the midnormal of p_i and p_j have two points with the current arcs. For each arc in the side with p_i of the midnormal, the position of p_j in the kNN candidate list will be decreased (for example, change from the second nearest into the third). The position of p_i will go forward (for example, the third near into the second). The final kCRNN results of the circle Ω will be obtained by scanning all the targets. The result of the kCRNN query also includes all the target objects in the circular area. So when the objects are scanned, the algorithm also needs to check whether they are in the circular area, and if so, they are added to the final kCRNN results.

In order to speed up the convergence rate of kCRNN candidate sets, we sort the objects and apply Theorem 1 to scan the nearest objects of Ω, which is most likely to appear in the final kCRNN results.

Theorem 1. *The target is sorted and scanned according to its minimum distance from the circle Ω. It does not scan those whose minimum distance from Ω is $2r$ (r is the radius of the circle Ω) farther than the kth nearest target point.*

According to Theorem 1, we can get a terminating condition for the query: stop scanning when the minimum distance of the target point distance is $2r$ farther than the kth nearest target point. Algorithm 1 describes the specific processes of the EkCRNN algorithm. The target points are sorted ascendingly according to the minimum distance to the circle Ω. Firstly, the first target p_1 is scanned and then the next target p_i in accordance with the order of the queue scanning target. Secondly, if p_i is in the circle, it will be added to the result set. If it is outside the circle, we will have to find out the midnormals, which divides circular area into several arcs. Each arc corresponds to a target point. This process will continue until enough target points are found or the minimum distance from the circle of the target point of the next scan is $2r$ farther than the kth nearest target point.

Next, we analyzed the complexity of the algorithm. For a kCRNN query with M single objects, the while loop traverses at most M times. Each scan increases 2M arcs at most, so that the number of arcs of all candidate kCRNN results set is limited to $O(M^2)$. Each arc can appear at most k objects in the arc group. Therefore, the worst storage complexity is $O(kM^2)$. For time complexity, each $\Phi(p_i, \widehat{ab})$ is updated at most M times in each scan, and the worst case is $O(kM^3)$. Fortunately, the worst case rarely occurs because the kCRNN candidate result set is not very large, and we have already set the terminating condition.

3.4 Experimental Analysis

We used a test bed [4] to evaluate the EkCRNN algorithm. We run our experiments on RAM 2GByte and GPU 2.66 GHz computers. We assume that the user side and the server side communicate through the wireless network at the rate of 110 kbps. In the experiment, we use a real set of data, which contains the location data of 104857 targets.

In this paper, we compare the performance of our EkCRNN algorithm and the PkCRNN algorithm in the literature [6]. EkCRNN forms a kCRNN candidate after the end of the query, while PkCRNN judges whether it can become a candidate result set in the query process. That is to say, after each scan, the LBS server will return the result to the user. Figure 8 shows the result of the comparison of the response time of the two algorithms on the user side. We can see that the corresponding time of the two algorithms is almost the same when k or r (the radius of the circle Ω) is relatively small. However, when they become larger, PkCRNN is obviously better than our EkCRNN. This is because PkCRNN returns the result to the user after each scan, and the EkCRNN will return the result set to the user after scanning all the target points. Figure 9 shows the comparison of the accuracy of the results of the two algorithms. We use the utilization of query results to measure the accuracy of the algorithm results. The higher the utilization rate is, the more accurate the algorithm is.

Algorithm 1. EkCRNN

Input: the circle Ω, the radius r and the target set S
Output: the nearest k targets of Ω
Sort the target points in S according to their minimum distances to Ω, represented by $minDist(p_i, \Omega)$;
Pop the first target p_1;
$\Phi(p_i, \widehat{ab})$ represents the distance between target point p_i and arc $\widehat{ab}$;
$max\_KNN\_dist = \infty$;
$cand\_kCRNN\_results = \{p_1\}$;
Pop the next target p_i;
do
  if p_i *is in* Ω **then**
    $in\_circle\_results = in\_cirlcle\_results \cup p_i$;
  initialize each arc $\widehat{ab} : \Phi(p_i, \widehat{ab}) = |cand\_kCRNN\_results| + 1$;
  for *each point* p_j *in* $cand\_kCRNN\_results$ **do**
    divide each arc by $\perp p_i p_j$;
    for *for each arc* $\widehat{ab}$ *at the side of* p_i **do**
      if $\Phi(p_j, \widehat{ab})$ *exist* **then**
        $\Phi(p_j, \widehat{ab}) + +$;
      $\Phi(p_i, \widehat{ab}) - -$;
    end
  end
  S stores the set of scanned targets $cand\_kCRNN\_results = \{p | p \in S, \exists anarc\widehat{ab}, \Phi(p, \widehat{ab}) \leq k\}$;
  remove the entity whose $\Phi(p, \widehat{ab}) > k, p \in S$;
  if $i = k$ **then**
    $max\_kNN\_dist = minDist(p_i, \Omega)$;
  pop the next target p_i;
while $minDist(p_i, \Omega) < 2r + max\_kNN\_dist$;
return The final results: $in\_circle\_results \cup cand\_KNN\_results$;

From Fig. 9(a) and (b), we can see that the results of EkCRNN are obviously more accurate. The purpose of our algorithm is to find the corresponding target points of each arc, and then find the result points by the server according to the arcs corresponding to the real positions of the user.

4 Summary

In this article, we gives the candidate results set refining algorithm at the anonymous server side. We proposed an extented kCRNN algorithm, in which the anonymous server can find the target points that meet the user's needs according to the query request, the real location and the algorithm. We also verify the performance of the algorithm by experiments. How to reduce response time

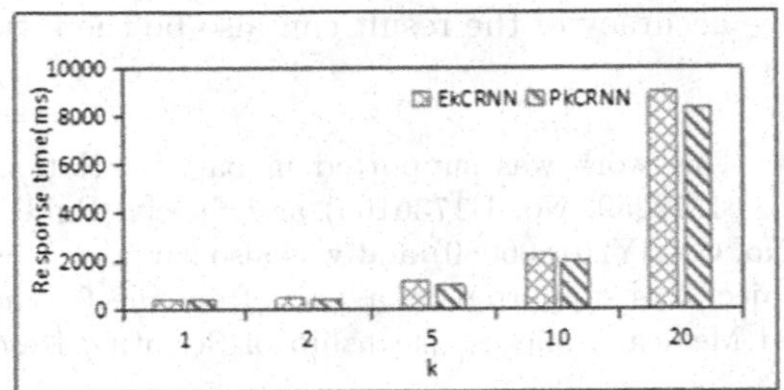

(a) Response time to different number of query targets

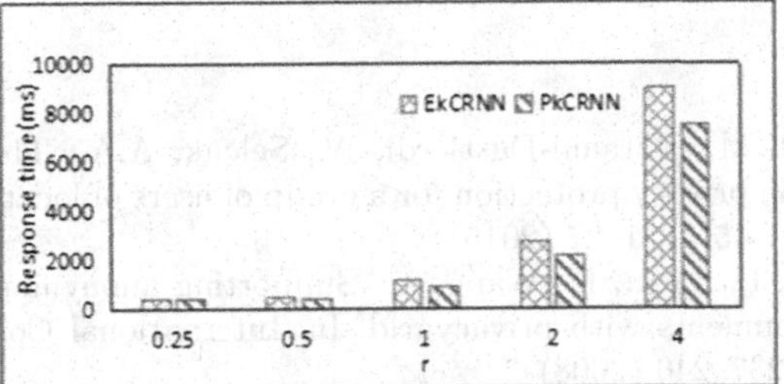

(b) Response time of the circular area with different sizes

Fig. 8. Response time contrast diagram of two algorithms

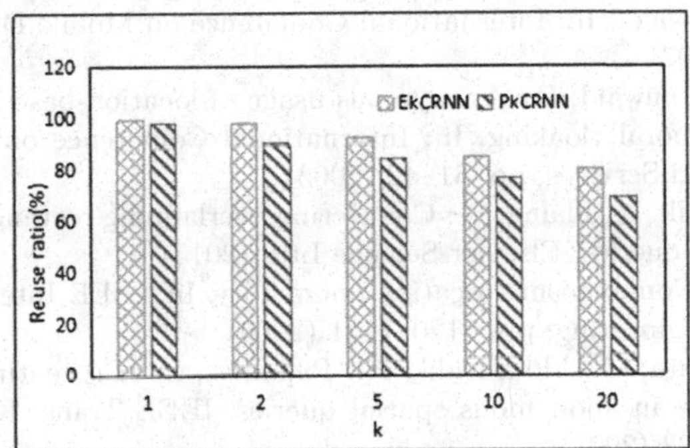

(a) Query result utilization under different query target number

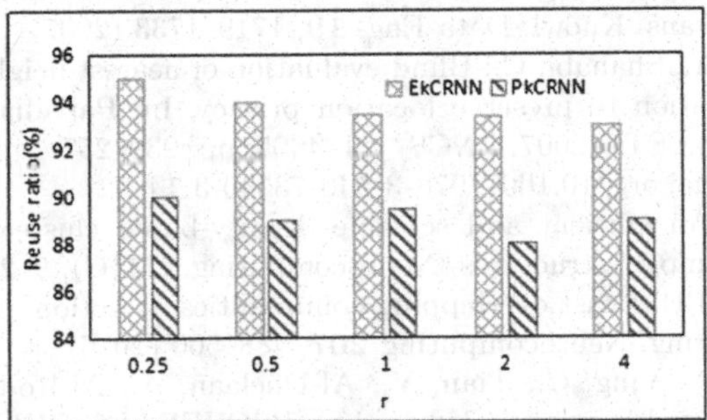

(b) Query result utilization under different size of circular areas

Fig. 9. Query result utilization contrast diagram of two algorithms

without reducing the accuracy of the result can also be the future research content.

Acknowledgement. This work was supported in part by National Science Foundation of China (No. 61572259, No. U1736105) and Special Public Sector Research Program of China (No. GYHY201506080) and was also supported by PAPD.

This research project was supported by a grant from the Research Center of the Female Scientific and Medical Colleges, Deanship of Scientific Research, King Saud University.

References

1. Ashouri-Talouki, M., Baraani-Dastjerdi, A., Selçuk, A.A.: The cloaked-centroid protocol: location privacy protection for a group of users of location-based services. Knowl. Inf. Syst. **45**(3), 1–27 (2015)
2. Bamba, B., Liu, L., Pesti, P., Wang, T.: Supporting anonymous location queries in mobile environments with privacygrid. In: International Conference on World Wide Web, pp. 237–246 (2008)
3. Chow, C.Y., Mokbel, M.F., Aref, W.G.: Casper*: query processing for location services without compromising privacy. ACM Trans. Database Syst. **34**(4), 1–48 (2009)
4. Du, J., Xu, J., Tang, X., Hu, H.: iPDA: supporting privacy-preserving location-based mobile services. In: International Conference on Mobile Data Management, pp. 212–214 (2007)
5. Gruteser, M., Grunwald, D.: Anonymous usage of location-based services through spatial and temporal cloaking. In: International Conference on Mobile Systems, Applications, and Services, pp. 31–42 (2003)
6. Hashem, T., Kulik, L., Zhang, R.: Countering overlapping rectangle privacy attack for moving kNN queries. Elsevier Science Ltd. (2013)
7. Hu, H., Xu, J.: Non-exposure location anonymity. In: IEEE International Conference on Data Engineering, pp. 1120–1131 (2009)
8. Kalnis, P., Ghinita, G., Mouratidis, K., Papadias, D.: Preventing location-based identity inference in anonymous spatial queries. IEEE Trans. Knowl. Data Eng. **19**(12), 1719–1733 (2007)
9. Kalnis, P., et al.: Preventing location-based identity inference in anonymous spatial queries. IEEE Trans. Knowl. Data Eng. **19**, 1719–1733 (2007)
10. Khoshgozaran, A., Shahabi, C.: Blind evaluation of nearest neighbor queries using space transformation to preserve location privacy. In: Papadias, D., Zhang, D., Kollios, G. (eds.) SSTD 2007. LNCS, vol. 4605, pp. 239–257. Springer, Heidelberg (2007). https://doi.org/10.1007/978-3-540-73540-3_14
11. Lv, Y., et al.: An efficient and scalable density-based clustering algorithm for datasets with complex structures. Neurocomputing **171**(C), 9–22 (2016)
12. Ma, T., et al.: LED: a fast overlapping communities detection algorithm based on structural clustering. Neurocomputing **207**, 488–500 (2016)
13. Ma, T., Ying, C., Ying, C., Tian, Y., Al-Dhelaan, A., Al-Rodhaan, M.: Detect structural-connected communities based on BSCHEF in C-DBLP. Concurr. Comput. Pract. Exp. **28**(2), 311–330 (2016)
14. Ma, T., et al.: KDVEM: a k-degree anonymity with vertex and edge modification algorithm. Computing **97**(12), 1165–1184 (2015)

15. Ma, T., et al.: Social network and tag sources based augmenting collaborative recommender system. IEICE Trans. Inf. Syst. **98**(4), 902–910 (2015)
16. Mokbel, M.F., Chow, C.Y., Aref, W.G.: The new Casper: query processing for location services without compromising privacy. In: International Conference on Very Large Data Bases, pp. 763–774 (2006)
17. Niu, B., Zhu, X., Li, Q., Chen, J., Li, H.: A novel attack to spatial cloaking schemes in location-based services. Future Gener. Comput. Syst. **49**(C), 125–132 (2015)
18. Niu, B., Zhu, X., Li, W., Li, H., Wang, Y., Lu, Z.: A personalized two-tier cloaking scheme for privacy-aware location-based services. In: International Conference on Computing, Networking and Communications, pp. 94–98 (2015)
19. Pan, X., Xu, J., Meng, X.: Protecting location privacy against location-dependent attack in mobile services. In: ACM Conference on Information and Knowledge Management, pp. 1475–1476 (2008)
20. Rong, H., Ma, T., Tang, M., Cao, J.: A novel subgraph k^{+}-isomorphism method in social network based on graph similarity detection. Soft Comput. **22**(8), 2583–2601 (2018)
21. Shokri, R., Theodorakopoulos, G., Le Boudec, J.Y., Hubaux, J.P.: Quantifying location privacy. In: Security and Privacy, pp. 247–262 (2011)
22. Stenneth, L., Yu, P.S., Wolfson, O.: Mobile systems location privacy: MobiPriv a robust k anonymous system. In: IEEE International Conference on Wireless and Mobile Computing, Networking and Communications, pp. 54–63 (2010)
23. Um, J.H., Kim, Y.K., Lee, H.J., Jang, M., Chang, J.W.: k-Nearest neighbor query processing algorithm for cloaking regions towards user privacy protection in location-based services. J. Syst. Archit. **58**(9), 354–371 (2012)
24. Wang, H.S., Zhou, H.Y.: Development of tourism geographic information system based on Baidu map API. Mod. Comput. **23**, 16 (2012)
25. Xu, J., Tang, X., Hu, H., Du, J.: Privacy-conscious location-based queries in mobile environments. IEEE Trans. Parallel Distrib. Syst. **21**(3), 313–326 (2010)

Fast Detection of Heavy Hitters in Software Defined Networking Using an Adaptive and Learning Method

Zhiliang Wang[1](✉), Changping Zhou[1], Yang Yu[2], Xingang Shi[1], Xia Yin[2], and Jiangyuan Yao[3]

[1] Institute for the Network Sciences and Cyberspace, Tsinghua University, Beijing, China
wzl@cernet.edu.cn

[2] Department of Computer Science and Technology, Tsinghua University, Beijing, China

[3] College of Information Science and Technology, Hainan University, Haikou, China

Abstract. Heavy Hitters refer to the set of flows that represent a significantly large proportion of the link capacity or of the active traffic. Identifying Heavy Hitters is of particular importance in both network management and security applications. Traditional methods are focusing on sampling in the middle box and analyzing those packets using streaming algorithms. The paradigm of Software Defined Network (SDN) simplifies the work of flow counting. However, continuously monitoring the network will introduce overhead, which needs to be considered as a tradeoff between accurate measurement in real-time. In this paper, We propose a novel method that stamps each suspicious flow with a weight based on an online learning algorithm. The granularity of measurement is dynamically changed according to the importance of each flow. We take advantage of history flows to make the procedure of finding a heavy hitter faster so that applications can make decisions instantly. Using real-world data, we show that our online learning method can detect heavy hitters faster with less overhead and the same accuracy.

Keywords: Software-defined-network · Heavy hitter · Online learning

1 Introduction

It is very critical for anomaly detectors [25] to identify network anomalies such as DDoS attacks, heavy hitters, port scan and worms in real-time with high precisions and take actions to adapt to those network changes in time. A heavy hitter (HH) [15,28] refers to the entities whose number of distinct network elements is at least a specific fraction of the total number of distinct network elements. A straightforward indicator for a HH is the flows whose volumes are larger than certain thresholds. With the development of the Internet, different kinds of applications bring huge scale and diversity of traffic, which makes it

X. Sun et al. (Eds.): ICCCS 2018, LNCS 11065, pp. 44–55, 2018.
https://doi.org/10.1007/978-3-030-00012-7_5

difficult for monitoring network activities and measuring network traffic. Identifying HHs in real-time has become significant for network applications such as traffic engineering and anomaly detection.

Traditional attempts usually adopt different streaming algorithms such as [9] based on summary structures to analyze network activities or sample the traffic randomly in the network routers to achieve a better overhead/accuracy balance. Despite the statistical methods in packet-sampling have been optimized to improve accuracy and reduce overhead, those approaches will still miss small flows and deployment cost is typically high. Whereas, collecting statistical data about network flows can be greatly simplified in SDN [6]. SDN is a breakthrough in both the academy and industry world and provides potential benefits to the network measurement. The control plane functions have been nicely decoupled from the data plane due to the SDN enabler, OpenFlow [3]. SDN switches can be purely used for monitoring purpose with separate wildcard rules installed, while SDN controller can pull flow statistics from any switch at any time by maintaining the global network view, which also simplifies the detection of HHs.

Although SDN introduces programmability to reduce the complexity of network measurement tasks, there still exists challenges. Firstly, all of the monitoring traffic flow information has to be forwarded to the controller, which is likely to result in a bandwidth bottleneck. Secondly, switches usually have relatively small TCAMs, whose resources are limited so the number of flow rules are under hard constraint. Tradeoff exists among real-time analysis and communication overhead between the switches and the controller. A measurement framework in SDN was proposed in [30] that measures large scale traffic aggregation in commodity switches by taking advantage of switches match packets against a small collection of wildcard rules available in TCAM. However, this sketch-based method requires an upgrade or replacement of all network nodes. Therefore, these methods not only increase the overhead in the network, but also cannot guarantee the timeliness of detection. In contrast, pull-based algorithms have been proposed in [8,11,27,32] which collect statistical data by querying switches without modifying data plane. Although they have some advantages, they still cannot guarantee the timeliness of detection. In [32], an adaptive flow collection method was proposed for anomaly detection. This approach can reduce overhead by allowing flexible specification of the spatial and temporal properties of counting units. However, in this method, large-stream data that has been measured is not used, so the detection effect is not optimal. In our opinion, it can be improved to identify the heavy hitter faster without loss of accuracy.

In this paper, we propose an approach to detect heavy hitters faster based on an online learning model. We make fully use of the collected flow information by recording them in the controller, and build an online learning model to track and measure the most suspicious traffic flows (i.e., a possibly potential heavy hitter) under different aggregation levels in order to deal with unknown network conditions. Flows are stamped for faster measurement than the others if they are deemed to be important. In order to guarantee the accuracy and reduce overhead, we do not sample packets in the data plane and make full use of control messages sent by switches.The main contributions of our paper are:

(1) We introduce an online learning model to label flows. The main goal is to identify the heavy flows timely.
(2) We implemented our architecture in the POX [4] and design a high-level RESTful API on top of existing Northbound Interface (NBI), which is the communication interface between the controller and applications. Additionally, We give the user access to defining initial parameters or selecting important flows based on their specific scenarios.
(3) Using real network traffic, we compare our techniques with the adaptive method in [32]. The experimental results show that our method reduces roughly 10% time to identity a heavy hitter in average without loss of accuracy and also reduce overhead.

The remainder of this paper is structured as follows. Related work is presented in Sect. 2. Section 3 presents our proposed learning techniques. Section 4 reports the performance evaluation of our mechanism using real network traffic. Conclusion is given in Sect. 5.

2 Related Work

Identifying heavy hitters has been studied in many previous works. Before the emergence of SDN, some sampling and analyzing tools are developed such as sFlow [5] and NetFlow [12]. They introduce less overhead than processing on each packet basis, however, the accuracy has been compromised due to the probability of missing small flows and the mechanism is typically implemented in a customized hardware. The efficiency of algorithms has been discussed in the work [14]. Additionally, optimization on both spatial and temporal has been studied to the streaming algorithm in the work [10,13,15,20].

The state-of-the-art in SDN has provided a relatively light-weight and easy way of monitoring flow statistics. According to whether changing the data plane or not, monitoring framework can be classified into two categories. As a typical representative of the first category, OpenSketch [30] reconfigured data plane using sketch and adopted the match-and-count algorithm to reduce overhead, and controller could periodically update these rules according to different configurations. [22] also studied the tradeoff to achieve a happy zone between the accuracy and the overhead. In [17,23], data plane is also changed to reduce overhead. In particular, progME [31] introduced the concept of FlowSet and provided a platform to measure any set of flows. All of those mechanism require ISPs making large investment to modify the commodity hardware.

To avoid modifying data plane, pull-based method is widely used to work with OpenFlow switches. Network flows are continuously monitored in [8,11,19,24,26,27], most of which sent requests to switches to attain accurate information of each flow. For example, OpenTM [26] selected the switch to query flow information based on a heuristic algorithm. An adaptive flow aggregation mechanism has been used in [11,32] for the purpose of anomaly detection, or providing a RESTful API of flow statistics. Although the accuracy is higher than the sampling method, the overhead is unavoidable. There is also a push-based design which performs monitoring only by using control messages sent from the switch. FlowSense [29] adopted this design and measured the network link utilization with zero overhead at discrete points in time, however, the long delay determines that it can not meet the real-time monitoring requirement.

There are also some work combining advantages of traditional methods and SDN methods. In the work [16], A mechanism was presented for online detection of bidimensional Hierarchical Heavy Hitters (HHHs) in networks based on OpenFlow switches. The collector is called by the controller every time a monitored prefix achieves the defined threshold and then a streaming approximation algorithm runs on top of it. It leverages port mirror in switches to exact measurement statistics of network flows. Identifying a heavy hitter can be faster but traffic volume may exceed the capacity of ports, causing the switch to drop packets.

Our work is inspired by the learning method proposed in [21], which used a (de)aggregation measurement mechanism to allow fine-grained or course-grained measurement tasks of incoming flows. Instead of modifying data plane, we propose an online learning method to label the obtained flow information and also stamp each flow according to its informative level. Our work also builds on top of the existing proposals of SDN [32] to identify heavy hitters using the pull-based design without changing the data plane.

3 Methodology

Identifying HHs timely is essential to many network monitoring or network security applications so that instant reactions could be made. Our method neither changes data plane, nor samples packets in switches. We leverage an online learning algorithm to speed up detecting HH. Leveraging the collected information, we find out informative flows and stamp each flow with an weight, so the controller can tell which aggregated flow is more suspicious and pay more attention to it by reducing the pulling time interval or dividing it into fine-grained aggregation in the following interactive rounds with the OpenFlow switches.

3.1 Overview

We design an online learning architecture served as an application in SDN as shown in Fig. 1. In general, there are four main parts: Switch Monitor, Learning Model, Flow Rule Installer and GUI. The Switch Monitor pulls switches to attain flow statistics and transfer these information to the Learning Model, which is the heart of our detection framework. The Learning Processor inside the model calculates the informative level of every flow in terms of the weight defined by the administrator based on the characteristics of the flow and a historical dataset. The output of the Learning Model will give feedback to the historical dataset if identified to be HH, otherwise, the result of the Learning Model will be interpreted as new flow rules and these rules can be sent to switches though the Flow Rule Installer. Finally, the network administrators can define the initial parameters in our model and change the priority of the flow that they pay more attention to through the GUI part.

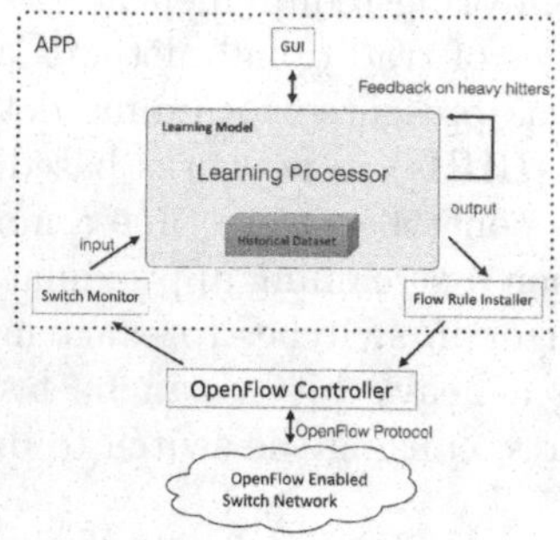

Fig. 1. Architecture of online learning heavy hitter detection

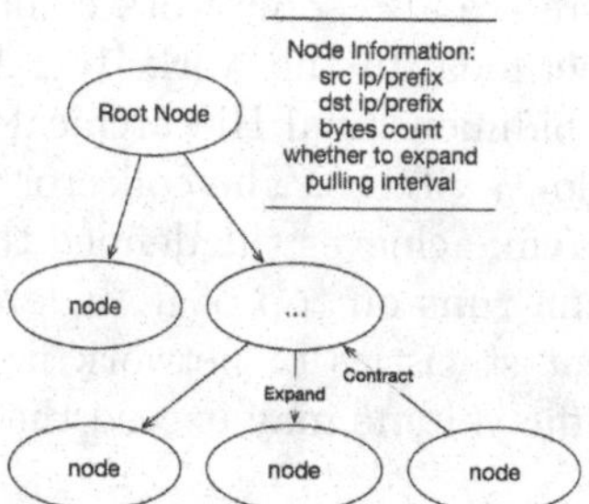

Fig. 2. The trie tree

3.2 Learning Model

In this section, we will discuss the design of our adaptive online learning model.

The adaptive technique proposed in [32] leverages the statistics information of all flows in switches to construct a trie tree, as shown in Fig. 2. Each node in a tree contains not only basic flow information such as src ip or dst ip, bytes count, but also the flag indicating whether to expand the node or not. With the help of linear perfection formula, a range of predicted values for aggregated flows were defined using previous flow entries, and they can determine whether the incoming flow is suspicious. So the controller will decide how to change the period of collecting statistics, at the same time, coarse-grained or fine-grained rules will be sent to the switch as a zoom-out or zoom-in of existing rules.

Leveraging the adaptive method mentioned above and the existing algorithm in machine learning, we can make a decision for expanding or contracting nodes in a tree. The heavy hitters are unknown previously, so we can consider this process as unsupervised learning. The machine learning view of the Heavy Hitter Detection is shown as in Fig. 3. Given a training set, which in the current scenario is the flow statistics, ω represents two underlying status of a network.

$$\omega = \begin{cases} 1, & \text{heavy hitter network state.} \\ 0, & \text{normal network activity.} \end{cases} \tag{1}$$

Our goal is to learn mapping f(.) using the flow set, where f(.): Flow Set $\rightarrow \{\omega\}$. The online learning model can be formulated as follows: We build a map leveraging the flow statistics gathered in the history. Let X be an n-dimensional random feature vector at time t, and each dimension represents a different method of spatial aggregation, such as source or destination ip with different mask length, the range of the port or the type of the protocol.

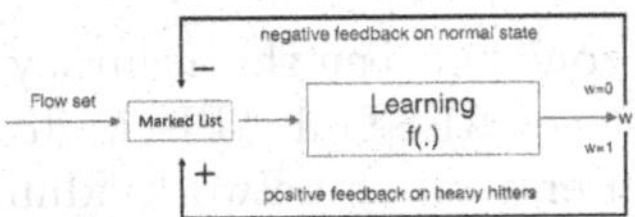

Fig. 3. Online learning model of HH detection

The learning process works as follows: the input to our model is the flow statistics received from switches. A marked list M stores heavy hitters already identified. The main learning algorithm maps every incoming flow to a network state according to the change of its bytes and its weight which is calculated using M. The output of the model can act as feedback to the list, so that M can be updated based on the available feedback.

The positive feedback works as follows, for example, if flow A whose source ip is 10.1.0.0/16 is identified to be a heavy hitter, then A will be inserted to M when M does not contain any flow who has a larger ip range than A, else if flow B with source ip 10.0.0.0/8 has already been inserted to M, then A will replace B in M. In contrast, if the flow is neither a heavy hitter nor suspicious, then it will be removed from M, which is the negative feedback in our model.

Algorithm 1 shows steps for learning control. The basic idea of the algorithm is to query suspicious flows frequently or slowly otherwise. The marked list M serves as the input in the learning process. The threshold Δ_1 and Δ_2 is predetermined, which satisfies $\Delta_1 < \Delta_2$, and d in line 25 and 30 is a constant variable predetermined too.

The main part of our algorithm is from line 3–33. Firstly, we construct a trie tree using records requested from switches with the spatial aggregation property X. The attributes of each node is shown in Fig. 2. Secondly, we rate each node in the tree according to its performance in the history, and calculate change in bytes count compared to the old records. If the difference is above a threshold, say Δ_1, then the node is suspicious and should be expanded. Moreover, if the difference is above a heavy hitter threshold, say Δ_2, then it is a HH and should be inserted into M in line 11 acting as a positive feedback. In the procedure GETSCORE, isSubNet() judges whether the flow is a bigger group containing an identified heavy hitter under certain aggregate. The output of GETSCORE is a rating for the node. If the rating r > 0, the node is to be expanded and the pulling interval T will be divided by r. The larger r is, the shorter the pulling interval will be. Lastly, the node will be removed from the list and contracted to its parent, which is considered as a negative feedback in Fig. 3.

The main loop iterates for $\mathcal{O}(n)$ time, where n = $|S|$. The rating can be got in $\mathcal{O}(m)$ time by iterating M, so m = $|M|$. But the maximum number of M is

1/threshold. For example, If the threshold is 5%, the maximum number of HHs is 20. So the computational complexity of the algorithm is $\mathcal{O}(n)$.

3.3 User Interface

In order to achieve a happy zone between the accuracy and overhead in different scenarios, we provide high-level RESTful APIs built on top of the controller, which not only allows the user such as network administrator to define initial parameters, but also give them access to the heavy hitters already found and let them select and mark flows that should be paid more attention to.

We use a Django-based architecture [2] to build the user interface upon the existing Northbound Interface since Django is a popular framework which builds better web app more quickly. The basic request API is designed as Table 1: The network administer can set initial parameter in our model through set config method. They can also check the heavy hitters already found and drill down to a specific flow' details. If a flow is in the subnet that the users care more than others, they can mark the flow and raise its priority so that the controller will pay more attention to it, as shown in Algorithm 1 from line 43–45.

The GUI part is an MVC (Model-View-Controller) architecture, Firstly, we define models representing the database, for example, the Flow model stores information of every flow, the Config model stores the initial general configurations of our learning algorithm. Then we define the specific url for every API. Finally, the view serves a specific function and generates output in JSON format.

Table 1. User interface

API	URI	Method	Description
flow list	/v1.0/web/flow/list/	GET	check the list of heavy hitters already found
flow detail	/v1.0/web/flow/detail/<flow id>/	GET	provide the insight to the user into the specific flow information of a heavy hitter
set config	/v1.0/web/config/	POST	set initial parameter in our model
drill down	/v1.0/web/flow/mark/<flow id>/	POST	mark a flow if the user cares more

4 Evaluation

In this section we describe the performance evaluation of our proposal. We compare it with OpenWatch [32]. We have implemented our work using POX, which is a SDN control plane for rapid development of network control applications. The underlying network was emulated by Mininet [18], which is an emulator to reproduce an environment with virtual hosts, switches, and links between them. Our topology contains one OpenFlow switch with two hosts connected to it. We download real packet trace from CAIDA [1] and use the tool called tcprelay [7] to inject the traffic into the OpenFlow switch in our topology. The flow set we use in

Algorithm 1. Online learning algorithm

```
Input Marked List M, Flow Set S, Spatial Aggregation X.
Output At each epoch t, the set of new rules to be installed in switches
procedure ONLINE_LEARNING
    for each flow in S do
        find node in TRIE corresponding this flow
        diff_byte_count=flow.byte_count−node.byte_count
        node.ratings = GETSCORE(node);
        if diff_byte_count>Δ1 then
            node.flag = EXPAND;
            if diff_byte_count>Δ2 then
                M.update(node);
            end if
        else if node.ratings>0 then
            node.flag = EXPAND
        else
            node.flag = CONTRACT;
            M.remove(node);
        end if
    end for
    for each node in TRIE do
        if node.flag==EXPAND then
            if ratings>0 then
                node.T = node.T / ratings;
            else
                node.T = node.T / d;
            end if
            expand node to match more precisely
        else
            remove rule for node and contract to its parent
            parent(node).T=parent(node).T∗d;
        end if
    end for
end procedure
procedure GETSCORE(node)
    rating = 0;
    for each m in M do
        if isSubNet(m, node) then
            rating ++;
        end if
    end for
    return rating
end procedure
procedure MODIFY(M)
    modify M through user interface
end procedure
```

our testbed is a part of "The CAIDA Anonymized 2015 Internet Traces Dataset", which contains anonymized passive traffic traces from CAIDA's equinix-chicago monitor on high-speed Internet backbone links. We use two input sets each of which contains 5 min of data with traffic volume size 320 Mbps in average. The first set is from 13:00 to 13:05 and the second set is from 14:00 to 14:05, both in February 19, 2015. The threshold Δ_1 is configured to 3% and Δ_2 is 5%. We evaluate our method from three aspects: the accuracy, the timeliness and the overhead for heavy hitter detection.

4.1 Accuracy

The accuracy can represent the effectiveness of the heavy hitter detection result. For example, a heavy hitter whose source ip is 10.0.0.0/8 is less precise than a more specific heavy hitter whose source ip is 10.1.2.3/24. In order to prove that our method can find the more precise aggregate than OpenWatch given the same detection time, we evaluate the accuracy using the average mask length of all heavy hitters found at the same time in each method. In Fig. 4, it show us that the online learning method reports a more specific prefix in the whole time.

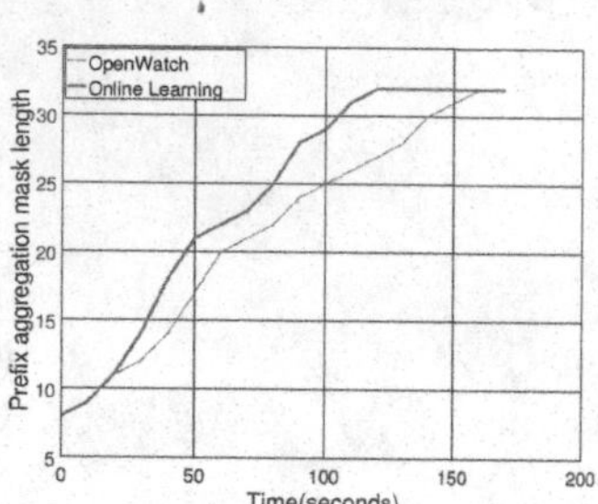

Fig. 4. Average prefix length

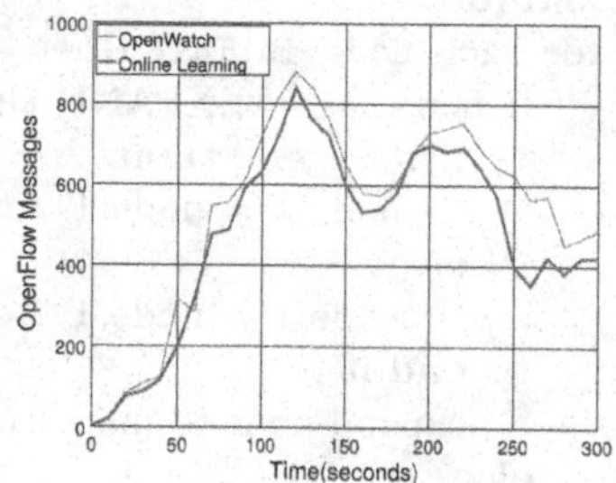

Fig. 5. Messaging overhead

4.2 Timeline

In order to prove our method can identify heavy hitters more duly and faster than OpenWatch, we measure the time it takes to identify the first heavy hitter and the average time it takes to find all heavy hitters. The number of true heavy hitters reported over the total number of answers reported in both of these methods is almost the same around 80%. The result is shown in Table 2. It can be seen that compared to OpenWatch, our method keeps the detection time low.

Therefore, the online learning method proposed in this article can dramatically decrease the time of detecting heavy hitters. With this method, people can find the heavy hitters much faster and deal with them in time.

Table 2. Timeliness of online learning heavy hitter detection

	Duration of identifying the first heavy hitter(s)	Average time of identifying all heavy hitters(s)
Our method	116	180
OpenWatch	156	200

4.3 Overhead

We elaborate the communication cost of our proposal and compare it with OpenWatch. Figure 5 shows the total number of OpenFlow messages between the switch and the controller. The horizontal axis represents measurement time while the yxis represents OpenFlow messages the controller received every interval. The initial pulling interval is set to 20 s. Compared with OpenWatch, our method saves up to 10% of the total number of OpenFlow messages. For example, 110 s after the start, switches send 710 messages every interval to the controller in our method while in OpenWatch about 820 messages are sent. Figure 7 plots the Commutative Distribution Function (CDF) of the difference in number of OpenFlow messages. For most of the time, the difference in control messages remains above 10% of the total number of communication messages.

Since the size of the TRIE tree can decide the complexity of our algorithm, we compare the number of tree nodes during the detection time. As is shown in Fig. 6, with the expansion of the tree, the number of nodes shows an exponential growth at the beginning. Then it reaches a stabilized status after finding the first heavy hitter. Within the dynamic change in the tree size, our method manipulates a smaller tree than OpenWatch in memory, which results in lower overhead in our algorithm.

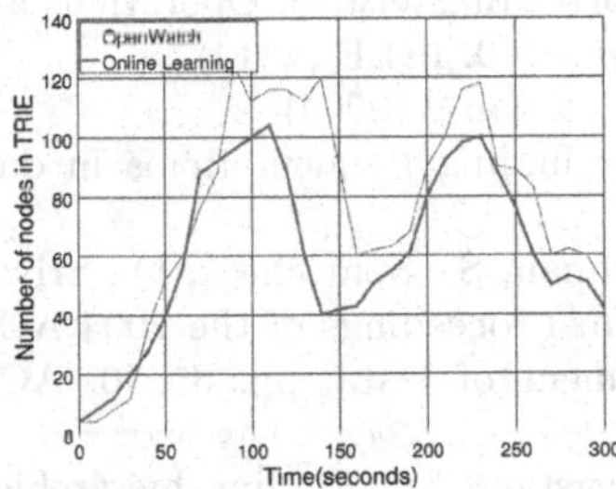

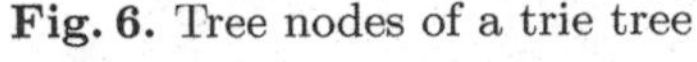

Fig. 6. Tree nodes of a trie tree

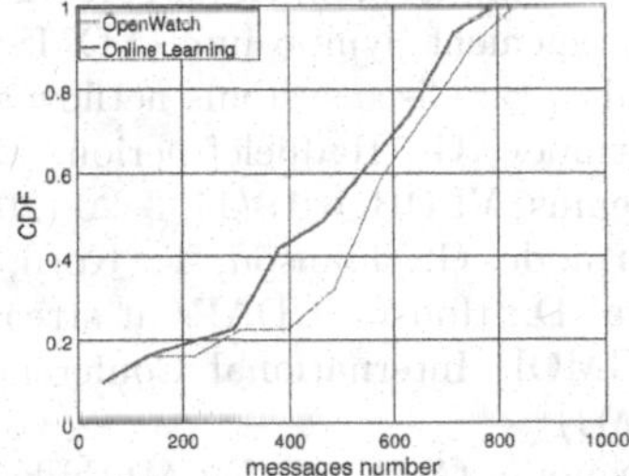

Fig. 7. Difference in number of messages

5 Conclusion

In this work, we present an online learning model for identifying heavy hitters in SDN. Our method can make the process of identifying heavy hitters faster.

Based on an existing adaptive algorithm, our proposal employs a learning model to memorize the identified heavy hitters in order to change the strategy of sending new flow rules. For future work, we plan to optimize our rule replacement algorithm and change our learning model based on different scenarios.

Acknowledgments. This work is supported by Hainan Provincial Natural Science Foundation of China (618QN219) and the National High Technology Research and Development Program of China (863 Program) No. 2015AA016105.

References

1. The CAIDA UCSD anonymized internet traces 2013. http://www.caida.org/data/passive/passive_2013_dataset.xml
2. Django. https://www.djangoproject.com/
3. Openflow. https://www.opennetworking.org
4. Pox. https://github.com/noxrepo/pox
5. sflow. www.sow.org
6. Software defined networks: the new norm of networks. https://www.opennetworking.org/sdn-definition/
7. Tcpreply. http://tcpreplay.synfn.net/
8. Argyropoulos, C., Kalogeras, D., Androulidakis, G., Maglaris, V.: PaFloMon-a slice aware passive flow monitoring framework for openflow enabled experimental facilities. In: 2012 European Workshop on Software Defined Networking (EWSDN), pp. 97–102. IEEE (2012)
9. Bandi, N., Metwally, A., Agrawal, D., El Abbadi, A.: Fast data stream algorithms using associative memories. In: Proceedings of the 2007 ACM SIGMOD international conference on Management of data, pp. 247–256. ACM (2007)
10. Cho, K.: Recursive lattice search: hierarchical heavy hitters revisited. In: Proceedings of the 2017 Internet Measurement Conference, pp. 283–289. ACM (2017)
11. Chowdhury, S.R., Bari, M.F., Ahmed, R., Boutaba, R.: Payless: a low cost network monitoring framework for software defined networks. In: Network Operations and Management Symposium (NOMS), 2014 IEEE, pp. 1–9. IEEE (2014)
12. Claise, B.: Cisco systems netflow services export version 9 (2004)
13. Cormode, G., Hadjieleftheriou, M.: Methods for finding frequent items in data streams. VLDB J. **19**(1), 3–20 (2010)
14. Cormode, G., Johnson, T., Korn, F., Muthukrishnan, S., Spatscheck, O., Srivastava, D.: Holistic UDAFs at streaming speeds. In: Proceedings of the 2004 ACM SIGMOD International Conference on Management of Data, pp. 35–46. ACM (2004)
15. Cormode, G., Korn, F., Muthukrishnan, S., Srivastava, D.: Finding hierarchical heavy hitters in data streams. In: Proceedings 2003 VLDB Conference, pp. 464–475. Elsevier (2003)
16. Da Cruz, M.A., e Silva, L.C., Correa, S., Cardoso, K.V.: Accurate online detection of bidimensional hierarchical heavy hitters in software-defined networks. In: 2013 IEEE Latin-America Conference on Communications (LATINCOM), pp. 1–6. IEEE (2013)
17. Curtis, A.R., Mogul, J.C., Tourrilhes, J., Yalagandula, P., Sharma, P., Banerjee, S.: DevoFlow: scaling flow management for high-performance networks. In: ACM SIGCOMM Computer Communication Review, vol. 41, pp. 254–265. ACM (2011)

18. Handigol, N., Heller, B., Jeyakumar, V., Lantz, B., McKeown, N.: Reproducible network experiments using container-based emulation. In: Proceedings of the 8th International Conference on Emerging Networking Experiments and Technologies, pp. 253–264. ACM (2012)
19. Huici, F., Di Pietro, A., Trammell, B., Gomez Hidalgo, J.M., Martinez Ruiz, D., d'Heureuse, N.: Blockmon: a high-performance composable network traffic measurement system. ACM SIGCOMM Comput. Commun. Rev. **42**(4), 79–80 (2012)
20. Locher, T.: Finding heavy distinct hitters in data streams. In: Proceedings of the Twenty-third Annual ACM Symposium on Parallelism in Algorithms and Architectures, pp. 299–308. ACM (2011)
21. Malboubi, M., Wang, L., Chuah, C.N., Sharma, P.: Intelligent SDN based traffic (de) aggregation and measurement paradigm (iSTAMP). In: INFOCOM, 2014 Proceedings IEEE, pp. 934–942. IEEE (2014)
22. Moshref, M., Yu, M., Govindan, R.: Resource/accuracy tradeoffs in software-defined measurement. In: Proceedings of the Second ACM SIGCOMM Workshop on Hot topics in Software Defined Networking, pp. 73–78. ACM (2013)
23. Shirali-Shahreza, S., Ganjali, Y.: Flexam: flexible sampling extension for monitoring and security applications in openflow. In: Proceedings of the Second ACM SIGCOMM Workshop on Hot topics in Software Defined Networking, pp. 167–168. ACM (2013)
24. Su, Z., Wang, T., Xia, Y., Hamdi, M.: Flowcover: Low-cost flow monitoring scheme in software defined networks. In: Global Communications Conference (GLOBECOM), 2014 IEEE, pp. 1956–1961. IEEE (2014)
25. Thottan, M., Liu, G., Ji, C.: Anomaly detection approaches for communication networks. In: Cormode, G., Thottan, M. (eds.) Algorithms for Next Generation Networks. Computer Communications and Networks, pp. 239–261. Springer, London (2010). https://doi.org/10.1007/978-1-84882-765-3_11
26. Tootoonchian, A., Ghobadi, M., Ganjali, Y.: OpenTM: Traffic matrix estimator for openflow networks. In: Krishnamurthy, A., Plattner, B. (eds.) PAM 2010. LNCS, vol. 6032, pp. 201–210. Springer, Heidelberg (2010). https://doi.org/10.1007/978-3-642-12334-4_21
27. Van Adrichem, N.L., Doerr, C., Kuipers, F.A.: Opennetmon: network monitoring in openflow software-defined networks. In: Network Operations and Management Symposium (NOMS), 2014 IEEE, pp. 1–8. IEEE (2014)
28. Yang, L., Ng, B., Seah, W.K.: Heavy hitter detection and identification in software defined networking. In: 2016 25th International Conference on Computer Communication and Networks (ICCCN), pp. 1–10. IEEE (2016)
29. Yu, C., Lumezanu, C., Zhang, Y., Singh, V., Jiang, G., Madhyastha, H.V.: FlowSense: monitoring network utilization with zero measurement cost. In: Roughan, M., Chang, R. (eds.) PAM 2013. LNCS, vol. 7799, pp. 31–41. Springer, Heidelberg (2013). https://doi.org/10.1007/978-3-642-36516-4_4
30. Yu, M., Jose, L., Miao, R.: Software defined traffic measurement with opensketch. In: NSDI, vol. 13, pp. 29–42 (2013)
31. Yuan, L., Chuah, C.N., Mohapatra, P.: ProgME: towards programmable network measurement. IEEE/ACM Trans. Netw. (TON) **19**(1), 115–128 (2011)
32. Zhang, Y.: An adaptive flow counting method for anomaly detection in SDN. In: Proceedings of the Ninth ACM Conference on Emerging Networking Experiments And Technologies, pp. 25–30. ACM (2013)

Focused Crawler Framework Based on Open Search Engine

Jiawei Liu[1,2(✉)] and Yongfeng Huang[1,2(✉)]

[1] Department of Electronic Engineering, Tsinghua University, Beijing 100084, China

[2] Tsinghua National Laboratory for Information Science and Technology, Beijing, China

jw-liu15@mails.tsinghua.edu.cn

Abstract. When users need to analyze webpages related to some specific topics, generally they use crawlers to acquire webpages, and then analyze the results to extract those match the users' interests. However, in data acquisition stage, users usually have customize demand on acquiring data. Ordinary crawler systems are very resource-constrained so they cannot traverse the entire internet. Meanwhile, search engines can satisfy these demand but it relies on many manual interactions. The traditional solution is to constrain the crawlers in some limited domain, but this will lead to the problem of low recall rate as well as inefficiency. In order to solve the problems above, this paper does some research on focused crawlers framework based on open search engine. It takes advantage of open search engine's information gather and retrieval capabilities, and can automatically/semi-automatically generate the topic model to interpret and complete users search intents, with only a few seed keywords need to be provided initially. Then it uses open search engine interfaces to iteratively crawl topic-specific webpages. Compared with the traditional ways, the focused crawler based on open search engine proposed in this paper improves the recall rate and efficiency under the premise of ensuring the accuracy.

Keywords: Focused crawlers · Topic models · Search engine

1 Introduction

With the advent of big data era, the value of data has been greatly highlighted in business world. With huge amount data distributed on the entire cloud of internet, lots of users do data retrieving every seconds. The security of data have been paid lots of attention recently. Traditionally users care more about data confidentiality and completeness, but as said with huge amount of data on the cloud, nowadays users care more

This work is supported by the National Key Research and Development Program of China (No. 2016YFB0800402) and the National Natural Science Foundation of China (No. U1536201, U1705261).

X. Sun et al. (Eds.): ICCCS 2018, LNCS 11065, pp. 56–68, 2018.
https://doi.org/10.1007/978-3-030-00012-7_6

about the usability of data, which is, the users are more concern about how to express their demand to gather the most precise data they need.

Webpage crawlers have been widely used in academic institutions, firms and other organizations. They can be divided into standard crawlers and focused crawlers. The basic idea of standard crawlers is to use the connectivity among webpages to traverse the internet. As for focused crawlers, they estimate the correlation between target webpage and the topic users interested in, so as to only visit the relevant webpages.

At early ages users used standard crawlers to gather webpages, when the crawlers were mostly applied to search webpages for search engines, with several manners using to evaluate the importance of webpages [1, 2]. But for users' customized data acquisition demand, obviously this kind of manners are not efficient. Chakrabarti et al. firstly introduced focused crawlers [3] to give crawlers a differentiated purpose. Then still due to user side limited resources, many researchers began to study different search strategies to improve the crawlers' efficiency and recall rate. De Bra and Post proposed the Fish Search algorithm [4], Vieira et al. proposed a way to select better seed set [5]. Rawat and Patil proposed a way of using best first search manner to make the crawler more efficient [6]. But these strategies need to construct the crawler from zero. However, open search engines have already been built based on large scale crawlers, and they have great webpages retrieve capability and efficiency, which can be well utilized here. On the other hand, the accuracy of the search results is of same importance. Researchers have studied different measures to better estimate the correlation between webpages and target topic. Hersovici et al. proposed Shark Search algorithm [7]. Aggarwal et al. proposed a way of using content, URL structure and other behaviors to estimate the correlation [8]. But these manners all use previous webpage' information to estimate the correlation, rather than use the target webpage itself. So the assumption here is not that precise. There also exist some manners that estimate the correlation after accessing the potential webpages, which lead to huge resources consuming. The full-text search engines have index mechanism, which can naturally match target webpages with the users' search demand in a very efficient way. Meanwhile the webpage results returned by search engines are relatively reliable.

This paper researches how to build a focused crawler framework with better performance. The traditional focused crawler frameworks have low recall rate due to resource constraints, crawl strategies and other reasons. In order to solve the above problem, this paper propose a focused crawler framework based on open search engines, it combines search engines with focused crawlers, with using topic models to interpret users search intent.

2 Related Work

2.1 Focused Crawler

Focused crawlers are topic-specific search robots. They can be used to search relevant webpages under the situation when users have the demand of acquiring topic-specific webpages. The core idea of focused crawlers is when they confront an URL, they shall decide whether or not to access the URL based on the correlation between the target webpage and user-specific topic. Normally focused crawlers use information on current webpage (such as context, hyperlinks, anchor text, etc.) to compute the correlation, then access target webpage and continuously crawl other webpages based on the connectivity among all the webpages [9].

There are many search strategies for focused crawlers. The Fish Search algorithm [1] achieves dynamic access by maintaining a URL queue that simulates the herd multiplication characteristics of fishes, the fish that find food (refer to webpages that related to the topic) can reproduce more offspring, and the fish at the top of the queue are easier to get reproduce (prioritized access), while the fish at the bottom of the queue die when resources is constrained. The main disadvantage of the Fish Search algorithm is that it uses a discrete variable 'potential_score' to represent webpage correlation, which reflects only three discrete states, related, unrelated, and others. Based on Fish Search algorithm, Hersovici et al. proposed Shark Search algorithm [7]. Shark Search algorithm introduces a space vector model that allows for more accurate description of the correlation in Fish Search algorithm, with a highlight on the impact of the anchor text and context on correlation. Best first algorithm [6] uses TF · IDF model to describe webpages, further to estimate the correlation between two webpages, the candidate links in more relevant webpages will have a higher priority, which are more likely to be accessed.

Both Fisher Search and Shark Search algorithms are derived from the standard crawler algorithms, such as PageRank algorithm [1] and Authorities and Hubs algorithm [2]. The traditional standard crawlers are mostly for the purpose of acquiring more webpages, while focused crawlers are for more specific purpose. However, for ordinary users, no matter build a standard or a focused crawler system, a large amount of resources like storage, bandwidth and electricity are required. Therefore, it is very difficult for an ordinary user to implement a crawler that traverses the entire internet.

Second, focused crawlers traverse among webpages relying on the connectivity of webpages, so they can only reach the webpages which have direct or indirect connection with current webpage. So crawling start form few seed webpages can cause the boundedness issues. In some case, the search domain could be very limited. Some solution are proposed to improve this problem, Vieira et al. [5] proposed a new framework for seed set selection, in order to improve the coverage of focused crawler.

Third, as to the focused crawler search strategies, the way estimating the correlation of the target webpage with the topic is based on the information within current webpage. But in fact the hyperlinks, context and the anchor text in the current webpage cannot appropriately represent the topic of the target webpage. Therefore, there might lead to misjudged and decrease the accuracy of focused crawlers.

The above three factors lead to the low recall rate and low accuracy of focused crawlers, this paper designs a new framework, which uses open search engine as the entrance to construct a new focused crawler, and takes advantage of search engine's real-time information update and webpages retrieval capabilities, to solve traditional focused crawlers' problem due to resource constraints and search strategies.

2.2 Open Search Engine Technology

Search engines can be divided into full-text search, directory index, meta-search engines [10]. Search engines like Baidu, Google are belong to full-text search engines. The retrieval algorithm of full-text search engine is based on the inverted index mechanism. Search engines build indexes for each term in webpages to track down which article the term belong and where the location is in the webpages.

Also, full-text search engine like Baidu provides user interfaces that include amount of search constraints and can automatically receive and interpret users' search intents. Meanwhile, the search results are being well filtered and sorted.

According to the ideas of Authorities and Hubs algorithm mentioned in Sect. 2.1, Search engines can be considered as a huge hub node. So use search engine results pages as the seed webpages for focused crawlers might have better features, this paper will do some research on this topic.

2.3 Topic Models

Topic models are ways of modeling the implied topics of text, which format as a series of topics related terms. In this way topics can be regard as the distribution of these terms [11]. The TF-IDF model is an algorithm that can extract keywords from a large amount of text [12]. TF-IDF refers to term frequency - invert document frequency. The main idea of it is for those which frequently appear in the document, but infrequently appear in the entire corpus, should be assigned a greater weight, because these words often carry more important semantic information of the document. The main disadvantage of TF-IDF model is that it can't solve the problem of synonyms and its essential assumption is not that appropriate for describing the topics of a document.

LDA topic model is a classic topic model algorithm, it simulates a document generation process based on the probability theory. Be more specific, first it selects a topic with a certain probability, and then selects lexical terms under this topic with another certain probability, repeat the above two steps and eventually generate a complete document. Then in order to solve the distribution of the lexical terms under each topic and the topic probability distribution of each document, the algorithm reverses the process to estimate the parameters [13]. The obtained keywords and the corresponding probability distributions consist the topic models. Then the model can compute new document distribution on these topics. Due to the extended feature of LDA topic model, it has been widely used to solve document classification problem.

Based on the TF-IDF and LDA topic models, this paper introduces a focused crawler system based on topic model construction, which the process can be done automatically or semi-automatically.

3 Focused Crawler System Framework Based on Open Search Engine

3.1 System Framework Design

This paper constructs a focused crawler system based on open search engine, the overall framework is as follows:

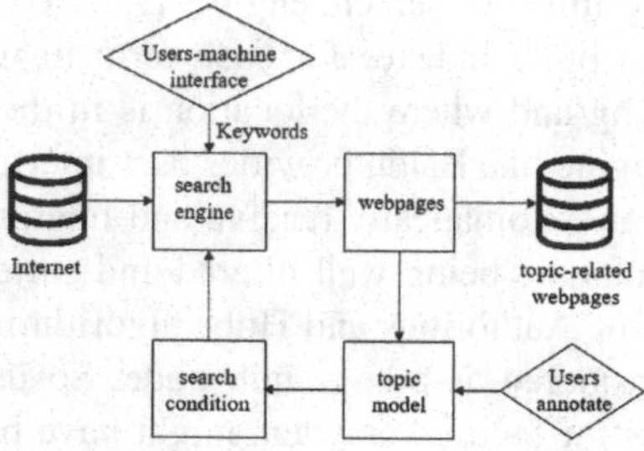

The first step is users input few seed search conditions match with target topic. Then the system interprets these conditions to the search engine interface specified format, call the interface and gather the result webpages. After that, build a topic model according to these webpages then generate appropriate search conditions based on the topic model, call search engine interface again and update the topic model according to the new search result. Iterate the above process and build up the final topic-related webpages database.

3.2 Open Search Engine Interface Analysis

Baidu, Google and other search engines provide full-scale search interfaces. Users usually manually enter a line of keywords or sentences in the search box on main page and then it goes to the results page where displays the information users need. But besides this, there are also many other search conditions or constraints.

There are two main ways to call search engines interface: call API or access through URL. The former is a synchronous access way. API provide functions, which the input and output represent the search conditions and the results returned respectively. Whereas access through URL is an asynchronously way. Users need get the HTML of the corresponding webpage by accessing the URL and then parse the HTML to get the information they need.

This paper uses of Baidu search engine and deploys an URL asynchronous search manner. The search conditions of the search engine can be mapped to the search URL within search engine site, the search engine will automatically parse the URL to generate the search conditions match with its own interface, and finally returns the specific results correspond to the search conditions.

For Baidu search engine, the basic format of search condition is:
http://www.baidu.com/s?q1=<keywords>

Where the above <keyword> term is basic search keywords or sentences, just like what users input in the search box on search engine main page.

Other main search conditions are as the Table 1 below:

Table 1. URL attached conditions and description

URL attached conditions	Values and functions
q2 = <keywords_complete>	Append keywords that must be contained in the search results. The search engine will not do words segmentation
q3 = <keywords_partial>	Append keywords that only need be partially contained
q4 = <keywords_cannothave>	Append keywords that can't be contain in the search result. Search engine will filter the webpages which contain these words
q6 = <keyword_sitetype>	Restrict domain type of websites such as '.edu'
lm = <parameter>	Restrict the timestamp of webpages, when the parameter is 0 it represents entire time, 1 represents latest 1 day, 7 represents latest 7 days, etc.
ct = <parameter>	Restrict language of the webpages, 0 represents all the language, 1 represents Chinese Simplified, 2 represents Chinese Traditional. Default value is 0

If more than one conditions are to be specified, these conditions should be linked with '&'. And only some of the main conditions terms are listed above.

According to the above, user side search interface can be well defined. The framework proposed in this paper requires users to enter a basic search keyword <keywords> at least, it will be modified during subsequent iterative search steps meanwhile other conditions are optional and remain the same. The process simulates users using different keywords to describe the topic and do iteratively searching.

3.3 Build Topic Model and Iterative Search Process

Generally, the topic models often contain lots of keywords, but normally only few keywords can be provided by a user in the initial stage to describe the topic. Obviously these keywords cannot cover all the dimensions related to the topic.

Build and expend topic model through text parsing can be described as follows:

Seed Keywords Search. Initially users should give some seed keywords or sentences describing the target topic, as the search engine input. Meanwhile multiple search condition options are provided to users based on the search engine's interface. And turn all the conditions into corresponding search URL. The URL leads to the results page, where each result webpages within is organized as a link, a title and a brief of webpage.

Find Keywords. Due to search results returned from search engine have already been sorted, to some extend the rank can be used to represent the correlation between webpages and the target topic. Webpages with top rank refer to higher correlation with the topic. So it can be inferred that the keywords in these webpages are more relevant and they can be more appropriate to describe the users-concerned topic.

The way how to find keywords in the results webpages is as blow:

First do words segmentation to the text in webpages then this extract the noun and verb as candidate keywords. Meanwhile the frequency of the words can be initially regard as the weight. After this use the blow formula to update all keywords' weight:

$$\{Keywords_{cluster}\} = \frac{1}{N} * \sum\nolimits_{i}^{N} \left(\{Keywords_{page_i}\} * \{IDF\} * \frac{(N-2i) * b + N}{2N} \right) \quad (1)$$

Where N is the quantity of webpages searched for the first time, $i \in \{1, 2, 3, \ldots, N\}$. $b \in [0, 1]$ is the smoothing coefficient, which affects the influence of the search engine's rank i on the correlation of webpages and target topic. $\{\mathrm{Keywords_{cluster}}\}$ is a set of key-value pairs consisting of keywords and weights of the whole search results cluster. $\left\{\mathrm{Keywords_{page_i}}\right\}$ is the potential keywords extracted from a single webpage page.

$\{IDF\}$ is the invert document frequency, which is trained by $\mathrm{TF} \cdot \mathrm{IDF}$ algorithm with a large amount of historical data. The term $\left\{\mathrm{Keywords_{page_i}}\right\} * \{IDF\}$ represent the weight multiple of the corresponding words. It can be calculated as:

$$IDF(t) = \log_2 \frac{N_{idf}}{TF(t) + 1} \quad (2)$$

Where TF is term frequency, TF(t) is the frequency of specific feature word t, N_{idf} is the quantity of document in the train data set. IDF(t) is the weight of feature word t.

Build Topic Model. This paper introduces two modes used to build topic models: automatic mode and semi-automatic mode. For automatic mode, the search conditions are generated directly by the system and the iteratively search process can be proceed automatically. For semi-automatic mode, users need to interact with the system in different stages.

First ensure nothing changes in search condition besides the basic search <keyword> term described in Sect. 3.2. Then segment <keywords> term, and define this keywords set as variable '*target_topic*'.

Automatic Mode. Select the Top 5 key-value pairs with the highest weights in $\{\mathrm{Keywords_{cluster}}\}$ and multiply the weights for the five key-value pairs by an attenuation factor α. Combine the '*target_topic*' with the 5 words in the highest weighted key-value pairs, there can generate a new words set {search_words}. Joint the words in this set into a string and make it replace the old <keywords> term in search conditions, with the newly generated search conditions, do the second search process.

When the second search process above is done, a new document set D can be obtained, first remove the duplicated webpages in D, then update the topic model according to the formula:

$$\{\text{Keywords}_{cluster}\} = \{\text{Keywords}_{old}\} + \frac{1}{\mathrm{N_D}} * \sum_i^N (\{\text{Keywords}_{\text{new}}\} * \{IDF\}) * \frac{(N_D - 2i) * b + N_D}{2N_D} \quad (3)$$

Where $\{\text{Keywords}_{cluster}\}$ is the new set of candidate keywords. Then repeatedly select the Top 5 key-value pairs with the highest weight and do the same operations above. Until the terminal conditions are satisfied, which can be defined as when the number of news meets the needs of users' demand, or when the number of newly valid obtained webpages is less than a threshold.

Semi-automatic Mode. First use a large corpus train LDA topic model, in this paper we use over 500 thousand historical Chinese news data as train data. Then users should give the appropriate parameter, assume the number of topics to be trained is N.

After each search loop has completed, put the newly obtained webpages into the trained LDA topic model, it will generate N topic sets. Each topic set is consisted by key-value pairs with the form like <keyword, weight>. After all the topic sets have been clustered by the model, display those N topics to the user and make the user annotate each topic set with label 'relevant' or 'irrelevant'. With the information of these annotated topic sets, search conditions can be updated:

First define an empty set as target topic model. Then merge all the relevant topic sets with the keywords set '*target_topic*'. For the word k which already exists in both '*target_topic*' and the 'relevant' topic set at the same time, assume the weight is w_1 and w_2 respectively. The new weight in '*target_topic*' can be updated as:

$$Weight_k = \frac{b}{\sqrt{\sum_i Weight_i^2}} * \mathrm{w}_1 + \frac{1}{\sqrt{\sum_j Weight_j^2}} * \mathrm{w}_2 \quad (4)$$

Where the two coefficient for w_1 and w_2 are the normalized coefficients, $Weight_i$ is the weight of the i-th order word in the '*target_topic*. b is the constant coefficient, which indicates the influence by the user annotation.

For the 'irrelevant' topic sets, use them to attenuate the '*target_topic*'. For each word k which exists in both '*target_topic*' and the 'irrelevant' topic set at the same time, assume the weight is w_1 and w_2 respectively. The new weight in '*target_topic*' can be updated as:

$$Weight_k = \begin{cases} \frac{b}{\sqrt{\sum_i Weight_i^2}} * \mathrm{w}_1 - \frac{1}{\sqrt{\sum_j Weight_j^2}} * \mathrm{w}_2, & \text{if } Weight_k > 0 \\ 0, & \text{if } Weight_k \leq 0 \end{cases} \quad (5)$$

So for those irrelevant keywords, when they occur in the 'irrelevant' topic sets, and according to the formula (5), when the calculate result is less than 0, the framework could eliminate the irrelevant keywords.

For words that only exist in '*target_topic*', the weights can be normalized and updated as:

$$Weight_k = \frac{1}{\sqrt{\sum_i Weight_i^2}} * w_1 \quad (6)$$

Then select the Top 5 key-value pairs with the highest weights in the final updated '*target_topic*' and multiply the weight for these five key-value pairs by an attenuation factor α. Then joint the words into a string and make it replace the old <keywords> term in search conditions, with the newly generated search conditions, repeat the same operations above.

4 Experiment

In this section, this paper designs an experiment to verify the accuracy and efficiency of the focused crawler framework proposed in this paper. The experiment designs based on search engine BAIDU, and natural language applied is Chinese. First, construct a system correspond to the focused crawler framework. Put serval of keywords into the system, of which match with users' interested topic. Also, the system does a second filter to the search result, eliminate the webpages which are not available or obviously irrelevant. First we define 10 topics for this experiment (Table 2):

Table 2. Define 10 topics and corresponding keywords

#	Target topic	Initial keywords
1	南海军事事件 (South China sea military event)	南海军事 舰艇 美国 中国 (South China sea military, vessels, America, China)
2	美国大选 (American election)	美国 总统选举 特朗普 希拉里 (America, president election, Trump, Hillary)
3	乐视"诈骗"事件 (LeTV fraud event)	乐视 贾跃亭 资本 (LeTV, Jiayueting, Capital)
4	AlphaGo	AlphaGo 谷歌 围棋 李世石 (AlphaGo, Google, Game go, Lee Sedol)
5	"90后" (The 90s)	90后 中年危机 00后 头发 (90s, mid-age crisis, 00s, hair)
6	马航事件 (Malaysia Airlines event)	马航 坠毁 飞机 (Malaysia Airlines, crash, airplane)
7	游戏领域事件 (Game domain event)	腾讯 网易 王者荣耀 吃鸡 (Tecent, Netease, 'Strike of Kings', 'Battlegrounds')
8	十九大 (the 19th National Congress)	十九大 北京 中国 (the 19th National Congress, Beijing, China)
9	比特币 (Bitcoin)	比特币 以太坊 炒币 区块链 (Bitcoin, Ethererum, invest in digital coin, blockchain)
10	苹果手机 (Iphone)	苹果 apple 手机 发布会 iphone 电池 (Apple, iphone, conference, battery)

Where the field 'target topic' represents users' interested topic, and the field 'initial keywords' represents the keywords provided to the search engine at the initial stage, which are defined by users manually.

Then we apply the focused crawler system on the 10 topics to record the accuracy and how many webpages it can gather (recall rate) (Table 3).

Table 3. Experiment result on different topics

#	Target topic	Auto mode		Semi-auto mode	
		Accuracy	# webpages	Accuracy	# webpages
1	South China sea military event	84.1%	8326	94.2%	5064
2	American election	85.6%	3872	93.7%	2932
3	LeTV fraud event	84.7%	4991	92.1%	3092
4	AlphaGo	92.2%	3034	95.4%	2078
5	The 90s	72.3%	6764	83.6%	4833
6	Malaysia Airlines event	79.6%	9027	93.5%	7282
7	Game domain event	82.5%	10129	88.9%	8837
8	The 19th National Congress	83.5%	7587	91.2%	6247
9	Bitcoin	87.8%	11224	93.4%	9177
10	Iphone	83.3%	9665	91.1%	7994
	Average	83.6%	7462	91.7%	5754

It can be observed that the focused crawler framework proposed in this paper has relatively high accuracy and generally can satisfied the users' demand. Under the semi-auto mode, the main noise is the advertisement in the search results caused by the biding rank algorithm. As well as under the auto mode, which is unsupervised, there is more noise when more irrelevant keywords are added to the target topic. And this eventually makes the overall accuracy get lower than that of semi-auto mode.

In the meantime, this experiment designs a directional harvesting crawler as a benchmark, it crawled 471k webpages from main Chinese news portals, in this experiment we extract webpages related to the defined 'target topic' above, and simply match the words term in webpages with the 'initial keywords', if a webpage contains one or more keywords in the 'initial keywords' set, then consider it as relevant (Table 4).

Also, pay attention to the results with the focused crawler in the previous part, we compare the total number of relevant webpages (Fig. 1)

The directional harvesting crawler can only crawl new webpages until the websites release them, so usually the recall rate is much lower than standard or focused crawlers, which can continuously crawl webpage. And the accuracy is also much lower, among which the webpages are just keywords level matched rather than topic level matched. Also, the directional harvesting crawler can only reach very limited range of websites. Therefore the former way is time-consuming and can't gather that much related webpages compared to the manner proposed in this paper.

Table 4. Comparing focused crawler with directional harvesting crawler

#	Target topic	# of matched webpages	Accuracy
1	South China sea military event	21734	4.61%
2	American election	18337	3.89%
3	LeTV fraud event	21275	4.52%
4	AlphaGo	12580	2.67%
5	The 90s	57329	7.30%
6	Malaysia Airlines event	36711	7.80%
7	Game domain event	67321	10.66%
8	The 19th National Congress	45143	8.65%
9	Bitcoin	32001	5.80%
10	Iphone	39754	7.44%
	Average	35219	6.33%

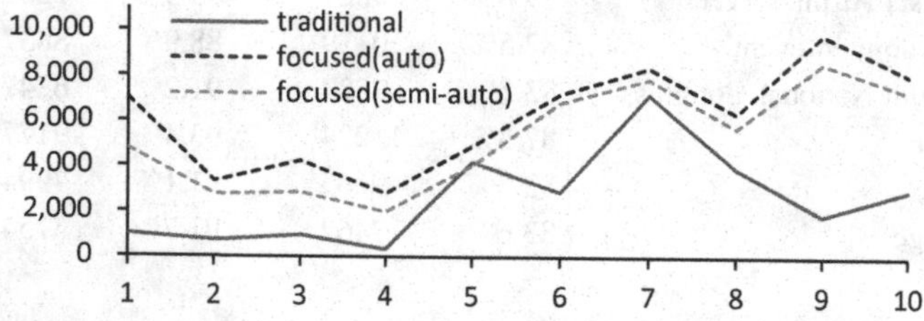

Fig. 1. The total related webpages comparison between traditional crawler and focused crawler

Then, this section analyzes how the topic semantics influence the experiment result. Among the 10 'target topic', we manually sort the topic by how concentration they are. Then compare these topic with the accuracy and recall rate (Fig. 2):

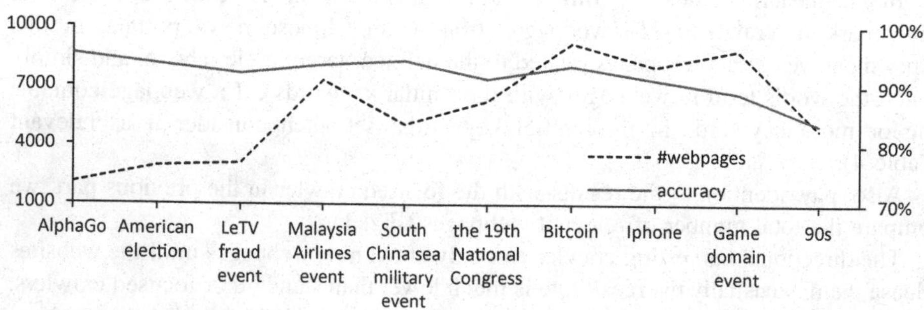

Fig. 2. Number of webpages and search accuracy influenced by the topic concentration

Where the topic 'Alpha Go' is defined as the most concentrated topic as well as '90s' is defined as the least concentrated topic. It can be inferred that with a topic gets more concentrated, the accuracy gets higher and the recall rate gets lower. This is because more specific a topic is, then it will cover less webpages through the entire internet. So when the crawler walking through among the webpages, the hit rate will be low and eventually lead to less results return from the search engine. Meanwhile, it will be harder for the search engine or the crawler system to understand the users' intention if a topic described by the users is vaguer or say it is less concentrated.

5 Conclusion

This paper researches the focused crawler framework based on open search engine, and take advantage of the topic model. This framework only needs users provide a few topic-related seed keywords or sentences initially, then it will use topic models to generate appropriate search conditions which match the open search engine interfaces to acquire as much related webpages as possible within user side limited resources. The crawler can be deploy on either single PC or server with stable network situation.

Meanwhile this framework exists some defects. The topic model may occur the semantically shift during the iterative searching process, which means the newly updated topic model continuously lose the correlation with the initial topic. This situation may be improved by combining the newly generated subtopic with previous information. Be more specific, when new keywords are going to be added into the target topic model, the crawler should examine the correlation between these candidate keywords and the current target topic, so that to eliminate the irrelevant keywords. Also it may help by introducing more supervision.

References

1. Page, L.: The PageRank citation ranking: bringing order to the web. Stanf. Dig. Libr. Work. Paper **9**(1), 1–14 (1999)
2. Kleinberg, J.M.: Hubs, authorities, and communities. ACM Comput. Surv. **31**(4es), 5 (1999)
3. Chakrabarti, S., Berg, M.V.D., Dom, B.: Focused crawling: a new approach to topic specific resource discovery. Comput. Netw. **31**(11–16), 1623–1640 (2000)
4. Bra, D.P.M.E.D.: Searching for arbitrary information in the www: the fish-search for mosaic. In: World Wide Web Conference Series (1994)
5. Vieira, K., Barbosa, L., Silva, A.S.D., Freire, J., Moura, E.: Finding seeds to boot-strap focused crawlers. World Wide Web-Internet Web Inf. Syst. **19**(3), 449–474 (2016)
6. Rawat, S., Patil, D.R.: Efficient focused crawling based on best first search. In: Advance Computing Conference, pp. 908–911 (2013)
7. Hersovici, M., Jacovi, M., Maarek, Y.S., Dan, P., Shtalhaim, M., Ur, S.: The shark-search algorithm. An application: tailored web site mapping. In: International Conference on World Wide Web, pp. 317–326 (1998)
8. Aggarwal, C.C., Al-Garawi, F., Yu, P.S.: Intelligent crawling on the world wide web with arbitrary predicates. In: International Conference on World Wide Web, pp. 96–105 (2001)
9. Novak, B.: A survey of focused web crawling algorithms (2004)
10. Baidu Encyclopedia: Meta-search engine. https://baike.baidu.com/item/%E5%85%83%E6%90%9C%E7%B4%A2%E5%BC%95%E6%93%8E/205513?fr=aladdin. Accessed 27 Feb 2018

11. Blei, D.M., Lafferty, J.D.: Topic models. In: Text Mining, pp. 101–124. Chapman and Hall/CRC (2009)
12. Robertson, S.: Understanding inverse document frequency: on theoretical arguments for IDF. J. Doc. **60**(5), 503–520 (2013)
13. Blei, D.M., Ng, A.Y., Jordan, M.I.: Latent Dirichlet allocation. J. Mach. Learn. Res. Arch. **3**, 993–1022 (2003)

Identity Based Privacy Information Sharing with Similarity Test in Cloud Environment

Faguo Wu[1,2,3], Wang Yao[1,2,3], Xiao Zhang[1,2,3(✉)], Zhiming Zheng[1,2,3], and Wenhua Wang[4]

[1] School of Mathematics and Systems Science, Beihang University, Beijing 100191, China
09621@buaa.edu.cn

[2] Key Laboratory of Mathematics, Informatics and Behavioral Semantics, Ministry of Education, Beijing 100191, China

[3] Beijing Advanced Innovation Center for Big Data and Brain Computing, Beihang University, Beijing 100191, China

[4] AVIC Economics and Technology Research Establishment, Beijing 100029, China

Abstract. In recent years, great progress has been made in global digital construction, various kinds of methods, such as encryption, isolated storage and firewall, are used to prevent information from stealing. However, the above mentioned technologies severely hinder information sharing, especially in some special areas, such as medical industries in which doctors need to share similar patient's information to improve the effectiveness of treatment. The premise of sharing information is to find the desired information on encrypted data, although identity based encryption scheme with equality test (IBEET) has been defined as a viable solution, it can only search for the ciphertext formed by the exact same plaintext. In this paper, we firstly propose an efficient identity based privacy information sharing with similarity test in cloud environment. Our scheme can search out similar data of the target data on encrypted content. Besides, we use advanced Locality-Sensitive Hashing function to generate index for data to protect the privacy information of users.

Keywords: Identity-based · IBEET · Equality test · Similarity test Locality-Sensitive Hashing

1 Introduction

In recent years, as more and more countries and industries place the center of future construction on the construction of information industry, the issue of information security has received unprecedented attention which is the key to the success of information construction. Countries and industries use a variety of methods, such as firewall, physical isolation and encryption, to prevent information from stealing. While these methods bring security protection, they also

X. Sun et al. (Eds.): ICCCS 2018, LNCS 11065, pp. 69–78, 2018.
https://doi.org/10.1007/978-3-030-00012-7_7

have a serious impact on the sharing of information. Many industries, especially the medical industry, need to take both information security and information sharing into consideration. For example, when a doctor encounters a patient with a serious illness, he/she wants to know whether the same patient in the encrypted database, if any, could be referenced to greatly improve the treatment effect. The premise of sharing information is to find the desired information on encrypted data. Unsurprisingly, efficient searchable encryption schemes have been proposed [3,4,6,11,14]. Equality Test is viewed as one popular technique for keyword searching.

Public Key Encryption Scheme with Equality Test (PKEET), firstly proposed by Yang et al. [16], has been defined as a viable solution to check whether two ciphertexts are encryptions of the same message. Ma et al. design a flexible PKEET scheme supporting four types of authorization at the same time [10]. Afterwards, in order to specify who can preform equality test, Tang et al. proposed PKEET with Fine-Grained Authorization [13], their formulation provides fine-grained authorization policy enforcements for users. In order to eliminate certificate management, Ma firstly proposed identity-based encryption with equality test (IBEET) [9]. They firstly combine the concept of PKEET and IBE, and inheriting the advantage of IBE, their scheme is very suitable for the client with minimal computation resource, such as handhold mobile device. In 2017, Wu et al. pointed out that Ma's scheme is inefficient due to Hash function and a number of bilinear map operations used [15]. Their scheme achieved a huge reduction in computation cost during the encryption and test phase by reducing the need for HashToPoint function.

The above mentioned equality test schemes only focused on the cipertexts which are totally identical in plaintexts. However, it is not common in realistic situations. For example, one doctor wants to search out if there are other doctors who have the same patients whose conditions are as same as his/hers. However, patients with the same disease will have a little different information recorded in the database due to the number of complications, severity of the disease and so on. Therefore, the above mentioned schemes don't apply to these types of situations. In view of this challenge, Locality-Sensitive Hashing (LSH) technique, firstly proposed by Indyk [5], is recruited in this paper to achieve similarity test and privacy sharing in cloud environment. The LSH technique is being used in numerous applied settings [1,2,7,8,17]. In this paper, we propose the notion of identity based privacy information sharing with similarity test in cloud environment and its construction by combining identity based encryption scheme, re-encryption scheme [12] and Locality-Sensitive Hashing technique. As far as we know, our scheme is the first time to share privacy information by searching over similar data and our scheme can be seen as an expansion of IBEET. The proposed scheme achieves a desirable security which guarantees that although being searched, cloud server cannot decrypt cipertext. Furthermore, being implemented with the concrete parameters, it would be a useful tool for searching encrypted data on resource constrained service.

The remainder of our paper is organized as follow. In Sect. 2, we present the motivation of this paper and we provide necessary preliminaries of our scheme in Sect. 3. In Sect. 4, we describe give the security model of our Identity Based Privacy Information Sharing with Similarity Test in Cloud Environment scheme. In Sect. 5, we use LSH to generate index. In Sect. 6, we present the detail construction of our scheme.

2 Motivation

An example is presented in Fig. 1 to demonstrate the motivation of our paper. In a system where information needs to be protected, especially in the medical system. Various information protection methods, such as encryption, firewall and so on, seriously hindered the sharing of information. However, The medical industry is a special industry that needs a high degree of information sharing. Therefore, we want to construct a system as shown in Fig. 1. In Fig. 1, there are two doctors, i.e., Doctor A and Doctor B, both doctors store their patient information safely in the cloud, such as diseases, symptoms and complications, and treatment methods. Suppose that Doctor A has a patient with a certain type of disease which is accompanied by many symptoms and complications. Doctor A wants to treat the patient more precisely, therefore, he wants to know if there was a patient who had the same disease and had similar complications in the database. Doctor A generates the index corresponding to disease, symptoms and complications, then proposes a request to the Cloud Service Provider (CSP) for similar patient. Upon receiving this request, according to preset similar definition, Cloud Service Provider could search and check whether there exist any other patients with similar diseases, symptoms and complications to Doctor A's patient. It needs to be emphasized that during the query, the Cloud Service Provider cannot know any actul information of patient. Then the Cloud Service Provider sends the search result to Doctor A and Doctor B. Doctor B adopt re-encryption to send the similar patient treatment information to Doctor A. Such a scheme also can be extended to multiple users setting, For example, one or more doctors can generate such indexes and propose matching request to Cloud Service Provider, then they obtain feedback indicating whether there are any patients on the system having similar diseases, symptoms and complications.

3 Preliminaries

3.1 Bilinear Pairing

Let $\mathbf{G_1}$, $\mathbf{G_2}$ be additive cyclic groups, whose order are large prime p. g is a generator of $\mathbf{G_1}$. The map $e : \mathbf{G_1} \times \mathbf{G_1} \rightarrow \mathbf{G_2}$ is said to be an admissible bilinear map if it satisfies the following conditions:

- Bilinearity: For all $g_1, g_2 \in \mathbf{G_1}$, $a, b \in \mathbb{Z}_p^*$, there is $e(g_1^a, g_2^b) = e(g_1, g_2)^{ab}$
- Non-degeneracy: $\exists\ g_1, g_2 \in \mathbf{G_1}$ such that $e(g_1, g_2) \neq \mathbf{1}_{\mathbf{G_2}}$ where $\mathbf{1}_{\mathbf{G_2}}$ is identity element of $\mathbf{G_2}$.
- Computability: $\forall\ g_1, g_2 \in \mathbf{G_1}$, there is an polynomial time algorithm to compute $e(g_1, g_2)$.

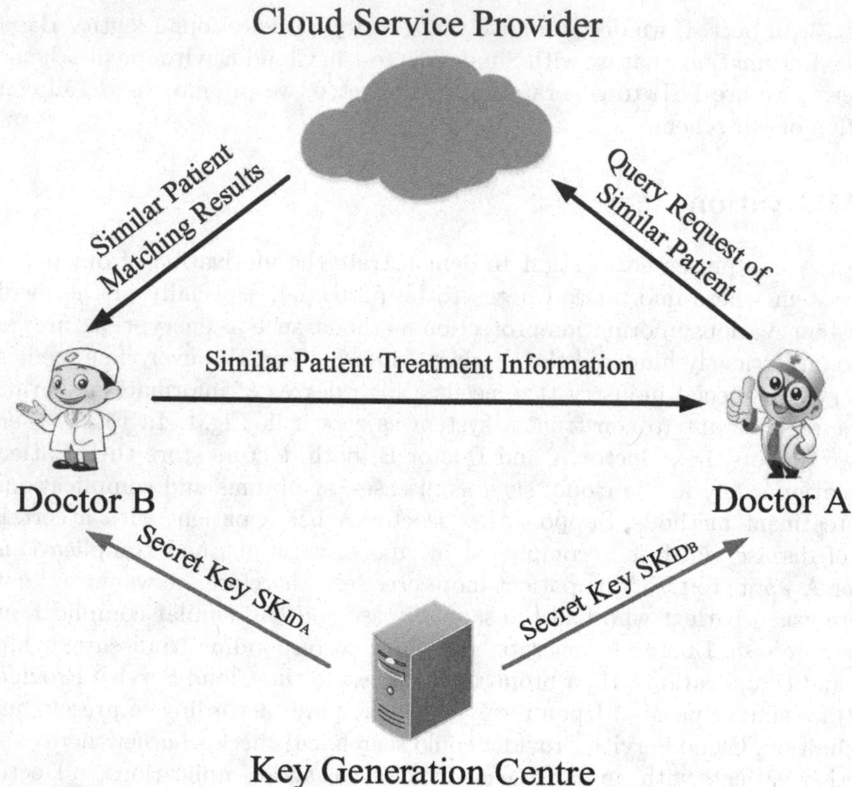

Fig. 1. Application scenario of privacy information sharing with similarity test

3.2 Hardness Assumption

Definition 1. Decisional Bilinear Diffie-Hellam Problem (DBDH): Let $\mathbf{G_1}$, $\mathbf{G_2}$ be additive cyclic groups, whose order are large prime p. Given a triple $(g, g^a, g^b, g^c, Q) \in \mathbf{G_1} \times \mathbf{G_2}$ where a, b, c are randomly and independently chosen from $\mathbb{Z}_p^*$, Decision if $Q = e(g, g)^{abc}$ is established or not.

We define the advantage of an algorithm $\mathcal{A}$ in solving the Decisional Bilinear Diffie-Hellman (DBDH) problem as follows:

$$Adv_{\mathbf{G_1}}^{DBDH}(\mathcal{A}) =\mid Pr[\mathcal{A}(g, g^a, g^b, g^c, e(g, g)^{abc}) = 1] - Pr[\mathcal{A}(g, g^a, g^b, g^c, Q) = 1] \mid$$

where the probability is over the random choice of generator $g \in \mathbf{G_1}$. We say that the $(k, t, \epsilon)-$DBDH assumption holds in $\mathbf{G_1}$ if no t-time algorithm has advantage at least ϵ in solving the DBDH problem in $\mathbf{G_1}$ under a security parameter $k = log(p)$.

3.3 Locality-Sensitive Hashing

Local Sensitive Hash (LSH) function is a function that measures the similarity of the original vector. The main idea of LSH function is to select a specific hash function (or a hash function family). In this way, two neighboring points in original data space still neighbors after hash with large probability. More formally, for two points p, q which are randomly and independently chosen from $\mathbb{R}^d$, a hash function H(.) is called $(\mathbf{R}, \mathbf{cR}, P_1, P_2) - \textit{Sensitive}$ if following conditions satisfied:

$$\begin{aligned} if \parallel p - q \parallel \leq \mathbf{R} &\Longrightarrow Pr[H(x) = H(y)] \geq P_1 \\ if \parallel p - q \parallel \leq \mathbf{cR} &\Longrightarrow Pr[H(x) = H(y)] \leq P_2 \end{aligned} \tag{1}$$

LSH function is the most popular of the nearest neighbor search algorithms. It has a solid theoretical basis and performs well in the data space. Its main function is to find similar data from massive data and can be applied to text similarity detection, web search, and other fields.

4 Privacy Information Sharing with Similarity Test in Cloud Environment

Syntax model of our Privacy Information Sharing with Similarity Test in Cloud Environment scheme is proposed in this section. In our Privacy Information Sharing with Similarity Test scheme, there are four participants: Key Generation Centre (KGC), Doctor A with ID_A who want to obtain similar patient information from the cloud, such as diagnostic methods, Cloud Service Provider (CSP), Doctor B with ID_B who have similar patient information. This scheme can be defined by the following eight polynomial-time algorithms (Setup, KeyGen, IndexGen, Enc, Test, RKGen, Reencrypt, Decrypt), where:

1. Setup: Given a security parameters k, and select appropriate parameters and functions. Outputs both the master key msk, and the master public parameters par, that is, $(msk, par) \leftarrow Setup(1^k)$.
2. KeyGen: Given the Doctor identity ID, public parameters par, this algorithm outputs the secret key SK_{ID} of Doctor, that is, $SK_{ID} \leftarrow KeyGen(par, msk, ID)$.
3. IndexGen: Given the pathological features of patient. Choose a LSH function to project the user into corresponding buckets, based on the patient's observed pathological features W. Then the bucket W can be regard as the index of patient, that is, $Index \leftarrow IndexGen(LSH, W)$.
4. Enc: Given the public parameters par, doctor's secret key SK_{ID}, and a plaintext M which is patient's condition and treatment information, this algorithm output the first level ciphertext C_{ID} which can be re-encrypted by the re-encryption key, that is, $C_{ID} \leftarrow Enc(par, ID, M)$.
5. Test: Given the index W_A of Doctor A's patient, this algorithm output 1 if there exist indexes which are similar to A in the Cloud Storage Server (CSS), otherwise, output 0. That is, $\{0, 1\} \leftarrow Test(W_A)$.

6. RKGen: Given the public key PK_{ID_A} of data requester, secret key SK_{ID_B} of similarity data owner, this algorithm generates the re-encryption key $rk_{ID_B \to ID_A}$, that is, $rk_{ID_B \to ID_A} \leftarrow RKGen(PK_{ID_A}, SK_{ID_B})$.
7. Reencrypt: Given the re-encryption key $rk_{ID_B \to ID_A}$, first level ciphertext C_{ID_A}, this algorithm outputs the second level re-encryption ciphertext C_{ID_B}, that is $C_{ID_B} \leftarrow Reencrypt(rk_{ID_B \to ID_A}, C_{ID_A})$.
8. Decrypt: Given the $i - th$ level cipertext C_{ID_i}, the corresponding secret key SK_{ID_i}, this algorithm outputs the plaintext M, that is, $M \leftarrow Decrypt(C_{ID_i}, SK_{ID_i})$.

5 Index Generation and Similar Definition

As we mentioned above, index generation and similar definition are important parts of our scheme, in this section, we provide the index construction and define the similar relationship.
1. Index Generation Based on LSH: First, all the doctors in this system should choose preselected LSH function h(.) to build indexes for all the patients. Concretely, for a patient P, doctor can model her/his diseases, symptoms and complications as an n-dimensional vector $W = (W_1, W_2, \cdots, W_n)$. For example, the patient got diabetes (severe), accompanied by retinopathy (mild), uveitis (mild), cataract (moderate) and no arteriosclerosis. The doctor classifies each disease and his complications into three levels: mild, moderate, and severe, corresponding levels are 1, 2, and 3 respectively, furthermore, if the patient does not have a certain symptom, record it as 0. The above mentioned diabetes patients can be recorded as vector $W = (3, 1, 1, 2, 0, \cdots)$, we should point out that the length of the vector and the order of complications should be pre-agreed by the doctors. For vector W,its LSH function can be represented as following:

$$h(W) = \begin{cases} 1 & W \circ V > 0 \\ 0 & W \circ V \leq 0 \end{cases} \tag{2}$$

Where V is n-dimensional vector $V = (V_1, V_2, \cdots, V_n)$ and V_i is randomly chosen from [−1, 1]. $\circ$ is dot product between W and V. if there are two patient P_i and, P_j with an n-dimensional vector $W_i = (W_{i1}, W_{i2}, \cdots, W_{in})$ and $W_j = (W_{j1}, W_{j2}, \cdots, W_{jn})$, respectively. The above mentioned LSH means if W_i and W_j are located on the same side of V with both $W_i \circ V > 0$ and $W_j \circ V > 0$, or, both $W_i \circ V < 0$ and $W_j \circ V < 0$. Then W_i and W_j can be regarded as similar with high probability. However, a single LSH function often falls short in locating similarity. Therefore, we choose r LSH functions $h_1(.), h_2(.), \cdots, h_r(.)$ to generate an a tuple of vectors $H(W) = (h_1(W), h_2(W), \cdots, h_r(W))$. Finally, the patient $P's$ index can be represented as $H(W)$. Although above mentioned LSH functions have the advantage of searching similar vectors, they are inevitable to produce unsatisfactory search results (due to LSH is probability-based search function). Therefore, the following two kinds of wrong judgments will be formed

- Case 1: Similar patient P_i of the target patient P_j is regarded as dissimilar, that is, $W_i \approx W_j$, $H(W_i) \neq H(W_j)$.

- Case 2: Dissimilar patient P_i of the target patient P_j is regarded as similar, that is, $W_i \neq W_j$, $H(W_i) = H(W_j)$.

To overcome these shortcoming, we can adopt following techniques to redefine similarity.

Definition 2

- For Case 1, we use following definition to represent the similarity between the patient P_i and the target patient P_j

$$\exists l, satisfy \quad h_l(W_i) = h_l(W_j)(1 \leq l \leq r) \tag{3}$$

- For Case 2, we use the previous method to generate T LSH tables, that is $(H_1(W), H_2(W), \cdots, H_T(W))$ where $H_i(W) = (h_{i1}(W), h_{i2}(W), \cdots, h_{ir}(W))$. We use following definition to represent the similarity between the patient P_i and the target patient P_j

$$\forall x \in \{1, \cdots, T\}, \exists l, satisfy \quad h_{xl}(W_i) = h_{xl}(W_j)(1 \leq l \leq r) \tag{4}$$

Therefore, according to the above mentioned definition, the indexes of patients can be calculated as $H(W) = (h_1(W), h_2(W), \cdots, h_r(W))$. The patient P_i and the target patient P_j are similar if they satisfy (3) and (4).

6 Proposed Privacy Information Sharing with Similarity Test in Cloud Environment

We give a detailed account of our Privacy Information Sharing with Similarity Test in Cloud Environment scheme in this section. There are four participants: Key Generation Centre (KGC), Doctor A with ID_A who want to obtain similar patient information from the cloud, such as diagnostic methods, Cloud Service Provider, Doctor B with ID_B who have similar patient information. This scheme can be defined by the following eight polynomial-time algorithms (Setup, Key-Gen, IndexGen, Enc, Test, RKGen, Reencrypt, Decrypt), where:

1. Setup: Given the security parameter k of this system, we select $\mathbf{G_1}$, $\mathbf{G_2}$ be additive cyclic groups, whose order are large prime p. g is a generator of $\mathbf{G_1}$. The bilinear map $e : \mathbf{G_1} \times \mathbf{G_1} \rightarrow \mathbf{G_2}$. Select random $s \in \mathbb{Z}_p$, Symmetrical encryption and decryption (AES), then compute $\gamma = g^s$. Select two hash function $F_1 = \{0,1\}^* \rightarrow \{0,1\}^{128}$, $F_2 = \{0,1\}^* \rightarrow \mathbf{G_1}$, that is $mpk = (\mathbf{G_1}, \mathbf{G_2}, e, g, p, \gamma, F_1, F_2, AES)$, $msk = s$.
2. KeyGen: On input security parameter k, public parameter par. For any doctor's private key request on his identity ID $\in \{0,1\}^*$. Key Generation Centre (KGC) generates doctor's partial private key as $SK_{ID} = F_1(ID)^s$ and send it to doctor via secure channel. Then doctor with ID choose pseudo-random number function $f : \{0,1\}^* \times K_{prf} \rightarrow \mathbb{Z}_p$, let $k_{prf} \leftarrow K_{prf}$, then $ek_{ID} = (mpk, k_{prf})$, $dk_{ID} = (SK_{ID}, k_{prf})$.

3. IndexGen: Doctors model every patient's diseases, symptoms and complications as an n-dimensional vector $W = (W_1, W_2, \cdots, W_n)$. They use preselected LSH functions $\mathrm{H}(.) = (h_1(.), h_2(.), \cdots, h_r(.))$ to build indexes for all the patients $H(W) = (h_1(W), h_2(W), \cdots, h_r(W))$. They store these indexes in the CSP.
4. Enc: To encrypt patient information, especially diseases, symptoms, complications and treatment information. Doctor randomly chooses $\rho \in \mathbb{Z}_p$ $R \in \mathbf{G_2}$. $K_{AES} = F_1(R)$, $t = k_{prf}(j)$, $c_0 = AES(m)$, $c_1 = g^{\rho}$, $c_2 = R \cdot e(g^s, F_2(ID)^{\rho t})$, $C_{ID_i} = (c_0, c_1, c_2)$.
5. Test: Once Doctor have trouble in treating the patient, He/She proposes a request to CSP for searching similar patients of the target patient P_A. He/She generates index $H(W_A) = (h_1(W_A), h_2(W_A), \cdots, h_r(W_A))$ and sends $H(W_A)$ to CSP for searching similar patients. CSP use the Similar Definition in Sect. 5 to find similar patients. If there exist patient P_B of Doctor B who is similar to target patient, CSP sends $(1, ID_B, H(W_B))$ to Doctor A and $(1, ID_A, H(W_A), H(W_B))$ to Doctor B, otherwise, CSP send 0 to Doctor B.
6. RKGen: Once Doctor B received $(1, ID_A, H(W_A), H(W_B))$ from CSP, he/she computes and send $t = k_{prf}(j)$, $F_2(ID_A)^t$ to CSP, CSP computes $rk_{ID_A \to ID_B} = F_2(ID_A)^{-st} \bullet F_2(e(F_2(ID_A)^s, F_2(ID_B)))$.
7. Reencrypt: For cipertext $C_{ID_B} = (c_0, c_1, c_2)$ of Doctor B, CSP use $rk_{ID_A \to ID_B}$ and compute $c_2^* = c_2 e(c_1, rk_{ID_A \to ID_B})$. Afterwards, CSP send $e(F_2(ID_A)^s, F_2(ID_B))$ and (c_0, c_1, c_2^*) to Doctor A.
8. Decrypt: Once Doctor B received (c_0, c_1, c_2^*) from CSP, he/she compute $R = c_2 \bullet e(c_1, F_2(e(F_2(ID_A)^s, F_2(ID_B)))^{-1})$, $K_{AES} = F_1(R)$ then $m = Dec(K_{AES}, c_0)$.

7 Security Analysis

Identity based privacy information sharing with similarity test in cloud environment should achieve secure storage and secure sharing, that is, once Doctor send encrypted data or changed ciphertext to the CSP, even CSP can't decrypt it for plaintext.

Theorem 1. *If Decisional Bilinear Diffie-Hellam Problem is difficult, our privacy information sharing with similarity test in cloud environment scheme is existential unforgeable against adaptive chosen message and identity attacks in the random oracle model.*

Proof. The security proof is a security interactive game played between a adversary A and a challenger C, the following is the simulation. On input the (g, g^a, g^b, g^c, Q), adversary A should distinguish Q is randomly selected from $\mathbf{G_2}$ or $Q = g^{abc}$. Providing A with c_1, c_2, A needs to judge whether b = 0 or 1 in m_b, it's not difficult to prove that the advantage of making correct judgments is equal to solve DBDH, we omit the security proof for the above mentioned theorem, readers who are interested in security proof can contact the authors to get the full paper.

8 Conclusion

With the surprising development of global digital construction, both privacy information security and privacy information sharing should be taken into consideration. The core of information sharing is to search out desired information on encrypted data. Although PKEET and IBEET are efficient searching techniques, their applicability are limited in realistic scenario due to they can only search out exact same information as the target file. In this paper, as far as we know, we firstly proposed an efficient privacy information sharing on encrypted data using bilinear pairing with equality test, we can search out information which is similar to the target information. Our scheme is more suitable for realistic situation, such as medical industry. Furthermore, there is no certificate management problem in our scheme due to identity based concept used in our scheme. We will design more flexible privacy sharing scheme such as supporting different types of authorization at the same time in the future, besides, we will use different techniques to avoid key escrow issue in our scheme.

Acknowledgements. This work was supported by the Major Program of National Natural Science Foundation of China (11290141).

References

1. Ahle, T.D., Aumller, M., Pagh, R.: Parameter-free locality sensitive hashing for spherical range reporting, pp. 239–256 (2016)
2. Andoni, A., Razenshteyn, I.: Tight lower bounds for data-dependent locality-sensitive hashing. Computer Science (2016)
3. Cui, B., Liu, Z., Wang, L.: Key-aggregate searchable encryption (KASE) for group data sharing via cloud storage. IEEE Trans. Comput. **65**(8), 2374–2385 (2016)
4. Hahn, F., Kerschbaum, F.: Searchable encryption with secure and efficient updates, pp. 310–320 (2017)
5. Indyk, P.: Approximate nearest neighbors: towards removing the curse of dimensionality. Department of Computer Science, Stanford University (1998)
6. Khader, D.: Introduction to attribute based searchable encryption (2016)
7. Lizunov, P., Biloshchytskyi, A., Kuchansky, A., Biloshchytska, S., Chala, L.: Detection of near duplicates in tables based on the locality-sensitive hashing method and the nearest neighbor method. **6**(4(84)), 4–10 (2016)
8. Luo, Y., Zeng, J., Berger, B., Peng, J.: Low-density locality-sensitive hashing boosts metagenomic binning, p. 255 (2016)
9. Ma, S.: Identity-based encryption with outsourced equality test in cloud computing. Inf. Sci. Int. J. **328**(C), 389–402 (2016)
10. Ma, S., Huang, Q., Zhang, M., Yang, B.: Efficient public key encryption with equality test supporting flexible authorization. IEEE Trans. Inf. Forensics Secur. **10**(3), 458–470 (2015)
11. Miao, Y., Ma, J., Liu, Z.: Revocable and anonymous searchable encryption in multi-user setting. Concurr. Comput. Pract. Exp. **28**(4), 1204–1218 (2016)
12. Ming-Fu, L.I., Chen, L.W.: A secure cloud data sharing scheme from identity-based proxy re-encryption. Nat. Sci. J. Xiangtan Univ. (2017)

13. Tang, Q.: Towards public key encryption scheme supporting equality test with fine-grained authorization. In: Parampalli, U., Hawkes, P. (eds.) ACISP 2011. LNCS, vol. 6812, pp. 389–406. Springer, Heidelberg (2011). https://doi.org/10.1007/978-3-642-22497-3_25
14. Wang, Q., He, M., Du, M., Chow, S.S.M., Lai, R.W.F., Zou, Q.: Searchable encryption over feature-rich data. IEEE Trans. Dependable Secure Comput. **PP**(99), 1 (2016)
15. Wu, L., Zhang, Y., Choo, K.K.R., He, D.: Efficient and secure identity-based encryption scheme with equality test in cloud computing. Future Gener. Comput. Syst. **73**(C), 22–31 (2017)
16. Yang, G., Tan, C.H., Huang, Q., Wong, D.S.: Probabilistic public key encryption with equality test. In: Pieprzyk, J. (ed.) CT-RSA 2010. LNCS, vol. 5985, pp. 119–131. Springer, Heidelberg (2010). https://doi.org/10.1007/978-3-642-11925-5_9
17. Zhu, Z., Xiao, J., He, S., Ji, Z., Sun, Y.: A multi-objective memetic algorithm based on locality-sensitive hashing for one-to-many-to-one dynamic pickup-and-delivery problem. Inf. Sci. Int. J. **329**(C), 73–89 (2016)

Image Encryption and Compression Based on a VAE Generative Model

Xintao Duan(✉), Jingjing Liu, En Zhang, Haoxian Song, and Kai Jia

Henan Normal University, Xinxiang 453007, Henan, China
duanxintao@126.com, liujingjl012@163.com

Abstract. To solve the problem that the network security real-time transmits image, a new image encryption and compression method based on a variational auto-encoder (VAE) generative model is proposed in this paper. The algorithm aims to encrypt and compress images by using a variational auto-encoder generative model. Firstly, we use multi-layer perceptual neural network to train the VAE model, and set parameters of the model to get the best model. Then, the peak signal-to-noise ratio (PSNR) and mean square error (MSE) are used to measure the compression effect and Set the number of iterations of the model. Finally, we extract the data of based on a variational auto-encoder and perform division, then the data input the VAE generative model to encrypt image and analyze encryption images. In this paper, we use the standard image of 256 * 256 to do simulation experiments and use histogram and image correlation to analyze the results of encryption. The simulation results show that the proposed method can effectively compress and encrypt images, and then obtain better compression image than stacked auto-encoder (SAE), while the algorithm is faster and easier encrypting and decrypting images and the decrypted image distortion rate is low and suitable for practical applications.

Keywords: Image encryption · Image compression · VAE · Generative model

1 Introduction

Digital images have clearly become an important carrier of communication in the age of multimedia information, especially after the cloud storage emerging. The cloud storage not only stores large amounts of information such as files, videos and images, but also provides large enough online space to store the shared data. However, these data are so private, confidential, and commercially valuable, hencc people do not want data information to be maliciously attacked, leaked, and arbitrarily. In order to protect data security that encryption technology has became an urgent problem to be solved. At the same time, high-definition image data transmission in a limited bandwidth has also been limited. Therefore, the significance of the image compression and encryption is particularly prominent.

Image compression and encryption methods have become a hot topic in the era of big data. The main purpose of image compression [1–3] is to quickly transfer and store data on low bandwidth networks by removing redundant or irrelevant information. Classical compression methods are based on DCT transform data of JPEG and

X. Sun et al. (Eds.): ICCCS 2018, LNCS 11065, pp. 79–89, 2018.
https://doi.org/10.1007/978-3-030-00012-7_8

multi-scale orthogonal wavelet of JPEG 2000. In order to reduce the loss of image compression, the neural network is used to reduce the dimension such as auto-encoder compressed image [4], Stack auto-encoder image compression [5] and joint non-linear end-to-end optimization of image compression [6]. In image encryption, the researchers use different technologies to change images pixel value or location or the image hide in another image [7, 8]. Encryption technology can be divided into frequency domain and spatial domain image encryption algorithm. It is that changes the image data or the transform function in the frequency domain, such as DCT transform [9], Fourier transform, Wavelet transform, Chaotic transform [5, 10, 11] and so on. The spatial domain image encryption algorithm is the use of alternative or change the pixel position of the image replacement. In this paper, by using the generation model of variational auto-encoder (VAE) [12, 13] to encrypt and compress the image and compare with the stack auto-encoder image compression [5], which can compress and reconstruct the image more effectively and make image encryption more quickly.

Variational auto-encoder (VAE) is a generative model [14, 15] that generates similar images through unsupervised neural network learning and training. It was widely applied to inference of complex models in machine learning. It can generate faes [16, 17] and high-resolution digital images [12, 18, 19], and can also obtain state-of-the-art machine learning results in image generation and reinforcement learning [20]. In this paper, a data encryption method based on the variational auto-encoder generation model is proposed for the first time. The basic idea is to generate the unidentified noise image, that is, encrypted image by changing weights and bias of the generated model. Specifically, how do we change weights and bias in the generative model? In this paper, two different images are used to train weights and bias data of the variable auto-encoder until distinct images are generated, and the result of the two-divisional division of the data is loaded into the generated model to generate the encrypted image. The advantages of this method are simple and fast encryption, and the decryption effect is high quality. The simulation results and experimental analysis are also in this paper.

2 Related Works

VAE was proposed by Kingma and Max Welling in 2013 [12], and is called a variational auto-encoder because of its basic model structure similar to the auto-encoder (AE) [21, 22]. As shown in the basic structural model of VAE in Fig. 1, we can see the $\tilde{x}$ is generated by the latent variable z, that is, $z \rightarrow \tilde{x}$ is a generate model, which is the decoder from auto-encoder point of view. $x \rightarrow z$ is a kind of recognition model, and is similar to the auto-encoder's encoder, so called variational auto-encoder. But which has nothing to do with the mathematical theory of the auto-encoder. Instead of generating an implicit vector each time, variational auto-encoder generate two vectors, one is the mean (μ), one is the standard deviation (σ), and the latent variables for the two statistics. From a theory perspective, the unobserved variables z has an interpretation as a latent representation or code. In this paper, we will also refer to the recognition model $q_{\phi}(z|x)$ as a probabilistic encoder, since given a data-point x it produces a Gaussian distribution over the possible values of the code z from which the data-point x could have been generated. In a similar vein we will refer to $p_\theta(x|z)$ as a probabilistic decoder, since given a code z it produces a distribution over the possible corresponding values of x.

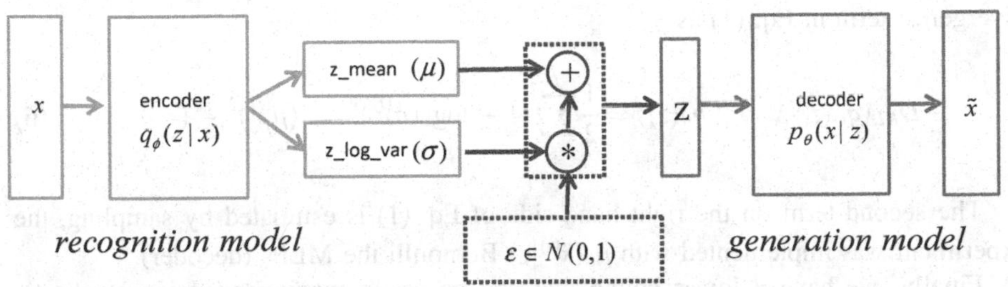

Fig. 1. The basic structural model of VAE.

The loss function of the variational auto-encoder is from the difference between the generated image data and the real image data, that is, the reconstruction loss and the posterior probability density in the encoder and the posterior probability density difference in the decoder. Therefore, in variational auto-encoders, the whole network uses gradient descent method to adjust and optimize the loss function. The reconstruction loss can be calculated using cross entropy, and the distribution of the encoder is close to the standard distribution, which is calculated by using the Kullback-Leibler divergence [28]. The KL divergence is the distance of two probability distributions. If the two distributions are closer, the KL divergence is smaller, and vice versa. From [12] we can see that the lower limit of variation is:

$$L(\theta, \phi; x^{(i)}) = -D_{KL}(q_\phi(z \mid x^{(i)}) \,||\, p_\theta(z)) + E_{q_\phi(z|x^{(i)})}[\log p_\theta(x^{(i)}|z] \tag{1}$$

$$p_\theta(z) = N(z; 0, \mathrm{I}) \tag{2}$$

$p_\theta(z)$ can be selected by the appropriate choice of analysis and integration. To do this, we first re-parameterize Z by introducing a differentiable transformation $g_\theta(\varepsilon, x)$ with a noise random variable ε.The analysis can be integrated with the right choice.

$$Z^{(il)} = g_\phi(\varepsilon, x^{(i)}), \varepsilon \sim p(\varepsilon) \tag{3}$$

Specifically, VAE [12] is used:

$$Z^{(i,l)} = g_\phi(\varepsilon, x^{(i)}) = \mu^{(i)} + \sigma^{(i)} \odot \varepsilon^{(l)}, \varepsilon^{(l)} \sim N(0, 1) \tag{4}$$

where l represents the lth noise ε, i represents the ith data point, and $\odot$ represents the product of the elements. $\mu^{(i)}$ and $\sigma^{(i)}$ are outputs of the non-linear map (encoder) from $x^{(i)}$. According to Eq. (4), there is

$$q_{\phi}(z \mid x^{(i)}) = N(z; \mu^{(i)}, \sigma^{2(i)} I) \tag{5}$$

In the meantime, supposing the prior over latent variables z are centred isotropic multivariate Gaussian Eq. (2). Therefore, we can derive the analytic form of the KL divergence term in Eq. (1) as

$$-D_{KL}(q_{\phi}(z \mid x^{(i)}) \,||\, p_{\theta}(z)) = \frac{1}{2}\sum_{j=1}^{J}(1 + \log((\sigma_j^{(i)})^2) - (\mu_j^{(i)})^2 - (\sigma_j^{(i)})^2)) \tag{6}$$

The second term on the right hand side of Eq. (1) is estimated by sampling, the experiment was implemented with $p_{\theta}(x^{(i)}|z)$ Bernoulli the MLPs (decoder).

Finally, we have a lower bound that can be easily maximized using stochastic gradient descent, which is referred to as Auto-Encoder Variational Bayes (AEVB) in [12]:

$$\begin{aligned} L(\theta, \phi; x^{(i)}) &\simeq \frac{1}{2}\sum_{j=1}^{J}(1 + \log((\sigma_j^{(i)})^2) - (\mu_j^{(i)})^2 - (\sigma_j^{(i)})^2) + \frac{1}{L}\sum_{l=1}^{L}\log p_{\theta}(x^{(i)} \mid z^{(i,l)}) \\ z^{(i,l)} &= \mu^{(i)} + \sigma^{(i)} \odot \varepsilon^{(l)}, \varepsilon^{(l)} \sim N(0, I) \end{aligned} \tag{7}$$

3 Proposed Scheme

The two images were trained using VAE respectively, and then the training data were correspondingly divided and encrypted on the generated model. Figure 2 shows the flow chart of encryption and decryption. Specific steps are described the follows.

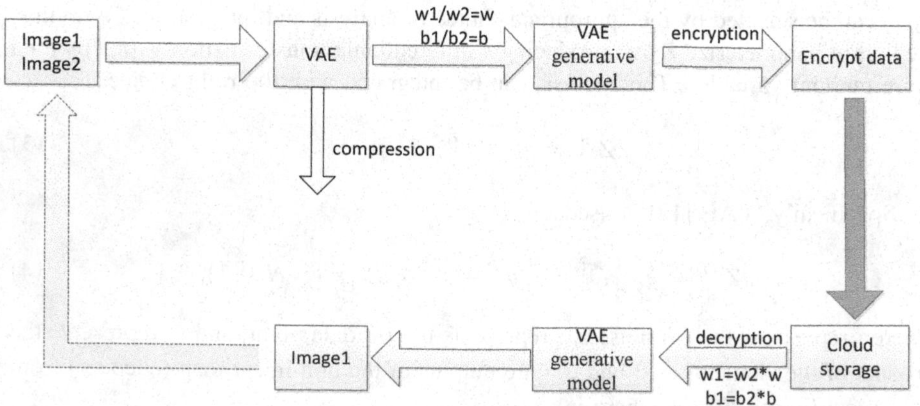

Fig. 2. Flow chart of encryption and decryption.

3.1 Training VAE Model

The VAE model is trained by a stochastic gradient descent method. The first is to set the learning rate and number of iterations of the model. Specific steps are as follows:

(1) Setting the basic parameters of the model and then input the image data normalized by the grayscale processing into the VAE.
(2) The data x through the encoder can output the mean and variance.
(3) The according to the Eq. (4), can get the latent variable z, so that the probability of coding $q_\phi(z \mid x^{(i)})$ obtained from Eq. (5).
(4) z input the decoder Via Bernoulli network output reconstruction Data, the probability of $p_\theta(x^{(i)} \mid z)$ will be known.
(5) Using the random gradient iteration training VAE network to automatically adjust the parameters and repeat steps (2)–(4), and calculate the minimum loss function by Eq. (7).

3.2 Image Compression and Encryption

In the generation model of VAE, f (•) is a non-linear activation function, and experimentally uses the sigmoid function as an activation function. By training the VAE model, we can get a compressed representation from any hidden layer. This is a form of image compression. In the experiment, we choose the second hidden layer to reconstruct the image compression effect.

The VAE is a generative model for generating images through neural network learning and training, it is possible to generate an encryption image by changing the data of the generated model. In this paper, two different image data are correspondingly divided to change the main data of the generated model, so that the generated model generates an unrecognized noise image, that is, image encryption. Experiments show that the last layer of the decoder (generation model) has a greater impact on encryption. When the image is decrypted, it is only necessary to load the data into the variational auto-encoder generation model to generate a clear image.

4 Experimental Results and Analysis

We train the VAE generative model with standard images of Lena, Baboon, Cameraman, and peppers. They have the same size as 256 * 256. The image is transformed into a 1 × 65536 pixel matrix and normalized, and means that the range of pixel values is between [0, 1]. The VAE of the first hidden layer dimension (*h_dim*) is 64, and the second hidden layer dimension (*z_dim*) is 16. The dimension of each layer in the decoder network corresponds to the encoder network. The training variable auto-encoder model is designed to get the best generation model, and the best form of the model is the variable self encoder generation model to reconstruct the image with high clarity. The gradient descent algorithm is used to update the weight and offset to reduce the error and reconstruct the clear image at the same time, and set different iterations and use two parameters as the criterion for measuring the reconstruction. These two parameters are the measurement of the mean square error (MSE) and the peak signal noise (PSNR).

The dimension of each layer in the decoder network and the encoder network correspond to each other. The training variational auto-encoder model is for obtaining the best generation model, and the generation model is the best, that is, the variational auto-encoder generation model to reconstruct the high-resolution image. Using the gradient descent algorithm to iteratively update weights and bias to reduce errors while reconstructing clear images, and setting different iteration times to reconstruct image and using two parameters to measure the effect of the reconstruction. The two parameters are the mean square error (MSE) and the peak signal noise (PSNR). The MSE [23] is the average of the square of the difference between the expected response and the actual output. It is also called squared error loss. The PSNR [24, 25] is the ratio of the maximum power signal and the power of noise, which is usually used to measure the reconstruction quality of the image compression. Their mathematical definitions are as follows:

$$MSE = \frac{1}{m \times n} \sum\nolimits_{i=0}^{n-1} \sum\nolimits_{j=0}^{n-1} [f(i,j) - g(i,j)]^2 \tag{10}$$

$$PSNR = 10 \log_{10}(\frac{255^2}{MSE}) \tag{11}$$

The largest of these is the maximum pixel value of the image, which in this experiment is 255, the image size is $m \times n$, f is the original image and g is the reconstructed image.

Figure 3 shows image reconstruction effect of the variational auto-encoder when iteration times are 10000, 20000, 30000, and 40000 respectively. It is known that the more iteration times, the clearer and higher the generated image, but the longer it takes. From the reduction of model training time and the visual effect of image reconstruction, the iteration times can be set to 30000.

The reconstruction quality under iteration times 30000 and 40000 is compared with respect to mean square error (MSE) and peak signal noise ratio(PSNR). The result is shown in Table 1.

We choose a second hidden layer to reconstruct the compressed image. Experimental results of decompressed images are shown in Fig. 4, which is use of mean square error and peak signal to noise ratio and finally determine the compression effect.

In order to verify the effect, this paper used the mean square error (MSE) and the peak signal to noise ratio (PSNR) to measure and compared with the literature [5].

Variational autoencoder image compression MSE and PSNR stack self-encoder (SAE) [5] calculated results are shown in Table 2.

And then use the trained Cameraman weight and bias in VAE to divide respectively with the weights and offsets of Lena and Baboon. The data is encrypted in the generated model framework. At the receiving end, the corresponding multiply is performed by the accepted data to the input VAE generated model to decrypt. Image encryption and decryption diagrams and histograms are shown Fig. 5.

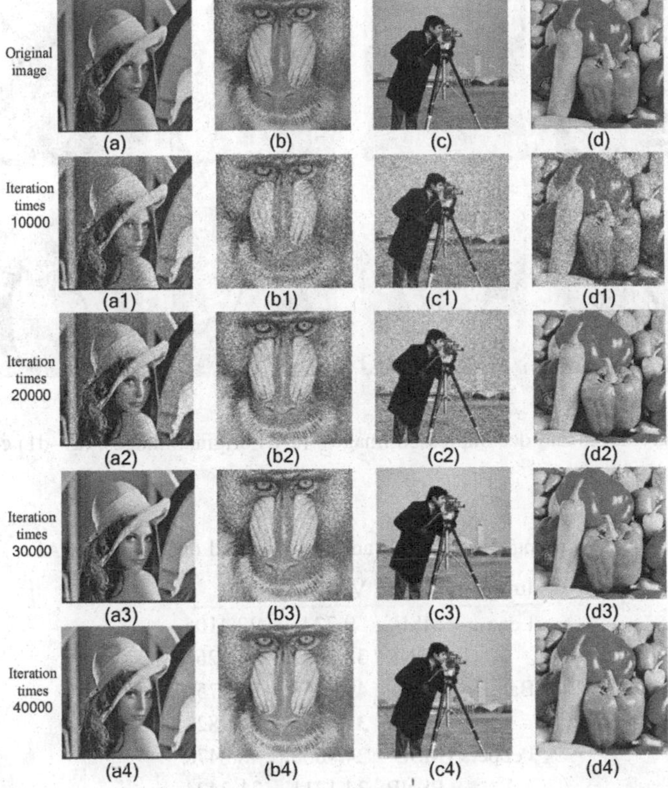

Fig. 3. The reconstruction results under different iteration times

Table 1. Image iteration times 30000, 40000 MSE and PSNR of compression

Image		Iteration times 30000	Iteration times 40000
Lena	MSE	7.5212	7.2853
	PSNR	39.3679	39.5063
Baboon	MSE	12.1928	4.2615
	PSNR	37.2698	41.8352
Cameraman	MSE	7.3107	7.6059
	PSNR	39.4912	39.3193
Peppers	MSE	16.8555	7.3107
	PSNR	35.8634	39.4912

In order to further evaluate the encryption and decryption effects, we carried out correlation coefficient analysis as shown in Table 3. The correlation coefficient is used to evaluate the correlation of a pair of adjacent pixels. The formula is as follows:

Fig. 4. Original images and decompressed images. (a–d) original images, (a1–d1) compression images.

Table 2. Comparison of MSE and PSNR based on VSE and SAE.

Image		VAE	SAE
Lena	MSE	9.7244	22.4105
	PSNR	38.2522	34.6263
Baboon	MSE	49.2058	130.2750
	PSNR	31.2106	26.9822
Peppers	MSE	24.8868	48.8470
	PSNR	34.1711	31.2424

$$\begin{aligned} E(x) &= \frac{1}{N}\sum_{i=1}^{N} x_i \\ D(x) &= \frac{1}{N}\sum_{i=1}^{N} (x_i - E(x))^2 \\ Cov(x,y) &= \frac{1}{N}\sum_{i=1}^{N} (x_i - E(x))(y_i - E(y)) \\ r_{xy} &= \frac{Cov(x,y)}{\sqrt{D(x)}\sqrt{D(y)}} \end{aligned} \tag{12}$$

Where r_{xy} is the correlation coefficient between variables x and y, E (•) is the mean function, D (•) is the variance function, x and y are the adjacent pixels.

The above experimental results show that the image correlation coefficient of the encryption method based on the variational auto-encoder generation model is significantly reduced, and the correlation coefficient between the decrypted image and the original image is also close to prove the low distortion rate. Therefore, an image

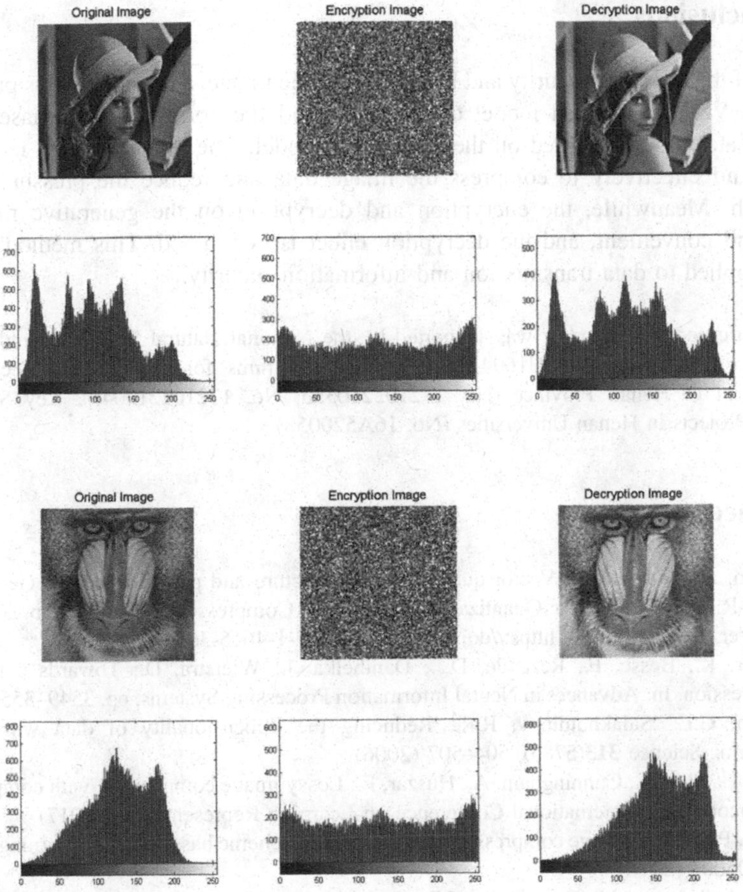

Fig. 5. Histograms of original, encryption and decryption images for Lena, Baboon on the VAE generated model

Table 3. Correlation analysis for original images, encrypted images and decrypted image

Image	Original	Ecrypte	Dcrypte
Lena	0.9755	0.1547	0.9716
Baboon	0.6671	0.1550	0.8153

encryption method based on a variational auto-encoder generation model is feasible for image encryption and can be applied to secure storage of protected images and network transmission.

5 Conclusions

In view of that privacy, security and bandwidth of the image, a new method is proposed based on VAE production model compression and the corresponding phase of the training data to be encrypted on the generation model. The feature of this method is quickly and effectively to compress the image data and reduce the pressure of the bandwidth. Meanwhile, the encryption and decryption on the generative model is simple and convenient, and the decryption effect is very good. This method can be widely applied to data transmission and information security.

Acknowledgment. This paper was supported by the National Natural Science Foundation of China (No. U1204606, No. U1604156), the Key Programs for Science and Technology Development of Henan Province (No. 172102210335, No. 172102210045), Key Scientific Research Projects in Henan Universities (No. 16A520058).

References

1. Gersho, A., Gray, R.M.: Vector quantization i: structure and performance. In: Gersho, A., Gray, R.M. (eds.) Vector Quantization and Signal Compression, vol. 159, pp. 309–343. Springer, Boston (1992). https://doi.org/10.1007/978-1-4615-3626-0_10
2. Gregor, K., Besse, F., Rezende, D.J., Danihelka, I., Wierstra, D.: Towards conceptual compression. In: Advances in Neural Information Processing Systems, pp. 3549–3557(2016)
3. Hinton, G.E., Salakhutdinov, R.R.: Reducing the dimensionality of data with neural networks. Science **313**(5786), 504–507 (2006)
4. Theis, L., Shi, W., Cunningham, A., Huszar, F.: Lossy image compression with compressive autoencoders. In: International Conference on Learning Representations (2017)
5. Hu, F., Pu, C.: An image compression and encryption scheme based on deep learning. arXiv: 1608.05001 (2016)
6. Ballé, J., Laparra, V., Simoncelli, E.P.: End-to-end optimized image compression. arXiv preprint arXiv:1611.01704 (2016)
7. Zhang, Y., Qin, C., Zhang, W.M., Liu, F.L., Luo, X.Y.: On the fault-tolerant performance for a class of robust image steganography. Sig. Process. **146**, 99–111 (2018)
8. Qin, C., Zhang, X.: Effective reversible data hiding in encrypted image with privacy protection for image content. J. Vis. Commun. Image Represent. **31**, 154–164 (2015)
9. Fan, J., Wang, J., Sun, X., Li, T.: Partial encryption of color image using quaternion discrete cosine transform. Int. J. Sig. Process. Image Process. Pattern Recognit. **8**, 171–190 (2015)
10. Ahmad, J., Khan, M.: A compression sensing and noise-tolerant image encryption scheme based on chaotic maps and orthogonal matrices. Neural Comput. Appl. (2016)
11. Fridrich, J.: Symmetric ciphers based on two-dimensional chaotic maps. Int. J. Bifurcat. Chaos. **8**, 1259–1284 (1998)
12. Kingma, D.P., Welling, M.: Auto-encoding variational bayes. arXiv preprint arXiv:1312. 6114 (2013)
13. Doersch, C.: Tutorial on Variational Autoencoders. arXiv preprint. arXiv:1606.05908 (2016)
14. Kingma, D.P., Mohamed, S., Rezende, D.J., Welling, M.: Semisupervised learning with deep generative models. In: Advances in Neural Information Processing Systems, pp. 3581–3589 (2014)

15. Lamb, A., Dumoulin, V., Courville, A.: Discriminative regularization for generative models. arXiv preprint arXiv:1602.03220 (2016)
16. Rezende, D.J., Mohamed, S., Wierstra, D.: Stochastic backpropagation and approximate inference in deep generative models. In: ICML (2014)
17. Kulkarni, T.D., Whitney, W.F., Kohli, P., Tenenbaum, J.: Deep convolutional inverse graphics network. In: NIPS (2015)
18. Salimans, T., Kingma, D., Welling, M.: Markov chain monte carlo and variational inference: bridging the gap. In: ICML (2015)
19. Gregor, K., Danihelka, I., Graves, A., Rezende, D., Wierstra, D., Draw: a recurrent neural network for image generation. In: ICCV (2015)
20. Sohn, K., Lee, H., Yan, X.: Learning structured output representation using deep conditional generative models. In: NIPS (2015)
21. Gonzalo, L., Giraldo, S.: Revisiting denoising auto-encores. In: International Conference on Learning Representations (2017)
22. Kan, M., Shan, S., Chang, H., Chen, X.: Stacked progressive auto-encoders (SPAE) for face recognition across poses. In: IEEE Conference on Computer Vision and Pattern Recognition (CVPR), pp. 1883–1890 (2014)
23. Tiwari, M., Gupta, B.: Image denoising using spatial gradient based bilateral filter and minimum mean square error filtering. Procedia Comput. Sci. **54**, 638–645 (2015)
24. Karamchandani, S.H., Gandhi, K.J., Gosalia, S.R., Madan, V.K., Merchant, S.N., Desai, U. B.: PCA encrypted short acoustic data inculcated in digital color images. Int. J. Comput. Commun. Control **10**(5), 678–685 (2015)
25. Horé, A., Ziou, D.: Image quality metrics: PSNR vs. SSIM. In: International Conference on Pattern Recognition, pp. 2366–2369 (2010)

Improved Two-Factor Authentication Protocol Based on Biometric Feature and Password for Cloud Service

Jian Song[1], Bo-ru Xu[2], Guo-chao Zhang[3], Guang-song Li[1](✉), Chuan-gui Ma[4], and Ai-jun Ge[1]

[1] State Key Laboratory of Mathematical Engineering and Advanced Computing, Zhengzhou 450001, China
lgsok@163.com
[2] University of Space Engineering, Beijing 101416, China
[3] Institute of Science, Information Engineering University, Zhengzhou 450001, China
[4] Aviation Institute, Beijing 101116, China

Abstract. Secure and efficient authentication protocols are necessary for cloud service. Multi-factor authentication protocols taking advantage of smart card, user's password and biometric, are more secure than password-based single-factor authentication protocols which are widely used in practice. However, almost all the existed two-factor authentication protocols and multi-factor authentication protocols are based on smart cards, which will inevitably lead to a series of security problems caused by the loss of smart cards. Recently, Li et al. proposed a two-factor authenticated key agreement protocol based on biometric feature and password innovatively without using smart card. But we demonstrate that Li et al.'s protocol can't resist the privileged-insider attack and the stolen verifier attack. Moreover, their protocol failed to provide user anonymity. To overcome the weaknesses of Li et al.'s scheme, we then proposed an improved two-factor authentication protocol based on the extended Chebyshev chaotic mapping. To illustrate the security of our scheme, we give a standard formal proof with the sequence of games (SOG) technique. Furthermore, we also present a comprehensive heuristic security analysis to demonstrate that the proposed protocol is capable of withstanding all the possible various attacks and provides the desired security features. Compared with other schemes, ours is more secure and efficient.

Keywords: Cloud service · Chebyshev polynomial · Anonymity Two-factor authentication protocol

1 Introduction

With the rapid developing of Cloud computing [1], now a variety of cloud servers have stored massive sensitive data of users. When users want to access the data, they need to log in the server through the public channel. However, in this process, an adversary could intercept, tamper, and forgery the information between the user and the server by

X. Sun et al. (Eds.): ICCCS 2018, LNCS 11065, pp. 90–100, 2018.
https://doi.org/10.1007/978-3-030-00012-7_9

some technical means. When users access some privacy services, they don't even want other people to know their identity. In order to provide secure and efficient services for a valid user, authentication protocols were proposed [2].

In practice, there are three basic methods to verify the identity of users: (1) What the user knows, such as user password; (2) What the user has, such as smart card; (3) The user's unique biological information, such as fingerprint and iris. As single factor authentication protocols are based on password which are easy to operate, scalable and cheap, most people prefer to use this authentication scheme. Therefore, the most commonly used authentication scheme in the current network is still single factor authentication protocols based on password [3]. However the single factor authentication protocol has the following inherent defects: (1) The limitation of human memory capacity leads to low entropy of password selection; (2) The development of password cracking hardware and algorithm makes the efficiency of off-line dictionary attack greatly improved [4].

To solve the problem, Chang et al. proposed a two-factor authentication scheme based on password and smart card [5]. After that, a number of new two-factor authentication protocols had been proposed [6–8]. But the smart card is easily lost or stolen, then the multi-factor authentication protocols combined with biological information were proposed [9–11]. However, the lost smart card attack still exists.

In 2017, Li et al. proposed a new two-factor authenticated key agreement protocol based on biometric feature and password innovatively [12]. The protocol took advantages of the user's biological information and password to achieve the secure communication without the smart card, which radically solves a series of security problems that can be caused by the loss of smart cards. But we found that Li et al.'s scheme cannot resist the privileged-insider attack and the stolen verifier attack, and does not achieve user anonymity. What's more, password change phase is not provided in their protocol.

In order to overcome the aforementioned weaknesses, and achieve user anonymity, we propose an improved two-factor authentication protocol based on biometric feature and password. The new scheme adds the password change phase, and in order to design more efficient and secure authentication protocols, the extended Chebyshev chaotic mapping [13] is introduced in this paper. The computational cost of extended Chebyshev polynomials is lower, compared to the traditional modular exponentiation operation and the point addition operation of elliptic curve [13]. In addition, the proposed scheme hides the real identities of users by exploiting the semigroup property and commutativity under composition in extended chaotic maps. It not only resists all possible attacks but also has a lower computational cost compared with the previous scheme. Moreover, the proposed scheme is proven to be secure using the sequence of games (SOG) technique [14].

The remainder of this paper is organized as follows. The preliminaries of enhanced Chebyshev chaotic maps and fuzzy extraction are given in Sect. 2. Review and cryptanalysis of Liu et al.'s protocol is present in Sect. 3. Then we propose an improved two-factor authentication protocol based on biometric feature and password for cloud service in Sect. 4. Sections 5 and 6 present security and efficiency analyses of the new protocol. Section 7 concludes the paper.

2 Preliminaries

2.1 Enhanced Chebyshev Chaotic Maps

The Enhanced Chebyshev polynomial $T_n(x)$ is a polynomial in x of degree n and is defined by the following relation:

$$T_n(x) \equiv \begin{cases} 1, & n = 0 \\ x \bmod p, & n = 1 \\ (2x \cdot T_{n-1}(x) - T_{n-2}(x)) \bmod p, & n \geq 2 \end{cases}$$

where $x \in (-\infty, +\infty)$, and p is a large prime number.

The Enhanced Chebyshev polynomial satisfies the semigroup property and satisfies

$$T_r(T_s(x)) = T_{rs}(x) = T_s(T_r(x))$$

for $s, r \in \mathbb{Z}^+$.

2.2 Difficulty Assumptions

Enhanced Chebyshev polynomials are associated with three hard problems, which are the extended chaotic-map-based discrete logarithm problem (DLP), the computational Diffie–Hellman problem (CDHP), and the decisional Diffie–Hellman problem (DDHP), described as follows.

(1) Extended Chaotic-Map-Based DLP: Given x, y, $T(\cdot)$ and p, p is a large prime number, finding the integer r satisfying

$$y = T_r(x) \bmod p$$

is computationally infeasible.

(2) Extended Chaotic-Map-Based CDHP: Given $T_r(x)$, $T_s(x)$, x, $T(\cdot)$ and p, where $r, s \geq 2$, $x \in (-\infty, +\infty)$, and p is a large prime number, calculating

$$T_{rs}(x) \equiv T_r(T_s(x)) \equiv T_s(T_r(x)) \bmod p$$

is computationally infeasible.

(3) Extended Chaotic-Map-Based DDHP: Given $T_r(x)$, $T_s(x)$, $T_z(x)$, x, $T(\cdot)$ and p, p is a large prime number, deciding whether

$$T_{rs}(x) \equiv T_z(x) \bmod p$$

holds or not is computationally infeasible.

2.3 Notions

Table 1 lists the notations that are used in this paper.

Table 1. Notations

Notation	Description
ID_X	The identity of the entity X
U_i	User
S_j	Server
p	A big prime number
G	The group of points on the elliptic curve E
P	A generating element of group G
PW_i	The password of user U_i
B_i	The biological information of user U_i
sP, s	The public/private key of sever in Li et al.'s protocol
$r/T_r(x)$	The private/public key of sever in the proposed protocol
l	The security length parameter
H	A secure hash function
$h(\cdot)$	Cryptographic one-way hash function, satisfying $h : \{0,1\}^* \to \{0,1\}^l$
MAC	A secure message authentication code
$A \xrightarrow{M} B$	A sends message M to B
$\|$	String concatenation
$\oplus$	Exclusive-or operation

3 Cryptanalysis of Li et al.'s Protocol

In this section, we analyze the weaknesses of Li et al.'s two-factor authenticated key agreement protocol based on biometric feature and password.

Privileged Insider Attacks. In the user registration phase, users directly send identity information, password and biological information to the server in plaintext. The privileged insider in the server can easily get users' login password and biological information. What's more, if users use the same password and biological information to register with other servers, then the privileged insider can compute the secrecy $W_i = H(R_i \| PW_i)$ and a valid $Auth_i = H(K \| W_i)$ to impersonate users accessing other servers.

Stolen Verifier Attacks. If the adversary A steals a copy of the server S_j's data base, then A can get (ID_i, P_i, W_i). Next, A chooses a random number $a^* \in Z_p^*$, and computes $T_A^* = a^*P$, $K^* = H(a* \cdot sP \| T_A^* \| sP)$ and $Auth_i^* = H(K^* \| W_i)$. Finally, the adversary A sends the login message $< ID_i, T_A^*, Auth_i^* >$ to the server S_j. It is easy to verify that $< ID_i, T_A^*, Auth_i^* >$ is a valid login message. Therefore, the adversary A successfully impersonates the user U_i accessing the server S_j.

In addition, Li et al.'s scheme doesn't provide anonymity and password change phase. Users' identity information and the auxiliary string are transmitted in plaintext through the open channel. Thus the adversary can track users' identity and analyze users' privacy information such as the surfing internet schedule, which will threat the privacy of users. Moreover, users cannot change the password once completing registration phase in Li et al.'s scheme. It means that the adversary can guess users' password until it's correct without worrying about the time. And once the password is cracked, the adversary can impersonate the user accessing the server forever even if the user realizes that his/her password has been cracked.

4 Our Proposed Authentication Protocol

In order to overcome the security flaws existed in Li et al.'s scheme and achieve user anonymity, we designed an improved two-factor authentication protocol based on biometric feature and password. Our scheme contains there phases, namely user registration phase, authentication phase and password change phase.

First, the server needs to generate a large prime number p and a random number $x \in \mathbb{R}$ with the security parameter l. Also, it selects a secure hash function $h(\cdot)$ and the public/private key $(T_r(x), r)$, where r is a high entropy random number to ensure the security of the server's private key. Then the server makes $<p, x, l, h(\cdot), T_r(x)>$ known to the public as the system parameters of our protocol.

User Registration. In this phase, first, the server distributes a new ID_i to the user U_i who wants to register, ensuring that the identity information of the different users won't be the same. Then, the user U_i computes the required registration information (SID_i, SP_i, X_i) and sends it to the server through another secure channel, so that the server cannot associate U_i's real identity with (SID_i, SP_i, X_i), which protects users' privacy.

Step 1. User U_i sends a registration request to the server S_j through a secure channel.

Step 2. After receiving the registration request from U_i, S_j selects a new identity ID_i, and sends $<ID_i>$ to U_i through the secure channel.

Step 3. After receiving $<ID_i>$ from S_j, U_i selects a password PW_i, and inputs biological information B_i through biological feature extractor. Then, U_i inputs B_i into the algorithm $Gen(\cdot)$, which outputs a random bit strings R_i with length l and an auxiliary string P_i. Finally, U_i computes $X_i = h(ID_i \| PW_i \| R_i)$, $SID_i = ID_i \oplus h(PW_i) \bmod l$ and $SP_i = P_i \oplus h(ID_i \| PW_i) \bmod l$, and then sends $<SID_i, SP_i, X_i>$ to the server S_j through another secure channel.

Step 4. After receiving $<SID_i, SP_i, X_i>$ from U_i, S_j computes $SX_i = X_i \oplus h(r) \bmod l$ with private key r. Then S_j stores (SID_i, SP_i, SX_i) into the data base.

Authentication. Because the user does not have a smart card in our scheme, it is assumed that the user cannot store any information. In this phase, the user has to firstly retrieve the auxiliary string from the server to restore the random string R_i generated by his/her biological information. The user then calculates the secret value X_i for the following mutual authentication.

Step 1. The user U_i enters the identity ID_i, password PW_i and biological information B_i^*. Then, U_i chooses a random number a, and computes $K_i = T_a(x)$, $K_{is} = T_a(T_r(x))$,

$SID_i = ID_i \oplus h(PW_i) \bmod l$, $PID_i = SID_i \oplus K_{is}$ and $Auth_1 = h(SID_i \parallel ID_j \parallel K_{is})$. Finally, U_i sends the message $< PID_i, ID_j, K_i, Auth_1 >$ to the server S_j.
Step 2. After receiving the message $< PID_i, ID_j, K_i, Auth_1 >$ from U_i, S_j uses the private key r to compute $K'_{is} = T_r(K_i)$, and then restores $SID'_i = PID_i \oplus K'_{is}$. Next, S_j verifies whether $Auth_1 = h(SID'_i \parallel ID_j \parallel K'_{is})$. If not, S_j rejects U_i's login request; otherwise, S_j matches (SID_i, SP_i, SX_i) in the data base. If don't success, S_j returns "Wrong identity information." to U_i; otherwise, S_j computes $Auth_2 = h(SID'_i \parallel ID_j \parallel K'_{is} \parallel SP_i)$, and then sends message $< SP_i, Auth_2 >$ to U_i.
Step 3. After receiving the message $< SP_i, Auth_2 >$ from S_j, U_i verifies whether $Auth_2 = h(SID_i \parallel ID_j \parallel K_{is} \parallel SP_i)$. If not, U_i terminates the session; otherwise, U_i computes $P'_i = SP_i \oplus h(ID_i \parallel PW_i) \bmod l$. Then U_i inputs P'_i and B^*_i into the algorithm $Rep(\cdot,\cdot)$, which outputs the random bit strings R'_i. Next, U_i computes $X'_i = h(ID_i \parallel PW_i \parallel R'_i)$ and $Auth_3 = h(SID'_i \parallel ID_j \parallel K'_{is} \parallel X'_i)$, and then sends the login message $< PID_i, ID_j, Auth_3 >$ to S_j.
Step 4. After receiving the login message $< PID_i, ID_j, Auth_3 >$ from U_i, S_j computes $X_i = SX_i \oplus h(r) \bmod l$ with private key r. Then S_j verifies whether $Auth_3 = h(SID'_i \parallel ID_j \parallel K'_{is} \parallel X_i)$. If not, S_j terminates the session; otherwise, S_j chooses a random number b, then computes $K_j = T_b(x)$, $K_{ij} = T_b(K_i)$, $k_{session} = h(ID_j \parallel X_i \parallel K_{ij})$ and $Auth_4 = h(SID'_i \parallel ID_j \parallel X_i \parallel K_{ij} \parallel k_{session})$. Finally, S_j sends the confirmation message $< PID_i, ID_j, K_j, Auth_4 >$ to U_i.
Step 5. After receiving the confirmation message $< PID_i, ID_j, K_j, Auth_4 >$ from S_j, U_i computes $K'_{ij} = T_i(K_j)$ and $k'_{session} = h(ID_j \parallel X'_i \parallel K'_{ij})$. Then U_i verifies whether $Auth_4 = h(SID'_i \parallel ID_j \parallel X_i \parallel K'_{ij} \parallel k'_{session})$. If not, U_i refuses the message and requests the server S_j to resend a confirmation message; otherwise, U_i computes the confirmation message $Auth_5 = h(ID_j \parallel SID_i \parallel K'_{ij} \parallel X'_i \parallel k'_{session})$ of the session key, and then sends message $< PID_i, ID_j, Auth_5 >$ to S_j.
Step 6. After receiving the confirmation message $< PID_i, ID_j, Auth_5 >$ from U_i, S_j verifies whether $Auth_5 = h(ID_j \parallel SID'_i \parallel K_{ij} \parallel X_i \parallel k_{session})$. If not, S_j terminates the session; otherwise, U_i and S_j complete mutual authentication successfully. And then a session is established with $k_{session}$ as the session key.

Password Change. In this phase, if the user U_i wants to change his/her password after logging in the server successfully, U_i needs to input the original password and new password. If and only if the information calculated by the original password is matched with the information stored in the data base, the server will accept the password change. The transmission information is encrypted by the established session key $k_{session}$.

Step 1. User U_i sends a password change request to the server S_j.
Step 2. After receiving the password change request from U_i, S_j sends $< SP_i >$ to U_i.
Step 3. After receiving $< SP_i >$ from S_j, U_i enters the identity ID_i, the original password PW_i, biological information B^*_i and new password PW^{new}_i. Then U_i inputs P'_i and B^*_i into the algorithm $Rep(\cdot,\cdot)$, which outputs the random bit strings R'_i. Next, U_i computes $SID_i = ID_i \oplus h(PW_i) \bmod l$, $X_i = h(ID_i \parallel PW_i \parallel R'_i)$, $SID^{new}_i = ID_i \oplus h(PW^{new}_i) \bmod l$, $SP^{new}_i = P'_i \oplus h(ID_i \parallel PW^{new}_i) \bmod l$ and $X^{new}_i = h(ID_i \parallel PW^{new}_i \parallel R'_i)$. Finally, U_i sends the message $< SID_i, X_i, SID^{new}_i, SP^{new}_i, X^{new}_i >$ to the server S_j.

Step 4. After receiving the message $<SID_i, X_i, SID_i^{new}, SP_i^{new}, X_i^{new}>$ from U_i, S_j computes $SX_i' = X_i \oplus h(r) \bmod l$ with private key r. Then S_j matches (SID_i, SX_i') with the information stored in the data base. If don't success, S_j rejects the password change; otherwise, S_j replaces (SID_i, SP_i, SX_i) with $(SID_i^{new}, SP_i^{new}, SX_i^{new})$ in the data base.

5 Security Analysis

In this section, we first analyze that the proposed protocol provides AKE security [16]. Then we demonstrate the proposed protocol can withstand privileged insider attacks and stolen-verifier attacks, and provides user anonymity and perfect forward secrecy. Finally, we compared the security features of the proposed protocol with another two two-factor authentication protocols.

5.1 Security Analysis

We assume that the adversary is able to have complete control over all message exchanges between the protocol participants. That is, the adversary can intercept, insert, modify, delete, and eavesdrop on messages exchanged among the two parties at will. The following descriptions analyze that the proposed protocol has AKE security.

Theorem 1: The probability that an adversary breaks the AKE security of the proposed authentication scheme P satisfies

$$\mathrm{Adv}_P^{\mathrm{ake}}(\mathrm{A}_{\mathrm{ake}}) \leq \frac{1}{2^{l-1}} + 2 \cdot \mathrm{Adv}^{\mathrm{ddh}}(\mathrm{A}_{\mathrm{ddh}})$$

where $\mathrm{Adv}^{\mathrm{ddh}}(\mathrm{A}_{\mathrm{ddh}})$ is the advantage that an extended chaotic-map-based DDH attacker solves the extended chaotic-map-based DDHP and l is a secure parameter size.

Proof: (The detailed proof is shown in the appendix.)

If the extended chaotic-map-based DDH assumption holds and the hash function is secure, then $\frac{1}{2^{l-1}} + 2 \cdot \mathrm{Adv}^{\mathrm{ddh}}(\mathrm{A}_{\mathrm{ddh}})$ is negligible. By definition we can come to the conclusion that the proposed scheme has AKE security.

5.2 Withstanding the Replay Attack

In our protocol, The user U_i guarantees the freshness of communicating messages by verifying $Auth_2$ and $Auth_4$ containing a generated by U_i. Similarly, the server S_j guarantees the freshness of communicating messages by verifying $Auth_5$ containing b generated by S_j. Therefore, our new protocol can withstand the replay attack.

5.3 Anonymity

In the proposed protocol, the user U_i's identity ID_i is involved in the $PID_i = SID_i \oplus K_{is}$ and $Auth_i(i = 1, \ldots, 5)$, where $K_{is} = T_a(T_r(x))$. The adversary can't derive SID_i from PID_i without knowing the random number a, and the S_j's private key r, because $K_{is} = T_a(T_r(x))$ is computationally infeasible based on the hardness of the extended chaotic-map-based CDHP. Also, the adversary can't derive SID_i from $Auth_i(i = 1, \ldots, 5)$ due to the one-way property of the hash function. What's more, because $SID_i = ID_i \oplus h(PW_i) \bmod l$, even the server S_j cannot retrieve the user's real identity ID_i. Therefore, the proposed protocol achieves user anonymity.

5.4 Withstanding the Stolen Verifier Attack

In the proposed protocol, if the adversary steals a copy of the data base, that is (SID_i, SP_i, SX_i), and tries to impersonate a user to log in the server S_j, but he/she can't compute $X_i' = h(ID_i \,||\, PW_i \,||\, R_i')$ and $Auth_3 = h(SID_i' \,||\, ID_j \,||\, K_{is}' \,||\, X_i')$ without ID_i, PW_i and R'. Also, he/she can't compute $X_i = SX_i \oplus h(r) \bmod l$ without the server S_j's private key r. Thus, the adversary can't compute a valid $Auth_3$, and a fail login will be detected by the server S_j. Therefore, the proposed protocol withstands the stolen verifier attacks.

5.5 Withstanding the Privileged Insider Attack

From the registration stage of the proposed protocol, it is easy to see that even the privileged insiders who own the private key of the server cannot retrieve the real identity information ID_i of the user, and he/she can only get limited information (SID_i, SP_i, X_i) about the user, where $SID_i = ID_i \oplus h(PW_i) \bmod l$, $SP_i = P_i \oplus h(ID_i \,||\, PW_i) \bmod l$ and $X_i = h(ID_i \,||\, PW_i \,||\, R_i)$. Therefore, through these information, the privileged insiders can't retrieve the user's identity, password or biological information due to the one-way property of the hash function.

In addition, the X_i^* corresponding with the user stored in other servers will be definitely different. Therefore, the privileged insiders can't compute a valid $Auth_3$ without X_i^*, and a fail login will be detected by other servers. That is, the privileged insiders cannot impersonate legitimate users to access other servers. Thus, the proposed protocol withstands the privileged insider attacks.

5.6 Perfect Forward Secrecy

In the proposed protocol, the established session key is $k_{session} = h(ID_j \,||\, X_i \,||\, K_{ij})$, where $K_{ij} = T_{ab}(x)$, a and b are random numbers selected by the user and the sever respectively. Previously established session keys remain secure even when the long-term keys of the server and the user are disclosed, because the adversary is computationally infeasible to compute the session key with $T_a(x)$ and $T_b(x)$ because of the hardness of the extended chaotic-map-based CDHP.

5.7 Security Features Comparisons

Because there are only a few two-factor authentication protocols based on biometric feature and password proposed, so we compared the security features of the proposed protocol with Li et al.'s [12] and a new two-factor authentication protocol [8] based on smart card with high efficiency.

Table 2 shows the results of the security features comparisons. From Table 2, we note that Li et al.'s protocol doesn't achieve user anonymity. Wang et al.'s protocol doesn't provide perfect forward secrecy. And both of them cannot withstanding the stolen verifier attack and the privileged insider attack. Table 2 shows that the proposed protocol is the only one that is free from security attacks and provides anonymity and perfect forward secrecy.

Table 2. Comparison of security features

	Wang et al.'s [8]	Li et al.'s [12]	Proposed protocol
Withstanding the replay attack	✓	✓	✓
Withstanding the man-in-the-middle attack	✓	✓	✓
Withstanding the lost password attack	✓	✓	✓
Withstanding the lost biological feature attack	✓	✓	✓
Withstanding the stolen verifier attack	✖	✖	✓
Withstanding the privileged insider attack	✖	✖	✓
Mutual authentication	✓	✓	✓
Anonymity	✓	✖	✓
Perfect forward secrecy	✖	✓	✓

6 Efficiency Analysis

This section compares the efficiency of the proposed protocol with that of Li et al.'s [12] and Wang et al.'s [8]. Table 3 shows the results the efficiency comparisons.

Table 3. Efficiency comparisons

	User	Server	Computational cost
Wang et al.'s [8]	$2T_E + 8T_H + T_S$	$2T_E + 4T_H + T_S$	$4T_E + 12T_H + 2T_S$
Li et al.'s [12]	$3T_{EcM} + 6T_H$	$3T_{EcM} + 6T_H$	$6T_{EcM} + 12T_H$
Proposed protocol	$3T_{Che} + 9T_H$	$3T_{Che} + 6T_H$	$6T_{Che} + 15T_H$

To simplify the presentation, the following symbols are defined. T_{Che}, T_{EcM}, T_H, T_S, T_M and T_{QR} respectively denote the time for executing the $T_n(x) \bmod p$ in Chebyshev polynomial, ECC point multiplication, the hash, the symmetric encryption/decryption, the modular exponentiation modulo n respectively. To be more precise, on an Intel Pentium4 2600 MHz processor with 1024 MB RAM, where n and p are 1024 bits long, T_{Che}, T_{EcM}, T_H, T_S is 21 ms, 63.1 ms, 0.5 ms, 8.7 ms respectively [13]. The computational time of the bit XOR operation and multiplication operation can be ignored compared with the above operations.

Table 3 shows that the computational cost of Wang et al.'s protocol and Li et al.'s protocol is equivalent. However, the computational cost of the proposed protocol is greatly reduced.

7 Conclusion

It is still challenging to propose more secure and efficient authentication protocols for cloud service. Though a dozen of authentication protocols have been suggested in recent years, most are based on smart cards, which will inevitably lead to a series of security problems caused by the loss of smart cards. In this paper, We have analyzed the two-factor authentication protocol based on biometric feature and password of Li et al. and we have shown its security drawbacks. Then, we proposed an improved two-factor authentication protocol based on biometric feature and password with fuzzy extractor, which adopts the extended Chebyshev chaotic mapping as a cryptographic algorithm. We have proven the proposed protocol has AKE security based on the extended chaotic-map-based DL and DDH assumptions by the sequence of games (SOG) technique. Furthermore, we also present a comprehensive heuristic security analysis to demonstrate that the proposed protocol is capable of withstanding all the possible various attacks including the weaknesses revealed in Li et al.'s protocol, and we further show that the proposed protocol supports all the desired security features. Most importantly, the proposed protocol solves the security problems caused by the stolen/loss of smart card fundamentally. Efficiency analysis shows compared with the existing schemes, the new protocol achieves higher efficiency. Therefore, the proposed scheme is more suitable for practical applications.

Acknowledgments. This paper is supported by National Key Research and Development Program (Nos. 2016YFB0800101 and 2016YFB0800100), Innovative Research Groups of the National Natural Science Foundation of China (Grant Nos. 61521003), National Natural Science Foundation of China (Grant Nos. 61379150 and 61309016).

References

1. Armbrust, M., Fox, A., Griffith, R., et al.: A view of cloud computing. Commun. ACM **53** (4), 50–58 (2010)
2. Takabi, H., Joshi, J.B.D., Ahn, G.J.: Security and privacy challenges in cloud computing environments. IEEE Secur. Priv. **8**(6), 24–31 (2010)
3. Bonneau, J., Herley, C., Oorschot, P.C.V., et al.: The quest to replace passwords: a framework for comparative evaluation of web authentication schemes. In: Security and Privacy, pp. 553–567. IEEE (2012)

4. M. Adeptus, Hashdumps and Passwords. http://www.adeptus-mechanicus.com/codex/hashpass/hashpass.php (2014)
5. Chang, C.C., Wu, T.C.: Remote password authentication with smart cards. IEE Proc. E – Comput. Digit. Techn. **138**(3), 165–168 (2005)
6. Xie, Q., Wong, D., Wang, G., et al.: Provably secure dynamic ID-based anonymous two-factor authenticated key exchange protocol with extended security model. IEEE Trans. Inf. Forensics Secur. **12**(6), 1382–1392 (2017)
7. Ding, W., Ping, W.: Two birds with one stone: two-factor authentication with security beyond conventional bound. IEEE Trans. Depend. Secur. Comput. **PP**(99), 1 (2016)
8. Wang, D., Wang, N., Wang, P., et al.: Preserving privacy for free: efficient and provably secure two-factor authentication scheme with user anonymity. Inf. Sci. **321**, 162–178 (2015)
9. He, D., Zeadally, S., Kumar, N., et al.: Anonymous authentication for wireless body area networks with provable security. IEEE Syst. J. **PP**(99), 1–12 (2016)
10. Jiang, Q., Zeadally, S., Ma, J., et al.: Lightweight three-factor authentication and key agreement protocol for internet-integrated wireless sensor networks. IEEE Access **5**, 3376–3392 (2017)
11. Wu, F., Xu, L., Kumari, S., et al.: An improved and provably secure three-factor user authentication scheme for wireless sensor networks. Peer-to-Peer Netw. Appl. **11**, 1–20 (2016)
12. Li, X.W., Yang, D.Q., Chen, B.X., et al.: Two-factor authenticated key agreement protocol based on biometric feature and password. J. Commun. **38**(7), 89–95 (2017)
13. Kocarev, L., Lian, S.: Chaos-based Cryptography: Theory Algorithms and Applications. Springer, Heidelberg (2011). https://doi.org/10.1007/978-3-642-20542-2
14. Shoup, V.: Sequences of games: a tool for taming complexity in security proofs. IACR Cryptology ePrint Archive, p. 332 (2004)
15. Dodis, Y., Reyzin, L., Smith, A.: Fuzzy extractors: how to generate strong keys from biometrics and other noisy data. In: Cachin, C., Camenisch, Jan L. (eds.) EUROCRYPT 2004. LNCS, vol. 3027, pp. 523–540. Springer, Heidelberg (2004). https://doi.org/10.1007/978-3-540-24676-3_31
16. Kanso, A., Yahyaoui, H., Almulla, M.: Keyed hash function based on a chaotic map. Inf. Sci. **186**(1), 249–264 (2012)
17. Boyko, V., MacKenzie, P., Patel, S.: provably secure password-authenticated key exchange using Diffie-Hellman. In: Preneel, B. (ed.) EUROCRYPT 2000. LNCS, vol. 1807, pp. 156–171. Springer, Heidelberg (2000). https://doi.org/10.1007/3-540-45539-6_12

Mass Discovery of Android Malware Behavioral Characteristics for Detection Consideration

Xin Su[1,2,3], Weiqi Shi[3], Jiuchuan Lin[4(✉)], and Xin Wang[5]

[1] Hunan Provincial Key Laboratory of Network Investigational Technology, Hunan Police Academy, Changsha, China
[2] Key Laboratory of Network Crime Investigation of Hunan Provincial Colleges, Hunan Police Academy, Changsha, China
[3] Department of Information Technology, Hunan Police Academy, Changsha, China
[4] Key Lab of Information Network Security of Ministry of Public Security, The Third Research Institute of Ministry of Public Security, Shanghai, China
linjiuchuan@stars.org.cn
[5] College of Computer Science and Electronics Engineering, Hunan University, Changsha, China

Abstract. Android malware have surged and been sophisticated, posing a great threat to users. The key challenge of detect Android malware is how to discovery their behavioral characteristics at a large scale, and use them to detect Android malware. In this work, we are motivated to discover the discriminatory features extracted from Android APK files for Android malware detection. To achieve this goal, firstly we extract a very large number of static features from each Android application (or app). Secondly, we explain the importance of each kind of feature in Android malware detection. Thirdly, we fed these features into three different classifiers (e.g., SVM, DT, RandomFoerst) for the detection of Android malware. We conduct extensive experiments on large real-world app sets consisting of 6,820 Android malware and 37,581 Android benign apps. The experimental results and our analysis give insights regarding what discriminatory features are most effective to characterize Android malware for building an effective and efficient Android malware detection approach.

1 Introduction

Android platform dominates the smartphone operating system market, and has become the main attack target for Android malware. According to the report from IDC [2]. Android takes the first place again with 87.6% market share in the second quarter of 2016. However, this rapid deployment and extensive availability of Android apps has made them attractive targets for various malware. Malware authors generally take advantage of the update mechanism of mobile apps to infect existing Android apps with malicious code and thus compromise the security of the smartphone. Recent statistical data show that malware based

X. Sun et al. (Eds.): ICCCS 2018, LNCS 11065, pp. 101–112, 2018.
https://doi.org/10.1007/978-3-030-00012-7_10

on Android platform accounts for 97% of mobile malware [1]. The private data of the users, such as IMEI, contacts list, and other user specific data are the primary target for the attackers, which is a serious threat for the security and privacy of Android users. Consequently, there is an urgent need to identify and cope with the malware for the Android platform.

This ever-growing malware threat has stimulated research into Android app security. Existing work mainly focused on (i) permission security model analysis [8,16], (ii) app vulnerability mitigation [9,11], and (iii) malware behavior analysis and detection [6,19] based on static or dynamic analysis.

As the number of apps and malapps as well as their variants explosively increases in the market, it is crucial to discovery and precisely characterize the behavior of an app, so as to develop methods for Android malware detection at a large scale. The main challenge of characterizing apps is threefold as follows. First, apps running on Android have distinct characteristics compared to traditional desktop software. Second, Android malware is becoming increasingly sophisticated by leveraging legitimate apps and system vulnerabilities to evade detection systems. Third, some unprotected data on smartphone such as sensor data can be exploited to steal confidential information.

In order to better characterize the behavior of Android apps for malware classification, in this work, we aim at discovering discriminatory features of apps. We first extract 11 kind feature sets from Android APK files. Then, we explain the importance of each kind of feature to understand better how the features perform differently, how to select features in detection tasks and when to retrain the classification models. Extensive experiments are conducted with different feature sets and feature groups. First, in order to study the discriminative power of each feature set, we feed them into four classifiers to compare the classification performance. Second, the composition of relevant features selected by Random Forest classifier is thoroughly analyzed to reveal the most useful features of each feature set for Android malware analysis and detection.

In summary, the main contributions of this work are listed as following:

- We explore eleven kind of Android app feature sets to discovery and characterize behaviors of Android apps based on static analysis. We propose to employ three classifiers, namely, linear Support Vector Machine (SVM), J.48, and Random Forest (RF), and compare the discriminative power of different feature sets and the performance of different classifiers.
- We analyze the composition of relevant features and discover the usage patterns of features in the Android malware. These patterns help to understand the behaviors of malapps with the most suitable features for automated Android malware detection.
- We conduct extensive experiments with a very large Android benign app and malware sets. The experimental results demonstrate the effectiveness of our methods and models

The rest of this paper is organized as follows. Section 2 describes the feature sets. Section 3 describes four different classifiers in this study. Section 4 provides a detailed evaluation and results analysis. Section 5 describes the related work, and Sect. 6 concludes this paper.

2 Behavioral Characteristics Description

As the first step, our approach performs a lightweight static analysis of a given Android app. The behavioral characteristics we extracted can be categorized into 11 behavioral characteristic sets (abbreviated as BC). Then, we categorized the 11 behavioral characteristic sets into 2 types based on the extracted source. The first type of behavioral characteristic sets named configuration-based behavioral characteristic sets which extract from Android app configuration files, such as AndroidManifest.xml, rsa file. The second type of behavioral characteristic sets named dex-based behavioral characteristic sets which extracted from dex code. Next, we will describe these behavioral as following 9 aspects.

2.1 Behavioral Characteristic Sets from Configuration File

Every Android app developed for Android must include a manifest file called AndroidManifest.xml which provides data supporting the installation and later execution of the app. The information stored in this file can be efficiently retrieved on the device using the Android Asset Packaging Tool that enables us to extract the following sets:

Component Name (BC_1): The majority of Android malapps are repackaged legitimate apps [18], in which the attackers insert the same malicious payload (usually in terms of components) into many different legitimate apps. We include component names as a behavioral characteristic set to capture the behavior of component reuse presented in both benign apps and malware.

Request Permission (BC_2) and Hardware and Software Requirement (BC_3): In Android system, the two behavioral characteristics indicate the demands of the apps for system resources. Permission request patterns can characterize the apps intents of resource accessing. In this paper, we use all the permissions defined by Android platform and the Android apps. Moreover, Android apps signal their hardware and software requirements to devices in their manifest files with <uses-feature> elements. We thus extract the hardware and software feature descriptors defined in Android documents as the third behavioral characteristic set.

Filter Intent (BC_4): Android platform uses intent as a messaging object an app and the platform can send to another apps component for requesting an action or process. Android malware often declare with an intent filter to receive specific system events, e.g., *BOOT_COMPLETED*, for activating malicious activity. In this work, we extract all the intent filters in the manifest files of the samples as a feature set.

Besides the AndroidManifest.xml file, rsa is another configuration file of Android app, we also extract one behavioral characteristic set from this file as following description.

Certificate Information (BC_5): App developers must sign their APK files with a certificate, the private key of which is held by themselves. This certificate helps to distinguish a developer from others. Developer information such as the country, email address, organization, state or province, as well as the SHA-1 thumbprint, can be extracted from the certificate.

2.2 Behavioral Characteristic Sets from Dex File

Android apps are developed in Java and compiled into optimized bytecode for the Dalvik virtual machine. This bytecode can be efficiently disassembled and provides our approach with information about API calls and data used in an app. To achieve a low run-time, we implement a lightweight disassembler based on the dex libraries of the Android platform that can output all API calls and strings contained in an app. We use this information to construct the following behavioral characteristic sets.

Restricted API Calls (BC_6) and Used Permissions (BC_7): Requesting a permission does not mean that the app actually accesses to the corresponding resources. We scan the disassembled code of the app samples and record whether they invoke API calls protected by some permissions. Additionally, we use the API-permission mapping provided by PScout [4] to obtain the used permissions. Used permissions and restricted API calls reflect the resources an app actually access at different levels of granularity.

String (BC_8): By matching with regular expression patterns, we collect all the URLs, IP addresses, file path strings, and numbers (with more than three digits) in the disassembled code as a feature set. These strings may involve many malicious behaviors.

Payload Information (BC_9): Payload indicates the files inside the APK archive file. We include payload information as a behavioral characteristic set, since some Android malware contain extra .apk files in the host apps that tricks users to install these malicious .apk files, and since Android malware can change the file name extension from .apk or .dex into .png, so as not to arouse suspicion.

Code Patterns (BC_{10}): In this behavioral characteristic set, we check whether an app dynamically loads .dex file or Linux native code, whether an app executes shell commands, whether an app use Java reflection techniques, and whether an app invokes cryptographic functions, etc.

Suspicious API Calls (BC_{11}): Inspired by Drebin [6], we extract certain API calls that allow access to sensitive smartphone resources such as accessing device ID, sending and receiving SMS messages, which are frequently used by Android malware.

3 Approach

The purpose of our study is to find discriminatory behavioral characteristics to effectively classify Android malware based on a variety of behavioral characteristics which are directly extracted from APK files with static analysis techniques. Thus, we treat the Android malware detection as a binary classification problem.

The framework of our approaches is shown in Fig. 1 consisting of four steps. First, we collect a large amount of apps from Google Plat, third-party Android app markets and Android malware in the wild. Second, we extract as many behavioral characteristics from the apps as possible, in order to characterize each app with a vector. Finally, we conduct comprehensive experiments including: (A) comparing the performance of different feature sets, (B) classifier comparison.

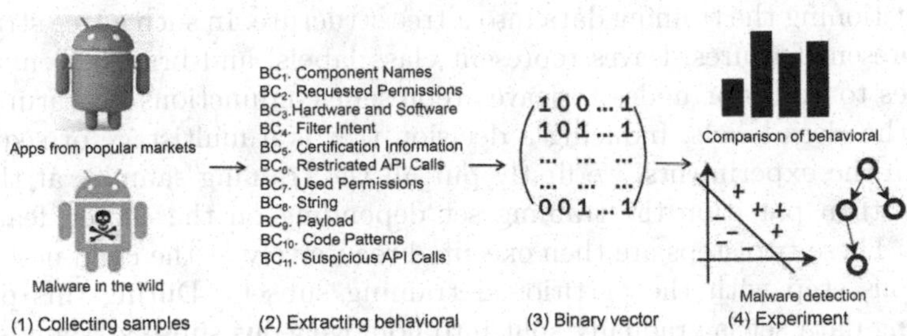

Fig. 1. Overview of our approach

We already discussed the behavioral characteristic sets extracted from Android apps, and the dataset we used will be discussed in Sect. 4. In this section, we mainly discuss the machine learning classifiers we use in this work.

3.1 Classification Models

Linear Support Vector Machine (SVM): SVM is one of the machine learning classifiers receiving the most attention currently, and its various applications are being introduced because of its high performance. The SVM could also solve the problem of classifying nonlinear data. Of the input features, unnecessary ones are removed by the SVM machine learning classifier itself and the modeling is carried out, so there is some overhead in the aspect of time. However, it could be expected to perform better than other machine learning classifiers in the aspect of complexity or accuracy in analysis.

Figure 2 shows how to find hyperplanes which are criteria for the SVM to do the learning process to classify data. All hyperplanes (a), (b) and (c) classify two things correctly, but the greatest advantage of the SVM is that it selects hyperplane (c) which maximizes the margin (the distance between data) and accordingly maximizes the capability of generalization.

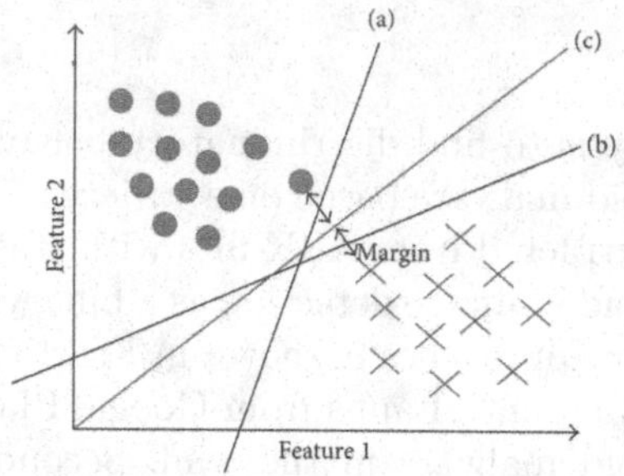

Fig. 2. classification method of SVM

Decision Tree (DT): Decision tree is a classification model defined by recursively partitioning the training data into a tree structure. In such a tree structure, nodes represent features, leaves represent class labels, and branches emanating from nodes to nodes or nodes to leaves represent conjunctions of features that generate the class labels. Inducing a decision tree is a multistage or sequential process. In the experiments, we firstly put all the training samples at the root node, and then partition the training set depending on the chosen feature at this node. These two steps are then executed recursively at the child nodes from the previous step with the partitioned training subsets. During this process, the training data set is gradually split into homogeneous subsets. Many specific decision tree algorithms have been proposed. We employ C4.5 in this work.

Random Forest (RF): Random forest is a combined classifier consisting of a collection of decision trees where each tree is learned independently on a randomly selected subset of training data. A subset for training each decision tree is selected by randomly sampling from both features and objects. The final classification will be done by voting within all the generated trees.

3.2 Embedded into Vector

Because the majority of classification models process data with numerical vectors, we need to map our extracted behavioral characteristics into a joint feature vector. To address this, we define the behavioral characteristic vector as follows:

$$F = \{f_1, f_2, ..., f_n\}, F^a = \{f_1^a, f_2^a, ..., f_m^a\} \tag{1}$$

First, all of behavioral characteristics from Android apps are contained in F, for each given app a, it can be defined with the features it contains. As shown in Eq. 1, n is the size of the feature set and m is the number of different behavioral characteristics in a. Then we define behavioral characteristic vector of an Android app as V in Eq. 2.

$$V = \{v_1, v_2, ..., v_i\}, v_i = \begin{cases} 1 & f_i \in F \text{ and } f_i^a \in F^a, 1 \leq i \leq n \\ 0 & \text{otherwise} \end{cases} \tag{2}$$

Thus a behavioral characteristic vector can be translated into $V = \{0, 1, 0, ...\}$, 1 indicates that the behavioral characteristic is contained in this app, whereas 0 indicates not. However, V is often a sparse vector, in order to reduce the storage overhead, we transform V to a compressed format V^*. Assuming that the behavioral characteristics are arranged in a fixed order, then we can index a feature by its position, and V^* is defined as follow:

$$V^* = \{1, 4, 6, ...\} \tag{3}$$

in Eq. 3, the positions of non-zero elements in V are stored in V^*, which saves a great amount of memory space when modeling. Unlike Drebin's high-dimensional vector, V only contains several hundreds typical behavioral characteristics benefiting from the extracted behavioral characteristics. According to our experiments, algorithm like SVM used in Drebin takes more than one hour to build a model on such a high-dimensional vectors.

4 Evaluation

4.1 Dataset

We collect a very large data set in order to comprehensively evaluate our methods. The data sets consist of two parts, benign apps collected from Google Play and popular third-party Android app markets and Android malware collected from different sources.

For benign apps, we first download 150 top popular (150 top rating score) Android apps from each of 31 most popular categories, which cover most of the app categories which are defined in Google Play, such as Game, Book, etc. Then, we collect 42,602 Android apps from four popular third-party Android app markets, such as *Anzhi, hiapk, mi, ZOL*. We use *ViruaTotal* to verify these apps, and find 32,931 apps are labeled as benign app. Therefore, we collect 37,581 Android benign apps.

For Android malware, we collect 1,260 malware from *Android Malware Genome Project* [18], and 5,560 Android malware from the dataset used by *Drebin* [6]. In total, the Android app dataset contains 37,581 Android benign apps and 6,820 Android malware.

4.2 Behavioral Characteristic Set Comparison

In this experiment, we first evaluate detection accuracy based on different single behavioral characteristic set, and to find importance of each single behavioral characteristic set in Android malware detection. Table 1 shows the detail results of this experiment.

From Table 1, we can find that the results of *Requested perimission* (BC_1) can achieve the best performance when using single type of behavioral characteristic set. This result means *Requested permission* is an important behavioral characteristic for Android malware detection. However, the results of using every

Table 1. Comparison results of single behavioral characteristic set (the order of classifiers results is SVM/DT/RF)

BC	Precision	Recall	F-Measure	ROC Area
Code	0.686/0.697/0.694	0.685/0.695/0.694	0.685/0.69/0.69	0.684/0.725/0.724
Hardware and software	0.563/0.563/0.564	0.548/0.548/0.548	0.411/0.411/0.413	0.507/0.503/0.547
Intent	0.762/0.839/0.854	0.629/0.827/0.84	0.723/0.823/0.837	0.69/0.879/0.892
Requested permission	0.876/0.916/0.938	0.876/0.916/0.937	0.876/0.916/0.937	0.868/0.938/0.975
Suspicious API	0.752/0.773/0.779	0.753/0.773/0.779	0.752/0.772/0.777	0.749/0.842/0.861
Used permission	0.841/0.853/0.867	0.837/0.853/0.867	0.835/0.852/0.867	0.83/0.917/0.943
Restricted API	0.859/0.901/0.916	0.843/0.873/0.904	0.851/0.887/0.91	0.905/0.915/0.927
Payload	0.755/0.684/0.699	0.555/0.685/0.7	0.407/0.684/0.698	0.512/0.74/0.779
Cert information	0.796/0.754/0.806	0.744/0.759/0.807	0.769/0.756/0.807	0.8/0.805/0.834
String	0.731/0.751/0.736	0.724/0.74/0.762	0.727/0.745/0.763	0.76/0.65/0.784
Component name	0.84/0.861/0.893	0.839/0.86/0.847	0.839/0.86/0.87	0.851/0.865/0.875

single type of behavioral characteristic set cannot achieve good performance, which means only use single type of behavioral characteristic set cannot characterize Android malware, and cannot obtain good detection results.

Second, we divide these behavioral characteristic sets into two categories based on extracted source as we mentioned in Sect. 1, and fed both of categories into three classification models to compare detection results. Figure 3 shows the detail results.

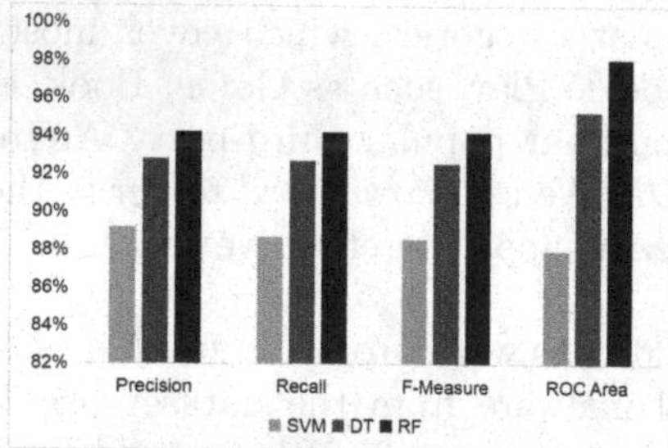

(a) Results of configuration-based behavioral characteristic sets

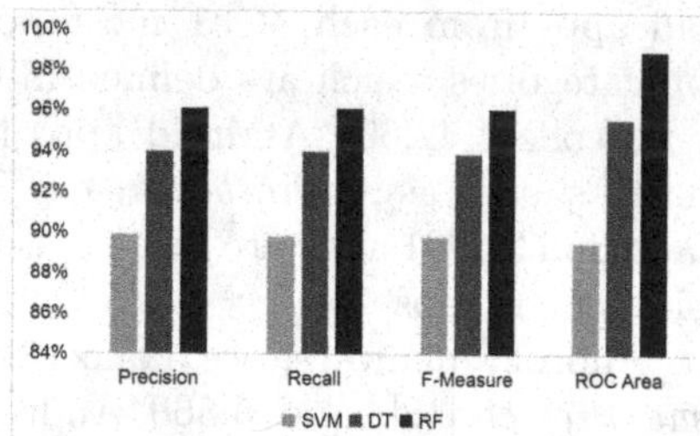

(b) Results of dex-based behavioral characteristic sets

Fig. 3. The comparison results of two categories behavioral characteristic sets

From Fig. 3, we can find that using dex-based behavioral characteristic set can achieve better performance than configuration-based one. This results means Android malware contain more distinct behaviors in dex code.

4.3 Detection Results

In this section, we fed all 11 behavioral characteristic sets into three classification models, and Fig. 4 shows the detail results. From this figure, we can find that using all behavioral characteristic sets can achieve better results than single or each category. Because all 11 behavioral characteristic sets can cover more behaviors of Android malware, which could obtain better detection results.

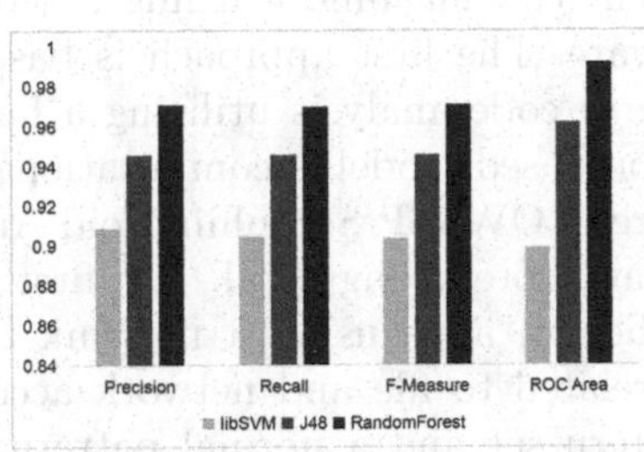

Fig. 4. classification results of all 11 behavioral characteristic sets

Moreover, we find *RF* could achieve best results among three classification models, which means *RF* is the most suitable classifier for the dataset we used in this work.

5 Related Work

The analysis and detection of Android malware have been a vivid area of research in the past several years. Several categories of researches have been proposed to cope with the growing amount of more and more sophisticated Android malware. We divide these researches into two categories which are described as follows.

5.1 Extract Behavioral Characteristics from Android App

Wang et al. [15] extract static behavioral characteristics, such as requested permission. Intent, component to characterize Android app, and use ensemble learning algorithm to build classification model to detect Android malware. Feizollah et al. [7] evaluate the effectiveness of Android Intents (explicit and implicit) as a distinguishing behavioral characteristic for identifying Android malware. This work also shows that Intents are semantically rich behavioral characteristic that are able to encode the intentions of malware when compared to other well-studied features such as permissions. Wu et al. [17] adopts a machine learning approach that leverages the use of dataflow application program interfaces (APIs) as classification features to detect Android malware. The authors conduct a thorough analysis to extract dataflow-related API-level features and improve the k-nearest neighbour classification model. Saracino et al. [13] present MADAM, a novel host-based malware detection system for Android devices which simultaneously analyzes and correlates features at four levels: kernel, application, user and package, to detect and stop malicious behaviors. Chen et al. [5] study the problem of learning and verifying unwanted behaviours abstracted as automata from malware.

5.2 Detection of Android Malware

Milosevic et al. [12] present two machine learning aided approaches for static analysis of Android malware. The first approach is based on permissions and the other is based on source code analysis utilizing a bag-of-words representation model. The permission-based model is computationally inexpensive, and is implemented as the feature of OWASP Seraphimdroid Android app that can be obtained from Google Play Store. Tong et al. [14] first collect execution data of sample malware and benign apps using a net link technology to generate patterns of system calls related to file and network access. Then, the authors build up a malicious pattern set and a normal pattern set by comparing the patterns of malware and benign apps with each other. At last, they compare them with both the malicious and normal pattern sets offline in order to detect Android malware from unknown app. Flowdroid [3] detected malware by building a precise model of Androids lifecycle, which helped to reduce missed leaks or false positives. Jiang et al. [10] propose a novel multi-channel intelligent attack detection method based on LSTM-RNNs.

6 Conclusions

In this work, we aim to discovery and characterize Android app behavioral characteristics, and combine them with three well-known classification models to detect Android malware at a large scale. To achieve this goal, we first extract 11 single kind of static behavioral characteristic sets from Android app, and category them into two groups: congiguration-based and dex-based behavioral characteristic. Then, we explain the importance of extracted behavioral characteristic sets from 9 aspects for purpose of Android malware detction. Third, we fed the 11 types of behavioral characteristics into three classification models to detect Android malware. Finally, we conduct two kinds of experiments to evaluate the efficiency of our approach, namely behavioral characteristic comparison experiment and Android malware detection experiment. The experiment results show that use single behavioral characteristic to detect Android malware cannot achieve high accuracy, and Random Forest can obtain the highest detection accuracy among three classification models.

Acknowledgement. This work is supported by the Science and Technology Projects of Hunan Province (No. 2016JC2074), the Research Foundation of Education Bureau of Hunan Province, China (No. 16B085), the Open Research Fund of Key Laboratory of Network Crime Investigation of Hunan Provincial Colleges (No. 2017WLZC008), the National Science Foundation of China (No. 61471169), the Key Lab of Information Network Security, Ministry of Public Security (No. C16614).

References

1. Mobile malware. http://www.forbes.com/sites/gordonkelly-/2014/03/24/report-97-of-mobile-malware-is-on-android-this-is-the-easy-way-you-stay-safe/
2. Smartphone OS market share, Q2 2016. http://www.idc.com/prodserv/smartphone-os-market-share.jsp, http://www.idc.com/prodserv/smartphone-os-market-share.jsp
3. Arzt, S., et al.: FlowDroid: precise context, flow, field, object-sensitive and lifecycle-aware taint analysis for android apps. In: Proceedings of the 35th ACM SIGPLAN Conference on Programming Language Design and Implementation, pp. 259–269 (2014)
4. Au, K.W.Y., Zhou, Y.F., Huang, Z., Lie, D.: PScout: analyzing the android permission specification. In: Proceedings of the 2012 ACM Conference on Computer and Communications Security, pp. 217–228 (2012)
5. Chen, W., Aspinall, D., Gordon, A.D., Sutton, C., Muttik, I.: On robust malware classifiers by verifying unwanted behaviours. In: Ábrahám, E., Huisman, M. (eds.) IFM 2016. LNCS, vol. 9681, pp. 326–341. Springer, Cham (2016). https://doi.org/10.1007/978-3-319-33693-0_21
6. Arp, D., Spreitzenbarth, M., Hübner, M., Gascon, H., Rieck, K.: DREBIN: effective and explainable detection of android malware in your pocket. In: Network and Distributed System Security Symposium, pp. 23–26 (2014)
7. Feizollah, A., Anuar, N.B., Salleh, R., Suarez-Tangil, G., Furnell, S.: AndroDialysis: analysis of android intent effectiveness in malware detection. Comput. Secur. **65**, 121–134 (2017)
8. Felt, A.P., Ha, E., Egelman, S., Haney, A., Chin, E., Wagner, D.: Android permissions: user attention, comprehension, and behavior. In: Proceedings of the Eighth Symposium on Usable Privacy and Security, pp. 1–14 (2012)
9. Felt, A.P., Wang, H.J., Moshchuk, A., Hanna, S., Chin, E.: Permission re-delegation: attacks and defenses. In: Proceedings of the 20th USENIX Conference on Security, pp. 22–22 (2011)
10. Jiang, F., et al.: Deep learning based multi-channel intelligent attack detection for data security, pp. 1–1 (2018)
11. Lu, L., Li, Z., Wu, Z., Lee, W., Jiang, G.: CHEX: statically vetting android apps for component hijacking vulnerabilities. In: Proceedings of the 2012 ACM Conference on Computer and Communications Security, pp. 229–240 (2012)
12. Milosevic, N., Dehghantanha, A., Choo, K.K.R.: Machine learning aided android malware classification. Comput. Electr. Eng. **61**, 266–274 (2017)
13. Saracino, A., Sgandurra, D., Dini, G., Martinelli, F.: MADAM: effective and efficient behavior-based android malware detection and prevention. IEEE Trans. Depend. Secur. Comput. **15**(1), 83–97 (2018)
14. Tong, F., Yan, Z.: A hybrid approach of mobile malware detection in android. J. Parallel Distrib. Comput. **103**, 22–31 (2017)
15. Wang, W., Li, Y., Wang, X., Liu, J., Zhang, X.: Detecting android malicious apps and categorizing benign apps with ensemble of classifiers. Future Gener. Comput. Syst. **78**, 987–994 (2018)
16. Wang, W., Wang, X., Feng, D., Liu, J., Han, Z., Zhang, X.: Exploring permission-induced risk in android applications for malicious application detection. In: IEEE Transactions on Information Forensics and Security, pp. 1869–1882 (2017)
17. Wu, S., Wang, P., Li, X., Zhang, Y.: Effective detection of android malware based on the usage of data flow apis and machine learning. Inf. Softw. Technol. **75**, 17–25 (2016)

18. Zhou, Y., Jiang, X.: Dissecting android malware: characterization and evolution. In: S&P, pp. 95–109 (2012)
19. Zhou, Y., Wang, Z., Zhou, W., Jiang, X.: Hey, you, get off of my market: detecting malicious apps in official and alternative android markets. In: Network and Distributed System Security Symposium, pp. 50–52 (2012)

Medical Information Access Control Method Based on Weighted Information Entropy

Lijuan Zheng[1,2(✉)], Linhao Zhang[2], Meng Cui[2], Jianyou Chen[3], Shaobo Yang[4], and Zhaoxuan Li[2]

[1] Beijing Key Laboratory of Security and Privacy in Intelligent Transportation, Beijing Jiaotong University, Beijing 100044, China
zhenglijuan@stdu.edu.cn

[2] School of Information Science and Technology, ShiJiaZhuang TieDao University, Shijiazhuang 050043, China
{1187907444,1084324590,970116648}@qq.com

[3] Hebei Coal Safety (Security) Training Center, Qinhuangdao 066100, China
chenjy9898@163.com

[4] The Sunzhuang Mining Company of Handan City, Handan 056200, China
yzredfox@163.com

Abstract. With the rapid popularization of the Internet and the Information Office of medical institutions, a large amount of electronic medical information has been generated. Medical information involves the privacy of the patient. At present, many lawless use various means to obtain the patient's privacy information and take advantage of it for benefits. At present, there are many research methods of medical data access control, but the structure of medical data is complex, and the amount of data is huge. The contradiction between privacy protection and data utilization is still difficult to balance. A method of medical information access control based on weighted information entropy is proposed for the privacy protection and data utilization of electronic medical information. This method uses information entropy to measure the amount of information that a medical information visitor possesses, and sets different weights for different kinds of privacy information to assist in computing information contents. Method sets the tolerance of information and compares the amount of information the visitor has with the tolerance. The access strategy decides whether to feed back the requested medical information according to comparison result. After security analysis and comparison, this method can effectively protect the patient's privacy information and meet the needs of the legitimate visitors.

Keywords: Medical information · Information entropy · Access control

1 Introduction

In recent years, the Internet has developed rapidly. The popularity of digital and information systems has caused the rapid expansion of information. Big data and cloud computing have gained momentum in recent years and have gradually touched various fields. Cloud computing technology has greatly promoted the improvement of informationization in all walks of life. Massive data generated by the information system

X. Sun et al. (Eds.): ICCCS 2018, LNCS 11065, pp. 113–122, 2018.
https://doi.org/10.1007/978-3-030-00012-7_11

can also be stored in cloud service platform, which saves local storage resources. In particular, many unexpected research results have been obtains in the medical field [1, 2]. It also injects a greater impetus to China's medical reform [3]. Big medical data are mainly used to discover new laws of disease and carry out precise medical treatment. A few weeks before the outbreak of H1N1 flu in 2009, Google's engineers published a paper on influenza prediction. The concept of precise treatment of cancer by sequencing big data genes is also gradually being widely accepted.

According to the source, big medical data can be divided into 4 categories: pharmaceutical enterprises and Life Sciences, clinical care and laboratory data, medical expenses/utilization, and health management software/social networking [4]. According to the role of data analysis, it can be divided into disease diagnosis, precision medical treatment and disease research [5]. Big medical data are mainly used to discover new laws of disease and to carry out precise medical treatment. Medical data are continuing to grow, and data types are complex and diverse. It contains a lot of structured data, unstructured documents, medical images, and so on [6], and the problems associated with them are also prominent. The risk of disclosure of privacy data is the common concern of patients and medical institutions. From the website vulnerability report published over the years, the amount of information leaked from medical website vulnerability is the largest [7]. So we can see the harm of medical data leakage. The disclosure of medical data is not only caused by the external risks of the medical institutions, but also the internal leakage. Inaccurate management of medical institutions and unclear access rights are common. Some internal personnel of a medical institution occur in exchange for rich and unlawful interests at the expense of the patient's privacy information [8]. Under the impetus of the Internet and cloud computing technologies, data integration has become an inevitable trend in the development of information technology, due to the rationalization of medical resource allocation [9]. However, data sharing makes the privacy of medical data more difficult to guarantee security. Many medical institutions have authority to access or operate the same medical resource, causing it difficult to make effective privacy protection of medical privacy information without affecting to use it.

In order to solve the problem of privacy disclosure in medical information access, a medical information access control method based on weighted information entropy is proposed in this paper. The information entropy obtained by the weighted calculation describes the amount of information about the privacy information in the information accessed by the visitor. Whether to respond to the access request is according to the amount of privacy information which the visitor has already mastered.

2 Related Work

Medical information is a relatively special information. The timeliness limitation is invalid and the type of data is very complex. It causes huge volume of medical information and complex processing. It is difficult to use privacy protection without affecting its use.

In order to avoid leakage of electronic medical information, the corresponding researchers proposed a solution based on traditional access control policies for protecting medical privacy information. At present, most of the methods are based on data anonymity. Ensure the availability of data at the same time, these methods properly losing some sensitive information to protect the information security of medical privacy. Access control is also a more applied method of privacy information protection which is used more. Zhou et al. proposed a hierarchical authorization based on role-based access control model for electronic medical record storage cloud system access control strategy [10]. According to the degree of patient's privacy protection needs of their own information, Huo et al. proposed a patient-oriented privacy protection access control mechanism [11]. Khan and Mckillop propose a patient-centered access control scheme based on consent. It mainly solves the problem that, when different management domains exchange medical information access systems, traditional access control models cannot effectively achieve privacy protection for patient who has privacy preference in the treatment process. In order to ensure that privacy preferences are properly understood and applied, this system adopts a logic-based approach to infer access control decisions and expresses them by ontologies-based knowledge [12]. Li et al. proposed a novel patient-centered framework and a set of mechanisms for data access control of personal health records stored on servers. The solution allows dynamic modification of access policies and file attributes. In emergencies, it will cancel and interrupt access in case of need [13]. Qu proposed a purpose-based management privacy protection access control model for medical information systems [14]. Combining access control, key and certificate management, Zhang et al. proposed an access control scheme based on purpose and identity encryption technology [15]. Secondly, there was still a part of research aimed at improving the encryption mechanism in access control. Hu et al. proposed a contract based on hybrid public key infrastructure (PKI) solution to achieve privacy and security requirements [16]. Because of the static nature of the decision-making, traditional access control strategies have certain limitations in the actual access control, and it is often difficult to meet the privacy data protection and data utilization requirements.

Some people have also proposed a dynamic access control strategy suitable for the type of medical information data. Hui et al. proposed risk adaptive self-adaptive access control model for medical big data [17]. It can dynamically control access control behavior and meet certain utilization requirement of data. However, this method only considers the complexity of the doctor's access to the data. It does not consider the value of the data itself in the process of use. Different types of data occupy different proportions in the data analysis, which should also be considered when formulating an access control strategy. So it can make the data to be utilized to the maximum extent under the premise of privacy protection.

According to the traditional access control model, the information entropy method used for private information access control has been relatively mature. As an effective tool for measuring information, not only can information entropy represent the amount of information, but it can also measure the private information [18]. Information entropy has many applications in location privacy protection and data anonymity. According to the traditional access control model, it is more mature that information entropy is used in the access control of privacy information. In the privacy information access control, the system intuitively understands the amount of private information held by visitors can assist in the formulation of strategies and the execution of decisions. Liu et al. proposed a privacy-based data access control and medical document sharing mechanism, which uses information entropy to calculate private information and identifies an integrated pattern with a large amount of information. Finally, it uses integrated patterns to query distributed medical documents [4]. However, privacy information has different degrees of sensitivity. In the process of data utilization, the use of data is often limited by privacy information protection requirements and the utilization rate is greatly reduced. In this paper, a medical information access control method based on weighted information entropy is proposed in view of the sensitivity of access control and the sensitivity of privacy information.

3 Access Control of Medical Privacy Protection

3.1 Basic Concepts

Medical Information. Medical information is the data generated by medically relevant behaviors. The types of medical information data are complex. According to their sources, it can be divided into 4 categories: pharmaceutical and Life Sciences, clinical care and laboratory research, medical expenses, and health management software. According to the role of data analysis, it can be divided into disease diagnosis, precision medical treatment and disease research.

Medical Data Access Behavior. Medical data access behavior is the operation refers to medical information which includes inquiry, processing, utilization and so on. The main operation object is the patient, the doctor and the data manager.

3.2 Access Control Model

In this paper, the user privacy information is divided into 3 levels according to the privacy protection sensitivity.

The first type of privacy information is the basic information about the patient, such as the name, ID card number, address and contact way. Its' level is represented L_1;

The second type of privacy information is the patient's medical record. Its' level is represented L_2;

The third type of privacy information is the patient's detection and test data. Its' level is represented L_3.

The first type of privacy information is the information that is directed to the patient. It is non-health privacy data. The leakage of such privacy information will cause great harm to patients., and the harm caused to patients will be more serious if the leaked privacy information is combined with medical records. So this kind of information will require higher privacy sensitivity. The second type of privacy information is the medical record of the patient, which is related to the diagnosis and treatment of the disease, including the patient's history, symptoms and treatment. This kind of information is health data, and has no directivity to patients, but it will cause indirect leakage of privacy information when it reaches a certain amount of data. The third type of privacy information is patient's test record. It is purely medical data and has no directivity information for patients. But it helps to analyze and diagnose diseases when it is combined with patient's diagnosis and treatment. It has research value and does not require high-level privacy protection sensitivity.

It is assumed that the patient's single medical data are expressed as d_i, and $p(d_i)$ represents the single medical data's quantitative ratio of the patient's total medical information. There are:

$$\begin{pmatrix} D \\ P(D) \end{pmatrix} = \begin{pmatrix} d_1 & d_2 & d_3 & \cdots\cdots & d_n \\ p(d_1) & p(d_2) & p(d_3) & & p(d_n) \end{pmatrix} \tag{1}$$

$$0 \leq p(d_i) \leq 1, \sum\nolimits_{i=1}^{n} p(d_i).$$

The patient's medical information entropy is expressed as:

$$H(X) = -\sum_{i=1}^{n} p(d_i)\log_2 p(d_i) \tag{2}$$

H(X) represents the average amount of information of patient medical information. It can be regarded as the uncertainty of patient medical information. For the information source, the greater the H(X) is, the less likely the privacy is to be compromised. For a malicious visitor, the smaller the information entropy of the information it obtains, the better it is to protect the private information. Using information entropy to measure the degree of protection of privacy information can be more directly understand the privacy leakage.

The first type of privacy information is defined as q_1. The second type of privacy information is q_2, and the third type of privacy information is q_3.

The form of access information is defined as access = {id, a_1, a_2, a_3… a_n}, a_i is the access information entry. The number of access information is n. When the weight is not included in the calculation, the amount of information of each request is calculated according to the definition of entropy as follows:

$$E_{a_1} = -\frac{1}{n}\log_2\frac{1}{n} \tag{3}$$

Each item in the access information will be classified and counted. The number of requests for three categories of privacy information is defined as s_1, s_2, and s_3. According to the enumeration and the weight set by privacy information classification, the formula of the amount of information that the access request will be obtained is as follows:

$$E_s = -q_1\sum_{i=1}^{s_1}\frac{1}{n}\log_2\frac{1}{n} - q_2\sum_{j=1}^{s_2}\frac{1}{n}\log_2\frac{1}{n} - q_3\sum_{k=1}^{s_3}\frac{1}{n}\log_2\frac{1}{n} \tag{4}$$

E_s is the amount of information that the entire access request will obtain. After calculating the amount of information for each access information entry, the system classifies all kinds of privacy information based on its type of privacy information. Then the amount of information that the entire access request will be obtained is calculated according to the weight of each kind of privacy information. The amount of information tolerance for each access request is set to E_t, which can be set according to specific conditions of different systems.

3.3 Access Control Scheme

Role Assignment. Visitors to medical information are diverse in identity and their needs are different. It needs to set different levels of access permissions according to different visitors. That is, the ability to access is defined according to the role.

Visitors to medical information are divided into patients, doctors, data administrators and external visitors. The patient can be either the patient himself or a patient agent. The role of doctors is divided into attending doctors, general doctors, and nurses. Data administrators are no longer subdivided. External visitors are divided into medical insurance agencies, public security agencies, and judicial authorities. Four types of visitors have different needs for medical information.

Permission Assignment. Patients should have full access rights to their own medical information and are not restricted (Patients with major illnesses may be given appropriate access rights). Patient agent has the same access rights as the patient; Doctors mainly use medical information to help medical diagnosis and medical research. The attending doctor needs to have a very detailed grasp of the patient's information. It should set the highest access rights for attending doctors to edit, modify and access electronic medical records. Also, the attending doctor should have authority to file the electronic medical record. Other general doctors should have limited access to medical information. They should only be able to access the medical data information related to the treatment tasks. Nurses should have lower access rights to do daily nursing records.

Data administrators manage medical data and make human intervention for access rights to meet the special needs of medical visits. However, administrators should perform data read privacy protection. Administrators, however, have limited operations on data and limited information access.

External visitors have low privileges and fewer medical information.

Weight Settings. Medical data relates to health data and non-health data. Health data is about a person's physical condition, such as medical information. Non-health data is a kind of information that is not directly related to an individual's health status. Different levels of privacy for data are different from the patient. After the visitor obtains the data, the value of different private information in use is not the same. Accordingly, the amount of private information obtained by the visitor can't be measured in terms of quantity. Different weight should be set for different privacy information, and the different levels of weight should be set according to the interest of the patient's private information.

According to the analysis of the data definition, the sensitivity of the three types of private information is different. The first type of privacy information has the highest sensitivity, and the corresponding weight value should be the largest, and the weights of the second and third types of private information are successively reduced.

The privacy protection settings for the three types of privacy information are shown in Table 1.

Table 1. Privacy information weight setting table

Privacy information category	Weight
L_1	$q_1 = 0.6$
L_2	$q_2 = 0.3$
L_3	$q_3 = 0.1$

Access Control Scheme. The access control method proposed in this paper is mainly aimed at the doctor's visit behavior. When the visitor submits the medical information access request, it abides by the following strategies to achieve access control.

① The system receives an access request, extracts the patient id and the specific request entry a_i;
② The request entry is classified according to L_1, L_2, L_3. All kinds of private information entries are recorded as s_1, s_2, s_3;
③ Calculate access request information entropy E_s;
④ Compare E_s and E_t. If $E_s < E_t$, access will be allowed. If $E_s > E_t$, access will be denied.

4 Security Analysis

4.1 Access Control Analysis

Hypothesis 1. Suppose 3 peer visitors have 3 privacy information requests: $access_1 = \{1, a_{11}, a_{12}, a_{13}\}$, $access_2 = \{2, a_{21}, a_{22}, a_{23}, a_{24}\}$, $access_3 = \{3, a_{31}, a_{32}, a_{33}, a_{34}\}$, $E_t = 0.5$. The privacy information request classification is shown in Table 2 as follows:

Table 2. Privacy information request classification table

Privacy information category	Category
L_1	a_{11}, a_{12}, a_{21}
L_2	a_{22}, a_{23}, a_{31}
L_3	a_{13}, a_{24}, a_{32}, a_{33}, a_{34}

Get the following data according to Formula 4:
$E_{s1} = 0.6864$, $E_{s2} = 0.6501$, $E_{s3} = 0.264$

$E_{s1} > E_t$, $E_{s2} > E_t$, $E_{s3} < E_t$, $access_1$ and $access_2$'s request will be rejected and $access_3$'s request will be accepted. From the assumptions, it can be seen that $access_1$ has the minimum number of request messages, but it has the largest amount of private information requested. $Access_2$ and $access_3$ have the same number of request messages, but the amount of private information requested by $access_2$ is much larger than that of $access_3$. The result shows that the method proposed in this paper can distinguish different requests for privacy access control, instead of using the same standard for all requests, achieving dynamic privacy information access control. Also, privacy information can be measured by the amount of information which is calculated according to the weight. So the sensitive information can be better protected.

Hypothesis 2. Suppose that a general practitioner and two external visitors have three access requests: $access_4 = \{4, a_{41}, a_{42}, a_{43}, a_{44}, a_{45}\}$, $access_5 = \{5, a_{51}, a_{52}, a_{53}, a_{54}, a_{55}\}$, $access_6 = \{6, a_{61}, a_{62}, a_{63}, a_{64}\}$. $E_{t4} = 0.7$, $E_{t5} = 0.5$, $E_{t6} = 0.5$. The privacy information request classification is shown in Table 3 as follows:

Table 3. Privacy information request classification table

Privacy information category	Category
L_1	a_{41}, a_{51}
L_2	a_{42}, a_{43}, a_{52}, a_{53}, a_{61}, a_{62}, a_{63}
L_3	A_{44}, a_{45}, a_{54}, a_{55}, a_{64}

Get the following data according to Formula 4:

$E_{s4} = 0.6501$, $E_{s5} = 0.6501$, $E_{s6} = 0.4$.

$E_{s4} < E_{t4}$, $E_{s5} > E_{t5}$, $E_{s6} < E_{t6}$, $access_4$ and $access_6$'s request will be accepted and $access_5$'s request will be rejected. From the assumptions, $access_4$, $access_5$ have the same number of access information entries, and $access_6$ requests less access information entries. From the classification table, it can be seen that the privacy information classifications of requests for $access_4$ and $access_5$ are the same completely, and the requests of $access_6$ are mostly low sensitivity information. Correspondingly, the amount of private information contained in the $access_4$, $access_5$ request information is also the same, and the amount of private information contained in the $access_6$ request information is less. However, the access rights levels of the two different visitors are different. The general doctor's access level is higher than external visitors. Therefore, the same amount of information is requested for private information, the amount of private information requested by the general doctor is lower than the standard value, and normal access is possible. Instead, the privacy information obtained by external visitor's requests is high than the standard value, so it is rejected. Similarly, when the amount of private information requested by the external visitor is lower than the tagged value, it can be accessed normally.

4.2 Comparative Analysis

Compared with role access control based on Hierarchical Authorization, this access control scheme can achieve access control more flexibly by setting access information standards, instead of assigning fixed access rights to the hierarchy. The access control scheme proposed by Huo Chengyi et al. is based on the role based access control model. It increases the personalized intention of the patients to the data access control policy. Patients' privacy preferences for data are not the same. It causes operational requirements of the medical system are higher, and makes the difficulty of data utilization increase. In contrast, the access control scheme proposed in this paper can achieve the privacy protection of data by controlling the amount of accessed data information on the basis of hierarchical authorization of roles. At the same time, scheme accepts access requests while ensuring privacy is not compromised. It does not affect the use of medical data.

Compared with the purpose-based access control method, this method quantifies the amount of information of the access requests. It makes the access behavior easier to distinguish and realizes dynamic control. The access control scheme proposed by Qu Shiyan et al. adds the access control scheme based on the purpose-based management to the role-based access control scheme. Scheme sets the corresponding relationship between the role and the access purpose, and implements the fine-grained access control. However, the corresponding relationship enables the corresponding role to have unrestricted access operation rights to certain data. It makes the disclosure of private information inevitable if a malicious visitor appears. The access control scheme proposed in this paper increases the control of the amount of access information on the basis of detailed user roles. It controls the total amount of information on a fine-grained basis. This can prevent private information from leaking due to malicious access.

In summary, the method proposed in this paper is based on information entropy to quantify medical privacy information. It divides the sensitivity of different types of medical privacy information, and increases the weight setting link to meet the protection requirements of medical privacy information. Access behavior is divided and controlled according to the amount of private information. So it has certain practicality and advantages, and more universal.

Acknowledgment. This research was supported by Beijing Key Laboratory of Security and Privacy in Intelligent Transportation, Beijing Jiaotong University.

References

1. Wang, X.Y., Tian, L.Y., Han, X., et al.: Big data with precision and moderate health care. Commun. CCF **12**(10), 10–12 (2016)
2. Cai, J.H., Zhang, T., Zong, W.H.: Challenges and considerations of the big data of medicine. Chin. J. Health Inf. Manag. **10**(4), 292–295 (2013)
3. Shen, F.J.: The exploration and practice of cloud computing in the information of medical industry. Inf. Commun. **10**, 152–153 (2016)
4. Zhang, Z., Zhou, Y., Du, S.H., et al.: Medical big data and the facing opportunities and challenges. J. Med. Inf. **35**(6), 2–8 (2014)

5. Zou, B.J.: Bid data analysis and its application in the medical field. Comput. Educ. **7**, 24–29 (2014)
6. Bi, D., Dong, K.N., Xue, L.N., et al.: Big data analytics in healthcare: promise and potential. Big Data Time **4**, 6–20 (2017)
7. China Website Security Report in 2015. http://zt.360.cn/1101061855.php?dtid=1101062368&did=11015364902018/3/11
8. Zhao, Y.Y., Huang, X., Li, J.J.: Contribution title. In: 9th International Proceedings (2017). Prevention and control of internal auditing risk in medical institutions under big data environment. Times Financ. **2**, 15–21
9. Chen, B.: Integration and application of information technology for industrial integration – the application of cloud computing technology in medical and health fields. China Eng. Consul. **2**, 37–41 (2015)
10. Zhou, K., Jiang, X.H., Sun, T.F.: Study on EMR system based on cloud storage and access control policy. Inf. Secur. Commun. Priv. **4**, 86–89 (2012)
11. Huo, C.Y., Wu, Z.Q.: Patient-oriented privacy protection access control model for HIS. Comput. Appl. Softw. **31**(11), 75–77 (2014)
12. Khan, A., Mckillop, I.: Privacy-centric access control for distributed heterogeneous medical information systems. In: IEEE International Conference on Healthcare Informatics, vol. 7789, no. 1, pp. 297–306. IEEE (2013)
13. Li, M., Yu, S., Zheng, Y., et al.: Scalable and secure sharing of personal health records in cloud computing using attribute-based encryption. IEEE Trans. Parallel Distrib. Syst. **24**(1), 131–143 (2012)
14. Qu, S., Sun, T., Zhou, X.: Purpose management-based privacy access control model for his. Comput. Appl. Softw. **28**(3), 74–76 (2011)
15. Zhang, Y.T., Fu, Y.C., Ming, Y., et al.: Access control scheme for medical data based on PBAC and IBE. J. Commun. **36**(12), 200–211 (2015)
16. Hu, J.K., Chen, H.H., Hou, T.W.: A hybrid public key infrastructure solution (HPKI) for HIPAA privacy/security regulations. Comput. Stand. Interfac. **32**(5), 274–280 (2009)
17. Hui, Z., Li, H., Zhang, M., et al.: Risk-adaptive access control model for big data in healthcare. J. Commun. **36**(12), 190–199 (2015)
18. Peng, C.G., Ding, H.F., Zhu, Y.J., et al.: Information entropy models and privacy metrics methods for privacy protection. J. Softw. **27**(8), 1891–1903 (2016)

Modeling and Analysis of a Hybrid Authentication Protocol for VANET

Yang Xu[1,2(✉)], Ziwang Wang[1], Lei Huang[2], and Xiaoyao Xie[1]

[1] Key Laboratory of Information and Computing Science of Guizhou Province, Guizhou Normal University, Guiyang 550001, Guizhou, China
xy@gznu.edu.cn

[2] Guiyang Public Security Bureau Joint Research Centre for Information Security, Guizhou Normal University, Guiyang 550001, Guizhou, China

Abstract. A policy mechanism of pseudonym exchange was established in VANET. The group signature is introduced as the identity attribute tag of the message which be used as a supplement to pseudonym. A white list mechanism is also proposed to avoid generate huge storage and cancellation overhead in the pseudonym signature scheme. The security and performance analysis show that the proposed protocol is feasible. In the storage overhead, authentication speed and robustness are superior to the traditional scheme. However, the increase of message length has little effect on packet loss rate and end-to-end delay. Compared to its performance in privacy protection and saving computational overhead, these effects can be ignored.

Keywords: VANET · Pseudonym exchange · Group signatures Privacy preserving

1 Introduction

Vehicular ad-hoc network (VANET) is kind of wireless ad hoc network, which can offer vehicle connect with other vehicles (Vehicles to Vehicles, V2V) or roadside unit (Vehicles to Infrastructure, V2I) through On-Board Units (OBU) [1]. As a kind of mobile ad-hoc network in the field of intelligent transportation, it has a broad application prospect in the fields of cooperative driving, accident warning and traffic route optimization. As an open and wide area wireless network, information security is the primary problem in the application of ad hoc network technology. The security requirements of VANET include the data integrity, anonymity, non-repudiation and non-relevance [2–5]. With the gradual application of VANET, the issues of security are becoming more and more diverse, such as eavesdropping, tracking, deception, etc., of which privacy preserving and authentication are essential, as a participant in the vehicle communication, the security of vehicular communicate will directly affect the user's

Supported in part by Science and Technology Cooperation Program of Guizhou Province, China under Grant LH20157763, in part by Science and technology plan project of Ministry of Housing and Urban-Rural Development, China under Grant 2016-K3-009.

X. Sun et al. (Eds.): ICCCS 2018, LNCS 11065, pp. 123–137, 2018.
https://doi.org/10.1007/978-3-030-00012-7_12

privacy. At present, the protection of the privacy in VANET is mainly through the deployment of public key infrastructure (PKI), using a pseudonym and certificate revocation list (CRL) certificate management authorization mechanism to achieve anonymous communication.

In 2007, Raya, etc. proposed [6] the pseudonym verification mechanism which being applicable to VANET. The specific method of the protocol is: vehicles in VANET apply to trusted authority (TA) for a large number of randomly generated pseudo numbers as anonymous credentials, TA persists the binding of anonymous credentials and identity information, vehicles change pseudonym message issued in certain period and receiver checks message through the matching of the legality of anonymous credential. The message encryption is meaningless in broadcast networks. In VANET communications, a vehicle uses plain text transmission to send heartbeat packet payload. The message transmission will produce serious context leaks. When the position information is known, pseudonym replacement cannot achieve the non-relevance, the eavesdropper can easily associate the pseudonym that change before and after. So in the anonymous authentication scheme based on pseudonym, the pseudonym replacement strategy is very important [19].

Definition 1. Strong location privacy means that an attacker can't complete the location tracking of the vehicle long time when he has a certain understanding of the identity information of the vehicle.

Definition 2. The replacement of the pseudonym in the VANET meet the non-connectivity called an effective replacement.

Reference [3] points out that the location privacy can be quantified by the real location and uncertainty of attacker. Reference [7] suggests that each node of the vehicle replaces pseudonym in the cycle of a minute. According to the standard of dedicated short range communication (DSRC) [9], a vehicle will send a heartbeat packet in every 300 ms, if it achieves the strong location privacy, it is required at least two cars exchange the signature at the same time in the next heartbeat time. In theory, it needs 200 nodes at the same time in this position. If the error of GPS location information in the data packet is 20 m, considering vehicles in the road of tubular distribution and the distance between the vehicles, there are six traveling in the same direction nodes at most. That is, the probability of achieving strong location privacy is only 0.003. Combining with speed and other characteristics of information, it is impossible effective only one time replacement pseudonym.

Reference [10] proposed a scheme to replace pseudonym in the mixed zone (Mix-zone). Figure 1 demonstrates the working mechanism of the Mix-zone protocol. Node P1, P2 is changed to P3 and P4 after mix-zone. The message is not detected in the time of going through mix-zone. Thus, it achieves non-connectivity between (P1, P2) and (P3, P4). In the Mix-zone, the attacker cannot monitor vehicle heartbeat message, the Mix-zone is usually built at the crossroads or tunnels and other infrastructure. However, if the vehicle flow is less or the road is smooth, the time of the vehicles through mix-zone is predictable [11–13]. Reference [17] suggests that in the process of driving, the vehicle can choose the random time as the silent period, and to realize the effective replacement. However, the length of the silent period in the most security protocols is strictly restricted.

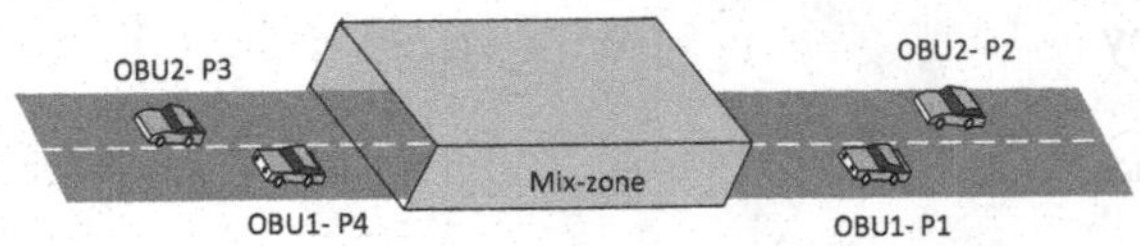

Fig. 1. Mix-zone demo

Authors in [8] suggested a conditional privacy preservation protocol GSIS of using the group signature and identity signature, through the non-relevance of group signature, while achieving vehicle pseudonymous and the true identity of the corresponding. In Literature [15], it is proposed a distributed group key distribution mechanism [18], each RSU (roadside unit) as the group manager of covered area distributed group key to the legitimate vehicles coming into the area, and there is a minimum of CRL distribution mechanism, which greatly increased the efficiency of authentication information, but in VANET default semi trusted RSU can't provide absolute non-repudiation to nodes. In Literature [16], scheme Dynamic Short Signature Group (DSGS) is proposed. The scheme can effectively shorten the length of signature, and allow the group member to join dynamically without the need to change the parameters.

Authentication protocol based on collaboration refers to the vehicle in the running process realize non-relevance in the vehicle location and the true identity cooperatively with the surrounding vehicles or the road side unit. Reference [20] proposed the vehicle in the certain region can consist of a group, through a trusted node to the message of proxy signature. The defect of the protocol is unable to guarantee the reliability of the agent. Lin et al. [21] proposed the authentication scheme of TESLA in VANET. TESLA provides an effective symmetric key signature scheme. It can realize identity verification by time slicing and synchronization technology and key technology. The scheme exist the availability based on the attack risk. Ring signature is a spontaneous group to generate the signature. Reference [22] proposes the vehicles around exchange each other's identity certificate randomly.

Based on the research of pseudonym and group signature protocol, this paper presents a mixed authentication based on the pseudonym exchange. We use group signature as identity tags for the non-repudiation and auditable. A white list is proposed, which can solve the replay attack. Analysis shows the pseudonym exchange protocol can also resist the man-in-the-middle attacks and collusion attack. At last, using of MOVE, SUMO to simulate the real environment, then import the results into the NS2. The experimental results showed that, the model is effective and has good performance in the packet average arrival rate and the end-to-end average delay.

2 Preliminary

2.1 Threat Model

In vehicular ad hoc networks based on wireless communication, TA is considered to be the only absolutely reliable, and vehicle and RSU are considered to be captured. The possible presences of malicious attacks in vehicular networks include:

(1) *Fake message attack.* An attacker which affects the judgment of other receivers.
(2) *Impersonation attack.* An attacker disguised as a vehicle or RSU to deceive the other vehicles or RSU, to hide the true identity and thus escape punishment.
(3) *Sybil attack.* An attacker who uses different identities to sign the same message, resulting in a false impression of many people.
(4) *Tracking Multi-target attack (MIT).* The attacker through the screening of a single user's mobile trajectory, infringe the user's location privacy and identity privacy.

Available Attacks. Include the available attack of the routing protocol and the Dos attack against the node.

2.2 Dynamic Group Signature Model of BSZ

Reference [14] proposed to introduce two groups authority of opener and group manager (GM) in Dynamic group signature model. The opener is used to reveal the true identity of the signer and the GM generates a group signature private key and reserved the corresponding tables (CTs) for members and their private keys which has the group management key. Specific models are as follows:

Initialization: Input security parameter 1^k generation group public key K_{gp}, *GM* private key K_i and opener private key K_o.
Join operations: The member i and the GM are input with the private key $K_{s,i}$ and the K_i, output member private key $K_{gs}[i]$, update the relationship between $K_{gs}[i]$ and the member's ID to the table CTs.
Message signature: The member i input $K_{s,i}$, group signature private key $K_{gs}[i]$ and message m generation group signature σ.
Authentication: Get the Signature pair (m, σ) of the verifier, using group public key K_{gp}, message m and group signature σ to Verify the message is effective. The output equals 1 and 0 are valid and invalid, respectively.
Open operations: Opener run open algorithm with K_o, m and σ, the result is like (i, τ), inside, τ is the part which signature with $K_{s,i} \cdot \sigma$. It is verified whether the signer is member i when $i \neq 0$, otherwise, no member will be found.

3 Hybrid Authentication Protocol

In public key cryptosystem, the user identify equivalent to user public key, users need to exchange the right to use the public key when the pseudonym is exchanged. In this paper, a policy mechanism of pseudonym exchange was established in VANET, which has stronger non traceability in the case of the same vehicle density. And the group signature is introduced as the identity attribute tag of the message. The group signature tag can be used as a supplement to pseudonym, which ensures the non-forgery and the audit. In this paper, the new protocol is called Hybrid Authentication Protocol for VANET (HAP) which using the pseudonym signature for authentication, and group signature is used for identity.

A white list (WL) mechanism is proposed to avoid generate huge storage and cancellation overhead in the pseudonym signature scheme. In HAP, VANET maintain a small amount of pseudonym, the WL is more suitable for pseudonym exchange which group signature as secondary authentication. On the one hand, when the WL delete the pseudonym could be used by legal nodes which has been exchanged for evil nodes and then delete with the evil is exposed, we cannot refuse the nodes using. On the other hand, WL does not require highly real-time, the WL is feasible.

3.1 System Model

Our system model has 4 types of participants: master authority (MA), regional authority (RA), roadside unit (RSU) and OBU, as shown in Fig. 2. Different from the traditional three tier architecture which set up by trustable authority, RSU and OBU, we divide TA into MA and RA to get more computing power and communication abilities, the three of them have the same credibility.

(1) MA&RA:The completely trusted units in VANET, and its main task is to manage RSU, offer authentication to OBU and distribution and maintenance key. In this paper, the TA is divided into a global management center MA and regional based management center RA.
(2) RSU: One of the VANET main infrastructures, through the wired network connects other roadside units and TA for communication. It usually as OBU and TA communication relay exists. In Literature [15], RSU also is responsible for the generation and management of signature key.
(3) OBU: A communication module installed on each vehicle node, communication with RSU and other OBU via wireless signal.

In order to facilitate the statement, firstly, we still use TA to replace MA and RA. In the following discussion, we will distinguish MA and RA. The notations used in the following scheme are listed in Table 1.

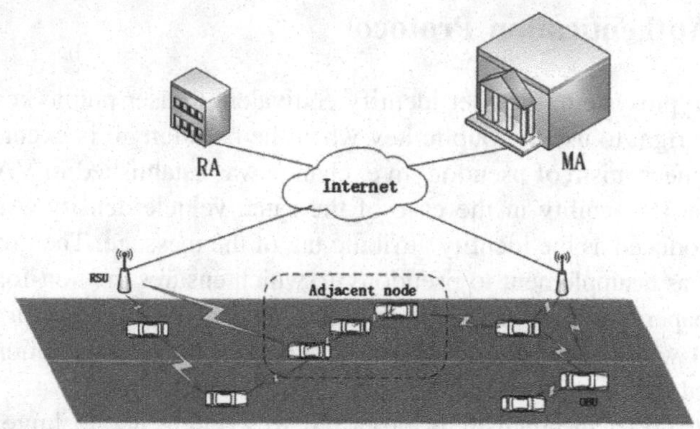

Fig. 2. System model

Table 1. Notations and symbols

Notation	Descriptions
TA	Trusted authority
M	A message
m	A payload of message
$Cert(V_i)$	V_i's certificate
WL	White list
WL_j	The white of area j
CRL	Certificate revocation list
CRL_j	Certificate revocation list of area j
ERL	Exchange record list
$K^P_{V_i}$	V_i's public key
$K^s_{V_i}$	V_i's key
K^P_{TA}	TA's public key
$K^P_{P_{V_i}}$	V_i's pseudonym public key
$K^S_{P_{V_i}}$	V_i's pseudonym private key
$K_{gs}[i]$	V_i's group private key
$K_{gp}[i]$	V_i's group public key
G_{id}	Group ID
$Hash(*)$	Hash function

3.2 Pseudonym Exchange with Trusted Authority

When the node V_A needs to replace the pseudonym $K_{P_{V_A}}$, V_A gets a key $\left\{K^P_{C_{V_A}}, K^S_{C_{V_A}}\right\}$ for the exchange of pseudonym and a short pseudonym pair $\left\{K^P_{P^t_{V_A}}, K^S_{P^t_{V_A}}\right\}$ from TA with $Cert(V_i)$, and then if TA find the Node list contains node V_B has acquired a certificate pair $\left\{K^P_{C_{V_B}}, K^S_{C_{V_B}}, K^P_{Pt_{V_B}}, K^S_{Pt_{V_B}}\right\}$ which V_A submitted, the public key $K^P_{C_{V_B}}$ will be send to V_A, and V_A encrypted message $(K^P_{C_{V_B}}, K^P_{C_{V_A}}, T)$ with $K^P_{C_{V_B}}$ only can be decrypt by V_B who has $K^S_{C_{V_B}}$, V_B will shared $K^P_{C_{V_B}}$ in the same way. And now V_B is default deemed to accept exchange with V_A, V_A send the pseudonym $K_{P_{V_B}}$ to V_B and turn into silence state until received $K_{P_{V_A}}$. If the exchange is complete, the change will be submitted to TA. The specific protocol as follows.

$$B \to TA : \{K^P_{P_{V_B}}, T\}K^P_{TA} \tag{1}$$

$$TA \to B : \{K^P_{C_{V_B}}, K^S_{C_{V_B}}, K^P_{Pt_{V_B}}, K^S_{Pt_{V_B}}, T\}K^S_{TA} \tag{2}$$

$$A \to TA : \{K^P_{P_{V_A}}, T\}K^P_{TA} \tag{3}$$

$$TA \to A : \{(K^P_{P_{V_A}}, K^P_{P_{V_B}}, K^P_{C_{V_A}}, T)K^P_{C_{V_B}}, K^P_{C_{V_A}}, K^S_{C_{V_A}}, K^P_{Pt_{V_A}}, K^S_{Pt_{V_A}}, T\}K^S_{TA} \tag{4}$$

$$A \to B : (K^P_{P_{V_A}}, K^P_{P_{V_B}}, K^P_{C_{V_A}}, T)K^P_{C_{V_B}} \tag{5}$$

$$B \to A : (K^P_{P_{V_A}}, K^S_{P_{V_B}}, (K^P_{C_{V_B}})K^P_{P_{V_A}}, T)K^P_{C_{V_A}} \tag{6}$$

$$A \to B : (K^S_{P_{V_A}}, T)K^P_{C_{V_B}} \tag{7}$$

$$B \to A : (M, T)K^S_{P_{V_A}} \tag{8}$$

$$A \to B : (M, T)K^S_{P_{V_B}} \tag{9}$$

$$B \to TA : \left(K^P_{P_{V_A}}, K^S_{P_{V_A}}, T\right)K^P_{TA} \tag{10}$$

$$A \to TA : \left(K^P_{P_{V_B}}, K^S_{P_{V_B}}, T\right)K^P_{TA} \tag{11}$$

Vehicle A and B certificate and submit exchange pseudonym application in TA respectively in step 3 and 1. Encryption information $\left(K^P_{P_{V_A}}, K^P_{P_{V_B}}, K^P_{C_{V_A}}, T\right)K^P_{C_{V_B}}$ is used to ensure that the node V_A sent to V_B information is from TA in step 5, and $K^P_{C_{V_B}}$ send in step 6 only can be decrypt by V_A. If the exchange process interrupt in step 6, 7, 8 or 9, the temporary pseudonym certificate $\left\{K^P_{Pt_{V_A}}, K^S_{Pt_{V_A}}\right\}$ or $\left\{K^P_{Pt_{V_B}}, K^S_{Pt_{V_B}}\right\}$ will be used according to need. In step 10 and 11, the new pseudonym information will be update into exchange record list (ERL).

3.3 System Initialization

In system initialization, TA needs to complete the open parameters establishment and registration for RSU, OBU. In this paper, TA first generates more than one group for different regions, such as, a city a group. In addition, TA needs to generate a number of public private key pairs in advance as a pseudonym certificate pool.

3.4 Vehicle Registration

To achieve confidentiality, identity integrity, authentication and non-repudiation, any vehicle node that is connected to the VANET network must registered in the authorization manage center TA, and then TA issued identity certificate to complete vehicle registration. In the scheme of this paper, vehicle node V_i registered and get certificate $Cert(V_i)$ at TA, the $Cert(V_i) = \left\{ID_{V_i}, PK_{V_i}, K_{S_{V_i}}, PK_{TA}\right\}$ will be transmission in secure channel. Inside, PK_{V_i} is the public key itself, $K_{S_{V_i}}$ is the secret private key used for authentication with TA. PK_{TA} is TA's public key.

TA will update the nodes to the database which obtain the latest certificate. TA needs to maintain a WL of pseudonym and a CRL of group signatures. CRL_j means the information need to save by current area nodes which is part of CRL.

3.5 Vehicle Wake up

In this paper, every time the nodes wake up need to complete a TA certification to update the certificate information. After the vehicle wakes up, as shown in Fig. 3, need to have the following information:

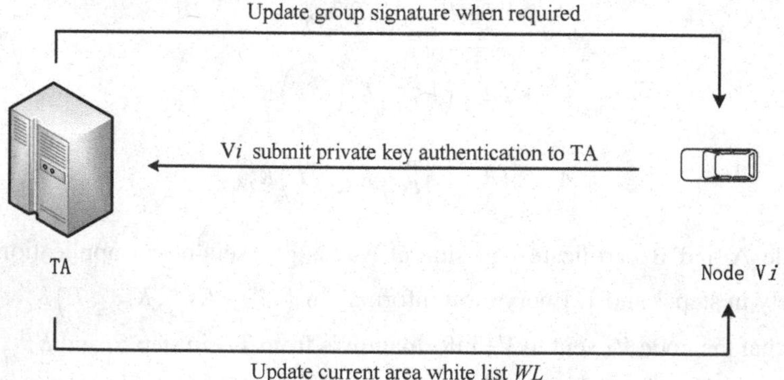

Fig. 3. Vehicle wake up

(1) A pseudonym $K_{P_{Vi,p}}$ in the short term and the corresponding private key $K_{P_{Vi,s}}$.
(2) Key pair $\left\{K_{gs}, K_{gp}\right\}_i$ for group g_j in the current region j.
(3) A WL of pseudonym which is complete update.
(4) Certificate revocation list CRL_j for group g_j which is complete update.

3.6 Message Signing

Before any OBU broadcasts a message M, it must signs M first with its pseudonym and group private key. Table 2 shows the message format carrying complete signature. M is the payload of current message which contains information about the position, direction and speed of the vehicle; timestamp T used to prevent replay attacks; Pseudonym certificate $K_{P_{Vi,p}}$ used to verify the corresponding pseudonym signature $Sign_{K_{P_{Vi,s}}}\{Hash(M,T)\}$; Group signature $Sign_{K_{gs}[i]}\{Hash(M,T)\}$ is the Signature of message M and T from group private key $K_{gs}[i]$. In our scheme, the numbers of group is limited quantity, thus, in a message broadcast, the index G_{id} to replace group public key is feasible.

Table 2. Message structure

Id	Message M	Timestamp T	Pseudonym signature	Pseudonymous certificate	Group signature	Group ID

For example, the node A message is as follows:

$$M, T, Sign_{K^S_{P_{V_i}}}\{Hash(M,T)\}, K^P_{P_{V_i}}, Sign_{K_{gs}[i]}\{Hash(M,T)\}, G_{id}$$

3.7 Authentication

In our scheme, the message was quickly verified by pseudonymous $K^P_{P_{V_i}}$ authentication which has complete certificate information

$$\{Sign_{K^S_{P_{V_i}}}\{Hash(M,T)\}, K^P_{P_{V_i}}, Sign_{K_{gs}[i]}\{Hash(M,T)\}, K_{gp}[i]\}$$

If the pseudonymous is not in WL, the group certificate $K_{gp}[i]$ will be checked. The Authentication phase as follows.

If ($K^P_{P_{V_i}}$ *is contained in WL) then*
Access
Exit
Else if ($K^P_{P_{V_i}}$ *is not contained in WL and* $K_{gp}[i]$ *is not contained in CRL)*
then
Access
Send $K_{gp}[i]$ *to TA*
Exit
Else if ($K^P_{P_{V_i}}$ *is not contained in WL and* $K_{gp}[i]$ *is not contained in CRL)*
then
Reject
End if

3.8 Verification with Pseudonym and Group Signature

If the malicious node V_e is exposed, TA filters out all used pseudonym that are still in the life cycle through ERL, And remove those pseudonym from the local pseudonym WL_j. In the end, the corresponding group signature will be added to the local CRL. When all the pseudonym of the nodes V_e that have been retained by the node is beyond the life cycle, it won't be able to get a new pseudonym from TA. Temporality, the group signature by the node V_e can be removed to reduce the length of the revocation list from CRL_j.

4 Security Analysis

HAP protocol can accomplish the non-link of pseudonym and identity well by implementing the pseudonym exchange of neighboring nodes. Location hiding only needs to complete an effective exchange. Commonly, after more than 2 times the exchange can ensure the effective exchange of existence in each driving.

Pseudonym after exchange cannot guarantee that non repudiation, a pseudonym private key will be retained in any one node who once exchange to the pseudonym, the malicious node used to exchange pseudonym times, it means that he can resume the pseudonym without authentication, occupancy the pseudonym may be performed by any node that participation in the be attacked pseudonym exchange, that is, there may be legitimate users who are using an attack. Under this circumstance, a WL for the pseudonym has a higher value than CRL, when an pseudonym is removed from the WL by TA, it is using his legal vehicle to complete the authentication through the group signature, at the same time, they can reapply for legal pseudonym from TA who not being revoked.

When a malicious node is playing a replay attack, it collects the pseudonym that will complete the life cycle in a period of time, means that we can remove the malicious node's group information from the CRL, because the malicious node does not have the pseudonym in the life cycle to enter the validation. In the collusion attack, the malicious node can only obtain the current area pseudonym which is being used can be implemented to cheat. Two nodes of the same pseudonym will be generated in the current region. It's easy to identify the risk pseudonym for TA and RSU. TA determines the malicious node by group signature or identity information, and enforces revocation of the pseudonym.

In this protocol, RSU is only used as a data transmission relay, and its computing performance will be redundant. So, we proposed that RSU can be used to monitor the revocation nodes re-enter the network, RSU's CRL will be suspended for a long time to the group signature is revoked, even if the corresponding pseudonym has lost the life cycle. Compare the protocol structures, HAP use a 2 layer trust model, RSU only as TA to node message relay, reduced the risk of the system being attacked. The method of replace the group signature public key with a identifier which is also applicable to the pseudonym public key, storage, distribute and query for a small number of signatures is simple, the group signature public key can be used in the first broadcast to improve the feasibility of the identifier.

In this paper, the Mix-zone protocol [10], GSIS protocol [8] and our new protocol, HAP are compared and analyzed. The elliptic curve digital signature algorithm (ECDSA) is used in the Mix-zone protocol and HAP to signature. From Table 3, we can see HAP has better property on privacy preserving.

Table 3. Security comparisons

Protocol	Trust model	Strong unforgeability	Robustness	Strong location privacy
Mix-zone	3 layer	√	Low	×
GSIS	3 layer	×	High	√
HAP	2 layer	√	High	√

5 Performance Analysis

CRL in HAP is dynamically updated. Not only it can greatly save the verification time of a single message, but also its group signature information will no longer occupy the space of CRL, when the pseudonym of a vehicle node expires. In the GSIS of using the group signature, the length of CRL is one way to grow. Group signature requires more than two operations to complete a signature matching. Thus, when matching a long CRL, the verification time of a single message will be far greater than that of the verification time. In HAP, using a white list to cancel the match, the matching cost of a legitimate message is smaller than using pseudonym mechanism.

In Table 4 L is length of CRL, means the number of group signature. T_p represents time of one pair operation. L′ means length of CRL current time. Table 5 shows the cost comparison of three protocols for message signature and verification. T_m represents the time consumption of a modular operation or power operation, T_p means represents time of one pair operation.

Table 4. Approval a certificate consume

Protocol	Legitimate message	Attack information
Mix-zone	0	0
GSIS	$3 * T_p * L$	$3 * T_p * L$
HAP	0	$3 * T_p * L'$

When illegal information accounts for a very small portion of the traffic flow, HAP can effectively improve the verification speed and reduce cancellation cost.

In order to verify the effectiveness of HAP, the simulation experiment is carried out. MOVE and SUMO are used to simulate the real environment of road and traffic nodes, then the results output imported into the NS2 network simulation, at last, by programming the experiment network data for two indicators packet loss rate and the end-to-end delay. Table 6 shows the experimental environment. The simulation parameters showed in Table 7.

Packet Loss Rate

Packet loss rate is the key parameter that affects the quality of network communication. The data of packet loss rate and time delay are obtained under different packet lengths.

Table 8 shows that in the same simulation environment, the impact of packet length of different protocols on packet loss rate. With the increase of message length, packet loss rate will be increased. Thought the packet loss rate of HAP (5.22%) is a little higher than that of Mix-zone (4.67%), it is almost the same with that of GSIS (5.21%).

End-to-End Delay

In VANET, the timeliness of the message has a very high demand. Mobile speed, dynamic topology and message encryption algorithm can increase the end-to-end delay. Table 9 shows that in the same simulation environment, the impact of packet length of different protocols on end-to-end delay.

From Table 9, we can see that message length increases by 100 bytes, the average end-to-end delay is increased from 0.8 ms to 1.8 ms. According to the standard of the DSRC protocol, the maximum end to end delay in the actual vehicular wireless communication environment can be accepted by the 100 ms. From the average end to end delay analysis, the impact of packet increase on end-to-end delay is very small.

That the packet loss rate and the end to end delay are increased by 0.12% and 0.18% respectively compared with the centralized group signature scheme GSIS. These effects can be ignored for improving the efficiency of anonymous authentication.

Figure 4 shows the distribution of end to end delay of single message at different message lengths. Red indicates the time delay of a single message under GSIS

Table 5. Signing overhead and cancellation cost

Protocol	signature length (bytes)	Signing overhead	verification overhead
Mix-zone	187	$2 * T_m$	$3 * T_m$
GSIS	192	$9 * T_m + 1 * T_p$	$12 * T_m + 2 * T_p$
HAP	301	$9 * T_m + 11 * T_p$	$3 * T_m$

Table 6. Experimental environment

Experimental component	Name
Server hardware	Intel Core I5CPU 4 GB Memory
OS	Linux Ubuntu 15.10 wily
Road and traffic nodes simulation	MOVE by National University of Taiwan v 2.92
Network simulation	SUMO by German Aerospace Center v 0.12.3 NS2 by Monarch 2.34

Table 7. Simulation parameters

Simulation parameters	Reference value	Simulation parameters	Rreference value
Scene size	500×20 m^2	Channel	WirelessChannel
Number of roads	2	Transmission mode	TwoRayGround
Number of nodes	40	Routing protocol	AODV
Max speed	60 km/h	Mac protocol	IEEE802.11p
Min speed	40 km/h	Simulated time	600 s
Packet size	362/480/554 bit	Transmission speed	3 Mbps

Table 8. Packet loss rate

Protocol	Message length (bytes)	Number packet	Number packet loss	Packet loss rate
Mix-zone	362	42478	1983	0.046683
GSIS	480	42418	2164	0.051016
HAP	554	42458	2218	0.05224

Table 9. Average end-to-end delay

Protocol	Mix-zone	GSIS	HAP
Packet length	362	480	554
Average end-to-end delay	0.017	0.0178	0.0196

protocol. Blue represents the time delay of a single message delay under Mix-zone protocol. Green represents that under HAP. From the graph, we can see that the increase of message length has little effect on the time consumption of processing message queue when the network gets congested.

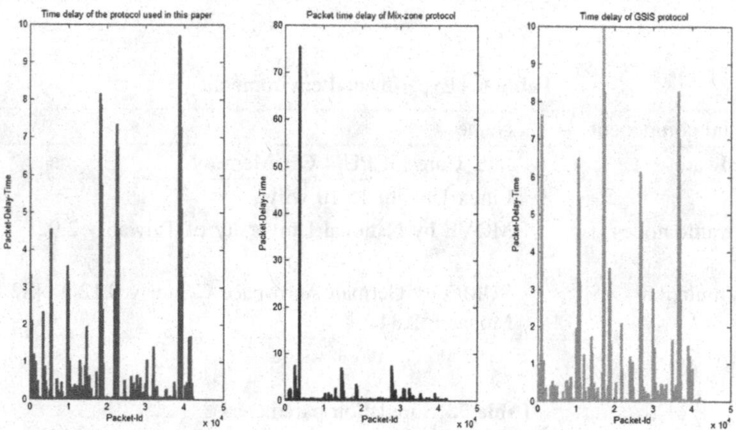

Fig. 4. Packet delay time comparison (Color figure online)

6 Conclusion

According to the privacy protection authentication problem in vehicle network, this paper proposes a hybrid authentication protocol based on trusted exchange pseudonym, constructs an exchange policy for the interchange between neighboring nodes. The pseudonym is used to implement the signature and authentication of TA.

The Mix-zone protocol, GSIS protocol and our new protocol, HAP are compared and analyzed. In the security analysis, we can find that HAP has better properties on authentication and privacy preserving than pseudonym protocol. In the performance analysis, HAP is far superior to the existing group signature schemes in terms of the computation overhead of packet verification and the stability of group signature schemes. Furthermore, we simulate and analyze the increase message length. We can see that the increase of message length has little effect on packet loss rate and end-to-end delay. Compared to its performance in privacy protection and saving computational overhead, these effects can be ignored.

References

1. Zhang, H.G., Han, W.B., Lai, X.J., et al.: Survey on cyberspace security. Sci. China Inf. Sci. **58**(11), 1–43 (2015)
2. Mokhtar, B., Azab, M.: Survey on security issues in vehicular ad hoc networks. AEJ – Alex. Eng. J. **54**(4), 1115–1126 (2015)

3. Mohammed, N.H.A., El-Moafy, H.N., Abdel-Mageid, S.M., et al.: Mobility management scheme based on smart buffering for vehicular networks. Int. J. Comput. Netw. Appl. **4**(2), 35–46 (2017)
4. Liu, X., Zhang, Y., Wang, B., et al.: Mona: secure multi-owner data sharing for dynamic groups in the Cloud. IEEE Trans. Parallel Distrib. Syst. **24**(6), 1182–1191 (2013)
5. Joe, M.M., Ramakrishnan, B.: Review of vehicular ad hoc network communication models including WVANET (Web VANET) model and WVANET future research directions. Wirel. Netw. **22**(7), 1–18 (2015)
6. Raya, M., Hubaux, J.: Securing vehicular ad hoc networks. J. Comput. Secur. **15**(1), 39–68 (2007)
7. Haas, J., Hu, Y., Laberteaux, K.: Design and analysis of a lightweight certificate revocation mechanism for VANET. In: Proceedings of 6th ACM International Workshop on Vehicular Inter-networking, New York, pp. 89–98 (2009)
8. Lin, X., Sun, X., Ho, P.H., et al.: GSIS: a secure and privacy-preserving protocol for vehicular communications. IEEE Trans. Veh. Technol. **56**(6), 3442–3456 (2007)
9. Dedicated short range communications (DSRC) [EB/OL] (2011). http://grouper.ieee.org/groups/scc32/dsrc/index.html
10. Freudiger, J., Raya, M., Félegyházi, M., et al.: Mix-zones for location privacy in vehicular networks. In: ACM Workshop on Wireless Networking for Intelligent Transportation Systems (2007)
11. Zhu, X., Donghui, H., Hou, Z., et al.: A location privacy preserving solution to resist passive and active attacks in VANET. China Commun. **11**(9), 60–67 (2014)
12. Dahl, M., Delaune, S., Steel, G.: Formal analysis of privacy for vehicular mix-zones. In: Gritzalis, D., Preneel, B., Theoharidou, M. (eds.) ESORICS 2010. LNCS, vol. 6345, pp. 55–70. Springer, Heidelberg (2010). https://doi.org/10.1007/978-3-642-15497-3_4
13. Freudiger, J., Shokri, R., Hubaux, J.P.: On the optimal placement of mix zones. In: PETS 2009, 216–234 (2009)
14. Boneh, D., Boyen, X., Shacham, H.: Short group signatures. In: Franklin, M. (ed.) CRYPTO 2004. LNCS, vol. 3152, pp. 41–55. Springer, Heidelberg (2004). https://doi.org/10.1007/978-3-540-28628-8_3
15. Hao, Y., Cheng, Yu., Chi, Z., et al.: A distributed key management framework with cooperative message authentication in VANETs. IEEE J. Sel. Areas Commun. **29**(3), 616–629 (2011)
16. Jung, Y.H., Li, Q.: Short dynamic group signature scheme supporting controllable linkabilityp. IEEE Trans. Inf. Forensics Secur. **32**(6), 1–14 (2013)
17. Sampigethaya, K., Li, M., Huang, L., Poovendran, R.: AMOEBA: robust location privacy scheme for VANET. IEEE J. Sel. Areas Commun. **25**(8), 1569–1589 (2007)
18. Liu, Z., Liu, J., Wu, Q., et al.: Secure and efficient distributed pseudonym generation in VANET. J. Commun. **36**(11), 33–40 (2015)
19. Chow, C.Y., Mokbel, M.F., Liu, X.: A peer-to-peer spatial cloaking algorithm for anonymous location-based service. In: Proceedings of the 14th Annual ACM International Symposium on Advances in Geographic Information Systems, pp. 171–178. ACM (2006)
20. Li, M., Sampigethaya, K., Huang, L., et al.: Swing & swap: user-centric approaches towards maximizing location privacy. In: Proceedings of ACM WPES, pp. 19–28 (2006)
21. Lin, X., Sun, X., Wang, X., et al.: TSVC: timed efficient and secure vehicular communications with privacy preserving. IEEE Trans. Wirel. Commun. **7**(12), 4987–4998 (2009)
22. Zeng, S., Huang, Y., Liu, X.: Privacy-preserving communication for VANETs with conditionally anonymous ring signature. Int. J. Netw. Secur. **17**(2), 135–141 (2015)

Modeling and Data Analysis of the Balise System

Shuai Zhang(✉), Zhiwei Gao, and Li Cui

School of Information Science and Technology, Shijiazhuang Tiedao University, Shijiazhuang, China
stduzs@163.com, 466069161@qq.com, 1040745658@qq.com

Abstract. As the key components of the train control system, Balise and Balise Transmission Module (BTM) cooperate with each other and fulfill the ground-train information transmission to ensure the safety and reliability of train operation. However, Balise is a transmission point device which is based on electronic coupling, the up-link signal easily affected by surrounding electromagnetic field. Aiming at the requirements for developments of high-speed railway, this paper builds the model for the dynamic transmission process of the Balise up-link signal using finite integral method (FIT) and electromagnetic field theory, respectively. It is proved that the model has sufficient accuracy for presenting the desired characteristics. Then, the effects of electromagnetic pulse (EMP) on the Balise up-link is studied using electromagnetic field theory, and the time domain waveform of the Balise system induced current is derived. The simulation analysis shows that the electromagnetic pulse belongs to transient electromagnetic interference. Its duration is usually shorter than the communication time of the Balise up-link, but its spectrum distribution is wider and its pulse energy is larger. When the spectral range of the electromagnetic pulse overlaps the operating band of the Balise up-link, in-band interference will occur, and it can cause bit errors in the Balise up-link signal, which will influence the safety of high-speed railway operation.

Keywords: CST · BTM · Balise system · Up-link · EMP

1 Introduction

The Balise system is one kind of high-rate point-mode data transmission equipment based on electromagnetic coupling [1, 2], which includes two parts, the on-board BTM devices and the ground Balise [3], as shown in Fig. 1.

When the train passes through the ground Balise, the train antenna arrives at the effective induction area of the ground Balise signal, BTM Receiving Antenna will radiate a 27.095 MHz signal to the ground continuously. When the ground Balise receives enough energy, it will transmit the energy wave to its working power and starts to work. The ground Balise will send the intended telegram at a frequency of 4.234 MHz as the up-link signal to the BTM Receiving Antenna via the air gap. The BTM processes the signal received, parses the Balise telegram inside and forwards it to vital computer [4, 5]. This paper mainly carries on the simulation research to the Balise up-link process.

X. Sun et al. (Eds.): ICCCS 2018, LNCS 11065, pp. 138–150, 2018.
https://doi.org/10.1007/978-3-030-00012-7_13

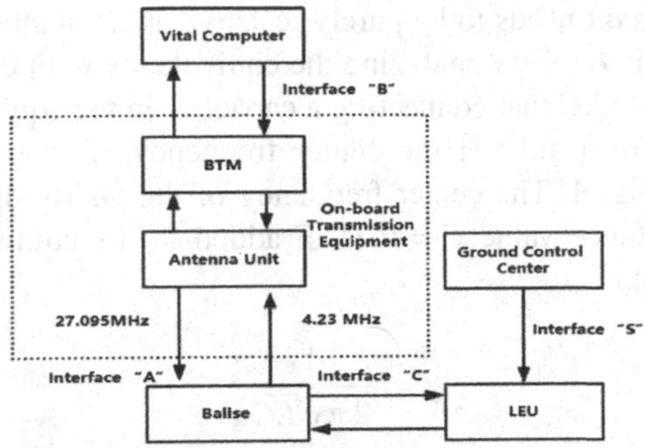

Fig. 1. The system diagram of Balise system

2 Architecture and Design

2.1 Modeling and Simulation of the Balise Up-Link Model

2.1.1 Tuning and Impedance Matching of the Balise Antenna

The Balise Antenna is the transmitting end of the Balise up-link model. According to the European Balise specification SUBSET-036, Balise are divided into standard Balise and compact Balise, of which the size of the standard Balise is 358 mm × 488 mm (5 mm × 20 mm in cross section) and the size of the compact Balise is 200 mm × 390 mm (5 mm × 20 mm in cross section) [6]. This paper uses standard Balise dimensions for modeling and simulation. The CST model of a standard Balise Antenna is shown in Fig. 2. Its shape is a ring-shaped slice. The material of the model is solid copper and the conductivity of the material is 5.8×10^7 S/m. Figure 2 shows a 10 mm wide feed port in the notch. This paper uses a discrete port to feed the Balise Antenna. The self-impedance of the Balise antenna is calculated by CST software as Z = 0.02 + 16.48j, and the equivalent circuit diagram of Balise Antenna is shown in Fig. 3.

Fig. 2. Model of the Balise antenna

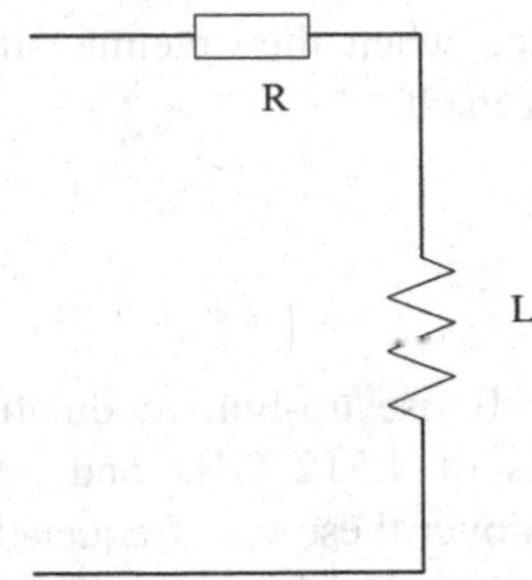

Fig. 3. Equivalent circuit diagram of Balise antenna

The R resistance is the self-resistance of the Balise antenna, and the L inductance is the equivalent inductance of the Balise antenna. According to the circuit resonance principle [7, 8], the circuit needs to be purely resistive at resonance, and the imaginary part of the impedance is zero. By analyzing the equivalent circuit diagram of the Balise antenna, it can be concluded that connecting a capacitor in the equivalent circuit so that the circuit can reach resonance at the center frequency. The antenna of the Balise antenna is shown in Fig. 4. The center frequency of the Balise up-link is 4.23 MHz, and the tuning capacitance value $C = 9.31\text{nF}$ added in the equivalent circuit can be obtained by formula (1).

$$f = \frac{1}{2\pi\sqrt{LC}} \tag{1}$$

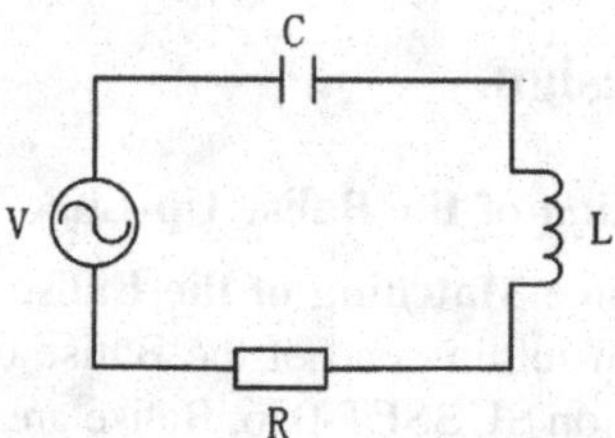

Fig. 4. Resonant circuit of Balise antenna

To make the antenna to reach the maximum power and avoid the occurrence of energy reflection, impedance matching is needed.

Q value is the quality factor of the antenna and is an important reference for impedance matching [9, 10]. It determines the operating bandwidth and transmission efficiency of the antenna. The relationship between the operating bandwidth B, the center frequency f, and the Q value is: $Q = f/B$.

The relation between the Q value and the resistance and inductance of the antenna is shown in formula (2), where R is the resistance of the antenna itself, R_1 is the resistance when the antenna impedance is matched, and L is the inductance of the antenna itself

$$Q = \frac{2\pi fL}{R + R_1} \tag{2}$$

The Balise up-link modulation signal needs to transmit signals with carrier frequencies of 4.512 MHz and 3.948 MHz. The operating bandwidth of the antenna should cover these two frequencies. Therefore, the bandwidth of the antenna designed in this paper is 1.05 MHz. Therefore, the Q value is about 2.3, and R_1 value can be obtained from the formula (2).

The integrated matching circuit of the Balise antenna is shown in Fig. 6. When the R value is relatively small, then there is a formula (3), and it is known that Z_0 is 50 Ω, and a matched inductor L_1 and capacitance value C_1 can be obtained (Fig. 5).

$$Z_0 = \frac{(R + R_1) + w^2(L + L_1)^2}{R + R_1} \tag{3}$$

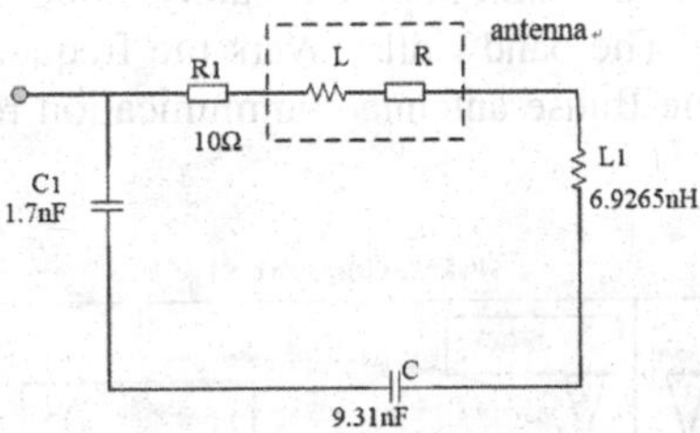

Fig. 5. The matching circuit of Balise antenna

C is resonant capacitor and L_1, C_1, R_1 are components added to the antenna impedance matching process in the matching circuit of Balise Antenna. After impedance matching, the real and imaginary simulation results of the Balise Antenna impedance are shown in Fig. 6.

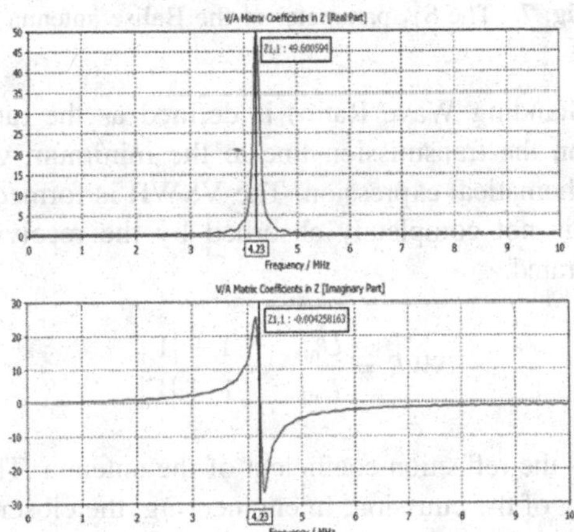

Fig. 6. The real and imaginary parts of the Balise antenna impedance

From the picture, we can see that the impedance of Balise Antenna is Z = 49.6 − j0.004, the real part of the impedance is 49.6 Ω and is close to 50 Ω, and the imaginary part is close to 0. So, the Balise antenna basically reaches the impedance matching state.

2.1.2 S Parameter and VSWR of the Balise Antenna

S parameter means the scattering parameter. The resonant frequency of the Balise antenna is 4.23 MHz. The S_{11} simulation result is shown in Fig. 7. The curve of the S_{11} shows that the Balise antenna reaches resonance at 4.23 MHz. The S_{11} value is about −35.69 dB less than −20 dB. The Balise antenna has a −10 dB bandwidth of approximately 1.2 MHz, a minimum of approximately 3.606 MHz, and a maximum of approximately 4.802 MHz. The bandwidth covers the frequencies of 3.948 MHz and 4.512 MHz and satisfies the Balise antenna communication requirements.

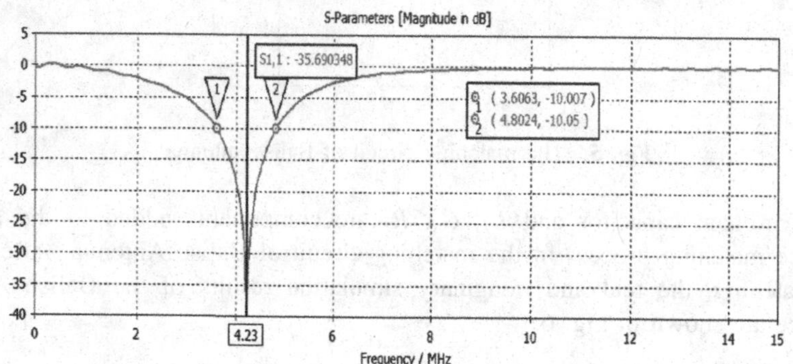

Fig. 7. The S_{11} parameter of the Balise antenna

VSWR (Voltage Standing Wave Ratio) is defined as the ratio of the maximum value of the voltage on the transmission line to the minimum value of the voltage. Formula (4) is the mathematical expression. The VSWR is formed because the energy of the incident wave is not completely absorbed by the receiving end, and then a reflected wave is generated.

$$VSWR = \frac{U_{\max}}{U_{\min}} = \frac{1 + |\Gamma|}{1 - |\Gamma|} \tag{4}$$

In the formula, Γ is the reflection coefficient of the antenna. The smaller the value, the higher the efficiency of the emission. In engineering, the closer its value is to 1, the better. But the ideal traveling wave state is not easy to achieve. The actual antenna design requires that its VSWR is less than 1.5. The simulation results of the VSWR of the Balise antenna is shown in Fig. 8. The Balise antenna designed in this paper has a VSWR of approximately 1.333 at the center frequency of 4.23 MHz, which is close to 1 and meets the antenna design standards.

2.1.3 Modeling and Simulation of the BTM Antenna

The BTM antenna is the receiving antenna of the Balise up-link. Its shape is similar to the model of the Balise antenna. It is a ring-shaped piece with a size of 200 mm × 200 mm (5 mm × 20 mm in cross section) and adopts a conductivity of

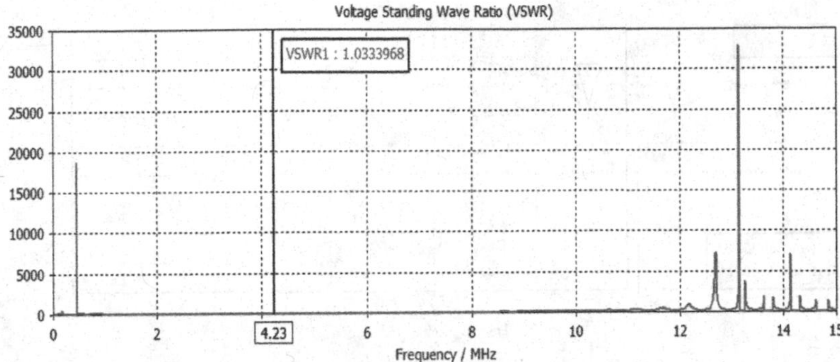

Fig. 8. The VSWR of the Balise antenna

5.8×10^7. S/m brass material. In order to receive signals from the Balise antenna with the maximum efficiency, the BTM antenna also requires circuit tuning and impedance matching.

After tuning and impedance matching, the BTM antenna model is shown in Fig. 9. In the BTM antenna model, port 2 is the feed port. The tuning capacitance and matching inductor capacitance and resistance are added to the port. The method of BTM antenna tuning and impedance matching is the same as the Balise antenna. The concrete parameters are shown in Fig. 10 of the matching circuit of the BTM antenna. The purpose is to make the BTM antenna resonant at a frequency of 4.23 MHz, where C is a resonant capacitor. C_1, L_2, and R_2 are to ensure that the impedance of the BTM antenna matches the transmission impedance.

Fig. 9. The BTM antenna model

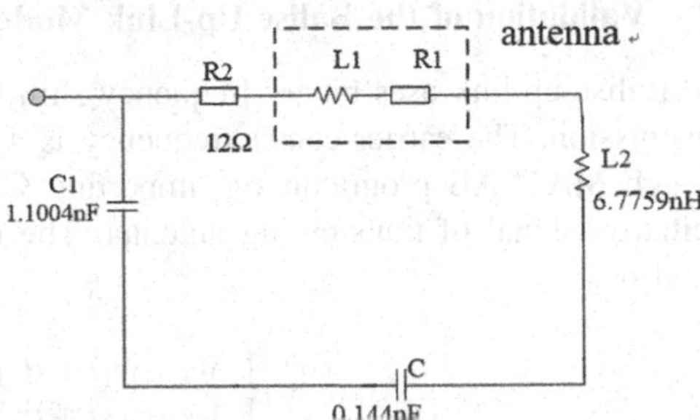

Fig. 10. The matching circuit of BTM antenna

The simulation results of the S-parameter and VSWR of the BTM antenna are shown in Figs. 11 and 12. The results show that the BTM antenna achieves resonance at a frequency of 4.23 MHz and the bandwidth covers 3.948 MHz to 4.512 MHz, which meet the requirements of uplink bandwidth. The VSWR of the BTM antenna is 1.025 at a frequency of 4.23 MHz, which conforms to the design requirements of t antenna.

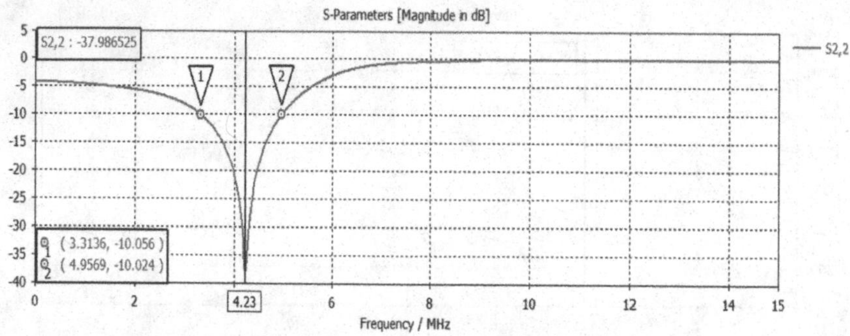

Fig. 11. The S_{22} parameter of BTM antenna

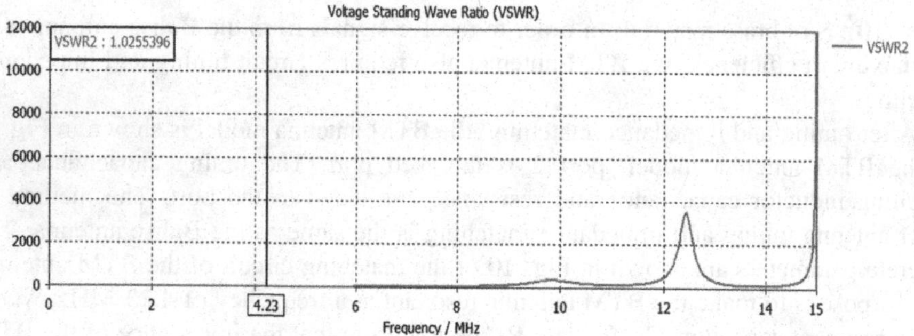

Fig. 12. The VSWR of BTM antenna

2.2 Validation of the Balise Up-Link Model

The Balise up-link uses binary frequency shift keying signals (2FSK) for information transmission. The carrier center frequency is 4.23 MHz. We realize the 2FSK signal through MATLAB programming, importing CST software with TXT format, as the excitation signal of transmitting antenna. The mathematical expression of the 2FSK signal is

$$S_{2FSK} = \begin{cases} Acos(w_1 t + \theta_1) \ when\, send \text{ "1"} \\ Acos(w_2 t + \theta_2) \ when\, send \text{ "0"} \end{cases} \tag{5}$$

In the formula, the amplitude A is a constant.

The initial phase of the signal is θ_1 and θ_2;

$\omega_1 = 2\pi f_1$ and $\omega_2 = 2\pi f_2$ are the angular rate of the upper frequency and the angular rate of the lower frequency.

The FSK signal's waveform imported into the CST is shown in Fig. 13.

Comparing Fig. 13 with Fig. 14, it can be obtained that when the BTM receives the FSK signal, the waveform is not distorted and the signals can be normally transmitted between the two antennas. The Fourier transform of the time-domain waveform in

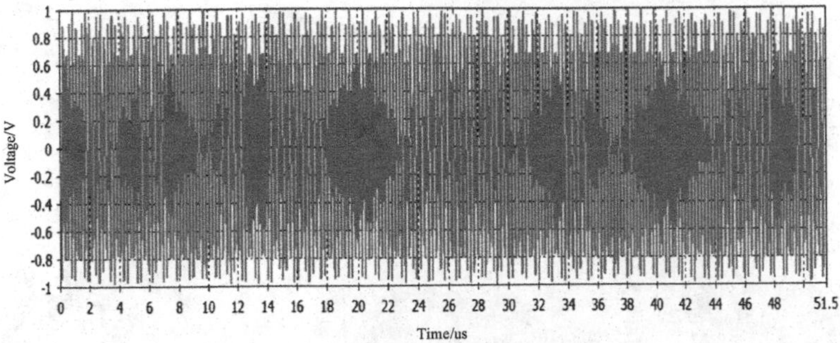

Fig. 13. The time domain waveform of the FSK signal Balise antenna transmitted

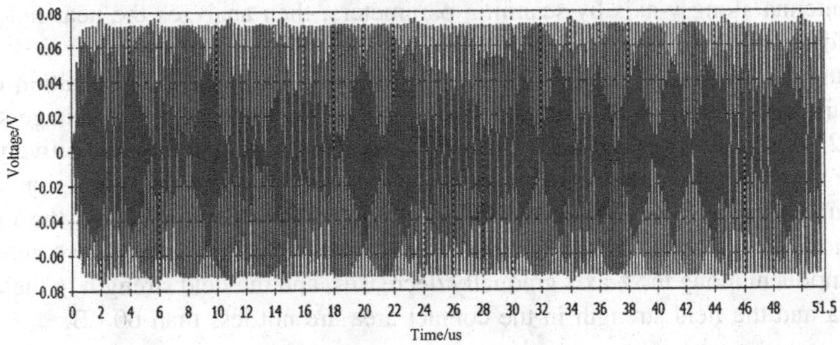

Fig. 14. The time domain waveform of the FSK signal received by BTM antenna

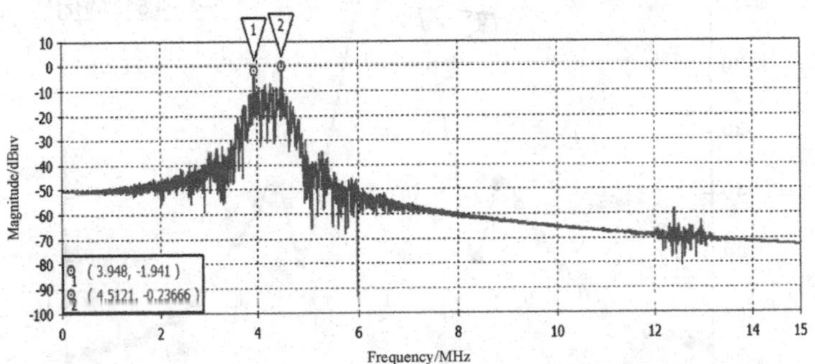

Fig. 15. The spectrum of the FSK signal received by BTM antenna

Fig. 15 gives the spectrum (as shown in Fig. 15). From the Fig. 16, we can see that the received signal has two peaks, corresponding to the frequency of the upper frequency of the signal of 4.512 MHz and the frequency of the lower frequency of 3.948 MHz. So the bandwidth of the Balise up-link model is verified and it complies with the Balise communication requirement.

Fig. 16. Shape and architecture of the coil antennas of the BTM and the Balise.

This paper simulates the dynamic change process of the Balise antenna and the BTM antenna along y-axis by scanning parameters, then analyzes the near-field lobe and field intensity difference of the up-link.

Figure 17 depicts the process of a 500 mm change in the relative position of the Balise antenna, and the BTM antenna along the y axis by adding a 1 V voltage source with 4.23 MHz, 3.948 MHz, and 4.512 MHz to the Balise antenna respectively. We can see that the difference between the peak intensity in the sidelobe region of the Balise up-link model and its main lobe peak is greater than 35 dB, and the up-link magnetic field increases with the horizontal relative distance between the two antennas. The component along the z-axis gradually decreases, and the field strength in the cross-talk area and the field strength in the contact area are not less than 60 dB.

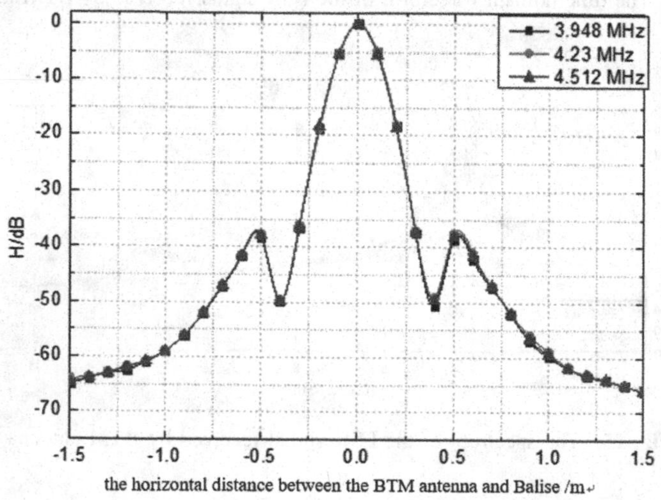

Fig. 17. The near-field lobe plots of the up-link at frequencies of 3.948 MHz, 4.23 MHz, and 4.512 MHz

3 The Effect of EMP on the Balise Up-Link Model

3.1 The Time-Domain Characteristics of Typical Electromagnetic Pulses

Electromagnetic pulse is a transient electromagnetic phenomenon [11]. According to relevant standard [12–14], a double exponential function is used here to describe the electromagnetic pulse. Its mathematical expression is

$$E = E_0 k\left(\mathrm{e}^{-\alpha t} - \mathrm{e}^{-\beta t}\right) \tag{6}$$

E_O is the peak factor of the pulse, k is the normalization factor of the pulse waveform, and it is related to the rising and falling edges of the pulse waveform.

By adjusting the pulse parameter values α and β, different types of electromagnetic pulse sources can be obtained.

In this paper, three representative electromagnetic pulses are selected to illustrate and study the frequency domain characteristics (Table 1 and Figs. 18 and 19).

Table 1. The waveform parameters of three typical electromagnetic pulses

EMP	Double exponential function parameter		
	α	β	k
EMP1	5.210×10^7	2.580×10^9	1.110
EMP2	4.000×10^7	6.000×10^8	1.300
EMP3	7.714×10^4	2.489×10^5	2.330

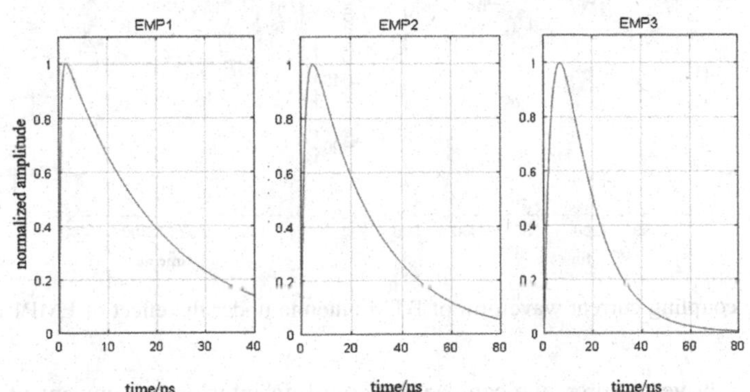

Fig. 18. Time-domain waveforms of three types of electromagnetic pulses

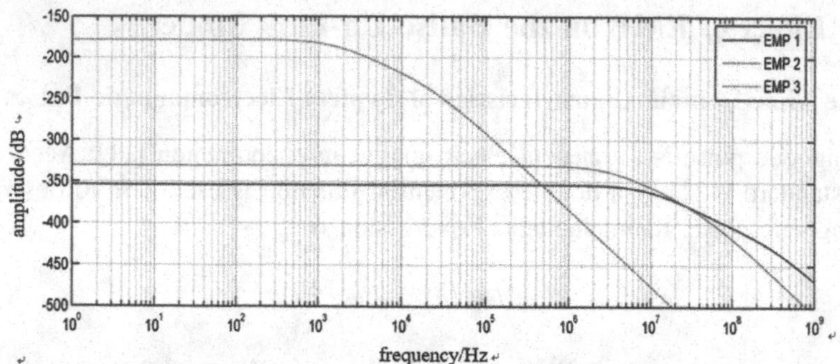

Fig. 19. Time-domain waveforms of three types of electromagnetic pulses

3.2 The Effect of Different Types of Electromagnetic Pulse on Balise Up-Link

Three different types of electromagnetic pulses, EMP1, EMP2, and EMP3, were added to a simulation model in the form of plane waves to perform interference experiments.

The incident directions of the three electromagnetic pulses are set to be the same, the pitch angle is 90°, the azimuth angle is 0°, and the polarization modes are all vertical polarizations, and the peak values of the pulses are all set at 50 kV/m (Figs. 20 and 21).

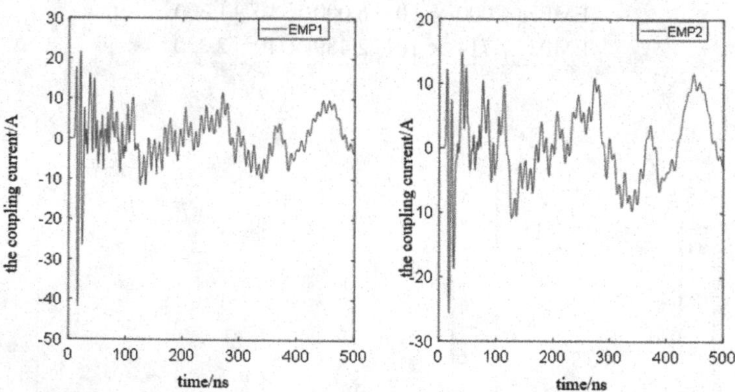

Fig. 20. The coupling current waveform of BTM antenna under the effect of EMP1 and EMP2

From the above pictures, we can see the coupling interference current of the BTM antenna has exceeded the current amplitude (mA level) of the Balise up-link signal under the influence of EMP1 and EMP2, while the coupling current is very small caused by EMP3. So EMP1 and EMP2 at this incident angle will interfere with the BTM antenna receiving signals from the Balise antenna.

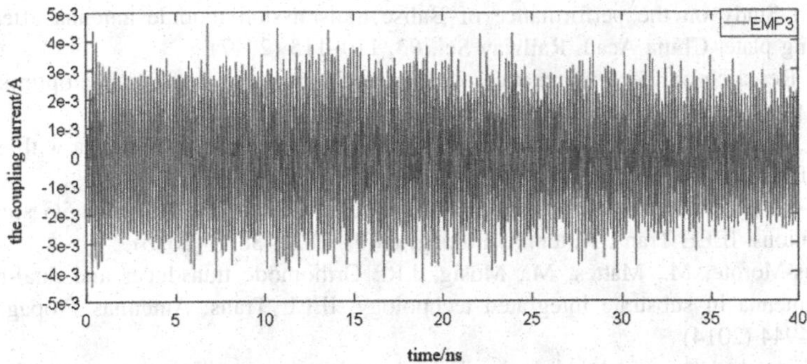

Fig. 21. The coupling current waveform of BTM antenna under the effect of EMP3

4 Conclusion

In this paper, a Balise up-link model is established according to the technical requirements of the Balise up-link. The coupling laws of different types of electromagnetic pulses on the Balise uplink are studied, and it is expected to provide a certain help for the Balise system protection. The major jobs are as follows:

- A simulation model of the Balise up-link is established using the CST electromagnetic simulation software. Add rail and train body to optimize the model.
- The FSK signal is implemented by MATLAB programming and imported into CST software. The simulation results show that the Balise up-link model meets the requirements of the communication standard.
- Electromagnetic pulses are transient electromagnetic interferences. Its duration is usually shorter with respect to the Balise uplink communication time. While its spectral distribution range is wide and the pulse energy is large. When the spectral range of the electromagnetic pulse overlaps the operating band of the Balise uplink (3.948 MHz to 4.512 MHz), there will be in-band interference and error codes in the Balise up-link signals.

References

1. Qian, J.: Research on the limit of interference warning for BTM antenna ports. Beijing Jiaotong University (2017)
2. Meng, Y.: Research on electromagnetic interference of ballast-less track slab to the transmission of Balise. In: Proceedings of 2013 International Conference on Electrical, Control and Automation Engineering (ECAE 2013). Advanced Science and Industry Research Center (2013)
3. Guo, Y., Zhang, J.: Analysis of electromagnetic compatibility of EMU onboard BTM equipment. J. China Railway Soc. **11**, 75–79 (2016)
4. Li, X., Liu, Z.: Study on influence of Balise installation angular deflection on transmission performance. J. China Railway Soc. **01**, 83–89 (2017)

5. Xu, N.: Study on the performance of Balise transmission module antenna after adding shielding plate. China Acad. Railway Sci. **03**, 110–115 (2017)
6. Di, L.: Research on electromagnetic coupling mechanism and performance optimization of Balise transmission system. Beijing Jiaotong University (2017)
7. Liu, H., Liu, Y., Gong, S.: Design of a compact dual-polarised slot antenna with enhanced gain. IET Microwaves Antennas Propag. **11**(6), 892–897 (2016)
8. Li, M.-Y., et al.: Eight-port orthogonally dual-polarized antenna array for 5G smartphone applications. IEEE Trans. Antennas Propag. **64**(9), 3820–3830 (2016)
9. Esquius-Morote, M., Mattes, M., Mosig, J.R.: Orthomode transducer and dual-polarized horn antenna in substrate integrated technology. IEEE Trans. Antennas Propag. **62**(10), 4935–4944 (2014)
10. Zhu, F., et al.: Ultra-wideband dual-polarized patch antenna with four capacitively coupled feeds. IEEE Trans. Antennas Propag. **62**(5), 2440–2449 (2014)
11. Liu, S., Liu, W.: Progress of relevant research on electromagnetic compatibility and electromagnetic protection. High Volt. Eng. **40**(06), 1605–1613 (2014)
12. Jia, M.: The analysis and anti-interferences measures of the transient pulse interference of the railway signal equipment. Railw. Sig. Commun. Eng. **10**(01), 87–89 (2013)
13. Sheng, S., Bi, Z., Tian, M., et al.: A new analytical expression of current waveform in standard IEC 61000-4-2. High Power Laser Part. Beams **15**(5), 464–466 (2003)
14. IEC. IEC61000-4-6: Electromagnetic compatibility (EMC)-Part 4-6: Testing and measurement techniques -Immunity to conducted disturbances, induced by radio-frequency fields (2008)

Network Attack Prediction Method Based on Threat Intelligence

Junshe Wang[1], Yuzi Yi[1], Hongbin Zhang[1,2(✉)], and Ning Cao[3]

[1] School of Information Science and Engineering, Hebei University of Science and Technology, Shijiazhuang, People's Republic of China
hbzhang@live.com

[2] Hebei Key Laboratory of Network and Information Security, Hebei Normal University, Shijiazhuang 050024, China

[3] College of Information Engineering, Qingdao Binhai University, Qingdao 050000, People's Republic of China

Abstract. The increasing number of Advanced Persistent Threat (APT) and compound attacks have brought greater challenges to network security issues. In order to effectively prevent and respond to compound attacks, a method of cyber-attack prediction based on threat intelligence is proposed. Firstly, a threat intelligence matching method is used to extract high-quality threat intelligence from the external threat intelligence, and then predicting the attack behavior based on the context data in high-quality threat intelligence. In the absence of high-quality threat intelligence, the mixed strategy Nash equilibrium is used to predict the attack behavior. According to the game relationship between attack strategy and defense strategy.

Keywords: Threat intelligence · Advanced Persistent Threat
Nash equilibrium · Attack prediction

1 Introduction

With the continuous expansion of computer network applications, network attacks have become increasingly complicated and accompanied by a strong purpose. In recent years, APT has caused serious losses in defense, finance, and energy industries. The capabilities, persistence, and complexity of adversarial attacks in the present threat landscape result in a speed race between security analysts, incident responders, and threat actors. Security analysts and incident responders need the skills to recognize attacks before performing defense efforts [1]. Traditional IDS, IPS and other devices are passive defense methods, and they always identify security events after an attack occurs. Lacking the ability to predict attacks, they simply relies on traditional detection equipment leads to delays in defensive actions and failure to respond to attacks in a timely manner.

At this stage, it is of urgent practical significance to study effective cyber-attack prediction methods, and it has become one of the research hotspots. Threat intelligence is referred to as the task of gathering evidence-based knowledge, including context,

X. Sun et al. (Eds.): ICCCS 2018, LNCS 11065, pp. 151–160, 2018.
https://doi.org/10.1007/978-3-030-00012-7_14

mechanisms, indicators, implications and actionable advice, about an existing or emerging menace or hazard to assets that can be used to inform decision regarding the subject's response to that menace or hazard [2]. Threat intelligence contains the information about existing or potential threats, which can provide defense basis. In order to reduce the harm of attacks on the network and take targeted defense measures in advance, the attack prediction method based on threat intelligence is proposed in this paper, in this method, based on the game relationship between the attacker and the defender, the combination of contextual data in high-quality threat intelligence and the hybrid strategy Nash equilibrium between offense and defense is used to predict the attack behavior.

The rest of the paper is organized as follows: Sect. 2 describes the relating work, Sect. 3 introduces the AP-TI model, and elaborates on each module of the model. Section 4 verifies the feasibility of the proposed method by experiment. In Sect. 5, we make the conclusion of the whole paper.

2 Related Work

In attack prediction, [3] Combined time series analysis techniques with probabilistic models, data mining and other techniques to analyze DDoS attack characteristics and behavior changes. Through the events that occur at time T, predict T+1, T+2, …, T+n events. Although this method can reduce the training overhead, it cannot effectively handle a large number of data sets, and the method requires strict assumptions for the data generation process. [4] proposed a pseudo-Bayesian network method to model the attack behavior and analyze its possible changes. This machine learning method has good convergence and fault tolerance. However, this method requires proper training to obtain the corresponding parameters, and during the classification process, the marker data need to be obtained. [5] based on the statistical characteristics of the alarm, the concept of alarm quality was introduced to ensure the validity of the data source, by improving the accuracy of the prediction. However, the sampling period is small and it is suitable for short-term prediction. [6] proposed a combination of fuzzy clustering and game theory, which improved the efficiency of forecasting. But it required high level of attack and defense modeling of the network. There are many factors to be considered.

The goal of the attack behavior prediction is to determine the attack action and identifies the attack route to help the defender reinforce the attack target. In this paper, using threat intelligence to predict attack behavior in response to the multiple and aggressive nature of APT and compound attacks. The concept of high-quality threat intelligence is introduced, and the attack intention is judged based on the context data in high-quality threat intelligence. The defender can reinforce the target system based on the tactics, techniques and procedures (TTP) used by the attacker, which was contained in high-quality threat intelligence. In the absence of high-quality threat intelligence, based on the game between attack and defense, the mixed strategy Nash equilibrium in game theory is used to predict the attack behavior.

3 APM-TI

Attack prediction model based on threat intelligence (APM-TI) is divided into two modules: threat intelligence matching, attack-defense game modeling. Threat intelligence matching is based on the security status of the target system. The process of extracting contextual data from threat intelligence can use contextual data to analyze attack intent and predicts attack behavior. Attack-defense game modeling is based on the game between attack and defense in the target system and uses the mixed strategy Nash equilibrium to predict the attack behavior. In this section, the threat intelligence matching method and attack-defense game modeling are elaborated.

3.1 Threat Intelligence Matching

Threat intelligence contains a large amount of security event information (threat intelligence model is presented in Fig. 1). However, not all security event information is applied to the current system state. In order to improve data accuracy, and obtain the relevant context data of security events, the concept of high-quality threat intelligence is introduced in this paper, simultaneously, the internal and external threat intelligence matching method is proposed to obtain high-quality threat intelligence. The definition of internal threat intelligence, external threat intelligence and high-quality threat intelligence are as follows:

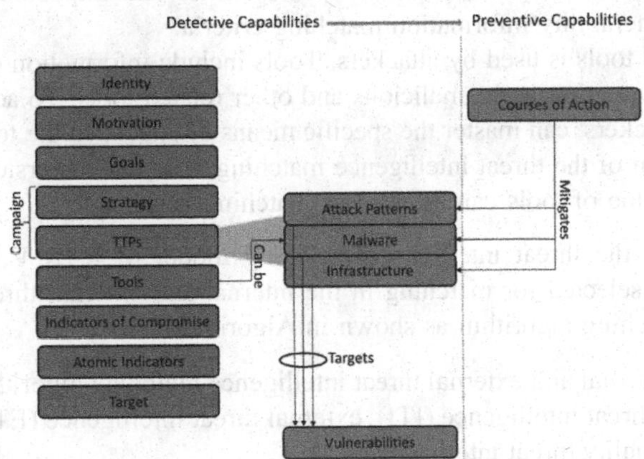

Fig. 1. Threat intelligence model

Definition 1: Internal threat intelligence. The internal threat intelligence originates from security event information in the target system and is obtained by integrating related data in security devices such as security information and event management (SIEM) tools and intrusion detection systems (IDS).

Definition 2: External threat intelligence. Open source intelligence (OSINT) or threat intelligence provided by intelligence providers.

Definition 3: High-quality threat intelligence. The external threat intelligence that exists context data or related information about security events, it is of guiding significance to the defense.

In order to facilitate data matching, the internal and external threat intelligence formats are unified before threat intelligence matching. We select Structured Threat Information Expression (STIX) [7] as the internal and external threat intelligence format. STIX is a language and serialization format used to exchange cyber threat intelligence, STIX architecture is comprised of several cyber threat information such as cyber observables, indicators, incidents, adversaries' TTP, exploit targets, courses of action, cyber-attack campaigns, and threat actors.

Obtain host privileges by exploiting system vulnerabilities is a common method used by attackers. Based on vulnerability information, combined with attack patterns and tools used in the attack, the threat intelligence matching model is established. The model can be expressed as $\mathrm{M} = \{A, V, T\}$, among:

(1) A represents attack patterns. Attack patterns are a type of TTP that describe ways the adversaries utilize to compromise targets. The attack pattern is used as the first matching object, and the similar attack behavior can be screened from the macro. Common Attack Pattern Enumeration and Classification (CAPEC) is selected [8] as the standard of attack pattern.
(2) V represents the vulnerabilities exploited by attacks. Vulnerability exploits are common attacks by attackers. The vulnerability information is matched to further filter the attack behavior. Common Vulnerabilities and Exposures (CVE) [9] is used as vulnerability information matching criteria.
(3) T represents tools is used by attackers. Tools include information detection tools, vulnerability exploit tools, malicious and other related tools. To acquire the tools used by attackers, can master the specific means of attack, so the tools are used as the condition of the threat intelligence matching. The name, version information, and hash value of tools can be used as matching basis.

According to the threat intelligence matching model $\mathrm{M} = \{A, V, T\}$, the corresponding data is selected for matching in the internal and external threat intelligence respectively, matching algorithm as shown in Algorithm 1.

```
Algorithm 1. internal and external threat intelligence matching algorithm:
Input: Internal threat intelligence (ITI), external threat intelligence (ETI)
Output: High-quality threat intelligence
1.  if (ITI.capec_id = ETI.capec_id)
        continue
    else END
2.  if (ITI.cve_id = ETI.cve_id)
        continue
    else END
3.  if (ITI.malware.hash = ETI.malware.hash && TI.tool.name = ESTI.tool.name)
     ITI matched with ETI
    else END
```

High-quality threat intelligence obtained through threat intelligence matching contains the security event context data in the target system, including key information such as attacker, TTP, attack target and attack intent, the defender can take targeted reinforcement of the target system based on the threat information.

3.2 Attack-Defense Game Modeling

In the attack and defense of cyberspace, the target of the attacker and the defender is opposed, and the strategies adopted by both parties are targeted. This paper uses the non-cooperative zero-sum game model to model the attack and defense of the network based on the characteristics of the relationship between the two sides. The network attack-defense game model can be expressed as $\mathrm{AD-GM} = \left\{P^a, P^d, \left(S_i^a, S_j^d\right), \left(U^a, U^d\right)\right\}$, among them: P^a and P^d represent the attacker and defender respectively, S_i^a and S_j^d represent the attacker and defender strategy respectively, U^a and U^d represent the utility of the attacker and defender respectively.

First, according to the vulnerability information in the target system, obtaining the tactics that attacker may adopt, and then use the corresponding defense method as the set of defense policy. By calculating the utility of the different strategies of the attacker and the defender, the prediction of the attacking action can be realized according to the probability distribution of the mixed strategy that achieves the Nash equilibrium [10].

In the course of the game, both sides of the attack and defense are pursuing the maximization of their own benefits. The utility of both parties is determined by the strategies adopted by both parties. Either party adopts an action strategy to generate reward and cost, and the utility is the difference between reward and cost.

Definition 4: Attack cost (AC). The cost incurred by an attacker to take attack action, including hardware and software resources, time, labor costs, and possible sanctions. The higher the threat degree of the attack, the higher the cost of the attack. Refer to the Lincoln laboratory attacks classification [11] to quantify the AC, specific values are shown in Table 1.

Table 1. Attack classification

Classification	Description	AL/AC
Root	Get administrator permissions	10
User	Get normal user permissions	5
Data	Unauthorized access or read and write data	3
DoS	Denial of service attack	2
Probe	Probe attack	0.5
Other	Other	*

Definition 5: Defense cost (DC). The cost of taking defensive measures. According to the category of defense strategy, the defense strategy is divided into: no defense $\emptyset$,

monitoring protection measures D_S, prevent protection measures D_F, repair protection measures D_R [6], defense cost $DC\left(S_j^d\right)$ respectively is 0, 4, 8, 10.

Definition 6: Attack reward (AR). The impact of the attack action on the system. It is derived from the attack success rate, the degree of attack threat (AL), and the degree of damage to the target system K_a. The attack success rate is obtained by statistical analysis of historical data. The values of AL are shown in Table 1, and the K_a calculation methods are shown in Eq. (1).

K_a is determined by asset weight W and attack damage T. W is affected by the confidentiality C, integrity I and availability A of the target system, can be represented as $W = (\mathrm{C}, \mathrm{I}, \mathrm{A})$, $\mathrm{C}, \mathrm{I}, \mathrm{A}$ according to important, general and unimportant three degrees, the values are 10, 5 and 1 respectively. T can be represented as $T = (\mathrm{L}, \mathrm{M}, \mathrm{H})$, $\mathrm{L}, \mathrm{M}, \mathrm{H}$ represent low, medium, high, three levels of destruction, $\mathrm{L}, \mathrm{M}, \mathrm{H}$ values for 1, 2, 3. To sum up, K_a can be represented as an one-dimensional vector:

$$K_a = W \times T \tag{1}$$

In the zero-sum game, the utility of both parties is relatively equal, that is $U^a = -U^d$. Among them:

Attacker utility is:

$$U^a = AR + DC - AC \tag{2}$$

Defender utility is:

$$U^d = AC - DC - AR \tag{3}$$

In the network attack-defense game, the strategic choices of both attacker and defender are independent and simultaneous. Under the mixed strategy, the two parties' profit expectation are:

$$\mathrm{E_a}(\mathrm{P_a}, \mathrm{P_d}) = \sum_{\mathrm{i}}^{\mathrm{m}} \mathrm{P_{ai}} \left[\sum_{\mathrm{j}}^{\mathrm{n}} \mathrm{P_{dj}} \mathrm{U_a}(\mathrm{S_i^a}, \mathrm{S_j^d}) \right] = \sum_{\mathrm{i}}^{\mathrm{m}} \sum_{\mathrm{j}}^{\mathrm{n}} \mathrm{P_{ai}} \mathrm{P_{dj}} \mathrm{U_a}(\mathrm{S_i^a}, \mathrm{S_j^d}) \tag{4}$$

$$\mathrm{E_d}(\mathrm{P_a}, \mathrm{P_d}) = \sum_{\mathrm{j}}^{\mathrm{n}} \mathrm{P_{dj}} \left[\sum_{\mathrm{i}}^{\mathrm{m}} \mathrm{P_{ai}} \mathrm{U_d}(\mathrm{S_i^a}, \mathrm{S_j^d}) \right] = \sum_{\mathrm{j}}^{\mathrm{n}} \sum_{\mathrm{i}}^{\mathrm{m}} \mathrm{P_{ai}} \mathrm{P_{dj}} \mathrm{U_d}(\mathrm{S_i^a}, \mathrm{S_j^d}) \tag{5}$$

According to the principle of non-cooperative game theory, using Brouwer's fixed point theorem [10], it can be concluded that there exists a Nash equilibrium in the AD-GM model. That is, the mixed strategy $\left(P_a^*, P_d^*\right)$ in the AD-GM model reaches the Nash equilibrium, where $\left(P_a^*, P_d^*\right)$ satisfies:

$$\begin{cases} \forall P_{ai}, \sum_{i=1}^{m}\sum_{j=1}^{n} U_a\left(S_i^a, S_j^d\right) P_{ai}^* P_{dj}^* \geq \sum_{i=1}^{m}\sum_{j=1}^{n} U_a\left(S_i^a, S_j^d\right) P_{ai} P_{dj}^* \\ \forall P_{dj}, \sum_{i=1}^{m}\sum_{j=1}^{n} U_d\left(S_i^a, S_j^d\right) P_{ai}^* P_{dj}^* \geq \sum_{i=1}^{m}\sum_{j=1}^{n} U_d\left(S_i^a, S_j^d\right) P_{ai}^* P_{dj} \\ \sum_{i=1}^{m} P_{ai} = 1, P_{ai} \geq 0 \\ \sum_{j=1}^{n} P_{dj} = 1, P_{dj} \geq 0 \end{cases} \quad (6)$$

In summary, mixed strategy $P_{ai}^* = \left(P_{a1}^*, P_{a2}^*, \ldots, P_{am}^*\right)$ is the best choice for the attacker and is the most likely strategy that the attacker adopts. The defender can take defensive measures based on the attacker's optimal strategy.

4 Experimental Verification

In order to verify the threat intelligence matching algorithm and the AD-GM model, two experiments were used to prove its validity. This section describes two experiments and experimental results.

4.1 Threat Intelligence Matching Algorithm

In the aspect of threat intelligence matching algorithm, the challenge1 data source [12] in the honeynet project challenges is used as the security event. The key process for the security event is:

(1) Obtain the port information of the host.
(2) Invasion system by the LSASS buffer overflow vulnerability.
(3) Establish a TCP session with the target host and download the malware.
(4) Execute malicious.

We generate threat intelligence based on the complete information of the data source, adding it to a number of other threat intelligence as the external threat intelligence. In this paper, we select the attack after the exploit as the predict object, and use the vulnerability and the previous information of the security event to make the internal threat intelligence as the matching basis. In the security event, attack pattern is capec-185, vulnerability is CVE-2003-0533, the attacker establishes a connection with the target host through the TCP session, so the TCP session is one of the tools used by the attacker. The matching results of the three stages are shown in Table 2:

Table 2. Threat intelligence matching results

Matching elements	Matched successful number/total number	Remaining ratio
Attack pattern	(14/80)	18%
Vulnerability	(3/80)	4%
Tools	(1/80)	1%

The experiment shows that the threat intelligence matching method proposed in this paper can be used to screen relevant external threat intelligence and extract the high-quality threat intelligence to some extent.

4.2 AD-GM Model

In order to verify the proposed AD-GM model attack prediction method, the topology of Fig. 2 was used to simulate attack and defense scenarios.

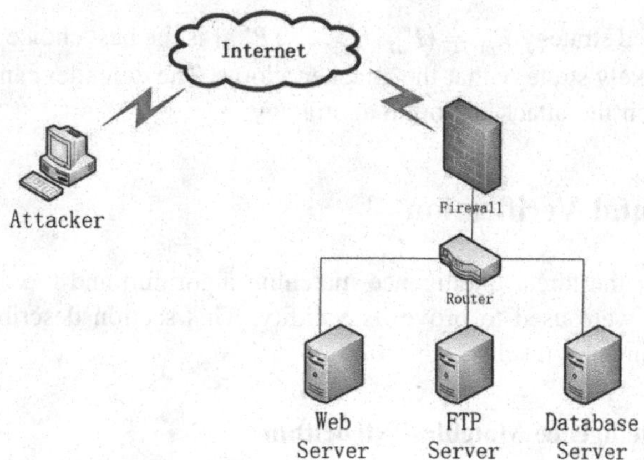

Fig. 2. Network topology

Web Server, FTP Server, and Database Server are located on the intranet. Attackers are located on the external network. Firewalls allow external hosts to access Web Servers and FTP Servers. Only Web Servers and FTP Servers can access Database Servers.

The vulnerability information of each server in the experimental environment is shown in Table 3. According to the vulnerability information, the defensive party's optional defense measures are shown in Table 4.

We analyze the selectable strategies and defensive success ratios of both attack and defensive players, and obtain the utility matrix of both parties through Eqs. (2) and (3):

$$\begin{bmatrix} 26.8, -26.8 & 133, -133 & 80.5, -80.5 \\ 62, -62 & 54, -54 & 115.5, -115.5 \\ 30.5, -30.5 & 129.6, -129.6 & 145.2, -145.2 \\ 14.9, -14.9 & 151.9, -151.9 & 116.8, -116.8 \end{bmatrix}$$

Calculating the Nash Equilibrium to obtain a mixed strategy probability distribution for both sides: $P_a^* = (0, 0.31, 0.69)$, $P_d^* = (0.54, 0.46, 0, 0)$. The mixed strategy $P_a^* = (0, 0.31, 0.69)$ is a prediction of attack behavior. According to the prediction, the attacker's most likely strategy is to exploit the Wu-Ftpd SockPrintf() vulnerability.

Table 3. Vulnerability information

Host	Vulnerability information	Result	AC
FTP server	1. Ftp.rhosts	User	5
Web server	2. Apache Chunked Enc.	Root	10
	3. Wu-Ftpd SockPrintf()	Root	10
Database server	4. Oracle TelCommand Execute	Root	10

Table 4. Defensive strategy

Defensive strategy	Strategy category	DC
No access to the port	Prevent protection measures D_F	8
Install Apache patch	Repair protection measures D_R	10
Install Oracle patch	Repair protection measures D_R	10
Stop the FTP service	Prevent protection measures D_F	8

5 Conclusion and Future Work

This paper proposes a network attack prediction method based on threat intelligence, which predicts the security events in the target system according to the context information in the threat intelligence. When threat intelligence is not applicable, the Nash equilibrium is used to predict the attack behavior according to the utility during the game of attack and defense. This method fully considers the system vulnerability information, from this, we can determine the attack actions that the attacker may take and the reinforcement measures that the defense can take. Threat intelligence matching method, which is proposed in this paper, removes useless information, and ability to capture TTP information and attack intent based on relevant context data in high-quality threat intelligence, TTP describes the attacker's attack method, and the attack intention reflects the fundamental purpose of the attacker, both can provide direct and effective help for the defender. The method of calculating the Nash equilibrium to predict attack action analyzes the impact of the game process between the attack and the defense on the network state, and predicts the attack behavior according to the optimal utility under the attacker's mixed strategy. This paper proposes a preliminary method for predicting attacks using threat intelligence and Nash equilibrium. In the next step, improves match accuracy by optimizing threat intelligence matching algorithms. Adding the framework proposed in this paper to the threat intelligence sharing session, and obtain the latest threat intelligence in a timely manner. Meanwhile, we generate new threat intelligence from security events in the target system and provide threat intelligence sharing. Finally, testing the proposed method in the actual environment and improve the deficiencies.

Acknowledgments. This research was supported in part by the National Natural Science Foundation of China under grant numbers 61672206, 61572170. Hongbin Zhang is the corresponding author of this article.

References

1. Mavroeidis, V., Bromander, S.: Cyber threat intelligence model: an evaluation of taxonomies, sharing standards, and ontologies within cyber threat intelligence. In: European Intelligence and Security Informatics Conference IEEE Computer Society, pp. 91–98 (2017)
2. Definition of Threat Intelligence. https://www.gartner.com/doc/2487216/definition-threat-intelligence. Accessed 21 Dec 2017
3. Fachkha, C., Bou-Harb, E., Debbabi, M.: Towards a forecasting model for distributed denial of service activities. In: Proceedings of the IEEE International Symposium on Network Computing and Applications, pp. 110–117 (2013)
4. Ramaki, A.A., Khosravi-Farmad, M., Bafghi, A.G.: Real time alert correlation and prediction using Bayesian networks. In: Proceedings of the ISCISC, pp. 98–103 (2015)
5. Xi, R.R., Yun, X.C., Zhang, Y.Z., et al.: An improved quantitative evaluation method for network security. Chin. J. Comput. **38**(4), 749–758 (2015)
6. Wu, J., et al.: Big data analysis based security situational awareness for smart grid. IEEE Trans. Big Data **PP**(99), 1 (2016)
7. Barnum, S.: Standardizing Cyber Threat Intelligence Information with the Structured Threat Information Expression (STIX^{TM}), vol. 11. MITRE Corporation (2012)
8. MITRE: Common Attack Pattern Enumeration and Classification. https://capec.mitre.org/. Accessed 11 Jan 2018
9. MITRE: Common Vulnerabilities and Exposures. https://cve.mitre.org. Accessed 11 Jan 2018
10. Nash, J.: Non-cooperative games. Ann. Math. 286–295 (1951)
11. Gordon, L.A., Loeb, M.P., Lucyshyn, W., et al.: 2006 CSI/FBI computer crime and security survey. Comput. Secur. J. **22**(3), 1–29 (2006)
12. Honeynet Project Challenges. http://honeynet.org/challenges. Accessed 01 Feb 2018

Network Security Situation Assessment Approach Based on Attack-Defense Stochastic Game Model

Jianyi Liu[1(✉)], Fangyu Weng[1], Ru Zhang[1], and Yunbiao Guo[2]

[1] Beijing University of Posts and Telecommunications, Beijing, China
liujy@bupt.edu.cn
[2] Beijing Institute of Electronics Technology and Application, Beijing, China

Abstract. To analyze the influence of threat propagation on network system and accurately evaluate system security, this paper proposes an approach to improve the awareness of network security, based on Attack-Defense Stochastic Game Model (ADSGM). The variety of network security elements collected by multi-sensors are fused into a standard dataset such as assets, threats and vulnerabilities. For every threat, it builds a threat propagation network and propagation rule. By using the game theory to analyze the network offensive and defensive process, it establishes the ADSGM. The ADSGM can dynamically evaluate network security situation and provide the best reinforcement schema. Experimental results on a specific network indicate that the approach is more precise and more suitable for a real network environment. The reinforcement schema can effectively prevent the propagation of threats and reduce security risks.

Keywords: Network security situation awareness · Stochastic game model
Mixed strategy Nash equilibrium · Threat propagation

1 Introduction

Network security situation awareness has received much attention in recent years, and its core is network security situation assessment. Assessment technique qualitatively and quantitatively analyzes, obtains and understands the network security situation from the massive security data. It can provide the evidence and guidance for the security administrator's decision-making, and improve the initiative of network defense, so as to reduce the harm of network attack as much as possible. At present, there are many valuable research works in network security situation assessment, which include analytic hierarchy process, data fusion method and so on [1].

Chen et al. [2] proposed a quantitative and hierarchical model to evaluate security situation. The model adopts the evaluation from bottom to top and from local to global, calculates the risk indexes of host, service and the structure of the network system. The data fusion method mainly aims at integrating the massive and heterogeneous information produced by different security devices, so as to obtain global network security situation. Steinberg et al. put forward JDL data fusion model. Endslay [3] divided

X. Sun et al. (Eds.): ICCCS 2018, LNCS 11065, pp. 161–173, 2018.
https://doi.org/10.1007/978-3-030-00012-7_15

network security situational awareness into: perception, understanding and prediction. Time Base [4] proposed to integrate the network intrusion detection system with multi-sensor information and proposed the concept of network situation awareness. Xie et al. [5] applied neural network to evaluate and predict the network security situation. Qu [6] used the data fusion method based on D-S evidence theory to evaluate the network security situation, this method fuses multi-source alert information through D-S evidence theory, associates with nodes vulnerability information and severity of threats. Liu [7] proposed a method of fusing attack graph model and Hidden Markov model (HMM). Hu [8] fused the situation factors of attacker, defender and network environment to evaluate the capability of attacker and the exploitability rate of vulnerability.

The above research focuses on the impact of network security events from attacker but does not take into account the impact of defense strategies from administrator and did not take into account the potential impact of threat propagation. The offensive and defensive confrontation of network security has the characteristics of goal antagonism, strategy dependence and noncooperation. Game theory is a common method to solve such problems. Game theory has been widely used in the space situation awareness, network situation awareness and so on [9–12]. Dan [13] used the Markov game model to estimate the network security situation and analyze the attack effect. Ryutov et al. [14] designed a three-party game theory framework including attacker, defender and user. Shandilya et al. [15] established an imperfect information stochastic game model that describes the game state between user and administrator and established a cooperative game model framework based on interaction between honeypot and suspicious users. Liu et al. [16] proposed a new dynamic game method of attack and defense strategy for distributed network attacks. Zhang [17] proposed network security situation awareness method based on Markov three party game model, which includes attackers, administrators and users, but the method did not consider the cost in the calculation of participant's revenue calculation and did not consider the mixed strategy Nash equilibrium.

Based on the above research results, this paper divides network security situation into inherent situation and potential situation. The inherent situation indicates that network security events have the direct impact on network security situation, and the potential situation is the influence of threat propagation on network security situation. An attack-defense stochastic game model (ADSGM) method was proposed to evaluate the network security situation. The method integrates a variety of safety elements data, calculates the mixed strategy Nash equilibrium considering the impact of the implementation of protective measures and threat propagation and then provides the best reinforcement schema. The reinforcement schema can effectively prevent the propagation of threats and reduce security risks.

2 Network Security Situation

Network security situation means the comprehensive status and trends of the entire network security data including asset data, basic running information data, threat data, vulnerability data, security event data.

2.1 Definitions

Definition 1 (Asset data). Assets refer to resources that are valuable to the network system, such as hosts, routers, firewalls, and so on. Each asset consists of services, data, software, and hardware. The asset data set S_{asset} is composed of all the asset information in the network. Individual asset is represented as Asset = $(id_a, name, type, V_a, serv, os, id_r, V_r)$, id_a is asset identifier; *name* is asset name; *type* is asset type which includes host, server, router, and other network devices. V_a represents the importance or sensitivity of an asset. Confidentiality, integrity, and availability are three security attributes of asset evaluation, $V_a = (val_c, val_i, val_a)$ represents the value component of three security attributes [18]. *serv* is asset runtime service information. *os* is operating system type. id_r represents the asset runtime information identification. V_r represents the asset operating value.

Definition 2 (Basic running information data). It represents the performance of various aspects of assets, divided into host operating information and network components running information. The host running information is represented as $Run_h = (id_r, id_a, V_{rh}, \rho_m, \rho_{cpu}, flow)$, id_r is base running information ID, id_a is the ID for corresponding asset, V_{rh} is running value for host assets, ρ_m is memory utilization, ρ_{cpu} is CPU utilization, *flow* is network flow.

The components running information is represented as $Run_e = (id_r, id_a, V_{re}, type, \beta, \theta)$, id_r is base running information ID, id_a is the ID for corresponding asset, V_{re} is running value for components assets, *type* is component type, β represents ability of detect and defend, θ represents traffic for components.

Definition 3 (Vulnerability data). The vulnerability is represented as $Vul = (id_v, id_a, name, p_t, V_v)$, id_v is identification of the vulnerability; id_a is the ID for corresponding asset; *name* is the name of vulnerability; p_t indicates the probability that the vulnerability will be exploited successfully; V_v represents the extent of damage after vulnerability is exploited.

Definition 4 (Threat data). Each threat is represented as $Threat = (id_v, id_a, id_t, name, type, p_t, V_t)$, id_t is identification of the threat; id_a identifies the asset where the threat occurred; id_v identifies vulnerabilities of the threats; *name* is the name of the threat; *type* is the threat type; p_t r represents the possibility of exploiting vulnerabilities; V_t indicates the damage value caused by the threat.

Definition 5 (Security event data). If the vulnerability of assets is exploited by the threat, the security event will be produced. A security event is represented as $SE = (id_a, id_v, id_t, p_{se}, V_{se})$, id_a identifies the asset; id_t identifies the threat that cause security event; id_v identifies exploited vulnerabilities. p_{se} is the occurrence possibility of security event: $p_{se} = p_v \cdot p_t$.

2.2 Attack-Defense Stochastic Game Model

The network offensive and defensive environment includes three parties: attackers, defenders and users. Attackers always want to destroy the security attributes of assets to get the maximum benefits, and defenders take security schema to prevent attackers from damaging the security attributes in the hope of minimizing security damage. Both the offensive and defensive goals are totally antagonistic and will not reach a cooperation agreement. Users want to pay less to get as much network services and will not cooperate with other parties. Therefore, the problem of network security is essentially a kind of multi-person non-cooperative game, which is the game process in which all participants pursue the maximization of benefits. All participants want to select the appropriate strategy to get the maximum benefit with the least cost. The selection process of the strategy not only depends on its own situation, but also the influence of the tripartite behavior. Attackers and defenders usually prioritize strategies that are cost-effective for the network. Under normal circumstances, the impact of users is relatively small, so this paper does not consider the impact of user's behavior. Offensive and defensive benefits are not exactly equal to each other, it is non-zero-sum game. So, ADSGM is a two-person non-cooperative non-zero-sum game offensive and defensive stochastic game model, which can be represented as:

$$ADSGM = (I, S, A, D, \pi, P, R, \delta)$$

(1) I denotes participant in a game. $I = \{i_a, i_d\}$ represents attackers and defenders.
(2) S denotes state space. It refers to the state of threat propagation access network. The transition of status is determined by the behaviors of both parties.
(3) A indicates attacker's action set. In the state S_k, $A_k = (a_1, a_2, \ldots, a_m)(A_k \in A)$ represents the action set of an attacker at the status K. An attacker's actions are defined as threats spread to uninfected adjacent nodes: $A_k = (a_1, a_2, \ldots, a_m)$. $A_k(i) = m$ denotes the threat's propagation to node m at the state K moment. An attacker's set of actions at state k can be calculated from the threat propagation algorithm.
(4) D represents the defender's action set. $D_k = (d_1, d_2, \ldots, d_n)$, $(D_k \in D)$ represents the action set of a defender at the status K. The defender's actions include eliminating the vulnerability and cutting off the transmission path. $D_k(j) = n$ means to eliminate the vulnerability on node n. $D_k(j) = e(m, n)$ means cut off propagation path $e(m, n)$. The action set of the defender is obtained according to the current state of the threat propagation access network and propagation algorithm.
(5) π denotes attack-defense strategies. It said the offensive and defensive sides to take action rules. In the state S_k, the attackers and defenders take the action of the rule called offensive and defensive strategy, denoted as π_k^a, π_k^d. The attacker's strategy is expressed as $\pi_k^a = (\pi_k^a(a_1), \pi_k^a(a_2), \ldots, \pi_k^a(a_m))$. $\pi_k^a(a_i)$ indicates the probability that the attacker take action a_i in the status S_k. $\pi_k^a(a_i) \in [0, 1]$, $\pi_k^a(a_i) \in [0, 1]$, $\sum_{a_i \in A_k} \pi_k^a(a_i) = 1$. $\pi_k^d(d_i)$ indicates the probability that the defender take action d_i in the status S_k, $\pi_k^d(d_i) \in [0, 1]$, $\sum_{d_i \in D_k} \pi_k^d(d_i) = 1$.
(6) $P: \mathrm{S} \times \mathrm{A} \times \mathrm{D} \times \mathrm{S} \rightarrow [0, 1]$ indicates state transition probability. The probability that participants choose action $A_k(i)$, $D_k(j)$ in a certain state and make the state of the system move to other states.

(7) R^i: S × A × D × S → R($i = a, d$), it represents an attacker or defender's revenue function. In the status k, the attacker takes action $A_k(i)$, the defender takes action $D_k(j)$, and the gains of both offensive and defensive sides are:

$$r_i^a(i,j) = R^a(S_k, A_k(i), D_k(j))$$
$$r_k^d(i,j) = R^d(S_k, A_k(i), D_k(j))$$

(8) Discount factor $\delta(0 < \delta < 1)$ represents the impact on the future.

3 Network Security Situation Assessment Based on ADSGM

3.1 Assessment Framework

The frame diagram of the network security situation assessment method based on attack-defense stochastic game model (ADSGM-NSSA) is shown in the Fig. 1:

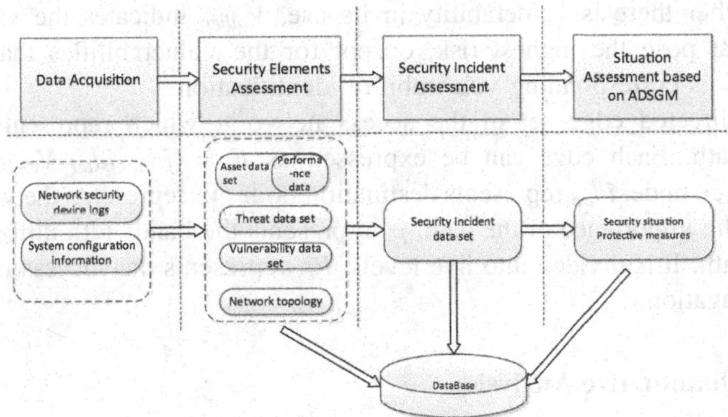

Fig. 1. ADSGM-NSSA frame diagram.

As shown above, the method (ADSGM-NSSA) includes the following steps:

Step one: Data acquisition. Network security situation assessment technology can analyze all aspects of security elements, including network security events such as hacker attacks, the vulnerability of the system itself, services and other information. In order to evaluate network security situation comprehensively, data sources include system configuration information, system operation information and network traffic information.

Step two: After the data acquisition, the framework will integrate heterogeneous data to the safety factor data set: asset data set, assets running data set, the threat data set, vulnerability data set and network topology.

Step three: Security events are analyzed based on safety factor data set. Threats can cause damage to assets by taking advantage of vulnerabilities that bring about security events. Threat is the external reason; vulnerability is the internal reason, and the combined effect of both results in risks.

Step four: Build offensive and defensive stochastic game model. The model takes security incident information as input data, evaluates the situation of network security and obtains network security protection schema.

3.2 Threat Propagation Analysis

After the network node A was hacked, the attackers can exploit the access relationship between node A and node B and continue attack node B. This process is called threat propagation [19]. Because of threat propagation, the risk of assets is divided into two parts: inherent risk and potential transmission risk. In order to evaluate the network security situation more accurately, the influence of threat propagation on the situation should be taken into account. According to paper [20], an access network that describes threat propagation for each threat to the collection U_t was constructed, which was expressed as TPAN $= (V, E)$. V is the network nodes set, including assets that have been attacked. According to S_{asset}, S_{vul} and S_{threat}, nodes are represented as $V_i = (id_a, V_a, V_r, e_t, e_v, V_{other}, id_{ov})$, e_t indicates whether the node has a threat t, e_v indicates whether there is vulnerability in its use, V_{other} indicates the value of vulnerabilities that pose the highest risk, except for the vulnerabilities that threaten t utilization, id_{ov} is corresponding vulnerability identification.

E is the directed edge set of the access network, which represents a threat's propagation path. Each edge can be expressed as $E_i = (id_{ar}, id_{ad}, V_e, \rho_e, P_{es})$. id_{ar} represents source node. id_{ad} represents destination node. V_e represents the weight of the edge, that is, the importance of the path, ρ_e represents the bandwidth utilization of the propagation path. It is divided into five levels. P_{es} represents the success rate of using the edge propagation.

3.3 Game Quantitative Analysis

(1) Quantification of offensive and defensive income

In the offensive and defensive environment, attackers always want to destroy the security attributes of the assets to maximize profits, while defenders take security schema to prevent attackers from damaging security attributes, hoping to minimize security damage. The gains of both offensive and defensive sides are determined by the choice of both strategies. The direct benefits of threats are determined by the threat of security damage and threat costs to the system. The damage to the system includes damage to the asset and its associated links. The direct benefits of both the asset i and related edges that threaten t in the K state are represented as:

$$ua_i(t,k) = Sdam_i(t) - Acost_i(t) \tag{1}$$

$Sdam$ represents damage to the system, and $Acost_i$ denotes the cost of the attack. According to the actual experience, if the cost is larger than a threshold, then the threat's benefits is regarded as zero, else the cost is ignored.

$$Sdam_i(t) = Vdam_i(t) + \sum\nolimits_{e \in E} Edam_{ei}(t) \tag{2}$$

E is the relative path edge set, $Vdam$ represents a loss of assets, proportional to the severity of the vulnerability. $Edam_{ei}$ represents the loss of the link.

$$Vdam_i(t) = (V_a, V_v)p_t p_v \tag{3}$$

$$Edam_{ei}(t) = V_e \cdot \Delta\rho \cdot p_{es} \tag{4}$$

Defenders implement security schemas on asset nodes or links to reduce the damage caused by attacks. However, security schemas may have a negative impact on node and propagation link performance. Defenders' benefits are expressed as:

$$ud_i(t,k) = -Sdam_i(t) + \sum\nolimits_{i \in N, e \in E} Dcost_i(t)) \tag{5}$$

Security schema reduce the threat of security damage to the system, expressed as $Sdam$, $Dcost$ represents the cost of security schemas, including the implementation of security schemas, operating costs, negative costs, and so on. Negative cost includes losses caused by security schemas, resulting in reduced quality of service, and other losses. When the cost is larger than a threshold, the profit is regarded as zero. Negative costs are expressed as:

$$Dcost_i(t) = \theta_{node}(i,j) val_{ai} \cdot V_r + \theta_{edge}(i,j) V_e \cdot \rho_e \tag{6}$$

$\theta(i,j)$ represents the damage factor to the availability of the attack i generated by the attack strategy j. When the guard policy is the repair node, $\theta_{node} = 0.2, \theta_{edge} = 0.2$. When the protective measure is truncated propagation path, $\theta_{node} = 0, \theta_{edge} = 1$.

(2) Quantization of game matrix

The bi matrix game and the Markov decision process are synthesized and extended to get the attack-defense stochastic game model. The attacker uses each row in the matrix to represent the selected attack action, and the defender use each column to indicate optional protection. Therefore, in each game state S_k, for the threat t, the game behavior of the attack and defense sides can be regarded as a $m \times n$ bi-matrix game.

The network security situation assessment method based on ADSGM divides the situation into the inherent situation and the potential situation. The inherent situation is expressed by the direct benefit of the offensive and defensive, and the potential benefit of the future state is represented by the situation discount value. The matrix game elements on both sides of the attack and defense are represented as $\left(s^a_{ij}(t,k), s^d_{ij}(t,k)\right)$, details are as follows:

$$s^a_{ij}(t,k) = r^a_{ij}(t,k) + \delta \sum\nolimits_{i=1}^{K} p^{kl}_{ij}(S_l(t)|S_k(t)), S_k(t), A_k(i), D_k(j))S_l(t) \tag{7}$$

$$s_{ij}^{d}(t,k) = r_{ij}^{d}(t,k) + \delta \sum\nolimits_{i=1}^{K} p_{ij}^{kl}(S_l(t)|S_k(t)), S_k(t), A_k(i), D_k(j)) S_l(t) \tag{8}$$

$$i = 1, 2, \ldots, m; j = 1, 2, \ldots, n; P_{ij}^{kl} \geq 0; \forall i, j, k, l, \sum\nolimits_{k=1}^{k} P_{ij}^{kl} < 1$$

$s_{ij}^{a}(t,k)$ represents the gain earned by an attacker in status S_k when the attacker takes action $A_k(i)$, and the defender uses the action $D_k(j)$. It consists of two parts, the former represents the direct gain, and the latter represents the potential gain.

$s_{ij}^{d}(t,k)$ represents the gain earned by the defender in status S_k when an attacker takes action $s_{ij}^{d}(t,k)$ and the defender uses the action $D_k(j)$. It consists of two parts, the former $r_{ij}^{d}(t,k)$ represents the direct gain, and the latter represents the potential gain.

The game process is shown in Fig. 2. S_i expresses the state of the game, and the game matrix under each game state is constructed. The choice of action between the attacker and the defender determines the state of the game at the next moment.

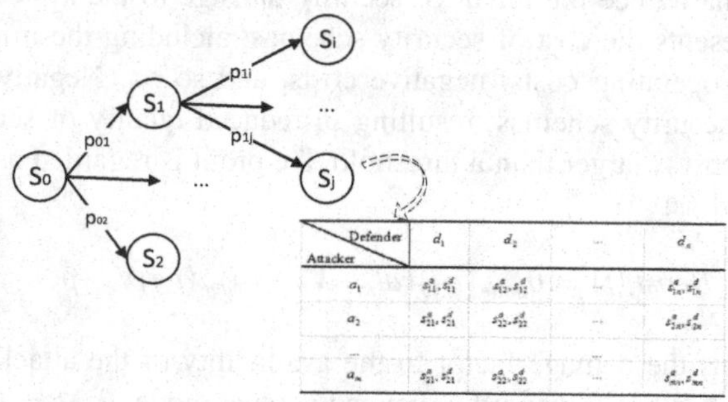

Fig. 2. State diagram of game.

According to formulas (5) and (8), the quantification of direct benefit is divided into two cases. If i is equal to j, that is, the attacker attacks the node i, and the defender protects node i: $r_{ij}^{a} = -Acost_i + Dcost_j$, $r_{ij}^{d} = Dcost_j - Acost_i$. If i is not equal to j, the attacker attacks i, and the defender protects j: $r_{ij}^{a} = Sdam_i - Acost_i + \delta Dcost_i$, $r_{ij}^{d} = -\delta \cdot Sdam_j + \delta Dcost_j - Acost_j$.

(3) Situation assessment

The algorithm firstly constructs TPAN according to the network security data after data fusion, and then evaluates the network security situation of the current state of S_0 based on TPAN. Consider the $K = 2, 3, 4, 5$ step propagation of threat, the game state under each step is obtained, which is expressed as $S_k = (S_{k1}, S_{k2}, \ldots, S_{kl},)$, $k = 1, 2, 3, \ldots, K$. For each game state, a bi-matrix game is constructed and the expected benefit and equilibrium strategy are calculated. According to the iteration algorithm, the step k's results are substituted into the step $k - 1$, and finally the Nash equilibrium of status S_1 and the strategy set are obtained. According to the Nash equilibrium of the attack and defense states of S_1, the network security situation value is calculated, and the reinforcement strategy is given. The following is the Nash equilibrium solving algorithm:

(1) According to bi-matrix, determine whether the payoff matrix has saddle point;
(2) If the saddle point exists, the Nash equilibrium of the pure strategy is solved. Pure strategy Nash equilibrium is a special case of mixed strategy Nash equilibrium.
(3) If there is no saddle point, the mixed strategy Nash equilibrium is solved in accordance with the following formula

$$maxF\left(\pi^a, \pi^d, R^a, R^d\right) = \sum_{i=1}^{m}\sum_{j=1}^{n} p_i^a p_j^d s_{ij}^a + \sum_{i=1}^{m}\sum_{j=1}^{n} p_i^a p_j^d s_{ij}^d - v^a - v^d$$

$$s.t. \sum\nolimits_{j=1}^{n} p_j^d s_{ij}^a \le v^a, i = 1, 2, \ldots, m, \sum\nolimits_{i=1}^{m} p_i^a s_{ij}^d \le v^d, j = 1, 2, \ldots, n$$
$$\sum\nolimits_{i=1}^{m} p_i^1 = 1, \sum\nolimits_{j=1}^{n} p_j^2 = 1$$

4 Experimental Analysis

In order to verify the effectiveness of the method proposed in this paper, an experimental network was constructed and as shown below (Fig. 3).

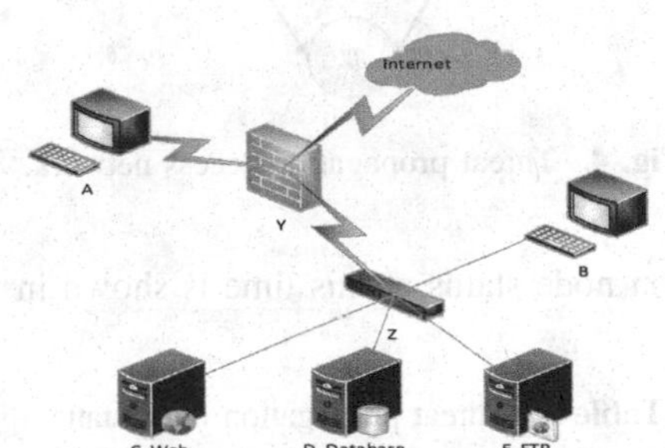

Fig. 3. Experimental network structure diagram.

Given the network topology, there are the following requirements. Firewall protection strategy is to allow external access to web services and without restrictions from the network to the outside network. Node A can login node B remotely through the SSH protocol. Node B can manage nodes C, D, E through the RSH protocol and the SNMP protocol. The node C can read and write the data in the node D and upload the data in the download node E through the FTP protocol. Network security data is collected from IDS, NNAMP, and other vulnerability scanning tools deployed at each node and network exit. Integrate security data into asset data sets, asset operation data sets, vulnerability data sets, and threat data sets, and determine network security events. For each threat network security situation was evaluated based on ADSGM.

The set of assets at a certain time is obtained, as shown in the Table 1:

Table 1. Partial asset data information table

id_a	V_a	*type*	*ser*	*os*	V_r
A	(3, 3, 3)	Person	None	Windows	3
B	(3, 3, 5)	Person	None	Windows	3
C	(3, 3, 5)	Server	http	Linux	4
D	(5, 5, 2)	Server	MySQL	Linux	4
E	(4, 5, 2)	Server	FTP	Linux	3

Threat propagation access network based on network topology and other information was constructed, as shown in the following Fig. 4:

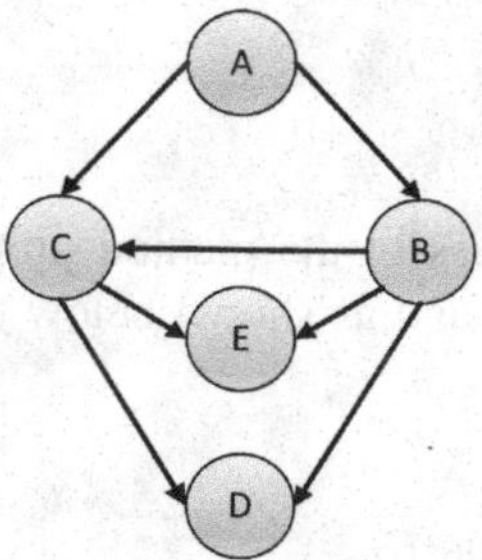

Fig. 4. Threat propagation access network.

The threat propagation node status at this time is shown in the Table 2:

Table 2. Threat propagation node status

id_a	e_t	e_v	id_{ov}
A	Y	Y	2
B	N	N	4
C	N	N	6
D	N	N	8
E	N	N	9

At the s moment, the propagation path of the threat t is shown in the Table 3:

Consider the k-step propagation of threat t, the state of moment s is denoted as S_0. According to the propagation nodes and the propagation path information, the strategies of both offensive and defensive sides are obtained, and the game matrix under one-step propagation is calculated according to the proceeds, as shown in Table 4.

Table 3. Propagation path information table

E	V_e	ρ_e	p_{es}
$e(A,C)$	4	3	0.3
$e(A,B)$	3	2	0.3
$e(B,C)$	3	2	0.3
$e(B,D)$	3	2	0.3
$e(B,E)$	3	2	0.3
$e(C,D)$	5	4	0.3
$e(D,E)$	5	4	0.3
$e(E,D)$	2	2	0.7

Table 4. Game matrix of attack and defense

Attacker	Defender				
	1A	2B	3C	$4e(A,C)$	$5e(A,B)$
1B	s_{11}^a, s_{11}^d	s_{12}^a, s_{12}^d	s_{13}^a, s_{13}^d	s_{14}^a, s_{14}^d	s_{15}^a, s_{15}^d
2C	s_{21}^a, s_{21}^d	s_{22}^a, s_{22}^d	s_{23}^a, s_{23}^d	s_{24}^a, s_{24}^d	s_{25}^a, s_{25}^d

Each element in the matrix is calculated by formulas (7) and (8), and the transfer status according to the offensive and defensive actions are obtained. Consider the threat of $k\,(k = 2, 3, \ldots, K)$ step propagation, for each step of the propagation process, a game matrix is respectively build.

In the experiment environment, the network attack is carried out, and the network security data of five times are sampled. Based on the proposed ADSGM based algorithm and the game model based on maximum and minimum strategies, the network security situation values are calculated, as shown in the Fig. 5.

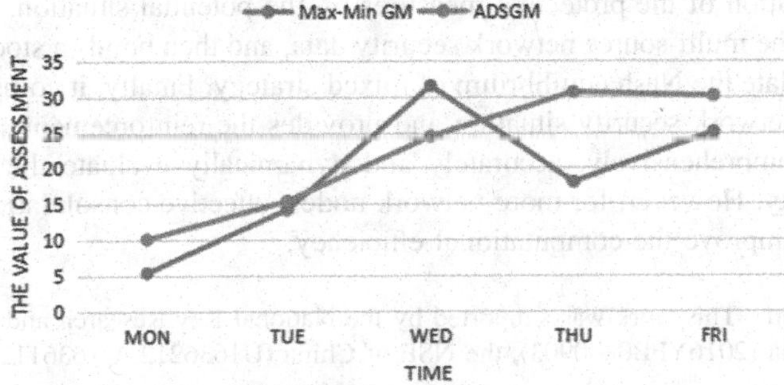

Fig. 5. Results of network security situation assessment

At the start of the sampling data node, the A host is hacked. And then the node C and B are attacked by taking advantage of threat propagation, and finally node D is attacked through node B. Security schemas were implemented at the nodes on Thursday. As a result, there will be no security consolidation measures from Wednesday to Thursday, so there will be no downward movement. On Thursday to Friday, the situation will be lowered as a result of the reinforcement of the network. The situation value based on ADSGM has a downward trend, but the algorithm based on Max-min GM has a slight increase. In summary, compared with the actual network security environment, the network security situation assessment algorithm based on ADSGM is more accurate. Mixed strategy Nash equilibrium can be acquired by ADSGM algorithm. $\pi_a = (0.37, 0.63)$ represents the attacker's mixed strategy Nash equilibrium, that is, the probability of selecting each strategy, and the greater the probability, the more likely it is to be chosen. $\pi_d = (0.26, 0.20, 0.40, 0.09, 0.05)$ represents the defender's mixed strategy Nash equilibrium. The probability that the defender chooses the protection node C strategy is 0.40, and the probability of selecting A protection strategy is 0.26.

Through the experiment analysis, we can see that the network security situation assessment approach based on ADSGM is effective in this network environment. Threat information, vulnerability information, network topology and on the basis of confidentiality, integrity, availability of three security attributes are integrated to obtain more accurate network security situation assessment results which are predictive of security risks. The protection strategy obtained by the algorithm can reduce the security damage, thereby reducing the risk of the spread of risk, and effectively curb the occurrence of network security incidents.

5 Conclusion

The paper proposes an approach based on ADSGM for network security situation awareness, which considers the potential impact of threat propagation caused by node relevance on the current assessment. The method divides the security situation into the inherent situation and potential situation, and comprehensively calculates the impact of the implementation of the protective measures on the potential situation. The method firstly merges the multi-source network security data, and then builds a stochastic game model to calculate the Nash equilibrium of mixed strategy. Finally, it comprehensively evaluates the network security situation and provides the reinforcement schema. This method can comprehensively, accurately and dynamically evaluate the situation of network security. However, for more network nodes, effective consolidation should be carried out to improve the computational efficiency.

Acknowledgment. This work was supported by the National Key Research and Development Program of China (2016YFB0800903), the NSF of China (U1636212, U1636112).

References

1. Xuan, Z.: Survey of network security situation awareness and key technologies. In: Li, S., Jin, Q., Jiang, X., Park, J.J. (eds.) Frontier and Future Development of Information Technology in Medicine and Education. LNEE, vol. 269, pp. 3281–3286. Springer, Dordrecht (2014). https://doi.org/10.1007/978-94-007-7618-0_423
2. Chen, X., Zheng, Q., et al.: Study on evaluation for security situation of networked systems. J. Xi'an Jiao Tong Univ. **38**, 404–408 (2004)
3. Trusted Computing Group: TCG Specification architecture overview specification revision 1.2. [EB/OL], 15 April 2011
4. Trusted Computing Group: TCG Specification Architecture Overview, pp. 5–40. Trusted Computing Group, Oregon (2007)
5. Xie, L., Wang, Y.: New method of network security situation awareness. J. Beijing Univ. Posts Telecommun. 31–35 (2014)
6. Qu, Z.Y., Li, Y.Y.: A network security situation evaluation method based on D-S evidence theory. In: International Conference on Environmental Science and Information Application Technology, pp. 496–499. IEEE (2010)
7. Liu, S.C., Liu, Y.: Network security risk assessment method based on HMM and attack graph model. In: IEEE/ACIS International Conference on Software Engineering, Artificial Intelligence, Networking and Parallel/distributed Computing, pp. 517–522. IEEE (2016)
8. Hu, H., Zhang, H., Liu, Y., et al.: Quantitative method for network security situation based on attack prediction. Secur. Commun. Netw. 1–19 (2017)
9. Dang, D.: Assessment of information security risk by support vector machine. J. Huazhong Univ. Sci. Technol. **38**(3), 46–49 (2010)
10. Liang, X., Xiao, Y.: Game theory for network security. IEEE Commun. Surv. Tutor. **15**(1), 472–486 (2013)
11. Chen, Y., Wu, X., et al.: Network security evaluation of stochastic game and network based on entropy. J. Beijing Univ. Posts Telecommun. **1**, 92–96 (2014)
12. Wang, Y., et al.: Modeling and security analysis of enterprise network using attack–defense stochastic game Petri nets. Secur. Commun. Netw. **6**(1), 89–99 (2013)
13. Shen, D., Chen, G., Haynes, L., et al.: A Markov game theoretic data fusion approach for cyber situational awareness. In: Proceedings of SPIE - The International Society for Optical Engineering, vol. 6571, no. 48, pp. 65710F–65710F-12 (2007)
14. Ryutov, T., Orosz, M., Blythe, J., von Winterfeldt, D.: A game theoretic framework for modeling adversarial cyber security game among attackers, defenders, and users. In: Foresti, S. (ed.) STM 2015. LNCS, vol. 9331, pp. 274–282. Springer, Cham (2015). https://doi.org/10.1007/978-3-319-24858-5_18
15. Shandilya, V., Shiva, S.: A Network Security Game Model, pp. 159–161 (2015)
16. Liu, X., Yuan, Y.: A novel dynamic method in distributed network attack-defense game. Math. Probl. Eng. 1–7 (2015)
17. Zhang, Y., Tan, X., Cui, X.: Network security situation awareness approach based on Markov game model. J. Softw. **22**, 495–508 (2011)
18. GB/T 20984-2007: Information security technology, information security risk assessment specification
19. Feng, N., Wang, H.J., Li, M.: A security risk analysis model for information systems: causal relationships of risk factors and vulnerability propagation analysis. Inf. Sci. **256**, 57–73 (2014)
20. Zhang, Y., Fang, B.X., Chi, Y., Yun, X.: Research on network node correlation in network risk assessment. J. Comput. Res. **30**, 234–240 (2007)

Preservation Mechanism of Electronic Record Based on Erasure Code and Multi Copies in Cloud Storage

Yongjun Ren[1,2(✉)], Lin Zhou[1,2], Yepeng Liu[1,2], and Xiaorui Zhang[1,2]

[1] Jiangsu Collaborative Innovation Center of Atmospheric Environment and Equipment Technology (CICAEET), Nanjing University of Information Science and Technology, Nanjing 210044, China
renyjl00@126.com

[2] School of Computer and Software, Nanjing University of Information Science and Technology, Nanjing, China

Abstract. With the rapid growth of cloud storage center, the cumulative volume of data reaches EB and even ZB from PB. As a result, both network size and the number of storage nodes continue to grow explosively, while the data failure rate is still increasing. Cloud storage centers encode the raw data into erasure codes, to save the system overhead as much as possible meanwhile guarantee the reliability of data. However, the state-of-art erasure codes techniques still rely on a conventional centralized model which results in unaffordable encoding/decoding cost, and thus cannot adapt to the data-intensive processing requirements for distributed cloud storage environments. In the paper, the preservation mechanism of combining erasure code and copy backup is proposed, to improve the reliability of electronic records in cloud storage. This paper focuses on the erasure code archiving of electronic documents and puts forward the ability aware erasure code filing of electronic documents. Moreover, the corresponding implementation algorithm and steps are described.

Keywords: Cloud storage · Electronic record · Multi copies

1 Introduction

With the acceleration of information digitization and network service, digital resources have developed rapidly, and extensive electronic records have been produced. The acquisition, use, and sharing of electronic documents have unique advantages over traditional documentary resources, making them play an increasingly important role in people's lives, learning, and work. However, people have found that the long-term preservation of electronic records is very tricky. First of all, electronic documents are stored on a physical carrier in the form of digital codes, mainly based on light, electricity, and magnetism. The transport of these materials has a very high requirement for the storage environment. The effects of high temperature, humidity, and magnetic fields all contribute to the loss of information, and the longevity of these carriers is far shorter than that of the traditional carrier papers, which is hundreds of years. The magnetic carrier storage time is about ten years, and the storage time of the optical disk is 10–20

X. Sun et al. (Eds.): ICCCS 2018, LNCS 11065, pp. 174–183, 2018.
https://doi.org/10.1007/978-3-030-00012-7_16

years [1–3]. Second, the reading of electronic records depends on computer software. As technology continues to evolve, operating systems and software upgrades will no longer support traditional record formats, which will lead to embarrassing situations in which electronic records cannot be used. Electronic files stored in computers are bound to be subject to security threats. Nowadays, electronic records have reached a tremendous amount and are continuing to develop, which makes it impossible to estimate the cost of saving electronic records [4]. Moreover, the preservation cost of electronic records not only includes the physical space and environmental control costs required for the preservation of traditional paper records but also relates to other expenses necessary to ensure the reproduction of electronic files, such as technical updating and digital migration. Also, the long-term preservation of electronic records still lacks public standards and legal difficulties [5, 6].

Long-term preservation of electronic records can only be guaranteed by a secure storage environment to ensure the long-term validity and availability of records. The proposal of cloud storage provides a new possibility for the long-term preservation of electronic records. Compared with traditional preservation strategies, cloud storage has a reliable storage architecture, perfect backup measures, and an efficient migration mechanism that reduces initial investment, saves management costs, reduces maintenance expenses. So cloud storage is suitable for large-scale digital storage, providing a one-to-one portable service which can efficiently guarantee the continuity of service, and the speed of website access response is fast. It is a better way for current electronic records to be stored for a long time [7, 8].

However, under the cloud storage environment, electronic records are stored in the cloud server for a long time. The electronic record is completed under the control of the cloud server. The record manager entirely loses the physical control of the electronic record. Once a problem occurs with the cloud service provider, the organization may not be able to retrieve electronic records and electronic records. In 2014, the international CodeSpace cloud company was hacked. All the records in the Apache Subversion collection and Elastic Block collection on the company's cloud service platform were all permanently deleted, and the records could not be recovered. This situation is disastrous for electronic records and archives that require permanent preservation and retention as human history [9, 10]. With the aim of enhancing the reliability of electronic records, this paper proposes a combination of erasure codes and copy backup for electronic records stored in the cloud. Based on this, the technical implementation problem was studied.

2 Related Work

Currently, magnetic disks are the key and core of electronic record storage systems in both centralized and distributed electronic record storage systems. However, due to the limitations of the mechanical characteristics of the disk itself, although some researchers have proposed RAID (Redundant Arrays of Inexpensive Disks) technology, its reliability has not been substantially improved. However, in large-scale electronic record storage systems, disk failure or storage node failure has become a regular behavior. For example, in an electronic record center with a scale of approximately

4,000 nodes, an average of four disks will fail each day. Google researchers counted disk corruption in its electronic record center, and about 1.7% to 8.6% of disks in the system would fail each year [11]. According to statistics from Carnegie Mellon University, the annual replacement rate of the disk in some systems is about 13% [12]. Each year, dozens or even hundreds of disk corruptions are commonplace for a PB-class system consisting of tens of thousands of disks. For larger EB-class storage systems, tens or even tens of thousands of disks are destroyed every year. At the same time, the magnetic media on a portion of the surface of the disk platter is often damaged or occurs read and write errors, resulting in inaccessibility or loss of data on some sectors of the disk. Net App has made statistics on disk sector errors. Within 32 months, the proportion of such errors in the disk system with a size of 1.53 million reached 3.45% [13].

In addition to regular disk damage, the storage node's network card is damaged, and memory, CPU, and other hardware are damaged. Alternatively, the whole rack in the storage system is damaged due to the system power off, and the electronic records in the entire rack are temporarily unavailable. There are also unreliable electronic records due to system software errors. Kroll Ontrack conducted a systematic statistical study of the reasons for the loss of electronic records, of which system failures or hardware device damage caused approximately 56% of electronic record losses; about 26% was due to human-induced system failures. Software failures or virus intrusion cause the resulting loss of about 16% of electronic records; about 2% of electronic records are lost due to natural causes such as earthquakes and tsunamis. That is, one out of every 500 electronic record centers have an electronic record disaster [14].

On the one hand, the exploding storage capacity of electronic records has increased the demand for primary storage devices. On the one hand, it is the frequent failure of large-scale mass electronic record storage systems. On the other hand, the loss of electronic records to their owners and users is enormous. All of this makes the reliability of the electronic record storage system an critical challenge.

Increasing redundancy is a standard way to realize the reliability of electronic records. When an electronic record partially fails, customers can satisfy their own needs by accessing redundant data. Under the distributed storage environment such as GFS, HDFS and Amazon S3, three-replica redundancy is used, which can well meet the reliability of electronic records and load balancing requirements. The original intention of the three-copy strategy adopted by GFS/HDFS is to ensure that no more electronic record lost under the condition that keeps the node hardware performance [15].

The electronic record storage cluster mainly consists of the following components: cluster manager nodes, access nodes, and storage nodes. The cluster management node is responsible for the metadata information in the system such as the configuration of the cluster and the system's namespace. When a block of electronic records in a cluster needs to undergo a block redundancy change, the cluster management node also concurrently manages the work of encoding record blocks. The visiting node is mainly responsible for responding to the I/O access request sent by the user. After the user request arrives at the access node, the access node first interacts with the management node to obtain the state information of the accessed record block and the address information of the record block on the production node. Then returns corresponding information from the corresponding storage node according to the address information of the electronic record block to the user. The storage node is responsible for the actual storage of the data and saves the original content and the associated verification data. A large number of storage nodes are deployed on multiple racks and interconnected by switches. The three copies of the electronic record block are distributed in the cluster in a rack-aware, random layout, specifically, two copies are placed on two nodes in the same rack, and a third copy is placed on the other rack.

When the cluster size is small, the consumption of storage space of three copies is not particularly significant. However, in a large-scale application cluster, the utilization rate of nodes is often too high, and the needs of cost control cannot be entirely satisfied only by increasing the storage space of the nodes. More importantly, in the multi-copy mode, the cluster's scalability is limited due to the limitations of cluster metadata management [13–15].

The reliability enhancement technology based on multiple backups is intuitive and straightforward, easy to implement, and is the simplest and most widely used type of data redundancy mode in distributed storage systems. This strategy requires the sharing of multiple copies of the same electronic record to different storage nodes. Apparently, this strategy has a significant storage space overhead. Redundant electronic records are multiple copies of the original record. With the explosive growth of electronic records and the ever-increasing scale of storage devices, the management and operation of hardware devices will bring enormous costs. The choice of electronic record reliability preservation strategy needs to consider the record redundancy problem of the backup strategy, load balancing issues, and additional energy consumption issues.

3 Problem Statement

For the data reliability problem of storage systems, in recent years, scholars at home and abroad have conducted exploration and research and opened up a new storage path based on encoding redundancy strategy. Erasure codes are widely used in storage clusters, such as archiving systems, data centers, cloud storage, and so on. Among them, Solomon coding has become a typical data organization solution in fault-tolerant clusters because of its smooth operation and increased fault tolerance. Solomon coding guarantees data availability with extremely low storage overhead. Compared to data copies, erasure codes can provide equivalent fault tolerance with less storage overhead [14]. Most of the data is accessed for a short period throughout its life cycle. For example, more than 90% of data access in the Yahoo M45 Hadoop cluster occurs on the first day of data creation [15]. Therefore, it is economical to use erasure code to archive data copies. Today, some practical storage systems (for example, WAS [16], GFSII) adopt a mixed redundancy strategy, use a copy strategy for newly created data, and use an erasure code for archiving when the data access frequency is reduced.

Archiving improves storage utilization by reducing the storage overhead of infrequently accessed data. Existing distributed storage systems such as HDFS, and GFS. To ensure data availability, improve the degree of parallelism of operations, and use more copies to store data. The size of the default data block is 64 MB or 128 MB. With the exponential growth of data, the storage pressure of existing data centers is increasing. In the application scenario where multiple reads are written at once, after the data is generated, the frequency of use is negatively related to the time. The data with low access frequency is archived from multiple copies into an erasure code storage format, which can ensure data availability, improve storage space utilization, and relieve data center pressure.

4 Preservation Mechanism of Electronic Record Based on Erasure Code and Multi Copies

4.1 Erasure Code

RS-type erasure codes are the primary erasure coding techniques applied in distributed storage systems [17]. Its earliest application in distributed record system dates back to 1989. Rabin proposed an information splitting algorithm based on Rabin code for network server faults and bandwidth problems. Its core is the RS type erasure code. Reed-Solomon Coding [18] uses Galois Field operations for encoding/decoding, where the Galois Field addition operation is an XOR operation, and the multiplication operation is usually performed by searching for a corresponding Galois Field table.

RS code is a block-based MDS error correction coding, which is widely used in the field of communications and storage. In general, the $(k + r, k)$-type RS code indicates that each band of the code is composed of k data blocks and r check blocks. It uses data and a generation matrix to generate redundant data. The generation matrix consists of a $k \times k$ identity matrix and a $k \times r$ redundancy matrix. The RS coding process is actually about the linear operation of the data block, and the redundant block is calculated by the multiplication of the k data blocks and the $k \times r$ generating matrix. The encoding process of the Andermonde-RS $(k + r, k)$ algorithm is as follows.

$$\begin{bmatrix} r_{1,1} & r_{1,2} & \cdots & r_{1,k} \\ r_{2,1} & r_{2,2} & \cdots & r_{2,k} \\ \vdots & \vdots & & \vdots \\ r_{n,1} & r_{n,2} & \cdots & r_{nk} \end{bmatrix} \otimes \begin{bmatrix} d_1 \\ d_2 \\ \vdots \\ d_k \end{bmatrix} = \begin{bmatrix} 1 & 0 & \cdots & 0 \\ 0 & 1 & \cdots & 0 \\ \vdots & \vdots & & \vdots \\ 1 & 2^{r-1} & \cdots & k^{r-1} \end{bmatrix} \otimes \begin{bmatrix} d_1 \\ d_2 \\ \vdots \\ d_k \end{bmatrix} = \underbrace{\begin{bmatrix} d_1 \\ d_2 \\ \vdots \\ d_k \\ p_1 \\ \vdots \\ p_r \end{bmatrix}}_{\text{E}} \quad (1)$$

If r-blocks in the E-matrix are lost, the corresponding rows of the r-blocks in the A-matrix and the E-matrix are deleted at the time of recovery, and a new $(n \times n)$-order matrix A′ and an $(n \times 1)$-order matrix E' are obtained. A' is non-singular, and inverts A' to get A'^{-1} recovery data: $D = A'^{-1} \cdot E'$. Extract the calculation part in which the redundant data $\mathrm{p}_1 \sim \mathrm{p}_\mathrm{r}$ is generated, that is, the process of generating redundancy check for the code, as shown below.

$$\begin{bmatrix} f_{1,1} & f_{1,2} & \cdots & f_{1,k} \\ f_{2,1} & f_{2,2} & \cdots & f_{2,k} \\ \vdots & \vdots & & \vdots \\ f_{n,1} & f_{n,2} & \cdots & f_{nk} \end{bmatrix} \otimes \begin{bmatrix} d_1 \\ d_2 \\ \vdots \\ d_k \end{bmatrix} = \begin{bmatrix} 1 & 0 & \cdots & 0 \\ 0 & 1 & \cdots & 0 \\ \vdots & \vdots & & \vdots \\ 1 & 2^{r-1} & \cdots & k^{r-1} \end{bmatrix} \otimes \begin{bmatrix} d_1 \\ d_2 \\ \vdots \\ d_k \end{bmatrix} = \begin{bmatrix} p_1 \\ p_2 \\ \vdots \\ p_r \end{bmatrix} \quad (2)$$

There are two drawbacks to using Disk Reduce directly: (1) Read performance in multi-copy mode is better, multiple pieces of data services at the same time, and load balancing is possible. (2) Under the erasure code storage mode, the degraded read of the failed data block and reconstruction of data blocks will bring about a large amount of disk IO and network data transmission, while only need transmit one data block in the multiple copy mode.

By using hybrid storage of copy and erasure codes, only data with a low frequency of access is encoded to improve storage space. In a real large-scale cluster, the data is used very shortly after it is generated. In this way, when the data heat is reduced, archival storage of the three-copy data using the erasure correction code can ensure data reliability and considerably save storage space without affecting the data access speed.

4.2 Preservation Mechanism of Electronic Record Based on Erasure Code and Multi Copies

Heterogeneous Storage Cluster

With the arrival of the era of big data, the scale of the system is getting bigger and bigger. Because the old system cannot meet the increasing demands of users on capacity and performance, the system must be upgraded. In this case, if a one-time hardware upgrade is performed on the system hardware, many resources will be wasted. With the system's multiple upgrades, and the masses will have a variety of different models, different performance hardware devices. The different performances of the nodes are specifically: the computing power of different CPUs, memory capacity, network bandwidth, and disk speed. Also, the scale of the system is expanded to increase the number of nodes, which are usually located in different racks, resulting in different bandwidths and delays between different nodes. In general, as the system and hardware upgrades, the increase in the size of the storage system makes the performance of different storage nodes heterogeneous.

On the other hand, User access requests are unbalanced, which also makes the heterogeneity between nodes more complicated. When a node is storing more hot data, a large number of users request access to the node over a period. Also, some nodes have better performance and may not have user's requests. This condition will timeout in an idle state, thereby reducing the quality of the service system, mainly when the nodes perform poorly. This situation not only does not share resources but also causes a waste of system resources due to too large pressures on another node.

The heterogeneity between large-scale storage system nodes is an unavoidable issue that must be taken into account. What needs to be emphasized is that due to the existing enterprise-class data centers, to improve the utilization efficiency of resources and the user experience, the clusters often provide 24-h services, so that the heterogeneity of clusters will become more and more prominent as time passes.

Competence-Aware Erasure Record Archiving

In the process of online storage degradation, the performance problems caused by uneven distribution of electronic records and uneven distribution of node user loads will occur, which cannot be solved by traditional data locality scheduling methods. This paper proposes a mechanism to balance the preservation of electronic records according to nodes' capabilities. According to the core metrics of the node bandwidth and its storage capacity, more coding tasks are allocated to nodes with robust capabilities, and fewer are assigned to nodes with weaker capabilities. So that when the heterogeneous hardware in the node, uneven distribution of electronic records, and different user load distribution occurs, people can more fully use the resources of the entire cluster, rather than that of a single node.

For the heterogeneity of node performance and the difference in I/O capacity on nodes, the bandwidth, and storage capacity. Ability value = I/O capability * time period/electronic record block size + remaining bandwidth. The capability value represents the maximum number of data blocks that can be transmitted by the network during a period. The size of the point capability value determines how much of the coded electronic record block is allocated to that node. The system allocates less coding tasks to the weaker nodes and allocates more coding tasks to the more capable nodes. This strategy can effectively prevent the nodes whose encoding speed is too slow from becoming the shortboard of the entire coding process. The node that encodes the user's heavy load allocates less coding tasks, and the nodes with lighter user loads allocate more coding tasks, which can effectively reduce the resources competition between the coding process and the user's access, thereby improving the work efficiency of the cluster.

Based on the capability values, the assignment of coding tasks takes place in a short period. The period divides a long massive job into small jobs within a plurality of time slices and predicts a load of a time window with the user load at the beginning of the small job, that is, the load is constant. The system also converts dynamic node loads to static encoding task schedules. Combine the completion of encoding tasks for each period on each node and correct the ability value of the node's current period. This capability value feedback method can continuously update the node's capabilities over the last period.

Ability Value Initialization

According to each node's current capability value as the primary factor in the selection of coding nodes. Each node's capability value is the remaining bandwidth of the node, and it is I/O capability. Individually, firstly, the number of processing tasks of the node i per unit time in the cluster is calculated. The value can be obtained by dividing the number of the code storage completed by the node in a certain time period by the consumed time. Second, calculate the remaining bandwidth of the nodes in the cluster.

Coding Task Assignment

The allocation of coding tasks mainly depends on the current capability value of each node and electronic record blocks distribution. Assume that W_i corresponds to the number of record blocks expected to be processed by node i within a unit of time. Let B_i denote the current remaining bandwidth of node i, sorting from the largest to the smallest according to the W and B values of each node, picking the node to which the encoding is to be assigned. If the remaining bandwidth of the node is insufficient or its capacity value does not meet the coding requirements, the node will not get a new coding task. This encoding task assignment process ensures that the sum of the encoding tasks and user loads for each node does not exceed the throughput of each node itself. In addition, in the case that the task of each node is not overloaded, the locality of the record can be combined, so that the resource consumption of the network bandwidth in the encoding process is as small as possible.

Update of Ability Value

Because the load of the task on each node changes dynamically, the value of the node's capabilities is obsolete after each task assignment. When a coding operation task is completed, the number of coded task records R_{ti} and the coding task processing time T_i in the time period are obtained. Therefore, the new I/O capability value is R_{ti}/T_i. In addition, the remaining bandwidth of the node during the calculation of the time period will also be evaluated. Such capability value updating process can correct and reflect the idle bandwidth and I/O capability of the node in real time when the user load of the node changes, so as to achieve the task of assigning codes accurately.

The total encoding time T of each stripe is determined by the longest one of all the nodes participating in the stripe encoding.

$$T = \max\nolimits^{p''}_{p=1'',p\neq En}\{T_{PDisk} + T_{PNet}, T_{EnDisk} + T_{EnNet} + T_{Encode}\} \tag{3}$$

The p'' nodes participating in the encoding process of band i are $(SN1'', \ldots, SNp'')$, SN_{En} is the node for encoding nodes and receiving data blocks. T_{PDisk} is the time for node SN_p to read a strip of p_q data blocks on the storage medium, T_{PNet} is the time for the transmission of p_q data blocks in the node SN_p network. For non-coded nodes that participate in the coding of this band, reading p_q data blocks on the storage medium and sending p_q data blocks on the network card can be performed concurrently. The network transmission speed is slower than the storage medium reading speed. So, this time formula can be equivalent to:

$$T = \max_{p=1'',p\neq En}^{p''}\{T_{PNet}, T_{EnNet} + T_{Encode}\} \tag{4}$$

Because the encoding calculation is not very time-consuming for network transmission, so this time formula (3) can be equivalent to:

$$T \approx \max_{p=1'',p\neq En}^{p''}\{T_{PNet}, T_{EnNet} + T_{Encode}\} \tag{5}$$

For node p, measurement method according to the weight value W:

$$T_{PNet} \approx \frac{P_q}{W_i} \tag{6}$$

For coding nodes, the node reads En_q blocks of local storage media, while the network card accepts $\sum_{p=1^n, p \neq En}^{p^n} p_q (= k_{Enq})$ blocks of data. In a rack-aware random distribution of three copies, when $k \geq 6$, k_{PEn}, this allows the reception of network data blocks to account for the primary time of the code compute node:

$$T_{EnDisk} + T_{EnNet} \approx T_{EnNet} \tag{7}$$

The measurement method according to the weight value W:

$$T_{EnNet} = \sum\nolimits_{p=1'', p \neq En}^{m} \frac{p_q}{W_{En}} = \frac{(K - P_{En})}{W_{en}} \tag{8}$$

Substituting the Formula mentioned above can be derived:

$$T \approx \max_{p=1'', p \neq En}^{p''} \left\{ \frac{p_q}{W_p}, \sum\nolimits_{p=1'', p \neq En}^{m} \frac{p_q}{W_{En}} = \frac{(K - P_{En})}{W_{en}} \right\} \tag{9}$$

5 Conclusion

With the aim of ensuring the safety and reliability of the electronic record in the cloud storage servers, the preservation mechanism of electronic record based on erasure code and multi copies are proposed in the paper. This paper focuses on the erasure code archiving of electronic records and puts forward the ability aware erasure code archiving of electronic records. Moreover, the corresponding implementation algorithm and steps are described.

Acknowledgment. This work is supported by the NSFC (No. 61772280 and 61702236), Jiangsu Province Natural Science Research Program (BK20130809, BK2012461), the Project of six personnel in Jiangsu Province (2013-WLW-012), the research fund from Jiangsu Technology & Engineering Center of Meteorological Sensor Network in NUIST under Grant (No. KDXG1301), the Changzhou Sci&Tech Program (No. CJ20179027), and the PAPD fund from NUIST. Prof. Xiaorui Zhang is the corresponding author.

References

1. Xie, L., Wang, J., Ma, L.: Trusting records: findings of team Asia InterPARES. Arch. Sci. Study **2017**(4), 8–13 (2017)
2. Qian, Y.: Study on the long-term preservation standard of trusted electronic records in China. Arch. Sci. Bull. **2014**(3), 75–79 (2014)

3. Ren, Y., Shen, J., Wang, J., Han, J., Lee, S.: Mutual verifiable provable data auditing in public cloud storage. J. Internet Technol. **16**(2), 317–323 (2015)
4. He, D., Kumar, N., Wang, H., Wang, L., Choo, K.: Privacy-preserving certificateless provable data possession scheme for big data storage on cloud. Appl. Math. Comput. **314** (12), 31–43 (2017)
5. Jiang, Q., Zeadally, S., Ma, J., He, D.: Lightweight three-factor authentication and key agreement protocol for internet-integrated wireless sensor networks. IEEE Access **5**, 3376–3392 (2017)
6. Shen, J., Zhou, T., Chen, X., Li, J., Susilo, W.: Anonymous and traceable group data sharing in cloud computing. IEEE Trans. Inf. Forensics Secur. (2017). https://doi.org/10.1109/TIFS.2017.2774439
7. Fu, Z., Huang, F., Ren, K., Weng, J., Wang, C.: Privacy-preserving smart semantic search based on conceptual graphs over encrypted outsourced data. IEEE Trans. Inf. Forensics Secur. **12**(8), 1874–1884 (2017)
8. Wei, F., Zhang, R., Ma, C.: A provably secure anonymous two-factor authenticated key exchange protocol for cloud computing. Fundam. Inf. **157**(1–2), 201–220 (2018)
9. Li, X., Niu, J., Kumari, S., Wu, F., Sangaiah, A., Kim, C.: A three-factor anonymous authentication scheme for wireless sensor networks in internet of things environments. Netw. Comput. Appl. **103**, 194–204 (2018)
10. Chao, L.: Research on electronic record migration model in cloud computing environment. Arch. Sci. Bull. **2013**(1), 53–56 (2013)
11. Ren, Y., Shen, J., Liu, D., Wang, J., Kim, J.: Evidential quality preserving of electronic record in cloud storage. J. Internet Technol. **17**(6), 1125–1132 (2016)
12. Fu, Z., Wu, X., Guan, C., Sun, X., Ren, K.: Toward efficient multi-keyword fuzzy search over encrypted outsourced data with accuracy improvement. IEEE Trans. Inf. Forensics Secur. **11**(12), 2706–2716 (2016)
13. Jiang, H., Fan, M., Wang, X.: Low complexity array codes for random triple failures in distributed storage system. J. Converg. Inf. Technol. **7**(23), 247–250 (2012)
14. Xia, M., Saxena, M., Blaum, M.: A tale of two erasure codes in HDFS. FAST **2015**, 213–226 (2015)
15. Huang, J., Liang, X., Qin, X.: PUSH: a pipeline reconstruction I/O for erasure-coded storage clusters. IEEE Trans. Parallel Distrib. Syst. **26**(2), 516–526 (2015)
16. Huang, J., Zhang, F., Qin, X.: Exploiting redundancies and deferred writes to conserve energy in erasure-coded storage clusters. ACM Trans. Storage **9**(2), 1–29 (2013)
17. Wang, Y., Zhao, Y., Hou, F.: Minimum bandwidth regeneration code of distributed storage system. J. Chin. Comput. Syst. **33**(8), 1710–1714 (2012)
18. Hao, J., Lu, Y., Liu, X., Xia, S.: Survey for regenerating codes for distributed storage. J. Chongqing Univ. Posts Telecommun. (Nat. Sci. Ed.) **25**(1), 30–38 (2013)

Privacy-Preserved Prediction for Mobile Application Adoption

Changxu Wang(✉) and Jing Chu(✉)

School of Software, Tsinghua University, Beijing, China
{wangcxl5, j-zhul6}@mails.tsinghua.edu.cn

Abstract. As the increasing quantity of mobile applications brings all kinds of benefits to smartphone users, people are more difficult to pick a new suitable mobile application (also known as app) out of hundreds in an app store. Thus, predicting which app will be installed by a specific user can help both users and app store operators. Existing works have focused on this problem and tried to use various features and algorithms to help recommend apps to users. However, some of them suffer from privacy and security issues, i.e. the system requires too much personal information about the user, such as detailed location series, social network information or even age, gender and other personality traits. And most of the content-based filtering methods only take the apps that have similar topics or functions to the already-used ones into consideration but ignore the *demand saturation* situation and the facts that users may explore new topics according to their personality. In this paper, we put forward a novel method, which uses limited user information to recommend new apps to individuals. It protects user privacy and achieves high accuracy at the same time. Experiments show that the proposed model achieve 23.5% precision and 19.3% recall in top-5 (out of 577 apps) prediction result.

Keywords: Mobile application · Recommendation · User privacy
Adoption prediction

1 Introduction

In the past five years, the number of mobile apps in Apple Store and Google Play increases from 1.4 million to 5.7 million. The prosperity of app market draws significant challenges for app store operators. Given explosively numerous apps available to users, it is necessary for app store operators to recommend suitable app to every specific user. The need for accurate application recommendation has triggered extensive research on prediction of user interests based on their behaviors and environments. Previous works not only transplanted and improved traditional recommendation algorithms such as collaborative filtering [1] and content-based filtering [2] but also utilize the unique feature of smart device to obtain context information or even the personality traits of the target user, achieving better performance of prediction and recommendation.

However, two challenges hinder the application of these recommendation approaches in practical use. First, some of the extra information is difficult to obtain in practice, especially in the context of privacy protection. Specifically, users who cares

X. Sun et al. (Eds.): ICCCS 2018, LNCS 11065, pp. 184–194, 2018.
https://doi.org/10.1007/978-3-030-00012-7_17

more about privacy than service may refuse to give access to his personal data. Second, most of the content-based approaches use the topic similarity between applications to calculate the score of adoption possibility and fail to address the "demand saturation" situation where users are more likely not to use them at the same time. That is, If the currently used application already cover the needs of users, the high similarity of a new app won't be a positive factor but a negative one.

This paper seeks to advance the state-of-the-art by achieving accurate apps recommendation with limited user information and "demand saturation" problem. Specifically, we only use the snapshot of apps and coarse location (which city the user stays in and if the region is urban area or rural area). The coarse location information could be inferred from the users' IP address and the getting the snapshot of an android device doesn't need any user permission, which makes it more feasible and privacy-friendly. Moreover, we verify the assumption of "demand saturation" and consider the situation in apps recommendation.

In summary, the main contributions of our work are:

1. We only require coarse location information and two snapshots of the applications for prediction of future apps adoption, which is far less personal and sensitive data of users than existing approaches.
2. We verify the "demand saturation" where users may not likely use too many apps with very similar topics or functions at the same time, and improve the predict model according to this observation, which is necessary for predicting the user interest in similar apps.
3. Experiment results show that our model achieves 23.5% top-5 precision and 19.3% top-5 recall, which is much higher than models which don't use location information or "demand saturation" factor. It proves that our work has good performance.

The rest of this article is arranged in the following order: Sect. 2 shows research areas and achievements related to our work. Section 3 describes the main methodology of this article. Section 4 reports and analyzes the experiment results. Section 5 summarizes the contribution of our work.

2 Related Works

Mobile Application Recommendation. The explosive growth of mobile application makes application recommendation a popular issue. While collaborative filtering (CF) [1] and content-based filtering (CBF) [2] are two well-known and well-studied methods to deal with traditional recommendation issues, such as news recommendation and commodity recommendation, there is still different issues and new ideas in application recommendation area. [3, 4] exploited modern portfolio theory (MPT) to recommend mobile apps using users' detailed usage information. [5] took privacy constraints of a user into consideration and recommends apps with the proper permission requirements. [6] investigated how versions of an application influence user's preference. [7] used contextual factors from phone sensors together with usage information. Though previous work achieves good results, this paper is different from other articles. We use as little user information as we can while some of the previous works need personal and sensitive data of users. And we improve the prediction model with the user's coarse location and the observation of demand saturation situation. Our work also related to the following areas of studies:

Inference of User Identity from Application Usage. Previous researches showed that users with different attributes may behave differently in terms of mobile application usage. Thus, by analyzing application usage history, one's gender, revenue, age etc. could be inferred. [8, 9] demonstrated that the user's personal profile could be predicted only by analyzing his or her adoption list. [10] used app snapshot together with installation data like adoption time to derive the Big Five Personality Traits.

Application Usage Prediction. Understanding the usage pattern of how mobile users use their smart device could help the mobile system to predict the user's next operation and to further provide better service, such as personalized icon layout, content pre-loading and even new application suggesting etc. [11] used APPM, a transplanted and improved algorithm of "Prediction by Partial Match" (PPM) to predict the next app to be used without requiring either additional sensor context or long overhead training. [12] used users' spatiotemporal contexts and detailed application usage context to reach a high accuracy in predicting the next opened app. [13] predicted users' future adoption using their social network connectivity.

3 Methodology

3.1 System Structure

Figure 1 shows how the proposed predicting system works. In order to predict apps that a user would install, the already used apps, coarse location together with the topic distribution of apps are fed into the model. The model calculates installation possibility of each app, and then output the rank list of most likely applications to be installed. There are three sub-models inside: user relation model, app relation model and location model. The outputs of these sub-models are combined to predict app installation.

The model also considers the situation that a new app is published or a new user requests a prediction. The corresponding sub-model will update when a new app or a new user appears is added in.

3.2 Model Components

User Relation Model. This model is used to predict app installation from relation-ship between users. User-based CF is a common approach in recommendation systems as interests of a user can be inferred from their app installation history. Users with similar interests may install similar apps. To model this, we define relationship between two users as follow, where $A(u, a)$ is the adoption of users and apps, 1 means the user installed the app, 0 means not installed, # means the count of the items in the set:

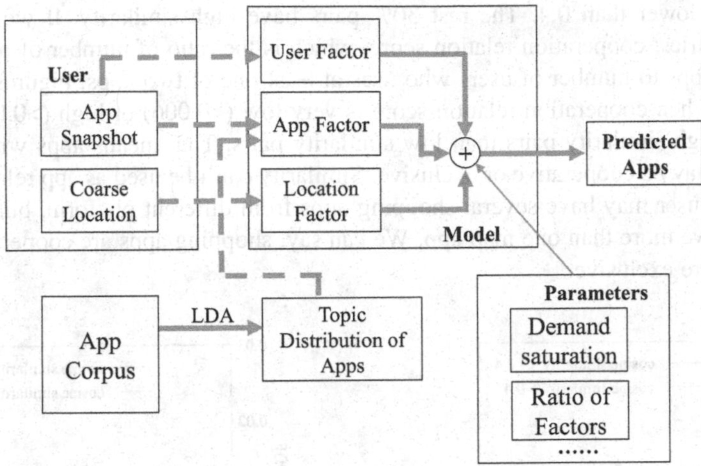

Fig. 1. System structure

$$R_u(u_1, u_2) = \#\{a|A(u_1, a) = 1 \; and \, A(u_2, a) = 1, a \in Apps\}$$

Then the factor of user relation is:

$$F_u(u, a) = \sum\nolimits_{u' \in Users} R_u(u, u')A(u', a)$$

The popularity of the whole users may be very large. It will cost too much time to calculate F_u, making it impossible to process. In practical, we choose first k users who are in top k relationship to u, in which k is much smaller than the count of users. It reduces cost dramatically.

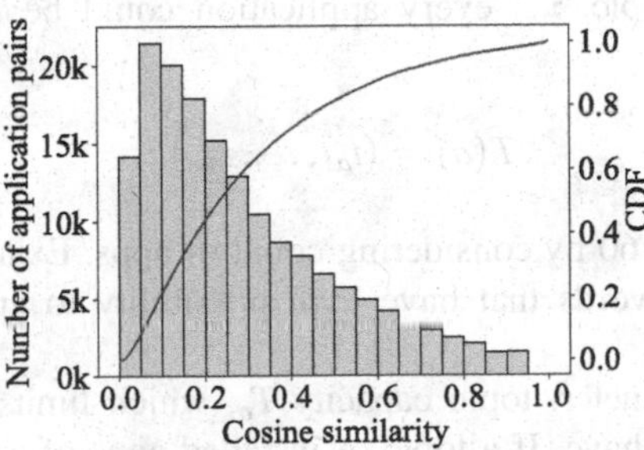

Fig. 2. Cosine similarities of pairs of apps

App Relation Model. Another insight is that installed apps reflect interests of a user. Thus, we can predict what apps the user will install in the future. Unlike user relations, app relations are more complex, which may be cooperative, exclusive, or irrelevant. Figure 2 shows cosine similarities of all pairs of apps. 70% of the pairs have similarities lower than 0.4. The rest 30% pairs have high similarity. If we consider another metrics: cooperation relation score, which is the ratio of number of users who uses both apps to number of users who uses at least one of two apps. Figures 3 and 4 show that when cooperation relation score is very low (<0.006) or high (>0.06), there are more high similarity pairs than low similarity pairs. That means apps with higher similarity may be cooperative or exclusive. Similarity can't be used as app relation. For example, a user may have several shopping apps from different platform, but the user may not have more than one map app. We can say, shopping apps are cooperative and map apps are exclusive.

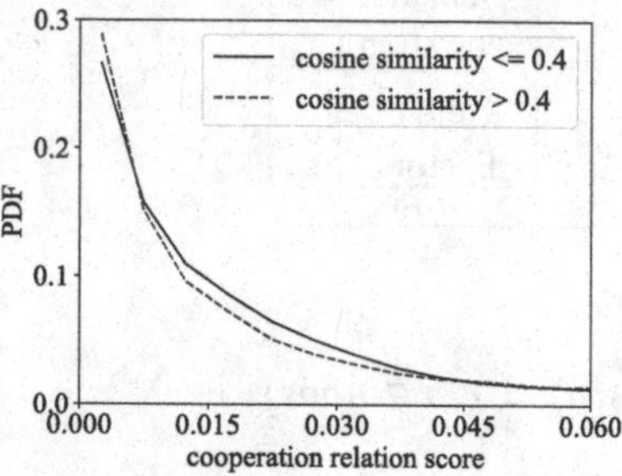

Fig. 3. PDF of cooperation relation score (<0.06)

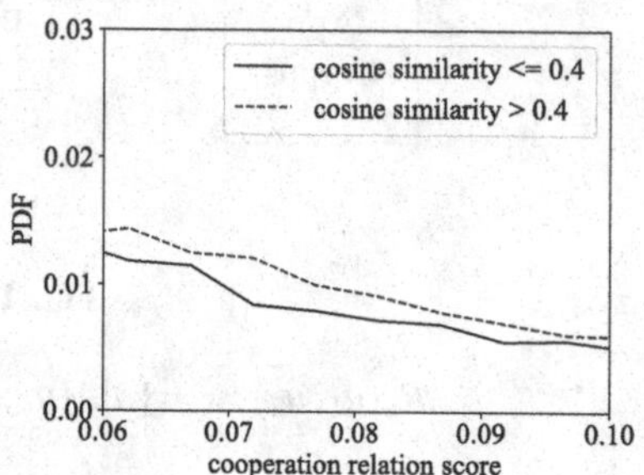

Fig. 4. PDF of cooperation relation score (0.06–0.10)

We utilize topic models to estimate app relations. Though Topic models (e.g. Latent Dirichlet Allocation (LDA)) was designed as a generative statistical model, it has been used to extract low-dimension feature for recommendation systems in content-based filtering in recent years. In this paper, we expand each application to a content document by concatenating the webpage content related to the app name. Then applying LDA to the corpus to extract m topics together with relevance between every application and every topic, i.e. every application could be represented by a topic vector $T(a)$:

$$T(a) = (t_{a1}, \ldots, t_{am})$$

Here we choose $m = 60$ by considering count of apps. Examples of the topics and the represented words (words that have high possibility to appear in the topic) are shown in Table 1.

We introduce a parameter: topic capacity T_c, which limits how many apps with same topic a user would have. If a topic of installed apps of a user exceeds the limit, new apps with same topic are more unlikely to be installed. We use $T_u(u)$ to denote topic of all apps that the user installed:

$$T_u(u) = \sum\nolimits_{a \in Apps} T(a)A(u,a) = (t_{u1}, \ldots, t_{um})$$

Table 1. Sample topics and represented words

Open class, live, study abroad, Ai, intelligence, internet, stock	Beauty, fashion, hairstyles, brands, women, weddings, makeup
Forum, original, lottery, zodiac, sticker, master, featured	Music, download, theme, dance, guitar, play
Plot, variety, film, complete works, theater, video, starring	Beijing, address, chaoyang, information, education network, haidian, users

Factor of topic $F_t(u,a)$ is defined as follow. If a topic of the user doesn't exceed topic capacity, this factor will be positive, making user more likely to install the app, otherwise, the factor will be negative, reducing the score that user installing the app.

$$F_t(u,a) = \sum_{i=1}^{m} t_{ai}\left(\frac{2}{1+e^{t_{ui}-t_{ci}}} - 1\right)$$

Thus, we define the app factor F_a as follow, where R_a is the static relation between apps, α is a value between 0 and 1. The reason why we add R_a is that F_t can only model dynamic app relations from user installed apps and topics, but a static relation is also needed. Both R_a and α are parameters, and they will be trained to get proper values.

$$F_a(u,a) = \alpha F_t(u,a) + (1-\alpha) \sum_{a' \in Apps} R_a(a,a')A(u,a)$$

Location Model. As mentioned in [8], there is relation between user's profile and application usage preference. Since one's gender could be inferred from the app list and one's interest could be influenced by nearby people, we make the assumption that the quantity distribution of applications with specific topic could be influenced by the economic condition of regions.

In order to verify this hypothesis, we calculate the adoption ratio in urban and rural area for each app. And in order to measure the degree of dispersion of app installation rates in different cities, we calculate the coefficient of variation (CV) for each app. CV is a common metric to measure dispersion, which is defined as the ratio of the standard deviation to the mean.

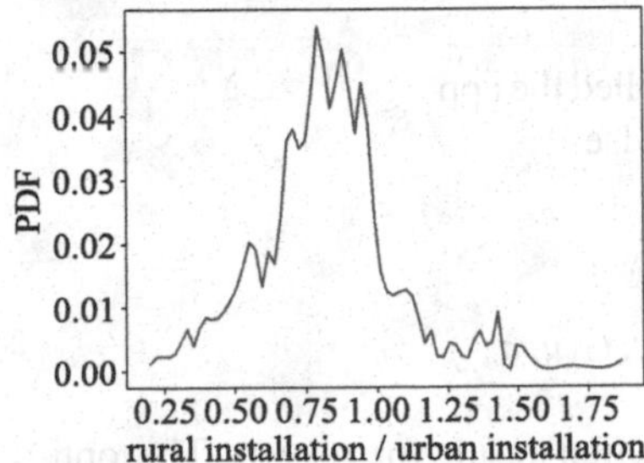

Fig. 5. PDF of rural/urban installation ratio

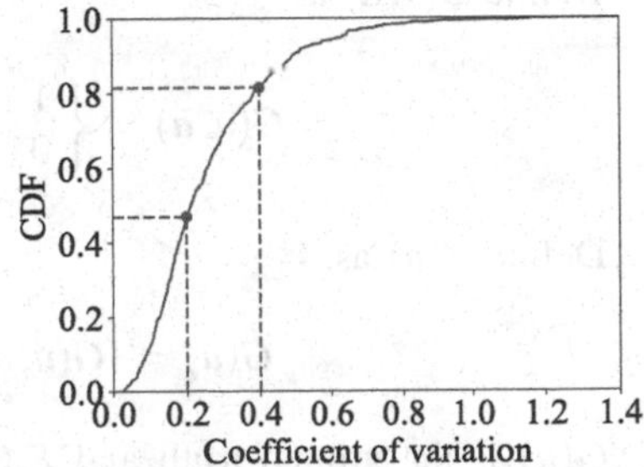

Fig. 6. Variation of application distribution in cities

Figure 5 shows that for some applications there is an uneven distribution in urban and rural areas. For example, applications associate with recruitment or financial get a higher installation rate in urban area. And applications associate with funny joke are more likely to be installed in rural areas. That might be explained by the reason that urban area has more job opportunities or it's more relaxed to live in rural area.

Figure 6 shows that more than 50% of the apps have a CV more than 0.2, and there are even 19% of the apps have a CV larger than 0.4. That means the distribution of installation in each city is uneven for these apps. For example, huaban is an app about fashion and design. Its installation rate is twice of other cities in Dalian and Shenyang, which are the top 2 cities in terms of GDP per capita in Liaoning.

In order to reflect the regional differences, we calculate factor of location as follow:

$$F_c(u,a) = a_{city}(a, u_{city})$$
$$F_{ur}(u,a) = a_{urban}(a, u_{urban})$$

3.3 Model Combination and Training

In previous sections, we define four factors, F_u, F_a, F_c and F_{ur}. The linear combination of the factors is defined as $F(u,a)$, where p_i are parameters, and $A(u,a)$ is adoption function:

$$F(u,a) = \begin{cases} p_1F_u(u,a) + p_2F_a(u,a) + p_3F_c(u,a) + p_4F_{ur}(u,a) & A(u,a) = 0 \\ -\infty & A(u,a) = 1 \end{cases}$$

We normalized the predicted app vector using softmax function for training:

$$F_s(u) = softmax(F(u,a_0), F(u,a_1), \ldots, F(u,a_n))$$

Where softmax is:

$$softmax(z) = \frac{e^{z_i}}{\sum_{j=1}^{n} e^{z_j}} \text{ for } i = 1, 2, \ldots, n$$

Define $G(u,a)$ as:

$$G(u,a) = \begin{cases} 1 & \text{if the user installed the app} \\ 0 & \text{otherwise} \end{cases}$$

Define $G(u)$ as:

$$G(u) = (G(u,a_0), G(u,a_1), \ldots, G(u,a_n))$$

$G(u)$ is the ground truth and $F_s(u)$ is the prediction result for user u. The optimization goal is cross entropy of them:

$$P = \text{argmin}_P - \sum_{i=0}^{n} G(u,i)\log F_s(u,i)$$

P include p_i and parameters defined in F_a. They are optimized after training process.

Cross entropy is usually used as optimization goal in classification with one-hot encoding. Although $G(u)$ is not one-hot encoded, and there might be multiple 1 on the vector, we still use it here for the following reason. It can be proved that the cross entropy will still be minimal when $F_s(u,i)$ is as close as $G(u,i)$ for every app a_i, i.e. the ideal output is that for every i, $F_s(u,i) = \frac{1}{\sum_{i=0}^{n} G(u,i)}$ when $G(u,i)$ is 1, where $\sum_{i=0}^{n} G(u,i)$ is just the adoption number. Thus, we are able to use cross entropy as optimization goal.

The parameters are optimized by Adam optimizer, which is similar to gradient descent optimizer, but has better performance. Once the model is trained, the system is ready to predict or recommend apps to users.

4 Evaluation

4.1 Data Set

Our dataset contains coarse locations and application snapshots of 10000 anonymous devices in Liaoning province aggregated from mobile flow records (MFR). Coarse locations include the city and urban/rural information. For each device, there are two snapshots in the data set. One for apps used within first 4 weeks, the other lists the new apps adopted within 2 weeks afterwards. No detailed usage information or accurate location involved.

After filtering out seldom-used applications (adopted by less than 10 users) and inactive users (who didn't adopt any new applications), there are 7745 devices involving 577 different mobile applications left. The users are distributed in urban or rural region in 14 cities.

We use only such coarse data because it's less privacy-sensitive and easy to acquire. Thus, our model is more feasible for in practice usage while showing respect to privacy. For app store operators, the coarse location of a user could be inferred from IP address and the installed-application list could be requested by the following Android API: PackageManager.getInstalledPackages [14]. It does not require any user permission, which means any application can get it so as app store.

4.2 Metrics

The model outputs a vector in which are scores that user will install an app. Since the number of apps installed by a user is very small compared to all apps, top-k metrics is suitable. Here're the metrics we used to evaluate the model.

- Top-*k* precision. The ratio of the number of the apps with top-*k* scores are actually installed to *k*.
- Top-*k* recall. The ratio of the number of the apps with top-*k* scores are actually installed to the number of all actually installed apps.
- Top-*k* F1-Score. Calculated from $2 \times \frac{\text{precision} \times \text{recall}}{\text{precision} + \text{recall}}$.

4.3 Experiments

We divide the dataset into training set and test set with ratio 0.6:0.4, i.e. 4647 and 3098 users. Apps they used in first 4 weeks are model input and next 2 weeks are prediction. We build and train 4 models: (1) Only user factors (baseline). (2) Without location information. (3) Without demand saturation factor. (4) Proposed model.

The models are built and trained using TensorFlow [15]. We evaluated each of the models. Table 2 shows the result of these models.

Table 2. Experiment result

Model	K = 5			K = 10		
	Precision	Recall	F1-score	Precision	Recall	F1-score
User only	0.1776	0.1501	0.1627	0.1482	0.2505	0.1862
w/o location	0.1981	0.1676	0.1816	0.1627	0.2752	0.2045
w/o DS	0.2030	0.1718	0.1861	0.1634	0.2764	0.2054
Proposed	0.2348	0.1933	0.2120	0.1865	0.3216	0.2361

As shown in the above table, our model achieves the highest precision and recall in all models. It proves that the demand saturation assumption is reasonable and it helps improve the prediction result. Compared with the model without location information, the proposed model, even with coarse location information, has better performance. Thus, the factors we selected are helpful in predicting adoption action, and the predicting performance could be pretty good though only using limited user information.

It is worth noting that we have a total of 577 apps in our data set and randomly select 5(10) apps out of 577 could only reach a very low precision. A precision of 0.2348 for top-5-ranking means that averagely more than one app out of 5 is correctly predicted, which is a quite good performance in practice.

5 Conclusion

5.1 Contributions

In this paper, we design and implement a predicting model to recommend apps to users. The model can achieve a pretty good accuracy while utilizing very limited information. The main contributions of our work are: (1) We only require coarse location information and two snapshots of the users' apps to predict user adoption in the next two weeks. (2) We notice "demand saturation" phenomenon that apps with similar topics of functions may be exclusive. (3) We also find that there are plenty of apps distributed unevenly in different regions. The predicting model is improved based on these observations.

5.2 Future Work

As users' interests may change over time, we consider doing sequence analysis on long period data in the future work, avoiding a possible hysteresis during prediction. Furthermore, currently we only consider 577 applications as candidates and predict the future adopted ones within them. However, there are even millions of applications in an app store today, which makes it much more difficult to predict the users' future installation action. Thus, we also consider obtaining more applications and trying to get more insight into user preference in the future.

References

1. Breese, J.S., Heckerman, D., Kadie, C.: Empirical analysis of predictive algorithms for collaborative filtering. In: Proceedings of the Fourteenth Conference on Uncertainty in Artificial Intelligence, Morgan Kaufmann Publishers Inc. (1998)
2. Pazzani, M.J.: A framework for collaborative, content-based and demographic filtering. Artif. Intell. Rev. **13**(5–6), 393–408 (1999)
3. Yan, B., Chen, G.: AppJoy: personalized mobile application discovery. In: Proceedings of the 9th International Conference on Mobile Systems, Applications, and Services, ACM (2011)
4. Zhu, K., Liu, Z., Zhang, L., Gu, X.: A mobile application recommendation framework by exploiting personal preference with constraints. Mob. Inf. Syst. **2017**, 9 (2017). Article ID 4542326
5. Zhu, H., et al.: Mobile app recommendations with security and privacy awareness. In: Proceedings of the 20th ACM SIGKDD International Conference on Knowledge Discovery and Data Mining, ACM (2014)
6. Lin, J., et al.: New and improved: modeling versions to improve app recommendation. In: Proceedings of the 37th International ACM SIGIR Conference on Research and Development in Information Retrieval, ACM (2014)
7. Karatzoglou, A., et al.: Climbing the app wall: enabling mobile app discovery through context-aware recommendations. In: Proceedings of the 21st ACM International Conference on Information and Knowledge Management, ACM (2012)
8. Seneviratne, S., et al.: Predicting user traits from a snapshot of apps installed on a smartphone. ACM SIGMOBILE Mob. Comput. Commun. Rev. **18**(2) 1–8 (2014)
9. Seneviratne, S., et al.: Your installed apps reveal your gender and more! In: Proceedings of the ACM MobiCom Workshop on Security and Privacy in Mobile Environments, ACM (2014)
10. Xu, R., et al.: Towards understanding the impact of personality traits on mobile app adoption-a scalable approach. In: Proceedings ECIS 2015 (2015)
11. Parate, A., et al.: Practical prediction and prefetch for faster access to applications on mobile phones. In: Proceedings of the 2013 ACM International Joint Conference on Pervasive and Ubiquitous Computing, ACM (2013)

12. Baeza-Yates, R., et al.: Predicting the next app that you are going to use. In: Proceedings of the Eighth ACM International Conference on Web Search and Data Mining, ACM (2015)
13. Pan, W., Aharony, N., Pentland, A.: Composite social network for predicting mobile apps installation. In: AAAI, vol. 7, no. 7.4, p. 2 (2011)
14. PackageManager|Android Developers. https://developer.android.com/reference/android/content/pm/PackageManager.html. Accessed 18 May 2018
15. Abadi, M., et al.: TensorFlow: a system for large-scale machine learning. In: OSDI, vol. 16 (2016)

Privacy-Preserving Credit Scoring on Cloud

Jilin Wang, Yingzi Chen, and Xiaoqing Feng(✉)

School of Information, Zhejiang University of Finance and Economics, Hangzhou 310018, China
fenglinda@zufe.edu.cn

Abstract. Credit scoring needs comprehensive data to achieve accurate assessment. However, these data often lie in the different places such as banks and financial institutions, internet firms, and almost all the data contain privacy information. Meanwhile, the acquisition of big data and privacy protection influence the rapid development of big data for credit scoring. And the introduction of big data for credit scoring proposes a lot of requirements for computing and storage capabilities. Cloud servers can provide powerful computing and storage services, but it also accompanies with higher privacy requirements. In this paper, we designed an additively homomorphic based secure multiparty computation scheme to collect and calculate credit data shared by different parties and at the same time preserve privacy in the cloud computing. We introduced two scenarios for credit scoring in this paper: one is to collect statistic information of relevant variables (such as a user's overdue information in all banks) based on the existing credit model. The other is to collect a large amount of data for training to get credit evaluation model, but the efficiency of this scenario will be significantly lower due to the need of lots of multiplication operations. Finally, we analyzed the security and performance of our scheme, and proved that our scheme is safe and does not reveal the privacy of data in the cloud server.

Keywords: Credit scoring · Cloud computing · Privacy
Homomorphic encryption

1 Introduction

The application of big data technology in credit scoring has solved many problems [1]. Large of data related to credit is analyzed by big data technology to obtain a more accurate evaluation model [2–4]. However, the presence of the big data has brought a huge challenge on enterprise's computing and storage capacity. At the same time, the data related to credit comes from different institutions like banking financial institutions, internet financial enterprises and public utilities. And they are not willing to share these data because of privacy concerns. Cloud computing provides a strong support on data storage and computing services currently and it is intelligent to out-source large data to the cloud server to for data computing and storage. Meanwhile, protecting the privacy of the data shared by data owners will greatly improve the willingness to share data.

X. Sun et al. (Eds.): ICCCS 2018, LNCS 11065, pp. 195–205, 2018.
https://doi.org/10.1007/978-3-030-00012-7_18

How to protect the privacy of data is an important topic in the process of outsourcing to cloud [5–7]. The data providers may not want anyone to learn their data, and credit bureaus may also not want anyone else to learn the results or model of credit scoring. Anonymity is used to preserve the privacy of data shared by data owners. It is widely used for privacy-preserving data mining [8, 9]. In order to deal with privacy concerns, Stecking et al. [10] use a microaggregation procedure to anonymize data over personal credit client feature information before classification of credit scoring data using support vector machines. But it seems that it is difficult to refined control of the degrees of privacy when clustering original data.

The securest way to protect the privacy of the data is to encrypt it before outsourcing to cloud, but the encryption is difficult to be processed. Homomorphic encryption can deal with encrypted data and it needn't to decrypt the ciphertexts before performing specific algebraic operations on ciphertexts. Generally, there are three types of homomorphic encryption, multiplicatively, additively and fully homomorphic encryption. Multiplicatively and additively homomorphic encryption only support one homomorphic operation but the fully homomorphic encryption can support both [11]. But the efficiency of fully homomorphic encryption is lower. Many researches proposed a framework for privacy preserving in cloud based on fully homomorphic encryption, such as secure storage, secure calculation, privacy-preserving data mining. [12–14]. Yan et al. [15] proposed two schemes of privacy-preserving trust evaluation based on additively homomorphic encryption. One scheme assumed a third party responsible for evidence access control and management is trusted and the other assumed it untrusted. But it can only deal with trust evaluation that contains evidence summation and cannot deal with other situations. Liu et al. [16] proposed a privacy-preserving framework for trust-oriented Point-of-Interest recommendation, it solves that a user wants to share its current locations with a recommender but forbids it to disclose these data to any other third party. That framework uses partially homomorphic encryption to preserve the privacy of every party involved in the recommendation. The two papers both aim to solving the trusted data sharing using additively homomorphic encryption to preserve the privacy data, but they only support trust aggregation. Besides, those methods cannot directly apply to solving the credit scoring problem due to the difference of the system.

In this paper, we designed an additively homomorphic based secure multiparty computation scheme to collect and calculate credit data shared by different parties and at the same time preserve privacy in the cloud computing. We didn't consider the fully homomorphic encryption because of the current technical limitations and its high computational complexity. Our scheme can also perform the multiplication without interaction with the data providers, but it needs an interaction between two cloud servers. Our contributions can be summarized as follows:

- We show how to preserve privacy of credit data providers when outsourcing credit data to cloud. This encourages the data providers to share their privacy data and thereby improve the credit scoring.
- Our scheme use additively homomorphic encryption to preserve privacy. We also designed a multiplication protocol to support multiplication while at the same time there is no interaction between data provider and the cloud.

- We proved the security and performance of our scheme theoretically. We introduced two application scenarios of our scheme and we concretely showed the more efficient scenario.

The rest of this paper is organized as follows. Section 2 introduces the system and threat model, as well as the goals of our scheme. The detail of our scheme and two concrete applications of our scheme in credit scoring will be described in Sect. 3. Section 4 analyses the security and performance of our scheme. Finally, we summarize the paper in Sect. 5.

2 Problem Statement

2.1 System Model

In our PPCS scheme, we consider four types of entities. They are data providers like banking financial institutions, internet financial enterprises and public utilities, which have many data related to credit, an evaluator serviced as a cloud service provider, credit bureaus which provide credit information service and an authorized center which is responsible for access control and management and also provides online encryption/decryption and cloud computing service. The concrete system model is described as follows (illustrated in Fig. 1):

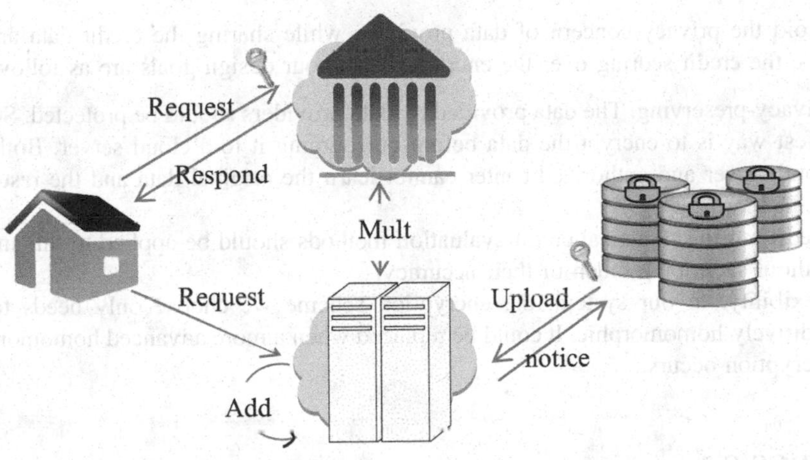

Fig. 1. An overview of the system model.

In the credit scoring system, a credit bureau may need to access a personal credit for personal loan or other service. The credit bureau neither has enough data to establish a credit evaluating model nor a specific user's credit data. They send requests to authorized center and evaluator for credit scoring. The authorized center which is semi-honest in this model is responsible for receiving requests and checking the request. It also provides computing power and encryption/decryption services. The evaluator announces the corresponding data providers to upload the relevant data and services as a cloud service provider which processes the encrypted data uploaded from the data providers. It undertakes the work of machine learning to establish a credit evaluating model. It can be seen that there needs two cloud server in this paper to provide computing service. The data providers own the data related to credit, but this information is usually privacy. This system considers the concern of the data providers about their privacy and collects the data in encrypted form. Each data providers use the public key of the authorized center to encrypt their data before uploading them to the evaluator.

2.2 Adversary Model

In this paper, we will discuss our model in the semi-honest model which means that all participants of the model is semi-honest and they will perform the protocol honestly but try to deduce the messages of others from the output and intermediate message, or reveal the output results to attackers. We deem the authorized center and evaluator will always perform the tasks honestly for credibility and long-term business interests. But they are both not fully trusted. We assume that both the authorized center and evaluator do not collude with each other. We also assume that the channel between evaluator and data providers is secure so that the authorized center cannot eavesdrop the data.

2.3 Design Goals

To avoid the privacy concern of data providers while sharing the credit data and to achieve the credit scoring over the encrypted data, our design goals are as follows.

- Privacy-preserving. The data provided by data providers should be protected. So the safest way is to encrypt the data before outsourcing it to a cloud server. Both the cloud server and authorized center cannot learn the original data and the result of credit scoring.
- Credit scoring. Practical credit evaluation methods should be applied to this model without sacrificing much of their accuracy.
- Flexibility. In our system, the encryption scheme we choose only needs to be additively homomorphic. It could be replaced when a more advanced homomorphic encryption occurs.

3 PPCS Scheme

3.1 Preliminaries and Notations

Homomorphic Encryption. The concept of homomorphic encryption was first proposed by Rivest et al. in 1978. An public key encryption scheme is homomorphic if it is allowed to operate the encrypted data without decryption. And it is called additively homomorphic if it holds that

$$E(m_1 + m_2) = E(m_1) \cdot E(m_2) \quad (1)$$

where m_1 and m_2 are the plaintext messages to be encrypted. And we use *E*(*m*) to represent encrypting plaintext *m* under a key here for simplicity.

Notations. The notations used in this paper are presented in Table 1.

Table 1. Notations

Notations	Description
keyGen(k)	A key generation use parameter *k*
PK_x	The public key of *x*
SK_x	The secret key of *x*
$Sign\{SignK_x, m\}$	A signature of *x* on message m
E(*k*, *m*)	To encrypt *m* with *k*
$Add(m_1, m_2)$	To get the encryption of the sum of the plaintexts which correspond to m_1 and m_2.
$Mult(m_1, m_2)$	To get the encryption of the product of the plaintexts which correspond to m_1 and m_2.
k	The security parameter of Paillier's cryptosystem
n	The number of the data providers

3.2 Scheme Description

This paper chooses additive homomorphism to design our scheme. Recent fully homomorphic encryption (FHE) schemes lack efficiency although FHE supports both additive homomorphism and multiplicative homomorphism. Our designed scheme can both perform addition and multiplication operations but the multiplication operation needs one interaction between two cloud servers.

In our scheme, the credit bureaus may have its own credit evaluation model like FICO in America but doesn't have a specific user's credit data, or lacks enough data to establish a credit evaluating model. We deal with it by preserving the privacy of data so the data owners are comfortable sharing their data with credit bureaus. The scheme contains the following steps, and it is presented in Fig. 2.

Registration. In this step, all credit bureaus should first ran n(k) to generate its public key PK_c and register with their public key in the authorized center.

Request. The credit bureau sends a request and its public key to the authorized center for credit data. After checking the registration information the authorized center signs PK_c: $Sign\{SignK_a, PK_c\}$ and sends $Sign\{SignK_a, PK_c\}$ together with a signed public key $PK_a : Sign\{SignK_a, PK_a\}$ to the credit bureau. Then credit bureau sends them to the evaluator for Evaluation Request.

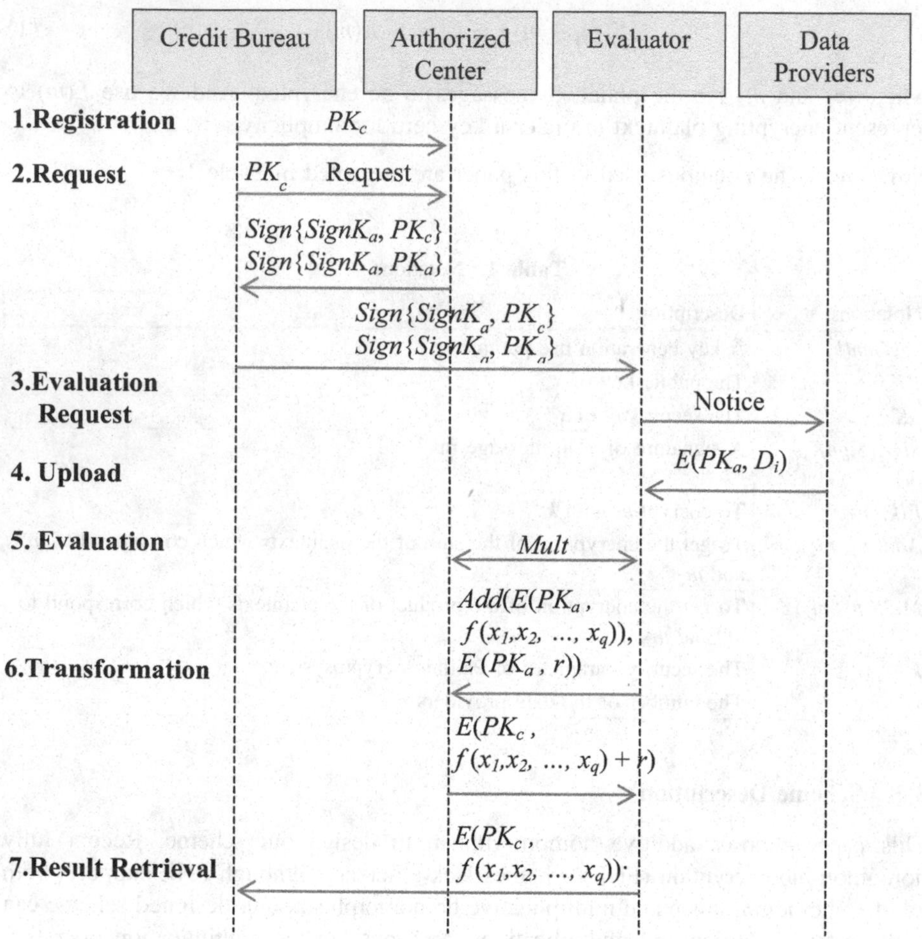

Fig. 2. The concrete process of PPCS

Evaluation Request. After receiving $\{Sign\{SignK_a, PK_c\}, Sign\{SignK_a, PK_a\}\}$ from credit bureau, evaluator verifies them and then notice the data providers to upload the relevant data.

Upload. Data provider P_i uploads the relevant data D_i encrypted with PK_a .

Evaluation. The evaluator collects the relevant data and then computes the function $f(x_1, x_2, \ldots, x_q)$ asked by credit bureau in the encrypted domain, such as calculating the statistics of each independent variable in the model, or training classifier over the encrypted domain to obtain a credit evaluating model.

We consider the function *f* to be represented as an arithmetic circuit. The addition gates are evaluated non-interactively in the evaluator as the cryptosystem in our scheme is additively homomorphic. We can compute the product of two ciphertexts when we actually need to get the sum of them in clear. Here we use *Add* to represent addition operation and *Mult* to represent multiplication operation. The multiplication needs the interaction between evaluator and authorized center. First we send the blinded version of the ciphertexts to authorized center and the authorized center decrypts them with its private key. Then the authorized center multiplies them in clear and re-encrypts them to evaluator. Finally the evaluator remove the blinding to obtain the result of multiplication of the original ciphertexts in the form of encryption. The Fig. 3 shows the detail of Multiplication.

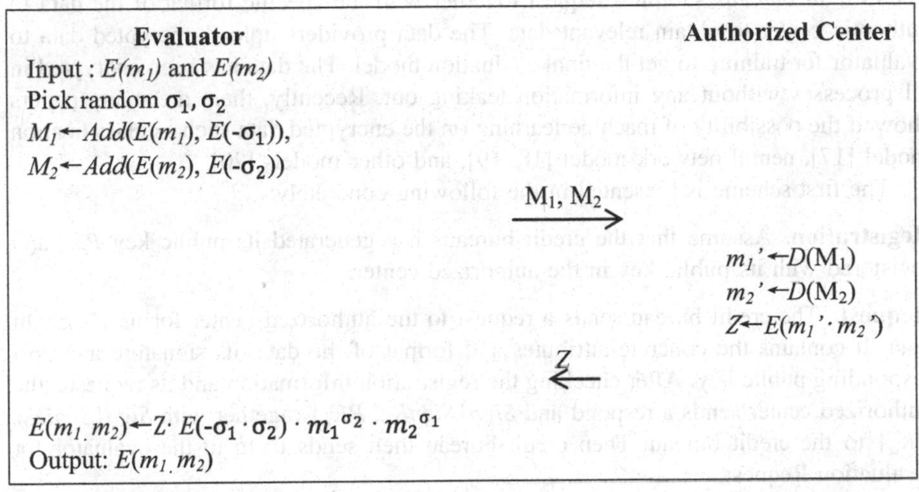

Fig. 3. For two ciphertexts $E(m_1)$ and $E(m_2)$, it generates the encryption of the multiplication of their corresponding plaintexts.

Transformation. The task of this part is to transform the result of evaluation encrypted under PK_a to encryption under credit bureau's public key PK_c. The evaluator first randomly chooses r and computes $Add(E(PK_a, f(x_1, x_2, \ldots, x_q)), E(PK_a, r))$. The the evaluator sends it to authorized center. The authorized center decrypts it with SK_a to get $f(x_1, x_2, \ldots, x_q) + r$ and then re-encrypts it with PK_c. Authorized center sends $E(PK_c, f(x_1, x_2, \ldots, x_q) + r)$ back to evaluator. In this way, the authorized center can't learn the plaintext of result in the part of Evaluate.

Result Retrieval. Finally the evaluator computes $E(PK_c, f(x_1, x_2, \ldots, x_q) + r) \cdot E(PK_c, -r)$ and sends it to credit bureau. The credit bureau receives it and decrypts it with SK_c to get the result of $f(x_1, x_2, \ldots, x_q)$.

3.3 Credit Scoring

Here we present two application scenarios of our scheme to show how credit scoring model and results are generated in this scheme. The first one is applied to solve such a scenario: the credit bureau has its own credit scoring model, such as $f(x_1, x_2, \ldots, x_q)$, but the data corresponding to the variables of the model comes from different enterprises, for example the loan and overdue information from different banking institutions, payment information from different platforms. Furthermore, these enterprises do not want to reveal the data to anyone else. In our scheme, the credit bureau sends a request to authentic center for user's relevant data in the model and gets the credit score of the user. But it can only get the statistics information of the variables, such as the sum of the all data belongs to the variable.

The second application addresses the need of the credit bureau for enough credit data to be trained by machine learning algorithms to obtain credit evaluation models. Then credit bureaus submit a request together with the specific format of the data to authentic center to obtain relevant data. The data providers upload encrypted data to evaluator for training to get the final evaluation model. The data has been encrypted in all processes without any information leaking out. Recently, there are many papers showed the possibility of machine learning on the encrypted data such as classification model [17], neural network model [18, 19], and other models [20].

The first scheme is presented in the following concretely.

Registration. Assume that the credit bureaus has generated its public key PK_c and registered with its public key in the authorized center.

Request. The credit bureau sends a request to the authorized center for user's credit data. It contains the concrete attributes and format of the data, its signature and corresponding public key. After checking the registration information and its requests, the authorized center sends a respond and $Sign\{SignK_a, PK_c\}$ together with $Sign\{SignK_a, PK_a\}$ to the credit bureau. Then credit bureau then sends them to the evaluator for Evaluation Request.

Evaluation Request. The evaluator verifies $\{Sign\{SignK_a, PK_c\}, Sign\{SignK_a, PK_a\}\}$ and then notice the data providers to upload the relevant data.

Upload. Data provider P_i uploads the relevant data D_i encrypted with PK_a in a fixed format. In this phase the evaluator doesn't know identity of a specific data provider.

Evaluation. After collecting the credit data, the evaluator perform the calculations including *add* operation and *mult* operation over the encrypted data, such as the summation of all the delinquencies attributes.

Transformation. In this part the evaluator transforms the result of evaluation encrypted under PK_a to encryption under credit bureau's public key PK_c.

Result Retrieval. The credit bureau receives the result from the evaluator and decrypts it with SK_c to get the final result. Then the credit bureau applies the result to its credit evaluating model.

4 Security and Performance Analysis

4.1 Security Analysis

The confidentiality of data in our model is achieved by the additively homomorphic encryption scheme such as Paillier's cryptosystem, then the security of the data follows from the semantic security of Paillier's cryptosystem. Besides, the security of our scheme relies on the how we design it. Based on the adversary model of this paper, we now analyze the attacks for privacy from the parties involved in our scheme.

Firstly, the evaluator can't get the raw data of data providers and the plaintext result in Evaluation and Transformation phases. The evaluator collects and computes the data from data providers encrypted with PK_a and it doesn't have the corresponding secret key. In the phase of Transformation the evaluator receives the result from authorized center encrypted with PK_c and it also doesn't have the corresponding secret key.

For the authorized center, although it has the secret key of PK_a, it only gets fresh ciphertexts of blinded messages in Multiplication and Transformation phases.

As for the credit bureau, it only receives a result encrypted with its own public key. And it cannot infer the data of a specific data provider because the result is calculated from different data providers.

4.2 Performance Analysis

We now analyze the performance of our scheme under the situation of Paillier's cryptosystem [21] of security parameter k, and n data providers. An overview of complexity of our scheme is presented in Table 2, and the traffic we simply count the ciphertexts in communication. The efficiency of our scheme relies on the performance of homomorphic algorithm as the homomorphic encryption and decryption occupy most of the computing resource. The computation complexity of the recent additively homomorphic encryption is presented in [22–24].

Table 2. The complexity of the scheme

Procedures	Traffic in bits	Round trips
Upload	nk	0.5
Add	0	0
Mult	$4k$	1
Transformation	$(n+1)k$	1
Result retrieval	nk	0.5

5 Conclusions

In this paper, we proposed a scheme for credit scoring which only used additively homomorphic encryption, but it can both deal with addition and multiplication. We then applied two scenarios to our scheme. One scheme one is to collect statistic information of relevant variables (such as a user's overdue information in all banks) based on the existing credit model. The other is to collect a large amount of data for training to get credit evaluation model, but the efficiency of this scenario will be significantly lower due to the need of lots of multiplication operations. Our scheme is secure for all the parties involved, and the computation complexity is mostly relied on the recent additively homomorphic encryption. It is more efficient than fully homomorphic encryption in some special situation (as our multiplication is achieved at the cost of communication) at present. The full homomorphic encryption can replace the additively homomorphic encryption of this paper to achieve higher efficiency when tan effective full homomorphic encryption appears.

Acknowledgments. This work is supported by the Planning Fund Project of Ministry of Education (12YJAZH136), the Natural Science Fund of China (NSFC-61202197), and the Public Welfare Technology and Industry Project of Zhejiang Provincial Science Technology Department (No. 2016C31081).

References

1. Aitken, R.: All data is credit data: constituting the unbanked. Compet. Chang **21**(309), (2017). https://doi.org/10.1177/1024529417712830
2. Zhao, Z., Xu, S., Kang, B.H., Kabir, M.M.J., Liu, Y., Wasinger, R.: Investigation and improvement of multi-layer perceptron neural networks for credit scoring. Expert. Syst. Appl. **42**(7), 3508–3516 (2015)
3. Abellán, J., Castellano, J.G.: A comparative study on base classifiers in ensemble methods for credit scoring. Expert. Syst. Appl. **73**, 1–10 (2016)
4. Yap, B.W., Seng, H.O., Husain, N.H.M.: Using data mining to improve assessment of credit worthiness via credit scoring models. Expert Syst. Appl. **38**(10), 13274–13283 (2011)
5. Singh, S.: State-of-the-art survey on security issues in cloud computing environment. In: IEEE International Conference on Futuristic Trends in Computational Analysis and Knowledge Management, IEEE (2015)
6. Bommala, H.: Security issues in service model of cloud computing environment. In: International Conference on Computational Science (2016)
7. Yan, Z., Deng, R.H., Varadharajan, V.: Cryptography and data security in cloud computing. Inf. Sci. **387**, 53–55 (2017)
8. Ilavarasi, A.K., Sathiyabhama, B.: An evolutionary feature set decomposition based anonymization for classification workloads: privacy preserving data mining. Clust. Comput. **20**(Suppl. 1), 1–11 (2017)
9. Li, X., Miao, M., Liu, H., et al.: An incentive mechanism for K -anonymity in LBS privacy protection based on credit mechanism. Soft. Comput. **21**(14), 3907–3917 (2017)
10. Stecking, R., Schebesch, K.B.: Classification of credit scoring data with privacy constraints. Intell. Data Anal. **19**(s1), S3–S18 (2015)
11. Brakerski, Z., Vaikuntanathan, V.: Efficient fully homomorphic encryption from (standard) LWE. In: Foundations of Computer Science, vol. 2011, pp. 97–106 (2011)
12. Mr, M.M.P., Dhote, C.A., Mr, D.H.S.: Homomorphic encryption for security of cloud data. Procedia Comput. Sci. **79**, 175–181 (2016)
13. Kumar, V., Kumar, R., Pandey, S.K., Alam, M.: Fully homomorphic encryption scheme with probabilistic encryption based on euler's theorem and application in cloud computing. In: Aggarwal, V.B., Bhatnagar, V., Mishra, D.K. (eds.) Big Data Analytics. AISC, vol. 654, pp. 605–611. Springer, Singapore (2018). https://doi.org/10.1007/978-981-10-6620-7_58

14. Hammami, H., Brahmi, H., Brahmi, I., Ben Yahia, S.: Using homomorphic encryption to compute privacy preserving data mining in a cloud computing environment. In: Themistocleous, M., Morabito, V. (eds.) EMCIS 2017. LNBIP, vol. 299, pp. 397–413. Springer, Cham (2017). https://doi.org/10.1007/978-3-319-65930-5_32
15. Yan, Z., Ding, W., Niemi, V., Vasilakos, A.V.: Two schemes of privacy-preserving trust evaluation. Futur. Gener. Comput. Syst. **62**(C), 175–189 (2016)
16. Liu, A., Wang, W., Li, Z., Liu, G., Li, Q., Zhou, X., et al.: A privacy-preserving framework for trust-oriented point-of-interest recommendation. IEEE Access **99**, 1 (2017)
17. Li, P., Li, J., Huang, Z., Gao, C.Z., Chen, W.B., Chen, K.: Privacy-preserving outsourced classification in cloud computing. Clust. Comput. **1**, 1–10 (2017)
18. Bu, F., Ma, Y., Chen, Z., Xu, H.: Privacy preserving back-propagation based on BGV on cloud. In: IEEE, International Conference on High Performance Computing and Communications, 2015 IEEE, International Symposium on Cyberspace Safety and Security, and 2015 IEEE, International Conference on Embedded Software and Systems, pp. 1791–1795. IEEE Computer Society (2015)
19. Li, P., Li, J., Huang, Z., Li, T., Gao, C.Z., Yiu, S.M., et al.: Multi-key privacy-preserving deep learning in cloud computing. Futur. Gener. Comput. Syst. **74**(C), 76–85 (2017)
20. Bost, R., Popa, R.A., Tu, S., Goldwasser, S.: Machine learning classification over encrypted data. In: Network and Distributed System Security Symposium (2014)
21. Paillier, P.: Public-Key cryptosystems based on composite degree residuosity classes. In: Stern, J. (ed.) EUROCRYPT 1999. LNCS, vol. 1592, pp. 223–238. Springer, Heidelberg (1999). https://doi.org/10.1007/3-540-48910-X_16
22. Catalano, D., Gennaro, R., Howgrave-Graham, N., Nguyen, P.Q.: Paillier's cryptosystem revisited. In: ACM Conference on Computer and Communications Security, pp. 206–214 (2001)
23. Jurik, M.J.: Extensions to the paillier cryptosystem with applications to cryptological protocols (2003)
24. Nishide, T., Sakurai, K.: Distributed paillier cryptosystem without trusted dealer. In: Chung, Y., Yung, M. (eds.) WISA 2010. LNCS, vol. 6513, pp. 44–60. Springer, Heidelberg (2011). https://doi.org/10.1007/978-3-642-17955-6_4

QS-Code: A Quasi-Systematic Erasure Code with Partial Security for Cloud Storage

Chong Wang, Ke Zhou(✉), and Ronglei Wei

School of Computer, Wuhan National Laboratory for Optoelectronics, HuaZhong University of Science and Technology, Wuhan, China
{c_wang,k.zhou,Ronglei_Wei}@hust.edu.cn

Abstract. To address the reliability and privacy concerns in cloud storage systems, we present a quasi-systematic erasure code with partial security, referred to as QS-code. As a new family of maximum distance separable (MDS) codes, it has a number of advantages, privacy-preserving, efficient and reliable in data access and storage. In QS-code, the coded data maintain the originality of one of the two data blocks in the original file, allowing for efficient data accessing, while preserving the privacy of the other. Results of our experiment showed that QS-code outperforms encryption technology in computational efficiency.

Keywords: Erasure codes · Weak security · Cloud storage
Data-intensive application · Systematic codes

1 Introduction

Cloud storage is known for its massive storage capacity and on-demand data access and has received much attention in recent literature. Generally, there have been two major concerns in the data outsourcing to the cloud. The first is data reliability, commonly achieved by maximum-distance separable (MDS) codes. MDS codes are able to achieve a prescribed level of reliability at the sacrifice of minimum redundancy. Typically, a source file of k data fragments is encoded into n coded blocks such that any k out of the n blocks are adequate to reconstruct the original file. However, erasure codes in DSSs are systematic in the sense that the original data form part of the encoded data. Hence, systematic codes in data-intensive application, for instance, are cost-effective in that the original data are readily available, avoiding the lengthy decoding process.

To address the second concern, the privacy problem, non-systematic codes have been adopted to reinforce the security in a proliferation of studies [19,21]. In non-systematic codes, instead of encrypting the file overall, coding schemes are exploited to secure distributed storage systems (DSS) [6,14]. Such schemes can achieve perfect (Shannon) secrecy by mixing the original file with a specific number of inserted random keys [7,14] before encoding. As a result, the adversary

X. Sun et al. (Eds.): ICCCS 2018, LNCS 11065, pp. 206–216, 2018.
https://doi.org/10.1007/978-3-030-00012-7_19

gains no information about the source file. However, since part of the original file is replaced by randomly generated variables, the construction of perfectly secure code incurs a loss in storage capacity. Furthermore, strict perfect secrecy in many occasions becomes entirely unnecessary. By reason of the luxury nature of perfect secrecy, costless weak secrecy would be adequate and more preferable in most practical circumstances [2,18]. By weak secrecy, the adversary can get only partial and meaningless information about the source file, (e.g. one bit of information a or b in $a \bigoplus b$), but he is unable to recover the source bits on this basis. In multi-cloud system, where coded data are distributed into different clouds, weak security is enough for preserving data privacy for each individual cloud.

Additionally, non-systematic codes, though simpler computationally and more efficient in data access, undermine the data access because a decoding process prior to it is still required in data-intensive application. In practice, often, not all the private information uploaded needs to be secured. For instance, information in medical big data includes user name, ID number, age, gender, illness condition and prescription, among other things. For most big data analyses, the valuable information that needs to be accessed is merely age, gender, illness condition and prescription to the exclusion of other privacy information like name and ID number, etc. Consequently, in data-intensive applications, it is reasonable and cost-effective to know which information needs to be encrypted and which do not so that the privacy-preserving cost can be significantly reduced by only securing the important and sensitive information [22,23].

In pursuit of an enhanced storage reliability and a reasonable privacy-preserving service for cloud storage, we propose a quasi-systematic erasure code, QS-code with weak security. In this current framework, the original file is split into two parts, one for data analysis and efficient sharing, the other for the privacy-preserving purpose. The coded data maintain the originality of the former data block and guarantee the security of the latter data block in the meantime. Furthermore, additional redundant information is created so that the data reliability is well obtained. The contribution of the paper is summarized below:

- A QS-coding mechanism is postulated for cloud storage system to achieve privacy preservation, efficient data access and reliable storage;
- Satisfying MDS properties, QS-code achieves optimal storage efficiency;
- Compared to encryption technology, QS-codes improve computational efficiency.

The remainder work is organized as follows. In Sect. 2 we present necessary notation and definitions as foundations for the following discussions. A construction of QS-code is introduced in Sect. 3. Section 4 gives the evaluation results. Related works are reviewed in Sect. 5. Finally, Sect. 6 concludes the paper.

2 Preliminaries

2.1 Erasure Codes in DSS

We denote by $\mathbb{F}_q$ the Golois filed with cardinality q. Let $[n]$ denote the set $\{1, 2, \ldots, n\}$. For any $n \geq 1$,let I_n denote a $n \times n$ identity matrix, and $\mathbf{0}$ denote the all-zero matrix of certain size. We also use $M_{m \times n}$ to denote any submatrix of $\mathbf{M}$. Finally, we denote the transpose of a vector $u \in \mathbb{F}_q^n$ as u^T.

Let the original file be $\mathbf{f} = (f_1, f_2, \ldots, f_k)^T$, and $\mathbf{F} = (F_1, F_2, \ldots, F_k)^T$ be $\mathbf{f}$'s corresponding vector, where F_is are independent and identically uniformly distributed random variables over $\mathbb{F}_q$. Similarly, the file the file in the coded from is $\mathbf{c} = (c_1, c_2, \ldots, c_n)^T$ and the corresponding vector is $\mathbf{C} = (C_1, C_2, \ldots, C_n)^T$ of random variables over $\mathbb{F}_q$. In a $[n, k, d]_q$ code, the file $\mathbf{f}$ is encoded into $\mathbf{c} = G\mathbf{f}$, where G is a generator matrix with size $n \times k$ and d is the minimum distance of this code. A code attaining the Singleton bound ($d \leq n - k + 1$) is called MDS. The following lemma specifies a necessary and sufficient condition for the MDS code.

Lemma 1 ([13], *Ch11*). *Let $\mathcal{C}$ be an $[n, k, d]$ code over $\mathbb{F}_q$. $\mathcal{C}$ is MDS if and only if every k rows of a generator matrix G are linearly independent.*

In addition, the code is call systematic, if the generator matrix G is in the following form:

$$\begin{pmatrix} I_k \\ A \end{pmatrix}$$

where A is a certain matrix of size $(n - k) \times k$. We propose a quasi-systematic code defined as r out of k original chunks are maintained in the storage systems, where $1 \leq r < k$.

2.2 Adversary Model and Security Level

As the cloud system consists large amounts of varieties of storage nodes that are widely spread in different locations, some nodes may be susceptibly compromised by an unauthorized intruder. The adversary can access λ nodes in the storage system, in order to learn the content of the file stored by the storage system and even to maliciously corrupt the data. Roughly, two types of intruders can be distinguished in distrusted storage systems, depending on their capacities [14]. (1) An active adversary can control the node, completely get the knowledge of the stored data and modify them. (2) A passive adversary can only read the data on the observed node, but he does not have the right to modifying them.

In this work, we focus on the passive adversary of strength λ, which can access up to λ nodes among all the storage nodes. Recall that C_i presents the chunk storage node i. Let $E \subseteq [n]$ denote the set of indices of the nodes the adversary can access. Therefore, the coded chunks the adversary can observe are $\bigcup_{i \in E} C_i$, where $|E| \leq \lambda$. Given the adversary model above, there are two different levels of security for erasure coded storage systems.

1. **Perfect security** [17]: A $[n, k]$ code for a DSS is called perfect security against an adversary of strength $\lambda < k$ if the adversary gets *no information* about the original file $\mathbf{F}$ from the intercepted chunks, which could be formulated as:

$$H(\mathbf{F}|\bigcup_{i\in E} C_i) = H(\mathbf{F}), \forall E \subseteq [n], |E| \leq \lambda.$$

2. **Weak security** [2]: A $[n, k]$ code for a DSS is called weak security against an adversary of strength $\lambda < k$ if the adversary gets *no meaningful information* about any individual data chunks, which could be formulated as:

$$H(\mathbf{F}_j|\bigcup_{i\in E} C_i) = H(\mathbf{F}_j), \forall j \in [k]; \forall E \subseteq [n], |E| \leq \lambda.$$

Different levels of security are illustrated in Fig. 1. For instance, a systematic code in Fig. 1(a) is insecure because the adversary can directly get the data chunk f_2. A non-systematic code in Fig. 1(b) is weak secure, as long as the adversary accesses encoded chunk $f_1 + 2f_2$, it cannot get any meaningful information of individual data chunks f_1 and f_2. A code scheme using randomly generated variable r in Fig. 1(c) is perfectly secure, since the adversary get no information at all from node 2.

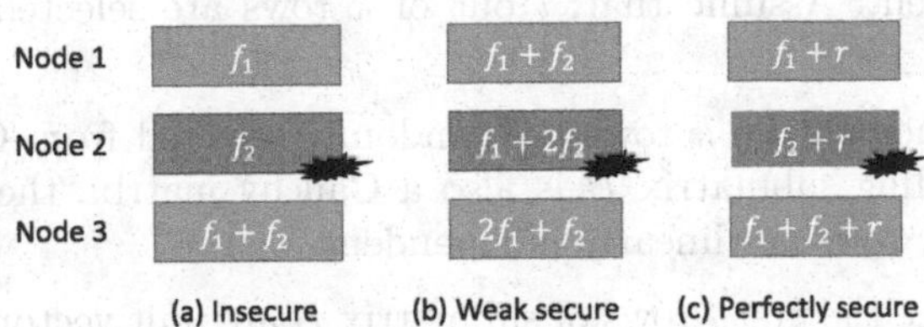

Fig. 1. Different levels of security for distributed storage systems

3 Code Construction

In this section, we present a general construction for QS-code. In our scheme the corresponding vector $\mathbf{F} = (F_1, F_2, \ldots, F_k)^T$ of of the original file is divided into two parts, $\mathbf{R}$ for efficient data access and $\mathbf{S}$ for privacy-preserving. Without loss of generality, let $\mathbf{R} = (F_1, F_2, \ldots, F_r)^T$ and $\mathbf{S} = (F_{r+1}, F_2, \ldots, F_k)^T$, where $|\mathbf{R}| = r$ and $|\mathbf{S}| = s$, thus $r + s = k$. Our goal is to propose an encoding scheme, that satisfies:

(P1) the set of coded blocks contains r original chunks, $F_1, F_2, \ldots, F_r$;

(P2) the adversary with strength $\lambda < k$ gets no meaningful information about any individual data chunks about $F_{r+1}, \ldots, F_k$, that is

$$H(\mathbf{F}_j|\bigcup_{i\in E} C_i) = H(\mathbf{F}_j), \forall j \in \{r+1, \ldots, k\}; \forall E \subseteq [n], |E| \leq \lambda.$$

3.1 Construction of Generator Matrix

Establishing a certain coding scheme is to construct a corresponding generator matrix. The generator matrix $G_{n\times k}$ of QS-code is written in the following block form.

$$\begin{pmatrix} I_r & 0_{r\times s} \\ \hline & A_{(n-r)\times s} \end{pmatrix}$$

where A is a $(n-r)\times k$ Cauchy matrix whose component (i,j) is of the type $1\backslash(\alpha_i+\beta_j), i\in[n-r], j\in[k]$ and $\alpha_i\neq\beta_j$. Cauchy matrix is a supperrgular matrix [16], where any of its square submatrices is nonsingular. The property of supperrrguar matrix is critical in both MDS and weak security.

The following lemmas assert that a coding scheme based on generator matrix G satisfying satisfies P1 and P2.

Lemma 2. *The first r coded blocks are the original data chunks $F_1, F_2, \ldots, F_r$.*

Proof. Since each vector in first r rows of G is a unit vector, it is clear that, the coded chunk $C_i = F_i, i\in[r]$. □

Lemma 3. *The generator matrix G generates an $[n,k]$ MDS code.*

Proof. According to Lemma 1, we should prove that, every k rows of G are linearly independent. Assume that, l out of k rows are selected in the first r rows, where $0\leq l\leq r$.

Case 1: $l=0$. Since all the k rows are randomly selected from Cauchy matrix A, the corresponding submatrix B is also a Cauchy matrix, then $det(B)\neq 0$. Therefore, these k rows are linearly independent.

Case 2: $l>0$. Since the first l rows of submatrix B are unit vectors, without loss of generality, we perform elementary column operations, and could obtain B' in the following block form.

$$B' = \begin{pmatrix} I_l & 0 \\ - & A' \end{pmatrix}$$

Submatrix A' of Cauchy matrix A is nonsigular, then $det(B')\neq 0$. Thus, $det(B)\neq 0$. Consequently, the generator matrix G generates an $[n,k]$ MDS code. □

3.2 Security Analysis

We now perform the security analysis of our scheme. Since the first r coded blocks are in the original form, and publicly shared in the cloud, the linear combination can be easily deduced by them. Therefore, we should eliminate these blocks and analyze the weak secure property of the remainder coded blocks. Let G' be the submatrix with the last $n-r$ rows and the last s columns of the generator matrix G. Thus, G' generates an $[n-r,s]$ MDS code. Then we need to prove the following lemma.

Lemma 4. *The $[n-r, s]$ code with generator matrix G' is weak security against adversary with strength $\lambda(\lambda < s)$.*

Proof. In this $[n-r, s]$ code, $\mathbf{S} = (F_{r+1}, F_2, \ldots, F_k)^T$ is the corresponding vector of the original file, and $\mathbf{C}' = (C'_{r+1}, \ldots, C'_{n-r})^T$ corresponds to the coded blocks. Let MS present the coded units that the adversary obtains by observing λ storage nodes, where M is a submatrix with any λ row vectors of generator matrix G'. So M is also a Cauchy matrix with size $\lambda \times s$. Then the rank of submatrix M is λ. Moreover, since each vector F_i in S is a random selected uniformly and independently from $\mathbb{F}_q$, it holds that:

$$I(\mathbf{F}_j, \bigcup_{i\in E} C'_i) = 0, \forall j \in \{r+1, \ldots, k\}; \forall E \subseteq [n-r], |E| \leq \lambda.$$

where $I(X, Y)$ is the mutual information between X and Y. Thus

$$H(\mathbf{F}_j | \bigcup_{i\in E} C'_i) = H(\mathbf{F}_j), \forall j \in \{r+1, \ldots, k\}; \forall E \subseteq [n-r], |E| \leq \lambda.$$

□

Theorem 1. *The generator matrix G generates an $[n, k]$ MDS code satisfying both (P1) and (P2).*

Proof. According to Lemmas 2, 3 and 4, the coding scheme satisfying both (P1) and (P2). □

Remark. Due to the structure of Cauchy matrices, the encoding complexity of one vector takes $O(n \log^2 n)$ operations [10]. Identically, decoding of one vector also has the resulting complexity of $O(n \log^2 n)$, as shown in [10]. Since the first r coded blocks are the original data chunks, QS-codes need $(n-r)/n$ operations compared to non-systematic codes based on Cauchy matrix.

Example. Let $k = 6, n = 9, r = 4$, and $q = 11$. Let $\mathbf{f} = (f_1, f_2, \ldots, f_6)^T \in \mathbb{F}_{11}^6$. The following is the generator matrix.

$$G = \begin{pmatrix} 1 & 0 & 0 & 0 & 0 & 0 \\ 0 & 1 & 0 & 0 & 0 & 0 \\ 0 & 0 & 1 & 0 & 0 & 0 \\ 0 & 0 & 0 & 1 & 0 & 0 \\ 2 & 1 & 6 & 3 & 7 & 9 \\ 8 & 6 & 4 & 9 & 5 & 2 \\ 7 & 4 & 3 & 2 & 10 & 8 \\ 10 & 9 & 2 & 7 & 1 & 5 \\ 4 & 5 & 10 & 1 & 9 & 6 \end{pmatrix}$$

This code is designed to be resilient against $n - k = 3$ node failures. According to the generator matrix, it is easy to verify that this $[9, 6]$ code is MDS and the first 4 coded data is in the original from. Consequently, these 4 chunks can be access publicly. Since $s = 2$ an adversary who accesses any one coded block, can get no meaningful information from f_5 and f_6.

Table 1. Test environment

Components	Parameters
CPU	Intel XeonE3v3/3.4 GHZ processors
RAM	DDR3, 8 GB
OS	Ubuntu 16.04
Hard disk	WDC, 500G, 7200 rpm
Network	1 Gbps

4 Evaluation

Data upload and download are basic operations in cloud storage systems. To meet system reliability and privacy protection, data to be uploaded need to be encoded or encrypted firstly. Corresponding decode and decryption occurs after the download. Since our motivation lies in encrypting the data blocks selectively, the focus of the experiment is to examine the encoding and decoding time of QS-code and the private data selected. The encoding/decoding time was obtained by averaging 30 trials. Our test environment is shown in Table 1:

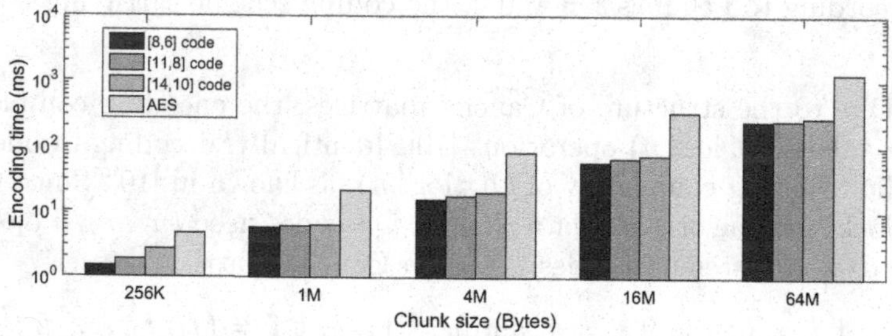

Fig. 2. Encoding time of 2 privacy-protected data blocks

In the experiment evaluation, Advanced Encryption Standard(AES) encryption in CBC mode from Openssl library at version 1.1.1 was used. We chose [8,6], [11,8] and [14,10] codes with redundancy of 2, 3 and 4, respectively. The number of corresponding protected data blocks were 2 and 3, respectively. In the experiment, selected data blocks were 256 kB, 1M, 4M, 8M and 64M in size. Figures 2 and 3 show the decoding time of each code and the encrypted time in the privacy-protected data blocks (number of data blocks equals 2 and 3 respectively). From Figs. 2 and 3, it can be seen that the encoding time and encryption time increase linearly with redundancy and the data blocks. Since the encoding process is a linear operation in a finite field, the total time for encoding and generating redundant information for privacy-protected data blocks is much less than the encryption time. For a 4M data block, the encoding time of different codes is about 15–120 ms, but the encryption time needs about 80–120 ms.

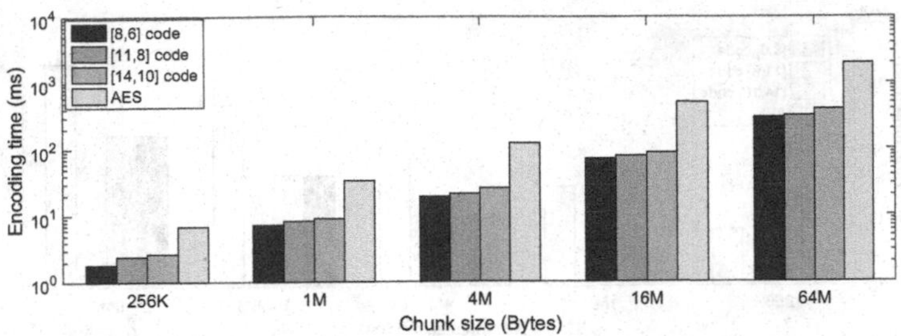

Fig. 3. Encoding time of 3 privacy-protected data blocks

Figures 4 and 5 show the decoding time of each code and the decryption time in the privacy-protected data blocks (number of data blocks equals 2 and 3 respectively). From Figs. 4 and 5, it can be seen that the decryption time also positively correlating with the number of data blocks. Given the fact that QS-code contains part of the original data, the decoding time mainly deals with the calculation of privacy-protecting data blocks. Therefore, the decoding time remains roughly intact when dealing with equal number of data blocks. For a 4M-size data block, the encoding time of different codes is about 7 ms and 10 ms, but the encryption time needs about 80–120 ms.

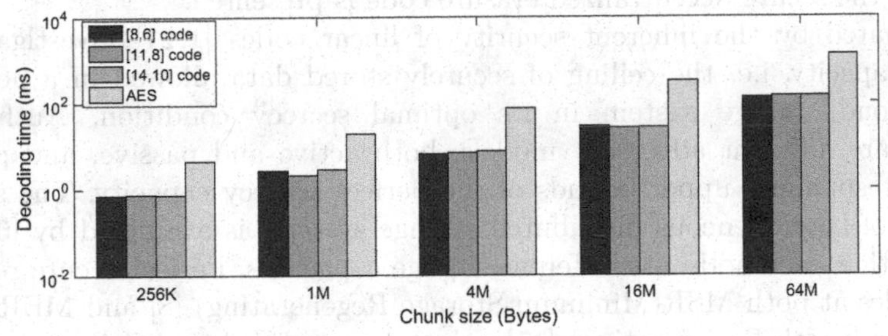

Fig. 4. Decoding time of 2 privacy-protected data blocks

In short, regardless of encoding and decoding, the computation speed presented here is far more efficient than the encryption and decryption algorithm. Although QS coding only implements weak security compared to AES encryption, in certain application environments (e.g. the strength of the adversary is limited below a specified threshold), QS-code enables a more efficient data access.

5 Related Work

Encrypting the whole file stored in the cloud is a straightforward solution for securing privacy-sensitive information, but for data-intensive applications, the

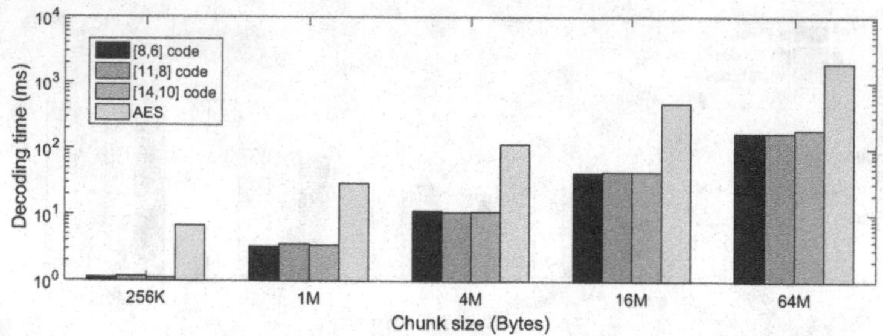

Fig. 5. Decoding time of 3 privacy-protected data blocks

cost spent in en/decrypting the files repeatedly is generally not affordable. To lower the privacy-preserving cost while satisfying the data holders privacy demands, a novel upper bound privacy leakage constraint-based approach is provided by [22,23]. It reduces the amount of encrypted data sets by differentiating the intermediate data sets that need to be encrypted from those that need not. With the aim of reinforcing privacy and reliability, Lin et al. [11] construct a secure decentralized erasure code, combining encryption with erasure code. During encoding, the linear operation is replaced by modular multiplications, yielding a more efficient decryption process before decoding in the retrieval of the original file. In a more recent work by [12], a secure data forwarding scheme based on the secure decentralized erasure code is presented.

Motivated by the inherent security of linear codes [1,21] investigate the secrecy capacity, i.e. the ceiling of securely stored data allowed in a network-coded cloud storage system in its optimal secrecy condition. Authors in [14]compare different adversary models, both active and passive, and provide their corresponding upper bounds of the perfect secrecy capacity. The secrecy capacity of heterogeneous distributed storage systems is examined by [6], who consider that each node has different storage capacities. Perfect secure regenerating codes at both MSR(Minimum Storage Regenerating) [8] and MBR (Minimum Bandwidth Regenerating) [15] points are proposed in distributed storage systems. Similarly, MSR [9] and MBR [4] codes on weak security are studied recently. Dau et al. [5] present a p-decodable μ-secure erasure coding scheme, which satisfies partially decodability and MDS property. Such code scheme can achieve perfect secrecy with threshold and weak secrecy with threshold from μ to $\mu + p$. Besides, weak security codes have been also adopted to address other problems, such as indexing coding [3] and cooperating data exchange [20].

6 Conclusions

A Quasi-systematic erasure code, referred to as QS-code, is presented in this paper. In the proposed scheme, two different data blocks are identified in the original file. The originality of one of them is maintained faithfully and the security of the other is preserved by applying a weak security mechanism. The binary operation enables a more efficient data access and protects the privacy of sensitive information. An enhanced data stability is also observed. Given these merits, it is argued that the present scheme is potentially applicable in cloud storage in general.

Acknowledgments. Our research is supported in part by the National Natural Science Foundation of China under Grants 61502189, and the National Key Research and Development Program of China (No. 2016YFB0800402).

References

1. Adeli, M., Liu, H.: On the inherent security of linear network coding. IEEE Commun. Lett. **17**(8), 1668–1671 (2013)
2. Bhattad, K.: Weakly secure network coding. In: The Workshop on Network Coding, pp. 281–285 (2005)
3. Dau, S.H., Skachek, V., Chee, Y.M.: On the security of index coding with side information. IEEE Trans. Inf. Theory **58**(6), 3975–3988 (2012)
4. Dau, S.H., Song, W., Yuen, C.: On block security of regenerating codes at the MBR point for distributed storage systems. In: IEEE International Symposium on Information Theory, pp. 1967–1971 (2014)
5. Dau, S.H., Song, W., Yuen, C.: Secure erasure codes with partial decodability. In: IEEE International Conference on Communications, pp. 388–394 (2014)
6. Ernvall, T., Rouayheb, S.E., Hollanti, C., Poor, H.V.: Capacity and security of heterogeneous distributed storage systems. IEEE J. Sel. Areas Commun. **31**(12), 2701–2709 (2013)
7. Hu, P., Sung, C.W., Ho, S., Chan, T.H.: Optimal coding and allocation for perfect secrecy in multiple clouds. IEEE Trans. Inf. Forensics Secur. **11**(2), 388–399 (2016)
8. Huang, K., Parampalli, U., Xian, M.: On secrecy capacity of minimum storage regenerating codes. IEEE Trans. Inf. Theory **PP**(99), 1 (2015)
9. Kadhe, S., Sprintson, A.: Universally weakly secure coset coding schemes for minimum storage regenerating (MSR) codes. arXiv preprint arXiv:1710.06753 (2017)
10. Lacan, J., Fimes, J.: Systematic mds erasure codes based on vandermonde matrices. IEEE Commun. Lett. **8**(9), 570–572 (2004)
11. Lin, H.Y., Tzeng, W.G.: A secure decentralized erasure code for distributed networked storage. IEEE Trans. Parallel Distrib. Syst. **21**(11), 1586–1594 (2010)
12. Lin, H.Y., Tzeng, W.G.: A secure erasure code-based cloud storage system with secure data forwarding. IEEE Trans. Parallel Distrib. Syst. **23**(6), 995–1003 (2012)
13. Macwilliams, F.J., Sloane, N.J.A.: The Theory of Error-correcting Codes. North-Holland (1977)
14. Pawar, S., Rouayheb, S.E., Ramchandran, K.: Securing dynamic distributed storage systems against eavesdropping and adversarial attacks. IEEE Trans. Inf. Theory **57**(10), 6734–6753 (2011)
15. Rashmi, K.V., Shah, N.B., Ramchandran, K., Kumar, P.V.: Information-theoretically secure erasure codes for distributed storage. IEEE Trans. Inf. Theory **64**(3), 1621–1646 (2018)
16. Roth, R.M., Lempel, A.: On mds codes via cauchy matrices. IEEE Trans. Inf. Theory **35**(6), 1314–1319 (1989)
17. Shannon, C.E.: Communication theory of secrecy systems. Bell Labs Tech. J. **28**(4), 656–715 (1949)

18. Silva, D., Kschischang, F.R.: Universal weakly secure network coding. In: IEEE Information Theory Workshop on Networking and information theory, ITW 2009, pp. 281–285 (2009)
19. Tang, H., Liu, F., Shen, G., Jin, Y., Guo, C.: UniDrive: synergize multiple consumer cloud storage services. In: Middleware Conference, pp. 137–148 (2015)
20. Yan, M., Sprintson, A., Zelenko, I.: Weakly secure data exchange with generalized reed solomon codes. In: IEEE International Symposium on Information Theory, pp. 1366–1370 (2014)
21. Zhang, P., Jiang, Y., Lin, C., Fan, Y., Shen, X.: P-coding: secure network coding against eavesdropping attacks. In: Conference on Information Communications, pp. 2249–2257 (2010)
22. Zhang, X., Liu, C., Nepal, S., Chen, J.: An efficient quasi-identifier index based approach for privacy preservation over incremental data sets on cloud. J. Comput. Syst. Sci. **79**(5), 542–555 (2013)
23. Zhang, X., Liu, C., Nepal, S., Pandey, S., Chen, J.: A privacy leakage upper bound constraint-based approach for cost-effective privacy preserving of intermediate data sets in cloud. IEEE Trans. Parallel Distrib. Syst. **24**(6), 1192–1202 (2013)

Research and Application of Traceability Model for Agricultural Products

Xiaotong Wu[1], Pingzeng Liu[1(✉)], Jianrui Ding[2], Changqing Song[3], Bangguo Li[1], and Xueru Yu[1]

[1] Shandong Agricultural University, Tai'an 271018, China
lpz8565@126.com
[2] Department of Computer Science, Utah State University, Logan, USA
[3] Agricultural Big-data Engineering Laboratory of Shandong Province, Tai'an 271018, China

Abstract. Aiming at the problem of strong decentralization, poor compatibility and low sharing in the traceability system of domestic agricultural products, combined with the industrial chain of agricultural products, three general traceability models of agricultural products were proposed and established. Through the research of the model, it is concluded that the establishment of the traceability information flow model of agricultural products ensures seamless connection of all links in the agricultural product chain, and facilitates the traceability of agricultural products smoothly. The information sharing model of the traceability information of agricultural products improves the sharing of traceability information and is beneficial to the establishment of a comprehensive traceability system. The traceability function model of agricultural products provides a more general model for the traceability system. The validity of the model was proved by applying the model to the traceability system of winter jujube, providing a theoretical basis and a feasible solution for the construction of agricultural products.

Keywords: Traceability model · Industry chain · Information sharing Traceability system

1 Introduction

In recent years, the quality of life and food safety awareness of Chinese residents has been improving. The consumption demand for agricultural products has been rising. With the increase of consumption space, the quality and safety of agricultural products is becoming more and more prominent, which has aroused great concern from the government and consumers. Therefore, the voice of the traceability system established and implemented in our country is getting higher and higher. The relevant laws and regulations and documents all clearly propose the construction of traceability systems for the promotion of the quality of agricultural products. The establishment of a traceability system for agricultural products provides a guarantee of the quality and safety of agricultural products, which not only meets consumers' demand for

X. Sun et al. (Eds.): ICCCS 2018, LNCS 11065, pp. 217–226, 2018.
https://doi.org/10.1007/978-3-030-00012-7_20

traceability of agricultural products, but also improves the level of information and competitiveness of agricultural products in China [1, 2].

Foreign countries have done relatively well in the traceability of agricultural products. Many countries are actively building agricultural products/food traceability systems. The European Union is an important force in promoting the traceability system. Because the European Union has a good effect in controlling the quality of agricultural products, traceability system of agricultural products has been widely recognized and promoted by many countries. For example, both the United States and Canada are active practitioners of the traceability system and strive to promote the construction of the traceability system. Countries such as Brazil, Chile, and other large agricultural countries, as well as South Africa and other African countries, also have reports of promoting the traceability system of agricultural products. In addition, the Global Standards 1, the International Codex Alimentarius Commission, the International Standards Organization and other international organizations have developed relevant standards and implementation manuals, aiming at promoting the global food, agricultural products and commodity traceability system [3–8].

Compared with foreign countries, the research on the traceability of agricultural products is relatively late in China, and the construction of the traceability system of agricultural products is in its infancy, although the traceability systems of various regions, industries, and types continue to emerge in an endless stream, the research on the versatility of traceability systems mainly focuses on traceability coding, product identification, and information collection, etc., less research on the research of general models and the representation of traceability methods. Therefore, most of the traceability systems in the current construction lack a general model, and it is difficult to achieve mutual compatibility and information sharing among multiple traceability systems. Within the system, it is difficult to achieve rapid expansion and timely traceability when the agricultural industry chain and distribution channels change, which directly leads to the high construction cost of traceability systems, narrow application scope, inflexible use methods, and the "Isolated Information Island" problem in traceability field [9–13]. Therefore, from the perspective of the industrial chain of agricultural products, this article further abstracts and formalizes the traceability system, focusing on the main links and traceability methods of the agricultural product industry chain. The agricultural product traceability information flow model, the traceability information sharing model of agricultural products and the traceability function model of agricultural products were put forward, which solved the problems of strong dispersion in the industry chain, poor compatibility between the systems, difficult information sharing, and inconsistent source tracing methods. It ensures the effectiveness of traceability system and traceability information, and establishes a more general traceability model for the traceability system of agricultural products, which lays the foundation for the future construction of traceability system of general agricultural products.

2 Hypothesis

To design a traceability system for agricultural products, we first need to determine a traceability information flow model, through the information flow model, the traceability system of agricultural products runs through the entire agricultural product industry chain, and the key information such as planting, processing, and sales of the industrial chain is properly identified, recorded, transmitted, and monitored. Secondly, through the establishment of information sharing model, the traceability system of multiple industries and regions can be combined to achieve traceability information sharing, and strengthen the links and cooperation between related enterprises. The function model enables the system to track, trace and early warning, and effectively control the product. In terms of hindsight control, it could quickly identify and control the links of problems, and recycle agricultural products that are harmful and not yet consumed, so as to achieve the purpose of eliminating hazards and reducing losses [14], realize the risk management of the whole industry chain and reflect the significance of the traceability of agricultural products.

3 Establishment

3.1 Information Flow Model

The link between the various links of the traditional agricultural chain of our country is not close, and the government departments lack effective supervision on such industrial chain. Some agricultural products have serious safety problems when they are produced. However, due to the strong dispersion, regulatory difficulties make it difficult to find such problems. The problems that arise in the circulation process are also difficult to detect because of this dispersity. These are not conducive to agricultural products traceability, hinder the effective management of agricultural products.

In view of the above problems, a relatively comprehensive model of agricultural product information flow must be established to achieve the quality of agricultural products, through close links with planting, logistics, sales and other links, the complex production process can be linked together, facilitating the transmission of product information flow, and also facilitating the seamless connection of all links in the industrial chain, ensure the smooth progress of the industry chain and reverse traceability, general agricultural product traceability information flow model, as shown in Fig. 1.

In the model, the information transmission of the industrial chain is achieved by tracing the source code, for example, in the planting link, enterprises and plots information and planting information are added to the initial tracing source code, and the traceability code attached to the product is passed to the picking link through the transmission of product flow, in the picking process, the picking information is added to the source code, and the source code is passed to the next link. By analogy, the seamless link of the industrial chain is achieved.

It can be seen from the model that agricultural products from farmland to dining table undergo a series of complex processes, such as planting, picking, testing,

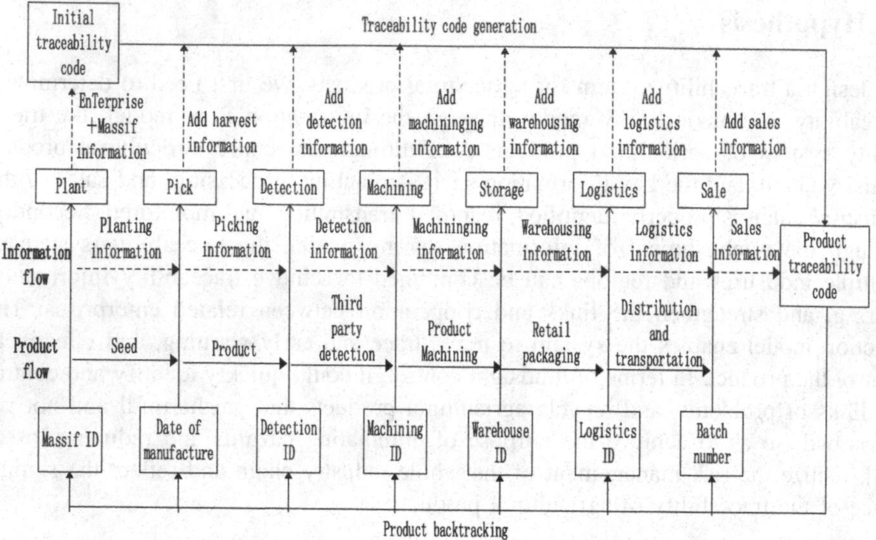

Fig. 1. Information flow model of agricultural product traceability.

processing, warehousing, logistics and sales, and have experienced different circulation entities such as farms, farmers markets, supermarkets, consumers and so on, the system uses product codes as the source code of agricultural products for identification. Through establishing links between various labels, all relevant information on agricultural products from planting to sales can be retrieved through the source code traceability, so as to achieve true traceability.

3.2 Information Sharing Model

At present, our country pays more and more attention to the traceability of agricultural products. The traceability system of agricultural products is also considered to be one of the effective means to control and manage the safety of agricultural products. Many related industries and departments are also actively investing in traceability work to separately implement safety traceability of agricultural products and establish independent databases and information query platforms. However, due to the lack of a globally-unified identity system, databases of various industries and departments are incompatible and inconsistent, forming an information "island". It can be seen that the exchange and cooperation in the current quality and safety information of agricultural products is far from enough, and it is difficult to meet the requirements for the implementation of traceability systems for agricultural products. Therefore, strengthening information exchange, cooperation and sharing, and forming the information sharing system of agricultural products quality and safety as soon as possible, which is shared, coordinated, unified and consistent in the whole city and across the country, is an urgent problem to solve, Fig. 2 is the information sharing model of the traceability of agricultural products.

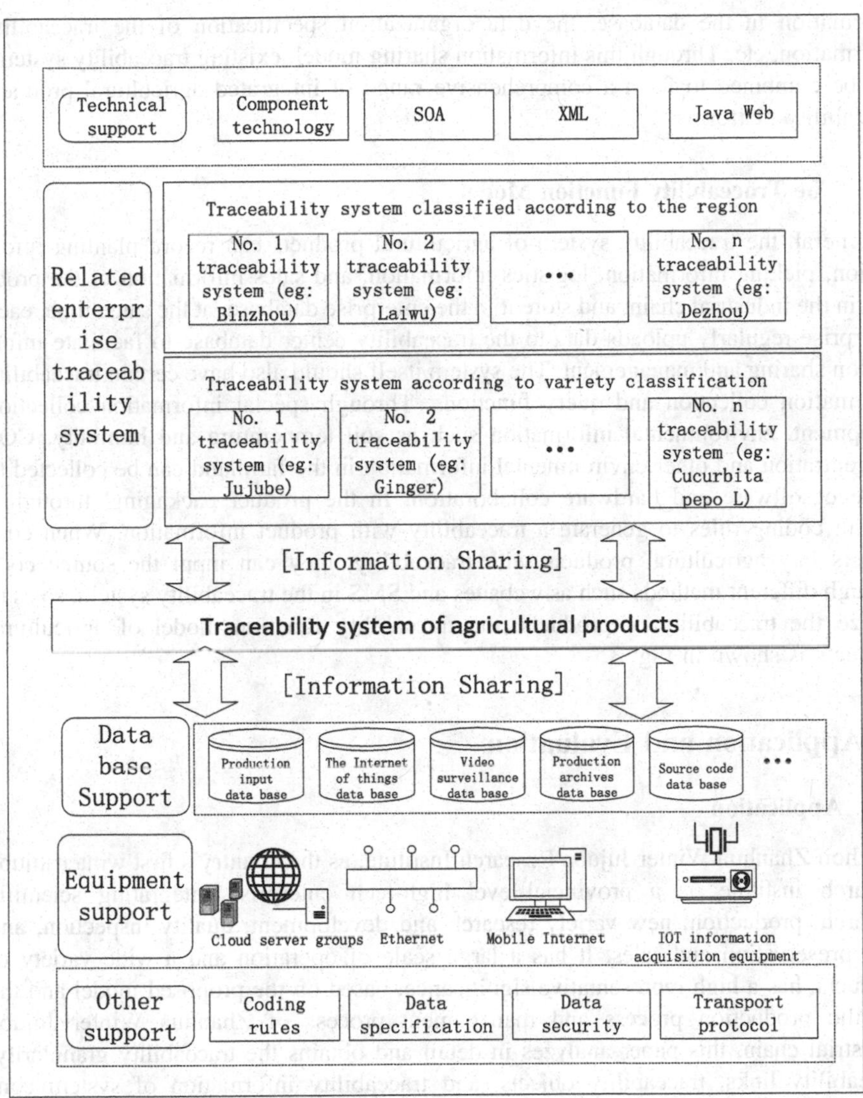

Fig. 2. Information sharing model of agricultural products traceability.

The shared model is based on the traceability system and is supported by component technologies such as SOA and XML, upload the traceability information in the database to the central database through devices such as cloud server groups, allow traceability information from relevant areas of other regions and other industries, to achieve the purpose of information sharing. The model not only combines all kinds of advanced software design patterns and design ideas, and new data exchange methods and services, but also puts forward other support to achieve traceability of agricultural products, such as the coding rules of the source code, the access rules of the traceability information in the database, the data organization specification of the traceability information, etc. Through this information sharing model, existing traceability systems can be combined to form a comprehensive range of integrated agricultural products traceability platforms.

3.3 The Traceability Function Model

In general, the traceability system of agricultural products can record planting information, picking information, logistics information, and sales information of the products in the industrial chain, and store it in the enterprise database, at the same time, each enterprise regularly uploads data to the traceability center database to facilitate information sharing and management. The system itself should also have certain traceability information collection and query functions. Through special information collection equipment, environmental information such as soil temperature and humidity, CO2 concentration and other environmental information in the farmland can be collected to achieve software and hardware collaboration. In the product packaging, through a certain coding rules to generate a traceability with product information. When consumers buy agricultural products with traceability, they can input the source code through different methods such as websites and SMS in the traceability system, so as to realize the traceability of products, the traceability function model of agricultural products is shown in Fig. 3.

4 Application and Evaluation

4.1 Application

Binzhou Zhanhua Winter Jujube Research Institute, as the country's first winter jujube research institute, is a provincial-level high-tech enterprise integrating scientific research, production, new variety research and development, quality inspection, and fruit preservation and sales. It has a large scale of operation and a wide variety of products, has a high representative significance. based on the proposed model and the specific production process and management process of Zhanhua Winter Jujube industrial chain, this paper analyzes in detail and obtains the traceability granularity, traceability links, traceability objects, and traceability information of system construction, and establishes supporting information collection equipment and traceability management system. The system optimizes the entire product chain process of the product, ensures the authenticity of the traceable information and the reliability of transmission, satisfies the consumers with a reliable understanding of the whole process of product information, and improves the management ability and competitiveness of the enterprise, an empirical test of the model proposed in this paper is made, and the system screenshot is shown as shown in Fig. 4.

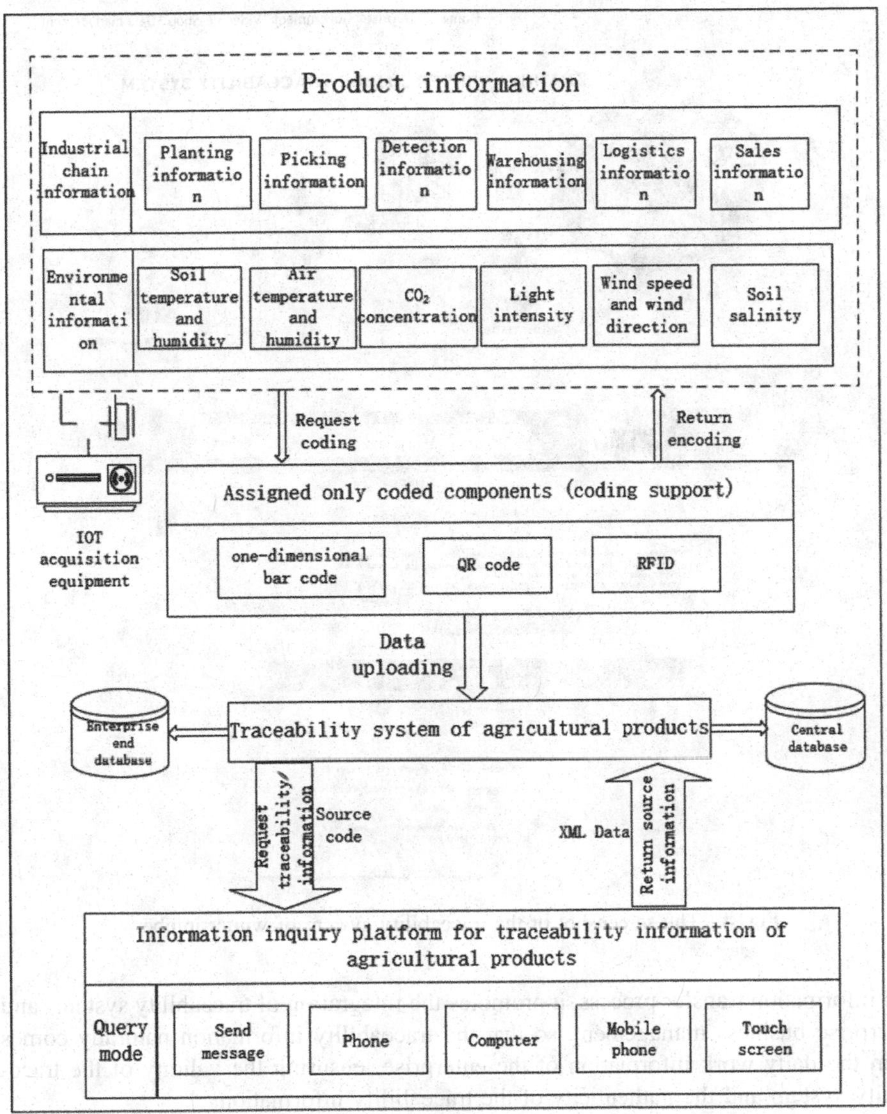

Fig. 3. The traceability function model of agricultural products.

4.2 Significance

(1) Ensure the validity of the traceability system and the authenticity of the traceability information

The three traceability models proposed in this paper simplify the development process, lock the research content of developers to the traceability links, granularity, and information, and realize the close integration of the model with the business logic

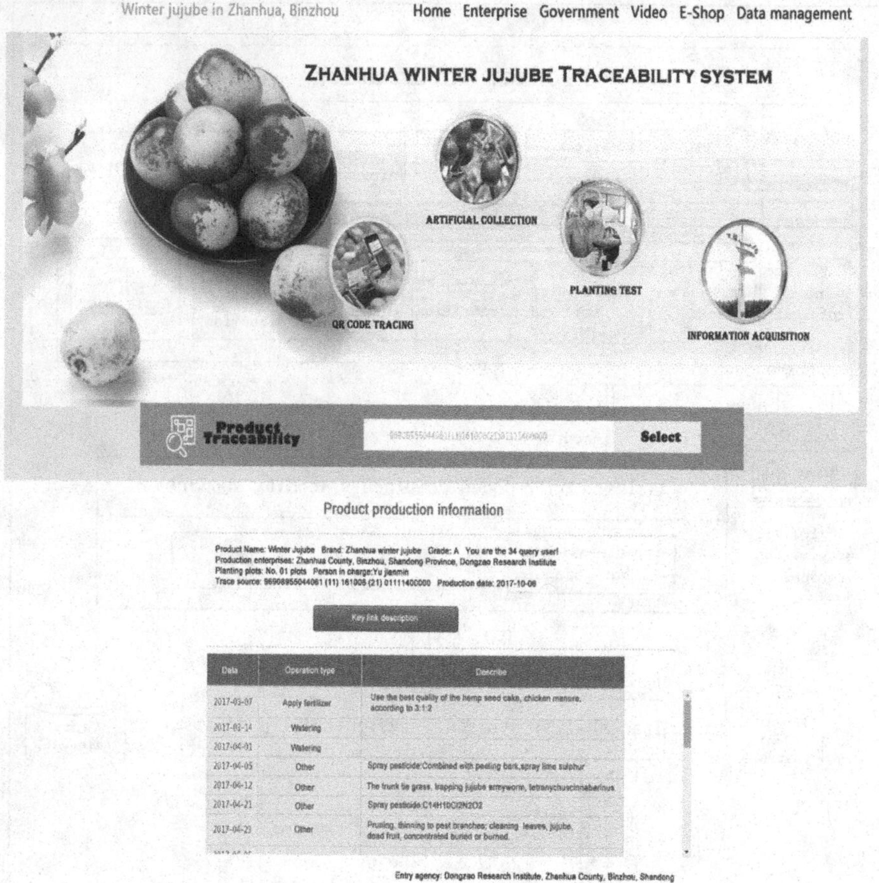

Fig. 4. The screenshot of the traceability system of winter jujube.

and information transfer process, it promotes the integration of traceability systems and enterprise business management, so that the traceability information naturally comes from the daily work information of the enterprise, ensuring the validity of the traceability system and the authenticity of the traceability information.

(2) To realize the exploration of the theoretical and partial standardization of the traceability system

The traceability system based on the traceability model has a more rigorous theoretical basis than the traceability system, and is the inevitable trend of the development of the traceability system. At the same time, the exploration of traceability representation theory will provide the basis for traceability best practices and traceability standardization, which will better promote the healthy development of traceability systems and promote the standardization process of traceability construction.

(3) Improve R&D efficiency of traceability systems and reduce R&D risk

The core implementation of the traceability model has a wide range of compatibility and versatility, which greatly reduces the technical difficulties and software design and implementation difficulties of the new traceability system R&D, on the other hand, the core of a stable and reliable traceability system also reduces the cost of software testing. It reduces costs during the entire process of software development and testing, improves work efficiency, and reduces system risk.

(4) Improve the versatility of traceability system peripheral software systems

The unified product information traceability method avoids the need to separately develop web and mobile client programs in previous traceability programs. With a stable data structure, various types of clients can basically become common clients, improving the versatility of peripheral software systems.

4.3 Deficiency

(1) In the practical application process of the traceability information flow model proposed in this paper, it is difficult for different enterprises to achieve a perfect fit. It is necessary to make some changes to the model to meet the actual needs of different industries.
(2) The traceability information sharing model may have issues such as inconsistent product identification and inconsistent information transparency in the actual application process. Therefore, it is necessary to put forward a set of relatively uniform operating and system construction specifications.
(3) In the traceability function model, this article does not provide in-depth description and research on the combination of information acquisition equipment and software, item coding rules, and information recording standards, this is also a question that needs further study.

5 Summary

The development status of traceability system of agricultural products at home and abroad is summarized in this paper. Aiming at the problems of poor compatibility, low sharing and "isolated islands" of traceability system in China, a design idea suitable for traceability and traceability of agricultural products is put forward.

(1) In view of the problem of strong dispersion of domestic traceability systems, the design idea of the traceability information model of agricultural products was proposed, and the links of the industrial chain were linked to ensure the smooth progress of the traceability of agricultural products.
(2) Aiming at the current situation of the construction and application of agricultural products traceability system and their independent information sharing, a traceability information sharing model of agricultural products is designed, which lays the foundation for forming a large-scale comprehensive traceability platform.

(3) Analyzed and described the functions of traceability system, including production process record, information collection and management, software and hardware cooperation, coding rule, bar code printing, tracing information query, data upload and feedback, data statistics and so on, the design idea of a more general agricultural product traceability function model has been put forward, which has perfected the shortage of domestic agricultural products traceability function.

Acknowledgements. This work was financially supported by The Yellow River Delta (Binzhou) National Agricultural Science and Technology Park.

References

1. Bai, H.W., Sun, C.H., Weirong, D., et al.: Research progress on traceability system of agricultural products. Jiangsu Agric. Sci. **41**(4), 1–4 (2013). https://doi.org/10.15889/j.issn.1002-1302.2013.04.050
2. Yang, X.T., Qian, J.P., Sun, C.H., et al.: Design and application of safe production and quality traceability system for vegetable. Trans. CSAE **24**(3), 162–166 (2008)
3. Wang, D.T., Rao, X.Q., Ying, Y.B.: Development of agri-products traceability in main developed agriculture region of the world. Trans. Chin. Soc. Agric. Eng. **30**(8), 236–250 (2014). https://doi.org/10.3969/j.issn.1002-6819.2014.08.028
4. Schwägele, F.: Traceability from a European perspective. Meat Sci. **71**(1), 164–173 (2005)
5. Smith, G.C., Tatum, J.D., Belk, K.E., et al.: Traceability from a US perspective. Meat Sci. **71**(1), 174 (2005)
6. Meisinger, J.L., Pendell, D.L., Morris, D.L., et al.: REVIEW: swine traceability systems in selected countries outside of North America. Prof. Anim. Sci. **24**(4), 295–301 (2008)
7. Viana, J.G.A., Cartes, G.S., Fornazier, A., et al.: Perception of producers facing the bovine traceability: comparative study between Brazil and Chile. Arch. De Zootecnia. **60**(231), 825–828 (2011)
8. Zheng, H.G.: Study on food safety traceability system. Chinese Academy of Agricultural Sciences, Beijing (2012). https://doi.org/10.13304/j.nykjdb.2015.265
9. Zhang, Y.F., Liu, P.Z., Ma, H.J., et al.: Study of flexible traceability model for agricultural industry chain. Agric. Netw. Inf. **4**, 46–51 (2014)
10. Cao, Q.Q.: Research and application of vegetable quality safety prediction and traceability model based on support vector machine. South China University of Technology (2014)
11. Huang, X.: Design and implementation of agricultural product traceability model based on electronic transaction. Northeast Agricultural University (2009)
12. Pu, Y.X.: Research and implementation of encoding technology for traceability system of fruit and vegetable products based on internet of things. Jiangsu Agric. Sci. **44**(08), 414–418 (2016). https://doi.org/10.15889/j.issn.1002-1302.2016.08.120
13. Yang, X.T., Qian, J.P., Sun, C.H., et al.: Key technologies for establishment agricultural products and food quality safety traceability systems. Trans. Chin. Soc. Agric. Mach. **45**(11), 212–222 (2014). https://doi.org/10.6041/j.issn.1000-1298.2014.11.033
14. Bi, X.: Agricultural product quality tracing system model and its application. Tianjin University (2014)

Research on Risk Aversion Enterprise Financial Crisis Warning Based on Support Vector Data Description

Xiang Yu[1(✉)], Shuang Chen[3], Yanbo Li[1], Hui Lu[2(✉)], and Le Wang[2]

[1] College of Computer Science and Technology, Heilongjiang Institute of Technology, Harbin 150050, China
1267013@qq.com, liyanbo210@126.com

[2] Cyberspace Institute of Advanced Technology, Guangzhou University, Guangzhou 510006, China
{luhui,wangle}@gzhu.edu.cn

[3] School of Economics and Management, Heilongjiang Nongken Vocational College, Harbin 150050, China

Abstract. Enterprise financial crisis warning is on the basis of the existing financial index to construct and run mathematical model to predict the possibility of enterprise financial crisis. Due Based on reviewing research situation of enterprise financial crisis warning both domestic and foreign, a new financial crisis warning model based on support vector data description for risk aversion enterprise is proposed which aims at the ignorance of loss differences caused by model errors from the angle of the usage of financial crisis model by the manager of risk aversion enterprises. The theoretical analysis and empirical study show that the proposed model can reduce the second class of financial crisis warning model errors.

Keywords: Financial crisis warning · Support vector · Data description
Index system

1 Introduction

When an enterprise loses the ability of paying expired debt, it means that the enterprise has fallen into a financial crisis, which is also called financial failure or financial difficulty. The appearance of financial crisis will greatly influence the commercial credit of the enterprise and incorrect measures which are taken by the enterprise might lead to bankruptcy. Thus, it is necessary to research on the model of enterprise financial crisis deeply and further to distinguish the possibility of financial crisis with precaution model, then we can not only get the corresponding countermeasures of controlling financial crisis for enterprise, but also improve the level of controlling risk and operating performance of the enterprises.

X. Sun et al. (Eds.): ICCCS 2018, LNCS 11065, pp. 227–233, 2018.
https://doi.org/10.1007/978-3-030-00012-7_21

2 Relevant Research Summary

In 1966, American professor Beaver from Stanford University first predict enterprise financial crisis with single financial index. In the process of building financial crisis predict model with single index, seventy-nine operating failed enterprises and seventy-nine normal operating enterprises are first selected, and the warning model are built based on five financial indexes for empirical research. The results finally shows that the predict results of warning model which is built on cash flow/total debts index are better than the results from other warning model. The advantages of financial crisis warning model with single index is easy to build model, however, there also has the problem that conflicts do exist between the results from different warning model built with different financial indexes. In order to solve such problem, professor Altman tried to reflect enterprise financial situations comprehensively by linearly combining a set of financial indexes, based on this, Z-score model, the famous financial crisis precaution model with multiple variables is proposed [1]. Since multiple financial indexes are comprehensively considered at precaution stage, the predict accuracy of Z-score model is higher than the precaution model with single variable, unfortunately, the precaution results are still seriously influenced by thresholds.

The research on enterprise financial crisis precaution starts later in China, in 2001, scholar Shinong Wu carry on his financial crisis precaution research on Fisher linear discriminant analysis method and multivariate linear regression analysis method and logistic regression analysis respectively, and the results show that the accuracy of logistic regression analysis model is the highest.

With the continuous development of artificial intelligence and machine learning technology, some scholars construct financial crisis precaution model with support vector machine, decision tree and BP neural network which show good precaution results. In 2007, by comparing the results of various intelligent decision methods applied to the enterprise financial crisis precaution, Sun Jie found that support vector machine method have good fitting ability, generalization ability and model stability, and support vector machine method can get the best balance of the three aspects [2].

However, an important question which is ignored in the researches mentioned above is that the accuracy of all financial crisis precaution models cannot reach 100% when precaution enterprise crisis. If errors exist, the first kind of error is to predict the enterprises whose finances are normal into the enterprises with financial crisis, which is called the first kind of precaution model error. Another kind of error is to predict the financial crisis enterprises into normal enterprises, which is called the second kind of precaution model error. The loss caused by the two kinds of errors are totally different, the latter will cause more damage obviously. Thus, as the manager of risk aversion enterprise, when there are errors exist in financial crisis precaution model, they would rather deal with the second kind of precaution model error. Most of the precaution models proposed by scholars before are based on the purpose of finding the prediction with the highest accuracy, and these kinds of models cannot meet the requirements of the managers of risk aversion enterprises. To solve the problems above, a risk aversion financial crisis precaution model based on support vector data description is proposed.

3 Support Vector Data Description

The method of support vector description construct model with classified hyperplane by using data from single class or unbalanced data form two classes [3, 4], it construct a hypersphere as classified hyperplane. As shown in Fig. 1, symbol circle represents target data, symbol star represents the others, the goal of support vector data description algorithm is to surround all target data with the smallest hypersphere which is far away from the other data as much as it can. It can be described by mathematics formula as follows:

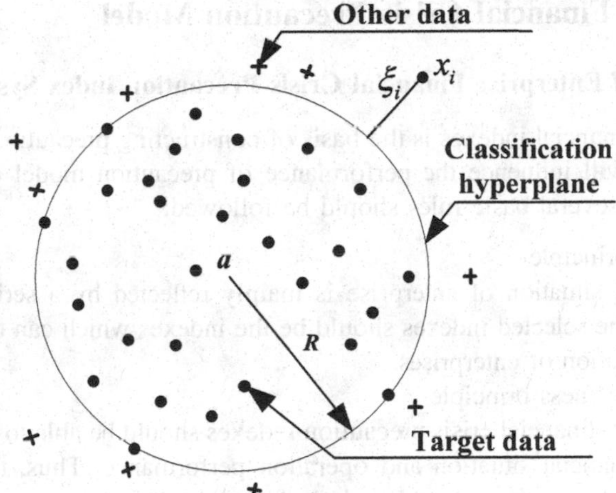

Fig. 1. The diagram of support vector data description

$$\begin{cases} \min \quad R^2 + C\sum_{i}^{n} \xi_i \\ s.t. \quad \|K(x_i) - a\|^2 \le R^2 + \xi_i \\ \qquad \xi_i \ge 0,\ i = 1, \cdots, n \end{cases}$$

In the mathematics formula, x_i denotes arbitrary target data, a denotes the center of the hypersphere, and ξ_i denotes the slack variable of x_i. When data x_i lies out of the hypersphere, $\xi_i > 0$, otherwise $\xi_i = 0$. $K(\bullet)$ denotes the core function, C denotes the penalty coefficient, and the dual problem above is:

$$\max \quad \sum_{i}^{n} \alpha_i K(x_i, x_i) - \sum_{i=1}^{n} \sum_{j=1}^{n} \alpha_i \alpha_j K(x_i, x_j)$$

$$s.t. \quad \begin{cases} \sum_{i}^{n} \alpha_i = 1 \\ 0 \le \alpha_i \le C \end{cases}$$

The final classification function is obtained by solving the equation:

$$f(x) = K(x,x) - 2 \sum_{i}^{n} \alpha_i K(x_i, x) + \sum_{i=1}^{n} \sum_{j=1}^{n} \alpha_i \alpha_j K(x_i, x_j)$$

4 Enterprise Financial Crisis Precaution Model

4.1 Selection of Enterprise Financial Crisis Precaution Index System

The selection of financial indexes is the basis of constructing precaution model whose selecting results will influence the performance of precaution model directly. When selecting indexes several basic rules should be followed:

(1) Objectivity principle
The business situation of enterprise is mainly reflected by a series of financial indexes, so the selected indexes should be the indexes which can truly reflect the financial situation of enterprises.
(2) Comprehensiveness principle
The enterprise financial crisis precaution indexes should be able to fully reflect all aspects of financial situation and operation performance. Thus, the constructed evaluation index system should include four important aspects, solvency, profitability, operation ability and development ability.
(3) Significance principle
The selection of enterprise financial crisis precaution indexes should be able to reveal and maximize the differences between the enterprises with normal financial condition and those with abnormal financial condition. Those similar indexes or indexes with similar index values and has less impact on financial condition can be ignored appropriately, in order to reduce the redundancy indexes.
According to the three principle of constructing financial crisis precaution system and the relevant research literature at home and abroad, four aspects, involving the ability of solvency, profitability, operation and development, are adopted to select the financial crisis precaution indexes of enterprises in our country, as shown in Table 1 [5].

Table 1. Enterprise financial crisis precaution indexes system

Enterprise financial crisis precaution indexes system	Principle	Index	Calculation formula
	Ability of solvency	Flow ratio	Current assets/current liabilities
		Quick ratio	(Current assets - inventory)/current liabilities
		Asset-liability ratio	Total assets/liabilities
	Ability of profitability	Net profit margin on sales	Net profit/main business income
		Net interest rates	Net profit/total assets
		Main business profit margin	Main business profit/main business income
	Ability of operation	Inventory turnover ratio	Main business cost/average inventory
		Accounts receivable turnover ratio	Main business income/average accounts receivable
		Total assets turnover rate	Main business income/average total assets
	Ability of development	Net profit growth rate	Final net profit/net profit of the same period last year-1
		Main business revenue growth rate	Final main business income/main business income of the same period last year-1
		Total asset growth	Final total assets/total assets over the same period last year-1

4.2 Sample Data Acquisition

Relative research shows that, influenced by industry characteristics, the probability of financial crisis occurring of two enterprises in different industry is different, even their financial indexes data are of the same [6–8], so 447 listed companies in manufacturing industry are selected as the research data in this paper. Since the financial report disclosure time of China's listed companies is the second year, the 2008 annual report data is selected as sample data, which is used to predict the 2010 financial situation of listed manufacturing companies in China, and the ST enterprises are identified as the enterprises in financial crisis, all data are from RESSET database.

4.3 Construction of Precaution Model Based on the Data Description on Support Vector

According to data description of the modeling process of support vector, the core idea of the modeling method is mapping the training data into a high dimensional space by kernel function method [9, 10]. In the high dimensional space, all target data will be involved in a hypersphere with minimum radius, and all non-target data will be excluded out of the hypersphere. Therefore, in this paper, the data of all the normal enterprises are selected as the target data in training support vector data description model, and a minimum of hypersphere containing all the data of normal enterprises. When precaution an enterprise for financial crisis, as long as the enterprise financial index data is excluded out of the hypersphere, the outbreak of the financial crisis can be predicted.

Obviously, the optimal goal of the model is not the precaution accuracy, as long as there exist great difference between the financial indexes data and training precaution model of enterprise waiting to precaution, precaution can be sent out, so the second type of model precaution errors will be reduced to meet the requirements of the manager of risk aversion enterprise.

4.4 Experiments Results Test

The precaution performance of support vector data description method is greatly influenced by the setting of model parameter, when the penalty coefficient C is small, the precaution model generated by training can avoid appearing overfitting phenomenon, but the classifier generated by training will has more samples which are mistaken classified. Due to the precaution model proposed in this paper is mainly to meet the requirements of the managers of risk aversion enterprises, a larger value of $C = 1000$ is set.

In order to verify the precaution performance of model, the financial index data of the 282 normal financial enterprises from the top 300 enterprises are selected as training data, the financial index data from 1 to 300, together with the data from 301 to 447 are selected as test data, the precaution performance are shown in Table 2.

Table 2. Table of precaution performance of precaution model on the test set

Test data set	The first kind of precaution model error rate	The second kind of precaution model error rate	Total precaution error rate
1–300 enterprises	16/282 (5.67%)	1/12 (8.33%)	17/300 (5.66%)
301–447 enterprises	22/136 (16.18%)	1/11 (9.09%)	23/147 (15.65)

Drawn from the precaution results, when the test set consists of the enterprises from 1 to 300, the model has the best performance. The main reason is that the training set and the test set are the same data set, and the precaution model will not have the classification error caused by overfitting, while the second type errors of the precaution model are far less than the first type errors in both two test sets, so the precaution model can meet the requirements of the managers of risk aversion enterprises.

5 Conclusion

To the enterprises in our country, establishing the efficient precaution system of financial crisis timely, forecasting and diagnosing the financial crisis signals accurately and effectively, taking corresponding measures correctly and nipping the financial crisis in the bud, have become an important part of strengthening the enterprise financial management and establishing modern enterprise system. Due to the current financial crisis precaution model does not distinguish the difference between the damages caused by the first and the second type of precaution errors, starting from the perspective of risk aversion, a new kind of enterprise financial crisis precaution modeling method based on support vector data description is proposed, theoretical analysis and experimental results show that this method can effectively reduce the second kind of precaution error, and meet the requirements of the managers of risk aversion enterprises.

Acknowledgment. This work was supported by the National Key research and Development Plan (Grant No. 2018YFB0803504), the National Natural Science Foundation of China under Grant No. 61572153, and the key research topics of economic and social development in Heilongjiang province under Grant No. WY2017048-B.

References

1. Altman, E.: Financial ratios: discriminant analysis and the prediction of corporate bankruptcy. J. Financ. **23**, 589–609 (1986)
2. Jie, S.: Research on intelligent decision making method of enterprise financial crisis precaution. Doctoral Dissertation of Harbin Institute of Technology (2007)
3. Tax, D., Duin, R.: Support vector domain description. Pattern Recognit. Lett. **20**(11–13), 1191–1199 (1999)
4. Shawe-Taylor, J., Cristianini, N.: Kernel Methods for Pattern Analysis. Cambridge University Press, Cambridge (2004)
5. Chandola, V., Banerjee, A., Kumar, V.: Anomaly detection: a survey. ACM Comput. Surv. (CSUR) **41**(3), 15 (2009)
6. Fiolet, V., Toursel, B.: Distributed data mining. Scalable Comput.: Pract. Exp. **6**(1), 99–109 (2005)
7. Perez, M.S., Sanchez, A., Robles, V., et al.: Design and implementation of a data mining grid aware architecture. Futur. Gener. Comput. Syst. **23**(1), 42–47 (2007)
8. Baoan, Y., et al.: The application of BP neural network in enterprise financial crisis precaution. **2**(2), 50–56 (2001)
9. Tax, D.M.J., Duin, R.P.W.: Support vector data description. Mach. Learn. **54**(1), 45–66 (2004)
10. Markou, M., Singh, S.: Novelty detection: a review-part 1: statistical approaches. Signal Process. **83**(12), 2481–2497 (2003)

Research on Trust Management Model in Cloud Manufacturing

Xiaolan Xie[1,2], Xiao Zhou[3(✉)], and Tianwei Yuan[1]

[1] College of Information Science and Engineering, Guilin University of Technology, Guilin, Guangxi Zhuang Autonomous Region, China

[2] Guangxi Universities Key Laboratory of Embedded Technology and Intelligent Information Processing, Guilin University of Technology, Guilin, China

[3] College of Mechanical and Control Engineering, Guilin University of Technology, Guilin, Guangxi Zhuang Autonomous Region, China

zhouxiao@glut.edu.cn

Abstract. For security and trust issues in cloud manufacturing systems, trust management issues in the trust system are analyzed. An effective trust management model was proposed and introduced in detail. The model considers multiple trust-related factors. The model adds a time period to the calculation of direct trust. The reputation information of the node, the attenuation of the trust recommendation transmission, and the weight of the trust level are taken into consideration. The model combines weighted tightness with trust. This method implements traversal of the recommended node. Ultimately, indirect trust is derived. Based on the values of direct trust, indirect trust, and the weight of the overall trust assessment, a comprehensive degree of trust is derived. Trust values are saved and updated. Experiments show that the research is credible and practical. The model improves the overall safety performance of cloud manufacturing systems.

Keywords: Cloud manufacturing · Safety · Trust · Trust management model

1 Introduction

The manufacturing industry in China has the problem of repeated construction and unbalanced manufacturing capacity [1]. There are problems of idle resources and resource bottlenecks. In order to fundamentally solve these problems. Academician Li Bohu [2] proposed a new model of smart manufacturing based on the network and services. It is cloud manufacturing.

Cloud Manufacturing is a new networked manufacturing model that provides users with various on-demand manufacturing services [3]. It uses network and cloud manufacturing service platforms to organize online manufacturing resources according to user needs. In cloud manufacturing [4], service providers transform various types of manufacturing resources and manufacturing capabilities into manufacturing cloud services through cloud technology. A large number of cloud services aggregate according to certain rules to form a manufacturing cloud [5]. The service user

X. Sun et al. (Eds.): ICCCS 2018, LNCS 11065, pp. 234–244, 2018.
https://doi.org/10.1007/978-3-030-00012-7_22

establishes a corresponding demand model based on the application requirements. Users can select and use various types of manufacturing services dynamically and agilely [6]. Cloud manufacturing achieves win-win results and universalization. It also enables efficient sharing and collaboration.

Like the challenges that cloud computing faces, security is also a major challenge for cloud manufacturing [7]. From the point of view of cloud manufacturing resources and service providers, it ensures that the secure access of resources and the accessed resources are not maliciously accessed or damaged. From the perspective of cloud manufacturing resources and service users [8], it must ensure that the resources and services accessed are credible. It ensures that the submitted task will not be destroyed and executed correctly and will not be provided with malicious results [9]. From the point of view of cloud manufacturing resources and service providers [10], it must provide a secure and trusted payment and transaction environment to prevent cloud service data centers from being damaged and attacked [11]. The above problems are all due to the issue of cloud manufacturing security and credibility [12]. Only by solving the above problems can cloud manufacturing be better developed.

At present, most of the researches on the trust management model in cloud manufacturing are focused on one aspect of trust quantification and trust calculation [13]. It lacks a complete solution. Based on the above issues, this paper proposes a trust management model in cloud manufacturing. The management model takes into account such factors as the reputation information of the node [14], the attenuation of the trust recommendation transmission, and the weight of the trust level. Based on the characteristics of multiple nodes [15], this model derives comprehensive trust based on the values of direct trust and indirect trust and the weights in the comprehensive trust assessment [16]. It established a comprehensive trust evaluation mechanism to suppress the behavior of malicious nodes [17]. At the same time, the model preserves and updates the trust. The model improves the transaction success rate of the trust node and enhances the performance of the cloud manufacturing system. The model is feasible through theoretical analysis and experimental proof.

2 Trust Management System

A cloud manufacturing system usually includes a physical resource layer, a cloud manufacturing service platform layer, an application layer, and standard specifications and security systems required for each layer. The perception layer, virtual resource layer, service layer, and interface layer constitute the cloud manufacturing service platform layer. The sensing layer connects physical manufacturing resources and capabilities to the cloud manufacturing system. It uses intelligence devices, adaptation tools, and the like. The virtual resource layer uses virtualization technology to separate the physical resources and capabilities from the physical environment in which they are located to form virtual manufacturing resources and capabilities. The service layer uses service technology to encapsulate numerous virtual manufacturing resources and capabilities into a cloud service pool. And through the appropriate management tools for integrated management. It manages the entire lifecycle of cloud services and uses cloud services to conduct various manufacturing activities. The interface layer uses ordinary human-computer interaction technology to provide personalized services for information exchange.

Trust and security issues exist at all levels of the cloud manufacturing service platform. Trust management has become an important functional module of the cloud manufacturing service platform. The schematic diagram of the trust management system in this paper is shown in Fig. 1:

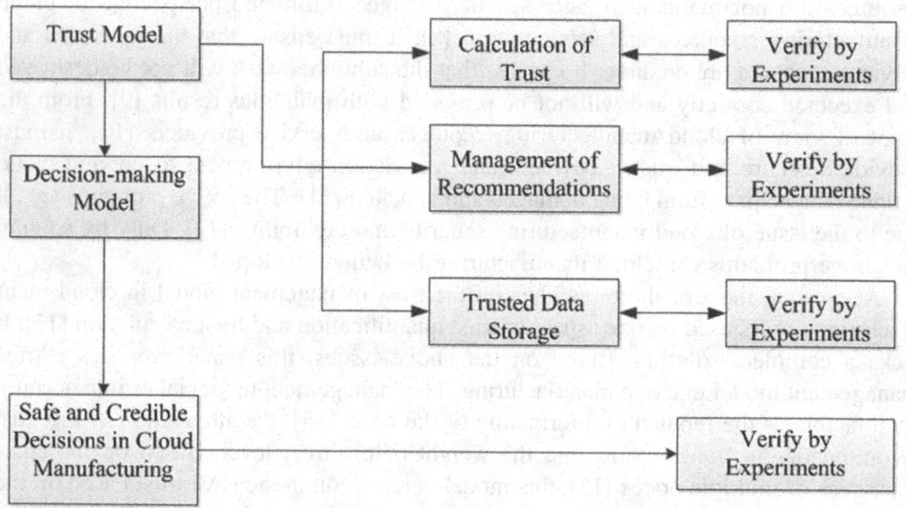

Fig. 1. Trust management system solution

The system consists of two parts: trust management model and interactive decision model. The system has a certain degree of versatility. The main task of the interactive decision model is to provide interactive decisions on the nodes specified in the cloud manufacturing environment. The main task of the trust management model is to evaluate the trust of designated nodes in the cloud manufacturing environment. It includes three aspects.

1. Trust calculation. Calculate the trust value of the specified node. Calculate the trust value of other nodes (for example, the request of the corresponding other node for trust data).
2. Trust data storage.
3. Management of recommendations. A trust score is generated and recommended for the interacted nodes. Manage trust scores and recommendations submitted by other nodes.

3 Research on Trust Management Model

Trust management is an important method to solve the security problems in cloud manufacturing. The core part of the trust management model is the calculation of trust values. The trust management model in this paper derives direct trust through the direct transaction history between the subject node and the target node. Indirect trust is obtained through indirect experience information provided by the recommender. Ultimately, the degree of comprehensive trust is calculated. The cloud manufacturing system saves and updates the trust obtained in the trust management model.

3.1 Calculation of Direct Trust

Direct trust is the degree of subjective trust between two nodes that have had direct interaction. The subjective approval degree of the subject node to the target node after the node directly interacts. It is a measure of trustworthiness. The level of direct trust directly reflects the subjective impressions between nodes. The node interaction trust value has time correlation. Therefore, this paper uses the combination of historical trust and periodic trust to calculate the direct trust between nodes.

The success rate of the node transaction history describes the credibility of the service provided by the node in the long-term transaction process. The definition formula is as follows:

$$Q_{AB} = \frac{S_{AB}}{S_{AB} + F_{AB}} \tag{1}$$

Where A represents the subject node and B represents the target node. F_{AB} represents the number of failures between nodes in the course of historical transactions. S_{AB} is the number of success.

The transaction success rate of the time period t represents the proportion of the number of successful interactions between the interacting nodes in the current cycle. It can reflect the credibility of the service provided by the node at intervals. The definition formula is as follows:

$$Q_{AB}(t) = \frac{S_{AB}(t)}{S_{AB}(t) + F_{AB}(t)} \tag{2}$$

Where $F_{AB}(t)$ represents the number of times that node A and node B failed to trade within the current time period. $S_{AB}(t)$ is the number of successful transactions in the current time period.

The model defines the direct trust rate through the historical successful transaction rate between the interaction nodes and the transaction success rate within the cycle. The definition formula is as follows:

$$Dt_{AB} = \begin{cases} \delta Q_{AB} + (1-\delta) Q_{AB}(t) & \text{A and B have interactive history} \\ 0.5 & \text{else} \end{cases} \tag{3}$$

$\delta \in (0, 1)$. In general, δ takes 0.6. The default is $Dt_{AB} = 0.5$ if the two nodes have no interaction experience.

3.2 Indirect Confidence Calculation

When selecting an interactive object, the user considers the direct interaction experience and also considers the recommendation of other nodes on the object to be selected. The user can more comprehensively and concretely understand the comprehensive trust degree of the interactive object to be selected. This is the recommended meaning. It makes the cloud manufacturing environment more secure and improves the success rate of transactions.

In an indirect-trust network, the two nodes are wired together if the two nodes interact directly. The user issues a transaction request. A recommendation chain is formed between the subject node and the target node. It is a path connected by lines and points. The trust of two adjacent nodes in the recommendation chain is established at the beginning of the history of direct interaction. There can be multiple paths between two nodes. The interaction between nodes in a certain period of time is shown in Fig. 2:

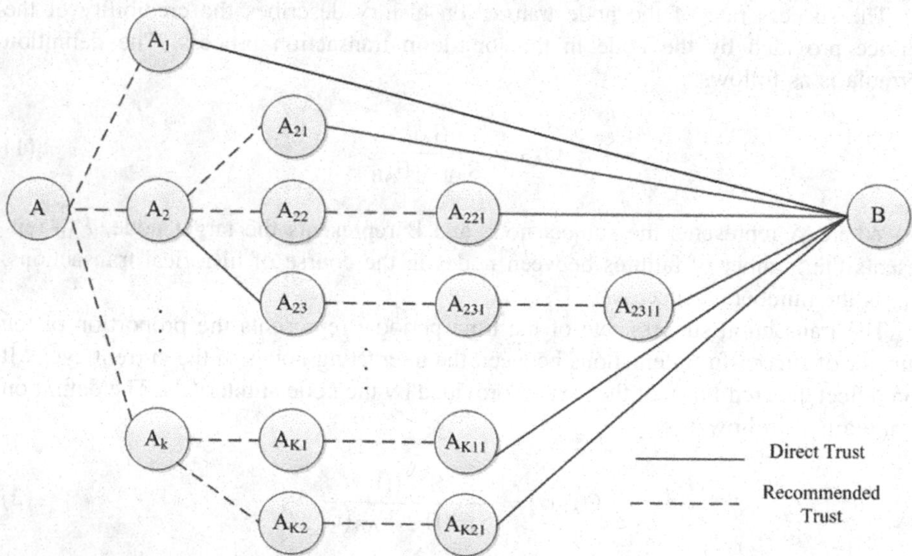

Fig. 2. Schematic diagram of trust consolidation based on weighted compactness

The indirect trust value comes from the recommended trust value for the target node. The more recommenders and recommended paths associated with two nodes in a cloud manufacturing environment, the higher the objective reality of the relationship between them. The closeness of the tightness between the reaction nodes. The use of weighted compactness to achieve the merger of the trust path fully considers the path between the trusting subject and the trusting object. When considering trust path consolidation, factors such as reputation information of the node, attenuation of trust recommendation transmission, and weight of trust level are taken into consideration to make the trust value truly reflect the objective credibility of the target node.

The number of hops for multiple paths that may exist in the recommended chain is the same. An ordered set of real numbers I is defined, and I is used as a representation of each path set with the same number of hops. If all paths belonging to P have different hop counts then $I = \{1, 2, 3, \cdots, n\}$. In a set of paths with the same hop count, use $N_k (k \in I)$ to mark the number of hops for the path in the set. The tightness formula is as follows:

$$cl(A, B) = \sum_{k \in I} \frac{1}{N_k \sqrt{|P_k| + 1 \cdot k}} \tag{4}$$

Among them, A represents the main node and B represents the target node. P represents an ordered set of selectable paths between node A's neighbor and target nodes. $|P_1|$ is the number of hops in the shortest path. $|P_2|$ indicates the number of hops in the shortest path, and so on.

In the calculation of trust, different trust levels have different effects on the credibility evaluation. It is unreasonable to treat all trust levels to the trust value in the same way. In order to make the trust value more in line with the objective situation, the model uses weights with different levels of trust. The weight of the trust degree of path P_k is defined as:

$$W_{P_k} = \frac{\sum_{j=1}^{|P_k|} w_{P_{kj}}}{|P_k| + 1} \tag{5}$$

$j = 1, \cdots, |P| + 1$. $w_{P_{kj}}$ represents the weight corresponding to the trust degree between the j node and the $j + 1$ node in the path $P_k (w_{P_{kj}} \in \{W_1, W_2, W_3\})$. The trust relationship corresponds to the weight W_1. The critical trust relationship corresponds to the weight W_2. The form of the weighted compactness $wcl(A, B)$ between node A and node B is as follows:

$$wcl(A, B) = \sum_{k \in I} \frac{W_{P_k}}{N_k \sqrt{|P_k| + 1 \cdot k}} \tag{6}$$

The final recommendation trust value is obtained by the integration of the weighted average and the weighted closeness of all neighbor node recommendation trust values of A. It can be calculated according to Eq. (7):

$$Rt_{AB} = wcl(A, B) \times \sum_{i=1}^{n} \frac{C_{Ai}}{\sum_{j=1}^{i} C_{Aj}} \times Rt_{Ai} \tag{7}$$

$wcl(A, B)$ is the weighted compactness between node A and node B. C_{Ai} is the credibility of node A's recommendation of the trust value to the neighbor node A_i. Rt_{Ai} is the recommendation trust value corresponding to the neighbor node A_i. Rt_{Ai} is iterated according to Eq. (7). When A_i is the last recommended node on the recommended path, $Rt_{Ai} = Rt_{iB}$. n is the number of recommended nodes in the neighbor node of the main node A.

Calculate the trust value of each neighbor node using a trust consolidation method based on weighted compactness. The traversal search is then performed on all nodes in the cloud manufacturing trust network. Select the node that best meets the requirements as the target node. It is the selected node that will be traded.

3.3 Comprehensive Confidence Calculation

The degree of comprehensive trust is derived from direct trust, indirect trust, and the weight of both in integrated trust assessment. The trust value T_{AB} of node *A* to node *B* depends on the direct trust value Dt_{AB} and the indirect trust value Rt_{AB}. It can be calculated as (8):

$$T_{AB} = \alpha Dt_{AB} + \beta Rt_{AB} \tag{8}$$

α and β are weight factors. $\alpha + \beta = 1(\alpha,\ \beta \in [0,\ 1])$. The values of α and β are set by the node according to its own trust policy and strictness. Direct trust is more rational than indirect trust. Usually $\alpha > \beta$, $\alpha > 0.5$.

3.4 Saving and Updating Trust

In the cloud manufacturing environment, the information of each node dynamically changes in real time. Therefore, relevant information of entities in the public storage area must be saved and updated in a timely manner after each transaction. Related nodes can participate in the next transaction or recommendation better and more accurately. The updated data content includes the relevant degree of trust after each transaction, the associated trust after the referring entity obtains the feedback evaluation, and the related information changes due to other changes.

In addition to the need to consider conventional factors, the judgment of the trust value needs to consider many other factors. In a cloud manufacturing environment, if you have not interacted with a node for a long time. The value of trust in it will not stay at the original level and the trust value will decrease. Therefore, we must consider the time influence factor.

The trust evaluation is updated based on the evaluation obtained from the multiple interactions of the subject node and the target node. The trust value is updated according to whether the subject node evaluates the target node. It is shown in formula (9):

$$T_N = T_O \pm \gamma \cdot \Delta t \tag{9}$$

Δt is the time difference between two updated trust values. γ is a parameter. T_O is the trust value before the change is updated. T_N is the current trust value obtained after the change is updated.

The model saves and updates trust. The model fully considers the influence of time factors in this process. The results can be shared by other nodes in real time. After the interaction ends, the trust-related information of each node participating in the interaction is updated. If each evaluation is a good level of satisfaction, the recommended nodes in the trust transfer process are all nodes with higher degrees of trust. The trust-related value of this node will be gradually strengthened. If the interaction is successful, the trust value of the interacting node will be updated to the trust related value of this time. If the interaction fails, the interactive node is punished. Then the trust correlation value is updated. Update all trust-related values to the cloud manufacturing environment and use them at the next interaction.

4 Experiment and Result Analysis

4.1 The Value of Trust Varies with the Number of Transactions

According to the node's trust value, the model divides the nodes in the network into three categories. When the node's corresponding trust value meets $0 \leq T \leq T_1$, the node is an untrusted node. When the corresponding trust value of the node satisfies $T_1 \leq T \leq T_2$, the node is a critical trust node. When the node's corresponding trust value satisfies $T_2 \leq T \leq 1$, the node is a trusted node. Among them, $0 \leq T_1 \leq T_2 \leq 1$. Table 1 shows the weight values corresponding to the setting of T_1 and T_2 values and the degree of trust:

Table 1. Related parameters and their values

Parameter	Value
W1	0
W2	0.5
W3	0.9
T1	0.5
T2	0.7

The initial trust value of each intra-domain node in the experiment is 0.5. Trusted nodes have little deceptive interaction. When the critical trust node is good or bad, malicious referrals will be made. The recommendation and the services provided by the untrusted nodes are completely untrustworthy. The node trust value changes as the number of interactions increases as shown in Fig. 3:

The trust degree of the trust node increases upward as the number of interactions increases. The credibility of critical trust nodes is good and bad, with undulating waves. The degree of trust of untrustworthy nodes decreases with the number of interactions. Experiments show that the degree of change in the degree of trust of the three types of nodes is consistent with the model's rule thinking and expectation analysis.

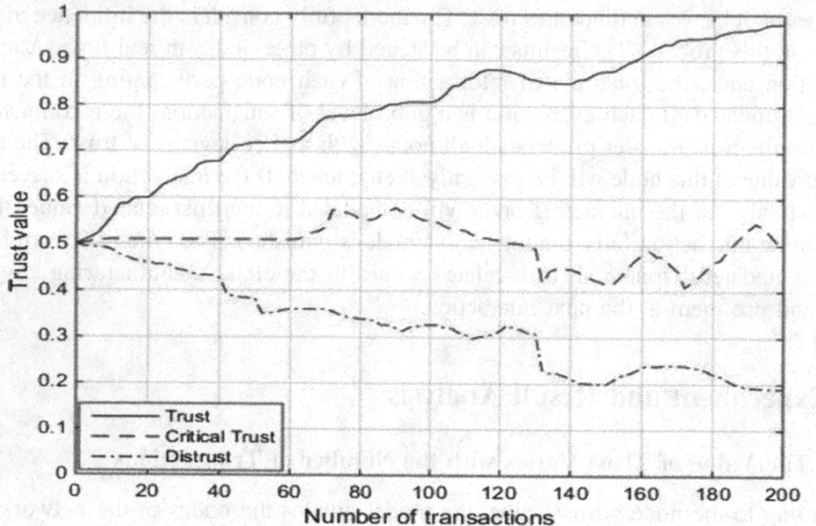

Fig. 3. The figure of the node's trust value as the number of transactions increases

4.2 Analysis of the Credibility of the Model

In the experiment, 50 nodes were set and the task amount was 500. Randomize these 500 tasks to all 50 nodes. Experiments ensure that each file is owned by at least one

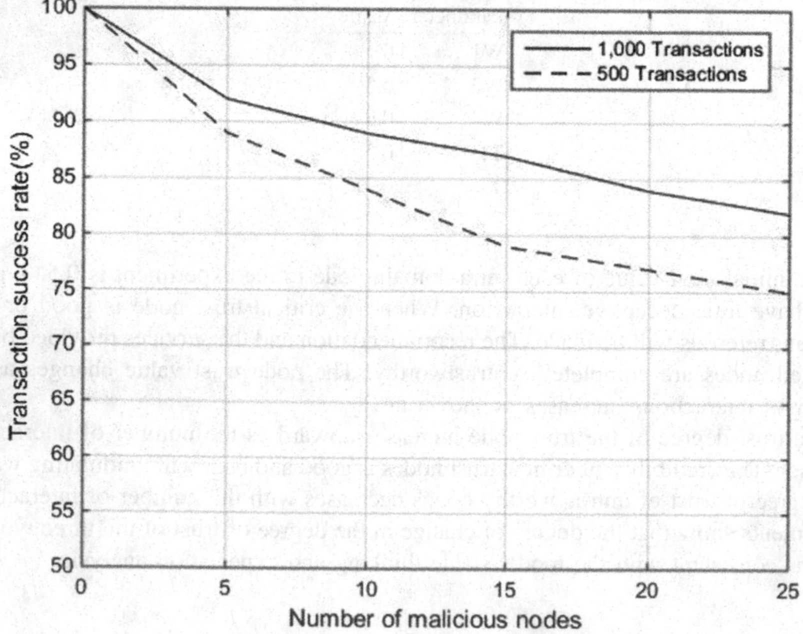

Fig. 4. Diagram of trading success rates at different trading volumes

trusted node. Each node needs to complete 20 interactions throughout the experiment. The trading volume is 1000. The experiment simulates the change of transaction success rate with the increase in the number of malicious nodes under the condition that malicious nodes participate. It is shown in Fig. 4:

It can be seen from Fig. 4 that the success rate of the transaction in the model is directly related to the transaction volume and the number of malicious nodes. As the volume of transactions increases, the success rate of transactions increases. When the transaction volume is 500, the transaction success rate drops faster with the increase in the number of malicious nodes. When the malicious node is 50%, the transaction success rate is 75%. The trading volume is 1000. When the malicious node reaches 50%, the impact on the trading results is not significant. The transaction success rate remained at around 82%. This fully shows that as more and more transactions are made, the model's assessment of trust values is becoming more and more accurate. The node makes the right judgment. This can improve the overall performance of the cloud manufacturing environment. Therefore, the model has feasibility and credibility.

5 Conclusion

In the cloud manufacturing environment, this paper studies the trust management system based on the analysis of the cloud manufacturing system framework for cloud manufacturing security. Considering multiple factors related to trust, this paper proposes a trust management model for trust management. The model passes the historical success rate of node transaction history and the direct trust degree of transaction cycle success rate. Indirect trust is obtained by combining weighted compactness with trust. This method implements traversal of all target nodes. This method reflects the objective credibility of the target node more realistically. Finally, based on the obtained direct trust degree and the weight of the two in the comprehensive trust evaluation, the comprehensive trust degree is obtained. The model stores and updates trust values. It can increase the success rate of transactions while ensuring higher real-time performance and accuracy. It enables the node to better participate in the work process of the cloud manufacturing environment. It also allows the platform to develop healthily. The study provides a more secure, reliable and efficient environment for cloud manufacturing. Subsequent studies will be conducted on the security performance of the scheme against malicious evaluation attacks.

Acknowledgement. This research work was supported by the National Natural Science Foundation of China (Grant No. 61762031), Guangxi Key Research and Development Plan (No. 2017AB51024), Guangxi Key Laboratory of Embedded Technology and Intelligent System.

References

1. Butala, P., Sluga, A.: Decentralised network architecture for cloud manufacturing. Int. J. Comput. Integr. Manuf. **30**(4–5), 395–408 (2017)
2. Xu, X.: From cloud computing to cloud manufacturing. Robot. Comput. Integr. Manuf. **28** (1), 75–86 (2012)

3. Li, B.-H., Zhang, L., Ren, L.: Further discussion on cloud manufacturing. Comput. Integr. Manuf. Syst. **17**(03), 449–457 (2011)
4. Laili, Y., Tao, F., Zhang, L.: A study of optimal allocation of computing resources in cloud manufacturing systems. Int. J. Adv. Manuf. Technol. **63**(5–8), 671–690 (2012)
5. Ren, L., Zhang, L., Wang, L.: Cloud manufacturing: key characteristics and applications. Int. J. Comput. Integr. Manuf. **30**(6), 501–515 (2017)
6. Wang, X.V., Wang, L., Mohammed, A.: Ubiquitous manufacturing system based on Cloud. Robot. Comput.-Integr. Manuf. **45**(C), 116–125 (2017)
7. Golightly, D., Sharples, S., Patel, H.: Manufacturing in the cloud: a human factors perspective. Int. J. Ind. Ergon. **55**, 12–21 (2016)
8. Cheng, W.S., Zhu, M.N.: Cloud manufacturing—Advanced manufacturing informationization. J. Syst. Simul. **23**(10), 2253–2258 (2011)
9. Wang, J., Zhang, L., Duan, L.: A new paradigm of cloud-based predictive maintenance for intelligent manufacturing. J. Intell. Manuf. **28**(5), 1125–1137 (2017)
10. Zhang, Y., Zhang, G., Liu, Y.: Research on services encapsulation and virtualization access model of machine for cloud manufacturing. J. Intell. Manuf. **28**(5), 1109–1123 (2017)
11. Meng, W., Li, S., Yang, G.: Reputation-based multi-dimensional trust model in cloud manufacturing service platform. Multiagent Grid Syst. **10**(4), 233–246 (2014)
12. Gan, J., Duan, G.J.: Method of cloud manufacturing service trust evaluation. Comput. Integr. Manuf. Syst. **18**(7), 1527–1535 (2012)
13. Niu, P., Zhou, D.J., Xie, X.L.: Trust model based on reputation propagation mechanism in cloud manufacturing environment. Adv. Mater. Res. **722**(722), 420–423 (2013)
14. Yu, D., Nan, C., Tan, C.: Research on trust cloud-based subjective trust management model under open network environment. Inf. Technol. J. **10**(4), 10–12 (2011)
15. Yan, K., Cheng, Y., Tao, F.: A trust evaluation model towards cloud manufacturing. Int. J. Adv. Manuf. Technol. **84**(1–4), 1–14 (2016)
16. Jin, H., Yao, X., Chen, Y.: Correlation-aware QoS modeling and manufacturing cloud service composition. J. Intell. Manuf. **28**(8), 1947–1960 (2017)
17. Kai, W.: Cloud model-based subjective trust management model for grid users. J. South China Univ. Technol. **39**(2), 80–81 (2011)

Resource Allocation Based on Reverse Auction Algorithm in Edge Computing Environment

Xinfeng Zhu[1(✉)], Zhihao Zhang[1], Yanling Wang[2], and Guohai Wang[3]

[1] College of Information Engineering, Yangzhou University, Yangzhou 225127, China
xfzhu@yzu.edu.cn, 1046911153@qq.com

[2] School of Information Science and Technology, Zhejiang Sci-Tech University, Hangzhou, China

[3] China Electronics Technology Company Avionics Ltd., Chengdu, China

Abstract. With the exploding growth in the number of devices and data traffic, cloud networks face challenges such as high speeds and low latency. The traditional edge calculation is to send data that can't be processed by the local edge server to the remote cloud for processing. This will put great pressure on the remote cloud server, and the data will have relatively large transmission delay through the intermediate device. For this problem, this paper proposes an edge calculation method based on reverse auction algorithm to process the data nearby, and adopts the idea of reverse auction to distribute the overloaded data to the edge server with less load, reduce the transmission delay, improve the user experience, and balance the server load. The final simulation results show that allocating overloaded data to adjacent edge server for processing can make server load balance and significantly reduce transmission delay compared to sending to remote cloud.

Keywords: Edge calculation · Auction · Balanced load · Decrease delay

1 Introduction

Currently, with the explosive growth of wireless devices, the quality of service required by users has been constantly improving. Mobile edge computing technology can provide users with high-speed, high-quality computing services, and does not need to send data to the remote cloud., greatly reduce the transmission delay, has received more and more attention in recent years. However, the traditional edge computing mode will send unprocessable data to the remote cloud, which will greatly increase the transmission delay, thus affecting the user experience (Fig. 1).

Mobile Edge Computing (MEC) can use wireless access networks to provide services and cloud computing functions needed by telecom users and provide high-performance, low-latency and high-bandwidth carrier-grade service environments to accelerate various items in the network. Fast download of content, services, and applications gives consumers an uninterrupted, high-quality web experience.

X. Sun et al. (Eds.): ICCCS 2018, LNCS 11065, pp. 245–252, 2018.
https://doi.org/10.1007/978-3-030-00012-7_23

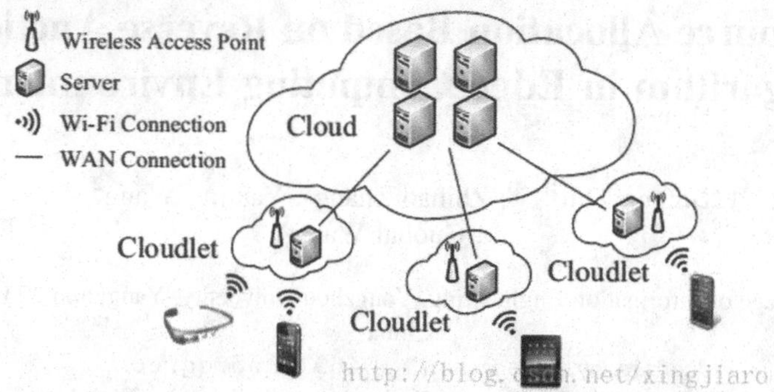

Fig. 1. Traditional mobile edge computing service model

The mobile edge computing (MEC) effectively integrates wireless network and Internet technologies, and adds functions such as computing, storage, and processing at the wireless network side, builds an open platform for application, and opens wireless networks and services through wireless APIs. Information exchange between servers, the integration of wireless networks and services, upgrades traditional wireless base stations into intelligent base stations. For the business level (Internet of things, video, medical, retail, etc.), mobile edge computing can provide customized and differentiated services to the industry, which in turn increases the efficiency of network utilization and value-added value. At the same time, the deployment strategy of mobile edge computing (especially geographical location) can achieve the advantages of low latency and high bandwidth. MEC can also obtain wireless network information and more accurate location information in real time to provide more accurate services.

In the mobile edge computing environment, when a large number of users access an edge server, a mobile edge computing server with limited computing resources may suffer from overloaded workload. Mobile Edge Computing relieves the load on the server through Group Intelligence collaboration technology [1]. Group Intelligence collaborative technology accomplishes tasks that cannot be accomplished by individual users through a large number of users, and the edge servers can also perform collaborative tasks to balance the network load. The cooperation between edge servers, because the edge server's computing resources are much larger than a single user, can reduce the node's access, relatively speaking, the allocation algorithm is relatively simple. In this paper, the reverse auction algorithm is used to achieve the cooperation between the edge servers to balance the load of the edge servers and reduce the delay.

The sealed-bid auction is also known as Open Descending Bid (ODB), and the process is the opposite of the English auction process: auctions are descending from high to low until the first buyer's price is filled. This article adopts a sealed-bid auction, arranges tasks from big to small, and bids by edge servers. When the edge server resource reaches the threshold or the task is all auctioned, the auction algorithm ends.

2 Related Works

The literature [2] is based on the resource trading model to plan the cooperation between the edge cloud service providers as a cooperative game framework, and proposes a coalition game method to use the price mechanism and user requirements to stimulate resource cooperation between the edge cloud service providers. Literature [3] proposed a random portfolio auction mechanism to minimize the social costs of mobile terminal collaboration. This mechanism is mainly divided into perceptual task assignment and payment determination. Derive the upper boundary of the integrity gap and design an ellipsoid method to determine the set of configuration files and the corresponding weights.

The literature [4] proposes an ad hoc mobile group intelligence collaborative framework in which mobile users can recruit workers in real time, can actively crowdsource their tasks to other people, and propose an online multiple stop planning problem to design an optimal online worker. Recruitment strategies to use the method of backward induction to maximize the sum of expected service quality. In order to motivate users to participate in tasks while ensuring fair trade. Literature [5] proposed a multi-market dynamic two-way auction mechanism, MobiAuc, to motivate and promote user collaboration and benefit from the service, and solved the fair trade problem in multi-market dynamic two-way auctions in the re-mobile wireless environment.

The literature [6] uses the multidimensional design space method to obtain an optimal solution that minimizes the total cost of the terminal collaboration. In order to obtain the best strategy to minimize the terminal cooperation cost, we need to search for a huge solution space, so the literature [6] obtains an approximate solution based on dimensionality reduction techniques and proves the bounded approximation ratio of the approximate solution and the optimal solution. A lightweight online heuristic algorithm was proposed.

3 System Model

This article uses reverse auction ideas. The edge server acts as a bidder. There are G bidders, the bidder set is define as $ES = \{ES_1, ES_2, ES_3, \ldots\ldots ES_G\}$, and the user task is acts as a auctioneer, there are Q auctioneers, the auctioneer set is define as $T = \{T_1, T_2, T_3, \ldots\ldots T_Q\}$. Bid by ES, when the task T is auctioned off, completes the distribution. Different from the traditional auction algorithm, this paper considers the load balancing problem of the edge server. The reverse auction method can make the server's maximum idle resources decrease, and the overall idle resources of the system are relatively reduced, showing superior performance.

According to the Shannon formula, the throughput of the local edge server and the nth edge server is as follows:

$$c_n = B_n * \log_2(1 + \sigma_n * p_n) \tag{1}$$

Where B_n is the bandwidth of the local edge server and the *n*th edge server. p_n denotes the average transmitted power between the local edge server and the *n*th edge server, and σ_n is stand for the *CINR* of the local edge server and the *n*th edge server. σ_n is define as follows:

$$\sigma_n = \frac{d_n * h_0}{B_0 * N_0} \tag{2}$$

Where d_n is the path loss between the local edge server with *n*th edge server and h_0 denotes the channel incremental. h_0 have different values for different channel conditions and remain unchanged in the same time slot. N_0 is the power spectral density and the value is $1 * 10^{-7}$.

When obtaining an available edge server, because the edge server has certain restrictions, in order to reduce the transmission time and improve the overall performance, a threshold is set for the remaining resources of the edge server, and when the edge server is less than the threshold, the edge server is discarded. Another threshold is set for the channel capacity between the edge server and the local edge server. When the channel capacity is less than the threshold, the edge server is discarded. According to the above description, a constraint condition is obtained:

$$a_n = \{0, 1\} \tag{3}$$

If the edge server is available, $a_n = 1$, and if the edge server is not available, $a_n = 0$.

The auction is based on a weighted sum of the channel capacity between the edge servers and the remaining resources of the edge server itself. It's define as follows:

$$b_n = \gamma * c_n + (1 - \gamma) * M_n \tag{4}$$

Where c_n is the throughput of the local edge server and the *n*th edge server. Then M_n denotes the remaining resources of *n*th edge server.

According to (3) and (4), calculate the maximum available auction price, the specific formula is as follows:

$$bid = \max\{a_n * b_n\} \tag{5}$$

Calculate the above conditions, obtain the auction bid, edge server get the task with the highest bid price, and calculate the transmission time of the task data to the edge server, the specific expression is as follows:

$$t_i = \frac{D_i}{c_n} \tag{6}$$

Where t_i denotes the data transmission time between *i*th task with *n*th edge server.

Finally, according to (6) find the total transmission time from the local edge server to other edge servers:

$$\sum t_i \tag{7}$$

Based on the above formula, a single resource allocation algorithm NSBA based on reverse auction is obtained, as shown in the following table:

single resource allocation algorithm NSBA based on reverse auction
Step1: Initialize B、h、N0、pm、G、Q and other parameters **Step2:**Generate the number of tasks and the amount of resources they request, generate edge servers and their remaining resources. **Step3:**Generate channel capacity $cc = \{c_n\}$ and calculate all bids $b = \{b_n\}$ **Step4:**Calculate the maximum bid, $bid = \max\{a_n * b_n\}$ and obtain the maximum amount of task to be calculated $D = \max\{D_i\}$ **Step5:**Perform an auction, update the bidding table, and update the amount of tasks. The auctioned task is blank. **Step6:**Repeat step 4, step 5 until all tasks are empty. **Step7:**The auction is completed.

4 Results and Comparison

In order to verify the performance of this algorithm, we use the MATLAB to simulate the Compare the transmission delay calculated in this paper with the transmission delay directly transmitted to the remote cloud, and compare the server idle resources before and after using this algorithm. The specific simulation conditions are as follows: the bandwidth between edge servers is $B = 500\,\text{MHz}$ and the power spectral density between edge servers is $N = 10^{-7}$, average power is $pm = 10\,\text{dbm}$.

The number of edge server is 40, and the number of the task is 8000, and the algorithm complexity is $O(n)$.

From Fig. 2 we can see that as the number of tasks increases, the maximum amount of resource left in the edge server is a more gradual curve because the free resources in the edge server are allocated as the number of tasks increases. With fewer and fewer resources, the load tends to balance, so the curve tends to be flat.

Comparing Fig. 3 with Fig. 4, Fig. 4 is relatively balanced compared to Fig. 3. Figure 3 shows a large fluctuation, indicating that the workload of each edge server is extremely uneven and has a large gap, which affects the overall performance of the edge server network. While using the auction algorithm to distribute tasks to each edge server, the curve is shown in Fig. 4. The remaining resources of the edge server are relatively balanced. Due to the algorithm restriction conditions, the channel capacity and the remaining resources of the server are less than a certain threshold, so the figure appears. The 13th server has higher remaining resources and some other edge servers have relatively low remaining resources.

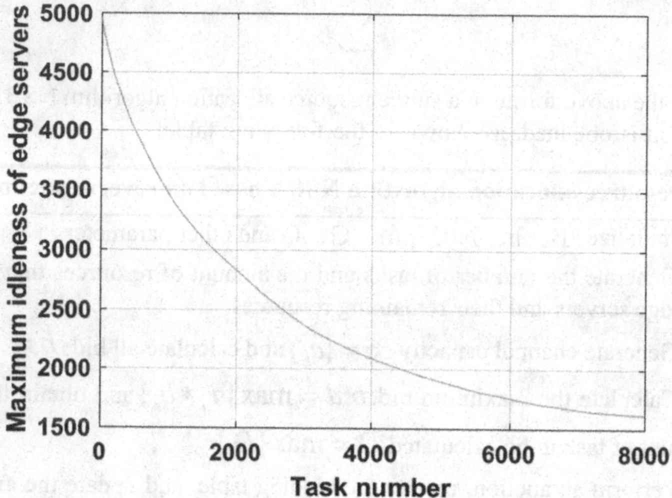

Fig. 2. Relationship between the maximum amount of resource left in the edge server and the number of users

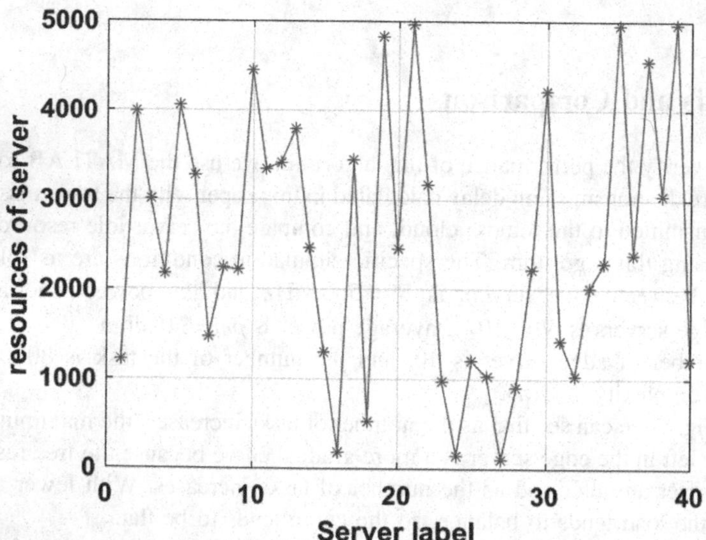

Fig. 3. The number of remaining resources of the edge server before using the auction algorithm

As shown in Fig. 5, using the auction algorithm can greatly reduce data transmission delay, reduce latency, and improve user experience. If the data is transmitted to the remote cloud for processing, the transmission delay will be increased because the link is far away, and the data will be transmitted to the neighboring edge server for processing, which can balance the network load and reduce the edge server with a large amount of free resources. Quantity, improve the overall utilization of the network.

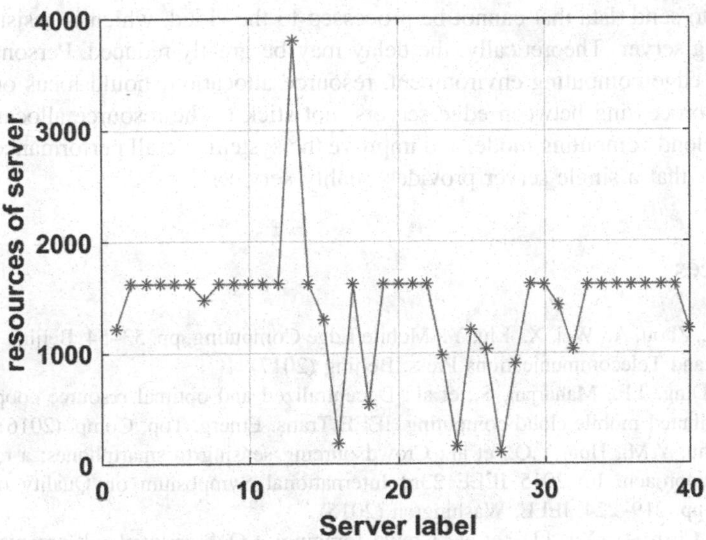

Fig. 4. The number of remaining resources of the edge server after using the auction algorithm

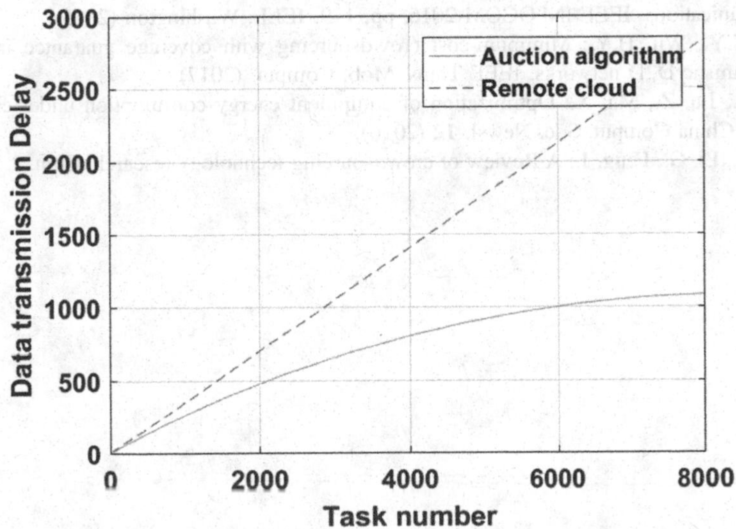

Fig. 5. Relationship between task number and data transfer time

5 Conclusion

For the first time, this paper uses reverse auction thinking to use Edge Server as a bidder and the pending task as an auction object to effectively balance network load and reduce network delay. In this way, it is possible to avoid situations in which a single server has excessive traffic data during a certain period of time, and it is not necessary to send data that cannot be processed to the cloud, which is assisted by the neighboring server. Theoretically, the delay may be greatly reduced. Personally think that in the edge computing environment, resource allocation should focus on the collaborative processing between edge servers, not stick to the resource allocation ways under the cloud computing mode, and improve the system overall performance more on the premise that a single server provides quality services.

References

1. Wang, S., Zhou, A., Wei, X., Liu, Y.: Mobile Edge Computing, pp. 53–54. Beijing University of Posts and Telecommunications Press, Beijing (2017)
2. Yu, R., Ding, J.F., Maharjan, S., et al.: Decentralized and optimal resource cooperation in geo-distributed mobile cloud computing. IEEE Trans. Emerg. Top. Comp. (2016)
3. Li, J., Zhu, Y.M., Hua, Y.Q., et al.: Crowdsourcing sensing to smartphones: a randomized auction approach. In: 2015 IEEE 23rd International Symposium on Quality of Service, IWQoS, pp. 219–224. IEEE, Washington (2015)
4. Pu, L.J., Chen, X., Xu, J.D., et al.: Crowd foraging: a QoS-oriented self-organized mobile crowdsourcing framework over opportunistic networks. IEEE J. Sel. Areas Commun. (2017)
5. Zhang, H.G., Liu B.Y., Susanto, H., et al.: Incentive mechanism for proximity-based mobile crowed service systems. In: The 35th Annual IEEE International Conference on Computer Communications, IEEE INFOCOM 2016, pp. 1–9. IEEE, Washington (2016)
6. Han, Y.Y., Wu, H.Y.: Minimum-cost crowdsourcing with coverage guarantee in mobile opportunistic D2D networks. IEEE Trans. Mob. Comput. (2017)
7. Cao, C., Lu, Z., Ma, X.: Optimization of equipment energy consumption under cloud-end fusion. China Comput. Soc. Newsl. **12** (2016)
8. Feng, J., Li, G., Feng, J.: A Review of crowdsourcing technology research. Chin. J. Comput. (2015)

RITS: Real-Time Interactive Text Steganography Based on Automatic Dialogue Model

Zhongliang Yang[1,2(✉)], Pengyu Zhang[3], Minyu Jiang[3], Yongfeng Huang[1,2], and Yu-Jin Zhang[1]

[1] Department of Electronic Engineering, Tsinghua University, Beijing 100084, China
{yangzl15@mails.tsinghua.edu.cn}

[2] Tsinghua National Laboratory of Information Science and Technology, Beijing 10084, China

[3] Fan Gongxiu Honor College, Beijing University of Technology, Beijing 100022, China

Abstract. Steganography based on texts has always been a hot but extremely hard research topic. Due to the high coding characteristics of the text compared to other information carriers, the redundancy of information is very low, which makes it really difficult to hide information inside. In this paper, combined with the recurrent neural network (RNN) and reinforcement learning (RL), we designed and implemented a real-time interactive text steganography model (RITS). The proposed model can automatically generate semantically coherent and syntactically correct dialogues based on the input sentence, through the reasonable encoding of the text in the dialog generation process to realize secret information hiding and transmission. We trained our model using publicly collected datasets which contains 5808 dialogues and evaluated the proposed model from several perspectives. Experimental results show that the proposed model can be very efficient to implement the embedding and extraction of information. The generated dialogue texts are of high quality which shows high concealment.

Keywords: Text steganography
Recurrent neural network · Reinforcement learning

1 Introduction

Information hiding, as known as steganography, is an ancient but still important and challenging subject, which can be traced back to early civilizations [1]. It can

This work is supported by the National Key Research and Development Program of China (No. 2016YFB0800402) and the National Natural Science Foundation of China (No. U1405254, U1536201, U1705261).

X. Sun et al. (Eds.): ICCCS 2018, LNCS 11065, pp. 253–264, 2018.
https://doi.org/10.1007/978-3-030-00012-7_24

embed secret information into multimedia data on the premise of not affecting the sensory characteristics of multimedia files, thereby realizing the transmission of secret information through open channels. Now, steganography has been widely used in many areas of our lives, including covert communication, storage and transmission of confidential information, copyright protection of digital media, etc.

The carrier media used for information hiding can be varied, such as image [2,3], audio [4,5], text [6,7] and so on [8]. Text is one of the most common and widely used digital carriers in the daily life of the Internet and human beings. Research on text steganography is of great significance to covert communications and copyright protection, and the extremely small data redundancy space and the completely different data characteristics from other media bring more challenges to the research of text steganography.

Previous text information hiding methods can be classified into two categories according to information embedding methods: format based method [9] and content based method [10]. Format-based methods mainly using format information such as a paragraph format, the font format, and the storage format of different document types for information hiding. For example, some of the previous works show that they can conceal information by adjusting the format of the text, like inter-character space [11], word-shifting [6], character-coding [12], etc. This kind of method mainly satisfies the invariance of the documents' appearance, that is, visually concealed. The main disadvantage is that its robustness is not high enough and hidden information can be easily destroyed.

Content based method, also known as natural language information hiding [13], is mainly based on linguistic and statistical knowledge, using Natural Language Processing (NLP) technology to automatically generate content similar to natural texts or make modifications to the existing normal texts, and try to keep the text of local and global semantic invariant, grammatically correct, syntactic structure reasonable to achieve information hiding. For example, Chapman and Davida [14,15] use information such as probabilistic context-free grammars and syntactic substitution strategies, sentence templates, and extensions of dictionary libraries to generate information-hiding text. Such methods require the support of complex natural language processing techniques such as syntax analysis, disambiguation, and automatic generation, to make the text with information embedded in satisfies many requirements, such as the rationality of words, the accuracy of word collocation, the correctness of syntactic structure, and the language statistical characteristics. However, currently there is no text steganography that can fully satisfy all these requirements.

In this paper, combined with the recurrent neural network (RNN) and reinforcement learning (RL), we propose a real-time interactive text steganography model (RITS). The proposed method can automatically and efficiently generate semantically coherent and syntactically correct dialogues based on the input sentence. At the same time, in generation process, we embed the information by effectively coding the text and choosing different words according to the different code streams embedded. Through this way, the proposed model can guarantee high concealment and large hidden capacity at the same time.

2 Related Work

2.1 Text-Generated Steganography

Text-generated steganography is a kind of content-based text steganography that automatically generates corresponding text based on a bits stream of secret information, rather than modifying a pre-given text carrier. Because of this advantage, in recent years, there is plenty of works in the content based approach that utilize text generation algorithms to realize information hiding [7,16–18]. Method proposed in [16] used Huffman tree to generate texts, their model has the ability to resist statistical attacks but still has a poor concealment, because the text it generates is completely unreadable. The work in [17] uses Markov chain model to generate English texts, by taking each word as a transfer state in first-order Markov model and then outputting English words sequence based on embedding message. Model proposed in [18] used Markov model to generate poetries, and then selects different words in different positions according to the template of the poem to realize information hiding. But due to that poetry is a kind of special-genre text and not often used in daily life, which may lead to arouse the suspicions of listeners and make it less concealed if it was transmitted in an open channel.

Through the above analysis, we can find that, limited by the technology of text automatic generation, the existing text-generated steganography can hardly generate high-quality readable natural text, leading to low concealment. At the same time, the existing method can only ensure the complete dissemination of information, but it's not real-time which limits its application scope. The algorithm proposed in this paper, which is called RITS, will effectively solve these two problems.

2.2 Automatic Dialogue System

Natural language conversation is one of the most challenging artificial intelligence problems, which involves language understanding, reasoning, and the utilization of common sense knowledge. In recent years, with the extensive application of deep neural network technology in natural language processing, more and more automatic dialogue models based on neural networks have emerged [19,20]. Most of these works treat the response generation as a translation problem, in which the model is trained on a parallel corpus of post-response pairs. Method proposed in [19] takes a probabilistic model to address the response generation problem, and propose employing a neural encoder-decoder for this task. They first summarize the post as a vector representation, then feed this representation to a recurrent neural network to decode and generate responses. But they only consider one round of conversation, in which each round is formed by two short texts, with the former being an input (referred to as post) from a user and the latter a response given by the computer. The model proposed in [21] consider a more specific scenario. It simulate a trading scene for the purpose of negotiating and ultimately reaching a transaction, they design an automatic dialogue system that can conduct multiple rounds of dialogue. They use recurrent neural network to generate dialogue texts and combine with reinforcement learning to train the entire network, rewarding or punishing every behavior in the negotiation to achieve a final transaction. Based on their works, in this paper, we propose the RITS algorithm, which can effectively encode texts during the negotiation process as well as the automatic dialogue process, enabling the completion of multiple rounds of dialogue while embedding covert information in real time.

3 RITS Methodology

The proposed RITS algorithm, on the one hand, takes advantage of RNN's powerful ability in text feature extraction and expression. On the other hand, we use the reinforcement learning to train the proposed model so as to ensure the generated text context is logically consistent. In this section, we first describe how we implement automatic dialogue in these two aspects. Then based on these, we further introduce our information hiding algorithm.

Recurrent neural network is a kind of artificial neural network where connections between units form a directed cycle, which makes it very suitable for modeling sequential information. Theoretically, a simplest RNN can deal with arbitrary length sequence signals. But in fact, due to the gradient vanish problem [22], it cannot deal with the problem of long-range dependence effectively. But its improved algorithm, Long short-term memory (LSTM) model [23], can effectively solve this problem by elaborately designed unit nodes. The main improvement of LSTM is the hidden layer unit, it's composed of four components: a cell, an input gate, an output gate and a forget gate. It can store the input information of the past time into the cell unit, so as to overcome the problem of long distance dependence, and realize the modeling of long time series. An LSTM unit can be described using following formulations:

$$\begin{cases} Input_t = \sigma(W_i \cdot [h_{t-1}, x_t] + b_i), \\ Forget_t = \sigma(W_f \cdot [h_{t-1}, x_t] + b_f), \\ Cell_t = Forget_t \cdot Cell_{t-1} + \sigma(W_c \cdot [h_{t-1}, x_t] + b_c) \\ Out_t = \sigma(W_o \cdot [h_{t-1}, x_t] + b_o), \\ h_t = Out_t * tanh(Cell_t). \end{cases} \tag{1}$$

For simplicity, we denote the transfer function of LSTM units by $f_{LSTM}(*)$. We need to notice that when we calculate the output at time step t, the information we use, according to Eq. (1), besides the input vector at time step t, also includes the information stored in the cells at the previous $t-1$ moments. Therefore, the output at time step t can be written as

$$Out_t = f_{LSTM}(x_t \mid x_1, x_2, ..., x_{t-1}). \tag{2}$$

To help the computer understand the content of the conversation context in order to further generate the corresponding conversation, we use a bidirectional recurrent neural network and attention mechanism [24] to encode the input text.

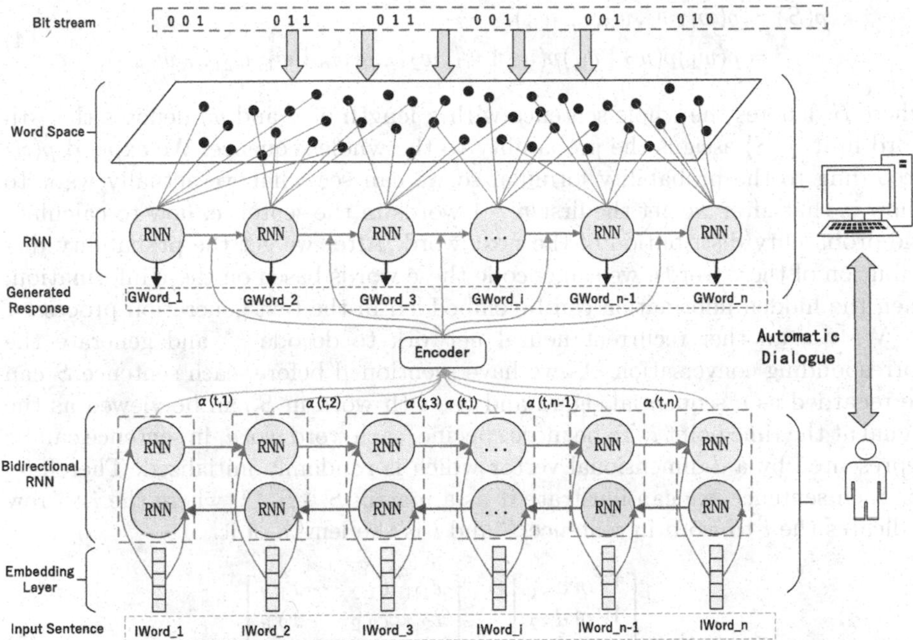

Fig. 1. A detailed explanation of the proposed model and the information hiding algorithm. The top of the figure is the bits stream that needs to be embedded, and the middle sentence is a response automatically generated based on the input sentence below. We use a bidirectional recurrent neural network and attention mechanism to encode the input text. The encoded information is then input to another RNN to decode and generate a corresponding response. During the generation, the distribution of the word space is effectively encoded so that the generated sentence contains the bit stream that needs to be hidden.

$$\begin{cases} \overrightarrow{h_t} = LSTM_r(\overrightarrow{h}_{t-1}, [Ex_t, h_t]), \\ \overleftarrow{h_t} = LSTM_r(\overleftarrow{h}_{t+1}, [Ex_t, h_t]), \\ h_t = [\overrightarrow{h_t}, \overleftarrow{h_t}], \\ h_t^o = W[tanh(W' \cdot h_t)], \\ \alpha_t = \frac{exp(w \cdot h_t^o)}{\sum exp(w \cdot h_t^o)}, \\ h^s = tanh(W^s \sum \alpha_t h_t). \end{cases} \tag{3}$$

Through the above process, we encode the entire information of the input text into a vector h^s, where α_t represents the importance of the t-th word for understanding the entire text.

A sentence can be regarded as a kind of sequential signal, which is composed of a group of sequentially connected words, and each word can be viewed as a signal of a time point. Our text generation algorithm is actually hoping to get a good language model through training process. A language model is a probability distribution over sequences of words, it is usually modeled as follows

$$\begin{aligned} p(S) &= p(w_1, w_2, w_3, ..., w_n) \\ &= p(w_1)p(w_2 \mid w_1)p(w_3 \mid w_1, w_2)...p(w_n \mid w_1, w_2, ..., w_{n-1}), \end{aligned} \quad (4)$$

where S denotes the whole sentence with a length of n and w_i denotes the i-th word in it. $p(S)$ assigns the probability to the whole sequence. We expend $p(S)$ according to the probability formula, so we can see what we actually want to know is that after we get the first $n-1$ words in the sentence, how to calculate the probability distribution of the next word. After we get the probability distribution of these words, we can encode these words based on these information, then the hidden information can be embedded in the text generation process.

We use another recurrent neural network to decode h^s and generate the corresponding conversation. As we have mentioned before, each sentence S can be regarded as a sequential signal and the i-th word in S can be viewed as the signal at the time point i. To be more specific, each word $word_i$ in sentence can be represented by a d-dimensional vertor which is randomly initialized. Therefore, for each sentence, we can illustrate it as a matrix $S \in \mathbb{R}^{l \times d}$, where the i-th row indicates the i-th word in sentence S and l is the length of it.

$$S = \begin{bmatrix} Words_{S1} \\ Words_{S2} \\ \vdots \\ Words_{SL} \end{bmatrix} = \begin{bmatrix} x_{1,1} & x_{1,2} & \cdots & x_{1,d} \\ x_{2,1} & x_{2,2} & \cdots & x_{2,d} \\ \vdots & \vdots & \ddots & \vdots \\ x_{l,1} & x_{l,2} & \cdots & x_{l,d} \end{bmatrix} \quad (5)$$

We use n_i indicates the LSTM units number of i-th hidden layer, so the units of i-th layer can be represented as

$$U_i = \{u_{i,1}, u_{i,2}, \cdots, u_{i,n_i}\}. \quad (6)$$

When we use LSTM to generate sentences, at time step t, we input the t-th word of sentence S, that is the t-th row of matrix S to our model. For the j-th LSTM layer, the output value of $u_{j,i}$ at time step t is

$$o_{i,t}^j = f_{LSTM}(u_{i,t}^j) = f_{LSTM}(\sum_{k=1}^{d} w_{i,k}^j \cdot x_{j,k} + b_{i,t}^j). \quad (7)$$

Where $W_{\cdot}^j$ and $b_{\cdot}^j$ are learned weight matrices and biases.

We can use a vector Out_t^j to represent the output of the j-th layer at time step t, each element in Out_t^j indicates the output value of each unit in the j-th layer at time step t, that is

$$Out_t^j = f_{LSTM}(x_t) = [o_{1,t}^j, o_{2,t}^j, ..., o_{n_j,t}^j]. \quad (8)$$

As we have mentioned before, the output at time step t is not only based on the input vector of the current time x_t, but also the information stored in the cells at the previous $t-1$ moments according to Eq. (1). Therefore, the output of the hidden layer at time step t can be regarded as a summary of all previous t moments, that is, the information fusion of the previous t words $\{Word_1, Word_2, ..., Word_t\}$.

Based on these features, after all the hidden layers, we add a softmax layer to calculate the probability distribution of the $(t+1)$-th word. To be more specific, we define the Prediction Weight (PW) as matrix W_P, and then use this learned matrix W_P to calculate the score for each word in the dictionary, that is

$$y_i = \sum_{k=1}^{n_j} w_{k,i}^p \cdot o_{i,t}^j + b_{i,t}^p, \tag{9}$$

where W_P and b^p are learned weight matrix and bias. The dimension of the output vector y is N, which is the size of dictionary D. We then pass the vector y through the softmax classifier to get the predicted probability of next word:

$$p(Word_{Di} \mid Word_{S1}, Word_{S2}, ..., Word_{St}) = \frac{\exp(y_i)}{\sum_{j=1}^{N} \exp(y_j)}. \tag{10}$$

$p(Word_{Di})$ shows the probability distribution of the next word according to all the words generated in the previous steps.

The process of information embedding mainly occurs in the process of generating conversations. Our thought is mainly based on the fact that when our model is well trained, there is actually more than one feasible solution at each time point. That is, for the same input sentence, there can be different dialogues. At the same time, the same meaning can be expressed differently. We encode all the words in the dictionary D based on the probability distribution, and then select the corresponding word according to the secret bits stream, so as to achieve the purpose of hiding the information.

Here we consider a very simple but effective enough coding method. We first sort all the words in the dictionary D in descending order of probability distribution, and then we choose the top m sorted words to build the Candidate Pool (CP). Then we use a perfect binary tree to encode all the words in the candidate pool. We represent each word in the candidate pool with each leaf node of the tree, the edges connecting each non-leaf node (including the root node) and its two child nodes are then encoded with 0 and 1, respectively, with 0 on the left and 1 on the right, which has been shown in Fig. 2.

Through the above method, we can automatically generate semantically coherent and syntactically correct dialogues, and through the reasonable coding of the probability distribution of the words in the dialog generation process, the secret information can be embedded at the same time.

4 Experiments and Analysis

4.1 Experimental Setting and Training Details

In this work, we trained our model using the dataset collected by [21], which contains a total of 5808 dialogues. For each word in the dictionary, we embedded it to a 64-dimensional vector. For the bidirectional RNN, we seted the size of hidden layer to be 256, and for the sentence generation RNN we set it to be 128.

In order to make the generated text consistent with the context semantics, we use reinforcement learning to train and update the network parameters. During reinforcement learning, we use two of the above models to simulate the dialogue between the two parties, named Computer A and Computer B. The text produced by each other is taken as an input, and the corresponding conversation is alternately output until one of the parties gives a symbol indicating the termination of the conversation. For example, when Computer A reads the sentence generated by B as a start, after encoding the text using bidirectional RNN according as described previously, it generates a small set of candidate responses. Then Computer B generates a corresponding dialogue based on each response until one of them considers the conversation to be over. Finally, our model calculates corresponding scores for each candidate's dialogue, and gives corresponding rewards or penalties based on scores, and finally outputs the dialogue with the highest reward. Specifically, let r^A be the score that Computer A achieved, T be the length of the dialogue, γ be a discount factor that rewards actions at the end of the dialogue more strongly, and μ be a running average of completed dialogue rewards so far. We define the future reward R for an action $x_t \in \mathbb{X}^A$ as follows:

$$R(x_t) = \sum_{x_t \in \mathbb{X}^A} \gamma^{T-t}(r^A(o) - \mu). \tag{11}$$

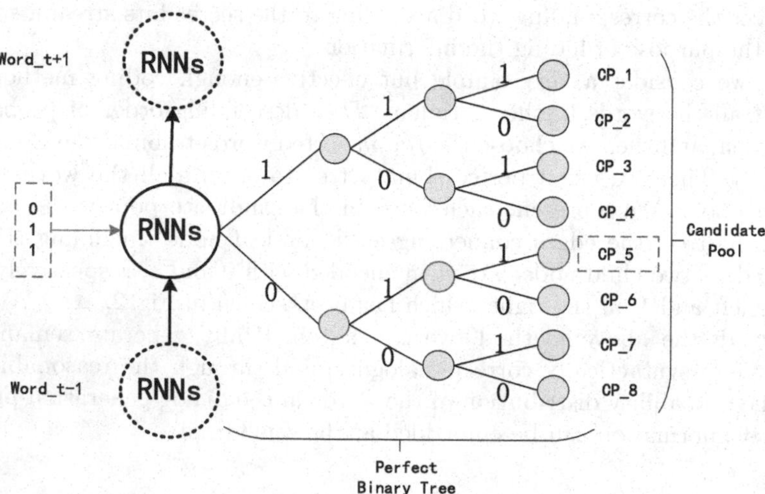

Fig. 2. Encoding words in candidate pool using perfect binary tree. We represent each word in the candidate pool with each leaf node of the tree. The edges connecting each non-leaf node (including the root node) and its two child nodes are then encoded with 0 and 1, respectively, with 0 on the left and 1 on the right.

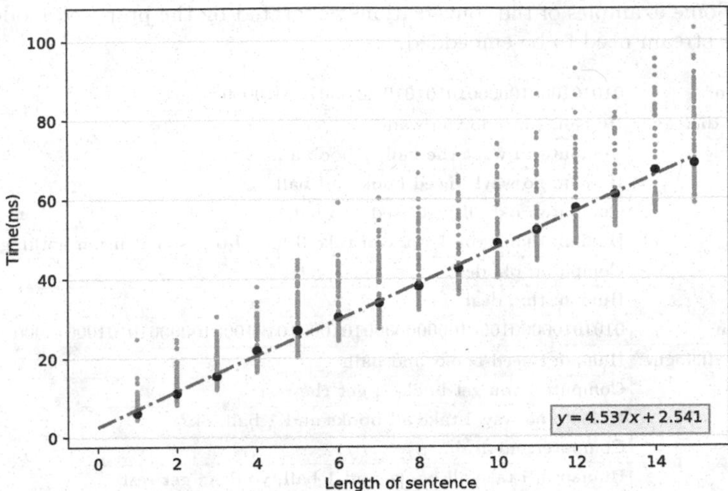

Fig. 3. The relationship between the time required to generate a response and the length of it. The blue point indicates the time required for each record to generate a specific length of response. The black point is its average value and the red line is the result of the fitting. (Color figure online)

We then optimise the expected reward of each action $x_t \in \mathbb{X}^A$:

$$L_\theta^{RL} = \mathbb{E}_{x_t \sim p_\theta(x_t|x_0 \ldots, x_{t-1}, g)}[R(x_t)]. \tag{12}$$

The gradient of L_θ^{RL} is calculated as in REINFORCE [25]:

$$\nabla_\theta L_\theta^{RL} = \sum_{x_t \in X^A} [R(x_t) \nabla_\theta \, log(p_\theta(x_t \mid x_0 \ldots, x_{t-1}, g))]. \tag{13}$$

During reinforcement learning, we use a learning rate of 0.1, clip gradients above 1.0, and use a discount factor of $\gamma = 0.95$. After every 4 reinforcement learning updates, we make a supervised update with mini-batch size 16 and learning rate 0.5, and we clip gradients at 1.0.

4.2 Evaluation Results and Discussion

In this section, we tested and analyzed the performance of the proposed model from several aspects. We tested the efficiency of the proposed model, which

Table 1. The average time our model takes to embed information and generation response varies with the length of it.

Length	4	6	8	10	12	14
Time(ms)	21.946 ± 5.303	30.336 ± 6.592	38.122 ± 7.084	48.894 ± 9.110	57.759 ± 9.945	67.215 ± 11.927

Table 2. Some examples of the conversations generated by the proposed model based on the bits stream need to be embedded.

Bits stream:	01010100010000010101010100000101010000
Generated dialogue:	Human: what do you want?
	Computer: i want the ball, 1 book and a hat
	Human: no way! i need book and ball
	Computer: ok, i'll just need two hats
	Human: thank you ! you can take 3 hats because hat mean nothing to me!
	Computer: ok, deal
	Human: thx, deal
Bits stream:	0101010000010001000000000101000101010001000001010100010000
Generated dialogue:	Human: i need books and balls
	Computer: you get books, i get the rest
	Human: no way, i take all books and 1 ball, ok?
	Computer: no deal
	Human: if i take all books and 1 ball, you can get rest
	Computer: no, i want 2 balls and 2 hats
	Human: no way, 1 ball for you
	Computer: ok, 1 ball and 1 book
	Human: you can take 1 ball and all hats
	Computer: deal

calculates how much time the proposed model takes to generate a fixed length response with secret information embedded in it. Figure 3 and Table 1 show the relationship between the time required to generate a response and the length of it. The blue point indicates the time required for each record to generate a specific length of response. The black point is its average value and the red line is the result of the fitting. As you can see from Fig. 3, the time needed to generate a response and the length of it have a linear growth relationship. It is worth noting that the time needed to generate a reply is only tens of milliseconds. For example, if a sentence with 14 words length is generated, the average time spent on it is only 67.215 ms. This shows the efficiency and real time of our model, which can embed secret information in the real-time human-machine automatic dialogue.

Table 2 shows some examples of the conversations generated by the proposed model based on the bits stream need to be embedded. The entire conversation environment we simulate is a trading scenario. Where "Human" represents text entered by the user and "Computer" represents the corresponding conversation generated by the proposed model. From the examples shown in Table 2, we can see that the proposed model can automatically generate syntactically correct and semantically coherent dialogues based on the input text. It is worth noting that, after embedding enough secret information, the generated dialogue still maintains a sufficiently high degree of naturalness and shows a high degree of concealment.

5 Conclusion

In this paper, we propose a real-time interactive text steganography model (RITS). It can automatically generate semantically coherent and syntactically correct dialogues based on the input sentence with high information hiding efficiency. At the same time, in the process of generation, we embed the information by effectively coding the text and choosing different words according to the different code streams embedded. We trained our model using publicly collected datasets which contains 5808 dialogues and evaluated the proposed model from several perspectives. Experimental results show that the proposed model can be very efficient to implement the embedding and extraction of information. The generated dialogue texts are of high quality which shows high concealment. We hope that this paper will serve as a reference guide for researchers to facilitate the design and implementation of better text steganography.

References

1. Kipper, G.: Investigator's Guide to Steganography. CRC Press, Inc., Boca Raton (2003)
2. Zhou, Z., Sun, H., Harit, R., Chen, X., Sun, X.: Coverless image steganography without embedding. In: Huang, Z., Sun, X., Luo, J., Wang, J. (eds.) ICCCS 2015. LNCS, vol. 9483, pp. 123–132. Springer, Cham (2015). https://doi.org/10.1007/978-3-319-27051-7_11
3. Nikolaidis, N., Pitas, I.: Robust image watermarking in the spatial domain. Sig. Process. **66**, 385–403 (1998)
4. Peng, X., Huang, Y., Li, F.: A steganography scheme in a low-bit rate speech codec based on 3D-sudoku matrix. In: IEEE International Conference on Communication Software and Networks, pp. 13–18 (2016)
5. Avcibas, I.: Audio steganalysis with content-independent distortion measures. IEEE Sig. Process. Lett. **13**(2), 92–95 (2006)
6. Shirali-Shahreza, M.H., Shirali-Shahreza, M.: A new approach to Persian/Arabic text steganography. In: IEEE/ACIS International Conference on Computer and Information Science and IEEE/ACIS International Workshop on Component-Based Software Engineering, Software Architecture and Reuse, pp. 310–315 (2006)
7. Majumder, A., Changder, S.: A novel approach for text steganography: generating text summary using reflection symmetry. Procedia Technol. **10**(10), 112–120 (2013)
8. Cox, I.J., Miller, M.L.: The first 50 years of electronic watermarking. Eurasip J. Adv. Signal Process. **2002**(2), 1–7 (2001)
9. Zou, D., Shi, Y.Q.: Formatted text document data hiding robust to printing, copying and scanning. In: IEEE International Symposium on Circuits and Systems, vol. 5, pp. 4971–4974 (2005)
10. Bennett, K.: Linguistic steganography: survey, analysis, and robustness concerns for hiding information in text (2004)
11. Chotikakamthorn, N.: Electronic document data hiding technique using inter-character space. In: The 1998 IEEE Asia-Pacific Conference on Circuits and Systems, IEEE APCCAS 1998, pp. 419–422 (1998)
12. Low, S.H., Maxemchuk, N.F., Lapone, A.M.: Document identification for copyright protection using centroid detection. IEEE Trans. Commun. **46**(3), 372–383 (1998)

13. Desoky, A.: Comprehensive linguistic steganography survey. Int. J. Inf. Comput. Secur. **4**(2), 164–197 (2010)
14. Chapman, M., Davida, G.I., Rennhard, M.: A practical and effective approach to large-scale automated linguistic steganography. In: Davida, G.I., Frankel, Y. (eds.) ISC 2001. LNCS, vol. 2200, pp. 156–165. Springer, Heidelberg (2001). https://doi.org/10.1007/3-540-45439-X_11
15. Chapman, M., Davida, G.I.: Plausible Deniability Using Automated Linguistic Stegonagraphy. In: Davida, G., Frankel, Y., Rees, O. (eds.) InfraSec 2002. LNCS, vol. 2437, pp. 276–287. Springer, Heidelberg (2002). https://doi.org/10.1007/3-540-45831-X_19
16. Wayner, P.: Mimic functions. Cryptologia **16**(3), 193–214 (1992)
17. Ge, X., Jiao, R., Tian, H., Wang, J.: Research on information hiding. US-China Educ. Rev. **3**(5), 77–81 (2006)
18. Luo, Y., Huang, Y., Li, F., Chang, C.: Text steganography based on CI-poetry generation using Markov Chain model. KSII Trans. Internet Inf. Syst. **10**, 4568–4584 (2016)
19. Shang, L., Lu, Z., Li, H.: Neural responding machine for short-text conversation, pp. 52–58 (2015)
20. Pascual, B., Gurruchaga, M., Ginebra, M.P., Gil, F.J., Planell, J.A., Goñ, I.: A neural network approach to context-sensitive generation of conversational responses. Trans. R. Soc. Trop. Med. Hyg. **51**(6), 502–504 (2015)
21. Lewis, M., Yarats, D., Dauphin, Y.N., Parikh, D., Batra, D.: Deal or no deal? End-to-end learning for negotiation dialogues (2017)
22. Hochreiter, S.: The vanishing gradient problem during learning recurrent neural nets and problem solutions. Int. J. Uncertain., Fuzziness Knowl.-Based Syst. **06**(02), 107–116 (1998)
23. Hochreiter, S., Schmidhuber, J.: Long short-term memory. Neural Comput. **9**(8), 1735–1780 (1997)
24. Bahdanau, D., Cho, K., Bengio, Y.: Neural machine translation by jointly learning to align and translate. Comput. Sci. (2014)
25. Williams, R.J.: Simple statistical gradient-following algorithms for connectionist reinforcement learning. Mach. Learn. **8**(3–4), 229–256 (1992)

Searchable Encryption Scheme Based on CPABE with Attribute Update in a Cloud Medical Environment

Sun Jingzhang[1], Cao Chunjie[1,2(✉)], and Li Hui[1,2]

[1] College of Information Science and Technology, Hainan University, Haikou 570228, China
{jingzhang_sun,lihui}@hainu.edu.cn, chunjie_cao@126.com

[2] State Key Laboratory of Marine Resource Utilization in the South China Sea, Hainan University, Haikou 570228, China

Abstract. With the development in cloud storage, hospitals outsource the encrypted electronic medical records to the cloud services for economic saving. A cloud medical environment where the attribute is frequently updated, the existing searchable encryption schemes cannot support both ciphertext search and fine-grained access control. Therefore, combining ciphertext policy attribute-based encryption with searchable encryption technology, a cryptographic retrieval scheme supporting attribute update is proposed. Attributes can be updated frequently and partial decryption is transferred to the cloud storage server. Security analysis shows that the scheme can protect security and privacy under the DBDH assumption and the experimental results with real data show that the scheme is an efficient and practical application.

Keywords: Could medical storage · Attribute-based encryption
Searchable encryption · Attribute update

1 Introduction

In an uncontrolled public cloud environment, encrypting data is a good method of ensuring the confidentiality of private data, yet it also reduces the possibility of performing computations on the ciphertexts, such as searching for keywords or specific items within the data. Searchable encryption provides a solution to this problem by selectively retrieving data matching a query without revealing either the private data or keywords to the honest-but-curious server.

Most existing schemes are mostly oriented to the one-to-one scenario. However, in such an information-sharing background, those schemes are inapplicable [1]. For example, in the electronic health systems, there are numerous hospitals, doctors, nurses, patients and other staff. A patient may wish that the orthopedist doctor can only have access to his or her orthopedist electronic health record, whereas the infectious disease record is invisible to that doctor or others. At the same time, all medical staff may need to write data to the private records. This requires attribution division in more detail.

X. Sun et al. (Eds.): ICCCS 2018, LNCS 11065, pp. 265–276, 2018.
https://doi.org/10.1007/978-3-030-00012-7_25

Moreover, the suggested system has the function to add and revoke user or user's attributes.

Existing methods cannot meet the demand of ciphertext search and provide fine-grained access control mechanism, thus cannot be used in a many-to-many environment. Aiming at solving these problems, attribute-based encryption (ABE) could be used. ABE is a kind of public-key encryption in which the private key and the ciphertext are labeled with attributes, and the decryption of a ciphertext is enabled only if the attributes of the key match the attributes of the ciphertext. It widely used in a fine-grained access control system for outsourced private records. CP-ABE with access control is suitable for that scenario. Data owners allocate specific and flexible access policy on their data, and only those users that have attributes satisfying the access policy are authorized to read private records.

Over the extensively studied literature, the attribute-based encryption is h-regarded. In 2001, Boneh [2] designed the first semantic security identity-based encryption by using bilinear pairing. A novel approach to searchable encryption for multi-user proposed by Shamir [3]. In that scheme, data owners define as an identity, and people who match identity can decrypt the private. To improve error tolerance property, Sahai [4] proposed fuzzy identity-based encryption in 2005 and was applied in the case that an encrypted document can only be decrypted by the user who has a certain set of attributes. Later, Bethencourt et al. [5] represented the CP-ABE scheme, and the scheme was proved in the random oracle model. Waters [6] proposed a selective-attribute CPA secure CP-ABE with ciphertext size, encryption, and decryption time scales linearly with the complexity of the access formula using linear secret share scheme (LSSS). Lewko et al. [7] presented a first fully secure CP-ABE under 3 assumption using composite-order bilinear groups. However, there are many composite operations, leading to a low efficiency.

As for attribute updating, Boldyreva [8] gave an identity-based encryption scheme with revocation scheme. There is a key management center which contains a user revocation list. Hur [9] proposed an encrypting attribute scheme which supporting attribute update. Qiang [10] presented a scheme combined CPABE with broadcast encryption supporting user revocation. Begum [11] applied a scheme, in which only the ciphertext associated with the attribute update needs to be updated, thus it reduces the consumption of computing and communicating. Naruse [12] proposed a CPABE with revocation scheme based LSSS, while it cost too much computation and bandwidth consumption. Piretti [13], Zu [14] and Tao [15] also showed some solutions to handle the previous problems.

In this work, we put forward a cryptographic retrieval scheme combining ciphertext policy attribute-based encryption with searchable encryption technology, which supports attribute update. In this paper, attributes can be updated frequently and partial decryption was transferred to the cloud storage server. In the standard model, the scheme has been proved to be secure on the basis of DBDH assumption.

2 Preliminaries

In this part, we describe some formal definitions for scheme.

Definition 1 (Bilinear Pairing). Let G and G_T be two multiplicative cyclic groups with the same prime order p, and g is the generator of G. A bilinear map $e : G \times G \rightarrow G_T$ has the following properties:

(1) Bilinear: $\forall a, b \in \mathbb{Z}_p$, $u \in G$ and $v \in G_T$, existing $e(u^a, v^b) = e(u, v)^{ab}$.
(2) Non-degeneracy: There exist $e(g, g) \neq 1$.
(3) Computability: There exist $u, v \in G$, e can be computed in a polynomial time algorithm.

Definition 2 (Access Structure). Let $P = \{P_1, P_2, \ldots, P_n\}$ be a set of entities. $A \subseteq 2^P$ is one of non-empty subset in 2^P. If for each B and C, $B \in A$ and $B \subseteq C$, then $C \in A$ and $A \subseteq 2^P$ is monotonic. If access structure A is one of non-empty subset in $P = \{P_1, P_2, \ldots, P_n\}$, then the subsets of A are called authorized sets, otherwise, unauthorized sets.

Definition 3 (Access Control Tree). Every privacy records in the scheme corresponds with an access control tree. A leaf node represents an attribution, and a non-leaf node stands for *AND* or *OR*. Figure 1 describes the access control tree. In this tree, the record only allow patient U, medical faculty and doctor A belongs to provincial hospital to access.

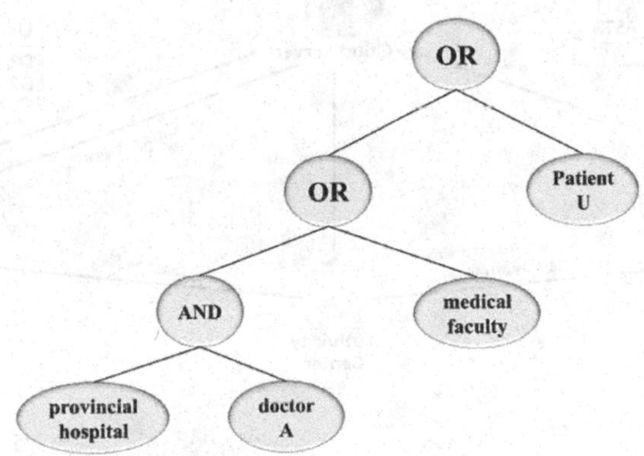

Fig. 1. Access control tree

Definition 4 (Linear Secret Sharing Schemes). If a LSSS scheme $\prod$ over a set of entities P meet following conditions, it can be called linear:

(1) Each entities' shares form a vector over $\mathbb{Z}_p$.
(2) In $\prod$, there has a matrix M called the share-generating matrix. $M_{l \times n}$ has l rows and n columns. The function $p : \{1, \ldots, l\} \rightarrow p_i$ map the i-th row of M to an entity. Let $s \in \mathbb{Z}_p$ is the secret to be shared, and randomly chosen $r_2, \ldots, r_n \in \mathbb{Z}_p$, forms a column vector $v = (s, r_2, \ldots, r_n)$. Mv is the vector of l shares of the secret s. $\lambda_i = (Mv)_i$ is the share of entity $p(i)$.

Linear secret sharing scheme meet the linear reconstruction property: Let $\prod$ is a LSSS scheme for the access structure $A = (M_{l \times n} \times p)$ and $S \in A$ is authorized set. Let set I be defined as $I = \{i : p(i) \in S\}$, there exit constants $\{w_i \in \mathbb{Z}_p\}_{i \in I}$ such that for any share $\{\lambda_i\}$ of s, there has $\sum_{i \in I} w_i \lambda_i = s$ and $\{w_i\}$ can be computed in time polynomial.

Definition 5 (Decision Bilinear Diffie-Hellman Assumption). Let G be a multiplicative cyclic groups with the same prime order p, and g is the generator of G. Let $x, y, z, u \in \mathbb{Z}_p$ be randomly chosen. If an adversary is given $y = (g, g^x, g^y, g^z, e(g, g)^{xyz})$, it must be hard to distinguish a valid tuple $e(g, g)^u \in G_T$.

3 Formal Definition and Security Model

3.1 System Model

Figure shows the system model of AU-CPABE-SE. There are four entities in this system: Authority center (Hospital), Data owner (patient), Data user (doctor), Cloud server (Fig. 2).

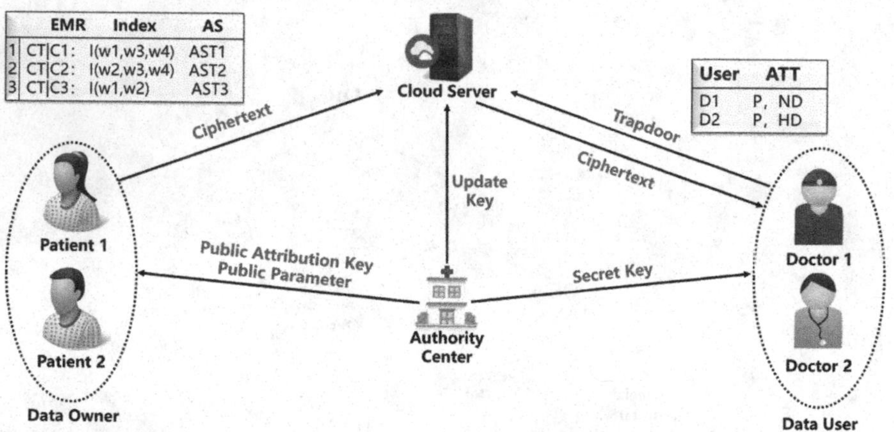

Fig. 2. Overview of the system.

Authority Center (CA): This entity generates public attribute keys, public parameters and version attribute keys for the system, also, it generates and assigns private keys for doctors. CA is always able to generate new update keys and new update ciphertext.

Data Owner (DO): Firstly, data owners use the traditional scheme to encrypt the private medical record. Then, set up the access control policies and use it to encrypt symmetric encrypted key. Lastly, DO send record ciphertext C and ciphertext CT to CS.

Data User (DU): DU is associated with a set of attributes according his or her identity. DU can generate search trapdoor to query, if his or her set of attributes satisfy with the access structure of ciphertext, the CS will return C and CT to it. Then, DU decrypt and read it.

Cloud Server (CS): A remote CS (pay-as-you-go cloud server) stores the encrypted data like medical records and provides data access services to DUs. Also, CS is responsible for ciphertext updating.

3.2 Security Model

In a medical cloud storage system, authority center such as hospitals, research institutes and medical schools are credible, cloud s server that provide storage servers are semi-trusted and curious. The CS will strictly execute the DU's query and return the corresponding ciphertext, but at the same time, it will try to collect the content of the encrypted data or the received message in order to get any privacy information about the medical record. We now describe the security model for AU-CPABE-SE system by the following game between a challenger and an adversary as follows.

Setup: The challenger performs algorithm and outputs system public parameter PP and public attribute key $\{PK_x\}$.

Phase 1: The adversary submits the attribute list Att to oracle. Then, it returns secret keys SK as well as update keys UK.

Challenge: Adversary submits two messages with the same length M_0 and M_1. Also, the adversary submits a challenge access structure A'. There not SK and UK in period of Phase 1 satisfy this access structure. The challenger randomly selects a coin $b \in \{0, 1\}$ and performs encrypting operation for M_b under A'. Finally, the challenger gives it back to the adversary.

Phase 2: Adversary continued queried to oracle in Phase 1. The new query attributes do not satisfy the access structure.

Guess: The adversary guesses and outputs b'. If $b' = b$, the adversary wins.

Definition: The scheme will meet the chosen-ciphertext secure, if the adversary holds a negligible advantage $\Pr[b' = b] - 1/2 < \varepsilon$ in polynomial time.

3.3 Outline of Our Scheme

The AU-CPABE-SE consists following algorithms:

ACInit: This algorithm is running by AC. It inputs security κ and the set of attributes ATT. It outputs system master secret key MSK, system public parameter PP and the set of public attribute key $\{PK_x\}$.

DUKey: This algorithm is also running by AC. It takes system master secret key MSK, system public parameter PP and DU's identity, then it outputs DU's secret key SK.

DOEnc: This algorithm is running by DO like patient. It inputs system public parameter PP, the set of public attribute key $\{PK_x\}$, medical record m and access control structure A. It outputs record ciphertext C and ciphertext CT.

DUTrap: This algorithm is running by DU like doctor. It inputs secret key SK, system public parameter PP and attribute set of patients K'_w, then it output the trapdoor.

CSTest: This algorithm is running by CS. It inputs and ciphertext CT, system public parameter PP and trapdoor. If the doctor's attribute satisfies the access structure of symmetric key ciphertext, CS will return the record ciphertext C and ciphertext CT to DU. Otherwise, it will output $\perp$.

DUDec: This algorithm is running by DU. It takes ciphertext CT and his or her secret key SK as input. It outputs the symmetric key. Then, DU decrypt record ciphertext C by using symmetric key to get the medical record.

DUKeyU: This algorithm is also running by AC. It takes system master secret key MSK, current version key $vk_{x'}$ set of public attribute key $\{PK_x\}$ as input. Then, it outputs a new version key $v'_{x'}$, update key $UK_{x'}$ and DU's new secret key SK'.

CSCTU: This algorithm is running by CS. It inputs ciphertext CT and DU's new secret key SK'. It outputs a new ciphertext CT'.

4 Searchable Encryption Scheme with Revocation

In this section, we describe the detailed construction of our scheme.

Let ATT be the universe of possible attributes that can be described as $ATT = \{att_1, att_2, \ldots, att_n\}$, where n is the number of attributes. Let G and G_T be the multiplicative groups with the same prime order p and generator g, $e : G \times G \rightarrow G_T$ is a bilinear map. Hash function $H : \{0, 1\}^* \rightarrow \mathbb{Z}_p$ map attribute to group G.

ACInit(1^κ,ATT): This algorithm is running by AC. ATT be universe of attributes for AC like hospital and κ is security parameter. Then AC randomly chooses $a, b, c \in \mathbb{Z}_p$ as the master key MSK and keeps secret.

$$MSK = (a, b, c) \tag{1}$$

The AC chooses $\{h_x \in \mathbb{Z}_p\}(i \in [1, n])$. For each attribute $\forall x \in [1, n]$, AC also randomly choose $v_x \in \mathbb{Z}_p$ to initialize attribute version number and calculates public attribute key and publishes

$$PK_x = \left\{PK_{1,x} = g^{v_x}, PK_{2,x} = h_x^{1/v_x}\right\} \tag{2}$$

Then, it generates the public parameters and publishes

$$PP = \left\{g, g^a, g^b, g^c, e(g,g)^a, \{h_i\}_{i\in[1,n]}, G, G_T, H\right\} \tag{3}$$

DUKey($\boldsymbol{MSK}, \boldsymbol{PP}, \boldsymbol{Att}$)**:** This algorithm is running by AC. When a DU (doctor) joints the hospital, the AC would assign a set of attributes $Att \subseteq ATT$ to him or she according to its identity. Then AC randomly chooses $u \in \mathbb{Z}_p$ and calculates $DU = g^u$, $U = g^{ac} \cdot g^{bu}$ and $U_x = h^{u/v_x}$ for each attributes $x \in Att$. SK is issued as the DU private key.

$$SK = \left\{DU, U, \{U_x\}_{x\in Att}\right\} \tag{4}$$

DOEnc($\boldsymbol{PP}$, $\{\boldsymbol{PX_x}\}, \boldsymbol{m}, \boldsymbol{A}$)**:** This algorithm is running by DO. When a DO (patient) go to hospital for treating and generating a medical record. Before outsourcing record m to the CS, privatized processing method is implemented by DO. Firstly, DO extract medical record's attribute set K_w and hash it $H(K_w)$. DO encrypts the plaintext m into medical ciphertext C according symmetric key K, then using CPABE scheme to encrypt K. Then, let M be a $l \times n$ matrix which l represents the number of attributes. The function p map attribute to matrix. Next, DO chooses $t \in \mathbb{Z}_p$, secret value $k \in \mathbb{Z}_p$ and a vector $v = (k, y_2, \ldots, y_n) \in \mathbb{Z}_p^n$ randomly, where $y_2, \ldots, y_n$ is the share of secret k. For any i from 1 to l, it computes $\lambda_i = v \cdot M_i$. Meanwhile, DO randomly chooses vector $r = \{r_1, r_2, \ldots, r_l\}$ and calculates $W = g^{ct}$, $W_0 = g^{(t+k)} \cdot g^{H(K_w)t}$, $W_1 = g^k$, $K' = K \cdot e(g,g)^k$. For $i \in [1, l]$, it calculates $\left\{C_i = g^{b\lambda_i} h_{p(i)}^{-r_i}, D_i = g^{v_x r_i}\right\}$, the symmetric key ciphertext CT is

$$CT = \left\{W, W_0, W_1, K', \{C_i, D_i\}_{i\in[1,l]}\right\} \tag{5}$$

Finally, DO uploads the encrypted medical record to CS. Figure 3 is the format of ciphertext.

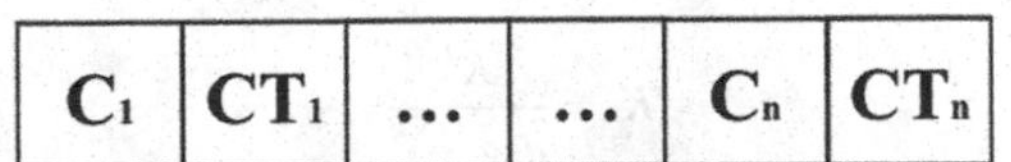

Fig. 3. Storage format for ciphertext

DUTrap($\boldsymbol{PP}, \boldsymbol{SK}, \boldsymbol{W'}$)**:** This algorithm is running by DU. When a doctor would like to read a patient's record. DU input his or her SK and attribute set of patients K'_w. The algorithm firstly randomly chooses $s \in \mathbb{Z}_p$ and calculates $DUT_1 = \left(g^a \cdot g^{H(K'_w)}\right)^s$, $DUT_2 = g^{cs}$, $DUT_3 = \left(g^{ac} \cdot g^{bt}\right)^s$, $DU' = g^{us}$. Then for any $x \in Att$, it calculates $K'_x = \left(h_x^{u/v_x}\right)^s$. The trapdoor is

$$Trap = \left\{DUT_1, DUT_2, DUT_3, DU', \left\{K'_x\right\}_{x \in Att}\right\} \tag{6}$$

Finally, DU will do the search operation.

CSTest$(\boldsymbol{CT}, \boldsymbol{PP}, \boldsymbol{Trap})$**:** This algorithm is running by CS. If the doctor's attribute satisfies the access structure of symmetric key ciphertext. Then there must exist $\left\{w_i \in \mathbb{Z}_p\right\}_{i \in I}$ such that $\sum_{i \in I} w_i \lambda_i = k$ and $I = \{i, p(i) \in Att\}$. Next, the CS calculates

$$Test_1 = e(W_0, DUT_2) \cdot \prod\nolimits_{i \in I} \left(e(C_i, DU')e\left(D_i, K_{p(i)}\right)\right)^{w_i} \tag{7}$$

$$Test_2 = (W, DUT_1) \cdot e(W_1, DUT_3) \tag{8}$$

If $Test_1 = Test_2$, DU will find the medical ciphertext, otherwise CS outputs $\perp$.

DUDec$(\boldsymbol{CT}, \boldsymbol{SK})$**:** When DU receive the ciphertext C and CT from CS. The doctor runs the *DUDec* algorithm. It input private key SK containing attribute set and ciphertext CT with access control (M, p). Only the attribute set match the access control, doctor would decrypt the ciphertext. The decrypt algorithm calculates

$$\begin{aligned}
&\frac{\prod\limits_{i \in I} \left(e(C_i, U)e\left(D_i, K_{p(i)}\right)\right)^{w_i}}{e(W_0, DU)} \\
&= \frac{\prod\limits_{i \in I} \left(e\left(g^{b\lambda_i} h_{p(i)}^{-r_i}, g^{ac} \cdot g^{bu}\right) e\left(g^{v_x r_i}, H(K_w)^t\right)\right)^{w_i}}{e\left(g^{a(t+k)}, g^u\right)} \\
&= \frac{e(g,g)^{au(t+k)\sum\limits_{i \in I} \lambda_i w_i}}{e(g,g)^{au(t+k)}} \\
&= e(g,g)^k
\end{aligned} \tag{9}$$

Then

$$K = \frac{K'}{e(g,g)^k} \tag{10}$$

Finally, the doctor can use the symmetric key K to decrypt the encrypted record C, so that he or she can read the medical record m.

DUKeyU$(\boldsymbol{v_x}, \boldsymbol{PK_x})$**:** This algorithm is running by AC. There are two parts in this case. One is when a DO promote or leave the hospital, he or she must update the access privileges of all the record in the CS. Another is that a patient would update his or her record's attribute. Firstly, it randomly chooses a number $v'_x \in \mathbb{Z}_p\left(v'_x \neq v_x\right)$ for new attribute version number. The AC calculates $UK'_{1,x} = v'_x / v_x$ and $UK'_{2,x} = v_x / v'_x$ for DO to update his or her SK, $UK'_x = \left\{UK'_{1,x}, UK'_{2,x}\right\}$. Next, AC calculates the public attribute key $PK'_{1,x} = g^{v'_x}$ and $PK'_{2,x} = g^{1/v'_x}$, $PK'_x = \left\{PK'_{1,x}, PK'_{2,x}\right\}$. The DU's new SK is $K''_x = (K_x)^{v_x/v'_x} = h_x^{t/v'_x}$ and $K'''_x = (K'_x)^{v_x/v'_x} = h_x^{ts/v'_x}$.

CSCTU$(\boldsymbol{MK}, \boldsymbol{UK}_{x'})$**:** This algorithm is running by CS. To reduce the burden of calculating, the system uses proxy re-encryption technical to update the ciphertext. CS randomly chooses $y \in \mathbb{Z}_p$ and calculates $W'_0 = W_o \cdot g^{ay} = g^{a(t+(k+y))}$, $W'_1 = W_1 \cdot g^y = g^{(k+y)}$. For any i from 1 to l and $p(i) \neq x$, it calculates $D'_i = D_i \cdot p(i) = (D'_i)^{UK'_{2,x}} = g^{v'_x r_i}$, $C'_i = C_i \cdot g^{bs'} \cdot M$

$$CT' = \left\{W'_0, W'_1, \{D'_i, C'_i\}_{i \in [1,l]}\right\} \quad (11)$$

5 Analysis of AU-CPABE-SE

5.1 Security Analysis

We conclude the security analysis as the following Theorems:

Theorem 1. AU-CPABE-SE is secure against the forward security and backward security.

Proof. In this scheme, the user's private key is generated randomly, that is, even if two distinguishing users have the same attribute set, the private key is also different. So unauthorized users are not able to decrypt private medical records by trying to collide the private key. Meanwhile, if a user is revoked with an attribute, the AC will generate a new version of the secret key and update the ciphertext associated with the revoked attribute. Since the version key is generated using different values, the revoked user cannot decrypt the ciphertext with the previous key (backward security). As for new DU, the system will assign a set of attributes according his or her identity and generate secret key for DU, such that DU who has t attributes can decrypt the ciphertexts which were published before it joined the system (forward security).

Theorem 2. AU-CPABE-SE is secure against the record ciphertext security.

Proof. The scheme first uses traditional symmetric encryption methods to encrypt medical record into encrypted form, and then encrypts the symmetric keys by CPABE scheme, which ensures the security of record ciphertext. At the same time, the secret sharing value related to symmetric key is embed into the key ciphertext. Attacker needs operate many bilinear pairing operations to recover this value. Also, the system master key and the secret key of the user are generated randomly, so the conspiracy of the malicious users and the attackers cannot get any information about private medical record.

Theorem 3. When the decision bilinear diffie-hellman assumption holds, there not polynomial time adversary can break AU-CPABE-SE with a non-negligible advantage.

Proof. Support there is an adversary A with non-negligible advantage ε in the selective security game against the AU-CPABE-SE and chooses a challenge access structure *AS*. We also build a challenger C which plays the DBDH difficulty with non-negligible advantage [16].

5.2 Performance Analysis

The performance of the scheme is analyzed by the overhead of computing performance and communication performance. At the same time, the simulation experiment was carried out to verify the protocol which compared with the Hur's scheme.

Compare the encryption time of the data owner, the decryption time of the data user and the time of the ciphertext update. x is the number of attributes, *num* represents the number of data users in the system, num_x is the number of attributes that a data user has (Table 1).

Table 1. Computing performance.

	DOEnc	DUDec	CSCTU
Hur's scheme	O(x + log num)	O(numx)	O(numx)
Our scheme	O(x)	O(1)	O(1)

Compare the communication overhead of attribute update and ciphertext update. n_1 is the number of data users whose attribute x is not update, n_2 represents the number of ciphertext containing attribute x, $|p|$ is the number of ciphertext (Table 2).

Table 2. Communication performance.

	DUKeyU	CSCTU
Hur's scheme	N/A	$(n_2 + n_1)\|p\|$
Our scheme	$n_1\|p\|$	$\|p\|$

In order to prove the above theoretical analysis and evaluate the actual efficiency of the scheme, we have simulated the DUKeyU algorithm and CSCTU algorithm of this scheme. The simulation platform is Inter Pentium Inter® Pentium® CPU G4000 @ 3.30 GHz, 8 GB, Ubuntu 16.04. The PBC library is used to initialize operation, and the prime number is chosen as the 512 bits. The A-type elliptic curve is used and set the order of the elliptic curve to be 160 bits. Then, using the CPABE library to encrypt symmetric key and enforce access control. Compare with the Hur's scheme as the following figure (Figs. 4 and 5).

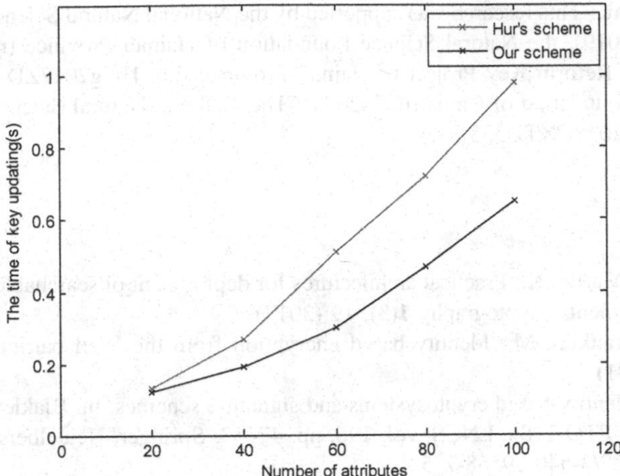

Fig. 4. The time of key updating

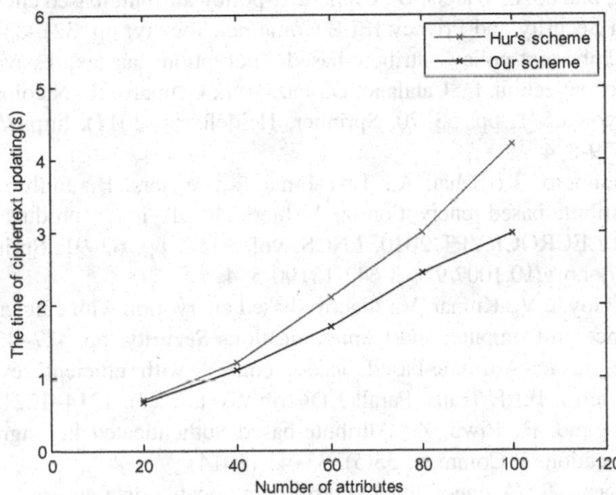

Fig. 5. The time of ciphertext updating

6 Conclusion

We give a cryptographic retrieval scheme combining ciphertext policy attribute-based encryption with searchable encryption technology, which supports attribute update. In this scheme, attributes can be updated frequently and partial decryption was transferred to the cloud storage server. Security analysis shows that the scheme can protect security and privacy under the DBDH assumption and the experimental results with real data show that the scheme is efficient and practical application.

Acknowledgement. This research was supported by the National Natural Science Foundation of China (no. 61661019), the Natural Science Foundation of Hainan Province (no. 617079), the Higher Education Reform Key Project of Hainan Province (no. Hnjg2017ZD-1), the National Natural Science Foundation of China (61762033); The National Natural Science Foundation of Hainan (617048, 2018CXTD333).

References

1. Renwick, S., Martin, K.: Practical architectures for deployment of searchable encryption in a cloud environment. Cryptography **1**(3), 19 (2017)
2. Boneh, D., Franklin, M.: Identity based encryption from the Weil pairing. Crypto **32**(3), 213–229 (2001)
3. Shamir, A.: Identity-based cryptosystems and signature schemes. In: Blakley, G.R., Chaum, D. (eds.) CRYPTO 1984. LNCS, vol. 196, pp. 47–53. Springer, Heidelberg (1985). https://doi.org/10.1007/3-540-39568-7_5
4. Sahai, A., Waters, B.: Fuzzy identity-based encryption. In: Cramer, R. (ed.) EUROCRYPT 2005. LNCS, vol. 3494, pp. 457–473. Springer, Heidelberg (2005). https://doi.org/10.1007/11426639_27
5. Bethencourt, J., Sahai, A., Waters, B.: Ciphertext-policy attribute-based encryption. In: IEEE Symposium on Security and Privacy IEEE Computer Society, pp. 321–334 (2007)
6. Waters, B.: Ciphertext-policy attribute-based encryption: an expressive, efficient, and provably secure realization. In: Catalano, D., Fazio, N., Gennaro, R., Nicolosi, A. (eds.) PKC 2011. LNCS, vol. 6571, pp. 53–70. Springer, Heidelberg (2011). https://doi.org/10.1007/978-3-642-19379-8_4
7. Lewko, A., Okamoto, T., Sahai, A., Takashima, K., Waters, B.: Fully secure functional encryption: attribute-based encryption and (hierarchical) inner product encryption. In: Gilbert, H. (ed.) EUROCRYPT 2010. LNCS, vol. 6110, pp. 62–91. Springer, Heidelberg (2010). https://doi.org/10.1007/978-3-642-13190-5_4
8. Boldyreva, A., Goyal, V., Kumar, V.: Identity-based encryption with efficient revocation. In: ACM Conference on Computer and Communications Security, pp. 417–426. ACM (2008)
9. Hur, J., Dong, K.N.: Attribute-based access control with efficient revocation in data outsourcing systems. IEEE Trans. Parallel Distrib. Syst. **22**(7), 1214–1221 (2011)
10. Qiang, L., Dengguo, F., Liwu, Z.: Attribute-based authenticated key agreement protocol supporting revocation. J. Commun. **35**(5), 33–43 (2014)
11. Begum, S.J., Yasin, S.: A fine-grained control of revocable data access for multi-authority cloud storage. Int. J. Comput. Sci. Mechatron. 86–90 (2015)
12. Naruse, T., Mohri, M., Shiraishi, Y.: Provably secure attribute-based encryption with attribute revocation and grant function using proxy re-encryption and attribute key for updating. Hum.-Centric Comput. Inf. Sci. **5**(1), 8 (2015)
13. Pirretti, M., Traynor, P., Mcdaniel, P., et al.: Secure attribute-based systems, pp. 99–112. IOS Press (2006)
14. Zu, L., Liu, Z., Li, J.: New ciphertext-policy attribute-based encryption with efficient revocation. In: IEEE International Conference on Computer and Information Technology, pp. 281–287. IEEE (2014)
15. Tao, Q., Huang, X.F.: Multi-authority ciphertext-policy attribute-based encryption scheme. J. Wuhan Univ. (Nat. Sci. Ed.) **61**(6), 545–548 (2015)
16. Jung, T., Li, X.Y., Wan, Z., et al.: Privacy preserving cloud data access with multi-authorities. In: Proceedings of the 32nd IEEE International Conference on Computer Communications (INFOCOM 2013), pp. 2625–2633. IEEE (2013)

Secure File Storage System Among Distributed Public Clouds

Li Ximing, Chen Weizhao, Guo Yubin(✉), Zhang Senyang, and Huang Qiong

College of Mathematics and Informatics, South China Agricultural University, Guangzhou, China
guoyubin@scau.edu.cn

Abstract. This paper studies the technology of file storage and retrieval in multiple public clouds based on secret sharing. The research is based on a local storage and multiple public cloud storage to achieve the exchange of data between local storage and public cloud storage. Users can view files, upload files, download files, delete files, and retrieve files through local clients. A file storage directory tree is provided which records the file nodes. Through this storage directory tree, users can examine the structure of file storage on the client, add nodes, that is the simulation of deleting files, and delete nodes, that is the simulation of downloading files. After symmetric encryption, the source file which users upload through the client is stochastically deposited into multiple cloud-storage spaces in the form of encrypted file. Based on the idea of Shamir secret sharing, as the original secret, the storage directory tree is divided into several sub-secrets each of which is deposited individually into a specified cloud-storage space. During the separation, the key data which used for the reconstruction of the original secret is preserved in the local-storage space. The symmetric key is generated by an algorithm, and the seed of the key is preserved in the simulated local storage. The purpose of the study is to improve the data security of public cloud storage, reduce the risk of user data leakage, and provide users with convenient and practical system services.

Keywords: Secret sharing · Secure File Storage System
Distributed Public Clouds

This work is supported by Demonstration on the Construction of Guangdong Survey and Geomatics Industry Technology Innovation Alliance (2017B090907030), The Demonstration of Big Data Application for Land Resource Management and Service (2015B010110006). Qiong Huang is supported by Guangdong Natural Science Funds for Distinguished Young Scholar (No. 2014A030306021), Guangdong Program for Special Support of Top-notch Young Professionals (No. 2015TQ01X796), Pearl River Nova Program of Guangzhou (No. 201610010037), and the National Natural Science Foundation of China (Nos. 61472146, 61672242).

X. Sun et al. (Eds.): ICCCS 2018, LNCS 11065, pp. 277–289, 2018.
https://doi.org/10.1007/978-3-030-00012-7_26

1 Introduction

The public cloud in this study consists of a number of cloud platforms that are available from multiple cloud service providers, such as Baidu Cloud, Google Cloud, Amazon Cloud and so on. Each public cloud server consists of cloud engines, cloud disks, cloud databases, and applications.

Public cloud data storage is user-friendly, space-saving, money-saving, so public cloud storage services are becoming more and more popular. The traditional method currently used for public cloud storage is uploading data in the form of clear text to one public cloud platform provided by one cloud service provider.

Each user uploads, deletes, downloads, and views the file through methods provided by one public cloud provider. While cloud services are increasingly widely accepted, data security is facing more and more challenges. The existing approach of public cloud storage exposes many shortcomings and threats. If the data is preserved on one public cloud platform, and the system of this public cloud platform fails or the data is lost, the user will not be able to obtain the uploaded data. Current storage service of public cloud is based on the reliance on public cloud providers, but the cloud storage provider may be untrustworthy, and the provider may compromise user's data and violate user's privacy for profit. In addition, when data is stored in foreign servers, the security of the data is also affected by local policies. If there is a policy requirement, the public cloud service provider may provide the user's data to the relevant agencies. Besides, with the continuous advance of learning algorithm and its application, it will be of great risks if there is a leakage of the directory tree of data storage, as each file node contains its basic but valuable information. As long as the directory tree is maliciously taken advantage of, a lot of loss will be caused towards users of public-cloud service.

1.1 Our Contribution

We explored the application of conveying files to multi-cloud servers and technical solutions. In this paper, we propose a Secure File Storage System among Distributed public Clouds(SFSS_DC) scheme. The public cloud in this scheme consists of a number of cloud platforms that are available from multiple cloud service providers, such as Baidu Cloud, Google Cloud, Huawei Cloud and so on. Each public cloud server consists of cloud engines, cloud disks, cloud databases, and software applications.

In SFSS_DC, a file storage directory tree is provided which documents the storage structure. Through this storage directory tree, users can examine the structure of file storage on the client, add nodes, that is uploading files, and delete nodes, that is deleting files. After AES encryption, the source file which users upload through the client is stochastically deposited into two cloud servers in the form of encrypted file. Based on the idea of Shamir secret sharing, as the original secret, the storage directory tree is divided into several sub-secrets each of which is deposited individually into a specified cloud storage.

1.2 Organization

This paper is organized as follows. Section 1 explains the background of our scheme and our contributions. Section 2 briefly reviews the related work. Section 3 proposes the SFSS DC 's system model and basic ideas. Section 4 details the process of the system including uploading and querying files. Section 5 discusses the security and computing cost issues of SFSS DC. Section 6 summarizes and concludes the paper.

2 Related Work

Recent work proposed outsourcing schemes based on Shamir's secret sharing algorithm [1] and concentrated on the confidentiality of outsourced data against untrusted servers. Benaloh et al. [2] proposed schemes by which a secret can be divided into many shares which can be distributed to mutually suspicious agents.

Hadavi et al. [3–6] explored the DAS model and proposed a series of solutions using (k, n) threshold secret sharing for preserving data confidentiality, which execute queries over encrypted data in the outsourcing database. In their early solutions [3,4], searchable attribute values are encrypted using an order preserving encryption scheme with the help of a B^{+}-tree index structure to build indexes at the index server. And in their lately solutions [5,6], their client-aware partitioning approach subdivides the domain of shares so that the clients can efficiently search within distributed shares.

An order preserving polynomial building technique was proposed by Emekci et al. [7] which uses hash functions to generate random coefficients.

Attasena et al. proposed a novel approach to securing cloud data warehouses by flexible verifiable secret sharing (fVSS) [8]. The main novelty of fVSS is that, to optimize shared data volume and thus cost, they share a piece of data fewer than n times by using pseudo shares to construct a polynomial and then enforce data integrity with the help of both inner and outer signatures.

Some research activities to protect database structure have been done. Ferretti et al. [9] proposed SecureDBaas architecture that integrates cloud database services with data confidentiality and the possibility of executing concurrent operations on encrypted data. SecureDBaaS is designed to allow multiple and independent clients to connect directly to the untrusted cloud DBaaS without any intermediate server.

Dolev et al. proposed the accumulating automata structure to solve the problem of data hiding in the distribution phase [10,11]. They also proposed the idea in which the concept of accumulating automata is used to constructed secret sharing data tables, as well as some simple ideas to verify data architecture.

Dautrich et al. concluded in [12], that some secret sharing outsourcing schemes are not simultaneously secure and practical in the honest-but-curious server model, where servers are not trusted to keep data private. Their attack is to align shares based on their order and then map the aligned shares onto actual secret values relying upon servers' prior knowledge of original data distribution.

3 System Model and Basic Idea of SFSS_DC

3.1 System Model

As with most cloud models of client-server interaction, SFSS_DC also contains three parts: (1) the data owner, (2) data user and (3) cloud servers providers, which is depicted in Fig. 1. Each part is detailed as follows:

(1) Data Owner: The data owner encrypts the files by AES and then generates the storage directory tree based on the file storage structure. Each node of the storage directory tree contains basic information about its corresponding file, such as the storage path of this file on cloud servers. The encrypted files are randomly uploaded to the cloud servers in the form of ciphertext files. The whole storage directory tree is secretly shared to the cloud servers.
(2) Data Users: Only authorized users can access uploaded files under their authority. Authorized users download and reconstruct the storage tree by using the Lagrangian interpolation, and then achieve the secret information of files by searching the tree node of storage directory tree. After retrieving the targeted file path in cloud, the user downloads the file from cloud servers and decrypts the file.
(3) Cloud Servers Providers: The cloud servers provide limited services to store and manage the uploaded files. It can only be achieved by simply retrieving the file through file name. The cloud server is honest but curious.

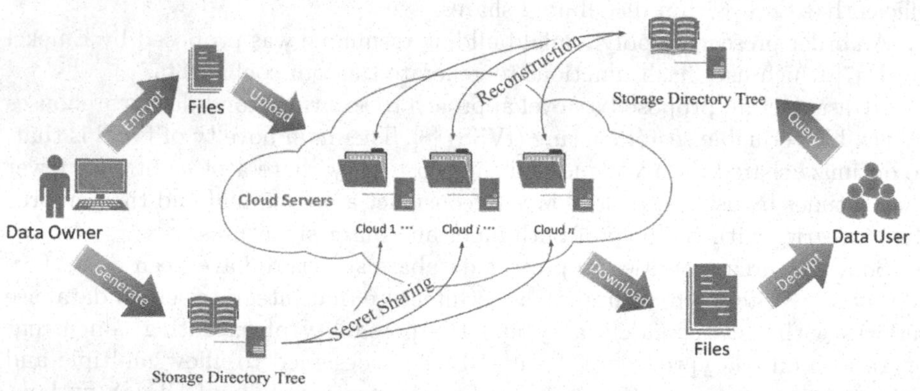

Fig. 1. SFSS_DC Model

As shown in Fig. 1, there are n public clouds, $Cloud_1, Cloud_2, ..., Cloud_n$, and enough storage space is applied for the cloud disk and enough memories are applied for the cloud engine in each public cloud. A software application is running in every cloud engine. The function of the application is to search data in the cloud disk, download data from the cloud disk towards the Client and uploads data from the Client towards the cloud disk. Another software application is running in the Client.

3.2 Secret Sharing for SFSS_DC

Shamir's secret sharing scheme [1] is designed to share a single secret value V among n servers such that shares from at least k servers must be obtained in order to reconstruct V. Such a scheme is called (k, n) threshold scheme. We utilize a simple (k, n) threshold scheme [1] which is based on Lagrange polynomial interpolation. To divide the data V into n pieces, we randomly pick $k-1$ coefficients: $a_{k-1}, ..., a_1$ to construct a random $k-1$ degree polynomial $f(x) = a_{k-1}x^{k-1} + a_{k-2}x^{k-2} + \cdots + a_1 x + a_0$ in which $f(x_0) = a_0 = V$, and evaluate: $Share_1 = f(s_1)$, $\cdots$, $Share_n = f(s_n)$. Given any subset of k of these $Share_i$ values (together with their identifying indices), one can evaluate $V = f(0)$ by interpolation. Knowledge of at most $k-1$ of these values does not suffice to calculate V.

3.3 Encrypting Files

The client generates a key and encrypts the uploaded file with this key. Upload each encrypted file towards two corresponding public clouds. We utilize Shamir's secret sharing scheme [1] to share the key on cloud servers. Authorized user can retrieve files based on the information of the storage directory tree. Then authorized users can get shares of key from cloud servers and use the Lagrange interpolation method to reconstruct the key, and then decrypt the file.

3.4 Storage Directory Tree

As it is shown in Fig. 2, each node of the tree contains important information about the corresponding file. The file storage directory tree is the storage structure of all nodes and allows the user to retrieve the file based on the keyword. Because the storage directory tree contains sensitive information about the file, and the memory capacity of storage directory tree is very small, we utilize Shamir's secret sharing scheme [1] to share Storage Directory Tree towards cloud servers, and it would not reduce the efficiency of querying files. Authorized users can get shares of Storage Directory Tree from cloud server and use the Lagrange interpolation method to reconstruct the Storage Directory Tree, thus they can search node to get the path of file in cloud servers.

4 Process of Uploading Files, Querying and Updating

This section details the process of uploading and querying files of SFSS_DC. Assume that, there are n cloud servers. In Table 1 we give some parameters which will be used throughout this section.

4.1 Uploading Process

Each public cloud has a number from 1 to n, and the numbers of $x_1, x_2, ..., x_n$ correspond to the numbers of $Cloud_1, Cloud_2, ..., Cloud_n$. According to the (k, n)

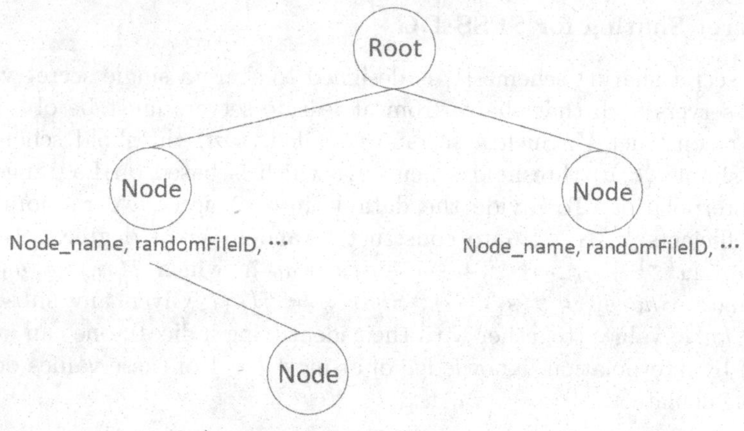

Fig. 2. The Structure of storage directory tree

Table 1. SFSS_DC parameters

Parameters	Definitions
Obj_{sdTree}	Object of storage directory tree
key	The key used to encrypt the files
$file_k$	The original file
B_j	Byte after dissect Obj_{sdTree} or key_i, $j = 1, 2, 3..., max$
$share_{B_j}^{x_i}$	Share of B_j, $j = 1, 2, 3..., max$
n	The total number of cloud server
$x_1, \cdots, x_n$	Abscissa value of $f(x)$, indicating for each cloud server
F_i	The i-th file used to store byte $(1 < i < n)$
$Cloud_i$	i-th cloud server $(1 < i < n)$
max	The total number of B_j
MAX	The total number of files

threshold scheme, we assume that at least k secrets are needed to reconstruct the original secret. The client generates a key and encrypts all source files that are needed to be uploaded. Then, the client uploads each encrypted file to the corresponding cloud servers. The Obj_{sdTree} is indicated as the Storage Directory Tree. The Obj_{sdTree} and key will be performed each with the algorithm 1 $ALGO_{SharingCon}$.

After algorithm 1 $ALGO_{SharingCon}$, each F_i will be uploaded to corresponding servers: $server_1$ to $server_n$, respectively. Then the client only needs to hold $x_1, \cdots, x_k$ as the key of decryption.

At the same time, all data owner's encrypted files are uploaded to corresponding clouds. Algorithm 2 $ALGO_{UploadingFile}$ shows that how one of the files is uploaded to the corresponding cloud server. Execute algorithm 2 for all files.

Algorithm 1. $ALGO_{SharingCon}$

Input:
Obj_{sdTree} or key;
Output:
F_i, $(i = 1, 2, ..., n)$;
Dissect Obj_{sdTree} or key in bytes , B_j, $j = 1, 2, 3..., max$;
Randomly generate a set of $x_1, ..., x_n$, which will be stored to data owner,
for $j = 1; j <= max; j++$ **do**
  Randomly generate a set of $a_1, a_2, ..., a_{n-1}$;
  Construct a polynomial, $f(x) = B_j + a_1x + a_2x^2 + ... + a_{k-1}x^{k-1}$;
  for $i = 1; i <= n; i++$ **do**
    Compute $share^{x_i}_{B_j} \leftarrow f(x_i) = B_j + a_1x + a_2x^2 + ... + a_{k-1}x^{k-1}$;
  end for
end for
for $i = 1; i <= n; i++$ **do**
  for $j = 1; j <= max; j++$ **do**
    $share^{x_i}_{B_j}$ are written into the file F_i in sequence;
  end for
end for
return F_1, ...,F_i, ..., F_n;

Algorithm 2. $ALGO_{UploadingFile}$

Input:
$file_k$;
Output:
Success or *Fail*;
Randomly generate an unique identifier named $randomFileID$ for $file_k$;
Obtain the encryption *key* to encrypt $file_k$, then get $Efile_k$;
Read $randomFileID$ bit by bit. Every three bits are collected together. For the last collection, if there are less than three bits, fill the vacant position with zero
Calculate the corresponding decimal result for each collection above;
For all the decimal results above, calculate both the summation and multiplication of them, and mark summation result as *sum_result* and multiplication result as *mul_result*;
if $sum\_result\%n == mul\_result\%n$ **then**
  Upload $Efile_k$ towards $Cloud_{sum\_result\%n+1}$ and $Cloud_{(mul\_result+1)\%n+1}$;
  Record the *Cloud* index number into the node corresponding with the uploaded file;
else $\{sum\_result\%n \neq mul\_result\%n\}$
  Upload $Efile_k$ towards $Cloud_{sum\_result\%n+1}$ and $Cloud_{mul\_result\%n+1}$;
  Record the *Cloud* index number into the node corresponding the uploaded file of Obj_{sdTree};
end if
return *Success* or *Fail*;

4.2 Query Process

The algorithm 3 $ALGO_{SecretRecon}$ shows how to reconstruct the key and the directory tree from cloud. According to the (k, n) threshold scheme, we assume that at least k secrets are needed to reconstruct the original secret. Based on the directory tree, users choose files that they need to download. Then, the decryption key is used to decrypt the encrypted files.

Algorithm 3. $ALGO_{SecretRecon}$

Input:
  $F_1, ..., F_i, ..., F_k$;
Output:
  Obj_{sdTree} or key;
Download an k of F_i from clouds;
Obtain $x_1, \cdots, x_k$ form data owner;
for $j = 1; j <= max; j++$ **do**
  for $i = 1; i <= k; i++$ **do**
    Read $share_{B_j}^{x_i}$ from the file F_i in sequence;
  end for
end for
for $j = 1; j <= max; j++$ **do**
  for $i = 1; i <= k; i++$ **do**
    Construct a polynomial, $f(x) = B_j + a_1x + a_2x^2 + ... + a_{k-1}x^{k-1}$, with the help of $(x_i, share_{B_j}^{x_i})$ by Lagrange Interpolation Formula;
  end for
  Compute $B_j \leftarrow f(0)$
end for
Combine all bytes, B_j, $j = 1, 2, 3..., max$, to reconstruct the Obj_{sdTree} or key;
return Obj_{sdTree} or key;

4.3 Updating Files

The execution of updating includes inserting and deleting.

Suppose that only one file is inserted, and inserting multiple files is similar to this method, which is shown in Inserting algorithm 4 $ALGO_{InsertFile}$.

Suppose that only one file is deleted, and deleting multiple files is similar to this method, which is shown in Deleting algorithm 5 $ALGO_{DeleteFile}$.

5 Security, Performance Analysis and Experiment Result

5.1 Security, Performance Analysis

Below we analyze the security and the performance of our scheme, and we have the following lemmas. Proofs will be shown in the full version.

Algorithm 4. $ALGO_{InsertFile}$

Input:
An authorized user submits an inserting request to data owner, 'INSERT $file_k$';
Output:
Success or *Fail*;

```
Perform algorithm 3 ALGO_SecretRecon, then obtain the key and the Obj_sdTree ;
Perform algorithm 2 ALGO_UploadingFile for file_k;
Insert a new node of file_k in the Obj_sdTree;
For the key and updated Obj_sdTree, perform algorithm 1 ALGO_SharingCon;
return Success or Fail;
```

Algorithm 5. $ALGO_{DeleteFile}$

Input:
An authorized user submits a deleting request to the data owner, 'DELETE $file_k$';
Output:
Success or *Fail*;

```
Perform algorithm 3 ALGO_SecretRecon, then obtain Obj_sdTree ;
Search Obj_sdTree, then obtain the node information of file_k;
Obtain the index number of file_k from the node, index number indicate in which cloud file_k was stored ;
Delete file_k in corresponding cloud, according to the index number;
Delete node of file_k in the Obj_sdTree;
Perform algorithm 1 ALGO_SharingCon for updated Obj_sdTree;
return Success or Fail;
```

Lemma 1. *In the proposed SFSS_DS scheme, assuming less than n servers collude, the system will not leak any secret information.*

Lemma 2. *SFSS_DS query efficiency does not depend on the size of the file system, but only is related to the number of nodes in the Storage directory tree.*

5.2 Experiment Result

In this section, the feasibility of our method is demonstrated through evaluating the performance of whole sharing and querying execution. We implemented the whole system and examined sharing computation and query cost.

We implemented whole system in C# with about 300 lines of code supporting all our methods. The whole system is implemented on Win10 with a Core i7-6700 3.40 GHz processor and 8 GB of memory. This is a C# program executed on behalf of the data owner over the original relation. The following experimental results only compute the time of SFSS DC, excluding the time of AES encryption and network transmission. The files for test in the experiment are all randomly generated by the system.

Sharing Process Cost. The first series of experiments evaluate the cost of time of sharing processing scenario. Figures 3 and 4 show the comparison of the processing time of sharing different amounts of files for client, where the abscissa indicates number of files in the system. For example, when there are 20,000 files in the system, that is, there are 20,000 nodes in the storage directory tree, executing the algorithm 1 $ALGO_{SharingCon}$ costs 39.827 s. With the increase of the number of files, the time of sharing process is gradually increasing.

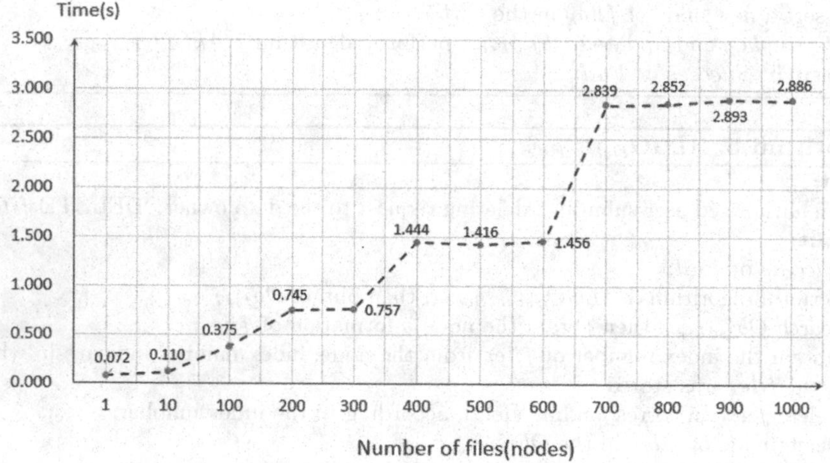

Fig. 3. The processing time of client-side sharing (1 – 1000 files)

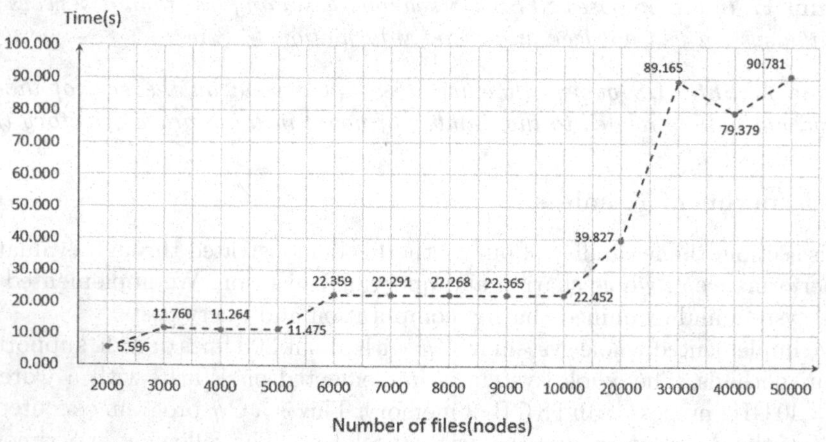

Fig. 4. The processing time of client-side sharing (2000 – 50000 files)

Reconstruction Process Cost. The second series of experiments evaluate the cost of time of query processing scenario. We issued equality query to the system and obtained the processing time of reconstruction of different amounts of files. Each processing time of reconstruction is recorded after 12 tests, where we remove the longest-time record and the shortest-time record, then get the average.

The Figs. 5 and 6 suggests that the process of reconstruction of SES_FS is efficient. For example, when there are 20,000 files in the system, that is, there are 20,000 nodes in the storage directory tree, executing the algorithm 3 $ALGO_{SecretRecon}$ costs 5.097 s.

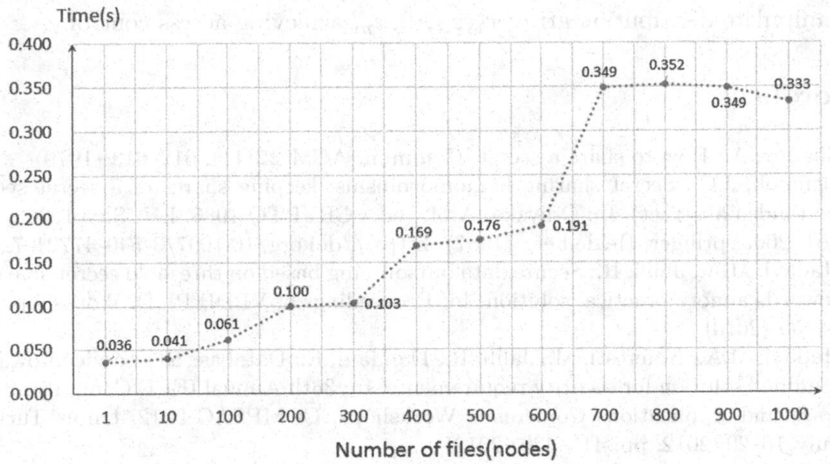

Fig. 5. The processing time of client-side reconstruction (1 – 1000 files)

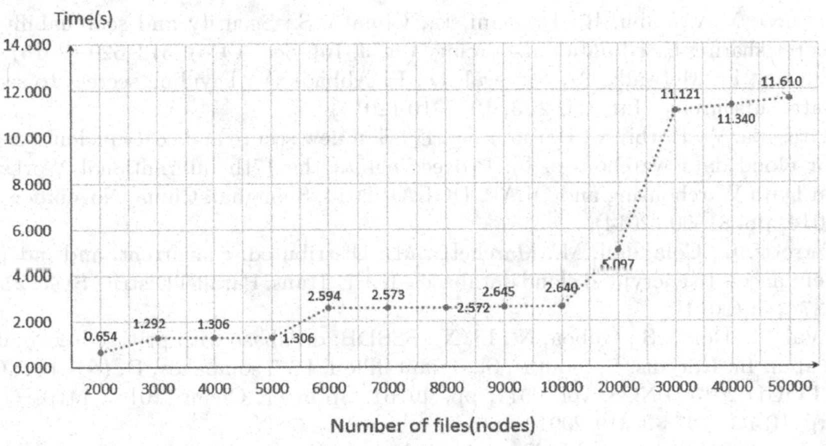

Fig. 6. The processing time of client-side reconstruction (2000 – 50000 files)

6 Discussion

In this paper, we propose a data secure storage scheme based on multi-public clouds. We can expand our scheme in two aspects: (1) The Client can be any electronic equipment qualified for the operation of the application in the Client. After uploading data through one of these electronic equipment, users can copy the newest local variables towards another one to search and download data from the cloud; (2) SFSS_DC is applicable to few users in this scenario, but it can be extended to multi-user environments if we use Chinese remainder theorem [13] 's to manipulate distribution array $x_1, x_2, ..., x_m$ achieving access control.

References

1. Shamir, A.: How to share a secret. Commun. ACM **22**(11), 612–613 (1979)
2. Benaloh, J.C.: Secret sharing homomorphisms: keeping shares of a secret secret (extended abstract). In: Odlyzko, A.M. (ed.) CRYPTO 1986. LNCS, vol. 263, pp. 251–260. Springer, Heidelberg (1987). https://doi.org/10.1007/3-540-47721-7_19
3. Hadavi, M.A., Jalili, R.: Secure data outsourcing based on threshold secret sharing; towards a more practical solution. In: Proceedings of VLDB Ph.D. Workshop, pp. 54–59 (2010)
4. Hadavi, M.A., Noferesti, M., Jalili, R., Damiani, E.: Database as a service: towards a unified solution for security requirements. In: 36th Annual IEEE Computer Software and Applications Conference Workshops, COMPSAC 2012, Izmir, Turkey, July 16–20, 2012, pp. 415–420 (2012)
5. Hadavi, M.A., Damiani, E., Jalili, R., Cimato, S., Ganjei, Z.: AS5: a secure searchable secret sharing scheme for privacy preserving database outsourcing. In: Di Pietro, R., Herranz, J., Damiani, E., State, R. (eds.) DPM/SETOP -2012. LNCS, vol. 7731, pp. 201–216. Springer, Heidelberg (2013). https://doi.org/10.1007/978-3-642-35890-6_15
6. Hadavi, M.A., Jalili, R., Damiani, E., Cimato, S.: Security and searchability in secret sharing-based data outsourcing. Int. J. Inf. Sec. **14**(6), 513–529 (2015)
7. Emekçi, F., Metwally, A., Agrawal, D., El Abbadi, A.: Dividing secrets to secure data outsourcing. Inf. Sci. **263**, 198–210 (2014)
8. Attasena, V., Harbi, N., Darmont, J.: fVSS: a new secure and cost-efficient scheme for cloud data warehouses. In: Proceedings of the 17th International Workshop on Data Warehousing and OLAP, DOLAP 2014, Shanghai, China, November 3–7, 2014, pp. 81–90 (2014)
9. Ferretti, L., Colajanni, M., Marchetti, M.: Distributed, concurrent, and independent access to encrypted cloud databases. IEEE Trans. Parallel Distrib. Syst. **25**(2), 437–446 (2014)
10. Avni, H., Dolev, S., Gilboa, N., Li, X.: SSSDB: database with private information search. In: Karydis, I., Sioutas, S., Triantafillou, P., Tsoumakos, D. (eds.) ALGOCLOUD 2015. LNCS, vol. 9511, pp. 49–61. Springer, Cham (2016). https://doi.org/10.1007/978-3-319-29919-8_4
11. Dolev, S., Gilboa, N., Li, X.: Accumulating automata and cascaded equations automata for communicationless information theoretically secure multi-party computation: extended abstract. In: Proceedings of the 3rd International Workshop on Security in Cloud Computing, SCC@ASIACCS 2015, Singapore, Republic of Singapore, April 14, 2015, pp. 21–29 (2015)

12. Dautrich, J.L., Ravishankar, C.V.: Security limitations of using secret sharing for data outsourcing. In: Cuppens-Boulahia, N., Cuppens, F., Garcia-Alfaro, J. (eds.) DBSec 2012. LNCS, vol. 7371, pp. 145–160. Springer, Heidelberg (2012). https://doi.org/10.1007/978-3-642-31540-4_12
13. Hadavi, M.A., Jalili, R., Karimi, L.: Access control aware data retrieval for secret sharing based database outsourcing. Distrib. Parallel Databases **34**(4), 1–30 (2016)

Security Strategy of Campus Network Data Center in Cloud Environment

Ge Suhui(✉), Wan Quan, and Sun Wenhui

Qingdao Institute of Technology, Qingdao, ShanDong, China 266300
suhuige@126.com, wanlibaidu@foxmail.com, swhtongxin@163.com

Abstract. In the campus network security strategy, the traditional university data center only considers traffic safety as the consideration factor, in the cloud computing environment, the security model of the virtualization data center is transformed from 2d to 3d. This paper proposes four security strategies and designs the security and equipment deployment of campus network data center under the cloud environment, thus improving the security of campus network data center in the cloud environment.

Keywords: Cloud environment · Data center · Security strategy

1 Introduction

With the rapid development of cloud technology, the use of virtualization technology in the data center, integrate the various physical resources such as servers, storage and network realization of elastic cloud service mode, to apply for the traditional campus offers a variety of cloud service platform, including data storage cloud services, research cloud computing service, desktop virtualization cloud services and so on. Despite the vertical and horizontal security strategies, the security strategy of the traditional university data center in campus network is to regard traffic safety as the only consideration. However, in order to adapt to the new technology, the campus network security model of the virtualization data center in the cloud environment should be changed, and the security strategy of the other one-dimensional space should be added, and the two-dimensional plane can be transformed into three-dimensional space. After the authorization, the host joins or leaves the computing cluster, the virtual machine dynamic migration, and the isolation of a large number of users among various businesses. But these traditional data centers can't be implemented. Security as a service in the cloud environment, how to adapt to the basic network architecture and the application services of virtualization, realize virtual delivery, is the focus of campus network security policy. To solve the above problems, based on the cloud data center virtualization of campus network security construction must draw lessons from the new ideas and new methods, such as extending the virtual local area network, security policy, security strategy moves along with the virtual machine live migration.

X. Sun et al. (Eds.): ICCCS 2018, LNCS 11065, pp. 290–297, 2018.
https://doi.org/10.1007/978-3-030-00012-7_27

2 Security Strategy of Campus Network Data Center of Cloud Environment

A. *VLAN extension*

Virtualization campus data center as a centralized resource of foreign service, in front of the user have multiplied, bearing service is huge, especially operating cloud platform for users of the general public, should be allowed to teachers and students, parents and users anywhere from any terminal access to the school of public service information resources, and make students learn not only the school computer room or a classroom, but in any place can log on to the campus network for the construction of a learning environment resources and services, enhance the flexibility and agility of network learning, learning resources of "On demand, it is On demand". At the same time, parents can grasp the students' learning status in time, and the society can fully understand the development status of the school. So, cloud platform logic (virtual machine or physical) of safety, reliability, and the platform mass users, all kinds of clear separation between the business and security identification, is the data center managers need to consider factors. To identify and isolate a large number of users, for each user based on the cloud is the best way to provide them with different VLAN ID, but can provide virtual local area network (LAN) is the greatest number of 4096, a cloud environment to a large number of business, so you need to expand the VLAN [1].

Because the cloud is flexible, dynamic, elastic, agile, and adaptable, it requires a flexible, dynamic, flexible architecture as the basis for cloud computing. Consider support virtualization firewall, is the inevitable choice of network infrastructure point of view, different users can be based on the VLAN mapped to different instances of virtualization, each virtual instances have independent security control strategy and management functions [2]. Figure 1 shows the use of VLAN technology to map different users to different instances of virtualization.

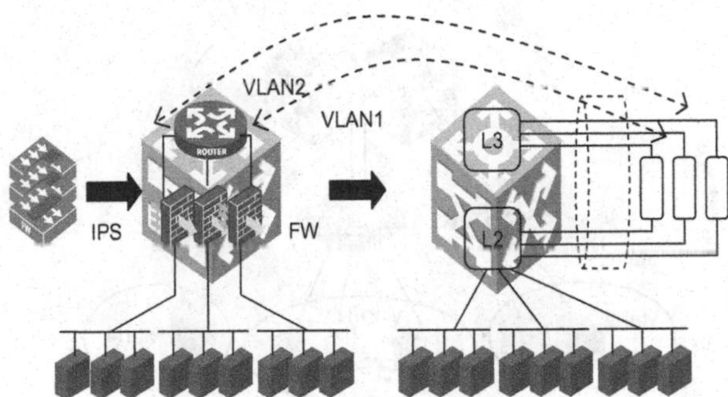

Fig. 1. Different users based on VLAN mapping to different instances of virtualization

B. *Selection of secure deployment boundaries*

The basic principle of the traditional campus network security protection strategy is different regions adopt different strategies, namely, the so-called border isolation and access control strategy, but this method is based on the pre-demarcated boundaries between regions. But in cloud computing environment, unified the basic network architecture, realize the high integration of computing and storage resources, therefore the deployment of the boundary between safety equipment completely disappear, this will mean safety equipment deployment mode is no longer like the construction pattern of traditional security, based on cloud computing environment need to find a new model of security deployment.

Use IRF2 strategy of gathering cut-off switch is the second and third layer, the campus server belong to three layers model, and the network side belong to the second mode, this is the working characteristics of browser/server data center. Various services on campus, such as Web, AP, DB. Corresponding to a VLAN, exchange of visits between the VLAN ACL to control, a variety of services to the outside world by a firewall security control, and the three layers of gathering switches as a gateway, control access to the data flow [3]. Both the firewall and the switch will be divided into the virtual route, and the unified business will be divided into the same VRF, and the WEB/AP/DB will be divided into the same VRF and different two-tier partitions [4]. The three-layer routing function of the switch realizes the communication between the same business Web, AP and DB, and use ACL to control access business. The communication between different businesses is achieved through a VRF firewall. Second, three layer interface on campus need to the corresponding network firewall access to another network, you can configure a "weak policy routing", the routing of the next-hop as the firewall, the firewall is working correctly determines the normal use of the routing, therefore can be equipped with a bypass firewalls, so as to ensure the normal operation of the routing [5]. This method is suitable for the virtual machine based on virtual environment of migration, and the use of switches, access control lists (ACL to isolate different application, relative to the frequent adjustment of the client is a better way to deal with, so suitable for the low required security isolation, host deployment flexibility higher environment [6] (Fig. 2).

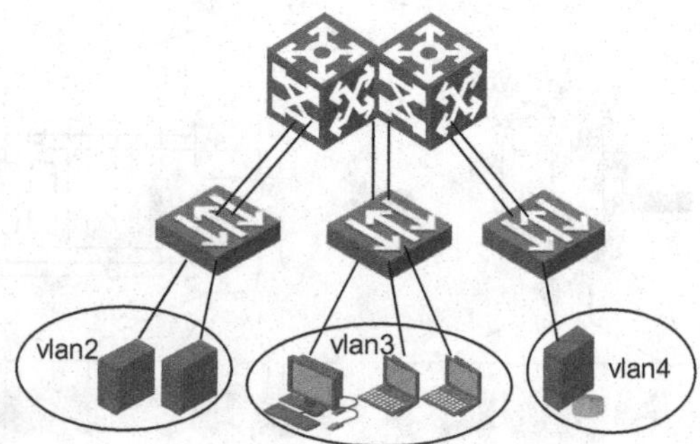

Fig. 2. Selection of secure deployment boundaries

C. *Centralized security service center*

Traditional security construction model pays attention to the boundary of different protection strategy, the height of the storage resource and computing resource integration, so different users in the campus network application of cloud computing services, can only achieve logical isolation, there can be no physical security boundary. Therefore, it is no longer possible to gather user traffic and deploy independent security boundary system according to the classification of campus network users. Therefore, the service deployment based on the security protection of each subsystem should be transformed into the protection of the whole cloud computing environment and the centralized security center to adapt to the logical isolation of the physical model [7]. Cloud service providers or cloud administrators can through the appropriate method request security service user traffic is introduced into the focus of security service center, after complete the security service forward again to return to the original path. The centralized security service center can not only complete the individual configuration of user security services, but also save construction cost. The deployment diagram for providing security services on a certain convergence ratio is shown in Fig. 3.

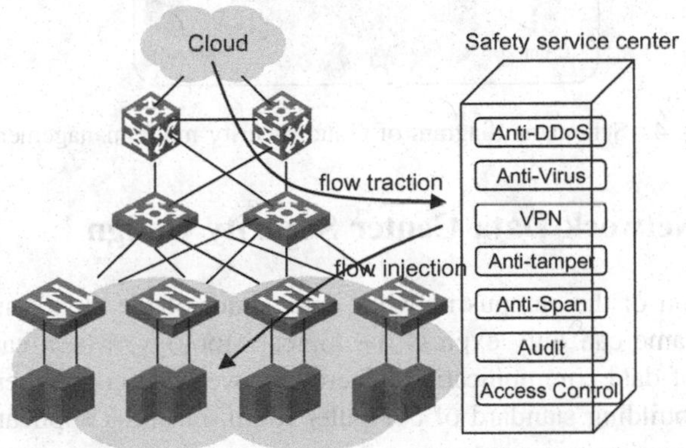

Fig. 3. Centralized security service center deployment

D. *Coupling of cloud security patterns*

It is an important development direction of campus network to realize the security detection and protection of cloud mode by using the powerful computing power in the campus network. Compared with the traditional security model of cloud environment security model not only requires the cloud of local customers have basic threat detection and protection function, more emphasis on their threat to unknown or suspicious sensing detection ability [8]. For suspicious traffic that cannot be correctly judged, the users in the campus network can send it to the cloud detection center. The high speed and accurate detection ability of the cloud can correctly locate and remove the threat. Can also use these suspicious traffic data sent to all customers, gateway, even let the cloud customer and gateway possess the ability to detect the unknown threat, so as to achieve the security of customer model of security defense system closed-loop strategy (Protection, Detectiong, Reaction, Restore) [9]. In Fig. 4, is the essence of cloud detection mode.

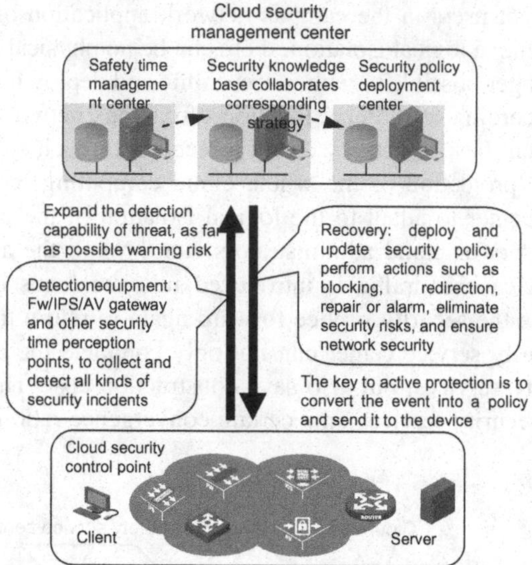

Fig. 4. Schematic diagram of cloud security mode management

3 Campus Network Data Center Security Design

In the construction of the campus network data center of the cloud environment, the simple picture frame can only express the logical topology, which can not meet the security design of data communication. Therefore, we need comprehensive consideration, including building standard of computer room, business application model and so on. The following requirements are used to design the equipment, structure model and network deployment of the campus network data center machine room using the tia-942 standard. 500 sets of data center servers, server gigabit network card access, server access switches by Wan Zhao cascade to convergence layer switches, power 300 W for each server, and each network cabinet maximum power 3 kw, each storage racks biggest power 2 kw, the storage network has a separate cabinet [10].

A. *Logical topology*

According to the application demand of campus network, all the business can be divided into Web, AP, DB three logical access area, each area is a standard three layer model, access layer using H3C S7510E equipment, convergence layer using S9512E equipment, core layer using S12508 equipment. This kind of flat network structure changed according to the application before the dividing method of "sugar-coated berry string" type, the maximum meet the demand of mass user's access, facilitate campus data center room scalability [11]. Campus data center as shown in Fig. 5, the client access to the data center through special FW process, improve the external security of data centers, inside the campus network, access between all kinds of information gathered by the data center layer of FW to control, so as to improve safety [12].

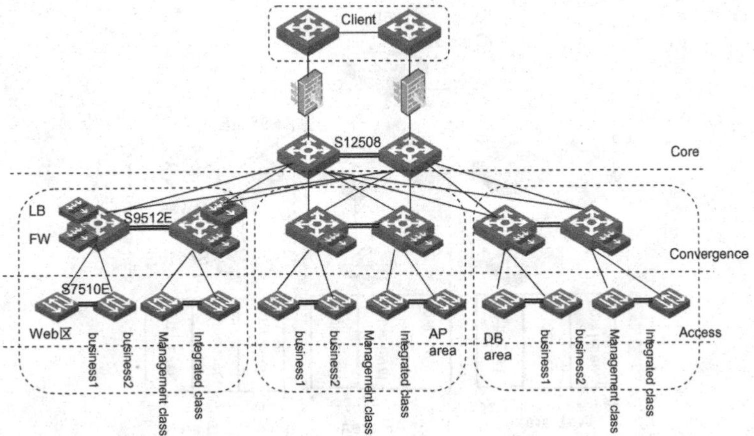

Fig. 5. Topology of campus network data center

Four S7510E device connection servers were placed in the three logical access areas of the Web, AP and DB, and each S7510E was connected to the sink layer by 2 * 10GE, and two 4 * 10GE single boards were configured. The convergence layer USES the S9512E device, and the FW plug-in is deployed to improve the security. Areas based on Web application type, load balancing is essential, so we need in the Web configuration on S9512E LB card, use 2 * 10 GE cascade to the two core funnel switch S12508, use 4 * 40 GE is connected with another S9512E convergence layer the same area, using 4 * 10 GE S7510E interconnected with the access layer. The core layer is placed with 2 S12508, each of which USES 2 pieces of 4 k * 10GE single board, which is connected with another S12508 by 3 * 10GE, and connects with S9512E of the aggregation layer through 2 * 10GE, which meets the communication between each layer of business.

B. *Network security and equipment deployment*

The deployment of the campus network data center depends on the importance of different levels of the business, from security and application considerations, to setting the gateway on different devices. There are two types of business access patterns: vertical access is the same business accessed in different areas; Horizontal access is the access between different applications in the same level [13]. Depending on the application requirements, the business level is distinguished and the deployment plan is shown in Fig. 6.

Low-level application services set up gateways on the S9512E of the aggregation layer switch and achieve vertical and horizontal access through ACL access control policies. For intermediate application services, horizontal access USES the switch ACL access control list implementation, and vertical access is controlled by the firewall. For advanced applications, both horizontal and vertical access are controlled by the firewall [14]. For the virtualization of the above three businesses, using MCE technology and binding VPN instances to achieve mutual business isolation will greatly reduce ACL configuration and resource consumption. Server 2 switching between controlled by

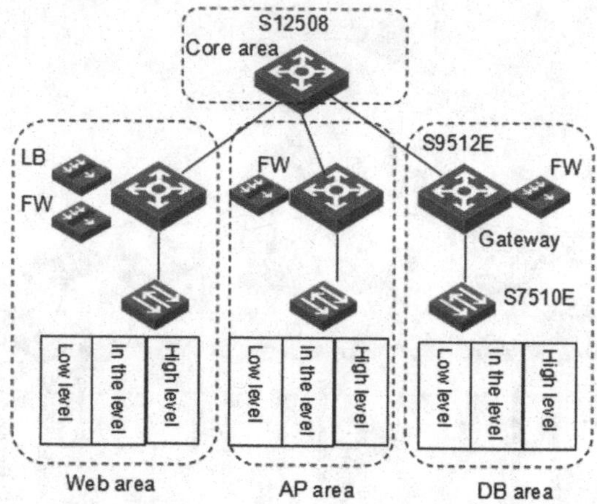

Fig. 6. Data center security deployment

access layer S7510E, convergence layer S9512E exchanged with FW, and implement and core layer S12508 cross-regional routing forwarding, core layer S12508 switch control business communication between different areas.

4 Conclusion

Cloud environment of the campus network security is the important factor in the development of informationization in university, as the bottom of the base platform will face many challenges, on the one hand, to improve technology to optimize the previous safe mode now, on the other hand should continuously adopt new technology to meet the challenge. Further explore new security model, based on the cloud data center network architecture embedded security policy, using more safe way of interaction, improve the campus data center cloud environment certification identification ability, and can provide real-time control strategy, so as to avoid the disadvantages of traditional security strategy, improve the campus data center cloud environment security.

Acknowledgements. I want to take this chance to thanks to Wang Bin and Wan Quan. In the process of composing this paper, they give me many academic and constructive advices and help me to correct my paper.

At the same time, I would like to appreciate my research team for the approved fund project, ShanDong University Science and Technology Project (J16LN54) and Qingdao University of Technology Project (2016JY007/2017KY008).

References

1. Cook, G., Horn, J.V.: How dirty is your data? A look at the energy choices that power cloud computing. Greenpeace International Technology report, April 2015
2. Qureshi, A.: Power-demand routing in massive geo-distributed systems. Ph.D. dissertation. Massachusetts Institute of Technology (2016)

3. Gao, P.X., Curtis, A.P., Wong, B., Keshav, S.: It's not easy being green. In: Proceeding of the ACM SIGCOMM 2012, Helsinki, Finland, pp. 211–222 (2012)
4. The theory and practice of the new generation of network construction. Electronic Industry Press, Beijing, October 2015
5. Xu, X., Lei, H.: Discussion on the technology of virtualization technology in the construction of university informatization. J. Southwest Univ. Natl. Nat. Sci. Ed. **34**(4), 818–822 (2014). Chengdu
6. Joysula, V., Orr, M., Page, G., Jun, Z.: Automation of cloud computing and data center. People's Post and Telecommunications Press, Beijing, July 2016
7. Xue, L., Xu, K.: The utility maximization model of cloud virtual machine resource allocation. J. Comput. Sci. (2), 252–262 (2015)
8. Qin, X., Zhang, W., Wei, J., et al.: Status and challenges of distributed cache technology under cloud computing environment. J. Softw. **24**(1), 50–66 (2017)
9. Zhang, T.: Management of cloud management from data center. IP Pilot. (4), 121–123 (2016)
10. Yu, S., Lu, Y., Wang, F.: Research and design of data deletion architecture based on cloud storage. Comput. Syst. Appl. **22**(1), 208–211 (2015)
11. Liu, X., Yang, S., Guo, L.: Snowflake structure: a new data center network structure. J. Comput. Sci. (1), 76–86 (2014)
12. Deng, W., Liu, F., Jin, H.: New energy application in cloud computing data center: research status and trends. J. Comput. Sci. (3), 582–588 (2013)
13. Ye, K., Wu, Z., Jiang, X., He, Q.: Energy consumption management of virtualization cloud computing platform. J. Comput. Sci. (6), 1262–1285 (2016)
14. Feng, Zhang, M., Zhang, Y., et al.: Research on cloud computing security. J. Softw. **22**(1), 71–83 (2015)

SLIDE: An Efficient Secure Linguistic Steganography Detection Protocol

Linghao Zhang[1(✉)], Sheng Wang[1], Wei Gan[2], Chao Tang[1], Jie Zhang[1], and Huihui Liang[1]

[1] State Grid Sichuan Electric Power Research Institute, Chengdu 610072, China
zlh_sgcc@163.com

[2] State Grid Sichuan Electric Power Company, Chengdu 610041, China

Abstract. Linguistic steganography detection aims at distinguishing between normal text and stego-text. In this paper, based on homomorphic cryptosystem, we propose an efficient secure protocol for linguistic steganography detection. The protocol involves a vendor holding a private detector of linguistic steganography and a user in possession of some private text documents consisting of stego-text and normal text. By cooperatively performing the secure two-party protocol, the user can securely obtain the detection results of his private documents returned by the vendor's remote detector while both vendor and user learn nothing about the privacy of each other. It is shown the proposed protocol is still secure against probe attack. Experiment result and theoretical analysis confirm the efficiency, correctness, security, computation complexity and communication overheads of our scheme.

Keywords: Information hiding · Privacy-preserving · Detection Correlations between words · N-window mutual information

1 Introduction

Recent advances of flexible and ubiquitous transmission mediums, such as wireless networks and Internet, have opened the way towards a new type of services in which individual and organization could sell their knowledge and ability to process and analyze data remotely through an internet web service. Some existing examples include remote diagnostics [2,18], face detection [4,21], neural-network-based computation [1,11], similar document detection [3,10,12] and so on. The purpose of linguistic steganography detection schemes is to distinguish stego-text and normal text. Placing a detector of linguistic steganography on the Internet allows users to enjoy the power of the detector without having to design and construct it themselves. However, it presents privacy risk to both the user and the party holding the detector. The vendor, holding the private detector of linguistic steganography, would be reluctant to release his detector, as he has spent much time, money and energy in designing and constructing it. The user may like to employ the remote detection service, but he is also reluctant to

X. Sun et al. (Eds.): ICCCS 2018, LNCS 11065, pp. 298–309, 2018.
https://doi.org/10.1007/978-3-030-00012-7_28

reveal his privacy, such as the content of his texts. In this paper, we introduce a secure two-party protocol, named SLIDE, whereby a user may ask a remote linguistic steganography detection service provider to run his private detector on a set of secret text documents consisting of stego-text and normal text in a secure manner. By cooperatively performing the privacy-preserving protocol, the user can obtain nothing but the detection results returned by a vendor's private remote detector, but the vendor learns nothing about the user's documents and his private detector will also be securely protected. That is, the user can enjoy the power of a remote detector of linguistic steganography, and the privacy of both vendor and user will be well preserved. The privacy-preserving protocol relies on the semantically secure homomorphic encryption system [13] by which $E(x+y)$ and $E(k*x)$ (x and y are any plaintext, k is a positive integer) can be computed from $E(x)*E(y)$ and $E(x)^k$ respectively. Here, $E(\cdot)$ is the encryption function. The properties of homomorphic cryptosystem open the possibility that a vendor holding a private detector and a user having private text documents collaboratively detect the latter's private documents without disclosing any privacy of both.

So far, some schemes for linguistic steganography detection have been proposed. Using the idea of conceptual graph, [16] presented a detecting algorithm by measuring the correlation between sentences, and the accuracy of the simulation detection using this scheme is 76%. An attack against the systems based on synonym substitution was proposed by Taskian *et al.* [14]. The experimental accuracy of Taskian's scheme on classification of steganographically modified sentences is 84.9% and that of unmodified sentences is 38.6%. To improve the accuracy, Chen *et al.* [5–7] put forward a new type of detection scheme using the measurement of the statistical characteristics of the correlations between the general service words, such as the mutual information. The experimental results show the accuracy of this scheme is 97.19% [6,7] and that of the simple version of the scheme is still as high as 96.3% [5]. However, all the above schemes can only detect the text documents locally. In this paper, we propose a practical, provably secure interactive protocol for privacy-preserving linguistic steganography detection by which a remote user's documents can been detected by a vendor's private detector while no privacy of both is disclosed. To the best of our knowledge, there has not been any method for privacy-preserving linguistic steganography detection. Some privacy-preserving protocols have been proposed for various applications, such as remote diagnostics [2,20], face detection [?],[19], neural-network-based computation [1,17], similar document detection [10,12], but their settings are restricted to respective special service and the protocols cannot deal with the remote linguistic steganography detection.

Our Main Contributions: We propose an efficient secure two-party protocol for linguistic steganography detection. The protocol involves a vendor holding a private detector of linguistic steganography and a user in possession of some private text documents consisting of stego-text and normal text. By collaboratively performing the privacy-preserving protocol, the user will securely obtain the detection results of his private text documents returned by the vendor's remote detector while both vendor and user learn nothing about the privacy of each other. Experiment result and theoretical analysis confirm the efficiency, correctness, security, computation complexity and communication overheads of the new scheme.

The rest of the paper is organized as follows. Section 2 reviews the notions and schemes of homomorphic encryption system and linguistic steganography detection using statistical characteristics of correlations between words. We propose the privacy-preserving protocol for linguistic steganography detection in Sect. 3, and then present the theoretical analysis of its correctness, security, communication overheads and computation complexity. Section 4 describes the experiment results and gives some discussions. Section 5 concludes this paper.

2 Preliminaries

2.1 Homomorphic Encryption System

There is a public cryptosystem (E, D) where E is the encryption function and D is the decryption function. If the following condition holds on,

$$D(E(m_1) * E(m_2)) = m_1 + m_2, \tag{1}$$

where m_1 and m_2 are any plaintext, then, the public encryption system is homomorphic. It is obvious that $E(m_1)*E(m_2)$ is the corresponding ciphertext of m_1+m_2 in a homomorphic cryptosystem, that is to say, $E(m_1) * E(m_2) \mathrel{\mathring{=}} E(m_1+m_2)$, where $\mathrel{\mathring{=}}$ denotes that they hide the same plaintext item. Therefore, using homomorphic cryptosystem, $E(m_1 + m_2)$ can be computed from $E(m_1)$ and $E(m_2)$ without decrypting them. As an obvious inference, there is

$$E(m_1)^k \mathrel{\mathring{=}} E(m_1 * k) \tag{2}$$

where k is a positive integer.

Paillier [13] proposed an efficient and semantically secure (IND-CPA secure) homomorphic cryptosystem. Another significant feature of Pallier's homomorphic encryption system is that it does not encrypt a plaintext unit into the same ciphertext item everytime. The encryption function E has two inputs a secret message m and a random parameter r. For an arbitrary plaintext item m, we have $E(m, r_1) \neq E(m, r_2)$ $(r_1 \neq r_2)$. However, the decryption does not depend on the random parameter at all and $D(E(m, r_1)) \equiv D(E(m, r_2)) \equiv m$. The encryption scheme that satisfies the property is called a probabilistic encryption scheme which was first introduced in [9]. This property is especially important in the application. For example, when the plaintext samples are integer in the interval $[0, \mathcal{N} - 1]$, a non-probabilistic cryptosystem will produce only $\mathcal{N}$ possible ciphertexts, then an adversary could easily break the system by traversing each possible ciphertext. Whereas a probabilistic encryption scheme can produce a great more different ciphertexts, therefore the brute force attack would be impossible. We briefly describe Pallier's cryptosystem as follows. See [13] for more details.

Key Generation: Select two large enough primes p and q. Then, the secret private key sk is $\lambda = lcm(p-1, q-1)$ which is the least common multiple of $p-1$ and $q-1$. The public key pk is (n, g), where $n = p*q$ and $g \in \mathbb{Z}^*_{n^2}$ such that $gcd(L(g^\lambda \bmod n^2), n) = 1$, that is, the maximal common divisor of $L(g^\lambda \bmod n^2)$ and n is equivalent to 1 where $L(x) = (x-1)/n$ and the same below.

Encryption: Let $m \in \mathbb{Z}_n$ be the plaintext. Select a random number $r \in \mathbb{Z}_n$ as the secret parameter for probabilistic encryption. Then the cryptograph c of the message m is

$$c = g^m r^n \bmod n^2. \tag{3}$$

Decryption: Let $c \in \mathbb{Z}_{n^2}$ be a ciphertext. The plaintext m hidden in c is

$$m = \frac{L(c^\lambda \bmod n^2)}{L(g^\lambda \bmod n^2)} \bmod n. \tag{4}$$

3 Efficient Secure Linguistic Steganography Detection Protocol

3.1 System Definition and Security Model

We consider the scene consisting of a vendor, named Alice, and the user, called Bob. Alice holds a private detector of linguistic steganography and Bob privately has w text documents consisting of stego-text and normal text: $\mathbf{d}_1$, $\mathbf{d}_2$, $\cdots$, $\mathbf{d}_w$. Alice has obtained the training N-WMI matrix $\mathbf{T} = [t_{ij}]_{m\times m}$, the threshold $\mathcal{V}_0$ and other essential parameters. Bob holds the sample N-WMI matrixes ${}^1\mathbf{S}$, ${}^2\mathbf{S}$, $\cdots$, ${}^w\mathbf{S}$, of which ${}^k\mathbf{S} = [{}^k s_{ij}]_{m\times m}$ $(k = 1, 2, \cdots, w)$ is the corresponding N-WMI matrix of document $\mathbf{d}_k$. Assume $\sum_{i=1}^m \sum_{j=1}^m t_{ij}^2$, $\sum_{i=1}^m \sum_{j=1}^m {}^k s_{ij}^2$, $\sum_{i=1}^m \sum_{j=1}^m t_{ij} * {}^k s_{ij}$, $\mathcal{V}_0 \in (0, m^2\mathcal{K})$, where $\mathcal{K}$ is a positive integer and $(0, m^2\mathcal{K})$ denotes the open interval from 0 to $m^2\mathcal{K}$. Their goal is that by collaborative computation, Bob obtains the detection result of each text document returned by Alice's detector and both participants learn nothing about the privacy of each other.

Similar to many existing privacy-preserving protocols [2],?,[1,10,12,15], we also assume the participants are semi-honest [8], also called honest-but-curious. That is, a participant will correctly follow the protocols while trying to find out potentially confidential information from his legal medium records. It is remarkable that the semi-honest assumption is reasonable and practicable, as the participants, in reality especially in the situation of privacy-preserving linguistic steganography detection, may strictly follow the protocols to exactly obtain the profitable outputs. Actually, our protocol is still secure in some potential malicious behaviors.

Protocol 1. Efficient Secure for LInguistic Steganography DEtection Protocol (SLIDE)

Input: Alice has a private detector of linguistic steganography and Bob privately holds a set of text documents consisting of stego-text and normal text: $\mathbf{d}_1$, $\mathbf{d}_2$, $\cdots$, $\mathbf{d}_w$. Alice is in possession of the training matrix $\mathbf{T}= [t_{ij}]_{m\times m}$, the threshold $\mathcal{V}_0$ and other parameters. Bob has the sample N-WMI matrixes ${}^1\mathbf{S}$, ${}^2\mathbf{S}$, $\cdots$, ${}^w\mathbf{S}$, of which ${}^k\mathbf{S} = [{}^k s_{ij}]_{m\times m}$ $(k = 1, 2, \cdots, w)$ is the sample N-WMI matrix of $\mathbf{d}_k$. Assume $\sum_{i=1}^{m}\sum_{j=1}^{m} t_{ij}^2$, $\sum_{i=1}^{m}\sum_{j=1}^{m} {}^k s_{ij}^2$, $\sum_{i=1}^{m}\sum_{j=1}^{m} t_{ij} * {}^k s_{ij} \in (0, m^2\mathcal{K})$ where $\mathcal{K}$ is integer.

Output: Bob obtains the detection result of each document, and Alice learns nothing.

Step 1: Alice computes the private vector $\mathbf{A}= (a_1, a_2, \cdots, a_n)$ where $n = m^2$, each element of the vector $\mathbf{A}$ is integer and $a_{m(i-1)+j} = 10^4 * t_{ij}$ $(i, j = 1, 2, \cdots, m)$.

for $k = 1$ to w **do**

According to the secret matrix ${}^k\mathbf{S}$, Bob locally computes his private vector ${}^k\mathbf{B} = ({}^k b_1, {}^k b_2, \cdots, {}^k b_n)$ where $n = m^2$, each element of the vector ${}^k\mathbf{B}$ is integer and ${}^k b_{m(i-1)+j} = 10^4 * {}^k s_{ij}$ $(i, j = 1, 2, \cdots, m)$.

end for

Step 2: Alice generates the homomorphic encryption key pairs (pk_A, sk_A). Here pk_A is the public key, and sk_A is the corresponding private key. Then Alice encrypts her secret vector $\mathbf{A}$, obtains the vector $\mathbf{C}= (c_1, c_2, \cdots, c_n)$ in which $c_i = E_{pk_A}(a_i)$ $(i = 1, 2, \cdots, n)$, and sends $c_1, c_2, \cdots, c_n$ and the public key pk_A to Bob.

Step 3: Bob locally generates another homomorphic cryptosystem key pairs (pk_B, sk_B) where pk_B and sk_B are the public key and secret key respectviely.

for $k = 1$ to w **do**

Bob randomly chooses an integer $v_k \in (0, 10^8 m^2\mathcal{K})$, and computes

$$x_k = E_{pk_A}(v_k) * \prod_{i=1}^{n} c_i^{\,{}^k b_i},$$

$$y_k = E_{pk_B}(2 * v_k + \sum_{i=1}^{n} {}^k b_i^2).$$

Then, he sends x_k, y_k and the public key pk_B to Alice.

end for

Step 4:

for $k = 1$ to w **do**

Alice decrypts x_k, and obtains $u_k = D_{sk_A}(x_k)$. Then, Alice generates three random integers ${}^k r_1$, ${}^k r_2$ and ${}^k r_3$ which meet $25*10^8 m^2\mathcal{K} \leqslant {}^k r_1$, ${}^k r_1 \leqslant {}^k r_2 \leqslant {}^k r_1 + \lfloor \frac{{}^k r_1}{5*10^8 m^2\mathcal{K}} \rfloor$ and $0 \leqslant {}^k r_3 \leqslant 5 * 10^8 m^2\mathcal{K}$, and computes

$$z_k = y_k^{\,{}^k r_1} * E_{pk_B}(({}^k r_1 * \sum_{i=1}^{n} a_i^2) - {}^k r_2 * (2 * u_k + 10^8 m^2\mathcal{V}_0) + {}^k r_3).$$

Send z_k to Bob.

end for

Step 5:

for $k = 1$ to w **do**

Using his private key sk_B, Bob decrypts z_k, and obtains $\mathcal{V}_k' = D_{sk_B}(z_k)$. Then, he classifies $\mathbf{d}_k$ as a stego-text if $\mathcal{V}_k' > 5 * 10^8 m^2\mathcal{K}$ and a normal text otherwise.

end for

// $E_{pk}(\cdot)$ and $D_{sk}(\cdot)$ respectively denotes encryption and decryption function.

3.2 Our Scheme

Suppose $\mathcal{V}_k$ is the N-WVMI of document $\mathbf{d}_k$ $(k = 1, 2, \cdots, w)$, then, $\mathcal{V}_k = \frac{1}{m^2} * \sum_{i=1}^{m} \sum_{j=1}^{m} ({}^k s_{ij} - t_{ij})^2$. To remotely and securely detect Bob's secret text documents, the privacy-preserving protocol should enable Bob to learn whether $\mathcal{V}_k > \mathcal{V}_0$ holds or not.

It is a simple way that Bob receives the value $\Delta_k = \mathcal{V}_k - \mathcal{V}_0$ by privacy-preserving collaborative computation. However, Alice's privacy will be violated if probe attack happens. For example, Bob may furtively generate two fictitious N-WMI matrixes $\mathbf{S}_{pseudo} = [p_{ij}]_{m \times m}$ and $\mathbf{S}'_{pseudo} = [p'_{ij}]_{m \times m}$ which meet $p_{i_0 j_0} + 0.5 = p'_{i_0 j_0}$ and $p_{ij} = p'_{ij}$ $(i, j = 1, 2, \cdots, m$, and $1 \leqslant i_0, j_0 \leqslant m, i \neq i_0,\ j \neq j_0)$. If Bob obtains the corresponding $\Delta_{pseudo} = \mathcal{V}_{pseudo} - \mathcal{V}_0$ and $\Delta'_{pseudo} = \mathcal{V}'_{pseudo} - \mathcal{V}_0$, then, he could compute

$$\begin{aligned} m^2 * (\Delta_{pseudo} - \Delta'_{pseudo}) &= m^2 * (\mathcal{V}_{pseudo} - \mathcal{V}'_{pseudo}) \\ &= (p_{i_0 j_0} - t_{i_0 j_0})^2 - (p'_{i_0 j_0} - t_{i_0 j_0})^2 \\ &= p^2_{i_0 j_0} - p'^2_{i_0 j_0} + 2 * (p'_{i_0 j_0} - p_{i_0 j_0}) * t_{i_0 j_0}. \end{aligned}$$

Consequently,

$$t_{i_0 j_0} = m^2 * (\Delta_{pseudo} - \Delta'_{pseudo}) - p^2_{i_0 j_0} + p'^2_{i_0 j_0}. \qquad (5)$$

Therefore, Bob will infer Alice's private data $t_{i_0 j_0}$ through the above attack.

Here, we propose a more intricate but efficient method, named efficient Secure for LInguistic steganography DEtection protocol (SLIDE), such that the protocol is still secure and no privacy will be disclosed even if a malicious participant modifies his data for some unholy sake. The details of our protocol are presented in Protocol 1.

3.3 Correctness

In this section, we will show that the detection results by performing SLIDE is equivalent to the output of the simple version of linguistic steganography detection using statistical characteristics of correlations between words [5–7].

That is, SLIDE is correct and it is exactly the privacy-preserving version of the linguistic steganography detection scheme in [5].

Lemma 1. *Assume that the integers z_1, z_2, r_1, r_2 and r_3 meet the conditions, $0 < z_1 < 4X$, $0 < z_2 < 5X$, $25X \leqslant r_1$, $r_1 \leqslant r_2 \leqslant r_1 + \lfloor \frac{r_1}{5X} \rfloor$ and $0 \leqslant r_3 \leqslant 5X$, then $r_1 * z_1 - r_2 * z_2 + r_3 > 5X$ if and only if $z_1 > z_2$. (Here, X is a positive integer and $\lfloor x \rfloor$ represents the largest integer that is not more than x.)*

Proof

(I) If $r_1 * z_1 - r_2 * z_2 + r_3 > 5X$, then $r_1 * z_1 - r_2 * z_2 > 5X - r_3$. That is,

$$r_1 * z_1 - r_2 * z_2 > 0.$$

Therefore, we have

$$r_1 * z_1 > r_2 * z_2.$$

As $r_1 \leqslant r_2$, then, the inequality $z_1 > z_2$ holds.

(II) If $z_1 > z_2$, then $z_1 - z_2 > 0$. Further,

$$z_1 - z_2 \geqslant 1, 4X - 2 \geqslant z_2.$$

Because $r_2 \leqslant r_1 + \lfloor \frac{r_1}{5X} \rfloor$, then $r_1 * z_1 - r_2 * z_2 + r_3 > r_1 * z_1 - (r_1 + \frac{r_1}{5X}) * z_2 + r_3$. That is,

$$r_1 * z_1 - r_2 * z_2 + r_3 > r_1 * (z_1 - z_2) - \frac{r_1}{5X} * z_2 + r_3.$$

Consequently,

$$r_1 * z_1 - r_2 * z_2 + r_3 > r_1 - \frac{r_1}{5X} * (4X - 2) + r_3.$$

There is

$$r_1 - \frac{r_1}{5X} * (4X - 2) + r_3 = \frac{r_1}{5} + \frac{2 * r_1}{5X} + r_3, r_1 \geqslant 25X.$$

Then,

$$r_1 - \frac{r_1}{5X} * (4X - 2) + r_3 > \frac{r_1}{5} \geqslant 5X.$$

Therefore, $r_1 * z_1 - r_2 * z_2 + r_3 > 5X$ holds too.

The above (I) and (II) complete the proof of Lemma 1 together.

Lemma 2. *Suppose* $\mathcal{M} = 10^8 m^2 \mathcal{K}$. $\mathcal{V}_k = \frac{1}{m^2} * \sum_{i=1}^{m} \sum_{j=1}^{m} ({}^k s_{ij} - t_{ij})^2$ *is the corresponding N-WVMI of document* $\mathbf{d}_k$ $(k = 1, 2, \cdots, w)$. *Then, in the protocol 1,* $\mathcal{V}_k^{'} > 5\mathcal{M}$ *if and only if* $\mathcal{V}_k > \mathcal{V}_0$.

Proof

According to the properties of homomorphic cryptosystem in Sect. 2.1, we have $E(m_1) * E(m_2) \mathring{=} E(m_1 + m_2)$ and $E(m_1)^k \mathring{=} E(m_1 * k)$. In step 2, $c_i = E_{pk_A}(a_i)$. Then,

$$x_k = E_{pk_A}(v_k) * \prod_{i=1}^{n} E_{pk_A}(a_i)^{{}^k b_i} \mathring{=} E_{pk_A}(v_k + \sum_{i=1}^{n}(a_i * {}^k b_i)),$$

and

$$z_k = y_k^{{}^k r_1} * E_{pk_B}(({}^k r_1 * \sum_{i=1}^{n} a_i^2) + {}^k r_3 - {}^k r_2 * (2 * u_k + 10^8 m^2 \mathcal{V}_0))$$

$$= E_{pk_B}(2 * v_k + \sum_{i=1}^{n} {}^k b_i^2)^{{}^k r_1} * E_{pk_B}(({}^k r_1 * \sum_{i=1}^{n} a_i^2) + {}^k r_3 - {}^k r_2 * (2 * u_k + 10^8 m^2 \mathcal{V}_0))$$

$$\mathring{=} E_{pk_B}\Big({}^k r_1 * (2 * v_k + \sum_{i=1}^{n}(a_i^2 + {}^k b_i^2)) - {}^k r_2 * (2 * u_k + 10^8 m^2 \mathcal{V}_0) + {}^k r_3\Big).$$

There is $u_k = D_{sk_A}(x_k)$ in step 4 of protocol 1 and $\mathcal{V}_k^{'} = D_{sk_B}(z_k)$ in step 5. Consequently,

$$u_k = v_k + \sum_{i=1}^{n}(a_i * {}^k b_i), \tag{6}$$

and

$$\mathcal{V}_k^{'} = {}^k r_1 * (2 * v_k + \sum_{i=1}^{n}(a_i^2 + {}^k b_i^2)) - {}^k r_2 * (2 * u_k + 10^8 m^2 \mathcal{V}_0) + {}^k r_3. \tag{7}$$

We set ${}^k\mathcal{T}_1 = 2 * v_k + \sum_{i=1}^{n}(a_i{}^2 + {}^k b_i{}^2)$ and ${}^k\mathcal{T}_2 = 2 * u_k + 10^8 m^2 \mathcal{V}_0$ $(k = 1, 2, \cdots, w)$. Then,

$$\mathcal{V}_k^{'} = {}^k r_1 * {}^k\mathcal{T}_1 - {}^k r_2 * {}^k\mathcal{T}_2 + {}^k r_3 \tag{8}$$

and

$$\begin{aligned} {}^k\mathcal{T}_1 - {}^k\mathcal{T}_2 &= \sum_{i=1}^{n}(a_i{}^2 + {}^k b_i{}^2) - 2 * (u_k - v_k) - 10^8 m^2 \mathcal{V}_0 \\ &= \sum_{i=1}^{n}(a_i{}^2 - 2 * a_i * {}^k b_i + {}^k b_i{}^2) - 10^8 m^2 \mathcal{V}_0 \\ &= \sum_{i=1}^{m}\sum_{j=1}^{m}(10^4 * t_{ij} - 10^4 * {}^k s_{ij})^2 - 10^8 m^2 \mathcal{V}_0 \\ &= 10^8 m^2 * (\frac{1}{m^2} * \sum_{i=1}^{m}\sum_{j=1}^{m}({}^k s_{ij} - t_{ij})^2 - \mathcal{V}_0) \\ &= 10^8 m^2 * (\mathcal{V}_k - \mathcal{V}_0). \end{aligned}$$

Therefore, ${}^k\mathcal{T}_1 > {}^k\mathcal{T}_2$ if and only if $\mathcal{V}_k > \mathcal{V}_0$.

There are $\sum_{i=1}^{m}\sum_{j=1}^{m} t_{ij}^2, \sum_{i=1}^{m}\sum_{j=1}^{m} {}^k s_{ij}^2, \sum_{i=1}^{m}\sum_{j=1}^{m} t_{ij} * {}^k s_{ij} \in (0, m^2\mathcal{K})$, thus

$$\sum_{i=1}^{n} a_i^2, \sum_{i=1}^{n} {}^k b_i^2, \sum_{i=1}^{n} a_i * {}^k b_i \in (0, \mathcal{M}) \; (\mathcal{M} = 10^8 m^2 \mathcal{K}).$$

In Step 3 of protocol 1, $\mathcal{V}_k$ is randomly selected from the interval $(0, \mathcal{M})$. Then,

$$\begin{aligned} 0 < u_k &= v_k + \sum_{i=1}^{n}(a_i * {}^k b_i) < 2\mathcal{M}, \\ 0 < {}^k\mathcal{T}_1 &= 2 * v_k + \sum_{i=1}^{n}(a_i{}^2 + {}^k b_i{}^2) < 4\mathcal{M}, \\ 0 < {}^k\mathcal{T}_2 &= 2 * u_k + 10^8 m^2 \mathcal{V}_0 < 5\mathcal{M}. \end{aligned}$$

There are $25\mathcal{M} \leqslant {}^k r_1$, ${}^k r_1 \leqslant {}^k r_2 \leqslant {}^k r_1 + \lfloor \frac{{}^k r_1}{5\mathcal{M}} \rfloor$ and $0 \leqslant {}^k r_3 \leqslant 5\mathcal{M}$ in step 4 of SLIDE. In Eq. 8, $\mathcal{V}_k^{'} = {}^k r_1 * {}^k\mathcal{T}_1 - {}^k r_2 * {}^k\mathcal{T}_2 + {}^k r_3$ holds.

According to Lemma 1, then $\mathcal{V}_k^{'} > 5\mathcal{M}$ if and only if ${}^k\mathcal{T}_1 > {}^k\mathcal{T}_2$.

Therefore, in protocol 1, $\mathcal{V}_k^{'} > 5\mathcal{M}$ if and only if $\mathcal{V}_k > \mathcal{V}_0$. Lemma 2 holds.

Theorem 1 (Correctness of SLIDE). SLIDE *is correct. That is, SLIDE is the exact privacy-preserving version of the simple version of linguistic steganography detection using statistical characteristics of correlations between words.*

Proof: According to Lemma 2, in protocol 1, $\mathcal{V}_k^{'} > 5\mathcal{M}$ if and only if $\mathcal{V}_k > \mathcal{V}_0$. That is, the detection results by running SLIDE is equivalent to the output of the simple version of linguistic steganography detection using statistical characteristics of correlations between words [5–7].

Therefore, SLIDE is exactly the privacy-preserving version of the linguistic steganography detection scheme and it is correct.

3.4 Security

To confirm SLIDE is secure, we need to consider:

During the execution of protocol 1, Alice receives nothing but the intermediate data $x_k = E_{pk_A}(v_k) * \prod_{i=1}^{n} c_i^{{}^k b_i}$ and $y_k = E_{pk_B}(2 * v_k + \sum_{i=1}^{n} {}^k b_i^2)$ $(k = 1, 2, \cdots, w)$ from Bob. She could deduce nothing from y_k $(k = 1, 2, \cdots, w)$, as Pallier's homomorphic encryption system [13] is semantically secure. Decrypting x_k $(k = 1, 2, \cdots, w)$, Alice obtains $u_k = D_{sk_A}(x_k) = v_k + \sum_{i=1}^{n}(a_i * {}^k b_i)$ (see the Eq. (6) in the proof of Lemma 2). However, v_k and ${}^k b_i$ $(i = 1, 2, \cdots, n)$ are privately holden by Bob, and then Alice could not learn any confidential number of Bob. That is, none of Bob's privacy is disclosed.

In step 2, Bob receives $c_1, c_2, \cdots, c_n$, of which $c_i = E_{pk_A}(a_i)$ $(i = 1, 2, \cdots, n)$. However, a_i $(i = 1, 2, \cdots, n)$ is well protected by the homomorphic cryptosystem. In step 4, Alice send $z_k = y_k^{{}^k r_1} * E_{pk_B}(({}^k r_1 * \sum_{i=1}^{n} a_i^2) - {}^k r_2 * (2 * u_k + 10^8 m^2 \mathcal{V}_0) + {}^k r_3)$ to Bob. Using the secret key sk_B, Bob computes and gets $\mathcal{V}_k^{'} = D_{sk_B}(z_k) = {}^k r_1 * (2 * v_k + \sum_{i=1}^{n}(a_i^2 + {}^k b_i^2)) - {}^k r_2 * (2 * u_k + 10^8 m^2 \mathcal{V}_0) + {}^k r_3$ $(k = 1, 2, \cdots, w)$ (see the Eq. (7) in the proof of Lemma 2). Yet he cannot obtain Alice's private data from $\mathcal{V}_k^{'}$, as ${}^k r_1$, ${}^k r_2$ and ${}^k r_3$ are locally and securely selected by Alice. Therefore, Alice's private information will also be well preserved.

To sum up, while each participant is semi-honest (see Sect. 3.1), no privacy of both Alice and Bob is revealed in protocol 1, and SLIDE is secure.

Probe Attack: It has shown that Alice gets the $u_k = v_k + \sum_{i=1}^{n}(a_i * {}^k b_i)$ and Bob obtains $\mathcal{V}_k^{'} = {}^k r_1 * (2 * v_k + \sum_{i=1}^{n}(a_i^2 + {}^k b_i^2)) - {}^k r_2 * (2 * u_k + 10^8 m^2 \mathcal{V}_0) + {}^k r_3$ $(k = 1, 2, \cdots, w)$. Firstly, The randomness of v_k guarantees that Bob's private number cannot be deduced. Secondly, Alice reselects the random factors ${}^k r_1$, ${}^k r_2$ and ${}^k r_3$ for each document $\mathbf{d}_k$, then, even if Bob modifies his sample N-WMI matrix, the private data of Alice is still well preserved. Therefore, SLIDE is also secure against probe attack.

3.5 Computation Complexity and Communication Overheads

In protocol 1, Alice's computation time in step 1 is $O(m^2)$, and she has a running time of $O(\mathcal{H}_E * m^2)$ in step 2 and $O(w * \mathcal{H}_E + w * m^2)$ in step 4. Here, $\mathcal{H}_E$ denotes the computation time of encryption function of homomorphic cryptosystem, and the time cost of decryption is $\mathcal{H}_D$. Accordingly, Bob has an executing time of $O(w * m^2)$ in step 1, $O(w * m^2 + w * \mathcal{H}_E)$ in step 3 and $O(w * \mathcal{H}_D)$ in step 5. Therefore, the computation complexity of SLIDE is $O(w * m^2 + \mathcal{H}_E * m^2 + w * \mathcal{H}_E + w * \mathcal{H}_D)$.

Assume $\mathcal{L}$ is the bit length of a ciphertext item in homomorphic cryptosystem. Then, the following contributes to the communication overheads: (1) $\mathcal{L} * m^2$ bits in step 2, (2) $2 * \mathcal{L} * w$ bits in step 3, (3) $\mathcal{L} * w$ bits in step 4. Overall, the total communication overheads of SLIDE are about $\mathcal{L} * m^2 + 3 * \mathcal{L} * w$ bits.

4 Experiment Results

To intuitively illustrate the efficiency of SLIDE, we implement the protocol and Paillier's homomorphic cryptosystem [13]. The experiments are performed on the Windows XP operating system with 2.60 GHz CPU and 2.0 GB memory. As we have analyzed the exact communication bit overheads in Sect. 3.5 and different network performance will make a great deal of difference in communication time, then in our simulation, each participant is simply action as a thread and the exchange data is directly shared in memory. That is, the runtime in the experimental results are the computation time. Two participants are in parallel as much as possible.

In the simulation experiment, it is set that Bob has 100 private text documents ($w = 100$) and the key of homomorphic cryptosystem has 512 bits. Table 1 records the time cost of each sub-procedure of homomorphic encryption system. The count of words in **D** is respectively set to five different values: 100, 200, 500, 800 and 1000, and the corresponding average time cost of privacy-preserving operations while remotely detecting a text document by SLIDE is given in Table 2.

Table 1. Runtime of homomorphic cryptosystem

Procedure	Key generation	Encryption	Decryption
Time (s)	0.309	0.063	0.024

As can be seen from Table 2, Alice distinctly spends more time than Bob on encryption. It is reasonable and sensible. As the vendor, Alice should bear the major computation task. Even the number of words in **D** reaches up to 1000, Bob just spends about 20 s on a document. While the general service word dictionary **D** contains 1000 words ($m = 1000$), the average cost for a document is about 656.803 s totally. However, the time cost will be declined if performing the privacy-preserving protocol in a more power platform. Additionally, the execution time could be drastically reduce through the way that they complete as much as preparation work before executing the remote detection task, such as Alice pre-produces the homomorphic cryptosystem key pairs and encrypts her private data in the idle time.

Table 2. Each document's average time cost of secure operations while remotely detecting them by SLIDE

Number of words in **D**	100	200	500	800	1000
Alice (s)	6.602	26.029	160.989	413.275	645.137
Bob (s)	0.407	1.151	5.092	12.653	20.176
Total time of SLIDE (s)	6.821	26.991	163.795	419.312	656.803

5 Conclusion

In this paper, a privacy-preserving scheme for linguistic steganography detection, SLIDE, has been proposed. The protocol takes place between a vendor holding a private detector of linguistic steganography and a user in possession of some private text documents consisting of stego-text and normal text. By performing the privacy-preserving protocol, the user could securely obtain the detection results of his private documents returned by the vendor's remote detector while both vendor and user learn nothing about the privacy of each other. Experiment result and theoretical analysis confirm the efficiency, correctness, security, computation complexity and communication overheads of the new scheme.

Many interesting and new challenges are involved in the privacy-preserving linguistic steganography detection, but our research show that it is feasible to run a remote detector on private text documents in a secure manner.

Acknowledgment. This work was supported by the Science and Technology Project of State Grid Sichuan Electric Power Company (No. 521997170017 and No. 52199717001P).

References

1. Barni, M., Orlandi, C., Piva, A.: A privacy-preserving protocol for neural-network-based computation. In: the 8th Workshop on Multimedia and Security, pp. 146–151. ACM (2006)
2. Brickell, J., Porter, D., Shmatikov, V., Witchel, E.: Privacy-preserving remote diagnostics. In: the 14th ACM Conference on Computer and Communications Security, pp. 498–507 (2007)
3. Chang, W., Wu, J.: Privacy-preserved data publishing of evolving online social networks. J. Inf. Privacy Secur. **12**(1), 14–31 (2016)

4. Chang, W., Wu, J., Tan, C.C.: Friendship-based location privacy in mobile social networks. Int. J. Secur. Netw. **6**(4), 226–236 (2011)
5. Chen, Z., Huang, L., Yu, Z., Li, L., Yang, W.: Text information hiding detecting algorithm based on statistics. J. Chin. Comput. Syst. **29**(12), 2199–2201 (2008)
6. Chen, Z., et al.: Linguistic steganography detection using statistical characteristics of correlations between words. In: Solanki, K., Sullivan, K., Madhow, U. (eds.) IH 2008. LNCS, vol. 5284, pp. 224–235. Springer, Heidelberg (2008). https://doi.org/10.1007/978-3-540-88961-8_16
7. Chen, Z.: Research on analysis and design of linguistic steganography. Ph.D. thesis, University of Science and Technology of China (2009)
8. Goldreich, O.: Foundations of Cryptography: Volume II, Basic Applications. Cambridge University Press, Cambridge (2004)
9. Goldwasser, S., Micali, S.: Probabilistic encryption. J. Comput. Syst. Sci. **28**(2), 270–299 (1984)
10. Jiang, W., Murugesan, M., Clifton, C., Si, L.: Similar document detection with limited information disclosure. In: Proceedings of 24th IEEE ICDE, pp. 735–743 (2008)
11. Li, X., Zhu, Y., Wang, J.: Efficient encrypted data comparison through a hybrid method. J. Inf. Sci. Eng. **33**(4), 953–964 (2017)
12. Murugesan, M., Jiang, W., Clifton, C., Si, L., Vaidya, J.: Efficient privacy-preserving similar document detection. VLDB J. **19**(4), 457–475 (2010)
13. Paillier, P.: Public-key cryptosystems based on composite degree residuosity classes. In: Stern, J. (ed.) EUROCRYPT 1999. LNCS, vol. 1592, pp. 223–238. Springer, Heidelberg (1999). https://doi.org/10.1007/3-540-48910-X_16
14. Taskiran, C., Topkara, U., Topkara, M., Delp, E.: Attacks on lexical natural language steganography systems. Proc. SPIE **6072**, 97–105 (2006)
15. Zhao, Y., Li, W., Lu, S.: Navigation-driven handoff minimization in wireless networks. J. Netw. Comput. Appl. **74**, 11–20 (2016)
16. Zhou, J., Niu, X., Yang, Y.: Research on the detecting algorithm of text document information hiding. J. Commun. **25**(12), 97–101 (2004)
17. Zhou, L., Zhu, Y., Castiglione, A.: Efficient k-NN query over encrypted data in cloud with limited key-disclosure and offline data owner. Comput. Secur. **69**, 84–96 (2017)
18. Zhou, L., Zhu, Y., Choo, K.K.R.: Efficiently and securely harnessing cloud to solve linear regression and other matrix operations. Future Gen. Comput. Syst. **81**, 404–413 (2018)
19. Zhu, Y., Huang, L., Yang, W.: Relation of PPAtMP and scalar product protocol and their applications. In: IEEE Symposium on Computers and Communications (ISCC), pp. 184–189 (2010)
20. Zhu, Y., Huang, Z., Takagi, T.: Secure and controllable k-NN query over encrypted cloud data with key confidentiality. J. Parallel Distrib. Comput. **89**, 1–12 (2016)
21. Zhu, Y., Li, X., Wang, J., Liu, Y., Qu, Z.: Practical secure naïve bayesian classification over encrypted big data in cloud. Int. J. Found. Comput. Sci. **28**(06), 683–703 (2017)

Study on the Development of U.S. Intercontinental Alliance Clean Renewable Energy Based on CA-DEA Model

Yazhou Dong[1,2], Mengxing Huang[1,2(✉)], Di Wu[1,2], Xijun He[1,2], Zhaoqing Wang[3], and Uzair Aslam Bhatti[1,2]

[1] State Key Laboratory of Marine Resource Utilization in South China Sea, Hainan University, Haikou 570228, China
514953505@qq.com, huangmx09@163.com

[2] College of Information Science and Technology, Hainan University, Haikou 570228, China

[3] College of Humanities and Communication, Hainan University, Haikou 570228, China

Abstract. This paper establishes a data envelopment analysis model to assess the sustainable development of energy in each state. At the same time, we use the principal component analysis method to select renewable energy indicators and form an evaluation system. Calculate and rank the clean renewable energy development index for each state and assess the development of clean energy in the four states. At the same time, we use the Corresponding analysis method, taking time and selected indicators as variables, and conducted a differentiated analysis of the development of energy indicators at each stage. Through a comprehensive analysis of indicators and factors such as the population, the geography, the climate, the industry, etc., we compared the development of each state, determined the choice of the best development area, and the similarities and differences between the development forecasts of the states in 2025 and 2050, and formulated proposal for faster and more effective development of the Intercontinental Union.

Keywords: Intercontinental alliance · Renewable energy · DEA CA

1 Introduction

In recent years, with the continuous development of the world economy, energy has become the basis of human survival. Energy plays a crucial role in the development of modern society and the sustainable development of society can't be separated from the energy security. With the increasing demand for energy, more and more countries have taken energy conservation. In the United States, many aspects of energy policy are decentralized to the state level. Additionally, the varying geographies and industries of different states affect energy usage and production. Therefore, the intercontinental contract came into being. Interstate Compact is a contractual arrangement between two or more states, between the two states or more states, those states to reach an agreement

X. Sun et al. (Eds.): ICCCS 2018, LNCS 11065, pp. 310–321, 2018.
https://doi.org/10.1007/978-3-030-00012-7_29

on specific policy issues, and to take on a set of criteria or a particular region or cooperate with each other on national issues [1].

The production and consumption of energy affect the people's livelihood and the environment, and the concept of clean renewable energy and sustainable development has gradually emerged. Since 1987, the World Commission on Environment and Development formally proposed sustainable development in its report "Our Common Future". Since the concept, sustainable development has become an ideal development model and a policy goal. At the "Environment and Development" conference held at the United Nations in June 1992, the participating countries unanimously promised to regard sustainable development as a long-term common development strategy. Through the sorting of relevant literatures at home and abroad, scholars have conducted research on clean renewable energy from four aspects: development trend and status quo, policy research, development strategy, and evaluation index system.

The first international study started with the 1995 United Nations Sustainable Development Work Plan (WPISD). At present, there is no unified evaluation system for the assessment indicators and quantitative models for regional clean renewable energy. But there are more representative examples: the International Atomic Energy Agency (IAEA) Sustainable Development Energy Indicator System, the World Energy Council (WEC) Energy Efficiency Indicator System, the European Union (EU) Energy Efficiency Indicator System, and the British Energy Industry Indicator System. The indicator system measures energy use and its capabilities of sustainable development and status from different perspectives. Some scholars based on meteorological data have evaluated the development and utilization of renewable energy in Bangladesh and its resource potential, or used GIS, NASA's surface meteorological information, and solar radiation information data to create a renewable electricity mix. The system optimization model measures the power generation potential of different renewable energy sources such as solar energy, wind energy, biomass energy, and hydropower in Bangladesh. It also indicates the future ways of using renewable energy, and some scholars are based on renewable energy. Development and utilization of renewable energy resources have been studied. Sahir and Qureshi (2008) evaluated the potential of Pakistan's solar, wind, biomass, and other renewable energy sources in terms of installed capacity and generation capacity.

Domestic scholars also explored the development of renewable energy. Han Fang (2010) started with the development of renewable energy in China and the development trend of renewable energy in the world, and analyzed the problems existing in the development of renewable energy in China. And put forward the corresponding countermeasures and suggestions, and on this basis, the prospects for the development of renewable energy in China are forecasted. Ran and Li [7] proposed the SEE-2R model for evaluating the sustainability of renewable energy development under the premise of fully considering the characteristics of renewable energy sources, energy substitution, especially the availability and regenerability of resources. This method distinguishes traditional fossil energy assessment methods. Li, Dong and Duan [6] build a comprehensive evaluation module for renewable energy based on the Analytic Hierarchy Process (AHP), and set core indicators from four aspects of economy, technology, resources, and the environment. Finally, all levels of indicators are coupled into renewable energy synthesis.

2 System Architecture

2.1 Data Filtering

To comply with the completeness and practicality of data, we selected data from the State Energy Data System (SEDS). Dataset consists of 605 variables of last 50 years that belongs to the production and consumption of energy in California (CA), Arizona (AZ), New Mexico (NM), and Texas (TX). Firstly, the index that has not changed more than 50% of the data has been deleted. This part of the data has little effect on the overall assessment; secondly, the indicator that the statistical year does not start from 1960 is deleted, and only the indicator that has complete 50-year data is retained. To facilitate subsequent analysis and calculations; finally, 32 indicators that describe the total amount are selected based on energy consumption and supply.

2.2 Data Classification

From the 32 selected indicators, we can see that some indicators may have strong correlation. For this purpose, each of the four states will be normalized index R cluster analysis, and polymerized in a similar relationship between the variables into five categories. The concrete results are shown in the following Fig. 1. Based on the fluctuation characteristics of each variable and the characteristics of energy development in each state, we select the five indicators from the 32 energy indicators of the five clustering results to conduct a comprehensive analysis.

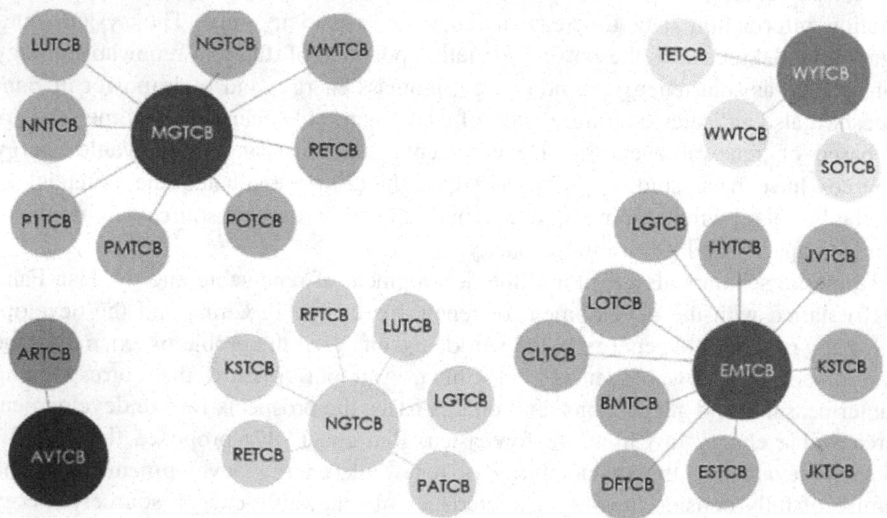

Fig. 1. Pedigree chart

2.3 Energy Overview

We mainly select five indicators (AVTCB, MGTCB, WYTCB, EMTCB, NGTCB) to analyze the energy status of the four states.

As of 2009, total energy consumption in California was at the forefront of the nation, increasing by about 2.4 times in 2009 over 1960. In particular, natural gas and petrol accounted for the majority of the country's energy consumption, the state's most populous country State. As a result, the number of motor vehicles in California, where transportation is dominant, is larger than in other states, and according to statistical analysis, car gasoline use in California continues to rise year by year, which is inextricably linked to the population and policies in the area. At the same time, natural gas consumption rises over time and accounts for a large proportion of total energy consumption in the United States. As almost two-thirds of California households use natural gas for household heating and half of California's utility-scale net generation is Natural gas is the fuel, so the output of natural gas is far less than 50% of the consumption [2]. However, California is also the lowest per capita energy consumption area in the United States. California is the first country to generate electricity from renewable sources and leads the country in solar energy, geothermal energy and biomass. California is also the nation's third-largest traditional hydroelectric power plant, the fifth largest wind power plant. The state views cost-saving energy efficiency as an important resource to meet the nation's clean energy goals.

Arizona's annual total energy consumption average growth rate was about 3.39% from 1996 to 2009, with a predominately 61% of coal consumption in 2009's energy consumption composition. Second, the consumption of renewable energy is slightly lower than that of coal. Fossil fuel resources, natural gas reserves less, but with rich solar and geothermal energy, rich renewable resources. Most of the consumption of energy such as gasoline and natural gas depends on imports and is supplied and transported through pipelines. As engaged in economic activities do not belong to the energy-intensive, mainly the development of real estate, commerce and trade and other fields. Therefore, it is the state with the lowest per capita energy consumption. At the same time, the state uses more hydropower and solar energy consumption which is mainly used in the transport sector, followed by the residential sector.

In New Mexico's energy consumption structure, natural gas dominated, accounting for 65%, followed by coal and crude oil accounting for 19% and 15%, respectively, and only 1% of renewable energy consumption. New Mexico, accounting for about 5% of the total natural gas reserves in the United States, is the first of the ten largest natural gas producers in the United States, accounting for about 4% of the country's total natural gas production and has a small population base. Therefore, the total energy consumption is relatively small. New Mexico contains a wealth of renewable energy such as fossil fuels, minerals, wind and solar. This state's unit GDP and per capita energy consumption were higher than the national average. With the highest energy consumption in the industrial sector, followed by the transport sector and the commercial sector. The state's net generating capacity depends mainly on coal-fired power plants, followed by gas-fired power plants. And mainly for the southern and western United States.

Texas is the second largest population and second largest economy, the total energy consumption of the United States ranked first, with a large number of crude oil and natural gas reserves in the production of energy ahead of the other three states. Where the power generated by wind energy is much higher than other states several times. At the same time, Texas is also the largest coal-consuming state and the largest consumer of gasoline. As of 2009, natural gas consumption accounts for 70% of the energy consumption structure, crude oil consumption accounts for about one-third of natural gas consumption, and renewable resources and coal resources consume about 3% [3]. The state has great potential in the field of solar energy development. As the major economic sectors in Texas are energy-intensive industries, the industrial sector consumes the most energy and the residential sector consumes less energy (Figs. 2 and 3).

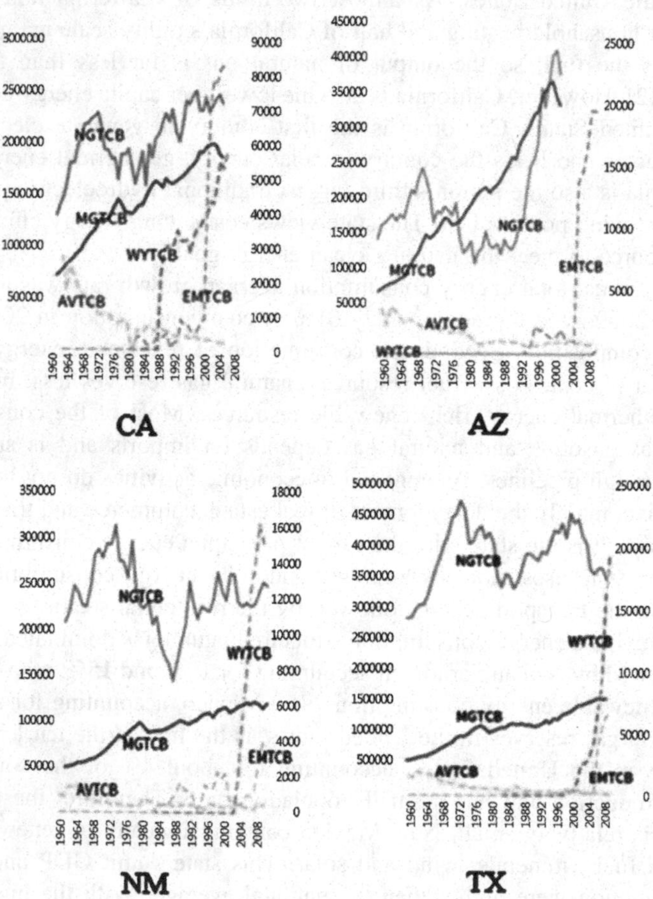

Fig. 2. Trends of five main indicators in each state

Note: The solid line variable in the figure refers to the Y axis to the left of the reference figure and the dashed variable refers to the Y axis to the right of the figure.

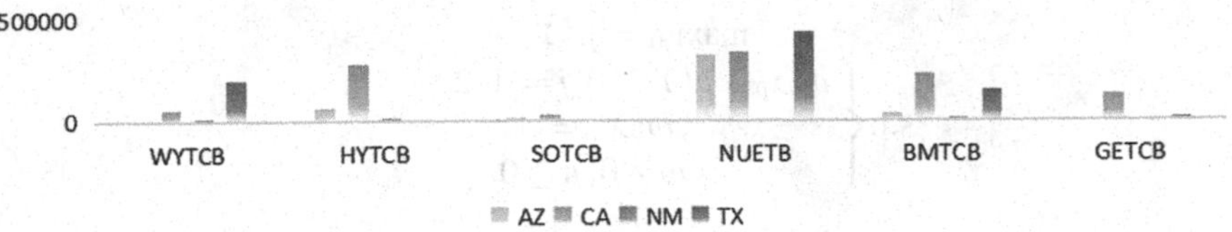

Fig. 3. The total renewable energy consumption in each state [2]

3 The Model

3.1 Data Envelopment Analysis Model

We want to establish a model to describe the energy profiles of each state with a number of variables and indicators. Therefore, we choose data envelopment analysis to measure the relative benefits of energy development, so as to analyze and evaluate the sustainable development of energy in each state. There are n DMU, and each DMU has m input and s outputs, let $x_{ij}(i = 1, \cdots, m; j = 1, \cdots, n)$, denote the i input quantity of the J. DMU represents the ith input amount of the Jth DMU, $y_{rj}(r = 1, \cdots, s; j = 1, \cdots, n)$ represents the rth output of the jth DMU, $v_i(i = 1, \cdots, m)$ denote the weight of the ith input, $u_r(r = 1, \cdots, s)$ denote the weight of the rth output.

The vectors $X_J, Y_j(j = 1, \cdots, n)$ denote the input and output vectors of decision unit j, v and u denote the vector of input and output weights, respectively, then

$$X_j = (x_{1j}, x_{2j}, \cdots, x_{nj})^T,$$
$$Y_j = (y_{1j}, y_{2j}, \cdots, y_{nj})^T,$$
$$\mathrm{u} = (u_1, u_2, \cdots, u_m)^T,$$
$$\mathrm{v} = (v_1, v_2, \cdots, v_s)^T.$$

The definition of decision-making unit j efficiency evaluation index is

$$h_j = \frac{u^T Y_j}{v^T x_j}, \mathrm{j} = 1, 2, \cdots,$$

The mathematical model to evaluate the efficiency of decision unit j_0 is

$$\max \frac{u^T Y_{j0}}{v^T x_{j0}},$$
$$\text{s.t.} \begin{cases} \frac{u^T Y_j}{v^T X_j} \leq 1, j = 1, 2, \cdots, n \\ u \geq 0, v \geq 0, u \neq 0, v \neq 0. \end{cases}$$

Through the Charnes-Copper change: $\omega = tv$, $\mu = tu$, $t = \frac{1}{v^T x_{j0}}$, The model can be transformed into an equivalent linear programming problem

$$\max v_{j0} = \mu^T Y_{j0},$$
$$\text{s.t.} \begin{cases} \omega^T x_j - \mu^T Y_j \geq 0, j = 1, 2, \cdots, n, \\ \omega^T X_{jo} = 1, \\ \omega \geq 0, \mu \geq 0. \end{cases}$$

The dual linear programming model of linear programming has clear economic significance.

$$\text{s.t.} \begin{cases} \sum_{j=1}^{n} \lambda_j X_j \leq \theta X_{j0}, \\ \sum_{j=1}^{n} \lambda_j Y_j \geq Y_{j0}, \\ \lambda_j \geq 0, j = 1, 2, \cdots, n \end{cases}$$

3.2 Indicator Selection

The DEA method is used to evaluate the development of energy status in each state. The representative indexes are selected here, and the average five-year indicators of each index are used as input variables and output variables. Variable selection and interpretation as shown in Table 1.

The calculation results are shown in Table 3 below. The optimal target value is represented by θ. Obviously, both AZ and NM were non-DEA effective from 1950–2005, and the economies of scale were increasing. As a result, it can be seen that New Mexico and Arizona are advancing toward sustainable development, with economies of scale increasing in the 1960s and 1980s and economies of scale remaining unchanged in the first 15 years of 1981. Based on a case study of CA, we found that California's population growth accelerated at this stage, resulting in a limit to the state's renewable energy development. And from 1996 to 2009, the scale of California showed a volatile state, showing the scale of the first decrease and then increase the trend. The economies of scale in Texas are growing year by year with good development. However, due to the fact that the major economic industries in Texas are industrial, environmental pollution is more serious and hinders the progress of sustainable development to a certain extent.

Table 1. Results evaluation by DEA method

Year	• AZ	• CA	• NM	• TX
1960–1965	• 0.169	• 0.103	• 0.236	• 0.240
1966–1970	• 0.432	• 0.412	• 0.378	• 0.287
1971–1975	• 0.586	• 0.559	• 0.233	• 0.336
1976–1980	• 0.613	• 0.835	• 0.332	• 0.445
1981–1985	• 0.664	• 1	• 0.340	• 0.551
1986–1990	• 0.795	• 1	• 0.413	• 0.664
1991–1995	• 0.766	• 1	• 0.567	• 0.989
1996–2000	• 0.896	• 0.784	• 0.727	• 1
2001–2005	• 0.947	• 0.675	• 0.828	• 1

4 Correspondence Analysis

The basic idea of correspondence analysis is to represent the scale structure of each element in the row and column of a co-list in the form of a point in a lower dimensional space. It is the most prominent feature of the large number of samples and many variables at the same time make the same diagram, the sample categories and their attributes on the map intuitive and clear that, with intuitive.

We consider annual and energy variables as two attribute variables, annual for each decade from 1960–2009 [4], and energy variables for each of the four variables extracted by principal component analysis from each state. We draw the joint classification map by correspondence analysis and draw it out on the same scatter plot.

In the joint classification diagram, different points represent different variables. The values of the variables are directly labeled in the Fig. 4. By observing the relative positions of the values of the variables, the strength of the relevance of the values of the variables can be analyzed. For ease of observation, a reference line is added to the graph and divided into four quadrants. It can be considered that there is a stronger correlation between the values of variables in the same quadrant with relatively close relative positions.

In 50 years, California and Texas biomass energy development is better, at the same time, hydropower development in California and Arizona during this period trend is also better than the other two states, the use of wood and its waste is also better. The use of [6] New Mexico's renewable energy development is poorer than the other three states.

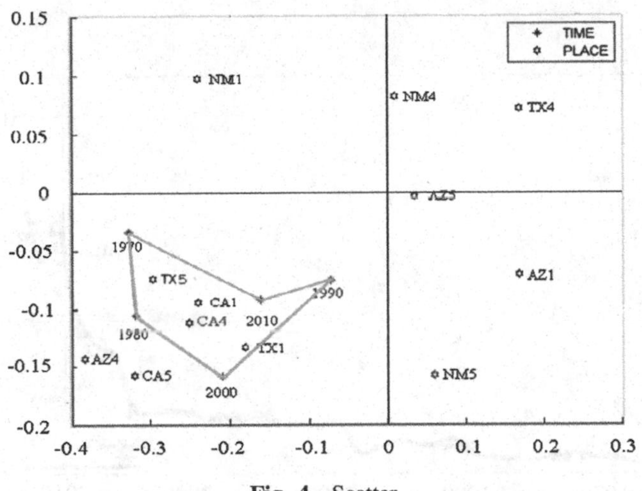

Fig. 4. Scatter

Note: The y-axis is dimension one, and the x-axis is dimension two.

5 State Development Forecasts for 2025

We use two methods, time series forecasting and regression forecasting, to predict the energy development in each of the states in 2025 [10]. By analyzing the errors of these two forecasting methods and optimizing them, we select more accurate forecasting methods and their results to analyze the specific conditions of the four states.

5.1 Time Series Model

The basic idea of time series forecasting method is as follows: When forecast the future change of a phenomenon, predict the future with the past behavior of the phenomenon, that is, reveal the law of the phenomenon with time through the historical data of time series, extend this rule to the future, Thus predicting the future of the phenomenon.

We tried multivariate linear regression analysis model to predict. Using the least squares method, we obtained the linear relationship between the selected BMTCB (X1), EMTCB (X2), GETCB (X3), HYTCB (X4) and clean renewable energy (Z). The hypothesis test is made by the linear relationship between the variable Z and the independent variables X1, X2, X3 and X4. The F statistic rejects the null hypothesis at the significance level of 99% and the model as a whole passes the test. Further, we conducted a T-test on each variable, and each variable had a significant impact on the model, so our model setting is reasonable.

Predicting the index Z of the development status of clean renewable energy by using two prediction methods, we can see that the model results of the time series are closer to the actual situation. Therefore, we choose the time series model to predict the results for analysis and explanation [11] (Fig. 5).

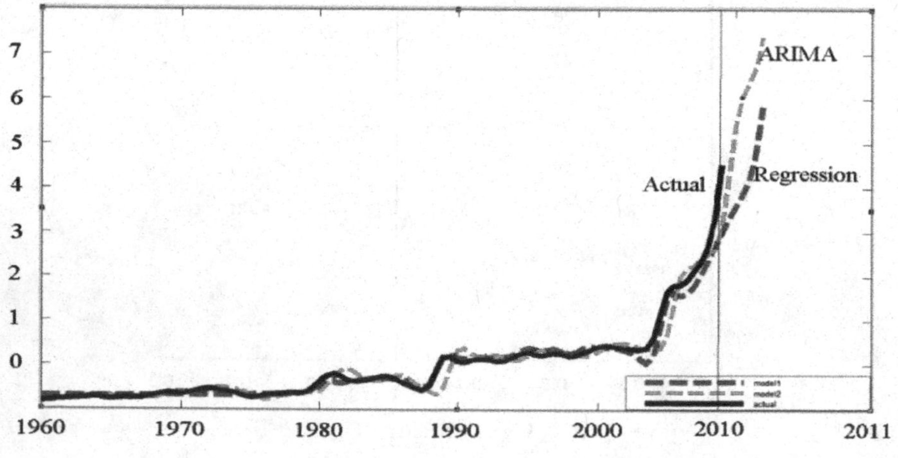

Fig. 5. Fitting comparison chart

According to projections for the Clean Renewable Energy Index (Z) for 2009, 2025 we can clearly see that the indicators of each state are increasing in value over time, which shows that the four states the development of renewable energy is moving in the better direction [12]. And Arizona has always maintained its advantage (Fig. 6).

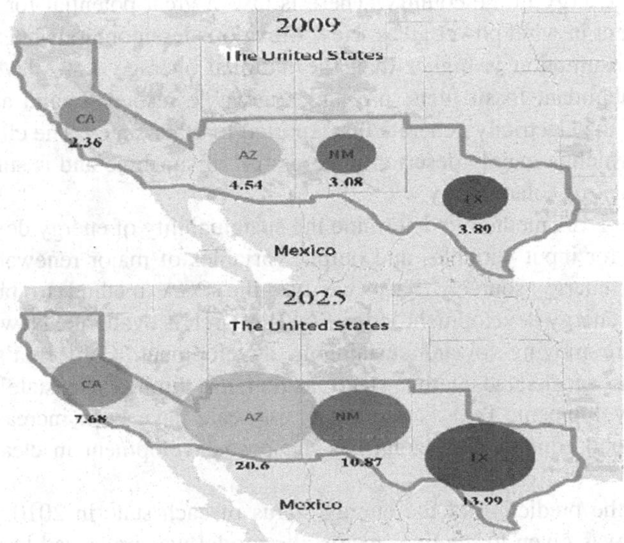

Fig. 6. 2009, 2025 state Z indicator forecast value

6 Conclusion

In this paper, the relevant indicators of the output and consumption of energy in the four states of California, Arizona, New Mexico, and Texas are selected to study the intercontinental alliance contract policy [13].

(a) Through cluster analysis, this paper clusters and analyzes the indicators that describe the total amount of energy, selects representative data, and describes the energy profiles of the states. Renewable energy development in California, Arizona, Texas, and New Mexico has achieved a certain degree of progress and development. Clean, renewable energy has become a precursor to sustainable social development. California is the region with the largest share of renewable energy in the United States. It mainly relies on wind and nuclear power, and it has a leading position in solar energy, geothermal energy, and biomass energy because of its superior geographical position. The main energy consumption is for the transportation sector, with the lowest proportion of energy consumption in the residential sector. Arizona has the lowest per capita energy consumption. The advantages of the northern Grand Canyon and the deserts in the south promote the rapid development of solar energy and wind energy in the state. The average annual growth rate of electricity generated by wind power reaches 6.8%, and the development of geothermal energy further optimizes energy. Structure, reduce energy consumption, and improve energy efficiency. Texas is rich in crude oil and natural gas resources, and has convenient conditions for oil production. The state mainly uses energy-intensive industries as the dominant economic development, ranking first in the total energy consumption in the United States, and the first in renewable energy in the country. There is also a great potential for solar energy development in wind power areas. New Mexico is less populous but its per capita energy consumption is higher than the national average water level. The state contains abundant fossil fuels, ore and renewable resources, and a certain percentage of the electricity generated is exported to other states. The climate in New Mexico, which is mainly desert climate, is full of sunshine and is suitable for the development of solar energy.

(b) We use the DEA method to determine the sustainability of energy development in each state for input variables and output variables of major renewable and non-renewable energy sources. Then we use the PCA method to build a clean renewable energy development index (Z). Research is available. New Mexico and Arizona are moving toward sustainable development. California's population growth has accelerated at this stage, which has limited the state's renewable energy development. Texas's economies of scale have been increasing year by year. In good condition, Arizona has the best development in clean renewable energy.

(c) Based on the prediction of the energy status of each state in 2010, further consideration was given to the time factor, the model was improved to a time series model, and the clean renewable energy generation index (Z) was used as a dependent variable for prediction using ARMIA and regression prediction methods. Compare the accuracy of the two prediction methods and optimize the selection of the ARIMA model.

Future Work

Our system had the opportunity to add in future IoT devices whose demand is growing day to day for medical purposes which will automate those 100% unattended HIS system model which can be replicated everywhere. Also, distributed model for HIS is also need to be improved for the vast areas where connectivity for internet is a big issue otherwise recommendation results will not be fruitful for everyone. This system still needs time to grow as most of the diseases are related with the other body parts, so it takes more time in future to build a comprehensive system which will be more intelligent in predicting the diseases and diagnosis.

Acknowledgments. This research received financial support from the National Natural Science Foundation of China (Grant #: 61462022), the National Key Technology Support Program (Grant #: 2015BAH55F04, Grant #:2015BAH55F01), Major Science and Technology Project of Hainan province (Grant #: ZDKJ2016015), Natural Science Foundation of Hainan province (Grant #:617062, Grant #:20156235), Scientific Research Staring Foundation of Hainan University (Grant #: kyqd1610).

References

1. Li, Y.: Enlightenment of the United States in ensuring energy security. Outlook (8–9), 74–75 (2007)
2. Fan, Y., Fan, H.: Political and economic analysis of the United States 2007 new energy bill. Asia-Pacific Econ. Forum **31**(1), 55–71 (2008)
3. DufoLopez, R., BernalAgustín, J.L., Contreras, J.: Optimization of control strategies for standalone renewable energy systems with hydrogen storage. Renew. Energy **32**(7), 1102–1126 (2007)
4. Sudhakar, R., Painuly, J.P.: Diffusion of renewable energy technologies—barriers and stakeholders' perspectives. Renew. Energy **29**(9), 1431–1447 (2004)
5. Chynoweth, D.P., Owens, J.M., Legrand, R.: Renewable methane from anaerobic digestion of biomass. Renew. Energy **22**(1–3), 1–8 (2001)
6. Li, H., Dong, L., Duan, H.X.: Research on comprehensive evaluation and structural optimization of renewable energy development in China. Resour. Sci. **03**, 431–440 (2011)
7. Ran, W., Li, M.: Sustainability evaluation of renewable energy development based on SEE-2R model. China Popul. Resour. Environ. **06**, 34–40 (2010)
8. Moore, T.: Electricity in the global energy future. EPRI-J. **24**(3), 9–17 (1999)
9. Zhang, L.F.: Analysis of China's economic growth and the impact of industrial structure on energy consumption. Econ. Probl. **5**, 1–6 (2008)
10. Huang, X.J., Zhong, T.Y.: China's carbon emission characteristics and its dynamic evolution analysis. China's Popul. Resour. Environ. **18**(3), 38–42 (2008)
11. Song, D.Y., Lu, C.B.: Decomposition of China's carbon emissions and its periodic fluctuation study. China's Popul. Resour. Environ. **19**(3), 18–24 (2009)
12. Ma, Z.H.: Comparative evaluation of several major energy greenhouse gases emission coefficients in China. China Inst. Atomic Energy 152–361 (2003)
13. Xu, G.Q., Liu, Z.Y., Jiang, Z.H.: The factorization model and empirical analysis of carbon emissions in China: 1995–2004. China Popul. Resour. Environ. **16**(6), 158–161 (2006)

SU-IDS: A Semi-supervised and Unsupervised Framework for Network Intrusion Detection

Erxue Min[1(✉)], Jun Long[1], Qiang Liu[1], Jianjing Cui[1], Zhiping Cai[1], and Junbo Ma[2]

[1] College of Computer, National University of Defense Technology, Changsha 410073, China
{minerxue12,junlong,qiangliu06,cuijianjing16,zpcai}@nudt.edu.cn
[2] Institute of Natural and Mathematical Sciences, Massey University, Palmerston North, New Zealand
J.Ma1@massey.ac.nz

Abstract. Network Intrusion Detection Systems (NIDSs) are increasingly crucial due to the expansion of computer networks. Detection techniques based on machine learning have attracted extensive attention for their capability to detect novel attacks. However, they require a large amount of labeled training data to train an effective model, which is difficult and expensive to obtain. To this effect, it is critically important to build models which can learn from unlabeled or partially-labeled data. In this paper, we propose an autoencoder-based framework, i.e., SU-IDS, for semi-supervised and unsupervised network intrusion detection. The framework augments the usual clustering (or classification) loss with an auxiliary loss of autoencoder, and thus achieves a better performance. The experimental results on the classic NSL-KDD dataset and the modern CICIDS2017 dataset show the superiority of our proposed models.

Keywords: Semi-supervised · Unsupervised · Autoencoder Reconstruction loss

1 Introduction

Due to the advance in Internet technologies, communication, sensors, numerous devices and application are connected to networks. As a result, protecting security and integrity of Internet-based infrastructures and services from network attacks has become an important issue. Network intrusion detection systems (NIDSs) monitor, detect and identify anomaly behaviors in network traffics. The mainstream detection methods used in NIDSs are misuse-based detection and anomaly-based detection. Misuse-based IDSs design a set of rules or signatures by domain experts to describe attacks. The advantages of misuse-based IDSs are high efficiency and low false alarm, thus this category of IDSs have been widely used in real scenarios. However, the shortcoming is that they require manually

X. Sun et al. (Eds.): ICCCS 2018, LNCS 11065, pp. 322–334, 2018.
https://doi.org/10.1007/978-3-030-00012-7_30

updating the rules and signatures frequently to catch up with the development of network intrusion. Besides, they cannot detect unknown attacks (also called zero-day attacks).

In recent years, anomaly-based detection methods have attracted extensive attention for its capability of detecting novel attacks. They build a model of normality and identify deviation from this model as an attack. Data mining-based and machine learning-based methods are the mainstream methods of anomaly-based detection because they can learn complex models. A great deal of related algorithms have been proposed for intrusion detection, including decision trees [1], support vector machine [2], bayesian network [3], neural network [4] and so on. Most of these methods are completely supervised and rely on massive labeled data to build an effective model. However, labeling network traffic is non-trivial and requires expert knowledge, thus generating a labeled up-to-date dataset of malicious traffic is expensive in terms of time and cost.

To this effect, semi-supervised models using partial-labeled data [5,6] and unsupervised methods using unlabeled data [7–9] have been applied to intrusion detection. Nevertheless, these methods can only perform unsupervised clustering or semi-supervised learning respectively, i.e., there is a gap between unsupervised and semi-supervised learning. In addition, most of these methods are based on the original data, thus their performance may be deteriorated when handling high-dimensional data. In recent years, deep learning algorithms become prevalent for their powerful ability of learning from high-dimensional and large-scale data. Studies in deep neural networks also made impressive progress in semi-supervised and unsupervised learning. Generative-like approaches such as Ladder Networks [10], Stacked What-Where Autoencoders (SWWAE) [11] and many others show superior performance in semi-supervised image classification. These network architectures typically augment the classification loss with a reconstruction loss of autoencoder, and train jointly. Among researches in unsupervised learning, deep clustering algorithms [12] become popular as they maps original feature space into a clustering-friendly one, and thus achieve a better clustering result. Most deep clustering algorithms are also based on autoencoder and they train a clustering loss with a reconstruction loss simultaneously. Inspired by these deep learning algorithms, in this paper, we propose a general framework of both unsupervised clustering and semi-supervised learning for intrusion detection. The framework is built on top of the autoencoder, which can learn effective latent representation of different feature sets. The rest of this paper is organized as follows: Sect. 2 provides an overview of related work. Section 3 describes the framework in detail. Section 4 show the settings of the experiments and the results. Finally, Sect. 5 concludes the paper.

2 Related Work

2.1 Semi-supervised Methods for Intrusion Detection

In general, semi-supervised classification methods can be divided into five categories: self-training, co-training and multi-view learning, generative models and graph-based methods, and many of them have been applied to intrusion detection. Wagh et al. [5] proposed a self-training method for intrusion detection, which iteratively exploits the most confident testing samples to refine the existing training set. Mao et al. [13] proposed a co-training-based IDPS, which trains two classifiers using different views of the training data. Chen et al. [14] proposed two graph-based methods, Spectral Graph Transducer and Gaussian Fields Approach, and one semi-supervised clustering method, the MPCK-means. Xiang et al. [6] proposed an incremental semi-supervised framework for intrusion detection, making use of the low space complexity merit of topology learning. Many other remarkable attempts were made in [15,16]. Most of the existing methods are based on classic machine learning algorithms.

2.2 Unsupervised Methods for Intrusion Detection

A large amount of unsupervised anomaly detection techniques have been proposed. Guan et al. [7] proposed a variant of K-means named Y-means. It removes the outliers and merges overlapped areas into a new cluster. Apart from clustering-based approaches. PSO-KM [8] combines Particle Swamp Optimization (PSO) algorithm with K-means for intrusion detection to overcome the impact of initial cluster selection. Local out Factor (LOF) [9] compares the local density of an sample with its neighbors, and the areas which have a relatively lower density are considered as the outliers. Statistical-based, distance-based, density-based methods have also been applied to intrusion detection [17–19]. These methods are also not capable to deal with high-dimensional data.

2.3 Deep Learning Methods for Intrusion Detection

Many attempts have been made to apply deep learning to intrusion detection. Ma et al. [20] evaluated deep neural network on the KDDCUP99 dataset. Niyaz et al. [21] ran deep belief network on NSL-KDD dataset. Some methods handling raw packets have been proposed in recent years. Wang et al. [22] applied convolutional neural network to learn spatial features of raw malware traffic, Torres et al. [23] used RNN to learn the temporal features of network traffic, Wang et al. [24] combined CNN with LSTM to learn both spatial and temporal features. Although these methods acquire impressive performance on intrusion detection, they are completely supervised and require ample labeled training samples.

3 SU-IDS

In this section, we describe the architecture and training objectives of the proposed framework, i.e., SU-IDS. The key idea of SU-IDS is jointly training a classification or clustering network along with an autoencoder network, which can learn representative features from data in a unsupervised manner. The procedure of our method can be summarized as follows: We first pretrain an autoencoder using the unlabeled samples. Then, the features extracted by the encoder network are fed into a clustering module (or classification module). Afterwards, we jointly optimize the clustering loss (or classification loss) with the reconstruction loss, i.e., we jointly train the parameters of clustering module (or classification module) with the autoencoder network. As is illustrated in Fig. 1, the feature extraction network for clustering (or classification) shares the same parameters and architecture with the encoder part of the autoencoder network.

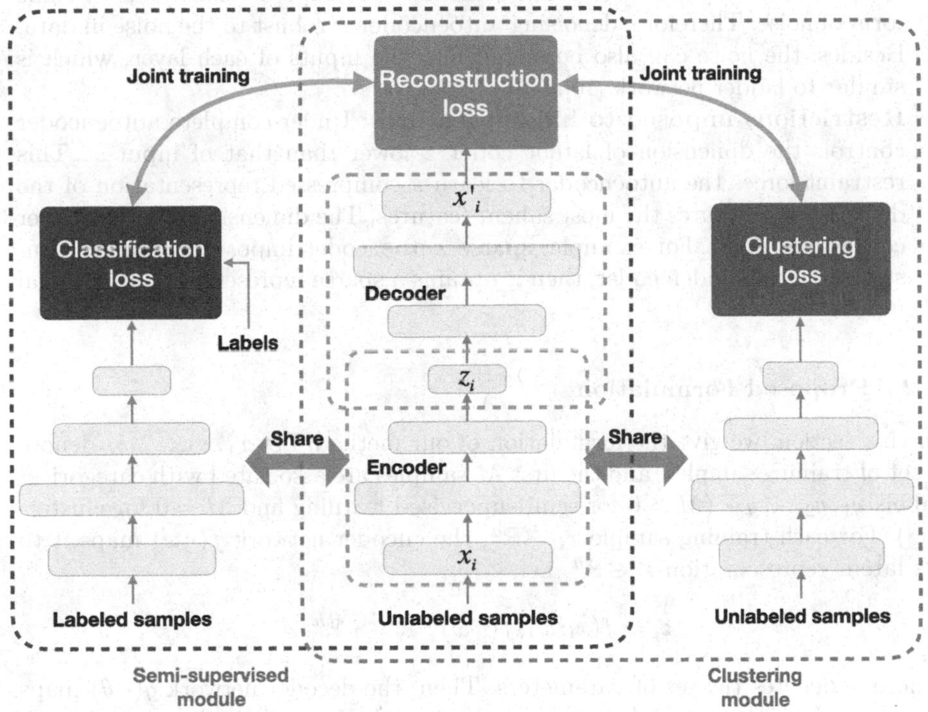

Fig. 1. This figure illustrates the architecture of SU-IDS

3.1 Autoencoders

An autoencoder is a feed-forward neural network that attempts to reconstruct the input x. It is usually a symmetric architecture consisting of two parts: an encoder part, which maps the input x into a hidden representation (or latent representation) z, and an decoder part, which converts z to $\hat{x}$, an approximate reconstruction of x. After the training of autoencoder, the encoder part can be used as a feature extractor. No labeled samples are required throughout the training, thus it is an unsupervised algorithm of representation learning. In recent years, extensive work [10–12, 25] demonstrates that adding the auxiliary task of training an autoencoder to a usual classification task or clustering task can significant improve its performance, which is the essence of our framework.

There are many variants of autoencoder, and we can improve the autoencoder according to specific applications from the following three perspectives:

- **The architecture of each layer:** The original autoencoder is composed of multiple fully-connected perception layers. However, in order to deal with data with spatial invariance, we can construct an autoencoder with convolutional and pooling layers.
- **Robustness:** Instead of reconstructing x given a clean x, denoising autoencoder tries to reconstruct x from $\tilde{x}$, which is a corrupted version of x by some form of noise. Therefore, denoising autoencoder is robust to the noise in data. Besides, the noise can also be added into the inputs of each layer, which is similar to ladder network [10].
- **Restrictions imposed to hidden features:** Under-complete autoencoder controls the dimension of latent coder z lower than that of input x. This restraint forces the autoencoder to learn a compressed representation of the data, i.e., it captures the most salient features. The dimension of latent coder can also be high. For example, sparse autoencoder imposes a sparsity constraint on the hidden coder, then it obtains a sparse representation of original inputs.

3.2 Proposed Formulation

In this section, we give the formulation of our method. Let $x_1, x_2, ..., x_N$ denote a set of training samples, and the first M samples are associated with categorical labels $y_1, y_2, ..., y_M$ ($M > 0$ for semi-supervised learning and $M = 0$ for clustering). For each training sample $x_i \in \mathbb{R}^d$, the encoder network $f(\cdot;\omega)$ maps it to its latent representation $z_i \in \mathbb{R}^h$, i.e.,

$$z_i = f(x_i;\omega), f(\cdot;\omega) : \mathbb{R}^d \rightarrow \mathbb{R}^h,$$

where ω denotes the set of parameters. Then, the decoder network $g(\cdot;\theta)$ maps the z_i back to the original space and requires that $g(z_i;\theta)$ and x_i match each other well under some metric, e.g., least squares measures or cross entropy. By the above reasoning, we obtain the reconstruction loss:

$$L_{rec} = \sum_{i=1}^{N} l(g(f(x_i)), x_i) \tag{1}$$

where $l(\cdot) : \mathbb{R}^d \rightarrow \mathbb{R}$ is a certain loss function that measures the reconstruction error.

For unsupervised clustering task, since there is no label for any sample, we come up with the following cost function:

$$L_{cls} = \sum_{i=1}^{N} l(g(f(x_i)), x_i) + \lambda \Phi(f(X), S, M) \tag{2}$$

where $\Phi(\cdot)$ is the clustering loss, X denotes all training samples, S is the assignments of each sample, M is other parameters of the clustering algorithm (e.g., cluster centroids), and $\lambda \geq 0$ is a regularization parameter which makes a balance between feature reconstruction and clustering.

For semi-supervised learning task, we have M labeled samples, the cost function is formulated as follows:

$$L_{ssl} = \sum_{i=1}^{N} l(g(f(x_i)), x_i) + \lambda \sum_{j=1}^{M} c(f(x_j), y_j, \sigma) \tag{3}$$

where $c(\cdot)$ denotes the classification loss of each sample, σ is the parameters of the classification algorithm, e.g., σ is the weights of the softmax layer when the classification algorithm is softmax.

Note that our framework is general and can be incorporated with many advanced clustering (or classification) algorithms, as long as their loss function can be optimized with the reconstruction loss jointly.

3.3 Optimization Procedure

Optimizing the cost functions is non-trivial since they are non-convex. In addition, the clustering loss may contains discrete variables and non-convex constrains, which requires alternating optimization. In this section, we describe our optimization procedure for both tasks. In our work, we assume that the classification algorithm is softmax and the clustering algorithm is K-means.

Initializing the Network via Layer-Wise Pre-training. A good initialization is critical to optimize highly non-convex objective functions. Therefore, we first adopts the layer-wise pre-training method to initialize the parameters of the autoencoder. Then, we fine-tune the all parameters of the autoencoder to obtain a better initialization. After that, for clustering task, we have to additionally perform K-means to the outputs of the encoder part to obtain initial cluster centroids and sample assignments.

Optimization for Semi-supervised Tasks. Assuming the classification algorithm is a softmax layer, optimizing the semi-supervised cost function is relatively simple. It is similar to the supervised training of neural networks, which calculates a mini batch gradient to update the network in each iteration. The difference is that in the semi-supervised case, in each iteration, we have to sample a labeled mini-batch with an unlabeled mini-batch to optimize the network.

Optimization for Clustering Tasks. In our work, we adopt K-means loss as the clustering loss, so the cost function can be formulated as follows:

$$L_{cls} = \sum_{i=1}^{N} (l(g(f(x_i)), x_i) + \lambda \parallel f(x_i) - Ms_i \parallel_2^2) \tag{4}$$
$$\text{s.t. } s_{j,i} \in \{0,1\}, \mathbf{1}^T s_i = 0, \forall i, j$$

where s_i is the one-hot assignment vector of sample i, $s_{j,i}$ is the jth element of s_i, and M is the centroid matrix, the k-th column of which denotes the kth cluster centroid, i.e., m_k. We cannot directly apply stochastic gradient descent (SGD) or its variants [26–28] to optimize all parameters because $\{s_i\}$ is a discrete variable, so we adopt alternating optimization to the cost function. To be specific, in each iteration, we first fix the assignment $\{s_i\}$ and M, then update the network parameters using SGD. Secondly, we fix the network parameters and M, then update s_i as follows:

$$s_{j,i} = \begin{cases} 1, & \text{if } j = \underset{k=\{1,\ldots,K\}}{\text{argmin}} \parallel f(x_i) - m_k \parallel \\ 0, & \text{otherwise} \end{cases} \tag{5}$$

Thirdly, we fix the network parameters and $\{s_i\}$, then we apply the following step to update M:

$$m_k = m_k - (1/c_k^i)(m_k - f(x_i))s_{k,i} \tag{6}$$

where c_k^i is the number of samples assigned to cluster k before dealing with the incoming sample x_i. This update method is more reasonable than simply averaging all assigned samples, because it update centroids with many assigned samples more gracefully while updating others more aggressively.

4 Performance Evaluation

We evaluate both clustering and semi-supervised performance of SU-IDS on two datasets, NSL-KDD [29] and CICIDS2017[1]. NSL-KDD is a widely-used dataset suggested to settle some inherent shortcomings of KDDCUP'99 dataset which are mentioned in [29]. It has the following advantages compared with the original one: (1) no redundant records in the training set, (2) no duplicate records in the testing set and (3) reasonable number of records in both training and testing set. However, it is too old-fashioned and cannot reflect the behavior of modern attacks, so we also choose another up-to-date dataset, CICID2017, which is published by the Information Security Center of Excellence (ISCX) of the University of New Brunswick (UNB) in Canada in 2017.

4.1 Data Specification

The NSL-KDD dataset has 41 input features and a class label. These features can be classified into four categories: basic features, content features, time-based traffic features and host-based traffic features. The basic features were extracted from individual TCP connections without inspecting the payload. Content features within a connection were extracted from the payload segments by domain knowledge. Time-based traffic features were calculated using a two-second time

[1] http://unb.ca/cic/research/datasets/index.html.

window. Host-based traffic features were calculated through a historical window instead of time. For preprocessing, we encoded each categorical features as one-hot vector and then scale each feature into range [0, 1].

The CICID2017 contains updated attacks such as DoS, DDoS, Brute Force, XSS, SQL Injection, Infiltration, Port scan and Botnet. Raw pcap files are available along with a processed one (CSV files). The processed one is completely labeled and contains 80 network traffic features which are calculated and extracted for all benign and attack flows by CICFlowMeter Software. The network traffic features includes ample statistical information about traffic conditions, such as packets number, packets length, bytes numbers, transmission speed, flag numbers, duration of one flow. In our experiment, we evaluated our methods on the processed version. Since all features are continuous value, the preprocessing step is just the [0, 1] normalization.

4.2 Evaluation Metrics

We used three metrics to evaluate the semi-supervised classification performance of SU-IDS: accuracy (ACC), detection rate (DR) and false alarm rate. They are widely used to evaluate the performance of intrusion detection techniques. ACC reflects the overall performance, DR shows the percentage of attack traffics detected, and FAR is an evaluation of misclassification of normal traffic. They are formulated as follows:

$$\begin{aligned} Accuracy(ACC) &= \frac{TP+TN}{TP+FP+FN+TN} \\ DetectionRate(DR) &= \frac{TP}{TP+FN} \\ FalseAlarmRate(FAR) &= \frac{FP}{FP+TN}. \end{aligned} \tag{7}$$

Note that TP denotes the number of samples correctly classified as A, TN denotes the number of samples correctly classified as Not-A, FP denotes the number of samples incorrectly classified as A, and FN denotes the number of samples incorrectly classified as Not-A. For evaluation of clustering performance of SU-IDS, we choose the unsupervised clustering accuracy (cACC). It is formulated as:

$$cACC = \max_m \frac{\sum_{i=1}^{n} 1\{y_i = m(c_i)\}}{n}.$$

where y_i is the ground-truth label, c_i is the cluster assignment generated by the algorithm, and m is a mapping function which perform one-to-one mapping between clusters and labels.

4.3 Experimental Setup

Pytorch and Scikit-learn are the software frameworks for our implementation. In the autoencoder network, encoder and decoder have a symmetry architecture.

For NSL-KDD dataset, we set the dimensions of encoder as $d - 100 - 50 - 10$, where d is the dimension of input data. For CICIDS2017 dataset, the dimensions are $d - 100 - 80 - 10$. All internal layers are activated by ReLU nonlinearity function. For clustering task, a clean autoencoder is used, while for classification task, we use the same architecture as ladder network, i.e., layer-wise noise and reconstruction loss are added. The autoencoder network pretraining is required. With respect to optimization, the batch size is 100 for all experiments and the optimizer Adam is applied with default parameters of pytorch. We implemented all other methods with scikit-learn and all parameters are default.

Table 1. Clustering results of SU-IDS on NSL-KDD dataset

Methods	cACC (2 clusters)	cACC (5 clusters)
K-means	0.8104	0.6024
GMM	0.6551	0.5158
PCA (5 dims)+K-means	0.8202	0.6072
PCA (15 dims)+K-means	0.8104	0.6072
SU-IDS	0.9102	0.6582

Table 2. Clustering results of SU-IDS on CICID2017 dataset

Methods	cACC (2 clusters)	cACC (9 clusters)
K-means	0.5689	0.4385
GMM	0.5781	0.3814
PCA (5 dims)+K-means	0.5702	0.4702
PCA (15 dims)+K-means	0.5784	0.4812
SU-IDS	0.7102	0.5137

4.4 Clustering Results

In this section, we test SU-IDS on unsupervised clustering tasks. For NSL-KDD dataset, we first labeled all classes of anomaly traffic as "Attack" then conduct 2-clusters (Normal-versus-Attack) clustering. After that, we divided attack samples into four main categories and performed 5-clusters clustering. For CICID2017 dataset, we choose 40000 samples from normal samples and choose 5000 samples per class from 8 classes of attacks. Both 2-clusters and 9-clusters clustering were conducted. We compare our method with four other clustering algorithms: K-means, GMM, PCA(5 dimensions)+K-means and PCA(15 dimensions)+K-means. Some other popular algorithms such as Spectral Clustering and DBSCAN were not tested because they cannot deal with large-scale datasets. As shown in Tables 1 and 2, SU-IDS has better clustering performance than other methods, which demonstrates that the joint training of clustering loss and reconstruction loss learns a better representation for clustering.

Table 3. Results of SU-IDS and NN on NSL-KDD dataset with 3000 samples per class for attack traffic and 12000 samples for normal traffic. The number of labeled samples are varied from 0.5% to 100%.

Percentage	SU-IDS			NN (no AE loss)		
	ACC%	DR	FAR	ACC%	DR	FAR
0.5%	97.30	0.9550	0.009	95.60	0.9273	0.016
1%	98.34	0.9743	0.007	98.19	0.9791	0.015
5%	98.75	0.9839	0.009	98.40	0.9808	0.013
10%	99.02	0.9908	0.010	98.54	0.9886	0.018
20%	99.50	0.9934	0.003	99.21	0.9909	0.007
100%	99.59	0.9954	0.004	99.55	0.9944	0.004

Table 4. Results of SU-IDS and NN on CICID2017 dataset with 5000 samples per class for attack traffic and 40000 samples for normal traffic. The number of labeled samples are varied from 0.5% to 100%.

Percentage	SU-IDS			NN (no AE loss)		
	ACC%	DR	FAR	ACC%	DR	FAR
0.5%	93.68	0.9238	0.05	89.74	0.9014	0.106
1%	95.99	0.9672	0.047	92.09	0.9504	0.109
5%	98.05	0.9838	0.022	95.78	0.9765	0.061
10%	98.55	0.9878	0.017	97.32	0.9866	0.040
20%	98.93	0.9944	0.016	97.91	0.9929	0.034
100%	99.13	0.9965	0.014	98.35	0.9938	0.026

4.5 Semi-supervised Classification Results

In this section, we evaluate the semi-supervised classification performance of SU-IDS. For NSL-KDD, we randomly chose 3000 samples per class for 5 classes of attack traffic and 12000 samples for normal traffic. For CICID2017, we randomly chose 5000 samples per class for 8 classes of attack traffic and 40000 samples for normal traffic. For both datasets, we split the chosen samples into a training set and a testing set using a ratio of 60% and 40% . Five tests varying the number of examples required for each class, i.e., 0.5%, 1%, 5%, 10%, 20% and 100% were run. We also implemented another neural network for comparison, which has the same architecture with the encoder part of autoencoder, and it was trained only on the labeled samples. The results are illustrated in Tables 3 and 4. It can be found that our method is obviously superior to completely supervised neural network with the same number of labeled samples. Besides, it is capable to achieve similar performance as supervised learning with only 20% labeled samples.

5 Conclusion

In this paper, we propose a novel intrusion detection framework, i.e., SU-IDS, which builds effective model from unlabeled or partial-labeled data. The semi-supervised module of SU-IDS augments the task of supervised classification with the auxiliary unsupervised training of an autoencoder, achieving a significant performance improvement with the same number of labeled samples. The unsupervised clustering module of SU-IDS jointly trains the clustering loss and reconstruction loss of autoencoder to obtain a more clustering-friendly feature representation, resulting in a better clustering result. We provide the general mathematical formulation of the framework and present an example of the optimization procedure. Extensive experiments illustrate the feasibility and effectiveness of our method.

Acknowledgment. This work is partially supported by National Natural Science Foundation of China (Grant No. 61702539, 60970034).

References

1. Kruegel, C., Toth, T.: Using decision trees to improve signature-based intrusion detection. In: Vigna, G., Kruegel, C., Jonsson, E. (eds.) RAID 2003. LNCS, vol. 2820, pp. 173–191. Springer, Heidelberg (2003). https://doi.org/10.1007/978-3-540-45248-5_10
2. Li, Y., Xia, J., Zhang, S., Yan, J., Ai, X., Dai, K.: An efficient intrusion detection system based on support vector machines and gradually feature removal method. Expert Syst. Appl. **39**(1), 424–430 (2012)
3. Jemili, F., Zaghdoud, M., Ahmed, M.B.: A framework for an adaptive intrusion detection system using Bayesian network. In: 2007 IEEE Intelligence and Security Informatics, pp. 66–70. IEEE (2007)
4. Cannady, J.: Artificial neural networks for misuse detection. In: National Information Systems Security Conference, Baltimore, vol. 26 (1998)
5. Wagh, S.K., Kolhe, S.R.: Effective intrusion detection system using semi-supervised learning. In: 2014 International Conference on Data Mining and Intelligent Computing (ICDMIC), pp. 1–5. IEEE (2014)
6. Xiang, Z., Xiao, Z., Wang, D., Georges, H.M.: Incremental semi-supervised kernel construction with self-organizing incremental neural network and application in intrusion detection. J. Intell. Fuzzy Syst. **31**(2), 815–823 (2016)
7. Guan, Y., Ghorbani, A.A., Belacel, N.: Y-means: a clustering method for intrusion detection. In: Canadian Conference on Electrical and Computer Engineering, IEEE CCECE 2003, vol. 2, pp. 1083–1086. IEEE (2003)
8. Li, Z., Li, Y., Xu, L.: Anomaly intrusion detection method based on k-means clustering algorithm with particle swarm optimization. In: 2011 International Conference on Information Technology, Computer Engineering and Management Sciences (ICM), vol. 2, pp. 157–161. IEEE (2011)
9. Campos, G.O., et al.: On the evaluation of unsupervised outlier detection: measures, datasets, and an empirical study. Data Mining Knowl. Discov. **30**(4), 891–927 (2016)

10. Rasmus, A., Berglund, M., Honkala, M., Valpola, H., Raiko, T.: Semi-supervised learning with ladder networks. In: Advances in Neural Information Processing Systems, pp. 3546–3554 (2015)
11. Zhao, J., Mathieu, M., Goroshin, R., Lecun, Y.: Stacked what-where auto-encoders. Comput. Sci. **15**(1), 3563–3593 (2015)
12. Yang, B., Fu, X., Sidiropoulos, N.D., Hong, M.: Towards k-means-friendly spaces: simultaneous deep learning and clustering (2016). arXiv preprint arXiv:1610.04794
13. Mao, C.-H., Lee, H.-M., Parikh, D., Chen, T., Huang, S.-Y.: Semi-supervised co-training and active learning based approach for multi-view intrusion detection. In: Proceedings of the 2009 ACM symposium on Applied Computing, pp. 2042–2048. ACM (2009)
14. Chen, C., Gong, Y., Tian, Y.: Semi-supervised learning methods for network intrusion detection. In: IEEE International Conference on Systems, Man and Cybernetics, SMC 2008, pp. 2603–2608. IEEE (2008)
15. Meng, Y., Kwok, L.: Intrusion detection using disagreement-based semi-supervised learning: detection enhancement and false alarm reduction. In: Xiang, Y., Lopez, J., Kuo, C.-C.J., Zhou, W. (eds.) CSS 2012. LNCS, vol. 7672, pp. 483–497. Springer, Heidelberg (2012). https://doi.org/10.1007/978-3-642-35362-8_36
16. Fitriani, S., Mandala, S., Murti, M.A.: Review of semi-supervised method for intrusion detection system. In: 2016 Asia Pacific Conference on Multimedia and Broadcasting (APMediaCast), pp. 36–41. IEEE (2016)
17. Goldstein, M., Dengel, A.: Histogram-based outlier score (hbos): a fast unsupervised anomaly detection algorithm. In: KI-2012: Poster and Demo Track, pp. 59–63 (2012)
18. Ramaswamy, S., Rastogi, R., Shim, K.: Efficient algorithms for mining outliers from large data sets. In: ACM Sigmod Record, vol. 29, pp. 427–438. ACM (2000)
19. Fan, H., Zaïane, O.R., Foss, A., Wu, J.: A nonparametric outlier detection for effectively discovering top-n outliers from engineering data. In: Ng, W.-K., Kitsuregawa, M., Li, J., Chang, K. (eds.) PAKDD 2006. LNCS (LNAI), vol. 3918, pp. 557–566. Springer, Heidelberg (2006). https://doi.org/10.1007/11731139_66
20. Ma, T., Wang, F., Cheng, J., Yang, Y., Chen, X.: A hybrid spectral clustering and deep neural network ensemble algorithm for intrusion detection in sensor networks. Sensors **16**(10), 1701 (2016)
21. Javaid, A., Niyaz, Q., Sun, W., Alam, M.: A deep learning approach for network intrusion detection system. In: Proceedings of the 9th EAI International Conference on Bio-inspired Information and Communications Technologies (formerly BIONETICS), pp. 21–26. ICST (Institute for Computer Sciences, Social-Informatics and Telecommunications Engineering) (2016)
22. Tan, Z., Jamdagni, A., He, X., Nanda, P., Liu, R.P., Hu, J.: Detection of denial-of-service attacks based on computer vision techniques. IEEE Trans. Comput. **64**(9), 2519–2533 (2015)
23. Torres, P., Catania, C., Garcia, S., Garino, C.G.: An analysis of recurrent neural networks for botnet detection behavior. In: 2016 IEEE Biennial Congress of Argentina (ARGENCON), pp. 1–6. IEEE (2016)
24. Wang, W., et al.: Hast-ids: learning hierarchical spatial-temporal features using deep neural networks to improve intrusion detection. IEEE Access **6**, 1792–1806 (2018)
25. Xie, J., Girshick, R., Farhadi, A.: Unsupervised deep embedding for clustering analysis. In: International Conference on Machine Learning, pp. 478–487 (2016)

26. Min, E., Zhao, Y., Long, J., Wu, C., Li, K., Yin, J.: SVRG with adaptive epoch size. In: 2017 International Joint Conference on Neural Networks (IJCNN), pp. 2935–2942. IEEE (2017)
27. Min, E., Cui, J., Long, J.: Variance reduced stochastic optimization for PCA and PLS. In: 2017 10th International Symposium on Computational Intelligence and Design (ISCID), vol. 1, pp. 383–388. IEEE (2017)
28. Min, E., Long, J., Cui, J.: Analysis of the variance reduction in SVRG and a new acceleration method. IEEE Access **6**, 16165–16175 (2018)
29. Tavallaee, M., Bagheri, E., Lu, W., Ghorbani, A.A.: A detailed analysis of the KDD cup 99 data set. In: IEEE Symposium on Computational Intelligence for Security and Defense Applications, CISDA 2009, pp. 1–6. IEEE (2009)

Using Blockchain for Data Auditing in Cloud Storage

Chunhua Li(✉), Jiaqi Hu, Ke Zhou, Yuanzhang Wang, and Hongyu Deng

Wuhan National Lab for Optoelectronics, Huazhong University of Science and Technology, Wuhan 430074, China
li.chunhua@hust.edu.cn

Abstract. Cloud storage is one of the most important service of cloud computing. Since cloud service providers can not be completely trusted, traditional auditing methods can't guarantee the security of data sources. This paper proposes a security framework for cloud data audit using blockchain technology. User's operational information on the file is formed to a block after validated by all checked nodes in the blockchain network, and then to be put into the blockchain. Any modification or fake to the operational information can be inspected through the chain structure of block, thus ensuring the security of auditing data source. We construct a prototype in an Ethereum-based blockchain using Aliyun as data storage service, then test the time overhead of uploading file, broadcasting operation information and packing information into block chain. The results show that the time for packaging block remains unchanged from an overall viewpoint, and as the file size increasing, packaging block occupies less percentage in the entire process of file uploading or downloading.

Keywords: Cloud storage · Behavior auditing · Customizable log
Blockchain

1 Introduction

In the cloud environment, data owner and user often rely on a trusted third party for authentication and authorization. However, a third party is not secure by nature. Some security incidents have occurred repeatedly in recent years, such as data leakage and data tampering. A third party may reveal user's data for economy benefit actuation, on the other hand, some users may maliciously declare data loss for high compensation. Due to the lack of mutual trust, more than 70% of companies are not planning to adopt cloud storage services in the near future. Therefore, an audit scheme based on a trusted architecture becomes increasing important in the cloud [2, 3].

Log analysis is a common method in many auditing schemes [4], which track data through extracting users' operation events from system log. However, it is inefficiency to analyze users' operation from large amounts of system log records. Itani et al. used hash chains to maintain the order consistency of operation records [5]. All these methods count on system log to provide them reliable data operation records. In fact, it is hard to guarantee cloud server provider (CSP) believable. Ateniese et al. proposed a

X. Sun et al. (Eds.): ICCCS 2018, LNCS 11065, pp. 335–345, 2018.
https://doi.org/10.1007/978-3-030-00012-7_31

called PDP (provable data possession) approach, which can verify the integrity of outsourced data in untrusted cloud environments by introducing third-party auditors (TPA) and supports sample auditing [6]. Tian et al. proposed a public auditing for users' operation behaviors in cloud storage [7], in which a trusted third party is introduced to verify the integrity of operation behavior logs to enhance the credibility of forensic results. But, TPA is not as dependable as you might expect, it may collude with CSP or users, or be prone to attacks such as tampering and forgery.

The emergence of blockchain technology provides a new research idea to solve the problem of mutual trust. It utilizes cryptography rather than centralized architecture to build trust in peers for safeguarding interactions of them [8]. Meanwhile, it employs consensus algorithm to generate and update data between peers to ensure that block data is not changed, thus very suitable for data security in Cloud. In the past two years, some cloud security schemes based on blockchain have been proposed. Sengupta et al. proposed a scheme called Retricoin which replaces the heavy computational proof-of-work of Bitcoin by proofs of retrievability [9]. To guarantee the availability of an important but large file, they distributed the file segments among the users in the Bitcoin network. Ramachandran et al. used blockchain to develop a secure and immutable scientific data provenance management framework [10], in which utilizes smart contacts to record immutable data, and efficiently prevent any malicious modification to the captured data. Yang et al. proposed a public verifiable data deletion scheme for cloud storage based on blockchain, which uses the idea of blockchain to guarantee that any malicious deletion operation can be verified [11]. Dagher et al. proposed a blockchain-based framework for secure, interoperable and efficient access to medical records, which utilizes smart contracts in an Ethereum-based blockchain for heightened access control, and employs advanced cryptographic techniques for further security [12]. Ghoshal et al. proposed an auditing mechanism using the blockchain data structure of Bitcoins [13], any user can perform the validation of selected files efficiently. Fu et al. proposed a blockchain-based secure data-sharing protocol under decentralized storage architecture [14]. The mentioned schemes above can be regarded as application trial of blockchain in cloud security. Since the capacity of a block is limited in the blockchain, only very important security information is considered to store into the block, or system performance will not be acceptable.

In this paper, we try to use blockchain to ensure the security of audit data source. We construct a security analysis framework in an Ethereum-based blockchain, and use Aliyun as data storage service. The key contributions of this paper can be summarized as follows:

- We design a block structure for auditing users' operation. The file metadata and operation information is put into a block called log block, which is broadcasted among peers in the network and validated by all checked nodes with a lightweight consensus algorithm. All verified log blocks is chained through the hash of adjacent blocks. The chained metadata information can later be used for data integrity verification, the chained operation record can later be used for tracing access to file.
- We design a security architecture based on blockchain network which includes four components: blockchain layer, proxy layer, user layer and cloud storage layer. We implement a prototype in an Ethereum-based blockchain using Aliyun as data storage service. The results of analysis and tests demonstrate that our scheme is feasible and can resist repudiation attacks and replay attacks.

Paper organization is as follows: Sect. 2 introduces the related knowledge of blockchain technology, and analyzes its architecture and security. Section 3 describes our design in detail, and gives a simple security analysis. The performance evaluation is shown in Sect. 4. The conclusion is drawn in Sect. 5.

2 Backgrounds

2.1 Blcokchain's Characteristics and Security

Blockchain is a novel distributed technology of verifying and storing data using an encrypted chain block structure [1, 3]. It is a public distributed ledger that can be shared, replicated, and synchronized among different nodes. Combining cryptographic algorithms, decentralized consensus mechanism and P2P network, blockchain provides a way for all nodes in the network to reach the same state in a secure and verifiable manner.

Decentration**:** The blockchain network adopts P2P network in which all nodes are in the equal status. All data distributed in blockchain network is available for any node, and newly added node can select to download all or part of the block data from the old nodes to query or verify the block data. Each transaction which generated in the network is broadcasted to all nodes and verified and updated by the miner nodes. With the support of blockchain technology, the storage of cloud data is no longer dependent on a small number of data centers, it can be distributed into much more nodes, thus preventing one or more data centers from being attacked or improperly managed. At the same time, bad behavior such as data loss or disclosure can be discovered in time.

Tamper-Resistant**:** The block structure in the blockchain network is shown in Fig. 1. Each block contains the hash value of the previous block, thus forming a complete chain structure in the network. The pre-hash in block header is computed from the previous block using a specific hash function. Some necessary information is also stored in the block header for the purpose of security verification, such as timestamp, the difficulty of the puzzle and the Merkle root. Suppose a malicious user change the data of the previous block, it will inevitably cause the hash change of this block, furtherly result in the inconsistency between the hash of previous block and the pre-hash of current block. When two miners construct a new block at the same time, both blocks will be linked to the current block. Once the blockchain network is forked, the blockchain always trusts the longest chain. Generally speaking, unless malicious node has mastered more than 51% power of the entire network for a long time, it is impossible to replace the normal chain and complete data modification, otherwise resulting in extremely high tampering costs. Therefore, blockchain can rely on proof of work (POW) and consensus algorithms to safeguard the system.

2.2 Merkle Hash Tree

A Merkle Hash Tree (MHT) [15] is a well-studied authentication structure. It is often constructed as a binary tree where the leaf nodes store the hashes of data elements (a file or a collection of files) and the non-leaf nodes store the hashes of its two children. Generally, MHT is used to identify whether the data has been altered or not by comparing the computed root hash and the one verifier holds. In blockchain network, MHT is also employed to store transaction's hash so as to check transaction's authenticity.

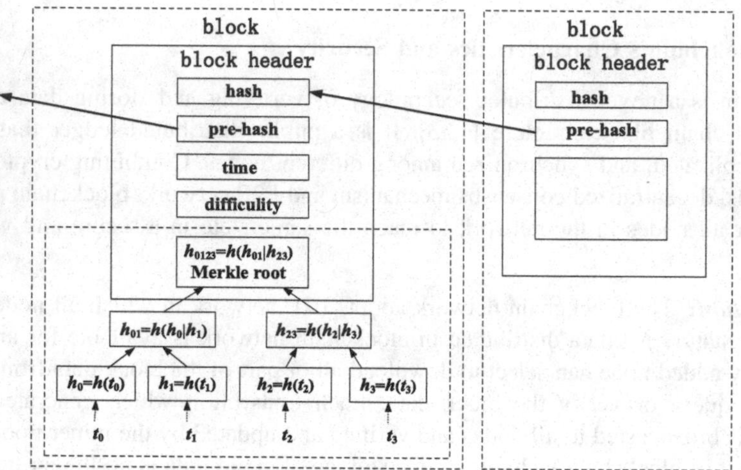

Fig. 1. Block structure in blockchain

As Fig. 1 shows, each block header saves the root hash of all transaction data in this block. When the verifier with a root h_{0123} wants to verify the transaction t_1, the prover will send him the auxiliary verification information $\{h_0, h_{23}\}$. Then the verifier computes $h_1 = h(t_1)$, $h_{01} = h(h_0| h_1)$, $h_{0123} = h(h_{01}| h_{23})$, and check if the computed root h_{0123} is the same as the one he holds. If there are an odd number of transactions, the remaining one is hashed with itself. Further, root hash participates in the hash operation of block header, thus any modification to transaction data will lead to the change of the root hash, which will result in the hash change of the block header. In this paper, we further utilize MHT to construct a hash tree for file metadata and file operation respectively, and make use of blockchain's decentralized architecture to ensure the security of audit data source.

3 Design and Implementation

The goals of our auditing framework is mainly to prevent log information from being modified by attackers or CSP. In addition, the process of adding a new block into the block chain will consume a lot of time, we'll try our best to reduce the latency.

3.1 System Architecture

We use blockchain to store user's operation on the file and metadata information when the file is uploaded. The system does not care about the actual location of a file, it only stores a file URL in file metadata. We utilize the tamper-resistant nature of blockchain to ensure the reliability of operation logs and file metadata. Metadata information can later be used to conduct integrity auditing, behavior auditing can be conducted by analyzing the operation logs.

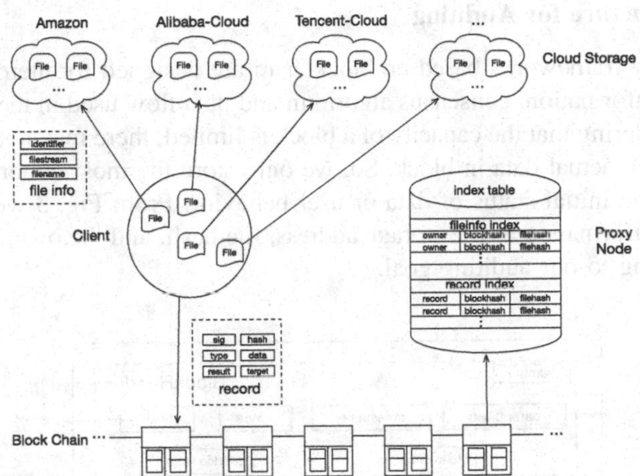

Fig. 2. System architecture

In order to accelerate the query of block data, we introduce a proxy layer. The proxy layer stores the index of block data. Users can quickly locate the requested block by interacting with the proxy layer. Of course, the proxy layer is not necessary, and a user can also traverse the block chain to get information. In order to accelerate block packaging, we plan to introduce lightning network into our system. Lightning network is a newly proposed technology which is scalable off-chain instant payments. However we are still finding a way to make it do with lightning network.

Figure 2 shows our system architecture, it is composed of four parts: blockchain layer, proxy layer, user layer and cloud storage layer.

Blockchain Layer: It consists of various nodes on the blockchain network, each node equally accepts the operation information broadcasted by the user node. The record information is packaged into the block by the mining algorithm. In the system, we use lightweight consensus protocol, that is, only a part of the miner is designated to participate in mining operation, while the mining interface is accessible to all nodes.

Proxy Layer: It is a node in the network used to keep the index of all blocks to speed up the query. When a newly generated block is put to the proxy node, it will analyze the content of block and forms a record index. When users need to get their own files or historical operation records, the proxy node can quickly locate the corresponding blocks according to the index.

User Layer: It is responsible for sending requests to the cloud and broadcasting operation information to each miner node of blockchain layer. When the operation record needs to be reviewed, the block index can also be obtained from the proxy node to retrieve related data.

Cloud Storage Layer: It also called persistent storage, namely, an actual storage location of data. In my system, only data is stored in cloud, file metadata is kept in the blockchain.

3.2 Data Structure for Auditing

Existing security frameworks based on blockchain are designed for their own security goal, so block information, consensus algorithm and data flow used in these system are different. Considering that the capacity of a block is limited, there may not have enough space to store the actual data in block. So, we only store the most important metadata which reflects the initial status of data or user behavior. From Fig. 3 we can see that such metadata information as file storage address, file hash, and the owner of a file will be kept according to our auditing goal.

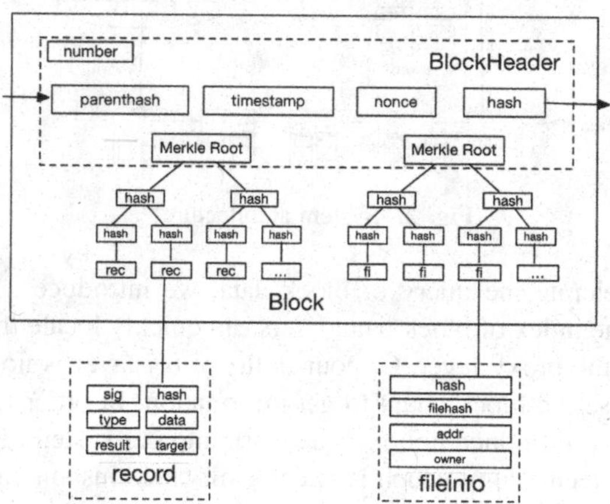

Fig. 3. Data structure for auditing

Different from blockchain in electronic currency, our system changes the original transaction structure to record user's operations on file. As shown in Fig. 3, the record structure retains the fields of user's signature (sig) and the hash in the original translation structure. The field of type is added to specify the user's operation type, and the field of result is used to store the hash value of data after being operated by users. Data field can't be empty if and only if the user manipulates new data. The encoded data will be stored in the data field, and the other operation types are empty. The field of target holds the hash address of data and is used to locate the data. In addition, we have added an array in the block body to save the file metadata information. Correspondingly, a Merkle root hash is added to the block header to verify the integrity of file information.

The fileinfo field is used to save the metadata information of user data. It contains the data owner, the filehash which is used to verify data integrity, the actual storage address of the data, and the hash of the fileinfo structure.

3.3 Auditing Description

Most of traditional behavior audit scheme uses logs to record the behavior, the log data is not only numerous but also easy to be modified. In this system, we build two Merkel trees in the block body. One is used to save user behavior records, and the other is used to save metadata information of a file. If the block data is tampered, an error will be discovered while verifying the block information and then the block will be rejected.

***Data Source Audit*:** One of the core elements of audit is to ensure the accuracy of the data source. If the data source is not trustworthy, the result of auditing is suspect. In this system, any operation on the file will automatically generate a corresponding operation record in client. These operation records are signed by user with their private key and then broadcasted to the blockchain network. The miner nodes in the blockchain layer accept record. They first verify the record integrity and then pack the valid record into a block, thus ensuring the security of data source.

***Integrity Audit*:** The files' metadata stored in the block body can be used for integrity auditing. The hash value of file has been recorded when upload the file. In other words, the initial state of a file has been recorded. When the file is obtained through the corresponding URL, its hash value is recalculated. If it is not equal to the hash value stored in the block body, the file is considered to be damaged.

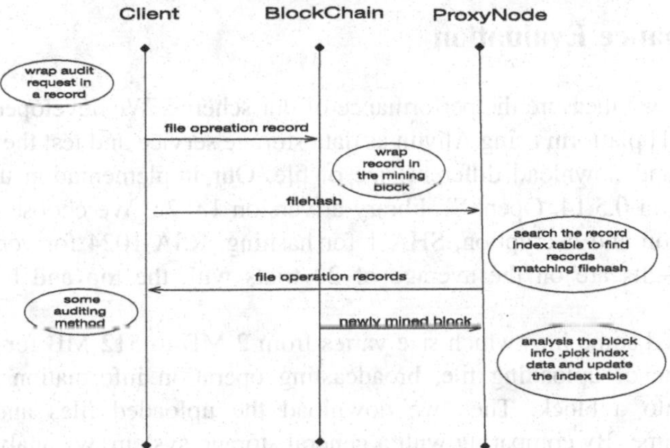

Fig. 4. The process of behavior auditing

***Behavior Audit*:** Figure 4 displays the process of behavior auditing. The file operation record stored in the block body can be used for behavior auditing. Since the audit data is stored in the block and the number of block is gradually increasing with the time, acquiring the block data directly will be a time-consuming operation. Therefore, a proxy node is added to our system for keeping the index of block data to accelerate the locating block. When the block is dug out by miner, it will be broadcasted to all nodes in the network. The proxy node will perform preliminary analysis, it stores the user's identification information into the file table, and saves the operation record into the record table. When we want to locate the file, we need first access to proxy node's file table, query the relevant records to find out which block the metadata is stored, and then we get the corresponding block from the block chain to take file metadata information. For the audit request, we also send a request to the proxy node so that we can find out the location of block where all historical records are stored, and then achieve the corresponding record information for subsequent audit and analysis operations.

3.4 Security Analysis

In this section, we analyze the security of our scheme through two common attacks.

Repudiation Attacks**:** The records are stored in block chain, and the copies are stored in various nodes in blockchain network. As the record chain is growing all the time, modifying some nodes' copies can not repudiate what he has done.

Replay Attacks**:** Every time a record is broadcasted to the miner, miner will check the hash of the record which contains a property named nonce. Nonce is a unique mark to identify a record generated by the blockchain network. When user wants to replay a record, he would construct a record, however the nonce is generated automatically, so the two records are different.

4 Performance Evaluation

In this section, we measure the performance of our scheme. We developed a prototype on Ethereum [1] platform using Aliyun as data storage service and test the performance of uploading and download different size of file. Our implementation uses the PBC library at version 0.5.14, OpenSSL library at version 1.0.2n. We choose AES-128 for block encryption and decryption, SHA-1 for hashing, RSA-1024 for verification. All experiment results are on the average of 20 trials with the top and bottom results excluded.

We prepared some files which size varies from 2 MB to 512 MB for this test. We record the time of uploading file, broadcasting operation information and packing information into a block. Then we download the uploaded files and record the downloading time. By comparing with a general storage system, we analyzed the time overhead of this system.

4.1 Time Overhead of Uploading File

The uploading process is divided into three steps. First, the user uploads files to cloud storage server, then the user broadcasts the request of storing files to the network, finally, the user waits for the system to pack this record into a block. The percentages of the time for uploading, broadcasting, and packing into blocks are shown in Fig. 5.

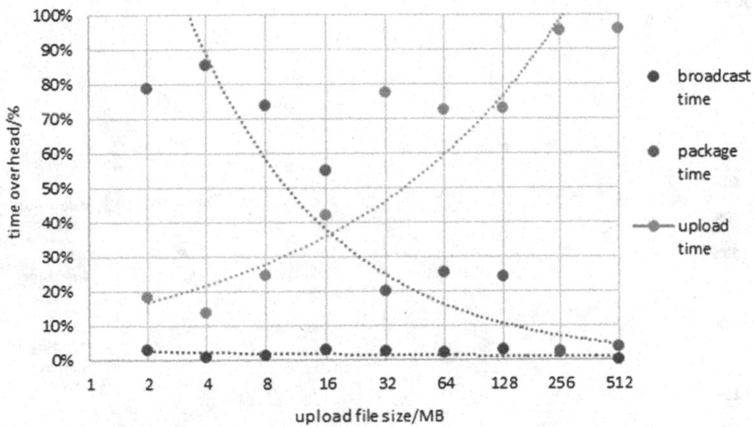

Fig. 5. Time overhead for upload download file

From the Fig. 5, we can see that the broadcast operation occupies a small time in the entire file upload process, and gradually decreases as the data increases. After adding the waiting time of packing into a block, we can see that the time delay has a remarkable rise when the uploading file data is small, and the percentage of time spent packing into a block in the entire operation is also high. However, as the size of data increases, the time allocation of packing into a block in the total operating time shows a decreasing trend. When the file size is up to 512 MB, the time allocation is even lower than 2%.

From the Fig. 5, we can see the waiting time of packing into a block is not fixed, for that mining is a process of calculating random numbers, so there may be some cases where the speed of mining is too fast or too slow for some test cases. However, on the whole, when the file is small, the time spent waiting for packing into a block takes a high proportion. When the file is large, the network I/O, that is, the upload time takes a high proportion.

4.2 Time Overhead of Downloading File

The downloading process is also divided into three steps. First, the user accesses the agent node to obtain the metadata information of the file, then the user could obtain the file from cloud storage server according to the file URL, and finally broadcasts this operation to the blockchain network waiting for the network to pack this operation into blocks. The percentage of total time for these three periods is shown in the Fig. 6.

As can be seen from the Fig. 6, obtaining the file's metadata information only exists in the process of interacting with the proxy node, and the time-consuming tends to be stable. The downloading time increases as the size of the file increases, and the proportion of the downloading time to the total downloading time is also increasing, however, the proportion of time spent broadcasting and packing into a block to the total downloading time is decreasing. This shows that with the increase of files' sizes, the impact of the network's I/O on the system is greater than that of waiting for packing into a block.

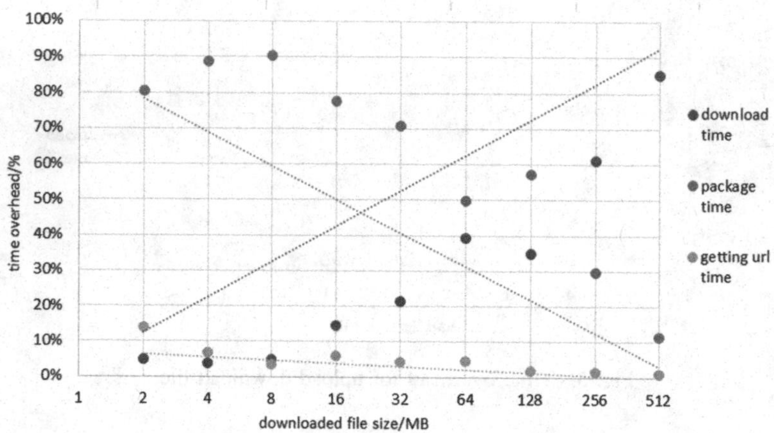

Fig. 6. Time overhead for download file

5 Conclusions

This paper builds a blockchain-based behavior audit framework that uses blockchain to store files' metadata information and users' behavior information. The framework implements operations such as auditing the integrity of files and auditing users' behaviors. Compared with the traditional logging-based audit method, the security of the audited data is guaranteed. Although the proxy node is used to speed up the query of operations on the block, due to the problem of packing delay in the blockchain system, the file records may be packed into the block for a long time, resulting in a long waiting time for the user to confirm that the operation is recorded in the log. In the meantime, it takes a long time waiting for packing into a block when files are stored, which may lead to that users successfully upload files but cannot immediately query their own files. Through the test we have found that when the file size is increased, the total time spent on packing records into the block gradually decreases.

Acknowledgments. This work is supported by the National Key R&D Program of China (2016YFB0800402), partially supported by the National Natural Science Foundation of China under Grant No. 61232004 and the Fundamental Research Funds for the Central Universities (2016YXMS020).

References

1. G Wood Ethereum: a secure decentralised generalised transaction. http://www.ethereum.Org
2. Dong, C., Wang, Y., Aldweesh, A., et al.: Betrayal, Distrust, and Rationality: Smart Counter-Collusion Contracts for Verifiable Cloud Computing, ACM CCS. ACM, New York (2017)
3. Li, X., Jiang, P., Chen, T., Luo, X., Wen, Q.: A survey on the security of blockchain systems. Future Gen. Comput. Syst. (2017)
4. Oliner, A., Stearley, J.: What supercomputers say: a study of five system logs. In: IEEE/IFIP International Conference on Dependable Systems and Networks, pp. 575–584. IEEE Computer Society (2007)
5. Itani, W., Kayssi, A., Chehab, A.: Privacy as a service: privacy-aware data storage and processing in cloud computing architectures. In: The 8th IEEE International Conference on Dependable, Autonomic and Secure Computing, DASC (2009)
6. Ateniese, G., Burns, R., Curtmola, R., et al.: Provable data possession at untrusted stores. In: ACM Conference on Computer and Communications Security, pp. 598–609. ACM (2007)
7. Tian, H., Chen, Z., Chang, C.C., et al.: Enabling public auditability for operation behaviors in cloud storage. Soft. Comput. **21**(8), 1–13 (2016)
8. Nakamoto, S.: Bitcoin: a peer-to-peer electronic ash system. Technical report (2009). https://bitcoin.org/bitcoin.pdf
9. Sengupta, B., Bag, S., Ruj, S., et al.: Retricoin: bitcoin based on compact proofs of retrievability. In: The 17th International Conference on Distributed Computing and Networking (2016)
10. Ramachandran, A., Kantarcioglu, D.: Using Blockchain and smart contracts for secure data provenance management (2017)
11. Yang, C., Chen, X., Xiang, Y.: Blockchain-based publicly verifiable data deletion scheme for cloud storage. J. Netw. Comput. Appl. **103** (2017)
12. Dagher, G.G., Mohler, J., Milojkovic, M., et al.: Ancile: privacy-preserving framework for access control and interoperability of electronic health records using blockchain technology, sustainable cities & society (2018)
13. Ghoshal, S., Paul, G.: Exploiting block-chain data structure for auditorless auditing on cloud data. In: Ray, I., Gaur, M.S., Conti, M., Sanghi, D., Kamakoti, V. (eds.) ICISS 2016. LNCS, vol. 10063, pp. 359–371. Springer, Cham (2016). https://doi.org/10.1007/978-3-319-49806-5_19
14. Fu, Y.: Meta-key: a secure data-sharing protocol under blockchain-based decentralised storage architecture (2017)
15. Merkle, R.C.: Protocols for public key cryptosystems. In: Proceedings of IEEE Symposium on Security and Privacy (1980)

Encryption

A Chaotic Searchable Image Encryption Scheme Integrating with Block Truncation Coding

Mingfang Jiang[1] and Guang Sun[2(✉)]

[1] Department of Information Science and Engineering, Hunan First Normal University, Changsha 410205, China
bingyuejiang@126.com

[2] Research Institute for Finance and Economics Big Data, Hunan University of Finance and Economics, Changsha 410073, China
simon5115@163.com

Abstract. In order to provide secure retrieval for encrypted digital images in cloud-based system, a secure searchable image encryption algorithm based on Block Truncation Coding (BTC) and Henon chaotic map is presented. Henon Chaotic map is used to encrypt two quantization levels of BTC compressed images, and a pseudo random sequence is created by chaotic map to scramble the bit plane of each sub-block. The feature value of each sub-block is computed according to the relationship between the number of 1s and 0s in the corresponding bit plane. The encrypted image retrieval can be achieved by comparing the normalized correlation coefficients between the feature vectors. Experimental results show that the proposed scheme has satisfactory retrieval accuracy and security. Meanwhile, it has low computational cost and can be used for encrypted images retrieval in the cloud.

Keywords: Searchable image encryption · Henon chaotic map
Block Truncation Coding

1 Introduction

In recent years, with rapid development and extensive popularity of cloud computing, the Internet of Things and big data, more and more digital data are stored in cloud service. However, users are very afraid of the confidentiality and privacy of their data in the remote cloud if they are not processed before storage. To provide security protection for their outsourced data in the cloud, these data should be stored in the cloud in a secure manner. This makes the indexing and searching over outsourced encrypted data a challenge. Searchable Encryption (SE) provides an effective solution to search on encrypted data [1]. Currently the digital trend and the demand of multimedia application become much stronger than ever before, searchable encryption technology over encrypted images have received more and more attention [2, 3].

Several SE approaches which support similarity search over encrypted images have been proposed in the literature [4–6]. These SE solutions exploiting homomorphic encryption strategy are hard to realize on the resource constrained mobile devices.

X. Sun et al. (Eds.): ICCCS 2018, LNCS 11065, pp. 349–358, 2018.
https://doi.org/10.1007/978-3-030-00012-7_32

To reduce the amount of computation on the client side, Zou et al. [7] proposed a novel image encryption search scheme by using comparable encryption. Hyma et al. [8] have proposed a new searchable medical image encryption method to provide secrecy or authentication for medical images in a third-party server, which allows the authorized user to retrieve the most relevant cluster of images from the database in the third part server. Wang et al. [9] designed a novel search scheme for encrypted image by combining K-means and secure modular hashing, and the results show that the scheme can achieve satisfactory privacy-preserving image search while providing a comparable search efficiency and accuracy. Kamal et al. [10] devised and realized a non-keyword based searchable encryption algorithm by using secret sharing scheme. It achieves lower computational overhead than conventional searchable encryption methods. Zhang et al. [11] employ DWT-DCT to develop a searchable encryption scheme for medical images. The image was encrypted in DCT domain using Henon mapping, and the perceptual hash sequence of the image was extracted by combining DWT and DCT for similarity search on encrypted medical images. The above-mentioned SE methods can achieve secure retrieval and storage over encrypted images in the cloud server, but they are not suitable for compressed images in cloud storage system. This makes traditional searchable image encryption schemes unpractical since digital image usually are stored in the cloud in compressed manner for the sake of reducing server load and saving communication bandwidth. Considering the simplicity and effectiveness of BTC, we propose a novel searchable image encryption scheme for BTC compressed images in this paper.

The paper is organized as follows: Sect. 2 provides background information including BTC and Henon chaotic map. Section 3 describes the proposed searchable image encryption method. The experimental results and analysis of the proposed algorithm are given in Sect. 4. Finally, the conclusions are drawn in Sect. 5.

2 Preliminaries

2.1 Block Truncation Coding

Block Truncation Coding (BTC) is a block-adaptive binary encoding technology proposed by Delp and Ritcell for grayscale image compression [12]. It is also called the moment-preserving block truncation coding (MPBTC) scheme because the first and second moments of image blocks remain unchanged before and after compression. In 1984, the absolute moment block truncation coding (AMBTC) [13] that preserves the sample mean and the sample first absolute central moment is introduced, and it can provide better reconstructed image quality than conventional MPBTC.

In the encoding process of AMBTC, each grayscale image is divided into non-overlapping sub-blocks of $s \times s$ pixels, which can be viewed as an image vector of k dimensions, where $k = s \times s$. Each sub-block is then compressed by using two quantization levels, i.e., higher mean h and lower mean l, and one bit-plane B. Given any sub-block $O = (o_1, o_2, \cdots, o_k)$, two quantization levels are calculated by

$$\begin{cases} l == \frac{1}{k-q} \sum\limits_{o_j < \bar{o}} o_j \\ h = \frac{1}{q} \sum\limits_{o_j \geq \bar{o}} o_j \end{cases} , j = 1, 2, \cdots, k \tag{1}$$

where q is the number of pixels having a value greater than or equal to the block mean $\bar{o}$.

The bit-plane B can be constructed by investigating the relationship of pixel values o_j and the block mean $\bar{o}$. So, each compressed image sub-block forms a trio (h, l, B). An example for AMBTC encoding procedure of sub-block with 4×4 pixels is shown in Fig. 1.

128	134	150	133
143	142	150	152
152	157	160	158
144	146	147	140

(a) original sub-block ($\bar{o}$ =146)

0	0	1	0
0	0	1	1
1	1	1	1
0	1	1	0

(b) bit-plane (q=9, h=152, l=137)

137	137	152	137
137	137	152	152
152	152	152	152
137	152	152	137

(c) reconstructed sub-block

Fig. 1. Example of AMBTC encoding

2.2 Henon Chaotic Map

Henon map is a chaotic dynamical system with good nonperiodicity, ergodicity and randomicity, which is described as following,

$$\begin{cases} x_{i+1} = 1 - ax_i^2 + y_i \\ y_{i+1} = bx_i \end{cases} , i = 0, 1, 2, \cdots \tag{2}$$

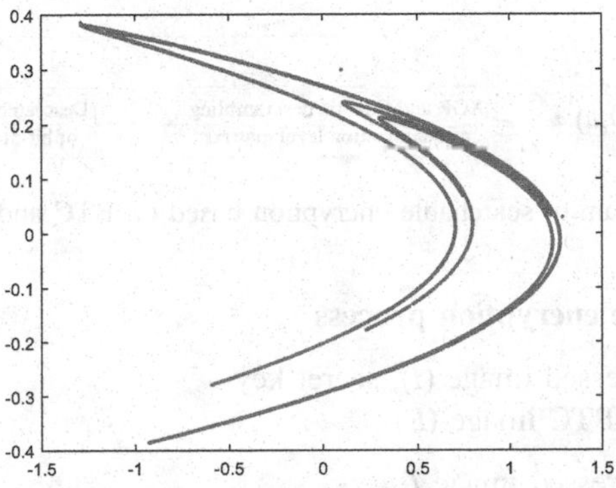

Fig. 2. Chaotic nature of Henon map.

Henon map shows chaotic behavior for a = 1.4 and b = 0.3, and it can be seen in Fig. 2.

Since the second equation in Eq. (2) can be written as $y_i = bx_{i-1}$, the 2-D Henon map can be converted into 1-D chaotic map which can be written as

$$x_{i+1} = 1 - ax_i^2 + bx_{i-1} \tag{3}$$

The parameter a, the parameter b, initial value x_0 and initial value x_1 may represent the key.

3 Searchable Image Encryption

In the proposed searchable image encryption method, Henon chaotic map is employed to encrypt the quantization levels and the bit plane during image encryption. Image decryption is inverse process of encryption. Normalized correlation coefficient is used to find matches from encrypted images. The image encryption process, decryption process and retrieval process for encrypted images are described in the following subsections.

3.1 Image Encryption and Decryption Process

The block diagram of the proposed searchable image encryption scheme is shown in Fig. 3 and main steps of the proposed image encryption method is given below.

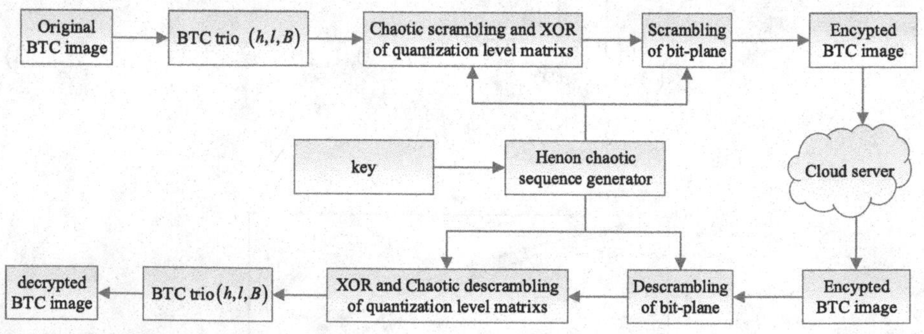

Fig. 3. Diagram of searchable encryption based on BTC and Henon map

Algorithm: image encryption process

Input: BTC compressed image (*I*), secret key
Output: encrypted BTC image (*E*)

(1) Read BTC compressed image *I*.

(2) Divide BTC compressed image I into non-overlapping sub-blocks with size $s \times s$, and obtain the trio (h, l, B) of each image sub-block.
(3) Construct higher mean matrix H and lower mean matrix L according to higher mean h and lower mean l.
(4) Apply 1-D Henon chaotic map in Eq. (3) to generate two random permute sequences PH and PL, which have same size with H and L.
(5) Scramble higher mean matrix H and lower mean matrix L with sequences PH and PL, respectively. The scrambled higher mean matrix and lower mean matrix are denoted by H' and L' respectively.
(6) Similarly produce two sequences GH and GL with 8-bit grayscale value using 1-D Henon chaotic map.
(7) Apply bit-XOR to the scramble H',L' and GH, GL, respectively and get encrypted higher mean H'' and encrypted lower mean L''.
(8) Scramble the bit-plane of each sub-block by using a chaotic sequence generated by 1-D Henon map. Finally, the encrypted BTC image E is generated after all the sub-blocks are processed.
(9) Extract feature vector F from each sub-block according to the relationship of the number of 1s and 0s in each bit-plane,

$$F(i) = \begin{cases} 0 & if\ q<k-q \\ 1 & else \end{cases}, i = 0, 1, 2, \cdots \tag{4}$$

where $F(i)$ is the feature value of the image sub-block.

During decryption, given the same secret key and parameters as used in encryption process, the original image can be decrypted by using the inverse of encryption process.

3.2 Encrypted Image Retrieval

Retrieval over encrypted images consist of the following steps.

(1) The user sends query image for retrieval.
(2) The cloud computes the feature vector F of query image and feature vectors F' of encrypted images in the cloud. It can be seen that feature vector remain unchanged since the number of 1s is not modified after scrambling.
(3) Return the corresponding encrypted images from encrypted image database according to Normalized Correlation Coefficient of feature vectors F and F'.

4 Experimental Results

Extensive experiments have been conducted over the USC-SIPI Image Database. Some test images from the USC-SIPI Image Database are shown in Fig. 4 and the corresponding encrypted images are shown in Fig. 5.

(a) Lena (b) Baboon

(c) Boat (d) Houses

Fig. 4. Some test images

Histogram Analysis. Take Lena image as an example, Fig. 6 shows the histograms of original BTC compressed image and encrypted BTC compressed image.

From Fig. 6, it can be observed that encrypted image yields uniform histogram while original image has non-uniform histogram, which makes it hard for an unauthorized user to correlate between the original image and its corresponding encrypted version.

Correlation Coefficient Analysis. The correlation between neighborhood pixels are shown in Fig. 7. It can be concluded that the correlation between neighborhood pixels in encrypted image is diffused completely, the encrypted image has poorer correlation than corresponding original image.

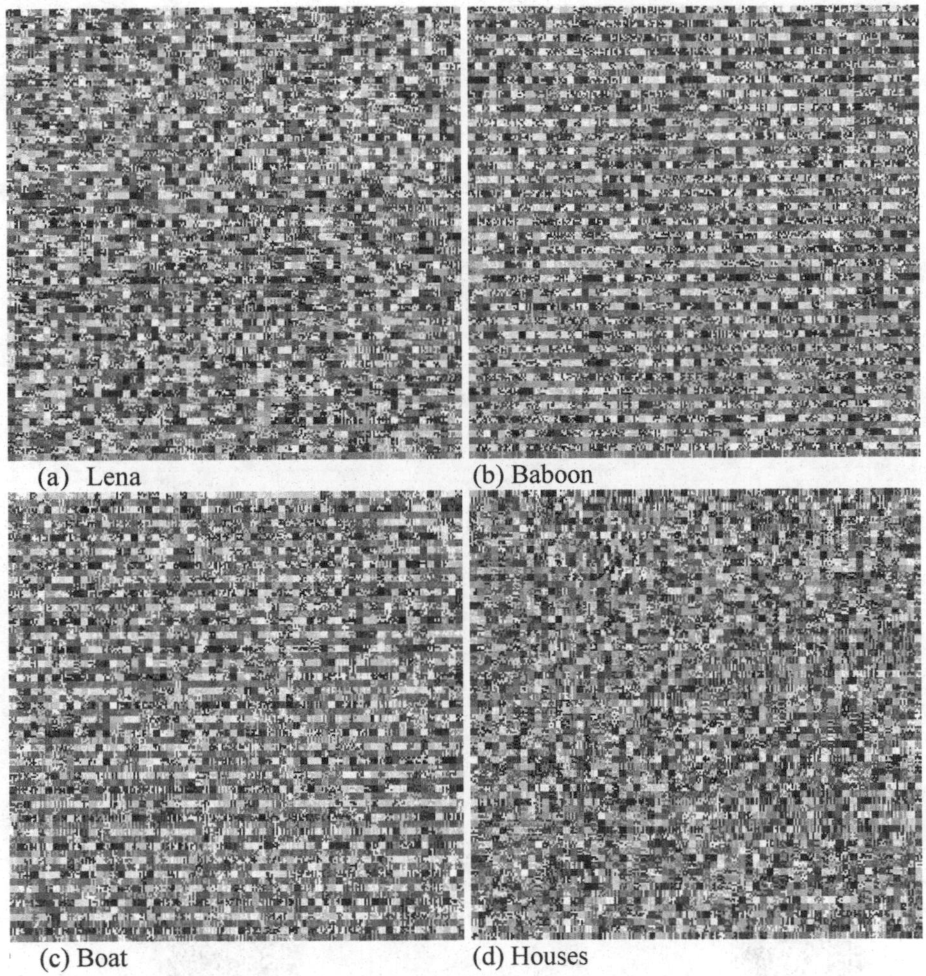

Fig. 5. Encrypted images.

Feature Similarity. The NC value (see Eq. 5) after encryption is not changeable since the number of 1s in the bit-plane. Figure 8 shows the feature image before and after encryption. In the fact, for the same picture, regardless of before and after encryption the NC values of the feature vectors are 1.00.

$$NC = \frac{\sum_{i} F'(i) \oplus F(i)}{\sum_{i} F(i) \oplus F(i)} \quad (5)$$

So, it is not difficult to find that this encryption algorithm maintains homomorphic features and supports similarity search over encrypted images.

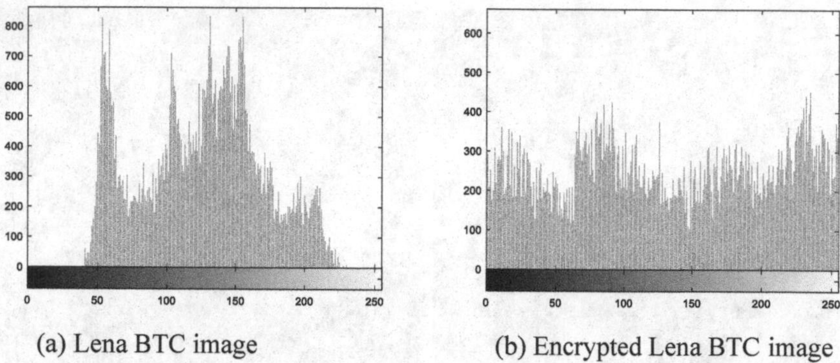

(a) Lena BTC image (b) Encrypted Lena BTC image

Fig. 6. Histogram of Lena BTC compressed image and its encrypted image.

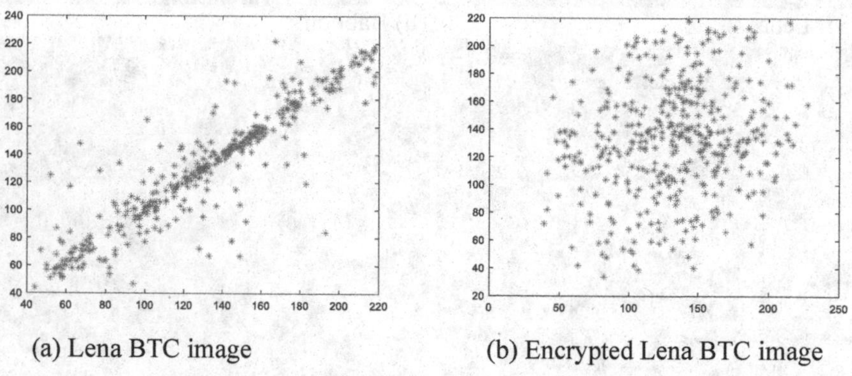

(a) Lena BTC image (b) Encrypted Lena BTC image

Fig. 7. Correlation coefficient of Lena image

(a) Before encryption (b) After encryption

Fig. 8. Feature vector of Lena image before and after encryption

In addition, 4800 encrypted images are generated based the USC-SIPI Image Database. To evaluate the retrieval effectiveness of the proposed searchable encryption scheme, the precision ratio is compared with that of existing methods [8, 11]. The test results are given in Table 1. From this table, it can be concluded that our searchable encryption scheme has higher precision than other SE methods, which indicates better retrieval performance of the proposed searchable encryption scheme compared with previous searchable encryption methods.

Table 1. Retrieval precision of different searchable encryption methods.

Methods	Precision
Hyma et al.'s method [8]	80.23
Zhang et al.'s method [11]	87.04
Proposed method	89.51

5 Conclusion

In this paper, a novel searchable image encryption algorithm by employing BTC and Henon chaotic map is proposed, which allows both ranked and similarity searches on the encrypted image stored in the cloud. The secure retrieval for encrypted digital images in cloud-based system is guaranteed by Henon chaotic map. The encryption process does not change the Feature vector. Experimental results prove that the proposed scheme can provide good retrieval accuracy and security. Meanwhile, it provides good feasibility in cloud computing environment because of the low computational cost of BTC compression method.

Acknowledgements. This work was supported in part by the National Social Science Fund of China under Grant No. 17BTQ084, the Social Science Fund of Hunan Province under Grant No. 16YBA102, and the Research Fund of Hunan Provincial Key Laboratory of informationization technology for basic education under Grant No. 2015TP1017.

References

1. Poh, G.S., Chin, J.J., Yau, W.C., Choo, K.K.R., Mohamad, M.S.: Searchable symmetric encryption: designs and challenges. ACM Comput. Surv. **50**(3), 1–37 (2017)
2. Yuan, J., Yu, S., Guo, L.: SEISA: secure and efficient encrypted image search with access control. In: Jiannong, C., Jie, W. (eds.) 2015 IEEE Conference on Computer Communications (INFOCOM), pp. 2083–2091. IEEE, New York (2015)
3. Lu, W., Varna, A.L., Wu, M.: Confidentiality-preserving image search: a comparative study between homomorphic encryption and distance-preserving randomization. IEEE Access **2**, 125–141 (2014)
4. Xia, Z., Zhu, Y., Sun, X., et al.: A similarity search scheme over encrypted cloud images based on secure transformation. Int. J. Future Gener. Commun. Netw. **6**(6), 71–80 (2013)
5. Zhu, Y., Sun, X., Xia, Z., et al.: Enabling similarity search over encrypted images in cloud. Inf. Technol. J. **3**(5), 824–831 (2014)
6. Zhu, Y., Sun, X., Xia, Z., et al.: Secure similarity search over encrypted cloud images. Int. J. Secur. Appl. **9**(8), 1–14 (2015)
7. Zou, Q., Wang, J., Ye, J., et al.: Efficient and secure encrypted image search in mobile cloud computing. Soft. Comput. **21**(11), 2959–2969 (2017)
8. Hyma, J., Kumar, D.S.S., Anand, A., et al.: An efficient privacy preserving medical image retrieval using ROI enabled searchable encryption. Int. J. Appl. Eng. Res. **11**(11), 7509–7516 (2016)
9. Wang, Y., Miao, M., Shen, J., et al.: Towards efficient privacy-preserving encrypted image search in cloud computing. Soft. Comput. **7**(11), 1–12 (2017)

10. Kamal, A.A.A.M., Iwamura, K., Kang, H.: Searchable encryption of image based on secret sharing scheme. In: Furui, S., Liu, R., et al. (eds.) 2017 Asia-Pacific Signal and Information Processing Association Summit and Conference, pp. 1495–1503. APSIPA, Hawaii (2017)
11. Zhang, C., Li, J., Wang, S., et al.: An encrypted medical image retrieval algorithm based on DWT-DCT frequency domain. In: 2017 International Conference on Software Engineering Research, Management and Applications, pp. 135–141. ACM, New York (2017)
12. Delp, E.J., Mitchell, O.R.: Image compression using block truncation coding. IEEE Trans. Commun. **27**(9), 1335–1342 (1979)
13. Lema, M., Mitchell, O.R.: Absolute moment block truncation coding and its application to color images. IEEE Trans. Commun. **32**(10), 1148–1157 (1984)

A Face Privacy Protection Algorithm Based on Block Scrambling and Deep Learning

Wei Shen[1], Zhendong Wu[2(✉)], and Jianwu Zhang[1]

[1] School of Communication Engineering, Hangzhou Dianzi University, Hangzhou, China
shenweiluck@126.com, jwzhang@hdu.edu.cn

[2] School of Cyberspace, Hangzhou Dianzi University, Hangzhou, China
wzd@hdu.edu.cn

Abstract. In recent years, with the widespread use of face recognition authentication technology, the phenomenon that a large number of face photos are stored on a third-party server is very common, and the problem of face privacy protection is very prominent. This paper presents a face privacy protection algorithm based on deep convolutional neural network (CNN), FBSR (Face Block Scrambling Recognition). The algorithm uses Arnold random scrambling to segment key face images and key parts. The server directly verifies scrambled face images through CNN model. The FBSR algorithm enables the server to save the original face template throughout the entire process, thus it achieves effective scrambling protection of the original face image. Experimental results show that the proposed algorithm has a recognition rate of 97.62% after CNN recognition, which strengthens face privacy protection to some extent.

Keywords: Arnold transform · FBSR algorithm · CNN
Face privacy protection

1 Introduction

With the rapid development of network technology and multimedia technology, digital image is gradually becoming the carrier of information exchange. At present, face recognition has been exerting force in all areas of people's daily lives, ushering in the "blowout period" of applications. But facial features, compared with fingerprints and irises, are a relatively weak biometric feature. Face images can be obtained through a variety of channels, forging other people's three-dimensional avatar is not difficult. For example, many people are photographed, and this is a relatively open feature. Facing this situation, how to protect the user's data security is particularly critical [1].

Therefore, biometric encryption technology came into being, aiming to solve the problem of privacy and security resulted from traditional biometrics technology by integrating biometrics and cryptography. Biometric encryption technology was firstly proposed by Bodo in 1994 in a patent. The complete concept was proposed by Tomko et al. [2]. The research on biometric encryption technology is mainly biometric template protection, which can be divided into two categories based on help data theory

X. Sun et al. (Eds.): ICCCS 2018, LNCS 11065, pp. 359–369, 2018.
https://doi.org/10.1007/978-3-030-00012-7_33

and biometric hash. In help data theory, Lee et al. used a feature extraction algorithm based on ICA (Independent Component Analysis), proposed a pattern clustering method, and built a new fuzzy safety box scheme based on iris feature. In biological hash research, Teoh and his team [3–5] proposed biological hashing algorithms to ensure the safety and revocability of biological templates. In 1999, Tian Jie, a researcher of the Institute of automation, Chinese Academy of Sciences, introduced Wang Xingming's concept of biometric encryption and developed an authentication system based on fingerprint encryption. The existing biometrics template protection method has been widely studied in the field of fingerprint recognition. However, there is relatively little research on face recognition, which is mainly due to the difference between faces and fingerprint features.

The traditional encryption technology has a long history of development. Classical cryptography can provide very good protection for one-dimensional content data, so as to protect the information security. However, digital image is a kind of two-dimensional structured data, which has the characteristics of high correlation between neighboring pixels, high redundancy and large amount of data. Conventional encryption technology encrypts digital images to convert the images into one-dimensional data, the unique characteristics of image data, which makes the classical cryptography encryption efficiency and encryption efficiency has dropped significantly, therefore, the digital image encryption should use a special method of digital image encryption [6, 7]. Pandey et al. presented a framework for secure identification using deep neural networks, and applied it to the task of template protection for face password authentication [8]. The existing digital image encryption algorithms are mainly divided into two categories: digital image encryption based on chaotic dynamics and digital image encryption based on matrix transformation.

Deep learning simulates the neural connections of the human brain by simulating human brain visual perception [9], performs multi-level abstraction and analysis, characterizes the data, and gives an explanation of the data. It can automatically learn features, be trained through massive data, get more essential features of the data to improve the accuracy of recognition. In recent years, deep learning has made breakthrough progress in many kinds of applications, such as speech recognition and computer vision. It is one of the hot topics in the field of machine learning [10]. Convolution neural network is one of the basic models of deep learning. Since LeCun et al. used the BP network to train deep network structures in 1989, the LeNet-5 system based on convolutional neural network has a recognition rate of 99.1% on the handwritten digital identification data set MNIST. This method has been successfully applied to bank handwritten check recognition in the 90s of last century. In 1998, LeCun et al. Further optimized the convolutional neural network using an error gradient-based algorithm [11]. In 2012, Hinton et al. constructed the convolutional neural network into deep convolutional neural network (Deep Convolutional Neural Network, DCNN) [12]. This method has gained the best results in the world at the time in recognizing famous ImageNet data set, which has become an important breakthrough in the field of image recognition.

At present, the recognition network models proposed on the basis of convolutional neural networks include [13]: LeNet-5, AlexNet, DeepID-Net, GoogleNet, and so on. Among them, (1) LeNet-5 consists of 7 layers, with layers 1, 3 and 5 as convolution layers, and 2 and 4 as down-sampling layers. This model is mainly used for digital classification [11]; (2) AlexNet consists of 8 layers. The first 5 layers are convolutional layers, the latter 3 layers are fully connected layers, which are mainly used for image classification. The model was the champion of ILSVRC 2012 [12]. (3) DeepID-Net is composed of 8 layers, the hidden layer the fourth layer and the third layer volume pool are connected, the model is mainly used for face verification [14]; (4) GoogleNet is made up of 22 layers and is mainly used for classification and detection. This model was the champion of ILSVRC 2014 [15].

In this paper, the digital image encryption based on matrix transformation is adopted, and the image is scrambled by using some matrix transformation method to realize the encryption of the digital image. On this basis, face block scrambing recognition based on convolutional neural network (FBSR) algorithm is proposed in this paper. Firstly, the Arnold transform is selected as the scrambling method. Secondly, the main part of human face, such as eyes, nose, mouth and other parts, branches and columns are scrambled for different times. Finally, we input the face image obtained by block scrambling into CNN to recognize it. Experimental results show that the proposed algorithm has better recognition rate and improves privacy protection to some extent.

2 Preliminary Research

2.1 Arnold Transform

Arnold transform is a transformation proposed by V. J. Arnold in ergodic theory, which is commonly known as Cat face transformation (Cat Mapping). It is assumed that a cat face image is drawn within the flat square of the plane by the following transformation:

$$\begin{bmatrix} x' \\ y' \end{bmatrix} = \begin{bmatrix} 1 & 1 \\ 1 & 2 \end{bmatrix} \begin{bmatrix} x \\ y \end{bmatrix} (\text{mod } 1) \tag{1}$$

The picture of the cat's face turns from clear to blur, and this is the Arnold transform. But when it comes to digital images, we need to rewrite the two-dimensional Arnold transform in formula (1) as:

$$\begin{bmatrix} x' \\ y' \end{bmatrix} - \begin{bmatrix} 1 & 1 \\ 1 & 2 \end{bmatrix} \begin{bmatrix} x \\ y \end{bmatrix} (\text{mod } N) \quad x, y \in \{1, 2, \cdots, N\} \tag{2}$$

Where (x, y) is the coordinates of pixels in the original image, (x', y') is the coordinates of the pixels in the new image after transformation. N is the order of the image matrix, that is, the size of the image, generally refers to the square image.

When performing Arnold transformation on an image, the pixel position of the image is moved according to formula (2) to obtain a chaotic image relative to the original image. An Arnold transformation of the image is equivalent to a scrambling of the image. Usually this process needs to be iterated over and over again to achieve satisfactory results.

Using Arnold transform to scramble the image, making the meaningful digital image into a meaningless image like white noise, realizing the preliminary hiding of the information, and arranging the number of times can provide a key for the watermarking system, thereby enhance the system's security and confidentiality.

Figure 1(a) is an original face image in the ORL database, and Fig. 1(b), (c), and (d) are the effects of one, two, five Arnold transformation respectively. It can be seen that after two and five transformations, the image has basically no outline or shape features of the original map. The visual presentation is out of order, similar to the distribution of noise.

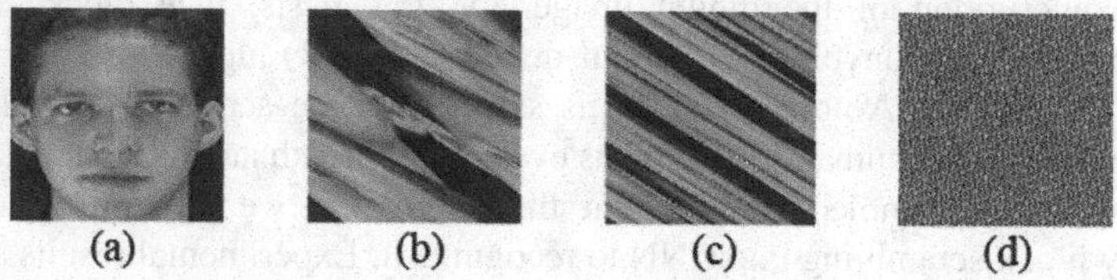

Fig. 1. Faces scrambling by Arnold transform effect

2.2 Convolutional Neural Network

As a model structure of deep learning, convolutional neural network (CNN) is a deep learning multilayer perceptron specially designed to recognize two-dimensional shapes. Because of its characteristics such as weight sharing and local perception, convolutional neural network is compared with other deep learning models such as deep belief network, it has the ability to extract features more efficiently and reduce the time spent in training and classification [16]. The basic CNN model structure includes convolutional layer, sub-sampling layer, fully connected layer, and end classification layer. The basic structure of CNN is shown in Fig. 2.

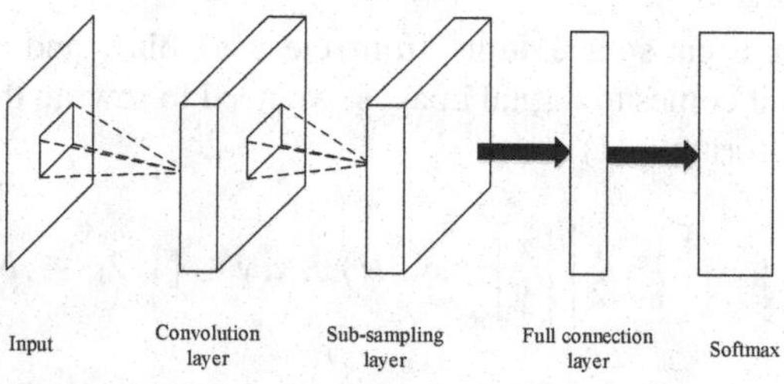

Fig. 2. CNN basic structure

Firstly, the convolution layer in CNN is convoluted by different training convolution kernel with all the feature maps of the first layer, plus the bias, and then the result is generated by the output of the activation function to form the current layer feature map. And then, to avoid dimensional disaster, it is common to reduce the number of features by using a sub-sampling layer after the convolution layer. Next, the two-dimensional array corresponding to each feature in the upper layer is transformed into a one-dimensional array, and all the converted one-dimensional arrays are concatenated into a feature length vector as the input of the full connection layer. In the end, The end classification layer softmax of CNN is a multi output competitive classifier. The classification results have multiple items, each item is divided by their cumulative sum, so that the output of all the sum of 1, and each corresponding to the number of representatives of the class of predictive probability value, select the maximum probability of correspondence. The output of the category as its final classification results.

3 FBSR Algorithm

3.1 Face Block

Different classes of images contain different features, which are the premise of classification. For example, different faces, such as faces, eyes, mouth and nose, are different from person to person in face images. Therefore, we firstly divide the image into segments, so that each segment can contain only one feature part. When extracting features from slices, it is equivalent to extract features from a single source, and the extracted features can be better classified.

Therefore, the basic principle of fragment size selection is that each segment should contain only one human face feature part, such as eye, mouth or mouth, too large or too small fragment, which will cause that the feature extracted from segmentation is not single source. In practical applications, the size of the fragment is mainly related to the size of the sample.

Assuming that the slice size is set to $m \times n$, it can be better guaranteed that each slice can contain only one image feature as far as possible. Then the two dimensional image X is overlapped and the moving step length is 1, then the total number of block is as follows:

$$s = (a - m + 1) \times (b - n + 1) \tag{3}$$

The original image X_i is divided into blocks:

$$X_i = \left[X_{i,1}, X_{i,2}, \cdots, X_{i,s}\right] \in R^{pq \times s} \tag{4}$$

In image processing, the traditional blocks are evenly divided into several parts, but this is not consistent with the human visual attention mechanism. Therefore, a new block method is presented in this paper, as shown in Fig. 3. At first glance, the picture will be concentrated in the middle area, then near the middle area, and the corner may be taken into account in the end.

Based on this idea, the paper firstly evenly divides the image into pieces and then divides it into three regions X, Y, and Z according to the visual attention mechanism, as shown in Fig. 3. Arnold random scrambling was then performed on the Y and Z sections containing eyebrows, eyes, nose, and mouth.

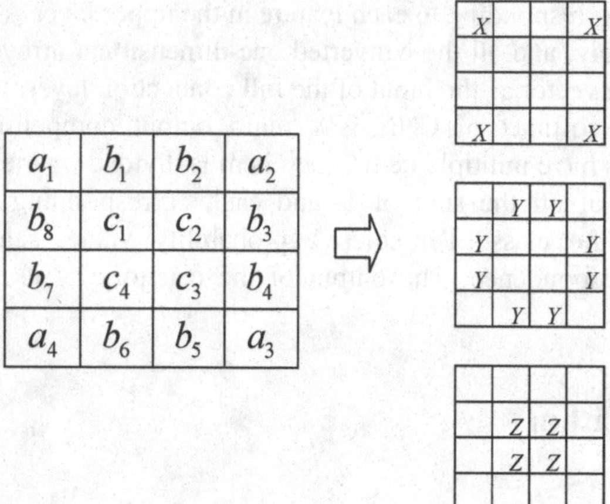

Fig. 3. Blocking method

3.2 CNN Design Build

Considering that the CNN designed in this paper needs to be applied to scrambling face recognition. After lots of tests, the paper determines that the network structure is 8 layers, without input and output, and each layer contains training parameters (weights and biases). The experimental model is shown in Fig. 4.

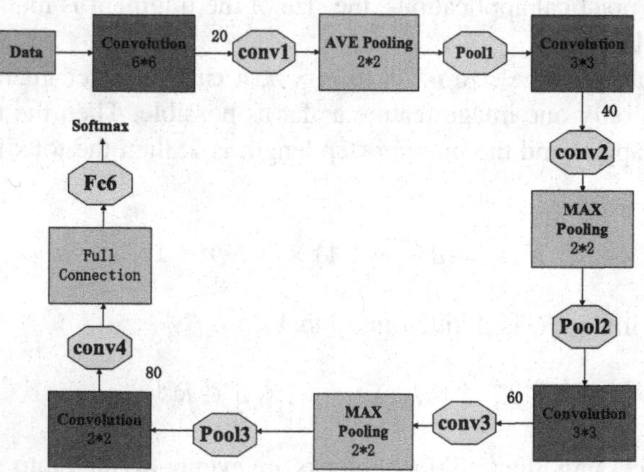

Fig. 4. Face recognition system model based on CNN

The first convolution layer is convoluted with a 6 * 6 convolution kernel and the input face image, and contains 20 feature maps. The next pooling layer, the principle of sampling is to use the local correlation of the image, the region selection of the image, can effectively retain the useful information in the image while reducing the training parameters. The size of the sub-region is 2 * 2. By the same token, the convolution layer and the pooling layer are calculated in the same way. Finally, the feature vector formed in series can be used as the input of the fully connected layer. Finally, the classification is done by softmax.

3.3 Implementation Process

A face recognition method based on block and scrambling of CNN based on Fig. 4 is designed. The specific implementation process is as follows: Firstly, the face image is pre-scaled according to the set block size, and then random key Arnold scrambling is performed according to importance referred by Sect. 3.1. The following formula is used to represent the production of a uniformly distributed random natural number:

$$R = Rand(Num, Seed) \tag{5}$$

Among them, *Seed* is a seed that generates random numbers. *Num* is the number of random numbers generated, and is also the upper limit of random numbers. That is, random natural numbers generated are less than Num, and the results are stored in a one-dimensional array *R*.

The above generated array *R* is brought into the Arnold transformation and applied to the major parts of the human face such as the eyes, the nose, the mouth, which are randomly scrambled.

In this paper, the ReLU (rectified linear units) function is used as the activation function, instead of the traditional Sigmoid function and tanh function as the activation function. The ReLU function is a non-saturated, non-linear function. The ReLU function will make the output of a part of the neuron 0, so that the sparseness of the network is achieved and the interdependence of parameters is reduced, over-fitting is alleviated.

The model is based on the softmax regression method to achieve different face classification detection work. The algorithm is based on existing face training. If there are 1000 categories of face in the library, the output of softmax is 1000 categories. In face recognition, according to different faces, the output is a vector with a length of 1000 in one dimension. Its maximum value indicates the most likely category. Because the model can accurately extract facial features, the use of softmax can achieve good recognition results in algorithm implementation. In logistic regression, the training set is $\{(x^{(1)}, y^{(1)}), \cdots, (x^{(m)}, y^{(m)})\}$. Where m is the number of samples, $y^{(i)} \in \{0, 1\}$. Assuming the model is:

$$h_\theta(x) = g(\theta^T x) = \frac{1}{1 + \exp(-\theta^T x)} \tag{6}$$

For softmax regression, the target result is multiple discrete values, which is a generalization of the logistic model for multi-classification problems. $y^{(i)} \in \{1, 2, 3, \cdots, k\}$, for a given test x, assume that the model estimates the probability value p for each class $p(y = j|x)$, so assume the form of the function $h_\theta(x)$ is:

$$h_\theta\left(x^{(i)}\right) = \begin{bmatrix} p(y^{(i)} = 1|x^{(i)};\theta) \\ p(y^{(i)} = 2|x^{(i)};\theta) \\ \cdots \\ p(y^{(i)} = k|x^{(i)};\theta) \end{bmatrix} = \frac{1}{\sum_{j=1}^{k} e^{\theta_j^T x^{(i)}}} \begin{bmatrix} e^{\theta_1^T x^{(i)}} \\ e^{\theta_2^T x^{(i)}} \\ \cdots \\ e^{\theta_k^T x^{(i)}} \end{bmatrix} \tag{7}$$

The corresponding cost function is:

$$J(\theta) = -\frac{1}{m}\left[\sum_{i=1}^{m}\sum_{j=1}^{k} 1\left\{y^{(i)} = j\right\} \log \frac{e^{\theta_j^T x^{(i)}}}{\sum_{l=1}^{k} e^{\theta_l^T x^{(i)}}}\right] \tag{8}$$

The probability that softmax classifies x into category j is:

$$p\left(y^{(i)} = j|x^{(i)};\theta\right) = \frac{e^{\theta_j^T x^{(i)}}}{\sum_{l=1}^{k} e^{\theta_l^T x^{(i)}}} \tag{9}$$

After that, the processed facial image is input into the trained CNN model for feature extraction. Finally, predict by the softmax at the end of the model and output the final recognition result.

3.4 Security Analysis

During the transmission, it is necessary to take into account that information is stolen by a third party. After the FBSR algorithm is applied, the second scrambling is performed on the face image to further enhance the privacy protection of the face.

As shown in Fig. 5, before transmitting the face picture, when the Arnold is scrambled to generate a key, the face image will appear as "snow-like" and the naked eye can't get any information, which greatly improves the security of face during transmission. Decryption is the reverse process of encryption. If the correct key is available to the other party, the real face image can be restored. Otherwise, the correct information cannot be obtained.

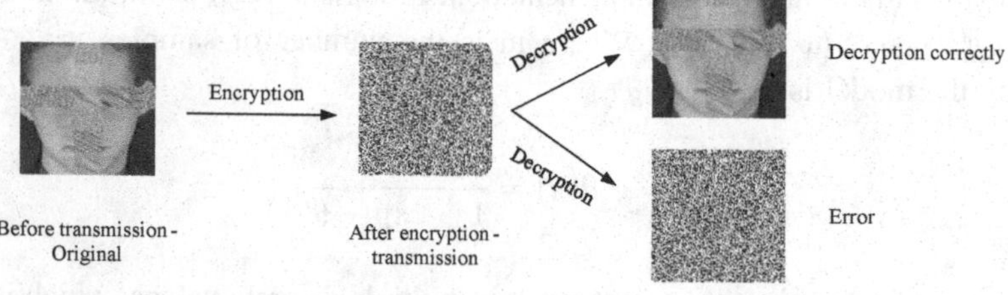

Fig. 5. Before and after transmission encryption and decryption analysis

4 Experimental Results and Analysis

4.1 Experimental Sample and Environment Configuration

In order to verify the effectiveness of the proposed algorithm, this paper experiments in Linux environment. Experimental equipment configuration: operating system ubuntu 16.04 LTS, processor Intel Core i7-6700K CPU, RAM 8G, SSD 256G.

The experimental data come from the ORL face database of the University of Cambridge, UK, which includes 400 face-grayscale images of 40 individuals and 10 images of each. The main background of the face is black, which contains the face angle, posture, facial expressions and facial details under different lighting conditions.

4.2 Experimental Process and Results

Firstly, the pictures in the ORL face database are divided and calculated according to a preset block size, and the block size is set to *height* = 20 and *width* = 20. Then round it down to get a new face image size of 120 × 100. The result is shown in Fig. 6(a). It can be seen that when the block size is taken as 20, the key parts of the face can be distinguished very well, and this block is still applicable when the expression changes. However, if the head is clearly rotated, if this method is still selected, the key parts of the face may not be selected. This requires adaptive selection. Then, according to Sect. 3.1, Arnold randomly scrambles the key parts of the face. The scrambled pictures are then merged together. The result is shown in Fig. 6(b).

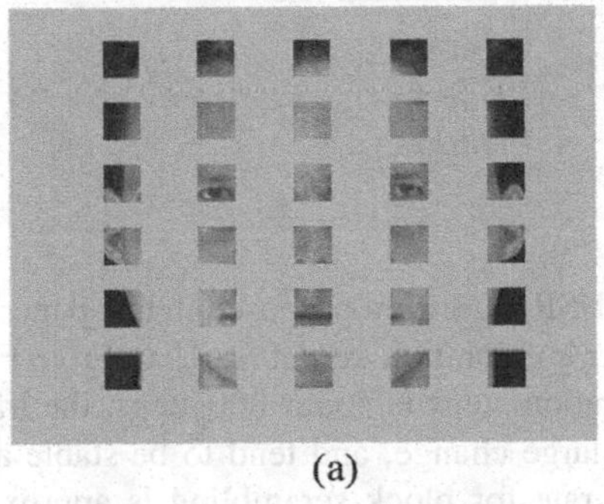

(a)

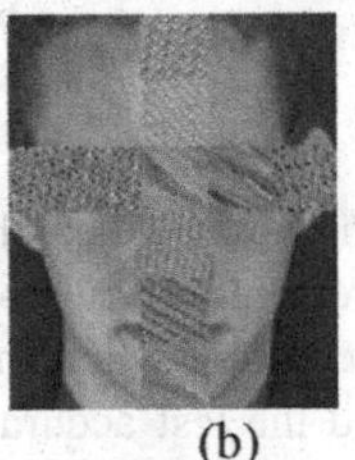

(b)

Fig. 6. (a) Face block effect; (b) Face block scrambling effect

As can be seen from Fig. 6(b), the eyes, nose and mouth of the face have been scrambled at different times. Moreover, since the Arnold transformation is periodic, for a certain size image block, after a limited number of transformations, the original image can be restored. In this paper, due to the large image block size of 20, and random number of scrambling, it is difficult to obtain the key for restoration, and the kind of scrambling is unknown, which largely protects the user's privacy. In addition, compared with global scrambling, the security of the FBSR algorithm adopted in this paper has been improved, and the operation process is relatively simple.

In the experiment, a 4-layer convolution is used, and the convolution kernel size of the first convolution layer is 6 * 6, as described in Sect. 3.2. The total number of iteration steps is 5000, the learning rate is set to 0.0001, and the GPU mode operation is selected. Finally, the train loss curve and the test accuracy curve are shown in Fig. 7 (a) and (b), respectively.

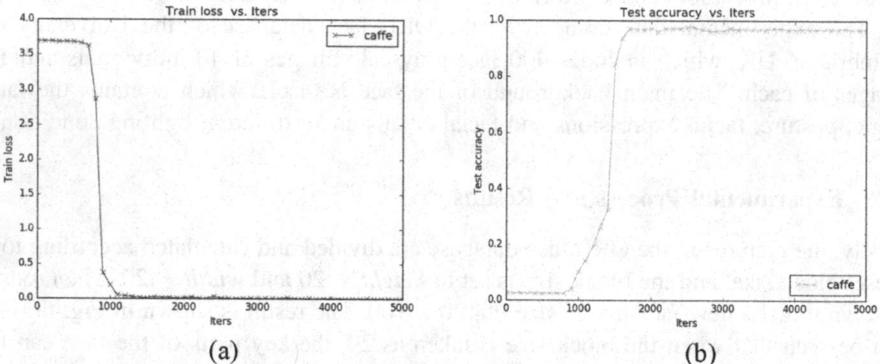

Fig. 7. (a) The relationship between train loss and number of iterations; (b) The relationship between test accuracy and number of iterations

Table 1. Comparison of recognition rates for different convolution kernel sizes

Convolution kernel size	Recognition rate
2 dpi × 2 dpi	97.5%
4 dpi × 4 dpi	95.84%
6 dpi × 6 dpi	97.62%
8 dpi × 8 dpi	96.32%

From Table 1, it can be seen that the FBSR algorithm proposed in this paper has the highest recognition rate when the first layer convolution kernel is 6 * 6. From Fig. 7, it can be seen that when the number of iteration steps is about 800 steps, the train loss value and the test accuracy value have a large change, and tend to be stable at about 1200 steps. Finally, the face recognition rate for block scrambling is approximately 97.62%, which verifies the effectiveness of the proposed FBSR algorithm.

5 Conclusion

This article describes the current limitations in the protection of face privacy and proposes an FBSR algorithm to improve this situation. In this paper, the face image is firstly processed by block preprocessing, then the critical parts of the face are scrambled randomly, and finally the CNN algorithm is used to classify the recognition. The experimental results show that the algorithm is simple and has high recognition rate. In the future work, we will further optimize the face block scrambling, deeper analysis of the CNN deep neural network, complete adjustments to the parameters and other aspects, and strive to achieve better security and higher recognition rate.

Acknowledgement. This research is supported by National Key R&D Program of China (No. 2016YFB0800201), National Natural Science Foundation of China (No. 61772162), Zhejiang Natural Science Foundation of China (No. LY16F020016).

References

1. Cunningham, S.J., Masoodian, M., Adams, A.: Privacy issues for online personal photograph collections. J. Theor. Appl. Electron. Commer. Res. **5**, 26–40 (2010)
2. Tomko, G.J., Soutar, C., Schmidt, G.J.: Fingerprint controlled public key cryptographic system: US, US 5541994 A[P] (1996)
3. Ngo, D.C.L., Teoh, A.B.J., Goh, A.: Biometric hash: high-confidence face recognition. IEEE Trans. Circuits Syst. Video Technol. **16**(6), 771–775 (2006)
4. Teoh, A.B.J., Goh, A., Ngo, D.C.L.: Random multispace quantization as an analytic mechanism for biohashing of biometric and random identity inputs. IEEE Trans. Pattern Anal. Mach. Intell. **28**(12), 1892–1901 (2006)
5. Jin, A.T.B., Ling, D.N.C., Goh, A.: Biohashing: two factor authentication featuring fingerprint data and tokenised random number. Pattern Recognit. **37**(11), 2245–2255 (2004)
6. Li, X.B., Sarkar, S.: Protecting Privacy Against Record Linkage Disclosure: A Bounded Swapping Approach for Numeric Data. INFORMS (2011)
7. Wang, P., Wang, J., Zhu, X.: Research on privacy preserving data mining. Adv. Mater. Res. **756–759**, 1661–1664 (2013)
8. Pandey, R.K., Zhou, Y., Kota, B.U., et al.: Deep secure encoding for face template protection. In: Computer Vision and Pattern Recognition Workshops, pp. 77–83. IEEE (2016)
9. Serre, T., Kreiman, G., Kouh, M., et al.: A quantitative theory of immediate visual recognition. Prog. Brain Res. **165**(6), 33–56 (2007)
10. Netzer, Y., Wang, T., Coates, A., et al.: Reading digits in natural images with unsupervised feature learning. In: NIPS Workshop on Deep Learning and Unsupervised Feature Learning (2011)
11. Lecun, Y., Bottou, L., Bengio, Y., et al.: Gradient-based learning applied to document recognition. Proc. IEEE **86**(11), 2278–2324 (1998)
12. Krizhevsky, A., Sutskever, I., Hinton, G.E.: ImageNet classification with deep convolutional neural networks. In: International Conference on Neural Information Processing Systems, pp. 1097–1105. Curran Associates Inc. (2012)
13. Dicecco, R., Lacey, G., Vasiljevic, J., et al.: Caffeinated FPGAs: FPGA framework for convolutional neural networks. In: International Conference on Field-Programmable Technology, pp. 265–268. IEEE (2017)
14. Sun, Y., Wang, X., Tang, X.: Deep learning face representation from predicting 10,000 classes. In: Computer Vision and Pattern Recognition, pp. 1891–1898. IEEE (2014)
15. Wu, C., Wen, W., Afzal, T., et al.: A Compact DNN: Approaching GoogleNet-Level Accuracy of Classification and Domain Adaptation, pp. 761–770 (2017)
16. Li, H., Lin, Z., Shen, X., et al.: A convolutional neural network cascade for face detection. In: Computer Vision and Pattern Recognition, pp. 5325–5334. IEEE (2015)

A General Two-Server Framework for Ciphertext-Checkable Encryption Against Offline Message Recovery Attack

Yunhao Ling, Sha Ma(✉), Qiong Huang, and Ximing Li

College of Mathematics and Informatics, South China Agricultural University, Guangzhou, Guangdong, China
yunhaolingyy@163.com, shamahb@163.com, csqhuang-c@my.cityu.edu.hk, liximing_cn@163.com

Abstract. In CT-RSA 2010, Yang et al. proposed a notion of public key encryption with equality test (PKEET), which allows a tester to check whether two ciphertexts encrypted under different public keys as well as the same public key contain the same message. Then various PKEET schemes are proposed to enforce authorization mechanisms for users to specify who can perform equality test on their ciphertexts. However, it is still an open problem for PKEET to resist offline message recovery attack until now. In this paper, we introduce a general two-server framework for ciphertext-checkable encryption scheme to withstand offline message recovery attack. Furthermore, it has a nice property of flexible authorization and supports checking two types of equations on the ciphertexts of M_i and M_j under different public keys as well as the same public key: $aM_i = bM_j$ and $M_i^a = M_j^b$, where a and b are integers.

Keywords: Ciphertext-checkable encryption
Offline message recovery attack · Smooth projective hash function

1 Introduction

With the remarkable advancement of cloud technology, an increasing number of users move their data to cloud server. To protect data security and privacy of users, the data are commonly stored in encrypted form. Unfortunately, traditional encryption schemes do not support to compute on ciphertexts. Therefore, searchable encryption is proposed, for example, [1,10–12]. In CT-RSA 2010, [22] proposed a notion of public key encryption with equality test (PKEET) as a type of searchable encryption, which allows a tester to check whether two ciphertexts encrypted under different public keys as well as the same public key contain the same message. PKEET has many interesting applications, for example, management of encrypted data in an outsourced database. However, almost all existing PKEET schemes [5,6,8,9,13–15,17,18,22] are very hard to overcome *offline message recovery attack* (OMRA), which is too risky for database applications. If

X. Sun et al. (Eds.): ICCCS 2018, LNCS 11065, pp. 370–382, 2018.
https://doi.org/10.1007/978-3-030-00012-7_34

actual plaintext space $\mathcal{M}$ is polynomial size, a malicious tester can mount the attack to recover plaintext hidden in ciphertext. Specifically, given a ciphertext $C = \mathsf{Enc}(pk_i, M)$, the tester can choose a guessing plaintext $M' \in \mathcal{M}$, and then uses ciphertext C' of the M' to test whether C' and C are equal. If so, the tester knows that the plaintext hidden in the ciphertext C is M', otherwise he chooses a new guessing plaintext to test until the correct plaintext is found. This type of attack is similar to *inside keyword guessing attack* (IKGA) in *public key encryption with keyword search* (PEKS), and is unavoidable due to the desired ciphertext equality test functionality. Until now resisting OMRA is still an open problem in PKEET.

1.1 Related Work

Resist IKGA. To withstand the attack, both [2,3,20] use two-server setting under the assumption that the two servers do not collude. Since the servers cannot independently check whether a PEKS ciphertext and a trapdoor of receiver are equal or not, their schemes can overcome IKGA. Different from them, [7] takes some secret information only known by the sender as input in PEKS encryption algorithm. Therefore, malicious servers cannot launch IKGA.

Resist ORMA. [21] takes some secret information shared by a small group as input in PKEET encryption algorithm. Since attackers cannot generate ciphertexts of the group, it can resist OMRA. Unfortunately, the secret information is known by everyone in the group, hence it is hard to ensure that the secret information is not leaked. [19] introduced a *new PKEET supporting fine-grained authorization* (FG-PKEET+) scheme, which uses a two-server setting to overcome OMRA. However, FG-PKEET+ requires pairing operations and a random number shared by two users in the token generation, which is not feasible in reality. [16] observed that the way of withstanding IKGA in [2,3] is useful to overcome OMRA in PKEET, so they improve it and then introduced a new scheme. The scheme can overcome OMRA and support checking two types of equation on the ciphertexts of M_1 and M_2: $aM_1 + bM_2 + c = 0$ and $M_1^a M_2^b c = 1$, where a, b and c are integers. However, the back server knowing the results of equality test in the scheme is probably not secure in some scenes. In addition, [16] lacks authorization mechanism for users to specify who can perform equality test on their ciphertexts, and does not support checking whether two ciphertexts encrypted under different public keys contain the same message.

1.2 Our Contributions

In this paper, we propose a new general two-server framework for ciphertext-checkable encryption supporting flexible authorization ($\mathcal{TS}$-$\mathcal{CCE}$-$\mathcal{FA}$) based on [16]. The contributions of this paper can be summarized as follows:

1. We introduce a general two-server framework named $\mathcal{TS}$-$\mathcal{CCE}$-$\mathcal{FA}$ to withstand offline message recovery attack and show its efficient instantiations without any paring.

2. Our scheme supports checking two types of equations on the ciphertexts of M_i and M_j: $aM_i = bM_j$ and $M_i^a = M_j^b$, where a and b are integers.
3. We propose a flexible authorization under the two-server setting, which can strengthen the privacy protection of users.

1.3 Paper Organization

In the next section we give a description of smooth projective hash function. Then we give the definition of $\mathcal{TS}$-$\mathcal{CCE}$-$\mathcal{FA}$ scheme and its security notion in Sect. 3 and its concrete construction in Sect. 4. In Sect. 5, we give the security proof of $\mathcal{TS}$-$\mathcal{CCE}$-$\mathcal{FA}$. In Sect. 6, we give instantiations of $\mathcal{TS}$-$\mathcal{CCE}$-$\mathcal{FA}$ from SPHF based on DDH assumption. Finally, we conclude the paper in Sect. 7.

2 Smooth Projective Hash Function

Smooth projective hash function (SPHF) was firstly introduced by Cramer and Shoup for constructing CCA-secure scheme [4]. An SPHF can be defined based on a domain $\mathcal{X}$ and an $\mathcal{NP}$ language $\mathcal{L}$, where $\mathcal{L}$ contains a subset of the elements of the domain $\mathcal{X}$, i.e. $\mathcal{L} \in \mathcal{X}$. Let $\mathcal{L}$ be a language as a certain subset of the domain $\mathcal{X}$, and an SPHF from a set $\mathcal{X}$ into a set $\mathcal{Y}$. An SPHF system on $\mathcal{L}$ is defined by the following five algorithms:

- $\mathsf{SPHFSetup}(1^k)$: It outputs a global parameters *param* and the description of an $\mathcal{NP}$ language instance $\mathcal{L}$;
- $\mathsf{HashKG}(\mathcal{L}, param)$: It outputs a hashing key hk for $\mathcal{L}$;
- $\mathsf{ProjKG}(hk, (\mathcal{L}, param), W)$: It outputs a projection key hp from the hk;
- $\mathsf{Hash}(hk, (\mathcal{L}, param), W)$: It outputs the hash value $hv \in \mathcal{Y}$ for the word $W \in \mathcal{X}$ from the hashing key hk;
- $\mathsf{ProjHash}(hp, (\mathcal{L}, param), W, w)$: It outputs the hash value $hv' \in \mathcal{Y}$ for the word $W \in \mathcal{L}$ from the projection key hp and the witness w.

Properties

1. *Correctness*: For any point $W \in \mathcal{L}$ with the witness w, $\mathsf{Hash}(hk, (\mathcal{L}, param), W) = \mathsf{ProjHash}(hp, (\mathcal{L}, param), W, w)$;
2. *Smoothness*: For any point $W \in \mathcal{X} \backslash \mathcal{L}$, the hash vale hv of the word W is statistically indistinguishable from a random element in $\mathcal{Y}$.
3. *Pseudo-Randomness*: For any point $W \in \mathcal{L}$, without the knowledge of witness w, the hash value hv of the word W is computational indistinguishable from a random element in $\mathcal{Y}$.

Note that we will omit $(\mathcal{L}, param)$ as input of the $\mathsf{ProjHash}$ and Hash algorithms in this paper for simplicity.

3 Definition

Note that $Q(M_i, M_j)$ represents one of the two types of equations: (1) $aM_i = bM_j$; (2) $M_i^a = M_j^b$, where a and b are integers.

3.1 Flexible Authorization

To support flexible authorization in PKEET, [6] introduced three types of authorizations and [15] proposed four types of authorizations. We describe our three types of authorization in this scheme as follows:

- *Type-I authorization*: Alice's all ciphertexts could be compared with all ciphertexts of any other receiver.
- *Type-II authorization*: An Alice's specific ciphertext could be compared with a specific ciphertext of any other receiver.
- *Type-III authorization*: An Alice's specific ciphertext could be compared with all ciphertexts of any other receiver, vice versa.

3.2 $\mathcal{TS}$-$\mathcal{CCE}$-$\mathcal{FA}$

Definition 1. *A $\mathcal{TS}$-$\mathcal{CCE}$-$\mathcal{FA}$ scheme is defined by the following ten algorithms* (Setup, KeyGen_{user}, KeyGen_{server}, Enc, Aut_1, Test_1, Aut_2, Test_2, Aut_3, Test_3):

- $\mathsf{Setup}(1^k)$: On input a security parameter 1^k, this algorithm runs $\mathsf{SPHFSetup}$ algorithm then outputs the global parameters *param* and the description of the language $\mathcal{L}$. We set the system parameter $P = \langle param, \mathcal{L} \rangle$
- $\mathsf{KeyGen}_{server}(P)$: On input the system parameter P, this algorithm generates public/secret key (pk_{LS}, sk_{LS}) of the left server and the public/secret key (pk_{RS}, sk_{RS}) of the right server, respectively.
  Let U_i and U_j be two users in the system. Note that $i = j$ is allowed.
- $\mathsf{KeyGen}_{user}(P)$: On input the system parameter P, this algorithm outputs public/secret key (pk_i, sk_i) of user U_i.
- $\mathsf{Enc}(P, pk_i, pk_{LS}, pk_{RS}, M)$: On input of the system parameter P, the public key (pk_i, pk_{LS}, pk_{RS}) of a user U_i, the left server and the right server and a plaintext M, this algorithm outputs ciphertext C of the plaintext M.

Type-I authorization:

- $\mathsf{Aut}_1(P, sk_i)$: On input of the system parameter P and the secret key sk_i of user U_i, this algorithm outputs trapdoor $td_{1,i}$ for user U_i.
- $\mathsf{Test}_1(\mathsf{LS}(P, C_i, C_j, td_{1,i}, Q), \mathsf{RS}(P, C_i, C_j, td_{1,j}, Q))$: On input of the system parameter P, the ciphertext C_i and the trapdoor $td_{1,i}$ of user U_i, the ciphertext C_j and the trapdoor $td_{1,j}$ of user U_j and Q, this algorithm outputs 1 if M_i and M_j satisfy the equation $Q(M_i, M_j)$ and 0 otherwise. Note that LS represents an algorithm run by the left server and RS represents an algorithm run by the right server.

Type-II authorization:

- $\mathsf{Aut}_2(P, sk_i, C_i)$: On input of the system parameter P, the secret key sk_i and the ciphertext C_i of user U_i, this algorithm outputs the trapdoor td_{2,C_i} for user U_i.
- $\mathsf{Test}_2(\mathsf{LS}(P, C_i, C_j, td_{2,C_i}, Q), \mathsf{RS}(P, C_i, C_j, td_{2,C_j}, Q))$: On input of the system parameter P, the ciphertext C_i and the trapdoor td_{2,C_i} of user U_i, the ciphertext C_j and the trapdoor td_{2,C_j} of user U_j and Q, this algorithm outputs 1 if M_i and M_j satisfy the equation $Q(M_i, M_j)$ and 0 otherwise.

Type-III authorization:

- $\mathsf{Aut}_{3,i}(P, sk_i)$: It outputs the trapdoor $td_{3,i}$ for user U_i.
- $\mathsf{Aut}_{3,j}(P, sk_j, C_j)$: It outputs the trapdoor td_{3,C_j} for user U_j.
- $\mathsf{Test}_3(\mathsf{LS}(P, C_i, C_j, td_{3,i}, Q), \mathsf{RS}(P, C_i, C_j, td_{3,C_j}, Q))$: On input of the system parameter P, the ciphertext C_i and the trapdoor $td_{3,i}$ of user U_i, the ciphertext C_j and the trapdoor td_{3,C_j} of user U_j and Q, this algorithm outputs 1 if M_i and M_j satisfy the equation $Q(M_i, M_j)$ and 0 otherwise.

Note that the Test_1, Test_2 and Test_3 algorithms are run interactively among the left server, the right server and users/a third party, respectively.

Correctness: A $\mathcal{TS}$-$\mathcal{CCE}$-$\mathcal{FA}$ scheme is correct if $P \leftarrow \mathsf{Setup}(1^k)$, $(pk_i, sk_i) \leftarrow \mathsf{KeyGen}_{user}(P)$, $(pk_j, sk_j) \leftarrow \mathsf{KeyGen}_{user}(P)$, $((pk_{LS}, sk_{LS}), (pk_{RS}, sk_{RS})) \leftarrow \mathsf{KeyGen}_{server}(P)$, for any ciphertexts C_i of user U_i and any ciphertexts C_j of user U_j, if plaintexts M_i and M_j satisfy the equation $Q(M_i, M_j)$, then

Type-I authorization: Given $td_{1,i} \leftarrow \mathsf{Aut}_1(sk_i)$ and $td_{1,j} \leftarrow \mathsf{Aut}_1(sk_j)$, it holds that

$$\mathsf{Test}_1(\mathsf{LS}(P, C_i, C_j, td_{1,i}, Q), \mathsf{RS}(P, C_i, C_j, td_{1,j}, Q)) = 1,$$

Type-II authorization: Given $td_{2,C_i} \leftarrow \mathsf{Aut}_2(sk_i, C_i)$ and $td_{2,C_j} \leftarrow \mathsf{Aut}_2(sk_j, C_j)$, it holds that

$$\mathsf{Test}_2(\mathsf{LS}(P, C_i, C_j, td_{2,C_i}, Q), \mathsf{RS}(P, C_i, C_j, td_{2,C_j}, Q)) = 1,$$

Type-III authorization: Given $td_{3,i} \leftarrow \mathsf{Aut}_{3,i}(sk_i)$ and $td_{3,C_j} \leftarrow \mathsf{Aut}_{3,j}(sk_j, C_j)$, it holds that

$$\mathsf{Test}_3(\mathsf{LS}(P, C_i, C_j, td_{3,i}, Q), \mathsf{RS}(P, C_i, C_j, td_{3,C_j}, Q)) = 1.$$

3.3 Security Models

Since the Aut algorithm of type-III authorization is a combination of type-I authorization and type-II authorization, we will omit type-III authorization query to adversary in following security games.

IND-CPA-I Security for Type-I Authorization Against Adversary Who Plays Left Server Role

We define following security model which ensures that the adversary who has the trapdoor of type-I authorization of the user U_t is not able to distinguish a ciphertext of U_t. Note that it also implys that IND-CPA security for type-II authorization against the adversary and IND-CPA security for both type-I and type-II authorization against adversary who plays right server role.

- Setup. The challenger runs the Setup algorithm, and then runs KeyGen_{user} algorithm to generate n public/secret key pairs of users $(pk_i, sk_i)(1 \leq i \leq n)$, runs KeyGen_{server} algorithm to generate two public/secret key pairs of two-server $(pk_{LS}, sk_{LS}, pk_{RS}, sk_{RS})$ and runs Aut algorithm to generate $td_{1,t}$. The challenger gives public parameter P, $(pk_{LS}, sk_{LS}, pk_{RS})$, $pk_i(1 \leq i \leq n)$ and $td_{1,t}$ to the adversary $\mathcal{A}$.

- Phase 1. The adversary $\mathcal{A}$ is allowed to issue the following kinds of query:
  - `Authorization query` $\langle i \rangle$: The challenger returns corresponding $td_{1,i}$.
  - `Test query` $\langle C_i, td_{1,i}, C_j, td_{1,j}, Q \rangle$: The adversary $\mathcal{A}$ can adaptively make test queries. The challenger returns 1 or 0 to the adversary $\mathcal{A}$ as a result.
- Challenge. The adversary $\mathcal{A}$ chooses two different plaintexts M_0 and M_1 and sends them to the challenger. The challenger picks a random bit b, and sends

$$C_t^* = \mathsf{Enc}(P, pk_t, pk_{LS}, pk_{RS}, M_b)$$

to the adversary $\mathcal{A}$.
- Phase 2. The adversary $\mathcal{A}$ is allowed to issue kinds of query as in Phase 1. The constraint is that C_t^* does not appear in the `Test query`.
- Guess. The adversary $\mathcal{A}$ outputs a guess b', and wins the games if $b' = b$.

We define the advantage of the adversary $\mathcal{A}$ as:

$$\mathsf{Adv}_{\mathcal{LS},\mathcal{A}}^{\mathsf{IND\text{-}CPA\text{-}I}}(1^k) = \mid \Pr[b = b'] - 1/2 \mid.$$

IND-CPA-II Security for Type-I Authorization Against Adversary Who Plays Two-Server Role

We define following security model which ensures that the adversary is not able to distinguish ciphertexts of user U_t without the type-I authorization trapdoor of user U_t. It implies that even if the two-server collude they cannot konw any information about an encrypted plaintext without the type-I trapdoor of the user.

- Setup. The challenger runs the Setup algorithm, and then runs Keygen_{user} algorithm to generate n public/secret key pairs of users $(pk_i, sk_i)(1 \leq i \leq n)$ and runs Keygen_{server} algorithm to generate two public/secret key pairs of two-server $(pk_{LS}, sk_{LS}, pk_{RS}, sk_{RS})$. The challenger gives public parameter P, $(pk_{LS}, sk_{LS}, pk_{RS}, sk_{RS})$ and $pk_i(1 \leq i \leq n)$ to the adversary $\mathcal{A}$.
- Phase 1. The adversary $\mathcal{A}$ is allowed to issue the following query. The constraint is that index t does not appear in the `Authorization query`:
  - `Authorization query` $\langle i \rangle$: The challenger returns corresponding $td_{1,i}$.
- Challenge. The adversary $\mathcal{A}$ chooses two different plaintexts M_0 and M_1 and sends them to the challenger. The challenger picks a random bit b, and sends

$$C_t^* = \mathsf{Enc}(P, pk_t, pk_{LS}, pk_{RS}, M_b)$$

to the adversary $\mathcal{A}$.
- Phase 2. The adversary $\mathcal{A}$ is allowed to issue `Authorization query` as in Phase 1.
- Guess. The adversary $\mathcal{A}$ outputs a guess b', and wins the games if $b' = b$.

We define the advantage of the adversary $\mathcal{A}$ as:

$$\mathsf{Adv}_{\mathcal{LS}-\mathcal{RS},\mathcal{A}}^{\mathsf{IND\text{-}CPA\text{-}II}}(1^k) = \mid \Pr[b = b'] - 1/2 \mid.$$

IND-CPA-III Security for Type-II Authorization Against Adversary Who Plays Two-Server Role

We define following security model which ensures that the adversary is not able to distinguish ciphertexts of user U_t without the type-II authorization trapdoor of user U_t. This implies that even if the two-server collude they cannot know any information about an encrypted plaintext without the type-II trapdoor of the user.

- Setup. The challenger runs the Setup algorithm, and then runs Keygen_{user} algorithm to generate n public/secret key pairs of users $(pk_i, sk_i)(1 \leq i \leq n)$ and runs Keygen_{server} algorithm to generate two public/secret key pairs of two-server $(pk_{LS}, sk_{LS}, pk_{RS}, sk_{RS})$. The challenger gives public parameter P, $(pk_{LS}, sk_{LS}, pk_{RS}, sk_{RS})$, $pk_i(1 \leq i \leq n)$ to the adversary $\mathcal{A}$.
- Phase 1. The adversary $\mathcal{A}$ is allowed to issue the following query:
  - Authorization query $\langle i, C_i \rangle$: The challenger returns corresponding td_{2,C_i}.
- Challenge. The adversary $\mathcal{A}$ chooses two different plaintexts M_0 and M_1 and sends them to the challenger. The challenger picks a random bit b, and sends

$$C_t^* = \mathsf{Enc}(P, pk_t, pk_{LS}, pk_{RS}, M_b)$$

  to the adversary $\mathcal{A}$.
- Phase 2. The adversary $\mathcal{A}$ is allowed to issue `Authorization query` as in Phase 1. The constraint is that C_t^* does not appear in the `Authorization query`.
- Guess. The adversary $\mathcal{A}$ outputs a guess b', and wins the games if $b' = b$.

We define the advantage of the adversary $\mathcal{A}$ as:

$$\mathsf{Adv}_{\mathcal{LS}-\mathcal{RS},\mathcal{A}}^{\mathsf{IND\text{-}CPA\text{-}III}}(1^k) = \mid \Pr[b = b'] - 1/2 \mid.$$

4 Generic Construction of $\mathcal{TS}$-$\mathcal{CCE}$-$\mathcal{FA}$ Scheme

Suppose the language $\mathcal{L}$ be hard-partitioned subset. Let SPHF = (SPHFSetup, HashKG, ProjKG, Hash, ProjHash) be an SPHF defined on $\mathcal{X} \to \mathcal{Y}$ for the language $\mathcal{L}$ under the security parameter k. Let $\mathcal{WS}$ be the witness space of the language $\mathcal{L}$. We describe the two types of operations as follow:

1. $* : \mathcal{Y} \times \mathcal{Y} \to \mathcal{Y}$. For any $y_1 \in \mathcal{Y}$, $y_2 \in \mathcal{Y}$, $y_1 * y_2 \in \mathcal{Y}$.
2. $\circ : \mathcal{WS} \times \mathcal{Y} \to \mathcal{Y}$. For any $w \in \mathcal{WS}$, $y \in \mathcal{Y}$, $w \circ y \in \mathcal{Y}$.

Note that if $h(M_i) \circ a = h(M_j) \circ b$ is hold, then M_i and M_j satisfy equation $Q(M_i, M_j)$. Our $\mathcal{TS}$-$\mathcal{CCE}$-$\mathcal{FA}$ scheme is described as follow:

- $\mathsf{Setup}(1^k)$: This algorithm generates the public parameter $param$ and the description of language $\mathcal{L}$. Set the system parameter $P = \langle param, \mathcal{L} \rangle$.

– KeyGen_{server} (P): This algorithm generates two pairs of public/secret keys (pk_{LS}, sk_{LS}) and (pk_{RS}, sk_{RS}) of the left server and the right server, respectively:

$$sk_{LS} = \mathsf{HashKG}(P), pk_{LS} = \mathsf{ProjKG}(sk_{LS}, P),$$
$$sk_{RS} = \mathsf{HashKG}(P), pk_{RS} = \mathsf{ProjKG}(sk_{RS}, P).$$

– KeyGen_{user} (P): This algorithm generates a pair of public/secret key (pk_i, sk_i) of user U_i:

$$sk_i = \mathsf{HashKG}(P), pk_i = \mathsf{ProjKG}(sk_i, P).$$

– $\mathsf{Enc}(P, pk_i, pk_{LS}, pk_{RS}, M)$: This algorithm randomly picks a word $W \in \mathcal{L}$ with the witness w, and then outputs ciphertext C of the plaintext M:

$$x = \mathsf{ProjHash}(pk_i, W, w), y = \mathsf{ProjHash}(pk_{LS}, W, w),$$
$$z = \mathsf{ProjHash}(pk_{RS}, W, w), C = (W, U) = (W, x * y * z * h(M)).$$

Note that we assume that ciphertext of M_i and ciphertext of M_j are C_i and C_j, respectively. And word W_i with the witness w_i and word W_j with the witness w_j are randomly picked, respectively.

$$C_i = (W_i, U_i) = (W_i, x_i * y_i * z_i * h(M_i)),$$
$$C_j = (W_j, U_j) = (W_j, x_j * y_j * z_j * h(M_j)).$$

Type-I authorization:

– Aut_1 (P, sk_i): This algorithm outputs trapdoor $td_{1,i} = sk_i$.

– $\mathsf{Test}_1(\mathsf{LS}(P, C_i, C_j, td_{1,i}, Q), \mathsf{RS}(P, C_i, C_j, td_{1,j}, Q))$: This algorithm is interactively run as follows:

(1) The left server and the right server randomly picks $r_{LS}, r_{RS} \in \mathcal{Y}$, respectively. The left server computes:

$$IV_{LS} = (\mathsf{Hash}(td_{1,i}, W_i) * \mathsf{Hash}(sk_{LS}, W_i))^{-1} * r_{LS},$$

and the right server computes:

$$IV_{RS} = (\mathsf{Hash}(td_{1,j}, W_j) * \mathsf{Hash}(sk_{RS}, W_j))^{-1} * r_{RS}.$$

Then IV_{LS} is sent to the right server and IV_{RS} is sent to the left server.

(2) The left server computes FV_{LS} using IV_{RS}, b and $r_{LS} \circ a$:

$$FV_{LS} = (U_j * \mathsf{Hash}^{-1}(sk_{LS}, W_j) * IV_{RS}) \circ b * (r_{LS} \circ a)$$
$$= (h(M_j) \circ b) * (r_{RS} \circ b) * (r_{LS} \circ a),$$

and the right server computes FV_{RS} using IV_{LS}, a and $r_{RS} \circ b$:

$$FV_{RS} = (U_i * \mathsf{Hash}^{-1}(sk_{RS}, W_i) * IV_{LS}) \circ a * (r_{RS} \circ b)$$
$$= (h(M_i) \circ a) * (r_{LS} \circ a) * (r_{RS} \circ b).$$

Both FV_{LS} and FV_{RS} are sent to users or the third party. Note that a and b are obtained by Q.

(3) The users or the third party learn 1 that indicating M_i and M_j satisfy the equation $Q(M_i, Mj)$ if $FV_{LS} = FV_{RS}$ and 0 otherwise.

Type-II authorization:

- Aut_2 (P, sk_i, C_i): This algorithm outputs the trapdoor $td_{2,Ci} = \mathsf{Hash}(sk_i, W_i)$.
- Test_2 $(\mathsf{LS}(P, C_i, C_j, td_{2,C_i}, Q)$, $\mathsf{RS}(P, C_i, C_j, td_{2,C_j}, Q))$: This algorithm and the Test_1 algorithm are the same except:
  - $IV_{LS} = (td_{2,C_i} * \mathsf{Hash}(sk_{LS}, W_i))^{-1} * r_{LS}$ is sent to the right server,
  - $IV_{RS} = (td_{2,C_j} * \mathsf{Hash}(sk_{RS}, W_j))^{-1} * r_{RS}$ is sent to the left server.

Type-III authorization:

- $\mathsf{Aut}_{3,i}$ (P, sk_i): This algorithm outputs the trapdoor $td_{3,i} = sk_i$.
- $\mathsf{Aut}_{3,j}$ (P, sk_j, C_j): This algorithm outputs the trapdoor $td_{3,C_j} = \mathsf{Hash}(sk_j, W_j)$.
- $\mathsf{Test}_3(\mathsf{LS}(P, C_i, C_j, td_{3,i}, Q)$, $\mathsf{RS}(P, C_i, C_j, td_{3,C_j}, Q))$: This algorithm and the Test_1 algorithm are the same except:
  - $IV_{LS} = (\mathsf{Hash}(td_{3,i}, W_i) * \mathsf{Hash}(sk_{LS}, W_i))^{-1} * r_{LS}$ is sent to the right server,
  - $IV_{RS} = (td_{3,C_j} * \mathsf{Hash}(sk_{RS}, W_j))^{-1} * r_{RS}$ is sent to the left server.

Correctness: The properties of the SPHF guarantee the correctness of the above construction. We give the correctness analysis as follow:

For the test algorithm, we have that:

$$
\begin{aligned}
IV_{LS} &= (\mathsf{Hash}(sk_i, W_i) * \mathsf{Hash}(sk_{LS}, W_i))^{-1} * r_{LS} = (x_i * y_i)^{-1} * r_{LS},\\
IV_{RS} &= (\mathsf{Hash}(sk_j, W_j) * \mathsf{Hash}(sk_{RS}, W_j))^{-1} * r_{RS} = (x_j * z_j)^{-1} * r_{RS},\\
FV_{LS} &= (U_j * \mathsf{Hash}^{-1}(sk_{LS}, W_j) * IV_{RS}) \circ b * (r_{LS} \circ a)\\
&= (x_j * y_j * z_j * h(M_j) * y_j^{-1} * (x_j * z_j)^{-1} * r_{RS}) \circ b * (r_{LS} \circ a)\\
&= (h(M_j) * r_{RS}) \circ b * (r_{LS} \circ a),\\
&= (h(M_j) \circ b) * (r_{RS} \circ b) * (r_{LS} \circ a),\\
FV_{RS} &= (U_i * \mathsf{Hash}^{-1}(sk_{RS}, W_i) * IV_{LS}) \circ a * (r_{RS} \circ b)\\
&= (x_i * y_i * z_i * h(M_i) * z_i^{-1} * (x_i * y_i)^{-1} * r_{LS}) \circ a * (r_{RS} \circ b)\\
&= (h(M_i) * r_{LS}) \circ a * (r_{RS} \circ b)\\
&= (h(M_i) \circ a) * (r_{LS} \circ a) * (r_{RS} \circ b).
\end{aligned}
$$

Therefore, if M_i and M_j satisfy $Q(M_i, M_j)$, then $FV_{LS} = FV_{RS}$.

5 Security Proof

Theorem 1. *Our $\mathcal{TS}$-$\mathcal{CCE}$-$\mathcal{FA}$ scheme is IND-CPA-I secure for type-I authorization against adversary based on the pseudo-randomness property of SPHF.*

Proof. That is, for any probatilistic polynomial time adversary $\mathcal{A}$, $\mathsf{Adv}^{\mathsf{IND\text{-}CPA\text{-}I}}_{\mathcal{LS},\mathcal{A}}(1^k)$ is a negligible function for security parameter 1^k. We consider the original game.

Game 0

This game is the same as original **IND-CPA-I** security game, and we write

$$x_t = \mathsf{ProjHash}(pk_t, W_t, w_t), y_t = \mathsf{ProjHash}(pk_{LS}, W_t, w_t),$$
$$z_t = \mathsf{ProjHash}(pk_{RS}, W_t, w_t), C_t^* = (W_t, x_t * y_t * z_t * h(M_b)).$$

to denote the challenge ciphertext. We define the advantage of $\mathcal{A}$ in Game 0 as $\mathsf{Adv}^{\mathsf{Game\ 0}}_{\mathcal{LS},\mathcal{A}}(1^k)$ and have that

$$\mathsf{Adv}^{\mathsf{Game\ 0}}_{\mathcal{LS},\mathcal{A}}(1^k) = \mathsf{Adv}^{\mathsf{IND\text{-}CPA\text{-}I}}_{\mathcal{LS},\mathcal{A}}(1^k). \tag{1}$$

Game 1

In this game, the challenger performs identically to that in **Game 0**, except that challenger chooses $z_t \leftarrow_R \mathcal{Y}$ instead of computing z_t as $\mathsf{ProjHash}(pk_{RS}, W_t, w_t)$. Because the *pseudo-randomness* property of SPHF, distribution $\{W_t, pk_{RS}, z_t \mid z_t = \mathsf{ProjHash}(pk_{RS}, W_t, w_t)\}$ is computationally indistinguishable from distribution $\{W_t, pk_{RS}, z_t \mid z_t \leftarrow_R \mathcal{Y}\}$. It is not difficult to have that:

$$|\mathsf{Adv}^{\mathsf{Game\ 1}}_{\mathcal{LS},\mathcal{A}}(1^k) - \mathsf{Adv}^{\mathsf{Game\ 0}}_{\mathcal{LS},\mathcal{A}}(1^k)| \leq \mathsf{Adv}^{\mathsf{PR}}_{\mathcal{SPHF},\mathcal{A}}(1^k). \tag{2}$$

Game 2

In this game, the challenger performs identically to that in **Game 1**, except that challenger chooses $C_t^* \leftarrow_R \mathcal{Y}$ instead of computing $C_t^* = x_t * y_t * z_t * h(M_b)$. Then we have that:

$$\mathsf{Adv}^{\mathsf{Game\ 2}}_{\mathcal{LS},\mathcal{A}}(1^k) = \mathsf{Adv}^{\mathsf{Game\ 1}}_{\mathcal{LS},\mathcal{A}}(1^k). \tag{3}$$

The adversary in **Game 2** can only win with probability 1/2 as C_t^* is independent of b. Hence, following inequation is obtained by (1), (2) and (3):

$$|\mathsf{Adv}^{\mathsf{Game\ 2}}_{\mathcal{LS},\mathcal{A}}(1^k) - \mathsf{Adv}^{\mathsf{IND\text{-}CPA\text{-}I}}_{\mathcal{LS},\mathcal{A}}(1^k)| \leq \mathsf{Adv}^{\mathsf{PR}}_{\mathcal{SPHF},\mathcal{A}}(1^k).$$

Since $\mathsf{Adv}^{\mathsf{Game\ 2}}_{\mathcal{LS},\mathcal{A}}(1^k) = 0$ and $\mathsf{Adv}^{\mathsf{PR}}_{\mathcal{SPHF},\mathcal{A}}(1^k)$ is negligible, we have that $\mathsf{Adv}^{\mathsf{IND\text{-}CPA\text{-}I}}_{\mathcal{LS},\mathcal{A}}(1^k)$ is negligible as well.

Theorem 2. *Our $\mathcal{TS}$-$\mathcal{CCE}$-$\mathcal{FA}$ scheme is IND-CPA-II secure for type-I authorization against adversary based on the pseudo-randomness property of SPHF.*

Proof. The proof of **Theorem 2** is similar to those of **Theorem 2.**

Theorem 3. *Our $\mathcal{TS}$-$\mathcal{CCE}$-$\mathcal{FA}$ scheme is IND-CPA-III secure for type-II authorization against adversary based on the pseudo-randomness property of SPHF.*

Proof. The proof of **Theorem 3** is similar to those of **Theorem 1**.

6 Instantiated $\mathcal{TS}$-$\mathcal{CCE}$-$\mathcal{FA}$ Schemes

We choose two types of equation $Q = (Q1, Q2)$ to define different mapping function h.
Q1: $h(M) = g^M \in \mathbb{G}_p$, where $M \in Z_p$. In the $Q1$, we can query whether M_i and M_j satisfy $aM_i = bM_j$ or not. If so, then $h(M_i) \circ a = h(M_j) \circ b$ is hold, thus

$$g^{aM_i} = g^{bM_j}.$$

Q2: $h(M) = M \in \mathbb{G}_p$. In the $Q2$, we can query if M_i and M_j satisfy $M_i^a = M_j^b$ or not. If so, then $h(M_i) \circ a = h(M_j) \circ b$ is hold, thus

$$M_i^a = M_j^b.$$

The description of instantiations of $\mathcal{TS}$-$\mathcal{CCE}$-$\mathcal{FA}$ from SPHF based on DDH assumption for $Q1$ and $Q2$ can be easily obtained by [16], and hence we omit it for the limit of number of pages.

7 Conclusion

In this paper, we introduced a $\mathcal{TS}$-$\mathcal{CCE}$-$\mathcal{FA}$ scheme to withstand offline message recovery attack. Furthermore, it also has the nice property of flexible authorization and supports checking two types of equations on the ciphertexts of M_i and M_j under different public keys as well as the same public key. Finally, we showed the efficient instantiations of $\mathcal{TS}$-$\mathcal{CCE}$-$\mathcal{FA}$.

Acknowledgements. This work is supported by the National Natural Science Foundation of China (No. 61872409, 61402184, 61472146), Guangdong Natural Science Funds for Distinguished Young Scholar (No. 2014A030306021), Guangdong Program for Special Support of Top-notch Young Professionals (No. 2015TQ01X796), Pearl River Nova Program of Guangzhou (No. 201610010037).

References

1. Boneh, D., Di Crescenzo, G., Ostrovsky, R., Persiano, G.: Public key encryption with keyword search. In: Cachin, C., Camenisch, J.L. (eds.) EUROCRYPT 2004. LNCS, vol. 3027, pp. 506–522. Springer, Heidelberg (2004). https://doi.org/10.1007/978-3-540-24676-3_30
2. Chen, R., Mu, Y., Yang, G., Guo, F., Wang, X.: A new general framework for secure public key encryption with keyword search. In: Foo, E., Stebila, D. (eds.) ACISP 2015. LNCS, vol. 9144, pp. 59–76. Springer, Cham (2015). https://doi.org/10.1007/978-3-319-19962-7_4
3. Chen, R., Mu, Y., Yang, G., Guo, F., Wang, X.: Dual-server public-key encryption with keyword search for secure cloud storage. IEEE Trans. Inf. Forensics Secur. **11**(4), 789–798 (2016)

4. Cramer, R., Shoup, V.: Universal hash proofs and a paradigm for adaptive chosen Ciphertext secure public-key encryption. In: Knudsen, L.R. (ed.) EUROCRYPT 2002. LNCS, vol. 2332, pp. 45–64. Springer, Heidelberg (2002). https://doi.org/10.1007/3-540-46035-7_4
5. Huang, K., Tso, R., Chen, Y.C., Li, W., Sun, H.M.: A new public key encryption with equality test. In: Au, M.H., Carminati, B., Kuo, C.C.J. (eds.) NSS 2014. LNCS, vol. 8792, pp. 550–557. Springer, Cham (2014). https://doi.org/10.1007/978-3-319-11698-3_45
6. Huang, K., Tso, R., Chen, Y.C., Rahman, S.M.M., Almogren, A., Alamri, A.: PKE-AET: public key encryption with authorized equality test. Comput. J. **58**(10), 2686–2697 (2015)
7. Huang, Q., Li, H.: An efficient public-key searchable encryption scheme secure against inside keyword guessing attacks. Inf. Sci. **403**, 1–14 (2017)
8. Lee, H.T., Ling, S., Seo, J.H., Wang, H.: Semi-generic construction of public key encryption and identity-based encryption with equality test. Inf. Sci. **373**, 419–440 (2016)
9. Lee, H.T., Ling, S., Seo, J.H., Wang, H., Youn, T.Y.: Public key encryption with equality test in the standard model. IACR Cryptology ePrint Archive 2016/1182 (2016)
10. Li, J., Lin, X., Zhang, Y., Han, J.: Ksf-oabe: outsourced attribute-based encryption with keyword search function for cloud storage. IEEE Trans. Serv. Comput. **10**(5), 715–725 (2017)
11. Li, J., Shi, Y., Zhang, Y.: Searchable ciphertext-policy attribute-based encryption with revocation in cloud storage. Int. J. Commun. Syst. **30**(1) (2017)
12. Li, J., Yao, W., Zhang, Y., Qian, H., Han, J.: Flexible and fine-grained attribute-based data storage in cloud computing. IEEE Trans. Serv. Comput. **10**(5), 785–796 (2017)
13. Lin, X.J., Qu, H., Zhang, X.: Public key encryption supporting equality test and flexible authorization without bilinear pairings. IACR Cryptology ePrint Archive 2016/277 (2016)
14. Ma, S.: Identity-based encryption with outsourced equality test in cloud computing. Inf. Sci. **328**, 389–402 (2016)
15. Ma, S., Huang, Q., Zhang, M., Yang, B.: Efficient public key encryption with equality test supporting flexible authorization. IEEE Trans. Inf. Forensics Secur. **10**(3), 458–470 (2015)
16. Ma, S., Ling, Y.: A general two-server cryptosystem supporting complex queries. In: Kang, B.B.H., Kim, T. (eds.) WISA 2017. LNCS, vol. 10763, pp. 249–260. Springer, Cham (2018). https://doi.org/10.1007/978-3-319-93563-8_21
17. Ma, S., Zhang, M., Huang, Q., Yang, B.: Public key encryption with delegated equality test in a multi-user setting. Comput. J. **58**(4), 986–1002 (2014)
18. Tang, Q.: Towards public key encryption scheme supporting equality test with fine-grained authorization. In: Parampalli, U., Hawkes, P. (eds.) ACISP 2011. LNCS, vol. 6812, pp. 389–406. Springer, Heidelberg (2011). https://doi.org/10.1007/978-3-642-22497-3_25
19. Tang, Q.: Public key encryption schemes supporting equality test with authorisation of different granularity. Int. J. Appl. Cryptogr. **2**(4), 304–321 (2012)
20. Wang, C.H., Tu, T.Y.: Keyword search encryption scheme resistant against keyword-guessing attack by the untrusted server. J. Shanghai Jiaotong Univ. (Science) **19**(4), 440–442 (2014)

21. Wu, T., Ma, S., Mu, Y., Zeng, S.: ID-based encryption with equality test against insider attack. In: Pieprzyk, J., Suriadi, S. (eds.) ACISP 2017. LNCS, vol. 10342, pp. 168–183. Springer, Cham (2017). https://doi.org/10.1007/978-3-319-60055-0_9
22. Yang, G., Tan, C.H., Huang, Q., Wong, D.S.: Probabilistic public key encryption with equality test. In: Pieprzyk, J. (ed.) CT-RSA 2010. LNCS, vol. 5985, pp. 119–131. Springer, Heidelberg (2010). https://doi.org/10.1007/978-3-642-11925-5_9

A Hash-Based Public Key Cryptosystem

Qian Yin(✉) and Gang Luo(✉)

College of Computer Science and Electronic Engineering, Hunan University, Changsha, China
{yinqian,l}@hnu.edu.cn

Abstract. In this paper, a new public key cryptosystem based on hash is proposed. The algorithm uses hash and time-memory trade-off to construct a trap-door one-way function. It can guarantee the security strength equivalent to the same length symmetric encryption algorithm. Meanwhile, our algorithm has a fast encryption speed and reasonable decryption time, which can be applied to message encryption on the occasions of limited resources such as wireless sensor network. Experimental and theoretical analysis proves that under the same encryption strength, our algorithm's packet length can be much lower than traditional encryption schemes such as RSA, and has an excellent performance in encryption.

Keywords: Time-memory trade-off · Hash function
Public-key cryptosystems · Digital signatures · Encryption

1 Introduction

Since Diffie and Hellman [1] explained how the public key cryptosystem could be created using a one-way function, various public-key encryption algorithms have been proposed. In 1978, the first public key encryption algorithm RSA [2] was proposed, which can apply data encryption and data signature. And it is widely applied to various fields such as transportation, medical science, environmental protection, industry, agriculture and so on. Other classic public key cryptosystems include the ECC [3] and NTRU [4], where the ECC relies on discrete logarithm and the NTRU [4] is based on lattice-based cryptography.

The security of these algorithms depends on the intractability of mathematical problems. Once they are completely cracked, and then the correspondent asymmetric encryption algorithm will be decrypted. Moreover, in the early stages, these encryption algorithms are not designed for wireless sensor networks with resource-constrained, so there are some problems in the application of wireless sensor networks. In addition, the common asymmetric encryption algorithm has higher computation capacity than symmetric encryption algorithm, which also limits its application in WSN nodes with limited computing capacity [5,6].

In this paper, we present a new public key cryptosystem that relies on the hash. It consists of two algorithms: encryption algorithms and signature algorithms. The latter is used for certification. The security of the algorithm comes

X. Sun et al. (Eds.): ICCCS 2018, LNCS 11065, pp. 383–392, 2018.
https://doi.org/10.1007/978-3-030-00012-7_35

from the difficulty of hash collision. It is very difficult to find any two distinct inputs that map to the same output. Meanwhile, for the same security level, the proposed algorithm has a shorter key length than RSA. Since the algorithm's decryption time will increase with the packet length, the packet length of our algorithm cannot be too long. Therefore, the proposed algorithm has a great value in the situation where the wireless sensor network and other computer resources are limited.

The rest of the paper is organized as follows. Section 2 shows the techniques involved in our algorithm. Section 3 describes the algorithm steps, as well as feasibility analysis. Section 4 presents the performance of the algorithm. And finally, we make a summary and discussion about the algorithm in Sect. 5.

2 Related Work

In this section, we introduce the technology involved in Sect. 3.

2.1 Hellman Time-Memory Trade-Off

In 1980, Martin Hellman [7] described a cryptanalytic time-memory trade-off and applied to DES. Given a fixed ciphertext C_0 and a plaintext P_0, the method tries to recovery the key K such that $C_0 = S_K(P_0)$ where S is an encryption function. Time-memory trade-off contains two parts, precomputation and cryptanalysis.

At the part of precomputation, the algorithm picking m starting points $SP_i\,(1 \leq i \leq m)$ and iterating the function f, defined by $f(K) = R(S_K(P_0))$, where R is a reduction function which creates a key from a ciphertext. At the same time, we set $X_{i0} = SP_i$ and define $X_i = f(X_i)$. By successively iterating the f we can generate chains of keys $SP_i = X_{i0} \xrightarrow{f} X_{i1} \xrightarrow{f} X_{i2} \xrightarrow{f} \cdots \xrightarrow{f} X_{it} = EP_i$.

For each SP_i that we choose, we perform t iterations, and then set $X_{it} = EP_i$. Then we will eventually obtain m pairs tuples like $(SP_i, EP_i)(1 \leq i \leq m)$ and stored in a table. It's worth nothing that all intermediate points will be discarded for reducing memory requirements.

In the cryptanalysis stage, if someone is given a ciphertext C, and the corresponding plaintext is P. We apply R to C for obtain a key Y_1, then we compare Y_1 with $EP_i\ (1 \leq i \leq m)$ and find the one that matches.

If $Y_1 = EP_i(1 \leq i \leq m)$, either the $K = X_{it-1}$, or a false alarm occurred. If Y_1 not an endpoint or a false alarm occurred, then compute $Y_2 = f(Y_1)$ and checks if is an endpoint until the key is finally found or all the table are searched.

2.2 Rainbow Table Algorithm

In 2003, Oechslin proposed the rainbow table algorithm based on Hellman's advantages of DP [8]. A rainbow table performs different reduction for each column of the table to construct different function f. At the cryptanalysis stage, first we apply R_t to C and check if it is an endpoint. If we match the endpoint we can regenerate the chain using the corresponding starting point. If we don't match the endpoint, we apply R_{t-1}, f_t to ciphertext and check if the key is in the second last column of the table, and so forth. In the worst case, the total number of calculations that we have to make it is $\frac{t(t-1)}{2}$. The cost of the rainbow table is less than half of Hellman table.

3 Description of the Algorithm

In this section, we present the details of algorithm design. We first carry out a feasibility analysis of our algorithm in theory. Then we describe the process of key creation, encryption and decryption. Finally, we show the method of signature and authentication. The corresponding definitions are then as follows:

Definition 1. *Let $\{0,1\}^*$ be a message space, $\{0,1\}^n$ be a space of the output message digest value, Then we define: $H : \{0,1\}^* \longrightarrow \{0,1\}^n$, $G = H(X)$, where X denotes an input of any length message, H is the hash function used, and G is the final output message digest value. The number n is called the hash length of H.*

Definition 2. *Suppose M to be a fixed text block, and define*

$$F(M) = T(H(Z(M)||k_p) \tag{1}$$

$$E(M) = T(H(M||k_p) \tag{2}$$

where k_p is public key, Z is a transform function from ciphertext to plaintext, H is a hash function, and T is a simple reduction function.

Now we have the following asymmetric encryption algorithm, which use parameters a, b and t. Figure 1 depicts the construction of F.

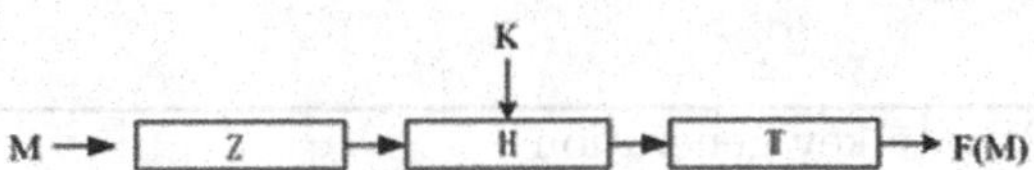

Fig. 1. Construction of the function F

3.1 Feasibility Analysis

The idea of public key cryptography is to design a trap-door one-way function. The public key of the trap-door one-way function is used for encryption, and the trap is the private key to recovery the plaintext from the ciphertext [9]. The inherent merits of hash, such as one-way, good diffusion and confusion and sensitivity to plain text, form the solid theoretical foundation for excellent trade-off one-way function construction.

The hash function H is a one-way function, and it is easy to compute from one direction but difficult to compute from the other direction. We apply the time-memory trade-off to the asymmetric encryption algorithm. The private key is equivalent to the pre-calculation phase of the time-memory trade-off, and the table is the trap door information. Once we decrypt the ciphertext, we only need to carry out the second stage of the time-memory trade-off.

3.2 Encryption Algorithm

Key Creation. In order to use the proposed cryptosystem, the sender and the receiver need to have their own key pairs. To create a key pair, the receiver will choose a random number to generate a fixed-length binary string as the public key and keeps it public. Algorithm 1 describes the procedure of public key generation.

Algorithm 1. Public key generation

Input: random number $k, k \in \{1, 2, .., N\}$, the length of public key is *klen*
Output: public key k_p
compute the value of $H(k)$
choose *klen* bytes as public key k_p
return k_p

$$\begin{array}{l} M_{1,0} \xrightarrow{E} M_{1,1} \xrightarrow{F_1} M_{1,2} \rightarrow \cdots \xrightarrow{F_b} M_{1,b} \\ M_{2,0} \xrightarrow{E} M_{2,1} \xrightarrow{F_1} M_{2,2} \rightarrow \cdots \xrightarrow{F_b} M_{2,b} \\ \vdots \\ M_{a,0} \xrightarrow{E} M_{a,1} \xrightarrow{F_1} M_{a,2} \rightarrow \cdots \xrightarrow{F_b} M_{a,b} \end{array} \tag{3}$$

Everyone can use the receiver's public key to encrypt the message and send it to the receiver. The receiver uses the private key to recover the message. Algorithm 2 shows the steps of private key generation.

Algorithm 2. Private key generation

Input: the number of chains a, the length of chains $b + 1$, the number of table t
Output: the private key
for $j \in [1, t]$ **do**
  Choose a different random plaintext M_{10}, M_{20},..., M_{a0}
  Compute a end points M_{ib} as depicted in Equation 3, where $i \in [1, a]$
  Store in table j: a (M_{i0}, M_{ib})-pairs, sorted on the end point, where $i \in [1, a]$
end
return private key

Encryption. Suppose that the message needs to be encrypted is M. In order to encrypt plaintext M, the following steps of Algorithm 3 should be implemented by the sender. Note that the length of ciphertext is two times than the length of the message.

Decryption. Suppose that the receiver has received the message C_0 from sender and wants to decrypt it using his private key. To do this efficiently, the receiver

Algorithm 3. Encryption

Input: public key k_p and plaintext M
Output: ciphertext C_0

Connect the public key k_p behind the plaintext M
Compute $h = H(M||k_p)$
Compute $C_0 = T(h)$
return C_0

first decrypts the message with the first private key table. If failed, then the receiver will use the next table until the message recover from ciphertext or all tables are retrieved. Since the decryption time will increase with the length of the key, the key length of our algorithm cannot be too long. Therefore, the proposed algorithm has a great value in the situation where the wireless sensor network and other computer resources are limited. The decryption algorithm of a single table as described in Algorithm 4.

Algorithm 4. Decryption

Input: private key and ciphertext C_0
Output: plaintext M

$Y \leftarrow C_0$
for $j \in [0, b]$ **do**
    if $Y \neq M_{i,b}$ **then**
        if $j \equiv b$ **then** return failure
        else $Y \leftarrow C_0$
        for $k \in [b-j-1, b-1]$ **do** compute $Y = F_k(Y)$

    end
    else
        $X \leftarrow E(M_{i,0})$
        if $X \equiv C_0$ **then** return plaintext M
        for $k \in [0, b-j-2]$ **do** compute $X = F_k(X)$
        if $F_{b-j-1}(X) \equiv C_0$ **then** $M \leftarrow Z(X)$
        else execute the content of step 4, step 5 and step 6
    end
end

3.3 Digital Signatures Scheme

A message can be signed using a private key. Anyone can verify this signature with the corresponding public key. Signatures cannot be forged, and a signer cannot deny the validity of his signature latterly.

The Signing Procedure. Assume user Bob send Alice a "signed"message m. Firstly, Bob will compute his "signature" S for message m using himself private key. Then he will encrypt the signature S using Alices public key and send it to Alice. The signing procedure is presented in Algorithm 5.

Algorithm 5. Signature

Input: private key and plaintext m

Output: signature S

```
1  Y ← m
2  for j ∈ [0, b] do
3      if Y ≠ M_{i,b} then
4          if j ≡ b then return failure ;
5          else Y ← m
6          for k ∈ [b − j − 1, b − 1] do compute Y = F_k(Y) ;
7          ;
8      end
9      else
10         X = E(M_{i,0})
11         if X ≡ m then return signature ;
12         for k ∈ [0, b − j − 2] do compute X = F_k(X) ;
13         if F_{b−j−1}(X) ≡ C_0 then S = Z(X) ;
14         else execute the content of step 4, step 5, and step 6 ;
15     end
16 end
```

The Verification Procedure. Firstly, Alice decrypts the ciphertext with her private key to obtain S. Then she extracts the message m using Bobs public key. Given S and k_p. It is easy to verify the authenticity of signature by computing $m' = E(S)$ and check that whether m is equal to m'. If $m' = m$, then we can make sure that the authenticity of the signature.

4 Analysis of the Algorithm and Experiment

This section includes three parts: the analysis of the correctness, security analysis and the implementation of the algorithm. First of all, we have made a brief theoretical proof in Sect. 4.1. Then, we describe the possible attack in next subsection. Finally, we present an implementation and discussion of the algorithm.

4.1 Correctness

Time-memory trade-off is a general inversion technique, which applies to any one-way function. In essence, our encryption algorithm is also a one-way function of the calculation process, so we can decode it by time-memory trade-off.

1. Assume that $E = T(H(M)||k_p))$. Given k_p, H and T , it is easy to compute E from M but very difficult to compute M from E. Hence, our encryption algorithm satisfies the condition of a one-way function.
2. Suppose $M_{i+1} = T(H(Z(M_i)||k_p))(1 \leq i \leq n)$. Given M_1 and M_n, and it is very easy to compute chain of $M_1 \to M_2 \to M_3 \to M_{n-1} \to M_n$. Thus, this is a trap-door and our algorithm is one-way trap-door function. Obviously, for all M_i, there exist a M_{i+1} to make $M_{i+1} = E$.
3. Suppose C to be a fixed cipher block, as described in Sect. 3.2, we have $C = T(H(M||k_p))$, where M denotes the plaintext. As shown in Eq. 3, $M_{i,j} = F_j(M_{i,j-1})$. Meanwhile, $F_j(M_{i,j-1}) = T(H(Z(M_{i,j-1})||k_p))$. If $C = M_{i,j}$, then we have $T(H(M||k_p)) = T(H(Z_j(M_{i,j-1})||k_p))$. Thus, we can recovery the plaintext $M = Z_j(M_{i,j-1})$.

4.2 Security Analysis

In the public key cryptography, the encryption key k_p is public and the decryption key k_s is required to be kept secret. Although the secret key k_s is determined by the public key k_p, the cryptographic key k_s cannot be calculated from the public key k_p. The one-way characteristic of hash function H, it is impossible to know some of the parameters to find the possibility of plaintext. In fact, any hash algorithm may be collided, but the existing security algorithm cannot be cracked within a limited time. For example, if a ciphertext crack time exceeds the confidential data of the confidentiality period, then it is meaningless to crack it, therefore it is considered safe. The following aspects are discussed for security.

Brute Force Attacks. An attacker can recover the plaintext by trying all possible ciphertext. An exhaustive attack is the simplest and straightforward way to calculate (second) the preimage, and the attacker randomly chooses an input and calculates its output value and then compares it with a given summary value. The hash function has a very large range. In theory, it is impossible to exhaust the entire hash value in the effective time. Assume that the probability of each output value is the same, the computational complexity of the attack output length of the n-bit hash function is 2^n. Since we are using k-bit plaintext packet input, and the input of the plaintext after a transformation in the encryption, the output of the n-bit hash value, so the exhaustive attack calculation complexity of 2^n.

Rainbow Table Attacks. The public key and private keys are paired. Assume that user A sends data to user B and user C respectively. Since the public key is generated randomly, the public keys sent to B and C are different, then the corresponding private keys are different. Each user's public key is different, then the attacker will have to generate a rainbow table for each user. Assume that you have ten thousand users, then his rainbow table will grow ten thousand times. The generated public key significantly increases the attacker's time and space costs, making the rainbow table attack no longer cost-effective. Assume that we encrypt a 64-bit plaintext, if the attacker wants to use Rainbow table to attack, at first, he need to generate a plaintext space, but the required time is much larger than 2^{64}. So within a certain period of time, the attacker is unable to crack, and we can guarantee that during this period of time our information is absolutely safe.

Security Level. The security level of our algorithm depends on the hash function H. Suppose that we choose MD5 [11,12] as the H function, if the attacker tries to find two messages producing the same ciphertext, then he needs 2^{64} operations to crack in 64-bit public key. Therefore, the security level of proposed algorithm is equivalent to 64-bit symmetrical encryption algorithm. Similarly, we assume that the the H function is SHA1 [13], then the attacker needs 2^{80} bit operations to crack. So the security level of proposed algorithm is equivalent to 80-bit symmetrical encryption algorithm. Table 1 shows the key length between different encryption algorithms at the same security level [15]. We can deduce that the key length of our algorithm can be shorter than other public key encryption algorithms under the same security level.

Table 1. Comparison of key length under the same security level

Algorithms	Proposed	Symmetrical	RSA	ECC	NTRU
Key length	80	80	1024	160	263

4.3 Experiments and Discussion

In this section, we present the implementation of the cryptosystem and evaluate the benefits of our cryptosystem.

Implementation. For implementing the proposed public key algorithm, we carried out a set of experiments on PC. PC is Dell machine runs Windows 7 Professional SP1 with 32-bit on Intel(R) Pentium(R), CPU 2.70 GHz, and 2.00 GB RAM. The program we used was written in C and not optimized for speed. In order to clearly explain the above encryption and decryption process, we have chosen 16 bits plaintexts as an example. In our experiment, we have chosen SHA1 as our hash function, T is a simple reduction function that select the first 32 bits of a 160-bit hash, and we have random chosen 16 bits as the public key.

In [10,14], the success probability of a rainbow that uses a single table written as

$$1 - \prod_{i=1}^{t}(1 - \frac{m_i}{N}) \tag{4}$$

where $m_1 = m$ and $m_{n+1} = N(1 - e^{-\frac{m_n}{N}})$. Suppose l to be the number of table, and we define $c = \frac{mt}{N}$, where c refers to the ratio of the calculations of a single table to N, which is used to measure the calculation cost required for pre-calculation. It is known from literature [6], Oechslin suggested that in the rainbow table should choose $m = N^{\frac{2}{3}}$, $t = N^{\frac{1}{3}}$, $l = 1$. In other words, $c = 1$. The success rate under both theory and experiment is 55%. Therefore, when we need

Table 2. Success rate (P_{succ}) with different calculations ratio (c) and number of tables (l)

P_{succ} (%)	49	59	63.5	70.6	77.3	86.1
l	1	1	1	1	2	3
c	1.02	1.61	2.0	3.17	1.66	1.66

to achieve a higher success rate, we need a larger single table or more tables. Table 2 is given the comparison of success rates under different c and l.

For each fixed l, this is a function of the single variable P_{succ}. Table 2 shows the success rate increases as the size of the table increases. From the data in Table 2, we can see that if we want to achieve a success rate of more than 70%, we need a larger table or multiple tables.

Comparison With Other Encryption Algorithms. There are currently a number of encryption algorithms in the literature, including the system of RSA based on the difficulty of factoring and the system of AES. We have tested the encryption speed of RSA cryptosystems and the encryption speed of AES. Proposed algorithm, RSA, AES and DES all work in units of message block. Numbers given for encryption are message blocks processed per second. The information is summarized in the following Table 3.

Table 3. Encryption speed with other algorithms

Algorithms	Proposed	RSA-512	AES-128	DES
Speed (blks/sec)	2252	303	1781	941

Comparing RSA-512, we find that proposed algorithm is 7.4 times faster than RSA-512, 1.2 times faster than AES, and 2.4 times faster than DES at encryption. Hence, we can observe that our cryptosystem takes less time for encryption compared to RSA, AES and DES cryptosystem for the given plaintext size. In Sect. 4.2, we discussed the security strengths of our algorithm and other encryption algorithms. According to Table 1, we can conclude that our algorithm has the same security strength as the RSA-1024. Thus, we can conclude that our algorithm is faster than RSA in encryption and the key length can be lower at the same level of security.

5 Conclusion

The paper described a public key cryptosystem, which is based on hash. At the same security strength, our encryption algorithm has a shorter key length than RSA. Meanwhile, there are deficiencies in our algorithm because the cost of decryption is too expensive. Therefore, the proposed algorithm is more suitable for super nodes in wireless sensor networks with unlimited energy.

References

1. Garg, S., Gentry, C., Halevi, S., et al.: Hiding secrets in software: a cryptographic approach to program obfuscation. Commun. ACM **59**(5), 113–120 (2016)
2. Nagaraj, S., Raju, G., Srinadth, V.: Data encryption and authetication using public key approach. Procedia Comput. Sci. **48**, 126–132 (2015)
3. Sasdrich, P., Güneysu, T.: Efficient elliptic-curve cryptography using Curve25519 on reconfigurable devices. In: Goehringer, D., Santambrogio, M.D., Cardoso, J.M.P., Bertels, K. (eds.) ARC 2014. LNCS, vol. 8405, pp. 25–36. Springer, Cham (2014). https://doi.org/10.1007/978-3-319-05960-0_3
4. Miri, J., Nsiri, B., Bouallegue, R.: Privacy group distance bounding protocol on TH-UWB based NTRU public key cryptosystem. In: 2017 Sixth International Conference on Communications and Networking, Hammamet, pp. 1–7 (2017)
5. Junli, F., Yawen, W., Haibin, S.: An improved energy-efficient routing algorithm in software define wireless sensor network. In: 2017 IEEE International Conference on Signal Processing, Communications and Computing, pp. 1–5. IEEE (2017)
6. Suryadevara, N.K., Mukhopadhyay, S.C., Kelly, S.D.T.: WSN-based smart sensors and actuator for power management in intelligent buildings. IEEE Trans. Mechatron. **20**(2), 564–571 (2015)
7. Hellman, M.: A cryptanalytic time-memory trade-off. IEEE Trans. Inf. Theory **26**(4), 401–406 (1980)
8. Lu, H., Zhu, X., Gan, Z.: A blocked rainbow table time-memory trade-off method. In: 12th Web Information System and Application Conference, Jinan, pp. 324–329 (2015)
9. Tian, Y., Gu, D., Gu, H., Ding, N.: Improved cryptanalytic of time-memory trade-off based on rainbow table. In: ICINS 2014, 2014 International Conference on Information and Network Security, Beijing, pp. 97–104 (2014)
10. Hong, J., Moon, S.: A comparison of cryptanalytic tradeoff algorithms. J. Cryptol. **26**(4), 559–637 (2013)
11. Gupta, P., Kumar, S.: A comparative analysis of SHA and MD5 algorithm. Architecture **1**, 5 (2014)
12. Shah, D.: Digital security using cryptographic message digest algorithm. Int. J. Adv. Res. Comput. Sci. Manag. Stud. **3**(10) (2015)
13. Lu, Y., Zhai, J., Zhu, R., et al.: Study of wireless authentication center with mixed encryption in WSN. J. Sens. **2016** (2016)
14. Lee, G.W., Hong, J.: Comparison of perfect table cryptanalytic tradeoff algorithms. Des. Codes Cryptogr. **80**(3), 473–523 (2016)
15. Date, W., Note, W.: Archived NIST Technical Series Publication. NIST Special Publication 800-26 (1992)

A Homomorphic Masking Defense Scheme Based on RSA Cryptography Algorithm

Juanmei Zhang[1], Zichen Li[2(✉)], Yafei Sun[1,3(✉)], Boya Liu[1], and Yatao Yang[1,3]

[1] Beijing Electronic Science and Technology Institute, Beijing 100070, China
yfsun0112@163.com

[2] Beijing Institute of Graphic Communication, Beijing 102600, China
lizc2020@163.com

[3] College of Communication Engineering, Xidian University, Xi'an 710071, China

Abstract. Aiming at the implement of RSA algorithm, the attack methods are variety. In order to ensure the algorithm can against the side channel attack, in this paper, we present a masking scheme for RSA decryption. Our scheme exploits the multiply-homomorphic property of the existing RSA encryption scheme to compute an multiply-mask as an encryption of a random message and randomly splits the secret key into two shares as the sub-calculate such that each share is statistically independent from the original value. Our solution differs in several aspects from the recent masking RSA implementation. According to encrypted random number, the original ciphertext is blinded and the splitting secret key can reduce the size of the key and speed up the calculation of the algorithm. During the decryption, all the operations are under the masking state, therefore, through multiply masking and secret key splitting, we can secure a RSA implementation, the scheme we proposed can against the timing attack, simple power attack and differential power attack. Compared with others, this scheme can reach a higher calculation and security level.

Keywords: RSA cryptographic algorithm · Side channel attack
Homomorphic · Side channel attack defense · Masking

1 Introduction

Paul Kocher has proposed the conception of timing attack [1] in 1996. From now on, it begins the research of side channel attack and defense. At present, the analysis of side channel is mainly containing the analysis method, the countermeasure method and the security evaluation index and other aspect at home and abroad. The side channel attack is mainly containing the timing attack, simple power attack, differential power attack, Cache attack, fault attack and electromagnetic analysis. Among them, the power attack is one of the most important and effective methods.

Power attack [2] was presented by Kocher in 1999, it can obtain the secret information through analysis the power consumption of the cipher device, and it belongs to

X. Sun et al. (Eds.): ICCCS 2018, LNCS 11065, pp. 393–402, 2018.
https://doi.org/10.1007/978-3-030-00012-7_36

the non-intrusive attack. Generally speaking, the instantaneous power consumption of the cipher device is related to its operations and the data which needed to be process. The attacker can use the statistical analysis method to analysis the power traces which are collected while the cipher is work, and obtain the secret key through the power traces finally.

The RSA cryptography algorithm is one of the most famous algorithm which was presented by Rivest et al. [3] in 1978. At present, the RSA algorithm is widely used in main industries and the research of it is quite mature. At the same time, because of its wide application, a large number of researchers have analyzed the vulnerability of the algorithm. The typical methods of mathematical analysis includes: the small index attack of RSA [4], the non-common mode attack and common mode attack [5], cyclic attack [6] and other methods. The methods [1, 2] which are presented by Kocher are different from the traditional attack method. From now on, it begins the research of side channel attack based on RSA.

At present, there are many articles of side channel attacks based on RSA cryptography. Based on the different time consumption and the different operation, Kocher [1] analysis the timing attack. Finke [7] according the power traces to decide the decompose of the prime, which is happened in the step of key generation. The method presented by Vuillaume [8] can effectively reconstructed the prime number generator of RSA, also in this paper, they proposed the template attack and fault attack based on RSA. Yen [9] through the special values −X and X to construct a method of Chosen Plaintext Attack and proved that the method is effective for most commonly used simple power attack protection measures. Through analysis the hardware implementation of RSA and combine the special chosen plaintext to implement the simple power attack, Miyamoto [10] finally get the secret key. Zhang [11] analysis the RSA signature implementation using Montgomerie multiplication, they make a successful attack on RSA protection scheme with a random fill function.

There are many defense measures corresponding to the attack method aimed at RSA. Fouque [12] aimed at the realization of software and hardware of modular power operation of RSA cipher algorithm, they proposed the software protection measures based on random probability and the hardware protection measures based on exponentiation of exponentiation in three binary system. In order to eliminate the power difference between operation units, the realization of equal power coding for power operation is proposed, and this method have achieved good results [13]. In order to solve the problem of slow speed and low efficiency in side channel attack defense scheme, Zhao [14] proposed an improved window sliding algorithm, which using the key iterative processing, while the Precalculation only produces the odd power of the remainder table, making the efficiency improved significantly. Also, through randomization the pseudo operation, while ensuring the security of the algorithm circuit, it can save power and time effectively [15]. Yen [16] proposed a method to defense the fault attack.

In this paper, we analysis the RSA cryptography algorithm, combined the homomorphic property of RSA with the key segmentation technology, a homomorphic masking defense scheme was proposed. This scheme is easy to implement and the security is higher than other schemes.

2 Knowledge

In this section, we first introduce the theory of RSA, and then we introduce the RSA algorithm.

Definition 1. Assume that a, b, m are integer. If $m|(a-b)$, then a and b is congruence while mode m, it can be written as $a \equiv b(\bmod m)$. m is called as the modulus of the congruence.

Theorem 1 (Chinese remainder theorem). Assume that $m_1, m_2, \cdots, m_n$ are inter prime with each other, $a_1, a_2, \cdots, a_n$ are integers, then the congruence equation $x \equiv a_i(\bmod m_i), i = 1, 2, \cdots, n \bmod M$, $M = m_1 m_2 \cdots m_n$ has only one result:

$$x = \sum_{i=1}^{n} a_i M_i y_i \bmod M \quad M_i = M/m_i, y_i = M_i^{-1} \bmod m_i, i = 1, 2, \cdots, n \tag{1}$$

Definition 2. Assume that n is an integer, the Euler function is defined as: $\phi(n) \underline{\underline{def}} |\{x | 0 \leq x \leq n-1, \gcd(x, n) = 1\}|$.

Theorem 2 (Eluer theorem). x and n are integers, if $\gcd(x, n) = 1$, then $x^{\phi(n)} \equiv 1 \bmod n$.

Theorem 3 (Fermat's little theorem). x and p are integers, if p is prime and $\gcd(x, p) = 1$, then $x^{p-1} \equiv 1 \bmod p$.

The RSA cryptography algorithm is based on the theory above, its essence is based on the problem of hard decomposition of large integers. The algorithm is contain three section: key generate algorithm, encryption algorithm, decryption algorithm. they are described as follows:

1. randomly chosen two different big prime p and q.
2. according to p and q, do the calculate $n = pq$, and the n is public.
3. calculate the $\varphi(n) = (p-1)(q-1)$, and the $\varphi(n)$ is secret.
4. randomly chosen integer $e \in Z, 1 < e < \varphi(n)$, and $(e, \varphi(n)) = 1$, then e is public.
5. calculate d according to e, and it is satisfied $ed = 1 \bmod \varphi(n)$, d is secret.
6. encryption: the input information is represented as an integer $m \in [0, n-1]$, calculate $c = m^e \bmod n$, output c as the ciphertext.
7. decryption: calculate $m = c^d = (m^e)^d \bmod n$.

In order to know more clearly the algorithm and explain the correctness of the algorithm, we analysis it as follow:

According to the construction of the algorithm, because of $ed = 1 \bmod \varphi(n)$, namely:

$$ed = r\varphi(n) + 1, \ m = c^d = (m^e)^d = m^{ed} \tag{2}$$

so, we can know that the core calculate of RSA is modular exponentiation.

3 Analysis of RSA Algorithm

In this section, we use the software jcryptool to make a simple power attack of RSA, and according this result to make an analysis of RSA.

Firstly, the parameters of RSA should be setting as follow (Fig. 1):

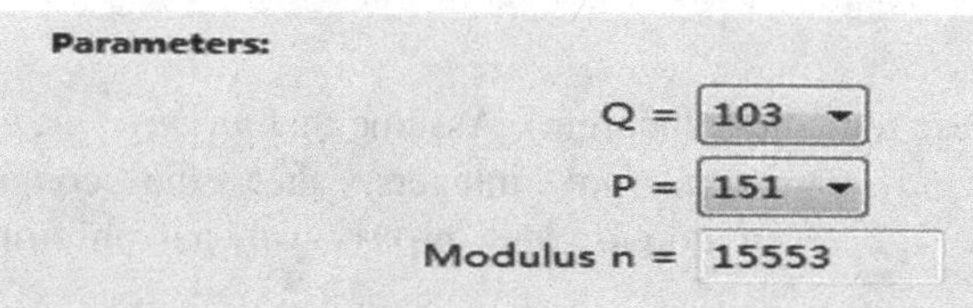

Fig. 1. The parameters of RSA

Then, we chose the ciphertext and the private key as follow (Fig. 2):

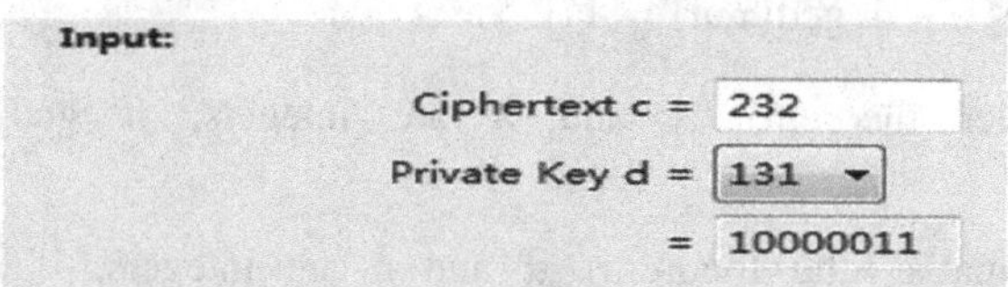

Fig. 2. The key of RSA

According to the setting of this algorithm, the calculate result is (Fig. 3):

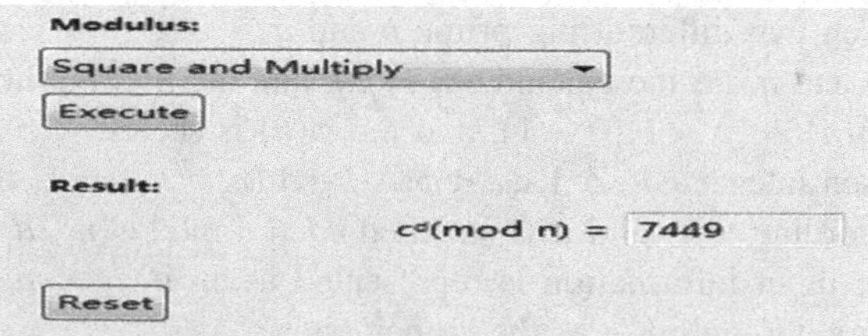

Fig. 3. The result of RSA calculate

The processing of peer bit is as follow (Fig. 4):

From this result we can know that when the bit is 0, the algorithm do the square calculate, and when the bit is 1, the algorithm do the square and multiply calculate. So the power consumption can be indicated as follow (Fig. 5):

Compared the result with the setting key, we can know that through the simple power attack, we can recovery the key clearly. From the result above, we can know that the different operation with the different bit leads to the information leakage. In order to

Round Counter(left to right)	Result after square	Result after multiply
Input: $R_1 = 1$	$S_i = R_i^2 \bmod n$	$R_{i+1} = S_i * c \bmod n$ if highest bit = 1
		$R_{i+1} = S_i$ if highest bit = 0
Process:		
1. highest bit = 1	$S_1 = 1^2 \bmod 15553 = 1$	$R_2 = 1 * 232 \bmod 15553 = 232$
2. highest bit = 0	$S_2 = 232^2 \bmod 15553 = 7165$	
3. highest bit = 0	$S_3 = 7165^2 \bmod 15553 = 12325$	
4. highest bit = 0	$S_4 = 12325^2 \bmod 15553 = 15027$	
5. highest bit = 0	$S_5 = 15027^2 \bmod 15553 = 12275$	
6. highest bit = 0	$S_6 = 12275^2 \bmod 15553 = 13714$	
7. highest bit = 1	$S_7 = 13714^2 \bmod 15553 = 6920$	$R_8 = 6920 * 232 \bmod 15553 = 3481$
8. highest bit = 1	$S_8 = 3481^2 \bmod 15553 = 1574$	$R_9 = 1574 * 232 \bmod 15553 = 7449$
Output:		
Final Result: 7449		

Fig. 4. The calculate of peer bit

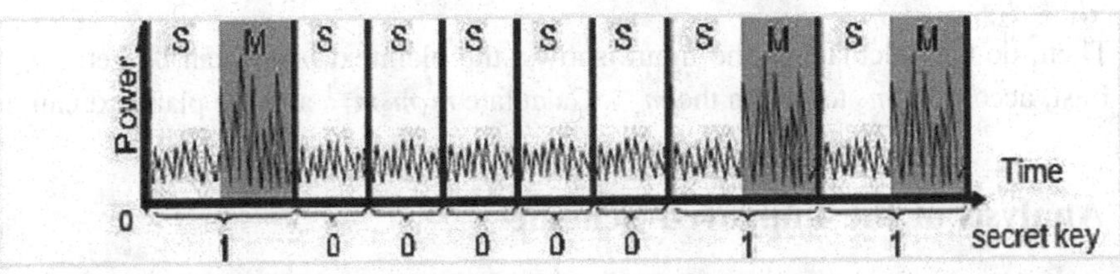

Fig. 5. The SPA result of RSA

defense the attacker obtain the information, the countermeasure we used is randomize the intermediate values.

4 Homomorphic Masking Scheme Based on RSA

Homomorphic property analysis of RSA:

The ciphertext c_1 and c_2 is corresponding to the plaintext m_1 and m_2. The cipher can be calculated as:

$$c_1 \cdot c_2 = (m_1)^e \cdot (m_2)^e = (m_1 m_2)^e = E(m_1 m_2) \tag{3}$$

According to the cipher, we can decryption as:

$$(c_1 \cdot c_2)^d = (c_1)^e \cdot (c_2)^e = (m_1)^{ed} (m_2)^{ed} = (m_1 m_2)^{ed} = m_1 m_2 \tag{4}$$

The algorithm can decryption correctly. So, we know the algorithm is multiply homomorphic property.

Masking scheme:

According to the homomorphic property of RSA and the key splitting technology, a homomorphic masking scheme is proposed as follow (Fig. 6):

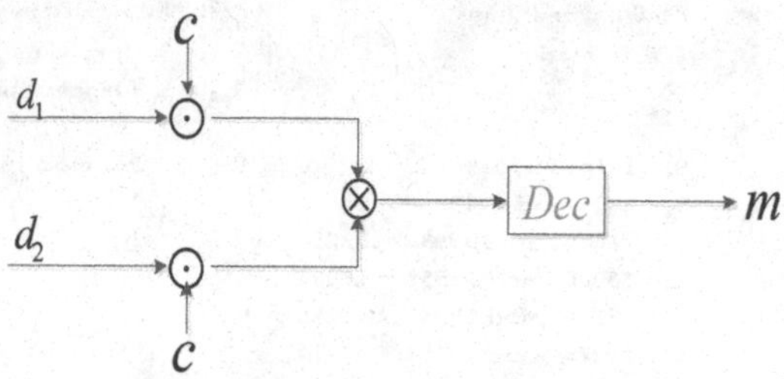

Fig. 6. The masking scheme of RSA

In this scheme, when a cipher c_1 is sending to do decrypt, a random number m_2 is generated and encrypted as c_2, then calculate the ciphertext as: $c = c_1c_2$.

Then, the secret key is randomly splitting into two parts, the sub key is satisfied as $d = d_1 + d_2$.

Then, do the calculate as the figure shows, the plaintext m_1m_2 can be get.

Last, according m_2 to obtain the m_2^{-1}. Calculate $m_1m_2m_2^{-1}$ and the plaintext can get.

5 Analysis of the Improved Scheme

Correctness: In this section, the correctness of RSA is verified. In the decryption processing, the calculate is:

$$m_1m_2 = ((m_1m_2)^e)^d = c^d = c^{d_1+d_2} = c^{d_1}c^{d_2} \tag{5}$$

So, when the m_2^{-1} is calculated, the real plaintext can be obtained. Namely, the improved scheme is correctness.

Security: In this scheme, the information m_2 is a random number, and the secret key d is randomly splitting, the timing and the power consumption can be confused. So the side channel attack can't be implemented, namely, the security of the scheme can be ensured.

Against timing attack: the core idea of timing attack is to judge the value of the key by the system's response time difference. In this scheme, the secret key is randomly splitting into two shares, the attack can't know the begin station of every sub key, so the attacker can't rebuild the key, even if the attacker can get some information of the secret key. The secret key is splitting in peer calculated, so it can enlarge the difficult to get obtain the key.

Against the power attack: the core idea of power attack is the different power consumption of the different bit, in order to against it, the masking technology is common countermeasure. In this scheme, the key splitting and homomorphic masking are all used to against the power attack. So the intermediate values are changed, the dependency between the data are eliminated.

If the algorithm is taking the serial calculation method, because of the key is randomly splitting, the attacker can't know the splitting position, namely, they can't rebuild the key. If the algorithm is taking parallel calculation method, the power consumption is superimposed, it is difficult to implement the simple power attack.

The key-splitting technology is a way to defend against first-order differential power attack, it can eliminate the dependency between data. While this scheme adding the homomorphic masking data, this scheme can against the second-order differential power attack. Because of every step is randomly calculate, the intermediate values of each calculation are different, it can be proved to against the second-order differential power attack.

Compare: in order to against the power attack, the modulus n can be blinded as nr, and the index d can be blinded as $d = d + r\phi$, among it the r is a random number [17]. Also, it can be designed as when the bit is 0, the system judge whether a random number is 0 or 1, if it is 1, then it do the same operation as the bit 1, this can reduce the amount of modular multiplication, it can improve the efficiency of the scheme [18]. In this scheme, the secret key splits into two shares, and the random number is encrypted as the masking data. Compared with the other schemes, our scheme has the following advantages:

1. The random number m_2 is generated by the decryption, the attacker can't control it, so it can ensure the system's security. Namely, this method can be used to against the first-order differential power attack.
2. The secret key is randomly splitting into two shares, the sub key calculate is c^{d_i}, compared with the original operation c^d, the size of the key is reduced, the timing consumption also can be reduced. In the same time, the key splitting technology can be used to against the first-order differential power attack, combined the random number above, this scheme can against the second-order differential power attack.
3. Homomorphic decryption. In this scheme, we used the property of the RSA algorithm, so it ensures that the program can decrypt correctly. Compared with the other masking scheme as boolean masking, this method needn't a lookup table. So it needn't used the lookup table repeat. All in all, this scheme can be implemented easily and quickly.

6 Experimental Simulation

In this section, the correctness of the improved scheme is verified through software programming. The experimental environment is the common computer (CPU is Inter Core i5-3470m 3.20 GHz) and the compiling environment is Dev-C++. Setting $p = 11, q = 13$ and the plaintext $m_1 = 47, m_2 = 19$, the result is as follows:

Firstly, the original algorithm is verified according to m_1, the result is as follows, we can know that the algorithm can correctness calculate (Figs. 7 and 8):

Then, the proposed scheme is verified, the sub key is manual mode setting, through calculate with the different sub key, the scheme can be correctness decryption (Figs. 9, 10 and 11):

```
please input the p,q: 11 13
the n is 143
the t is 120
please input the e: 13
then caculate out that the d is 37
Encryption please enter:  1
Decryption please enter:  2
1
Please enter plaintext m: 47
Result of encryption is:  60
```

Fig. 7. The original encryption of RSA

```
please input the p,q: 11 13
the n is 143
the t is 120
please input the e: 13
then caculate out that the d is 37
Encryption please enter:  1
Decryption please enter:  2
2
Please enter ciphertext c: 60
Result of decryption is:  47
```

Fig. 8. The original decryption of RSA

```
please input the p,q: 11 13
the n is 143
the t is 120
please input the e: 13
then caculate out that the d is 37
Please enter the random number:
19
Please enter the ciphertext:
60
Please enter the random sub-key 1:
17
Please enter the random sub-key 2:
20
The decryption result of sub-key 1:   68
The decryption result of sub-key 2:   133
The result of masking decryption is:   35
The final result of decryption is:  47
```

Fig. 9. Masking decryption 1

```
please input the p,q: 11 13
the n is 143
the t is 120
please input the e: 13
then caculate out that the d is 37
Please enter the random number:
19
Please enter the ciphertext:
60
Please enter the random sub-key 1:
14
Please enter the random sub-key 2:
23
The decryption result of sub-key 1:   81
The decryption result of sub-key 2:   94
The result of masking decryption is:   35
The final result of decryption is:   47
```

Fig. 10. Masking decryption 2

```
please input the p,q: 11 13
the n is 143
the t is 120
please input the e: 13
then caculate out that the d is 37
Please enter the random number:
19
Please enter the ciphertext:
60
Please enter the random sub-key 1:
18
Please enter the random sub-key 2:
19
The decryption result of sub-key 1:   27
The decryption result of sub-key 2:  139
The result of masking decryption is:   35
The final result of decryption is:   47
```

Fig. 11. Masking decryption 1

According to the above results, we can see that the time consumption of the improved implementation is same with the original scheme. To sum up, in the same experimental environment, the correctness of the proposed scheme is verified by programming, and the computation efficiency is almost equal to that of the non-masking scheme. Also, in the part 5, the security analysis has present that the scheme can against the side channel attack.

7 Conclusion

Based on the analysis of the RSA cipher algorithm, it is pointed out that it can't resist the characteristics of the side channel attack, analyze its multiplicative homomorphism characteristics, and combine this property with the key splitting technology, a homomorphic masking scheme is proposed. The security and correctness of the scheme can be proved, and this scheme can effectively against the timing attack, simple power attack and differential power attack. Compared with other scheme, this scheme has high security, low system overhead and easy implementation.

Acknowledgment. This work was supported by the National Natural Science Foundation of China (No. 61370188); The Scientific Research Common Program of Beijing Municipal Commission of Education (Nos. KM201610015002, KM201510015009); "13th Five-Year" National Cryptography Development Foundation (No. 20170110); The Beijing City Board of Education Science and technology key project (Nos. KZ201510015015, KZ201710015010); Project of Beijing Municipal College Improvement Plan (No. PXM2017_014223_000063); 2018 Academic innovation team of digital copyright protection (No. 041901180021093); BIGC Project (Nos. Ec201803, Ed201802, Ea201806).

References

1. Kocher, P.: Timing attacks on implementations of Diffie-Hellman, RSA, DSS, and other systems. In: Koblitz, N. (ed.) CRYPTO 1996. LNCS, vol. 1109, pp. 104–113. Springer, Heidelberg (1996). https://doi.org/10.1007/3-540-68697-5_9
2. Kocher, P., Jaffe, J., Jun, B.: Differential power analysis. In: Wiener, M. (ed.) CRYPTO 1999. LNCS, vol. 1666, pp. 388–397. Springer, Heidelberg (1999). https://doi.org/10.1007/3-540-48405-1_25

3. Rivest, R., Shamir, A., Adleman, L.: A method for obtaining digital signatures and public key cryptosystems. Commun. ACM **21**(2), 120–126 (1978)
4. Han, L., Wang, X., Xu, G.: On an attack on RSA with small CRT-exponents. Sci. China: Inf. Sci. **41**(2), 173–180 (2011)
5. Zou, H., Yu, M., Wang, J.: An prime generating scheme to avoid effectively common modulus attack on RSA. Comput. Eng. Appl. **27**, 88–89+153 (2004)
6. Jiang, Z., Huai, J., Wang, Y.: Investigation and analysis of the weakness and efficiency of genaralized cycling attacks on RSA modulus. J. Commun. **30**(6), 70–74 (2009)
7. Finke, T., Gebhardt, M., Schindler, W.: A new side-channel attack on RSA prime generation. In: Clavier, C., Gaj, K. (eds.) CHES 2009. LNCS, vol. 5747, pp. 141–155. Springer, Heidelberg (2009). https://doi.org/10.1007/978-3-642-04138-9_11
8. Vuillaume, C., Endo, T., Wooderson, P.: RSA key generation: new attacks. In: Schindler, W., Huss, S.A. (eds.) COSADE 2012. LNCS, vol. 7275, pp. 105–119. Springer, Heidelberg (2012). https://doi.org/10.1007/978-3-642-29912-4_9
9. Yen, S.M., Lien, W.C., Moon, S., Ha, J.: Power analysis by exploiting chosen message and internal collisions – vulnerability of checking mechanism for RSA-decryption. In: Dawson, E., Vaudenay, S. (eds.) Mycrypt 2005. LNCS, vol. 3715, pp. 183–195. Springer, Heidelberg (2005). https://doi.org/10.1007/11554868_13
10. Miyamoto, A., Homma, N., Aoki, T., et al.: Enhanced power analysis attack using chosen message against RSA hardware implementations. In: IEEE International Symposium on Circuits and Systems, pp. 3282–3285. IEEE (2008)
11. Zhang, B., Yin, X.: Secure and efficient implementation for RSA cryptographic algorithm. Acta Scientiarum Naturalium Universitatis Sunyatseni **47**(6), 22–26 (2008)
12. Fouque, P.A., Guillermin, N., Leresteux, D., et al.: Attacking RSA–CRT signatures with faults on montgomery multiplication. J. Cryptogr. Eng. **3**(1), 447–462 (2013)
13. Chen, Y., Wu, Z., Chen, J., et al.: Implementation of equivalent power consumption coding secure against side channel attack. J. Univ. Electron. Sci. Technol. China **37**(2), 168–171 (2008)
14. Zhao, Y., Zhao, J., Han, M.: An improved window algorithm for RSA against side channel attack. Comput. Eng. **39**(6), 150–154 (2013)
15. Han, J., Zeng, X., Tang, T.: Power trace analysis attack and countermeasures for RSA cryptographic circuits. Chin. J. Comput. **29**(4), 4590–4596 (2006)
16. Yen, S.M., Joye, M.: Checking before output may not be enough against fault-based cryptanalysis. IEEE Trans. Comput. **49**(9), 967–970 (2000)
17. Ren, Y., Wu, L., Li, X., et al.: Design and implementation of a side-channel resistant and low power RSA processor. J. Tsinghua Univ. (Sci. Technol.) **56**(1), 1–6 (2016)
18. Zhang, B., Zhong, W.: Improvement of RSA algorithm to resist side-channel attacks in PTM. Mod. Electron. Tech. **39**(19), 67–70+75 (2016)

A New Dependency Parsing Tree Generation Algorithm Based on the Semantic Dependency Relationship Between Words

Jin Han[(✉)], Wen Long Xu, and Yu Ting Jing

Nan Jin University of Information Science & Technology, Nanjin, China
hjhaohj@126.com

Abstract. In this paper it presents a new dependency parsing tree (DPT) generation algorithm. Different from other similar algorithms, which based on statistical probability model, the algorithm converts the dependency parsing tree generation problem into a semantic segments dividing problem. In this paper, the co-occurrence frequency of words is firstly analyzed, and it is pointed out that the co-occurrence frequency of words can be used as the basis for the judgment of semantic dependence relationship between words. Then it further analyzes the change of co-occurrence frequency entropy of words in a semantic unit (sentence is used as the basic semantic unit in this paper). And we present an algorithm to divide a sentence into semantic fragments in which words has tight semantic relationship with each other. Based on the above work, this paper divides the DPT generation algorithm into three steps. The first step is to divide the sentence into semantic fragments. The second step is to distinguish semantic core word and non-semantic core words according to the semantic dependency relationship between words in a semantic fragment. Then in the last step the DPT is generated according semantic dependency relationship between semantic core words. Based on court documents which collected from web, the experiments of our DPT generation algorithm are conducted in this paper. And the results show that the DPT generation algorithm in this paper maintains a high degree of consistency with the DPT tree generated by human.

Keywords: Dependency parsing tree · Semantic dependency relationship
Words co-occurrence relationship · Semantic fragments

1 The Introduction

Dependency parsing is a key research field in natural language processing research. The goal of dependency parsing research is to put forward an algorithm that can analysis the structure of sentences in texts and then construct the modification relationship between the words in the sentence. Dependency parsing can get structured information of the sentence. This information can not only describe components of a sentence and relationships between these components, but also be used to extract a certain amount of information on the level of sentence semantics. Thus, dependency parsing is a deep technique in natural language analysis. It is often used as underlying technology to support semantic analysis and pragmatic information analysis. And it

X. Sun et al. (Eds.): ICCCS 2018, LNCS 11065, pp. 403–411, 2018.
https://doi.org/10.1007/978-3-030-00012-7_37

also plays an important role in text semantic analysis, named entity recognition, text information extraction and other applications, and so on.

According to the Nivre's review article [1], the study of the dependency parsing started from the work of Tesniere [2]. Tesniere believes that each sentence has a complete internal structure, which consists of the central word of the sentence (called head) and the relationship between the head word with other words of the sentence. There are also many grammar theories about dependency parsing, such as word grammar [3], function generative description [4] and so on. In general, dependency parsing problem can be formulated as follows:

$$f : x \rightarrow y \tag{1}$$

In this formula, x represents an input text and y represents structured information which is produced by dependency parsing algorithm according to the input text. Usually the structured information which produced by a dependency parsing algorithm is defined as a tree, and it is called dependency parsing tree (DPT). Each nodes of a DPT represents a component of the input text, and the relationships between nodes in a DPT also represent the relationship between sentence components.

At present, the DPT generation algorithm can be divided into four kinds mainly, as shown in the following list:

- Dependency parsing algorithm based on graph, the algorithms are proposed mainly in [5–7]. In those works a text is mapped into a graph. The set of vertices of the graph represents the words of the sentence and directed edges of the graph indicate the dependency relationships between the words of the sentence. Then a function is used to get scores according to the edges of different graphs which mapped from a sentence. The graph which gets the highest score is the result of dependency parsing.
- Dependency parsing algorithm based on transition, the algorithms are proposed mainly in [8–10]. This class of algorithm is treat dependency parsing as transition from one status to another status. Using formal semantics to define conversion-based analyzers, analyzing words in sentences one by one by greedy algorithms strategy.
- Dependency parsing algorithm based on maximum entropy, the algorithms are proposed mainly in [11]. Those algorithms first need to mark the data sets of dependency relationship between words. According to the data sets, extract the features of train corpus. Then finishes the distributions of feature variables according to the maximum entropy theory. When doing dependency parsing on target text, first find two words from the text and extract the feature, then calculate the probability of all kinds of dependency relationship between the two words, and choose the dependency relationship with the highest probability. Conduct this process for a few times to complete the dependency calculation of the two words in the text. Then, sort the probability of dependencies between the two words, using the minimum spanning tree algorithm to construct the dependency parsing tree.
- Dependency parsing algorithm based on conditional random field (CRF), the algorithms are proposed mainly in [12]. Those Algorithms realizes dependency

parsing based on the CRF also needs a large number of marked training text set. CRF extracts feature functions by using the sequence of part-of-speech tagging in the text sentence, and uses CRF model to train the text set. Then sum up the counts of feature function in the sentence and figure out the parameter values in CRF model by gradient descent or other optimal iterations, so that P (X|Y) is the largest in the sequence of part-of-speech tagging. After the training, P(X|Y) can be used to predict the maximum probability of the dependency relationship between the two words in the sentence, and then build the dependency parsing tree. According to the literature [53], the accuracy rate can reach 76.6%.

Both of the dependency parsing algorithm based on maximum entropy and the dependency parsing algorithm based on (CRF) require a lot of tagged data sets, but the CRF considers the information brought by sequence of tagged words in the text, which is the difference between CRF based alforithm and maximum entropy based alforithm. This kind of information can help to make judgement on the dependency parsing between words and bring more features. However, organized training data set is a heavy task. Due to the complexity of the change of text word organization, the distribution model obtained through maximum entropy and CRF model is difficult to achieve satisfactory results. According to the experimental results in the literature [51], 87.42% accuracy was found. However, according to the experimental results in the text [52], the correct results of the experiment on the development test set was 65.98%.

This paper proposes a dependency parsing algorithm based on semantic dependency. Through the analysis of the co-occurrence relationship of words, the paper gives a method to judge the semantic dependency relationship of each word in the sequence of text words. Using this method, this paper presented the dependency parsing algorithm based on semantic dependency. This algorithm first cut the sentences in the text into segments that are closely semantically rely on each other so that realize the construction of dependency parsing tree of text. This paper carries out the experiment on dependency parsing tree construction using text data set of court documents. The experimental results show that the algorithm realized in this paper has good semantic segment classification accuracy. The results and artificial built dependency parsing tree are highly consistent.

2 The Algorithm of Word Semantic Dependency Relationship Judgment Based on Co-occurrence Frequency

2.1 The Semantic Correlation Relationship Between Words and the Semantic Dependency Relationship Between Words

As mentioned above, the dependency parsing is to find the modification relationship between the words in the text, and the words with the modifier relationship in the text must also be closely and semantically related. Therefore, if we can determine the segments of sequences in the text that are closely related, then every subtree of the dependency paring spanning tree, and the construction of dependency parsing tree can be completed by seeking further for the modified relation of segments of word sequence that are corresponding to the subtree. Therefore, the construction of dependency parsing actually consists of two problems: how to divide the text into the segments of word list that are semantic closely related, and how to judge the relationship between words.

This paper argues that the second problem can be resolved by the answer to the first question. If the semantic closely related segments of word list in the text can be analyzed, then the semantically related degree of the words in the text can be determined. Thus, it can be considered that there is a modification relationship between words with close semantic relevance. For the first question, this paper converts the semantic relativity analysis of words into semantic dependency relationship analysis.

This idea is very straightforward, because there must be a dependency on the semantic meaning of words that have semantic relevance in a sentence. Take sentence "red apple is delicious" as an example. After removing "red" or "delicious", the sentence is still semantically understandable. But if the word "apple" is removed, the meaning of the sentence becomes unintelligible. Therefore, the two words "red" and "delicious" in this sentence have semantic dependence on the word "apple". On the contrary, if a sentence can be divided into several word sequence segments, and each segment is semantic comprehensible, there is obviously no semantic dependency between the words of different segments. Hence, the semantic dependence of words can be used as the semantic correlation judgment basis of the segments of word list. In this paper, if the word wi forms a semantic dependency on the word wj, it is recorded as: $w_i \rightarrow w_j$

2.2 The Algorithm of the Semantic Dependency Relationship Judgment

Suppose there are two adjacent words w1, w2 in a word list L. How to judge whether w1 depends on w2 semantically or w2 depends on w1? This paper uses the co-occurrence frequency of words to realize the judgment on semantic dependency relationship between words. The co-occurrence frequency of words is derived from the co-occurrence relationship statistics of words. The co-occurrence relationship statistics of words is the number of times that the word w and other different words appear together in the same text semantic unit. Because there are many types of text semantic unit, including chapters, sections, paragraphs, sentences and components of sentences, etc., except from components of sentences which is not easy to divide, other semantic unit can be directly obtained from the corpus format. But considering the problem discussed in this paper, this paper uses sentences as semantic unit to count the co-occurrence relation in corpora.

Assuming that in corpora C, there is a word wi. Using sentences as semantic units, the co-occurrence of word wi and the word wj in all the sentences can be counted. We use X_{ij} to represent it. The co-occurrence of the word wi and all the other words in the corpus is denoted as X_i. It is clearly that $X_i = \sum_1^v X_{wij}$, in which v is the length of all the word set in the whole corpus. Says that $p(ij) = p(j|i) = X_{ij}/X_i$ is the co-occurrence of the word wi and word wj. It can be seen from the co-occurrence frequency of the words that if in a corpus $X_{ij} = X_{ji}$, $X_i \neq X_j$, then $p(ij) \neq p(ji)$.

By the definition of word co-occurrence frequency, if there is p (ij) > p (ji), then $X_i < X_j$, co-occurrence of word wj and other words in the corpus C is relatively bigger than the word wi. It also means that word wj have more opportunities to appear in different semantic unit. Therefore, from the perspective of semantic dependency, wj has more opportunities to form a semantic dependency relationship with other words.

This paper proposes a semantic dependency relationship judgment algorithm, as shown below:

The algorithm of words semantic dependency relationship Judgment

---

1. **Get the vocabulary V for Croup C**
2. **Constructs Matrix P**
   a) **For row_i in P which represents word W_i in the V**
      i. **Get Sentences in which w_i occurs**
      ii. **For each sentence, get a word collection W except for Wi**
      iii. **Update Xi and X_{ij} according to W**
   b) **Divides each X_{ij} in row_i by Xi**
3. **If there are two words w_i and w_j in a same semantic unit**
   a) **Get $P_{x_{ij}}$,$P_{x_{ji}}$ from the matrix P**
   b) **If $P_{x_{ij}}$>$P_{x_{ji}}$, then $w_i \rightarrow w_j$, else $w_j \rightarrow w_i$**

---

3 Semantic Parsing Algorithm Based on Semantic Dependency

3.1 The Core Words Solving Based on Word Co-occurrence Entropy

As mentioned in Sect. 2 above, each line in the P matrix constructed in the algorithm represents the co-occurrence frequency between one word and the other words in the text. It is denoted as the co-occurrence frequency vector V_i for the word w_i. Therefore, the co-occurrence frequency entropy of the word can be calculated according to the vector V_i:

$$H(w_i) = -\sum_{j}^{v} p_{ij} \log\left(p_{ij}\right) \tag{2}$$

According to the theory of information entropy, the greater the entropy value of w_i means the more words have a co-occurrence relationship with w_i. According to the semantic dependency relationship of the words in the second section, the larger the frequency entropy of a word in a sentence means that it has less semantic dependency of the other words in the sentence.

Considering the sentence: "The defendant Shang Senhua committed corruption and was sentenced to one year and eight months in prison, the probation for two years and a fine of one hundred and twenty thousand yuan (Payment shall be made within one month from the second day of the ruling)". After removing the function words in the sentence, according to the co-occurrence matrix obtained from the experiment in the fourth section of this paper, the notional word co-occurrence frequency entropy can be calculated. It is shown in Fig. 1.

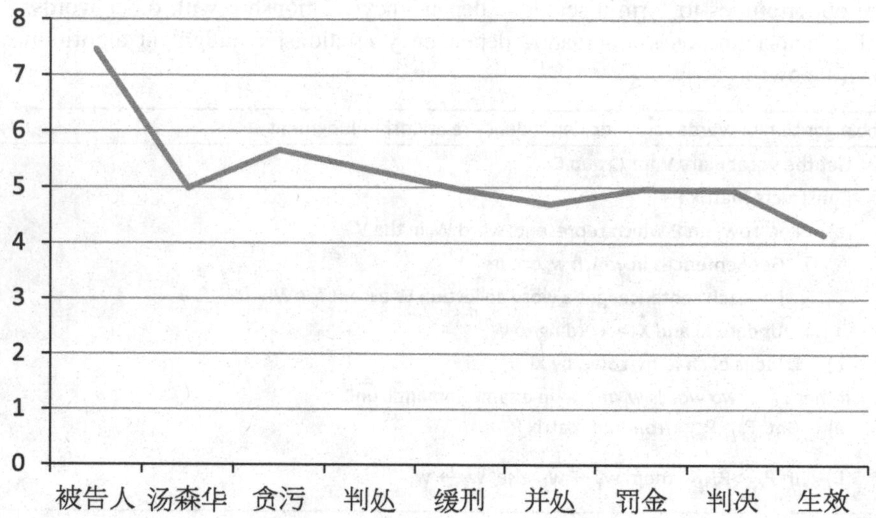

Fig. 1. The co-occurrence frequency entropy of the notional words in the examples.

Figure 1 shows the entropy sequence of the notional words that is sorted in according to the sentence order. It can be seen from the graph that the entropy sequence presents certain fluctuation. There are two turning points from decline to rise, in the position of notional word "汤森华" and "并处". As we mentioned before, the words with low entropy value has semantic dependency relationship to the words with high entropy value. That is to say, the inflection point of the entropy line graph is the semantical segmentation point of sentence, which divides sentences into different semantic related word sequence segments. But there is a problem with this division method, that is which word sequence segment the corresponding word at the inflection point should be attributed to. The solution this paper offers is to compare the word with the maximum entropy in two adjacent segments. The words corresponding to the inflection point belong to the segment with the largest entropy word. Therefore, the word "汤森华" in Fig. 1 should belong to in Sect. 1. After judgment, there are sometimes word sequences that contain only one word. In this case, the word attribution judgment can be performed once again until the last word sequence does not have a single word.

After completing the segmentation of the above semantic related word sequence segments, the dependency parsing tree can be constructed according to the semantic dependency relationship in the second section, which is shown in the following algorithm.

The DPT Construction Algorithm Based on Semantics Dependency Relationship

1. For a sentence S, filter all function words for S
2. Get the list of notional wordsof S according to the indexes of those words in S
3. Map the notional words list into a entropy curve by calculating word co-occurrence entropy of each word in the list
4. Find inflection points of the entropy curve and divide S in semantic segments by those points
5. Arrange words which are between two semantic segments to the segment in which a word has max word co-occurrence entropy.
6. If there are semantic segments have only one word, then arrange the word to other neighbour segments with same judge method
7. Repeat step 6, until there is no semantic segment has only one word.

4 The Experiment

The text data set in this paper is composed of 12, 000 adjudication documents in Fujian Provincc and Zhcjiang province. These 12, 000 documents are all from criminal offences. This paper uses these documents as text set to carry on the construction experiment of the dependency parsing tree since adjudication documents are normative legal documents which is highly professional and the terms and chapters are perfectly organized.

The text data is processed before the construction experiment of the dependency parsing tree. Some high frequency stop words and function words are filtered out. Only the notional words in the text are retained. After training, a total of 66,964 words were obtained. The co-occurrence frequency between each word and every other word was countcd. Statistical results show that most words have a lot of co-occurrence words, but they seldom occur with each other. In other words, the co-occurrence frequency so low that can be neglected when constructing dependency parsing. Therefore, when summing up the co-occurrence frequency of words, we sort the vector component of co-occurrence frequency of the words from biggest to smallest, and then accumulate each component in the sequence. After accumulating to 95%, discard the words with low co-occurrence frequency, excluding the word in the co-occurrence statistics.

According to the algorithm of dependency parsing tree construction, we constructed a dependency parsing tree corresponding to the sample sentences selected in the text data set, “ The defendant Wang Tong, committed the crime of drug trafficking, was sentenced to seven years and ten months in prison, fined ten thousand yuan (The term of imprisonment shall be counted from the date of execution of the judgment. If the sentence is held before the execution of the sentence, one day of custody shall be reduced to one day of imprisonment, namely since September 27, 2016 to July 26, 2024. The fine shall be paid to the court within one month after the judgment becomes effective.)” According to the above algorithm, the construction of the dependency parsing tree of the example sentence is realized, as shown in Fig. 2.

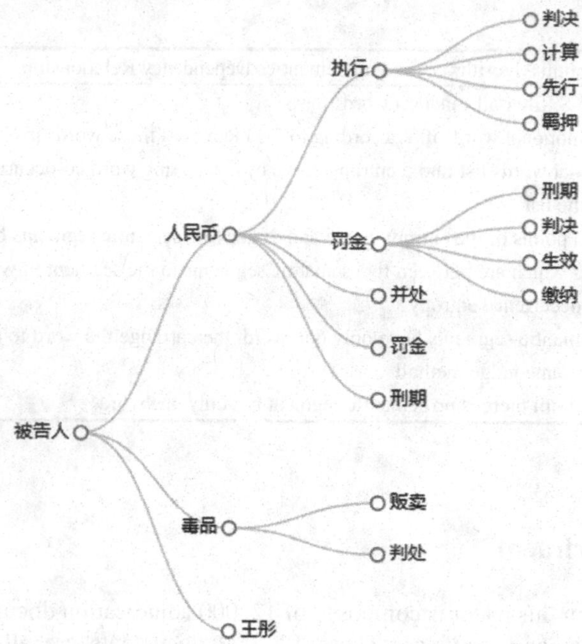

Fig. 2. The dependency parsing tree constructed by semantic dependency relationship according to the semantic dependency relationship.

5 Conclusion

This paper proposes a dependency parsing algorithm based on semantic dependency relationship, which mainly solves the problem of the minimum context. The minimum context is the smallest context, in which there is only one core word and the non-core word that modifies the core word. Because the minimum context is the underlying context unit, it is closer to the semantic of the text than other large scale contexts. Since the context is used to express the background knowledge of the text, the smaller the context is, the smaller the difference between the context and other contexts, the closer to the semantics of the text.

The minimum algorithm this paper uses also solves N-Gram which is a commonly used concept in the study of text analysis and information extraction. N-Gram is the substring with a fixed size in the text. A lot of semantic analysis algorithms use N-Gram as the basis of analyzing the context of words, sentences and word association analysis. The TEXTRANK algorithm described in this article also uses N-Gram to analyze word co-occurrence relation. But the length of the substring defined by N-Gram, that is, the value of N, has never been specified. It is determined according to the experimental results all the time. The solution to minimum pragmatic tree given by this paper also gives the judgment of the value of N. The text segment corresponding to the minimum contextual tree is the segment used in N-Gram to analyze the context of a word. Apparently, the word size that the minimum context tree contains is constantly changing but this paper solves this problem. This paper also gives the algorithm of dependency parsing tree construction. To be exact, dependency parsing tree express semantical modification relationship between each word in the sentence, while the algorithm of this paper expresses the connection in background knowledge of each word in the sentence. Similarly, because the scale of the sentence context is relatively small, and the smaller context is, the closer to the expression of semantics, the construction tree based on context can also be considered as the dependency parsing tree to some extent.

In total, the paper puts forward an algorithm of constructing dependency parsing tree, and make the experiments. From the experimental results, the tree constructed by in degree is slightly better.

References

1. Nivre, J.: Dependency grammar and dependency parsing. MSI Rep. **2005**(5133), 1–32 (1959)
2. Tesnière, L.: Eléments de syntaxe structurale (1965)
3. Hudson, R.A.: Word Grammar. Blackwell, Oxford (1984)
4. Sgall, P., Hajicová, E., Panevová, J.: The Meaning of the Sentence in its Semantic and Pragmatic Aspects. Springer, Heidelberg (1986)
5. Eisner, J.M.: Three new probabilistic models for dependency parsing: an exploration. In: Proceedings of the 16th Conference on Computational Linguistics, vol. 1, pp. 340–345. Association for Computational Linguistics (1996)
6. Carreras, X.: Experiments with a higher-order projective dependency parser. In: Proceedings of the 2007 Joint Conference on Empirical Methods in Natural Language Processing and Computational Natural Language Learning (EMNLP-CoNLL) (2007)
7. McDonald, R., Pereira, F.: Online learning of approximate dependency parsing algorithms. In: 11th Conference of the European Chapter of the Association for Computational Linguistics (2006)
8. Nivre, J., Scholz, M.: Deterministic dependency parsing of English text. In: Proceedings of the 20th International Conference on Computational Linguistics, p. 64. Association for Computational Linguistics (2004)
9. Yamada, H., Matsumoto, Y.: Statistical dependency analysis with support vector machines. In: Proceedings of IWPT, vol. 3, pp. 195–206 (2003)
10. Bohnet, B., McDonald, R., Pitler, E., et al.: Generalized transition-based dependency parsing via control parameters. In: Proceedings of the 54th Annual Meeting of the Association for Computational Linguistics (Volume 1: Long Papers), vol. 1, pp. 150–160 (2016)
11. Charniak, E.: A maximum-entropy-inspired parser. In: Proceedings of the 1st North American chapter of the Association for Computational Linguistics conference, pp. 132–139. Association for Computational Linguistics (2000)
12. Lafferty, J., McCallum, A., Pereira, F.C.N.: Conditional random fields: probabilistic models for segmenting and labeling sequence data (2001)

A Novel Hierarchical Identity-Based Encryption Scheme from Lattices

Qing Ye, Mingxing Hu, Wei Gao, and Yongli Tang(✉)

College of Computer Sciences and Technology, Henan Polytechnic University, Jiaozuo 454000, Henan, China
yltang@hpu.edu.cn

Abstract. Hierarchical identity based encryption is a powerful public key encryption scheme where entities are arranged in a directed tree. Each entity in the tree is provided with a secret key from its parent and can delegate this secret key to its children so that a child entity can decrypt messages intended for it. Aiming at the high complexity in user's private key extraction and large expansion ratio of trapdoor size in previous hierarchical identity-based encryption schemes, in this paper, we proposed a new HIBE scheme. We first used the implicit extension method to improve preimage sampling algorithm, and then we combined the improved algorithm with MP12 trapdoor delegation algorithm to construct an efficient hierarchical identity-based encryption user's private key extraction algorithm. Finally, we integrated the new extraction algorithm and the Dual-LWE algorithm to complete our scheme. Compared with the similar schemes, the efficiency of our scheme is improved in system establishment and user's private key extraction stage, the trapdoor size grows only linearly with the system hierarchical depth, and the improved preimage sample algorithm partly solves the Gaussian parameter increasing problem induced by MP12 trapdoor delegation. The security of the proposed scheme strictly reduces to the hardness of decisional learning with errors problem in the standard model.

Keywords: Lattice · Hierarchical Identity-Based encryption
Trapdoor function · Learning with errors

1 Introduction

Hierarchical identity-based encryption (HIBE) system [1, 2] is the extend version of identity-based encryption (IBE) [3–6], in the IBE cryptosystem, a single KGC can't meet in a large-scale network generated identity key for each user independently, because in a large number of user requests. To verify complete identity information for each user and for the establishment of private key security transfer channel is quite occupied system resources. Therefore, a hierarchical identity based encryption system is needed to complete the above problems. In the HIBE system, multiple KGC entities are distributed according to the structure of the directed tree. One of its characteristics is that each KGC trapdoor in the system is specified by its father KGC, which is called the

X. Sun et al. (Eds.): ICCCS 2018, LNCS 11065, pp. 412–422, 2018.
https://doi.org/10.1007/978-3-030-00012-7_38

trapdoor derivation. It should be noted that the trapdoor derivation is one-way, which means that each sub-KGC can't use its trapdoor to restore the parent KGC trapdoor.

In recent years, based on the new cryptosystem lattice theory because of its good asymptotic efficiency, simple operation, can be parallelized, anti-attack and quantum worst-case random instances has become a research hotspot after the era of quantum cryptography, and [7–11] made a series of achievements. In 2010, Cash et al. [12] Eurocrypt 10 proposed a trapdoor derivative algorithm, and this algorithm is based on lattice structure's first HIBE program, the program will be the identity of the user as consisting of a series of bits for each bit allocation and a uniform random matrix, which will lead to increased number of dimensional lattice with grading system the depth of significant growth, and the proposed algorithm derived trapdoor trapdoor derived size and depth is two times the classification system of power relations in the growth, high grade depth HIBE system will appear in the trapdoor size is too large and lead to the problem of normal. In addition, the scheme uses Gentry to [13] et al. STOC'08 proposed preimage sampling algorithm, the preimage sampling algorithm needs to perform high precision real orthogonal iteration, leads to the complexity of the user key extraction. The same year, Agrawal et al. [14] in Eurocrypt 10 to Cash et al's scheme is improved, will be in accordance with the user identity vector of each bit allocation matrix is improved by way of classification system in each stage of a distribution matrix, so that the lattice dimension only increases linearly with the depth of the grading system growth. But the trapdoor derivative algorithm and preimage sampling algorithm is still not changed, and the complexity of the trapdoor key size has not been fundamentally improved the extraction of user.

Micciancio et al. [15] (hereinafter referred to as MP12) in Eurocrypt'12 proposed a new lattice trapdoor generation algorithm and the corresponding preimage sampling algorithm, compared to the previous generation of trapdoor trapdoor generation algorithm [16], the process is simple, the complexity is equivalent to only two of a random matrix multiplication, and does not involve the high computation cost of HNF (Hermite normal form) and matrix inversion operation. Compared to the previous preimage sampling algorithm [13, 17], MP12 algorithm is relatively simple, preimage sampling algorithm, and support parallel computing and input for small integers, on line space demand is low. In addition, Micciancio et al. proposed trapdoor derived a new algorithm, the algorithm is compared with Cash et al. [12] algorithm is more efficient, because the algorithm does not need to Gauss sampling values are linearly independent detection, and the elimination of the ToBasis and HNF operation, more important is the size and grading system derived trapdoor depth only linearly growth. But at the same time, we note that the derived MP12 algorithm also has some shortcomings, the largest singular quality derived trapdoor trapdoor and derivative derivative algorithm compared to before the trapdoor trapdoor that matrix value will increase, resulting in the deterioration of the quality of the trapdoor, which led to a series of problems such as the growth parameters of Gauss. So using MP12 preimage sampling algorithm and trapdoor derivative algorithm to construct HIBE scheme, there will be a user key low extraction complexity and smaller size of the trapdoor expansion rate, but also should pay attention to avoid the growth of Gauss parameters derived from MP12 algorithm in the structure problem of the HIBE program. To optimize the preimage sampling algorithm using the implicit Cash method proposed by [12] et al. extended to a certain extent, can solve this problem, and can avoid unnecessary calculation and reduce the time complexity of the algorithm preimage sampling. Gentry et al. [13] pointed out that in the construction of HIBE scheme, the dual LWE algorithm should be used to complete the encryption and decryption stage of the scheme, which is more reasonable than the non-dual LWE algorithm. Subsequently, HIBE scheme [19–22] based on dual LWE algorithm has been proposed.

In order to make the HIBE scheme more practical and feasible, we must solve the problem of the complexity of user key extraction algorithm and the expansion rate of trapdoor size. Therefore, this paper proposes a new HIBE scheme on grid. The main contributions are: (1) to improve the MP12 preimage sampling algorithm in the HIBE scheme using implicit method, solves the Gauss parameters of the trapdoor derived after preimage sampling algorithm will increase the problem; (2) the improved preimage sampling algorithm and MP12 algorithm are combined to derive the trapdoor, construct a HIBE algorithm to extract the user key, and combined with dual LWE algorithm HIBE program structure. The security model is verified by the same security model similar to the same scheme. The proof results show that under the standard model, the security of the scheme can be reduced to the decisional learning with errors problem (DLWE).

2 Preliminaries

2.1 Lattice and Gaussian Distribution

Given n linearly independent vectors $\boldsymbol{B} = \{\boldsymbol{b}_1, \boldsymbol{b}_2, \ldots, \boldsymbol{b}_n\}$, a lattice Λ generated by $\boldsymbol{B}$ is defined as $\Lambda = \left\{\boldsymbol{Bk} = \sum_{i \in [n]} k_i \cdot \boldsymbol{b}_i : \boldsymbol{k} \in \mathbb{Z}^n\right\}$. We call $\boldsymbol{B}$ as basis of Λ. In this paper, our schemes work with a special class of integer lattices. Let $n \geq 1$ and modulus $q \geq 2$ be integers, where n is the main security parameter throughout this work, and all other parameters are implicitly functions of n. An m-dimensional lattice from the family is specified relative to the additive group $\mathbb{Z}_q^n$ by a parity check matrix $\boldsymbol{A} \in \mathbb{Z}_q^{n \times m}$. The associated lattice is defined as follows:

$$\begin{aligned} \Lambda^{\perp}(\boldsymbol{A}) &= \{\boldsymbol{x} \in \mathbb{Z}^m : \boldsymbol{Ax} = 0 \bmod q\} \\ \Lambda_{\boldsymbol{u}}^{\perp}(\boldsymbol{A}) &= \{\boldsymbol{x} \in \mathbb{Z}^m : \boldsymbol{Ax} = \boldsymbol{u} \bmod q\} \end{aligned} \tag{1}$$

Note that $\Lambda_{\boldsymbol{u}}^{\perp}(\boldsymbol{A})$ is a coset of $\Lambda^{\perp}(\boldsymbol{A})$.

For $\boldsymbol{y} \in \Lambda$, any $\sigma > 0$ and dimension $m \geq 1$, the Gaussian function $\rho_{\sigma,\boldsymbol{c}} : \mathbb{R}^m \to (0, 1]$ centered at $\boldsymbol{c} \in \mathbb{R}^m$ is defined as $\rho_{\sigma,\boldsymbol{c}}(\boldsymbol{y}) = \exp\left(-\pi\|\boldsymbol{y} - \boldsymbol{c}\|^2/\sigma^2\right)$. Let $\rho_{\sigma,\boldsymbol{c}}(\Lambda) = \sum_{\boldsymbol{y} \in \Lambda} \rho_{\sigma,\boldsymbol{c}}(\boldsymbol{y})$, and define the discrete Gaussian distribution over Λ as $D_{\Lambda,\sigma,\boldsymbol{c}}(\boldsymbol{y}) = \frac{\rho_{\sigma,\boldsymbol{c}}(\boldsymbol{y})}{\rho_{\sigma,\boldsymbol{c}}(\Lambda)}$.

2.2 The Learning with Errors Problem

Security of all our schemes reduces to the LWE (learning with errors) problem, a classic hard problem on lattices defined by Regev [7].

Definition 1 [7]: Consider these public parameters: a prime q, a positive integer n, and a distribution χ over $\mathbb{Z}_q$. An $(\mathbb{Z}_q, n, \chi)$-LWE problem instance is a challenge oracle $\mathcal{O}$ which consists of access to two types oracle, either, a noisy pseudo-random oracle $\mathcal{O}_s$ carrying some constant random secret key $s \in \mathbb{Z}_q^n$, or, a truly random oracle $\mathcal{O}_\$$, whose behaviors are respectively described as follows:

$\mathcal{O}_s$: outputs samples of the form $(u_i, v_i) = (u_i, u_i^T s + x_i) \in \mathbb{Z}_q^n \times \mathbb{Z}_q$, where $s \in \mathbb{Z}_q^n$ is a uniformly distributed persistent value invariant across invocations, u_i is uniform in $\mathbb{Z}_q^n$, and $x_i \in \mathbb{Z}_q$ is a fresh sample from χ.

$\mathcal{O}_\$$: outputs truly uniform random samples from $\mathbb{Z}_q^n \times \mathbb{Z}_q$.

The $(\mathbb{Z}_q, n, \chi)$-LWE problem allows repeated queries to the challenge oracle $\mathcal{O}$. We define that an attack algorithm $\mathcal{A}$ distinguishes the $(\mathbb{Z}_q, n, \chi)$-LWE problem if $\text{LWE - adv}[\mathcal{A}] = \left|\Pr\left[\mathcal{A}^{\mathcal{O}_s} = 1\right] - \Pr\left[\mathcal{A}^{\mathcal{O}_\$} = 1\right]\right|$ is non-negligible for a random $\mathbf{s} \in \mathbb{Z}_q^n$.

3 Algorithm Design and Scheme Construction

3.1 Optimized HIBE Preimage Sampling Algorithm

The implicit extension of preimage sampling algorithm of HIBE in [15] were optimized, and then the trapdoor derivative algorithm and Lemma 2 combined to construct an efficient HIBE algorithm to extract the user key.

Theorem 1. According to the conclusion of the 1 trapdoor derivative algorithm Lemma 2 the existence of Gauss parameter growth problems in the trapdoor derivation, the implicit method can be extended to optimize the Gauss parameters σ' in the preimage sampling process, and avoids the computation and storage of the derived matrix R'.

Proof. The output of MP12 derived known trapdoor $R' \in \mathbb{Z}_q^{m \times w}$ is not full rank matrix, compared to before the trapdoor expansion pie $R \in \mathbb{Z}_q^{\bar{m} \times w}$ matrix dimension $m - \bar{m}$, maximum singular $s_1(R') > s_1(R)$ and trapdoor trapdoor quality matrix, the relationship between Gauss parameters and trapdoor quality $s_1(R) \cdot \omega(\sqrt{\log n})$, therefore $\sigma' > \sigma$, the time complexity of the algorithm preimage sampling $v \leftarrow$ *SampleL*(R', u', σ') for trapdoor dimension expansion and derivative significantly, and Gauss parameters σ' of the growth of output norm vector algorithm becomes large. The implicit extension method can effectively solve the above problems. The concrete algorithms are as follows:

The matrix $A \in \mathbb{Z}_q^{n \times m}$ and the trapdoor matrix $R \in \mathbb{Z}_q^{\bar{m} \times w}$ of the TrapGen algorithm in the Lemma 1 are sum, the extended matrix of the matrix A, which is a homogeneous random matrix $A' = [A \| \bar{A}] \in \mathbb{Z}_q^{n \times m} \times \mathbb{Z}_q^{n \times w}$. It is the trapdoor matrix $\bar{A} \in \mathbb{Z}_q^{n \times w}$ of the matrix $R' \in \mathbb{Z}_q^{m \times w}$ output by the DelTrap algorithm in Lemma 2. An algorithm $\mathcal{O}(a, \sigma')$

for generating a vector, which is used to generate random and non-distinguishable vectors from the distribution $D_{\mathbb{Z}^w,\sigma'}$ statistics.

(1) Generation $\bar{\boldsymbol{v}} \leftarrow \mathcal{O}(\boldsymbol{a}, \sigma')$, judgment $\bar{\boldsymbol{v}}$ and statistical $D_{\mathbb{Z}^w,\sigma'}$ proximity, if not, then regenerate;
(2) Calculation $\bar{\boldsymbol{u}} = f_{\bar{A}}(\bar{\boldsymbol{v}}) = \bar{A}\bar{\boldsymbol{v}} \in \mathbb{Z}_q^n$;
(3) Execute the algorithm $\boldsymbol{v} \leftarrow SampleL(\boldsymbol{R}, \boldsymbol{u}' - \bar{\boldsymbol{u}}, \sigma)$, output $\boldsymbol{v}' = \boldsymbol{v}||\bar{\boldsymbol{v}}$.

Because the output $\mathcal{O}(\boldsymbol{a}, \sigma)$ is random, the non-homogeneous small integer solutions (ISIS, inhomogeneous small integer solution problem) is found to be statistically uniform, then by Theorem 3 in [15] shows the output vector preimage sampling algorithm is statistically homogeneous, therefore is also statistically uniform.

3.2 Efficient HIBE Identity Key Extraction Algorithm

This section uses MP12 optimization preimage trapdoor derivative algorithm and sampling algorithm described in Sect. 3.2 are combined to construct a efficient HIBE user key extraction algorithm. The algorithm mainly completes the HIBE user key extraction operation in the scheme.

Algorithm. The identity-key extracting algorithm for HIBE HIBE - ExtractSK (MPK, $\boldsymbol{A}_{\boldsymbol{id}_{\ell-1}}, \boldsymbol{R}_{\ell-1}, (\boldsymbol{id}_1||\ldots||\boldsymbol{id}_{\ell-1})||\boldsymbol{id}_\ell$)

Input. The master public key MPK, matrix $\boldsymbol{A}_{\boldsymbol{id}_{\ell-1}} \in \mathbb{Z}_q^{n\times[m+(\ell-1)w]}$, trapdoor matrix $\boldsymbol{R}_{\ell-1} \in \mathbb{Z}^{\bar{m}(\ell-1)\times w}$ and identity $(\boldsymbol{id}_1||\ldots||\boldsymbol{id}_{\ell-1})||\boldsymbol{id}_\ell \in \mathbb{Z}_q^{\ell n}$.

Output. Identity key $\boldsymbol{e}_{\boldsymbol{id}_\ell}$.

(1) Using the FRD (full-rank differences) function [14], the user identity $\boldsymbol{id}_\ell$ is mapped into a matrix $\boldsymbol{H}_{id_\ell}$, $\boldsymbol{A}_{\boldsymbol{id}_\ell} = [\boldsymbol{A}_{\boldsymbol{id}_{\ell-1}}||\boldsymbol{A}_\ell + \boldsymbol{H}_{\boldsymbol{id}_\ell}\boldsymbol{G}]$ which is a homogeneous random matrix $\boldsymbol{A}_\ell$.
(2) Implementation of trapdoor derivative algorithm $\boldsymbol{R}_\ell \leftarrow DelTrap^{\mathcal{O}}(\boldsymbol{A}' = [\boldsymbol{A}_{\boldsymbol{id}_{\ell-1}}|| \boldsymbol{A}_\ell + \boldsymbol{H}_{\boldsymbol{id}_\ell}\boldsymbol{G}], \boldsymbol{H}_\ell, \sigma_\ell)$, the details of the algorithm is the use of discrete Gauss distribution in Oracle $\mathcal{O}$ lattice coset $\Lambda^\perp(\boldsymbol{A})$ and Gauss parameters σ_ℓ is suitable on independent sampling, sampling results as a column vector of trapdoor matrix $\boldsymbol{R}_\ell$, and finally meet $\boldsymbol{A}_{\boldsymbol{id}}\boldsymbol{R}_\ell = \boldsymbol{H}_\ell\boldsymbol{G} - (\boldsymbol{A}_\ell + \boldsymbol{H}_{\boldsymbol{id}_\ell}\boldsymbol{G})$.
(3) After the execution optimization in Sect. 3.2 preimage sampling algorithm $\boldsymbol{e}_{\boldsymbol{id}_\ell} \leftarrow SampleL(\boldsymbol{R}_\ell, \boldsymbol{u}_\ell, \sigma_\ell)$, which $\sigma_\ell = s_1(\boldsymbol{R}) \cdot \omega(\sqrt{\log \ell n})$ meet $\boldsymbol{A}_{\boldsymbol{id}_\ell} \cdot \boldsymbol{e}_{\boldsymbol{id}_\ell} = \boldsymbol{u}_\ell$ and $||\boldsymbol{e}_{\boldsymbol{id}_\ell}|| \le \sigma_\ell\sqrt{m + \ell w}$, output $\boldsymbol{e}_{\boldsymbol{id}_\ell}$.

By Lemma 1 and the definition of FRD function [14] algorithm shows the first step of the matrix $[\boldsymbol{A}_\ell + \boldsymbol{H}_{\boldsymbol{id}_\ell}\boldsymbol{G}]$ is uniform random, by Lemma 2 shows that algorithm second step trapdoor matrix $\boldsymbol{R}_\ell$ derived to satisfy the unidirectional, by Theorem 3 in [14] shows that the output distribution of discrete Gauss dative third step preimage sampling algorithm, $\Lambda_{\boldsymbol{u}}^\perp(\boldsymbol{A}')$ are statistically indistinguishable.

With the HIBE grading depth increase, MP12 trapdoor trapdoor derived algorithm output size dimensions $\Lambda^\perp(\boldsymbol{A}')$ only dative linear growth relationship, rather than a power of two growth relations, linear independence and without trapdoor derived detection without high computational cost, operation ToBasis and HNF operation. To sum up, the user key extraction algorithm combined with the Sect. 3.2 algorithm is safe and feasible, and has lower time complexity and trapdoor size expansion.

3.3 HIBE Construction

In order to solve the problem of the complexity of user key extraction algorithm and the expansion rate of trapdoor size in HIBE scheme, we should start with the system establishment and user key extraction stage. The former mainly depends on the complexity of the trapdoor generation algorithm, the main complexity of the latter depends on the trapdoor derivation and preimage sampling algorithm. Compared with the existing lattice HIBE scheme of [12, 14, 19, 22], the characteristics of the scheme is first proposed by MP12 et al. the trapdoor generation, preimage sampling and trapdoor derivative algorithm to construct a scheme to enhance the system establishment and the user key extraction stage performance and efficiency; and the first method using implicit extended optimized sampling algorithm on MP12 preimage. As for the encryption and decryption phase of this scheme, the dual LWE algorithm is still used, similar to the other HIBE scheme [12, 14, 19, 22].

The concrete scheme is constructed as follows, including its basic parameters: uniform random matrix $\boldsymbol{A}_0 \in \mathbb{Z}_q^{n\times m}$ and the trapdoor $\boldsymbol{R}_0 \in \mathbb{Z}^{\bar{m}\times w}$, which n is safe and is supported by the system parameters, d is the maximum depth classification, user identity $\boldsymbol{id} = (\boldsymbol{id}_1||\ldots||\boldsymbol{id}_\ell)$, $1 \le \ell \le d$, and among them $\boldsymbol{id}_i \in \mathbb{Z}_q^n\backslash\{0\}$, $i \in [1, \ell]$, a structure $\boldsymbol{G} = \boldsymbol{I}_n \otimes \boldsymbol{g}^T \in \mathbb{Z}_q^{n\times nk}$, which is the unit matrix $\boldsymbol{I}_n$, FRD function $H : \mathbb{Z}_q^n \to \mathbb{Z}_q^{n\times n}$.

HIBE - Setup$(1^n, d)$: Input security parameters 1^n and system maximum classification depth d, run algorithm TrapGen$(1^n, q)$, output even random matrix $\boldsymbol{A}_0 \in \mathbb{Z}_q^{n\times m}$ and $\boldsymbol{A}_0$ trapdoor matrix $\boldsymbol{R}_0 \in \mathbb{Z}_q^{\bar{m}\times w}$, and select a uniform random matrix $s_1(\boldsymbol{R}_0) \le O(\sqrt{n \log q}) \cdot \omega(\sqrt{\log n})$, select dimension uniform random vector, output main public key MPK $= (\boldsymbol{A}_0, \boldsymbol{A}_1, \ldots, \boldsymbol{A}_d, \boldsymbol{G}, \boldsymbol{u})$ and main private key MSK $= \boldsymbol{R}_0 \in \mathbb{Z}_q^{\bar{m}\times w}$.

HIBE - Extract(MPK, $\boldsymbol{R}_{\ell-1}, (\boldsymbol{id}_1||\ldots||\boldsymbol{id}_{\ell-1})||\boldsymbol{id}_\ell$): Enter the main public key MPK, user identity $\boldsymbol{id}_\ell \in \mathbb{Z}_q^n$, $\mathbf{R}_{\ell-1}$ which represents the trapdoor corresponding to the user's public key matrix $\mathbf{A}_{\boldsymbol{id}_{\ell-1}}$ when the system classifying depth is $\ell - 1$, then $\boldsymbol{A}_{\boldsymbol{id}_{\ell-1}} = [\boldsymbol{A}_0||\boldsymbol{A}_1 + \boldsymbol{H}_{id_1}\boldsymbol{G}||\boldsymbol{A}_2 + \boldsymbol{H}_{id_2}\boldsymbol{G}||\ldots||\boldsymbol{A}_{\ell-1} + \boldsymbol{H}_{id_{\ell-1}}\boldsymbol{G}]$, the user key extraction algorithm HIBE - ExtractSK(MPK, $\boldsymbol{A}_{\boldsymbol{id}_{\ell-1}}, \boldsymbol{R}_{\ell-1}, (\boldsymbol{id}_1||\ldots||\boldsymbol{id}_{\ell-1})||\boldsymbol{id}_\ell$) of the Sect. 3.3 is invoked, and the user key $\boldsymbol{e}_{\boldsymbol{id}_\ell}$ is output.

HIBE - Encrypt(MPK, $\boldsymbol{id}, b$): Input the main public key MPK, the user identity $\boldsymbol{id} = (\boldsymbol{id}_1||\ldots||\boldsymbol{id}_\ell)$ of the hierarchical depth ℓ and the message $b \in \{0, 1\}$ to be encrypted. A matrix $\boldsymbol{A}_{\boldsymbol{id}_\ell} = [\boldsymbol{A}_0||\boldsymbol{A}_1 + \boldsymbol{H}_{id_1}\boldsymbol{G}||\boldsymbol{A}_2 + \boldsymbol{H}_{id_2}\boldsymbol{G}||\ldots||\boldsymbol{A}_\ell + \boldsymbol{H}_{id_\ell}\boldsymbol{G}] \in \mathbb{Z}_q^{n\times(m+\ell w)}$ is constructed, where $\boldsymbol{H}_{id_i} \leftarrow H(\boldsymbol{id}_i)$ a uniform random vector $\boldsymbol{s} \leftarrow \mathbb{Z}_q^n$ and a uniform random matrix $\bar{\boldsymbol{R}} \leftarrow \{-1, 1\}^{m\times \ell w}$ are selected, and the fault tolerance $x \xleftarrow{\bar{\Psi}_\alpha} \mathbb{Z}_q$, fault-tolerant vector $\boldsymbol{y} \xleftarrow{\bar{\Psi}_\alpha^m} \mathbb{Z}_q^m$, $\boldsymbol{z} = \bar{\boldsymbol{R}}^T\boldsymbol{y} \in \mathbb{Z}_q^{\ell w}$ and output ciphertext $\boldsymbol{CT} = (c_0, \boldsymbol{c}_1) \in \mathbb{Z}_q \times \mathbb{Z}_q^{m+\ell w}$ are calculated.

HIBE - Decrypt(MPK,e_{id_ℓ}, CT): Enter the main public key MPK, ciphertext $CT = (c_0, c_1)$ and user key e_{id_ℓ}, calculate $b' = c_0 - e_{id_\ell}^T c_1 \in \mathbb{Z}_q$, and compare b' with the integers $\lfloor q/2 \rfloor$ in the view $\mathbb{Z}$, if, output 1, otherwise output 0.

4 Security Proof

Agrawal et al. [14] INDr-sID-CPA security model lattice HIBE scheme in Eurocrypt 10 the standard model security proof by using the scheme, based on the security model of security proof and Yang et al. in 2014 [19] and 2016 Wang et al. [22] proposed HIBE scheme.

4.1 HIBE Correctness

The noise bound is the same as that of the document [14] HIBE scheme. The upper bound is $q\ell^2\sigma_\ell m\alpha_\ell \cdot \omega(\sqrt{\log m}) + O(\ell^2\sigma_\ell m^{3/2})$ to ensure that the system is running effectively and the noise is less than $q/5$ that in the document $1 \leq \ell \leq d$, we set the parameters as follows. The correctness of the proposed scheme is clearly established if we set $m{=}2n \log q$, $\sigma_\ell{=}w \cdot \omega(\sqrt{\log n})$, $\alpha_\ell{=}[wm \cdot \omega(\sqrt{\log n})]^{-1}$ and $q{=}w\sqrt{m^3} \cdot \omega(\sqrt{\log n})$.

4.2 Security Reduction

Theorem 2 Supposing that the LWE problem described in Definition 1 is hard under the parameters $(m, \sigma_\ell, \alpha_\ell, q)$ setting as is shown in Sect. 4.1, the proposed HIBE scheme is provable INDr-sID-CPA secure in the standard model.

Proof. The proof of theorem is used to prove the method that based on the sequence of games, used W_i to define the attacker Game i in the correct guess challenge bit events, namely, in the end, $r \in \{0, 1\}$ which is used as the random bit Challenger decided to challenge ciphertext types, $r' \in \{0, 1\}$ is speculation stage at the end of the game, the output of the attacker's bit challenge guess the solution, PPT proved that for any adversary to challenge the advantage of zero bit guess, an attacker cannot win with non negligible advantage in INDr-sID-CPA Game. The DLWE problem is used to prove that Game2 and Game3 are not distinguishable.

Game 0. Game 0 is a INDr-sID-CPA game between an attacker and a challenger to attack this program.

Game 1. The Game 1 is set $id^* = (id_1^* || \ldots || id_k^*)$ as an attacker to be attacked, if $k < d$ the zero vector $(d - k)$ is supplemented in the spare part. The generation mode of the change $A_1, \ldots, A_d$ is selected, and a random matrix $R_1^*, \ldots, R_d^* \leftarrow \{-1, 1\}^{m \times w}$ is selected and the structure matrix is constructed $A_i = \left[-H_{id_i^*} \cdot G - A_0 R_i^*\right]$. Set up to use to generate challenge ciphertext at the challenge stage. It is found that the $\bar{R}_k^* = (R_1^* || \ldots || R_k^*) \in \{-1, 1\}^{m \times kw}$ distribution $(A_0, A_0 R^*, z)$ and distribution (A_0, A_1', z) of the Lemma 4 in [14] can not be distinguished from the statistics, including the homogeneous matrix and the random matrix $R^* \in [-1,1]^{m\times kw}$. So the matrix $A_1,\ldots,A_d$ is statistically non - distinguishable in Game1 and Game0, and the attacker seems to be the same in Game0 and Game1.

Game 2. The difference between Game 2 and Game1 lies in the use of the TrapGen algorithm to generate the trapdoor matrix $G \in \mathbb{Z}_q^{n\times w}$ of the matrix R_G in Game2, and $A_i = \left[-H_{id_i^*}\cdot G - A_0 R_i^*\right]$ still remains the form in Game1. Query the user key response to the attacker, the attacker needs to set the query identity $id = (id_1||\ldots||id_\ell)$, the output matrix A_{id} of the trapdoor matrix, which $A_{id} = [A_1||\ldots||A_\ell||A_{\ell+1}] + [0||H_{id_1}\cdot G||\ldots||0||H_{id_\ell}\cdot G||0] = [G_{id} - A_0\bar{R}_\ell]$, $\bar{R}_\ell = [R_1^*||\ldots||R_\ell^*] \in \mathbb{Z}_q^{m\times \ell w}$, $G_{id} = \left[(H_{id_1} - H_{id_1^*})G||\ldots||\left(H_{id_\ell} - H_{id_\ell^*}\right)G\right] \in \mathbb{Z}_q^{n\times \ell w}$ by definition, FRD encoding function [14] that $\left[H_{id_i} - H_{id_i^*}\right]$ is invertible matrix, it can use the trapdoor Challenger matrix in response to the attacker's preimage sampling private key query prefix id, as defined by the security model know the query is not target identity of the attackers and, therefore, can use $e_{id_\ell} \leftarrow \text{SampleR}(A_0, \bar{R}_\ell, G_{id}, R_G, \sigma_\ell)$ the Challenger trapdoor matrix in response to user key attacker preimage sampling query. If the algorithm is called, the output is sent to the attacker; if $id \neq id^*$ the $\left[H_{id_i} - H_{id_i^*}\right]$ zero matrix is irreversible, the game terminates and returns a random bit. It is known from the Theorem 4 in [14] that the distribution $\sigma_\ell > s_1(R_\ell)\cdot\|\bar{R}_\ell\|\cdot\omega(\sqrt{\log n})$ of the distribution in the Game1 can not be distinguished from the statistics. So the private key query response e_{id} method in Game2 and the matrix and Game1 are not statistically different, so the attacker's advantages in Game2 and Game1 are the same.

Game 3. The difference between the Game 3 and the Game2 is that the challenge ciphertext (c_0^*, c_1^*) is no longer generated by the encryption algorithm, but is selected from the ciphertext space $\mathbb{Z}_q \times \mathbb{Z}_q^{\ell w+m}$ independently and randomly. Because the challenge of ciphertext is a random selection, the advantage of an attacker can be ignored.

Next, using the difficulty of the DLWE problem, it is proved that for the PPT enemy, Game3 and Game2 are undistinguishable.

Assuming that a PPT opponent $\mathcal{A}$ can distinguish between Game2 and Game3, we use an enemy $\mathcal{A}$ to construct an algorithm $\mathcal{B}$ to solve the problem of DLWE. The simulator $\mathcal{B}$ has a series of samples $(u_i, v_i) \in \mathbb{Z}_q^n \times \mathbb{Z}_q$, $i = 0, 1, \ldots, \bar{m}$. The enemy $\mathcal{A}$ announced $\mathcal{B}$ his identity id^* to the impersonator.

Setup. The simulator $\mathcal{B}$ generates random matrix $A_0 \in \mathbb{Z}_q^{n\times m}$ by sample. The first row of the matrix A is vector u_i. The sample vector is taken as a common random vector $u \in \mathbb{Z}_q^n$, and the rest parameters are the same as those generated in Game2.

Query. Analogous to Game2, the simulator $\mathcal{B}$ generates a polynomial key for the enemy $\mathcal{A}$.

Challenge. The opponent $\mathcal{A}$ submits the information $b^* \in \{0,1\}$. The simulator $\mathcal{B}$ operates as follows: $v_0, v_1, \ldots, v_m$ representing a sample component in the DLWE problem, making the blind message bits $\boldsymbol{v}^* = \begin{bmatrix} v_1 \\ \vdots \\ v_m \end{bmatrix} \in \mathbb{Z}_q^m$, so that we can select the random bits $c_0^* = v_0 + b^* \cdot \lfloor q/2 \rfloor \in \mathbb{Z}_q$, $\boldsymbol{c}_1^* = \begin{bmatrix} \boldsymbol{v}^* \\ \left(-\bar{\boldsymbol{R}}_k^*\right)^T \boldsymbol{v}^* \end{bmatrix} \in \mathbb{Z}_q^{m+kw}$, if we send them to the opponents, if we choose them randomly, and send them to the opponents.

If the distribution in the DLWE problem is pseudorandom, then the $\boldsymbol{A}_{id^*} = [\boldsymbol{A}_0 || -\boldsymbol{A}_0\bar{\boldsymbol{R}}_k^*]$ distribution is the same as that of Game2. At this point, it is known from the sample definition, $\boldsymbol{v}^* = \boldsymbol{A}_0^T \boldsymbol{s} + \boldsymbol{y}$ of which $\boldsymbol{y} \xleftarrow{\bar{\Psi}_\alpha^m} \mathbb{Z}_q^m$. Therefore, the above definition is satisfied

$$\boldsymbol{c}_1^* = \begin{bmatrix} \boldsymbol{A}_0^T \boldsymbol{s} + \boldsymbol{y} \\ -\bar{\boldsymbol{R}}_k^{*T} \boldsymbol{A}_0^T \boldsymbol{s} - \bar{\boldsymbol{R}}_k^{*T} \boldsymbol{y} \end{bmatrix} = \begin{bmatrix} \boldsymbol{A}_0^T \boldsymbol{s} + \boldsymbol{y} \\ \left(-\boldsymbol{A}_0^T \bar{\boldsymbol{R}}_k^*\right)^T \boldsymbol{s} - \bar{\boldsymbol{R}}_k^{*T} \boldsymbol{y} \end{bmatrix} = (\boldsymbol{A}_{id^*})^T \boldsymbol{s} + \begin{bmatrix} \boldsymbol{y} \\ -\bar{\boldsymbol{R}}_k^{*T} \boldsymbol{y} \end{bmatrix}$$

The upper right side is the Game2's challenge ciphertext $v_0 = \boldsymbol{u}_0^T \boldsymbol{s} + x$. It is also the satisfaction of the above definition, which is the $x \xleftarrow{\bar{\Psi}_\alpha} \mathbb{Z}_q$ challenge of the Game2. If the distribution $c_0^* = \boldsymbol{u}_0^T \boldsymbol{s} + x + b^* \lfloor q/2 \rfloor$ in the DLWE problem is really random, it is uniform in the upper and uniform in the upper. By the standard Left over hash Lemma [23], it is known that the above definition is independent and uniform $\boldsymbol{v}^*$. Therefore, the distribution of the challenge ciphertext is equally uniform $\mathbb{Z}_q \times \mathbb{Z}_q^{m+kw}$ in the Game3.

Guess. After the end of the polynomial sub-selective inquiry, the enemy $\mathcal{A}$ conjectures the interaction between Game2 or Game3. The conjecture $\mathcal{B}$ output of the simulator is used as a solution to the DLWE problem. Because there is no PPT algorithm to solve the DLWE problem effectively, this scheme is INDr-sID-CPA secure.

5 Conclusion

This paper presents a new lattice hierarchical identity based encryption scheme, the new scheme is based on the application of implicit method is extended to MP12 HIBE in the preimage sampling algorithm was improved to a certain extent to solve in combination with MP12 trapdoor algorithm derived Gauss parameters will increase in depression after birth of martial art, and saves unnecessary computation and storage. Then, an efficient HIBE user key extraction algorithm is constructed with MP12 trapdoor derivation algorithm. Finally, the HIBE scheme is constructed with dual LWE algorithm. Under the standard model, the security of the scheme can be reduced to the difficulty of the determinant fault-tolerant learning problem (DLWE), and a strict security proof is given. The comparative analysis shows that the efficiency of this scheme is better than that of the same scheme in the stage of system establishment and the user key extraction stage.

6 Acknowledgments

This work was supported by the "13th Five-Year" National Crypto Development Foundation (MMJJ20170122), the Project of science and Technology Department of Henan Province (142300410147), the Project of Education Department of Henan Province (12A520021, 16A520013), the Doctoral Fund of Henan Polytechnic University (B2014-044), the Natural Science Foundation of Henan Polytechnic University (No.T2018-1).

References

1. Gentry, C., Silverberg, A.: Hierarchical ID-based cryptography. In: Zheng, Y. (ed.) ASIACRYPT 2002. LNCS, vol. 2501, pp. 548–566. Springer, Heidelberg (2002). https://doi.org/10.1007/3-540-36178-2_34
2. Horwitz, J., Lynn, B.: Toward hierarchical identity-based encryption. In: Knudsen, Lars R. (ed.) EUROCRYPT 2002. LNCS, vol. 2332, pp. 466–481. Springer, Heidelberg (2002). https://doi.org/10.1007/3-540-46035-7_31
3. Boneh, D., Franklin, M.: Identity-based encryption from the Weil pairing. In: Kilian, J. (ed.) CRYPTO 2001. LNCS, vol. 2139, pp. 213–229. Springer, Heidelberg (2001). https://doi.org/10.1007/3-540-44647-8_13
4. Lai, J., Deng, R.H., Liu, S., Weng, J., Zhao, Y.: Identity-based encryption secure against selective opening chosen-ciphertext attack. In: Nguyen, P.Q., Oswald, E. (eds.) EUROCRYPT 2014. LNCS, vol. 8441, pp. 77–92. Springer, Heidelberg (2014). https://doi.org/10.1007/978-3-642-55220-5_5
5. Yamada, S.: Adaptively secure identity-based encryption from lattices with asymptotically shorter public parameters. In: Fischlin, M., Coron, J.-S. (eds.) EUROCRYPT 2016. LNCS, vol. 9666, pp. 32–62. Springer, Heidelberg (2016). https://doi.org/10.1007/978-3-662-49896-5_2
6. Wang, F., Liu, Z., Wang, C.: Full secure identity-based encryption scheme with short public key size over lattices in the standard model. Proc. Int. J. Comput. Math. **93**(6), 854–863 (2016)
7. Regev, O.: On lattices, learning with errors, random linear codes, and cryptography. J. ACM **56**(6), 84–93 (2009)
8. Nguyen, Phong Q., Zhang, J., Zhang, Z.: Simpler efficient group signatures from lattices. In: Katz, J. (ed.) PKC 2015. LNCS, vol. 9020, pp. 401–426. Springer, Heidelberg (2015). https://doi.org/10.1007/978-3-662-46447-2_18
9. Brakerski, Z., Perlman, R.: Lattice-Based fully dynamic multi-key FHE with short ciphertexts. In: Robshaw, M., Katz, J. (eds.) CRYPTO 2016. LNCS, vol. 9814, pp. 190–213. Springer, Heidelberg (2016). https://doi.org/10.1007/978-3-662-53018-4_8
10. Libert, B., Ling, S., Nguyen, K., Wang, H.: Zero-knowledge arguments for lattice-based accumulators: logarithmic-size ring signatures and group signatures without trapdoors. In: Fischlin, M., Coron, J.-S. (eds.) EUROCRYPT 2016. LNCS, vol. 9666, pp. 1–31. Springer, Heidelberg (2016). https://doi.org/10.1007/978-3-662-49896-5_1
11. Duan, R., Gu, C., Zhu, Y.: Efficient identity-based fully homomorphic encryption over NTRU. J. Commun. **38**(1), 66–75 (2017)

12. Cash, D., Hofheinz, D., Kiltz, E., Peikert, C.: Bonsai trees, or how to delegate a lattice basis. In: Gilbert, H. (ed.) EUROCRYPT 2010. LNCS, vol. 6110, pp. 523–552. Springer, Heidelberg (2010). https://doi.org/10.1007/978-3-642-13190-5_27
13. Gentry, C., Peikert, C., Vaikuntanathan, V.: Trapdoors for hard lattices and new cryptographic constructions. In: Proceedings of the Fortieth Annual ACM Symposium on Theory of Computing, STOC 2008, Victoria, British Columbia, Canada, pp. 197–206. ACM (2008)
14. Agrawal, S., Boneh, D., Boyen, X.: Efficient lattice (H)IBE in the standard model. In: Gilbert, H. (ed.) EUROCRYPT 2010. LNCS, vol. 6110, pp. 553–572. Springer, Heidelberg (2010). https://doi.org/10.1007/978-3-642-13190-5_28
15. Micciancio, D., Peikert, C.: Trapdoors for lattices: simpler, tighter, faster, smaller. In: Pointcheval, D., Johansson, T. (eds.) EUROCRYPT 2012. LNCS, vol. 7237, pp. 700–718. Springer, Heidelberg (2012). https://doi.org/10.1007/978-3-642-29011-4_41
16. Alwen, J., Peikert, C.: Generating shorter bases for hard random lattices. Theor. Comput. Syst. **48**(3), 535–553 (2011)
17. Peikert, C.: An efficient and parallel gaussian sampler for lattices. In: Rabin, T. (ed.) CRYPTO 2010. LNCS, vol. 6223, pp. 80–97. Springer, Heidelberg (2010). https://doi.org/10.1007/978-3-642-14623-7_5
18. Agrawal, S., Boyen, X., Vaikuntanathan, V., Voulgaris, P., Wee, H.: Functional encryption for threshold functions (or fuzzy IBE) from lattices. In: Fischlin, M., Buchmann, J., Manulis, M. (eds.) PKC 2012. LNCS, vol. 7293, pp. 280–297. Springer, Heidelberg (2012). https://doi.org/10.1007/978-3-642-30057-8_17
19. Yang, C., Zheng, S., Wang, L., Lu, X., Yang, Y.: Hierarchical identity-based broadcast encryption scheme from LWE. J. Commun. Netw. **16**(3), 258–263 (2014)
20. Katsumata, S., Yamada, S.: Partitioning via non-linear polynomial functions: more compact IBEs from ideal lattices and bilinear maps. In: Cheon, J.H., Takagi, T. (eds.) ASIACRYPT 2016. LNCS, vol. 10032, pp. 682–712. Springer, Heidelberg (2016). https://doi.org/10.1007/978-3-662-53890-6_23
21. Zhang, J., Chen, Yu., Zhang, Z.: Programmable hash functions from lattices: short signatures and IBEs with small key sizes. In: Robshaw, M., Katz, J. (eds.) CRYPTO 2016. LNCS, vol. 9816, pp. 303–332. Springer, Heidelberg (2016). https://doi.org/10.1007/978-3-662-53015-3_11
22. Wang, F., Wang, C., Liu, Z.: Efficient hierarchical identity based encryption scheme in the standard model over lattices. Front. Inf. Technol. Electron. Eng. **17**(8), 781–791 (2016)
23. Dodis, Y., Ostrovsky, R., Reyzin, L., Smith, A.: Fuzzy extractors: how to generate strong keys from biometrics and other noisy data. Proc. Soc. Ind. Appl. Math. (SIAM) **38**(1), 97–139 (2008)

A Novel Hierarchical Identity-Based Fully Homomorphic Encryption Scheme from Lattices

Mingxing Hu, Qing Ye, Wei Gao, and Yongli Tang(✉)

College of Computer Sciences and Technology, Henan Polytechnic University, Jiaozuo 454000, Henan, China
yltang@hpu.edu.cn

Abstract. Hierarchical identity-based fully homomorphic encryption (HIBFHE) scheme is a powerful scheme, as it aggregates the advantages of both fully homomorphic encryption and hierarchical identity-based encryption systems. In recent years, the construction of HIBFHE schemes were mainly based on lattices due to their conjectured resistance against quantum cryptanalysis, however, which makes these cryptosystems further unpractical. The first hierarchical identity-based fully homomorphic encryption scheme was presented by Gentry, Sahai and Waters (CRYPTO 2013). Their scheme however works with a not well performed trapdoor and delegation algorithm; that is, the trapdoor is conceptually and algorithmically complex, and the delegation algorithm's performance is sensitive with the lattice dimension. In this work, we substantially improve their work by using a novel trapdoor function and its relevant algorithms. Specifically, we first use that construct an efficient algorithm for sampling-invertible matrix, based on this we construct a novel delegation algorithm which can keep the lattice dimension unchanged upon delegation. Building on this result, we first construct a more efficient hierarchical identity-based encryption scheme, and then transform it to HIBFHE scheme by using eigenvector method. Under the hardness of Learning with Errors problem, the resulting scheme can be proven secure in the standard model. To the best of our knowledge, this is the first HIBFHE scheme in fixed dimension.

Keywords: Lattice
Hierarchical identity-based fully homomorphic encryption · Trapdoor function
Learning with errors

1 Introduction

Fully homomorphic encryption (FHE) is a powerful variant of public key encryption that facilitates arbitrary computation on encrypted data. Since Gentry's breakthrough realization in 2009 [1], many improved variants have appeared in the literature [2–6].

Hierarchical identity-based encryption (HIBE) is also a powerful variant of PKE where entities are arranged in a directed tree, which is an extend version of identity-based encryption (IBE). The notion of HIBE is more appropriate than standard IBE for large organizations, can isolate damage in the case of secret-key exposure, and has further applications such as forward-secure encryption [7] and broadcast encryption [8, 9].

X. Sun et al. (Eds.): ICCCS 2018, LNCS 11065, pp. 423–434, 2018.
https://doi.org/10.1007/978-3-030-00012-7_39

Naturally, the hierarchical identity-based fully homomorphic encryption (HIBFHE) cryptosystem has attracted much attention as it aggregates the advantages of both FHE and HIBE. The first HIBFHE scheme was presented by Gentry, Sahai and Waters [10] in CRYPTO'13, which we call GSW13. They designed a compiler which can transform any HIBE scheme that satisfying specified conditions to HIBFHE scheme. Moreover, Gentry et al. applied their compiler to the HIBE work [11] and obtained a HIBFHE scheme in standard model under Learning with Errors (LWE) problem [12], but do not gave a concrete security proof.

Because the HIBFHE scheme is converted from HIBE that make the security and efficiency are mainly dominated by the latter. The work GSW13 claimed the HIBE schemes [11, 13–15] all meet the properties needed for their compiler. However, these HIBE schemes are not efficient, because the trapdoor functions [16, 17] they based involves costly computations of Hermite normal forms and matrix inverses. Then, the resulting HIBFHE schemes are not very practical when transformed from these HIBE schemes. Not only that, these HIBFHE schemes will become extremely impractical when the hierarchical level raising, because the lattice dimension increased when the trapdoor delegated from the parent node to its child node. We note that the parameters of lattice based cryptosystems are all tightly related with the lattice dimension, namely the performance of the system is quite sensitive to even small changes in the lattice dimension.

Question: A natural important question is: *Can we construct a provably secure HIBFHE scheme from lattice assumption under standard model, which based on an efficient trapdoor and the trapdoor delegation does not increase the lattice dimension?*

A natural solution to solve the *Question* would be to apply the GSW13 compiler to transform Agrawal et al. *'s* work [15], we then can obtain a HIBFHE scheme whose lattice dimension are fixed across the levels of the hierarchy. However, the construction is direct and the GSW13 work mentioned it is immediate to use their compiler, more importantly the aforementioned problem, inefficiency of trapdoor function, still expose here.

Our contributions: Instead of taking the above approach, we almost thoroughly construct a new trapdoor delegation algorithm and the corresponding simulation tool, then based on that we design a novel HIBFHE scheme from lattices. To the best of our knowledge, this is the first HIBFHE scheme in fixed dimension. The core technical component of our construction is a novel trapdoor function, proposed by Micciancio and Peikert [18] at Eurocrypt'12, which is more efficient than previous work [16, 17]. We call this novel trapdoor function as MP12 trapdoor function. With the observations in [15], [14] and [18], we summarize our contributions as follows.

1: We first design an efficient algorithm for sampling $\mathbb{Z}_q$-invertible matrix (see Sect. 3.1) using the nice properties of MP12 preimage sampling algorithm [18], which is a fundamental algorithm for our novel trapdoor delegation algorithm (see Sect. 3.2).

2: Based on the above $\mathbb{Z}_q$-invertible matrix sampling algorithm, we construct an improved trapdoor delegation algorithm without increasing the lattice dimension, which can be seen as a combination of the MP12 trapdoor function with the trapdoor delegation algorithm in fixed dimension. Though the combination is not direct, we eliminate the difficult using a ToBasis [19] like algorithm.

3: Based on the above works, we construct the HIBE scheme (see Sect. 4.1) and then transform it to HIBFHE scheme by employing the GSW compiler [10]. We note that our HIBE scheme is efficiently transformable, and the resulting HIBFHE scheme has a smaller B-strongly-bound parameter without affecting the security level (i.e., error-to-modulus parameter q/B). It means our HIBFHE scheme has more room for the noise to grow as homomorphic operations are performed.

2 Preliminaries

2.1 Lattice and Gaussian Distribution

Given n linearly independent vectors $\boldsymbol{B} = \{\boldsymbol{b}_1, \boldsymbol{b}_2, \ldots, \boldsymbol{b}_n\}$, a lattice Λ generated by $\boldsymbol{B}$ is defined as $\Lambda = \left\{ \mathbf{B}\boldsymbol{k} = \sum_{i \in [n]} k_i \cdot \boldsymbol{b}_i : \boldsymbol{k} \in \mathbb{Z}^n \right\}$. We call $\boldsymbol{B}$ as basis of Λ. In this paper, our schemes work with a special class of integer lattices whose importance in cryptography was first demonstrated by Ajtai [20]. Let $n \geq 1$ and modulus $q \geq 2$ be integers, where n is the main security parameter throughout this work, and all other parameters are implicitly functions of n. An m-dimensional lattice from the family is specified relative to the additive group $\mathbb{Z}_q^n$ by a parity check matrix $\boldsymbol{A} \in \mathbb{Z}_q^{n \times m}$. The associated lattice is defined as follows:

$$\begin{aligned} \Lambda^{\perp}(\boldsymbol{A}) &= \{\boldsymbol{x} \in \mathbb{Z}^m : \boldsymbol{A}\boldsymbol{x} = 0 \bmod q\} \\ \Lambda_{\boldsymbol{u}}^{\perp}(\boldsymbol{A}) &= \{\boldsymbol{x} \in \mathbb{Z}^m : \boldsymbol{A}\boldsymbol{x} = \boldsymbol{u} \bmod q\} \end{aligned} \tag{1}$$

Note that $\Lambda_{\boldsymbol{u}}^{\perp}(\boldsymbol{A})$ is a coset of $\Lambda^{\perp}(\boldsymbol{A})$.

For $\boldsymbol{y} \in \Lambda$, any $\sigma > 0$ and dimension $m \geq 1$, the Gaussian function $\rho_{\sigma,\mathbf{c}} : \mathbb{R}^m \to (0, 1]$ centered at $\boldsymbol{c} \in \mathbb{R}^m$ is defined as $\rho_{\sigma,\mathbf{c}}(\boldsymbol{y}) = \exp\left(-\pi\|\boldsymbol{y} - \boldsymbol{c}\|^2/\sigma^2\right)$. Let $\rho_{\sigma,\mathbf{c}}(\Lambda) = \sum_{\boldsymbol{y} \in \Lambda} \rho_{\sigma,\mathbf{c}}(\boldsymbol{y})$, and define the discrete Gaussian distribution over Λ as $D_{\Lambda,\sigma,\mathbf{c}}(\boldsymbol{y}) = \frac{\rho_{\sigma,\mathbf{c}}(\boldsymbol{y})}{\rho_{\sigma,\mathbf{c}}(\Lambda)}$.

2.2 The Learning with Errors (LWE) Problem

Security of all our schemes reduces to the LWE (learning with errors) problem, a classic hard problem on lattices defined by Regev [12].

Definition 1 [12]: Consider these public parameters: a prime q, a positive integer n, and a distribution χ over $\mathbb{Z}_q$. An $(\mathbb{Z}_q, n, \chi)$-LWE problem instance is a challenge oracle $\mathcal{O}$ which consists of access to two types oracle, either, a noisy pseudo-random oracle $\mathcal{O}_s$ carrying some constant random secret key $\boldsymbol{s} \in \mathbb{Z}_q^n$, or, a truly random oracle $\mathcal{O}_\$$, whose behaviors are respectively described as follows:

$\mathcal{O}_s$: outputs samples of the form $(\boldsymbol{u}_i, v_i) = \left(\boldsymbol{u}_i, \boldsymbol{u}_i^T \boldsymbol{s} + x_i\right) \in \mathbb{Z}_q^n \times \mathbb{Z}_q$, where $\boldsymbol{s} \in \mathbb{Z}_q^n$ is a uniformly distributed persistent value invariant across invocations, $\boldsymbol{u}_i$ is uniform in $\mathbb{Z}_q^n$, and $x_i \in \mathbb{Z}_q$ is a fresh sample from χ.

$\mathcal{O}_\$$: outputs truly uniform random samples from $\mathbb{Z}_q^n \times \mathbb{Z}_q$.

The $(\mathbb{Z}_q, n, \chi)$-LWE problem allows repeated queries to the challenge oracle $\mathcal{O}$. We define that an attack algorithm $\mathcal{A}$ distinguishes the $(\mathbb{Z}_q, n, \chi)$-LWE problem if LWE $-$ adv$[\mathcal{A}] = \left|\Pr\left[\mathcal{A}^{\mathcal{O}_s} = 1\right] - \Pr\left[\mathcal{A}^{\mathcal{O}_\$} = 1\right]\right|$ is non-negligible for a random $s \in \mathbb{Z}_q^n$.

3 Improved Trapdoor Delegation Algorithm Without Dimension Increase

In this section, we describe a novel trapdoor delegation algorithm FixedTrapDel which could securely and efficiently delegate trapdoor dose not increase the lattice dimension.

3.1 An Efficient Algorithm for Sampling $\mathbb{Z}_q$-Invertible Matrix

As in [15], before construct the delegation algorithm, we also need an algorithm to sample the public "low norm" and non-singular matrix $\boldsymbol{R}$. Like [15], we also call it as $\mathbb{Z}_q$-invertible matrix. With the observation of the SampleR algorithm in [15], we have the novel MP12SampleR algorithm as following.

Algorithm 1 Efficient algorithm MP12SampleR$^{\mathcal{O}_G}(1^m)$ for sampling public $\mathbb{Z}_q$-invertible matrix from $\mathcal{D}_{m\times m}$.

Input: Integer $m = O(n \log q)$, an oracle $\mathcal{O}_G$ for Gaussian sampling over a desired coset $\Lambda^\perp(\boldsymbol{G})$ with Gaussian parameter $\sigma_G \geq \eta_\epsilon\left(\Lambda^\perp(\boldsymbol{G})\right)$.

Output: A public, full-rank and "low norm" matrix $\boldsymbol{R}$.

1) Let $\boldsymbol{G}$ be the primitive matrix, $\boldsymbol{G} = \boldsymbol{I}_n \otimes \boldsymbol{g}^T \in \mathbb{Z}_q^{n\times nk}$ where $\boldsymbol{I}_n$ is the $n\times n$ identity matrix, $\boldsymbol{g}^T = \left[1, 2, 2^2, \mathrm{K}, 2^{k-1}\right] \in ¢_q^k$, and $k = \lceil \log q \rceil$. Let $\boldsymbol{T_G}$ be the public trapdoor of $\boldsymbol{G}$. Randomly choose a uniform matrix $\bar{A} \in \mathbb{Z}_q^{n\times \bar{m}}$ where $\bar{m} = m - nk$.
2) Calling to oracle $\mathcal{O}_G$, generate $\bar{\boldsymbol{r}} \leftarrow \mathcal{D}_{\Lambda^\perp(G),\sigma_G}$,
   If $\bar{\boldsymbol{r}}$ is statistically close to the distribution $\mathcal{D}_{\mathbb{Z}^{nk},\sigma_G}$:
   a) Compute $\boldsymbol{u} = f_{\bar{A}}(\bar{\boldsymbol{r}}) = \bar{A}\bar{\boldsymbol{r}} \in \mathbb{Z}_q^{\bar{m}}$.
   b) Take $\boldsymbol{G}$, $\boldsymbol{T_G}$, $\boldsymbol{u}$ and σ_G as input, sample $\hat{\boldsymbol{r}} \leftarrow$ MP12Sample$(\boldsymbol{G}, \boldsymbol{T_G}, \sigma_G, \boldsymbol{u})$, output $\hat{\boldsymbol{r}} \in \mathbb{Z}^{nk}$.
   c) Let $\boldsymbol{r} = (\bar{\boldsymbol{r}} \mid \hat{\boldsymbol{r}}) \in \mathbb{Z}^m$ and output $\boldsymbol{r}$.
   else:
   a) Repeat 2).
3) By using the FRD encoding function, take $\boldsymbol{r} \in \mathbb{Z}^m$ as input, output a public, full-rank and "low norm" matrix $\boldsymbol{R}$.

We first analyse the security of Algorithm 1. Due to the output of $\mathcal{O}_{\mathbf{G}}$ is random and uniform, and $\bar{A}$ is a randomly chosen $n \times \bar{m}$ matrix. Consequently, by the assumption of inhomogeneous small integer solution (ISIS) problem, vector $\boldsymbol{u}$ is $negl(n)$-far from uniform. Hence, by the MP12 preimage sampling algorithm in [18], the output $\hat{r}$ of MP12Sample is statistically close to uniform. Then, the vector concatenated by $\hat{r}$ and $\bar{r}$ is also uniform. Finally, by the property of the FRD function, we can obtain the invertible and "low norm" matrix $\boldsymbol{R}$.

3.2 Construction of Delegation Algorithm

Based on the MP12SampleR algorithm in Sect. 3.1, we try to construct the efficient delegation algorithm that does not increase the dimension of the underlying matrices.

However, the combination of the MP12Sample algorithm from [18] with the trapdoor delegation algorithm in fixed dimension from [15] is not directly. We have an obstacle here.

Difficulty. The output of the MP12 trapdoor delegation algorithm is not a full rank trapdoor matrix, rather than the full rank trapdoor like [15] and [11]. And hence, we cannot directly instantiate our MP12SampleR algorithm with MP12 trapdoor function. Fortunately, we can remove this obstacle by the following lemma.

Lemma 1 [18]. There is an efficient polynomial time algorithm with the following properties: given an arbitrary $\boldsymbol{A} \in \mathbb{Z}_q^{n \times m}$ and its trapdoor $\boldsymbol{T}_{\mathbf{A}} \in \mathbb{Z}^{\bar{m} \times w}$ with tag $\boldsymbol{H} \in \mathbb{Z}_q^{n \times n}$, let $\boldsymbol{T}_{\mathbf{G}} \in \mathbb{Z}^{\bar{m} \times w}$ be any basis for lattice $\Lambda^{\perp}(\boldsymbol{G})$. Then we can obtain a full basis of lattice $\Lambda^{\perp}(\boldsymbol{A})$, $\boldsymbol{S} = \begin{bmatrix} \boldsymbol{I} & \boldsymbol{T_A} \\ \boldsymbol{0} & \boldsymbol{I} \end{bmatrix} \begin{bmatrix} \boldsymbol{I} & \boldsymbol{0} \\ \boldsymbol{W} & \boldsymbol{T_G} \end{bmatrix}$, where $\boldsymbol{W} \in \mathbb{Z}^{w \times \bar{m}}$ is an arbitrary solution to $\boldsymbol{G}\boldsymbol{W} = -\boldsymbol{A}[\boldsymbol{I}|\boldsymbol{0}]^T/\boldsymbol{H} \bmod q$. Moreover, the basis $\boldsymbol{S}$ satisfies $\|\tilde{\boldsymbol{S}}\| \leq s_1\left(\begin{bmatrix} \boldsymbol{I} & \boldsymbol{T}_{\mathbf{A}} \\ \boldsymbol{0} & \boldsymbol{I} \end{bmatrix}\right) \cdot \|\tilde{\boldsymbol{T}}_{\boldsymbol{G}}\| \leq (s_1(\boldsymbol{T_A})+1) \cdot \|\tilde{\boldsymbol{T}}_{\boldsymbol{G}}\|$, when $\boldsymbol{S}$ is orthogonalized in suitable order.

Algorithm 2 Efficient algorithm FixedTrapDel(A, T_A, B, R, σ) for delegating trapdoor without dimension increase.

Input: A parity check matrix $A \in \mathbb{Z}_q^{n \times m}$, a trapdoor matrix $T_A \in \mathbb{Z}^{\bar{m} \times w}$ of A, a Gaussian parameter $\sigma \geq \eta_\epsilon(\Lambda^\perp(A))$, a matrix $B = AR^{-1}$, a $\mathbb{Z}_q$-invertible matrix R obtained from the MP12SampleR algorithm in Section 3.1 Algorithm 1.

Output: A basis T_B of lattice $\Lambda^\perp(B)$.

1) By the algorithm described in Lemma 1, using the trapdoor matrix T_A as input, obtain the full rank basis $S \in \mathbb{Z}^{m \times m}$.
2) Let $S = \{s_1, \dots, s_m\} \subseteq \mathbb{Z}^m$. Compute $S' = \{Rs_1, \dots, Rs_m\} \subseteq \mathbb{Z}^m$.
3) For $i = 1, \dots, m$:
   a) Choose a perturbation $p_i = [p_{i,1}; p_{i,2}]$ for $p_{i,1} \in \mathbb{Z}_q^{\bar{m}}$, $p_{i,2} \in \mathbb{Z}_q^w$ from $D_{\mathbb{Z}^m, \sqrt{\Sigma_{p_i}} \cdot \omega(\sqrt{\log m})}$ where $\Sigma_{p_i} \geq 2[S'; I][S'^T \mid I]$.
   b) Compute $\bar{w}_i = \bar{A}(p_{i,1} - S'p_{i,2}) \in \mathbb{Z}_q^n$ and $w_i = Gp_{i,2} \in \mathbb{Z}_q^n$.
   c) Call $z_i \leftarrow$ MP12Sample$(G, T_G, \sigma_G, 0)$ and compute $v_i = H^{-1}Ap_i \in \mathbb{Z}_q^n$.
4) Transform the vectors $v_1, \dots, v_m$ to a basis S'' using ToBasis algorithm [].
5) Output the resulting basis $T_B = S''$ of lattice $\Lambda^\perp(B)$.

We now simply analyze the security of Algorithm 2. We note that the column vectors $\mathbf{s}'_1, \dots, \mathbf{s}'_m$ of S' lie in a non-full-rank subset of $\Lambda^\perp(A)$, and its distribution is non-spherical and could leak the information of S'. Fortunately, that does not influence the resulting output when we use the "convolution" technique in step 3) from [23] to correct for the statistical skew that arises in Rs_i.

4 An Efficient Hierarchical Identity-Based Fully Homomorphic Encryption from LWE

In Sect. 4.1, we will show how to combine the improved delegation algorithm FixedTrapDel presented in Sect. 3.2 with the MP12 trapdoor function [18], which can efficiently generate public parameters and delegate trapdoor to its child entities. We note that the combination does not affect to use the Dual-Regev algorithm [13] in the Encrypt & Decrypt stages. In Sect. 4.2, we transform the HIBE scheme to HIBFHE scheme by employing the eigenvector idea from [10]. We mention that our works all construct on a special modulus q which is a power of 2, which means we can employ the MPDec algorithm [10] to operate any messages over $\mathbb{Z}_q$.

4.1 Construction of HIBE

We can now describe the HIBE scheme. Let integers $\bar{m}, q, \beta$ be polynomials in the security parameter n. Set integers $k = \lceil \log q \rceil$, $w = nk, m = \bar{m} + w, m' = m + n$ that are fixed across the levels of the hierarchy. Now, for a hierarchy of maximum depth d the scheme works as follows:

HIBE – Setup($1^n, 1^d$): Given a security parameter n and a number of maximum depth d, compute $(\boldsymbol{A}, \boldsymbol{T_A}) \leftarrow$ MP12TrapGen$(1^n, 1^m, q)$ such that $\boldsymbol{A} \in \mathbb{Z}_q^{n \times m}$ and $\boldsymbol{T_A} \in \mathbb{Z}^{\bar{m} \times w}$. Randomly choose $\boldsymbol{U}_0 \leftarrow \mathbb{Z}_q^{n \times n}$. For each $(i, b) \in [d] \times \{0, 1\}$, use MP12SampleR algorithm to sample a $\mathbb{Z}_q$-invertible matrix $\boldsymbol{R}_{i,b} \in \mathbb{Z}^{m \times m}$. Return the master public key and master secret key (MPK,MSK) $= \left(\left(\boldsymbol{A}, \boldsymbol{U}_0, \{\boldsymbol{R}_{i,b}\} \right), \boldsymbol{T_A} \right)$.

HIBE – Derive(MPK, $\boldsymbol{id}|\boldsymbol{id}_\ell, \boldsymbol{TD_{id}}$): Given master public key MPK, a trapdoor $\boldsymbol{TD_{id}}$ corresponding to a parent identity $\boldsymbol{id}$ at depth $\ell - 1$ the algorithm finally returns a delegation trapdoor $\boldsymbol{TD}_{\boldsymbol{id}_\ell}$ for the identity $\boldsymbol{id}|\boldsymbol{id}_\ell$ at depth ℓ. Compute $\boldsymbol{A_{id}} = \boldsymbol{A}\left(\boldsymbol{R}_{\ell,\boldsymbol{id}_\ell}\right)^{-1}\left(\boldsymbol{R}_{\ell-1,\boldsymbol{id}_{\ell-1}}\right)^{-1} \ldots \left(\boldsymbol{R}_{1,1}\right)^{-1} \in \mathbb{Z}_q^{n \times m}$ and $\boldsymbol{A}_{\boldsymbol{id}_\ell} = \boldsymbol{A_{id}}\left(\boldsymbol{R}_{\ell,\boldsymbol{id}_\ell}\right)^{-1}$. Then compute FixedTrapDel($\boldsymbol{A_{id}}, \boldsymbol{T}_{\boldsymbol{A_{id}}}, \boldsymbol{A}_{\boldsymbol{id}_\ell}, \boldsymbol{R}, \boldsymbol{H}', \sigma'$) to delegate a trapdoor $\boldsymbol{T}_{\boldsymbol{A}_{\boldsymbol{id}_\ell}}$ for $\boldsymbol{A}_{\boldsymbol{id}_\ell}$ with tag $\boldsymbol{H}'$. Finally, return the delegated trapdoor $\boldsymbol{T}_{\boldsymbol{A}_{\boldsymbol{id}_\ell}}$.

HIBE - Encrypt(MPK, $\boldsymbol{id}, \bar{\boldsymbol{\mu}}$): Given master public key MPK, an identity $\boldsymbol{id} = (\boldsymbol{id}_1|\ldots|\boldsymbol{id}_\ell)$ at depth ℓ, and a message $\bar{\boldsymbol{\mu}} \in \mathbb{Z}_q^{m'}$ which is an all 0's vector except with $\boldsymbol{\mu} \cdot \lfloor q/2 \rfloor$ in the first n coefficients. Compute $\boldsymbol{R_{id}} = \boldsymbol{R}_{\ell,\boldsymbol{id}_\ell} \cdot \boldsymbol{R}_{\ell-1,\boldsymbol{id}_{\ell-1}} \cdot \ldots \cdot \boldsymbol{R}_{1,1} \in \mathbb{Z}^{m \times m}$ and encryption matrix $\boldsymbol{A_{id}} = \boldsymbol{A} \cdot \boldsymbol{R}_{\boldsymbol{id}}^{-1} \in \mathbb{Z}_q^{n \times m}$. Let $\boldsymbol{A}'_{\boldsymbol{id}} = \boldsymbol{U}_0|\boldsymbol{A_{id}} \in \mathbb{Z}_q^{n \times m'}$. Randomly choose $\boldsymbol{s} \leftarrow \mathbb{Z}_q^n$. Then, compute $\boldsymbol{c_{id}} = \boldsymbol{s}^T\boldsymbol{A}'_{\boldsymbol{id}} + \boldsymbol{x} + \bar{\boldsymbol{\mu}} \in \mathbb{Z}_q^{m'}$, where 'error-vector' $\boldsymbol{x}$ are chosen according to error distribution $\Psi_\alpha^{m'}$. Finally, output the ciphertext $\boldsymbol{c_{id}} \in \mathbb{Z}_q^{m'}$.

HIBE – Decrypt(MPK, $\boldsymbol{TD_{id}}, \boldsymbol{c_{id}}$): Given master public key MPK, a trapdoor $\boldsymbol{TD_{id}}$ corresponding to identity $\boldsymbol{id}$ at depth ℓ and a ciphertext $\boldsymbol{c_{id}}$. Compute $\boldsymbol{E_{id}} \leftarrow$ MP12Sample$(\boldsymbol{A_{id}}, \boldsymbol{TD_{id}}, \boldsymbol{U}_0, \sigma_\ell)$, let $\boldsymbol{I}_n$ be a $n \times n$ identity matrix, set $\boldsymbol{S_{id}} = [\boldsymbol{I}_n; -\boldsymbol{E_{id}}]$, note that $\boldsymbol{A}'_{\boldsymbol{id}} \cdot \boldsymbol{S_{id}} = \boldsymbol{0}$. Compute $\boldsymbol{\mu}' = \boldsymbol{S}_{\boldsymbol{id}}^T \cdot \boldsymbol{c_{id}}$. Then, compare μ'_i and treat them as integers in $\mathbb{Z}$, and set $\mu_i = 1$ if $|\mu'_i - \lfloor q/2 \rfloor| < \lfloor q/4 \rfloor$, otherwise $\mu_i = 0$, where $i \in \{1, \ldots, n\}$. Finally, output the plaintext $\boldsymbol{\mu} \in \{\mu_0, \ldots, \mu_n\}^T$.

4.2 Construction of HIBFHE

To preserve strong boundedness, a notion introduced in [10], under the security constraint, i.e., ensure the ratio q/B is at most subexponential in N, where B is introduced in Definition 2. It is necessary to introduce some facts and basic operations (BitDecomp $(\cdot)$, BitDecomp^{-1} $(\cdot)$, Powersof2 $(\cdot)$, Flatten $(\cdot)$) from [10] to help describe how strong boundedness is preserved, and serve as useful tools for HIBFHE constructions. Based on the basic operations and facts, we employ the eigenvector idea from [10] to transform our HIBE scheme to HIBFHE scheme. Set $\ell_q = \lfloor \log q \rfloor + 1$, $N = m' \cdot \ell_q$.

HIBFHE – Setup($1^n, 1^L, 1^d$): Given a security parameter n, a number of levels L (circuit depth to support) and a number of maximum depth d. Generate master public key and master secret key by running HIBE – Setup algorithm. Finally, return (MPK, MSK) $= \left(\left(\boldsymbol{A}, \boldsymbol{U}_0, \{\boldsymbol{R}_{i,b}\} \right), \boldsymbol{T_A} \right)$.

HIBFHE – KeyGen(MPK, MSK, $\boldsymbol{id}$): Given master public key MPK, master secret key MSK and a user identity $\boldsymbol{id}$ at depth ℓ. Compute $\boldsymbol{E_{id}} \leftarrow$ MP12Sample $(\boldsymbol{A_{id}}, \boldsymbol{TD_{id}}, U_0, \sigma_\ell)$, and set $\boldsymbol{S'_{id}} = [\boldsymbol{I}_{n\times n}| - \boldsymbol{E_{id}}]$, where $\mathbf{I}_{n\times n}$ denotes an $n \times n$ identity matrix. Finally, return $\boldsymbol{V_{id}} \leftarrow$ Powersof2($\mathbf{S'_{id}}$).

HIBFHE – Encrypt(MPK, $\boldsymbol{id}$, $\boldsymbol{\mu}$): Given master public key MPK, a user identity **id** at depth ℓ and a message $\boldsymbol{\mu} \in \mathbb{Z}_q^n$. Generates N encryptions of 0 using HIBE - Encrypt algorithm, sets $\boldsymbol{C'_{id}}$ to be the $nN \times m'$ matrix whose rows are these ciphertexts. Finally, return $\boldsymbol{C_{id}} = \text{Flatten}\left([\mu_1 \cdot \mathbf{I}_N; \ldots; \mu_n \cdot \mathbf{I}_N] + \text{BitDecomp}\left(\boldsymbol{C'_{id}}\right)\right) \in \mathbb{Z}_q^{nN\times N}$.

HIBFHE – MPDec($\boldsymbol{C_{id}}, \boldsymbol{V_{id}}$): Given $\boldsymbol{V_{id}} \leftarrow \text{Powersof2}\left(\boldsymbol{S'_{id}}\right)$ and a ciphertext $\boldsymbol{C_{id}}$ under identity $\boldsymbol{id}$. Let $\boldsymbol{v}_1, \ldots, \boldsymbol{v}_n$ to be the rows of $\boldsymbol{V_{id}}$. Set $\boldsymbol{C}_i = \text{Flatten}\left([\mu_i \cdot \mathbf{I}_N] + \text{BitDecomp}\left(\boldsymbol{C'_i}\right)\right) \in \mathbb{Z}_q^{N\times N}$, where $\mathbf{C}'_i \in \mathbb{Z}_q^{N\times m'}$ and $1 \leq i \leq n$. Observe that the first $\ell - 1$ coordinates of $\boldsymbol{v}_i$ are $1, 2, \ldots, 2^{\ell-2}$ and $q = 2^{\ell-1}$, and therefore if $\boldsymbol{C}_i \cdot \boldsymbol{v}_i = \mu_i \cdot \boldsymbol{v}_i + \text{BitDecomp}\left(\boldsymbol{C'_i}\right) \cdot \boldsymbol{v}_i = \mu_i \cdot \boldsymbol{v}_i + \boldsymbol{C}'_i \cdot \boldsymbol{s}_i$, then the first $\ell - 1$ coordinates of $\boldsymbol{C}_i \cdot \boldsymbol{v}_i$ are $\mu_i \cdot \boldsymbol{g} + \boldsymbol{C}'_i \cdot \boldsymbol{s}_i$, where $\boldsymbol{g} = \left(1, 2, \ldots, 2^{\ell-2}\right)$. Recover LSB$(\mu_i)$ from $\mu_i \cdot 2^{\ell-2} + \mathbf{C}'_i \cdot \boldsymbol{s}_i$, then recover the next least significant bit from $(\mu_i - \text{LSB}(\mu_i)) \cdot 2^{\ell-3} + \boldsymbol{C}'_i \cdot \boldsymbol{s}_i$, etc. Finally, return the plaintext $\boldsymbol{\mu} \in \{\mu_1, \ldots, \mu_n\}^T$.

HIBFHE – Eval(MPK,f, $\boldsymbol{C_{id,1}}, \boldsymbol{C_{id,2}}, \ldots, \boldsymbol{C_{id,t}}$) : Given MPK, an arbitrary t-ary function $f \in \mathcal{F}$ and ciphertexts $\boldsymbol{C_{id,1}}, \boldsymbol{C_{id,2}}, \ldots, \boldsymbol{C_{id,t}}$, where $\mathcal{F}$ is a set that consists of all circuits of depth L for some L, consisting of (e.g.) NAND gates. Then, compute and return $\boldsymbol{C_{id,f}} \leftarrow \text{Eval}(\text{MPK}, f, \boldsymbol{C_{id,1}}, \boldsymbol{C_{id,2}}, \ldots, \boldsymbol{C_{id,t}})$, where $\boldsymbol{C_{id,f}}$ is a ciphertext that satisfies HIBFHE – Decrypt$(\boldsymbol{C_{id,f}}, \boldsymbol{V_{id}}) = f(\boldsymbol{\mu}_1, \ldots, \boldsymbol{\mu}_t)$.

5 Analysis of the Proposed Schemes

5.1 Security Reduction

In this work, we use privacy property called indistinguishability from random in [14], which captures both semantic security and recipient anonymity by requiring the challenge ciphertext to be indistinguishable from a uniformly random element in the ciphertext space. Therefore, we use the security model to prove our HIBE scheme is INDr-sID-CPA secure under standard model.

Theorem 4. Supposing that the LWE problem described in Definition 1 is hard under the parameters $(m, \sigma_\ell, \alpha_\ell, q)$ setting as is shown in Sect. 4.1, the proposed HIBE scheme is provable INDr-sID-CPA secure in the standard model.

Proof. Suppose there is an adversary $\mathcal{A}$ against the selective identity CPA security with advantage $\in$. Then we first construct a distinguisher $\mathcal{B}$ with the advantage of at least $\in /2$ between two distributions, that is: $\left\{(\boldsymbol{A}, \boldsymbol{s}^T\boldsymbol{A} + \boldsymbol{x}) : \boldsymbol{A} \in \mathbb{Z}_q^{n\times m}, \boldsymbol{s} \in \mathbb{Z}_q^n, \boldsymbol{x} \leftarrow \bar{\Psi}_\alpha^m, \alpha < \left(m^{3.5} \cdot \omega(\sqrt{\log m})\right)^{-1}\right\}$ and uniform distribution $\left\{\mathbb{Z}_q^{m+n}\right\}$.

Recall from Definition 1 that an LWE problem instance is provided as a sampling oracle $\mathcal{O}$ which can be either truly random $\mathcal{O}_\$$ (i.e., uniform over $\mathbb{Z}_q^{m+n}$) or a noisy pseudo-random $\mathcal{O}_s$ (i.e., $(\boldsymbol{A}, \boldsymbol{s}^T\boldsymbol{A}+\boldsymbol{x})$) for some secret $\boldsymbol{s} \in \mathbb{Z}_q^n$. A selective identity adversary $\mathcal{A}$ outputs the challenge identity $\boldsymbol{id}^* = (\boldsymbol{id}_1^*, \boldsymbol{id}_2^*, \ldots, \boldsymbol{id}_\ell^*)$. The simulator $\mathcal{B}$ use the adversary $\mathcal{A}$ to distinguish between the two, and proceeds as follows:

Instance. $\mathcal{B}$ requests from $\mathcal{O}$ and receives, for each $i \in [m]$, a fresh pair $(\boldsymbol{u}_i, \boldsymbol{v}_i) \in \mathbb{Z}_q^n \times \mathbb{Z}_q$.

Simulation of the attack environment. $\mathcal{B}$ constructs the system's public parameters MPK as follows:

1. Assemble the random matrix $\boldsymbol{A}_0 \in \mathbb{Z}_q^{n\times m}$ from m of the previous given LWE instance by letting the i-th column of $\boldsymbol{A}_0$ be the n-vector $\boldsymbol{u}_i$ for $i \in [m]$.
2. Assign the zeroth LWE sample (so far unused) to become the public random n-vector $\boldsymbol{u}_0 \in \mathbb{Z}_q^n$.
3. Run SampleR algorithm (Sect. 3.1) to sample k $\mathbb{Z}_q$-invertible matrices $\boldsymbol{R}_{1,id_1^*}^*, \boldsymbol{R}_{2,id_2^*}^*, \ldots, \boldsymbol{R}_{\ell,id_\ell^*}^*$, then set $\boldsymbol{A} = \boldsymbol{A}_0\boldsymbol{R}_{1,id_1^*}^*\boldsymbol{R}_{2,id_2^*}^* \cdots \boldsymbol{R}_{\ell,id_\ell^*}^*$.
4. Consider the d matrices $\boldsymbol{A}_{id_i}$, for each matrix $\boldsymbol{A}_{id_i}$ the simulator $\mathcal{B}$ invokes SampleRwithTrap$(\boldsymbol{A}_{id_i})$ to obtain a matrix $\boldsymbol{R}_{i,1-id_i^*} \in \mathbb{Z}^{m\times m}$ and a trapdoor for $\boldsymbol{A}_{id_i} \cdot \boldsymbol{R}_{i,1-id_i^*}$.
5. Send to $\mathcal{A}$ the public parameters MPK $= (\boldsymbol{A}, \boldsymbol{u}_0, \boldsymbol{R}_{1,0}, \boldsymbol{R}_{1,1}, \boldsymbol{R}_{2,0}, \boldsymbol{R}_{2,1}, \ldots, \boldsymbol{R}_{d,0}, \boldsymbol{R}_{d,1},)$.

Queries. $\mathcal{A}$ makes identity key extraction queries on identities $\boldsymbol{id}$ that are not a prefix of $\boldsymbol{id}^*$. $\mathcal{B}$ answers a query on $\boldsymbol{id} = (\boldsymbol{id}_1, \boldsymbol{id}_2, \ldots, \boldsymbol{id}_\ell)$ of length $|\boldsymbol{id}| = \ell \in [d]$ as follows. To simplify the description assume $\ell = d$ (the case $\ell < d$ is just as easy). Note that the distinguisher $\mathcal{B}$ holds the trapdoor $\boldsymbol{T}_i$ for $\boldsymbol{A}_{id_i} \cdot \boldsymbol{R}_{i,1-id_i^*}$ by the SampleRwithTrap algorithm as mentioned in [15].

1. Call SampleRwithTrap algorithm to obtain a trapdoor $\boldsymbol{T}_i$ for $\Lambda^{\perp}(\boldsymbol{A}_{id_i} \cdot \boldsymbol{R}_{i,1-id_i^*})$, and $\|\tilde{\boldsymbol{T}}_i\| \leq O\sqrt{n \log q}$.
2. Run MP12Sample$(\boldsymbol{A}_{id_i} \cdot \boldsymbol{R}_{i,1-id_i^*}, \boldsymbol{T}_i, \boldsymbol{u}_0, \sigma_d)$ to generate a secret key for $\boldsymbol{id}$ from the trapdoor $\boldsymbol{T}_i$, and send the resulting secret key to the adversary.

Challenge. $\mathcal{A}$ outputs a message $\mu^* \in \{0, 1\}$ to be encrypted and $\mathcal{B}$ responds with an encryption of μ^* for the identity $\boldsymbol{id}^*$. By definition $\boldsymbol{A}_{id^*} = \boldsymbol{A}_0\boldsymbol{R}_{1,id_1^*}^*\boldsymbol{R}_{2,id_2^*}^* \cdots \boldsymbol{R}_{\ell,id_\ell^*}^* = \boldsymbol{A}$, and $\mathcal{B}$ proceeds as follows:

1. Retireve $v_0, v_1, \ldots, v_m \in \mathbb{Z}_q$ from the LWE instance and set $\boldsymbol{v}^* = (v_1, v_2, \ldots, v_m) \in \mathbb{Z}_q^m$.
2. Blind the message bit by letting $c_0^* = v_0 + \mu^*\lfloor q/2 \rfloor \in \mathbb{Z}_q$, and set $\boldsymbol{c}_1^* = \boldsymbol{v}^*$.

When $\mathcal{O}$ is a pseudo-random LWE oracle then $c_0 = \boldsymbol{u}_0^T\boldsymbol{s} + x + \mu\lfloor q/2 \rfloor$ and $\boldsymbol{c}_1 = \boldsymbol{A}_{id^*}^T\boldsymbol{s} + \boldsymbol{y}$ for some random $\boldsymbol{s} \in \mathbb{Z}_q^n$ and noise values x and $\boldsymbol{y}$. In this case $(c_0, \boldsymbol{c}_1)$ is a valid encryption of μ for $\boldsymbol{id}^*$. When $\mathcal{O}$ is a random oracle then $(v_0, \boldsymbol{v}^*)$ are uniform in $\left(\mathbb{Z}_q \times \mathbb{Z}_q^m\right)$ and therefore $(c_0, \boldsymbol{c}_1)$ is uniform in $\left(\mathbb{Z}_q \times \mathbb{Z}_q^m\right)$.

Queries (Phase 2). $\mathcal{A}$ can make more secret key queries are answered by $\mathcal{B}$ in the same manner as before.

Guess. $\mathcal{A}$ guesses whether (c_0^*, c_1^*) was an encryption of μ^* for $\boldsymbol{id}^*$. $\mathcal{B}$ outputs $\mathcal{A}'s$ guess and ends the simulation.

The distribution of the public parameters is identical to its distribution in the real system as are responses to private key queries. Finally, the challenge ciphertext is distributed either as in the real system or is independently random in $\left(\mathbb{Z}_q \times \mathbb{Z}_q^m\right)$. Therefore, $\mathcal{B}'s$ advantage in solving LWE is the same as $\mathcal{A}'s$ advantage in attacking the system, as required.

6 Conclusion

In this paper, we proposed an improved IBFHE scheme in the standard model from lattices. We took the first step in this direction by constructing an efficient HBFHE scheme which trapdoor delegation in a fixed method. The scheme was proven secure against the chosen-identity and chosen-plaintext attack without random oracle. The main contribution of our work was that we introduce the MP12 trapdoor function in the construction of trapdoor delegation algorithm, and then combine with other techniques to propose an improved HIBFHE scheme. Compared with the similar schemes, our HIBFHE scheme was asymptotically-faster.

Acknowledgments. This work was supported by the "13th Five-Year" National Crypto Development Foundation (No.MMJJ20170122), the Project of Science and Technology Department of Henan Province (No.142300410147), the Project of Education Department of Henan Province (No.12A520021, No.16A520013), the Doctoral Fund of Henan Polytechnic University (No.B2014-044), the Natural Science Foundation of Henan Polytechnic University (No.T2018-1).

References

1. Gentry, C.: Fully homomorphic encryption using ideal lattices. In: Proceedings of 41th ACM Symposium on Theory of Computing, STOC 2009, pp. 169–178. ACM, Bethesda (2009)
2. van Dijk, M., Gentry, C., Halevi, S., Vaikuntanathan, V.: Fully homomorphic encryption over the integers. In: Gilbert, H. (ed.) EUROCRYPT 2010. LNCS, vol. 6110, pp. 24–43. Springer, Heidelberg (2010). https://doi.org/10.1007/978-3-642-13190-5_2
3. Brakerski, Z., Vaikuntanathan, V.: Fully homomorphic encryption from ring-LWE and security for key dependent messages. In: Rogaway, P. (ed.) CRYPTO 2011. LNCS, vol. 6841, pp. 505–524. Springer, Heidelberg (2011). https://doi.org/10.1007/978-3-642-22792-9_29
4. Gentry, C., Halevi, S., Smart, N.P.: Fully homomorphic encryption with polylog overhead. In: Pointcheval, D., Johansson, T. (eds.) EUROCRYPT 2012. LNCS, vol. 7237, pp. 465–482. Springer, Heidelberg (2012). https://doi.org/10.1007/978-3-642-29011-4_28

5. Ducas, L., Micciancio, D.: FHEW: bootstrapping homomorphic encryption in less than a second. In: Oswald, E., Fischlin, M. (eds.) EUROCRYPT 2015. LNCS, vol. 9056, pp. 617–640. Springer, Heidelberg (2015). https://doi.org/10.1007/978-3-662-46800-5_24
6. Nuida, K., Kurosawa, K.: Fully homomorphic encryption over integers for non-binary message spaces. In: Oswald, E., Fischlin, M. (eds.) EUROCRYPT 2015. LNCS, vol. 9056, pp. 537–555. Springer, Heidelberg (2015). https://doi.org/10.1007/978-3-662-46800-5_21
7. Canetti, R., Halevi, S., Katz, J.: A forward-secure public-key encryption scheme. In: Biham, E. (ed.) EUROCRYPT 2003. LNCS, vol. 2656, pp. 255–271. Springer, Heidelberg (2003). https://doi.org/10.1007/3-540-39200-9_16
8. Dodis, Y., Fazio, N.: Public key broadcast encryption for stateless receivers. In: Feigenbaum, J. (ed.) DRM 2002. LNCS, vol. 2696, pp. 61–80. Springer, Heidelberg (2003). https://doi.org/10.1007/978-3-540-44993-5_5
9. Yao, D., Fazio, N., Dodis, Y., Lysyanskaya, A.: ID-based encryption for complex hierarchies with applications to forward security and broadcast encryption. In: ACM Conference on Computer and Communications Security, pp. 354–363. ACM, Washington (2004)
10. Gentry, C., Sahai, A., Waters, B.: Homomorphic encryption from learning with errors: conceptually-simpler, asymptotically-faster, attribute-based. In: Canetti, R., Garay, J.A. (eds.) CRYPTO 2013. LNCS, vol. 8042, pp. 75–92. Springer, Heidelberg (2013). https://doi.org/10.1007/978-3-642-40041-4_5
11. Cash, D., Hofheinz, D., Kiltz, E., Peikert, C.: Bonsai trees, or how to delegate a lattice basis. In: Gilbert, H. (ed.) EUROCRYPT 2010. LNCS, vol. 6110, pp. 523–552. Springer, Heidelberg (2010). https://doi.org/10.1007/978-3-642-13190-5_27
12. Regev, O.: On lattices, learning with errors, random linear codes, and cryptography. In: STOC 2005 Proceedings of the thirty-seventh annual ACM symposium on Theory of computing, pp. 84–93. ACM, Baltimore (2005)
13. Gentry, C., Peikert, C., Vaikuntanathan, V.: Trapdoors for hard lattices and new cryptographic constructions. In: Proceedings of 41th ACM Symposium on Theory of Computing, pp 197–206. ACM, Victoria (2008)
14. Agrawal, S., Boneh, D., Boyen, X.: Efficient lattice (H)IBE in the standard model. In: Gilbert, H. (ed.) EUROCRYPT 2010. LNCS, vol. 6110, pp. 553–572. Springer, Heidelberg (2010). https://doi.org/10.1007/978-3-642-13190-5_28
15. Agrawal, S., Boneh, D., Boyen, X.: Lattice basis delegation in fixed dimension and shorter-ciphertext hierarchical IBE. In: Rabin, T. (ed.) CRYPTO 2010. LNCS, vol. 6223, pp. 98–115. Springer, Heidelberg (2010). https://doi.org/10.1007/978-3-642-14623-7_6
16. Ajtai, M.: Generating hard instances of the short basis problem. In: Wiedermann, J., van Emde Boas, P., Nielsen, M. (eds.) ICALP 1999. LNCS, vol. 1644, pp. 1–9. Springer, Heidelberg (1999). https://doi.org/10.1007/3-540-48523-6_1
17. Alwen, J., Peikert, C.: Generating shorter bases for hard random lattices. Theor. Comput. Syst. **48**(3), 535–553 (2009)
18. Micciancio, D., Peikert, C.: Trapdoors for lattices: simpler, tighter, faster, smaller. In: Pointcheval, D., Johansson, T. (eds.) EUROCRYPT 2012. LNCS, vol. 7237, pp. 700–718. Springer, Heidelberg (2012). https://doi.org/10.1007/978-3-642-29011-4_41
19. Micciancio, D., Goldwasser, S.: Complexity of lattice problems: a cryptographic perspective. Siam J. Comput. **671**(6495), 220 (2002)
20. Ajtai, M.: Generating hard instances of lattice problems. In: STOC 1996 Proceedings of the Twenty-Eighth Annual ACM Symposium on Theory of Computing, pp. 99–108. ACM, Philadelphia (1996)
21. Micciancio, D., Regev, O.: Worst-case to average-case reductions based on Gaussian measures. SIAM J. Comput. **37**(1), 267–302 (2007)

22. Peikert, C.: An efficient and parallel Gaussian sampler for lattices. In: Rabin, T. (ed.) CRYPTO 2010. LNCS, vol. 6223, pp. 80–97. Springer, Heidelberg (2010). https://doi.org/10.1007/978-3-642-14623-7_5
23. Yamada, S.: Adaptively secure identity-based encryption from lattices with asymptotically shorter public parameters. In: Fischlin, M., Coron, J.-S. (eds.) EUROCRYPT 2016. LNCS, vol. 9666, pp. 32–62. Springer, Heidelberg (2016). https://doi.org/10.1007/978-3-662-49896-5_2

A Novel Privacy-Preserving Decentralized Ciphertext-Policy Attribute-Based Encryption with Anonymous Key Generation

Hongjian Yin[1], Leyou Zhang[1(✉)], and Yi Mu[2]

[1] Xidian University, Xi'an 710126, Shaanxi, China
xidianyhj@163.com, lyzhang@mail.xidian.edu.cn
[2] University of Wollongong, Wollongong, NSW 2522, Australia
ymu@uow.edu.au

Abstract. A privacy-preserving decentralized ciphertext-policy attribute-based encryption (CP-ABE) scheme is a variant of the multi-authority attribute-based encryption schemes where it requires neither a central authority nor cooperation among authorities for issuing secret keys. It also featured the privacy-preserving and resisting user collusion. However, previous privacy-preserving decentralized CP-ABE schemes can only hide user's partial information, such as global identifier (GID), but user's attribute information leaked to the authority may be sensitive which will lead to privacy disclosure. To overcome this shortcoming, we propose an improved privacy-preserving decentralized CP-ABE scheme with anonymous key generation protocol, where it can prevent authorities from learning any information about user's both GID and attributes. Theoretical analysis and simulation results demonstrate that the proposed scheme is secure and efficient. In the standard model, its security is reduced to a standard decisional bilinear Diffie-Hellman complexity assumption.

Keywords: Privacy-preserving · Multi-authority
Decentralized CP-ABE · Anonymous key generation protocol

1 Introduction

Attribute-based encryption (ABE) is one of flexible public key encryption that allows for fine-grained access control on encrypted data. In an ABE scheme, the data owner can specify an access policy over a set of attributes, where these users whose attributes satisfy the policy can access the encrypted data. Since the first ABE scheme was proposed by Sahai and Waters [1], it has been intensively researched and further developed. There are two types of ABE schemes, which are called ciphertext-policy attribute-based encryption (CP-ABE) [2] and key-policy attribute-based encryption (KP-ABE) [3]. In a CP-ABE scheme, ciphertext is related to access structure and the secret keys of user are associated with

X. Sun et al. (Eds.): ICCCS 2018, LNCS 11065, pp. 435–446, 2018.
https://doi.org/10.1007/978-3-030-00012-7_40

an attribute set. Only the user whose secret keys satisfy the access structure associated with the ciphertext will be able to decrypt the ciphertext successfully. In contrast, in a KP-ABE scheme, ciphertext is related to an attribute set and the secret keys of user are associated with access structure. The user will be able to decrypt ciphertext only if the attributes associated with the ciphertext satisfy the access structure of the private key.

Most of ABE proposals are issued from the single authority. The single authority generates the private keys of the users and verifies all the attributes by itself. So it is impractical in some cases especially large scale attributes set. Chase further developed the ABE scheme and proposed the notion of multi-authority ABE [4]. Compared with previous ABE schemes, Chase's scheme supports multiple authorities to distribute attributes instead of a single authority. Specifically, her multi-authority ABE scheme allows any polynomial number of independent authorities to monitor attributes and distribute secret keys. In order to resist user collusion attacks, user secret keys have to be tied to a global identifier (GID) and a fully trusted central authority is necessary to issue a unique key to each user. However, this central authority has ability to decrypt every ciphertext in this system. The whole system will fail if the central authority is corrupted.

To solve the above problem, Lewko and Waters proposed a new multi-authority ABE system named decentralized ABE [5]. In their scheme, the central authority is removed and each independent authority can create public key and issue attribute secret keys to different users. A user can encrypt data in terms of any boolean formula over attributes issued from any chosen set of authorities. In addition, authorities are completely independent, such that every authority can join or leave the system without the necessity of reinitializing the system. And some corruption authorities will not affect the other uncorrupted authorities.

Some recent works about decentralized ABE have focused on achieving privacy preserving [6,7,9,10]. Specially, Han et al. further developed the decentralized ABE and proposed the privacy-preserving decentralized KP-ABE [6]. In their scheme, each authority can issue secret keys to a user independently without knowing anything about the user's GID. In addition, their scheme is tolerant against maximum $(N-1)$ authorities colluding. It means that the scheme is secure if the number of the corrupted authorities is not more than $(N-1)$, where N is the number of the authorities in the whole system. However, Ge et al. [11] pointed out that it did not resist user collusion attack. Subsequently, a modified privacy-preserving decentralized KP-ABE scheme was proposed by Rahulamathavan et al. [9]. Their scheme mitigates the user collusion attack employing anonymous key issuing protocol and achieves user's GID hidden.

In 2014, Han et al. proposed another type privacy-preserving decentralized ABE, named privacy-preserving decentralized CP-ABE [7]. User privacy protection is further considered in this scheme where both users' GID and attribute information are hidden from the authorities. It means that a user can get his/her attribute secret keys from multiple authorities without revealing any information about his/her GID and attributes. Unfortunately, this scheme is also vulnerable to collusion attack [12], which means that some unauthorized users whose attributes do not satisfy the ciphertext policy combine their secret keys together and then decrypt the ciphertext successfully. Additionally, in this scheme, the authority can figure out the attributes information from key extract protocol by running the decisional Diffie-Hellman test (DDH-test) $e(\Theta_2, Z_x) \stackrel{?}{=} e(\Psi_x^2, g)$. Moreover, its security is reduced to q-strong Diffie-Hellman assumption which is a strong hardness assumption.

Until now, as described in [12], it is an open problem to construct a decentralized ABE scheme in which both GID and attributes are hidden to support privacy preserving. In this paper, a novel privacy-preserving decentralized ciphertext-policy attribute-based encryption is proposed to answer this open problem. In our scheme, both user's GID and attributes are hidden. Specifically, the proposed scheme can prevent authorities from learning any information about user's GID and attributes. Different authorities are able to issue secret key independently to users and need not even be aware of each other. The security of the proposed scheme is reduced to a standard decisional bilinear Diffie-Hellman complexity assumption. Furthermore, compared with some previously known multi-authority ABE schemes, our privacy-preserving decentralized CP-ABE scheme is efficient.

2 Preliminaries

2.1 Access Structure

Our construction will employ AND-gate on multi-valued attributes access structure, which is similar to what used in [15]. It is described as follows.

Let $\mathbb{U} = \{att_1, att_2, \cdots, att_n\}$ be a set of attributes. For $att_i \in \mathbb{U}$, $S_i = \{v_{i,1}, v_{i,2}, \cdots v_{i,m_i}\}$ is a set of possible values, where m_i is the number of possible values for each att_i. Let $L = [L_1, L_2, \cdots L_n]$ be an attribute list for a user where $L_i \in S_i$. Let $\mathbb{A} = [w_1, w_2, \cdots w_n]$ be an access structure where $w_i \in S_i$. The notation $L \models \mathbb{A}$ expresses that an attribute list L satisfies an access structure $\mathbb{A}$ and $\not\models$ refers to not satisfy symbol.

2.2 Commitment Scheme

A commitment scheme allows someone to commit a chosen value without leaking this value for a period of time and reveal the committed value later when it is needed. There are two properties in a commit scheme, *binding* and *hiding*. Binding: once the value has been committed to, its owner will not be able to change the value. Hiding: the value remains unreleased until its owner release it later. In our scheme, we will follow Pedersen's commitment scheme which is a perfect hiding commitment scheme introduced in [16], it is defined as follows.

- Setup: Let $\mathbb{G}$ be a group with prime order. $g_0, g_1, \cdots, g_l$ are the generators of group $\mathbb{G}$.
- Commit: This algorithm takes messages $(m_1, m_2, \cdots, m_l)$ and a random number $r \in_R \mathbb{Z}_p$ as input, returns the commitment $T = g_0^r \prod_{j=1}^{l} g_j^{m_j}$.

– Decommit: The algorithm decommits the commitment with the random value r. If the commitment is correct, it outputs 1, otherwise outputs 0.

2.3 Zero-Knowledge Proof

A zero-knowledge proof system is always run between prover and verifier. The prover wants to convince the verifier some knowledge is true, but without revealing the knowledge during the exchange. In our scheme, we will use the zero-knowledge proof scheme proposed by Camenisch and Stadler [17]. The scheme is defined as follows.

We denote a zero-knowledge proof of integers α, β and γ by $PoK\{(\alpha, \beta, \gamma) : y = g^{\alpha} h^{\beta} \wedge \tilde{y} = \tilde{g}^{\alpha} \tilde{h}^{\gamma}\}$, where g, h are the generators of group $\mathbb{G}$ and $\tilde{g}, \tilde{h}$ are the generators of group $\tilde{\mathbb{G}}$. The integers α, β and γ are the knowledge, while other values can be used to verify the equations by the verifier.

2.4 K-out-of-n Oblivious Transfer

A k-out-of-n oblivious transfer (denoted by OT_n^k) protocol involves two parties, the sender S and the receiver R. The sender S has n messages $m_1, m_2, \cdots, m_n$ and the receiver R wants to obtain some party of them $m_{\sigma_1}, m_{\sigma_2}, \cdots, m_{\sigma_j}$, where $j < n$. In doing this process, R only obtains the massages what he/she choices and S does not know which massages are chosen by R. In our construction, we will employ the efficient OT_n^k-II scheme which was proposed by Chu and Tzeng [18], the scheme is described in Algorithm 1. Let $\mathbb{G}_q$ be the subgroup of $\mathbb{Z}_p^*$ with prime order q, g be a generator of $\mathbb{G}_q$, and $p = 2q + 1$ is also prime. Let $H_1^* : \{0,1\}^* \rightarrow \mathbb{G}_q$, $H_2^* : \mathbb{G}_q \rightarrow \{0,1\}^l$ be two collision-resistant hash functions. Let messages be of l-bit length.

Algorithm 1. k-Out-of-n Oblivious Transfer

System parameters: $(g, H_1^*, H_2^*, \mathbb{G}_q)$;

1: R computes $w_{\sigma_j} = H_1^*(\sigma_j)$ and $A_j = w_{\sigma_j} g^{a_j}$, where $a_j \in_R \mathbb{Z}_q$ and $j = 1, 2, \cdots, k$
2: R sends $A_1, A_2, \cdots, A_k$ to S
3: S computes $y = g^x$, $D_j = (A_j)^x$, $w_i = H_1^*(i)$, and $c_i = m_i \oplus H_2^*(w_i^x)$, where $x \in_R \mathbb{Z}_q$, $i = 1, 2, \cdots, n$, and $j = 1, 2, \cdots, k$
4: R sends $y, D_1, D_2, \cdots, D_k, c_1, c_2, \cdots, c_n$ to S
5: R computes $K_j = D_j / y^{a_j}$ and gets $m_{\sigma_j} = c_{\sigma_j} \oplus H_2^*(K_j)$ for $j = 1, 2, \cdots, k$

3 Definition and Security Model

3.1 Definition of DCP-ABE

A definition of decentralized ciphertext-policy attribute-based encryption (DCP-ABE) scheme consists of the following five algorithms:

- Global Setup. This algorithm takes a security parameter λ as input and returns public parameters PP to the system.
- Authority Setup. This algorithm is run by each authority A_i to generate the relevant public key PK_i and secret key SK_i, where $i = 1, 2, \cdots, N$.
- KeyGen. Taking as input the public parameters PP, the secret keys SK_i, a user U's global identifier GID_U and a set of attributes $\tilde{U} \cap \tilde{A}_i$, this algorithm outputs a secret key SK_U^i. Here $\tilde{U}$ is used to indicate the set of attribute for user U, $\tilde{A}_i$ denotes the attributes monitored by the authority A_i.
- Encryption. It takes public parameters PP, a message $\mathcal{M}$, authority's public keys PK_i and an access structure W as input, returns the ciphertext CT.
- Decryption. Taking as input the global identifier GID, a collection of secret keys corresponding to user attributes and CT, then decryption algorithm outputs $\mathcal{M}$ when user attributes satisfy the access structure in ciphertext.

3.2 Security Model of DCP-ABE

Similar to [4,6,7], the selective access policy model is defined as follows.

- Instruction: The adversary $\mathcal{A}$ submits the set of challenge access structure W^* and a set of corrupted authorities $\mathfrak{U}$, where $|\mathfrak{U}| < N$.
- Global Setup: The challenger $\mathcal{B}$ runs the **Global Setup** algorithm and outputs the system parameters PP to $\mathcal{A}$.
- Authorities Setup: There are two different cases.
  - (i) For the corrupted authority, $\mathcal{B}$ runs the **Authority Setup** algorithm to get the secret public key pair (PK_i, SK_i) and sends them to $\mathcal{A}$.
  - (ii) For the uncorrupted authority, $\mathcal{B}$ runs the **Authority Setup** algorithm to get the secret public key pair (PK_i, SK_i) and sends PK_i to $\mathcal{A}$.
- Phase 1: $\mathcal{A}$ submits the user U^*'s attributes list L^* and global identifier GID_{U^*} to the challenger $\mathcal{B}$ for secret keys queries but $L^* \not\models W^*$. Then $\mathcal{B}$ runs the **KeyGen** algorithm and sends the corresponding SK_{U^*} to $\mathcal{A}$.
- Challenge: $\mathcal{A}$ submits two same-length messages $\mathcal{M}_0$, $\mathcal{M}_1$ and a challenge access structure W^* to $\mathcal{B}$. Then $\mathcal{B}$ flips an unbiased coin $\xi \in \{0, 1\}$ and runs the **Encryption** algorithm to encrypt $\mathcal{M}_\xi$ under access structure W^* and get the corresponding ciphertext CT^*. Finally, $\mathcal{B}$ sends CT^* to $\mathcal{A}$.
- Phase 2: Same as phase 1.
- Guess: Finally, $\mathcal{A}$ outputs the guess bit $\xi' \in \{0, 1\}$ for ξ and wins the game if $\xi' = \xi$.

Definition 1. *A DCP-ABE scheme is (t, q, ϵ) secure in the selective access policy model if all t-time adversary makes q secret key queries and succeeds in the above game with negligible advantage ϵ.*

3.3 Definition of Privacy-Preserving DCP-ABE

The definition of privacy-preserving DCP-ABE is similar as normal DCP-ABE except the KeyGen algorithm. In order to protect user privacy, the KeyGen algorithm is replaced by anonymous KeyGen algorithm in the DCP-ABE scheme. In the following, we will introduce the outline of our anonymous KeyGen algorithm.

- Anonymous KeyGen. The user U runs the commitment scheme proposed in Sect. 2.2, then he/she sends the *com* to authority A_i. From *com*, authority A_i can use the aforementioned zero-knowledge proof system in Sect. 2.3 to verify whether the user U has GID_U or not. If the proof is successful, A_i picks a random number $w_i^u \in_R \mathbb{Z}_p$ and computes partial secret keys for U. Again user U utilizes the aforementioned zero-knowledge proof system to verify whether these secret keys from A_i are correct or not. If the proof is successful and algorithm *Decommit* returns 1, the user U can compute his/her secret keys successfully and authority A_i gets empty. Otherwise, algorithm aborts and outputs $(\perp, \perp)$ for the authority and user.
  To obtain the attribute secret keys, the anonymous KeyGen algorithm will employ the *k-out-of-n* oblivious transfer protocol introduced in Sect. 2.4. Before running the *k-out-of-n* oblivious transfer protocol, the user should convince authority A_i that he/she has the possession of attributes anonymous. In order to achieve this goal, we employ the anonymous credential system, which is proposed by Zhang and Feng [19]. In this anonymous credential system, the user can prove the possession of attributes without leaking any attribute information. If the user runs the anonymous credential system successfully, then the anonymous KeyGen algorithm will run the *k-out-of-n* oblivious transfer protocol to get the attribute secret key. From anonymous credential system and OT_n^k, the authority A_i can issue the correct attribute secret keys without knowing what attributes the user has. Firstly, the user prove the possession of attribute set $\tilde{U}$ anonymous by employing the anonymous credential system. If this anonymous credential system runs successfully, then the authority A_i takes $(pp, SK_i, \tilde{A}_i)$ as input and computes a set of attribute secret keys $\widetilde{SK}^i_{att}$. Finally, user U runs the OT_n^k and gets the attribute secret keys which ones are in $\tilde{U} \cap \tilde{A}_i$.

3.4 Security Model of Privacy-Preserving DCP-ABE

Following Han et al.'s scheme in [7], the security model of our privacy-preserving DCP-ABE is same as the model of DCP-ABE. Besides, the anonymous KeyGen algorithm should satisfy two extract properties: *leak-freeness* and *selective-failure blindness* [6,7]. Leak-freeness requires that a malicious user cannot learn anything which he/she cannot know by executing the anonymous KeyGen algorithm with an honest authority. Selective-failure blindness requires that a malicious authority cannot learn anything about user's identifier and his/her attributes. We will use the following two experiments to define the leak-freeness game.

- Real experiment: The distinguisher $\mathcal{D}$ runs the Global Setup algorithm and Authority Setup algorithm as many as he/she wants. The malicious user U with global identifier GID_U and a set of attributes $\tilde{U}$ executes the anonymous KeyGen algorithm with the honest authority A_i.
- Ideal experiment: The distinguisher $\mathcal{D}$ runs the Global Setup algorithm and Authority Setup algorithm as many as he/she wants. The malicious user U'

with global identifier $GID_{U'}$ and a set of attributes $\tilde{U}'$, and requires a trusted party to obtain the outputs of KeyGen algorithm.

Definition 2. *An anonymous KeyGen algorithm is leak-freeness if for any efficient adversary U, there exists a simulator U' such that no distinguisher $\mathcal{D}$ can distinguish whether U is playing in the real experiment or in the ideal experiment with non-negligible advantage.*

The selective-failure blindness game is defined as follows.

(i) The malicious authority A_i outputs its public key PK_i and two pairs of global identifiers and attribute sets $(GID_{U_0}, \tilde{U}_0)$ and $(GID_{U_1}, \tilde{U}_1)$.
(ii) Randomly choose a bit $b \in \{0, 1\}$.
(iii) A_i is given comments com_b and com_{1-b}. Then it black-box accesses oracles $\mathcal{U}(params, GID_{U_b}, \tilde{U}_b, PK_i, decom_b)$ and $\mathcal{U}(params, GID_{U_{1-b}}, \tilde{U}_{1-b}, PK_i, decom_{1-b})$.
(iv) The algorithm U outputs the secret keys $SK^i_{U_b}$ and $SK^i_{U_{1-b}}$, respectively.
(v) If $SK^i_{U_b} \neq \perp$ and $SK^i_{U_{1-b}} \neq \perp$, the A_i is given $(SK^i_{U_b}, SK^i_{U_{1-b}})$; if $SK^i_{U_b} \neq \perp$ and $SK^i_{U_{1-b}} = \perp$, the A_i is given $(\epsilon, \perp)$; if $SK^i_{U_b} = \perp$ and $SK^i_{U_{1-b}} \neq \perp$, the A_i is given $(\perp, \epsilon)$; if $SK^i_{U_b} = \perp$ and $SK^i_{U_{1-b}} = \perp$, the A_i is given (ϵ, ϵ).
(vi) Finally, A_i outputs its guess b' on b. A_i wins the game if $b' = b$.

Definition 3. *An anonymous KeyGen algorithm is selective-failure blindness if no probably polynomial time adversary A_i can win the above game with non-negligible advantage.*

Definition 4. *A privacy-preserving DCP-ABE scheme is secure if and only if it satisfies the following conditions:*

(i) The privacy-preserving DCP-ABE scheme is secure in the selective access policy model;
(ii) The anonymous KeyGen algorithm is both leak-freeness and selective-failure blindness.

4 Our Construction

4.1 Decentralized Ciphertext-Policy Attribute-Based Encryption

- Global Setup. To generate the global system parameters, this algorithm takes a security parameter λ as input. Then it returns a bilinear group $\Theta = (e, p, \mathbb{G}, \mathbb{G}_T)$ with prime order p. It chooses random generators $g, h, h_1 \in \mathbb{G}$ and the collision-resistant hash function $H : \{0, 1\}^* \to \mathbb{Z}_p$ which takes the user U's global identifier GID_U as input. We denote the corresponding output by u. Suppose that there are N authorities $\{A_1, A_2, \cdots, A_N\}$ in the system and A_i monitors an attribute list $\tilde{A}_i = \{a_{i,1}, a_{i,2}, \cdots, a_{i,n_i}\}$, where $i = [1, N]$. Public parameters are $PP = \langle g, h, h_1, e, p, H, \mathbb{G}, \mathbb{G}_T \rangle$.

- Authorities Setup. Each authority A_i, where $i = [1, N]$, randomly chooses $\alpha_i, \beta_i \in_R \mathbb{Z}_p$ and $t_{i,j} \in_R \mathbb{Z}_p$ ($i = [1, n], j = [1, n_i]$). The authority computes $Y_i = e(g, g)^{\alpha_i}$, $E_i = g^{\beta_i}$ and $T_{i,j} = g^{t_{i,j}}$. Then A_i publishes the public keys $PK_i = \langle Y_i, E_i, \{T_{i,j}\}_{j=[1,n_i]}\rangle$ and keeps the master secret keys $SK_i = \langle \alpha_i, \beta_i, \{t_{i,j}\}_{j=[1,n_i]}\rangle$.
- KeyGen. To generate secret key for user U with GID_U and a set of attributes $\tilde{U}$, the authority A_i randomly picks $w_{i,j}^u \in_R \mathbb{Z}_p$ for each attribute $att_{i,j} \in \tilde{U} \cap \tilde{A}_i$ and sets $w_i^u = \Sigma_{att_{i,j} \in \tilde{U} \cap \tilde{A}_i} w_{i,j}^u$. Then A_i computes $D_{1,i} = g^{\alpha_i} h^{u\beta_i} h_1^{\beta_i w_i^u}$ and $D_{2,i,j} = h_1^{\frac{w_{i,j}^u \beta_i}{t_{i,j}}}$. Then the U's secret key is $SK_U^i = \langle D_{1,i}, D_{2,i,j}\rangle_{a_{i,j} \in \tilde{U} \cap \tilde{A}_i}$.
- Encryption. To encrypt a massage $\mathcal{M} \in \mathbb{G}_T$ under the access policy W, the encryptor randomly picks $s \in_R \mathbb{Z}_p$. Let $\mathcal{I}$ be a set which consists of the indexes of the authorities whose attributes are selected to $\mathcal{M}$. Then encryption algorithm computes $C_0 = \mathcal{M} \prod_{i \in \mathcal{I}} Y_i^s$, $C_1 = g^s$, $C_{2,i,j} = T_{i,j}^s$, $C_3 = \prod_{i \in \mathcal{I}} E_i^s$. The ciphertext is $CT = \langle C_0, C_1, C_{2,i,j}, C_3\rangle_{a_{i,j} \in W}$.
- Decryption. To decrypt a ciphertext CT, the user who have a attribute set L can compute A, B, and E as follows if $L \models W$:

$$A = \prod_{i \in \mathcal{I}} e(D_{1,i}, C_1) = \prod_{i \in \mathcal{I}} e(g^{\alpha_i} h^{u\beta_i} h_1^{\beta_i w_i^u}, g^s)$$
$$= \prod_{i \in \mathcal{I}} e(g, g)^{\alpha_i s} \cdot \prod_{i \in \mathcal{I}} e(g, h)^{\beta_i u} \cdot \prod_{i \in \mathcal{I}} e(g, h_1)^{w_i^u \beta_i s},$$
$$B = \prod_{a_{i,j} \in W} e(D_{2,i,j}, C_{2,i,j}) = \prod_{a_{i,j} \in W} e(h_1^{\frac{w_{i,j}^u \beta_i}{t_{i,j}}}, g^{t_{i,j} s})$$
$$= \prod_{i \in \mathcal{I}} e(g, h_1)^{w_i^u \beta_i s},$$
$$E = e(h, C_3)^u = e(h, \prod_{i \in \mathcal{I}} g^{s\beta_i})^u = \prod_{i \in \mathcal{I}} e(g, h)^{us\beta_i}.$$

Therefore, the user can get the massage $\mathcal{M} = \frac{C_0 B E}{A}$.

4.2 Anonymous KeyGen Protocol

$\tilde{U}$. On the other hand authority A_i cannot learn anything about GID_U and what attribute the user has.

Algorithm 2 shows the anonymous KeyGen protocol, where the user U and authority A_i combine to compute partial decryption keys for U. Firstly, U randomly chooses $\rho \in_R$ then U and A_i interact with each other using two-party multiplication protocol 2MPC. Following the 2MPC protocol [14], it takes (u, ρ) from U and β_i from A_i as input and outputs $x = \rho u \beta_i \bmod p$ to A_i. Because ρ is randomly picked in $\mathbb{Z}p$ by U, A_i cannot learn anything about user's global identifier u from x. Next, U computes $P = g^{\frac{1}{\rho}}$, $Q = h_1^{\frac{1}{\rho}}$, $R = g^{\frac{1}{\rho^2}}$ and sends them to A_i. To proof that U knows (u, ρ) in zero-knowledge protocol, U computes $PoK\{(u, \rho) : \Psi = g^{u\rho}\}$ and sends it to A_i. After that, the authority A_i

Algorithm 2. Anonymous KeyGen Protocol

U randomly picks $\rho \in_R \mathbb{Z}p$
$U \overset{2MPC}{\longleftrightarrow} A_i : x = \rho u \beta_i$
U computes $PoK\{(u, \rho) : \Psi = g^{u\rho}\}$, $P = g^{\frac{1}{\rho}}$, $Q = h_1^{\frac{1}{\rho}}$, $R = h^{\frac{1}{\rho^2}}$ and sends them to A_i
A_i verifies $g^x \stackrel{?}{=} \Psi^{\beta_i}$
if $g^x = \Psi^{\beta_i}$ **then**
    A_i chooses a random number $w_i^u \in_R \mathbb{Z}p$. Then A_i computes $\widetilde{D_{1,i}} = P^{\alpha_i} Q^{w_i^u \beta_i} R^x$, $PoK\{(\alpha_i, w_i^u \beta_i, x) : \widetilde{D_{1,i}} = P^{\alpha_i} Q^{w_i^u \beta_i} R^x\}$ and sends them to U
else
    Abort
A_i proofs it knows $(\alpha_i, w_i^u \beta_i, x)$ in zero knowledge to U
if the proof is successful **then**
    U computes $D_{1,i} = (\widetilde{D_{1,i}})^\rho$
else
    Abort
$U \overset{OT_n^k}{\longleftrightarrow} A_i$: U gets $D_{2,i,j} = h_1^{\frac{w_{i,j}^u \beta_i}{t_{i,j}}}$

verifies $g^x \stackrel{?}{=} \Psi^{\beta_i}$, if it is correctly verified, A_i randomly chooses $w_{i,j}^u \in_R \mathbb{Z}_p$ for each attribute $att_{i,j} \in \tilde{U} \cap \tilde{A}_i$ and sets $w_i^u = \Sigma_{att_{i,j} \in \tilde{U} \cap \tilde{A}_i} w_{i,j}^u$ and computes $\widetilde{D_{1,i}} = P^{\alpha_i} Q^{w_i^u \beta_i} R^x$. Then authority A_i sends them to U. At the same time, A_i needs to prove he/she knows the three-tuple $(\alpha_i, w_i^u \beta_i, x)$ in zero-knowledge to U. The detailed steps as follows.

(i) A_i randomly picks $b_1, b_2, b_3 \in_R \mathbb{Z}p$, computes $\widetilde{D_{1,i}^*} = P^{b_1} Q^{b_2} R^{b_3}$ and sends $\widetilde{D_{1,i}}$, $\widetilde{D_{1,i}^*}$ to U.
(ii) U chooses $c \in_R \mathbb{Z}p$ and sends it to A_i.
(iii) A_i computes $b_1' = b_1 - c\alpha_i$, $b_2' = b_2 - c w_i^u \beta_i$, $b_3' = b_3 - cx$ and sends b_1', b_2', b_3' to U.
(iv) U verifies $\widetilde{D_{1,i}^*} \stackrel{?}{=} P^{b_1'} Q^{b_2'} R^{b_3'} (\widetilde{D_{1,i}})^c$.

If the proof is successful, U uses ρ to compute $D_{1,i} = (\widetilde{D_{1,i}})^\rho$. During the whole algorithm we can get user U's partial secret keys about global identifier without leaking any identity information. By employing *k-out-of-n* oblivious transfer protocol, attribute secret keys can be obtained anonymously.

In the proposed scheme, each authority A_i is in charge of a set of attribute $\tilde{A}_i = \{att_{i,1}, att_{i,2}, \cdots, att_{i,n_i}\}$. Firstly, A_i uses its secret keys $\beta_i, t_{i,j}, w_i^u$ and the public parameters h_1 to compute $\{h_1^{w_i^u \beta_i / t_{i,j}}\}_{a_{i,j} \in \tilde{A}_i}$. Recalling the OT_n^k protocol, we put $\{h_1^{w_i^u \beta_i / t_{i,j}}\}_{a_{i,j} \in \tilde{A}_i}$ as massages m_i and let U run this protocol for obtaining $m_{\sigma_1}, m_{\sigma_2}, \cdots, m_{\sigma_{|\tilde{U}|}}$. During this process, A_i cannot known which attribute secret keys are chosen by U, therefore the user U can gets his/her attribute secret keys $\{D_{2,i,j} = h_1^{w_i^u \beta_i / t_{i,j}}\}_{a_{i,j} \in \tilde{U} \cap \tilde{A}_i}$ anonymously. In conclusion, U obtains his/her secret keys by interacting with A_i without leaking any information about GID_U and attributes to A_i.

5 Security of the Proposed Scheme

Theorem 1. *The proposed DCP-ABE is (t, q, ϵ) secure in the selective access policy model if all t-time adversary makes q secret key queries and succeeds in the following game with negligible advantage ϵ.*

Theorem 2. *The proposed anonymous KeyGen protocol is leak-free and selective-failure blind.*

Due to space limitations, detailed proofs of Theorems 1 and 2 will be given in the full version.

6 Performance Comparison

In this section, we will present the comparisons between previous different multi-authority CP-ABE schemes and ours with regard to security and efficiency.

Table 1. Security comparison among different multi-authority CP-ABE schemes.

Scheme	A_i cooperation	Attribute hidden	Tolerance	Access structure	Hardness
[7]	No	No	$N-1$	LSSS	q-PBDHE
[8]	Yes	Yes	$N-2$	Tree	DBDH
[13]	Yes	No	$N-2$	Threshold	DBDH
Ours	No	Yes	$N-1$	AND	DBDH

In Table 1, all of the schemes achieve the privacy protection for the global identifier, but only our scheme apparently achieves the privacy protection for the global identifier and attributes simultaneously. In addition, there is no cooperation among authorities in the initialization phase. Our construction is tolerant against maximum $(N-1)$ authorities colluding. And its security is reduced to a standard DBDH complexity assumption.

To simulate these schemes and get the computational costs, the Pairing-Based Cryptography (PBC) Library (version 0.5.14) is implemented. In the whole system, the PBC Library is implemented on a Windows machine with 2.67GHz Intel(R) Core(TM)2 Quad CPU and 4GB ROM. Without loss of generality, we assume that there are three authorities in these schemes. In Fig. 1(a), (c) and (d), the time complexity of all schemes increase linearly with the number of attributes in each authority. In Fig. 1(b), the key issuing time costs of [13] increases quadratically with the number of attributes because each pair of authorities must agree on a shared secret for a attribute. In Fig. 1, it is obvious to see that our scheme is efficient in computational costs comparing with among these schemes, especially in the key issuing phase.

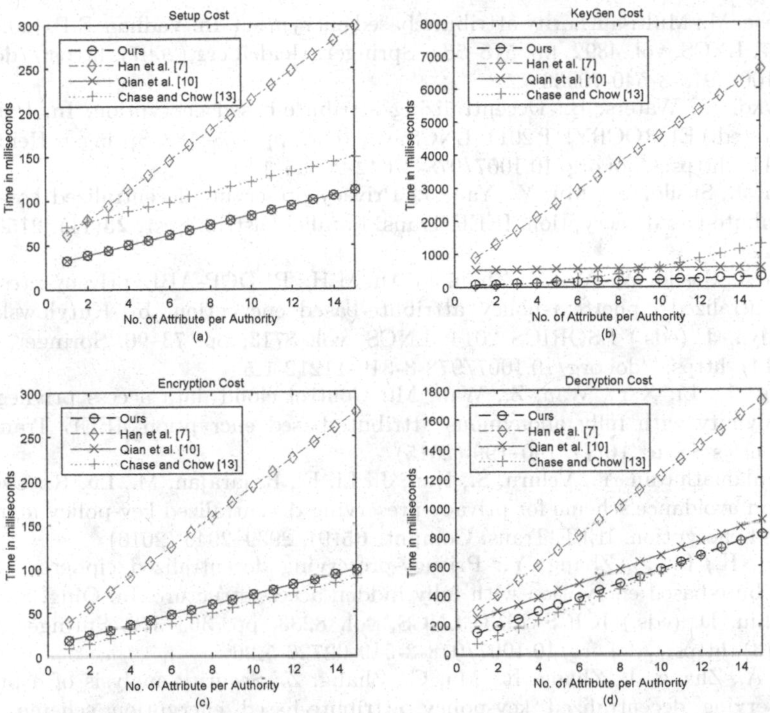

Fig. 1. Computational costs comparison among different multi-authority CP-ABE.

7 Conclusions

In this paper, we proposed a novel privacy-preserving DCP-ABE to answer the open problem in [12]. Due to our anonymous key generation protocol, the proposed scheme can protect user privacy by preventing authorities from learning any information about both GID and attributes. It requires neither a central authority nor cooperation among authorities for issuing secret keys. In addition, the proposed scheme achieves low computational costs and its security can be reduced to a standard DBDH assumption.

References

1. Sahai, A., Waters, B.: Fuzzy identity-based encryption. In: Cramer, R. (ed.) EUROCRYPT 2005. LNCS, vol. 3494, pp. 457–473. Springer, Heidelberg (2005). https://doi.org/10.1007/11426639_27
2. Bethencourt, J., Sahai, A., Waters, B.: Ciphertext-policy attribute-based encryption. In: 2007 IEEE Symposium on Security and Privacy, pp. 321–334. IEEE, Washington (2007)
3. Goyal, V., Pandey, O., Sahai, A., Waters, B.: Attribute-based encryption for fine-grained access control of encrypted data. In: 13th ACM Conference on Computer and Communications Security, pp. 89–98. ACM, New York (2006)

4. Chase, M.: Multi-authority attribute based encryption. In: Vadhan, S.P. (ed.) TCC 2007. LNCS, vol. 4392, pp. 515–534. Springer, Heidelberg (2007). https://doi.org/10.1007/978-3-540-70936-7_28
5. Lewko, A., Waters, B.: Decentralizing attribute-based encryption. In: Paterson, K.G. (ed.) EUROCRYPT 2011. LNCS, vol. 6632, pp. 568–588. Springer, Heidelberg (2011). https://doi.org/10.1007/978-3-642-20465-4_31
6. Han, J., Susilo, W., Mu, Y., Yan, J.: Privacy-preserving decentralized key-policy attribute-based encryption. IEEE Trans. Parallel Distrib. Syst. **23**(11), 2150–2162 (2012)
7. Han, J., Susilo, W., Mu, Y., Zhou, J., Au, M.H.: PPDCP-ABE: privacy-preserving decentralized ciphertext-policy attribute-based encryption. In: Kutyłowski, M., Vaidya, J. (eds.) ESORICS 2014. LNCS, vol. 8713, pp. 73–90. Springer, Cham (2014). https://doi.org/10.1007/978-3-319-11212-1_5
8. Jung, T., Li, X.Y., Wan, Z., Wan, M.: Control cloud data access privilege and anonymity with fully anonymous attribute-based encryption. IEEE Trans. Inf. Forensics Secur. **10**(1), 190–199 (2015)
9. Rahulamathavan, Y., Veluru, S., Han, J., Li, F., Rajarajan, M., Lu, R.: User collusion avoidance scheme for privacy-preserving decentralized key-policy attribute-based encryption. IEEE Trans. Comput. **65**(9), 2939–2946 (2016)
10. Qian, H., Li, J., Zhang, Y.: Privacy-preserving decentralized ciphertext-policy attribute-based encryption with fully hidden access structure. In: Qing, S., Zhou, J., Liu, D. (eds.) ICICS 2013. LNCS, vol. 8233, pp. 363–372. Springer, Cham (2013). https://doi.org/10.1007/978-3-319-02726-5_26
11. Ge, A., Zhang, J., Zhang, R., Ma, C., Zhang, Z.: Security analysis of a privacy-preserving decentralized key-policy attribute-based encryption scheme. IEEE Trans. Parallel Distrib. Syst. **24**(11), 2319–2321 (2013)
12. Wang, M., Zhang, Z., Chen, C.: Security analysis of a privacy-preserving decentralized ciphertext-policy attribute-based encryption scheme. Concurr. Comput. Pract. Exp. **28**(4), 1237–1245 (2016)
13. Chase, M., Chow, S.S.M.: Improving privacy and security in multi-authority attribute-based encryption. In: 16th ACM Conference on Computer and Communications Security, pp. 121–130. ACM, New York (2009)
14. Lindell, Y., Pinkas, B.: Privacy preserving data mining. J. Cryptol. **15**(3), 177–206 (2002)
15. Li, J., Yao, W., Zhang, Y., Qian, H., Han, J.: Flexible and fine-grained attribute-based data storage in cloud computing. IEEE Trans. Serv. Comput. **10**(5), 785–796 (2017)
16. Pedersen, T.P.: Non-interactive and information-theoretic secure verifiable secret sharing. In: Feigenbaum, J. (ed.) CRYPTO 1991. LNCS, vol. 576, pp. 129–140. Springer, Heidelberg (1992). https://doi.org/10.1007/3-540-46766-1_9
17. Camenisch, J., Stadler, M.: Efficient group signature schemes for large groups. In: Kaliski, B.S. (ed.) CRYPTO 1997. LNCS, vol. 1294, pp. 410–424. Springer, Heidelberg (1997). https://doi.org/10.1007/BFb0052252
18. Chu, C.-K., Tzeng, W.-G.: Efficient k-out-of-n oblivious transfer schemes with adaptive and non-adaptive queries. In: Vaudenay, S. (ed.) PKC 2005. LNCS, vol. 3386, pp. 172–183. Springer, Heidelberg (2005). https://doi.org/10.1007/978-3-540-30580-4_12
19. Zhang, Y., Feng, D.: Efficient attribute proofs in anonymous credential using attribute-based cryptography. In: Chim, T.W., Yuen, T.H. (eds.) ICICS 2012. LNCS, vol. 7618, pp. 408–415. Springer, Heidelberg (2012). https://doi.org/10.1007/978-3-642-34129-8_39

A Robust Fingerprint Identification Method by Deep Learning with Gabor Filter Multidimensional Feature Expansion

Jiajia Yang, Zhendong Wu(✉), and Jianwu Zhang

Hangzhou Dianzi University, Hangzhou, China
jjiayang@126.com, {wzd,jwzhang}@hdu.edu.cn

Abstract. Traditional fingerprint methods based on minutiae matching perform well for the acquisition of large area fingerprint. But the accuracy rate and the robustness of small area fingerprint decreases obviously when contains less minutia. Aiming at solving the above problem, a small area fingerprint matching method based on Convolution Neural Network (CNN) which selecting the center block of fingerprint as the region of interest (ROI) after preprocessing and using the Gabor filter to extract feature as multidimensional feature extension named ROIFE_CNN (ROI of fingerprint feature extension recognition of CNN) is proposed to enhance robustness. Experiments show that the accuracy of small area fingerprint classification based on CNN is enhanced.

Keywords: Robustness · Convolution Neural Network (CNN) Preprocessing · Gabor filter · Multidimensional feature extension

1 Introduction

With the improvement of social information and the increase of unstable factors, traditional identification methods, such as instructions and passwords, urgently require more reliable identification technologies to authenticate identities due to insecurity and complexity. Biometric Identification Technology (BIT) [1] adopts the characteristics of each biological entity and contains different physical or behaviors with the same species for identity authentication, which overcomes the shortcomings of the traditional authentication methods. Since Apple Inc. integrated Touch ID into smart phones in 2013, major internet giants have launched fingerprint payment solutions such as Apple Pay, Samsung Pay and Alipay. Therefore, the use of biometric identification has reached its the upsurge nowadays. Among them, fingerprint recognition is respected by scholars because of its convenience and reliability.

However, there are still some key problems that need to be solved in the fingerprint identification technology for small collection equipment due to the particularity of the application's environment and security. For example, collectors embedded in smart phones are typically smaller, such as Apple's Touch ID Fingerprint Reader [2], which are generally only 30% to 60% of the normal fingerprint area and contain fewer minutias [3]. Therefore, the traditional minutiae-based fingerprinting method will be affected.

X. Sun et al. (Eds.): ICCCS 2018, LNCS 11065, pp. 447–457, 2018.
https://doi.org/10.1007/978-3-030-00012-7_41

Fingerprint recognition techniques can be traced back to the work of Lee et al. [4]. From the precious achievements, we can find that scholars from different countries come up with many kinds of extraction algorithms about the details of features: Dario Maio proposed an algorithm that traced the ridges on the original grayscale image to obtain features [5]. The algorithm only enhances some parts of the image, which greatly reduces the redundancy caused by the previous processing, thus the efficiency is improved. Based on this algorithm, Xudong Jiang proposed an improved method [6] for adaptive steps and post-processing of detail points. In order to get smoother lines, Ratha tried three ways to deal with the discontinuities, glitches and endpoints of ridgelines in an effort to eliminate their effect on feature extraction [7]. Based on statistical pattern recognition and structural pattern recognition, Xiao and Raffa combined the two to extract features [8]. Jea et al. [9] achieved the small-size fingerprint matching by using the auxiliary features derived from the minutiae nodes in combination with the flow network-based matching technique. Girgis et al. [10] proposed a small-area fingerprint matching method based on graph matching theory, and used genetic algorithm to improve the adverse effects of ridge deformation and elastic deformation on fingerprint matching. In addition, pore-valley descriptors [11] and reconstruction of global features [12] are also used in the area of small area fingerprinting.

These methods can more accurately mark the fingerprint feature points, but the complexity of the process has greatly increased the cost of manpower and material resources and also faced with the "Orange peels to unlock the cell phone" crisis.

In this paper, we propose a method named ROIFE_CNN (ROI of fingerprint feature extension recognition of CNN) which extracts the centre block of fingerprint as region of interest (ROI) firstly, after that, we use Gabor filter to extract texture map of fingerprint thinning from different dimensions as feature extension to enhance the robustness of recognition. Experiment results show that our method really can improve the accuracy of small area fingerprint matching as well as robustness and it has no need to extract minutia. This paper is organized as following: Sect. 2 introduces the fingerprint image preprocessing process. Section 3 proposes the process of algorithm based on CNN. Section 4 presents the experiment process and obtains the experiment result. Section 5 summarizes the paper and puts forward the prospect.

2 Fingerprint Identification

In general, the Automated Fingerprint Recognition System (AFRS) consists of fingerprint image acquisition, fingerprint image preprocessing, feature extraction, fingerprint classification and fingerprint comparison of several parts, as shown in Fig. 1.

Preprocessing is a key part of the entire AFRS and is the basis for the proper feature extraction and matching. Preprocessing usually includes image segmentation, enhancement, binarization, refinement, etc. And the enhancement part is the most critical. In this paper, fingerprint image will be enhanced in the frequency domain, and the effect is better than the Gabor filter in the time domain. This paper describes the frequency domain enhancement process as below.

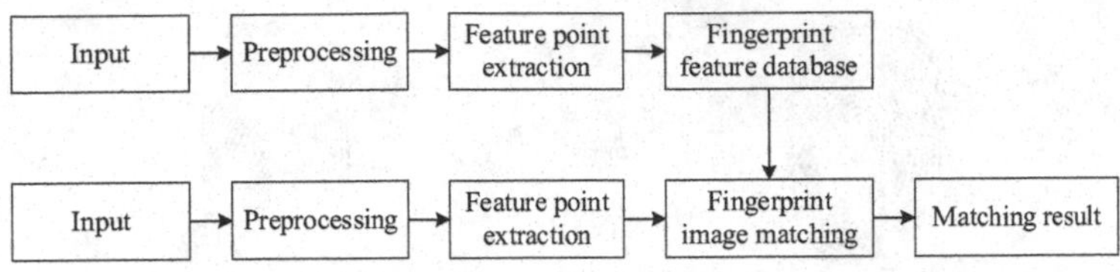

Fig. 1. The matching process of fingerprint automatically identify

The ridgeline of the fingerprint image varies greatly from the view of the global. However, from the point of local view, the ridgeline changes more smoothly besides the sharp change in the center of the fingerprint, and the frequency and the direction of the ridgeline can be considered unchanged. Therefore, the fingerprint is generally divided into blocks. By separately calculating the Fourier transform of each small block, the frequency and direction of the small block are estimated, and the obtained frequency and direction information is used for filtering.

Let a small block of size $W \times H$ centering on the (m, n) point be filtered through the angle-direction filter and get a result of $B'(m, n)$, the energy of the patch is:

$$E = \sum_{m} \sum_{n} \left| B'(m, n) \right|^2 \tag{1}$$

Since the edge part of the fingerprint image and the approximate blank area inside the fingerprint image have less energy, by setting an appropriate threshold value s can separate the background effectively. If $E \leq E_{threshold}$, regarded the small piece as the background, this method for the follow-up fingerprint feature extraction and removal of pseudo-feature point is very effective. Combining all $FFT^{-1}(B')$ at the center of non-overlapping region is the enhanced fingerprint images.

The filter is decomposed into a radial filter and an angle-direction filter. The radial filter selects the Butterworth bandpass filter to eliminate noise points in the fingerprint image. The bandwidth of the angular direction filter is related to the correlation coefficient. The filtering results have no effect on the fingerprint center structure. The ridge lines outside the center are enhanced, some isolated noise points are eliminated, and the broken ridge lines can be adhered. The whole algorithm is equally valid for low quality fingerprint images. The processed pieces are combined as both enhanced images (Fig. 2).

3 Proposed Method

Different from the fingerprint recognition model that inputs the fingerprint image directly for deep learning, the model proposed in this paper performs the preprocessing in favor of deep learning for fingerprint image, and uses the Gabor filter to extract feature information in different dimension directions specifically. It tries to extract the fingerprint feature information and improve the robustness of the recognition.

Fig. 2. (1) The left is the original fingerprint image; (2) the middle one is the thinning map enhanced using the time domain method; (3) the right is the thinning picture which use this paper's method to enhance the map

3.1 Extract Center of ROI

The singular feature points of human fingerprints refer to the center points and triangle points of fingerprint feature points. Extracting singular feature points can help people to classify fingerprints in fingerprint recognition and locate the relative coordinate system when be compared with fingerprints. The algorithm for extracting singular feature points of fingerprints needs to be referenced by discrete Poincare [13] to mathematically model them. The commonly used grid representations are 3 × 3 and 5 × 5 grid templates because it is convenient for computer computing.

The following Table 1 uses a 5 × 5 grid. The algorithm shows the calculation of the sum of field-direction field differences in the region where the point (i,j) is centered and the radius is d or D.

Table 1. Closed curve Poincare value 5 × 5 grid template algorithm

	D_{12}	D_{11}	D_{10}	
D_1	d_1	d_8	d_7	D_9
D_2	d_2	(i,j)	d_6	D_8
D_3	d_3	d_4	d_5	D_7
	d_4	d_5	D_6	

In the grid template shown in the above table, the point (i,j) is the centre of the region formed by closed curves $D_1, D_2, \ldots, D_{12}$ clockwise, and the Poincare value of the closed curve is calculated:

$$Poincare(i,j) = \sum_{1}^{12} \left| D_i - D_{(i+1)\text{mod}12} \right| \tag{2}$$

And in the 3 × 3 grid template, the Poincare value of the closed curved $d_1, d_2, \ldots, d_8$ formed clockwise from the centers point (i,j) is calculated:

$$Poincare(i,j) = \sum_{1}^{8} |D_i - D_{(i+1)\mathrm{mod}8}| \tag{3}$$

Among the plurality of neighboring candidate singular feature points obtained by the above method, the final singular feature point is further determined using a mean value algorithm. In order to remove noises which may generate pseudo singular feature points, the Poincare value of the closed curve needs to be calculated again. When the 3×3 square Poincare value is equal to the 5×5 square (0.5 or −0.5) It can be determined that the candidate singular feature point is a true fingerprint feature singularity point.

The specific steps for extracting the singular feature points of the fingerprint are:

1. Get the field value of the current point direction, determine whether the point is the background point, and if so, jump out of the loop;
2. Calculate the Poincare value of the counterclockwise closed curve formed in the 3×3 grid centered at this point, marked as SUM1;
3. Calculate the Poincare value of the counterclockwise closed curve formed within the 5×5 square centered at this point marked as SUM2;
4. If the SUM1 and SUM2 directions have the same field difference, it is determined that this point is a singular point.

After extracting the center point of the fingerprint in the fingerprint thinning map, the center point of the fingerprint is taken as the center to intercept the block diagram of the center point of the fingerprint. Shown as the following (Fig. 3):

Fig. 3. (1) The leftmost figure shows the original fingerprint image; (2) the middle part is the fingerprint refinement figure; (3) the right figure is the center fingerprint block extracted from the center point.

3.2 Filter ROI with Gabor

In image processing, the Gabor function is a linear filter for edge extraction. The study found that Gabor filter is very suitable for texture expression and separation. In addition, biological experiments have found that the Gabor filter can well approximate the single cell receptive field function (transfer function under light intensity stimulation), and the frequency and direction expression of the Gabor filter is similar to the human visual system.

The Gabor filter can be divided into two components, the real part and the imaginary part. The filtered image is:

$$S(x,y) = \sqrt{(h_R * I)(x,y)^2 + (h_I * I)(x,y)^2} \tag{4}$$

Among them, $(h * I)$ represents the convolution of the image I and the filter. $S(x,y)$ is the feature image extracted by the Gabor filter, which is undergoing Gaussian smoothing. If we use $h(x,y)$ as the main wavelet, we can get a set of self-similar filters called Gabor wavelets by performing proper scaling and rotation changes. The direction and scale of the Gabor wavelet are adjustable, and the kernel function is defined as follows:

$$\psi_{v,u}(\vec{z}) = \frac{||\vec{k}_{v,u}||^2}{\sigma^2} e^{\frac{||\vec{k}_{v,u}||^2||\vec{z}||^2}{2\sigma^2}} (e^{i\vec{k}_{v,u}\vec{z}}, -e^{-\sigma^2/2}) \tag{5}$$

$$\vec{k}_{v,u} = (k_v \cos\varphi_u, k_v \cos\varphi_u) \tag{6}$$

In the formula, φ_u and k_v respectively define the direction and scale of the wave vector $\vec{k}_{v,u} \cdot \vec{z} = (x,y)$, $||g||$ defines the vector norm. In formula (6), $k_v = k_{\max}/f^v$ and $\varphi_u = \pi u/8$. f is the sampling step in the frequency domain, usually $f = \sqrt{2}$. $k_{\max}$ corresponds to the maximum sampling frequency, taking $k = \pi/2$. The parameter m determines the ratio of the width of the Gaussian window to the length of the wave vector. In this paper, σ=2π.

Gabor filter filtering of the ROI obtained in the previous section to obtain the following processing picture (Fig. 4).

Fig. 4. Two graphs randomly choose for filtering effects. (1) The leftmost figure is the fingerprint thinning diagram; (2) the right one is the second dimension of the second direction obtained by the Gabor filter;

3.3 Convolution Neural Network

The CNN is shown in Fig. 5. It includes four basic layers: the input layer, the convolution layer, the down-sampling layer (the pooled layer), and the output layer. The input layer which unified the size of the images of different sizes is input into the model to ensure the convolution process of the convolution layer. The convolution layer [14] uses several convolution kernels with different weights to perform convolution with the input image to extract different features. A class of features can form a Feature Map [15]. Therefore, several convolution kernels can get the same number of feature maps. The down-sampling layer refers to the pooling layer. It includes two operations: maximum pooling and average pooling. The process of each operation is different, but the final result is to reduce the dimensionality of the convolution layer feature map. Reduce the number of parameters. Before the output layer, a classifier is usually connected, and the recognition result is finally obtained at the output layer. Of course, the parameter adjustment still depends on the back propagation algorithm.

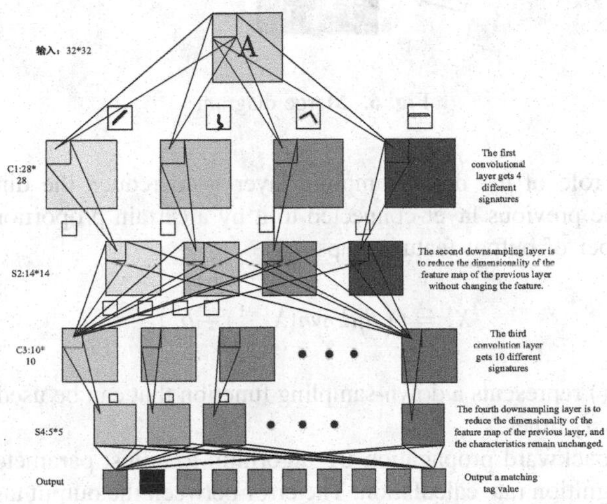

Fig. 5. The structure of CNN

3.4 Convolution Process Using ROIFE_CNN

After the above two steps are extracted, in order to make full use of all the information, we need to adjust the center point block diagram and the Gabor filtering feature map and remove the blank edges of the two images properly. After splicing up and down, some blank splicing parts are removed to become one. The map is input to the input layer, as shown in Fig. 6.

The first few layers are mainly connected locally, while the last layer is fully connected. Parameters and weights are adjusted using the BP algorithm. The algorithm is described in detail as follows:

Step 1: On a convolution layer, the characteristic diagram is convolved by several different convolution kernels with the output characteristics of the previous layer, and then obtained by an activation function which indicates by $f(\cdot)$. Each output graph may be a weighted sum of convolved multiple input graphs:

$$X_j^\ell = f\left[\sum_{i \in M_j} X_i^{\ell-1} * K_{ij}^\ell + b_j^\ell\right] \tag{7}$$

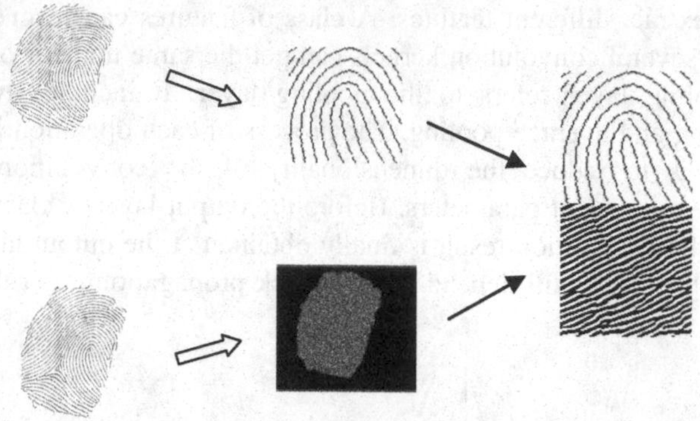

Fig. 6. Merge diagram

Step 2: The role of the down-sampling layer is to reduce the dimension of the output map of the previous layer connected to it by a certain proportion, but does not change the number of output feature maps:

$$X_j^\ell = f\left(\beta_j^\ell down(X_i^{\ell-1}) + b_j^\ell\right) \tag{8}$$

Where $down()$ represents a down-sampling function that can be used to reduces the output image by n_2 times.

Step 3: Use backward propagation BP algorithm to adjust parameters;

Step 4: Recognition rate calculation: The error between the output tag value and the ideal tag can be expressed as: $\varepsilon = ||O - T||$. Where T is the ideal tag value.

Find the sample with $\varepsilon \leq 0.1$ and count the number to get the recognition rate, as in Eq. (7):

$$correct = \sum x/M \tag{9}$$

Among them, when $\varepsilon \leq 0.1$, x takes 1 and when $\varepsilon > 0.1$, x takes 0. Denominator M is the total number of test data pictures.

4 Experiment Results

The test fingerprint library of this experiment comes from the SF database and has undergone blind alignment processing. The fingerprint database is in the laboratory environment, randomly selects 40 individuals as sample sources, and each person has 20 fingerprint images, and the fingerprinting pretreatment is performed during the collection process, such as coloring and watering as shown in Fig. 7. No center point refinement diagram is deleted, as shown in Fig. 8. Usually, a 3:1 ratio is used to randomly select fingerprint images for training and testing. The size of the original image is 328 × 356, and the size of ROI is 121 × 121.

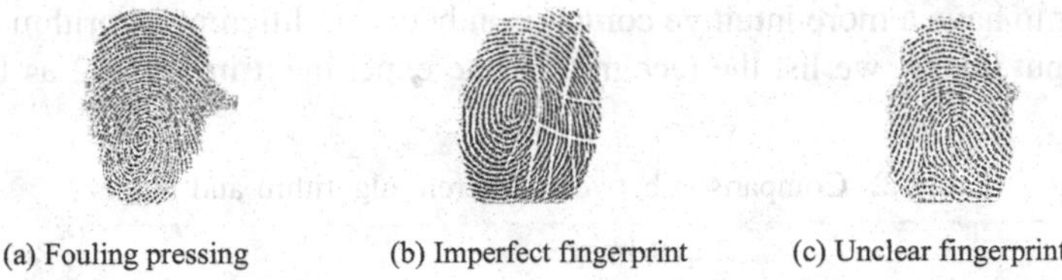

(a) Fouling pressing (b) Imperfect fingerprint (c) Unclear fingerprint

Fig. 7. Several types of fingerprint

Fig. 8. Abandoned images after pre-process

According to this algorithm, the experiment is divided into four steps:

1. Preprocess the fingerprint image and obtain a thinning image;
2. After blind alignment processing, extract dimensional and direction features using Gabor filters for thinning image;
3. Extracting the central part of the intercepted fingerprint which resizes 121*121;
4. Synthesize a picture and input it to the CNN for training and recognition to obtain the recognition rate;

In addition, we also have a rough study of the effect of the number of iterations on the loss function values during the training process. The results of the experiment are shown in Fig. 9(a). From the experimental results, it can be seen that the increase of the number of iterations makes the loss decrease, and both of them have a nonlinear relationship. Therefore, in order to get smaller losses and shorter training time, we need to choose the appropriate number of iterations. And we also get the relationship between the number of iterations and accuracy shown in Fig. 9(b).

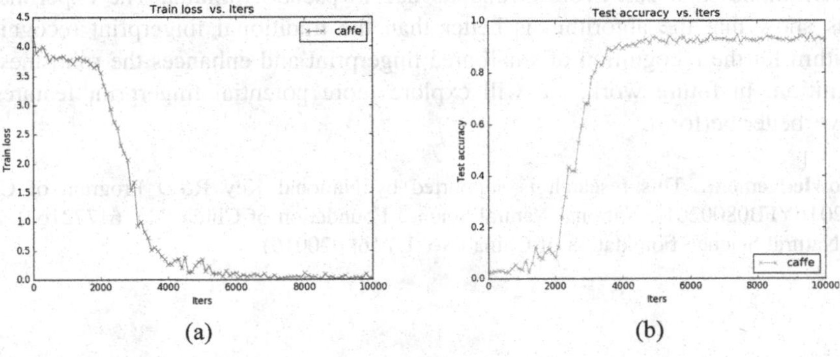

(a) (b)

Fig. 9. (a) The relationship between the number of iterations and the loss; (b) The relationship between the number of iterations and the accuracy

In order to have a more intuitive comparison between different algorithm as well as different input image, we list the recognition rate experiment in Table 2 as following:

Table 2. Comparison between different algorithm and inputs

Algorithm	Input image	Recognition rate
CNN	Original fingerprint image	68.18%
	Pre-processed original fingerprint image	90.12%
	Pre-processed original centre block fingerprint image	92.37%
Traditional minutia matching algorithm	Original fingerprint image	72.86%
	Pre-processed original fingerprint image	88.32%
	Pre-processed original centre block fingerprint image	–
ROIFE_CNN	Gabor filtering image of ROI	95.10%

From the data in the table, we find that when the extracted fingerprint area is small, the recognition rate of the traditional minutia matching method is reduced to 88.32%. However, ROIFE_CNN can achieve better performance by extending the feature which Gabor filtering obtained, and do not rely on the minutiae. In addition, the robustness of our algorithm is enhanced.

5 Summary

In this paper, the fingerprint classification of small area blocks which contain fewer minutias is studied by using feature extension. The central block image is obtained when the original fingerprint image is intercepted and the fingerprint dimension feature map extracted by Gabor filter is used as training image. Finally, ROIFE_CNN algorithm is applied to classify and recognize the image. Our method does not need to extract minutia so it can avoid erroneous due to pseudo minutia. The experimental results show that the algorithm is better than the traditional fingerprint recognition algorithm for the recognition of small area fingerprint and enhances the robustness of recognition. In future work, we will explore more potential fingerprint features to achieve better perform.

Acknowledgement. This research is supported by National Key R&D Program of China (No. 2016YFB0800201), National Natural Science Foundation of China (No. 61772162), Zhejiang Natural Science Foundation of China (No. LY16F020016).

References

1. Zhai, L., Hu, Q.: The research of double-biometric identification technology based on finger geometry & palm print. In: 2011 2nd International Conference on Artificial Intelligence, Management Science and Electronic Commerce (AIMSEC), pp. 3530–3533. IEEE (2011)
2. Fernandez-Saavedra, B., Sanchez-Reillo, R., Ros-Gomez, R., et al.: Small fingerprint scanners used in mobile devices: the impact on biometric performance. Iet Biom. **5**(1), 28–36 (2016)
3. Mathur, S., Vjay, A., Shah, J., et al.: Methodology for partial fingerprint enrollment and authentication on mobile devices. In: International Conference on Biometrics, 1–8. IEEE (2016)
4. Lee, H.C., Gaensslen, R.E.: Advances in Fingerprint Technology. Elsevier, New York (2001)
5. Maio, D., Maltoni, D.: Direct gray-scale minutiae detection in fingerprints. IEEE Trans. Pattern Anal. Mach. Intell. **19**(1), 27–40 (1997)
6. Jiang, X., Yau, W.Y., Ser, W.: Detecting the fingerprint minutiae by adaptive tracing the gray-level ridge. Pattern Recogn. **34**(5), 999–1013 (2001)
7. Ratha, N.K., Bolle, R.: Automatic Fingerprint Recognition Systems. Springer, New York (2003). https://doi.org/10.1007/b97425
8. Schulingkamp, R.J., Pagano, T.C., Hung, D., et al.: Insulin receptors and insulin action in the brain: review and clinical implications. Neurosci. Biobehav. Rev. **24**(8), 855–872 (2000)
9. Liu, Y., Ma, Y., Feng, X., et al.: Fingerprint identification preprocessing algorithms based on gabor filter. Comput. Meas. Control **1**, 48 (2007)
10. Girgis, M.R., Sewisy, A.A., Mansour, R.F.: A robust method for partial deformed fingerprints verification using genetic algorithm. Expert Syst. Appl. **36**(2), 2008–2016 (2009)
11. Zhao, Q., Zhang, D., Zhang, L., et al.: High resolution partial fingerprint alignment using pore–valley descriptors. Pattern Recogn. **43**(3), 1050–1061 (2010)
12. Wang, Y.A., Hu, J.: Global ridge orientation modeling for partial fingerprint identification. IEEE Trans. Pattern Anal. Mach. Intell. **33**(1), 72–87 (2010)
13. Selvarani, S., Jebapriya, S., Mary, R.S.: Automatic identification and detection of altered fingerprints. In: 2014 International Conference on Intelligent Computing Applications (ICICA), pp. 239–243. IEEE (2014)
14. Nakashika, T., Garcia, C., Takiguchi, T.: Local-feature-map integration using convolutional neural networks for music genre classification (2012)
15. Lavin, A.: maxDNN: an efficient convolution kernel for deep learning with maxwell GPUs. Computer Science (2015)

A Survey on the New Development of Medical Image Security Algorithms

Yun Tan[1(✉)], Jiaohua Qin[1], Ling Tan[2], Hao Tang[2], and Xuyu Xiang[1]

[1] Central South University of Forestry and Technology, Changsha 410004, China
tantanyun@hotmail.com, qinjiaohua@163.com, xyuxiang@163.com

[2] Second Xiangya Hospital of Central South University, Changsha 410011, China
{dr.tanling,dr.tanghao}@csu.edu.cn

Abstract. With the development of big data, cloud computing and artificial intelligence, smart healthcare based on Internet plus has become a highly attractive application area. Medical image storage and analysis are progressively becoming cloud-based, providing the preconditions for the efficient cooperation of remote diagnostics and the full sharing of research resources. However, the frequent medical data breach events have greatly infringed on the privacy of users and brought about huge social losses. Therefore, how to strengthen medical images security and privacy protection during transmission, storage and use is very urgent. In this paper, the security requirements of medical images in cloud computing are analyzed. And a survey is introduced focusing on the development status of medical images security techniques in recent 5 years. The open issues of medical image security are also analyzed in this paper, which point out the possible directions for future research.

Keywords: Security · Cryptography · Information hiding
Medical image

1 Introduction

With the development of big data, cloud computing, and artificial intelligence, smart medical service based on the Internet plus has become a highly attractive application area. For diagnosis and research needs, medical images, as the most important part of medical data, are frequently transmitted and exchanged between different hospitals and research institutions around the world through internet and mobile communications. Medical image storage and analysis are gradually becoming cloud-based, providing preconditions for efficient coordination of remote diagnosis and full sharing of scientific research resources. At the

Supported by the National Natural Science Foundation of China (Grant No.61772561) and the Key Research & Development Plan of Hunan Province (Grant No.2018NK2012).

X. Sun et al. (Eds.): ICCCS 2018, LNCS 11065, pp. 458–467, 2018.
https://doi.org/10.1007/978-3-030-00012-7_42

same time, the problem of security encryption and privacy protection of medical data is increasingly vital and urgent.

How to effectively protect the privacy of patients and related information, the most widely used internationally is HIPAA (Health Insurance Portability and Accountability Act) [1] which is signed by the U.S. government. The act was originated in 1991 and has undergone several amendments. In 2013, the final rule for HIPAA Omnibus was introduced to strengthen the privacy and security protection of electronic medical information. Due to the complexity of medical activities and the high cost of system upgrades, the safety issues of the widely used PACS (Picture Archiving and Communication Systems) have not been well resolved. Although cloud platform services typically provide dynamic, scalable, resource-encapsulated virtualization services, the online operating environment makes it difficult to realize complete and robust security. In recent years, the leakage of medical data has frequently occurred [2,3], which has greatly infringed on the privacy of users and caused huge social losses. Therefore, many researchers have begun to work on the security issues of medical images and made a lot of improvements.

In this paper, we focus on the development status of medical images security techniques in recent 5 years. The literatures are reviewed and their performances are analyzed. This paper is organized as follows. In Sect. 2, the security requirements of medical images in cloud computing are analyzed. Section 3 introduces the recent proposed security techniques and their functionalities. Section 4 analyzes the special features of medical images that are different with natural images and also points out the possible directions for future research. We conclude this paper with some discussions in Sect. 5.

2 Security Requirements

In smart healthcare applications and medical image cloud platform, the security requirements of medical images usually include following features [4,5].

2.1 Reliability

The reliability of medical images is the basic condition for smart healthcare implementation. For image cloud platforms, reliability requirement includes both the safety of the medical image cloud platform and the reliability of the image source. This is the basic requirement for cloud image system design. Therefore, the medical image security algorithm must have strong anti-attack capability to ensure the safe transmission and reliable storage of images.

2.2 Privacy

The medical image involves the patient's privacy and personal information and can't be freely leaked or stolen. It cannot be misused or abused, otherwise it will bring huge losses to the country and individuals, and even cause irreparable harm. The requirement of privacy is an extremely important aspect of medical image security, and it is also the first point that should be considered during security algorithms research.

2.3 Authenticity

As being an important basis for intelligent medical diagnosis and treatment planning, medical images must be true and cannot be tampered with. Authenticity is an important condition to ensure the normal operation of smart healthcare services. Therefore, the medical image security algorithm should have the ability to verify the image authenticity and tamper recovery capabilities.

2.4 Integrity

For a patient or a disease case, there are usually many different types of medical images. There will also be different information in different diagnostic and treatment stages. When remote transmission and storage are performed, the medical images should be guaranteed to be complete and reliable. Therefore, it is meaningful to implement multi-image fusion encryption and multiple information hiding in the security algorithms.

In summary, the security of medical images is based on reliability, privacy, authenticity, and integrity. With modern digital image system, the medical images usually have the characteristics of big size and high redundancy. While in smart healthcare and image cloud environment, real-time and resource-constrained security algorithms are required and traditional algorithms can't meet these requirements. Therefore, many new algorithms emerged, which are reviewed in the next section.

3 Security Techniques

There are two categories of medical security techniques as information hiding and cryptography (see Fig. 1) [6]. Usually the general process of information hiding is to use the redundancy of the carrier information and hide the secret through the hidden algorithms and keys. The secret information is embedded into the original carrier and transmitted finally. While the basic idea of cryptography is to transform the meaningful original image into disorder and lose its original appearance, then the information becomes similar to random noise on the channel in case of illegally obtained by a third party.

In recent years, based on these two types of techniques, many new algorithms for medical image security have been proposed. In smart healthcare applications, usually only watermarking or cryptography is not sufficient to ensure the security of medical images. Therefore, information hiding and cryptography are always combined together and embedded each other in most security systems. Here we will review the new security algorithms according to their different methodology.

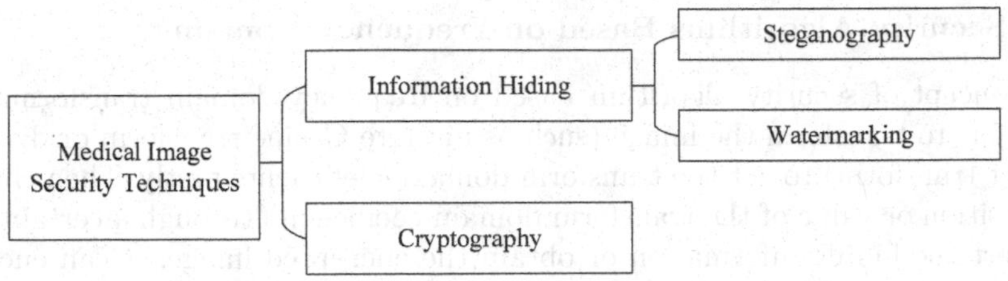

Fig. 1. Medical image security techniques overview

3.1 Security Algorithms Based on Matrix Transformation

The cryptography algorithm based on matrix transformation is to perform a limited number of elementary matrix transformations on the image matrix and disrupt the order of entered image data. Then the original image is covered up effectively. This kind of cryptography method is simple and easy to be implemented. But it only scrambles the position of the pixels and does not change the pixels value. The histogram of the image before and after scrambling does not change, and it is difficult to resist statistical attacks. In addition, the key space of this type of algorithm is small and also unable to resist key exhausting attacks.

Therefore, in recent works, matrix transformation is combined with other techniques to overcome the shortcomings and achieve better performance. In [7], the Fresnelet transform is employed along with appropriate handling of the Arnold transform and the discrete cosine transform to provide secure distribution of medical images. The experimental results exhibit significant encryption of information images and high imperceptibility for embedded images. In [8], a method that combines Arnold and Knights Tour algorithm is proposed. It can get the advantages of good scrambling and high security. In [9], an efficient image encryption scheme is proposed, which is based on Arnold transformation and pairing-free identity based authenticated key agreement protocol. The results show that the histogram of encrypted images is distributed uniformly and is robust against histogram analysis attack.

For information hiding, an algorithm combining DWT-DFT and Arnold scrambling is proposed in [10], where the Arnold scrambling is employed to preprocess original watermarking. Combined with cryptography sense, this algorithm provide double protection for medical images. The experimental results show that the algorithm can achieve a true embedded zero-watermarking. It also has satisfactory robustness and invisibility under common attacks and geometrical attacks in different levels. In [11], Venkateswarlu et al. propose a multi-transform domain security model based on Arnold transform, which implements spatial de-correlation of the cover image followed by Discrete Wavelet Transform domain based watermark insertion. Structural Similarity Index (SSIM), Normal Cross Correlation (NCC) and Peak Signal-to-Noise Ratio (PSNR) are measured in the experiments and show enhanced robustness.

3.2 Security Algorithms Based on Frequency Domain

The concept of security algorithm based on frequency domain transformation usually is to transform the image (such as discrete Cosine transform or discrete wavelet transform) to get the transform domain coefficients firstly. Then change the position or value of the transform domain coefficients through a certain rule to insert the hiding information or obtain the encrypted image. It can encrypt or insert information in only part of the image based on the security requirement, which can significantly reduce the amount of encrypted data and improve algorithm efficiency. It has been widely used in medical image watermark.

In [12], a security scheme is proposed based on DWT-DCT and logistic map, where DWT-DCT is used to obtain the visual feature vectors of the medical image. The watermarking image is encrypted by Logistic Map to strengthen its security. Good invisibility and robustness are demonstrated in the simulation results. A combination of DCT-DWT based watermarking for copyright protection and honey encryption for security of images is used against different types of attacks as compression, salt and pepper noise, Gaussian noise etc. The effect of different attacks on the robustness and imperceptibility of the watermark is also studied. In [13], a multiple watermark scheme for medical images is proposed, which apply 2-level DWT in the region of interest (ROI). The watermark is embedded using the low-frequency sub-band (LL2) of the DWT. While for the region of non-interest (RONI), DCT is used and the intermediate frequency coefficients are selected to embed watermark. This scheme meets the different requirements of multiple watermarks and the results show the advantages of lower error rate, strong robustness and high capacity. Singh [14] further proposes a hybrid multiple watermarking technique using fusion of DWT, DCT, and singular value decomposition (SVD). The cover image is decomposed into first level discrete wavelet transforms, where the lower frequency subband is transformed by DCT and SVD. The watermark image is transformed by DWT, DCT and SVD. Before embedding into the cover, the text watermark is encrypted to enhance the security. Good performance of robustness, capacity and reduced storage and bandwidth requirements are demonstrated in the experimental results.

3.3 Security Algorithms Based on Chaotic Theory

With the development of chaos theory, some researchers proposed chaos theory based encryption algorithm. Fu et al. [15] propose a chaos-based medical image encryption scheme, which introduces a substitution mechanism in the permutation process through a bit-level shuffling algorithm. Comparing to original substitution process, this method achieves some progress on efficiency problem.

The algorithm based on one-dimensional chaotic sequence has the problem of small key space and the security performance is not good enough. Zhang et al. [16] propose a watermark medical image encryption algorithm based on hyperchaotic systems, which embeds medical information into the image target area, and then uses chaotic system encryption to achieve greater information hiding.

Chai et al. [17] propose a medical image encryption algorithm based on four-dimensional memristive hyperchaotic system, which has a large key space and is very sensitive to keys. The results show that it can resist the brute force attack, known plain text attack, chosen plain text attack and differential cryptanalysis attack.

Chaos image encryption is also combined with other techniques in recent research works. In [18] a chaotic medical image encryption algorithm based on bit-plane decomposition is presented. The experimental results show that it satisfies the desired effect on histogram, pixel correlation and number of pixels change rate. Chen et al. [19] propose a medical image encryption algorithm that combines multiple chaotic maps and wavelet transforms. Firstly, the pixels are shuffled using Arnold and wavelet transforms. Kent map is then introduced to generate the parameters of Arnold map, and keys are generated using Logistic maps for higher security.

In order to meet the flexibility and efficiency of smart healthcare requirement, some adaptive and selective encryption algorithms for medical images are proposed recently. In [20], Logistic-sine chaos map is used to scramble the plain image and then the scrambled image is divided into 2-by-2 sub blocks. The sub blocks are adaptively encrypted by using the hyperchaotic system. The experimental results show that the proposed algorithm overcomes the shortcoming of lack of diffusion in single direction encryption and has the ability to effectively resist all kinds of attacks. In [21], a selective chaotic encryption scheme is proposed. Block-based chaotic cat mapping is used for image shuffling and concealment, which has strong robustness to resist cryptanalysis attacks.

3.4 Security Algorithms Based on Secret Share

The concept of secret sharing scheme [22] is to encode a secret image into several shares and distribute them to multiple participants. Every sub-image itself does not represent any information. Any k or more sub-images can be reconstructed into the original image, but less than k portion cant get any information of the original image, so as to ensure image safety. Sangeetha et al. [23] present threshold visual cryptographic schemes and use half toning method to provide color image as a secret image. Shares are generated using Zigzags scanning method and embedded in the original image. Experimental results of proposed system provide robust security than conventional visual cryptographic schemes. In order to ensure the good quality of the stego image, Ahmad et al. [24] propose a method to protect the medical image by using the shared secret mechanism and steganography, which shows good quality in terms of PSNR. In [25], an approach based on the Shamir's Secret Sharing method and multi-cloud environment is proposed, which is applied to gray-level images. And the results show that it is an appropriate method to store and share patients medical images in a secure and efficient manner.

3.5 Security Algorithms Based on DNA Computing

DNA computing is a new computational method that uses the enormous parallel computing ability and high memory density of bio-molecules. The encryption algorithm based on DNA computing is a new field of cryptography by using DNA molecular as information medium [26,27].

In recent years, the DNA cryptography for medical images has also inspired the interest of researchers. In [28], difference pair mapping method is used to embed the message into the cover image. And DNA based encryption algorithm is used to resist the statistical and exhaustive attacks. The proposed algorithm provides high embedding capacity and high security. Later Ravichandran et al. [29] propose a hybrid encryption scheme based on deoxyribo nucleic acid and chaotic maps, which uses multiple chaotic maps to generate random keys to encrypt the medical images. The results show the resistance toward statistical, differential, and brute force attacks. In [30], an approach is proposed based on Chao's theories and DNA encoding. The input medical image is transformed into two DNA encoded matrices based on intensity levels firstly. Then Chens hyper chaotic map and Lorenz chaotic map are used to produce the chaotic sequences separately. ADD operation is used to attain the encrypted image. This method achieves the integrity, robustness and efficiency for medical image encryption.

In [31], a hybrid watermarking and encryption technique for copyright protection and authentication of medical images is introduced. The medical image is watermarked in wavelet domain. A Composite algorithm for improved image security is proposed by taking the advantages of DNA based image encryption and genetic algorithms (GA). It uses logistic map function and DNA conversion rules to generate the deoxyribonucleic acid masks, where genetic algorithm is applied to find the best DNA mask in iterative manner. Then encryption is performed on the watermarked image. The results of proposed scheme show the security attributes in both frequency and encryption domain and also minimization of image distortion.

Besides, there are still some other new image security algorithms based on the methods such as optical theory or compressive sensing theory. It is expected to be also applied in medical image security systems in the near future.

4 Open Issues of Medical Images Security

The security of medical images has gradually become one of the bottlenecks that restrict the development of smart healthcare and cloud image platforms. How to enhance the security encryption and privacy protection of medical images in transmission, storage, and use has become an urgent task. At the same time, because the features of medical images are different from natural images, many algorithms and research on natural images cannot be directly transplanted into medical images. Therefore, there are still some open issues on the medical images security as follows:

(1) Most medical images are gray scale images, and the background is mostly black. Different image contents may have similar gray scale information. More

noise, artifacts, and geometric distortions may be introduced during medical imaging. Therefore, these characteristics need to be fully considered during the research of medical security.

(2) Medical image is an important basis for doctors to obtain patients pathological information and perform diagnosis and treatment. Therefore, the data quality requirements are extremely strict, and no modification is allowed. Therefore, the security algorithms should be more resistant to the attack and have the good ability of tamper recovery.

(3) Most encryption algorithms do not consider the image compression problem at the same time, and the amount of encryption data generated is often greater than or equal to that of plain text. For the massive data of medical cloud image platform, the cost of encryption, decryption, and data transmission cannot be ignored.

(4) There is some correlation between different types of medical images of the same patient, and the existing security techniques do not take this into account. The security algorithms that infuse multiple types of images and multiple features will be meaningful, which will improve the efficiency of the cloud-based security system and also ensure the integrity and reliability of the patient's various types of information.

In a summary, the future research work should pay more attention on the new security requirements of cloud based environment. The algorithm efficiency and calculation cost are important factors that need to be considered.

5 Conclusion

In this paper, we have introduced the latest development of medical image security algorithms in recent five years. The open issues of medical images security are also analyzed. With the development of smart healthcare and image cloud platform, we can expect the rapid development of medical image encryption techniques in the near future.

References

1. United States Department of Health and Human Services. HIPPA: medical privacy national standards to protect the privacy of personal health information. http://www.hhs.gov/ocr/privacy/
2. Kromtech Security Discovers Health Data Breach of 150K Patients. http://healthitsecurity.com/news/kromtech-security-discovers-health-data-breach-of-150k-patients/
3. Hacker Might Have Stolen the Healthcare Data for Half of Norway's Population. http://www.bleepingcomputer.com/news/security/hacker-might-have-stolen-the-healthcare-data-for-half-of-norways-population/
4. Kavitha, P.K., Saraswathi, P.V.: A survey on medical image encryption. In: 1st International Conference on Applied Soft Computing Techniques, International Journal of Scientific Research in Science and Technology, vol. 3, pp. 1–8. India (2017)

5. Umamageswari, A., Ferni Ukrit, M., Suresh, G.R.: A survey on security in medical image communication. Int. J. Comput. Appl. **30**(3), 41–45 (2011)
6. Mousavi, S.M., Naghsh, A., Abu-Bakar, S.A.: Watermarking techniques used in medical images: a survey. J. Digit. Imaging **27**(6), 714–729 (2014)
7. Nazeer, M., Kim, D.G., Nargis, B., Malik, Y.M.: A Fresnelet-based encryption of medical images using Arnold transform. Int. J. Adv. Comput. Sci. Appl. **4**(3), 131–140 (2013)
8. Xing, Y.L., Han, B.R., Shi, F.U.: A medical image scrambling method based on Arnold and Knights tour algorithm. J. Suzhou Vocat. Univ. **4**(3), 20–25 (2015)
9. Wahballa, O., Wahaballa, A., Li, F., Idris, I.I., Xu, C.: Medical image encryption scheme based on Arnold transformation and ID-AK protocol. Int. J. Netw. Secur. **19**(5), 76–78 (2017)
10. Sui, M., Li, J., Dong, C., Bai, Y.: The encrypted watermarking for medical image based on Arnold scrambling and DWT. J. Converg. Inf. Technol. **8**(5), 893–902 (2013)
11. Venkateswarlu, L., Reddy, B.E., Rao, N.V.: Arnold-wavelet based robust watermarking technique for medical images. In: International Conference on ICT in Business Industry & Government, pp. 1–5. IEEE, Indore (2016). https://doi.org/10.1109/ICTBIG.2016.7892689
12. Liu, Y., Li, J.: The medical image watermarking algorithm using DWT-DCT and logistic. In: International Conference on Computing & Convergence Technology, vol. 3(2), pp. 599–603. IEEE, Seoul (2012)
13. Lu, J., Wang, M., Dai, J., Huang, Q., Li, L., Chang: C.-C.: Multiple watermark scheme based on DWT-DCT quantization for medical images. J. Inf. Hiding Multimed. Signal Process. **6**(3), 458–472 (2015)
14. Singh, A.K.: Improved hybrid algorithm for robust and imperceptible multiple watermarking using digital images. Multimed. Tools Appl. **76**(6), 1–18 (2017)
15. Fu, C., Meng, W.H., Zhan, Y.F., Zhu, Z.L., Lau, F.C.: An efficient and secure medical image protection scheme based on chaotic maps. Comput. Biol. Med. **43**(8), 1000–1010 (2013)
16. Zhang, S., Gao, T., Gao, L.: A novel encryption frame for medical image with watermark based on hyperchaotic system. Math. Probl. Eng. **1**(8), 1–11 (2014)
17. Chai, X., Cheng, Y.: A novel medical image encryption algorithm based on four-dimensional memristive hyper-chaotic system. Comput. Era **5**(1), 53–58 (2016)
18. Kanso, A., Ghebleh, M.: An efficient and robust image encryption scheme for medical applications. Commun. Nonlinear Sci. Numer. Simul. **24**(3), 98–116 (2015)
19. Chen, X., Hu, C.J.: Medical image encryption based on multiple chaotic mapping and wavelet transform. Biomed. Res. **28**(20), 9001–9008 (2017)
20. Dai, Y., Wang, H., Wang, Y.: Chaotic medical image encryption algorithm based on bit-plane decomposition. Int. J. Pattern Recognit. Artif. Intell. **30**(4), 643–660 (2016)
21. Xiao, C., Hu, C.J.: Adaptive medical image encryption algorithm based on multiple chaotic mapping. Saudi J. Biol. Sci. **24**(8), 62–70 (2017)
22. Shamir, A.: How to share a secret. Commun. ACM **22**(11), 612–613 (1979)
23. Sangeetha, M., Arumugam, C., Senthilkumar, K.M.: Encryption for sharing of secret medical images. Res. J. Biotechnol. **10**(2), 19–21 (2015)
24. Ahmad, T., Studiawan, H., Ahmad, H.S., Ijtihadie, R.M., Wibisono, W.: Shared secret-based steganography for protecting medical data. In: International Conference on Computer, pp. 1–5. IEEE, Bandung (2014). https://doi.org/10.1109/IC3INA.2014.7042606

25. Marwan, M., Kartit, A., Ouahmane, H.: Secure cloud-based medical image storage using secret share scheme. In: International Conference on Multimedia Computing & Systems, pp. 1–5. IEEE, Marrakech (2016). https://doi.org/10.1109/ICMCS.2016.7905649
26. Adleman, L.M.: Molecular computation of solutions to combinatorial problems. Science **266**(11), 1021–1024 (1994)
27. Cui, G., Qin, L., Wang, Y., Zhang, X.: Information security technology based on DNA computing. In: IEEE International Workshop on Anti-counterfeiting, pp. 1–3. IEEE, Xiamen (2007). https://doi.org/10.1109/IWASID.2007.373746
28. Kumar, C.V., Natarajan, V., Poonguzhali, P.: Secured patient information transmission using reversible watermarking and DNA encryp-tion for medical images. Appl. Math. Sci. **9**(48), 2381–2391 (2015)
29. Ravichandran, D., Praveenkumar, P., Rayappan, J., Amirtharajan, R.: DNA Chaos blend to secure medical privacy. IEEE Trans. Nanobiosci. **16**(8), 850–858 (2017)
30. Akkasaligar, P.T., Biradar, S.: Secure medical image encryption based on intensity level using Chaos theory and DNA cryptography. In: IEEE International Conference on Computational Intelligence & Computing Research, pp. 1–10. IEEE, Chennai (2016). https://doi.org/10.1109/ICCIC.2016.7919681
31. Anusudha, K., Venkateswaran, N., Valarmathi, J.: Secured medical image watermarking with DNA codec. Multimed. Tools Appl. **2**(8), 1–22 (2016)

Adaptively Chosen Ciphertext Secure Lattice IBE Based Programmable Hash Function in the Standard Model

Yongli Tang, Mingming Wang, Zongqu Zhao, and Qing Ye(✉)

College of Computer Science and Technology, Henan Polytechnic University, Jiaozuo 454000, Henan, China
yeqing@hpu.edu.cn

Abstract. In order to increase security of identity-based encryption (IBE) scheme in the standard model from lattice, and reduce the size of master public key, we propose a new lattice-based IBE scheme. This scheme mainly uses the identity-based lossy trapdoor function to generate trapdoor, and get the master public key, master private key and ciphertext from programmable hash function. Comparative analysis shows that, compared to MP12 trapdoor delegation algorithm, identity-based lossy trapdoor function is directly related to user's identity, at the same time the trapdoor is lossy, each different identity corresponds to a different trapdoor, it is impossible to distinguish that the master public key whether is lossy or injective for the adversary, so that the adversary is unable to obtain complete information about how to construct the trapdoor functions, this feature makes the trapdoor function more secure than other trapdoor functions. In addition, the size of master public of previous scheme is $O(n)$ (n denotes the length of the user's identity), using programmable hash function constructs master public key of our scheme, so that our scheme master public key size is reduced to $O(\log n)$, the size of the master public key of our scheme is reduced and the efficiency of our scheme is improved. Finally, we can prove our scheme is indistinguishability from random under adaptive chosen ciphertext and chosen-identity attacks (INDr-ID-CCA) secure based on learning with error hard problem in the standard model.

Keywords: Lattice · Identity-based encryption · Programmable hash function

1 Introduction

Shamir [1] introduced identity-based encryption (IBE) in 1984, In this new paradigm users' public key can be any string which uniquely identifies the user, For example email or phone number can be public key. As a result, it significantly reduces system complexity and cost of establishing public key infrastructure. Although Shamir constructed an identity-based signature scheme using RSA function but he could not construct an identity-based encryption and this became a long-lasting open problem. Until 2001, Boneh and Franklin [2] define a security model for identity-based encryption and give a construction based on the Bilinear Diffie-Hellman (BDH) problem. Once this proposal was put forward, it caused a great response, since then, IBE has

X. Sun et al. (Eds.): ICCCS 2018, LNCS 11065, pp. 468–478, 2018.
https://doi.org/10.1007/978-3-030-00012-7_43

attracted widespread attention of many scholars, many identity-based encryption and signature schemes have been proposed [3, 4]. In recent years, a new cryptography system based on Lattice because of its high asymptotic efficiency, simple operation, anti-quantum attacks, worst-case random instances and other features has become a research focus in the field of cryptography in the post quantum age, and lattice Identity-based encryption has also developed rapidly. Gentry et al. [5] proposed the first IBE scheme based on the learning with errors (LWE) assumption in the random oracle model, later, several works were dedicated to the study of lattice-based (hierarchical) IBE schemes also in the random oracle model [6]. Cash et al. [7] and Agrawal et al. [8] recently showed how to construct secure IBE in the standard model from the LWE problem, at this point, the identity-based encryption scheme under the standard model has developed rapidly.

In 2008, Peiker and Waters [12] proposed a new general primitive called lossy trapdoor functions (lossy TDFs). Lossy TDFs have quickly proven to be a powerful tool, we can further demonstrate standard trapdoor functions and a CCA-secure (chosen ciphertext attack) cryptosystem, and proof the security of this scheme. In 2012, Bellare and Kiltz [13] defined and constructed identity-based TDFs (IB-TDFs), and also provide IB-TDFs based on LWE, whose hardness follows from the worst-case hardness of certain lattice-related problems, at the same time based on the indistinguishable of the master public key in the constructed scheme, we can proof the scheme is CCA security.

In 2012, as a primitive capturing the partitioning proof techniques, programmable hash function introduced by Hofheinz and Kiltz [9] is a powerful tool to construct provably secure cryptographic schemes in the standard model. Since its introduction, PHFs have attracted much attention from the research community, and had been used to construct many cryptographic schemes (such as short signature schemes [10]) in the standard model. However, both the definition and the constructions of traditional PHFs seem specific to hash functions defined over groups where the “DL problem” is hard. This might be the reason why almost all known PHFs were constructed from “DL groups”. Until 2016, Zhang et al. [11] proposed the concept of PHF on the lattice, This concept not only inherited the characteristics of the traditional PHF, but also using the partitioning proof techniques of lattice, and obtain a new short signature scheme and a new fully secure IBE scheme.

In order to get the CCA security IBE scheme under the standard model, our scheme builds a new IBE scheme with the help of PHF, which mainly contributes to the following aspects: (1) Using PHF to build our framework for IBE scheme, one of the advantages about IBE based PHF is reducing the size of the master public key, with keys consisting of a logarithmic number of matrices/vectors in the security parameter. (2) Trapdoor function is generated by IB-TDFs, compared to MP12 [14], IB-TDFs are relevant to user identities, in other words, each different identity corresponds to a different trapdoor, due to the addition of the concept of lossy trapdoor function, it is impossible to distinguish that the master public key whether is lossy or injective for the adversary, so that the adversary is unable to obtain complete information about how to construct the trapdoor functions, and protect users’ trapdoor. Although this trapdoor construction process is relatively complicated, this change greatly improves the safety of our scheme. (3) Finally, we proof our scheme is INDr-ID-CCA security.

2 Preliminaries

2.1 Lattice and Gaussian Distribution

Definition 1. An m-dimensional full-rank lattice $\Lambda \subset \mathbb{R}^n$ is the set of all integral combinations of m linearly independent vectors $B = \{\boldsymbol{b}_1, \boldsymbol{b}_2, \ldots, \boldsymbol{b}_n\}$, i.e.,

$$\Lambda = \{Bc|Bc = c_1\boldsymbol{b}_1 + c_2\boldsymbol{b}_2 + \ldots + c_n\boldsymbol{b}_n,\ c_i \in Z,\ i = 1, 2, \ldots, n\} \tag{1}$$

Let $\boldsymbol{A} \in \mathbb{Z}_q^{n\times m}$, $n, m, q \in \mathbb{Z}$, consider the following two lattices

$$\boldsymbol{\Lambda}_q^{\perp}(\boldsymbol{A}) = \{\boldsymbol{e} \in \mathbb{Z}^m s.t. \boldsymbol{Ae} = \boldsymbol{0} \bmod q\} \tag{2}$$

$$\boldsymbol{\Lambda}_q(\boldsymbol{A}) = \{\boldsymbol{y} \in \mathbb{Z}^m s.t. \exists \boldsymbol{s} \in \mathbb{Z}^n, \boldsymbol{A}^t\boldsymbol{s} = \boldsymbol{y} \bmod q\} \tag{3}$$

Definition 2. For $\boldsymbol{x} \in \Lambda$, define the Gaussian function $\rho_{\sigma,\boldsymbol{c}}(\boldsymbol{x})$ over $\Lambda \in \mathbb{Z}^m$ centered at $\boldsymbol{c} \in \mathbb{R}^m$ with parameter $\sigma > 0$ as

$$\rho_{\sigma,c}(\boldsymbol{x}) = \exp\left(-\frac{\pi\|\boldsymbol{x} - \boldsymbol{c}\|^2}{\sigma^2}\right) \tag{4}$$

Let $\rho_{\sigma,c}(\Lambda) = \sum_{\boldsymbol{x}\in\Lambda} \rho_{\sigma,\boldsymbol{c}}(\boldsymbol{x})$, and define the discrete Gaussian distribution over Λ as $D_{\Lambda,\sigma,\boldsymbol{c}}(\boldsymbol{y}) = \frac{\rho_{\sigma,c}(\boldsymbol{y})}{\rho_{\sigma,c}(\Lambda)}$ where $\boldsymbol{y} \in \Lambda$.

2.2 Algorithm

The trapdoor generation algorithm based on the identity-based lossy trapdoor function of our scheme is described as Lemma 1; the preimage sampling algorithm is described as Lemma 2; Definition 3 mainly describes two specific algorithms of hash function; Definition 4 introduces the basic concept of PHF.

Lemma 1. Let $c > 1$, $b \geq 2$, $\hat{n} = cn$, $q = q(n)$, $\bar{m} = \hat{n}\log_b q + \omega(\log n)$, and $m = \bar{m} + 2\hat{n}\omega$. $C : IDSp \rightarrow \mathbb{Z}_q^{\hat{n}\times\hat{n}} \times \{0, 1\}^{\hat{n}}$ denote an injective encoding of identities that will be instantiated for a specific scheme, The identity space is $id \in \{0, 1\}^{\hat{n}}$. We define the algorithm for generating user trapdoor functions as *TrapGen*, given input $\boldsymbol{A} \in \mathbb{Z}_{\mathrm{q}}^{\hat{n}\times\bar{m}}$, and auxiliary input $\boldsymbol{H} = (\boldsymbol{H}[1], \ldots, \boldsymbol{H}[\hat{n}]) \in \left(\mathbb{Z}_{\mathrm{q}}^{\hat{n}\times\hat{n}}\right)^{\hat{n}}$, run the algorithm $TrapGen(\boldsymbol{A}, \boldsymbol{H}, id)$, the output is $\boldsymbol{A}(id) \in \mathbb{Z}_q^{\hat{n}\times(\bar{m}+\hat{n}\omega)}$ and trapdoor is $\boldsymbol{R}(id) \in \mathbb{Z}_q^{\bar{m}\times\hat{n}\omega}$, trapdoor matrix size for all identities is $s_1(\boldsymbol{R}(id)) = O(\hat{n}b\sqrt{m}) \bullet \omega(\sqrt{\log n})$, $\boldsymbol{A}(id)$ is uniformly random in $\mathbb{Z}_q^{\hat{n}\times(\bar{m}+\hat{n}\omega)}$.

Lemma 2. The parameter is same as Lemma 1. Select a uniformly random matrix $\boldsymbol{U} \leftarrow_r \mathbb{Z}_q^{\hat{n}\times\hat{n}}$, and user identity is id, we have the algorithm $SampleD(\boldsymbol{R}(id), \boldsymbol{F}(id),$

$I_{\hat{n}}$, U, $s) \to D(id)$, $I_{\hat{n}}$ is a tag matrix for $F(id)$, where $F(id) = (A(id)|H_K(id)) \in \mathbb{Z}_q^{\hat{n}\times m}$, ($H_K(id)$ is described in Definition 3), s is the system parameter, $s = \Theta(\hat{n}b^2\sqrt{m}) \bullet \omega(\sqrt{\log n})^2$.

Definition 3. Given the security parameter n, m, $\bar{m}$ be some polynomials in the security parameter n. A hash function consists of two algorithms ($\mathcal{H}.Gen$ and $\mathcal{H}.Eval$), the probabilistic polynomial time (PPT) key generation algorithm $\mathcal{H}.Gen$ outputs a key K, i.e. $\mathcal{H}.Gen \to K$, the efficiently deterministic evaluation algorithm $\mathcal{H}.Eval(K, X)$ outputs a hash value $Z \in \mathbb{Z}_q^{n\times m}$, i.e. $H_K(X) = \mathcal{H}.Eval(K, X)$.

Definition 4 (Programmable Hash Functions from Lattices). The parameter is the same as Definition 3, given a uniformly random $A \in \mathbb{Z}_q^{n\times\bar{m}}$ and a (public) trapdoor matrix $B \in \mathbb{Z}_q^{n\times m}$, there exist a PPT trapdoor key generation algorithm $(K', td) \leftarrow \mathcal{H}.TrapGen(1^n, A, B)$, and an efficiently deterministic trapdoor evaluation algorithm $\mathcal{H}.TrapEval(td, K', X) = (V_X, W_X)$, $V_X \in \mathbb{Z}_q^{n\times\bar{m}}$, $W_X \in \mathbb{Z}_q^{n\times n}$.

3 Our Construction

Our construction consists of the four algorithms listed in this section, we have that, security parameter is $n, c > 1, b \geq 2$, define $\hat{n} = cn, q = q(n), \bar{m} = \hat{n}\log_b q + \omega(\log n)$, $m = \bar{m} + 2\hat{n}\omega$, where $\omega = \lceil \log_b q \rceil$, the specific plan is as follows.

Setup: Given input $A \in \mathbb{Z}_q^{\hat{n}\times\bar{m}}$, auxiliary input $H = (H[1], \ldots, H[\hat{n}]) \in \left(\mathbb{Z}_q^{\hat{n}\times\hat{n}}\right)^{\hat{n}}$, and user identity $id \in \{0, 1\}^{\hat{n}}$, run the algorithm $TrapGen(A, H, id)$ to generate $A(id) \in \mathbb{Z}_q^{\hat{n}\times(\bar{m}+\hat{n}\omega)}$ with the corresponding trapdoor $R(id) \in \mathbb{Z}_q^{\bar{m}\times\hat{n}\omega}$, run the algorithm $\mathcal{H}.Gen(1^n)$ to generate K. Randomly choose $U \leftarrow_r \mathbb{Z}_q^{\hat{n}\times\hat{n}}$, Finally, return $mpk = (A(id), K, U)$ and $msk = R(id)$.

Extract: This is a PPT algorithm that takes as inputs user identity $id = \{0, 1\}^{\hat{n}}$, and msk, run the algorithm $\mathcal{H}.Eval(K, id)$ to generate $H_K(id) \in \mathbb{Z}_q^{\hat{n}\times\hat{n}\omega}$ with the identity, and let $F(id) = (A(id)|H_K(id)) \in \mathbb{Z}_q^{\hat{n}\times m}$, run the algorithm Sample$D(R(id), F(id), I_{\hat{n}}, U, s) \to D(id)$, let $sk_{id} = D(id) \in \mathbb{Z}_q^{m\times\hat{n}}$, sk_{id} is the user's private key, output the private key.

Enc: Given mpk, user id $id = \{0, 1\}^{\hat{n}}$, and message $M \in \{0, 1\}^{\hat{n}}$, randomly choose $s \leftarrow_r \mathbb{Z}_q^{\hat{n}}$, $x_0 \leftarrow_r D_{\mathbb{Z}^{\hat{n}},\alpha q}$ and $x_1 \leftarrow_r D_{\mathbb{Z}^{\bar{m}+\hat{n}\omega},\alpha q}$, where $\alpha \in \mathbb{R}$, and compute $\mathcal{H}.TrapGen(1^n, A(id), B)$ for some trapdoor matrix $B \in \mathbb{Z}_q^{\hat{n}\times\hat{n}\omega}$ to get V_{id} and W_{id}. Finally, compute and return the ciphertext $C = (c_0, c_1)$, where

$$c_0 = U^{\mathrm{T}}s + x_0 + \frac{q}{2}M \tag{5}$$

$$c_1 = F^{T}(id)s + \begin{pmatrix} x_1 \\ V_{id}^{T} x_1 \end{pmatrix} \tag{6}$$

Dec: Given $C = (c_0, c_1)$, and $sk_{id} = D(id)$, compute $b = c_0 - D(id)^{T} c_1$, then, treat each coordinate of $b = (b_1, \ldots, b_n)^{T}$, as an integer in $\mathbb{Z}$, and set $M_i = 1$ if $\left|b_i - \lfloor \frac{q}{2} \rfloor\right| \leq \lfloor \frac{q}{4} \rfloor$, else $M_i = 0$.

4 Security

The standard IBE security model of defines the indistinguishability of ciphertexts under an adaptive chosen-ciphertext and chosen-identity attack(IND-ID-CCA2). A weaker notion of IBE security given by Canetti, Halevi, and Katz [15] forces the adversary to announce ahead of time the public key it will target, which is known as a selective-identity attack (IND-sID-CCA2). As with regular public-key encryption, we can deny the adversary the ability to ask decryption queries (for the target identity), which leads to the weaker notions of indistinguishability of ciphertexts under an adaptive chosen-identity chosen-plaintext attack (IND-ID-CPA) and under a selective-identity chosen-plaintext attack (IND-sID-CPA) respectively.

We define IBE adaptively security using a game that captures a strong privacy property called indistinguishable from random which means that the challenge ciphertext is indistinguishable from a random element in the ciphertext space. This property implies both semantic security and recipient anonymity, and also implies that the ciphertext hides the master public key used to create it. We also use the concept of indistinguishable from random to expand on the basis, and improve INDr-ID-CPA security to INDr-ID-CCA security. The specific solution is as follows.

4.1 Building a Security Model

Setup. The challenger $\mathcal{C}$ first runs $Setup(1^n)$ with the security parameter n. Then, it gives the adversary $\mathcal{A}$ the master public key mpk, and keeps the master secret key msk to itself.

Phase 1. The adversary is allowed to query the user private key for any identity. The challenger $\mathcal{C}$ runs $sk_{id} \leftarrow Extract(msk, id)$ and sends sk_{id} to the adversary $\mathcal{A}$. The adversary can repeat the user private key query any polynomial times for different identities. At the same time the attacker can make decryption queries. The challenger runs $m \leftarrow Dec(sk_{id}, C)$ and sends m to the adversary. The adversary can repeat the decryption query any polynomial times for different identities.

Challenge. The adversary $\mathcal{A}$ outputs a challenge plaintext M^* and a challenge identity id^*, with a restriction that id is not used in the user private key query id^* in phase 1. The challenger chooses a uniformly random ciphertext C_0 from the ciphertext space. Then, it computes $C_1 \leftarrow Enc(mpk, id^*, M^*)$. Finally, it randomly chooses a bit $b^* \leftarrow_r \{0, 1\}$, and sends C_{b^*} as the challenge ciphertext to $\mathcal{A}$.

Phase 2. The adversary $\mathcal{A}$ can adaptively make more user $id \neq id^*$ private key queries with any identity. The challenger $\mathcal{C}$ responds as in Phase 1. The adversary $\mathcal{A}$ can adaptively make more decryption queries with any identity. The challenger $\mathcal{C}$ responds as in Phase 1.

Guess. Finally, $\mathcal{A}$ outputs a guess $b \in \{0, 1\}$. If $b = b^*$, the challenger outputs 1, else outputs 0.

Compared to INDr-ID-CPA, INDr-ID-CCA increases the attacker's decryption query for users who are not challenged identities both in Phase 1 and Phase 2, this is also the essential difference between CCA security and CPA security. To prove the safety of our scheme, we make our security proof based on the hardness of LWE problem on lattices. We assume that $\hat{n}$, q, $m \in \mathbb{Z}$ and α, $\beta \in \mathbb{R}$ be polynomials in the security parameter n. For large enough $v = poly(n)$, $\mathcal{H} = (\mathcal{H}.Gen,\ \mathcal{H}.Eval)$ let be any with high min-entropy, range is $\{0, 1\}^{\hat{n}} \rightarrow \mathbb{Z}_q^{\hat{n}\times m}$, where $\gamma = negl(n)$ and $\delta > 0$ is noticeable. Then, if there exists a PPT $\mathcal{A}$ breaking the INDr-ID-CPA security of IBE with non-negligible advantage ε and making at most $Q < v$ user private key queries $Q < v$, there exists an algorithm $\mathcal{B}$ solving the $LWE_{q,\alpha}$ problem with advantage at least $\varepsilon' \geq \varepsilon\delta/3 - negl(n)$.In the following, we use a sequence of games from Game 0 to Game 5. Informally, Game 0 is exactly the real security game where the challenger honestly encrypts the challenge plaintext, while Game 5 is a random game where the challenge ciphertext is independent from the challenge plaintext. The security is established by showing that if $\mathcal{A}$ can succeed in Game 0 with non-negligible advantage, then it can succeed in Game 5 with non-negligible advantage ε, which is contradictory to the fact that Game 5 is a random game. It is impossible to achieve, thus our solution is INDR-ID-CCA security.

4.2 Security

Game 0. The challenger $\mathcal{C}$ honestly simulates the INDr-ID-CPA security game for $\mathcal{A}$ as follows:

Setup. First compute $TrapGen(\boldsymbol{A}, \boldsymbol{H})$, such that $\boldsymbol{A}(id) \in \mathbb{Z}_q^{\hat{n}\times(\bar{m}+\hat{n}\omega)}$ and $\boldsymbol{R}(id) \in \mathbb{Z}_q^{\bar{m}\times\hat{n}w}$. Then, randomly choose $\boldsymbol{U} \leftarrow_r \mathbb{Z}_q^{\hat{n}\times\hat{n}}$, and compute $K \leftarrow H.Gen(1^n)$. Finally, send the master public key $mpk = (\boldsymbol{A}(id),\ K,\ \boldsymbol{U})$ to the adversary $\mathcal{A}$, and keep the master secret key private $msk = \boldsymbol{R}(id)$.

Phase 1. Upon receiving the user private key query with identity $id \in \{0, 1\}^{\hat{n}}$, compute the hash value $\boldsymbol{F}(id) = (\boldsymbol{A}(id)|\boldsymbol{H}_K(id)) \in \mathbb{Z}_q^{\hat{n}\times m}$, where $\boldsymbol{H}_K(id) = H.Eval(K,\ id)$. Then, compute Sample$D(\boldsymbol{R}(id),\ \boldsymbol{F}(id),\ \boldsymbol{I}_{\hat{n}},\ \boldsymbol{U},\ s)$, and send the user private key $sk_{id} = \boldsymbol{D}(id) \in \mathbb{Z}_q^{m\times\hat{n}}$ to the adversary. At the same time, the $\mathcal{A}$ sends the randomly selected ciphertext $\boldsymbol{C}(c_0,\ c_1)$ to the challenger, and compute $\boldsymbol{b} = \mathbf{c}_0 - \boldsymbol{D}^t(id)\mathbf{c}_1$, and make a judgment, send the judgment result to $\mathcal{A}$.

Challenge. At some time, the adversary $\mathcal{A}$ outputs a challenge identity id^* and a plaintext $M^* \in \{0, 1\}^n$ with the restriction that it never obtains the user private key of

id^* in Phase 1. The challenger first randomly chooses $s \leftarrow_r \mathbb{Z}_q^{\hat{n}}$, $x_0 \leftarrow_r D_{\mathbb{Z}^{\hat{n}},\alpha q}$ and $x_1 \leftarrow_r D_{\mathbb{Z}^m,\alpha q}$. Then, it computes $H.TrapGen(1^n, A(id), B) \rightarrow (K', td)$, $H.TrapEval(td, K', id) = (V_{id}, W_{id})$, and sets $C_1 = (c_0^*, c_1^*)$, where

$$c_0^* = U^t s + x_0 + \frac{q}{2} M_{b^*} \tag{7}$$

$$c_1^* = A_{id^*}^t s + \begin{pmatrix} x_1 \\ V_{id^*}^t x_1 \end{pmatrix} \tag{8}$$

Finally, it randomly chooses a bit $b^* \leftarrow_r \{0, 1\}$, and sends the challenge ciphertext C_{b^*} to the adversary.

Phase 2. $\mathcal{A}$ can adaptively make more user private key queries with any identity $id \neq id^*$, and many times $(id, C) \neq (id^*, C_{b^*})$ decryption queries. The challenger responds as in Phase 1.

Guess. Finally, $\mathcal{A}$ outputs a guess $b \in \{0, 1\}$. If $b = b^*$, the challenger $\mathcal{C}$ outputs 1, else outputs 0.

Denote F_i be the event that $\mathcal{C}$ outputs 1 in Game i for $i \in \{0, 1, \ldots, 5\}$.

From Game 0, we can get

$$\left|\Pr[F_0] - \frac{1}{2}\right| = \varepsilon \tag{9}$$

Game 1. This game is identical to Game 0, except $K \leftarrow \mathcal{H}.Gen(1^n)$ is replaced by $(K', td) \leftarrow \mathcal{H}.TrapGen\,(1^n, A(id), G)$, the corresponding master public key is $mpk = (A(id), K', U)$, and send this master public key to $\mathcal{A}$, the master private key is unchanged, and keep the master secret key R and the trapdoor td private. At the same time, in the challenge, the challenger uses (K', td) directly to generate the ciphertext.

If $\mathcal{H}$ is a PHF with high min-entropy, then

$$|\Pr[F_1] - \Pr[F_0]| \leq negl(k) \tag{10}$$

Game 2. This game is identical to Game 1 except that $\mathcal{C}$ changes the guess phase as follows.

Guess. Finally, the adversary $\mathcal{A}$ outputs a guess $b \in \{0, 1\}$. Let $id_1, \ldots, id_Q$ be all the identities in the user private queries, and let id^* be the challenge identity. Denote $I^* = \{id_1, \ldots, id_Q, id^*\}$, the challenger $\mathcal{C}$ first defines the following function.

$$\tau\left(\widehat{td}, \widehat{K}, I^*\right) = \begin{cases} 0, & \text{if } \hat{S}_{id^*} = \mathbf{0}, \text{ and } \hat{S}_{id^*} \text{ is invertible for all } i \in \{1, \ldots, Q\} \\ 1, & \text{otherwise} \end{cases} \tag{11}$$

where $(\hat{R}_{id^*}, \hat{S}_{id^*}) = \mathcal{H}.TrapEval\left(\widehat{td}, \widehat{K}, id^*\right)$ and $(\hat{R}_{id_i}, \hat{S}_{id_i}) = \mathcal{H}.TrapEval\left(\widehat{td}, \widehat{K}, id_i\right)$. Then, $\mathcal{C}$ proceeds the following steps:

Abort check: Let (K', td) be produced in the setup phase when generating the master public key $mpk = (\boldsymbol{A}, K', \boldsymbol{U})$, the challenger $\mathcal{C}$ computes the value of $\tau(td, K', I^*)$. If $\tau(td, K', I^*) = 1$, the challenger $\mathcal{C}$ aborts the game, and outputs a uniformly random bit.

Artificial abort: Fixing $I^* = \{id_1, \ldots, id_Q, id^*\}$, let p be the probability $p = \Pr\left[\tau\left(\widehat{td}, \widehat{K}, I^*\right) = 0\right]$ over the random choice of $\left(\widehat{td}, \widehat{K}\right)$. Then, challenger $\mathcal{C}$ samples $O(\varepsilon^2 \log(\varepsilon^{-1})\delta^{-1}\log(\delta^{-1}))$ times the probability p by independently running $\left(\widehat{td}, \widehat{K}\right) \leftarrow \mathcal{H}.TrapGen(1^n, \boldsymbol{A}, \boldsymbol{G})$ to compute an estimate p'. Let δ be the parameter for the well-distributed hidden matrices property of $\mathcal{H}$, if $p' > \delta$, the challenger $\mathcal{C}$ aborts, and outputs a uniformly random bit.

Finally, if $b = b^*$, the challenger $\mathcal{C}$ outputs 1, else outputs 0.

For $i \in \{2, 3, 4, 5\}$, let $\tilde{p}_i$ be the probability that $\mathcal{C}$ does not abort in the abort check stage in Game i, and let p_i be the probability in the artificial abort stage of Game i defined by $p_i = \Pr\left[\tau\left(\widehat{td}, \widehat{K}, I^*\right) = 0\right]$. Since the adversary might obtain some information of td from the challenge ciphertext, the probability $\tilde{p}_i$ might not be equal to the probability p. However, we will show later that the two probabilities can be very close under the LWE assumption. Formally, let Γ_i be the absolute difference between $\tilde{p}_i$ and p_i (i.e., $\Gamma_i = |\tilde{p}_i - p_i|$). If $\mathcal{H}$ is a $(1, v, \beta, \gamma, \delta) - PHF$ and $Q < v$, we have

$$\left|\Pr[F_2] - \frac{1}{2}\right| \geq \frac{1}{2}\varepsilon(\delta - \Gamma_2) \tag{12}$$

Game 3. This game is identical to Game 2 except that the challenger changes the way of generating the user private keys and the challenge ciphertext as follows. For generating user private keys, the different place is that we need to run $(\boldsymbol{R}_{id}, \boldsymbol{S}_{id}) = \mathcal{H}.TrapEval(td, K', id)$, then determine whether the matrix $\boldsymbol{S}_{id}$ is invert, if $\boldsymbol{S}_{id}$ is invert, then $\mathcal{C}$ outputs a uniform random bit and aborts the game. Otherwise, the challenger $\mathcal{C}$ executes the algorithm $SampleD(\boldsymbol{R}(id), \boldsymbol{F}(id), \boldsymbol{S}_{id}, \boldsymbol{U}, s)$, sends the user private key to $\mathcal{A}$. For challenge, the different is $(\boldsymbol{R}_{id^*}, \boldsymbol{S}_{id^*}) = \mathcal{H}.TrapEval(td, K', id^*)$, if $\boldsymbol{S}_{id^*} \neq \boldsymbol{0}$, Challenger outputs a uniform random bit and aborts the game at the same time, if $\boldsymbol{S}_{id^*} = \boldsymbol{0}$, then, follows the original steps.

If $\mathcal{H}$ is a $(1, v, \beta, \gamma, \delta) - PHF$ and $Q < v$, then

$$\Pr[F_3] = \Pr[F_2] \text{ and } \Gamma_3 = \Gamma_2 \tag{13}$$

Game 4. This game is identical to Game 3 except that the challenger changes the setup and the challenge phases as follows. The change to Setup is that the trapdoor generation algorithm is not used to generate $\boldsymbol{A}(id)$ and $\boldsymbol{R}(id)$, instead, the challenger randomly chooses $\boldsymbol{A}(id)$ and computes $(K', td) \leftarrow \mathcal{H}.TrapGen(1^n, \boldsymbol{A}(id), \boldsymbol{G})$, send master public key $mpk = (\boldsymbol{A}(id), K, \boldsymbol{U})$ to $\mathcal{A}$, keep hash trapdoor td. In Challenge, this changed the way ciphertext was generated, randomly choose vector $\boldsymbol{b}_0 \leftarrow_r \mathbb{Z}_q^{\hat{n}}$, $\boldsymbol{b}_1 \leftarrow_r \mathbb{Z}_q^m$, and compute $\boldsymbol{c}_0^* = \boldsymbol{b}_0 + \frac{q}{2}M_{b^*}$, $\boldsymbol{c}_0^* = \boldsymbol{b}_0 + \frac{q}{2}M_{b^*}$.

If the advantage of any PPT algorithm $\mathcal{B}$ in solving the $LWE_{q,\alpha}$ problem is at most ε', then we have that

$$|\Pr[F_4] - \Pr[F_3]| \leq \varepsilon' \text{ and } |\Gamma_4 - \Gamma_3| \leq \varepsilon' \tag{14}$$

Game 5. Compared to Game 0, in the setup phase, the challenger computes $(K', td) \leftarrow \mathcal{H}.TrapGen(1^n, \boldsymbol{A}(id), \boldsymbol{G})$, and sends the master public key to the adversary, and keep $(\boldsymbol{R}, K', td)$ private. Phase 1 is the same as Game 0. The Challenge phase is identical to Game 4, except that the challenger generates the ciphertext $C_1 = (\boldsymbol{c}_0^*, \boldsymbol{c}_1^*)$ by randomly choosing $\boldsymbol{c}_0^* \leftarrow_r \mathbb{Z}_q^{\hat{n}}$ and $\boldsymbol{c}_1^* \leftarrow_r \mathbb{Z}_q^m$.

If $\mathcal{H}$ is a $(1, v, \beta, negl(k), \delta) - PHF$ with min-entropy, then we have

$$|\Pr[F_5] - \Pr[F_4]| \leq negl(k) \text{ and } |\Gamma_5 - \Gamma_4| \leq negl(k) \tag{15}$$

From (12) and (13) we have $|\Pr[F_3] - \frac{1}{2}| \geq \frac{1}{2}\varepsilon(\delta - \Gamma_3)$, by (14) and (15) we can get $\Pr[F_4] \leq \frac{1}{2} + negl(k)$ and $\Gamma_4 \leq negl(k)$, from (14), we have $\frac{1}{2}\varepsilon(\delta - \varepsilon') - negl(k) \leq |\Pr[F_3] - \frac{1}{2}| \leq \varepsilon' - negl(k)$, this shows that $\varepsilon' \geq \varepsilon\, \delta/3 - negl(n)$ it is established. Based on the above analysis, we prove that our solution is INDr-ID-CCA security.

5 Analysis

Comparing our schemes with several other IBE schemes under the standard model of lattice in trapdoor generation functions, etc. In terms of efficiency in our system, the trapdoor generation function is an identity-based lossy trapdoor function, compared with MP12 used by other system, our trapdoor function is based on MP12, user's identity is used as an element to generate trapdoors, therefore, different identities correspond to different matrices $\boldsymbol{A}(id)$ [16] and their corresponding trapdoor matrices $\boldsymbol{R}(id)$, and because it is lossy, that is $g_{A(id)}$, the generated function is lossy, loss means information hiding, that is, the information about $g_{A(id)}$ is incomplete to the adversary and make it impossible for an adversary to easily obtain complete information about the master public key, this advantage is very important for the CCA security of our program. As far as security is concerned, our solution is based on the INDr-ID-CCA security under the LWE problem compared to other solutions, and its security is higher than that of INDr-ID-CPA security.

In Table 1, we give a (rough) comparison of lattice-based IBEs in the standard model. For simplicity, the identity length is set to be $\hat{n}$, we compare the size of master public keys and ciphertexts in terms of the number of "basic" elements, on general

Table 1. Rough comparison of lattice-based IBEs in the standard model.

Scheme	Size of master public key	Size of ciphertext	Trapdoor function	Security
ABB10a [16]	$\hat{n}^3$	$\hat{n}^2$	MP12 [14]	Selective
ABB10b [17]	$1, n$	1	MP12	Selective, full
[11]	$\log \hat{n}$	1	MP12	$INDr - ID - CPA$
Our scheme	$\log_b \hat{n}$	1	IB-TDF	$INDr - ID - CCA$

lattices, the "basic" element in the master public keys is a matrix, while the "basic" element in the ciphertexts is a vector. We ignore the constant factor in the table to avoid clutter.

Acknowledgements. This work is supported by "13th Five-Year" National Crypto Development Fund under Grant (No. MMJJ20170122), the Project of Education Department of Henan Province (No. 18A413001, No. 16A520013), Natural Science Foundation of Henan Polytechnic University (No. T2018-1).

References

1. Shamir, A.: Identity-based cryptosystems and signature schemes. In: Blakley, G.R., Chaum, D. (eds.) CRYPTO 1984. LNCS, vol. 196, pp. 47–53. Springer, Heidelberg (1985). https://doi.org/10.1007/3-540-39568-7_5
2. Boneh, D., Franklin, M.: Identity-based encryption from the weil pairing. In: Kilian, J. (ed.) CRYPTO 2001. LNCS, vol. 2139, pp. 213–229. Springer, Heidelberg (2001). https://doi.org/10.1007/3-540-44647-8_13
3. Boneh, D., Raghunathan, A., Segev, G.: Function-private identity-based encryption: hiding the function in functional encryption. In: Canetti, R., Garay, Juan A. (eds.) CRYPTO 2013. LNCS, vol. 8043, pp. 461–478. Springer, Heidelberg (2013). https://doi.org/10.1007/978-3-642-40084-1_26
4. Tessaro, S., Wilson, D.A.: Bounded-collusion identity-based encryption from semantically-secure public-key encryption: generic constructions with short ciphertexts. In: Krawczyk, H. (ed.) PKC 2014. LNCS, vol. 8383, pp. 257–274. Springer, Heidelberg (2014). https://doi.org/10.1007/978-3-642-54631-0_15
5. Gentry, C., Peikert, C., Vaikuntanathan, V.: Trapdoors for hard lattices and new cryptographic constructions. In: STOC 2008 Proceedings of the Fortieth Annual ACM Symposium on Theory of computing, pp. 197–206. ACM, New York (2008)
6. Zhandry, M.: Secure identity-based encryption in the quantum random oracle model. Int. J. Quantum Inf. **13**(04), 1484–1510 (2015)
7. Cash, D., Hofheinz, D., Kiltz, E., Peikert, C.: Bonsai trees, or how to delegate a lattice basis. In: Gilbert, H. (ed.) EUROCRYPT 2010. LNCS, vol. 6110. Springer, Heidelberg (2010). https://doi.org/10.1007/978-3-642-13190-5_27
8. Agrawal, S., Boyen, X.: Identity-based encryption from lattices in the standard model. Manuscript (2009)

9. Hofheinz, D., Kiltz, E.: Programmable hash functions and their applications. J. Cryptol. **25** (3), 484–527 (2012)
10. Hofheinz, D., Jager, T., Kiltz, E.: Short signatures from weaker assumptions. In: Lee, D.H., Wang, X. (eds.) ASIACRYPT 2011. LNCS, vol. 7073, pp. 647–666. Springer, Heidelberg (2011). https://doi.org/10.1007/978-3-642-25385-0_35
11. Zhang, J., Chen, Yu., Zhang, Z.: Programmable hash functions from lattices: short signatures and IBEs with small key sizes. In: Robshaw, M., Katz, J. (eds.) CRYPTO 2016. LNCS, vol. 9816, pp. 303–332. Springer, Heidelberg (2016). https://doi.org/10.1007/978-3-662-53015-3_11
12. Peikert, C., Waters, B.: Lossy trapdoor functions and their applications. In: STOC 2008 Proceedings of the Fortieth Annual ACM Symposium on Theory of Computing, pp. 187–196. ACM, New York (2008)
13. Bellare, M., Kiltz, E., Peikert, C., Waters, B.: Identity-based (lossy) trapdoor functions and applications. In: Pointcheval, D., Johansson, T. (eds.) EUROCRYPT 2012. LNCS, vol. 7237, pp. 228–245. Springer, Heidelberg (2012). https://doi.org/10.1007/978-3-642-29011-4_15
14. Micciancio, D., Peikert, C.: Trapdoors for lattices: simpler, tighter, faster, smaller. In: Pointcheval, D., Johansson, T. (eds.) EUROCRYPT 2012. LNCS, vol. 7237, pp. 700–718. Springer, Heidelberg (2012). https://doi.org/10.1007/978-3-642-29011-4_41
15. Canetti, R., Halevi, S., Katz, J.: A forward-secure public-key encryption scheme. In: Biham, E. (ed.) EUROCRYPT 2003. LNCS, vol. 2656. Springer, Heidelberg (2014). https://doi.org/10.1007/3-540-39200-9_16
16. Agrawal, S., Boneh, D., Boyen, X.: Efficient lattice (H)IBE in the standard model. In: Gilbert, H. (ed.) EUROCRYPT 2010. LNCS, vol. 6110, pp. 553–572. Springer, Heidelberg (2010). https://doi.org/10.1007/978-3-642-13190-5_28
17. Agrawal, S., Boneh, D., Boyen, X.: Lattice basis delegation in fixed dimension and shorter-ciphertext hierarchical IBE. In: Rabin, T. (ed.) CRYPTO 2010. LNCS, vol. 6223, pp. 98–115. Springer, Heidelberg (2010). https://doi.org/10.1007/978-3-642-14623-7_6

An Efficient and Secure Key Agreement Protocol Preserving User Anonymity Under Chebyshev Chaotic Maps

Hong Lai[1(✉)], Mingxing Luo[2], Li Tao[1], Fuyuan Xiao[1], Cheng Zhan[1], and Xiaofang Hu[1]

[1] School of Computer and Information Science and Centre for Research and Innovation in Software Engineering (RISE), Southwest University, Chongqing 400715, China
hlai@swu.edu.cn

[2] Information Security and National Computing Grid Laboratory, School of Information Science and Technology, Southwest Jiaotong University, Chengdu 610031, China

Abstract. A type of key agreement protocol based on chaotic maps was proposed in 2009. Soon after the proposal, it was analyzed and improved. Unfortunately, there are still two weaknesses in the two improved protocols. To strengthen the performance of the focused type of protocol, a new improved protocol based on Niu et al.'s protocol is proposed in this paper. Theoretical analysis shows that our improved protocol is immune to denial of service attacks through the keyed hashed digests with either the secret key or the session key. Moreover, modified protocol is more cost-efficient by shifting most computations from on-line to off-line.

Keywords: Key agreement protocol · Chaotic maps
Denial of service attacks · The keyed hashed digests

1 Introduction

In recent years, some chaotic maps have been used to design key agreement protocols [1–9], and these schemes mainly aim at improving security and reducing computational and storage overhead. Unfortunately, these protocols cannot protect user anonymity while establishing a shared secret session key, which is a crucial issue in a lot of e-commence application.

To address the problem, in 2009, Tseng et al. [10] presented a novel key agreement protocol based on chaotic maps. They claimed that their proposed protocol could preserve user anonymity. However, in 2010, Niu et al. [11] proved that Tseng et al.'s protocol could not guarantee user anonymity or provide perfect forward secrecy, and their protocol cannot prevent insider attack. They further proposed an anonymous key agreement protocol based on chaotic maps. Later, Yoon [12] found out that Niu et al.'s protocol had computational efficiency problems when a trusted third party decrypts message sent by the user

X. Sun et al. (Eds.): ICCCS 2018, LNCS 11065, pp. 479–489, 2018.
https://doi.org/10.1007/978-3-030-00012-7_44

and was susceptible to Denial of Service (DoS) attack based on illegal message modification by an attacker. Yoon analyzed the efficiency and secure problems appearing in Niu et al.'s protocol. However, Yoon argued that it was difficult to enhance the Niu et al.'s protocol with moderately modifications to remove the following two weaknesses: (1) It is low efficient for the TTP to decrypt the message from user. (2) It cannot avoid the Denial of Service attack. As a matter of fact, we are able to propose an efficient and secure key agreement protocol preserving user anonymity under Chebyshev chaotic maps to cope with demerits mentioned above. The proposed scheme can successfully better the computation efficiency by shifting most computations from on-line to off-line. At the same time, through the keyed hashed digests with either the secret key or the session key, our protocol can provide the integrity of the transmitted message, which can avoid Denial of Service attack observed by Yoon [12].

This paper is organized as follows. Section 2 gives the description of Chebyshev chaotic map, and some hard problems concerning the Chebyshev chaotic map and review of Niu et al.'s key agreement protocol. Section 3 applies Chebyshev chaotic maps to hammer out an efficient and security key agreement protocol. Section 4 provides security analysis of our proposed scheme and performance analysis of our proposed scheme are given in Sect. 5. Finally, we conclude this paper in Sect. 6.

2 Background

In this section, we review some basic definitions regarding Chebyshev chaotic map, and some hard problems based on the Chebyshev chaotic map [6] and go over Niu et al.'s key agreement protocol and its drawbacks.

Definition 1 (Chebyshev polynomials). Let n be an integer, and x be a variable taking values over the interval $[-1, 1]$. Chebyshev polynomial maps $T_n : R \to R$ of degree n is defined using the following recursive relation:

$$T_n(x) = 2xT_{n-1}(x) - T_{n-2}(x) \tag{1}$$

Where $n \geq 2, T_0(x) = 1$, and $T_1(x) = x$.

The first few Chebyshev polynomials are:

$$T_2(x) = 2x^2 - 1 \tag{2}$$

$$T_3(x) = 4x^3 - 3x \tag{3}$$

$$T_4(x) = 8x^4 - 8x^2 + 1 \tag{4}$$

The interval $[-1, 1]$ is invariant under the action of the map T_n : $T_n([-1, 1]) \to [-1, 1]$. Therefore, the Chebyshev polynomials restricted to the interval $[-1, 1]$ is a well-known chaotic map for all $n > 1$. It has a unique absolutely continuous invariant measure with positive Lyapunov exponent in n. For $n = 2$, the Chebyshev map reduces to the well-known logistic map.

Definition 2. Let n be an integer, and let x be a variable taking value over the interval $[-1,1]$. The polynomial $T_n(x):[-1,1]\rightarrow[-1,1]$ is defined as:

$$T_n(x) = cos(n \times arccos(x)) \tag{5}$$

If we only know one pair $(x, T_n(x))$, where $T_n(x)$ is a polynomial of order n, not just a power x, it is very difficult to compute the order of the polynomial n. The just potential way is to compute $T_k(x)$ for all $k = 2,\ldots,n$, and find whether $T_k(x) = T_n(x)$ one by one. However, if n is large enough number, it is impossible to do so.

Definition 3 (Semi-group property). One of the most important properties of Chebyshev polynomials is the so called semi-group property which establishes that:

$$T_r(T_s(x)) = T_{rs}(x) \tag{6}$$

An immediate consequence of this property is that Chebyshev polynomials commute under composition

$$T_r(T_s(x)) = T_s(T_r(x)) \tag{7}$$

Definition 4 (Enhanced Chebyshev polynomials). In order to enhance the property of the Chebyshev chaotic map, Zhang [13] proved that the semi-group property holds for Chebyshev polynomials defined on interval $[-\infty,+\infty]$. This paper uses the following enhanced Chebyshev polynomials:

$$T_n(x) = 2xT_{n-1}(x) - T_{n-2}(x)(modN) \tag{8}$$

Where $n \geq 2, x \in [-\infty,+\infty]$, and N is a large prime number. Obviously,

$$T_r(T_s(x)) = T_s(T_r(x)) = T_{rs}(x) \tag{9}$$

So the semi-group property still holds and the enhanced Chebyshev polynomials also commute under composition.

Definition 5 (The discrete logarithm problem(DLP)). DLP is explained by the following. Given an element α, find the integer r, such that $T_r(x) = \alpha$.

Definition 6 (The Diffie-Hellman problem(DHP)). DHP is explained by the following. Given an element x, and the values of $T_r(x)$, $T_s(x)$, what is the value of $T_{rs}(x)$?

It is widely believed that there is no polynomial-time algorithm to solve DLP and DHP with non-negligible probability.

3 Review of Niu et al.'s Key Agreement Protocol

This section reviews Niu et al.'s key agreement protocol [10], which is shown in Fig. 1. For easy of presentation, we list following notations in Table 1.

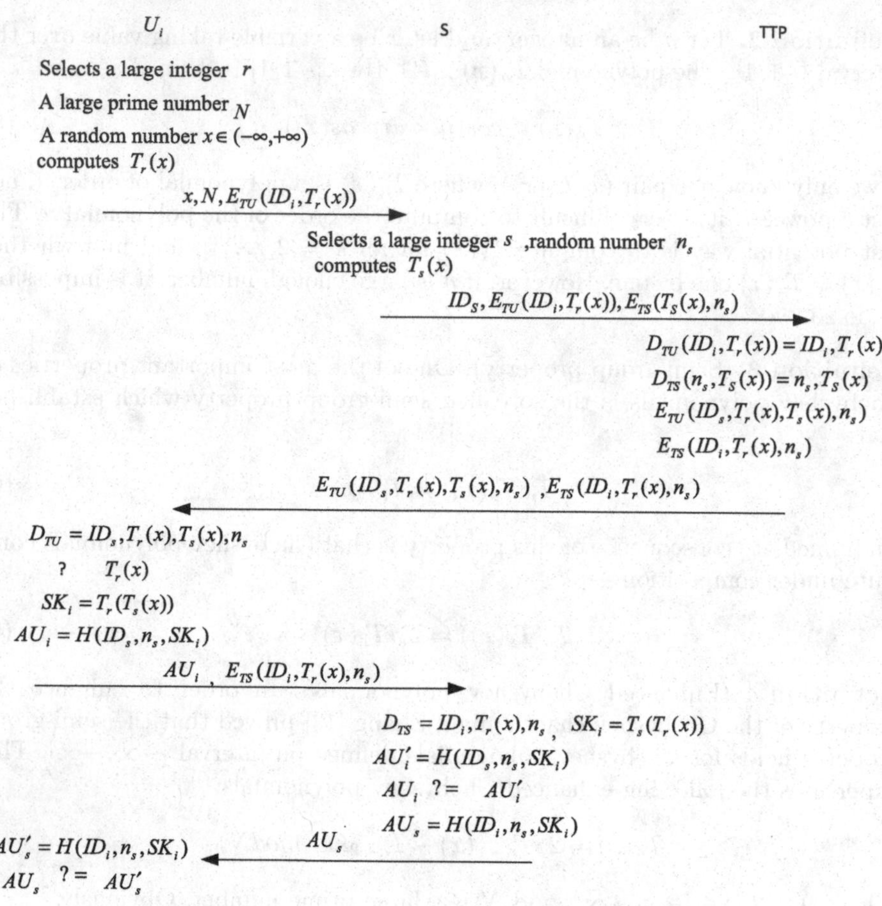

Fig. 1. Niu et al.'s anonymity key agreement protocol.

Table 1. Some of the notations used in Niu et al.'s protocol.

Symbol	Definition
ID_i, ID_s	Identities of user i and server, respectively
$D_T(\cdot)/E_T(\cdot)$	Encryption/Decryption algorithm of the secret key T
TU	Shared secret key between User U_i and TTP
TS	Shared secret key between Server and TTP
r, s	Fresh chaotic random integers chosen by U_i and server
N	Large prime number chosen by U_i

Suppose U_i and Server are two participants of the key agreement process and TTP is a trusted third party in the network such as key distribution center, a trusted server. In the network system, TTP shares a different secret key with each participant. All of these keys are in place before protocol begins. The steps of the Niu-Wang's anonymous key agreement protocol is outlined in Fig. 1 and explained as follows.

(1) $U_i \rightarrow Server$: $\{x, N, E_{TU}(ID_i, T_r(x))\}$. U_i first randomly selects a large integer r, a large prime number N and a random number x, and then computes $T_r(x)$, where $x \in (-\infty, +\infty)$ is the seed of the enhanced Chebyshev polynomial in Definition 4. Next U_i encrypts ID_i and $T_r(x)$ with the key K_{TU} shared with TTP. Finally, he sends to Server message $(x, N, E_{TU}(ID_i, T_r(x)))$.

(2) $Server \rightarrow TTP$: $\{ID_s, E_{TU}(ID_i, T_r(x)), E_{TS}(n_s, T_s(x))\}$.
On receiving the message, Server chooses a large integer s and calculates $T_s(x)$. Then, Server concatenates $T_s(x)$ and a nonce n_s, and encrypts it with the shared secret key TS with TTP. Finally, Server sends it to TTP together with his/her identity ID_s and $E_{TU}(ID_i, T_r(x))$.

(3) $TTP \rightarrow U_i$: $\{E_{TU}(ID_s, T_s(x), T_r(x), n_s), E_{TS}(n_s, T_r(x), ID_i)\}$.
When receiving the message, TTP decrypts them and generates two new messages. The first is Server's identity $ID_s, T_s(x), T_r(x)$ and n_s, all encrypted with K_{TU}. The second is $ID_i, T_r(x)$ and n_s, all encrypted with K_{TS}. Finally, TTP transmits both messages to U_i.

(4) $U_i \rightarrow server$: $\{AU_i, E_{TS}(n_s, T_r(x), ID_i)\}$.
U_i decrypts the message $(E_{TU}(ID_s, T_s(x), T_r(x), n_s)$ with his/her key TU and checks whether $T_r(x)$ has the same values as he/she did in step (1). If not, U_i stops here; otherwise, U_i calculates the shared session key SK_i and AU_i as follows:

$$SK_i = T_r(T_s(x)) \tag{10}$$

$$AU_i = H(ID_s, n_s, SK_i) \tag{11}$$

Finally, U_i sends to Server AU_i and the message $E_{TS}(n_s, T_r(x), ID_i)$.

(5) $server \rightarrow U_i$: AU_s.
Upon receiving the message, Server firstly extracts $T_r(x), ID_i$ and n_s from $E_{TS}(n_s, T_r(x), ID_i)$. Then, he/she checks whether ID_i and n_s is valid, and calculates SK_i and AU_i' as follows:

$$SK_i = T_s(T_r(x)) \tag{12}$$

$$AU_i' = H(ID_s, n_s, SK_i) \tag{13}$$

Then, Server checks whether AU_i equals AU_i'. If so, the identity of U_i is authenticated. Next, Server computes AU_s as follows:

$$AU_s = H(ID_i, n_s, SK_i) \tag{14}$$

Finally, Server transmits AU_s to U_i.

(6) After receiving the message, U_i computes $AU_s' = H(ID_i, n_s, SK_i)$ and checks whether AU_s equals AU_s'. If so, the identity of Server is authenticated. As a result, U_i and Server can use the shared common session key SK_i in their subsequent communications.

3.1 The Weaknesses of Niu et al.'s Key Agreement Protocol

According to Yoon's [8] analysis, there are main following two weaknesses.

(1) Niu et al.'s key agreement protocol has computational efficiency problem when a trusted third decrypts the user sending message.
(2) Niu et al.'s key agreement protocol is susceptible to Denial of Service(DoS) attack based on illegal message modification by an attacker.

4 The Improved Key Agreement Protocol

To remedy the weaknesses pointed out in [8], we propose an efficient and secure key agreement protocol preserving user anonymity under Chebyshev chaotic maps (See Fig. 2.). The protocol is described as follows:

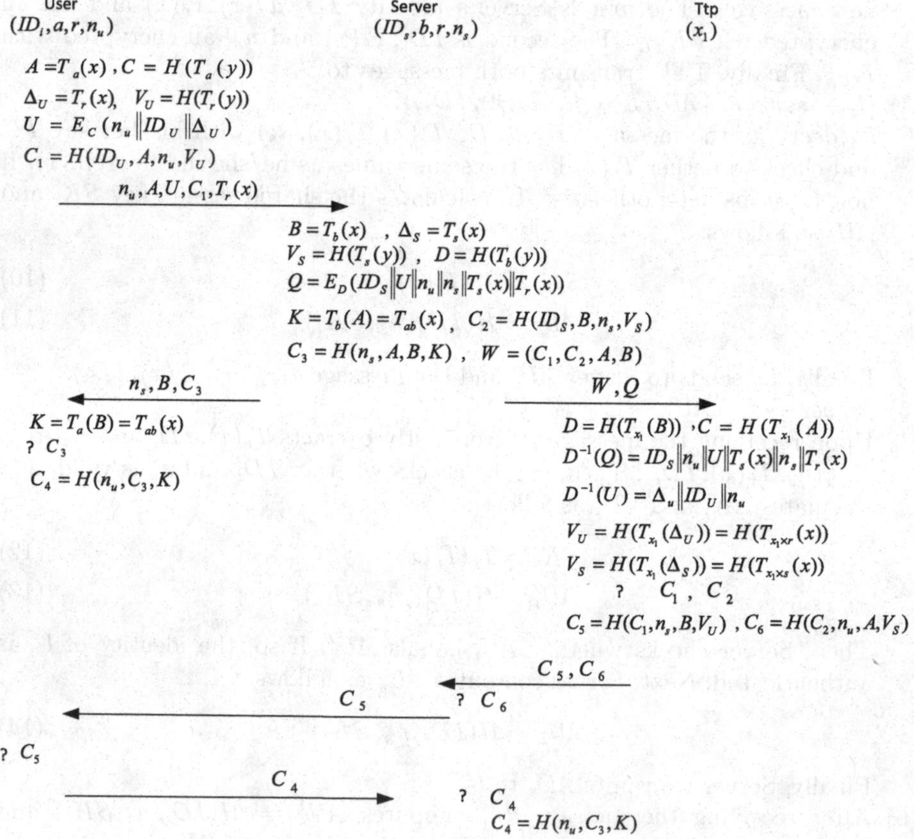

Fig. 2. Our proposed key agreement protocol preserving user anonymity.

First, TTP chooses public parameters (x, N), where x is the seed of the Chebyshev polynomial and N is a large prime. TTP also selects a private key x_1 and computes its public key $y = T_{x_1}(x)$.

(1) $U_i \rightarrow server$: $\{n_u, A, U, C_1, T_r(x)\}$.
U_i first selects two large integers a, r and a random number n_u.Then he calculates $A = T_a(x), C = H(T_a(y)), \Delta_U = T_r(x), V_U = H(T_r(y)), U = E_C(n_u \| ID_U \| \Delta_U)$ and $C_1 = H(ID_U, n_u, A, V_U)$. Finally, he sends $n_u, A, U, C_1, T_r(x)$ to Server. Note A is the user's ephemeral public key and $C = H(T_a(y))$ is the (hashed) Diffie-Hellman key with TTP, and A, C, Δ_U, V_U can be pre-computed off-line.

(2) $server \rightarrow Ttp$: W, Q.
$server \rightarrow U_i$: n_s, B, C_3.
On receiving the message from U_i, Server first selects two large integers b, s, a random number n_s and then does as follows:
(2.1) Compute $B = T_b(x), K = T_b(A) = T_{ab}(x), C_3 = H(n_s, A, B, K)$ for the key agreement with U_i if and only if U_i calculates the same result in a one-way hash function.
(2.2) Compute $\Delta_S = T_s(x), V_S = H(T_s(y)), D = H(T_b(y))$. Then concatenate $ID_S, U, n_u, n_s, T_r(x), T_s(x)$ and encrypt with D. Finally, compute $C_2 = H(ID_S, n_s, B, V_S)$ and $W = (C_1, C_2, A, B)$ and $Q = E_D(ID_S \| U \| T_s(x) \| T_r(x) \| n_u \| n_s)$ to TTP for mutual authentication and prove the integrity of the transmitted message.
Note B is the Server's ephemeral public key and $D = H(T_b(y))$ is the (hashed) Diffie-Hellman key with TTP, and B, D, Δ_S, V_S can be pre-computed off-line.

(3) Upon receiving the message n_s, B, C_3 from Server, U_i computes $K = T_a(B) = T_{ab}(x)$ to test whether C_3 is valid, then compute $C_4 = H(n_u, K, C_3)$.

(4) $Ttp \rightarrow Server$: C_5, C_6.
Upon receiving the message W, Q from Server, TTP first computes $D = H(T_b(y)), C = H(T_a(y))$. Then, he decrypts Q with D to recover $ID_S, U, T_s(x), T_r(x), n_u, n_s$ and decrypts U with C to recover n_u, ID_U, Δ_U. Then TTP computes $V'_U = H(T_{x_1}(\Delta_U)), V'_S = H(T_{x_1}(\Delta_S))$, then he computes C_1, C_2 and tests whether C_1, C_2 are valid. If so, he calculates $C_5 = H(C_1, n_s, B, V'_U), C_6 = H(C_2, n_u, A, V'_S)$. Finally, he sends C_5, C_6 to Server. It is worthwhile note that D, C can be pre-computed off-line.

(5) On receiving the message from TTP, the Server tests whether C_6 is valid, if so, he transmits C_5 to U_i.

(6) When receiving the message from Server, U_i tests whether C_5 is valid, if so, he transmits C_4 to Server. Hence, U_i with Server can use the shared session key K in the subsequent communication.

5 Security Analysis

In the section, we define the security goals that proposed key agreement protocol based on chaotic maps should achieve, followed by the studied treat model main design purposes incudes:

User anonymity: any other entity except the TTP cannot reveal the real identity of user.

Mutual authentication: the user, Server and TTP, can authenticate one another, which implies resistance against impersonation attacks.

Confidentiality and fairness of the session key: the U_i and Server can securely establish a random session key, which should be just revealed to them and contain contribution from both of them.

5.1 Protection of User Anonymity

Our protocol is able to preserve the identity anonymity for any user. This can be explained from following three aspects:

1. ID_U is hidden in $U = E_C(n_u \| ID_U \| \Delta_U)$. Because the Diffie-Hellman problem stops adversary $\mathcal{A}$ from deriving $D = H(T_{ab}(x))$ from $A = T_a(x)$, even if he also knows $B = T_b(x)$ (It happens when $\mathcal{A}$ is an insider $U_\mathcal{A}$). Hence, $\mathcal{A}$ cannot decrypt U to recover ID_U.
2. ID_U is hidden in $C_1 = H(ID_U, ID_S, n_s, V_U)$. He still cannot infer ID_U from C_1, because the hash function has collision-free and irreversible properties.

5.2 The Proposed Protocol Can Provide a Mutual Authentication Among Three Parties

We analysis this point from three aspects: authentications among U_i, Server, and TTP.

Case 1: U_i and Server.

To authentication U_i, Server needs to suppose that they own the same session key. In the protocol, TTP shoulders the responsibility of confirming both the origin and integrity of the received message in step (2) to help them to authenticate each other. TTP ensures that the received message ID_U, n_u, A, V_U and ID_S, n_s, B, V_S have indeed been sent from U_i and Server respectively, and that no modification has occurred. Meanwhile, TTP sends the respective evidence C_5 and C_6 for the origin and the integrity of (n_u, A), and (n_s, B). Based on the premise that TTP is trustworthy, U_i/Server is convinced that the origin of $(n_s, B)/(n_u, A)$ is Server/U_i when the validity of C_5/C_6 is verified. As only U_i/Server knows the secret a/b of A/B, the common session key is generated by U_i/Server as $T_a(B)/\ T_b(A)$. Because the session key is only known by U_i and Server, no one can forge a valid $C_3 = H(n_s, A, B, K)$ or $C_4 = H(n_u, K, C_3)$. Therefore, mutual authentication between U_i and Server is achieved while the session key confirmation is guaranteed.

Case 2: U_i and TTP.

To identify U_i, on the one hand, TTP has to verify the validity of the evidence $C_1 = H(ID_U, n_u, A, V_U)$. On the other hand, U_i must test the validity of $C_5 = H(C_1, n_s, B, V'_U)$ to authenticate TTP. These evidences are computed with the common secret key. Because only U_i and TTP know the common secret key V_U, where V_U equals V'_U derived from $T_{x_1}(\Delta_U)$ by TTP, no one can counterfeit the evidence. When validity of C_1 and C_5 is tested by TTP and U_i respectively, the integrity of the transmitted message from U_i, contains ID_U, n_u, A is confirmed by TTP and the integrity of evidence C_5 from TTP is confirmed by U_i. Thus, mutual authentication between U_i and TTP is achieved.

Case 3: Server and TTP.

The analysis of the mutual authentication between Server and TTP is done likewise. Except Server and TTP, no one knows the secret key V_S. Therefore, mutual authentication between Server and TTP is achieved by verifying the validity of $C_2 = H(ID_S, n_s, B, V_S)$ and $C_6 = H(C_2, n_u, A, V'_S)$ respectively.

5.3 Neither the Shared Secret Key nor the Generated Session Key Will Be Made Known

Given the confidentiality of the secret key, the secret key is hidden in $T_a(x), T_b(x)$. In order to obtain a or b, the attacker has to solve the DLP. However, according to Definition 5, it is believed infeasible in polynomial time.

5.4 The Proposed Protocol Can Provide Integrity of the Transmitted Messages

In our protocol, integrity of the transmitted message is guaranteed by the keyed hashed digests with either the secret key or the session key. Without knowing the secret key or the session key, the attacker cannot modify the transmitted without perception.

5.5 The Proposed Protocol Can Prevent Denial of Service Attack

Due to 4.3, and 4.4, our protocol can provide integrity of the transmitted messages, the attacker cannot modify the transmitted message without perception. Therefore, our proposed protocol can prevent Denial of Service attack.

5.6 The Proposed Protocol Meets the Freshness of the Transmitted Messages

A random number is attached to guarantee the freshness of the transmitted messages. Because the random number is not self-generated, but also self-verified in the protocol. According to this knowledge, the freshness can be guaranteed by testing whether the random is acceptance.

5.7 The Contribution Property

Our mutual authentication and key agreement protocol ends up with U_i and Server agree on $K = T_a(B) = T_b(A) = T_{ab}(x)$, a session key containing equal contribution from both parties.

5.8 Performance Analysis of Proposed Scheme

As is shown in Xue et al.'s protocol [9] that T_{cheb} (denotes the time for Chebyshev polynomial computing) is nearly 32.2 ms on average. Instead, T_{hash} is below 0.2 ms on average. In Niu et al.'s protocol, TTP has to compute two Chebyshev polynomial computing, which leads to low efficient. We successfully address the efficiency problem by shifting the two computations from the on-line side to off-line. Compared with Niu et al.'s protocol, our proposed protocol not only is in need of fewer rounds to perform the key agreement protocol but also enjoys considerably lower computational cost.

The detailed comparison is showed in Table 2.

Table 2. Comparison of computation overhead.

	P1	P2
R-N (U_i/S/TTP)	2/2/0	2/2/0
S-E/D (U_i/S/TTP)	2/2/4	0/0/1
A-E/D (U_i/S/TTP)	0/0/0	1/1/2
H-O (U_i/S/TTP)	2/2/2	2/4/4
C-P-C (U_i/S/TTP)	2/2/2	1+2Pre/1+2Pre/4Pre

Note: "P1" means Niu et al.'s protocol and "P2" symbolizes Our protocol. "S" denotes server and "Pre" denotes pre-computed operation, "R-N" stands for Random number, "S-E/D" represents Symmetric encryption/decryption, "A-E/D" means Asymmetric encryption/decryption, "H-O" stands for Hash operation, and "C-P-C" symbolizes Chebyshev polynomial computing.

6 Conclusion

In this paper, we have shown that we can propose an efficient and secure key agreement protocol preserving user anonymity under Chebyshev chaotic map to address the problems observed by Yoon. By shifting majority of computations from the on-line side to off-line, we address the computational efficiency problem. Through the keyed hashed digests with either the secret key or the session key to guarantee the integrity of the transmitted messages, our protocol can prevent Denial of Service attack. Moreover, our proposed protocol is not only in need of fewer rounds to perform the key agreement protocol, but also enjoys considerably lower computational cost in comparison with Niu et al.'s protocol. Analysis shows that our protocol is resilient to various attacks, and achieves user anonymity and the contribution property.

Acknowledgments. Hong Lai is supported by the National Natural Science Foundation of China (No. 61702427) and the Doctoral Program of Higher Education (No. SWU115091), the Fundamental Research Funds for the Central Universities (XDJK2018C048), and the financial support in part by the 1000-Plan of Chongqing by Southwest University (No. SWU116007). Mingxing Luo is supported by the National Natural Science Foundation of China (No. 61772437), and Sichuan Youth Science & Technique Foundation (No. 2017JQ0048). Li Tao is supported by the Fundamental Research Funds for the Central Universities (XDJK2018C045), and the CERNET Innovation Project (NGII20170110). Cheng Zhan is supported by the National Natural Science Foundation of China (No. 61702426) Xiaofang Hu is supported by National Natural Science Foundation of China (Grant No. 61601376), Fundamental Science and Advanced Technology Research Foundation of Chongqing (cstc2016jcyjA0547), Chongqing Postdoctoral Science Foundation Special Funded (Xm2017039), Doctoral foundation of Southwest University (SWU116005).

References

1. Xiao, D., Liao, X.F., Deng, S.: A novel key agreement protocol based on chaotic maps. Inf. Sci. **177**(4), 1136–1142 (2007)
2. Mason, J.C., Handscomb, D.C.: Chebyshev Polynomials. CRC Press, Boca Raton (2002)
3. Han, S.: Security of a key agreement protocol based on chaotic maps. Chaos Solitons Fractals **38**(3), 764–768 (2008)
4. Han, S., Chang, E.: Chaotic map based key agreement with/out clock synchronization. Chaos Solitons Fractals **39**(3), 1283–1289 (2009)
5. Wang, X., Zhao, J.: An improved key agreement protocol based on chaos. Commun. Nonlinear Sci. Numer. Simul. **15**(12), 4052–4057 (2010)
6. Yoon, E.J., Jeon, I.S.: An efficient and secure DiffieCHellman key agreement protocol based on Chebyshev chaotic map. Commun. Nonlinear Sci. Numerical Simul. **16**(6), 2383–2389 (2011)
7. Xue, K.P., Hong, P.: Security improvement on an anonymous key agreement protocol based on chaotic maps. Commun. Nonlinear Sci. Numerical Simul. **17**(7), 2969–2977 (2012)
8. Lai, H., Xiao, J.H., Li, L.X., Yang, Y.X.: Applying semigroup property of enhanced Chebyshev polynomials to anonymous authentication protocol. Math. Probl. Eng., 1–17 (2012)
9. Wang, X.Y., Yang, L., Liu, R., Kadir, A.: A chaotic image encryption algorithm based on perceptron model. Nonlinear Dyn. **62**(3), 615–621 (2010)
10. Tseng, H.R., Jan, R.H., Yang, W.: A chaotic maps-based key agreement protocol that preserves user anonymity. In: IEEE International Conference on Communications, ICC 2009, pp. 1–6. IEEE (2009)
11. Niu, Y., Wang, X.: An anonymous key agreement protocol based on chaotic maps. Commun. Nonlinear Sci. Numer. Simul. **16**(4), 1986–1992 (2011)
12. Yoon, E.J.: Efficiency and security problems of anonymous key agreement protocol based on chaotic maps. Commun. Nonlinear Sci. Numer. Simul. **17**(7), 2735–2740 (2012)
13. Zhang, L.: Cryptanalysis of the public key encryption based on multiple chaotic systems. Chaos Solitons Fractals **37**(3), 669–674 (2008)

An Efficient Privacy-Preserving Handover Authentication Scheme for Mobile Wireless Network

Jiaqing Mo[1(✉)], Zhongwang Hu[1], and Yuhua Lin[2]

[1] School of Computer Science and Software, Zhaoqing University, Zhaoqing 526061, China
mojiaqing@126.com

[2] Education Technology and Computer Center, Zhaoqing University, Zhaoqing 526061, China

Abstract. An efficient and secure authentication protocol is essential to enable the mobile devices handover seamlessly to a different access point. However, due to the limited computation resource and battery capacity in mobile devices as well as the openness and insecurity of wireless channel, designing an efficient and secure handover scheme for wireless network is a challenging task. Furthermore, most of the existing handover schemes are vulnerable to various kinds of attacks and cannot yield good performance. According to the analysis of the current schemes, we summarize the security goals that should be fulfilled by the handover authentication scheme. In this paper, we present a new handover authentication and key agreement scheme on elliptic curve cryptosystem for mobile wireless networks which does not involve the trusted third party and provides privacy-preserving mutual authentication between mobile devices and the access point. The proposed scheme consists of three phases: system setup, handover preparation, handover authentication. We give the details of each phase. The theoretical analysis indicates that the proposed scheme achieves universal security features. The secrecy of the generated session key and mutual authentication of the proposed scheme are verified by ProVerif. In addition, performance comparison shows that the proposed scheme outperforms the related schemes in terms of computation cost and communication overhead.

Keywords: Handover authentication · Anonymity · Privacy · Efficiency
Mobile wireless networks

1 Introduction

With the development of wireless communication technology (e.g. WiFi, WiMax, LTE) and the popularity of mobile intelligent terminal (e.g., smartphone, tablet PC), the network brings more and more convenience to the people. The requirement of users on network mainly in mobility support and business diversification have become an increasingly high demand, especially the real-time services such as interactive

X. Sun et al. (Eds.): ICCCS 2018, LNCS 11065, pp. 490–505, 2018.
https://doi.org/10.1007/978-3-030-00012-7_45

streaming and voice also bring challenges to the mobile wireless networks (MWN). Compared with the limitation of the traditional wired networks, the MWN arouses the interest in industry and academia for its deploying flexibility, easy installation, low cost and mobility [1, 2]. A typical MWN involves three kinds of entities, i.e. many mobile terminals (MTs), a lot of access points (APs), an authentication server (AS). Each *AP* has limited geographic coverage, when a MT moves out of the current AP's coverage, it needs to handover to the new *AP* to continue the ongoing sessions. As discussed in [3], the total handover time should be limited to 50 ms, and the ideal time of the authentication module should not exceed 20 ms. In order to provide seamlessly continuous access services for the mobile terminals, it is essential to design a secure and efficient handoff authentication protocol to reduce communication latency and improve Quality-of-Service (QoS).

A handover authentication overview is showed in Fig. 1. In the authentication process, a *MT* first submits relevant information to the *AS* for registration, then connects to an *AP* and subscribes services or starts a session with other MT. In the course of the session, if the *MT* moves from the current *AP* (e.g., *AP1*) to another *AP* (e.g., *AP2*)'s coverage, the handover authentication mechanism should be performed between the *MT* and the *AP2*. By this way, the *MT* and the *AP2* can authenticate each other and generate a session key in order to provide integrity and confidentiality for the future communication. Meanwhile, the illegal users are prevented from unauthorized access.

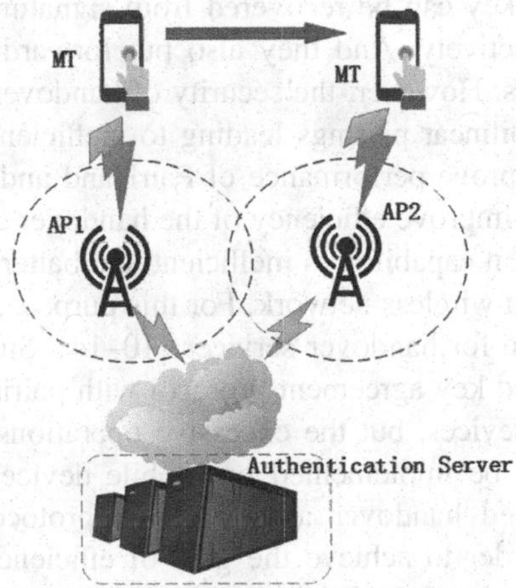

Fig. 1. A typical handover authentication scenario in mobile wireless networks

1.1 Related Works

Since the messages are transmitted between the related parties in a wireless channel instead of a wired connection, this provides an opportunity for an adversary to eavesdrop the transferred messages and temper with them. Thus, security and privacy are serious issues in handover authentication services. In particular, mobile users are extremely concerned about the protection of sensitive information such as their identity and location. Therefore, the handover authentication should achieve the user anonymity and untraceability.

For the purpose of improving efficiency and preserving user privacy, a number of handover authentication schemes using different methods have been proposed for MWN. In these schemes, elliptic curve cryptosystem (ECC), provides the same security level with smaller keys and faster computation compared with the other public key cryptography such as RSA, e.g., a 160-bit ECC based public key can provide security level of 1024-bit RSA based public key. Thus, the authentication schemes based on ECC are more beneficial for mobile devices than other cryptosystems.

To achieve efficiency and handover seamlessly, He et al. [3] proposed a handover authentication scheme named PairHand on bilinear pairing, in which they introduced the concept of short-lived unlinkable pseudonyms and the corresponding private keys to preserve user privacy. Moreover, considering to reduce the communication overhead and alleviate the heavy burden on *AS*, their scheme just requires two handshakes for handover authentication and key agreement between the mobile client and the *AP*. However, He et al. [4] and Yeo et al. [5] pointed out that PairHand is insecure since the private key of mobile client can be recovered by adversary from the signature in the transferred message, and they presented an improved version to fix the security weakness respectively. Later, Tsai et al. [6] and Wang et al. [8] found that the enhanced version of PairHand cannot withstand an attack named algorithm of Pohlig and Hellman [7], and the private key can be recovered from signature by employing linearly combining method, respectively. And they also put forward the countermeasures to eliminate the security risks. However, the security of handover protocols [3, 4, 6, 8, 9] rely on time-consuming bilinear pairings leading to inefficient with regard to computation cost and cannot improve performance of PairHand and its improved version.

It is very important to improve efficiency of the handover authentication for mobile client in which computation capability is inefficient and battery power is limited while maintaining the security in wireless network. For this purpose, some studies have been proposed with pairing-free for handover services [10–14]. Sun et al. [10] described a certificateless authenticated key agreement protocol with pairing-free and claimed it is practical for low-power devices, but the excessive operations of elliptic curve multiplication make it hard to be implemented on mobile devices. Islam and Khan [11] presented an identity-based handover authentication protocol with pairing-free for WMW. In addition, in order to achieve the goal of efficiency, their protocol adopts light-weight hash function instead of time-consuming map-to-point hash function. In 2012, Cao et al. [15] proposed a handover authentication schemes with pairing-free for mobile networks to decrease the system complexity and computation cost. However, Li et al. [16] found that Cao et al.'s protocol failed to achieve true user anonymity and untraceablity, then put forward a privacy-aware identity-based scheme for mobile devices without pairing operation, and argued that their new scheme can provide user anonymity, resistance to replay attack and mutual authentication. Unfortunately, Xie et al. [13] pointed out that Li et al. [16]'s scheme is suffered from impersonation attack in the response of the handover authentication phase and cannot provide mutual authentication. As a remedy, Xie et al. presented an improved handover authentication scheme. However, both Li et al. [16] and Xie et al. [13] suffered from impersonation attack, because in their authentication phase, the request message contains all the parameters to construct verified expression in the *AP* side, and this request message transferred in public channel can be intercepted by the adversary, as a result, the adversary can select some parameters satisfying the form of verified expression and fake a request message and send it to *AP*, thus the *AP* would consider the adversary as a legal user. In the same year, Chaudhry et al. [14] also showed that the scheme in [16] is suffered from access point impersonation attack and proposed an improved scheme. However, there is a mistake in the authentication phase of their scheme, that is when the *AP* computes the parameter Z_j, the *AP* does not know m_j in advance. There are some other recent studies [17–21] proposed the user authentication schemes with privacy preservation using different techniques for mobile devices. Unfortunately, these schemes are found neither satisfy some security requirement nor be practical for mobile environment [22–26].

As the analysis aforementioned, due to their different inherent design weakness, most of the current handover authentication schemes are either insecure to withstand some serious attacks [13, 15, 16], or inefficient to be implemented in MWN [10]. As pointed out in [25], to date, how to develop a privacy-preserving handover authentication scheme which can withstand various known attacks while maintaining efficiency, is still an open problem.

1.2 Our Contribution

Motivated by above observation, we propose a new efficient and robust handover authentication protocol making use of ECC algorithm in MWN context. In short, our protocol has the following features:

- The proposed protocol is more efficient than the other related works with regard to computation cost and communication overhead.
- The proposed protocol not only achieves user anonymity and user untraceablity, but also provides mutual authentication and fast handover authentication with two handshakes between the *MT* and the *AP* in heterogeneous wireless network environment.
- The proposed protocol is proved to be secure with cryptographic protocol verifier ProVerif.

The rest of the paper is organized as follows: In Sect. 2, we give a brief view of preliminary and security goals. Details of our handover authentication protocol for WMN are described in Sect. 3, the security analysis and formal security verification are incorporated in Sect. 4. Next, the performance comparison is introduced in Sect. 5. Finally, conclusions are drawn in Sect. 6.

2 Preliminary and Security Goals

In this section, we provide a brief description of mathematical problems on elliptic curve and the security goals.

2.1 Mathematical Problems

An elliptic curve E/F_p is defined by the equation $y^2 \bmod p = x^3 + ax + b \ mod\ p$, where p is a big prime number, and $a, b \in F_p$ with $(4a^3 + 27b^2)\ mod\ p \neq 0$. Two important mathematical problems that rely on the elliptic curve are described below.

Elliptic Curve Discrete Logarithm Problem (ECDLP): Given $Q, P \in G$, find an integer $a \in [1, p - 1]$ such that $Q = aP \in G$ is hard.
Computational Diffie-Hellman Problem (CDHP): Given (P, aP, bP) for any $a, b \in [1, p - 1]$, finding $abP \in G$ is hard.

2.2 Security Goals

A secure handover protocol should achieve the following goals:

Anonymity: Except *AS*, the *MT*'s identity should be unknown to other entities including *AP*.
Untraceability: No strong global adversaries can track the actions of *MTs*.
Mutual authentication: Both *MT* and *AP* should authenticate each other over insecure channels without disclosing their identities.
Key agreement: The *MT* and *AP* should establish a symmetric session key to encrypt the messages in their future conversations. Additionally, the session key should not be compromised to compute previous keys and the future ones. This means the scheme can provide backward and forward secrecy.
Robustness: The protocol should be able to withstand various kinds attacks like impersonation attack, replay attack, man-in-middle attack, etc.
Integrity: The transferred messages via open channels should not be tempered, replayed, altered by adversaries. Also, the eavesdropped messages should prevent the adversaries from getting plaintext.

3 The Proposed Protocol

In this section, we present a new efficient mutual authentication protocol for WMN. Our protocol consists of three phases, i.e., system setup phase, handover preparation phase, handover authentication phase.

3.1 System Setup Phase

The *AS* selects a security parameter n as an input to generate all the system parameter in the following ways:

(1) Chooses a t-bit prime number p and the field size q where $q = 2p + 1$ and generates an elliptic curve E/F_P which is defined on a finite field F_p with order p, an additive cyclic group G over E/F_P with order q and determines a generator P of G.
(2) Selects the master key $s \in Z_q^*$, and computes $K_{pub} = sP$ as the public key.
(3) Selects five one way hash functions $H_1(), H_2(), H_3(): \{0,1\}^* x\ G \rightarrow \{0,1\}^n$.
(4) Publishes system parameter $\{F_P, E/F_P, p, P, K_{pub}, G, H_1(), H_2(), H_3()\}$ and keeps s secretly.

Afterwards, the *AS* computes the private key and the public key for each *AP*:

(1) Assigns a unique ID_{AP} for each *AP*.
(2) Selects a random number $r_j \in Z_q^*$, computes $R_j = sH_1(ID_{AP}||r_j)$, sets the tuple (r_j, R_j) as the private key of *AP*. '||' is the concatenate operation.
(3) Assume that a pre-shared key has been built between *AP* and *AS* before. The *AS* encrypts the tuple (r_j, R_j) with the pre-shared key and emits them to the *AP*.

Upon receiving the encrypted message, the *AP* decrypts (r_j, R_j) and keeps (r_j, R_j) secret, and computes $K_{AP} = R_jP$ as his public key.

3.2 Handover Preparation Phase

When the *MT* registers to *AS* with his real ID, in order to provide user anonymity and untraceability, the *AS* selects a set of unlink-able pseudo-identifiers $(PID_1, PID_2,\ldots, PID_n)$ for the *MT*. For each pseudo-ID PID_i, *AS* computes a private key and the corresponding public key *AS* follows:

(1) *AS* selects $r_i \in Z_q^*$ at random, and computes $R_i = r_iP$.
(2) *AS* computes $d_i = r_i + sH_1(PID_i||R_i)$.
(3) *AS* sends (PID_i, d_i, R_i) to *MT* via a secure channel.

MT sets (d_i, R_i) *AS* his private key after receipt of the tuple (PID_i, d_i, R_i) from *AS*, and computes his public key $D_i = d_iP = R_i + H_1(PID_i||R_i)K_{pub}$.

3.3 Handover Authentication Phase

Assume the *AP* periodically broadcasts a beacon message with its identity, public key and other regular information to declare service existence. If *MT* moves out of the coverage of current *AP* and receives the beacon message of the new *AP*, he extracts the identity and the public key and performs handover authentication with the new *AP AS* follows:

(1) $MT \rightarrow AP$: $\{PID_i, h_{MT}, R_i, S, D_i\}$

MT selects a random number $a \in Z_q^*$, and computes $T_{MT} = AP$, then *MT* generates a signature $S = a/(d_i + h_{MT})$ with private key d_i, where $h_{MT} = H_2(T_{MT}||PID_i)$. Finally, *MT* sends the message $\{PID_i, h_{MT}, R_i, S, D_i\}$ to the target *AP*.

(2) $AP \rightarrow MT$: $\{ID_{AP}, PT_{AP}, MAC\}$

On receiving the message, *AP* computes $h_{AP} = H_2(PID_i||R_i)$, $(T_{MT'} = S(R_i + h_{AP}K_{pub} + h_{MT}P)$, and checks whether the equation $H(T_{MT'}||PID_i)\ ? = h_{MT}$ holds. If it is unsuccessful, *AP* aborts this session. Otherwise, *AP* selects a random number $b \in Z_q^*$, computes $T_{AP} = bP, K_{am} = D_i \cdot b \cdot K_{AP}, l_{AP} = H_2(ID_{AP}||r_j), PT_{AP} = T_{MT'} \oplus (l_{AP}||T_{AP})$, and the message authentication code $MAC = H_3(PID_i||K_{am}||T_{MT'}||ID_{AP})$. Finally, *AP* sends the message $\{ID_{AP}, PT_{AP}, MAC\}$ to *MT*. '$\oplus$' is the exclusive-or operation *(XOR)*.

(3) After receipt of message from *P*, *MT* computes $(l_{AP}||T_{AP}) = PT_{AP} \oplus T_{MT}$, the session key $K_{ma} = d_i \cdot T_{AP} \cdot l_{AP} \cdot K_{pub}$, $MAC' = H_3(PID_i||K_{ma}||T_{MT}||ID_{AP})$. *MT* further verifies the equation $MAC' = MAC$. If the result is unsuccessful, the *MT* terminates this session. Otherwise, *MT* treats the *AP AS* a legal service provider, and completes the mutual handover authentication. Finally, a secure channel is established with the session key K_{am} $(=K_{ma})$ between *MT* and *AP*.

The proposed handover authentication phase is shown in Fig. 2.

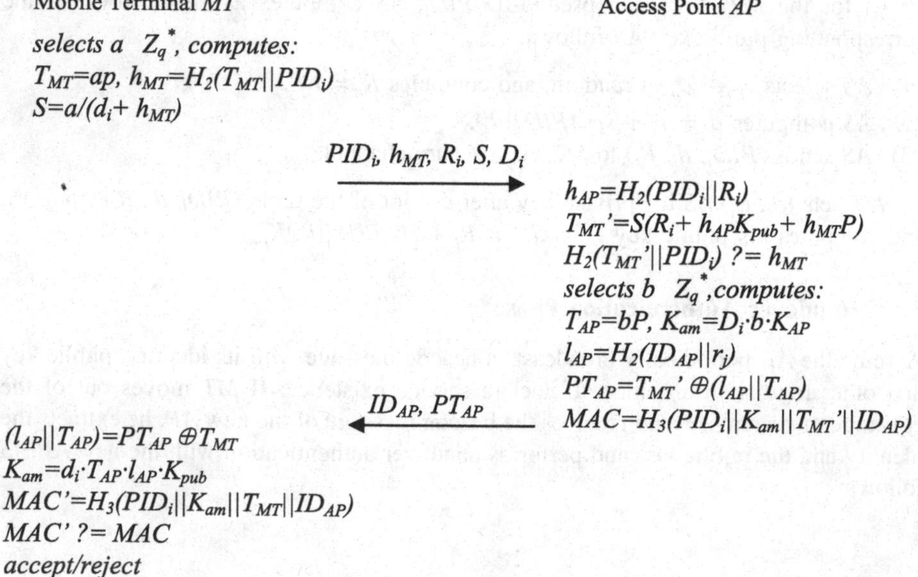

Mobile Terminal MT
Access Point AP
selects a Z_q^*, computes:
T_{MT}=ap, h_{MT}=$H_2(T_{MT}||PID_i)$
S=a/(d_i+ h_{MT})
PID_i, h_{MT}, R_i, S, D_i
h_{AP}=$H_2(PID_i||R_i)$
T_{MT}'=S(R_i+ $h_{AP}K_{pub}$+ h_{MT}P)
$H_2(T_{MT}'||PID_i)$?= h_{MT}
selects b Z_q^*,computes:
T_{AP}=bP, K_{am}=D_i·b·K_{AP}
l_{AP}=$H_2(ID_{AP}||r_j)$
PT_{AP}=T_{MT}' ⊕($l_{AP}||T_{AP}$)
MAC=$H_3(PID_i||K_{am}||T_{MT}'||ID_{AP})$
ID_{AP}, PT_{AP}
($l_{AP}||T_{AP}$)=PT_{AP} ⊕T_{MT}
K_{am}=d_i·T_{AP}·l_{AP}·K_{pub}
MAC'=$H_3(PID_i||K_{am}||T_{MT}||ID_{AP})$
MAC' ?= MAC
accept/reject

Fig. 2. Handover authentication phase

4 Security Analysis and Formal Security Verification

4.1 Security Analysis

we analyze the security of the proposed protocol with regard to security goals described in Subsect. 2.2.

4.1.1 Mutual Authentication and Key Agreement

In the handover authentication phase, *AP* verifies the legitimacy of *MT* based on the signature *S*, and *MT* verifies the legitimacy of *AP* based on his private key and *AP*'s public information issued by *AS*. If one of these two verifications is unsuccessful, the session would be aborted. Otherwise, the proposed protocol achieves mutual authentication between *MT* and *AP*.

It is easy to see that the session key K_{am} generated by *AP* and K_{ma} generated by *MT* are identical, which is shown *AS* follows:

$$
\begin{aligned}
K_{am} &= D_i \cdot b \cdot K_{AP} \\
&= d_i \cdot P \cdot b \cdot s \cdot H_2(ID_{AP} || r_j) \cdot P \\
&= d_i \cdot b \cdot P \cdot H_2(ID_{AP} || r_j) \cdot s \cdot P \\
&= d_i \cdot T_{AP} \cdot l_{AP} \cdot K_{pub} \\
&= K_{ma}
\end{aligned}
$$

4.1.2 Provide User Anonymity and Untraceability

In the proposed scheme, each *MT* will obtain a series of pseudo identifiers PID_i $(1 \le i \le n)$ and the corresponding secret key d_i when he registers in *AS*. And at the beginning of the handover authentication phase, *MT* picks an unused PID_i to replace his real identifier in order to preserve privacy. Therefore, only *AS* knows the relationship between pseudo identifier PID_i and the real *ID* of *MT*. Furthermore, the adversary, even the *AP* cannot discern the two sessions whether are initiated by the same *MT* because there is no link between these pseudo identifiers.

4.1.3 Resistance to Attacks

The design of a secure protocol needs to consider the ability to resist various attacks. Our protocol can meet this requirement. For replay attack, if the adversary intercepts the message $\{PID_i, h_{MT}, R_i, S, D_i\}$ and impersonate *MT* to replay this message to *AP*, but the adversary cannot compute a right MAC' to pass *MT*'s verification without the knowledge of *a* and T_{MT}. Moreover, if the adversary intends to impersonate the *AP* and replay $\{ID_{AP}, PT_{AP}, MAC\}$ to *MT*, it is infeasible because the random number *b* is different in each exchanged message. For man-in-the-middle attack, the key agreement of proposed protocol is based on the ECDLP and CDHP, and the session key between *MT* and *AP* is established with partial keys from each party which are long-term private keys so that the proposed protocol can prevent the attacker from eavesdropping the exchanged message to forge or replay the messages in the middle. It is also infeasible for the adversary impersonating the authorized *MT* or *AP* to receive data message owing to the fact that the long term secret key of participant is issued by the *AS*.

4.1.4 Provide Forward and Backward Secrecy

In the proposed protocol, the session key $K_{ma} = d_i \cdot T_{AP} \cdot l_{AP} \cdot K_{pub}$ is computed by *MT* and the session $K_{ma} = D_i \cdot b \cdot K_{AP}$ is computed on *AP* side. The forward secrecy and the backward secrecy is to say that if the private key d_i of *MT* and the private key r_j of *AP* are comprised, the adversary cannot breach the secrecy of the session key whether it is previous or subsequent. It is clear that if the private key d_i of *MT* and the private key r_j of *AP* are comprised, the adversary cannot compute K_{am} or K_{ma} without the knowledge of secret number *a* and *b*. Moreover, the random number *a* and *b* are selected by *MT* and *AP* when *MT* moves out of the coverage of current *AP* and performs the handover authentication mechanism everytime. Thus, the proposed protocol can provide forward and backward secrecy.

4.2 Formal Security Verification via ProVerif

ProVerif is an effective automatic cryptographic protocol verifier based on pi calculus in Dolev-Yao model [27] and implements many cryptographic primitives, such as symmetric encryption and asymmetric encryption, signatures, hash, mac, Diffie-Hellman key agreements. Many protocols have been tested by ProVerif to prove their secrecy, authentication and other correspondence properties [27]. Here, we use ProVerif to provide a formal security verification of the proposed protocol to ensure that our scheme can provide the secrecy and authentication property.

According to the protocol description, we introduce three channels, channel *ch1* is used for the secure (private) communication between *AP* and *AS*, channel *ch2* is used for secure communication between *MT* and *AS*. In particular, channel *ch3* models the public insecure communication between *MT* and *AP*.

```
(*Channels*)
free ch1:channel [private].
free ch2:channel [private].
free ch3:channel.
```

Next, we define two private variables *kma* and *kam*, which represent the session keys generated by *MT* and *AP*, respectively.

```
(*Session key*)
free kam,kma:bitstring [private].
```

The constants and variables are declared *AS* follows:

```
(*constants and varibles*)
const P: bitstring.
const p: bitstring.
const q: bitstring.
free IDi: bitstring.
free ID_AP: bitstring.
free IDj: bitstring.
free Kpub:bitstring.
free PIDi: bitstring.
free PIDx: bitstring.
```

The cryptographic functions are described as follows.

```
(*Constructor*)
fun concat(bitstring,bitstring):bitstring.
fun mult(bitstring,bitstring):bitstring.
fun add(bitstring,bitstring):bitstring.
fun syme(bitstring,bitstring):bitstring.
fun inverse(bitstring):bitstring.
fun xor(bitstring,bitstring):bitstring.
fun H1(bitstring):bitstring.
fun H2(bitstring):bitstring.
fun H3(bitstring):bitstring.
fun fp(bitstring):bitstring.(*former part*)
fun bp(bitstring):bitstring.(*back part*)
```

To model the symmetric decryption, the destructor is introduced.

```
(*destructor and equations*)
reduc forall m:bitstring,key:bitstring;symd(syme(m,key),key)=m.
```

Four events are introduced to verify the mutual authentication between *MT* and *AP*. For example, event *beginAP* represents that *AP* receives the authentication request from *MT*, the event *endAP* occurs says that *AP* sends the response to *MT*. In particular, we can use ProVerif to ensure the authenticity by testing whether the begin event occurs before the end event.

```
(*events*)
event beginAP(bitstring).
event endAP(bitstring).
event beginMT(bitstring).
event endMT(bitstring).
```

We define three distinct process macros *AServer*, *APoint*, *MTerminal* for participant *AS*, *AP*, *MT* in terms of the operations of *AS*, *AP*, *MT* during the proposed protocol execution, respectively. The macro *AServer* is modeled as follows.

```
(*Authentication Server*)
let AServer=
new s: bitstring;
let Kpub = mult(s, P) in
new rj: bitstring;
let Rj = mult(s,H1(concat(IDi,rj))) in
out (ch1,(rj,Rj));
new ri: bitstring;
let Ri = mult(ri,P) in
let di = add(ri,mult(s,H1(concat(PIDi,Ri)))) in
out(ch2,(PIDi,di,Ri)).
```

The macro *APoint* is modeled as follows.

```
(*Access Point*)
let APoint=
in(ch1,(Xrj:bitstring,XRj:bitstring));
   let K_AP=mult(XRj,P) in
event beginAP(IDi);
out(ch3, (XRj,IDj));
in(ch3,(XPIDi:bitstring,
      Xh_MT:bitstring,XRi:bitstring,XS:bitstring,XDi:bitstring));
let h_AP=H2(concat(XPIDi,XRi)) in
let T_MT' = mult(XS,add(XRi,add(mult(h_AP,Kpub),mult(Xh_MT,P)))) in
let  Xh_MT'=H2(concat(T_MT',XPIDi)) in
if (Xh_MT = Xh_MT') then
   new b:bitstring;
   let T_AP=mult(b,P) in
   let kam=mult(XDi,mult(b,K_AP)) in
   let l_AP=H2(concat(ID_AP,Xrj)) in
   let PT_AP=xor(T_MT',concat(l_AP,T_AP))  in
   let MAC_AP=H3(concat(XPIDi,concat(kam,concat(T_MT',ID_AP)))) in
   out(ch3,(ID_AP,PT_AP,MAC_AP));
   event endAP(IDi).
```

The macro *MTerminal* is modeled as follows.

```
(*Mobile Terminal*)
  let MTerminal=
  in(ch2,(XPIDi:bitstring,Xdi:bitstring,XRi:bitstring));
  let Di=mult(Xdi,P) in
  in(ch3,(XRj:bitstring, XIDj:bitstring));
  event beginMT(PIDx);
  new a:bitstring;
  let T_MT=mult(a,P) in
  let h_MT=H2(concat(T_MT,XPIDi)) in
  let S=mult(a,inverse(add(Xdi,h_MT))) in
  out(ch3,(XPIDi,h_MT,XRi,S,Di));
  in(ch3,(XID_AP:bitstring,XPT_AP:bitstring,XMAC_AP:bitstring));
  let lAP_TAP=xor(XPT_AP,T_MT) in
  let l_AP'=fp(lAP_TAP) in
  let T_AP'=bp(lAP_TAP) in
  let kma = mult(Xdi,mult(T_AP',mult(l_AP',Kpub))) in
  let MAC_MT=H3(concat(XPIDi,concat(kma,concat(T_AP',XIDj)))) in
  if (MAC_MT=XMAC_AP) then
    event endMT(PIDx).
```

The modeled protocol is emulated *AS* running in parallel for these three macros *AS* follows.

```
process((!AServer) | (!APoint) | (!MTerminal))
```

In order to verify the adversary's capabilities in breaching the secrecy of the session key K_{ma} generated by *MT* and K_{ma} generated by *AP* (K_{ma} and K_{ma} are actually equal), we define the queries as follows:

```
query attacker(kam).
query attacker(kma).
```

Furthermore, to verify the mutual authentication between *MT* and *AP*, we model the correspondence assertions as follows.

```
query id:bitstring;inj-event(endAP(id))==>inj-event(beginAP(id)).
query id:bitstring;inj-event(endMT(id))==>inj-event(beginMT(id)).
```

The output of these processes as running in ProVerif v1.98 (latest version) is showed as follows.

1 RESULT inj-event(endMT(id)) ==> inj-event(beginMT(id)) is true.
2 RESULT inj-event(endAP(id_1254)) ==> inj-event(beginAP(id_1254)) is true.
3 RESULT not attacker(kma[]) is true.
4 RESULT not attacker(kam[]) is true.

The experimental result in line 1–2 indicates that the proposed protocol can provide mutual authentication between *MT* and *AP*. Meanwhile, line 3–4 shows that the attacker cannot obtain the session key K_{am} or K_{ma}. In other words, because all these results are true, attacker can neither break the secrecy of the session key generated by each party nor break the authentication property that is verified by correspondence assertions in Dolev_Yao model.

5 Performance Comparison

In this section, we compare the computation cost and communication overhead in handover authentication phase with related protocols [13, 14, 28].

We set q to be the order of the super singular curve, p to be the order of non-super singular curve E over a finite field F_p, and their values are set to 512 bits and 160 bits, respectively. For brevity, let T_m, T_a be the execution time for an elliptic curve multiplication in G, the execution time for an elliptic curve addition in G, respectively. The execution time of other operations, e.g., a one-way hash function operation and a message authentication code operation, are ignored because they are much less than that of T_m or T_a. All of the cryptographic operations are benchmarked on environment *AS* follows: PBC library (version 0.5.14) on 32-bit [29], 3.4 GHz Intel i7 processor, 2 GB main memory, running Ubuntu desktop 14.04. In our experiment, T_m takes approximately 0.017 ms, while T_a takes 0.013 ms. The comparison of computation cost between our scheme and the related protocols is shown Table 1.

Table 1. Computation cost comparison

Scheme	Computation cost of *MT*	Computation cost of *AP*
[13]	$5T_m + 4T_a \approx 0.137$ ms	$6T_m + 4\ T_a \approx 0.154$ ms
[14]	$4\ T_m + 4\ T_a \approx 0.120$ ms	$7\ T_m + T_a \approx 0.171$ ms
[28]	$6\ T_m + 2\ T_a \approx 0.128$ ms	$6\ T_m + 2\ T_a \approx 0.128$ ms
Ours	$5\ T_m + T_a \approx 0.098$ ms	$5\ T_m + T_a \approx 0.098$ ms

To facilitate comparison in communication overhead, we set l_i, l_p, l_h, l_t, l_{mac} be the length of client's identifier, a point, an one-way hash value, a timestamp, a message authentication code, respectively. And their corresponding values are defined as 32 bits, 1024 bits, 160 bits, 32 bits, 160 bits, respectively. Table 2 demonstrates the comparison of communication overhead between our scheme and the related protocols.

Table 2. Communication overhead comparison

Scheme	Message components	Communication overhead
[13]	$2l_i + 6l_p + l_t + l_{mac}$	6400 bits
[14]	$2l_i + 4l_p + l_t + l_{mac}$	4352 bits
[28]	$2l_i + 4l_p + 2l_h$	4480 bits
Ours	$2l_i + 4l_p + l_h$	4320 bits

From Table 1, we can learn that on both *MT* and *AP*, the consumed time of the proposed scheme is 0.098 ms, which is much less than other related protocols [13, 14, 28]. Thus, the proposed scheme is more efficient than [13, 14, 28] both on *MT* side and *AP* side. Moreover, from Table 2, we can see that the communication overhead of our scheme is 4320 bits, which is slightly lower than that of [14] and decreases greatly *AS* compared with [13, 28]. Therefore, the proposed scheme has the advantage in communication overhead compared with [13, 14, 28]. Overall, the proposed scheme has better performance than [13, 14, 28].

6 Conclusion

In this paper, we summarize the current handover authentication schemes and put forward an efficient anonymous handover authentication protocol with privacy-preserving for mobile wireless network. Owing to the hardness of ECDLP and CDHP assumption, the proposed scheme has merits of efficiency and robust security. We also provide a formal security verification via the automatic cryptographic protocol verifier ProVerif to show that our scheme can preserve the secrecy of the session key and provide mutual authentication property. In particular, our protocol achieves excellent performance as compared with the related up-to-date handover protocols. Based on these merits, we are convinced that the proposed scheme provides a reasonable deployment solution for handover in mobile wireless network.

References

1. Fu, L., et al.: Joint optimization of multicast energy in delay-constrained mobile wireless networks. IEEE/ACM Trans. Netw. **99**, 633–646 (2018)
2. Pedersen, J., i Amat, A.G., Andriyanova, I., Brannstrom, F.: Distributed storage in mobile wireless networks with device-to-device communication. IEEE Trans. Commun. **64**, 4862–4878 (2016)
3. He, D., Chen, C., Chan, S., Bu, J.: Secure and efficient handover authentication based on bilinear pairing functions. IEEE Trans. Wirel. Commun. **11**, 48–53 (2012)
4. He, D., Chen, C., Chan, S., Bu, J.: Analysis and improvement of a secure and efficient handover authentication for wireless networks. IEEE Commun. Lett. **16**, 1270–1273 (2012)
5. Yeo, S.L., Yap, W.S., Liu, J.K., Henricksen, M.: Comments on "analysis and improvement of a secure and efficient handover authentication based on bilinear pairing functions". IEEE Commun. Lett. **17**, 1521–1523 (2013)

6. Tsai, J.L., Lo, N.W., Wu, T.C.: Secure handover authentication protocol based on bilinear pairings. Wirel. Pers. Commun. **73**, 1037–1047 (2013)
7. Pohlig, S.C., Hellman, M.E.: An improved algorithm for computing logarithms over GF(p) and its cryptographic significance. IEEE Trans. Inform. Theory **24**, 106–110 (1978)
8. Wang, W., Hu, L.: A secure and efficient handover authentication protocol for wireless networks. Sensors **14**, 11379–11394 (2014)
9. He, D., Khan, M.K., Kumar, N.: A new handover authentication protocol based on bilinear pairing functions for wireless networks. Int. J. Ad Hoc Ubiquitous Comput. **18**, 67–74 (2015)
10. Sun, H., Wen, Q., Zhang, H., Jin, Z.: A novel pairing-free certificateless authenticated key agreement protocol with provable security. Front. Comput. Sci. **7**, 544–557 (2013)
11. Islam, S.H., Khan, M.K.: Provably secure and pairing-free identity-based handover authentication protocol for wireless mobile networks. Int. J. Commun. Syst. **29**, 2442–2456 (2016)
12. Chang, C.C., Huang, Y.C., Tsai, H.C.: Design and analysis of chameleon hashing based handover authentication scheme for wireless networks. J. Inf. Hiding Multimedia Sig. Process. **5**, 107–116 (2014)
13. Xie, Y., Wu, L., Kumar, N., Shen, J.: Analysis and improvement of a privacy-aware handover authentication scheme for wireless network. Wirel. Pers. Commun. **93**, 523–541 (2017)
14. Chaudhry, S.A., Farash, M.S., Naqvi, H., Islam, S.H., Shon, T.: A robust and efficient privacy aware handover authentication scheme for wireless networks. Wirel. Pers. Commun. Int. J. **93**, 311–335 (2017)
15. Cao, J., Ma, M., Li, H.: An uniform handover authentication between E-UTRAN and non-3GPP access networks. IEEE Trans. Wirel. Commun. **11**, 3644–3650 (2012)
16. Li, G., Jiang, Q., Wei, F., Ma, C.: A new privacy-aware handover authentication scheme for wireless networks. Wirel. Pers. Commun. **80**, 581–589 (2015)
17. Wang, Y.Y., Liu, J.Y., Xiao, F.X., Dan, J.: A more efficient and secure dynamic ID-based remote user authentication scheme. Comput. Commun. **32**, 583–585 (2009)
18. Juang, W.S., Chen, S.T., Liaw, H.T.: Robust and efficient password-authenticated key agreement using smart cards. IEEE Trans. Ind. Electron. **55**, 2551–2556 (2008)
19. Wen, F., Li, X.: An improved dynamic ID-based remote user authentication with key agreement scheme. Comput. Electr. Eng. **38**, 381–387 (2012)
20. Tsai, J.L., Lo, N.W., Wu, T.C.: Novel anonymous authentication scheme using smart cards. IEEE Trans. Indus. Inform. **9**, 2004–2013 (2013)
21. Kim, K.-k., Kim, M.-H.: Retracted: an enhanced anonymous authentication and key exchange scheme using smartcard. In: Kwon, T., Lee, M.-K., Kwon, D. (eds.) ICISC 2012. LNCS, vol. 7839, pp. 487–494. Springer, Heidelberg (2013). https://doi.org/10.1007/978-3-642-37682-5_34
22. Khan, M.K., Kim, S.K., Alghathbar, K.: Cryptanalysis and security enhancement of a 'more efficient & secure dynamic ID-based remote user authentication scheme'. Comput. Commun. **34**, 305–309 (2011)
23. Ma, C.G., Wang, D., Zhao, S.D.: Security flaws in two improved remote user authentication schemes using smart cards. Int. J. Commun. Syst. **27**, 2215–2227 (2015)
24. Huang, X., Chen, X., Li, J., Xiang, Y., Xu, L.: Further observations on smart-card-based password-authenticated key agreement in distributed systems. IEEE Trans. Parallel Distrib. Syst. **25**, 1767–1775 (2014)
25. Wang, D., Wang, N., Wang, P., Qing, S.: Preserving privacy for free: efficient and provably secure two-factor authentication scheme with user anonymity. Inf. Sci. **321**, 162–178 (2015)

26. Ding, W., Ping, W.: Two birds with one stone: two-factor authentication with security beyond conventional bound. IEEE Trans. Dependable Secure Comput. **PP**, 1 (2016)
27. http://prosecco.gforge.inria.fr/personal/bblanche/proverif/
28. Yang, X., Huang, X., Liu, J.K.: Efficient handover authentication with user anonymity and untraceability for mobile cloud computing. Future Gen. Comput. Syst. **62**, 190–195 (2016)
29. https://crypto.stanford.edu/pbc/

Analysis and Improvement on an Image Encryption Algorithm Based on Bit Level Permutation

Bin Lu, Fenlin Liu, Ping Xu, and Xin Ge(✉)

China National Digital Switching System Engineering Technology Research Center, Zhengzhou 45000, Henan, China
gexin_er@126.com

Abstract. A modeling description of Ye algorithm is first presented in this paper. Then a chosen plaintext attack is proposed aiming at the drawback of Ye algorithm that the generation procedure of permutation vectors has no relation with plain image. With the attack, the permutation vectors (keystreams equivalent to secret key) can be correctly recovered with only ceil($\log_2$(8MN)) chosen plain images, which is proved by Proposition 1. Thirdly, an improvement of Ye algorithm is proposed. Experiments and analysis show the validity of chosen plaintext attack and the security of improved algorithm. Attack and improvement proposed in this paper provides concrete method of security analysis and "plain image related" design idea of secure permutation against chosen plaintext attack for analysis and design of chaos based image encryption algorithm.

Keywords: Image encryption · Bit level permutation · Chaos

1 Introduction

Presently, image encryption is one of the hottest research fields due to the rapid development and application of multimedia technology. The special characteristic of the image itself makes some traditional encryption algorithms difficult to apply. In recent years, chaos based encryption technology is favored due to the good property of chaos, such as the extreme sensitivity to parameters and initial value, ergodic property and so on.

Image encryption algorithm based on chaos can be divided into various types from different viewpoints [1–16]. From the viewpoint of algorithm structure, the pixel position permutation algorithms [1–8] can be called P structure algorithm (permutation structure algorithm), pixel value diffusion algorithms [9, 10] can be called D structure algorithm (diffusion structure algorithm), then the encryption algorithm based on the combination of pixel position permutation and pixel value diffusion can be called PD structure algorithm (permutation-diffusion structure algorithm) [13–16], and the pixel position permutation and pixel value diffusion combined with multi round encryption can be called PDR structure algorithm [11, 12]. At this point, we can divide the image encryption algorithm based on chaos into four kinds- P, D, PD and PDR structure algorithm.

X. Sun et al. (Eds.): ICCCS 2018, LNCS 11065, pp. 506–518, 2018.
https://doi.org/10.1007/978-3-030-00012-7_46

In P structure algorithm, encryption is achieved by permuting the location of the image pixels. Existing P structure algorithm can be divided into two categories: one based on bit permutation and the other based on pixel permutation. Recently, a bit level permutation algorithm is proposed by Ye in [7] (referred to as Ye algorithm). In Ye algorithm, pixels of plain image are firstly decomposed into bits and then are permuted to achieve the purpose of pixel position scrambling and pixel value encryption simultaneously. However, the key drawback of the algorithm is that the position permutation keystreams will keep unchanged if the secret key keeps unchanged. Based on this drawback and the construction property of permutation vectors, $s_m = ceil(\log_2 M)$ images of size $M \times 1$ and $t_m = ceil(\log_2 8N)$ images of size $1 \times N$ are constructed. With these peculiar images, a chosen plaintext attack is proposed, which can correctly recover the permutation vectors $H = (h_i)_{M\times 1}$ and $L = (l_j)_{1\times 8N}$ (keystreams equivalent to secret key). Then an improvement of Ye algorithm is proposed, in which the generation of permutation vectors is not only related with secret key but also related with the pixel values of plain image, so that tiny change in pixel value of plain image leads to completely different permutation vectors. As a result the permutation is sensitive not only to the key but also to the plain image. Experiments and analysis show the validity of chosen plaintext attack and the security of improved algorithm.

Since permutation is not only the component of P structure encryption algorithm, but also the important component of PD and PDR structure encryption algorithm. Attack algorithm proposed in this paper suggests that permutation in P, PD and PDR algorithm is insecure against chosen plaintext attack if the generation of permutation vectors only depends on the secret key. And the improvement of Ye algorithm provides "plain image related" idea for the design of secure permutation against chosen plaintext attack.

The rest of the paper is organized as follows. Ye algorithm is presented in Sect. 2. Chosen plaintext attack on Ye algorithm is proposed in Sect. 3. Improvement of Ye algorithm is proposed in Sect. 4. Experimental results and analyses are reported in Sect. 4. In the last section, a conclusion is drawn.

2 Ye Algorithm

An image of size $M \times N$ can be described by a matrix $P = (p_{i,j})_{M\times N}$, where $p_{i,j} \in \{0, 1, \cdots, 255\}$, the encryption procedure of Ye algorithm are as follows:

S1: Convert plain image $P = (p_{i,j})_{M\times N}$ into a binary matrix $B = (b_{i,j})_{M\times 8N}$ of size $M \times 8N$, where

$$b_{i,8(j-1)+k} = floor(p_{i,j}/2^{k-1}) \bmod 2,\ b_{i,j} \in \{0, 1\}, k = 1, 2, \ldots, 8 \qquad (1)$$

S2: Generate two permutation vectors $H = (h_i)_{M\times 1}$ and $L = (l_j)_{1\times 8N}$ with two chaotic sequences by two chaotic systems. Then construct matrix $E_H = (e(h_1), \cdots, e(h_M))^T$ of size $M \times M$, where $e(h_i) = (e_1, e_2, \ldots, e_{hi}, \ldots, e_M)$, $e_{hi} = 1$ and for all $k \neq h_i$ $e_k = 0$; and matrix $E_L = (e(l_1), \ldots, e(l_{8N}))$ of size $8N \times 8N$, where $e(l_j) = (e_1, e_2, \ldots, e_{lj}, \ldots, e_{8N})^T$, $e_{lj} = 1$ and $e_j = 0$ for all $s \neq l_i$ $e_s = 0$.

S3: Permute B with E_H and E_L by:

$$D = E_H \times B \times E_L, \tag{2}$$

S4: Convert the permuted matrix $D = (d_{i,j})_{M\times 8N}$ into a decimal matrix $C = (c_{i,j})_{M\times N}$, which is the ciphered image.

$$c_{i,j} = \sum_{k=1}^{8} 2^{k-1} \times d_{i,8(j-1)+k}, \text{ where } k = 1, 2, \ldots, 8 \tag{3}$$

In decryption procedure, ciphered image is firstly converted into a binary matrix $D = (d_{i,j})_{M\times 8N}$, then the plain binary image is obtained by performing inverse permutation on $D = (d_{i,j})_{M\times 8N}$ with Eq. (4) and converting into a decimal matrix.

$$B = E_H^{-1} \times D \times E_L^{-1} \tag{4}$$

3 Analysis on Ye Algorithm

According to encryption procedure of Ye algorithm, the generation of keystreams that are the permutation vectors $H = (h_i)_{M\times 1}$ and $L = (l_j)_{1\times 8N}$ is only related to the initial value of the chaotic system, and have nothing to do with plain image, so if the secret key keeps unchanged, the keystreams that are the permutation vectors $H = (h_i)_{M\times 1}$ and $L = (l_j)_{1\times 8N}$ will keep unchanged. Since the permutation vectors are determined only by the secret key, the recovery of the permutation vectors equals to the recovery of the corresponding secret key.

In this section, a chosen plaintext attack is proposed on Ye algorithm. Chosen plaintext attack is a common cryptanalysis method, in which the attacker can choose particular plaintext and get the corresponding ciphertext. The goal is to recover the secret key (or the keystreams which are equivalent to the secret key in Ye algorithm). For the ciphered image C of size $M \times N$, the chosen plain image attack is detailed as followed.

S1: Construct chosen plain images

Construct $s_m = ceil(\log_2 M)$ images $P^{(1)}, P^{(2)}, \cdots P^{(s_m)}$ of size $M \times 1$ and $t_m = 3 + ceil(\log_2 N)$ images $Q^{(1)}, Q^{(2)}, \cdots, Q^{(t_m)}$ of size $1 \times N$, where the pixel values of $P^{(s)} = (p_i^{(s)})_{M\times 1}$ satisfy $p_i^{(s)} = \sum_{k=1}^{8} 2^{k-1} \times a_{i,k}^{(s)}$, $a_{i,k}^{(s)} = floor((i-1)/2^{s_m - s}) \bmod 2$, the pixel values of $Q^{(t)} = (q_j^{(t)})_{1\times N}$ satisfy $q_j^{(t)} = \sum_{k=1}^{8} 2^{k-1} \times v_{8(j-1)+k}^{(t)}$, let $u = 8(j-1) + k$, $v_u^{(t)}$ satisfies $v_u^{(t)} = floor((u-1)/2^{t_m - t}) \bmod 2$, $i = 1, 2, \cdots, M$, $j = 1, 2, \cdots, N$, $k = 1, 2, \cdots, 8$, $s = 1, 2, \cdots, s_m$, $t = 1, 2, \cdots, t_m$, $ceil(\cdot)$ rounds to the nearest integer not less than the corresponding elements, $floor(\cdot)$ rounds to the nearest integer less than the corresponding elements.

S2: Encrypt chosen plain images

Encrypt image $P^{(1)}, P^{(2)}, \cdots, P^{(s_m)}$ and $Q^{(1)}, Q^{(2)}, \cdots, Q^{(t_m)}$ with Ye algorithm, and denote the corresponding ciphered image by $C^{(1)}, C^{(2)}, \cdots, C^{(s_m)}$ and $R^{(1)}, R^{(2)}, \cdots, R^{(t_m)}$.

S3: Convert the ciphered images

Convert the ciphered images $C^{(1)}, C^{(2)}, \cdots, C^{(s_m)}$ and $R^{(1)}, R^{(2)}, \cdots, R^{(t_m)}$ into binary matrix $D^{(1)}, D^{(2)}, \cdots, D^{(s_m)}$ of size $M \times 8$ and binary matrix $G^{(1)}, G^{(2)}, \cdots, G^{(t_m)}$ of size $1 \times 8N$ with Eqs. (5) and (6) respectively, where $D^{(s)} = (d_{i,j}^{(s)})_{M\times 8}$, $G^{(t)} = (g_j^{(t)})_{1\times 8N}$, $s = 1, 2, \cdots, s_m$, $t = 1, 2, \cdots, t_m$.

$$d_{i,8(j-1)+k}^{(s)} = floor(c_{i,j}^{(s)}/2^{k-1}) \bmod 2 \tag{5}$$

$$g_{8(j-1)+k}^{(t)} = floor(r_j^{(s)}/2^{k-1}) \bmod 2 \tag{6}$$

S4: Calculate vectors $\bar{H} = (\bar{h}_i)_{M\times 1}$ and $\bar{L} = (\bar{l}_u)_{1\times 8N}$

$$\bar{h}_i = 1 + \sum\nolimits_{s=1}^{s_m} 2^{s_m - s} \times d_{i,1}^{(s)} \tag{7}$$

$$\bar{l}_u = 1 + \sum\nolimits_{t=1}^{t_m} 2^{t_m - t} \times g_u^{(t)} \tag{8}$$

where $d_{i,1}^{(s)}$ is the i-th row 1-st column element of $D^{(s)}$, $i = 1, 2, \cdots, M$, $u = 1, 2, \cdots, 8N$.

S5: output $\bar{H}$ and $\bar{L}$.

Ye algorithm is a bit level permutation algorithm, the keystreams are the permutation vectors H and L. If the vectors $\bar{H}$ and $\bar{L}$ obtained from step S3 in the above attack algorithm equal to the permutation vectors H and L of Ye algorithm, it means that the keystreams of Ye algorithm are obtained through the attack algorithm, and all the images encrypted with the same secret key can be correctly recovered with $\bar{H}$ and $\bar{L}$, that is Ye algorithm cannot resist chosen plaintext attack. In fact, the following proposition is true.

Proposition 1. The vectors $\bar{H}$ and $\bar{L}$ obtained from the above attack algorithm satisfy $\bar{H} = H$ and $\bar{L} = L$.

Proof: According to the construction step of the above attack (step S1), the pixel values of $P^{(s)} = (p_i^{(s)})_{M\times 1}$ satisfy $p_i^{(s)} = \sum_{k=1}^{8} 2^{k-1} \times a_{i,k}^{(s)}$, $a_{i,k}^{(s)} = floor((i-1)/2^{s_m - s})$ mod2. Let $A^{(s)} = (a_{i,k}^{(s)})_{M\times 8}$, obviously, $A^{(s)}$ is the binary form of $P^{(s)}$. Thus, $D^{(s)}$ and $A^{(s)}$ in step S3 of chosen plaintext attack satisfy:

$$D^{(s)} = E_H \times A^{(s)} \times E_L \tag{9}$$

According to the definition of $A^{(s)}$, elements of each column in $A^{(s)}$ are the same, therefore, Eq. (9) can be rewritten as

$$D^{(s)} = E_H \times A^{(s)} \tag{10}$$

That is, the elements $d_{i,1}^{(s)}$ of $D^{(s)}$ satisfy

$$d_{i,1}^{(s)} = e(h_i) \times (a_{1,1}^{(s)}, a_{2,1}^{(s)}, \cdots, a_{M,1}^{(s)})^T \tag{11}$$

From the form of $e(h_i)$, $d_{i,1}^{(s)}$ satisfy:

$$d_{i,1}^{(s)} = a_{h_i,1}^{(s)} = floor((h_i - 1)/2^{s_m - s}) \bmod 2 \tag{12}$$

From the definition of $\bar{h}_i$ in Eq. (7), we have:

$$\bar{h}_i = 1 + \sum\nolimits_{s=1}^{s_m} 2^{s_m - s} \times d_{i,1}^{(s)} = 1 + \sum\nolimits_{s=1}^{s_m} 2^{s_m - s} \times (floor((h_i - 1)/2^{s_m - s}) \bmod 2) = h_i \tag{13}$$

That is

$$\bar{H} = H \tag{14}$$

Similarly, $\bar{L} = L$ can also be proved.
In summary, the proposition is proved.

4 Improvement of Ye Algorithm

4.1 Improvement of Ye Algorithm

The main reason that Ye algorithm cannot resist chosen plaintext attack is that the generation of permutation vectors $H = (h_i)_{M\times 1}$ and $L = (l_j)_{1\times 8N}$ is only related with the initial value of chaos system and has nothing to do with plain image. Aiming at this drawback, improvement of Ye algorithm is proposed in this subsection. In our improvement, the generation of permutation vectors is not only related with secret key but also related with the pixel values of plain image, so that tiny change in pixel value of plain image leads to completely different permutation vectors. As a result the permutation is sensitive not only to the key but also to the plain image. The improved algorithm is detailed as follows.

S0: Input plain image $P = (p_{i,j})_{M\times N}$, secret key (including initial value x_0 of chaotic system, parameters m, n for generation of pre-iteration times), initial value a of feedback (which is an open parameter), where $m, n, a \in Z^+$.

S1: Convert plain image $P = (p_{i,j})_{M\times N}$ into a binary matrix $B = (b_{i,j})_{M\times 8N}$, with size of $M \times 8N$ by Eq. (1);

S2: Iterate chaotic system with initial value x_0 and parameters m, n, generate row permutation vector $H = (h_i)_{M\times 1}$ and column permutation vector $L = (l_j)_{1\times 8N}$;

S2.1 For $i = 1, 2, \cdots M$, perform the following steps to generate row permutation vector $H = (h_i)_{M\times 1}$.

(1) Calculate x_0 and m_0:

$$x_0 = (x_0 + \frac{a}{256N}) - floor(x_0 + \frac{a}{256N}), m_0 = (floor(a^2 x_0) + a) \bmod m.$$

(2) Iterate chaotic system m_0 times with initial value x_0, denote the new state by x_i;
(3) Calculate $j = ceil((x_i \times 10^{15}) \bmod (M - i + 1))$. Let $h_i = T_j$ (where T_j is the j-th element of sequence $T = (1, 2, 3, \cdots, M)$), if $h_i \neq h_j$ for all $j = 1, 2, \cdots, i - 1$, goto (4); else let $x_0 = x_i$, and goto (2);
(4) Renew x_0 and m_0:

$$x_0 = (x_i + \sum_{j=1}^{ceil(N/2)} \frac{b_{h_i,j}}{256N}) - floor(x_i + \sum_{j=1}^{ceil(N/2)} \frac{b_{h_i,j}}{256N}), m_0$$
$$= (floor(a^2 x_i) + \sum_{j=ceil(N/2)}^{N} b_{h_i,j}) \bmod m;$$

S2.2 For $s = 1, 2, \cdots 8N$, perform the following steps to generate $L = (l_i)_{1\times 8N}$:

(1) Calculate x_0 and n_0:

$$x_0 = (x_0 + \frac{a}{256N}) - floor(x_0 + \frac{a}{256N}), n_0 = (floor(a^2 x_0) + a) \bmod n;$$

(2) Iterate chaotic system n_0 times with initial value x_0, denote the new state by x_i;
(3) Calculate $t = ceil((x_i \times 10^{15}) \bmod (8N - s + 1))$. Let $l_s = \Pi_t$ where Π_t is the t-th element of $\Pi = (1, 2, 3, \cdots, 8N)$, if $l_s \neq l_j$ for all $j = 1, 2, \cdots, s - 1$, goto (4); else let $x_0 = x_i$, and goto (2);
(4) Renew x_0 and n_0:

$$x_0 = (x_i + \sum_{r=1}^{ceil(M/2)} \frac{b_{h_r,l_s}}{256N}) - floor(x_i + \sum_{r=1}^{ceil(M/2)} \frac{b_{h_r,l_s}}{256N}), n_0$$
$$= (floor(a^2 x_i) + \sum_{r=ceil(M/2)}^{M} b_{h_r,l_s}) \bmod n;$$

S3: Construct $E_H = \{e(h_1), \cdots e(h_M)\}_{M\times M}$ and $E_L = \{e(l_1), \cdots e(l_{8N})\}_{8N\times 8N}$ with H and L, where $e(h_i)$ and $e(l_j)$ denote the unit row vector and unit column vector generated by h_i and l_j ($e(h_i) = (e_1, e_2, \ldots, e_{hi}, \ldots, e_M)$, $e_{hi} = 1$ and for all $k \neq h_i$ $e_k = 0$; and matrix $E_L = (e(l_1), \ldots, e(l_{8N}))$ of size $8N \times 8N$, where $e(l_j) = (e_1, e_2, \ldots, e_{lj}, \ldots, e_{8N})^T$, $e_{lj} = 1$ and $e_j = 0$ for all $s \neq l_i$ $e_s = 0$);

S4: Permute $B = (b_{i,j})_{M\times 8N}$ with E_H and E_L, denote the result by $D = (d_{i,j})_{M\times 8N}$: $D = E_H \times B \times E_L$;

S5: Convert matrix $D = (d_{i,j})_{M\times 8N}$ of size $M \times 8N$ into a decimal matrix $C = (c_{i,j})_{M\times 8N}$ of size $M \times N$ with Eq. (3).

S6: Output ciphered image $C = (c_{i,j})_{M\times N}$

The decryption procedure is the inverse procedure of encryption algorithm. Ciphered image $C = (c_{i,j})_{M\times 8N}$ is first converted into a binary matrix $D = (d_{i,j})_{M\times 8N}$ with Eq. (1); then permutation vectors L and H are generated with $D = (d_{i,j})_{M\times 8N}$ and secret key, and E_L and E_H are then constructed according to L and H; then matrix $B = (b_{i,j})_{M\times 8N}$ is calculated by $B = E_H^{-1} \times V \times E_L^{-1}$. Finally, the plain image $P = (p_{i,j})_{M\times 8N}$ is obtained by converting $B = (b_{i,j})_{M\times 8N}$ into a decimal matrix.

4.2 Analysis on Improvement of Ye Algorithm

For the improvement of Ye algorithm, if we have find chosen plain images $Q^{(1)}, Q^{(2)}, \cdots$ that can be used to recover vectors $\tilde{H} = (\tilde{h}_i)_{M\times 1}$ and $\tilde{L} = (\tilde{l}_j)_{1\times 8N}$ with the chosen plaintext attack proposed in Sect. 3 satisfying $\tilde{H} = H$ and $\tilde{L} = L$, we can conclude that the improved algorithm cannot resist chosen plaintext attack.

According to the improved algorithm, $H = (h_i)_{M\times 1}$ and $L = (l_j)_{1\times 8N}$ are sensitive not only to the key but also to the plain image. For any two plain images $R = (r_{i,j})_{M\times N}$ and $Q = (q_{i,j})_{M\times N}$ of size $M \times N$, if $\exists\, 1 \le i \le M, 1 \le j \le N$, $r_{i,j} \ne q_{i,j}$, then the permutation vectors H_R and L_R used to encrypt $R = (r_{i,j})_{M\times N}$ are completely different from H_Q and L_Q used to encrypt $Q = (q_{i,j})_{M\times N}$. So the permutation vectors used to encrypt Q and R are the same when and only when $Q = R$. So in order to obtain $\tilde{H} = H$ and $\tilde{L} = L$ by chosen plaintext attack, there must be a plain image $Q^{(j)}$ among the chosen plain images $Q^{(1)}, Q^{(2)}, \cdots$ satisfies $Q = P$ (P is the plain image to be recovered).

For any two image P and Q of size $M \times N$, the probability $Q = P$ is $\Pr(P = Q) = \frac{1}{2^{8MN}}$. Therefore the probability of finding the suitable chosen plain image to make $\tilde{H} = H$ and $\tilde{L} = L$ is $\frac{1}{2^{8MN}}$, and $\frac{1}{2^{8MN}}$ will reduce exponentially with the increase of the plain image size $M \times N$. For the image size of 256×256, the probability of finding the suitable plain image is $\frac{1}{2^{8\times 256\times 256}}$, which is very small, so the improved algorithm can effectively resist chosen plaintext attack.

5 Experimental Verification

In this section, we analyze the performance of chosen plaintext attack on Ye algorithm and the security of the improved algorithm. The chaotic system used in implementation is first given as follows. Calculation in implementation is performed in double precision floating point numbers represented by 64 bits specified in IEEE.

5.1 Chaotic Systems

Generally speaking, any chaotic system can be applied to Ye algorithm and its improvement. Here in order to keep in line with the original paper, Logistic map (see Eq. (15)) is applied to the experiments on Ye algorithm which is applied in [7], and

PWLM (piecewise linear map, see Eq. (16)) with more uniform distribution is applied to the experiments on improved algorithm.

$$x_{n+1} = \mu x_n(1 - x_n) \tag{15}$$

where $3.5699456 < \mu < 2$, $0 < x_n < 1$.

$$x_{k+1} = \begin{cases} x_k/p & x_k \leq p \\ (1 - x_k)/(1 - p) & x_k > p \end{cases} \tag{16}$$

where $x, p \in (0, 1)$.

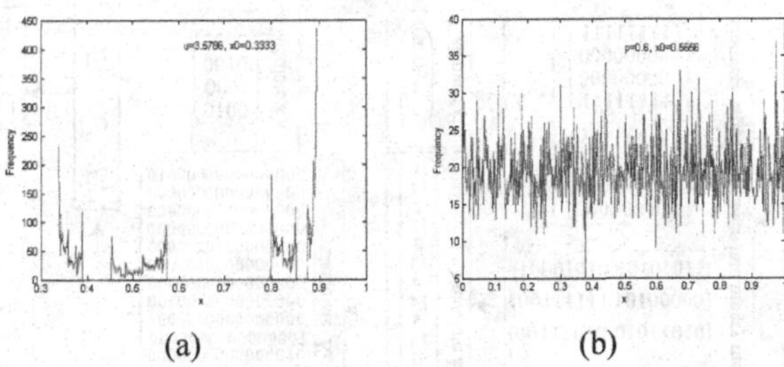

(a) (b)

Fig. 1. Comparison diagram of the distribution of Logistic map and PLCM map

Comparison of the distribution of Logistic mapping and PLCM mapping is shown in Fig. 1 where the number of iterations is 10^4. Distribution of Logistic mapping with control parameter $\mu = 3.5786$, initial value $x_0 = 0.3333$ is shown in Fig. 1(a); Distribution of PLCM with control parameter $p = 0.6$, initial value $x_0 = 0.5656$ is shown in Fig. 1(b). From the figures, we can see that the distribution of Logistic mapping is not uniform, and that of PLCM is relatively uniform.

5.2 Experiments on Chosen Plaintext Attack

From the previous analysis, we can know that Ye algorithm cannot resist chosen plaintext attack proposed in section. The results are verified by experiments in this section.In the implementation of the Ye algorithm, the two initial values of Logistic mapping are 0.1777 and 0.234567 respectively, and the control parameter is $\mu = 3.5786$.

(1) Analysis with numerical example

For ease of understanding, a simple numerical example is given to demonstrate the procedure of chosen plaintext attack. In this section, we take a plain image $P = \begin{pmatrix} 112 & 35 \\ 73 & 78 \\ 21 & 25 \\ 223 & 55 \end{pmatrix}$ of size 4×2 as an example, and obtain its ciphered image

$C = \begin{pmatrix} 115 & 254 \\ 165 & 190 \\ 106 & 80 \\ 22 & 52 \end{pmatrix}$ by encrypting it with Ye algorithm, the procedure of chosen plain image attack is shown as follows (Fig. 2).

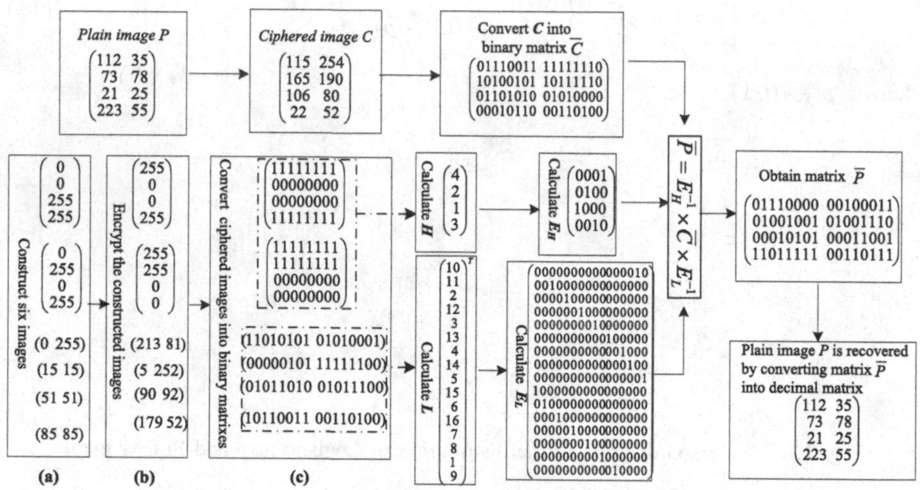

Fig. 2. The procedure of recovering a plain image of size 4×2 with chosen plaintext attack

Six chosen plain images are constructed according to the chosen plaintext attack in section (see (a) in the figure above); the corresponding six ciphered images are shown in (b); the six matrixes in (c) are the binary matrixes converted from the six ciphered images in (b); the row permutation vector H is calculated from the first two matrixes in (c) with Eq. (7), the column permutation vector L is calculated from the last four matrixes in (c) with Eq. (8); and then E_H and E_L are generated by H and L. Matrix $\bar{P}$ is calculated by Eq. (4) and $\bar{C}$, where $\bar{C}$ is the binary form of ciphered image C. Finally the recovered plain image P is obtained by convert $\bar{C}$ into binary matrix. It is from the figure that the recovered image by the chosen plaintext attack is the same as the plain image.

(2) **Experimental results**

Experiments are performed on the PC at CPU 1 GB, 3 GHz in the Matlab7.0 environment. Experiments on a plain image shown in Fig. 3 of size 256 × 256 are performed to shown the results of chosen plaintext attack.

For this plain image, we need to construct $s_m + t_m = ceil(\log_2 256) + ceil(\log_2 256) + 3 = 19$ images as the chosen plain image, including 8 images $P^{(1)}, P^{(2)}, \cdots, P^{(8)}$ of size 256 × 1 and 11 images $Q^{(1)}, Q^{(2)}, \cdots, Q^{(11)}$ of size 1 × 256, and $P^{(s)}$ satisfies $p_i^{(s)} = \sum_{k=1}^{8} 2^{k-1} \times a_{i,k}^{(s)}$, $a_{i,k}^{(s)} = floor((i-1)/2^{8-s}) \bmod 2$, $s = 1, 2, \cdots, 8$, $Q^{(t)} = (q_j^{(t)})_{1 \times N}$ satisfies $q_j^{(t)} = \sum_{k=1}^{8} 2^{k-1} \times v_{8(j-1)+k}^{(t)}$, let $u = 8(j-1) + k$, then $v_u^{(t)} = floor$

Fig. 3. Plain image

$((u-1)/2^{11-t}) \bmod 2$, $t = 1, 2, \cdots, 11$. The result of chosen plaintext attack on Ye algorithm is shown in Fig. 4, where Fig. 4(a) is the ciphered image of plain image shown in Fig. 3 encrypted by Ye algorithm. Figure 4(b) is the recovered image with chosen plaintext attack. From Fig. 4(b) we can see that Ye algorithm cannot resist the attack proposed in Sect. 3.

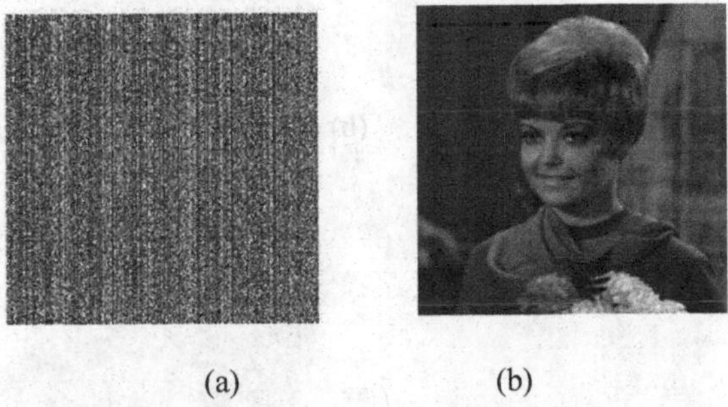

(a) (b)

Fig. 4. Result of chosen plaintext attack

(3) Experiments on improved algorithm

Experimental results on improvement of Ye algorithm is proposed in this section. The plain image shown in Fig. 3 is encrypted by improved algorithm and the result is shown in Fig. 5. In experiments, the two initial values of PLCM are 0.1777 and 0.234567, control parameter is $p = 0.6$, numbers of initial iteration are $m = 120$ and $n = 40$ respectively, feedback initial value is $a = 235$.

Fig. 5. Encryption result with improved algorithm

(1) Correlation analysis test

Generally, each pixel is highly correlated with its adjacent pixels in an ordinary image. And it is an ideal property of an encryption algorithm to produce the ciphered image without such correlation. In the experiments, we have randomly chosen 4096 pairs of horizontally, vertically and diagonally adjacent pixels respectively from plain image and ciphered image in Fig. 6. The figures of plain image are on the left side and those of ciphered image are on the right side.

According to Fig. 6, the 4096 pairs of pixels in plain image mainly concentrate on the diagonal line of the figure which show the highly correlation of adjacent pixels, and those in ciphered image distribute uniformly and show no correlation.

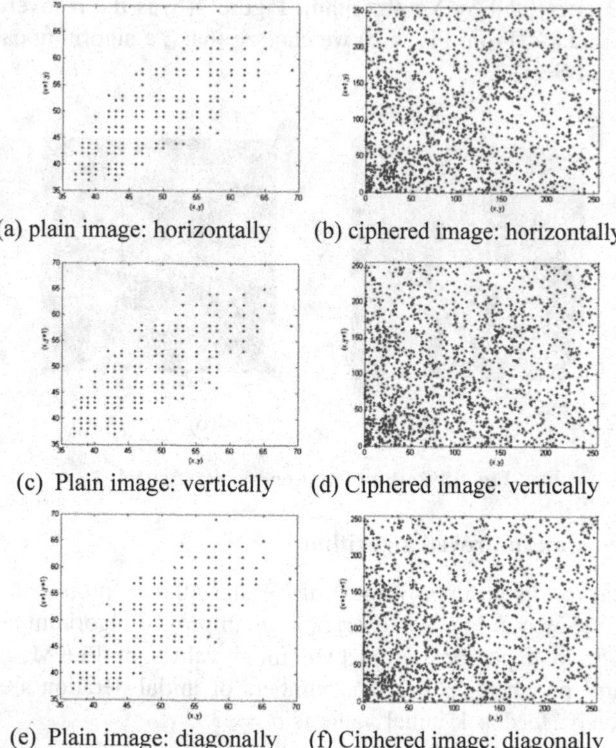

(a) plain image: horizontally (b) ciphered image: horizontally

(c) Plain image: vertically (d) Ciphered image: vertically

(e) Plain image: diagonally (f) Ciphered image: diagonally

Fig. 6. Correlation distribution of two horizontally adjacent pixels in plain and ciphered images

The correlation coefficients of plain image for horizontally, vertically and diagonally adjacent pixels are 0.837798, 0.808684 and 0.795863, respectively; and those of ciphered image are 0.091003, −0.035509 and −0.010317, respectively. According to the results, we find that the correlation coefficients between the pixels in different directions before and after encryption by the improved algorithm are greatly reduced, and the correlation is destroyed to a great extent.

(2) Key sensitivity test

For key sensitivity test, we make a tiny change in the secret key, change secret key 0.1777 into 0.17771 and keep 0.234567 unchanged, then decrypt the ciphered image with the changed key. The experimental results are shown in Fig. 7. Decryption result with the wrong key is shown in Fig. 7(a) and difference between decryption with the wrong and right key is shown in Fig. 7(b). The rate of different pixels in the two images is 95.91%. That means that nothing can be recovered as long as the attacker has tiny error in the user secret key. Therefore the algorithm is sensitive to the change of secret key.

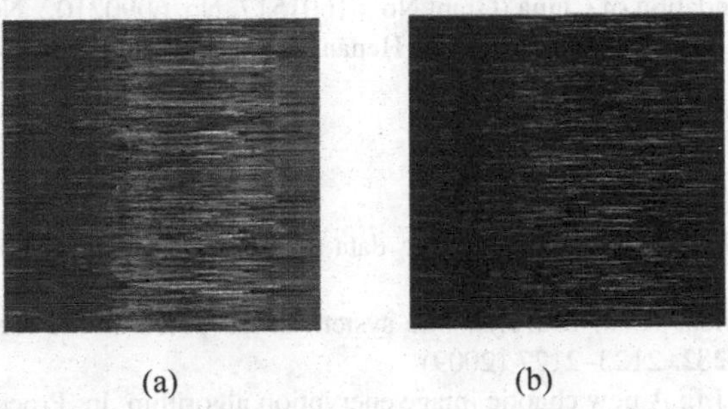

(a) (b)

Fig. 7. Key sensitivity test

(3) Histogram analysis test

Since in Ye algorithm, both position and value of pixels in plain image are encrypted, the histogram of ciphered image is different from that of plain image, see Fig. 8.

However, 0, 1 ratio in ciphered image does not change although the pixel value changes in Ye algorithm which is a bit-level permutation. For example, if all bits of the plain text image are all 0 or 1, all bits of the encrypted image are still 1 or 0. Therefore, even for a certain original plain image, one can make the pixel value distribution of ciphered image uniform by adjusting the parameters and secret key in encryption process. But there is no such parameters and secret key to make the result standing for all plain images. The experimental results of this section also verify this fact, as shown in Fig. 8(b), which shows that the distribution of the pixel value in ciphered image is not uniform enough.

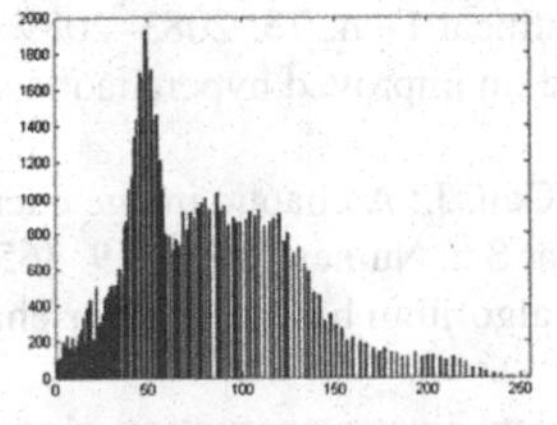

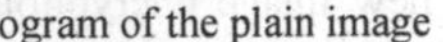

(a) Histogram of the plain image

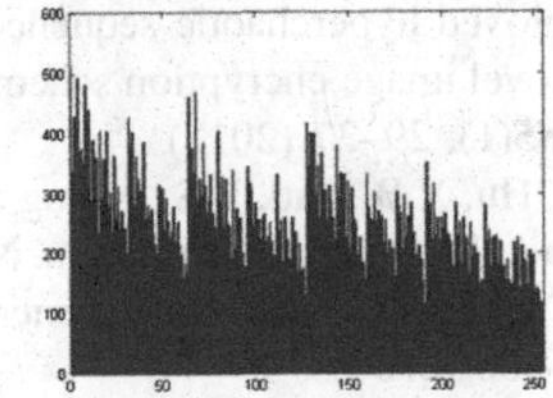

(b) Histogram of the ciphered image

Fig. 8. Histograms of the image before and after encryption

6 Conclusion

A chosen plaintext attack against Ye algorithm is proposed aiming at the drawback that the generation procedure of permutation vectors has no relation with plain image, which just need *ceil*($\log_2 8MN$) chosen plain images. Meanwhile, an improvement of Ye algorithm is proposed which can resist the chosen plaintext attack in Sect. 3. Finally, the validity of chosen plaintext attack and the security of improved algorithm are shown by experiments.

Acknowledgments. The work described in this paper was partially supported by the National Natural Science Foundation of China (Grant No. 61601517, No. 60902102, No. 60970141), basic and advanced technology research project of Henan Province, China (Grant No. 2014302703).

References

1. Scharinger, J.: Fast encryption of image data using chaotic Kolmogorov flows. Electron. Imaging **7**(2), 318–325 (1998)
2. Huang, C.K., Nien, H.H.: Multi chaotic system based pixel shuffle for image encryption. Opt. Commun. **282**, 2123–2127 (2009)
3. Yen, J.C., Guo, J.I.: A new chaotic image encryption algorithm. In: Proceedings of (Taiwan) National Symposium on Telecommunications, pp. 358–362 (1998)
4. Yen, J.C., Guo, J.I.: A new hierarchical chaotic image encryption algorithm and its hardware architecture. In: Proceedings of 1998 Ninth VLSI DESIGN/CAD Symposium (1998)
5. Guo, J.I., Yen, J.C.: The design and realization of a new hierarchical chaotic image encryption algorithm. In: Proceedings of 1999 International Symposium on Communications, pp. 210–214 (1999)
6. Yen, J.C., Guo, J.I.: Efficient hierarchical chaotic image encryption algorithm and its VLSI realization. In: IEE Proceedings-Vision, Image and Signal Processing, vol. 147, no. 2, pp. 167–175 (2000)
7. Ye, G.D.: Image scrambling encryption algorithm of pixel bit based on chaos map. Pattern Recogn. Lett. **31**(5), 347–354 (2010)
8. Li, C.Q., Lo, K.T.: Optimal quantitative cryptanalysis of permutation-only multimedia ciphers against plaintext attacks. Sig. Process. **91**, 949–954 (2011)
9. Lian, S.G.: Efficient image or video encryption based on spatiotemporal chaos system. Chaos Soliton Fractals **40**, 2509–2519 (2009)
10. Ge, X., Liu, F.L., Lu, B., Wang, W.: Cryptanalysis of a spatiotemporal chaotic image/videocryptosystem and its improved version. Phys. Lett. A **375**, 908–913
11. Li, C.Q., Liu, Y.S., Xie, T., ChenMichael, Z.Q.: Breaking a novel image encryption scheme basedon improved hyperchaotic sequences. Nonlinear Dyn. **73**, 2083–2089 (2013)
12. Zhu, C.: A novel image encryption scheme based on improved hyperchaotic sequences. Opt. Commun. **285**(1), 29–37 (2012)
13. Zhang, L.Y., Hu, X.B., Liu, Y.S., Wong, K.W., Gan, J.: A chaotic image encryption scheme owning temp-value feedback. Commun. Nonlinear Sci. Numer. Simul. **19**, 3653–3659 (2014)
14. Gao, T.G., Chen, Z.Q.: A new image encryption algorithm based on hyper-chaos. Phys. Lett. A **372**, 394–400 (2008)
15. Rhouma, R., Belghith, S.: Cryptanalysis of a new image encryption algorithm based on hyper-chaos. Phys. Lett. A **372**, 5973–5978 (2008)
16. Ge, X., Liu, F.L., Lu, B., Yang, C.F.: Improvement of Rhouma's attacks on Gao algorithm. Phys. Lett. A **374**, 1362–1367

Attribute-Based Encryption Scheme Supporting Tree-Access Structure on Ideal Lattices

Jinxia Yu, Chaochao Yang, Yongli Tang, and Xixi Yan(✉)

College of Computer Science and Technology, Henan Polytechnic University, Jiaozuo 454000, Henan, China
yanxx@hpu.edu.cn

Abstract. Attribute-based encryption (ABE) has been an active research area in cryptography due to its attractive applications. But almost all ABE scheme are based on bilinear maps, which leave them vulnerable to quantum cryptanalysis. The cryptographic system based on lattices is considered to be able to resist the quantum attack, and the computational efficiency is high. Therefore, the encryption scheme based on lattice theory has received wide attention in recent years. At present, the research of the attribute based encryption scheme on ideal lattices is lacking, and there are many problems need to be solved. Lots of existing schemes support only a single access policy and cannot support flexible expressions. For solving the problem of designing access structure in attribute-based encryption scheme under quantum environment, combined with Zhu's scheme, an attribute-based encryption scheme supporting tree access structures on ideal lattices is introduced. The scheme adopts tree-access structure to express access strategy, the leaf nodes of the tree represent attributes, and the non-leaf nodes represent logical operators. The access tree can express the access policy flexibly by Shamir threshold secret sharing technology, including "and", "or", "threshold" operation. The scheme is proved to be secure against chosen plaintext attack under the standard mode. The analysis shows that our scheme can resist the quantum attack and realize the flexible access strategy with the better performance.

Keywords: Attribute-based encryption · Ideal lattices · Tree-access structure

1 Introduction

Attribute based encryption (ABE) has the advantages of users' dynamic nature, flexibility of access strategy and privacy of user identity compared with traditional public key encryption. In 2005, Sahai and Waters [1] in Europe puts forward the concept of attribute based encryption cryptography meeting, it users a series of attributes to represent the user's identity, by the matching relationship between the attribute set and access structure determine its decryption ability, and give a support threshold structure ABE. In 2006, Goyal et al. [2] divided ABE system into two categories according to different encryption strategies, one is key-policy attribute based encryption (KP-ABE) which is characterized by embedding the access structure into the key and contains a

X. Sun et al. (Eds.): ICCCS 2018, LNCS 11065, pp. 519–527, 2018.
https://doi.org/10.1007/978-3-030-00012-7_47

specific set of attributes, another is cipher-text-policy attribute based encryption(CP-ABE) which is embedding the access structure into the cipher-text and contains a set of specific attributes that can be decrypted when the property set and access structure match. At the same time, the author proposes the KP-ABE scheme to support the tree access strategy. Compared with the threshold access structure, the tree access structure is more sophisticated, the expressive power is more abundant, and the logical operation is more practical. In 2007, Bethencourt et al. [3] proposed the first cipher-text strategy attribute base encryption scheme, and the access structure adopted the threshold structure. Compared with the key policy attribute base encryption mechanism, the attribute base encryption system of cipher-text strategy is more suitable for dynamic scenarios. The sender can design the access structure and control the scope of the receiver. In the same year, Ostrovshy [4] proposed the attribute base encryption scheme with non-gate access structure, which enriched the access strategy. In 2011, Waters [5] proposed a new cipher-text strategy attribute base encryption scheme using linear secret sharing scheme (LSSS). Compared with the tree access structure, LSSS has the same function, while the tree access structure is more intuitive, and the secret sharing matrix design in LSSS is more complex.

Attribute based encryption mechanism because of its characteristics such as the flexibility of access control is becoming a hot spot of scholars study, at the same time, the attribute based encryption mechanism has also been widely used, various related ABE scheme [6–8] have been proposed. However, most of the above scheme is based on bilinear pairings, encryption process requires several bilinear pairings computation, such as high computational complexity and could not resist quantum attack problem.

Based on the lattice, the cryptographic system is considered to be able to resist the quantum attack, and the operation efficiency is high. Therefore, the encryption scheme based on lattice theory has received wide attention in recent years. In 2012, Boyen [9] applied LSSS to the attribute base encryption scheme based on the standard grid, and proposed the first KP-ABE scheme to satisfy the safety of the random prediction model. In the same year, Zhang et al. [10] used the sampling algorithm to extract the property private key, embedded the threshold access structure in the cipher-text, and proposed the first CP-ABE scheme based on the LWE problem. In 2013, Wang [11] under the standard model is put forward, on the cipher-text strategies attribute based encryption schemes, this scheme implements the multivalued attribute threshold access structure, and under the hypothesis of LWE proves that the scheme of security.

Compared with the LWE password system on the standard grid, learning with error over ring(R-LWE) has the advantages of small key size and high encryption efficiency. In 2014, Zhu et al. [12] introduced the threshold access strategy to the ideal grid, and proposed a KP-ABE scheme based on R-LWE problem, and proved that it was safe to choose plaintext attack. In 2015, Tan et al. [13] proposed the CP-ABE scheme of LSSS access strategy based on the ideal grid based on R-LWE problem. In 2017, Chen et al. [14] pointed out that the scheme security of Zhu [12] could not satisfy the choice of plaintext attack security. Yan et al. [15] used LSSS access structure to propose the ideal multi-agency CP-ABE scheme. In the same year, Wang et al. [16] proposed an effective encryption scheme based on R-LWE to choose cipher-text security.

At present, the research of the attribute base encryption scheme on ideal lattices is lacking, and there are many problems need to be solved. Lots of existing schemes support only a single access policy and cannot support flexible expressions. In this paper, we propose a cipher-text policy ABE scheme based on the R-LWE problem, which supports arbitrary access structures using the access tree structure. The main innovation is that access tree structure is simple and support "and", "or", and "threshold" operation, and can achieve flexible access strategy. In this paper, the tree structure is used as the access policy to apply to the attribute base encryption scheme, which makes the access structure more flexible and diverse.

2 Preliminaries

2.1 Lattices

We denote the integer numbers by $\mathbb{Z}$ and the real numbers by $\mathbb{R}$. For a real number $x \in \mathbb{R}$, we let $\lceil x \rceil$ denote the largest integer not greater than x, $\lfloor x \rfloor$ denote $\lceil x \rceil - 1$, and $\text{Round}(x) = \lfloor x + 1/2 \rfloor$. We use the notation $[k]$ for an positive integer k to denote the set $\{1, \ldots, k\}$.

Column vectors are denoted by lower-case bold letters (e.g., $\boldsymbol{x}$) and row vectors by transpose (e.g., $\boldsymbol{x}^T$). We use bold capital letters (e.g., $\boldsymbol{A}$) to denote matrices, and sometimes identify a matrix with its ordered set of column vectors. The i-th column vector of a matrix $\boldsymbol{A}$ is denoted as $\boldsymbol{a}_i$. We denote the horizontal concatenation of matrices and/or vectors using a "|", e.g., $[\boldsymbol{A}|\boldsymbol{Ax}]$, and denote the vertical concatenation as $[\boldsymbol{A}; \boldsymbol{Ax}]$. We let $\|\tilde{\boldsymbol{A}}\|$ denote the maximal Gram-Schmidt length of $\boldsymbol{A}$.

The natural security parameter throughout the paper is n, which implies that all other quantities are polynomial functions of n. We use standard asymptotic notation $O(\cdot)$, $\Omega(\cdot)$, $o(\cdot)$, etc. Moreover, we use tildes $\tilde{O}(\cdot)$ to denote that logarithmic factors in the main parameter are suppressed. We use $poly(n)$ to denote an unspecified function $f(n) = O(n^c)$ for some constant c. We say that a function in n is negligible, denoted as $negl(n)$, if $f(n) = o(n^c)$ for every fixed constant c. We say that an event happens with overwhelming probability if it happens with probability at least $1 - negl(n)$.

The statistical distance between two distributions $\mathcal{X}$ and $\mathcal{Y}$ (or two random variables having those distributions), viewed as functions over a countable domain D, is defined as $\frac{1}{2}\sum_{d \in D} |\mathcal{X}(d) - \mathcal{Y}(d)|$. We say that two distributions (formally, two ensembles of distributions indexed by n) are statistically close (or statistically indistinguishable) if their statistical distance is negligible function of n.

Definition 1. Given n linearly independent vectors $b_1, b_2, \cdots, b_n \in R^m$, the lattice generated by them is defined as

$$\Lambda = L(b_1, \cdots, b_n) = \left\{ \sum_{i=1}^{n} x_i b_i : x_i \in Z \right\} \tag{1}$$

where $b_1, b_2, \cdots, b_n$ is a basis of the lattice.

Let $\boldsymbol{A} \in \mathbb{Z}_q^{n \times m}$, n, m, $q \in \mathbb{Z}$, consider the following two lattices:

$$\Lambda_q^{\perp}(\boldsymbol{A}) = \{e \in \mathbb{Z}^m \ s.t. \ \boldsymbol{A}e = \boldsymbol{0} \bmod q\} \tag{2}$$

$$\Lambda_q(\boldsymbol{A}) = \{\boldsymbol{y} \in \mathbb{Z}^m \ s.t. \ \exists \boldsymbol{s} \in \mathbb{Z}^n, \ \boldsymbol{A}^t\boldsymbol{s} = \boldsymbol{y} \bmod q\} \tag{3}$$

The standard worst-case approximation problem GapSVP is the approximating decision version of the shortest vector problem (SVP).

Definition 2. For $\mathbf{x} \in \Lambda$, define the Gaussian function $\rho_{\sigma,\mathbf{c}}(\boldsymbol{x})$ over $\Lambda \in \mathbb{Z}^m$ centered at $\boldsymbol{c} \in \mathbb{R}^m$ with parameter $\sigma > 0$ as

$$\rho_{\sigma,c}(\boldsymbol{x}) = \exp\left(-\frac{\pi\|\boldsymbol{x} - \boldsymbol{c}\|^2}{\sigma^2}\right) \tag{4}$$

Let $\rho_{\sigma,\boldsymbol{c}}(\Lambda) = \sum_{\boldsymbol{x} \in \Lambda} \rho_{\sigma,\boldsymbol{c}}(\boldsymbol{x})$, and define the discrete Gaussian distribution over Λ as $D_{\Lambda,\sigma,\boldsymbol{c}}(\boldsymbol{y}) = \frac{\rho_{\sigma,\boldsymbol{c}}(\boldsymbol{y})}{\rho_{\sigma,\boldsymbol{c}}(\Lambda)}$ where $\boldsymbol{y} \in \Lambda$.

2.2 R-LWE

For any positive integers n, $q \in \mathbb{Z}$, real $\alpha > 0$ and vector $\mathbf{s} \in \mathbb{Z}_q^n$, define the distribution $A_{\mathbf{s},\alpha} = \{(\mathbf{a}, \mathbf{a}^t\mathbf{s} + e \bmod q) : \mathbf{a} \leftarrow {}_r\mathbb{Z}_q^n, e \leftarrow {}_rD_{\mathbb{Z},\alpha q}\}$. For any m independent samples $(\mathbf{a}_1, b_1), \ldots, (\mathbf{a}_m, b_m)$ from $A_{\mathbf{s},\alpha}$, we denote it in matrix form $(\mathbf{A}, \mathbf{b}) \in \mathbb{Z}_q^{n \times m} \times \mathbb{Z}_q^m$, where $\mathbf{A} = (\mathbf{a}_1, \ldots, \mathbf{a}_m)$ and $\mathbf{b} = (b_1, \ldots, b_m)^t$. If for uniformly random $\mathbf{s} \leftarrow {}_r\mathbb{Z}_q^n$ and given polynomial many samples, no PPT algorithm can recover $\mathbf{s}$ with non-negligible probability, we say that the $\text{LWE}_{n,q,\alpha}$ problem is hard.

Consider these public parameters: a prime q, a positive integer n, and a distribution χ over $\mathbb{Z}_q$. An $(\mathbb{Z}_q, n, \chi)$-LWE problem instance is a challenge oracle $\mathcal{O}$ which consists of access to two types oracle, either, a noisy pseudo-random oracle $\mathcal{O}_s$ carrying some constant random secret key $\mathbf{s} \in \mathbb{Z}_q^n$, or, a truly random oracle $\mathcal{O}_\$$, whose behaviors are respectively described as follows:

$\mathcal{O}_s$: outputs samples of the form $(\boldsymbol{u}_i, v_i) = (\boldsymbol{u}_i, \boldsymbol{u}_i^T\boldsymbol{s} + x_i) \in \mathbb{Z}_q^n \times \mathbb{Z}_q$, where $\boldsymbol{s} \in \mathbb{Z}_q^n$ is a uniformly distributed persistent value invariant across invocations, $\boldsymbol{u}_i$ is uniform in $\mathbb{Z}_q^n$, and $x_i \in \mathbb{Z}_q$ is a fresh sample from χ.

$\mathcal{O}_\$$: outputs truly uniform random samples from $\mathbb{Z}_q^n \times \mathbb{Z}_q$.

The $(\mathbb{Z}_q, n, \chi)$-LWE problem allows repeated queries to the challenge oracle $\mathcal{O}$. We define that an attack algorithm $\mathcal{A}$ distinguishes the $(\mathbb{Z}_q, n, \chi)$-LWE problem if $\text{LWE - adv}[\mathcal{A}] = \left|\Pr\left[\mathcal{A}^{\mathcal{O}_s} = 1\right] - \Pr\left[\mathcal{A}^{\mathcal{O}_\$} = 1\right]\right|$ is non-negligible for a random $\mathbf{s} \in \mathbb{Z}_q^n$.

Let $f(x) = x^n + 1$, where the security parameter n is a power of 2, making $f(x)$ irreducible over the rational, and let $R = Z[x]/f(x)$ be the ring of integer polynomial modulo $f(x)$. Let $q = 1 \bmod 2n$ be a sufficiently large public prime modulus, and

$R_q = R/qR$ be the ring of integer polynomials modulo both $f(x)$ and q. Elements of R_q may be represented by polynomials of degree less than n, whose coefficients are in Z_q.

Analogously to standard LWE, the R-LWE problem can be described as follows. Let $s \in R_q$ be a uniformly random ring element. Define two distributions over $R_q \times R_q$ as follows. (1) $(a, b) = (a, as + e) \in R_q \times R_q$, where $a \leftarrow R_q$ is uniformly random, and e is some small random error term chosen from a certain distribution over R. (2) (a, c), where $a, c \leftarrow R_q$ is uniformly random. Then the two distributions described above are indistinguishable.

3 Construction of the CP-ABE Scheme

The proposed CP-ABE scheme is constructed based on the hardness of Ring-LWE problem. To construct a lattice CP-ABE scheme that capable to provide a fine grained access control on encrypted data, tree-access structure is built into the cipher-text. The proposed lattice CP-ABE scheme is formally defined as follows.

3.1 Setup

Setup(λ, U): Given a security parameter λ and a universe of attribute $U = \{u_1, u_1, \cdots, u_n\}$. Select a sufficiently large prime modulus $q = 1 \bmod (2\lambda)$, and a smaller positive integer p where $p < < q$ and $p < < q$. Let $R_q = Z_q[x]/ < f(x) >$ be the ring of integer polynomials modulo both $f(x)$ and q. Let χ be an error distribution over R_q.

(1) Select a uniformly random master secret key, $SK_0 \leftarrow R_q$ and random element $a \leftarrow R_q$. Compute $PK_0 = a \cdot SK_0 + pe_0 \in R_q$.
(2) For each attribute, select a pair of uniformly random $(SK_i, SK_i^{-1}) \leftarrow R_q$, where SK_i^{-1} is the inverse of SK_i in R_q. Compute $PK_i = SK_i + pe_i \in R_q$.
(3) Outputs the public parameters PP and a master key MSK as follows:

$$PP = \{a, PK_0, \{PK_i\}_{i=1}^n\} \text{ and } MSK = \{SK_0, \{SK_i\}_{i=1}^n, \{SK_i^{-1}\}_{i=1}^n\}.$$

3.2 Encryption

Encrypt(PP, M, T): Given the parameters PP, a tree-access structure T and a message M. The set of attributes in the tree is called. ω. Let's pick $s \in R_q$.

From top to bottom, select $d_{node} = k_{node} - 1$ polynomial $q_{node}(x)$ for every non-leaf node in the tree, where $q_{root}(0) = s$, and the polynomial of each node should satisfy $q_{node}(x) = q_{parent}(index(node))$, remember $q_{node}(0) = s_{node}$. The value of the leaf node is obtained from the parent node of the leaf node, denoted as $s_i \in R_q$, $i = attr(node)$.

(1) Select uniform random parameters $r \leftarrow R_q$ and noise parameters $e', e'_i \leftarrow \chi$. Let's calculate $C_0 = PK_0 \cdot r \cdot s + M + pe' \in R_q$ and $C_i = a \cdot PK_i \cdot r \cdot s_i + pe'_i \in R_q$.
(2) Output cipher-text $CT = (C_0, \{C_i\}_{i \in \omega}, T)$.

3.3 Key Generation

KeyGen(MSK, ω'): Enter the main private key *MSK* and the user attribute set ω'. Randomly select a pair of reciprocal elements $(t, t^{-1}) \in R_q$. Select the uniform random noise parameter $e'', e_i'' \leftarrow \chi$. Output the user private key: $K_0 = SK_0 \cdot t^{-1} + pe'' \in R_q$ and $K_i = SK_i^{-1} \cdot t + pe_i'' \in R_q$, $\forall i \in \omega'$.

3.4 Decryption

Decrypt(PP, CT, K): Obtain public parameter *PP*, user's private key *K* and cipher-text *CT*. If the user attribute set ω' matches the access structure *T*, it can be decrypted successfully. Define recursive decryption algorithm $DecNd(CT, K, node)$, where *CT* is cipher-text, *K* is the user's private key, and *node* is a node on the tree.

(1) If A is A leaf node, then

$$\begin{aligned} DecNd(CT, K, node) &= C_i \cdot K_i = a \cdot r \cdot s_i \cdot PK_i \cdot K_i + pe_i' \cdot K_i \\ &= a \cdot r \cdot s_i \cdot t + a \cdot r \cdot s_i \cdot p(SK_i^{-1} \cdot t \cdot e_i + SK_i \cdot e_i'' + pe_i \cdot e_i'') + pe_i' \cdot K_i, \end{aligned}$$

let $y_i = a \cdot r \cdot s_i \cdot (SK_i^{-1} \cdot t \cdot e_i + SK_i \cdot e_i'' + pe_i \cdot e'')$ and $y_i' = e_i' \cdot K_i$, then $DecNd(CT, K, node) = a \cdot r \cdot s_i \cdot t + p \cdot y_i + p \cdot y_i'$.

(2) If *node* is A non-leaf node, select I_{node}, which is *node* collection of the youngest child nodes that satisfy the access tree under node *node*, and the children of *node* are *z*, then

$$\begin{aligned} DecNd(CT, K, node) &= \sum_{z \in I_{node}} L_z \cdot C_z \cdot K_z \\ &= \sum_{z \in I_{node}} L_z \cdot a \cdot r \cdot s_z \cdot t + \sum_{z \in I_{node}} L_z \cdot p \cdot y_z + \sum_{z \in I_{node}} L_z \cdot p \cdot y_z' \\ &= a \cdot r \cdot t \cdot s_{node} + p \cdot \sum_{z \in I_{node}} L_z \cdot y_z + p \cdot \sum_{z \in I_{node}} L_z \cdot y_z' \end{aligned}$$

Among them $L_z = \frac{\prod_{i \in S_{node}, i \neq z} -i}{\prod_{i \in S_{node}, i \neq z} (z-i)}$, let $y_{node} = \sum_{z \in I_{node}} L_z \cdot s_z \cdot y_z$ and $y_{node}' = \sum_{z \in I_{node}} L_z \cdot y_z'$, then

$$DecNd(CT, K, node) = a \cdot r \cdot t \cdot s_{node} + p \cdot y_{node} + p \cdot y_{node}'.$$

To decrypt the root node *root* of the access tree, get $b = DecNd(CT, K, root) = a \cdot r \cdot t \cdot s + p \cdot y_{root} + p \cdot y_{root}'$, calculate $M^* = C_0 - K_0 b$, and output $M = M^* \bmod p$.

3.5 Correctness

The correctness of the proposed CP-ABE scheme is described as follows.

$$
\begin{aligned}
M^* &= C_0 - K_0 b \\
&= PK_0 \cdot r \cdot s + M + pe' - K_0 \cdot (a \cdot r \cdot t \cdot s + p \cdot y_{root} + p \cdot y'_{root}) \\
&= PK_0 \cdot r \cdot s + M + pe' - a \cdot r \cdot t \cdot s \cdot (SK_0 \cdot t^{-1} + pe'') - p \cdot y_{root} \cdot K_0 - p \cdot y'_{root} \cdot K_0 \\
&= PK_0 \cdot r \cdot s + M + pe' - a \cdot r \cdot s \cdot SK_0 - a \cdot r \cdot t \cdot s \cdot pe'' - p \cdot y_{root} \cdot K_0 - p \cdot y'_{root} \cdot K_0 \\
&= (a \cdot SK_0 + pe_0) \cdot r \cdot s + M + pe' - a \cdot r \cdot s \cdot SK_0 - a \cdot r \cdot t \cdot s \cdot pe'' - p \cdot y_{root} \cdot K_0 - p \cdot y'_{root} \cdot K_0 \\
&= pe_0 \cdot r \cdot s + M + pe' - a \cdot r \cdot t \cdot s \cdot pe'' - p \cdot y_{root} \cdot K_0 - p \cdot y'_{root} \cdot K_0
\end{aligned}
$$

and then $M = M^* \bmod p$.

Similar to most of lattice-based encryption schemes, the encryption algorithm of the proposed CP-ABE scheme involves adding a noise terms into cipher-text. To ensure the correctness of the decryption, the overall noise terms in cipher-text must be small enough compared to the ratio of q to p.

4 Analysis

4.1 Correctness

The correctness of the proposed CP-ABE scheme is described as follows.

$$
\begin{aligned}
M^* &= C_0 - K_0 b \\
&= PK_0 \cdot r \cdot s + M + pe' - K_0 \cdot (a \cdot r \cdot t \cdot s + p \cdot y_{root} + p \cdot y'_{root}) \\
&= PK_0 \cdot r \cdot s + M + pe' - a \cdot r \cdot t \cdot s \cdot (SK_0 \cdot t^{-1} + pe'') - p \cdot y_{root} \cdot K_0 - p \cdot y'_{root} \cdot K_0 \\
&= PK_0 \cdot r \cdot s + M + pe' - a \cdot r \cdot s \cdot SK_0 - a \cdot r \cdot t \cdot s \cdot pe'' - p \cdot y_{root} \cdot K_0 - p \cdot y'_{root} \cdot K_0 \\
&= (a \cdot SK_0 + pe_0) \cdot r \cdot s + M + pe' - a \cdot r \cdot s \cdot SK_0 - a \cdot r \cdot t \cdot s \cdot pe'' - p \cdot y_{root} \cdot K_0 - p \cdot y'_{root} \cdot K_0 \\
&= pe_0 \cdot r \cdot s + M + pe' - a \cdot r \cdot t \cdot s \cdot pe'' - p \cdot y_{root} \cdot K_0 - p \cdot y'_{root} \cdot K_0
\end{aligned}
$$

and then $M = M^* \bmod p$.

4.2 Proof

The Decision R-LWE problem instance is conditioned as sample oracle O, that can be either a noisy pseudo-random O_s, or truly random O'_s. First of all, the simulator asks the challenge oracle O to get $m+1$ sample $(\omega_k, v_k) \in R_q \times R_q$, where $k \in \{0, 1, 2, \ldots, m\}$. The process is as follows:

Init: The adversary submitted the simulator to challenge the access structure T^*.

Setup: The simulator performs initialization algorithm and defines $PK_0 = p\omega_0 \in R_q$. For $i \in U$, if $i \in T^*$ define $PK_i = p\omega_i \in R_q$, else, define $PK_i = SK_i + pe_i \in R_q$. The public parameter $PP = \{PK_0, \{PK_i\}_{i=1}^{n}\}$ is sent to the enemy.

Phase 1: The adversary asks the simulator for the private key, but the property set S cannot satisfy the access tree, that is, $S \notin T^*$. The execution *KeyGen* algorithm calculates the private key, $K_0 = SK_0 \cdot t^{-1} + pe'' \in R_q$, $K_i = SK_i^{-1} \cdot t + pe_i'' \in R_q$, $\forall i \in T^*$.

Challenge: The enemy hands send to the simulator randomly selected plaintext string $M \in \{0, 1\}^n$. The simulator randomly selects $b \in \{0, 1\}$, if $b = 0$, the simulator randomly selects $x_0 \leftarrow R_q$, calculates $C_0 = px_0 \in R_q$ and $C_i = px_i \in R_q$; If $b = 1$, you compute $C_0 = pv_0 + M \in R_q$ and $C_i = pv_i \in R_q$. Then send it to the enemy.

Phase 2: Repeat Phase 1.

Guess: The simulator accepts the enemy's guess b' about b. The simulator is based on b' return to DR-LWE oracle. If $b' = b$, output $O' = O_s$, otherwise output $O' = O_s'$. If O is a pseudo-random predictor O_s with noise, the enemy has an advantage ε, then $\Pr[b' = b | O = O_s] = 1/2 + \varepsilon$ and $\Pr[O' = O | O = O_s] = 1/2 + \varepsilon$. If the prediction machine is a true random predictor, the adversary has no advantage, and $\Pr[b' \neq b | O = O_s'] = 1/2$. Therefore, under the DR - LWE problem, the advantage of the simulator is $\frac{1}{2}\Pr[O' = O | O = O_s] + \frac{1}{2}\Pr[O' = O | O = O_s'] - \frac{1}{2} = \frac{\varepsilon}{2}$.

5 Conclusion

In this paper, we construct the CP-ABE scheme which supports access tree structure by using the R-LWE problem on the ideal lattice, which proves that the security is satisfied by choosing the access structure and choosing plaintext attack. The scheme adopts tree access structure with high flexibility, and the R-LWE problem on the ideal lattice can be used to encrypt the plaintext of a bit, and the system is more efficient. In practical applications, the attribute based encryption system properties will change, this can lead to attribute failure and change, etc., on the next step will be to attribute based encryption mechanism to study the properties of revocation problem.

Acknowledgements. This work is supported by "13th Five-Year" National Crypto Development Fund under Grant (No. MMJJ20170122), the Project of Education Department of Henan Province (No. 18A413001, No. 16A520013), Natural Science Foundation of Henan Polytechnic University (No. T2018-1).

References

1. Sahai, A., Waters, B.: Fuzzy identity-based encryption. In: Cramer, R. (ed.) EUROCRYPT 2005. LNCS, vol. 3494, pp. 457–473. Springer, Heidelberg (2005). https://doi.org/10.1007/11426639_27
2. Goyal, V., Pandey, O., Sahai, A., Waters, B.: Attribute-based encryption for fine-grained access control of encrypted data. In: Proceedings of the 13th ACM Conference on Computer and Communications Security, CCS 2006, pp. 89–98. ACM, New York (2006)
3. Bethencourt, J., Sahai, A., Waters, B.: Ciphertext-policy attribute-based encryption. In: IEEE Symposium on Security and Privacy, pp. 321–334 (2007)
4. Ostrovsky, R., Sahai, A., Waters, B.: Attribute-based encryption with non-monotonic access structures. In: Proceedings of the 14th ACM Conference on Computer and Communications Security, CCS 2007, pp. 195–203. ACM, New York (2007)

5. Waters, B.: Ciphertext-policy attribute-based encryption: an expressive, efficient, and provably secure realization. In: Catalano, D., Fazio, N., Gennaro, R., Nicolosi, A. (eds.) PKC 2011. LNCS, vol. 6571, pp. 53–70. Springer, Heidelberg (2011). https://doi.org/10.1007/978-3-642-19379-8_4
6. Goyal, V., Jain, A., Pandey, O., Sahai, A.: Bounded ciphertext policy attribute based encryption. In: Aceto, L., Damgård, I., Goldberg, L.A., Halldórsson, M.M., Ingólfsdóttir, A., Walukiewicz, I. (eds.) ICALP 2008. LNCS, vol. 5126, pp. 579–591. Springer, Heidelberg (2008). https://doi.org/10.1007/978-3-540-70583-3_47
7. Attrapadung, N., Imai, H.: Dual-policy attribute based encryption. In: Abdalla, M., Pointcheval, D., Fouque, P.-A., Vergnaud, D. (eds.) ACNS 2009. LNCS, vol. 5536, pp. 168–185. Springer, Heidelberg (2009). https://doi.org/10.1007/978-3-642-01957-9_11
8. Yanli, C., Huashan, Y.: CP ABE based searchable encryption with attribute revocation. J. Chongqing Univ. Posts Telecommun. (Nat. Sci. Edn.) **28**(4), 545–554 (2016)
9. Boyen, X.: Attribute-based functional encryption on lattices. In: Sahai, A. (ed.) TCC 2013. LNCS, vol. 7785, pp. 122–142. Springer, Heidelberg (2013). https://doi.org/10.1007/978-3-642-36594-2_8
10. Zhang, J., Zhang, Z., Ge, A.: Ciphertext policy attribute-based encryption from lattices. In: Proceedings of the 7th ACM Symposium on Information, Computer and Communications Security, ASIACCS 2012, pp. 16–17. ACM, New York (2012)
11. Wang, Y.: Lattice ciphertext policy attribute-based encryption in the standard model. Int. J. Netw. Secur. **16**(6), 444–451 (2014)
12. Zhu, W., Yu, J., Wang, T., Xie, W.: Efficient attribute-based encryption from R-LWE. Chin. J. Electron. **23**(4), 778–782 (2014)
13. Tan, S.F., Samsudin, A.: Lattice ciphertext-policy attribute-based encryption from Ring-LWE. In: International Symposium on Technology Management and Emerging Technologies, pp. 258–262. IEEE, Langkawi (2015)
14. Chen, Z., Zhang, P., Zhang, F., Huang, J.: Ciphertext policy attribute-based encryption supporting unbounded attribute space from R-LWE. KSII Trans. Internet Inf. Syst. **11**(4), 2292–2309 (2017)
15. Yan, X., Liu, Y., Li, Z., Huang, Q.: A privacy-preserving multi-authority attribute-based encryption scheme on ideal lattices in the cloud environment. In: Netinfo Security, no. 8, pp. 19–25 (2017)
16. Wang, T., Han, G., Yu, J., Zhang, P., Sun, X.: Efficient chosen-ciphertext secure encryption from R-LWE. Wirel. Pers. Commun. **95**, 1–16 (2017)

Big Data Security Framework Based on Encryption

Shaobing Wu[1,2(✉)] and Changmei Wang[2]

[1] Institute of Information Security, Yunnan Police College, Kunming 650223, China
1063093199@qq.com

[2] Solar Energy Institute, Yunnan Normal University, Kunming 650092, China

Abstract. The biggest challenge for big data era from a security point of view is the protection of user's privacy and data security. Big data analysis is a more complex process, especially if the data is unstructured. We must transfer the unstructured to the structured data if we query the information. Organizations will have to track down what pieces of information in their big data are ddata security and the related technologies for big data security, which includes Key Management for Access Control, Attribute-Based Access Control, Secure Search for Parties Involved, Searchable Encryption and Secure Data Processing.

Keywords: Big data security · Security framework · Encryption

1 Introduction

In big data era, data recorded the behavior of everyone. Banks, government agencies and even everyone around us have tagged us. Banks refuse to lend people with poor credit histories; Frequent job-hopping, the employer will have some concerns when hiring; Those who change their partners will be labeled with their hearts, and will be shunned by those around them. People with poor credit histories, such as high-speed trains and airplanes, are restricted to build a better system of integrity. To make everyone stand in awe of integrity and honor with good faith, we label the data based on different attributes. From the level of protection, there are public data and confidential data.

With the amount of data generated, collected, and analyzed by computing systems growing at an amazing rate, big data processing has become crucial to most enterprise and government applications.

The collected data often contains private information about individuals or corporate secrets that would cause great harm if they fell into the wrong hands. Criminal groups are creating under- ground markets where one can buy and sell stolen personal information [1]. Government intelligence services are targeting personal, corporate, and adversary government systems for espionage and competitive advantage [13].

The biggest challenge for big data era from a security point of view is the protection of user's privacy and data security. Big data frequently contains huge amounts of personal identifiable information (PII) and therefore privacy of users is a huge concern.

X. Sun et al. (Eds.): ICCCS 2018, LNCS 11065, pp. 528–540, 2018.
https://doi.org/10.1007/978-3-030-00012-7_48

In the past, large data sets were stored in highly structured relational databases. If you wanted to look for sensitive data such as the health records of a patient or the information of bank user, you knew exactly where to look and how to access the data. Also, removing any identifiable information was easier in relational databases. Big data makes this a more complex process, especially if the data is unstructured. We must transfer the unstructured to the structured data if we query the information. Organizations will have to track down what pieces of information in their big data are sensitive and they will need to carefully isolate this information to ensure compliance.

2 Literature Overview

In this section, we first review the literature for the following. In 2017, Custers i et al. [4] comparized data protection legislation and policies across the EU. They Pointed out that Significant differences exist in (the levels of) enforcement by the different data protection authorities, due to different legal competencies, available budgets and personnel, policies, and cultural factors in this paper.

Many methods were also proposed by researchers for big data security. In 2018, Singh et al. [2] proposed a cybersecurity framework to identify malicious edge device in fog computing and cloud-of-things environments. In this paper, proposed cybersecurity framework uses three technologies which are Markov model, Intrusion Detection System (IDS) and Virtual Honeypot Device (VHD) to identify malicious edge device in fog computing environment.

In 2012, Tankard et al. [3] introduced big data security. In this paper, they said that the centralized nature of big data stores creates new security challenges to which organizations must respond, which require that controls are placed around the data itself, rather than the applications and systems that store the data.

In 2017, Tankard et al. [4] proposed that encryption as the cornerstone of big data security and this paper expounded that data security is a must for any organization for protecting the business. Encryption should be a key part of any big data environment to ensure that sensitive information is adequately protected.

In 2015, Lafuente [5] discussed about the big data security challenge. Anonymising and encrypting data while also put in place proper access control and monitoring functions and effective policies and considering governance frameworks will have a positive impact for any company looking to take on a big data project.

In 2018, Anisettia et al. [6] proposed privacy-aware big data analytics as a service for public health policies in smart cities. In this paper, we focus on balancing quality of life and privacy protection in smart cities by providing a new Big Data-assisted public policy making process implement proposed approach is based on a Big Data Analytics as a service of privacy-by-design.

3 Big Data Security and Controls

3.1 The Basics of Data Security

We begin this section with an overview of some of the basic goals and tools of big data security. First, we discuss the typical adversary models used to capture the threats to data that need to be addressed. Then, we briefly review common security goals.

Having defined the adversary we want to protect against, we need to describe the big data security goals. The three most fundamental security goals are confidentiality, integrity, and availability, collectively known as the CIA triad.

Confidentiality: Confidentiality is the goal of keeping all sensitive data secret from an adversary. More formally, traditional definitions of confidentiality guarantee that an adversary should learn no information about the sensitive data, other than its length. Confidentiality is critical in big data applications to guarantee that sensitive data is not revealed to the wrong parties.

Integrity: Integrity is the goal that any unauthorized modification of data should be detectable. That is, a malicious adversary should not be able to modify such data without leaving a trace. This is very important to help guarantee the veracity of data collected in big data applications.

Availability: Availability is the goal of always being able to access one's data and computing resources. In particular, an adversary should not be able to disable access to critical data or resources. This is a very important security goal in big data processing, as the sheer volume and velocity of the data make guaranteeing constant access a difficult task. However, in today's big data systems, availability is typically guaranteed via non-cryptographic means such as replication and so on.

By analyzing big data, governments will be better able to understand the various threats that they face, the likely vectors of attack and the actors that might perpetrate them.

3.2 Security Issues for Big Data

One of the key security issues involved with big data aggregation and analysis is that organizations collect and process a great deal of sensitive information regarding customers and employees, as well as intellectual property, trade secrets and financial information.

3.2.1 Store and Process Data

As organizations look to gain value from such information, they are increasingly seeking to aggregate data from a wider range of stores and applications to provide more context in order to increase the value of the data.

Another potential problem relates to regulatory compliance, especially with data protection laws. Such laws are more stringent in some jurisdictions than others, particularly with regard to where data can be stored or processed. Organizations need to carefully consider the legal ramifications of where they store and process data to ensure that they remain in compliance with the regulations that they face.

3.2.2 Classify the Information

There are also security advantages to big data projects. When centralizing data stores, organizations should first classify the information and apply appropriate controls to it, such as imposing retention periods as specified by the regulations that they face. This will allow organizations to weed out data that has little value or that no longer needs to be kept so that it can be disposed of and is no longer available for theft or subject to litigation demanding presentation of records. Another security advantage is that large swathes of data can be mined for security events, such as malware, spear phishing attempts or fraud, such as account takeovers.

However, data classification can be a complex, long and arduous process – a factor that has been a significant struggle for many when attempting to implement technologies that rely on data classification. This is made worse by the fact that the data normally comes from external sources, often making it complicated to confirm its accuracy. What organizations need to do is to identify what information is of value for the business. If they spend too much time capturing all the information available, they risk wasting time and resources processing data that will add little or no value. Organizations also need to take into account industry standards and government regulations to which they must adhere, ensuring that records are retained and archived for the time periods specified and that data is protected according to the guidelines contained in some standards. To ease the classification process, organizations should look for automated database and network discovery tools, which can be used to scan networks to identify all data assets.

Data classification is also key for enabling sensitive data to be identified and therefore better protected. Data classification will help to determine which data is the most sensitive and where it is stored. This is something that should not just be left to the IT department, but should include the involvement of line-of-business personnel since they are likely to best understand the sensitivity of the data with which they work. It should also include compliance officers who are tasked with keeping abreast of new regulatory requirements. This is not a one-off process, but something that should be reviewed regularly.

3.3 Developing an Utility Program

For most enterprise or organizations, the volume of big data generated and stored can be a major challenge, with searching such vast Volume, Velocity, Variety, Value, amounts of data – most of which is unstructured – often taking weeks or more by using traditional tools.

Prior to the start of any big data management project, enterprise or organizations need to locate and identify all of the data sources in their network, from where they originate, who created them and who can access them. This should be an enterprise-wide effort, with input from security and risk managers, as well as legal and policy teams, that involves locating and indexing data. This also needs to be a continuous process so that not just existing data is uncovered, but also new data as it is created throughout the network.

As they go through the data classification process, organizations should also look to develop or update policies regarding data handling, such as defining what types of data must be stored and for how long, where they should be stored and how data will be accessed when they are needed. Enforcement of such policies will prevent users from creating their own data stores that are outside the control of the IT department. Data warehouses are popular technologies for managing large volumes of data. However, most rely on a relational format for storing data, which works fine for structured data. And unstructured data make up a high proportion of data contained in big data stores, as information is increasingly drawn from a wide range of sources beyond traditional enterprise applications.

In order to facilitate processing and analysis of the unstructured data, we developed an utility program for transferring the unstructured data into structured data by python and so the patent for this is applied.

3.4 Big Data Security Controls

In order to provide better control over big data sets, controls should be moved so that they are closer to the data store and the data itself, rather than being placed at the edge of the network, Data management department should be granular enough to ensure that only those authorized to access data can do so, in order to prevent sensitive information from being compromised.

Controls should also be set using the principle of least privilege, especially for those with greater access rights, such as administrators. Therefore companies can decide who can view the data or in the case of an administrator allow them physical access: but should they try to read the data it would be useless because the process would not have allowed decryption. Such an approach is highly effective in any multi-silo environment where any form of electronic data is stored.

To ensure that access controls are effective, they should be continuously monitored and should be modified as employees change role in the organization so that they do not accumulate excessive rights and privileges that could be abused. This can be done using existing technologies in use in many organizations such as database activity monitoring tools, the capabilities of which are being expanded by many vendors to deal with unstructured data in big data environments. Other useful tools include Security Information and Event Management (SIEM) technologies, which gather log information from a wide variety of applications on the network. To make SIEM tools more effective and manageable, many vendors, such as AlienVault, are expanding their solutions to provide capabilities called Network Analysis and Visibility (NAV), which capture and analyze network traffic to look for potential attacks and malicious insider abuse and are highly scalable across large networks. NAV tools provide useful add-ons to SIEM tools, such as metadata analysis, packet capture analysis and flow analysis. In the case of AlienVault, further steps have been taken in order to link the analyzed data and make proactive decisions in preventing or stopping the breach. Ensuring that data is archived as required and disposed of when no longer needed is another important security consideration so that the organization is not managing overly large volumes of data, and so the risk of sensitive data being breached is reduced. This can also be reduced through use of techniques that make sensitive data unreadable, such as encryption, tokenisation and data masking, so that only those with the keys to unlock the data can do so. This is a much easier task once data has been properly classified, but it is important that the legal department be involved in the development of policies related to data retention and disposal to ensure that they are in compliance with the requirements of industry standards and government regulations.

3.4.1 Anonymized Data

Anonymizing data is important to make certain that privacy concerns are addressed. In order to ensure the security of the data, it should be ensured that all sensitive information is removed from the set of records collected.

When producing information for big data, enterprise or organizations have to keep in mind keeping the right balance between utility of the data and privacy. Before the data is stored it should be adequately anonymized, removing any unique identifiers for a user. This in itself can be a security challenge as removing unique identifiers might not be enough to guarantee that the data will remain anonymous. The anonymized data could be could be cross-referenced with other available data following de-anonymization techniques. Therefore, in addition to anonymity, the data should be effectively encrypted.

3.4.2 Encrypt Data

When storing the data, enterprise or organizations will have to encrypt it. Because Encryption, so far, is the main solution to ensuring that data remains protected. At the same time, we must use intrusion detection techniques to identify external threats. "It is important that a threat intelligence system is in place to ensure that more sophisticated attacks are detected and that the organizations can react to known security threats". One of the problems is that a challenge they might face is that data cannot be sent encrypted by the users if the cloud needs to perform operations over the data. Some experts have come up with a solution for this is to use Fully Homomorphic Encryption (FHE), which allows data stored in the cloud to perform operations over the encrypted data so that new encrypted data will be created. When the data is decrypted, the results will be the same as if the operations were carried out over plain text data. Therefore, the cloud will be able to perform operations over encrypted data without knowledge of the underlying plain text data.

3.4.3 Access Control and Monitoring

Adequate access control mechanisms will be key in protecting the data. Access control has traditionally been provided by operating systems or applications restricting access to the information, which typically exposes all the information if the system or application is hacked. A better approach is to protect the information using encryption that only allows decryption if the entity trying to access the information is authorized by an access control policy. Big data solutions tend to rely on traditional Intrusion Detection System (IDS), firewalls or implementations at the application layer to restrict access to the information. Real-time security monitoring is also a key security component for a big data project. It is important that organizations monitor access to big data to ensure that no unauthorized access is being carried out. It is also important that a threat intelligence system is in place to ensure that more sophisticated attacks are detected and that the organizations can react to known security threats – such as malware, vulnerabilities, bugs and so on.

Another significant question is how to establish ownership of information. If the data is stored in the cloud, a trust boundary should be established between the data owners and the data storage owners. It should not be assumed that this is part of a contract, so any agreements must be sure to make this a consideration.

3.4.4 Encryption as the Basis and Premise of Big Data Security

Big data refers to huge data sets that have come about through the phenomenal growth being seen in the volume of information collected, produced, analyzed, shared and stored by organizations. By analyzing big data sets, valuable insights can be gained into how patterns of data are associated to enable better-informed decision-making, which can aid in competitiveness and drive innovation.

Big data sets harness information from multiple sources such as databases, data warehouses, log and event files, security controls such as intrusion prevention systems and user-generated data from sources such as emails and social media posts. The information collected can be in either structured form, such as in the columns of a database, or unstructured, such as information contained in a word-processing document.

3.4.4.1. The Information Stripping

All of this information is fed into a centralized big data management system so that the data can be correlated for analysis. Much of that data will be highly sensitive, including information related to customers, employees and suppliers, financial data, intellectual property and a vast array of other information. Breaches of sensitive information expose organizations to many risks, including theft of intellectual property, loss of revenue or reputational damage. Other risks include financial penalties and other sanctions for non-compliance with regulations demanding that high levels of security be applied to sensitive data. "It is more difficult to find all potentially sensitive information and to understand relationships among data sets. Tracking which users have access to sensitive data can also be difficult". especially where security controls are inconsistent, applied differently in traditional and big data environments and because access must be controlled across so many disparate data sources. For reasons such as these, security is a key consideration when designing big data analysis projects.

3.4.4.2. Secure Data Through Encryption

Encryption and key management should be considered the cornerstone of any data security strategy and big data projects are no exception. Encryption can dramatically lower the risks associated with data compromise. According to ENISA (European Union Agency for Network and Information Security), the following are essential for protecting data in big data environments:

- Encrypt data in transit and at rest, to ensure data confidentiality and integrity.
- Ensure a proper encryption key management solution is deployed, considering the vast amounts of devices that must be covered.
- Consider the timeframe for which data must be kept – data protection regulations might require that you dispose of some data due to its nature after a certain time period.

- Design databases with confidentiality in mind – for example, any confidential data could be contained in separate fields so that they can be easily filtered out and/or encrypted.

All sensitive data should be encrypted, including that in databases, spread-sheets, word documents, presentations and archives. At some point, data may move out of the organization, perhaps communicated among employees and business partners, or placed in the cloud for storage, where it can be accessed via mobile devices. When data is moved out of an organization, it is vital that the encryption keys remain within the organization to prevent anyone inappropriately accessing the keys, which will allow them to decrypt and read the data. If the keys are not protected, employees of the cloud service provider could potentially access data, or it could be subject to demands by government agencies that data be handed over, often without the knowledge of the organization that owns the data. Ensuring that encryption keys are not stored with encrypted data will also help to prevent the data being compromised by hackers.

While encryption will help to protect data from misuse, fraud or loss, it is essential that the ability to perform big data analysis is preserved. IBM has published some best practice guidelines for ensuring this. It recommends that data be masked both to protect the actual information from theft or loss and also so that there is a functional substitute for occasions when the real data is not required, in order to boost privacy. Sensitive data can be masked either at its source or within the big data platform. Unstructured information such as that found in textual, graphical and form-based documents should be redacted to protect it from misuse.

3.4.4.3. Integrated Security Platform

When dealing with big data environments that touch so many parts of the organization, encryption also needs to be pervasive. This requires that it is provided as a platform that offers granular controls, robust encryption and centralized management incorporating all data sources being used for big data analysis. This will help to optimize efficiency and ease security concerns, as all sensitive data sources will be included in the encryption programme, as well as making compliance easier to achieve. It will ensure that policies can be applied in a consistent manner, reducing the administrative effort associated with encryption.

For protecting big data environments, encryption technologies should also be integrated with other security controls, including endpoint security, which is especially required given the amount of access by mobile devices in most organizations. This will also become increasingly important as more IoT devices come into use, providing valuable data sources for big data environments. Integration with other security controls such as intrusion prevention systems and firewalls will help to reduce the possibility of big data breaches or the detection of any threats that have impacted the network.

Once deemed to be valuable primarily for compliance purposes, they have now come into their own for their usefulness in providing actionable intelligence required for improved decision-making and for improving security preparedness and defenses.

3.4.5 Data Protection Legislation and Policies

Big data is a relatively new concept and therefore there is no list of best practices yet that are widely recognized by the security community. We should focus on big data security by internet use, media attention and legislation and regulation.

3.4.5.1. Internet Use

When focusing more specifically on informational privacy and personal data protection, several relevant laws on the use and perception of personal data were selected to provide the general context and setting in this research.

3.4.5.2. Media Attention

Media attention should be paid to privacy and personal data protection. A typical indicator for media attention may also be the so-called Big Brother Awards, which are annual 'awards' for people, companies, or government institutions whose initiatives violate privacy. Obviously, the Big Brother Awards may either be the cause or the result of media attention for privacy and privacy violations.

3.4.5.3. Legislation and Regulations

We should have sectoral legislation that further protects the processing of personal data. Typical sectors include health care, telecommunications, finance, criminal law, and the public sector. and have sectoral legislation in these areas. And even if there is no sectoral legislation, in many cases there are guidelines, codes of conduct, or other forms of soft law regulations on the processing of personal data. Many laws that demand that affected parties and authorities be notified in the event of a breach provide a safe harbor if the data that is stolen has been adequately encrypted so that notification is not necessary. Even where a regulation does not provide this safe harbor, the use of encryption will be considered when the safeguards that an organization has put in place are investigated, potentially reducing the sanctions that could be applied.

4 The Related Technologies for Big Data Security

The key technology of big data security is encryption technology and access control. The difficulty is the distribution and management of key. So we now turn to cryptographic techniques to secure data in storage. The primary goal of these techniques is to enforce access control to data stored in potentially untrusted repositories. That is, we want to give authorized parties access to the data they need while ensuring that unauthorized parties, either outsiders trying to gain access or malicious insiders in the organization managing the repository, cannot access sensitive data. In this section we focus on systems where data is stored in blocks that are stored and retrieved by a unique identifier, such as in a file system. In such systems, we want authorized parties to be able to retrieve data by its identifier, but do not need to enable complex search queries to retrieve subsets of the data.

4.1 Secure Block Storage and Access Control

4.1.1 Key Management for Access Control

Key management includes generating and distributing cryptographic keys to system users in such a way that only authorized parties have the necessary keys to decrypt sensitive data. Most modern systems include some form of key management for controlling access to data in this way and there are many commercially available, standardized solutions for generating and managing keys. These typically use a trusted key management server to manage all keys in the system and to distribute the necessary keys to authorized parties. Here, we mainly discussed cryptographic technique called broadcast encryption or group keying which allows a data owner to encrypt data to a designated set of recipients without having to rely on a trusted key manager. This is particularly important in big data applications where the storage may be handled by an untrusted repository on which a trusted key manager may not be available.

4.1.2 Attribute-Based Access Control

Key management based solutions such as above have an inherent limitation. In order to share data with a set of users, it is necessary to know the identities (and keys) of all the authorized users. This is problematic in large systems or in systems with several organizational structures (as is very common in big data architectures where the data is collected, stored, and used in different environments) as the data owner is unlikely to know the identities of all the authorized users. An alternative approach to access control in such settings is a technique called attribute-based access control (ABAC). In ABAC, data is encrypted together with a policy describing the attributes of users authorized to access the data. The users receive keys for the attributes they possess and are able to access the data if and only if those attributes are authorized. This allows for enforcing access to data without knowing the full set of users with the authorized attributes.

4.2 Secure Search

The previous section dealt with security and access control for block storage where data can only be retrieved via its unique identifier. However, in any big data system, users rarely want to retrieve all available data and instead usually only fetch a subset of the available data based on some specified search criteria. We now switch topics to discuss cryptographic techniques to enable secure search allowing for complex, database-style queries to be performed on stored data.

4.2.1 Parties Involved

The standard model of searchable encryption considers three types of parties: an owner who initially possesses the data, a querier who wants to learn something about the data, and a server who handles the bulk of the storage and processing work. We note that in many scenarios, such as the publish-subscribe and email scenarios above, there may be multiple data owners or queriers.

We note that some scenarios envision only two parties, which we call the querier and server. For instance, the cloud outsourcing scenario above considers a client who acts as both the initial data owner and subsequent querier, and the secure database scenario considers a data owner who does her own server processing.

We can fit these scenarios into our three-party framework by thinking of them as instances of collusion4 between two of the three parties: in the cloud outsourcing scenario, the data owner colludes with the querier, and in the second scenario, the data owner colludes with the server.

4.2.2 Searchable Encryption

In 2000, Song, Wagner, and Perrig published the seminal work on searchable encryption [14]. They presented a cryptographic protocol in a two-party setting (with a querier and server) to search over encrypted data that provided the following four properties:

- Provable security for encryption: The untrusted server stores ciphertext data that has been encrypted using a semantically-secure encryption scheme, so the server cannot learn any information about the corresponding plaintexts.
- Controlled searching: The untrusted server can only perform searches that have been authorized by the querier. The server cannot make searches on her own.
- Hidden queries: Song et al. support keyword searches. During a query, the server does not learn the keyword. (This concept is later formalized by Goh [77] as "chosen keyword security" and defined in a similar style to semantic security.)
- Query isolation: While the server does learn which records are returned to the querier, the server learns nothing more about plaintexts than this information.

Additionally, the Song et al. protocol provides good performance by adhering to a few simple guidelines that subsequent works also follow:

The search protocols are simple and reminiscent of their insecure counterparts.

The scheme relies on faster symmetric-key cryptography rather than slower public-key cryptography. Song et al., in fact, use symmetric-key cryptography exclusively: schemes that follow their lead are collectively referred to as searchable symmetric encryption, or SSE. While some of the subsequent works described below do utilize public-key cryptography to provide additional functionality, they often use public-key cryptography as sparingly as possible.

Like most unprotected database search technologies, Song et al. bolster the performance of queries by pre-computing an index mapping keywords to records that match the query. While the bulk of Song et al.'s work is on non-indexed search, this observation foreshadows many of the subsequent works on SSE.

4.3 Secure Data Processing

In the previous section, we discussed performing secure searching on encrypted data. However, in many big-data applications it is not enough to be able to simply retrieve stored data. Instead, it is desirable to perform analytic computations over the data and return only the result of these computations rather than the original data. We stress that it is very important that the data and the computations be protected even while the processing is being performed. In this section, we describe four cryptographic techniques that enable generic secure computation: homomorphic encryption (HE), verifiable computation (VC), secure multi-party computation (MPC), and functional encryption (FE).

All of these can be used to securely outsource the processing of data but in different scenarios. Homomorphic encryption allows computing on encrypted data while maintaining confidentiality; it can be used to outsource processing of sensitive data to another entity that is trusted to perform the computation correctly but should not learn the data. Verifiable computation allows computing on data and allowing the integrity of the computation to be checked; it can be used to outsource processing of data to another entity that is allowed to learn the data but not trusted to perform the computation correctly. It is possible to combine homomorphic encryption and verifiable computation to achieve both confidentiality of the input and output and integrity of the computation. Secure multiparty computation allows performing a distributed computation on sensitive inputs held by multiple parties while maintaining confidentiality of each party's inputs from every other party and ensuring that the computation was performed correctly.

5 Conclusions

The main challenge introduced by big data is how to identify sensitive pieces of information that are stored within the unstructured data set. Organizations must make sure that they isolate sensitive information and they should be able to prove that they have adequate processes in place to achieve it. Organizations should run a risk assessment over the data they are collecting. They should consider whether they are collecting any customer information that should be kept private and establish adequate policies that protect the data and the right to privacy of their clients.

If the data is shared with other organizations, then it should be considered how this is done. Deliberately released data that turns out to infringe on privacy can have a huge impact on an organization from a reputational and economic point of view. Anyone using third-party cloud providers to store or process data will need to ensure that the providers are complying with regulations. Organizations should also carefully consider regional laws around handling customer data.

Organizations using big data will need to introduce adequate processes that help them effectively manage and protect the data. The traditional information life cycle management can be applied to big data to ensure that the data is not being stored once it is no longer needed. In addition, policies related to availability and recovery times will still apply to big data. However, organizations have to consider the volume, velocity and complexity of big data and amend their information life cycle management and policies accordingly.

Big data can often at first be viewed as a security nightmare. This needn't be the case. Security must always be thought of as a process and not a product. While there are plenty of 'big data solutions' on the market, it's vital for companies not to forget the process aspect. By all means, products can help manage all of the vast information that will be collected by the organization. But by also thinking about the steps outlined above along the big data journey, companies will be much better placed to handle the data in a way that balances the usefulness of it with the all important aspect of customer privacy.

While encryption should be the cornerstone of data security for any organization, it is not sufficient in isolation. Rather, it should be tightly integrated with other security controls, including endpoint security, network security, application security and physical security systems, which are increasingly being run over IP-based networks.

We believe that, as security becomes a critical requirement for sensitive big data processing, these techniques will become an integral part of the big data ecosystem. We hope that the exposition in this chapter will raise awareness of the latest types of tools and protections available for securing big data. We believe better understanding and closer collaboration between the data science and cryptography communities will be critical to enabling the future of big data processing.

Acknowledgements. This thesis is supported by the national social science foundation and supported by Yunnan Normal University postgraduate research Fund (Project number: 2017067).

References

1. Sohal, A.S., Sandhu, R., Sood, S.K., Chang, V.: A Cybersecurity framework to identify malicious edge device in fog computing and cloud-of-things environments. Comput. Secur. **74**, 340–351 (2018)
2. Tankard, C.: Digital Pathways. Big-data-security. Network-Security (2012)
3. The 2011 IDC digital universe. IDC (2011). www.emc.com/collateral/about/news/idc-emc-digital-universe-2011-infographic.pdf. Accessed 1 June 2012
4. Big data: the next frontier for innovation, competition and productivity. McKinsey Global Institute (2011). www.mckinsey.com/Insights/MGI/Research/Technology/Innovation/Big-data-The-next-frontier-for-innovation. Accessed 11 June 2012
5. Softserve Big Data Analytics Report. Softserve (2016). www.softserveinc.com/en-us-newsroom/knowledge-centre/softserve-big-data-analytics-report/. Accessed 11 May 2017
6. 2016 Global Encryption Trends Study. Thales e-Security/Ponemon Institute. www.thales-esecurity.com/knowl-edge-base/analyst-report-s/global-encryption-trends-study. Accessed 13 May 2017
7. Big data and infosecurity. Varonis (2012). http://blog.varonis.com/big-datasecurity/. Accessed 11 June 2012
8. Big data gap. MeriTalk (2012). www.meritalk.com/big-data-gap. Accessed 13 June 2013
9. Kajeepeta, S.: Strategy: Hadoop and big data. InformationWeek (2012). http://reports.informationweek.com/abstract/81/8670/Business-Intelligence-Information-Management/strategy-Hadoop-big-data.html. Accessed 13 Apr 2014
10. Tankard, C.: Digital Pathways. Encryption as the cornerstone of big data security. Netw. Secur. (2017)
11. Lafuente, G.: The big data security challenge. Netw. Secur. **2015**, 12–14 (2015)
12. Anisettia, M., Ardagnaa, C., Bellandia, V., et al.: Privacy-aware big data analytics as a service for public health policies in smart cities. Sustain. Cities Soc. **39**, 68–77 (2018)
13. Custers, B., Dechesne, F., Sears, A.M., Tani, T., van der Hof, S.: A comparison of data protection legislation and policies across the EU. Comput. Law Secur. Rev. Int. J. Technol. Law Pract. (2017). https://doi.org/10.1016/j.clsr.2017.09.001
14. Mandiant, February 2013. http://intelreport.mandiant.com/Mandiant-APT1-Report.pdf
15. Song, D.X., Wagner, D., Perrig, A.: Practical techniques for searches on encrypted data. In: 2000 IEEE Symposium on Security and Privacy, Berkeley, California, USA, 14–17 May 2000, pp. 44–55. IEEE Computer Society (2000)

Controlled Bidirectional Remote Preparation of Single- and Two-Qubit State

Yi-Ru Sun[1], Gang Xu[1(✉)], Xiu-Bo Chen[1,2(✉)], and Yi-Xian Yang[1,2]

[1] Information Security Center, State Key Laboratory of Networking and Switching Technology, Beijing University of Posts and Telecommunications, Beijing 100876, China
gangxu_bupt@163.com, flyover100@163.com

[2] Guizhou Provincial Key Laboratory of Public Big Data, Guizhou University, Guiyang 550025, Guizhou, China

Abstract. We propose two novel schemes for controlled bidirectional remote state preparation of single- and two-qubit state by using five- and nine-qubit entangled state as the quantum channel. First, our schemes are considered in two cases that the coefficients of prepared state are real and complex, respectively. Second, by virtue of appropriate measurement and the corresponding local unitary operations, we explicitly give how to accomplish these preparation tasks. Third, taking the first scheme as an example, we discuss our scheme in four kinds of noisy environments (bit-flip, phase-flip, amplitude-damping and depolarizing noisy environment). We calculate fidelity and find that it depends on the prepared state coefficients and decoherence rate. Eventually, some discussions are given.

Keywords: Controlled bidirectional remote preparation
Noisy environment · Fidelity

1 Introduction

Quantum teleportation, is a supernatural quantum information processing protocol presented by Bennett et al. [1] to achieve the teleportation of an unknown quantum state from one place to another by using a quantum channel and some classical communication. Later, Lo [2], Pati [3] and Bennett et al. [4] proposed a novel quantum communication scheme, which is called remote state preparation (RSP). It uses classical communication and a beforehand shared quantum channel to remotely prepare a known state. With the purpose of improving the security of RSP, the controlled remote state preparation (CRSP) schemes are introduced [5,6]. In CRSP, the information of the state could be transmitted only when the sender and the receiver cooperate with the controller.

Nevertheless, these schemes are all unidirectional RSP. Until 2014, Cao and Nguyen [8] devised a controlled bidirectional RSP (CBRSP)scheme. Two far-off parties can simultaneously exchange their single-qubit state. Then, three CBRSP

X. Sun et al. (Eds.): ICCCS 2018, LNCS 11065, pp. 541–553, 2018.
https://doi.org/10.1007/978-3-030-00012-7_49

schemes (probabilistic, deterministic and joint)were proposed by Sharma et al. [9]. They also gave a general way of analyzing the effects of two noise processes (amplitude-damping and phase-damping noise) on scheme. Peng et al. [10] presented a scheme for five-party controlled bidirectional joint RSP (CBJRSP) via an eight-qubit cluster state as quantum channel. In 2016, two CBJRSP schemes are presented by Zhang et al. [11], in which non-maximally and maximally six-qubit entangled state was used as the quantum channel, respectively. In practice, quantum noise seriously affect the security and reliability of the quantum communication, which is an unavoidable factor. So there are some schemes [9,13] discussed in the noisy environment.

In summary, these schemes all can accomplish the BRSP tasks by using various quantum channels, but all only prepare single-qubit state. Li [13] proposed a scheme to implement bidirectional quantum controlled teleportation, where Alice and Bob transmit a two-qubit state to each other. Inspired by Ref. [13], we present two schemes for CBRSP of single- and two-qubit state. Firstly, we consider our schemes in two cases that the coefficients of prepared state are real and complex, respectively. Secondly, the detailed measurement process and the corresponding local unitary operations are given. Thirdly, taking the first scheme as an example, we discuss our scheme in four kinds of noisy environment (bit-flip, phase-flip (phase-damping), amplitude-damping and depolarizing noisy environment) and calculate the fidelity of the output state. Finally, some discussions are given.

The article structure is as follows. In Sect. 2, we give the CBRSP scheme of single-qubit state. The proposed scheme is generalized to CBRSP of two-qubit state in Sect. 3. In Sect. 4, we discuss our first scheme in the noisy environment. Some discussions and conclusions are given in Sect. 5.

2 The CBRSP Scheme of Single-Qubit State

In this section, we propose a CBRSP scheme. There are three participants, Alice, Bob and the controller Charlie. We consider two cases where all the coefficients are real and complex, respectively.

The previous CBRSP schemes used various quantum channels, such as five-qubit cluster state [8], six-qubit non-maximally [12] and maximally entangled state [11] or eight-qubit entangled state [10], to accomplish the BRSP of single-qubit state. We use the construction method in Ref. [13] to construct five- and nine-qubit entangled state as quantum channel which can be used to CBRSP single- and two-qubit state. The quantum channels are in this form

$$|\varphi\rangle_{12345} = \frac{1}{\sqrt{2}}(|0\rangle_1|\Phi^+\rangle_{23}|\Phi^+\rangle_{45} + |1\rangle_1|\Psi^-\rangle_{23}|\Psi^-\rangle_{45}), \tag{1}$$

$$|\varphi\rangle_{123456789} = \frac{1}{\sqrt{2}}(|0\rangle_1|\Phi^+\rangle_{23}|\Phi^+\rangle_{45}|\Phi^+\rangle_{67}|\Phi^+\rangle_{89} + |1\rangle_1|\Psi^-\rangle_{23}|\Psi^-\rangle_{45}|\Psi^-\rangle_{67}|\Psi^-\rangle_{89}), \tag{2}$$

where $|\Phi^+\rangle = \frac{(|00\rangle+|11\rangle)}{\sqrt{2}}$ and $|\Psi^-\rangle = \frac{(|01\rangle-|10\rangle)}{\sqrt{2}}$.

In our scheme, Charlie constructs the quantum channel $|\varphi\rangle_{12345}, |\varphi\rangle_{123456789}$. Then, he sends the qubits 3, 5 (2, 4) to Alice (Bob) and holds qubit 1 in his hands. To insure that qubits of quantum channel are securely transmitted to Alice and Bob, participants should check eavesdropping by using the decoy qubits. The check process is the same as in Ref. [7]. Then we will introduce our CBRSP scheme of single-qubit state in detail.

Firstly, Alice, Bob and Charlie share the five-qubit entangled state as the quantum channel by Eq. (1), where qubit 3, 5 belong to Alice, qubit 2, 4 belong to Bob and qubit 1 owned by Charlie. With the control of Charlie, Alice (Bob) wants to prepare state $|\varphi\rangle_a = a_0|0\rangle + a_1|1\rangle$ ($|\varphi\rangle_b = b_0|0\rangle + b_1|1\rangle$) for Bob (Alice). Where $\sum_{i=0}^{1} |a|_i^2 = 1, \sum_{j=0}^{1} |b|_j^2 = 1$.

Secondly, Alice and Bob implement the single-qubit state measurements on their own qubit 5 and 2 simultaneously. Alice's (Bob's) single-qubit measurement bases are $\{|A_1\rangle, |A_2\rangle\}_5$ ($\{|B_1\rangle, |B_2\rangle\}_2$). Where

$$\begin{pmatrix} |A_1\rangle \\ |A_2\rangle \end{pmatrix}_5 = \begin{pmatrix} a_0 & a_1 \\ -a_1 & a_0 \end{pmatrix} \begin{pmatrix} |0\rangle \\ |1\rangle \end{pmatrix}_5, \begin{pmatrix} |B_1\rangle \\ |B_2\rangle \end{pmatrix}_2 = \begin{pmatrix} b_0 & b_1 \\ -b_1 & b_0 \end{pmatrix} \begin{pmatrix} |0\rangle \\ |1\rangle \end{pmatrix}_2. \quad (3)$$

After Alice's and Bob's measurements, we rewrite the Eq. (1):

$$\begin{aligned} |\varphi'\rangle_{12345} = \tfrac{1}{2\sqrt{2}}\{&|0\rangle_1 \otimes [|B_1\rangle_2(b_0|0\rangle + b_1|1\rangle)_3 + |B_2\rangle_2(-b_1|0\rangle + b_0|1\rangle)_3] \otimes [|A_1\rangle_5 \\ &(a_0|0\rangle + a_1|1\rangle)_4 + |A_2\rangle_5(-a_1|0\rangle + a_0|1\rangle)_4] + |1\rangle_1 \otimes [|B_1\rangle_2(b_0|1\rangle + b_1|0\rangle)_3 + |B_2\rangle_2 \\ &(-b_1|1\rangle - b_0|0\rangle)_3] \otimes [|A_1\rangle_5(-a_0|1\rangle + a_1|0\rangle)_4 + |A_2\rangle_5(a_1|1\rangle + a_0|0\rangle)_4]\}. \end{aligned} \quad (4)$$

Thirdly, Alice and Bob send their measurement results $|A_i\rangle_5|B_j\rangle_2, 1 \le i \le 2$ *and* $1 \le j \le 2$. to others through the classical channel. If Charlie permits, he will achieve single-qubit measurement in the basis $\{|0\rangle, |1\rangle\}$ on qubit 1 and tell his measurement results to Alice and Bob.

Finally, in order to facilitate the understanding of our scheme, we assume Alice's and Bob's measurement results are $|A_1\rangle|B_1\rangle$. If Charlie's result is $|0\rangle_1$, then Alice and Bob obtain the prepared state by applying the corresponding local unitary operators $I_3 \otimes I_4$ respectively. If Charlie's result is $|1\rangle_1$, then Alice and Bob apply the corresponding local unitary operators $X_3 \otimes -iY_4$. The whole corresponding unitary operations for Alice and Bob are shown in Table 1. Eventually, the success probability of our CBRSP scheme is 100%.

When the coefficients of the prepared state are complex, Alice's (Bob's) single-qubit projective measurement bases are $\{|A_1'\rangle, |A_2'\rangle\}_5$ ($\{|B_1'\rangle, |B_2'\rangle\}_2$). Where

$$\begin{pmatrix} |A_1'\rangle \\ |A_2'\rangle \end{pmatrix}_5 = \begin{pmatrix} a_0^* & a_1^* \\ -a_1 & a_0 \end{pmatrix} \begin{pmatrix} |0\rangle \\ |1\rangle \end{pmatrix}_5, \begin{pmatrix} |B_1'\rangle \\ |B_2'\rangle \end{pmatrix}_2 = \begin{pmatrix} b_0^* & b_1^* \\ -b_1 & b_0 \end{pmatrix} \begin{pmatrix} |0\rangle \\ |1\rangle \end{pmatrix}_2. \quad (5)$$

For satisfying the orthogonality, the coefficients should be restricted by $a_0^* a_1 = a_1^* a_0$ and $b_0^* b_1 = b_1^* b_0$. After Alice's and Bob's measurements, Eq. (1) becomes as:

$$|\varphi'\rangle_{12345} = \frac{1}{2\sqrt{2}}\{|0\rangle_1 \otimes [|B_1'\rangle_2(b_0|0\rangle + b_1|1\rangle)_3 + |B_2'\rangle_2(-b_1^*|0\rangle + b_0^*|1\rangle)_3] \otimes [|A_1'\rangle_5 (a_0|0\rangle + a_1|1\rangle)_4 + |A_2'\rangle_5(-a_1^*|0\rangle + a_0^*|1\rangle)_4] + |1\rangle_1 \otimes [|B_1'\rangle_2(b_0|1\rangle + b_1|0\rangle)_3 + |B_2'\rangle_2 (-b_1^*|1\rangle - b_0^*|0\rangle)_3] \otimes [|A_1'\rangle_5(-a_0|1\rangle + a_1|0\rangle)_4 + |A_2'\rangle_5(a_1^*|1\rangle + a_0^*|0\rangle)_4]\}. \tag{6}$$

Alice and Bob send their results $|A_i'\rangle_5|B_j'\rangle_2, 1 \leq i \leq 2$ *and* $1 \leq j \leq 2$ to others. If Charlie permits, he achieves single-qubit measurement in the basis $\{|0\rangle, |1\rangle\}$ on qubit 1 and tells his results to Alice and Bob. Alice and Bob can obtain the prepared state only when the results are $|A_1'\rangle_5|B_1'\rangle_2$. When Charlie's measurement result is $|0\rangle_1$, the corresponding local unitary operators of Alice and Bob are $I_3 \otimes I_4$ respectively. If Charlie's result is $|1\rangle_1$, the corresponding local unitary operators of Alice and Bob are $iY_3 \otimes -iY_4$ respectively. When the coefficients of the prepared state are complex, the success probability is 25%.

Table 1. The recovery operations for Alice and Bob

Alice's and Bob's result	Charlie's result	Unitary transformation
$\|A_1\rangle_5\|B_1\rangle_2$	$\|0\rangle_1$	$I_3 \otimes I_4$
$\|A_1\rangle_5\|B_2\rangle_2$	$\|0\rangle_1$	$iY_3 \otimes I_4$
$\|A_2\rangle_5\|B_1\rangle_2$	$\|0\rangle_1$	$I_3 \otimes iY_4$
$\|A_2\rangle_5\|B_2\rangle_2$	$\|0\rangle_1$	$iY_3 \otimes iY_4$
$\|A_1\rangle_5\|B_1\rangle_2$	$\|1\rangle_1$	$X_3 \otimes -iY_4$
$\|A_1\rangle_5\|B_2\rangle_2$	$\|1\rangle_1$	$I_3 \otimes -iY_4$
$\|A_2\rangle_5\|B_1\rangle_2$	$\|1\rangle_1$	$X_3 \otimes I_4$
$\|A_2\rangle_5\|B_2\rangle_2$	$\|1\rangle_1$	$I_3 \otimes I_4$

In summary, we can accomplish our schemes by four steps. Alice and Bob cooperate with Charlie to share five-qubit entangled state as quantum channel. Then, Alice and Bob make single-qubit state measurement on their own qubit and send results to other people via classical channel. After that, Charlie makes single-qubit measurement on his qubit and sends results to Alice and Bob. Finally, Alice and Bob can successfully prepare an arbitrary single-qubit state to each other by using the corresponding local unitary operations.

3 The CBRSP Scheme of Two-Qubit State

In this section, we will present another CBRSP scheme of arbitrary two-qubit state by using the nine-qubit entangled state as quantum channel. There are three participants, Alice and Bob are not only the sender but also the receiver. With the control of Charlie, Alice and Bob can transmit arbitrary two-qubit state to each other simultaneously. The details of scheme are described as below:

First, the quantum channel can be expressed by Eq. (2), where qubit 3, 5, 7, 9 belong to Alice, qubit 2, 4, 6, 8 belong to Bob and qubit 1 owned by Charlie. Alice, Bob and Charlie share this nine-qubit entangled state as the quantum channel. Alice wants to prepare $|\varphi\rangle_{ab} = a_{00}|00\rangle + a_{01}|01\rangle + a_{10}|10\rangle + a_{11}|11\rangle$ for Bob and Bob wants to prepare $|\varphi\rangle_{cd} = b_{00}|00\rangle + b_{01}|01\rangle + b_{10}|10\rangle + b_{11}|11\rangle$ for Alice, where $\sum_{i,j=0}^{1} |a_{ij}|^2 = 1, \sum_{i,j=0}^{1} |b_{ij}|^2 = 1$.

Second, when the coefficients of the prepared state are real, Alice and Bob implement two-qubit state measurements on their own qubit pairs (7, 9) and (2, 4) simultaneously. Alice's and Bob's two-qubit projective measurement bases are $\{|H_1\rangle, |H_2\rangle, |H_3\rangle, |H_4\rangle\}$ and $\{|K_1\rangle, |K_2\rangle, |K_3\rangle, |K_4\rangle\}$, respectively. Where

$$\begin{pmatrix}|H_1\rangle\\|H_2\rangle\\|H_3\rangle\\|H_4\rangle\end{pmatrix}_{79} = \begin{pmatrix}a_{00} & a_{01} & a_{10} & a_{11}\\ a_{01} & -a_{00} & -a_{11} & a_{10}\\ a_{10} & a_{11} & -a_{00} & -a_{01}\\ a_{11} & -a_{10} & a_{01} & -a_{00}\end{pmatrix}\begin{pmatrix}|00\rangle\\|01\rangle\\|10\rangle\\|11\rangle\end{pmatrix}_{79}, \begin{pmatrix}|K_1\rangle\\|K_2\rangle\\|K_3\rangle\\|K_4\rangle\end{pmatrix}_{24} = \begin{pmatrix}b_{00} & b_{01} & b_{10} & b_{11}\\ b_{01} & -b_{00} & -b_{11} & b_{10}\\ b_{10} & b_{11} & -b_{00} & -b_{01}\\ b_{11} & -b_{10} & b_{01} & -b_{00}\end{pmatrix}\begin{pmatrix}|00\rangle\\|01\rangle\\|10\rangle\\|11\rangle\end{pmatrix}_{24}. \quad (7)$$

After Alice's and Bob's measurements, we rewrite the Eq. (2):

$$\begin{aligned}
|\varphi'\rangle_{123456789} &= \tfrac{1}{\sqrt{2}}\{|0\rangle_1 \otimes \tfrac{1}{2}[|K_1\rangle_{24}(b_{00}|00\rangle + b_{01}|01\rangle + b_{10}|10\rangle + b_{11}|11\rangle)_{35}\\
&+|K_2\rangle_{24}(b_{01}|00\rangle - b_{00}|01\rangle + b_{11}|10\rangle - b_{10}|11\rangle)_{35} + |K_3\rangle_{24}(b_{10}|00\rangle - b_{11}|01\rangle\\
&-b_{00}|10\rangle + b_{01}|11\rangle)_{35} + |K_4\rangle_{24}(b_{11}|00\rangle + b_{10}|01\rangle - b_{01}|10\rangle - b_{00}|11\rangle)_{35}]\\
&\otimes\tfrac{1}{2}[|H_1\rangle_{79}(a_{00}|00\rangle + a_{01}|01\rangle + a_{10}|10\rangle + a_{11}|11\rangle)_{68} + |H_2\rangle_{79}(a_{01}|00\rangle - a_{00}|01\rangle\\
&+a_{11}|10\rangle - a_{10}|11\rangle)_{68} + |H_3\rangle_{79}(a_{10}|00\rangle - a_{11}|01\rangle - a_{00}|10\rangle + a_{01}|11\rangle)_{68}\\
&+|H_4\rangle_{79}(a_{11}|00\rangle + a_{10}|01\rangle - a_{01}|10\rangle - a_{00}|11\rangle)_{68}] + |1\rangle_1 \otimes \tfrac{1}{2}[|K_1\rangle_{24}(b_{00}|11\rangle\\
&-b_{01}|10\rangle - b_{10}|01\rangle + b_{11}|00\rangle)_{35} + |K_2\rangle_{24}(b_{01}|11\rangle + b_{00}|10\rangle - b_{11}|01\rangle - b_{10}|00\rangle)_{35}\\
&+|K_3\rangle_{24}(b_{10}|11\rangle + b_{11}|10\rangle + b_{00}|01\rangle + b_{01}|00\rangle)_{35} + |K_4\rangle_{24}(b_{11}|11\rangle - b_{10}|10\rangle\\
&+b_{01}|01\rangle - b_{00}|00\rangle)_{35}] \otimes \tfrac{1}{2}[|H_1\rangle_{79}(a_{00}|11\rangle - a_{01}|10\rangle - a_{10}|01\rangle + a_{11}|00\rangle)_{68}\\
&+|H_2\rangle_{79}(a_{01}|11\rangle + a_{00}|10\rangle - a_{11}|01\rangle - a_{10}|00\rangle)_{68} + |H_3\rangle_{79}(a_{10}|11\rangle + a_{11}|10\rangle\\
&+a_{00}|01\rangle + a_{01}|00\rangle)_{68} + |H_4\rangle_{79}(a_{11}|11\rangle - a_{10}|10\rangle + a_{01}|01\rangle - a_{00}|00\rangle)_{68}]\}.
\end{aligned} \quad (8)$$

Third, Alice and Bob send their measurement results $|H_i\rangle_{79}|K_j\rangle_{24}, 1 \le i \le 4$ *and* $1 \le j \le 4$ to others through the classical channel. If Charlie permits, Charlie achieves the single-qubit measurement in the basis $\{|0\rangle, |1\rangle\}$ on qubit 1 and tells his measurement results to Alice and Bob.

Finally, we assume Alice's and Bob's measurement results are $|H_1\rangle|K_1\rangle$, Charlie's result is $|0\rangle_1$, Alice and Bob can obtain the state $|\varphi\rangle_{cd}, |\varphi\rangle_{ab}$ by applying the unitary operators $I_3 \otimes I_5, I_6 \otimes I_8$ respectively. If Charlie's result is $|1\rangle_1$, Alice and Bob can apply the unitary operators $iY_3 \otimes iY_5, iY_6 \otimes iY_8$. By the analogical process, the other measurement results are all similar. The whole corresponding unitary operations for Alice and Bob are given in "Appendix". The success probability of our scheme is 100%.

When the coefficients of the prepared state are complex, Alice's and Bob's two-qubit projective measurement bases respectively are

$$\begin{pmatrix}|P_1\rangle\\|P_2\rangle\\|P_3\rangle\\|P_4\rangle\end{pmatrix}_{79}=\begin{pmatrix}a_{00}^* & a_{01}^* & a_{10}^* & a_{11}^*\\ a_{01}^* & -a_{00}^* & -a_{11}^* & a_{10}^*\\ a_{10} & a_{11} & -a_{00} & -a_{01}\\ a_{11} & -a_{10} & a_{01} & -a_{00}\end{pmatrix}\begin{pmatrix}|00\rangle\\|01\rangle\\|10\rangle\\|11\rangle\end{pmatrix}_{79},\begin{pmatrix}|Q_1\rangle\\|Q_2\rangle\\|Q_3\rangle\\|Q_4\rangle\end{pmatrix}_{24}=\begin{pmatrix}b_{00}^* & b_{01}^* & b_{10}^* & b_{11}^*\\ b_{01}^* & -b_{00}^* & -b_{11}^* & b_{10}^*\\ b_{10} & b_{11} & -b_{00} & -b_{01}\\ b_{11} & -b_{10} & b_{01} & -b_{00}\end{pmatrix}\begin{pmatrix}|00\rangle\\|01\rangle\\|10\rangle\\|11\rangle\end{pmatrix}_{24}. \tag{9}$$

The coefficients should be restricted as below in order to satisfy the orthogonality. $a_{00}^*a_{01}=a_{00}a_{01}^*, a_{10}^*a_{11}=a_{10}a_{11}^*$ and $b_{00}^*b_{01}=b_{00}b_{01}^*, b_{10}^*b_{11}=b_{10}b_{11}^*$. After Alice's and Bob's measurements, we will get

$$\begin{aligned}
|\varphi'\rangle_{123456789} &= \tfrac{1}{\sqrt{2}}\{|0\rangle_1\otimes\tfrac{1}{2}[|Q_1\rangle_{24}(b_{00}|00\rangle+b_{01}|01\rangle+b_{10}|10\rangle+b_{11}|11\rangle)_{35}\\
&+|Q_2\rangle_{24}(b_{01}|00\rangle-b_{00}|01\rangle+b_{11}|10\rangle-b_{10}|11\rangle)_{35}+|Q_3\rangle_{24}(b_{10}^*|00\rangle-b_{11}^*|01\rangle\\
&-b_{00}^*|10\rangle+b_{01}^*|11\rangle)_{35}+|Q_4\rangle_{24}(b_{11}^*|00\rangle+b_{10}^*|01\rangle-b_{01}^*|10\rangle-b_{00}^*|11\rangle)_{35}]\\
&\otimes\tfrac{1}{2}[|P_1\rangle_{79}(a_{00}|00\rangle+a_{01}|01\rangle+a_{10}|10\rangle+a_{11}|11\rangle)_{68}+|P_2\rangle_{79}(a_{01}|00\rangle-a_{00}|01\rangle\\
&+a_{11}|10\rangle-a_{10}|11\rangle)_{68}+|P_3\rangle_{79}(a_{10}^*|00\rangle-a_{11}^*|01\rangle-a_{00}^*|10\rangle+a_{01}^*|11\rangle)_{68}\\
&+|P_4\rangle_{79}(a_{11}^*|00\rangle+a_{10}^*|01\rangle-a_{01}^*|10\rangle-a_{00}^*|11\rangle)_{68}]+|1\rangle_1\otimes\tfrac{1}{2}[|Q_1\rangle_{24}(b_{00}|11\rangle\\
&-b_{01}|10\rangle-b_{10}|01\rangle+b_{11}|00\rangle)_{35}+|Q_2\rangle_{24}(b_{01}|11\rangle+b_{00}|10\rangle-b_{11}|01\rangle-b_{10}|00\rangle)_{35}\\
&+|Q_3\rangle_{24}(b_{10}^*|11\rangle+b_{11}^*|10\rangle+b_{00}^*|01\rangle+b_{01}^*|00\rangle)_{35}+|Q_4\rangle_{24}(b_{11}^*|11\rangle-b_{10}^*|10\rangle\\
&+b_{01}^*|01\rangle-b_{00}^*|00\rangle)_{35}]\otimes\tfrac{1}{2}[|P_1\rangle_{79}(a_{00}|11\rangle-a_{01}|10\rangle-a_{10}|01\rangle+a_{11}|00\rangle)_{35}\\
&+|P_2\rangle_{79}(a_{01}|11\rangle+a_{00}|10\rangle-a_{11}|01\rangle-a_{10}|00\rangle)_{35}+|P_3\rangle_{79}(a_{10}^*|11\rangle+a_{11}^*|10\rangle\\
&+a_{00}^*|01\rangle+a_{01}^*|00\rangle)_{35}+|P_4\rangle_{79}(a_{11}^*|11\rangle-a_{10}^*|10\rangle+a_{01}^*|01\rangle-a_{00}^*|00\rangle)_{35}]\}.
\end{aligned} \tag{10}$$

Their measurements results will be $|P_i\rangle_{79}|Q_j\rangle_{24}, 1\le i\le 4$ *and* $1\le j\le 4$. Alice and Bob send their result to others through the classical channel. If Charlie permits, Charlie achieves the single-qubit measurement in the basis $\{|0\rangle,|1\rangle\}$ on qubit 1 and tells his measurement results to Alice and Bob.

When the results are $|P_i\rangle_{79}|Q_j\rangle_{24}, 1\le i\le 2$ *and* $1\le j\le 2$, Alice and Bob can obtain the initial state. We assume Alice's and Bob's measurement results are $|P_1\rangle|Q_1\rangle$, Charlie's result is $|0\rangle_1$. Alice and Bob can obtain the prepared state by applying the unitary operators $I_3\otimes I_5, I_6\otimes I_8$ respectively. If Charlie's result is $|1\rangle_1$, Alice and Bob can apply the unitary operators $iY_3\otimes iY_5, iY_6\otimes iY_8$ respectively. The success probability of our scheme is 25%. The detailed recovery operations are shown in Table 2.

We accomplish our CBRSP task by four steps. Alice and Bob cooperate with Charlie to share nine-qubit entangled state as quantum channel. After that, Alice and Bob make two-qubit state measurement on their own qubits and send results to others. Then Charlie makes single-qubit measurement on his qubit and sends the result to Alice and Bob via classical channel. At last, Alice and Bob can successfully prepare arbitrary two-qubit state to each other by utilizing corresponding local unitary operations.

Table 2. The recovery operations of Alice and Bob

Alice's and Bob's result	Charlie's result	Unitary transformation
$\|P_1\rangle_{79}\|Q_1\rangle_{24}$	$\|0\rangle_1$	$I_3 \otimes I_5 \otimes I_6 \otimes I_8$
$\|P_1\rangle_{79}\|Q_2\rangle_{24}$	$\|0\rangle_1$	$I_3 \otimes I_5 \otimes I_6 \otimes -iY_8$
$\|P_2\rangle_{79}\|Q_1\rangle_{24}$	$\|0\rangle_1$	$I_3 \otimes -iY_5 \otimes I_6 \otimes I_8$
$\|P_2\rangle_{79}\|Q_2\rangle_{24}$	$\|0\rangle_1$	$I_3 \otimes -iY_5 \otimes I_6 \otimes -iY_8$
$\|P_1\rangle_{79}\|Q_1\rangle_{24}$	$\|1\rangle_1$	$iY_3 \otimes iY_5 \otimes iY_6 \otimes iY_8$
$\|P_1\rangle_{79}\|Q_2\rangle_{24}$	$\|1\rangle_1$	$iY_3 \otimes iY_5 \otimes iY_6 \otimes I_8$
$\|P_2\rangle_{79}\|Q_1\rangle_{24}$	$\|1\rangle_1$	$iY_3 \otimes I_5 \otimes iY_6 \otimes iY_8$
$\|P_2\rangle_{79}\|Q_2\rangle_{24}$	$\|1\rangle_1$	$iY_3 \otimes I_5 \otimes iY_6 \otimes I_8$

4 The CBRSP Scheme of Single-Qubit State in the Noisy Environment

In the reality, the effect of noisy environment on the communication scheme cannot be ignored. In this section, we consider our first scheme in four noisy environment, namely, bit-flip, phase-flip (phase damping), amplitude-damping and depolarizing noisy environment.

4.1 The Kraus Operators

The Bit-Flip Noise. There is a bit flip error with the probability p_b, while there is a probability $1 - p_b$ that nothing happens to the qubit. Where $p_b(0 \leq p_b \leq 1)$ is the decoherence rate. The Kraus operators of bit-flip noise are [17]

$$B_0 = \sqrt{1 - p_b}I, B_1 = \sqrt{p_b}X, \tag{11}$$

where I is identity matrix, X is the Pauli matrix.

The Phase-Flip (Phase Damping) Noise. The action of this noise is to flip the relative phase with the probability p_p and is left invariant otherwise. The Kraus operators of phase-flip noise are [17]

$$P_0 = \sqrt{1 - p_p}I, P_1 = \sqrt{p_p}Z, \tag{12}$$

where I is identity matrix, Z is the Pauli matrix and $p_p(0 \leq p_p \leq 1)$ is the decoherence rate.

The Amplitude-Damping Noise. The Kraus operators of this noise are [17]

$$A_0 = \begin{pmatrix} 1 & 0 \\ 0 & \sqrt{1 - p_a} \end{pmatrix}, A_1 = \begin{pmatrix} 0 & \sqrt{p_a} \\ 0 & 0 \end{pmatrix}, \tag{13}$$

here, $p_a(0 \leq p_a \leq 1)$ is the decoherence rate and refers to the probability of missing a photon. The amplitude-damping noise describes a system undergoing energy dissipation because of interaction with the noisy environment.

The Depolarizing Noise. In the depolarizing noisy environment, there is a probability $1 - p_d$ that the system is left invariant and a probability p_d that it is transformed into the completely mixed state $I/2$. The Kraus operators of depolarizing noise are [17]:

$$D_0 = \sqrt{1 - \frac{3p_d}{4}} I, D_1 = \frac{\sqrt{p_d}}{2} X, D_2 = \frac{\sqrt{p_d}}{2} Y, D_3 = \frac{\sqrt{p_d}}{2} Z, \tag{14}$$

where I is identity matrix, X, Y, Z are the Pauli matrix and $p_d (0 \leq p_d \leq 1)$ is the decoherence rate.

4.2 The Output State and the Fidelity

Charlie generates the five-qubit entangled state $|\varphi\rangle_{12345}$ as the quantum channel. He holds the qubit 1 in his hands. We consider the situation that the qubit 1 is not transmitted through noisy environment, so it is not affected by the noise. Charlie sends the qubits 3, 5 (2, 4) to Alice (Bob) through the channel 1 (channel 2). We discuss the case that the channel 1 and channel 2 are in the same noisy environment. So the qubits 3, 5 (2, 4) are affected by the same Kraus operator.

To analyze the effect of noise, we calculate the density matrix $\rho = |\varphi\rangle_{12345} \langle\varphi|_{12345}$. After the qubits are transmitted through the noisy environment, the density matrix ρ will be rewritten as $\varepsilon^{\Lambda}(\rho) = \sum_{m,n} \Lambda_m^5 \Lambda_m^3 \Lambda_n^4 \Lambda_n^2 \rho (\Lambda_m^5 \Lambda_m^3 \Lambda_n^4 \Lambda_n^2)^{\dagger}$, where $\Lambda \in \{B, P, A, D\}$. For $\Lambda \in \{B, P, A\}$, $m, n \in \{0, 1\}$, while for $\Lambda = D$, $m, n \in \{0, 1, 2, 3\}$. In these noisy environments, we will get the output state as:

$$\begin{aligned}
(\rho_{out}^B)_{34} &= (1-p_b)^4 (a_0b_0|00\rangle + a_0b_1|01\rangle + a_1b_0|10\rangle + a_1b_1|11\rangle)(a_0b_0\langle 00| \\
&+a_0b_1\langle 01| + a_1b_0\langle 10| + a_1b_1\langle 11|) + p_b^2(1-p_b)^2[(a_0b_0|01\rangle + a_0b_1|00\rangle + a_1b_0|11\rangle \\
&+a_1b_1|10\rangle)(a_0b_0\langle 01| + a_0b_1\langle 00| + a_1b_0\langle 11| + a_1b_1\langle 10|) + (a_0b_0|10\rangle + a_0b_1|11\rangle \\
&+a_1b_0|00\rangle + a_1b_1|01\rangle)(a_0b_0\langle 10| + a_0b_1\langle 11| + a_1b_0\langle 00| + a_1b_1\langle 01|)] + p_b^4(a_0b_0|11\rangle \\
&+a_0b_1|10\rangle + a_1b_0|01\rangle + a_1b_1|00\rangle)(a_0b_0\langle 11| + a_0b_1\langle 10| + a_1b_0\langle 01| + a_1b_1\langle 00|) \\
(\rho_{out}^P)_{34} &= [p_p^4 + (1-p_p)^4](a_0b_0|00\rangle + a_0b_1|01\rangle + a_1b_0|10\rangle + a_1b_1|11\rangle)(a_0b_0\langle 00| \\
&+a_0b_1\langle 01| + a_1b_0\langle 10| + a_1b_1\langle 11|) + 2p_p^2(1-p_p)^2(a_0b_0|00\rangle - a_0b_1|01\rangle - a_1b_0|10\rangle \\
&+a_1b_1|11\rangle)(a_0b_0\langle 00| - a_0b_1\langle 01| - a_1b_0\langle 10| + a_1b_1\langle 11|) \\
(\rho_{out}^A)_{34} &= (a_0b_0|00\rangle + (1-p_a)^2 a_0b_1|01\rangle + (1-p_a)^2 a_1b_0|10\rangle + (1-p_a)^4 a_1b_1|11\rangle) \\
&(a_0b_0\langle 00| + (1-p_a)^2 a_0b_1\langle 01| + (1-p_a)^2 a_1b_0\langle 10| + (1-p_a)^4 a_1b_1\langle 11|) \\
&+p_a^2(1-p_a)^2 a_1b_1(|10\rangle\langle 10| + |01\rangle\langle 01|) + a_1b_1p_a^8|00\rangle\langle 00| \\
(\rho_{out}^D)_{34} &= [5(p_d/4)^4 + (1-3p_d/4)^4](a_0b_0|00\rangle + a_0b_1|01\rangle + a_1b_0|10\rangle + a_1b_1|11\rangle) \\
&(a_0b_0\langle 00| + a_0b_1\langle 01| + a_1b_0\langle 10| + a_1b_1\langle 11|) + (1-3p_d/4)^2p_d^2/32(a_0b_0|01\rangle \\
&+a_0b_1|00\rangle + a_1b_0|11\rangle + a_1b_1|10\rangle)(a_0b_0\langle 01| + a_0b_1\langle 00| + a_1b_0\langle 11| + a_1b_1\langle 10|) \\
&+(1-3p_d/4)^2p_d^2/4^3(a_0b_0|00\rangle - a_0b_1|01\rangle - a_1b_0|10\rangle + a_1b_1|11\rangle)(a_0b_0\langle 00| \\
&-a_0b_1\langle 01| - a_1b_0\langle 10| + a_1b_1\langle 11|) + (1/2)(p_d/4)^4(a_0b_0|10\rangle - a_0b_1|11\rangle \\
&-a_1b_0|00\rangle + a_1b_1|01\rangle)(a_0b_0\langle 10| - a_0b_1\langle 11| - a_1b_0\langle 00| + a_1b_1\langle 01|)
\end{aligned} \tag{15}$$

And the fidelities of the output state can be calculated as

$$
\begin{aligned}
F^B &= (1-p_b)^4(a_0b_0+a_1b_1)^4 + 2p_b^2(1-p_b)^2(a_0a_1+b_0b_1)^2 + p_b^4(a_0b_1+b_0a_1)^4, \\
F^P &= [p_p^4+(1-p_p)^4](a_0b_0+a_1b_1)^4 + 2p_p^2(1-p_p)^2(a_0b_0-a_1b_1)^4, \\
F^A &= [a_0b_0+(1-p_a)^2a_1b_1]^4 + p_a^4(1-p_a)^4a_0^2a_1^2b_1^4 + p_a^4(1-p_a)^4a_1^4b_0^2b_1^2 + p_a^8a_0^2a_1^2b_0^2b_1^2, \\
F^D &= [5(p_d/4)^4+(1-3p_d/4)^4](a_0b_0+a_1b_1)^4 + (1-3p_d/4)^2(p_d^2/32)(a_0a_1+b_0b_1)^2 \\
&\quad +(1-3p_d/4)^2p_d^2/4^3(a_0b_0-a_1b_1)^4 + (1/2)(p_d/4)^4(-a_0a_1+b_0b_1)^2.
\end{aligned} \tag{16}
$$

We find that the fidelity of the output state depends on the coefficients of the prepared state and the decoherence rate. In Fig. 1, we assume that $p_b = p_p = p_a = p_d = p, a_0 = a$ and $b_0 = b_1 = \sqrt{2}/2$. In Fig. 2, we assume that $p_b = p_p = p_a = p_d = p$, and $a_0 = a_1 = b_0 = b_1 = \sqrt{2}/2$. In the bit-flip and phase-flip (phase-damping) noisy environment, the fidelities of the output state can reach 1 when the decoherence rate $p_b = p_p = 1$. Therefore, our scheme can be accomplished with unit fidelity in the noisy environment. Here we take the first scheme as an example. The effect of noise on the second scheme can also be analyzed by the same process which are omitted here.

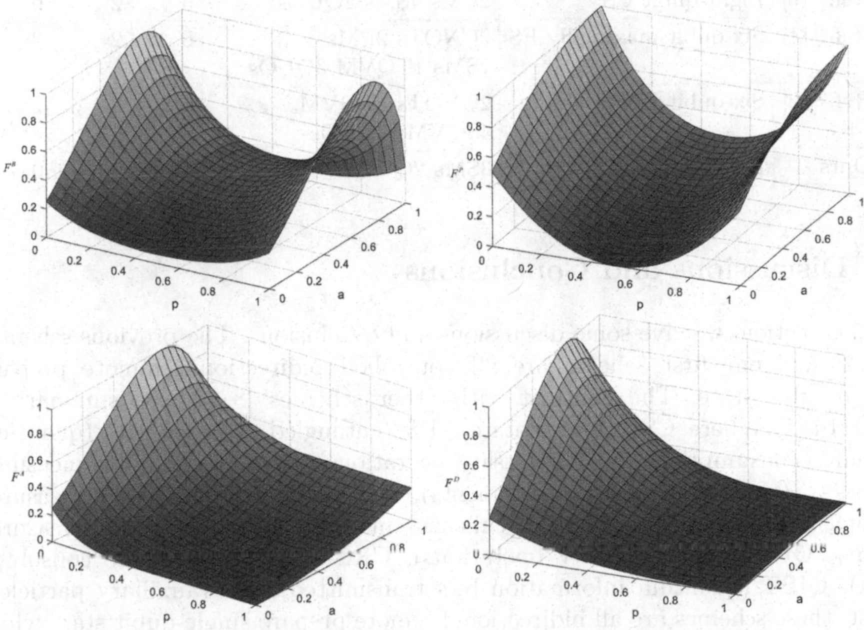

Fig. 1. Effect of four types of noise on our scheme is visualized through variation of the fidelities F^B(for bit-flip noise model), F^P (for phase-flip noise model), F^A (for amplitude-damping noise model), and F^D (for depolarizing noise model) with different coefficients of the prepared state and decoherence rate. We assume that four types of noise with $a_0 = a, b_0 = b_1 = \sqrt{2}/2, p_b = p_p = p_a = p_d = p$.

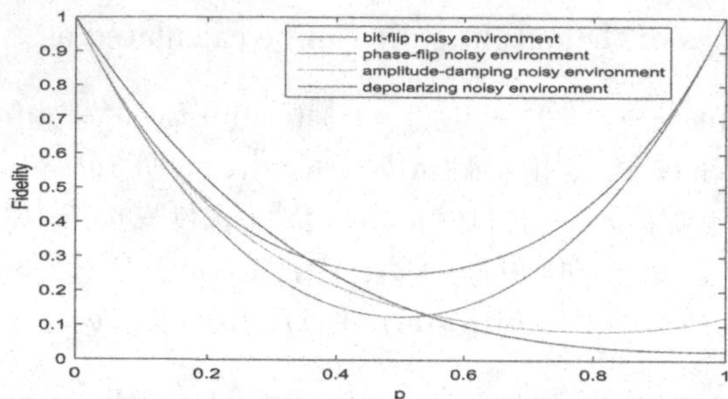

Fig. 2. Fidelities of the output state in bit-flip, phase-flip, amplitude-damping, depolarizing noisy environments assuming $a_0 = a_1 = b_0 = b_1 = \sqrt{2}/2, p_b = p_p = p_a = p_d = p$.

Table 3. Contrast with other schemes.

Scheme	QRC	NO	CRC	QIBT	AP
Ref. [8]	Five-qubit CS	2CNOTs 5SMs 2QUOs	5	2	2
Ref. [9]	Two-qubit CS	2SMs 2QUOs	3	2	1
Ref. [10]	Eight-qubit CS	2PMs 4SMs 2QUOs	5	2	0
Ref. [11]	Six-qubit maximally ES	2CNOTs 2PMs 2SMs 1TQVM 3QUOs	6	2	2
Ref. [12]	Six-qubit ES	2CNOTs 2TQVM 4SQVMs 3QUOs	6	2	2
Ours	Five-qubit ES	3SMs 2QUOs	3	2	0

5 Discussions and Conclusions

In this section, we give some discussions and conclusions. The previous schemes [8–12] and our first scheme are all controlled bidirectional remote prepare single-qubit state. The contrast with other schemes [8–12] are summarized in Table 3. Where CS (cluster state), ES (entangled state), QRC (quantum resource consumption), NO (necessary operations), SMs (single-qubit measurements), PMs (projective measurements), TQ-VM (two-qubit VoN measurement), SQVMs (sin-gle-qubit VoN measurements), TQM (two-qubit measurement), QUOs (qubit unitary operations), CRC (classical resource consumption), QIBT (quantum information bits transmitted), AP (auxiliary particle). First, these schemes are all bidirectional remote prepare single-qubit state while we present another CBRSP scheme of two-qubit state. Second, the quantum resource consumption (QRC) of our scheme is five-qubit entangled state which is never used in previous schemes. Third, the NO and the CRC of our scheme are relatively less than some schemes, while the other schemes need more operations resulting in excessive resource consumption. Finally, the Refs. [8,9,11,12] need the help of the auxiliary particles, whereas the Ref. [10] and our scheme do not need.

In conclusion, we have creatively presented two schemes for bidirectional prepare single- and two-qubit state by using the five- and nine-qubit entangled state as the quantum channel, respectively. However, the previous schemes are only bidirectional prepare single-qubit state. We firstly consider our schemes in two cases that the coefficients of prepared state are real and complex, respectively. Then, our first scheme is discussed in four kinds of noisy environment(bit-flip, phase-flip, amplitude-damping and depolarizing noisy environment) and the fidelity of the output state is calculated. The result shows that our scheme can be accomplished with unit fidelity in the noisy environment. Finally, we make a contrast with other schemes.

Acknowledgment. This work is supported by the NSFC (Grant Nos. 61671087, 61272514, 61170272, 61003287), the Major Science and Technology Support Program of Guizhou Province (Grant No. 20183001), the Fok Ying Tong Education Foundation (Grant No. 131067), and Open Foundation of Guizhou Provincial Key Laboratory of Public Big Data (2017BDKFJJ007).

Appendix

When the prepared state coefficients are real. Alice's and Bob's unitary operations are executed, respectively, where I, X, iY, Z are pauli operations.

Alice's and Bob's result	Charlie's result	Unitary operation
$\|H_1\rangle_{79}\|K_1\rangle_{24}$	$\|0\rangle_1$	$I_3 \otimes I_5 \otimes I_6 \otimes I_8$
$\|H_1\rangle_{79}\|K_2\rangle_{24}$	$\|0\rangle_1$	$I_3 \otimes I_5 \otimes I_6 \otimes -iY_8$
$\|H_1\rangle_{79}\|K_3\rangle_{24}$	$\|0\rangle_1$	$I_3 \otimes I_5 \otimes iY_6 \otimes -Z_8$
$\|H_1\rangle_{79}\|K_4\rangle_{24}$	$\|0\rangle_1$	$I_3 \otimes I_5 \otimes iY_6 \otimes -X_8$
$\|H_2\rangle_{79}\|K_1\rangle_{24}$	$\|0\rangle_1$	$I_3 \otimes -iY_5 \otimes I_6 \otimes I_8$
$\|H_2\rangle_{79}\|K_2\rangle_{24}$	$\|0\rangle_1$	$I_3 \otimes -iY_5 \otimes I_6 \otimes -iY_8$
$\|H_2\rangle_{79}\|K_3\rangle_{24}$	$\|0\rangle_1$	$I_3 \otimes -iY_5 \otimes iY_6 \otimes -Z_8$
$\|H_2\rangle_{79}\|K_4\rangle_{24}$	$\|0\rangle_1$	$I_3 \otimes -iY_5 \otimes iY_6 \otimes -X_8$
$\|H_3\rangle_{79}\|K_1\rangle_{24}$	$\|0\rangle_1$	$iY_3 \otimes -Z_5 \otimes I_6 \otimes I_8$
$\|H_3\rangle_{79}\|K_2\rangle_{24}$	$\|0\rangle_1$	$iY_3 \otimes -Z_5 \otimes I_6 \otimes -iY_8$
$\|H_3\rangle_{79}\|K_3\rangle_{24}$	$\|0\rangle_1$	$iY_3 \otimes -Z_5 \otimes iY_6 \otimes -Z_8$
$\|H_3\rangle_{79}\|K_4\rangle_{24}$	$\|0\rangle_1$	$iY_3 \otimes -Z_5 \otimes iY_6 \otimes -X_8$
$\|H_4\rangle_{79}\|K_1\rangle_{24}$	$\|0\rangle_1$	$iY_3 \otimes -X_5 \otimes I_6 \otimes I_8$
$\|H_4\rangle_{79}\|K_2\rangle_{24}$	$\|0\rangle_1$	$iY_3 \otimes -X_5 \otimes I_6 \otimes -iY_8$
$\|H_4\rangle_{79}\|K_3\rangle_{24}$	$\|0\rangle_1$	$iY_3 \otimes -X_5 \otimes iY_6 \otimes -Z_8$
$\|H_4\rangle_{79}\|K_4\rangle_{24}$	$\|0\rangle_1$	$iY_3 \otimes -X_5 \otimes iY_6 \otimes -X_8$
$\|H_1\rangle_{79}\|K_1\rangle_{24}$	$\|1\rangle_1$	$iY_3 \otimes iY_5 \otimes iY_6 \otimes iY_8$
$\|H_1\rangle_{79}\|K_2\rangle_{24}$	$\|1\rangle_1$	$iY_3 \otimes iY_5 \otimes iY_6 \otimes I_8$

Alice's and Bob's result	Charlie's result	Unitary operation
$\vert H_1\rangle_{79}\vert K_3\rangle_{24}$	$\vert 1\rangle_1$	$iY_3 \otimes iY_5 \otimes I_6 \otimes X_8$
$\vert H_1\rangle_{79}\vert K_4\rangle_{24}$	$\vert 1\rangle_1$	$iY_3 \otimes iY_5 \otimes I_6 \otimes Z_8$
$\vert H_2\rangle_{79}\vert K_1\rangle_{24}$	$\vert 1\rangle_1$	$iY_3 \otimes I_5 \otimes iY_6 \otimes iY_8$
$\vert H_2\rangle_{79}\vert K_2\rangle_{24}$	$\vert 1\rangle_1$	$iY_3 \otimes I_5 \otimes iY_6 \otimes I_8$
$\vert H_2\rangle_{79}\vert K_3\rangle_{24}$	$\vert 1\rangle_1$	$iY_3 \otimes I_5 \otimes I_6 \otimes X_8$
$\vert H_2\rangle_{79}\vert K_4\rangle_{24}$	$\vert 1\rangle_1$	$iY_3 \otimes I_5 \otimes I_6 \otimes Z_8$
$\vert H_3\rangle_{79}\vert K_1\rangle_{24}$	$\vert 1\rangle_1$	$I_3 \otimes X_5 \otimes iY_6 \otimes iY_8$
$\vert H_3\rangle_{79}\vert K_2\rangle_{24}$	$\vert 1\rangle_1$	$I_3 \otimes X_5 \otimes iY_6 \otimes I_8$
$\vert H_3\rangle_{79}\vert K_3\rangle_{24}$	$\vert 1\rangle_1$	$I_3 \otimes X_5 \otimes I_6 \otimes X_8$
$\vert H_3\rangle_{79}\vert K_4\rangle_{24}$	$\vert 1\rangle_1$	$I_3 \otimes X_5 \otimes I_6 \otimes Z_8$
$\vert H_4\rangle_{79}\vert K_1\rangle_{24}$	$\vert 1\rangle_1$	$I_3 \otimes Z_5 \otimes iY_6 \otimes iY_8$
$\vert H_4\rangle_{79}\vert K_3\rangle_{24}$	$\vert 1\rangle_1$	$I_3 \otimes Z_5 \otimes iY_6 \otimes I_8$
$\vert H_4\rangle_{79}\vert K_3\rangle_{24}$	$\vert 1\rangle_1$	$I_3 \otimes Z_5 \otimes I_6 \otimes X_8$
$\vert H_4\rangle_{79}\vert K_4\rangle_{24}$	$\vert 1\rangle_1$	$I_3 \otimes Z_5 \otimes I_6 \otimes Z_8$

References

1. Bennett, C.H., Brassard, G., Crpeau, C., Jozsa, R., Peres, A., Wootters, W.K.: Teleporting an unknown quantum state via dual classical and EinsteinCPodolsky-CRosen channels. Phys. Rev. Lett. **70**(1985), 13–29 (1993)
2. Lo, H.K.: Classical-communication cost in distributed quantum-information processing: a generalization of quantum-communication complexity. Phys. Rev. A **62**, 012313 (2000)
3. Pati, A.K.: Minimum classical bit for remote preparation and measurement of a qubit. Phys. Rev. A **63**, 014302 (2001)
4. Bennett, C.H., DiVincenzo, D.P., Shor, P.W., Smolin, J.A., Terhal, B.M., Wootters, W.K.: Remote state preparation. Phys. Rev. Lett. **87**, 077902 (2001)
5. Chen, X.B., Ma, S.Y., Su, Y., Zhang, R., Yang, Y.X.: Controlled remote state preparation of arbitrary two and three qubit states via the Brown state. Q. Inf. Process. **11**(6), 1653–1667 (2012)
6. Dakic, B.: Quantum discord as resource for remote state preparation. Nat. Phys. **8**(9), 666–670 (2012)
7. Chen, X.B., Sun, Y.R., Xu, G., Jia, H.Y., Qu, Z., Yang, Y.X.: Controlled bidirectional remote preparation of three-qubit state. Q. Inf. Process. **16**(10), 244 (2017)
8. Cao, T.B., Nguyen, B.A.: Deterministic controlled bidirectional remote state preparation. Adv. Nat. Sci. Nanosci. Nanotechnol. **5**(1), 015003 (2013)
9. Sharma, V., Shukla, C., Banerjee, S., Pathak, A.: Controlled bidirectional remote state preparation in noisy environment: a generalized view. Q. Inf. Process. **14**(9), 3441–3464 (2015)
10. Peng, J.Y., Bai, M.Q., Mo, Z.W.: Bidirectional controlled joint remote state preparation. Q. Inf. Process. **14**(11), 4263–4278 (2015)
11. Zhang, D., Zha, X., Duan, Y., Wei, Z.H.: Deterministic controlled bidirectional remote state preparation via a six-qubit maximally entangled state. Int. J. Theor. Phys. **55**(1), 440–446 (2016)

12. Zhang, D., Zha, X., Duan, Y., Yang, Y.: Deterministic controlled bidirectional remote state preparation via a six-qubit entangled state. Q. Inf. Process. **15**(5), 2169–2179 (2016)
13. Li, Y., Jin, X.: Bidirectional controlled teleportation by using nine-qubit entangled state in noisy environments. Q. Inf. Process. **15**(2), 929–945 (2016)
14. O'Brien, J.L., Pryde, G.J., White, A.G., Ralph, T.C., Branning, D.: Demonstration of an all-optical quantum controlled-NOT gate. Nature **426**, 264–267 (2003)
15. Bennett, C.H., Brassard, G.: Quantum crýptography: public key distribution and con Tos5. In: Proceedings of the International Conference on Computers, Systems and Signal Processing (1984)
16. Shor, P.W., Preskill, J.: Simple proof of security of the BB84 quantum key distribution protocol. Phys. Rev. Lett. **85**(2), 441 (2000)
17. Liang, X.T.: Classical information capacities of some single qubit quantum noisy channels. Commun. Theor. Phys. **39**(5), 537–542 (2003)

Efficient Group Signature Scheme Over NTRU Lattice

Qing Ye, Xiaomeng Yang, Xixi Yan, and Zongqu Zhao(✉)

College of Computer Science and Technology, Henan Polytechnic University, Jiaozuo 454000, Henan, China
zhaozong_qu@hpu.edu.cn

Abstract. Group signature schemes empower users to sign messages in the name of a group at the same time (1) keeping anonymity with respect to an outsider, and (2) guaranteeing traceability of a signer when needed. In this work we construct a new group signature scheme based on NTRU lattices. To achieve goals, we use a new algorithm for sampling a basis on NTRU lattice. Group signatures have many features, such as anonymity and traceability. They play an important role in the field of cryptography, and group-based group signatures are more resistant to quantum attacks. However, the unique advantages of lattice cryptography have the disadvantage of space consumption. At present the group signature schemes has high communication cost, and their size of system public key size is too large. Hence NTRU lattice is a kind of special lattice based on polynomial ring, and only involves polynomial ring small integer multiplication and modular arithmetic compared with the general case. NTRU lattice system shortens the length of public key, and has the faster computing speed. In order to reduce the size of the lattice key, this paper uses the Gaussian discrete distributed sampling algorithm on the NTRU lattice to construct a new NTRU lattice-based group signature. And provide relevant safety certification and efficiency analysis.

Keywords: Group signature · NTRU · Lattice-based cryptography

1 Introduction

In this work we construct a new group signature scheme based on NTRU lattices in the random oracle model. Now there are more and more lattice-based schemes in cryptography in recent years. First we recall some background on group signature. In 1991, Chaum and Heyst [1] built the first group signature. The group signature is in a group. Each legal member can sign on behalf of the group. The verifier can use the group public key to verify whether the signature is valid, but cannot determine the identity of the signer. Administrator can open the signature to find the identity of the signer. Subsequently, the literature [2, 3] constructed a group signature based on traditional knowledge of number theory, improved efficiency, and was more practical than the literature [1]. In recent years, the new cryptosystem constructed based on lattice theory has become a research hotspot in the era of quantum cryptography because of its

X. Sun et al. (Eds.): ICCCS 2018, LNCS 11065, pp. 554–562, 2018.
https://doi.org/10.1007/978-3-030-00012-7_50

advantages such as better progressive efficiency, simple operation, parallelization, resistance to quantum attacks, and the existence of worst-case random instances.

In 2010, Gordon et al. [4] proposed the first lattice-based group signature scheme (GKV) at the Asian Cryptography Society. The scheme uses a trapdoor sampling function to generate tracking keys, which is combined with basis of lattice proof technology. The scheme maintains anonymity and traceability, and constructed a zero-knowledge proof. In 2013, Laguillaumie et al. [5] constructed the first lattice-based group signature with a discrete logarithm size N with relatively large parameters. In 2015, Nguyen et al. [6] constructed a simpler and more efficient signature lattice-based group signature. The zero-knowledge argument systems arising in this paper carry out the framework of Stern's protocol. This protocol was at first proposed in the aspect of code-based cryptography, then adapted into the lattice setting by Kawachi et al. [7]. Subsequently, it was stimulated by Ling et al. [8] to dispose the matrix-vector relations associated with the SIS and LWE problems, and further developed to design several lattice-based schemes: group signatures [9–13], and group encryption [14]. In 2016, Bootle et al. [15] proposed a signature scheme that can quickly revoke group members' fully homomorphic group signatures, and provided strict security proofs.

NTRU lattice is a kind of special case based on polynomial ring. It involves only multiplication of polynomial ring and small integer modular arithmetic. Compared with the general lattice, NTRU lattice cryptosystem required shorter public key and private key, and its speed is faster. Hoffstein et al. [16] build give a kind of NTRU cryptosystem which parameter is flexible, and has work on the strict security certificate. In 2015, Lyubashevsky [17] proposed an algorithm which can quickly sample discrete in Gaussian distributions on NTRU lattice. And literatures [18, 19] are devoted to simplify the parameter and doing a lot of research on the reduction of dimensionality in the NTRU lattice. Our scheme adopts the algorithm of fast sampling and uses zero knowledge to construct a new group signature scheme based on NTRU lattice, which greatly improves the efficiency and makes relevant security certificate.

2 Preliminaries

2.1 Lattice and Gaussian Distribution

Now we give the formal definition of a lattice

We denote the integer numbers by $\mathbb{Z}$ and the real numbers by $\mathbb{R}$. For a real number $x \in \mathbb{R}$, we let $\lceil x \rceil$ denote the largest integer not greater than x, $\lfloor x \rfloor$ denote $\lceil x \rceil - 1$, and $\text{Round}(x) = \lfloor x + 1/2 \rfloor$. We use the notation $[k]$ for an positive integer k to denote the set $\{1, \ldots, k\}$.

Column vectors are denoted by lower-case bold letters (e.g., $\boldsymbol{x}$) and row vectors by transpose (e.g., $\boldsymbol{x}^T$). We use bold capital letters (e.g., $\boldsymbol{A}$) to denote matrices, and sometimes identify a matrix with its ordered set of column vectors. The i-th column vector of a matrix $\boldsymbol{A}$ is denoted as $\boldsymbol{a}_i$. We denote the horizontal concatenation of matrices and/or vectors using a "|", e.g., $[\boldsymbol{A}|\boldsymbol{Ax}]$, and denote the vertical concatenation as $[\boldsymbol{A}; \boldsymbol{Ax}]$. We let $\|\tilde{\boldsymbol{A}}\|$ denote the maximal Gram-Schmidt length of $\boldsymbol{A}$.

The natural security parameter throughout the paper is n, which implies that all other quantities are polynomial functions of n. We use standard asymptotic notation $O(\cdot), \Omega(\cdot), o(\cdot)$, etc. Moreover, we use tildes $\tilde{O}(\cdot)$ to denote that logarithmic factors in the main parameter are suppressed. We use $poly(n)$ to denote an unspecified function $f(n) = O(n^c)$ for some constant c. We say that a function in n is negligible, denoted as $negl(n)$, if $f(n) = o(n^c)$ for every fixed constant c. We say that an event happens with overwhelming probability if it happens with probability at least $1 - negl(n)$.

The statistical distance between two distributions $\mathcal{X}$ and $\mathcal{Y}$ (or two random variables having those distributions), viewed as functions over a countable domain D, is defined as $\frac{1}{2}\sum_{d \in D} |\mathcal{X}(d) - \mathcal{Y}(d)|$. We say that two distributions (formally, two ensembles of distributions indexed by n) are statistically close (or statistically indistinguishable) if their statistical distance is negligible function of n.

Definition 1 (LATTICE). Given n linearly independent vector $\mathrm{b}_1, \mathrm{b}_2, \cdots, \mathrm{b}_\mathrm{n} \in \mathbb{R}^\mathrm{m}$, the lattice generated by them is defined as

$$\mathcal{L}(\mathrm{b}_1, \mathrm{b}_2, \cdots, \mathrm{b}_\mathrm{n}) = \{\sum x_i b_i | x_i \in \mathbb{Z}\} \tag{1}$$

We refer to $\mathrm{b}_1, \mathrm{b}_2, \cdots, \mathrm{b}_\mathrm{n}$ as a basis of the lattice. Equivalently, if we define B as the $m \times n$ matrix whose columns are $\mathrm{b}_1, \mathrm{b}_2, \cdots, \mathrm{b}_\mathrm{n}$, then the lattice generated by B is

$$\mathcal{L}(B) = \mathcal{L}(\mathrm{b}_1, \mathrm{b}_2, \cdots, \mathrm{b}_\mathrm{n}) = \{Bx | x \in \mathbb{Z}\} \tag{2}$$

We say that the rank of the lattice is n and its dimension is m. If $n = m$, the lattice is called a full-rank lattice.

Let $\boldsymbol{A} \in \mathbb{Z}_q^{n \times m}$, $n, m, q \in \mathbb{Z}$, consider the following two lattices

$$\Lambda_q^{\perp}(\boldsymbol{A}) = \{e \in \mathbb{Z}^m s.t.\ \boldsymbol{A}\boldsymbol{e} = \boldsymbol{0} \bmod q\} \tag{3}$$

$$\Lambda_q(\boldsymbol{A}) = \{\boldsymbol{y} \in \mathbb{Z}^m s.t.\ \exists \boldsymbol{s} \in \mathbb{Z}^n, \boldsymbol{A}^t\boldsymbol{s} = \boldsymbol{y} \bmod q\} \tag{4}$$

Definition 2 (NTRU LATTICE). Let $N, q \in \mathbb{N}*$ and $f, g, F, G \in \mathbb{Z}_N[x]$ such that $fG - Fg = q \mod (x^N + 1)$. The NTRU lattice generated by f, g, F, G is the lattice generated by the rows of the block matrix

$$\begin{pmatrix} A(f) & A(g) \\ A(F) & A(G) \end{pmatrix} \tag{5}$$

Where $A(p)$ is the $N \times N$ matrix which i-th row is the coefficients of $x^{i-1} \cdot p(x) \mod (x^N + 1)$.

2.2 Gaussian Distribution and the Learning with Errors Problem

Definition 3 (Gaussian Distribution). For $\mathbf{x} \in \Lambda$, define the Gaussian function $\rho_{\sigma,\mathbf{c}}(\mathbf{x})$ over $\Lambda \in \mathbb{Z}^m$ centered at $\mathbf{c} \in \mathbb{R}^m$ with parameter $\sigma > 0$ as

$$\rho_{\sigma,c}(\mathbf{x}) = \exp\left(-\frac{\pi\|\mathbf{x}-\mathbf{c}\|^2}{\sigma^2}\right) \tag{6}$$

Let $\rho_{\sigma,\mathbf{c}}(\Lambda) = \sum_{\mathbf{x}\in\Lambda}\rho_{\sigma,\mathbf{c}}(\mathbf{x})$, and define the discrete Gaussian distribution over Λ as $D_{\Lambda,\sigma,\mathbf{c}}(\mathbf{y}) = \frac{\rho_{\sigma,\mathbf{c}}(\mathbf{y})}{\rho_{\sigma,\mathbf{c}}(\Lambda)}$ where $\mathbf{y} \in \Lambda$.

(The Learning with Errors Problem)

Security of all our schemes reduces to the LWE (learning with errors) problem, a classic hard problem on lattices.

Definition 4. Consider these public parameters: a prime q, a positive integer n, and a distribution χ over $\mathbb{Z}_q$. An $(\mathbb{Z}_q, n, \chi)$-LWE problem instance is a challenge oracle $\mathcal{O}$ which consists of access to two types oracle, either, a noisy pseudo-random oracle $\mathcal{O}_s$ carrying some constant random secret key $\boldsymbol{s} \in \mathbb{Z}_q^n$, or, a truly random oracle $\mathcal{O}_\$$, whose behaviors are respectively described as follows:

$\mathcal{O}_s$: outputs samples of the form $(\boldsymbol{u}_i, v_i) = (\boldsymbol{u}_i, \boldsymbol{u}_i^T\boldsymbol{s} + x_i) \in \mathbb{Z}_q^n \times \mathbb{Z}_q$, where $\boldsymbol{s} \in \mathbb{Z}_q^n$ is a uniformly distributed persistent value invariant across invocations, $\boldsymbol{u}_i$ is uniform in $\mathbb{Z}_q^n$, and $x_i \in \mathbb{Z}_q$ is a fresh sample from χ.

$\mathcal{O}_\$$: outputs truly uniform random samples from $\mathbb{Z}_q^n \times \mathbb{Z}_q$.

The $(\mathbb{Z}_q, n, \chi)$ - LWE problem allows repeated queries to the challenge oracle $\mathcal{O}$. We define that an attack algorithm $\mathcal{A}$ distinguishes the $(\mathbb{Z}_q, n, \chi)$ - LWE problem if LWE - adv$[\mathcal{A}] = \left|\Pr\left[\mathcal{A}^{\mathcal{O}_s} = 1\right] - \Pr\left[\mathcal{A}^{\mathcal{O}_\$} = 1\right]\right|$ is non-negligible for a random $\boldsymbol{s} \in \mathbb{Z}_q^n$.

Regev [12] shows that for certain noise distribution χ, denoted as $\bar{\Psi}_\alpha$, and modulus $q \geq (1/\alpha)\cdot\omega(\sqrt{n\log n})$, solving the LWE problem and its decisional version yields approximation factors of $\tilde{O}(n/\alpha)$ is as hard as the worst-case SIVP (shortest independent vectors problem) and GapSVP (a problem over lattice we stated later) under a quantum reduction.

The following lemma about the distribution $\bar{\Psi}_\alpha$ will be used to prove our schemes' correctness.

For an $\alpha \in (0,1)$ and a prime q, let $\bar{\Psi}_\alpha$ denote the distribution over $\mathbb{Z}_q$ of the random variable $Round(qX) \bmod q$ where X is a normal random variable with mean 0 and standard deviation $\alpha/\sqrt{2\pi}$.

Let $\bar{\boldsymbol{e}}$ be some vector in $\mathbb{Z}^{\bar{m}}$ and $\boldsymbol{y} \xleftarrow{\bar{\Psi}_\alpha^{\bar{m}}} \mathbb{Z}_q^{\bar{m}}$. Then the quantity $|\bar{\boldsymbol{e}}^T\boldsymbol{y}|$ treated as an integer in $[0, q-1]$ satisfies $|\boldsymbol{e}^T\boldsymbol{y}| \leq \|\boldsymbol{e}\|q\alpha\omega(\sqrt{\log n}) + \|\boldsymbol{e}\|\sqrt{\bar{m}}/2$ with all but negligible probability in n.

For lattice dimension parameter n and number d, GapSVP$_\gamma$ is the problem of distinguishing whether there is a n-dimensional lattice has a vector shorter than d or no vector shorter than $\gamma(n)\cdot d$. The two definitions below capture reductions, quantum and classical, from GapSVP to LWE for certain parameters. We present the result in terms of B-bounded distributions.

Definition 5 (*B*-bounded distributions). A distribution ensemble $\{\chi_n\}$, supported over the integers, is called *B*-bounded if $\Pr_{x \leftarrow \chi_n}[|x| > B] = negl(n)$.

Definition 6. Let $q = q(n)$ be a prime power, and let $B_\chi \geq \omega(\log n) \cdot \sqrt{n}$. Then there exists an efficient sample able *B*-bound distribution χ such that if there is an efficient algorithm that solves the average-case $\text{LWE}_{n,q,\chi}$ problem, then:

- There is an efficient quantum algorithm that solves the problem $\text{GapSVP}_{\tilde{O}(nq/B)}$ on any *n*-dimensional lattice.
- If $q \geq \tilde{O}(2^{n/2})$, then there is an efficient classical algorithm for solves $\text{GapSVP}_{\tilde{O}(nq/B)}$ on any *n*-dimensional lattice.

Fix a positive integer n, integers $m \geq n$ and $q \geq 2$, a vector $s \in \mathbb{Z}_q^n$, and a probability distribution χ on the interval $[0, q)^m$: Define the following two distributions over $\mathbb{Z}_q^{n \times m} \times [0, q)^m$:

Sampling $e \leftarrow \chi$, $LWE_{m,q,\chi}(s)$ is distribution acquired by choosing uniform $A \in \mathbb{Z}_q^{n \times m}$, and outputting $(A, A^T s + e \bmod q)$.

Uniform $y \in [0, q)^m$, $U_{m,q}$ is the distribution acquired by choosing uniform $A \in \mathbb{Z}_q^{n \times m}$, and outputting (A, y).

The decisional variant of the LWE problem (correlation to the distribution χ) can be guaranteed informally as the problem of distinguishing between $U_{m,q}$ and $LWE_{m,q,\chi}(s)$ for a uniform s. Formally, for m, q, and χ that could depend on n. We can say that $LWE_{m,q,\chi}$ scheme is hard if the following is insignificant for any probabilistic polynomial-time algorithm D:

$$|\Pr[s \leftarrow \mathbb{Z}_q^n; (\mathbf{A}, y) \leftarrow LWE_{m,q,\chi}(s) : D(\mathbf{A}, y) = 1] \\ \ldots\ldots \Pr[(\mathbf{A}, y) \leftarrow U_{m,q} : D(\mathbf{A}, y) = 1] \tag{7}$$

A standard setting for the LWE problem takes for the error distribution ψ_α^m over $[0, q)^m$ defined as follows: Sample m numbers $\eta_1, \cdots, \eta_m \leftarrow D_\alpha$, let $e_i := q \cdot \eta_i (\bmod q)$, and output $e_i := (e_1, \cdots, e_m)^T$. We write $LWE_{m,q,\alpha}(s)$ as an abbreviation for $LWE_{m,q,\psi_\alpha^m}(s)$.

2.3 Efficient NIWI Proofs for Lattice Problems

In this chapter we simply describe how it is allowable to structure a non-interactive witness-indistinguishable proof for the gap language $L_{s,\gamma} = (L_{YES}, L_{NO})$ defined by:

$$L_{YES} = \left\{ \begin{pmatrix} B_1, \cdots, B_N \\ z_1, \cdots, z_N \end{pmatrix} | \exists s \in \mathbb{Z}_q^n \text{ and } i \in [N] : \| z_i - B_i^T s \| \leq s\sqrt{m} \right\} \tag{8}$$

$$L_{NO} = \left\{ \begin{pmatrix} B_1, \cdots, B_N \\ z_1, \cdots, z_N \end{pmatrix} | \exists s \in \mathbb{Z}_q^n \text{ and } i \in [N] : \| z_i - B_i^T s \| > s\sqrt{m} \right\} \tag{9}$$

Here, L_{YES} is the gather of N points at least one of which is close to the corresponding lattice, and L_{NO} is the gather of N points all of which are removed from the corresponding lattices.

2.4 Trapdoor Sampling Function and GPV Signature

The GKV scheme uses a trapdoor sampling function to generate tracking keys and combines GPV signatures to achieve traceability of group signatures.

Lemma 1. There is a Probabilistic Polynomial Time (PPT) algorithm TrapSamp, given 1^n, 1^m and q (satisfy q $\geq$ 2 and $m \geq 8n \log q$) output matrices $A \in Z_q^{n\times m}$, $T \in Z_q^{n\times m}$ where the A statistic is close to a uniform distribution $Z_q^{n\times m}$, and the column vector of T is a set of bases $\Lambda^{\perp}(\mathbf{A})$.

Gentry, Peikert, and Vaikuntanathan [11] proposed a scheme for constructing a One-way Function sampling function using the TrapSamp algorithm, including the GPVGen and GPVInvert algorithms. For details, refer to the GKV scheme.

2.5 Efficient Discrete Gaussian Distribution Sampling Algorithm on NTRU Lattice

The algorithm for quickly sampling discrete Gaussian distributions on the NTRU grid is as follows:

Lemma 2. There is an efficient polynomial-time algorithm $CGS(B, c)$: performs the following operations: algorithm input $B = (b_0, \cdots, b_{n-1})$ and centroid c, sampling ϖ on the $D_{\Lambda(B),\sigma,c}$.

In order to reduce the physical parameters, the definition of the Kullback-Leibler divergence was introduced to characterize the "distance" between the two distributions.

Lemma 3. For any $\varepsilon < \frac{2^{-\frac{\lambda}{2}}}{4\sqrt{2n}}$. If $\sigma \geq \|\widetilde{B}\| \cdot \eta'_\varepsilon(Z)$, $\left(\eta'_\varepsilon(Z) \approx \frac{1}{\pi}\sqrt{\frac{1}{2}\ln(2+\frac{2}{\varepsilon})}\right)$ the KL divergence from the output of the CGS algorithm to the distribution $D_{\Lambda(B),\sigma,c}$ does not exceed $2^{-\lambda}$.

3 A Group Signature on NTRU Lattice

We let n be the security parameter, $q = poly(n)$, $m \geq 8nlogq$, and $s \geq C\sqrt{n \log q} \cdot \omega(\sqrt{\log m})$ be parameters of the system. We let $H : \{0,1\}^* \rightarrow \mathbb{Z}_q^n$ be a hash function, to be modeled as a random oracle. The distribution χ_1 is defined as the discrete Gaussian distribution D_{R_q,σ_1} with the standard deviation $\sigma_1 = 1.17\eta'_\varepsilon(Z)\sqrt{q}$ $(\varepsilon < \frac{2^{-\frac{\lambda}{2}}}{4\sqrt{2n}})$, the distribution χ_2 is defined as the discrete Gaussian distribution D_{Z,σ_2} with $\sigma = 8$, the plaintext space is $\{0,1\}$.

KenGen: First compute $(\mathbf{B}_1\mathbf{S}_1), \cdots, (\mathbf{B}_N\mathbf{S}_N) \leftarrow \text{TrapSamp}(1^n, 1^m, q)$, and then, for $1 \leq i \leq N$, compute $(\mathbf{A}_i, \mathbf{T}_i) \leftarrow \text{SuperSamp}(1^n, 1^m, q, \mathbf{B}_i)$. Output $TK = (S_i)_{i=1}^N$ as the tracing key.

And then generate polynomials f and g in D f, D g in NTRU lattice use the Lemma 2, respectively. Invert f in R_q to obtain f_q, invert f in R_p to obtain f_p, and check that g is invertible in R_q. The public key is $h_{i=1}^N = \{p * g * f_q (\text{mod } q)\}_{i=1}^N$. The private key is the pair $(f, f_p)_{i=1}^N$.

Sign: To sign message M using secret key $gsk[j] = T_j$, choose random $\gamma \leftarrow (0,1)^n$, set $\overline{M} = M \parallel \gamma$, and then compute $H_i = \overline{M} \parallel i$ for $1 \leq i \leq N$, Compute:
$e_j \leftarrow GPVI\text{nvert}(\mathbf{A}_j, \mathbf{T}_j, s, h_j)$.
For $1 \leq i \leq N$, sample $r_i \leftarrow \chi_2$, compute $z = r_i * h + e (\text{mod } q)$ and using the witness NIWI (r_i, i), and output $\sigma = (\gamma, Z_1, \cdots Z_n, \pi)$.

Vrfy: Parse the signature as $(r, z_1, \cdots, z_N, \pi)$ and set $\overline{M} = M \parallel r$ Output 1 if the proof π is correct, and $A_i Z_i = H(\overline{M} \parallel i) (\text{mod } q)$ for all i.

Open: Parse the signature as $(r, z_1, \cdots, z_N, \pi)$. Using the $\{S_i\}$, output the smallest index i for which $\text{dist}(\mathcal{L}(B_i^T, z_i) \leq s\sqrt{m}$.

We first check correctness. Let $(r, z_1, \cdots, z_N, \pi)$ be a signature produced by an honest signer. It is clear that π is a valid proof. Moreover, for any i we have

$$\begin{aligned} A_i Z &= A_i (r * h + m) \\ A_i Zf &= A_i (r * h + m) f \\ A_i Zf &= A_i r * h * f + Amf \\ A_i Zf &= A_i r * p * g * f_q * f + Amf \end{aligned} \tag{10}$$

the $r * p * g$ term vanishes, $f_q * f$ equal 1, then: $A_i Zf = Amf$. So we include: $A_i Z = Am = H(M)$.

4 Anonymity and Traceability

4.1 Anonymity

Anonymity means that if an attacker has the system public key and the secret signature key but do not have the matched tracking the key, the attacker is not feasible to get the identity of the signer from the signature. The anonymity of this scheme depends on the difficulty of the LWE problem, when compute $Z_i = h_i s_i + e_i (\text{mod } q)$, for $i \neq j$ and e_j is randomly selected from Z_q^m for $e_j \leftarrow D_{\wedge^\perp(A)+t,s}$, it is difficult to get the answer because the LWE problem is hard. So e_j is statistically indistinguishable from others; And sample $r_i \leftarrow Z_q^n$, this guarantee r_i and other is statistical indistinguishable. Namely, the attacker must know tracking key to get the identity of the signer. So our scheme is anonymous.

4.2 Traceability

Traceability of visualized definition is the manager of group can open the signature to determine the identity of the signer when necessarily. In our scheme it is mean that the attacker who have the system public key and tracking key but no signature key can't construct a valid signature. Traceability of the scheme depends on the unforgeability of GPV signature. You can see the detail in literature.

If there is a PPT algorithm A which can attack our new scheme, we can construct a falsify PPT algorithm F of GPV signature. If algorithm A counterfeit a untraceable signature successfully, the algorithm F then can counterfeit a untraceable signature. It is incompatible that the signature of GPV is unforgeable.

5 Conclusion

Reducing the signature key size and improving computational efficiency has become the focus of the research on quantum cryptography. This paper uses faster sample on NTRU lattice according to the algorithm of discrete Gaussian distribution, built a new group signature based on NTRU lattice. First, the scheme reduce the signature key size and space consumption and significantly improve computational efficiency. Secondly, it is properly to enlarge the Gaussian sampling bias f and g to eliminate the question assumptions of small polynomials to obtain stronger safety.

Acknowledgements. This work is supported by "13th Five-Year" National Crypto Development Fund under Grant (No. MMJJ20170122), the Project of Education Department of Henan Province (No. 18A413001, No. 16A520013), Natural Science Foundation of Henan Polytechnic University (No. T2018-1).

References

1. Chaum, D., van Heyst, E.: Group signatures. In: Davies, D.W. (ed.) EUROCRYPT 1991. LNCS, vol. 547, pp. 257–265. Springer, Heidelberg (1991). https://doi.org/10.1007/3-540-46416-6_22
2. Ateniese, G., Camenisch, J., Joye, M., Tsudik, G.: A practical and provably secure coalition-resistant group signature scheme. In: Bellare, M. (ed.) CRYPTO 2000. LNCS, vol. 1880, pp. 255–270. Springer, Heidelberg (2000). https://doi.org/10.1007/3-540-44598-6_16
3. Boneh, D., Boyen, X., Shacham, H.: Short group signatures. In: Franklin, M. (ed.) CRYPTO 2004. LNCS, vol. 3152, pp. 41–55. Springer, Heidelberg (2004). https://doi.org/10.1007/978-3-540-28628-8_3
4. Gordon, S.D., Katz, J., Vaikuntanathan, V.: A group signature scheme from lattice assumptions. In: Abe, M. (ed.) ASIACRYPT 2010. LNCS, vol. 6477, pp. 395–412. Springer, Heidelberg (2010). https://doi.org/10.1007/978-3-642-17373-8_23
5. Laguillaumie, F., Langlois, A., Libert, B., Stehlé, D.: Lattice-based group signatures with logarithmic signature size. In: Sako, K., Sarkar, P. (eds.) ASIACRYPT 2013. LNCS, vol. 8270, pp. 41–61. Springer, Heidelberg (2013). https://doi.org/10.1007/978-3-642-42045-0_3

6. Nguyen, P.Q., Zhang, J., Zhang, Z.: Simpler efficient group signatures from lattices. In: Katz, J. (ed.) PKC 2015. LNCS, vol. 9020, pp. 401–426. Springer, Heidelberg (2015). https://doi.org/10.1007/978-3-662-46447-2_18
7. Kawachi, A., Tanaka, K., Xagawa, K.: Concurrently secure identification schemes based on the worst-case hardness of lattice problems. In: Pieprzyk, J. (ed.) ASIACRYPT 2008. LNCS, vol. 5350, pp. 372–389. Springer, Heidelberg (2008). https://doi.org/10.1007/978-3-540-89255-7_23
8. Ling, S., Nguyen, K., Stehlé, D., Wang, H.: Improved zero-knowledge proofs of knowledge for the isis problem, and applications. In: Kurosawa, K., Hanaoka, G. (eds.) PKC 2013. LNCS, vol. 7778, pp. 107–124. Springer, Heidelberg (2013). https://doi.org/10.1007/978-3-642-36362-7_8
9. Langlois, A., Ling, S., Nguyen, K., Wang, H.: Lattice-based group signature scheme with verifier-local revocation. In: Krawczyk, H. (ed.) PKC 2014. LNCS, vol. 8383, pp. 345–361. Springer, Heidelberg (2014). https://doi.org/10.1007/978-3-642-54631-0_20
10. Ling, S., Nguyen, K., Wang, H.: Group signatures from lattices: simpler, tighter, shorter, ring-based. In: Katz, J. (ed.) PKC 2015. LNCS, vol. 9020, pp. 427–449. Springer, Heidelberg (2015). https://doi.org/10.1007/978-3-662-46447-2_19
11. Libert, B., Ling, S., Nguyen, K., Wang, H.: Zero-knowledge arguments for lattice-based accumulators: logarithmic-size ring signatures and group signatures without trapdoors. In: Fischlin, M., Coron, J.-S. (eds.) EUROCRYPT 2016. LNCS, vol. 9666, pp. 1–31. Springer, Heidelberg (2016). https://doi.org/10.1007/978-3-662-49896-5_1
12. Libert, B., Mouhartem, F., Nguyen, K.: A lattice-based group signature scheme with message-dependent opening. In: Manulis, M., Sadeghi, A.-R., Schneider, S. (eds.) ACNS 2016. LNCS, vol. 9696, pp. 137–155. Springer, Cham (2016). https://doi.org/10.1007/978-3-319-39555-5_8
13. Libert, B., Ling, S., Mouhartem, F., Nguyen, K., Wang, H.: Signature schemes with efficient protocols and dynamic group signatures from lattice assumptions. In: Cheon, J.H., Takagi, T. (eds.) ASIACRYPT 2016. LNCS, vol. 10032, pp. 373–403. Springer, Heidelberg (2016). https://doi.org/10.1007/978-3-662-53890-6_13
14. Libert, B., Ling, S., Mouhartem, F., Nguyen, K., Wang, H.: Zero-knowledge arguments for matrix-vector relations and lattice-based group encryption. In: Cheon, J.H., Takagi, T. (eds.) ASIACRYPT 2016. LNCS, vol. 10032, pp. 101–131. Springer, Heidelberg (2016). https://doi.org/10.1007/978-3-662-53890-6_4
15. Bootle, J., Cerulli, A., Chaidos, P., Ghadafi, E., Groth, J.: Foundations of fully dynamic group signatures. In: Manulis, M., Sadeghi, A.-R., Schneider, S. (eds.) ACNS 2016. LNCS, vol. 9696, pp. 117–136. Springer, Cham (2016). https://doi.org/10.1007/978-3-319-39555-5_7
16. Hoffstein, J., Howgrave-Graham, N., Pipher, J., Silverman, J.H., Whyte, W.: Performance improvements and a baseline parameter generation algorithm for ntrusign. IACR Cryptology ePrint Archive 2005, p. 274 (2005)
17. Lyubashevsky, V., Prest, T.: Quadratic time, linear space algorithms for Gram-Schmidt orthogonalization and Gaussian sampling in structured lattices. In: Oswald, E., Fischlin, M. (eds.) EUROCRYPT 2015. LNCS, vol. 9056, pp. 789–815. Springer, Heidelberg (2015). https://doi.org/10.1007/978-3-662-46800-5_30
18. Kirchner, P., Fouque, P.-A.: Revisiting lattice attacks on overstretched NTRU parameters. In: Coron, J.-S., Nielsen, J.B. (eds.) EUROCRYPT 2017. LNCS, vol. 10210, pp. 3–26. Springer, Cham (2017). https://doi.org/10.1007/978-3-319-56620-7_1
19. Yang, Z., Fu, S., Qu, L., Li, C.: A lower dimension lattice attack on NTRU. Sci. China Inf. Sci. **61**(5), 059101 (2018)

Error Tolerant ASCA on FPGA

Chujiao Ma[(✉)] and John Chandy

Computer Science and Engineering Department, School of Engineering,
University of Connecticut, Storrs, CT 06269-4155, USA
chujiao.ma@uconn.edu

Abstract. Algebraic Side-Channel Attack (ASCA) is a side-channel attack that models the cryptographic algorithm and side-channel leakage from the system as a set of equations, then solves for the secret key. Unlike pure side-channel attacks, ASCA has low data complexity and can succeed in unknown plaintext/ciphertext scenarios. However, past research on ASCA has been done on either 8-bit microcontroller data or simulated data. In this paper, we explore the application and feasibility of error tolerant ASCA on different platforms, such as field-programmable gate array (FPGA) and examines the error model of Hamming weights in terms of success of the attack. FPGA runs faster and is more difficult for encryption power trace to be isolated so it presents more of a challenge for the attacker. Since FPGA is as susceptible to ASCA as 8-bit micro-controllers, the attack could have widespread implications since it may be applicable to other hardware platforms as well.

Keywords: Algebraic Side-Channel Attack · AES · Cryptography
Block cipher · FPGA

1 Introduction

Attacks such as side-channel analysis (SCA) observe leakages from the system such as power consumption and use them to break the algorithm. The power analysis attack assumes that different data and operations consume different amount of power. Since the input to the cryptographic algorithms consists of plaintext and a secret key, there is a correlation between the secret key and the leakage of any intermediate values. Most smart card processors are implemented with CMOS circuits, where the switching of the gates causes a current flow that is observable. The Hamming weight model, which counts the number of switches, is used to model the relationship between the power trace and the intermediate variables which are correlated with the secret key. With enough data, the attacker is able to acquire the secret key using a divide-and-conquer strategy. The power analysis attack is first proposed by [6] and successfully performed on DES. Since then, it has also been proven to be successful on all common modes (ECB, CBC, CFB, OFB, and CTR) of AES [5] as well as XTS-AES, an advanced mode of AES for data protection that features two secret keys and an additional tweak for each data block [8]. Since the attack targets the implementation of the

X. Sun et al. (Eds.): ICCCS 2018, LNCS 11065, pp. 563–572, 2018.
https://doi.org/10.1007/978-3-030-00012-7_51

cryptographic algorithm, even the most mathematically secure algorithm may still be vulnerable to it.

However, the success of the attack depends on the quality and quantity of side-channel data. Due to measurement limitations and error from noise, side-channel attacks often require hundreds and thousands of traces even with elaborate signal processing methods [7,11,19,21]. One of the more recent methods is to combine SCA with algebraic analysis [15]. This attack models the cryptographic algorithm and the side-channel information as a system of equations. The equations are then put through a solver to solve for the secret key. Not only does ASCA requires less information than pure SCA, it can also succeed in the unknown plaintext/ciphertext scenario while SCA requires knowledge of the plaintext or ciphertext. ASCA can also exploit leakages from all rounds of the algorithm while SCA can only attack the first or last round. SCA employs a divide-and-conquer strategy and finds the key one byte at time while ASCA has low data complexity and recovers the whole key at once. The performance of SASCA, ASCA, and DPA-based on real data are compared in [4].

While most side-channel information is based on 8-bit micro-controllers, side-channel information can be acquired and used to attack most devices that use CMOS circuits. Previous works, [14,17,18], have shown that variations of power analysis attack can successfully break ECC, DES, and RSA on FPGA. The attack has also been performed on AES implemented on an ASIC [13], STC89C52 Microprocessor [3], and a Cortex-M3 CPU [1]. While ASCA has been successfully performed based on data from 8-bit microcontroller and on simulated data, it has not been attempted on other devices such as FPGA. While FPGA runs faster and is more difficult for encryption power trace to be isolated, if it is susceptible to SCA then it should be susceptible to ASCA as well.

The success of ASCA depends on the complexity of the algorithm being modeled, but more importantly, the amount and accuracy of the side-channel information. In this paper, we explore the application and feasibility of ASCA on different platforms, such as FPGA and examine the error model of Hamming weights in terms of success of the attack.

The rest of the paper is organized as follows: Sect. 2 explains previous research done in the area. Section 3 describes how the attack is performed. Section 4 describes the target algorithm. Section 5 describes the experiments performed. Section 6 analyzes the attack and Sect. 7 concludes the paper.

2 Background

Power consumption can be acquired as side-channel information and used to attack most devices that use CMOS circuits. The first successful power analysis attack on FPGA was done by [14] on ECC. They confirmed that the amount of power consumed is linear to the number of switched flip-flops. Power analysis attack was also successful on DES and RSA for FPGA [18,20] as well as AES [17,19]. However, the results are highly dependent on the measurement capabilities and context. Since ASCA uses information from power consumption, it should be feasible for any platform or algorithm where power analysis attack is successful as well with fewer traces from the target. However, most of the studies done on ASCA are either based on simulated data or 8-bit microcontrollers. Past research for power analysis attack has shown that there is indeed a difference in the amount of data required when using simulated data vs. real power traces, [4,13,21]. Thus, ASCA may not be practical or feasible for more complex cryptographic algorithms or different platforms despite the success it achieved with AES on 8-bit microcontrollers.

While the performance of ASCA depends on the model and solver used, the success of ASCA mostly depends on the amount and accuracy of the side-channel information. The inaccuracy of the side-channel information from 8-bit microcontroller has been explored in [10,12,22] and there are many ways to make the attack more error tolerant. This paper explores the feasibility and performance of the attack on FPGA. It is more difficult to acquire accurate power consumption data from FPGA than 8-bit microcontrollers due to the higher speed and the difficulty of isolating the power consumption for the encryption/decryption process. We use data from SASEBO-GII, which is a board designed for the purpose of side-channel cryptographic attack experiments. It contains a cryptographic FPGA (Xilinx Virtex-5), and a control FPGA (Xilinx Spartan-3A) as well as a stable power supply. With template attack, we extract the Hamming weights from the power consumption data of AES-128 on FPGA, then use that in our error tolerant ASCA model to solve for the key. We evaluate the feasibility as well as the error model for the attack.

3 Tolerant Algebraic Side-Channel Analysis (TASCA)

The TASCA attack assumes the attacker has access to a Device Under Test (DUT) which emits a measurable side-channel leakage, such as power consumption, during encryption or decryption. The power consumption should be capturable with an oscilloscope with an error rate that the solver can handle. The TASCA methodology recovers the secret key from the power trace using the following steps:

- **Identify potential leaks.** The side-channel leakages used are power consumption traces, more specifically from the first round of AES-128.
- **Profile DUT and devise a decoding process.** The target DUT is the FPGA running cryptographic algorithm, Xilinx Virtex-5. Template attack is used to decode or extract information from the target.
- **Acquire power traces from DUT and decode the Hamming weights.** In this phase, the attacker accesses the actual DUT to collect a few power traces from it with an oscilloscope. Hamming weights are then extracted using the templates.
- **Model the DUT and side-channel information as set of algebraic equations.** The formal description of the algorithm, AES-128, the Hamming weights from the side-channel information as well as error variables are represented as a system of equations.

- **Solve for the secret key.** Given the model, as well as plaintext or ciphertext if desired, the solver finds the solution that satisfies the model, which should be the correct secret key.

The objective of the attack is to acquire the key with a high success rate using the least amount of information and in a reasonable amount of time.

4 Attack Model

The target algorithm in this paper is the symmetric block cipher AES-128. It takes blocks of 128 bits as input (plaintext), arranges it into a state of 4 by 4 bytes, and then combines it with a secret key. The output goes through 10 rounds of operations to produce the final ciphertext as illustrated in Fig. 1. Each round of AES consists of the following four subrounds, as illustrated in Fig. 2.

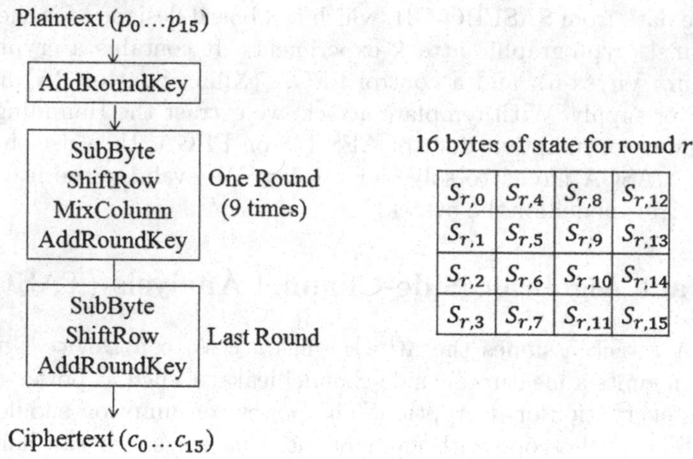

Fig. 1. AES-128.

For more details on the structure of AES, please refer to [2]. The AES algorithm as well as side-channel information are written using bit-vectors with a constraint programming model [9]. With this, we can adopt a more direct and natural formulation that does not require linearizations.

4.1 Template Attack

For template attack, the attacker records a large number of power traces on a copy of the target DUT for many different inputs (plaintext, keys). The attacker uses a multivariate Gaussian model to map the side-channel information to the Hamming weight of the intermediate values in the algorithm [12]. Instead of

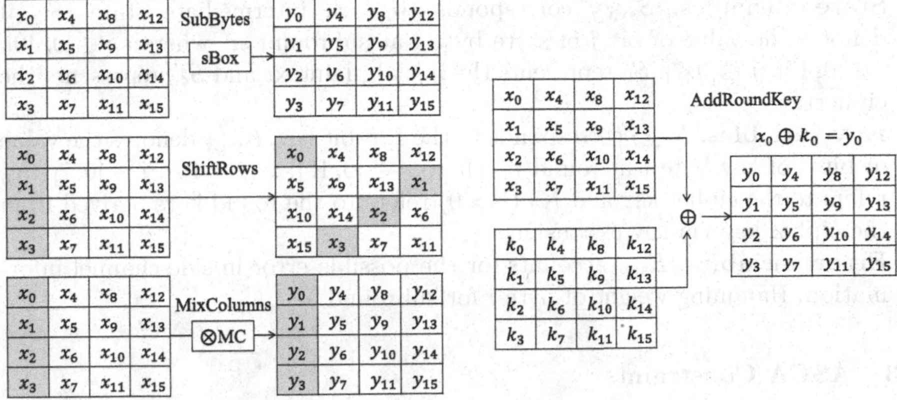

Fig. 2. The four subrounds of AES.

directly finding the key in a pure template attack, we are looking for Hamming weights instead.

Once we have a template for each possible Hamming weight value, then we match the power trace from the target during attack to each of the template. Thc power trace is modeled as $X_{measurement} = X_{actual} + N$, where the measured power trace is the actual power consumption plus noise. The noise is modeled as a Gaussian distribution with probability density function (PDF)

$$P(x) = \frac{1}{\sigma\sqrt{2\pi}} e^{-(x-\mu)^2 2\sigma^2}$$

where μ is the mean and σ is the standard deviation. This PDF is used to calculate how likely a certain measurement is. The one that matches the best is the most likely Hamming weight.

To increase accuracy, instead of just looking at Hamming weight at one point of the power trace, we look at multiple points of interest from the power trace to dctermine if the template is a match. Thus, for each possible Hamming weight value, we calculate a list of means and a matrix of covariance from the points of interest to use as the template. The points of interest are points that vary strongly between different operations and identified via sum of differences.

Once the Hamming weights are extracted, it is then added to the algebraic model of AES to perform ASCA.

4.2 ASCA Variables

Each state variable is represented by 16 bit-vectors that are 8-bit wide. Many of the AES subrounds, such as SubByte and MixColumns, operate over 8-bit values. Therefore, 8-bit wide bit-vectors are used for this model. The side-channel information and the state of the AES algorithm are modeled as decision variables below:

- **State variables.** $S_{sr,i,j}$ corresponds to each intermediate state. $S_{sr,i,j}$ denotes the value of bit j of state byte i at subround sr, where $sr \in [0, 40]$, $i \in [0, 15]$, $j \in [0, 7]$. S_0 represents the initial plaintext and S_{40} represents the ciphertext.
- **Key variables.** $K_{r,i,j}$ corresponds to the 128-bit key. $K_{r,i,j}$ denotes the value of bit j of key byte i at round r, where $r \in [0, 10]$, $i \in [0, 15]$, $j \in [0, 7]$. K_0 refers to the cipher key and K_r $(r > 0)$ refers to the round keys derived from the cipher key via key expansion.
- **Error variables.** $E_{sr,i}$ accounts for the possible error in side-channel information, Hamming weight of byte i for subround sr.

4.3 ASCA Constraints

- **AddKey/AddRoundKey** XOR the state with the round key.
- **SubByte** substitutes each byte of the state with another byte according to a look-up table or S-box.
- **ShiftRows & MixColumns** shifts each of the four rows of the state 0, 1, 2, and 3 bytes to the left then multiplies each column with a matrix of constants (MC). The two operations are combined together and the 8-bit efficient MixColumns implementation is used in the CP encoding.
- **Side-Channel Constraints** are created from the Hamming weight vector. The ***count*** constraint counts the number of bits with the value of 1 in a bit-vector and represents the actual Hamming weights. The constraint $M_{sr,i}$ is represented as Hamming weights with errors included:

$$count(S_{sr,i}) + e^{+}_{sr,i} - e^{-}_{sr,i} = M_{sr,i}$$

- **Objective Function** is modeled as the total number of errors, same as the IP model:

$$Min: \sum e^{+}_{sr,i} + \sum e^{-}_{sr,i}$$

In addition to providing a set of Hamming weights (HW) to account for errors, TASCA goes a step further and picks the most likely HW to branch/search first as part of the goal function.

5 Experiments

The side-channel information are power traces captured from a Xilinx Virtex-5 FPGA during encryption of AES-128. The template attack to create the template and extract Hamming weights are done using MATLAB. Once the Hamming weights are extracted from the template attack, it is then written as the constraint model together with the algorithm and error tolerance then solved with a CP solver. All experiments are done on a Mac with 3.1 GHz Intel Core i5 processor and 8 GB of memory.

5.1 Extracting Hamming Weights

We use 300,000 power traces from FGPA with different input and keys. The power traces are categorized by different Hamming weights (0 to 8). For each category or possible Hamming weight value, the mean trace as well as variances are calculated for the points of interest to form the template.

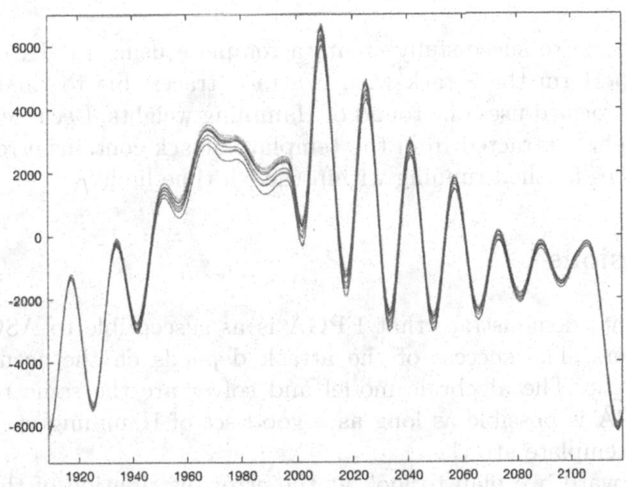

Fig. 3. Mean power consumption of the 9 possible Hamming weight values for one round of AES.

There is indeed a difference in power consumption between different Hamming weight values, as shown in Fig. 3. For each Hamming weight category, a template of the first round is created with the mean and variance for the points of interest with the greatest difference between categories.

It has been demonstrated in [16] that side-channel information such as Hamming weight can be acquired with 80% accuracy from 1 power trace by using **error detection** (rejecting side-channel information that gives rise to incoherent input/output values for the S-boxes) and **likelihood rating** (only uses a subset of all the Hamming weights extracted with the templates, starting with the most likely ones). IASCA in [10] explores the error tolerance of the Hamming weight by examining the distribution from 2000 attack traces. The distribution of error is illustrated in Table 1, which shows the accuracy of the template attack to extract Hamming weights from 8-bit microcontroller data of 2000 attack traces.

The error variable e_0 to e_4 denotes the set of Hamming weights with 0 to 4 errors. The error class e_0 contains only the correct Hamming weight (HW), e_1 is a set of Hamming weights with one error (HW, HW + 1), e_2 contains two errors (HW − 1, HW, HW + 1), e_3 contains 3 errors (HW − 1, HW, HW + 1, HW + 2), and e_4 contains 5 errors (HW − 2, HW − 1, HW, HW + 1, HW + 2). For all error classes, it is assumed that the correct Hamming weight is within the set.

Table 1. Error distribution from [10].

Error class	e_0	e_1	e_2	e_3	e_4
Occurrence	28%	44%	24%	4%	0%

6 Results

While we are able to successfully create a template using FPGA data, we are only able to perform the attack with 5 attack traces due to time constraint. The ASCA performed uses one round of Hamming weights. Because most of the Hamming weights extracted from the template attack contains error, only 3 of the attack traces finished running within the 5 h time limit.

7 Conclusions

The experiments demonstrate that FPGA is as susceptible to ASCA as 8-bit micro-controllers. The success of the attack depends on the accuracy of the Hamming weight. The algebraic model and solver are the same regardless of platform. ASCA is possible as long as a good set of Hamming weights can be extracted via template attack.

Moving forward, we plan to look at the error distribution of the Hamming weights as well as the noise distribution of each category since they are not evenly spaced. Because the success of ASCA depends on the accuracy of Hamming weight extracted from the template attack, it would also be interesting to see how to improve the template attack aspect. More specifically, how to choose points of interest and use statistical analysis to find correlation and improve accuracy.

References

1. Barenghi, A., Pelosi, G., Teglia, Y.: Improving first order differential power attacks through digital signal processing. In: Proceedings of the 3rd International Conference on Security of Information and Networks, SIN 2010, pp. 124–133. ACM, New York (2010). https://doi.org/10.1145/1854099.1854126
2. Daemen, J., Rijmen, V.: The Design of Rijndael: AES - The Advanced Encryption Standard. Springer, Heidelberg (2002). https://doi.org/10.1007/978-3-662-04722-4
3. Fei, H., Daheng, G.: Two kinds of correlation analysis method attack on implementations of advanced encryption standard software running inside STC89C52 microprocessor. In: 2016 2nd IEEE International Conference on Computer and Communications, ICCC, pp. 1265–1269, October 2016
4. Grosso, V., Standaert, F.-X.: ASCA, SASCA and DPA with enumeration: which one beats the other and when? In: Iwata, T., Cheon, J.H. (eds.) ASIACRYPT 2015. LNCS, vol. 9453, pp. 291–312. Springer, Heidelberg (2015). https://doi.org/10.1007/978-3-662-48800-3_12

5. Jayasinghe, D., Ragel, R., Ambrose, J.A., Ignjatovic, A., Parameswaran, S.: Advanced modes in AES: are they safe from power analysis based side channel attacks? In: 2014 IEEE 32nd International Conference on Computer Design, ICCD, pp. 173–180, October 2014
6. Kocher, P., Jaffe, J., Jun, B.: Differential Power Analysis. In: Wiener, M. (ed.) CRYPTO 1999. LNCS, vol. 1666, pp. 388–397. Springer, Heidelberg (1999). https://doi.org/10.1007/3-540-48405-1_25. http://dl.acm.org/citation.cfm?id=646764.703989
7. Lu, Y., O'Neill, M.P., McCanny, J.V.: FPGA implementation and analysis of random delay insertion countermeasure against DPA. In: 2008 International Conference on Field-Programmable Technology, pp. 201–208, December 2008
8. Luo, C., Fei, Y., Ding, A.A.: Side-channel power analysis of XTS-AES. In: Design, Automation Test in Europe Conference Exhibition, DATE, pp. 1330–1335, March 2017
9. Michel, L.D., Van Hentenryck, P.: Constraint satisfaction over bit-vectors. In: Milano, M. (ed.) CP 2012. LNCS, pp. 527–543. Springer, Heidelberg (2012). https://doi.org/10.1007/978-3-642-33558-7_39
10. Mohamed, M.S.E., Bulygin, S., Zohner, M., Heuser, A., Walter, M., Buchmann, J.: Improved algebraic side-channel attack on AES. J. Cryptograph. Eng. **3**(3), 139–156 (2013). https://doi.org/10.1007/s13389-013-0059-1
11. Mpalane, K., Gasela, N., Esiefarienrhe, B.M., Tsague, H.D.: Vulnerability of advanced encryption standard algorithm to differential power analysis attacks implemented on ATmega-128 microcontroller. In: 2016 Third International Conference on Artificial Intelligence and Pattern Recognition, AIPR, pp. 1–5, September 2016
12. Oren, Y., Weisse, O., Wool, A.: Practical template-algebraic side channel attacks with extremely low data complexity. In: Proceedings of the 2nd International Workshop on Hardware and Architectural Support for Security and Privacy, HASP 2013, pp. 7:1–7:8. ACM, New York (2013). https://doi.org/10.1145/2487726.2487733
13. Ors, S.B., Gurkaynak, F., Oswald, E., Preneel, B.: Power-analysis attack on an ASIC AES implementation. In: 2004 Proceedings of the International Conference on Information Technology: Coding and Computing, ITCC 2004, vol. 2, pp. 546–552, April 2004
14. Örs, S.B., Oswald, E., Preneel, B.: Power-analysis attacks on an FPGA – first experimental results. In: Walter, C.D., Koç, Ç.K., Paar, C. (eds.) CHES 2003. LNCS, vol. 2779, pp. 35–50. Springer, Heidelberg (2003). https://doi.org/10.1007/978-3-540-45238-6_4
15. Renauld, M., Standaert, F.-X.: Algebraic side-channel attacks. In: Bao, F., Yung, M., Lin, D., Jing, J. (eds.) Inscrypt 2009. LNCS, vol. 6151, pp. 393–410. Springer, Heidelberg (2010). https://doi.org/10.1007/978-3-642-16342-5_29
16. Renauld, M., Standaert, F.-X., Veyrat-Charvillon, N.: Algebraic side-channel attacks on the AES: why time also matters in DPA. In: Clavier, C., Gaj, K. (eds.) CHES 2009. LNCS, vol. 5747, pp. 97–111. Springer, Heidelberg (2009). https://doi.org/10.1007/978-3-642-04138-9_8
17. Standaert, F.-X., Mace, F., Peeters, E., Quisquater, J.-J.: Updates on the security of FPGAs against power analysis attacks. In: Bertels, K., Cardoso, J.M.P., Vassiliadis, S. (eds.) ARC 2006. LNCS, vol. 3985, pp. 335–346. Springer, Heidelberg (2006). https://doi.org/10.1007/11802839_42

18. Standaert, F.-X., van Oldeneel tot Oldenzeel, L., Samyde, D., Quisquater, J.-J.: Power analysis of FPGAs: how practical is the attack? In: Y. K. Cheung, P., Constantinides, G.A. (eds.) FPL 2003. LNCS, vol. 2778, pp. 701–710. Springer, Heidelberg (2003). https://doi.org/10.1007/978-3-540-45234-8_68
19. Standaert, F.-X., Örs, S.B., Preneel, B.: Power analysis of an FPGA implementation of Rijndael: is pipelining a DPA countermeasure? In: Joye, M., Quisquater, J.-J. (eds.) CHES 2004. LNCS, vol. 3156, pp. 30–44. Springer, Heidelberg (2004). https://doi.org/10.1007/978-3-540-28632-5_3
20. Standaert, F.-X., Örs, S.B., Quisquater, J.-J., Preneel, B.: Power analysis attacks against FPGA implementations of the DES. In: Becker, J., Platzner, M., Vernalde, S. (eds.) FPL 2004. LNCS, vol. 3203, pp. 84–94. Springer, Heidelberg (2004). https://doi.org/10.1007/978-3-540-30117-2_11
21. Standaert, O.X., Peeters, E., Rouvroy, G., Quisquater, J.J.: An overview of power analysis attacks against field programmable gate arrays. Proc. IEEE **94**(2), 383–394 (2006)
22. Zhao, X., et al.: MDASCA: an enhanced algebraic side-channel attack for error tolerance and new leakage model exploitation. In: Schindler, W., Huss, S.A. (eds.) COSADE 2012. LNCS, vol. 7275, pp. 231–248. Springer, Heidelberg (2012). https://doi.org/10.1007/978-3-642-29912-4_17

Fuzzy Identity-Based Signature from Lattices for Identities in a Large Universe

Yanhua Zhang[1(✉)], Yong Gan[2], Yifeng Yin[1], Huiwen Jia[3], and Yinghui Meng[1]

[1] Zhengzhou University of Light Industry, Zhengzhou 450002, China
{yhzhang,yinyifeng,yinghuimeng}@zzuli.edu.cn
[2] Zhengzhou Institute of Technology, Zhengzhou 450044, China
yongg@zzuli.edu.cn
[3] Guangzhou University, Guangzhou 510006, China
hwjia@gzhu.edu.cn

Abstract. A fuzzy identity-based signature (FIBS) is exactly like a traditional identity-based signature except that a signature issued under an identity id can be verified under any identity id′ that is "close enough" to id. This property allows FIBS having an efficient application in biometric authentication and three schemes over lattices exist, two constructions in the random oracle model and one in the standard model. However, the identities can only support binary vectors, i.e., $\{0,1\}^\ell$, which greatly limit the scope of its application. In this paper, a FIBS scheme from the hardness of lattice problems for identities living in a large universe, i.e., $(\mathbb{Z}_q^n)^\ell$, is proposed, so that they can capture more expressive attributes and the new construction is proved to be existentially unforgetable against adaptively chosen identity and message attacks (EU-aID-CMA) in the random oracle model.

Keywords: FIBS · Large universe · Lattice
Random oracle model

1 Introduction

Identity-based cryptosystem was introduced by Shamir [10] to reduce the complexity of managing the public key infrastructure (PKI). In this system, including identity based encryption (IBE) and identity-based signature (IBS), the identity is regarded as public key, and the private key generator (PKG) can generate a private key corresponding to that identity information. The concept of fuzzy identity-based encryption (FIBE) was first proposed by Sahai and Waters [9]. In a FIBE system, identities are regarded as a set of biometric attributes (e.g., fingerprints and irises) instead of an arbitrary string just like an email address in previous IBE system. Soon afterwards, a novel cryptographic primitive called fuzzy identity-based signature (FIBS) was introduced by Yang, Cao and Dong [14]. In a FIBS scheme, the signature issued by a signer with an identity id can be validly verified by identity id′ if and only if id and id′ are "close enough" and

X. Sun et al. (Eds.): ICCCS 2018, LNCS 11065, pp. 573–584, 2018.
https://doi.org/10.1007/978-3-030-00012-7_52

within a certain distance. Then, a large number of FIBS constructions based on the classic hardness of number-theoretic cryptographic problems (e.g., integer factorization and discrete logarithm) were proposed [12,13,15,18]. However, all of these constructions are insecure in a future with large-scale quantum computers [11].

As one of the most promising candidates for post-quantum cryptography, lattice-based cryptography has attracted significant interest in recent years, due to several potential benefits: asymptotic efficiency, worst-case hardness assumptions and security against quantum computers. To design secure and efficient lattice-based cryptographic schemes are interesting and challenging.

The first FIBS scheme over lattices was constructed by Yao and Li [17], and their construction is existentially unforgeable against adaptively chosen identity and message attacks (EU-aID-CMA) in the random oracle model. A lattice-based construction without random oracle (i.e., in the standard model) was proposed by Yang *et al.* [16] and achieves a strong unforgeability under selectively chosen identity and chosen message attacks (SU-sID-CMA). Recently, using the lattice basis delegation technique to keep the lattice dimension invariant, another FIBS scheme in the random oracle model was given [19]. However, all the constructions can only support identities in a small universe, namely, only considering identities as bit-vectors in $\{0,1\}^\ell$, where ℓ is the identities size.

1.1 Our Contributions

In order to have identities live in some large space, so that they can capture more expressive attributes and be used as an efficient tool in biometric authentication and attribute-based signatures, etc. In this paper, we present a FIBS scheme from the hardness of lattice problems for identities in a large universe, i.e., $(\mathbb{Z}_q^n)^\ell$, and then prove it to be EU-aID-CMA in the random oracle model.

1.2 Roadmap

The rest of this paper is organized as follows. In Sect. 2, we firstly introduce notations, the definition and security requirements for FIBS. Section 3 turns to recall several algorithms and hardness problems on lattices. Finally, a lattice FIBS scheme, the security and efficiency analysis are presented in Sect. 4.

2 Preliminaries

2.1 Notation

Vectors are in column form and denoted by bold lower-case letters (e.g., $\mathbf{a}$). The i-th component of $\mathbf{a}$ is denoted by a_i. Matrix is simply viewed as the set of its column vectors and denoted by bold upper-case letters (e.g., $\mathbf{A}$). The Euclidean norm of $\mathbf{a}$ is denoted as $\|\mathbf{a}\|$, and we define the norm of $\mathbf{A}$ as the norm of its longest column (i.e., $\|\mathbf{A}\| = \max_i \|\mathbf{a}_i\|$). The security parameter is n and all other quantities are implicit function of n. Let poly(n) denote an unspecified function $f(n) = O(n^c)$ for any constant $c > 0$. If $f(n) = O(g(n) \cdot \log^c n)$, it is denoted as $f(n) = \widetilde{O}(g(n))$. We use negl($n$) to denote a negligible function $f(n) = O(n^{-c})$ for all $c > 0$, and a probability is called overwhelming if it is $1-\text{negl}(n)$.

2.2 Syntax of FIBS

Here,. we formalize the definition and security model of FIBS as [15,17,19].

Definition 1. *A Fuzzy identity-based signature scheme consists of the following four probabilistic polynomial-time (PPT) algorithms:*

- ***FIBS.Setup***(1^n)*: A PPT algorithm that takes as input the security parameter n, and outputs a public parameters* PP *that contains an error tolerance parameter k and a master key* MK.
- ***FIBS.Extract****(PP, MK, id): A PPT algorithm that takes as input the public parameters PP, the master key MK, and an identity id, and outputs a private key associate with id, denoted by* SK_{id}.
- ***FIBS.Sign***(PP, SK_{id}, *m): A PPT algorithm that takes as input the public parameters PP, a private key* SK_{id} *associated with an identity id, and a message m, and outputs a signature* $\sigma_{\text{id,m}}$ *for identity id with message m.*
- ***FIBS.Verify****(PP, id', m,* $\sigma_{\text{id,m}}$*): A deterministic algorithm that takes as input the public parameters PP, an identity id' such that* $|id \cap id'| \geq k$*, the message m and the corresponding signature* $\sigma_{\text{id,m}}$*, and outputs "1" if the signature is valid or "0", otherwise.*

The correctness is that for any fixed identity id, and any id′ such that $|\text{id} \cap \text{id}'| \geq k$, if $\sigma_{\text{id,m}}$ is a valid signature generated by **FIBS.Sign**(PP,SK_{id},m), then it holds that **FIBS.Verify**(PP, id', m, $\sigma_{\text{id,m}}$) = 1.

We consider the security model of FIBS as existentially unforgeable against adaptively chosen identity and message attacks (EU-aID-CMA) as [17,19].

Let $\mathcal{A}$ be any PPT adversary, and $\mathcal{C}$ be a challenger assumed to be a probabilistic Turing machine taking as input the security parameter n. Consider the following game between $\mathcal{A}$ and $\mathcal{C}$.

Setup: $\mathcal{C}$ runs **FIBS.Setup** of FIBS and provides $\mathcal{A}$ the public parameters PP.

Queries 1: $\mathcal{A}$ is allowed to make poly-bounded queries as follows:

- **Extract query**: $\mathcal{A}$ issues private key queries for any identities id_i adaptively.
- **Sign query**: $\mathcal{A}$ issues sign queries for id_i on any message m_i adaptively.

Challenge: $\mathcal{A}$ declares the target identity id^* where $|\text{id}_i \cap \text{id}^*| < k$ for all id_i got from **Queries 1**.

Queries 2: $\mathcal{A}$ issues additional poly-bounded private key queries for any identities id_j, where $|\text{id}_j \cap \text{id}^*| < k$ and sign queries for any identity adaptively.

Forgery: Finally, $\mathcal{A}$ outputs $(\text{id}^*, \text{m}^*, \sigma^*_{\text{id},\text{m}^*})$. $\mathcal{A}$ is considered to be succeed if the following conditions hold:

1. **FIBS.Verify**$(\mathsf{PP}, \mathrm{id}^*, \mathrm{m}^*, \sigma^*_{\mathrm{id},\mathrm{m}^*}) = 1$.
2. For any $(\mathrm{id}, \mathrm{m}, \sigma_{\mathrm{id},\mathrm{m}})$ that is generated in **signquery**, we have i. $|\mathrm{id} \cap \mathrm{id}^*| \geq k$, $\mathrm{m} \neq \mathrm{m}^*$; or ii. $|\mathrm{id} \cap \mathrm{id}^*| < k$.
   The advantage is defined as $\mathsf{Adv}_{\mathcal{A}} = \Pr[\textbf{FIBS.Verify}(\mathsf{PP}, \mathrm{id}^*, \mathrm{m}^*, \sigma^*_{\mathrm{id},\mathrm{m}^*}) = 1]$.

Definition 2. *A FIBS scheme is said to be EU-aID-CMA if $\mathsf{Adv}_{\mathcal{A}}$ is negligible in the security parameter n for any PPT $\mathcal{A}$.*

3 Lattices

3.1 Integer Lattices

Definition 3. *Let $\boldsymbol{B} = \{\boldsymbol{b}_1, \boldsymbol{b}_2, \ldots, \boldsymbol{b}_m\} \in \mathbb{R}^{m\times m}$ be a matrix with m linearly independent vectors. The m-dimensional lattice Λ generated by $\boldsymbol{B}$ is as follows:*

$$\Lambda = \mathcal{L}(\boldsymbol{B}) = \{\boldsymbol{y} \in \mathbb{R}^m : \exists \boldsymbol{s} \in \mathbb{Z}^m, \boldsymbol{y} = \boldsymbol{B}\boldsymbol{s}\} \tag{1}$$

Definition 4. *For integer $q \geq 2$ and a matrix $\boldsymbol{A} \in \mathbb{Z}_q^{n\times m}$, define:*

$$\Lambda_q^{\perp}(\boldsymbol{A}) = \{\boldsymbol{e} \in \mathbb{Z}^m : \boldsymbol{A}\boldsymbol{e} = \boldsymbol{0} \bmod q\} \tag{2}$$

How to obtain a matrix $\mathbf{A}$ with a low Gram-Schmidt norm basis for $\Lambda_q^{\perp}(\mathbf{A})$ was introduced by Ajtai [3], and two improved algorithms investigated by [4,7].

Lemma 1. *Let integers $n \geq 1$, $q \geq 2$, and $m = \lceil 2n\log q \rceil$. There exists a PPT algorithm TrapGen(q, n, m) that outputs $\boldsymbol{A}$ and $\boldsymbol{T_A}$ such that $\boldsymbol{A}$ is statistically close to a uniform matrix in $\mathbb{Z}_q^{n\times m}$ and $\boldsymbol{T_A} \in \mathbb{Z}^{m\times m}$ is a short basis for $\Lambda_q^{\perp}(\boldsymbol{A})$, satisfying $\|\widetilde{\boldsymbol{T_A}}\| \leq O(\sqrt{n\log q})$ with all but a negligible probability in n.*

3.2 Discrete Gaussian Distributions

For any $s > 0$, a Gaussian function on $\mathbb{R}^m$, centered at $\mathbf{c}$ with parameter s is as follows: $\forall \mathbf{x} \in \mathbb{R}^m$, $\rho_{s,\mathbf{c}}(\mathbf{x}) = \exp(\frac{-\pi\|\mathbf{x}-\mathbf{c}\|^2}{s^2})$

Definition 5. *For any $\mathbf{c} \in \mathbb{R}^m$, real $s > 0$ and m-dimensional lattice Λ, define the discrete Gaussian distribution over Λ as:*

$$\forall \boldsymbol{x} \in \Lambda,\ D_{\Lambda,s,\mathbf{c}}(\boldsymbol{x}) = \frac{\rho_{s,\mathbf{c}}(\boldsymbol{x})}{\rho_{s,\mathbf{c}}(\Lambda)} = \frac{\rho_{s,\mathbf{c}}(\boldsymbol{x})}{\sum_{\boldsymbol{x}\in\Lambda}\rho_{s,\mathbf{c}}(\boldsymbol{x})} \tag{3}$$

The subscripts s and $\mathbf{c}$ are taken to be 1 and $\boldsymbol{0}$, respectively, when omitted.

Micciancio and Regev [8] defined a new quantity called smoothing parameter.

Definition 6. *For lattice Λ and a real $\epsilon > 0$, the smoothing parameter η_ϵ is the smallest real $s > 0$ such that $\rho_{1/s}(\Lambda^*\backslash\{0\}) \leq \epsilon$, where Λ^* is the dual of Λ.*

Lemma 2. *Assume that the columns of $\boldsymbol{A} \in \mathbb{Z}_q^{n\times m}$ generate $\mathbb{Z}_q^n$, let $\epsilon \in (0, 1/2)$, $s \geq \eta_\epsilon(\Lambda^\perp(\boldsymbol{A}))$. Then for $\boldsymbol{e} \leftarrow D_{\mathbb{Z}^m,s}$, the distribution of syndrome $\boldsymbol{u} = \boldsymbol{A}\boldsymbol{e}$ mod q is within statistical distance 2ϵ of uniform over $\mathbb{Z}_q^n$.*

Given a short basis, Gentry *et al.* [6] showed how to sample from a discrete Gaussian distribution over lattices.

Lemma 3. *Let integer $q \geq 2$, $\boldsymbol{A} \in \mathbb{Z}_q^{n\times m}$, and real $0 < \epsilon < 1$. Let $\boldsymbol{T_A}$ be a short basis for $\Lambda_q^\perp(\boldsymbol{A})$, parameter $s \geq \|\widetilde{\boldsymbol{T_A}}\| \cdot \omega(\sqrt{\log m})$. Then for $\boldsymbol{c} \in \mathbb{R}^m$, $\boldsymbol{u} \in \mathbb{Z}_q^n$:*

1. $Pr_{x \leftarrow D_{\Lambda,s,c}}[\|\boldsymbol{x} - \boldsymbol{c}\| > s\sqrt{m}] \leq \frac{1+\epsilon}{1-\epsilon} \cdot 2^{-m}$.
2. *A PPT algorithm SampleGau($\boldsymbol{A}, \boldsymbol{T_A}, s, \boldsymbol{c}$) returns $\boldsymbol{e} \in \Lambda_q^\perp(\boldsymbol{A})$ drawn from a distribution statistically close to $D_{\Lambda_q^\perp(\boldsymbol{A}),s,\boldsymbol{c}}$.*
3. *A PPT algorithm SamplePre($\boldsymbol{A}, \boldsymbol{T_A}, \boldsymbol{u}, s$) returns $\boldsymbol{e} \in \Lambda_q^{\boldsymbol{u}}(\boldsymbol{A})$ sampled from a distribution statistically close to $D_{\Lambda_q^{\boldsymbol{u}}(\boldsymbol{A}),s}$.*

3.3 Useful Facts

In this subsection, we recall several useful facts on lattices in literatures [1,5].

Lemma 4. *On input $\boldsymbol{A} \in \mathbb{Z}_q^{n\times m}$, whose columns generate the entire group $\mathbb{Z}_q^n$ and an arbitrary $\boldsymbol{A}' \in \mathbb{Z}_q^{n\times m'}$. Given a basis $\boldsymbol{T_A}$ of $\Lambda_q^\perp(\boldsymbol{A})$, there is a deterministic polynomial-time algorithm ExtBasis($\boldsymbol{T_A}, \hat{\boldsymbol{A}} = [\boldsymbol{A}|\boldsymbol{A}']$) that outputs a basis $\boldsymbol{T}_{\hat{\boldsymbol{A}}}$ for $\Lambda_q^\perp(\hat{\boldsymbol{A}}) \subseteq \mathbb{Z}^{m+m'}$ such that $\|\widetilde{\boldsymbol{T}_{y\hat{\boldsymbol{A}}}}\| = \|\widetilde{\boldsymbol{T_A}}\|$. Moreover, this statement holds even for any given permutation of the columns of $\hat{\boldsymbol{A}}$.*

Lemma 5. *On input $\boldsymbol{A} \in \mathbb{Z}_q^{n\times m}$, $s \geq \|\widetilde{\boldsymbol{T_A}}\| \cdot \omega(\sqrt{\log n})$. Given a basis $\boldsymbol{T_A}$ of $\Lambda_q^\perp(\boldsymbol{A})$, there is a PPT algorithm RandBasis($\boldsymbol{A}, \boldsymbol{T_A}, s$) that outputs a basis $\boldsymbol{T}'_{\boldsymbol{A}}$ for $\Lambda_q^\perp(\boldsymbol{A})$ such that $\|\boldsymbol{T}'_{\boldsymbol{A}}\| \leq s\sqrt{m}$ and no information specific to $\boldsymbol{T_A}$ is leaked.*

Lemma 6. *Let integer $n \geq 1$, suppose that $m > (n+1)\log q + \omega(\log n)$ and q is a prime. Let $\boldsymbol{A}$ and $\boldsymbol{B}$ be matrices chosen uniformly in $\mathbb{Z}_q^{n\times m}$, and $\boldsymbol{R}$ is an $m \times m$-matrix chosen uniformly in $\{-1,1\}^{m\times m}$mod q. Then, for all vectors $\boldsymbol{w}$ in $\mathbb{Z}_q^m$, the distribution $(\boldsymbol{A}, \boldsymbol{A}\boldsymbol{R}, \boldsymbol{R}^\top\boldsymbol{w})$ is statistically close to $(\boldsymbol{A}, \boldsymbol{B}, \boldsymbol{R}^\top\boldsymbol{w})$.*

Lemma 7. *Let $\boldsymbol{R}$ be an $m\times m$-matrix chosen at random from $\{-1,1\}^{m\times m}$. For vectors $\boldsymbol{e} \in \mathbb{R}^m$, $Pr[\|\boldsymbol{R}\boldsymbol{e}\| > \|\boldsymbol{e}\| \cdot \sqrt{m} \cdot \omega(\sqrt{\log m})] <$ negl(m).*

Lemma 8. *Let prime $q \geq 3$, integer n, and $m > n$, two matrices $\boldsymbol{A}$, $\boldsymbol{B} \in \mathbb{Z}_q^{n\times m}$ and a parameter $s \geq \|\widetilde{\boldsymbol{T_B}}\| \cdot \sqrt{m} \cdot \omega(\log m)$. There exists a PPT algorithm SampleRight($\boldsymbol{A}, \boldsymbol{B}, \boldsymbol{R}, \boldsymbol{T_B}, \boldsymbol{u}, s$) that given a short basis $\boldsymbol{T_B}$ of $\Lambda_q^\perp(\boldsymbol{B})$, a matrix $\boldsymbol{R} \in \{-1,1\}^{m\times m}$ and a vector $\boldsymbol{u} \in \mathbb{Z}_q^n$, outputs a vector $\boldsymbol{e} \in \mathbb{Z}^{2m}$ distributed statistically close to $D_{\Lambda_q^{\boldsymbol{u}}(\boldsymbol{F}),s}$, where $\boldsymbol{F} = [\boldsymbol{A}|\boldsymbol{A}\boldsymbol{R} + \boldsymbol{B}]$.*

3.4 The SIS Hardness Assumption

Definition 7. *The SIS problem in Euclidean norm is that given a integer q, a matrix $\boldsymbol{A} \in \mathbb{Z}_q^{n\times m}$ and a real β, find a non-zero vector $\boldsymbol{e} \in \mathbb{Z}^m$ such that $\boldsymbol{Ae} = \boldsymbol{0} \bmod q$ and $\|\mathbf{e}\| \leq \beta$.*

Lemma 9. *For poly-bounded m, $\beta = \mathrm{poly}(n)$ and prime $q \geq \beta \cdot \omega(\sqrt{n\log n})$, the average-case $SIS_{q,n,m,\beta}$ problem is as hard as approximating the shortest independent vector (SIVP) problem, among others, in worst-case to within certain $\gamma = \beta \cdot \widetilde{O}(\sqrt{n})$ factors.*

4 Lattice FIBS for Identities in a Large Universe

Inspired by the IBE scheme [1], we now construct a FIBS scheme from lattices for identities in a large universe. In the construction outlined, our identities are ℓ-vectors of attributes in $\mathbb{Z}_q^n$, so that they can capture more expressive attributes.

4.1 Our Construction

FIBS.Setup(1^n) : Take as input a security parameter n and set the parameters ℓ, k, q, m, s_1, s_2 as specified in the next subsection, where ℓ (ℓ depends on n) is the identity size, k ($k < \ell$) is an error tolerance parameter. Then, do the steps as follows:

1. For $i = 1, 2, \ldots, \ell$, run $\mathsf{TrapGen}(q, n, m)$ to generate a uniformly random $n \times m$-matrix $\mathbf{A}_{0,i} \in \mathbb{Z}_q^{n\times m}$ together with a short basis $\mathbf{T}_{\mathbf{A}_{0,i}} \in \mathbb{Z}^{m\times m}$ for $\Lambda_q^{\perp}(\mathbf{A}_{0,i})$ such that $\|\widetilde{\mathbf{T}_{\mathbf{A}_{0,i}}}\| \leq O(\sqrt{n\log q})$.
2. For $i = 1, 2, \ldots, \ell$, select two random matrices $\mathbf{A}_{1,i}$ and $\mathbf{B}_i$ in $\mathbb{Z}_q^{n\times m}$.
3. Let $H_1 : \{\mathbb{Z}_q\}^* \to \mathbb{Z}_q^{n\times n}$ and $H_2 : \{0,1\}^* \to \mathbb{Z}_q^n$ be two collision-resistance hash functions.
4. Output the public parameters PP and the master key MK,

$$\mathsf{PP} = (\{\mathbf{A}_{0,i}, \mathbf{A}_{1,i}, \mathbf{B}_i\}_{i=1,2,\ldots,\ell}, H_1, H_2),\ \mathsf{MK} = (\{\mathbf{T}_{\mathbf{A}_{0,i}}\}_{i=1,2,\ldots,\ell}).$$

FIBS.Extract$(\mathsf{PP}, \mathsf{MK}, \mathrm{id})$: Take as input the public parameters PP, the master key MK, and an identity $\mathrm{id} = (\mathrm{id}_1, \ldots, \mathrm{id}_\ell)$ where $\mathrm{id}_i \in \mathbb{Z}_q^n$ for $i = 1, 2, \ldots, \ell$, then do the steps as follows:

1. For id_i, $i = 1, 2, \ldots, \ell$, construct an $n \times 2m$-matrix $\mathbf{A}'_{i,\mathrm{id}_i} = [\mathbf{A}_{0,i}|\mathbf{A}_{1,i} + H_1(\mathrm{id}, \mathrm{id}_i, i)\mathbf{B}_i]$.
2. For id_i, $i = 1, 2, \ldots, \ell$, compute a matrix $\mathbf{T}_{\mathbf{A}'_{i,\mathrm{id}_i}} \in \mathbb{Z}^{2m\times 2m}$ using algorithm $\mathsf{RandBasis}(\mathsf{ExtBasis}(\mathbf{T}_{\mathbf{A}_{0,i}}, \mathbf{A}'_{i,\mathrm{id}_i}), s_1)$.
3. Output $\mathsf{SK}_{\mathrm{id}} = (\mathbf{T}_{\mathbf{A}'_{1,\mathrm{id}_1}}, \mathbf{T}_{\mathbf{A}'_{2,\mathrm{id}_2}}, \ldots, \mathbf{T}_{\mathbf{A}'_{\ell,\mathrm{id}_\ell}})$.

FIBS.Sign$(\mathsf{PP}, \mathsf{SK}_{\mathrm{id}}, \mathrm{m})$: Take as input the public parameters PP, a private key $\mathsf{SK}_{\mathrm{id}}$ associated with an identity $\mathrm{id} = (\mathrm{id}_1, \ldots, \mathrm{id}_\ell) \in (\mathbb{Z}_q^n)^\ell$ and a message $\mathrm{m} \in \{0,1\}^*$, then do the steps as follows:

1. Set an n-dimensional vector $\mathbf{v} = H_2(\text{m})$.
2. Construct ℓ shares of $\mathbf{v} = (v_1, \ldots, v_n) \in \mathbb{Z}_q^n$ using a Shamir Secret-Sharing scheme applied to each coordinate of $\mathbf{v}$ independently. Namely, for each $j = 1, \ldots, n$, choose a uniformly random polynomial $p_j \in \mathbb{Z}_q[x]$ of degree $k-1$ such that $p_j(0) = v_j$.
3. Construct the j-th share vector, $\hat{\mathbf{v}}_j = (p_1(j), p_2(j), \ldots, p_n(j)) \in \mathbb{Z}_q^n$. Thus for all $J \subseteq \{1, 2, \ldots, \ell\}$ satisfying $|J| \geq k$, there are fractional Lagrangian coefficients $L_j \in \mathbb{Z}_q$ such that $\mathbf{v} = \sum_{j \in J} L_j \cdot \hat{\mathbf{v}}_j \bmod q$.
4. For id_i, $i = 1, 2, \ldots, \ell$, compute a 2m-dimensional vector $\mathbf{e}_i \in \mathbb{Z}^{2m}$ using $\mathsf{SamplePre}(\mathbf{A}'_{i,\text{id}_i}, \mathbf{T}_{\mathbf{A}'_{i,\text{id}_i}}, q\hat{\mathbf{v}}_i, s_2)$.
5. Output the signature $\sigma_{\text{id,m}} = (\text{m}, \text{id}, \mathbf{e}_1, \ldots, \mathbf{e}_\ell)$.

FIBS.Verify$(\mathsf{PP}, \text{id}', \text{m}, \sigma_{\text{id,m}})$: Take as input the public parameters PP, identity $\text{id}' = (\text{id}'_1, \ldots, \text{id}'_\ell) \in (\mathbb{Z}_q^n)^\ell$, a message m, and a signature $\sigma_{\text{id,m}}$, then do the steps as follows:

1. Let $J \subseteq \{1, \ldots, \ell\}$ denote the set of matching elements in id and id$'$. If $|J| < k$, then output $\perp$. Otherwise, for $j \in J$, compute $\mathbf{A}'_{j,\text{id}_j} = [\mathbf{A}_{0,j} | \mathbf{A}_{1,j} + H_1(\text{id}, \text{id}_j, j)\mathbf{B}_j]$.
2. If $\|\mathbf{e}_i\| \leq s_2\sqrt{2m}$ and $\sum_{j \in J} L_j \cdot \mathbf{A}'_{j,\text{id}_j} \mathbf{e}_j = qH_2(\text{m})$, where $L_j = \prod_{j \in J, i \neq j} \frac{i}{i-j}$ is the Lagrangian coefficient, then output "1". Otherwise, "0".

4.2 Correctness

Let $\sigma_{\text{id,m}} = (\text{m}, \text{id}, \mathbf{e}_1, \ldots, \mathbf{e}_\ell)$ be a valid signature. To check the correctness, it is only need to consider the case $|J| \geq k$, where $J \subseteq \{1, 2, \ldots, \ell\}$ denotes the set of matching elements in id and id$'$. According to Lemma 3, for $i = 1, 2, \ldots, \ell$, $\mathbf{e}_i \in \mathbb{Z}^{2m}$ satisfies $\mathbf{A}'_{i,\text{id}_i} \mathbf{e}_i = q\hat{\mathbf{v}}_i$ and it is drawn from a distribution statistically close to $D_{\Lambda_q^{q\hat{\mathbf{v}}_i}(\mathbf{A}_{i,\text{id}_i}), s_2}$. Therefore, $\|\mathbf{e}_i\| \leq s_2\sqrt{2m}$ and $\sum_{j \in J} L_j \cdot \mathbf{A}'_{j,\text{id}_j} \mathbf{e}_j = \sum_{j \in J} L_j \cdot q\hat{\mathbf{v}}_j = qH_2(\text{m})$.

4.3 Parameters

The above construction depends on several parameters ℓ, k, q, m, s_1, s_2. The security parameter is n and all other parameters are determined as follows:

1. For $\mathsf{TrapGen}(q, n, m)$ in Lemma 1, we need $m = \lceil 2n\text{log}q \rceil$.
2. To ensure that the $\text{SIS}_{q,n,m,\beta}$ problem has a worst-case lattice reduction, according to Lemma 9, we set $q \geq \beta \cdot \omega(\sqrt{n\text{log}n})$. The parameter β is set in the next subsection.
3. The identity size $\ell = n^\epsilon$ for some constant $\epsilon \in (0, 1)$ and the error tolerance parameter $k < \ell$.
4. Due to Lemma 4, we set $s_1 = O(\sqrt{n\text{log}q}) \cdot \omega(\sqrt{\text{log}n})$.
5. Due to Lemmas 5 and 3, $\|\widetilde{\mathbf{T}_{\mathbf{A}'_{i,id_i}}}\| \leq \|\mathbf{T}_{\mathbf{A}'_{i,id_i}}\| \leq O(\sqrt{n\text{log}q}) \cdot \sqrt{2m} \cdot \omega(\sqrt{\text{log}n})$, $s_2 \geq \|\widetilde{\mathbf{T}_{\mathbf{A}'_{i,id_i}}}\| \cdot \omega(\sqrt{\text{log}2m})$, we set $s_2 = s_1 \cdot \sqrt{2m} \cdot \omega(\sqrt{\text{log}2m})$.

4.4 Proof of Security

The theorem below reduces the SIS problem to the EU-aID-CMA of our construction. The proof involves a forger $\mathcal{A}$ and a solver $\mathcal{B}$.

Theorem 1. *For a prime modulus $q = poly(n)$, if there is a PPT forger $\mathcal{A}$ that outputs an existential signature forgery with probability ε, in time τ, then there is a PPT algorithm $\mathcal{B}$ that solves the $SIS_{q,n,m\ell,\beta}$ problem in time $\tau' \approx \tau$, and with probability $\varepsilon' \geq (1-3^{-k}) \cdot \varepsilon/Q_{\text{id}} \cdot (1 - Q_{\text{e}}/Q_{\text{id}}) \cdot (1 - Q_{\text{s}}/Q_{\text{id}})$, where Q_{id}, Q_{e}, Q_{s} are the maximal number of hash queries, extract queries and sign queries made by $\mathcal{A}$, respectively, for $\beta = (\ell!)^3 \cdot (1 + \sqrt{m} \cdot \omega(\sqrt{\text{logm}})) \cdot s_2\sqrt{2m\ell}$.*

Proof. Suppose that there exists such a forger $\mathcal{A}$, we now construct a solver $\mathcal{B}$ that simulates the environment and uses the forgery to create its solution.

$\mathcal{B}$ is given a random instance of the $\text{SIS}_{q,n,m\ell,\beta}$ problem and asked to return an admissible solution.

i. $\mathcal{B}$ is given an $n \times m\ell$-matrix $\mathbf{A} \in \mathbb{Z}_q^{n \times m\ell}$ from the uniform distribution.
ii. $\mathcal{B}$ is requested any $\mathbf{e} \in \mathbb{Z}^{m\ell}$ such that $\mathbf{Ae} = \mathbf{0} \bmod q$ and $0 \neq \|\mathbf{e}\| \leq \beta$.

First of all, we assume that $\mathcal{B}$ begins by guessing which of the forger's id hash queries will correspond to the forger's forgery $(\text{id}^*, \text{m}^*, \sigma^*_{\text{id},\text{m}^*})$, furthermore, we assume that $\mathcal{A}$ has made all relevant hash queries before making extract queries, sign queries and outputting a forgery.

The operations performed by $\mathcal{B}$ are as follows:

Setup: $\mathcal{B}$ gives $\mathcal{A}$ the public parameters as follows:

1. Parse $\mathbf{A}$ as $\mathbf{A} = [\mathbf{A}_{0,1}, \mathbf{A}_{0,2}, \ldots, \mathbf{A}_{0,\ell}]$, where $\mathbf{A}_{0,i} \in \mathbb{Z}_q^{n \times m}$ for $i = 1, \ldots, \ell$.
2. For $i = 1, 2, \ldots, \ell$, pick a random $m \times m$-matrix $\mathbf{R}_i \in \{-1, 1\}^{m \times m}$, and compute $\mathbf{A}_{1,i} = \mathbf{A}_{0,i}\mathbf{R}_i$. According to Lemma 6, $\mathbf{A}_{1,i}$ is indistinguishable from that in the real scheme.
3. For $i = 1, 2, \ldots, \ell$, run algorithm $\mathsf{TrapGen}(q, n, m)$ to obtain a uniformly random $n \times m$-matrix $\mathbf{B}_i \in \mathbb{Z}_q^{n \times m}$ together with a short basis $\mathbf{T}_{\mathbf{B}_i} \in \mathbb{Z}^{m \times m}$ for $\Lambda_q^{\perp}(\mathbf{B}_i)$.
4. Pick a scalar $h \leftarrow \{1, 2, \ldots, Q_{\text{id}}\}$ uniformly.
5. Output the public parameters $\mathsf{PP} = (\{\mathbf{A}_{0,i}, \mathbf{A}_{1,i}, \mathbf{B}_i\}_{i=1,2,\ldots,\ell})$.

Queries: $\mathcal{B}$ maintains 3 lists ℓ_1, ℓ_2, ℓ_3 set to empty initially in its local storage to store the outputs of ***H_1* query**, ***H_2* query** and **Extract query**.

***H_1* query**. For a request of $\text{id} = (\text{id}_1, \ldots, \text{id}_\ell)$, $\mathcal{B}$ does as follows:

1. If id is in ℓ_1-list, $\mathcal{B}$ directly returns $(H_1(\text{id}, \text{id}_1, 1), \ldots, H_1(\text{id}, \text{id}_\ell, \ell))$.
2. If id is the h-th query, $\mathcal{B}$ computes $H_1(\text{id}, \text{id}_i, i)$ such that $H_1(\text{id}, \text{id}_i, i) \cdot \mathbf{B}_i = \mathbf{0} \bmod q$ for all $i = 1, 2, \ldots, \ell$, and then returns it.
3. Otherwise, $\mathcal{B}$ selects a uniformly random $n \times n$-matrix $\mathbf{K}_{\text{id}_i} \in \mathbb{Z}_q^{n \times n}$ for $i = 1, 2, \ldots, \ell$, if $\mathbf{K}_{\text{id}_i}\mathbf{B}_i = \mathbf{0} \bmod q$, $\mathcal{B}$ aborts and reselects it, then returns it as $H_1(\text{id}, \text{id}_i, i)$ and stores it into ℓ_1-list.

H_2 query. For a request of m $\in \{0,1\}^*$, $\mathcal{B}$ does as follows:

1. If m is in ℓ_2-list, $\mathcal{B}$ directly returns $H_2(\mathrm{m})$.
2. Otherwise, $\mathcal{B}$ selects a uniformly random vector $\mathbf{v} \in \mathbb{Z}_q^n$, returns as $H_2(\mathrm{m})$ and stores into ℓ_2-list.

Extract Query. For a request of private key of id, $\mathcal{B}$ constructs a private key for id, where $|\mathrm{id} \cap \mathrm{id}^*| < k$ (id* is the target identity) as follows:

1. If id is in ℓ_3-list, $\mathcal{B}$ directly returns $(\mathbf{T}_{\mathbf{A}'_{1,\mathrm{id}_1}}, \ldots, \mathbf{T}_{\mathbf{A}'_{\ell,\mathrm{id}_\ell}})$.
2. If id is the h-th query, $\mathcal{B}$ directly aborts.
3. Otherwise, $\mathcal{B}$ compute $\mathbf{A}'_{i,\mathrm{id}_i} = [\mathbf{A}_{0,i}|\mathbf{A}_{0,i} \cdot \mathbf{R}_i + H_1(\mathrm{id}, \mathrm{id}_i, i) \cdot \mathbf{B}_i]$ for $i = 1, 2, , \ldots, \ell$, and generate a short basis $\mathbf{T}_{\mathbf{A}'_{i,\mathrm{id}_i}} \in \mathbb{Z}^{2m \times 2m}$ for $\Lambda_q^\perp(\mathbf{A}'_{i,\mathrm{id}_i})$ using $\mathbf{T}_{\mathbf{B}_i}$. Then $\mathcal{B}$ returns $(\mathbf{T}_{\mathbf{A}'_{1,\mathrm{id}_1}}, \ldots, \mathbf{T}_{\mathbf{A}'_{\ell,\mathrm{id}_\ell}})$ and stores it into ℓ_3-list.

Sign Query. For a request of id and m, $\mathcal{B}$ does as follows:

1. If id is the h-th query, $\mathcal{B}$ aborts.
2. Otherwise, $\mathcal{B}$ simulates **Extract query** and **H_2query** to guarantee that $(\mathrm{id}, \mathbf{T}_{\mathbf{A}'_{1,\mathrm{id}_1}}, \ldots, \mathbf{T}_{\mathbf{A}'_{\ell,\mathrm{id}_\ell}})$ in ℓ_3-list and $(\mathrm{m}, H_2(\mathrm{m}))$ in ℓ_2-list.
3. Construct ℓ shares of $\mathbf{v} = H_2(\mathrm{m}) \in \mathbb{Z}_q^n$ by using a Shamir Secret-Sharing scheme applied to each coordinate of $\mathbf{v}$ independently. For $j = 1, 2, \ldots, n$, $\mathcal{B}$ chooses a uniformly random polynomial $p_j \in \mathbb{Z}_q[x]$ of degree $k-1$ such that $p_j(0) = v_j$. $\mathcal{B}$ constructs the j-th share vector, $\hat{\mathbf{v}}_j = (p_1(j), \cdots, p_n(j))$, and for all $J \subseteq \{1, 2, \ldots, \ell\}$ satisfying $|J| \geq k$, there are fractional Lagrangian coefficients $L_j \in \mathbb{Z}_q$ such that $\mathbf{v} = \sum_{j \in J} L_j \cdot \hat{\mathbf{v}}_j \bmod q$.
4. For id$_i$, $i = 1, 2, \ldots, \ell$, compute a 2m-dimensional vector $\mathbf{e}_i \in \mathbb{Z}^{2m}$ using algorithm $\mathsf{SamplePre}(\mathbf{A}'_{i,\mathrm{id}_i}, \mathbf{T}_{\mathbf{A}_{i,\mathrm{id}_i}}, q\hat{\mathbf{v}}_i, s_2)$, then return $(\mathrm{m}, \mathrm{id}, \mathbf{e}_1, \ldots, \mathbf{e}_\ell)$.

Forgery: Finally, $\mathcal{A}$ outputs a valid signature forgery $(\mathrm{id}^*, \mathrm{m}^*, \mathbf{e}_1^*, \ldots, \mathbf{e}_\ell^*)$, and the followings hold:

1. For $i = 1, 2, \ldots, \ell$, $\|\mathbf{e}_i^*\| \leq s_2\sqrt{2m}$.
2. There exists a set $J \subseteq \{1, 2, \ldots, \ell\}$ and $|J| \geq k$ satisfying that $\sum_{j \in J} L_j \cdot \mathbf{A}'_{j,\mathrm{id}_j^*} \cdot \mathbf{e}_j^* = qH_2(\mathrm{m}^*)$, where $\mathbf{A}'_{j,\mathrm{id}_j^*} = [\mathbf{A}_{0,j}|\mathbf{A}_{1,j} + H_1(\mathrm{id}^*, \mathrm{id}_j^*, j)\mathbf{B}_j]$.

Wlog, assume that $J = \{1, 2, \ldots, k\}$. The probability that $\mathcal{B}$ guesses right, i.e., id* is the h-th query to H_1, is at least $1/Q_{\mathrm{id}}$. If $\mathcal{B}$ guesses right, let scalar $D = (\ell!)^2$, for $j \in \{1, 2, \ldots, k\}$, $\mathcal{B}$ does as follows:

1. Parse $\mathbf{e}_j^* = (\mathbf{e}_{j,0}^*, \mathbf{e}_{j,1}^*)^\top$, where $\mathbf{e}_{j,0}^*, \mathbf{e}_{j,1}^* \in \mathbb{Z}^m$.
2. Return $\mathbf{e}^* = (D \cdot L_1 \cdot (\mathbf{e}_{1,0}^* + \mathbf{R}_1 \cdot \mathbf{e}_{1,1}^*), \ldots, D \cdot L_k \cdot (\mathbf{e}_{k,0}^* + \mathbf{R}_k \cdot \mathbf{e}_{k,1}^*), \mathbf{0}, \ldots, \mathbf{0})$ as a solution to the $\mathrm{SIS}_{q,n,m\ell,\beta}$ problem.

The detail analysis is as follows:

Because identity id* is the h-th query to H_1, for $j = 1, 2, \ldots, k$, we have $H_1(\mathrm{id}^*, \mathrm{id}_j^*, j)\mathbf{B}_j = \mathbf{0} \bmod q$, thus $\mathbf{A}'_{j,\mathrm{id}_j^*} = [\mathbf{A}_{0,j}|\mathbf{A}_{0,j}\mathbf{R}_j]$. So $\sum_{j \in J} L_j \mathbf{A}'_{j,\mathrm{id}_j^*} \mathbf{e}_j^* = qH_2(\mathrm{m}^*) = \mathbf{0} \bmod q$, that is to say,

$((\mathbf{A}_{0,1}|\mathbf{A}_{0,1}\mathbf{R}_1), \ldots, (\mathbf{A}_{0,\ell}|\mathbf{A}_{0,\ell}\mathbf{R}_\ell)) \cdot (L_1\mathbf{e}_1^*, \ldots, L_k\mathbf{e}_k^*, \mathbf{0} \ldots, \mathbf{0})^\top = \mathbf{0} \bmod q.$
So, $(\mathbf{A}_{0,1}, \ldots, \mathbf{A}_{0,\ell}) \cdot (L_1(\mathbf{e}_{1,0}^* + \mathbf{R}_1\mathbf{e}_{1,1}^*), \ldots, L_k(\mathbf{e}_{k,0}^* + \mathbf{R}_k\mathbf{e}_{k,1}^*), \mathbf{0}, \ldots, \mathbf{0})^\top = \mathbf{0}$.

We use the conclusion that for $i = 1, 2, \ldots, \ell$, $D \cdot L_i \in \mathbb{Z}$ and $|D \cdot L_i| \leq (\ell!)^3$ [2] to clear the denominators of L_i, thus

$$\mathbf{A} \cdot \underbrace{(D \cdot L_1(\mathbf{e}_{1,0}^* + \mathbf{R}_1\mathbf{e}_{1,1}^*), \ldots, D \cdot L_k(\mathbf{e}_{k,0}^* + \mathbf{R}_k\mathbf{e}_{k,1}^*), \mathbf{0}, \ldots, \mathbf{0})^\top}_{(\mathbf{e}^*)^\top} = \mathbf{0} \bmod q.$$

Since $\mathbf{R}_i$ is a low-norm matrix with coefficients ± 1, according to Lemma 7, we have $\Pr[\|\mathbf{R}_i\| > \sqrt{m} \cdot \omega(\sqrt{\log m})] < \text{negl}(m)$, and for $i = 1, \ldots, \ell$, $\|\mathbf{e}_i^*\| \leq s_2\sqrt{2m}$, thus with a overwhelming probability $\|\mathbf{e}^*\| \leq \beta$ for $\beta = (\ell!)^3 \cdot (1 + \sqrt{m} \cdot \omega(\sqrt{\log m})) \cdot s_2\sqrt{2m\ell}$.

Furthermore, $\mathcal{B}$ completes **Extract query** and **Sign query** without aborting with probability at least $(1 - Q_{\text{e}}/Q_{\text{id}}) \cdot (1 - Q_{\text{s}}/Q_{\text{id}})$. Therefore, we can deduce that $\mathbf{e}^*$ is with probability $\varepsilon' \geq (1 - 3^{-k}) \cdot \varepsilon / Q_{\text{id}} \cdot (1 - Q_{\text{e}}/Q_{\text{id}}) \cdot (1 - Q_{\text{s}}/Q_{\text{id}})$ a short non-zero preimage of $\mathbf{0}$ under $\mathbf{A}$, namely, $\mathbf{A}\mathbf{e}^* = \mathbf{0} \bmod q$ and $0 \neq \|\mathbf{e}^*\| \leq \beta$ for $\beta = (\ell!)^3 \cdot (1 + \sqrt{m} \cdot \omega(\sqrt{\log m})) \cdot s_2\sqrt{2m\ell}$.

4.5 Efficiency Analysis

The comparison with related lattice FIBS schemes in the random oracle model (ROM) in terms of public parameters size $\|\mathsf{PP}\|$, master key size $\|\mathsf{MK}\|$, private key size for id, $\|\mathsf{SK}_{\text{id}}\|$, signature size $\|\sigma_{\text{id,m}}\|$, private key extraction cost (Ext-Cost), signing cost (Sig-Cost) and verification cost (Ver-Cost) are shown in Table 1. Here, ℓ is the identity size and k is the error tolerance parameters.

For simplicity, T_1' denotes the time cost of RandBasis(ExtBasis) with a module pq [17], T_1 denotes it with module q and T_1'' denotes the cost of fixed dimension lattice basis delegation with module q [19]; T_2 denotes the cost of Shamir Secret-Sharing operation; T_3' denotes the cost of SamplePre with module pq and T_3 denotes it with module q; T_4' denotes the cost of inner product in $\mathbb{Z}_{pq}^{2m}$ and T_4 denotes it in $\mathbb{Z}_q^m$; T_5' denotes the cost of scalar multiplication in $\mathbb{Z}_{pq}^{2n}$, T_5 denotes it in $\mathbb{Z}_q^{2n}$.

Table 1. Comparison of lattice FIBS schemes in ROM

Scheme	[17]	[19]	This work
$\|\mathsf{PP}\|$	$2\ell nm\log pq$	$2\ell nm\log q$	$3\ell nm\log q$
$\|\mathsf{MK}\|$	$2\ell m^2\log pq$	$2\ell m^2\log q$	$\ell m^2\log q$
$\|\mathsf{SK}_{\text{id}}\|$	$4\ell m^2\log pq$	$\ell m^2\log q$	$4\ell m^2\log q$
$\|\sigma_{\text{id,m}}\|$	$2\ell m\log pq$	$\ell m\log q$	$2\ell m\log q$
Ext-Cost	$\ell T_1'$	$\ell T_1''$	ℓT_1
Sig-Cost	$nT_2 + \ell T_3'$	$mT_2 + \ell T_3 + n\ell T_4$	$nT_2 + \ell T_3$
Ver-Cost	$k(nT_4' + T_5')$	$(k+1)nT_4 + kT_5$	$k(2nT_4 + T_5)$
Universe	$\{0,1\}^\ell$	$\{0,1\}^\ell$	$(\mathbb{Z}_q^n)^\ell$

The results in Table 1 show that [19] has a slight advantage of $\|\mathsf{PP}\|$, $\|\mathsf{SK}_{\mathrm{id}}\|$, $\|\sigma_{\mathrm{id,m}}\|$ and Ver-Cost.

The results also show that our construction has a competitive advantages of $\|\mathsf{MK}\|$, Ext-Cost and Sig-Cost over [17,19]. Furthermore, our scheme can provide large universe entitles, i.e., identities $\mathrm{id} = (\mathrm{id}_1, \mathrm{id}_2, \cdots, \mathrm{id}_\ell)$ are ℓ-vectors of attributes in $\mathbb{Z}_q^n$, so that they can capture more expressive attributes and have a more efficient application in biometric authentication.

5 Conclusions

We present a FIBS schemes from the SIS problem over lattices which is proved to be EU-aID-CMA in the random oracle model for identities living in a large universe, i.e., $(\mathbb{Z}_q)^\ell$, so that it can capture more expressive attributes and has an efficient application in biometric authentication. Compared with the existing FIBS schemes over lattices in the random oracle model, the new construction has made a great improvement on enhancing the efficiency, namely, a faster signing operations. To construct an efficient FIBS over lattices in the standard model for identities living in a large universe over lattices will be our future work.

Acknowledgments. We thank the anonymous referees for their helpful comments and the research of authors is supported by the National Natural Science Foundation of China under Grant Nos. 61572445 and 61501405.

References

1. Agrawal, S., Boneh, D., Boyen, X.: Efficient lattice (H)IBE in the standard model. In: Gilbert, H. (ed.) EUROCRYPT 2010. LNCS, vol. 6110, pp. 553–572. Springer, Heidelberg (2010). https://doi.org/10.1007/978-3-642-13190-5_28
2. Agrawal, S., Boyen, X., Vaikuntanathan, V., Voulgaris, P., Wee, H.: Functional encryption for threshold functions (or fuzzy IBE) from lattices. In: Fischlin, M., Buchmann, J., Manulis, M. (eds.) PKC 2012. LNCS, vol. 7293, pp. 280–297. Springer, Heidelberg (2012). https://doi.org/10.1007/978-3-642-30057-8_17
3. Ajtai, M.: Generating hard instances of lattice problems (extended abstract). In: STOC, pp. 99–108 (1996)
4. Alwen, J., Peikert, C.: Generating shorter bases for hard random lattices. In: STACS, pp. 75–86 (2009)
5. Cash, D., Hofheinz, D., Kiltz, E., Peikert, C.: Bonsai trees, or how to delegate a lattice basis. In: Gilbert, H. (ed.) EUROCRYPT 2010. LNCS, vol. 6110, pp. 523–552. Springer, Heidelberg (2010). https://doi.org/10.1007/978-3-642-13190-5_27
6. Gentry, C., Peikert, C., Vaikuntanathan, V.: How to use a short basis: trapdoors for hard lattices and new cryptographic constructions. In: STOC, pp. 197–206 (2008)
7. Micciancio, D., Peikert, C.: Trapdoors for lattices: simpler, tighter, faster, smaller. In: Pointcheval, D., Johansson, T. (eds.) EUROCRYPT 2012. LNCS, vol. 7237, pp. 700–718. Springer, Heidelberg (2012). https://doi.org/10.1007/978-3-642-29011-4_41
8. Micciancio, D., Regev, O.: Worst-case to average-case reductions based on Gaussian measures. SIAM J. Comput. **37**(1), 267–302 (2007)

9. Sahai, A., Waters, B.: Fuzzy identity-based encryption. In: Cramer, R. (ed.) EUROCRYPT 2005. LNCS, vol. 3494, pp. 457–473. Springer, Heidelberg (2005). https://doi.org/10.1007/11426639_27
10. Shamir, A.: Identity-based cryptosystems and signature schemes. In: Blakley, G.R., Chaum, D. (eds.) CRYPTO 1984. LNCS, vol. 196, pp. 47–53. Springer, Heidelberg (1985). https://doi.org/10.1007/3-540-39568-7_5
11. Shor, P.W.: Polynomial-time algorithms for prime factorization and discrete logarithms on a quantum computer. SIAM J. Comput. **26**(5), 1484–1509 (1997)
12. Wang, C.J.: A provable secure fuzzy identity based signature scheme. Sci. China Inf. Sci. **55**(9), 2139–2148 (2012)
13. Wang, C.J., Kim, J.H.: Two constructions of fuzzy identity based signature. In: 2nd International Conference on Biomedical Engineering and Informatics, pp. 1–5. IEEE Press, New York (2009)
14. Yang, P.Y., Cao, Z.F., Dong, X.L.: Fuzzy identity based signature. IACR Cryptology ePrint Archive 2008/002 (2008)
15. Yang, P.Y., Cao, Z.F., Dong, X.L.: Fuzzy identity based signature with applications to biometric authentication. Comput. Electr. Eng. **37**(4), 532–540 (2011)
16. Yang, C.L., Zheng, S.H., Wang, L.C., Tian, M.M., Gu, L.Z., Yang, Y.X.: A Fuzzy identity-based signature scheme from lattices in the standard model. Math. Prob. Eng. **2014**(8), 1–10 (2014)
17. Yao, Y.Q., Li, Z.J.: A novel fuzzy identity based signature scheme based on the short integer solution problem. Comput. Electr. Eng. **40**(6), 1930–1939 (2014)
18. Zhang, L.Y., Wu, Q., Hu, Y.P.: Fuzzy biometric identity-based signature in the standard model. App. Mech. Mater. **44**(4), 3350–3354 (2011)
19. Zhang, X.J., Xu, C.X., Zhang, Y.: Fuzzy identity-based signature scheme from lattice and its application in biometric authentication. TIIS **11**(5), 2762–2777 (2017)

Improvement of STDM Watermarking Algorithm Based on Watson Model

Wenting Jiang(✉), Zhongmiao Kang, and Yan Chen

Guangdong Power Grid Corporation, Guangzhou 510000, China
jiangwenting@gddd.csg.cn

Abstract. In order to ensure the security of transmission data in the system, a secure transmission channel can be established by using steganography in order to ensure the security of transmission data in the system. STDM (Spread Transform Dither Modulation) watermarking algorithm has a good performance on robustness, capacity and blind detection. In order to make a balance between robustness and transparency, this paper make some improvements on the selection and construction of project vector of STDM based on research of Watson vision model, and then proposed an improvement STDM watermarking algorithm. The simulation results shows that this method can improve robustness performance when comes into JPEG attack.

Keywords: Improvement of STDM · Watson vision model

1 Introduction

With the rapid development of power information system, power information system has become a large communication network and are and more information is transmitted in this system. The transmission of information data must be confronted with security problems. Due to the interregional connectivity of the grid, the trade between the region and the region is increasingly frequent. As the most important civil product, the economic benefits of electricity are huge. Information greatly increases the dependence of power system on information system. The security of the information system may affect the safe and stable operation of the power system, and may even lead to a system shock and a large-scale power failure. Therefore, it is necessary to use steganography to establish a secure information transmission channel, so as to ensure the safety and reliability of transmission data of power system.

Digital watermarking used to protect copyright and identification by embedding secret information on text, image, audio or video. At present, the research of watermarking concentrate on transparency and robustness. According to the difference of ways that embedding watermark, the watermarking algorithm divided into two classes: spread spectrum and quantization algorithms.

In practical application, industry focus on how to achieve the balance of blind detection, robustness and transparency. The quantization-based algorithm has a good performance on blind detection and robustness. Therefore, many researchers combined STDM with the human visual characteristics, which can implement adaptive information using human visual redundancy effectively embedded in [1–5] to achieve this

X. Sun et al. (Eds.): ICCCS 2018, LNCS 11065, pp. 585–595, 2018.
https://doi.org/10.1007/978-3-030-00012-7_53

goal. Li [3] and Ma [5] have proposed many improvement algorithm of STDM based on vision model which these algorithms can still be improved [6] on selection of project vector [6–8]. This paper makes some research on selection and construction of project vector of STDM algorithm based on Watson vision model. On the basis of these work, we proposed an improvement STDM watermarking algorithm based on Watson.

This paper isorganized as follows. In Sect. 2, firstly, we use two steps: watermarking embedding and extracting watermarking to introduce traditional STDM algorithm. Then we introduced the improvement STDM algorithm. Section 3 contains experimental results and analyzes of the proposed method. And the finally Sect. 4 concludes the paper.

2 Algorithm Design

Firstly, we need to introduce the Watson vision model and the traditional STDM watermarking algorithm [9].

2.1 Watson Vision Model

In the field of digital watermarking, sensitivity, masking and merging used to reflect the perception of all the components.

The Watson vision model estimates the variable perception based on the block discrete cosine transform (DCT), then merge these estimates results into an single estimate of sensible distance [10]: firstly, divided an image C into multiple disjoint $8 * 8$ blocks, and use $C[i,j,k]$ to represent the (i,j) $(0 \leq i,j \leq 7)$ pixel of the kth block; secondly, apply DCT to every block, and use $c_0[i,j,k]$ to represent DCT block which corresponding to k^{th} block, $c_0[i,j,k]$ represent the average intensity of kth block. By using DCT, the energy of image be centralized at low frequency part. Thirdly, we calculate quantization step according to frequency and finally quantified all terms. Watson vision model based on the three perceptual phenomena mentioned above, and consists of a sensitivity function, two masking parts based on brightness and contrasts, and a merging part of [10].

(a) Sensitivity function. The model defines a frequency perception table (show in Table 1), every item $x[i,j]$ of Table 1 represent the minimum amplitude that DCT coefficient which can be detected under no masking noise.
(b) Brightness masking. If the average brightness of the $8 * 8$ pixel block is enough large, then the DCT coefficients are modified by larger values will not be detected. In order to solve this problem, the Watson model adjusts the sensitivity $x[i,j]$ of each $8 * 8$ pixel block according to its DC term, and the masking value can be obtained by the lower formula:
(c) $x_r[i,j,k] = x[i,j](c_0[0,0,j]/c_{0,0})^{\alpha_x}$
(d) Which, α_x are a constant, equals to 0.649; $c_0[0,0,k]$ is the DCT coefficients of kth block of image; $c_{0,0}$ is the average value of DC coefficients of image.

Table 1. Frequency sensitivity table based on 8 * 8 DCT block

	1	2	3	4	5	6	7	8
1	1.40	1.01	1.16	1.66	2.40	3.43	4.79	6.56
2	1.01	1.45	1.32	1.52	2.00	2.71	3.67	4.93
3	1.16	1.32	2.24	2.59	2.98	3.64	4.60	5.88
4	1.66	1.52	2.59	3.77	4.55	5.30	6.28	7.60
5	2.40	2.00	2.98	4.55	6.15	7.46	8.71	10.17
6	3.43	2.71	3.64	5.30	7.46	9.62	11.58	13.51
7	4.79	3.67	4.60	6.28	8.71	11.58	14.50	17.29
8	6.56	4.93	5.88	7.60	10.17	13.51	17.29	21.15

(e) Contrast masking. Contrast masking refers to the reduction of visibility in a frequency that can cause this frequency change. The relationship between the contrast masking threshold and the brightness masking threshold is as follows:

(f) $y_r[i,j,k] = \max\{xr[i,j,k], |c_0[i,j,k]^{w[i,j]}|x_r[i,j,k]^{1-w[i,j]}\}$

(g) Which, $w[i,j]$ is a constant between 0 and 1. In the Watson model, each $w[i,j]$ equals to 0.7.

2.2 Traditional STDM Watermarking Algorithm

In this part, we will introduce the traditional STDM watermarking algorithm from two parts: embed watermarking and extract watermarking.

(a) Embed watermark

The process of the embedding watermarking shown as Fig. 1:

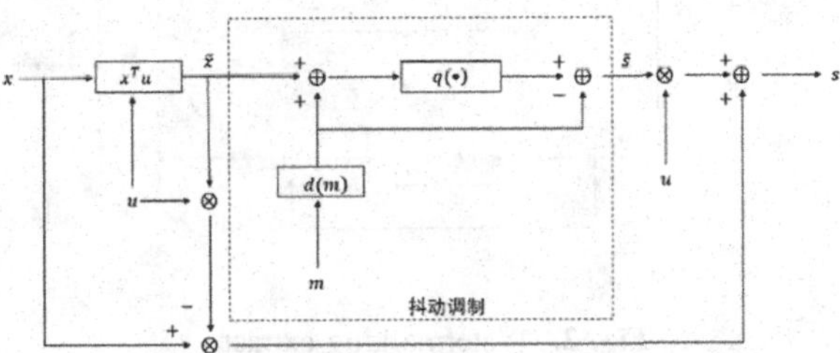

Fig. 1. Watermarking embedding

In the above figure:

(1) x represents the vector that extract from carrier signal;
(2) u represents the project vector;
(3) $m \in \{0, 1\}$ represents watermarking bits.

The whole process can be described as the following steps:

(1) Extract the vector x from the original signal, then use it and the project vector u to calculate the inner-product $x^T u$ to get the coefficients $\tilde{x}$ that will be quantify; after that, we transfer into dither modulation process;
(2) In the process of the dither modulation, firstly, we calculate the jitter according the watermarking bit to get data that will be quantify $w = \tilde{x} + d(m)$, then we apply the quantizer $q(\bullet)$ to w to get quantized value $\tilde{s}$ and finish the embed watermarking. This step can be described as the following formula:

$$\begin{cases} q(x) = \Delta * round(w/\Delta) \\ w = \tilde{x} + d(m) \end{cases}$$

where, Δ is quantization step, function $round(\bullet)$ used to rounding off $\bullet$, w represents data that need to be quantify.
(3) From the second step, we apply the following calculation to $\tilde{s}$ to finish the embedding watermarking process:

$$s = \tilde{s}u + x - \tilde{x}u$$

(b) Extract watermark

The extract watermarking of the traditional STDM algorithm is reverse process of embedding watermarking, that is, we extract the vector y from the signal that contains watermarking, then use minimum distance to decode. The whole process shown as Fig. 2:

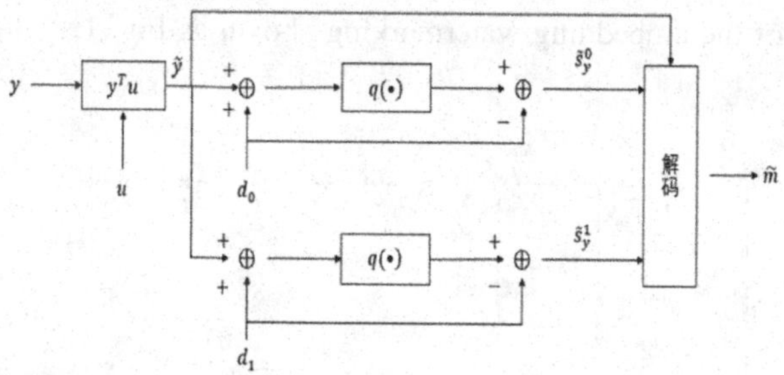

Fig. 2. Watermarking extract

In the above figure:

(1) y represents the vector that extract from the signal that contains watermarking;
(2) u represents the project vector.

The whole process can be described as following steps:

(1) Extract vector y from the signal that contains watermarking, then use it and project u to calculate inner-product to get coefficient $\tilde{y}$ that will be quantify, then move into the decode process;

(2) In the decode process, we calculate the data that to be quantify $w_0 = \tilde{y} + d_0$, $w_1 = \tilde{y} + d_1$, then we apply the quantizer $q(\bullet)$ to the data to get quantization values $\tilde{s}_y^0$, $\tilde{s}_y^1$. Finally, we decode the message according to the minimum distance to get watermarking bit $\tilde{m}$.

2.3 Research and Design

From the above parts, we can make a conclusion that the project vector u has a significant influence on the performance of STDM algorithm. This paper makes some research on the select of the project vector u to achieve the algorithm improvement.

Because of too many ways of select project vector to be described one by one, so we only select three project vector ways: random, balance, parallel, to make some research.

Firstly, we use X_0 to represents the original image of size $N * N$, $C_0[k, i, j]$ $(1 \leq i, j \leq m, 1 \leq k \leq (N * N)/(M * M))$ represents the element which coordinate is (i, j) in the kth block that calculated from X_0 which be applied $M * M$ block partition and DCT operations. $X_1[k, i]$ $(1 \leq i \leq M * M)$ represents the ith element of the vector that constructed by scan the $k^{th} M * M$ block by row. $P[k, i] (1 \leq i \leq M * M)$ represents the ith element of the kth project vector of $M * M$ block.

(1) Random project vector: every element of this vector is a random number, that is, if we use $V = (x_1, x_2, \cdots, x_n)$ to represent a vector, where x_i is a random number $(0 < x_i < 1,\ 1 \leq i \leq n)$, then the project vector is: $P = V/|V|$.
(2) Balance project vector: every element of this vector is equal number, that is, if we use $V = (1, 1, \cdots, 1)$ to represent a vector, then the project vector is: $P = V/\sqrt{N}$.
(3) Parallel project vector: $P[k] = X_1[k]/|X_1[k]|$.

After we get the project vector P and contrast threshold value $y_r[i, j, k]$ of Watson model, then we calculate coefficients screening vector:

$$w[k, n] = \begin{cases} 1 & y_r[i, j, k] > T \\ 0 & others \end{cases}$$

Where: $1 \leq n \leq M * M$, $1 \leq i, j \leq M * M$, T is a pre-set threshold value.
Finally, we calculate "the final project vector" u,$u = P \bullet w$.

3 Experiment and Analyze

3.1 Test Image

In order to make some simulation test on the algorithm of the this paper, we use the ten famous standard gray test images as carriers, the specific information shown as Table 2 and Fig. 3:

Table 2. Standard gray test images

Name	Size	Name	Size
Baboon	512 * 512	Barbara	512 * 512
Boat	512 * 512	Bridge	512 * 512
Couple	512 * 512	Goldhill	512 * 512
Lena	512 * 512	Peppers	512 * 512
Pirate	512 * 512	Plane	512 * 512

Fig. 3. Standard gray test images

3.2 Watermarking Message Bits

Without loss of generality, this paper use a random 01 sequence which length is 123 as the watermarking message bits.

3.3 Experiment Results and Analysis

In this part, we contrast the performance of the algorithm proposed (which based on Watson model) and the traditional STDM algorithm. Three parameters be used to evaluate the performance: Peak signal-to-noise ratio (PSNR), Bit error rate (BER) and the correlation coefficient (CORR). The following results are average value of ten test images under the same condition.

Table 3. The performance of different project vector under no attack

Project vector	Vision model	BER	CORR	PSNR
Balance	Watson	0	1	55.9138
	noWatson	0	1	56.9209
Parallel	Watson	0	1	56.2703
	noWatson	0	1	55.3766
Random	Watson	0	1	55.9400
	noWatson	0	1	56.2652

(1) **No Attack:** It is can be sawn from Table 3, the performances of the balance and parallel project vectors that based on Watson model are basically equals to the balance and parallel project vectors' of tradition algorithm. The random project vector has a poor performance compares to the balance project vector because of the former not take full advantage of carrier.

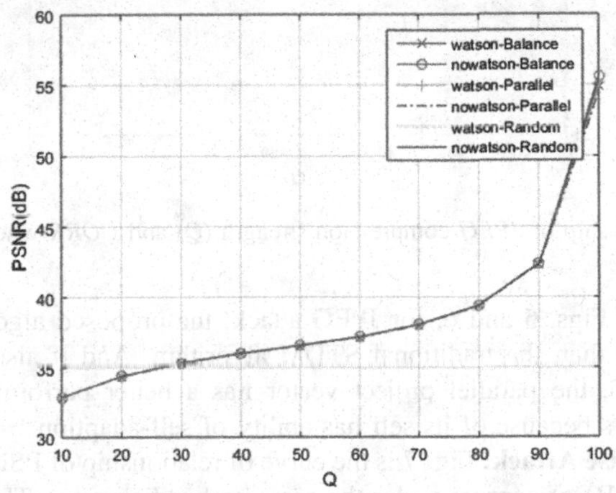

Fig. 4. The relationship of *PSNR(dB)* and *JPEG* compression strength (*Q*)

(2) **JPEG Attack:** Fig. 4 is the curve of relationship of PSNR and JPEG compression strength (Q) of carriers under the same embedding ratio. The relationship of BER, CORR and Q shown as Figs. 5 and 6 respectively when PSNR = 56 dB.

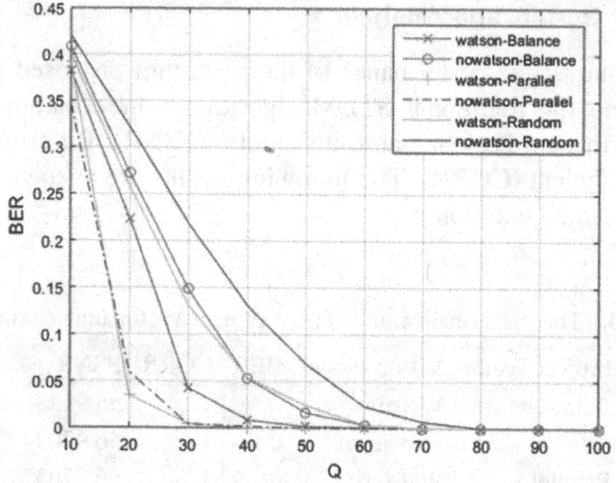

Fig. 5. The relationship of *JPEG* compression strength (*Q*) and *BER* when *PSNR = 56 dB*

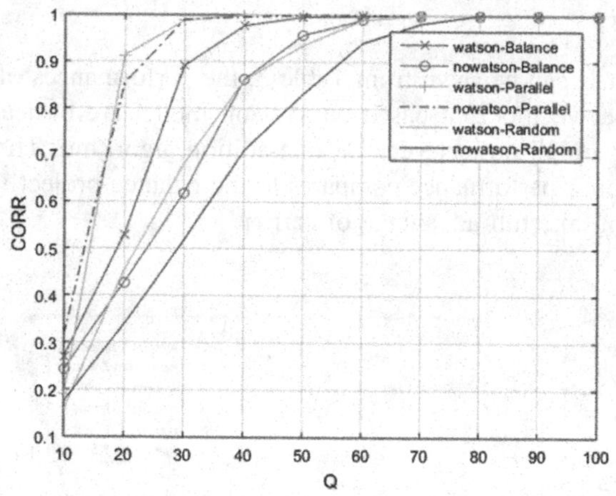

Fig. 6. The relationship of *JPEG* compression strength (*Q*) and *CORR* when *PSNR = 56 dB*

According to Figs. 5 and 6, for JPEG attack, the proposed algorithm has better performances than the traditional STDM algorithm. And It also can be seen at Figs. 5 and 6, the parallel project vector has a better performance than other project vectors because of its self has ability of self-adaption.

(3) **Gaussian Noise Attack:** Fig. 7 is the curve of relationship of PSNR and Gaussian Noise (0, VAR) of carriers under the same embedding ratio. The relationship of BER, CORR and Q shown as Figs. 8 and 9 respectively when PSNR = 56 dB. According to Figs. 8 and 9, for against Gaussian noise attack, the balance project vector based on Watson model has a compatible performance with the balance project vector of traditional algorithm, but has a better performance than other

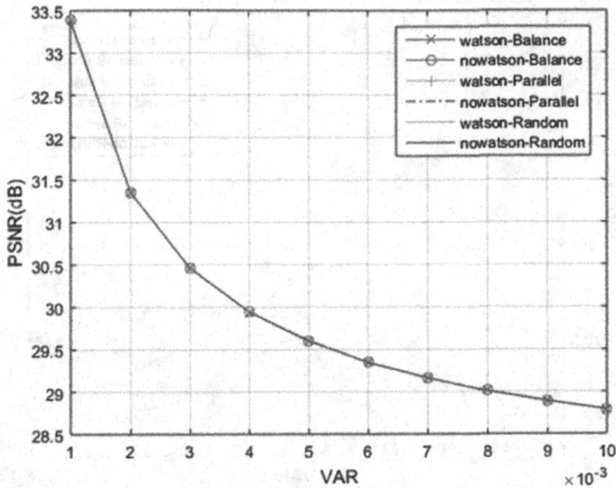

Fig. 7. The relationship of *PSNR (dB)* and *Gaussian Noise (0, VAR)*

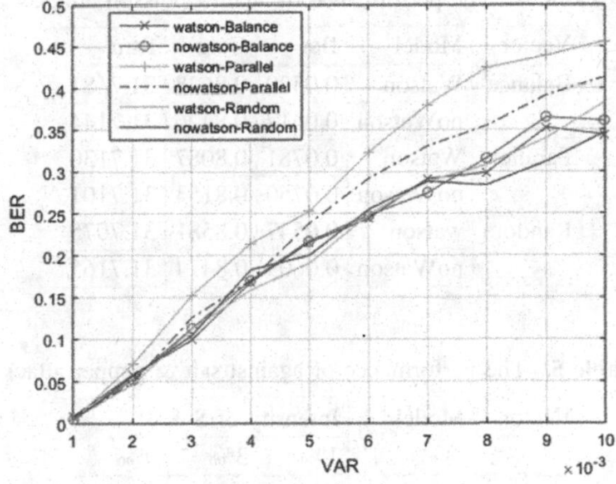

Fig. 8. The relationship of *Gaussian Noise (0, VAR)* and *BER* when *PSNR = 56Db*

project vectors. The reason for this phenomenon is that, the coefficients of the balance project are come from the low frequency part.

(4) **Poisson Attack and Salt & Pepper Attack:** The performances of algorithm that against poisson attack and salt & pepper attack are shown at Tables 4 and 5. It is can be seen, for poisson attack, the proposed algorithm has a better performance than traditional STDM algorithm; but for salt & pepper, it is a contrary conclusion.

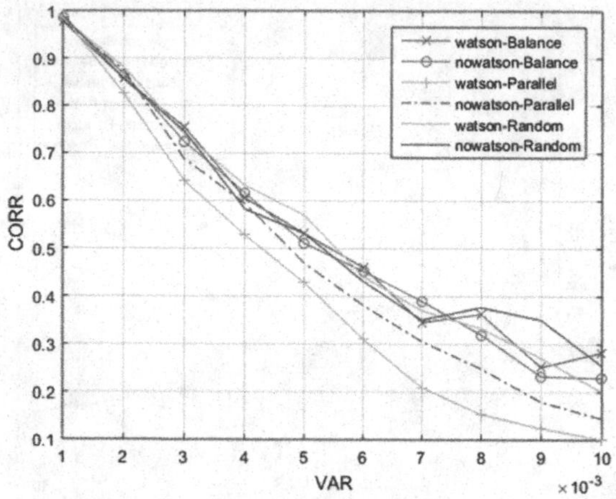

Fig. 9. The relationship of *Gaussian Noise (0, VAR)* and *CORR* when *PSNR = 56 dB*

Table 4. The performance of against poisson attack

Vector	Model	Ber	Corr	Psnr
Balance	Watson	0.0539	0.8628	31.7181
	noWatson	0.0617	0.8426	31.7144
Parallel	Watson	0.0781	0.8087	31.7130
	noWatson	0.0750	0.8154	31.7101
Random	watson	0.0547	0.8581	31.7075
	noWatson	0.0609	0.8474	31.7165

Table 5. The performance of against salt & pepper attack

Vector	Model	Intensity of S & P		
		1‰	3‰	5‰
Balance	Watson	0.0055	0.0297	0.0438
	noWatson	0.0023	0.0172	0.0227
Parallel	Watson	0.0156	0.0398	0.0602
	noWatson	0.0109	0.0367	0.0633
Random	Watson	0.0055	0.0297	0.0438
	noWatson	0.0047	0.0141	0.0383

4 Conclusion

In the practice application of digital watermarking technology, the balance of robustness, capacity and transparency is a problem that worthy to research and solve, and the improvement algorithm based on Watson model has a good performance for this. Theoretically, the Watson model could improve the system's performance. Therefore, this paper combines Watson model with the traditional STDM algorithm, improve the traditional STDM algorithm with optimize the design process of project vector. Then, the paper selects three project vectors based on Watson model: balance vector, parallel vector and random vector to test the proposed algorithm with quantization step equals to 90 under different attacks. The simulation results shows that, only for the JPEG and Poisson attacks, the proposed algorithm can observably improve the performances, but for Gaussian and Salt & Pepper attacks, the improvement is not obvious.

Acknowledgements. This work was supported by the science and technology project of Guangdong Power Grid Co., Ltd, (036000KK52170002).

References

1. Hong, B.B.: Research on robust digital image and video watermarking scheme. Beijing University of Posts and Telecommunications (2013)
2. Cox, I.J., Miller, M.I., Bloom, J.A.: Digital Watermarking, pp. 5–6. MordanKaufnann Publisher, San Francisco (2002)
3. Li, Q., Doerr, G., Cox, I.J.: Spread transform dither modulation using a perceptual model. In: IEEE Workshop on Multimedia Signal Processing, pp. 98–102. IEEE (2006)
4. Li, Q., Cox, I.J.: Improved spread transform dither modulation using a perceptual model: robustness to amplitude scaling and JPEG compression. In: IEEE International Conference on Acoustics, Speech and Signal Processing, pp. II-185–II-188. IEEE Xplore (2007)
5. Yu, D., Ma, L., Wang, G., et al.: Adaptive spread-transform dither modulation using an improved luminance-masked threshold. In: IEEE International Conference on Image Processing, pp. 449–452. IEEE (2008)
6. Li, X.C.: Digital Watermarking Based on Spread Transform Dither Modulation. Shandong University (2011)
7. Perez-Gonzalez, F., Balado, F., Martin, J.R.H.: Performance analysis of existing and new methods for data hiding with known-host information in additive channels. IEEE Trans. Signal Process. **51**(4), 960–980 (2003)
8. Chen, B., Wornell, G.W.: Provably robust digital watermarking. **3845**, 43–54 (1999)
9. Ma, Z.W., Man, C.T., Li, W.: Audio watermarking algorithm based on STDM and particle swarms optimizations. J. Harbin Univ. Sci. Technol. **5**, 73–78 (2016)
10. Sun, X.X., Cao, G.Z.: Discussion of perceptual model watermark based on Watson. Mod. Electron. Tech. **32**(7), 76–78 (2009)
11. Xiao, J., Wang, Y.: Project vector of spread transform dither modulation watermarking algorithm. J. Image Graph. **11**(12), 1799–1805 (2006)

Improving Privacy-Preserving CP-ABE with Hidden Access Policy

Leyou Zhang[1], Yilei Cui[1(✉)], and Yi Mu[2]

[1] School of Mathematics and Statistics, Xidian University, Xi'an 710071, Shaanxi, China
xidianzhangly@126.com, CYL_Study@163.com
[2] School of Computer Science and Software Engineering, University of Wollongong, Wollongong, NSW 2522, Australia
ymu@uow.edu.au

Abstract. User's privacy-preserving has become an urgent problem with the rapid development of cloud technologies. Anonymous ciphertext-policy Attribute Based Encryption (CP-ABE) not only protects the security of data, but also ensures that the privacy of the data user is not compromised. However, most of the known schemes have some shortcomings where those schemes either cannot achieve compact security or are inefficient in Encryption and Decryption. Additionally, recent works show the reality of the anonymity in some proposed schemes is doubtful. To address the problems above, we use the double exponent technique to construct an anonymous CP-ABE scheme which is more compact than the results at present. The proposed scheme with hidden access policy works in prime order groups. Meanwhile, we prove the security of our scheme under the decisional n-BDHE and decisional linear assumption.

Keywords: Privacy preserving · Cloud storage · Anonymity
Hidden access policy

1 Introduction

As an extension and development of cloud computing, cloud storage has solved the problems in big data storage and sharing, which allows users to store their data in cloud server and access data whenever and wherever through any networked device linking to the cloud. However, security and privacy problems are more and more serious at present. No users would like to share their documents containing sensitive information to a public cloud with no guarantee for security or privacy. It means that more flexible cryptosystem is demanded, where security and privacy protection must be both considered. Attribute-based encryption is one of the encryption techniques which can meet this requirement.

In 2005, Sahai and Waters introduced Attribute Based Encryption (ABE) [1], firstly. In attribute-based encryption, the ciphertext and decryption key are generated by the collection of attributes and data owner can establish a specific access control policy to limit who can decrypt the encrypted data. There are two categories of ABE schemes [2], one is ciphertext-policy ABE (CP-ABE) where user's attributes are used for key

X. Sun et al. (Eds.): ICCCS 2018, LNCS 11065, pp. 596–605, 2018.
https://doi.org/10.1007/978-3-030-00012-7_54

generation and the ciphertext is associated with a specific access policy, the other is the key-policy ABE (KP-ABE), in which the user can only decrypt encrypted data when his attributes satisfy the access policy embedded in the secret key. Because of the favorable feature of enabling data owner to set specific access policies to control who can decrypt the encrypted data, CP-ABE provides a novel way to solve the problem above. In 2007, Bethencourt et al. [3] proposed the first CP-ABE scheme with tree-access polices. To improve the efficiency, Emura [4] proposed a CP-ABE scheme with constant size ciphertexts with AND-gates on multi-valued attributes access structure. Then Waters [5] proposed an efficient and expressive CP-ABE scheme, by employing linear secret share scheme (LSSS). There have been many CP-ABE schemes [3–5] at present. However, in most of CP-ABE proposals, the access policy must be sent along with the ciphertext which means that anyone who can obtain the ciphertext will get the access policy. While, in some applications access policy may contain sensitive information of the users. For example, a data owner intends to upload a medical record to the cloud and wish that the record can only be accessed by a diabetologist in Central Hospital or a patient with the social security number NY12345678. If the data owner encrypts the record by a traditional CP-ABE scheme, with the access policy "(Patient: NY12345678 AND Hospital: Central Hospital) OR (Doctor: Diabetologist AND Hospital: Central Hospital)". Everyone who can get the access policy can infer that a patient with social security number NY12345678 is suffering diabetes. Obviously, the data owner would not like this as in Fig. 1. Thus, the CP-ABE schemes should not only guarantee the security of encrypted data but also must can satisfy the access structure protection.

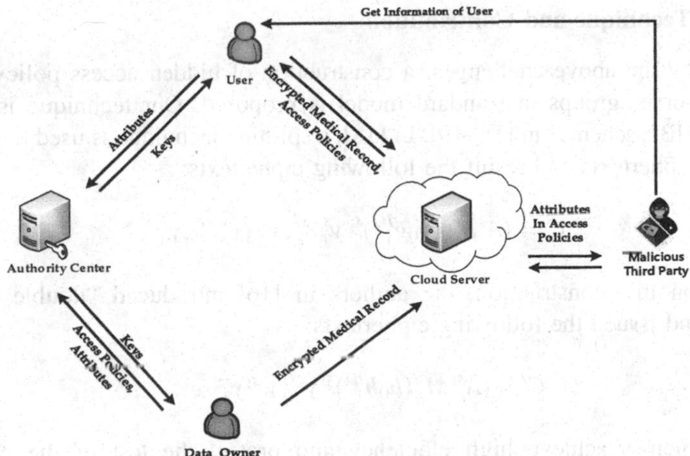

Fig. 1. Privacy leakage in traditional CP-ABE

For addressing the problem above, in 2008, Nishide et al. [6] proposed the idea of hiding the access policies of CP-ABE schemes and proposed two CP-ABE schemes partly hidden access policies with AND-gates on multi-valued attributes with wildcard access policy. However, both schemes have high computational complexity. Following Nishide, Li et al. [7] proposed an anonymous CP-ABE scheme with the ability of forbidden illegal key sharing among users, but the computational complexity in this scheme is still very high. Later, Lai et al. [8, 9] proposed two fully secure CP-ABE schemes with hidden access policy in standard model. The first one only supports AND-gates on multi-valued attributes with wildcards, while the other one supports any monotone access policy. In addition, the size of ciphertexts and secret keys is linearly growing with the number of attributes. In order to tackle the problem, in 2013, Rao et al. [10] proposed a fully secure scheme with constant size ciphertexts and secret keys. However, their scheme only supports restrict access structures. Additionally, these schemes [8–10] are all over composite-order groups. In 2013, Zhang et al. [11] proposed a novel anonymous CP-ABE scheme over prime order groups under standard assumptions with match phase to allow data users to test whether their attributes satisfy the access policy before decryption, which can decrease the computational overhead of users. However, it has been found that the match phase will reveal the attributes belonging to the access policy. In 2016, Li et al. [12] proposed a more efficient scheme with decryption test to decrease the computational complexity before successful decryption. But the decryption phase destroyed its anonymity. Recently, CP-ABE scheme with hidden access structure can also be constructed from attribute hiding Inner-product Predicate Encryption (IPE) [13, 14], nevertheless this transformation will cause a super-polynomial growth in size of arbitrary access policy, which is extremely inefficient. Phuong et al. [15] introduced a way to construct hidden access policy CP-ABE from IPE under standard assumptions, but the communication cost is too high as that the size of secret keys and ciphertexts are linear to the number of attributes.

1.1 Our Technique and Contribution

Motivated by the above challenges, a construction of hidden access policy CP-ABE over prime-order groups in standard model is proposed. Our technique is based on anonymous IBE schemes in [16–19]. In [18], a splitting technique is used to protect the privacy of ciphertexts and result the following ciphertexts:

$$C = (A^s M, (g_0 g_1^{ID})^s, v_1^{s-s_1}, v_2^{s_1}, v_3^{s-s_3}, v_4^{s_2}) \tag{1}$$

Based on this construction, the authors in [16] introduced "double exponent" technique and issued the following ciphertexts:

$$C = (A^{s_1} M, (h_0 h_1^{ID})^{s_1} y_2^{s_2}, w^{s_1} y_3^{s_2}, g^{s_2}) \tag{2}$$

Both schemes achieve high efficiency and protect the test of the ciphertexts. Inspired by these good features, they are used to construct anonymous CP-ABE, where we aim at both solving the shortcomings in existing works and reserving the high efficiency of original schemes in [16, 18]. Our contributions are given as follows.

1. The security of the proposed scheme is reduced to the decisional n-BDHE and decisional linear assumption in the standard model.
2. For the hidden control access policy, the user does not know whether his/her attributes satisfy the access policy, which makes him/her need to decrypt again and again to match the plaintexts. While, decryption in our scheme only needs four pairing computations, which can decrease the computation complexity efficiently. Moreover, the secret key size in our scheme achieves constant which is independent with the number of attributes.

2 Preliminaries

2.1 Complexity Assumptions

The Decisional n-Bilinear Diffie-Hellman Exponent (BDHE) Problem
Let g and h be two random generators of $\mathbb{G}$ and α be random element in $\mathbb{Z}_p^*$. The decisional n-BDHE assumption is defined as follows: given a tuple $(h, g, g^{\alpha}, \ldots, g^{\alpha^n}, g^{\alpha^{n+1}}, \ldots, g^{\alpha^{2n}}, Z)$, there is no probabilistic polynomial-time algorithm can distinguish whether $Z = e(g,h)^{\alpha^{n+1}}$ or Z is a random element in $\mathbb{G}_T$.

The Decisional Linear Assumptions
The D-Linear assumption was first proposed in [18]. The security of our scheme is reduced to Assumption 4. The confidence of these assumptions has been provided in [17, 19–21].

Assumption 1. Let $g \in_R \mathbb{G}$ be a random generator and $z_1, z_2, z_3, z_4 \in_R \mathbb{Z}_p^*$. When given a tuple $(g, g^{z_1}, g^{z_2}, g^{z_1 z_3}, g^{z_2 z_4}, Z)$, there is no probabilistic polynomial-time algorithm can distinguish whether $Z = g^{(z_3+z_4)}$ or Z is a random element in $\mathbb{G}$.

Assumption 2. Let $g \in_R \mathbb{G}$ be a random generator and $z_1, z_2, z_3 \in_R \mathbb{Z}_p^*$. When given $(g, g^{z_1}, g^{z_2}, g^{z_2^2}, \ldots, g^{z_2^n+1}, g^{z_2^n/z_1}, g^{z_2^{n+1} z_3}, g^{z_4}, Z)$, there is no probabilistic polynomial-time algorithm can distinguish whether $Z = g^{z_1(z_3+z_4)}$ or Z is a random element in $\mathbb{G}$.

Assumption 3. Let $g \in_R \mathbb{G}$ be a random generator and $z_1, z_2, z_3 \in_R \mathbb{Z}_p^*$. When given a tuple $(g, g^{z_1}, g^{z_2}, g^{z_2^2}, \ldots, g^{z_2^n}, g^{z_2^{n+2}}, g^{z_2^{2n}}, g^{z_3}, g^{z_4}, g^{z_2 z_4}, \ldots, g^{z_2^n z_4}, Z)$, there is no probabilistic polynomial-time algorithm can distinguish whether $Z = g^{z_1(z_3+z_4)}$ or Z is a random element in $\mathbb{G}$.

Assumption 4. Let $g \in_R \mathbb{G}$ be a random generator and $z_1, z_2, z_3 \in_R \mathbb{Z}_p^*$. When given a tuple $(g, g^{z_1}, g^{z_2}, g^{z_2^2}, \ldots, g^{z_2^n+1}, g^{z_2^n/z_1}, g^{z_2 z_3}, \ldots, g^{z_2^{n+1} z_3}, g^{z_4}, Z)$, there is no probabilistic polynomial-time algorithm can distinguish whether $Z = g^{z_1(z_3+z_4)}$ or Z is a random element in $\mathbb{G}$.

2.2 Definition and Security Model

2.2.1 Definition of Hidden Access Policy CP-ABE

A hidden access policy CP-ABE scheme consists of the following four algorithms:

- Setup $(\kappa, \mathcal{U}) \rightarrow (PK, MK)$: The setup algorithm takes security parameter κ and the universe of attribute $\mathcal{U}$ as input. Then it outputs the public parameters PK and the master key MK.
- KeyGen $(PK, MK, L) \rightarrow SK_L$: The keygen algorithm takes public parameters PK, the master key MK and a user's attribute set $L \subset \mathcal{U}$ as input. It outputs the secret keys SK_L associated with the attribute set L.
- Encrypt $(PK, M, W) \rightarrow CT$: The encrypt algorithm takes public parameters PK, a message M and an access policy W, then it generates the ciphertext CT as the encryption of M under W. Note that in a hidden access policy CP-ABE scheme, the access policy would not be included in the ciphertext.
- Decrypt $(SK_L, CT) \rightarrow M$ or $\perp$: The algorithm takes public parameters PK, secret keys SK_L and a ciphertext CT under a ciphertext policy W as input. If and only if the use's attribute set satisfies the access policy, it outputs the message M. Else it outputs $\perp$.

2.2.2 Security Model

Now we give the security model of the hidden access policy CP-ABE. It is presented as a security game between an adversary $\mathcal{A}$ and a simulator $\mathcal{B}$ as follows:

- **Init:** The adversary $\mathcal{A}$ submits two challenge ciphertext policies W_0^* and W_1^*.
- **Setup:** The simulator $\mathcal{B}$ runs the **Setup** algorithm and gives PK to the adversary $\mathcal{A}$.
- **Phase 1:** The adversary $\mathcal{A}$ submits the attribute list L, if $L \models W_0^* \wedge L \models W_1^*$ or $L \not\models W_0^* \wedge L \not\models W_1^*$, the simulator gives the secret key SK_L to $\mathcal{A}$. And $\mathcal{A}$ can repeat this for polynomial times.
- **Challenge:** The adversary $\mathcal{A}$ submits two equal length messages M_0 and M_1. If $L \models W_0^* \wedge L \models W_1^*$, then $M_0 = M_1$. Else $\mathcal{B}$ flips a random coin $b \in \{0, 1\}$, and sends **Encrypt** (PK, M_b, W_b^*) to $\mathcal{A}$.
- **Phase 2**: **Phase 1** is repeated.

Guess: The adversary outputs a guess $b' \in \{0, 1\}$ of b.

2.3 Access Policy

Assume that there are n categories of attributes as: $Att_1, Att_2, \ldots, Att_n$ and $Att_i = \{v_{i,1}, v_{i,2}, \ldots, v_{i,k_i}\} (\forall i \in [1, n])$ be the set of possible attributes belonging to Att_i. And each user has n attributes and different attribute belongs to different category. So that the universe of attributes can be donated as $\mathcal{U} = \bigcup_{i=1}^{n} Att_i$. For an access policy is donated as $W = \{W_1, W_2, \ldots, W_n\}$, in which $W_i \subset Att_i$ for $i \in [1, n]$. User's attribute set is donated as $L = \{L_1, L_2, \ldots, L_n\}$ in which $L_i \in Att_i$ for $i \in [1, n]$. If and only if $L_i \in W_i (\forall i \in [1, n])$ then it means that L satisfies W, denoted as $L \models W$, else it means that L does not satisfy W, denoted as $L \not\models W$.

3 The Proposed Construction

3.1 Construction

- **Setup** $\rightarrow (PK, MK)$: Let $\mathbb{G}$ and $\mathbb{G}_T$ be two cyclic groups of prime order p and $e : \mathbb{G} \times \mathbb{G} \rightarrow \mathbb{G}_T$ be a bilinear map. It picks a random generator $g \in \mathbb{G}$ and random elements $u, \omega, h_0, h_1, h_2, \ldots, h_n$ from $\mathbb{G}$. Then it chooses $z_1, z_2, z_3, a_{i,j} \in \mathbb{Z}_p$ randomly, where $i \in [1, n]$, $j \in [1, k_i]$ and sets $y_1 = g^{z_1}$, $y_2 = g^{z_2}$, $y_3 = g^{z_3}$, $A = e(u, y_1)$. The public parameters PK and master keys MK are given as:

$$PK = (g, \omega, h_0, h_1, h_2, \ldots, h_n, y_1, y_2, y_3, A),\ MK = (u, z_1, z_2, z_3, \{a_{i,j}\}_{i \in [1,n], j \in [1,k_i]}). \quad (3)$$

- **KeyGen** $(PK, MK, L) \rightarrow SK_L$: Let $L = \{L_1, L_2, \ldots, L_n\}(L_i \in Att_i)$ be a set of attributes of a user who is going to obtain secret keys corresponding to L. Let $k_i = h_0^{t_i} \cdot h_i^{a_{i,j}}$, where $\sum_{i=1}^{n} t_i = 1$. Last it picks r_1, r_2 at random from $\mathbb{Z}_p$ and constructs the secret keys as:

$$\begin{aligned} SK_L =& (\{k_i^{r_1}\}_{i \in [1,n]}, g^{r_1 z_1 z_2 + r_2 z_1 z_3}, g^{r_1 z_1}, g^{r_2 z_1}, u\omega^{r_2}) \\ =& (\{sk_{1,i}\}_{i \in [1,n]}, sk_2, sk_3, sk_4, sk_5). \end{aligned} \quad (4)$$

- **Encrypt** $(PK, M, W) \rightarrow CT$: The algorithm takes as input the public parameters PK, a message $M \in \mathbb{G}_T$ and a ciphertext policy $W = \{W_1, W_2, \ldots, W_n\}$, $W_i \subset Att_i$, the data owner chooses $s_{1,i}, s_{2,i} \in \mathbb{Z}_p$ randomly for $1 \leq i \leq n$ and sets $s_1 = \sum_{i=1}^{n} s_{1,i}$, $s_2 = \sum_{i=1}^{n} s_{2,i}$. Then the data owner computes

$$C_1 = y_1^{s_1},\ C_2 = g^{s_2},\ C_4 = \omega^{s_1} y_3^{s_2},\ C_5 = A^{s_1}.$$

If $v_{i,j} \in W_i$, $C_{i,j} = h_0^{s_{1,i}} h_i^{a_{i,j} s_1} y_2^{s_{2,i}}$, else $C_{i,j}$ is a random element in $\mathbb{G}$. Then C_3 is computed as: $C_3 = \{C_{i,j}\}_{\{1 \leq i \leq n, 1 \leq j \leq k_i\}}$. Finally, it outputs the ciphertexts as

$$CT = \{C_1, C_2, C_3, C_4, C_5\} \quad (5)$$

- **Decrypt** $(SK_L, CT) \rightarrow M$ or $\perp$: In this algorithm, user's secret key SK_L and ciphertext CT are taken as input. If user's attribute set satisfies the access policy then he/she can decrypt as follows:

$$M = C_5 / \frac{\prod_{i=1}^{n} e(sk_{1,i}, C_1) \cdot e(sk_5, C_1) \cdot e(sk_2, C_2)}{\prod_{i=1, v_{i,j} \in W_i}^{n} e(C_{i,j}, sk_3) \cdot e(sk_4, C_4)} \quad (6)$$

3.2 Correctness and Anonymity

Correctness

Assuming the ciphertext is well-formed for W and L. The verification is run as follows.

$$
\begin{aligned}
&\frac{\prod_{i=1}^{n} e(sk_{1,i}, C_1)\cdot e(sk_5, C_1)\cdot e(sk_2, C_2)}{\prod_{i=1, v_{i,j}\in W_i}^{n} e(C_{i,j}, sk_3)\cdot e(sk_4, C_4)}\\
&= \frac{e((h_0\prod_{i=1}^{n} h_i^{a_{i,j}})^{r_1},)e(u\omega^{r_2}, y_1^{s_1})\cdot e(g^{r_1z_1z_2+r_2z_1z_3}, g^{s_2})}{e(g^{r_1z_1}, (h_0\prod_{i=1}^{n} h_i^{a_{i,j}})^{s_1}\cdot y_2^{s_2})\cdot e(g^{r_2z_1}, \omega^{s_1}y_3^{s_2})}\\
&= \frac{e(u, g^{s_1z_1})\cdot e((h_0\prod_{i=1}^{n} h_i^{a_{i,j}})^{r_1}, g^{s_1z_1})\cdot e(\omega^{r_2}, g^{s_1z_1})}{e(g^{r_1z_1}, (h_0\prod_{i=1}^{n} h_i^{a_{i,j}})^{s_1})\cdot e(g^{r_1z_1}, g^{z_2s_2})\cdot e(g^{r_2z_1}, \omega^{s_1})}\cdot\frac{e(g^{r_1z_1z_2+r_2z_1z_3}, g^{s_2})}{e(g^{r_2z_1}, g^{z_3s_2})}\\
&= e(u, g^{z_1s_1})\cdot\frac{e((h_0\prod_{i=1}^{n} h_i^{a_{i,j}})^{r_1}, g^{s_1z_1})}{e(g^{r_1z_1}, (h_0\prod_{i=1}^{n} h_i^{a_{i,j}})^{s_1})}\cdot\frac{e(\omega^{r_2}, g^{s_1z_1})}{e(g^{r_2z_1}, \omega^{s_1})}\cdot\frac{e(g^{r_1z_1z_2+r_2z_1z_3}, g^{s_2})}{e(g^{r_1z_1}, g^{z_2s_2})\cdot e(g^{r_2z_1}, g^{z_3s_2})}\\
&= e(u, g^{z_1s_1}) = A^{s_1}.
\end{aligned}
\tag{7}
$$

Anonymity

By using the technique in [17] multiplying $h_0^{s_{1,i}}h_i^{a_{ij}s_1}$ by $y_2^{s_{2,i}}$, and ω^{s_1} by $y_3^{s_2}$, if an adversary intends to test whether an attribute $v_{i,j}$ is embed into $C_{i,j}$, he has to use C_1, C_2 and C_4, which are comprised in $C_{i,j}$ and C_4, respectively. It can resist the DDH-test. The specific proof will be given in Sect. 4.

4 Security Proof

Theorem 1. Under the decisional n-BDHE and Decisional Linear assumption, our scheme achieves selective secure and user's privacy protection.

Proof. In this section we will give the security proof using hybrid argument over a sequence of games as follows:

Game$_0$: This game is the real security game as described in security model, in which the challenge ciphertext is normal as $CT_0^* = \{C_1^*, C_2^*, C_3^*, C_4^*, C_5^*\}$.
Game$_1$: In this game C_5 is replaced by a random element $R_5 \in \mathbb{G}_T$, the challenge ciphertext is: $CT_1^* = \{C_1^*, C_2^*, C_3^*, C_4^*, R_5\}$.
Game$_2$: In this game both C_4 and C_5 are replaced by a random element $R_4 \in \mathbb{G}$ and a random element $R_5 \in \mathbb{G}_T$, the challenge ciphertext is: $CT_2^* = \{C_1^*, C_2^*, C_3^*, R_4, R_5\}$.

Then we modify *Game*$_2$ by changing the way to generate the components $\{C_{i,j}\}_{\{1\le i\le n, 1\le j\le k_i\}}$ and define a sequence of games as follows. For $v_{i,j}$ such that $(v_{i,j}\in W_{0,i}\wedge v_{i,j}\in W_{1,i})$ or $(v_{i,j}\notin W_{0,i}\wedge v_{i,j}\notin W_{1,i})$ the ciphertext component $C_{i,j}$ is obtained from the real game. But for $v_{i,j}$ such that $(v_{i,j} \in W_{0,i} \wedge v_{i,j} \notin W_{1,i})$ or $(v_{i,j} \notin W_{0,i} \wedge v_{i,j} \in W_{1,i})$, the ciphertext component $C_{i,j}$ which is generated normally in $Game_{2,\ell-1}$ is replaced by random value in $Game_{2,\ell}$. We will not define a new game by replacing ciphertext component $C_{i,j}$, until there is no $v_{i,j}$ satisfies $(v_{i,j} \in W_{0,i} \wedge v_{i,j} \notin W_{1,i})$ or $(v_{i,j} \notin W_{0,i} \wedge v_{i,j} \in W_{1,i})$.

Lemma 1. Under the decisional n-BDHE assumption, there is no adversary can distinguish the difference from $Game_0$ and $Game_1$ with non-negligible advantage in polynomial time.

Lemma 2. Under the Decisional Linear assumption, there is no adversary can distinguish the difference from $Game_1$ and $Game_2$ with non-negligible advantage in polynomial time.

Lemma 3. Under the Decisional Linear assumption, there is no adversary can distinguish the difference from $Game_{2,\ell-1}$ and $Game_{2,\ell}$ with non-negligible advantage in polynomial time.

Thus, the proposed scheme is IND-sCP-CPA secure under decisional n-BDHE assumption and Decisional Linear assumption.

5 Performance Comparison

In this section, the proposed construction will be compared with previous works. Tables 1 and 2 give the detailed comparisons between the proposed scheme in Sect. 3.1 and the others. For ease of expression the size of the public parameter, the secret key, and the ciphertext length excepting the access policy are denoted by *PK*, *SK*, and *CT*, respectively. Let N be the order of bilinear group, generally it is a big prime order number, but in some schemes, it is a composite number $N = pqr$, where p, q, r are prime order numbers. $|\mathbb{G}|, |\mathbb{G}_T|, |\mathbb{Z}_N|$ are the bit-length of the element belonging to each group, respectively. Let $\mathcal{U} = \{Att_1, Att_2, \cdots, Att_n\}$ be the universe of the attributes k_i is the number of attributes in Att_i and $K = \sum_{i=1}^{n} k_i$ is the number of all the attributes in $\mathcal{U}$.

Table 1. Security comparisons with previous works

Schemes	Order of bilinear groups	Fully hidden attribute	Assumption	Anonymity
[6]	$N = p$	✗	DBDH D-linear	✓
[8]	$N = pqr$	✗	Non-standard	✓
[11]	$N = p$	✗	DBDH D-linear	✗
[12]	$N = p$	✗	DDH	✗
Ours	$N = p$	✓	Decisional n-DBHE D-linear	✓

Table 2. Comparisons of the computation cost with others

Schemes	PK	SK	CT
[6]	$(2K+1)\|\mathbb{G}\|+\|\mathbb{G}_T\|$	$(3n+1)\|\mathbb{G}\|$	$(2K+1)\|\mathbb{G}\|+\|\mathbb{G}_T\|$
[8]	$(K+1)\|\mathbb{G}\|+\|\mathbb{G}_T\|$	$(n+1)\|\mathbb{G}\|$	$(K+1)\|\mathbb{G}\|$
[11]	$3\|\mathbb{G}\|+\|\mathbb{G}_T\|$	$(5n+2)\|\mathbb{G}\|$	$(3K+4)\|\mathbb{G}\|+2\|\mathbb{G}_T\|$
[12]	$(K+1)\|\mathbb{G}\|+\|\mathbb{G}_T\|$	$(2K+2)\|\mathbb{G}\|$	$(K+n)\|\mathbb{G}\|+\|\mathbb{G}_T\|$
Ours	$(n+6)\|\mathbb{G}\|+\|\mathbb{G}_T\|$	$(n+3)\|\mathbb{G}\|$	$(K+3)\|\mathbb{G}\|+\|\mathbb{G}_T\|$

Our scheme is efficient in commutation overhead where the size of *SK* and the size of *PK* and *CT* is relatively small.

6 Conclusion

We proposed an efficient hidden access policy CP-ABE scheme over prime-order groups. The security of the proposed scheme is selectively secure and anonymous under the decisional n-BDHE and the Decision Linear assumptions.

Unfortunately, the proposed scheme only supports AND gate and achieves selectively security. It is also desirable to construct a strong secure and more flexible CP-ABE scheme with fully hidden access structures using pairings in the prime-order groups.

Acknowledgement. This work was supported in part by the National Cryptography Development Fund under Grant (MMJJ20180209).

References

1. Sahai, A., Waters, B.: Fuzzy identity-based encryption. In: Cramer, R. (ed.) EUROCRYPT 2005. LNCS, vol. 3494, pp. 457–473. Springer, Heidelberg (2005). https://doi.org/10.1007/11426639_27
2. Goyal, V., Pandey, O., Sahai, A., Waters, B.: Attribute-based encryption for fine-grained access control of encrypted data. In: ACM Conference on Computer and Communications Security, pp. 89–98 (2006)
3. Bethencourt, J., Sahai, A., Waters, B.: Ciphertext-policy attribute-based encryption. In: IEEE Symposium on Security and Privacy, pp. 321–334. IEEE Computer Society (2007)
4. Emura, K., Miyaji, A., Nomura, A., Omote, K., Soshi, M.: A ciphertext-policy attribute-based encryption scheme with constant ciphertext length. In: Bao, F., Li, H., Wang, G. (eds.) ISPEC 2009. LNCS, vol. 5451, pp. 13–23. Springer, Heidelberg (2009). https://doi.org/10.1007/978-3-642-00843-6_2
5. Waters, B.: Ciphertext-policy attribute-based encryption: an expressive, efficient, and provably secure realization. In: Catalano, D., Fazio, N., Gennaro, R., Nicolosi, A. (eds.) PKC 2011. LNCS, vol. 6571, pp. 53–70. Springer, Heidelberg (2011). https://doi.org/10.1007/978-3-642-19379-8_4

6. Nishide, T., Yoneyama, K., Ohta, K.: Attribute-based encryption with partially hidden encryptor-specified access structures. In: Bellovin, S.M., Gennaro, R., Keromytis, A., Yung, M. (eds.) ACNS 2008. LNCS, vol. 5037, pp. 111–129. Springer, Heidelberg (2008). https://doi.org/10.1007/978-3-540-68914-0_7
7. Li, J., Ren, K., Zhu, B., Wan, Z.: Privacy-aware attribute-based encryption with user accountability. In: Samarati, P., Yung, M., Martinelli, F., Ardagna, Claudio A. (eds.) ISC 2009. LNCS, vol. 5735, pp. 347–362. Springer, Heidelberg (2009). https://doi.org/10.1007/978-3-642-04474-8_28
8. Lai, J., Deng, R.H., Li, Y.: Fully secure cipertext-policy hiding CP-ABE. In: Bao, F., Weng, J. (eds.) ISPEC 2011. LNCS, vol. 6672, pp. 24–39. Springer, Heidelberg (2011). https://doi.org/10.1007/978-3-642-21031-0_3
9. Lai, J., Deng, R.H., Li, Y.: Expressive CP-ABE with partially hidden access structures. In: Youm, H.Y., Won, Y. (eds.) Proceedings ACM Conference on Computer and Communications Security, ASIACCS 2012, pp. 18–19 (2012)
10. Rao, Y.S., Dutta, R.: Recipient anonymous ciphertext-policy attribute based encryption. In: Bagchi, A., Ray, I. (eds.) ICISS 2013. LNCS, vol. 8303, pp. 329–344. Springer, Heidelberg (2013). https://doi.org/10.1007/978-3-642-45204-8_25
11. Zhang, Y., Chen, X., Li, J., Wong, D.S., Li, H.: Anonymous attribute-based encryption supporting efficient decryption test. In: ACM Symposium on Information, Computer and Communications Security 2013, pp. 511–516. ACM, New York (2013)
12. Li, J., Wang, H., Zhang, Y., Shen, J.: Ciphertext-policy attribute-based encryption with hidden access policy and testing. Ksii Trans. Internet Inf. Syst. **10**(7), 3339–3352 (2016)
13. Katz, J., Sahai, A., Waters, B.: Predicate encryption supporting disjunctions, polynomial equations, and inner products. In: Smart, N. (ed.) EUROCRYPT 2008. LNCS, vol. 4965, pp. 146–162. Springer, Heidelberg (2008). https://doi.org/10.1007/978-3-540-78967-3_9
14. Lewko, A., Okamoto, T., Sahai, A., Takashima, K., Waters, B.: fully secure functional encryption: attribute-based encryption and (hierarchical) inner product encryption. In: Gilbert, H. (ed.) EUROCRYPT 2010. LNCS, vol. 6110, pp. 62–91. Springer, Heidelberg (2010). https://doi.org/10.1007/978-3-642-13190-5_4
15. Phuong, T.V.X., Yang, G., Susilo, W.: Hidden ciphertext policy attribute-based encryption under standard assumptions. IEEE Trans. Inf. Forensics Secur. **11**(1), 35–45 (2015)
16. Park, J.H., Lee, D.H.: Anonymous HIBE: compact construction over prime-order groups. IEEE Trans. Inf. Theory **59**(4), 2531–2541 (2013)
17. Seo, J.H., Kobayashi, T., Ohkubo, M., Suzuki, K.: Anonymous hierarchical identity-based encryption with constant size ciphertexts. In: Jarecki, S., Tsudik, G. (eds.) PKC 2009. LNCS, vol. 5443, pp. 215–234. Springer, Heidelberg (2009). https://doi.org/10.1007/978-3-642-00468-1_13
18. Boneh, D., Boyen, X., Shacham, H.: Short group signatures using strong Diffie Hellman. In: Franklin, M. (ed.) CRYPTO 2004. LNCS, vol. 3152, pp. 41–55. Springer, Heidelberg (2004). https://doi.org/10.1007/978-3-540-28628-8_3
19. Boyen, X., Waters, B.: Anonymous hierarchical identity-based encryption (without random oracles). In: Dwork, C. (ed.) CRYPTO 2006. LNCS, vol. 4117, pp. 290–307. Springer, Heidelberg (2006). https://doi.org/10.1007/11818175_17
20. Gentry, C.: Practical identity-based encryption without random oracles. In: Vaudenay, S. (ed.) EUROCRYPT 2006. LNCS, vol. 4004, pp. 445–464. Springer, Heidelberg (2006). https://doi.org/10.1007/11761679_27
21. Wu, Q., Wu, Q., Mu, Y., Zhang, J.: Privacy-preserving and secure sharing of PHR in the cloud. J. Med. Syst. **40**(12), 267 (2016)

Integral and Impossible Differential Cryptanalysis of RC6

Hongguo Zhu[1], Xin Hai[2], and Jiuchuan Lin[3(✉)]

[1] Hunan Provincial Key Laboratory of Network Investigational Technology, Hunan Police Academy, Changsha 410138, China
[2] College of Science, National University of Defense Technology, Changsha 410073, Hunan, China
[3] Key Lab of Information Network Security of Ministry of Public Security, Shanghai, China
linjiuchuan@stars.org.cn

Abstract. The block cipher RC6 is one of the finalists of the five candidates of AES for its security, simplicity and easy soft-hardware implementation. In view of its importance, the resistance of RC6 against integral cryptanalysis and impossible differential cryptanalysis is evaluated in this paper. The result shows that the complexities of both integral attack on RC6 reduced to 4 rounds and impossible differential attack on RC6 reduced to 5 rounds are lower than exhaustive search. Meanwhile, it is demonstrated that RC6 with more rounds is immune to the two kinds of cryptanalysis since the data-dependent cycle increases the diffusion immensely.

Keywords: Block cipher · RC6 · Integral attack · Impossible differential attack

1 Introduction

Block cipher algorithm is widely used in data encryption, digital signature and so on because of its fast speed and easy implementation. As a safe, complete and simple block encryption algorithm, RC6 algorithm [1] is developed by Rivest, Robshaw, Sidney, and Yin et al. RC6 inherits RC5's idea of simple operation and data related cyclic shift [2], and improves the number of bits shifted in RC5 without depending on all bits in registers.

The new feature of RC6 is that the plaintext is expanded from 2 blocks to 4. In addition, 32 bits integer multiplication is used in operation, which strengthens the effect of diffusion in every round of operations, so that fewer rounds can also ensure higher security.

It is a meaningful work to study effective block cipher analysis methods to provide more and better analysis tools for security evaluation of cryptographic algorithms. A present, the analysis methods of block ciphers can be divided into two categories. One is the attack method closely related to the components used in the algorithm, such as differential cryptanalysis and linear cryptanalysis. Evaluating the ability of the algorithm to resist such attacks requires one by one to quantify the related components. Another kind of method is only related to the internal structure of the algorithm. It is

X. Sun et al. (Eds.): ICCCS 2018, LNCS 11065, pp. 606–616, 2018.
https://doi.org/10.1007/978-3-030-00012-7_55

not associated with specific components, especially nonlinear components, such as integral attack and impossible differential attack.

The integral attack [3] is considered to be based on a variety of analytical ideas such as Square attacks [4], Saturation attacks [5], and Multiset attacks [6], etc. It separates the algorithm from the random displacement area by judging the XOR of the ciphertext corresponding to a special plaintext [7–11].

The impossible differential attack is independently proposed by Knudsen and Biham, which is applied to the DEAL algorithm and the skipjack algorithm. Unlike the classical differential cryptanalysis, which searches for high probability difference (difference feature), the impossible differential attack separates the algorithm from random replacement area by finding the impossible difference [12–16]. Up to now, integral attack and impossible difference attack are considered to be the most effective attack methods for AES algorithm [4, 17].

The design of RC6 adopts the fixed data cycle and the data dependence cycle, and there is no clear linear layer and nonlinear layer in the algorithm round function. Because of its special design idea, the analysis results of the algorithm are relatively small at present.

This paper will focus on the immune ability of low round number algorithm for integral attack and impossible difference attack. It shows that the use of the data dependence cycle does enhance the diffusion performance of the algorithm.

2 RC5 Block Cipher and RC6 Block Cipher

2.1 RC5 Description

RC5 is an iterative secret-key block cipher published by Rivest in1995 [2]. It has variable parameters such as the key size, the block size, and the number of rounds. A particular (parameterized) RC5 encryption algorithm is designated as RC5-*w*/*r*/*b*, where w is the word size (one block is made of two words), r is the number of rounds ($r = 2\ h$), and b is the number of bytes for the secret key. RC5 served as a model for the Advanced Encryption Standard (AES) candidate RC6.

Block ciphers in 1995 followed one of two generic models: Either they were based on a Feistel structure, or on a substitution-permutation network. RC5 is no exception and is a Feistel-like structure. It uses very few, very simple, and very fast operations in its round function; it is one of the first block ciphers using variable parameters and data-dependent rotations. Another novelty of RC5 is that it incorporates a complex one-way key scheduling procedure.

The "nominal" choice for the algorithm, RC5-32/12/64, has a 64-bit block size, 12 rounds, and a 128-bit key. The secret key is first expanded into a table of $2h + 2$ secret words S_i of w bits according to the key schedule. Let (L_0, R_0) denote the left and right halves of the plaintext. Note that a w-bit word is equivalently viewed as an integer modulo 2^w. Then the encryption algorithm is given by:

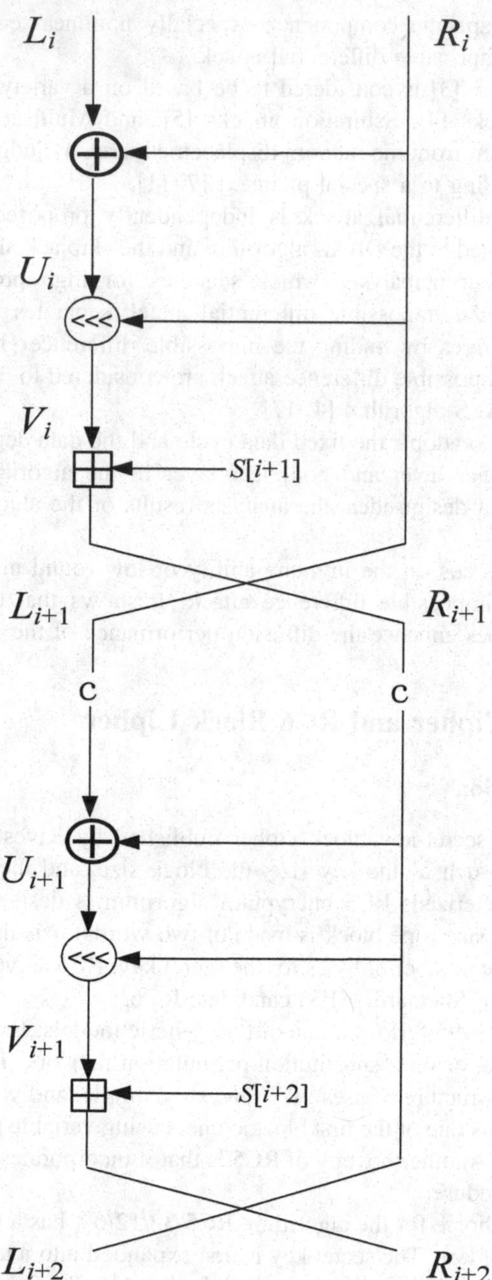

Fig. 1. The round transformation of RC5

$$
\begin{aligned}
&L_1 \leftarrow L_0 + S_0 \mod 2^w \\
&R_1 \leftarrow R_0 + S_1 \mod 2^w \\
&\text{for } i = 1 \text{ to } 2h \text{ do} \\
&\quad L_{i+1} \leftarrow R_i \\
&\quad R_{i+1} \leftarrow ((L_i \oplus R_i) \lll R_i) + S_{i+1} \mod 2^w
\end{aligned}
$$

where "$\oplus$" represents bit-wise exclusive-or, and "X $\ll$ Y" is the (data-dependent) rotation of X to the left by the $\log_2 w$ least significant bits of Y. The ciphertext is (L_{2h+1}, R_{2h+1}), and each half-round i involves exactly one subkey S_i. In Fig. 1 a graphical representation of one round is given.

Both differential and linear attacks on nominal RC5 have been studied [30, 31]. The best differential (chosen plaintext) and linear (known plaintext) attacks on RC5 are respectively the one breaks 12 rounds of RC5-32/12/16 with 2^{44} chosen plaintexts using partial differentials [27], and the one which breaks RC5 up to 10 rounds using multiple linear approximations [28]. Both results suggest that RC5 should be used with at least 16 to 20 rounds.

Following the new trend of side-channel attacks, RC5 was analyzed with respect to timing attacks and show that the existence of data-dependent rotations in RC5. It allows to recover the secretkey with a few thousands of timing measurements only. This suggests RC5 should be implemented in a time constant way.

2.2 RC6 Description

RC6 designed by Rivest et al. is one of the five final block ciphers which have go into the last round of AES plan. It is the improved vision of RC5 block cipher. The whole structure of RC6 is similar to Feistel structure.

The three "nominal" choices for the algorithm as submitted to the American Advanced Encryption Standard (Rijndael/AES) contest and to the European NESSIE contest are RC6 (32, 20, 16), RC6 (32, 20, 24) and RC6 (32, 20, 32). All three versions have a 128-bit block size, 20 rounds and only differ in the key-size which is respectively 128, 196 and 256 bits long.

Let the length of the message be w, the round number be r, the key number be b. We denote A, B, C, D as the w-bit word, S[i] as round key,$f(x) = (x(2x+1)) \lll 5$, where "$\lll$" denotes left rotation.

The encryption process of RC6 is described as follows.

Step 1: Input white process

Let the plaintext be (A, B, C, D), we have:

$$B = B + S[0] \qquad D = D + S[1]$$

Step 2: Iteration process

The round transformation is presented below and it is iterated r times:

$$\begin{cases} t = f(B) \\ u = f(D) \\ A = ((A \oplus t) \lll u) + S[2i] \\ C = ((C \oplus u) \lll t) + S[2i+1] \\ (A, B, C, D) = (B, C, D, A) \end{cases}$$

Step 3: Output white process

Let $A = A + S[2r+2]$, $C = C + S[2r+3]$. The output ciphertext is (A, B, C, D). Since the relationship of the round key is not studied in this paper, the details of the key schedule are not given in our paper. We refer to [6] for them. Moreover, the round transformation of RC6 is described in Fig. 2.

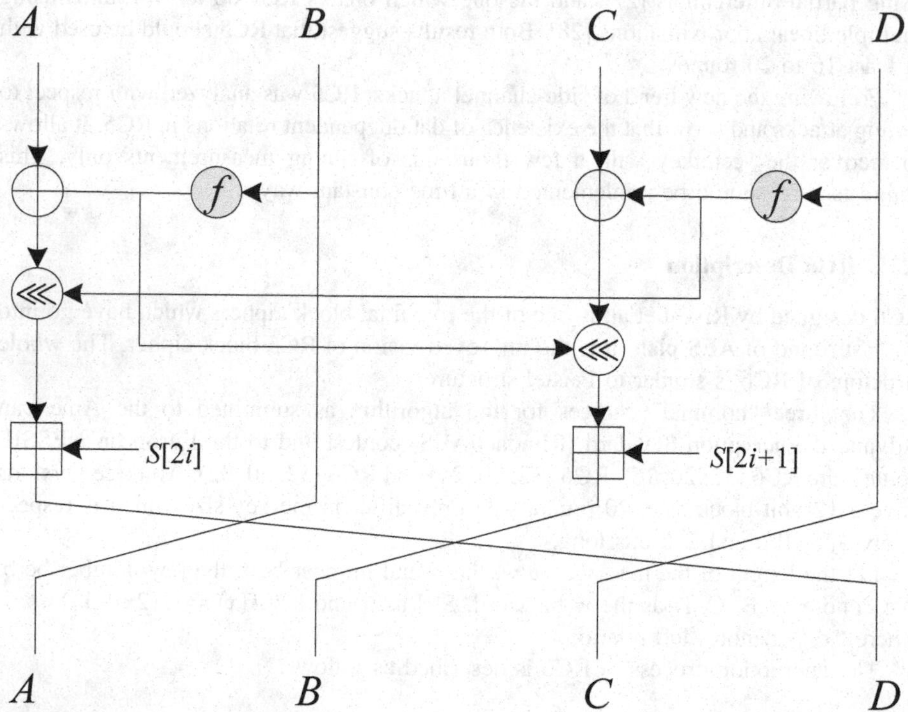

Fig. 2. The round transformation of RC6

2.3 Known Results on RC6

RC6 overcomes certain weaknesses of its predecessor RC5 by introducing fixed rotations as well as a quadratic function to determine the data-dependent rotations. A comprehensive analysis of the contribution of these features to the security of RC6 was given [32, 34].

So far, there are three kinds of effect attacks on RC6. One of them is statistical attack which is proposed by Gilbert et al. [18]. The attack breaks RC6 (32, 14, 16) and constructs a distinguisher by studying the statistical property of RC6. Furthermore, with the distinguisher, it can attack 14-round RC6. Another one is χ^2 attack which is presented by Knudsen and Meier [19]. It can attack 15-round and 17-round RC6 with the weak key. Moreover, Japanese scholars [20] have verified the experiment results from the theory view. The third one is multi-linear attack, which can attack 18-round RC6 with the weak key [21].

The more recent cryptanalysis results mainly apply on reduced-round versions without whitening keys (called RC6W), i.e., versions without the first-round and/or last-round key addition and suggest that it remains difficult to attack more than 17 or 18 rounds of RC6W.

Further results were obtained on several variants of RC6 such as ERC6 and MRC6, but the original nominal 20 round version of RC6 is still considered unbroken so far.

To our knowledge, for RC6, there are no results on integral and impossible differential attacks.

3 Integral Attack on Reduced RC6

3.1 4-Round Integral Distinguisher

Let the input of RC6 be (x, c, c, c), where c denotes the constant (c can be different in different positions). The output after input white process is still (x, c, c, c). Through the first round transformation, the output is $(c, c, c, x \oplus c)$, which can be viewed as (c, c, c, y), obviously, when x runs out $\{0, 1\}^w$, y also runs out $\{0, 1\}^w$. After the second round transformation, the output is (c, z, y, D), where D denotes the values that appear multiple times of $2^{32} \times 2^{-5} = 2^{27}$, then at the corresponding positions the values appear 32 different values at most. Similarly, when x runs out $\{0, 1\}^w$, y and z also run out $\{0, 1\}^w$, which is presented in Fig. 3.

Futhermore, the output after the third round is $(z, \alpha + m_1, D, \beta + m_2)$, where m_1 and m_2 are unknown values, α and β denote that the sum of all bits is zero for all words in the corresponding positions. According to the encryption process of RC6, the above distinguisher can be expanded to the following 4-round distinguisher naturally.

If the input of RC6 is (x, c, c, c), where c denotes the constant, and x runs out $\{0, 1\}^w$, the output of the fourth round is $(\alpha + m_1, ?, \beta + m_2, ?)$, where α and β are defined as before.

3.2 4-Round Integral Attack on RC6

Based on the above 4-round integral distinguisher, the 4-round integral attack is presented as below:

Step 1. Choose plaintexts as (x, c_1, c_2, c_3), where all of c_1, c_2 and c_3 are constant vectors in $\{0, 1\}^w$. We denote the first word of the ciphertext by $C(x)$.

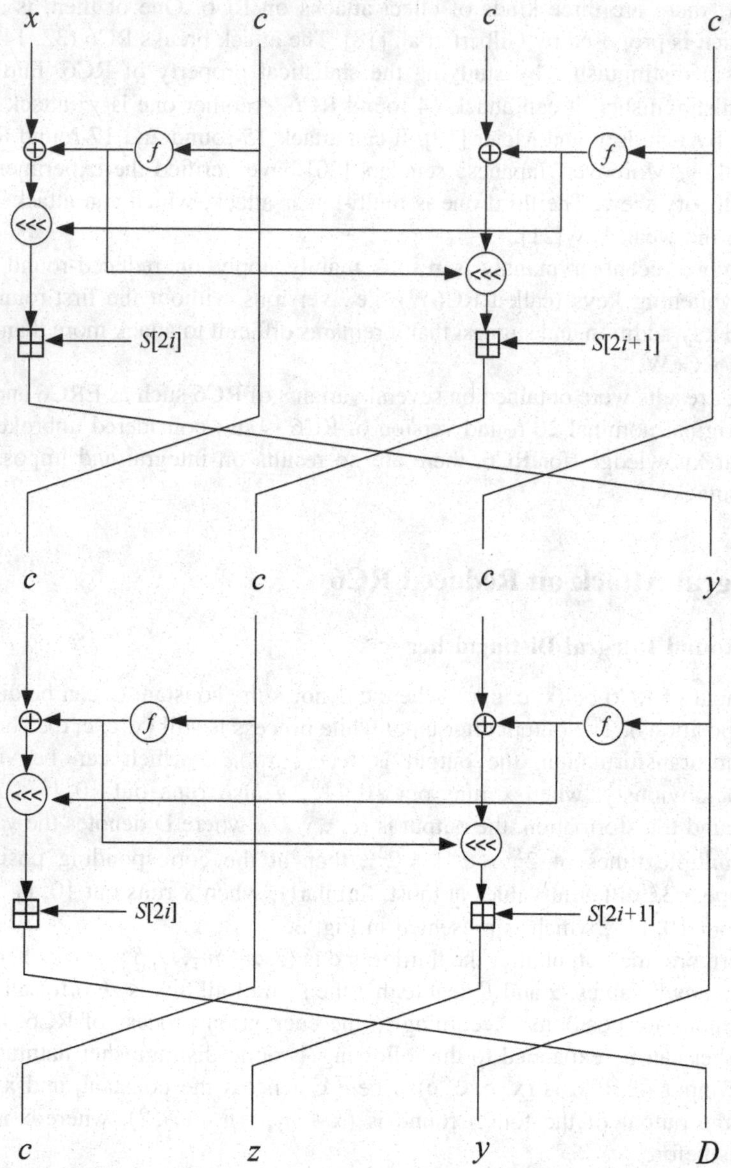

Fig. 3. 2-round integral propagations

Step 2. Guess the value of $S[10]+S[7]$, called K^*. First, we calculate $D(x) = C(x) - K^*$, and then calculate $s_{K^*} = \sum_x \sum_{i=0}^{w-1} D_i(x)$, where $D_i(x)$ denotes the i-th bit of $D(x)$.
Step 3. If $s_{K^*} = 0$, we view K^* as a candidate value. Otherwise, discard it.

Step 4. If it is necessary, repeat the above steps until K^* can be obtained with only one value.

Since the probability of $s_{K^*} = 0$ is 0.5, about 2^{w-1} wrong keys can be passed through the first plaintext and ciphertext pair. After t pairs of plaintext and ciphertext, there remain about 2^{w-t} wrong keys. Therefore, to get the only right key, we need $t = w+1$.

According to the above analysis, the data complexity of 4-round integral attack is $(w+1) \times 2^w$ chosen plaintexts.

4 Impossible Differential Attack on Reduced RC6

4.1 4-Round Impossible Differential

According to the analysis in 3.1 section, when the input difference of RC6 is $(a, 0, 0, 0)$, the output difference of the third round must be $(c, *, *, *)$, where $a \neq 0$, $c \neq 0$.

From the decryption direction, $(0, 0, d, 0) \leftarrow (0, b, 0, 0)$ is a 1-round truncated difference of RC6 with probability 1. Then, if $(a, 0, 0, 0) \rightarrow (0, b, 0, 0)$ is a possible difference $(a, 0, 0, 0) \rightarrow_3 (c, *, *, *) \neq (0, 0, d, 0) \leftarrow_1 (0, b, 0, 0)$

It contradicts with $c \neq 0$, so $(a, 0, 0, 0) \rightarrow_4 (0, b, 0, 0)$ is a 4-round impossible differential of RC6.

4.2 5-Round Impossible Differential Attack

Based on the above 4-round impossible differential, the 5-round integral attack is presented as follows.

Step 1. Choose plaintexts as (x, c_1, c_2, c_3), where all of c_1, c_2 and c_3 are constant vectors in $\{0,1\}^w$, x runs out $\{0,1\}^w$. Then, a pair of plaintexts contain $2^w(2^w - 1)/2 \approx 2^{2w-1}$ differences which are $(a, 0, 0, 0)$.
Step 2. Choose ciphertexts whose difference are $(b, \Delta_1, 0, \Delta_2)$, where $b \neq 0$. Guess the values of $S[10]$, $S[11]$, $S[12]$ and $S[13]$, then, calculate the difference value after 1-round decryption.
Step 3. If all difference values are $(0, \delta, 0, 0)$, where $\delta \neq 0$, the guessed values of $S[10]$, $S[11]$, $S[12]$ and $S[13]$ must be wrong, we discard them.
Step 4. If it is necessary, repeat the above steps until the candidate values of $S[10]$, $S[11]$, $S[12]$ and $S[13]$ can be obtained with only one value.

For an arbitrary guessed value, the probability that corresponding difference is $(0, \delta, 0, 0)$ is 2^{-2w}. Then, after a pair of ciphertexts whose difference is $(b, \Delta_1, 0, \Delta_2)$, the number of the wrong values remains $2^{4w}(1 - 2^{-2w})$. Therefore, after N pairs of ciphertexts whose differences are $(b, \Delta_1, 0, \Delta_2)$, the number of the wrong values remains $2^{4w}(1 - 2^{-2w})^N$. To get the only right key, we need $2^{4w}(1 - 2^{-2w})^N < 1$.

Then, $N \approx w \times 2^{2w+1}$. Since the probability that corresponding difference is $(b, \Delta_1, 0, \Delta_2)$ is 2^{-w}, the data complexity of the attack is $w \times 2^{w+2}$ pairs of chosen plaintexts, which totally is $w \times 2^{2w+2}$ chosen plaintexts.

5 Conclusion

As a widely used block cipher algorithm [22–32], RC6 adapts addition and rotation operations. It is Different from usual cipher which takes S-box. So, it is difficult to use classical cryptanalysis methods to attack RC6. This paper focuses on the ability of RC6 that resists against integral and impossible differential attacks. In our paper, we present 4-round integral attack and 5-round impossible differential attack. For these two attacks, they are better than the brute search. Moreover, it is difficult for us to attack more rounds. Our results show that the structure of RC6 significantly improves the diffusion.

Acknowledgement. This work is supported by the project of Hunan Province Department of Education (16B086) and Open Research Fund of Hunan Provincial Key Laboratory of Network Investigation al Technology. (No.2016WLZC018).

References

1. Rivest, R., Robshaw, M., Sidney, R., et al.: The RC6 Block Cipher. v1.1. AES Proposal (1998). http://www.rsa.com/rsalabs/aes
2. Rivest, R.L.: The RC5 encryption algorithm. In: Preneel, B. (ed.) FSE 1994. LNCS, vol. 1008, pp. 86–96. Springer, Heidelberg (1995). https://doi.org/10.1007/3-540-60590-8_7
3. Knudsen, L., Wagner, D.: Integral cryptanalysis. In: Daemen, J., Rijmen, V. (eds.) FSE 2002. LNCS, vol. 2365, pp. 112–127. Springer, Heidelberg (2002). https://doi.org/10.1007/3-540-45661-9_9
4. Daemen, J., Knudsen, L., Rijmen, V.: The block cipher square. In: Biham, E. (ed.) FSE 1997. LNCS, vol. 1267, pp. 149–165. Springer, Heidelberg (1997). https://doi.org/10.1007/BFb0052343
5. Lucks, S.: The saturation attack—a bait for twofish. In: Matsui, M. (ed.) FSE 2001. LNCS, vol. 2355, pp. 1–15. Springer, Heidelberg (2002). https://doi.org/10.1007/3-540-45473-X_1
6. Biryukov, A., Shamir, A.: Structural cryptanalysis of SASAS. In: Pfitzmann, B. (ed.) EUROCRYPT 2001. LNCS, vol. 2045, pp. 395–405. Springer, Heidelberg (2001). https://doi.org/10.1007/3-540-44987-6_24
7. Zhang, W., Su, B., Wu, W., Feng, D., Wu, C.: Extending higher-order integral: an efficient unified algorithm of constructing integral distinguishers for block ciphers. In: Bao, F., Samarati, P., Zhou, J. (eds.) ACNS 2012. LNCS, vol. 7341, pp. 117–134. Springer, Heidelberg (2012). https://doi.org/10.1007/978-3-642-31284-7_8
8. Sun, B., Zhang, P., Li, C., et al.: Higher order integral cryptanalysis of Zodiac. Chin. J. Electron. **22**(3), 589–593 (2013)
9. Li, R., Sun, B., Li, C.: A link between integrals and higher-order integrals of SPN ciphers. ETRI J. **35**(1), 131–141 (2013)
10. Pan, Z., Guo, J.: Bit-pattern based integral attack on LBlock. J. Inf. Eng. Univ. **14**(1), 30–35 (2013)

11. Dong, L., Wu, W., Wu, S., et al.: Another look at the integral attack by the higher-order differential attack. Chin. J. Comput. **35**(9), 1906–1917 (2012)
12. Knudsen, L.: DEAL: a 128-bit block cipher. Technical report 151, Department of Informatics. University of Bergen, Bergen, Norway (1998)
13. Biham, E., Biryukov, A., Shamir, A.: Cryptanalysis of skipjack reduced to 31 rounds using impossible differentials. In: Stern, J. (ed.) EUROCRYPT 1999. LNCS, vol. 1592, pp. 12–23. Springer, Heidelberg (1999). https://doi.org/10.1007/3-540-48910-X_2
14. Luo, Y., Lai, X., Wu, Z., et al.: A unified method for finding impossible differentials of block cipher structures. Inf. Sci. **263**, 211–220 (2014)
15. Wu, S., Wang, M.: Automatic search of truncated impossible differentials for word-oriented block ciphers. In: Galbraith, S., Nandi, M. (eds.) INDOCRYPT 2012. LNCS, vol. 7668, pp. 283–302. Springer, Heidelberg (2012). https://doi.org/10.1007/978-3-642-34931-7_17
16. Li, C., Wei, Y.: New impossible differential cryptanalysis of Zodiac. J. Natl. Univ. Def. Technol. **34**(5), 132–136 (2012)
17. Lu, J., Dunkelman, O., Keller, N., Kim, J.: New impossible differential attacks on AES. In: Chowdhury, D.R., Rijmen, V., Das, A. (eds.) INDOCRYPT 2008. LNCS, vol. 5365, pp. 279–293. Springer, Heidelberg (2008). https://doi.org/10.1007/978-3-540-89754-5_22
18. Gilbert, H., Handschuh, H., Joux, A., Vaudenay, S.: A statistical attack on RC6. In: Goos, G., Hartmanis, J., van Leeuwen, J., Schneier, B. (eds.) FSE 2000. LNCS, vol. 1978, pp. 64–74. Springer, Heidelberg (2001). https://doi.org/10.1007/3-540-44706-7_5
19. Knudsen, Lars R., Meier, W.: Correlations in RC6 with a reduced number of rounds. In: Goos, G., Hartmanis, J., van Leeuwen, J., Schneier, B. (eds.) FSE 2000. LNCS, vol. 1978, pp. 94–108. Springer, Heidelberg (2001). https://doi.org/10.1007/3-540-44706-7_7
20. Takenaka, M., Shimoyama, T., Koshiba, T.: Theoretical analysis of η^2attack on RC6. In: Safavi-Naini, R., Seberry, J. (eds.) ACISP 2003. LNCS, vol. 2727, pp. 142–153. Springer, Heidelberg (2003). https://doi.org/10.1007/3-540-45067-X_13
21. Shimoyama, T., Takenaka, M., Koshiba, T.: Multiple linear cryptanalysis of a reduced round RC6. In: Daemen, J., Rijmen, V. (eds.) FSE 2002. LNCS, vol. 2365, pp. 76–88. Springer, Heidelberg (2002). https://doi.org/10.1007/3-540-45661-9_6
22. Varshney, N., Raghuwanshi, K.: RC6 based data security and attack detection. In: Satapathy, S.C.C., Das, S. (eds.) Proceedings of First International Conference on Information and Communication Technology for Intelligent Systems: Volume 1. SIST, vol. 50, pp. 3–10. Springer, Cham (2016). https://doi.org/10.1007/978-3-319-30933-0_1
23. Hu, L., Li, Y., Li, T., et al.: The efficiency improved scheme for secure access control of digital video distribution. Multimed. Tools Appl. **75**(20), 12645–12662 (2016)
24. Helmy, M., El-Rabaie, E., Eldokany, I., et al.: 3-D image encryption based on Rubik's cube and RC6 algorithm. 3D Res. **8**, 38 (2017)
25. Manju, K., Shailender, G., Pranshul, S.: A survey of image encryption algorithms. 3D Res. **8**, 37 (2017)
26. Aljawarneh, S., Yassein, M., Talafha, W.: A resource-efficient encryption algorithm for multimedia big data. Multimed. Tools Appl. **76**(21), 22703–22724 (2017)
27. Biryukov, A., Kushilevitz, E.: Improved cryptanalysis of RC5. In: Nyberg, K. (ed.) EUROCRYPT 1998. LNCS, vol. 1403, pp. 85–99. Springer, Heidelberg (1998). https://doi.org/10.1007/BFb0054119
28. Borst, J., Preneel, B., Vandewalle, J.: Linear cryptanalysis of RC5 and RC6. In: Knudsen, L. (ed.) FSE 1999. LNCS, vol. 1636, pp. 16–30. Springer, Heidelberg (1999). https://doi.org/10.1007/3-540-48519-8_2
29. Handschuh, H., Heys, Howard M.: A timing attack on RC5. In: Tavares, S., Meijer, H. (eds.) SAC 1998. LNCS, vol. 1556, pp. 306–318. Springer, Heidelberg (1999). https://doi.org/10.1007/3-540-48892-8_24

30. Kaliski, Burton S., Yin, Y.L.: On differential and linear cryptanalysis of the RC5 encryption algorithm. In: Coppersmith, D. (ed.) CRYPTO 1995. LNCS, vol. 963, pp. 171–184. Springer, Heidelberg (1995). https://doi.org/10.1007/3-540-44750-4_14
31. Knudsen, L.R., Meier, W.: Improved differential attacks on RC5. In: Koblitz, N. (ed.) CRYPTO 1996. LNCS, vol. 1109, pp. 216–228. Springer, Heidelberg (1996). https://doi.org/10.1007/3-540-68697-5_17
32. Sun, B., Li, R., Qu, L., et al.: Square attack on block ciphers with low algebraic degree. Sci. China Ser. F Inf. Sci. **53**(10), 1988–1995 (2010)

Multi-class Imbalanced Learning with One-Versus-One Decomposition: An Empirical Study

Yanjun Song, Jing Zhang, Han Yan, and Qianmu Li(✉)

School of Computer Science and Engineering,
Nanjing University of Science and Technology, Nanjing 210094, China
qianmu@njust.edu.cn

Abstract. In supervised learning, the underlying skewed distribution of multiple classes poses extreme difficulties for learning good models. A common scheme to deal with the multi-class imbalanced problem is to decompose an original dataset into several binary-class subsets and incorporate some imbalanced learning techniques. This paper presents our empirical study on the state-of-the-art multi-class imbalanced learning algorithms which are based on One-versus-One (OVO) decomposition. We implemented six algorithms in literature, including SMOTEBagging, UnderBagging, OVO plus OVA, OVO plus SMOTE, One-Against-Higher-Order, and DynamicOVO, and evaluate their performance in terms of multi-class Area Under the ROC (MAUC) on eighteen datasets with different characteristics. Experimental results show that the OVO plus SMOTE algorithm is superior to other algorithms and it is quite stable.

Keywords: Multi-class learning · Imbalanced learning
One-versus-one decomposition · SMOTE

1 Introduction

Traditional machine learning classification algorithms usually perform well on balanced datasets because they work under an assumption that - class distribution of instances is approximately balanced. However, imbalanced class distribution often occurs in many real-word applications, such as disease diagnosis, fraud detection, and so on. The skewed class distribution of datasets makes the performance of conventional machine learning algorithms degrade, especially when predicting the unlabeled data belonging to the minority class. Therefore, learning from imbalanced data has become one of the most challenging issues in machine learning [1, 2]. During the past two decades, researchers have proposed a large number of methods to deal with the imbalanced issue, which can be divided into two categories: the data- and the algorithm-level methods. Data-level methods use some resampling strategies to reduce the imbalance rate of a dataset, including under-sampling of major class and over-sampling of minor class [2]. Algorithm-level methods, like the most widely used cost-sensitive learning [3], concentrate on modifying existing learners to alleviate their bias towards the major class. Previous studies [2] have shown that both of them can achieve good results on binary-class imbalanced datasets.

X. Sun et al. (Eds.): ICCCS 2018, LNCS 11065, pp. 617–628, 2018.
https://doi.org/10.1007/978-3-030-00012-7_56

In many real-world applications, multi-class learning occurs more naturally and frequently than binary-class one. An intuitive scheme for multi-class learning is to divide an original dataset into a series of sub-datasets that are easier to learn better models. Two common decomposition strategies are one-versus-one (OVO) and one-versus-all (OVA) [4]. The former creates all possible pairwise combinations of classes, while the latter selects one class as the positive class and combines the remaining ones as the negative class. However, when the class distribution exhibits imbalance, the situations of dealing with multi-class imbalanced problem become far more complicated. On the one hand, the relations among classes are no longer distinct, on the other hand, class overlapping may appear with more than two groups, class label noise may affect the problem, and borders between classes may be far from being well defined [23]. We focus on multi-class imbalanced problems with decomposition strategy. Advantages of such a strategy include simplifying sub-problems and alleviating of some data-level difficulties [5] (like overlapping and class noise). Note that training from the data processed by the OVA decomposition inherently suffers from the imbalance because OVA introduces an artificial class imbalance. It is not suitable for handling the problems with naturally skewed distributions. Also, OVO is the most mainstream approach and has been proved to be superior to OVA [6, 7].

The scheme of multi-class imbalanced learning with OVO decomposition usually consists of three steps. First, the multi-class dataset is decomposed into a series of binary-class sub-datasets. Second, multiple classifiers are built with some imbalanced learning techniques from those binary-class sub-datasets. Finally, an aggregation strategy is applied to combine the outputs of the multiple classifiers. Our work is to conduct a complete empirical study to investigate the performance of six OVO-decomposition-based multi-class imbalanced learning algorithms on the datasets with different characteristics. The main contributions of this paper are three-fold.

- We conduct a comprehensive horizontal comparison among six state-of-the-art multi-class imbalanced learning algorithms in literature. Although in previous studies [5, 6, 16] authors usually made comparisons among different methods, they usually compared their proposed algorithms with its variants while not those in other literature. Our study first focuses on those algorithms that are entirely reported in the six articles.
- Using eighteen multi-class imbalanced datasets with different characteristics, we make comparisons from different aspects, including the number of classes, imbalanced ratio, and the type of imbalance. The results show that a large number of classes can cause a decline in the performance of the classifier, and the degree of imbalance ratio also has negative effect on the algorithms.
- We publish the source code of these algorithms on GitHub, which is available at https://github.com/wisdomofcrowds/ImbalancedLearning.

The remainder of this paper is organized as follows. Section 2 briefly reviews the related work. In Sect. 3, we present the principles of six state-of-the-art multi-class imbalanced learning algorithms after the problem statement. Section 4 presents the experiments and our analysis of the results. Section 5 concludes the paper with some potential topics for future study.

2 Related Work

Decomposition strategies for addressing multi-class problems have been widely studied in [8]. The OVO and OVA decompositions are two commonly used approaches. Several studies on decomposition strategies showed that OVA exhibit inferior performance [5, 6] because it aggravates the imbalance rate between classes, which may further damage the learning process. For example, even for ten roughly equally sized classes, the imbalance rate will reach 9:1 between each binary class, nevertheless the skewed distributions. Hence, many studies primarily focused on the OVO strategy. Fernandez et al. [9] firstly decomposed an original dataset into binary classification sub-datasets and then rebalanced them by oversampling. Krawczyk [10] proposed to combine the OVO decomposition with ensemble learning and cost-sensitive learning. Ghanem et al. [11] further applied so-called A&O approach which integrates OVO with OVA in their algorithm to promote performance. Murphey et al. [12] proposed a method named One-Against-Higher-Order (OAHO). Galar et al. [7] proposed a dynamic classifier selection strategy in the voting phase for OVO scheme, which aims to avoid the non-competent classifiers. The algorithm mentioned above will be further introduced in detail in Sect. 3. Besides, Tan et al. [13] devised an ensemble machine learning approach named ensemble Knowledge for Imbalance Sample Sets, which integrates the classifiers generated from both OVO and OVA to improve the performance of the models learned from the multi-class imbalanced data. Vluymans et al. [14] considered the IFROWANN's extension to multi-class data by combining it with the OVO decomposition. Cerf et al. [15] proposed a One-Versus-Each (OVE) framework, where a rule has to be relevant for one class and irrelevant for every other class taken separately.

In the specialized literature, there exist some empirical studies comparing the decomposition strategies in solving the multi-class imbalanced problems from the different point of view. Galar et al. [6] focused on the ensemble methods by OVO and OVA decompositions, paying attention to the different ways in which the outputs of base classifiers are aggregated. Zhang et al. [16] conducted a study by combining OVO scheme with various ensemble learning approaches based on data processing. Fernández et al. [5] provided an experimental analysis of the optimal combination between the OVO and OVA decomposition strategies either with preprocessing approaches or with the utilization of cost-sensitive learning for multi-class imbalanced datasets. All studies mentioned above just replaced at a particular step throughout the entire learning process to find the best combination. Our motivation is to make a horizontal comparison between different algorithms with the OVO decomposition and evaluate their performance on diverse imbalanced datasets structures.

3 Multi-class Imbalanced Learning Algorithms

In this section, we first present the characteristics of multi-class imbalanced datasets, and then briefly introduce the principle of the six algorithms in the literature that are investigated in our empirical study.

3.1 Problem Statement

Imbalanced learning problems become more complicated when it comes to a multi-class scenario because the class structure in multi-class scenario exhibits different shapes. For an imbalanced multi-class dataset, there generally exist three types of imbalance cases: one majority class and multiple minority classes (multi-minority), one minority class and multiple majority classes (multi-majority), and multiple minority and multiple majority classes (defined as a mixed case). Different types may require different techniques, which exhibits the certain complexity of the multi-class imbalanced problem.

3.2 Algorithms with One-Vs-One Decomposition

To conduct a comprehensive empirical study, we selected six data-level algorithms with the OVO-based decomposition. We present their principles in this section.

Of the six algorithms, five use the OVO decomposition method, and the other uses OAHO decomposition (also based on OVO). The OVO decomposition strategy divides an m multi-class dataset into $m(m-1)/2$ binary-class sub-datasets. For each pair of corresponding classes, we train a classifier, ignoring the samples that do not belong to those two classes. When making predictions, unlabeled samples will be fed into all the classifiers. The output of a classifier given by (r_{ij}, r_{ji}) where $r_{ij} \in [0, 1]$ is the confidence of a binary classifier that discriminates classes i and j. All the confidence degrees can be represented by a score matrix R as follows:

$$R_{m,n} = \begin{pmatrix} - & r_{1,2} & \cdots & r_{1,m} \\ r_{2,1} & - & \cdots & r_{2,m} \\ \vdots & \vdots & \ddots & \vdots \\ r_{m,1} & r_{m,2} & \cdots & - \end{pmatrix}. \tag{1}$$

The final output of the system is derived from the score matrix R using a specific aggregation model. In this study, we consider the voting strategy (VOTE) as our aggregation approach. According to VOTE, the final class is assigned by computing the maximum vote as follows:

$$\mathrm{Class} = \arg\max_{\mathrm{i}=1,\cdots,\mathrm{m}} \sum\nolimits_{1 \le \mathrm{j} \ne \mathrm{i} \le \mathrm{m}} \mathrm{s_{ij}}, \tag{2}$$

where

$$\mathrm{s_{ij}} = \begin{cases} 1 & \mathrm{r_{ij}} > \mathrm{r_{ji}} \\ 0 & \text{otherwise} \end{cases}. \tag{3}$$

Two algorithms used in our empirical study are based on SMOTE [17]. The SMOTE algorithm creates artificial data based on the feature space similarities among existing minority samples. For minority class C_{min}, SMOTE considers

K-nearest neighbors for each sample $x_i \in C_{min}$. To create a synthetic sample with the original samples, the algorithm randomly selects one of its K-nearest neighbors and calculates a new sample by

$$x_{new} = x_i + \delta \times (x_i - \hat{x}_i), \tag{4}$$

where $x_i \in C_{min}$ is the minority instance under consideration, $\hat{x}_i$ is one of the K-nearest neighbors for x_i:$\hat{x}_i \in C_{min}$, and $\delta \in [0, 1]$ is a random number.

OVO + SMOTE (OSM). OSM is a method that uses the OVO binarization technique for decomposing the original data sets into binary classification problems and then oversample the imbalanced binary sub-problems by SMOTE. Using SMOTE preprocessing technique, the algorithm finds 5-nearest neighbors to generate synthetic samples and keep both classes in balance to roughly equal distribution. It should be noted that the original OSM method introduces a linguistic Fuzzy Rule-Based Classification System (FRBCSs) in which the Fuzzy Hybrid Genetics-Based Machine Learning (FH-GBML) algorithm is used as a base classifier. In our study, we replaced FH-GBML with a decision tree. On the one hand, FH-GBML is a particular classification algorithm that we cannot find its implementation. On the other hand, FH-GBML is independent with the imbalance treatment in their work. That is, replacement of FH-GBML does not affect the conclusion of our evaluation.

OVO + SMOTEBagging (OSB). OSB combines the OVO decomposition with SMOTEBagging algorithm. SMOTEbagging [18] is a combination of SMOTE and the Bagging ensemble algorithm, where SMOTE is involved in the process of Bagging, generating synthetic samples on the sub-dataset sampled from the bootstrap. In our study, SMOTEBagging and UnderBagging entirely use 40 base classifiers as suggested by a previous study [19]. As a base classifier, we still used the decision tree. The parameter settings of SMOTE algorithm are the same as OSM we mentioned before.

OVO + UnderBagging (OUB). OUB combines the OVO decomposition with the UnderBagging algorithm. UnderBagging applies the undersampling of the majority class conducted independently in each bag of the ensemble. The UnderBagging step also uses 40 decision tree algorithms as a base classifier. The method uses the Random Undersampling [10] to preprocess training datasets.

A&O + PRMs-IM (Multi-IM). Multi-IM is an approach that employs A&O strategy and PRMs-IM. A&O [20] is a combination of OVO and OVA, which takes the strengths of both methods and avoid the defects of each. For a K-class imbalance problem, A&O splits an original training dataset into K sub-training sets for OVA and $m(m-1)/2$ sub-training sets for OVO. Then, the base learners will be trained from these $m + m(m-1)/2$ sub-datasets. When predicting unlabeled samples, the A&O approach first classifies the test sample using the OVA approach to obtain the first and second output classes (C_i, C_j), and then uses the corresponding OVO binary classifier f_{ij} to determine the final class. As we explained before, the basic classifier does not matter with this experiment, hence we still replace the PRMs-IM with Gaussian Naive

Bayes algorithm. Because according to the previous experiments, the Gaussian Naive Bayes algorithm wins the highest accuracy in the training set of this method.

OAHO + BP Neural Network (OAHO). One-Against-Higher-Order (OAHO) is a decomposition strategy for multi-class pattern classification problem. OAHO constructs $m-1$ classifiers for m classes. OAHO first sorts the m classes based on the size of the training examples in their respective classes in descending order to obtain an ordered list of $\{C_1, C_2, \cdots, C_m\}$, and then constructs $m-1$ sub-datasets in the list. The method selects category ranked at the first place as positive class, all the other categories ranked behind the positive class are taken as a negative class until total $m-1$ classifiers are built. Specially, the authors also built an aggregation method named Integrated Prediction Decision (IPD) which is based on the idea how the classifiers in OAHO are modeled and train. According to the outputs of $m-1$ classifiers, IPD predicts class label with the largest probability. The base classifier used in the algorithm is one-hidden layer neural network trained with feed-forward back propagation (BP) learning algorithm. The parameter settings of BP NN are the same as their in the original article: testing various numbers of hidden nodes ranging from 3 to 30 on the training sets, and the number of nodes that get the best performance (In our experiment, it includes 15 or 20 nodes).

DynamicOVO (DYNO). DYNO is a dynamic classifier selection strategy for OVO that tries to avoid the non-competent classifiers when their outputs are probably not of interests. In the algorithm, the neighborhood of each instance decides whether a classifier is competent or not. Unlike the method we mentioned above, dynamicOVO is an aggregation strategy that acts primarily in the result prediction phase. For an unlabeled instance to be classified, the OVO creates a score-matrix about the prediction probability of each binary classifier (Eq. (1)). Then, the DynamicOVO algorithm computes the K-nearest neighbors by KNN and selects the subset of classes in the neighborhood. Finally, the algorithm removes from the score-matrix those classifiers which do not consider a pair of classes from this subset, and applies weighted voting (WV) procedure to the new score-matrix to predict the class as follows:

$$R(x) = \left(\begin{array}{ccccc|c} - & c_1 & c_2 & \cdots & c_m & wv \\ c_1 & - & r_{1,2} & \cdots & r_{1,m} & \sum r_{1,j} \\ c_2 & r_{2,1} & - & \cdots & r_{2,m} & \sum r_{2,j} \\ \vdots & \vdots & \vdots & \ddots & \vdots & \vdots \\ c_m & r_{m,1} & r_{m,2} & \cdots & - & \sum r_{m,j} \end{array}\right), \quad (5)$$

where WV does not count for the scores of classes not included in the subset classes.

The base classifier used is also Gaussian Naive Bayes. The value of K set in the KNN is 3 times the number of classes. If there is a unique class within the k nearest neighbor, the number of neighbors will increase to $2 \cdot k$.

4 Experiments

In this section, we present the experimental setup, evaluation metric, and results with some discussions.

4.1 Experimental Setup

We selected 18 multi-class imbalanced datasets from the KEEL and UCI dataset repository to evaluate the performance of the six methods. The detail information about these datasets is summarized in Table 1, which shows the number of samples (Size), the number of attributes (#Attr), the number of real values (#R), the number of integer values (#I), the number of classes (#CL), the class distribution of each dataset (CD), the imbalanced ratio (IR), and the multi-class imbalanced categories (MIC). In Table 1, we divided the datasets into three types according to the structure of imbalanced classes, including the number of classes, IR (calculated by dividing the majority class by the minority), and multi-class imbalanced categories. In column MIC, m-maj refers to multi-majority and m-min refers to multi-minority. Some of these data sets may be overlapped in the three types. All experimental procedures were conducted by employing 10-fold cross-validation with ten independent runs. Each fold follows the same distribution as the original dataset.

Table 1. Summary description of the used datasets

Dataset	Size	#Attr (#R/#I)	#CL	CD	IR	MIC
Balance	625	4(4/0)	3	288/49/288	5.88	m-maj
Contraceptive	1473	9(0/9)	3	629/333/511	1.88	m-maj
Hayes-roth	160	4(0/4)	3	64/64/31	2.1	m-maj
New-thyroid	215	5(4/1)	3	150/35/30	5	m-min
Vertebral column data (VCD)	310	6(6/0)	3	60/150/100	2.5	m-maj
User-knowledge-modelling (UKM)	403	5(5/0)	4	50/129/122/102	2.58	m-maj
Cleveland	297	13(13/0)	5	160/54/35/35/13	12.31	m-min
Pageblocks	5472	10(4/6)	5	4913/329/28/87/115	175.4	m-min
Breast-tissue	106	9(9/9)	6	21/15/18/16/14/22	1.57	m-min
Dermatology	358	34(0/34)	6	111/60/71/48	5.55	m-min
Ecoli	336	7(7/0)	6	143/77/35/20/5/52	28.6	m-min
Glass	214	9(9/0)	6	70/76/17/29/13/9	8.44	mixed
Winequality-red	1599	11(11/0)	6	10/53/681/638/199/18	68.1	mixed
Shuttle	2173	9(0/9)	4	1706/6/338/123	284.3	m-min
Winequalite-white	4898	11(11/0)	7	20/163/1457/2198/880/175/5	439.6	mixed
Marketing	6876	13(0/13)	9	1255/529/505/618/527/846/784/1069/743	2.48	mixed
led7digit	500	7(7/0)	10	45/37/51/57/52/52/47/47/53/49	1.54	m-maj
Yeast	1484	8(8/0)	10	244/429/463/44/35/51/163/30/5/20	92.6	mixed

4.2 Evaluation Metric

Considering the characteristics of imbalanced problems, accuracy is not a good metric because it often has a bias toward the majority [21]. Hence, we take a more comprehensive metric multi-class AUC (MAUC) [22], which is defined as follows:

$$A(i,j) = (A(i|j) + A(j|i))/2,$$
$$\mathrm{MAUC} = \frac{2}{k(k-1)}\sum\nolimits_{i<j} A(i,j), \quad (6)$$

where $A(i|j)$ is the probability that a randomly drawn member of class j has a lower estimated probability of belonging to class i than a randomly drawn member of class i. Note that for multi-class problems, $A(i|j)$ *and* $A(j|i)$ may not be equal.

4.3 Results and Discussion

Tables 2, 3 and 4 show the average MAUCs of six algorithms on three types of data sets,. In these tables, the best result is in bold, and the second best result is in italics.

Table 2 shows that OUB obtains the most times of the best and the second best results whereas the special decomposition approach OAHO is worse. Each algorithm performs best on at least one dataset except for Multi-IM and OAHO. For OAHO, it obtains the worse ranking with a much lower value and even a value as low as 21.55%. For the two algorithms OSB and OSM based on the SMOTE approach, the performance of OSM is very close to that of OSB, but the former is slightly better than the latter. As we can see, OUB is the best method on the multi-majority datasets. This may due to the fact that for the multiminority datasets, there is a balance between minority classes and undersampling for the only majority class has no effect on the minority classes.

Table 3 shows that OSB is the best algorithm on the multi-majority datasets. Compared with OSM, the average performance of OSB is slightly higher. The difference may lies in that OSB uses bagging strategy to combine several learners to improve performance. Although Multi-IM and DYNO do not have the most outstanding performance, they are also fairly stable and perform moderately. It is surprised that the performance of OAHO is extremely unstable and polarized, that is, performance on some datasets are superior and on other datasets are inferior. Compared with OUB, OSB has better results on the multi-majority datasets, while OUB outperforms OSB on the multi-majority datasets.

Table 4 shows that the performance of OSM is significantly better than that of all the compared methods on the mixed datasets. Unlike on the multi-majority datasets, the performance of OSB is much worse than that of OSM on the mixed datasets, averaging 8.9 points lower. Meanwhile, the performance of OUB is generally better than that of OSB. The performance of Multi-IM and DYNO on the mixed datasets is also not prominent. OAHO is still the worst performing algorithm and its average performance is 25.5 lower than OSM.

Table 2. Means of MAUC of six algorithms on the multi-minority datasets (in percent)

Dataset	OSB	OUB	Multi-IM	OAHO	OSM	DYNO
Ecoli	88.62	*91.03*	82.11	85.17	**93.51**	72.55
Pageblocks	*95.81*	**97.08**	87.72	83.58	95.52	90.56
New-thyroid	95.59	95.93	*96.61*	76.74	95.23	**96.62**
Cleveland	66.28	69.68	*70.59*	21.55	69.55	**73.03**
Shuttle	*99.82*	**99.87**	96.59	94.98	99.50	97.88
Dermatology	**99.60**	*99.54*	99.41	98.51	98.80	96.37
Average	90.95	**92.19**	88.84	75.76	92.02	87.84

Table 3. Means of MAUC of six algorithms on the multi-majority datasets (in percent)

Dataset	OSB	OUB	Multi-IM	OAHO	OSM	DYNO
Balance	*70.60*	66.90	69.92	**74.09**	64.44	69.92
Contraceptive	63.49	*66.57*	65.70	**70.99**	62.08	66.10
led7digit	**98.84**	*98.41*	97.53	94.11	95.57	95.00
Hayes-roth	**93.46**	92.48	85.79	60.86	*92.53*	86.04
Breast-tissue	82.25	82.25	84.57	60.11	**89.51**	*89.22*
UKM	*96.45*	96.26	94.29	71.44	**97.03**	96.34
VCD	*88.44*	**89.06**	87.62	86.12	86.54	87.92
Average	**84.79**	84.56	83.63	73.96	83.96	84.36

Table 4. Means of MAUC of six algorithms on the mixed datasets (in percent)

Dataset	OSB	OUB	Multi-IM	OAHO	OSM	DYNO
Yeast	77.83	*78.10*	75.85	66.90	**86.99**	76.31
Glass	82.43	*84.02*	66.17	29.26	**89.07**	81.05
Winequality-red	67.74	69.75	65.78	59.33	**78.17**	*71.44*
Winequalite-white	77.94	76.79	*81.56*	65.28	**83.96**	75.42
Marketing	58.88	*66.91*	54.09	61.05	**71.11**	64.43
Average	72.96	75.11	68.69	56.36	**81.86**	73.73

Table 5 presents the average results of these algorithms on the datasets with different number of class. It can be clearly seen that the performance of OSM is still the best, even on the datasets with different number classes. We can also observe that the performance of an algorithm will decrease to some extend as the number of classes increases, especially when the number of classes is greater than 10. At the same time, for the degree of imbalance, the algorithm shows a certain regular pattern on the datasets. As can be seen from Table 6, when the imbalance ratio is low, the MAUC value of the algorithm is generally higher, and when the imbalance ratio is high, the MAUC value of the algorithm is generally low.

In general, OSM is the best method and quite stable. OUS shows its superiority on the multi-minority datasets, while OSB works better on the multi-majority datasets.

And OSM shows its absolute dominance on the mixed datasets. A large number of classes can cause a decline in the performance of the classifiers, similarly the degree of imbalance ratio also has a negative affect on the algorithms.

Table 5. Means of MAUC on the datasets with different number of class (in percent)

Dataset	#CL	OSB	OUB	Multi-IM	OAHO	OSM	DYNO
yeast	10	77.83	*78.10*	75.85	66.90	**86.99**	76.31
Winequalite-white	7	77.94	76.79	*81.56*	65.28	**83.96**	75.42
Glass	6	82.43	*84.02*	66.17	29.26	**89.07**	81.05
Pageblocks	5	*95.81*	**97.08**	87.72	83.58	95.52	90.56
UKM	4	*96.45*	96.26	94.29	71.44	**97.03**	96.34
VCD	3	*88.44*	**89.06**	87.62	86.12	86.54	87.92
Average		86.48	86.89	82.20	67.10	**89.85**	84.6

Table 6. Means of MAUC of on datasets with different imbalanced rate (in percent)

Dataset	IR	OSB	OUB	Multi-IM	OAHO	OSM	DYNO
UKM	2.58	*96.45*	96.26	94.29	71.44	**97.03**	96.34
New-thyroid	5	95.59	95.93	*96.61*	76.74	95.23	**96.62**
Dermatology	5.55	**99.60**	*99.54*	99.41	98.51	98.80	96.37
Ecoli	28.6	88.62	*91.03*	82.11	85.17	**93.51**	72.55
Winequality-red	68.1	67.74	69.75	65.78	59.33	**78.17**	*71.44*
Yeast	92.6	77.83	*78.10*	75.85	66.90	**86.99**	76.31
Winequalite-white	439.6	77.94	76.79	*81.56*	65.28	**83.96**	75.42
Average		86.25	86.77	85.09	74.77	**90.53**	83.58

5 Conclusion and Future Work

This paper presented an in-depth empirical study on multi-class imbalanced learning with OVO decomposition strategy. We selected six state-of-the-art algorithms to explore their performance on different imbalanced data structure. From our experimental results, we concluded that OVO approach combines with SMOTE is the best method in multi-class imbalanced problems. In addition, the ensemble method has a siginificant effect on the improvement of the classification performance on imbalanced datasets. A large number of classes can cause a decline in the performance of the classifiers, and the imbalanced ratio has a siginificant impact on classification performance. That is, when the imbalanced ratio increases, the performance of the classifiers siginificantly decreases.

We have unexpectedly found that OSB algorithm using ensemble method does not perform better than the OSM algorithm that does not use ensemble method, which is a question worth further exploring. In our future work, we will try to deeply investigate this question and make a further study on more efficient ensemble methods.

Acknowledgment. This research has been supported by the National Natural Science Foundation of China under grant 61603186, the Natural Science Foundation of Jiangsu Province, China, under grant BK20160843, the China Postdoctoral Science Foundation under grants 2017T100370 and 2016M590457, the Postdoctoral Science Foundation of Jiangsu Province, China, under grant 1601199C, the Science Foundation (for Youth) of the Science and Technology Commission of the Central Military Commission (CMC), the national key research and development program under grant 2016YFE0108000, the CERNET next generation internet technology innovation project under grant NGII20160122, the project of ZTE cooperation research under grant 2016ZTE04-11, and Jiangsu Province Key Research and Development Program under grants BE2017739 and BE2017100.

References

1. Yang, Q., Wu, X.D.: 10 challenging problems in data mining research. Int. J. Inf. Technol. Decis. Mak. **5**(04), 597–604 (2006)
2. He, H.B., Garcia, E.A.: Learning from imbalanced data. IEEE Trans. Knowl. Data Eng. **21** (9), 1263–1284 (2009)
3. Zhou, Z.H., Liu, X.Y.: On multi-class cost-sensitive learning. Nat. Conf. Artif. Intell. **26**(3), 567–572 (2006)
4. Anand, R., Mehrotra, K., Mohan, C.K., Ranka, S.: Efficient classification for multiclass problems using modular neural networks. IEEE Trans. Neural Netw. **6**(1), 117–124 (1995)
5. Fernández, A., López, V., Galar, M., Del Jesus, M.J., Herrera, F.: Analysing the classification of imbalanced data-sets with multiple classes: binarization techniques and ad-hoc approaches. Knowl.-Based Syst. **42**(2), 97–110 (2013)
6. Galar, M., Ndez, A., Barrenechea, E., Bustince, H., Herrera, F.: An overview of ensemble methods for binary classifiers in multi-class problems: experimental study on one-vs-one and one-vs-all schemes. Pattern Recogn. **44**(8), 1761–1776 (2011)
7. Galar, M., Fernández, A., Ndez, A., Barrenechea, E., Bustince, H., Herrera, F.: Dynamic classifier selection for one-vs-one strategy: avoiding non-competent classifiers. Pattern Recogn. **46**(12), 3412–3424 (2013)
8. Lorena, A.C., Carvalho, A.C., Gama, J.M.: A review on the combination of binary classifiers in multi-class problems. Artif. Intell. Rev. **30**(1–4), 19–37 (2008)
9. Fernández, A., del Jesus, M.J., Herrera, F.: Multi-class imbalanced data-sets with linguistic fuzzy rule based classification systems based on pairwise learning. In: Hüllermeier, E., Kruse, R., Hoffmann, F. (eds.) IPMU 2010. LNCS (LNAI), vol. 6178, pp. 89–98. Springer, Heidelberg (2010). https://doi.org/10.1007/978-3-642-14049-5_10
10. Krawczyk, B.: Combining one-vs-one decomposition and ensemble learning for multi-class imbalanced data. In: Burduk, R., Jackowski, K., Kurzyński, M., Woźniak, M., Żołnierek, A. (eds.) Proceedings of the 9th International Conference on Computer Recognition Systems CORES 2015. AISC, vol. 403, pp. 27–36. Springer, Cham (2016). https://doi.org/10.1007/978-3-319-26227-7_3
11. Ghanem, A.S., Venkatesh, S., West, G.: Multi-class pattern classification in imbalanced data. In: IEEE 2010 International Conference on Pattern Recognition, pp. 2881–2884 (2010)
12. Murphey, Y.L., Wang, H., Ou, G., Feldkamp, L.A.: OAHO: an effective algorithm for multi-class learning from imbalanced data. In: IEEE 2007 International Joint Conference on Neural Networks, pp. 406–411 (2007)
13. Tan, A.C., Gilbert, D., Deville, Y.: Multi-class protein fold classification using a new ensemble machine learning approach. Genome Inf. **14**, 206–217 (2011)

14. Vluymans, S., Fernández, A., Saeys, Y., Cornelis, C., Herrera, F.: Dynamic affinity-based classification of multi-class imbalanced data with one-versus-one decomposition: a fuzzy rough set approach. Knowl. Inf. Syst. **1**, 1–30 (2017)
15. Cerf, L., Gay, D., Selmaoui-Folcher, N., Milleux, B., Boulicaut, J.F.: Editorial: parameter-free classification in multi-class imbalanced data sets. Data Knowl. Eng. **87**(9), 109–129 (2013)
16. Zhang, Z., Krawczyk, B., Garcìa, S., Rosales-Pérez, A., Herrera, F.: Empowering one-vs-one decomposition with ensemble learning for multi-class imbalanced data. Knowl. Based Syst. **106**(C), 251–263 (2016)
17. Chawla, N.V., Bowyer, K.W., Hall, L.O., Kegelmeyer, W.P.: SMOTE: synthetic minority over–sampling technique. J. Artif. Intell. Res. **16**, 321–357 (2002)
18. Wang, S., Yao, X.: Diversity analysis on imbalanced data sets by using ensemble models. In: IEEE 2009 Symposium on Computational Intelligence and Data Mining, vol. 1, no. 5, pp. 324–331 (2009)
19. Galar, M., Fernandez, A., Barrenechea, E., Bustince, H., Herrera, F.: A review on ensembles for the class imbalance problem: bagging-, boosting-, and hybrid-based approaches. IEEE Trans. Syst. Man Cybern.-Part C **42**(4), 463–484 (2012)
20. Garcia-Pedrajas, N., Ortiz-Boyer, D.: Improving multi-class pattern recognition by the combination of two strategies. IEEE Trans. Pattern Anal. Mach. Intell. **28**(6), 1001–1006 (2006)
21. Martino, M.D., Fernández, A., Iturralde, P.: Novel classifier scheme for imbalanced problems. Pattern Recogn. Lett. **34**(10), 1146–1151 (2013)
22. Hand, D.J., Till, R.J.: A simple generalisation of the area under the roc curve for multiple class classification problems. Mach. Learn. **45**(2), 171–186 (2001)
23. Krawczyk, B.: Learning from imbalanced data: open challenges and future directions. Prog. rtif. Intell. **5**(4), 1–12 (2016)

Multiple Schemes for Bike-Share Service Authentication Using QR Code and Visual Cryptography

Li Li[1], Jier Yu[1], Bing Wang[1], Qili Zhou[1](✉), Shanqing Zhang[1], Jianfeng Lu[1], and Chin-Chen Chang[2]

[1] School of Computer Science and Technology, Hangzhou Dianzi University, Hangzhou 310018, China
lili2008@hdu.edu.cn

[2] Department of Information Engineering and Computer Science, Feng Chia University, Taichung, Taiwan
alan3c@gmail.com

Abstract. With the growing application of quick response (QR) code on bike-share service, there is the possibility of tampering and replacing the QR code. Thus the security of the personal information and the property are fragile. To solve the problem, we propose the multiple QR code authentication schemes for bike-share service. The hierarchy visual cryptography system (HVCS) is combined with the error correction of QR code in Scheme I. Firstly, the secret image for authentication is encrypted into two shared images (referred to as shadows) according to improved (2, 2)-PVCS. Secondly, one of the shadows is stored in cloud server and the another shadow is encrypted into n sub-shadows based on probability. Then these sub-shadows are fused with QR codes to get the security QR codes which are posted on bikes. Finally, when users scan the security QR codes (shadows) by smartphone, the shadow stored in cloud server is downloaded and stack with the scanned QR code to decode the secret image for QR code authentication. Scheme II is a method of adapting multiply secret images for batter visual effect. The multi-secret visual cryptography system (MVCS) and the XOR mechanism of RS with Positives Basis Vector Matrix (PBVM) are combined. Firstly, a random grid is generated as the special shadow in cloud server. Secondly a series of shadows is generated according to the MVCS. Then these shadows are fused with QR code by XOR mechanism of RS code to obtain the security QR codes. Finally, secret images are decoded by stacking the special shadow and security QR codes. Experimental results show that our methods has great capacity and high security.

Keywords: Visual cryptography · Error correction mechanism
Positives Basis Vector Matrix · QR code

1 Introduction

Low-carbon transportation are gradually accepted by people with pressing green environmental protection. With increasing popularity of bike-share service, QR code is widely used on shared bikes for its accuracy and availability. However, lots of QR

X. Sun et al. (Eds.): ICCCS 2018, LNCS 11065, pp. 629–640, 2018.
https://doi.org/10.1007/978-3-030-00012-7_57

codes are tampered and replaced deliberately, and fake QR code was posted on the bike instead. Malicious Apps are downloaded when people scan the fake QR code with smartphone. Especially, personal user information can be stolen due to the tampered QR code.

Visual cryptography system (VCS) is a secure method, by which the secret image is encrypted into noise-like shadows. The original secret image cannot be decrypted only by one shadow. It has advantage that the decoding process of VCS scheme is simple. That is, the secret image can be decoded by the human visual system (HVS) without any complex calculation. The traditional VCS has problems of pixel expansion and contrast. To fix the pixel expansion, Biham [1] proposed a visual cryptography scheme based on XOR. Yang [2] proposed the probabilistic VCS (PVCS) with non-expandable shadow size.

There are some studies combining QR code and VCS. Researches [3–5] have been conducted on authentication only using VCS. Extended VCS (EVCS) has been used in [3, 4]. Cover image on shadow hides the encrypted data. Research [7], proposed a secure payment method. But the shadow combined with QR code makes no difference. It can be deciphered and tampered easily because of the single shadow. Security mechanism will be compromised in all scenarios when one of them is deciphered. A lot of shadows need to be stored in cloud server when several different secret images are needed. But storing so many shadows in cloud server waste the storing space and slow down matching speed. In our study, the shadow fused with QR code is different and it only need to store one shadow in cloud server when multi-secret images are needed.

Basing on the security technique of QR code combining with VCS, we propose two novel schemes. In Scheme I, hierarchy visual cryptography system (HVCS) and Error Correction Mechanism in QR code are combined. The secret image (*S*) is encrypted into two shadows (Shadow 1 and Shadow 2) according to improved (2, 2)-PVCS. Shadow 1 is stored in cloud server. Shadow 2 is encrypted into n different sub-shadows S_i (i = 1, 2, … n) by allocating the random probability of black and white pixels. Then these sub-shadows are encrypted by Arnold scrambling algorithm. And each sub-shadow is combined with the corresponding QR code. The new QR code is used as the security QR code stacked on the bike. Shadow 1 is downloaded and stacked with the security QR code after anti-Arnold when users scan the security QR code. Then, the secret image appears if the QR code is not tampered. Users can then use bikes securely. In Schema II, multi-secret visual cryptography system (MVCS) and XOR mechanism of RS code are combined to make secret image multiply. Each bike has its unique security QR code. It only has one special shadow stored in cloud server and other shadows are fused with original QR code. The special shadow and the security QR code are stacked together to obtain the secret image. The flow chart of bike-share service authentication is shown in Fig. 1.

The rest of this paper is organized as follows. Related techniques are introduced in Sect. 2. The detailed descriptions of proposed Schema I and corresponding experiments are presented in Sect. 3. Schema II is introduced in Sect. 4. And Sect. 5 is the conclusion.

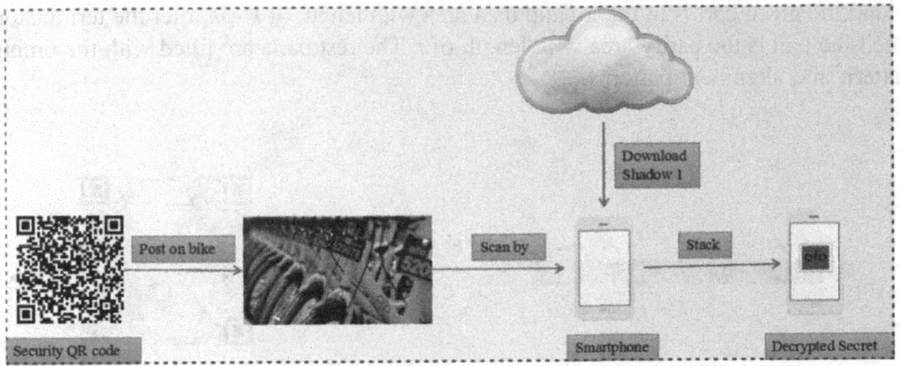

Fig. 1. One flow chart of bike-share service authentication

2 Preliminary

The related techniques are introduced in this section.

2.1 PVCS

The operation in Probabilistic VCS (PVCS) is "OR", which is the same as the traditional method. But it solves the problem of pixel extension by one pixel presenting one pixel in sub-shadows. The pixels in the encrypted image are allocated to sub-shadows in a certain black and white scale. The ratio of white pixel to white area is higher than that of white pixel in black pixels. The black and white pixels are distinguished by human visual system.

2.2 RS Code Encoding Mechanism

QR code has the characteristics of fast reading information and anti-rotation. QR code is encoded using RS code. It contains data area (*k* bits) and parity area (*t* bits). Data area contains valid data area and invalid data area. The valid data area is store embedded information streams, with length of *m*. And the rest of data area is called invalid data area.

The process of generating the QR code with RS code is presented as follows: Firstly, the input information is encoded based on the encoding rules of RS code. The region filled with those code words is valid data area. Valid data areas cannot be changed. Secondly, it is a terminator (0000) after the valid data region. The rest of the data area called the invalid data region, the length is *k-m*. Thirdly, the *t* parity bits is generated according to the data bits. It guarantees the robustness of QR codes. When data area is destroyed in a certain extent, the information also can be recovered according the parity bits. Finally, the generated RS code is combined with the timing pattern and alignment pattern [8]. Then the standard QR code is generated.

The distribution of RS code in QR code is shown in Fig. 2. Red and green parts are in the data area and the length is *k*. The red part is the valid data area with length of *m* and the green part is in the invalid data area with length of k - m after the terminator. The blue part is the parity area with length of t. The rest parts are filled with the timing pattern and alignment patterns.

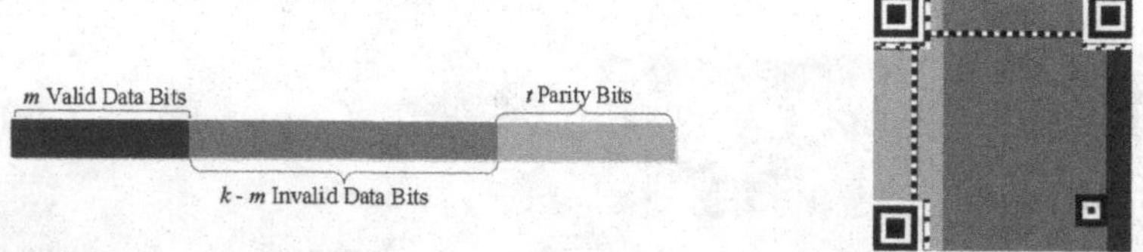

Fig. 2. The distribution of RS code in QR code (Color figure online)

2.3 Error Correction Mechanism of QR Code

QR code has 40 versions. There are four increased modules in each side of the higher version than in its immediate former version. There are four error correction levels (L, M, Q and H) in each version, the error correction capacity is 7%, 15%, 25% and 30% corresponding to level L, M, Q and H, respectively [9]. The principle of QR code is RS code encoding mechanism. One RS block is used as a unit of processing block. Its code words are sorted by data code words and error correction code words. The code words in QR code are arranged in special order, that is, from right to left, from bottom to top. Such a particular arrangement makes code words distributed uniformly inside QR code and can resist attacks to a certain extent.

2.4 Construction of PBVM

A series of RS codes obtained by Gauss Jordan elimination method [10] formulates a matrix (Fig. 3). The matrix is called Positive Basis Vector Matrix (PBVM). The front k bits form a unit vector matrix and represent data region. The rear t bits in each row of the matrix represent parity region. This PBVM can be used to modify RS code.

The appropriate basis vector matrix is selected when one bit of RS code needs to be modified. The process is shown in Fig. 4.

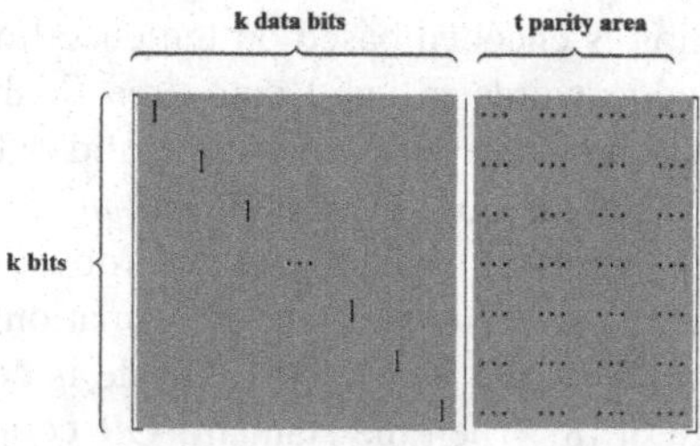

Fig. 3. PBVM

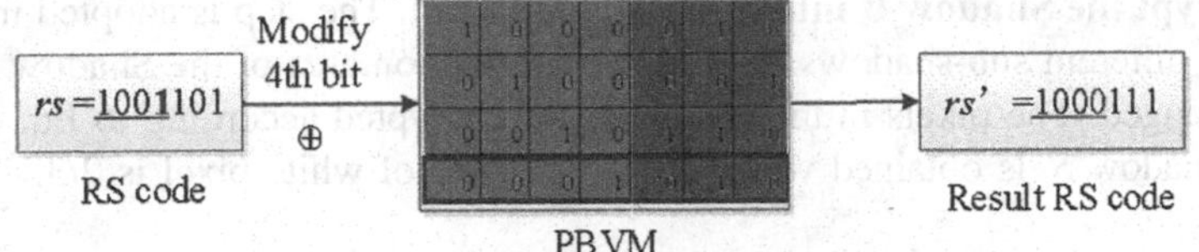

Fig. 4. Operation process with PBVM

3 Scheme I Based on HVCS and Error Correction Mechanism of QR Code

New security authentication for bike-sharing service is proposed in this study. HVCS is proposed to increase the complexity of QR codes. The capacity in this scheme is increased based on error correction mechanism. The flow chart of Scheme I is shown in Fig. 7.

The HVCS is combined with QR code in Sect. 3.1. The QR code based on error correction mechanism is used in Sect. 3.2. Section 3.3 is the experimental results.

3.1 HVCS

The hierarchy visual cryptography (HVCS) is designed to generate a series of shadows (Shadow A and S_i'). Shadow A is the specific shadow with highest weight and stored in cloud server, the rest shadows (S_i') are fused with QR code to get security QR codes (Q_i). The details are described as follows:

(1) **Generate two shadows (A and B).** The encrypted image (S) is processed by improved (2, 2)-PVCS, the result images are two no-extension shadows, Shadow A and Shadow B. Base matrices of write pixel and black pixel are shown below. C_0 (Eq. (1)) and C_1 (Eq. (2)) are two sets consisting of 2 * 1 column matrices (Fig. 5).

$$C_0 = \left\{ \begin{bmatrix} 1 \\ 1 \end{bmatrix}, \begin{bmatrix} 0 \\ 0 \end{bmatrix}, \begin{bmatrix} 0 \\ 0 \end{bmatrix} \right\}. \tag{1}$$

$$C_1 = \left\{ \begin{bmatrix} 0 \\ 1 \end{bmatrix}, \begin{bmatrix} 1 \\ 0 \end{bmatrix}, \begin{bmatrix} 1 \\ 0 \end{bmatrix} \right\}. \tag{2}$$

(a)Shadow A

(b)Shadow B

Fig. 5. Shadow A and Shadow B

(2) **Encrypt the Shadow B into n sub-shadows (S_i).** The step is adopted in order to get n different sub-shadows. The secret information area of the Shadow *B* remain unchanged. The pixels in the rest areas are encrypted according to Eq. (3). Then the shadow S_i is obtained which the probability of white pixel is 2/3.

$$C_3 = [1, 0, 0]. \tag{3}$$

(3) **Scrambling sub-shadows(S_i) by Arnold scrambling process.** In order to further enhance the randomness of shadows, Arnold scrambling is applied on the S_i. Rearrange of points in discrete sub-shadows (S_i) matrix, which increases the difficulty of cracking further and achieve the goal of increasing security. S_i are binary images in scrambling by Arnold scrambling in Eq. (4). Here, (x, y) is one pixel location in S_i, (x', y') is one pixel location of S_i, and *N* represents the transformation cycle. Four shadows after Arnold scrambling (S_i') are shown in Fig. 6.

$$\begin{pmatrix} x' \\ \overline{y'} \end{pmatrix} = \begin{bmatrix} 1 & 1 \\ 1 & 2 \end{bmatrix} \begin{pmatrix} x \\ \overline{y} \end{pmatrix} \bmod N. \tag{4}$$

Fig. 6. Four sub-shadows (S_i')

3.2 Fuse Shadows (S_i') with QR Code According the Error Correction Mechanism

(1) **Fuse original QR code (*Q*) and *S*.** The secret area in *S* is considered as the important area. Firstly the saliency map (*C*) should be obtained, the white region among saliency map (*C*) is corresponding changeable area of QR code. Secondly, *Qr* is calculated by QR code and saliency map (*C*) within the limit of successful error correction. Finally the saliency map on QR code is replaced by encrypted image, and security QR code (Q_2) is obtained.

(2) **Detect the Position of Shadow.** The image taken by smartphone will be distorted and rotated (Fig. 8(a)). In order to eliminate these distractions and get clear black and white modules, a pretreatment is executed. The pretreatment includes gray-scale, noise reduction, binarization and so on (Fig. 8(b)). Then the position of shadow is calculated based on the location function of QR code (Fig. 8(c)). The shadow is shown in (Fig. 8(d)).

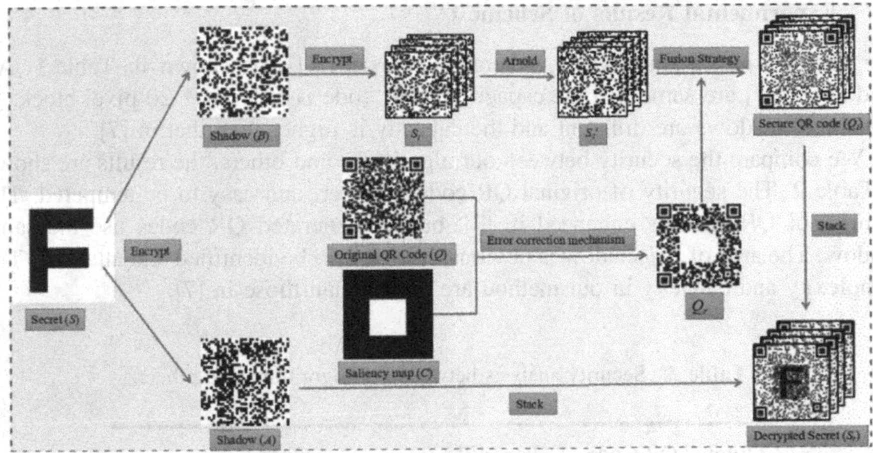

Fig. 7. Flow chart of Scheme I

Fig. 8. Positioning process

Table 1. The comparison of shadows between paper [7] and ours

	Paper [7]	Ours
Shadows		
Capacity	20*20 pixels	38*38 pixels

3.3 Experimental Results of Scheme I

The comparison of shadows in Schema I and paper [7] is shown in Table 1. All shadows in [7] are same and the capacity of QR code is only 20 * 20 pixel block. In Scheme I, shadows are different and the capacity is higher than that in [7].

We compare the security between our algorithms and others, the results are shown in Table 2. The security of original QR code is lower, and easy to be tempered. The security of QR code is enhanced in [7], but all generated QR codes use the same shadow. The area of the shadow is obvious, it is easy to be identified and attacked. The complexity and capacity in our method are higher than those in [7].

Table 2. Security analysis between our algorithms and others

Original QR Code	Paper[7]	Ours

4 Scheme II Based on MVCS and XOR Mechanism of RS

Multi-secret visual cryptography system (MVCS) is proposed in Scheme II in order to obtain multiply secret images. And the XOR mechanism of RS is used to make the region of the secret information larger and get better visual appearance of QR code.

The scheme of combining MVCS and QR code is introduced in this section. The process of generate one special shadow and other shadows by MVCS is shown in Sect. 4.1. The PBVM of QR code is used in Sect. 4.2. Section 4.3 is the experimental results.

4.1 MVCS

The method in Scheme I is only suitable for one secret image. Multi-secret images are beneficial for security and practicality. In this scheme, the secret images are different. Each QR code fused its corresponding shadow and the reconstructed images are not same. Each bike has a unique reconstructed image. The special shadow is stored in cloud server and is applicable to all security QR code when reconstructing the secret image.

(1) **Generate the specific shadow G_1.** G_1 is a random grid, each pixel in G_1 is either *0* or *1*. Each pixel is chosen by a random procedure and there is no relation among the pixels. The number of *0* is probabilistically equal to that of the *1* pixels because of randomness. Shadow G_1 is shown in Fig. 9.

Fig. 9. Shadow G_1.

(2) **Generate S_k.** For G_1 with size $h \times w$, S_k have the same size with G_1. Assuming there are k secret images, (k = 1, 2, 3 … n), S_k represents the K_{th} shadow corresponding the K_{th} secret image. Algorithm MVCS is used to generate S_k. The following operations is performing for each secret image.

Step 1: Compare the pixel in secret image (*S*) with G_1. If the pixel in *S* is *0*, the pixel in S_k is same as the pixel in G_1. If the pixel in *S* is *1*, the pixel in S_k is bit-inverse of G_1.
Step 2: Repeat Step 1 to all pixels in S_k.

Algorithm MVCS

Input: A binary secret image $S = \{S(i,j) \mid S(i,j) = 0 \text{ or } 1, 0 \le i < w, 0 \le j < h\}$ and random grid G_1
Output: A shadow S_k, $S_k = \{S_k(i,j) \mid S_k(i,j) = 0 \text{ or } 1, 0 \le i < w, 0 \le j < h\}$, where k=1,2,3...n
For(i and j , 0≤i<w and 0≤j<h),
  If(S(i,j)==0)
    $S_k(i,j) = G_1(i,j)$;
  Else
    $S_k(i,j) = \overline{G_1(i,j)}$; // $\overline{G_1(i,j)}$ represents "the bit-inverse of $G_1(i,j)$"
Output S_k

4.2 Fuse Shadows (S_k) with QR Code According XOR Mechanism of RS

The secret image (*S*) is divided into two shadows (G_1 and S_k) according MVCS introduced in Sect. 4.1. S_k is divided into blocks, the size is the same as the QR code (Q_1) module. The average value of each block is compared with the value of QR code module. If they are consistent after comparsion, the block in Q_1 is replaced by corresponding block in S_k. If not, the XOR mechanism of RS is used to make them same. Thus Qr is obtained. QR code is fused with S_k according to Qr and fusion strategy. The flowchart of Scheme II is shown in Fig. 10.

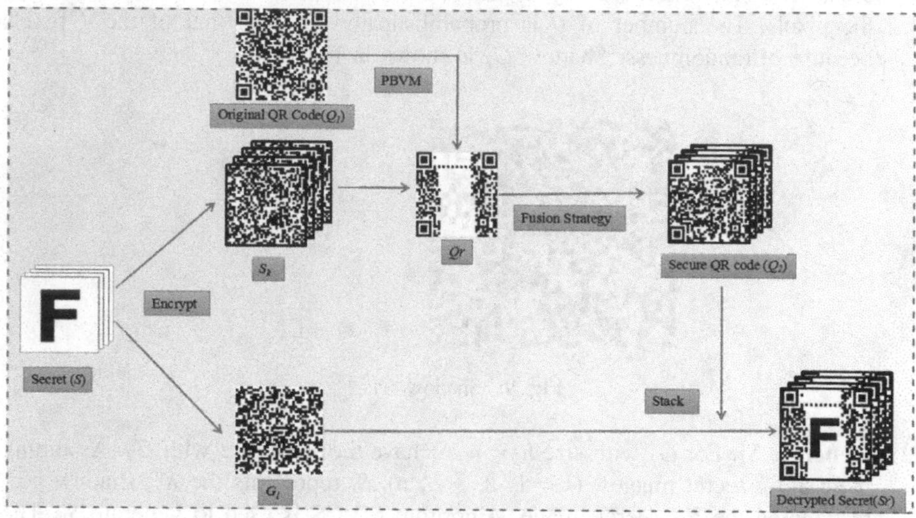

Fig. 10. Flowchart of Scheme II

Table 3. Experimental results of Scheme II

Shadow1	Security QR code ($Q2$)	Recovered secret	QR code in Paper 7

4.3 Experimental Results of Scheme II

The experimental results are shown in Table 3. The security QR code in Scheme II looks like similar to the normal QR code. In [7], the area of the shadow is obvious and same. It is easy to be identified and attacked. And there is only one secret image. However, the number of secret images is arbitrary in our method.

5 Conclusions

As QR codes are used widely, the tampering of QR code in bike-share service is possible. Combination of VCS and QR code are used in previous research on authentication. However, the security in previous proposed methods is not strong. The methods proposed in this paper enhance the security. In Scheme I, HVCS and QR code are combined together in order to get a series of different security QR code. MVCS is used in Scheme II to increase the diversity of secret images. The method of multiple-shadow generation is proposed in this paper. The multiple-shadow method not only increases the difficulty of cracking any individual bike, but also prevents all other bikes from illegal usage. Even if some bikes are cracked, it is safe because every bike has unique key sub-shadow. It increases crackers' difficulty to locate the needed shadow because the shadow is already combined with QR code. Our schemes and the other schemes are compared. The experimental results show that the security of QR code is enhanced and the complexity and capacity of shadows are increased.

Acknowledgments. This work was mainly supported by National Natural Science Foundation of China (No. 61370218) and Public Welfare Technology Project Of Zhejiang Pro.

References

1. Biham, E., Itzkovitz, A.: Visual cryptography with polarization. Dagstuhl Semin. Crypt. **23** (3), 2–12 (1998)
2. Yang, C.N.: New visual secret sharing schemes using probabilistic method. Pattern Recogn. Lett. **25**(4), 481–494 (2004)
3. Goel, M.: Authentication framework using visual cryptography. Int. J. Res. Eng. Technol. **2** (11), 271–274 (2013)
4. Jaya, Malik, S., Aggarwal, A., Sardana, A.: Novel authentication system using visual cryptography. In: Information and Communication Technologies (WICT), pp. 1181–1186 (2011)
5. Naor, M., Pinkas, B.: Visual authentication and identification. In: Kaliski, B.S. (ed.) CRYPTO 1997. LNCS, vol. 1294, pp. 322–336. Springer, Heidelberg (1997). https://doi.org/10.1007/BFb0052245
6. Yang, C.-N., Liao, J.-K., Wu, F.-H., Yamaguchi, Y.: Developing visual cryptography for authentication on smartphones. In: Wan, J., Humar, I., Zhang, D. (eds.) Industrial IoT 2016. LNICST, vol. 173, pp. 189–200. Springer, Cham (2016). https://doi.org/10.1007/978-3-319-44350-8_19
7. Lu, J., Yang, Z., Li, L.: Multiple schemes for mobile payment authentication using QR code and visual cryptography. Mob. Inf. Syst. Hindawi **2017**, 12 (2017)

8. Li, C., Zhang, T.Q., Liu, Y.: Blind recognition of RS codes based on Galois field columns Gaussian elimination. In: International Congress on Image and Signal Processing (2015)
9. Kim, S.H., Allebach, J.P.: Impact of HVS models on model-based halftoning. IEEE Trans. Image Process. **11**(3), 258–269 (2002)
10. R Cox – researchlrsc. http://research.swtch.com/qart. Accessed Oct 2010
11. Chen, T.H., Wu, C.S.: Efficient multi-secret image sharing based on boolean operations. Signal Process. **91**(1), 90–97 (2011)
12. Tuyls, P., Hollmann, H.D.L., Lint, J.H.V., Tolhuizen, L.: XOR-based visual cryptography schemes. Des. Codes Crypt. **37**(1), 169–186 (2005)
13. Zhi, Z., Arce, G.R., Crescenzo, G.D.: Halftone visual cryptography. IEEE Trans. Image Process. **15**(8), 2441–2453 (2006)
14. Li, L., Qiu, J., Lu, J., Chang, C.C.: An aesthetic QR code solution based on error correction mechanism. J. Syst. Softw. **116**(1), 85–94 (2016)

Power Network Vulnerability Detection Based on Improved Adaboost Algorithm

Wenwei Tao[1], Song Liu[1], Yang Su[1], and Chao Hu[2(✉)]

[1] CSG Power Dispatching Control Center, Guangzhou 510670, China
{taoww, liusong, suyang}@csg.cn

[2] NARI Information and Communication Technology Co., Ltd., Nanjing 210033, China
huchao@sgepri.sgcc.com.cn

Abstract. The impact of the Internet on the power industry is increasing, the detection of power network vulnerability becomes more and more important. Traditional power network vulnerabilities detection methods are relatively labor-intensive and inefficient, so, the power network vulnerability detection algorithm based on improved Adaboost is proposed in this paper. It is a kind of machine learning algorithm, which select C4.5 decision tree as weak classifier to integrate a strong classifier. Compared with neural network, KNN and other methods, the proposed algorithm is more efficient in power network vulnerability detection.

Keywords: Machine learning · Power network vulnerability detection Adaboost algorithm

1 Introduction

The power industry is one of the important sectors of the national economy. With the continuous development of modern industry, agriculture and the living standards of people, the demand of our society for electricity is increasing. The development level of the power industry will not only have a huge impact on other sectors of the national economy, but also the amount of primary energy consumption and investment. In recent years, the Internet developed rapidly, the life of people has become more informative and networked. All countries in the world have studied the smart grid. The power system has also gradually developed in this direction. The management of the power grid gradually adopts a management system based on market competition and constitutes a planned, targeted, and well structured power network. This is a necessary condition for taking advantage of market competition. However, with the continuous development of network information technology, the security risks it faces are also increasing. Hackers and viruses use network vulnerabilities to maliciously attack power network systems. it will bring irreparable damage to the construction of country, once the electricity network is attacked. Therefore, the detection of power network vulnerabilities has become a problem that we must consider.

The traditional power network vulnerability detection system is divided into three types: (1) manual inspection, (2) direct detection using a script or program, and (3) indirect search for evidence of the existence of a vulnerability. These power

X. Sun et al. (Eds.): ICCCS 2018, LNCS 11065, pp. 641–650, 2018.
https://doi.org/10.1007/978-3-030-00012-7_58

vulnerability detection methods are time-consuming and laborious, and it is difficult to accurately locate the source of power network vulnerabilities in a short period of time, which might result in significant losses. Therefore, using a more intelligent and efficient way to detect power network vulnerabilities has become an important part of ensuring network quality.

Machine learning is the core of artificial intelligence. It is a multi-disciplinary field that involves many disciplines such as probability theory, statistics, approximation theory, convex analysis, and so on. The application of artificial intelligence in the field of network vulnerability detection has pushed technology based on human expertise into the field of intelligence. The machine learning method is mainly to analyze the collected data to find possible network vulnerabilities, in recent years, machine learning methods have been widely used in the power industry. Power network vulnerability detection has the following process: (1) Data collection and update: Introduce external threat intelligence to form a threat intelligence database. According to external threat intelligence, the newly released power network security vulnerabilities are collected to form a vulnerability database. When there is new threat intelligence, the data of the threat intelligence database and vulnerability database is updated. (2) Construct model of network vulnerability detection algorithm: The use of threat intelligence database and vulnerability database data for the construction of network vulnerability detection algorithm model. (3) Application of the network vulnerability detection algorithm: Applying the algorithm model to practical problems, analyze the possible network security risk power monitoring system, and achieve effective identification of system network security vulnerabilities. Power network vulnerability detection based on machine learning algorithms includes two parts: (a) Construction of power network vulnerability detection algorithm: The selected marker data set is trained using a classification learning algorithm to obtain an algorithm model; (b) Application of power network vulnerability detection algorithm: Using algorithm model for power network vulnerability detection.

Conventional vulnerability detection methods include vulnerability detection based on immune analysis of virus infections, vulnerability detection based on web firewall interception, and vulnerability detection based on statistical information analysis, etc. [1]. Literature [2] proposed a network buffer vulnerability prediction algorithm based on meme group fusion to improve the performance of vulnerability detection through particle swarm clustering method. However, the algorithm has a large amount of calculations, which has little effect on the real-time security of network security. Literature [3] proposes a vulnerability detection algorithm based on time complexity prediction, through information fusion assessment of illegal invocation of hackers, the use of predictive link web crawler algorithm to implement vulnerability detection is of great significance in network security defense. However, this method is prone to distortion in phase matching of intrusion signals, resulting in poor detection accuracy. In [4], attack phase reorganization method is used to analyze and detect network vulnerability links. Due to the complexity of ports in complex random array networks, the vulnerability detection accuracy is not good.

The knowledge-based diagnosis method is based on the knowledge processing technology. By introducing the domain expert experience knowledge of the diagnosis object, the integration of dialectical logic and mathematical logic, the same process of symbol processing and numerical processing, and the unity of inference process and algorithm process are realized [4]. This method does not require a quantitative mathematical model and is the core of intelligent network vulnerability detection technology. Artificial Neural Network (ANN) and K-nearest neighbor (KNN) are common practices for network vulnerability detection and can achieve good results, for instance, ANN [5, 6] was exploited in several research works as a mechanism of clustering, diagnostic, detection and classification, Because neural network has the ability of self-learning and can fit any continuous nonlinear function, as well as the advantages of parallel processing and global action, it has strong advantages in dealing with nonlinear problems and online estimation. ANN is mainly used for network vulnerability detection in the following ways: (1) Using ANN to establish a diagnostic reasoning system [7, 8]. The ANN stores information in a distributed manner, uses the topology structure of the network and the distribution of weights to achieve non-linear mapping, and utilizes global parallel processing to achieve non-linear information transformation from the input space to the output space, so we can use the ANN algorithm as the comparison object of our power network vulnerability detection algorithm. The neural network power vulnerability detection system that is properly established for specific problems can directly introduce output data (representing power network vulnerability reasons) from its input data (representing the symptoms of power network vulnerabilities) so as to implement fault detection and diagnosis. (2) ANN is used to fit the normal characteristics of the system, resulting in residuals and network vulnerability detection [9, 10]. Residuals were clustered using ANN [11]. (3) Combining fuzzy logic with ANN to establish fuzzy neural network for detection reasoning [12]. The main disadvantage of neural networks is that their knowledge is distributed in the network structure and network weights, and the reasoning mechanism is not clear. In addition, ANN's learning algorithm requires higher training samples, it is easy to fall into local minimum, and its promotion ability is poor.

2 Framework of Adaboost Algorithm

Boosting is a method to improve the accuracy of any given learning algorithm. Its idea originated from the PAC (Probably Aperture Correct) learning model proposed by Valiant [13]. However, the Boosting algorithm has a major drawback in solving practical problems, that is, they all require that the lower limit of classification accuracy of the weak classification algorithm must be known in advance, which is difficult to achieve in practical problems. Later, Freund and Schapire [14] proposed a more practical algorithm framework based on Boosting, namely Adaboost (Adaptive Boosting) algorithm. The algorithm framework can be combined with many other types of learning algorithms. Weak learning algorithms combine different weights to synthesize strong classifiers (as shown in Fig. 1) to improve the performance of the classifier, so that it could be used to detecting the power network vulnerability.

The Adaboost method is an iterative algorithm that adds a new weak classifier in each round until a predetermined, sufficiently small error rate is reached. Each training sample is given a weight indicating the probability that it is selected into the training set. If a sample point has been accurately classified, the probability of being selected in the next training set is reduced; on the contrary, if a sample point is classified not accurate, its weight is increased. In this way, the Adaboost method can focus on samples which are harder to divide.

The classical Adaboost algorithm framework aims to train T weak classifiers with N labeled samples, and finally combine them into a strong classifier according to the accuracy to achieve accurate prediction. The whole algorithm is a promotion process for weak algorithm. The classification ability of data can be improved through continuous training, and the general steps are as follows:

(1) The N labeled samples which distributed according to the weight vector D, are trained to obtain a weak classifier.
(2) Obtain the weight error of the weak classifier, and the weight error reflects the classification ability of the weak classification algorithm.
(3) Then according to the weight error to get the speech right of the weak classifier, the speech rights and classification ability was positively correlated.
(4) Update the weight vector, the next round of labeled samples are distributed according to the weight vector; After being repeated T times, we can get T weak classifier, and they are combined into a strong classifier according to the speech rights.

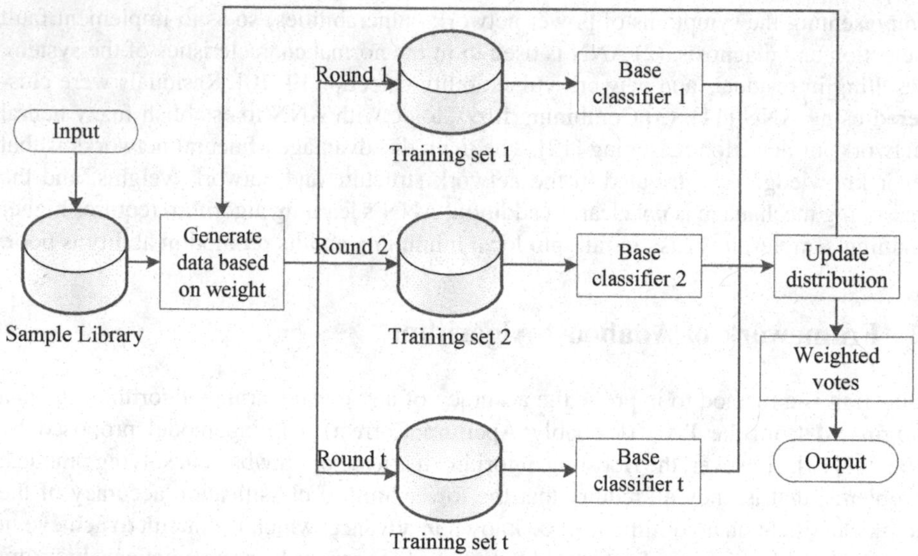

Fig. 1. Framework of Adaboost algorithm.

3 Power Network Vulnerability Detection Based on Improved Adaboost Algorithm

Power network vulnerability detection problem is a classification problem, and the classification problem in machine learning is often affected by dimensions, for example, neural network algorithms [15] and KNN [16]. As the dimension increases, or the less relevant features increase, their classification effect will be affected. Adaboost differs from them in that the training process only selects functions that are known to improve the model's predictive power, reduce the dimensions, and potentially improve execution time, because there is no need to calculate irrelevant features. Besides, Adaboost algorithm has good classification effect and can detect power network vulnerability well, the learning effects of individual learning algorithms used in the Adaboost algorithm may be weak, but as long as each learner performs slightly better than random guessing, the final model can be shown to converge to a strong learner, so the Adaboost algorithm can be used to detecting power network vulnerability. However, Adaboost algorithm is very sensitive to noisy data and outliers, so, how to reduce the impact of noise and outliers on the algorithm is also a problem that should be considered in power network vulnerability detection algorithms.

The C4.5 decision tree was proposed by Quinlan [17] in 1995. It is an improvement based on the ID3 decision tree. C4.5 overcomes the fact that when ID3 selects attributes with information gain, it prefers to select more attribute values, which is a property with many values, and the disadvantage of not being able to deal with continuous properties. The classification rules produced by the C4.5 algorithms are easy to understand and have a high accuracy. In addiction, the Adaboost algorithm is sensitive to noise, therefore, we use a parameter δ to reduce the effect of noise on the algorithm and propose an improved power network vulnerability detection algorithm.

The specific steps of the algorithm are as follows (as shown in Fig. 2):

(1) Data preprocessing

The preprocessing of the original data, including data quantification and normalization, enables the preprocessed data to be used to construct the weak classifier.

(2) Initialization of the algorithm

Given N labeled dataset $\{(x_1, y_1), (x_2, y_2), \cdots, (x_N, y_N)\}$, where $x_i \in X$ (X is called the sample space of the power network vulnerability data) and $y_i \in Y$ (Y is the class space of the power network vulnerability data), where $i = 1, 2, \cdots, N$. The data set is allocated, with about 80% of the samples as training set and the rest as test sets, the number of training times T has been given. The weight vector $D_1 = (w_1^1, w_2^1, \cdots, w_i^1, \cdots, w_N^1)$ of the training set is initialized, where $w_i^1 = 1/N$ and $i = 1, 2, \cdots, N$, it represents the weight of the $i-th$ sample in the first round, and the data set is distributed according to D_t.

(3) Construct weak predictor $h_t(t = 1, \cdots, T)$

We select the decision tree as the weak classifier. The t-round decision tree h_t is constructed based on C4.5 algorithm. Using the generated weak classifier h_t to calculate the weight error on the training data set, the formula is as follows:

$$\varepsilon_t = \sum\nolimits_{i=1}^{N} w_i^t |h_t(x) - y_i|, \tag{1}$$

It can be seen that the better the classification effect of the weak classifier is, the smaller the weight error ε_t is, and vice versa.

(4) Accuracy statistics

Statistics the accuracy of each sample point by using formula:

$$E_i(t) = \left(\sum\nolimits_1^t I[h_t(x_i) - y_i]\right)/t, \tag{2}$$

where $0 \leq E_i(t) \leq 1$. If $E_i(t) < \delta$, then $E_i(t) = 0$.

(5) Update weights

According to the weight error, the speech weight of weak classifier α_t is calculated. The smaller the weight error, the greater the speech weight, and vice versa, the formula is as follows:

$$\alpha_t = \frac{1}{2}\ln[(1 - \varepsilon_t)/\varepsilon_t]. \tag{3}$$

Then update the weight vector of the next round according to α_t, and the weight update formula is as follows:

$$D_{t+1} = (w_1^{t+1}, w_2^{t+1}, \cdots, w_N^{t+1}), \tag{4}$$

$$w_i^{t+1} = \frac{w_i^t[E_i(t)]^n}{Z_t}, \tag{5}$$

where $Z_t = \sum_{i=1}^N w_i^t \exp(-\alpha_t h_t(x_i) y_i)$ is the normalized constant, $i = 1, 2, \cdots, N$.

(6) Strong classifier

After T rounds of training, T weak classifiers are obtained. The weak classifiers are combined into a strong classifier according to a certain right of speech: α_t:

$$H(x) = sign\sum\nolimits_{t=1}^T \alpha_t h_t(x). \tag{6}$$

(7) Data Testing

The test samples were tested with the trained strong classifier to obtain the error rate of the power network vulnerability data.

In the improved Adaboost algorithm of this paper, a reasonable selection of δ value can effectively reduce the impact of noise on the classification results. Among them, the value of n restricts the unlimited expansion of the noise point to a certain extent. At the same time, the number of iterations of the classifier is also reduced, which improves the convergence speed of the algorithm. When $n = 0$, this algorithm is the traditional Adaboost algorithm.

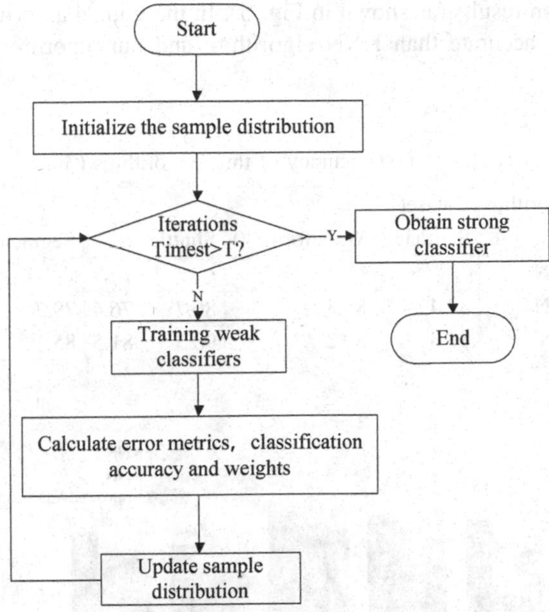

Fig. 2. Flowchart of our algorithm.

4 Experimental Analysis

To test the performance of the improved Adaboost-based power network vulnerability detection algorithm, we selected datasets from a representative set of five UCI benchmark databases [18], Comparing the efficiency of the proposed method, the neural network (ANN) method and the K-nearest neighbor (KNN) method. The basic parameters of the five UCI benchmark data sets are shown in Table 1.

Table 1. Brief description of five data sets.

Dataset	Category	Attributes	Number of samples	Training samples	Test samples
Setimage	6	36	6435	5148	1287
Waveform-40	3	40	5000	4000	1000
Shuttle	7	9	58000	46400	11600
Iris	3	4	150	120	30
Segment	7	19	2310	1848	462

First, five sets of datasets were used to compare the accuracy of the three algorithms (KNN, ANN, and ours). Firstly, data to be measured are divided the into n equal parts (in this article, $n = 5$), randomly take one copy as the test set, and the remaining $n - 1$ copies as the training set of the algorithm. Table 2 lists the accuracy of the three arithmetic operation results (as shown in Fig. 3). In the trained algorithm model, ANN algorithm is more accurate than KNN algorithm, and our algorithm has the highest accuracy.

Table 2. Test accuracy of three algorithms (%).

Algorithm	Dataset				
	Setimage	Waveform-40	Shuttle	Iris	Segment
KNN					
ANN	82.4	85.8	86.7	76.4	79.7
Ours	87.3	89.2	90.3	81.5	85.1

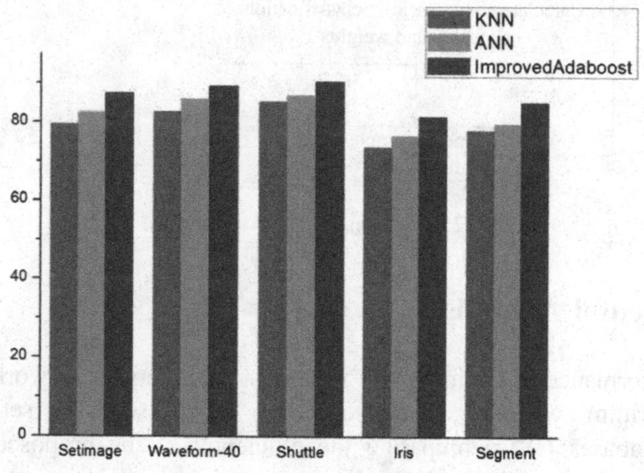

Fig. 3. The accuracy comparison among KNN, ANN and ours.

In addition, Table 3 shows the comparison of the generalization performance of the KNN, ANN and our algorithms and compares the error rates of the three algorithms (as shown in Fig. 4). In the error rate comparison, the ANN algorithm has a lower error rate than the KNN algorithm, and our algorithm has the lowest error rate.

Table 3. Test error rate of three algorithms (%)

Algorithm	Dataset				
	Setimage	Waveform-40	Shuttle	Iris	Segment
KNN	25.6	22.7	19.8	30.3	26.5
ANN	21.4	19.7	18.3	26.0	23.4
Ours	19.1	17.7	17.1	24.9	21.6

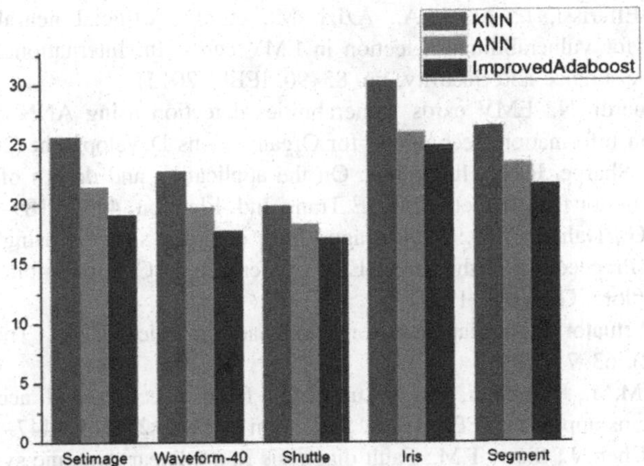

Fig. 4. The error rate comparison among KNN ANN and ours.

From the comparison of experimental data, In power network vulnerability detection, the proposed Adaboost algorithm has certain advantages than the other two algorithms in terms of accuracy and generalization performance.

5 Conclusion

With the development of machine learning technology, the use of machine learning methods to detect power network vulnerability has attracted more and more attention of scholars. In this paper, an improved multi-class Adaboost classifier is proposed to detect power network vulnerability. The advantage of this algorithm is, instead of converting multiple problems into multiple binary problems, it directly solves multi-class classification problems, greatly reducing the computational complexity. In addition, we introduced a variable A to solve the noise problem. So, it has better adaptability to noise and can adapt to the multiple vulnerabilities situation of power network. From the experimental results, this algorithm has a better classification effect than other algorithms and can achieve higher classification accuracy in a relatively short period of time.

References

1. Liu, Y., Che, W., Liu, T., Zhang, M.: A comparison study of sequence labeling methods for Chinese word segmentation, POS tagging models. J. Chin. Inf. Process. **27**, 30–36 (2013)
2. Feng, X.Z., Hao, P.: Information of product review mining based on analyzing of part of speech. Comput. Eng. Des. **34**(1), 283–288 (2013)
3. Juan, Y.U., Dang, Y.Z.: Chinese term extraction based on POS analysis & string frequency. Syst. Eng.-Theory Pract. (2010)
4. Wei, Y.G., Zhang, G.C., Chang, Y., Yuan, F.: Deep web semantic annotation method based on Chinese part-of-speech and domain knowledge. J. Zhengzhou Univ. (2009)

5. Ouerdi, N., Elfarissi, I., Azizi, A., Azizi, M., et al.: Artificial neural network-based methodology for vulnerabilities detection in EMV cards. In: International Conference on Information Assurance and Security, pp. 85–90. IEEE (2015)
6. Tarik, H., Ouerdi, N.: EMV cards vulnerabilities detection using ANN. In: International Conference on Information Technology for Organizations Development (2016)
7. Chow, M.Y., Sharpe, R.N., Hung, J.C.: On the application and design of artificial neural networks for motor fault detection. IEEE Trans. Ind. Electron. **40**(2), 189–196 (1993)
8. Tzafestas, S.G., Dalianis, P.J.: Fault diagnosis in complex systems using artificial neural networks. In: Proceedings of the Third IEEE Conference on Control Applications, pp. 877–882. IEEE Xplore, Glasgow (1994)
9. Wang, H.: Actuator fault diagnosis for nonlinear dynamic system. Trans. Inst. Meas. Control. **17**(2), 63–71 (1995)
10. Polycarpou, M.M., Helmicki, A.J.: Automated fault detection and accommodation: a learning systems approach. IEEE Trans. Syst. Man Cybern. **25**(11), 1447–1458 (1995)
11. Patton, R.J., Chen, J., Siew, T.M.: Fault diagnosis in nonlinear dynamic systems via neural networks. In: International Conference on Control, IET, vol. 2, pp. 1346–1351 (2002)
12. Smith, T.F., Waterman, M.S.: Identification of common molecular subsequences. Mol. Biol. **147**, 195–197 (1981)
13. Valiant, L.G.: A theory of the learnable. Commun. ACM **27**(11), 1134–1142 (1984)
14. Freund, Y., Schapire, R.E.: A desicion-theoretic generalization of on-line learning and an application to boosting. In: Vitányi, P. (ed.) EuroCOLT 1995. LNCS, vol. 904, pp. 23–37. Springer, Heidelberg (1995). https://doi.org/10.1007/3-540-59119-2_166
15. Pitts, W.: A logical calculus of the ideas immanent in nervous activity. Bull. Math. Biophys. **5**(4), 115–133 (1943)
16. Cover, T., Hart, P.: Nearest neighbor pattern classification. IEEE Press **13**(1), 21–27 (1967)
17. Quinlan, J.R.: C4.5: Programs for Machine Learning. Morgan Kaufmann Publishers Inc., Burlington (1993)
18. UCI repository of machine learning databases. http://www.ics.uci.edu

Privacy Preserving for Big Data Based on Fuzzy Set

Jun Wu[1,2] and Chunzhi Wang[1(✉)]

[1] Hubei University of Technology, Wuhan 430068, China
wujun.whut@gmail.com
[2] Wuhan University of Technology, Wuhan 430070, China

Abstract. Today Big Data is one of the major technology usages for every research areas in competitive world. There are many important aspects with Big Data which would be volume, velocity, variety and veracity. Furthermore it is necessary to optimize existing methods to be executable for privacy preserving of Big Data. In this paper, firstly analysis about Big Data and its associated privacy Preserving, then makes an overview of privacy preservation especially for the Location Privacy Data. Furthermore it proposes model for privacy preserving, and then gives formulation about the algorithm of Privacy Preserving Based on Fuzzy Set (PPFS) which can help to achieve privacy preserving.

Keywords: Big Data · Privacy preserving · Fuzzy set

1 Introduction

With the development of Internet information technology and economic society, mobile Internet, social networking, e-commerce would have greatly expanded the scope of application of the Internet to various industries and business. These functions of various types of data are going to have rapid expansion and accumulation. These kinds of a large amount of data from different areas are referred to Big Data which carry huge amounts of useful information and wide knowledge. So that Big Data has 4V characteristics as variety types, large volume, rapid velocity and great value. Today we are living in this Big Data era. And there is the emergence of data services which contain massive storage and powerful computing. That's why Cloud Computing is coming now, as the other generational invitation. Cloud computing is a model that allows for easy, on-demand network access to shared, configurable computing resources. In the cloud computing model, the data is stored and calculated compared to the traditional model in a large number of distributed computers, which is the traditional local computer or remote server mode is differentiated.

At present, there are three computing modes: software as a service, platform as a service, and infrastructure as a service. The three calculation modes can fully guarantee the demand of users. Big Data technology is mainly to solve the large-scale data storage, computing, analysis and other issues. With the advent of this era, on one hand, cloud computing represents data storage and computing power and requires Big Data to reflect its efficiency compared to other technologies. On the other hand, Big Data represents a data knowledge challenge which could support for accurate knowledge and

X. Sun et al. (Eds.): ICCCS 2018, LNCS 11065, pp. 651–659, 2018.
https://doi.org/10.1007/978-3-030-00012-7_59

security information. These services need cloud computing to reflect their innermost value. Cloud Computing and Big Data are the most talked about and most typical of the two representatives, and the combination of the two large cloud data platform has become the focus of attention in the field of science and technology, and more and more Of the penetration of real life, and the cloud of Big Data platform for the security of privacy preserving as an important guarantee of its value.

2 Overview of Big Data and Its Privacy Preserving

There are many Big Data security risks based on the cloud computing. As we know, if the security and privacy issues could not be solved, there would be a catastrophic crisis for the majority of users. Because these Big Data would carry so many personal important information for every user in the cloud platform, such as identity information, behavioral information, locational information, business information and so on. These above data and information about the value of information and forecasting information that is exploited by cloud computing technology on the cloud's Big Data platform can not only provide decision-making and services for the country, enterprises, and individuals but also to the government, enterprises and individuals.

Baruh et al. [1] focus on how the logic of big data analytics, and discuss how two possible individual strategies-withdrawal from the market and complete reliance on market-provided privacy preserving may result in less privacy options available to the society at large, which could provide more meaningful alternatives for privacy preserving. Goroff et al. [2] study big data through the Internet, and find out the lack of a clear legal framework and ethical guidelines for use of administrative data jeopardizes the value of important research. Then they provide strategies for organizations to minimize risks of reidentification and privacy violations for individual data subjects. Furthermore give the suggestion of privacy and ethical concerns which would best be managed by supporting the development of administrative data centers to lower transaction costs and increase the reproducibility of research conducted on administrative data. Madaan et al. [3] propose study of the privacy threat of information linkage, their paper illustrates and explains information linkage during the process of data integration in a smart neighborhood scenario, which could ensure stakeholders awareness and preserving of subjects about privacy breaches due to information linkage. For the purpose of the privacy or data preserving, Weichert [4] purposes binding and data transfer, on rights of the data subject, technical and organizational measures and procedural arrangements. Recently, codes of conduct and certification schemes have been added as instruments. The frame of privacy law is completed by the law on medical products and information security regulations.

Obviously, the research of Big Data security preserving based on the cloud computing is focused on cloud computing and Big Data which would be to reflect its scientific value and commercial value of the important preserving. If the cloud platform storage data security privacy is not guaranteed, which will greatly limit the cloud computing and Big Data in the future development. In order to ensure the security of Big Data stored in the cloud, we can add key technologies such as privacy preserving technology, data encryption technology, integrity verification technology, data dynamic update technology, data backup and data processing in Big Data storage and calculation processing. Recovery technology based on cloud computing Big Data security privacy preserving research is also worth further exploration.

This paper studies the Big Data security and privacy preserving based on the cloud computing. This paper starts from the two aspects of implicit security mechanism and displays security mechanism, so as to protect the data platform and data computing Security privacy. If we can achieve data security and privacy in the data storage and calculation, we will realize the security and privacy of the relevant computing information, which will be of great significance to our future research and practice.

Salah [5] has worked how to properly achieve elasticity for network firewalls deployed in a cloud environment. They develop the analytical model based on the principles of Markov chains and queuing theory to capture the behavior of a cloud-based firewall service comprising a load balancer, furthermore this model can be used in practice by cloud security engineers to achieve proper elasticity. Wu et al. [6] proposed an identity-based encryption with equality test scheme using bilinear pairing for cloud storage which is more suitable for cloud deployment, including in a mobile cloud environment. Mollah et al. [7] has worked the security and privacy requirements which are to avail the cloud services, the communications between mobile devices and clouds. Yu and Wang [8] have worked on how to deal with the cloud storage auditing security problem. They propose a paradigm named strong key-exposure resilient auditing for secure cloud storage, and built the security model for secure cloud storage and design a concrete scheme which has achieved desirable security and efficiency. Li et al. [9] focused on the data security and privacy issues on cloud computing platform, and proposes an intelligent cryptography approach, by which the cloud service operators cannot directly reach partial data. The proposed scheme is entitled Security-Aware Efficient Distributed Storage (SA-EDS) model which has assessed both security and efficiency performances and effectively defend main threats from clouds and requires with an acceptable computation time.

3 Privacy Concerns About Big Data Characters

3.1 Analysis on Big Data Characters

At present, Big Data can be divided into two categories as static data and dynamic data. The corresponding data encryption mechanism also has static data confidential mechanism and dynamic data encryption mechanism. There are two kinds of encryption algorithms for static data encryption mechanism, namely symmetric encryption algorithm and asymmetric encryption algorithm. Symmetric encryption algorithm refers to the same encryption key and decryption key, in the encryption and decryption process using the same key, such as DES, AES, IDEA, RC4, RC5, RC6. Asymmetric encryption algorithm has a private key and public key two different keys, common asymmetric encryption algorithm RSA, based on discrete logarithm EI Gamal algorithm.

3.2 Privacy Preserving Model Based on Big Data Lifecycle

Privacy preserving model based on Big Data lifecycle, need to work in many steps as following: data publishing, data storage, data mining and data using. As Fig. 1 shown, during every phase of Big Data lifecycle, data security and privacy preserving need to face different risks and solve by different technologies.

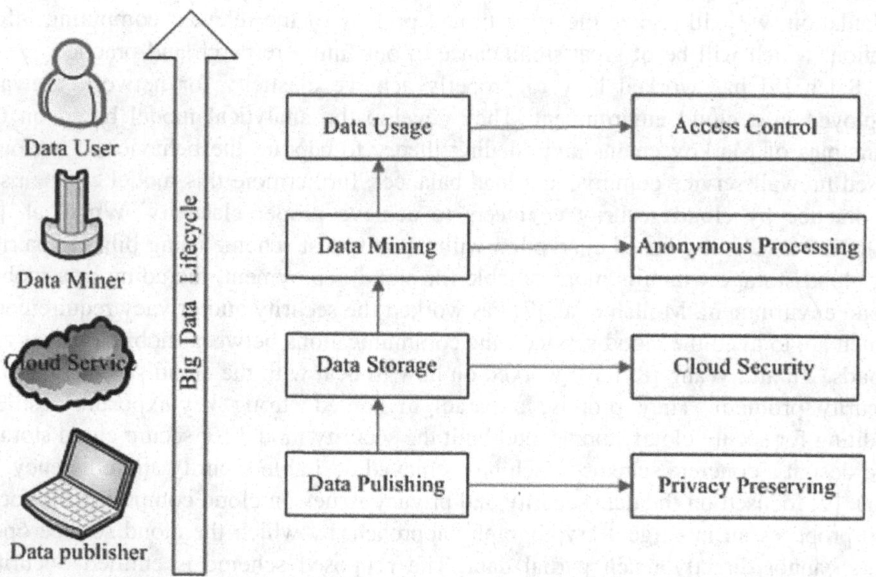

Fig. 1. Figure of big data lifecycle contains 4 different time periods.

Moor et al. [10] propose an investigation model supported by predictive, automated data collection actions and guided presentation of resulting information. And based this model on experience from security analysis working in the trench, and apply an iterative approach to tool building so that quick feedback from users can be incorporated into the model design and tool building continuously. Wald and Khoshgoftaar [11] applied mining and machine learning techniques to predict users' personality traits using only demographic and text-based attributes extracted from their profiles. Their experiment results have privacy implications in terms of allowing advertisers and other groups to focus on a specific subset of individuals based on their personality traits. Ayhan et al. [12] presented a novel analytics system that enables query processing and predictive analytics over streams of big aviation data. By their scalable service architecture, implementation and value, then analytics process to attain more accurate predictions. Agilex Technologies [13] team has presented an approach to attaining both high precision and high recall for name variant identification in large text collections which exploits latent semantic indexing. This significantly improves the precision of candidate name variant results and gets additional precision improvements. Bravo-Marquez et al. [14] purposed how to identify scenarios in which some of big social data resources, and then proposed a novel approach for sentiment classification based on meta-level features. Final results show that the combination of metal-level features provides significant improvements in performance. Zhang et al. [15] proposes a privacy preserving deep computation model by offloading the expensive operations to the cloud which would improve the efficiency of big data feature learning. And their scheme is highly scalable by employing more cloud servers, which is particularly suitable for big data. Sadhya [16] proposed a privacy preserving deep computation model based on homomorphic encryption. Their scheme improves the efficiency by offloading the expensive computation tasks on the cloud. During the Big Data era, Mass Distributed Storage (MDS) has been explored to scale up the data storage size in recent years. Obviously its benefits would be the high level performances of the scalable computation which needed in Big Data application. One aspect that needs improvements is to secure distributed data storage, in which the threats come from a variety of sides. The distributed storage manner can result in more chances of malicious attacks or abuse activities. Meanwhile, it is difficult to balance functionality and security performances due to cost concerns. This is the reason for our research of challenging issue to efficiently secure distributed data in cloud systems, since the risks deriving from different network layers are hardly fully addressed [17–20].

4 Model and Experimental Analysis

4.1 Analysis on Privacy Data

Privacy refers to individuals who are reluctant to let others know or do not want to disclose their own information. As following Fig. 2 shows that some kinds of App in our mobile phone have pushed massive privacy data.

And privacy is regarded as a basic right of individuals which have their own ability to isolate their privacy that can be selectively expressed, those individuals are proprietary, Sensitive information or things are usually treated as personal privacy. Personal privacy can be divided into information privacy, body privacy, communication privacy, and location privacy.

Location privacy is a special kind of information privacy, which refers to personal reluctance to be known outside the location-related information, and location information exposed personal information. Hospitals, bars, home addresses and other sensitive locations are usually regarded as the location of privacy, the user can decide when, how and what the extent their own location information to inform other people. Users are often more reluctant to reveal their current location or future location, but past location preserving is also important because the past location can help the attacker know who you are, where to live, what things are done; the user is willing to Friends reveal their location, and do not want the mobile terminal application software in its unknowingly automatically share their location; users are more willing to reveal its confused area, rather than reveal its true location. In location-aware applications, the server collects GPS location information and ambient awareness information uploaded by mobile devices, such as the natural environment, public infrastructure, and people's social activities.

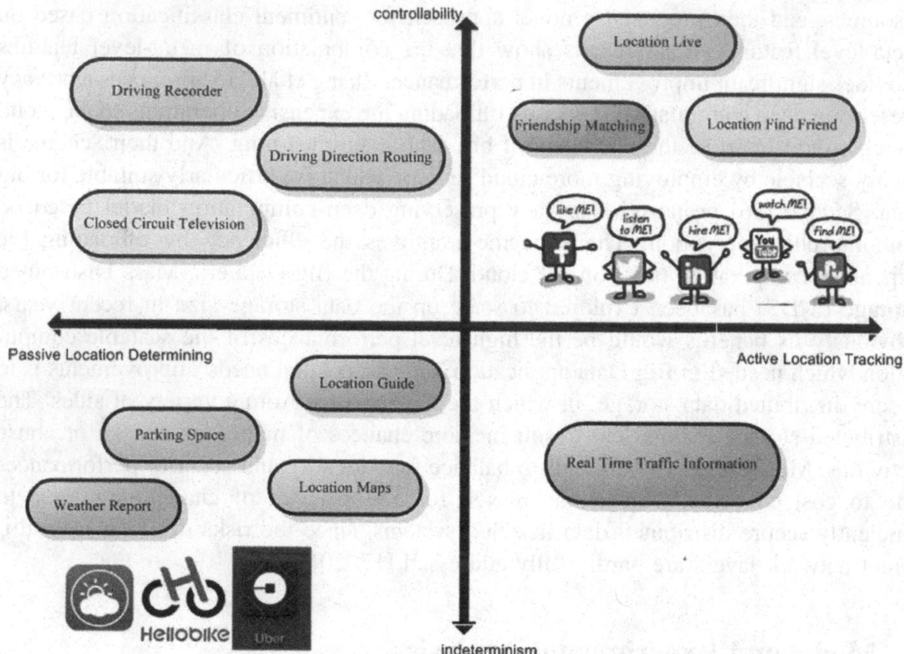

Fig. 2. The mobile phones post massive privacy data either passive side or active side.

4.2 Privacy Preserving Model for Location Big Data Based on Fuzzy Set

In the location-based service (LBS), the user will upload the location information to the service provider, the service provider according to the user location to provide business information query, advertising push, city friends, car navigation and other services. The service provider obtains the user's location when serving the user. Not only that, the service provider can also request the service continuously by the user to obtain the user's trajectory information. In addition, the attacker will attack the server to obtain the user's location information.

Xing et al. consider the problem of mutual privacy preserving in social participatory sensing in which individuals contribute their private information to build a community. Particularly, they propose a mutual privacy preserving k-means clustering scheme that neither discloses an individual's private information nor leaks the community's characteristic data (clusters). Our scheme contains two privacy-preserving algorithms called at each iteration of the k-means clustering which can resist collusion attacks, and can provide mutual privacy preserving even when the data analyst colludes with all except one participant [21]. Afzali et al. propose the model for big data mining based on data anonymization. Besides, special features of big data such as velocity make it necessary to consider each rule as a sensitive association rule with an appropriate membership degree which are embedded in the proposed model, but also can help to speed up data mining process [22]. Location trajectory data itself contains a lot of privacy information, the attacker through data mining analysis, can be inferred personal interests, behavior patterns, rough status, lifestyle and other privacy information; attackers may also be combined with payment records, news, blog, Social network equilateral information inferred track real owner.

The principle of Bayesian classification is to train sample data set for getting out the prior probability. The posterior probability is calculated by Bayes formula.

$$P(H_i \mid X) = \frac{P(H_i)P(X \mid H_i)}{\sum_{i=1}^{n} P(H_i)P(X \mid H_i)}$$

Select a class with a higher posterior probability value as the object's class

4.3 Algorithm of Privacy Preserving Based on Fuzzy Set

During Big Data lifecycle, data security and privacy preserving need to face different risks and solve by different technologies.

Input: Training data and being published data
Output: Privacy preserving data based on Fuzzy set

Step1: Build a linear regression modeling.

Step2: Determine the best classification points of sensitive attributes in training data, then make sure N as the number of Equivalence classes for the training data set.

Step3: Generalized train the training data set, then calculate $P(H_i)$ ***which is the prior probability of the training data set.***

Step4: Use Bayesian model to calculate $P(H_i \mid X)$ ***which is the posterior probability of the training data set.***

Step5: Choose the Max value of $P(H_i \mid X)$ ***as the best classification for this training data set. Then generalize the other being published data.***

Step6: While (i<n)

$$P(H_i \mid X) = \frac{P(H_i)P(X \mid H_i)}{\sum_{i=1}^{n} P(H_i)P(X \mid H_i)}$$

To calculate ;
end while

Although there are many third-party data platforms who will be collected to the user location track data released for researchers and business analysis and mining, used to assess the mobile network performance, urban planning or user behavior analysis.

When face the time of data publishing, it is important to work about privacy preserving. As 4.2 section preserved model, we would work about Algorithm of privacy preserving based on Fuzzy set (PPFS).

4.4 Experimental Execution and Analysis About Location Privacy Data

In this section, we choose the Location Data from "Kaggle Datasets" which contains Big Data about location information. Comparing these original data to privacy data with PPFS, it is easy to find the result in Table 1.

Table 1. Comparation between original data and PPFS result.

Data	Number of feature set	Classification
Original data set	2000	78
PPFS result set	866	31

5 Conclusion

In the location publishing application, the goal of privacy preserving is to reduce the risk of user location privacy leakage as far as possible, by dealing with the location trajectory data so that the processed data set satisfies the requirement of trace data analysis and mining application. While many privacy methods are proposed, such as anonymity, reduced recording data, and an addition of noise data, most of these methods focus on specific analysis and mining scenarios and less about how to choose the appropriate privacy preserving mechanism for different scenarios. It is difficult to determine the optimal privacy preserving mechanism under different application scenarios. However, the attacking strategy has some influence on the privacy preserving effect, and it is difficult to give the most impact on different attack strategies. Therefore, the choice of the privacy policy is a challenging scientific issue.

Acknowledgements. The research is supported by the National Science Foundation (NSF) under Grants (No. 61602161), Hubei Natural Science Foundation under Grants (No. 2014CFB590), Natural Science Foundation of Hubei University of Technology under Grant (No. BSQD13039), Wuhan University of Technology Hubei Key Laboratory of Transportation Internet of Things Foundation under Grants (No. 2015III015-A03).

References

1. Baruh, L., Popescu, M.: Big data analytics and the limits of privacy self-management. New Media Soc. **1**, 11–24 (2015)
2. Goroff, D., Polonetsky, J., Tene, O.: Privacy protective research: facilitating ethically responsible access to administrative data. Ann. Am. Acad. Polit. Soc. Sci. **675**(1), 46–66 (2018)
3. Madaan, N., Ahad, M.A., Sastry, S.M.: Data integration in IoT ecosystem: information linkage as a privacy threat. Comput. Law Secur. Rev. **34**, 125–133 (2017)

4. Weichert, T.: Health privacy in the age of digital networks. Bundesgesundheitsblatt - Gesundheitsforschung – Gesundheitsschutz, pp. 1–6 (2018)
5. Salah, K.P., Calyam, P., Boutaba, R.: Analytical model for elastic scaling of cloud-based firewalls. IEEE Trans. Netw. Serv. Manag. **14**(1), 136–146 (2017)
6. Wu, L., et al.: Efficient and secure identity-based encryption scheme with equality test in cloud computing. Future Gener. Comput. Syst. **73**(C), 22–31 (2017)
7. Mollah, M.B., Vasilakos, A., Vasilakos, A.: Security and Privacy Challenges in Mobile Cloud Computing. Academic Press Ltd., Cambridge (2017)
8. Yu, J., Wang, H.: Strong key-exposure resilient auditing for secure cloud storage. IEEE Trans. Inf. Forensics Secur. **12**(8), 1931–1940 (2017)
9. Li, Y., et al.: Intelligent cryptography approach for secure distributed big data storage in cloud computing. Inf. Sci. **387**(C), 103–115 (2016)
10. Moor, D., et al.: Investigative response modeling and predictive data collection. eCrime Researchers Summit, pp. 1–6. IEEE (2013)
11. Wald, R., Khoshgoftaar, T., Sumner, C.: Machine prediction of personality from Facebook profiles. In: IEEE International Conference on Information Reuse and Integration, pp. 109–115 (2012)
12. Ayhan, S., et al.: Predictive analytics with aviation big data. **54**(9), 1–13 (2013)
13. Bradford, R.B.: Use of latent semantic indexing to identify name variants in large data collections. In: IEEE International Conference on Intelligence and Security Informatics, pp. 27–32 (2013)
14. Bravo-Marquez, F., Mendoza, M., Poblete, B.: Meta-level sentiment models for big social data analysis. Knowl.-Based Syst. **69**, 86–99 (2014)
15. Zhang, Q., Yang, L.T., Chen, Z.: Privacy preserving deep computation model on cloud for big data feature learning. IEEE Trans. Comput. **65**(5), 1351–1362 (2016)
16. Sadhya, D., Singh, S.K., Chakraborty, B.: Review of key-binding-based biometric data preserving schemes. Iet. Biometrics **5**(4), 263–275 (2016)
17. Ateniese, G., Fu, K., Green, M., Hohenberger, S.: Improved proxy re-encryption schemes with applications to secure distributed storage. ACM Trans. Inf. Syst. Secur. **9**(1), 1–30 (2006)
18. Baek, J., Vu, Q., Liu, K., Huang, X., Xiang, Y.: A secure cloud computing based framework for big data information management of smart grid. IEEE Trans. Cloud Comput. **3**(2), 233–244 (2015)
19. Gai, K., Qiu, M., Zhao, H.: Security-aware efficient mass distributed storage approach for cloud systems in big data. In: 2016 IEEE 2nd International Conference on Big Data Security on Cloud (BigDataSecurity), IEEE International Conference on High Performance and Smart Computing (HPSC), and IEEE International Conference on Intelligent Data and Security (IDS), pp. 140–145. IEEE, New York (2016)
20. Gai, K., Qiu, M., Zhao, H., Dai, W.: Anti-counterfeit schema using monte carlo simulation for e-commerce in cloud systems. In: The 2nd IEEE International Conference on Cyber Security and Cloud Computing, pp. 74–79. IEEE, New York (2015)
21. Xing, K., et al.: Mutual privacy preserving k-means clustering in social participatory sensing. IEEE Trans. Indust. Informat. **PP**(99), 1 (2017)
22. Afzali, G.A., Mohammadi, S.: Privacy preserving big data mining: association rule hiding using fuzzy logic approach. IET Information Security (2016)

Quantum Private Comparison Based on Delegating Quantum Computation

Haibin Wang(✉), Daomeng Pan, and Wenjie Liu

Jiangsu Engineering Center of Network Monitoring,
NanJing University of Information Science and Technology,
Nanjing 210044, China
whb9741705@163.com

Abstract. Based on delegating quantum computation (DQC) model, a two-party quantum private comparison protocol with single photons is proposed, and it is also generalized to the multi-party case. In the protocols, the clients' inputs are firstly encrypted with the shared keys, and then sent to quantum center (QC) to perform quantum computation, i.e., the CNOT operations with which QC can get the comparison result. By utilizing the DQC model, clients with limited quantum resources can delegate semi-honest QC to perform quantum comparison of equality, besides their information sequences are encrypted and transmitted only once. Analysis shows that out protocols have very good security, low communication complexity and high efficiency.

Keywords: Delegating quantum computation · Quantum private comparison CNOT

1 Introduction

Quantum mechanics has achieved huge success in the information processing field in recent decades, quantum computation, especially quantum cryptography communication, has aroused more and more attention, and many important research findings are presented, including quantum key distribution (QKD) [1, 2], quantum secure sharing (QSS) [3, 4], quantum secure direct communication (QSDC) [5–7] quantum sealed-bid auction (QSBA) [8, 9], quantum remote state preparation (RSP) [10, 11], and quantum key agreement (QKA) [12–14].

And quantum private comparison (QPC) is just an attractive kind of quantum cryptographic protocols, it enables two distrustful parties to verify whether their secrets are identical without revealing their own secret to each other or outside. It is been widely discussed and studied in recent years. Based on the properties of quantum mechanics, the equality of private comparison can be easily achieved without any complex computation. It can be applied extensively in many application fields, including private bidding and auctions, secret ballot elections, commercial business, identification in a number of scenarios, and so on.

From 2009, Yang et al. [15] proposed the first QPC based on the Bell and hash functions, a large number of QPC protocol is progressively proposed [16–20] and in present, the two sides private information equal comparison is one of the most in-depth

X. Sun et al. (Eds.): ICCCS 2018, LNCS 11065, pp. 660–669, 2018.
https://doi.org/10.1007/978-3-030-00012-7_60

directions. In 2010, Chen et al. [16] proposed a QPC protocol using a triplet Greenberger-Horne-Zeilinger (GHZ) states. In their protocol, to construct a secure equality function in a two-party scheme, a semi-honest TP was introduced, where TP might try to steal the players' private inputs, which makes the protocol insecure. In 2012, Tseng et al. [17] based on decoy and two-photons entangled Bell states, proposing a two party QPC protocol with a third party TP. In their protocol, TP did not need to perform any local unitary operation or quantum measurement and only need to prepare the initial sates, the two party encoded their secrets on the particles of Bell states that TP produced. Subsequently, Sun et al. [18] proposed a new protocol for the private comparison of equal information based on the cluster entangled states. And Liu et al. [19] also proposed a non-maximally entanglement state W state based protocol for the private comparison of equal information. Recently, Liu et al. [20] employed single-photon interference providing a QPC protocol with lower communication complexity. In the above mentioned protocols, they all need a semi-honest TP to implement, because as a kind of multi-party secure computation, QPC cannot be securely achieved only with the participants themselves, a semi-honest party (TP) is necessary to accomplish private computation [21]. In fact, an unrestricted TP cannot help improve the security of QPC protocols, since if TP conspire with one of the participants; the protocol turns a two-party one, which has been proved insecure [22]. In QPC protocols, TP is usually considered as honest-but-curious, which means TP would strictly follow the procedure of the protocol but try to gain the clients' secrets according to the records during the protocols.

However, the truth is only a few institutions or companies could hold quantum computers over in the early era. Client with limited quantum resources cannot enjoy the benefits of the QPC protocols. In order to adapt this situation, we introduce DQC into QPC proposing two QPC protocols, clients only need to produce single photons, and then the rest work can be accomplished by a semi-honest quantum center. Through utilizing the feature of performing quantum computations on encrypted quantum data of DQC, private information sequences are encrypted and sent to QC to perform simple CNOT operation to obtain the comparison result. Private information of clients are encrypted and transmitted only once, security of the proposed protocols can be achieved perfectly, low communication complexity and efficiency can also be guaranteed.

The rest of this paper is organized as follows. In the following section, we will briefly review the DQC model. In Sect. 3, we present a two-party quantum private comparison protocol based on DQC model. In Sect. 4, we generalize the two-party QPC protocol to the Multi-party case. Then, the correctness and security of the proposed protocols is discussed, and conclusion is drawn in the last section.

2 Review of DQC

Delegating private quantum computation is first proposed by Broadbent et al. [23]. In DQC, quantum center (QC) performs universal quantum gates on encrypted data sent from the client, and the computation results can be decrypted by the client with secret key. This kind of client-server computation model enables an almost-classical client to delegate the execution of any quantum computation to a remote server without exposing his information. The brief process of DQC is as follows (also shown in Fig. 1).

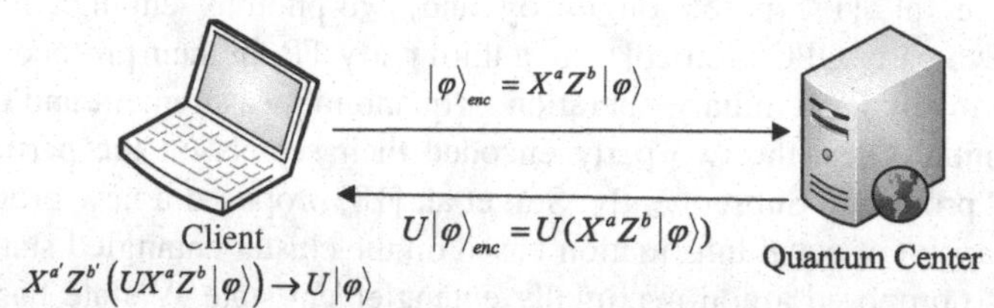

Fig. 1. DQC model.

(1) Quantum encryption: Client uses Pauli operations X and Z to encrypt $|\varphi\rangle$, and then obtains $|\varphi\rangle_{enc}= X^a Z^b|\varphi\rangle$, a and b are the secret keys randomly selected from. Then he sends $|\varphi\rangle_{enc}$ to the server QC.
(2) Quantum computation: QC implements the specific quantum computation (a certain unitary operation U) on the encrypted qubit $|\varphi\rangle_{enc}$.
(3) Quantum decryption: The server returns the output state $U|\varphi\rangle_{enc}$ to the client. The client decrypts the output state: $X^{a'} Z^{b'} \left(UX^a Z^b|\varphi\rangle\right) \to U|\varphi\rangle$ according to the decryption rules, and finally gets the quantum computation result.

As we know, the quantum gate set $\{X, Z, H, P, R, CNOT\}$ is universal [24], which means it can be used to simulate arbitrary unitary computation. The gates have following properties,

$$\begin{cases} X|j\rangle = |j+1\rangle \\ Z|j\rangle = (-1)^j|j\rangle \\ H|j\rangle = \left(|0\rangle + (-1)^j|1\rangle\right)/\sqrt{2} \\ P|j\rangle = (i)^j|j\rangle \\ R|j\rangle = \left(e^{i\pi/4}\right)^j|j\rangle \\ CNOT|j\rangle|k\rangle = |j\rangle|j\oplus k\rangle \end{cases} \quad j \in \{0,1\} \tag{1}$$

and their encryption and decryption can be completed as Fig. 2.

3 Two-Party Quantum Private Comparison Based on DQC

Suppose two parties Alice, Bob and QC agree that $|0\rangle(|1\rangle)$ represents information '0'('1'). Alice's private information is $X = \{x_1, x_2, \cdots, x_n\}$ and Bob's private information is $Y = \{y_1, y_2, \cdots, y_n\}$. And they want to know whether X is equal to Y without leaking any information of X and Y. The protocol process is as follows (also shown in Fig. 2):

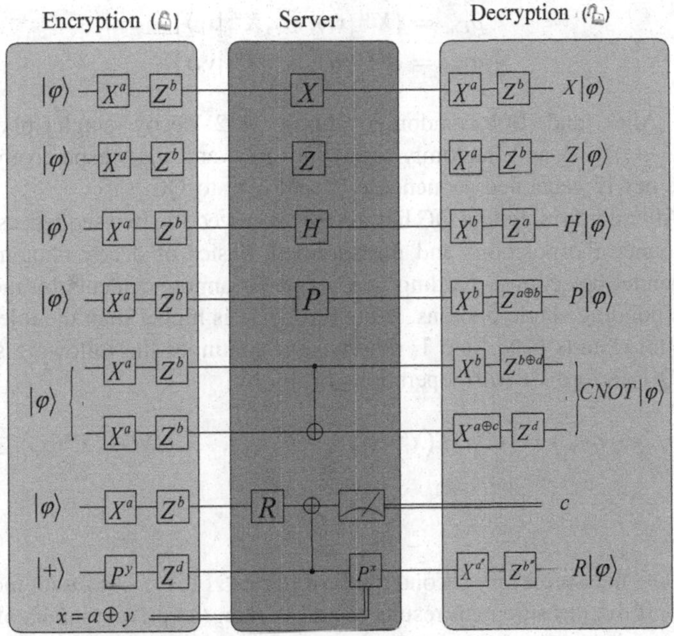

Fig. 2. Encryption and decryption process for universal gate set [25].

Step 1: Alice prepare single photons sequence $p = \{|x_1\rangle, |x_2\rangle, \cdots, |x_n\rangle\}$ according to private input X. And Bob prepare single photons sequence $q = \{|y_1\rangle, |y_2\rangle, \cdots, |y_n\rangle\}$ according to private input Y (Fig. 3).

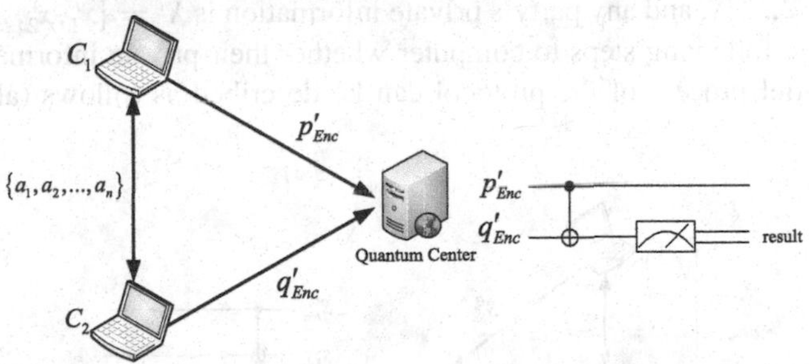

Fig. 3. The process of two-party quantum private comparison.

Step 2: Alice and Bob secretly shares encryption keys $K = \{a_1, a_2, \ldots, a_n\} a_i \in \{0, 1\}$ using a Verifiable Secret Sharing (VSS) scheme [29]. And then they use K to encrypt p, q

$$p_{Enc} = \{X^{a_1}|x_1\rangle, \ldots, X^{a_n}|x_n\rangle\},$$
$$q_{Enc} = \{X^{a_1}|y_1\rangle, \ldots, X^{a_n}|y_n\rangle\}. \quad (2)$$

Step 3: Alice and Bob randomly choose $n/2$ decoy single photons from $\{|0\rangle, |1\rangle, |+\rangle, |-\rangle\}$ and randomly insert into p_{Enc} and q_{Enc} respectively, and they sends the newly generated sequence p'_{Enc} and q'_{Enc} to QC.

Step 4: After confirming that QC has already received the two sequences, Alice and Bob announce the positions and measurement basics of decoy photons. QC performs channel detection according to C_1 and C_2 announcements by measurement the corresponding single photons. If the error rate is higher than the tolerable limit, the protocol restarts from Step 1, otherwise it continues the following step.

Step 5: QC performs *CNOT* operations bit by bit,

$$\begin{aligned} CNOT(p_{Enc} \otimes q_{Enc}) &= (CNOT(X^{a_1}|x_1\rangle \otimes X^{a_1}|y_1\rangle), \ldots, CNOT(X^{a_n}|x_n\rangle \otimes X^{a_n}|y_n\rangle)) \\ &= |\varphi_1\rangle|\varphi_2\rangle, \ldots, |\varphi_n\rangle \end{aligned} \quad (3)$$

and then QC measure every second qubit of $|\varphi_i\rangle i \in \{1, 2, \ldots, n\}$ with measurement $\{|0\rangle, |1\rangle\}$. If the measurement results are all 0, then the private inputs of Alice and Bob are equal, if there exiting 1 in the measurement result, the private inputs of Alice and Bob are not equal.

4 Multi-party Quantum Private Comparison Based on DQC

We also generalize the two-party protocol to the multi-party case. Suppose there are N client $C1$, $C2 \ldots CN$, and any party's private information is $X^i = \{x_1^i, x_2^i, \ldots, x_n^i\}$. Then they follow the following steps to computer whether their private information is equal or not. The brief process of the protocol can be described as follows (also shown in Fig. 4):

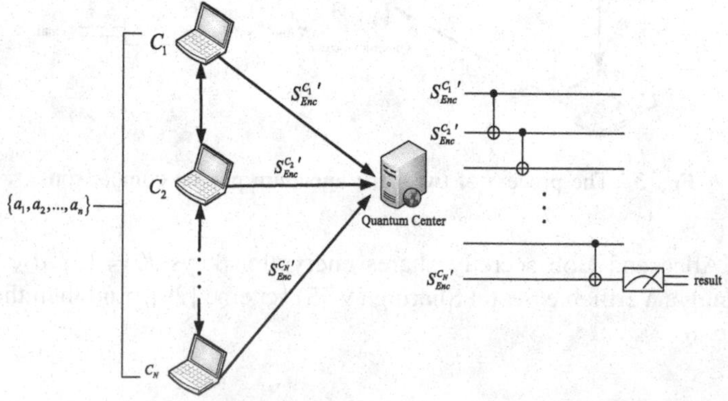

Fig. 4. The process of multi-party quantum private comparison.

Step 1: N clients $C_1, C_2, \ldots, C_N$ prepare single photons sequence $S^i = \{|x_1\rangle, |x_2\rangle, \cdots, |x_n\rangle\}$ according to their private input.
Step 2: $C_1, C_2, \ldots, C_N$ secretly shares the encryption keys $K = \{a_1, a_2, \ldots, a_n\} a_i \in \{0, 1\}$ using VSS scheme. then encrypt S^i:

$$S_{Enc}^{C_i} = (X^{a_1}|x_1^i\rangle, \ldots, X^{a_n}|x_n^i\rangle), \tag{4}$$

Step 3: $C_1, C_2, \ldots, C_N$ randomly choose from $\{|0\rangle, |1\rangle, |+\rangle, |-\rangle\}$ and randomly insert into $S_{Enc}^{C_i}$ respectively, they sends the newly generated sequence to QC.
Step 4: After $C_1, C_2, \ldots, C_N$ confirming that QC has already received the sequences, they announce the positions and measurement basics of decoy photons. QC performs channel detection according to C_1 and C_2 announcements by measurement the corresponding single photons. If the error rate is higher than the tolerable limit, the protocol restarts from Step 1, otherwise it continues the following step.
Step 5: QC performs *CNOT* operations bit by bit and obtain a finally state $|\varphi\rangle$, and then QC measures every second qubit of $|\varphi\rangle$ with measurement basis $\{|0\rangle, |1\rangle\}$. If the measurement results are all 0, then the private inputs of Alice and Bob are equal, if there exiting 1 in the measurement result, the private inputs of Alice and Bob are not equal.

5 Security and Correctness Analysis

5.1 Correctness

To verify the correctness of the proposed protocols, without loss of generality we take the two-party quantum private comparison as an example. we only need to consider the encrypted and disordered information sequence remained in QC:

$$p_{Enc} = \{X^{a_1}|x_1\rangle, \ldots, X^{a_n}|x_n\rangle\}, \tag{5}$$

$$q_{Enc} = \{X^{a_1}|y_1\rangle, \ldots, X^{a_n}|y_n\rangle\}. \tag{6}$$

QC performs *CNOT* operations bit by bit and measures the second qubit (shown in Fig. 5):

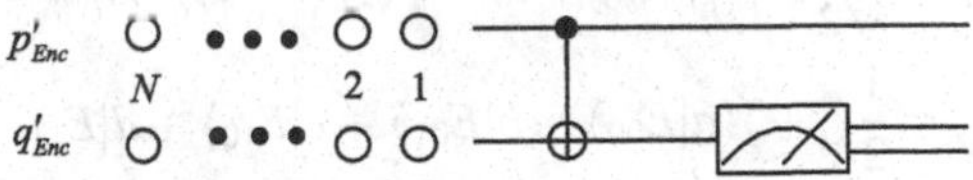

Fig. 5. Circuit for comparison.

If two photons are $|0\rangle \otimes |0\rangle$ and $|1\rangle \otimes |1\rangle$ in position 1, the result of *CNOT* operation will be $|00\rangle$ and $|10\rangle$, then measuring the second qubit will always get 0, if the two photons are $|0\rangle \otimes |1\rangle$ and $|1\rangle \otimes |0\rangle$, then measuring the second qubit will always get 1, which means if the private information are the same then the *CNOT* result are all 0. If 1 exist in the result of *CNOT*, it implies that Alice and Bob own the different private information. Therefore, out proposed protocol is correct.

5.2 Security

We show that the outside attack is invalid to our protocol. We also prove that dishonest QC cannot obtain any information about private information of participant based on the principle that QC cannot conspire with any participant. Besides dishonest participant also cannot obtain any information on private information of other participants.

Outside Attack

The DQC encryption scheme is introduced to the proposed protocols, since only single photons are used it can be simplified as $X^a|\varphi\rangle$. For an outside attacker it is impossible for him to get $|\varphi\rangle$ without knowing the secret key *a*. So our protocol is as secure as the BFK protocol to an outside attacker.

Participant Attack

We suppose that one client is malicious, and the other client's private information is not saved; so we introduce the decoy single photons to perform channel detection to check malicious client's eavesdropping.

We consider the situation that malicious client C_1 tries to obtain the private information of C_2 in second round encryption, and he performs intercept-resend attack. However decoy single photons are reordered and mixed with $\left(|\varphi\rangle_{Enc}^{C_1}\right)_{\text{Enc}}^{C_2}$, so C_1 cannot distinguish them and has to apply the same attack strategy to all of them. But any eavesdropping attempt by C_1 will inevitably modify the decoy photons states and expose him. Without loss of generality, the most general operation U_E C_1 employed is to cause the decoy photons to interact coherently with an auxiliary quantum system,

$$U_E|0\rangle|E\rangle = a|0\rangle|E_{00}\rangle + b|1\rangle|E_{01}\rangle \tag{7}$$

$$U_E|1\rangle|E\rangle = c|0\rangle|E_{01}\rangle + d|1\rangle|E_{11}\rangle \tag{8}$$

Here, $|a|^2 + |b|^2 = 1$ and $|c|^2 + |d|^2 = 1$. Since the decoy photons involved in our protocol are $\{|0\rangle, |1\rangle, |+\rangle, |-\rangle\}$, then operation U_E will be applied on the other two states as follows,

$$\begin{aligned} U_E|+\rangle|E\rangle &= \frac{1}{\sqrt{2}}(a|0\rangle|E_{00}\rangle + b|1\rangle|E_{01}\rangle + c|0\rangle|E_{10}\rangle + d|1\rangle|E_{11}\rangle) \\ &= \frac{1}{2}(|+\rangle(a|E_{00}\rangle + b|E_{01}\rangle + c|E_{10}\rangle + d|E_{11}\rangle)) \end{aligned} \tag{9}$$

$$\begin{aligned} U_E|-\rangle|E\rangle &= \frac{1}{\sqrt{2}}(a|0\rangle|E_{00}\rangle + b|1\rangle|E_{01}\rangle - c|0\rangle|E_{10}\rangle - d|1\rangle|E_{11}\rangle) \\ &= \frac{1}{2}(|-\rangle(a|E_{00}\rangle - b|E_{01}\rangle - c|E_{10}\rangle + d|E_{11}\rangle)) \end{aligned} \tag{10}$$

If Eve introduces no error in the eavesdropping detection, the above Eqs. ()–() must satisfy the following conditions,

$$a|E_{00}\rangle + c|E_{10}\rangle = b|E_{01}\rangle + d|E_{11}\rangle \quad (11)$$

$$a|E_{00}\rangle - c|E_{10}\rangle = -b|E_{01}\rangle + d|E_{11}\rangle \quad (12)$$

Then we can get that $a = d = 1$, $b = c = 0$, $|E_{00}\rangle = |E_{11}\rangle$, and then we get

$$U_E|0\rangle|E\rangle = |0\rangle|E_{00}\rangle, \quad (13)$$

$$U_E|1\rangle|E\rangle = |1\rangle|E_{11}\rangle. \quad (14)$$

We can summarize that only when decoy photons and message photons are $\{|0\rangle, |1\rangle\}$, C_1 would not be found which is impossible, so the private information of C_2 is secure.

QC Attack
Suppose a semi-honest QC wants to steal the participants' secret information, the most possible attack can be performed while QC is holding the encrypted single photons. But as we know, the secret information is encrypted by operation X. After performing the *CONT* operation the only information he can get is the comparison result, the control phase is still encrypted. But the *CNOT* result might disclose the difference between particular bits of information sequence. To solve this problem, the positions of the information sequence are disorder before sending to QC. The sequence all QCs can obtain is meaningless, so QC cannot obtain anything about participants' private information.

6 Conclusion

The two-party quantum private comparison protocol is proposed by using DQC model, and it also been introduced to multi-party quantum private comparison in this paper. Compared with previous QPC protocol, clients only need to be able to produce single photons which are more suitable for the early days of quantum cloud computation. And with the help of DQC, their information sequences are encrypted and transmitted only once, security of the proposed protocols can be achieved perfectly; low communication complexity and efficiency can also be guaranteed. It is well known that QPC and other quantum secure multi-party computation (QSMC) issues will continues to developed by leaps and bounds in the next few decades, and at the same time DQC provides an convenient and safe client-server computation model, it is nature to introduce DQC to QSMC fields, we believe DQC can provide solutions for more QSMC problems, the following step of our study is using DQC to solve more QSMC problems such as Quantum Sealed-Bid Auction [8, 26], quantum private query [27, 28] and so on.

Acknowledgements. This work is supported by the National Nature Science Foundation of China (Grant Nos. 61373131 and 61373016), the Priority Academic Program Development of Jiangsu Higher Education Institutions (PAPD), the University Science Research Project of

Jiangsu Province (Grant No. 16KJB520030), the National Training Program of Innovation and Entrepreneurship for Undergraduates (Grant No. 201610300024Z), the Natural Science Foundation of Jiangsu Province(Grant No. BK20171458), and the Six Talent Peaks Project of Jiangsu Province (Grant No. 2015-XXRJ-013).

References

1. Bennett, C.H., Brassard, G.: Quantum cryptography: public-key distribution and coin tossing. In: Proceedings of IEEE International Conference on Computers, Systems and Signal Processing, pp. 175–179. IEEE Press, New York (1984)
2. Ekert, A.K.: Quantum cryptography based on Bell's theorem. Phys. Rev. Lett. **67**(6), 661 (1991)
3. Hillery, M., Bužek, V., Berthiaume, A.: Quantum secret sharing. Phys. Rev. A **59**(3), 1829–1834 (1999)
4. Cleve, R., Gottesman, D., Lo, H.K.: How to share a quantum secret. Phys. Rev. Lett. **83**(3), 648 (1999)
5. Deng, F.G., Long, G.L., Liu, X.S.: Two-step quantum direct communication protocol using the Einstein-Podolsky-Rosen pair block. Phys. Rev. A **68**(4), 042317 (2003)
6. Liu, W.J., Chen, H.W., Ma, T.H., Li, Z.Q., Liu, Z.H., Hu, W.B.: An efficient deterministic secure quantum communication scheme based on cluster states and identity authentication. Chin. Phys. B **18**(10), 4105–4109 (2009)
7. Liu, Z.H., Chen, H.W.: Cryptanalysis and improvement of quantum broadcast communication and authentication protocol with a quantum one-time pad. Chin. Phys. B **25**(8), 080308 (2016)
8. Liu, W.J., Wang, F., Ji, S., Qu, Z.G., Wang, X.J.: Attacks and improvement of quantum sealed-bid auction with EPR pairs. Commun. Theor. Phys. **61**(6), 686–690 (2014)
9. Liu, W.J., et al.: Multiparty quantum sealed-bid auction using single photons as message carrier. Quantum Inf. Process. **15**(2), 869–879 (2016)
10. Liu, W.J., Chen, Z.F., Liu, C., Zheng, Y.: Improved deterministic N-to-one joint remote preparation of an arbitrary qubit via EPR pairs. Int. J. Theor. Phys. **54**(2), 472–483 (2015)
11. Wang, H.B., Zhou, X.Y., An, X.X., Cui, M.M., Fu, D.S.: Deterministic joint remote preparation of a four-qubit cluster-type state via GHZ states. Int. J. Theor. Phys. **55**(8), 3588–3596 (2016)
12. Zhou, N., Zeng, G., Xiong, J.: Quantum key agreement protocol. Electron. Lett. **40**(18), 1149–1150 (2004)
13. Chong, S.K., Tsai, C.W., Hwang, T.: Improvement on quantum key agreement protocol with maximally entangled states. Int. J. Theor. Phys. **50**(6), 1793–1802 (2011)
14. Chong, S.K., Hwang, T.: Quantum key agreement protocol based on BB84. Opt. Commun. **283**(6), 1192–1195 (2010)
15. Yang, Y.G., Wen, Q.Y.: An efficient two-party quantum private comparison protocol with decoy photons and two-photon entanglement. J. Phys. A: Math. Theor. **42**(5), 055305 (2009)
16. Chen, X.-B., Xu, G., Niu, X.-X., Wen, Q.-Y., Yang, Y.-X.: An efficient protocol for the private comparison of equal information based on the triplet entangled state and single-particle measurement. Opt. Commun. **283**, 1561–1565 (2010)
17. Tseng, H.Y., Jason, L., Tzonelih, H.: New quantum private comparison protocol using EPR pairs. Quantum Inf. Process. **11**(2), 373–384 (2012)
18. Sun, Z.S., Long, D.Y.: Quantum private comparison protocol based on cluster states. Int. J. Theor. Phys. **52**(1), 212–218 (2013)

19. Liu, W., Wang, Y.B., Jiang, Z.T.: An efficient protocol for the quantum private comparison of equality with W state. Opt. Commun. **284**(12), 3160–3163 (2011)
20. Liu, B., Xiao, D., Huang, W., et al.: Quantum private comparison employing single-photon interference. Quantum Inf. Process. **16**(7), 180 (2017)
21. Lo, H.K.: Insecurity of quantum secure computations. Phys. Rev. A: Atom., Mol. Opt. Phys. **56**(2), 1154–1162 (1997)
22. Yao, A.C.: Protocols for secure computations. In: Proceedings of 23rd IEEE Symposium on Foundations of Computer Science (FOCS 1982), Washington, DC (1982)
23. Broadbent, A.: Delegating private quantum computations. Can. J. Phys. **93**(9), 941–946 (2015)
24. Nielsen, M.A., Chuang, I.L.: Quantum Computation and Quantum Information 10th Anniversary Edition, vol. 21, no. 1, pp. 1–59 (2010)
25. Fisher, K.A., et al.: Quantum computing on encrypted data. Nat. Commun. **5**(2), 3074 (2013)
26. Zhao, Z.W., Naseri, M., Zheng, Y.Q.: Secure quantum sealed-bid auction with post-confirmation. Opt. Commun. **283**(16), 3194–3197 (2010)
27. Olejnik, L.: Secure quantum private information retrieval using phase-encoded queries. Phys. Rev. A **84**(2), 022313 (2011)
28. Jakobi, M., Simon, C., Gisin, N., et al.: Practical private database queries based on a quantum-key-distribution protocol. Phys. Rev. A **83**(2), 022301 (2011)
29. Pedersen, T.P.: Non-interactive and information-theoretic secure verifiable secret sharing. In: Feigenbaum, J. (ed.) CRYPTO 1991. LNCS, vol. 576, pp. 129–140. Springer, Heidelberg (1992). https://doi.org/10.1007/3-540-46766-1_9

Reversible Data Hiding in Partially-Encrypted Images

Haishan Chen[1(✉)], Wien Hong[1], Jiangqun Ni[2], and Tung-Shou Chen[3]

[1] Nanfang College of Sun Yat-sen University, Conghua, China
chenhsh3@mail3.sysu.edu.cn, wienhong@gmail.com

[2] School of Data Science and Computer Technology, Sun Yat-sen University, Guangzhou 510975, China
issjqni@mail.sysu.edu.cn

[3] National Taichung University of Science and Technology, Taichang, Taiwan
tschen@nutc.edu.tw

Abstract. This paper presents a novel reversible data hiding method for medical images with privacy protection in only partial of the image areas. Specifically, only those areas with privacy protection requirement are encrypted. Firstly, the cover image is segmented into two layers including the foreground layer where privacy information exists, and the background layer. Then, a parameter termed as shadowing factor is proposed to balance the requirements of privacy protection and embedding capacity. With the shadowing factor, the privacy area and the embedding area are obtained. Finally, location scrambling is employed to encrypt the privacy area, and data are embedded into the embedding area. The benefits of the proposed partial-encryption based RDH method are in three folds: improving the embedding capacity, providing implementation flexibility in choosing existing data hiding techniques, and presenting users with the capability of understanding some of the image content from the partially-encrypted image even without decryption.

Keywords: Reversible data hiding · Partially-encrypted image
Prediction-error expansion · Privacy content

1 Introduction

Reversible data hiding (RDH) is the technique to carry data bits within a cover signal (e.g. image, video etc.) while keeping both the embedded data and the cover signal completely recoverable. Among the various developments, RDH in encrypted images (RDH-EI) is particularly attractive in concealing data in full-encrypted images with capability of lossless data extraction and image recovery at the receiver side [1,2]. Therefore, RDH-EI is particularly valuable in cloud applications where privacy protection is critical but the content owner trust no cloud service providers.

X. Sun et al. (Eds.): ICCCS 2018, LNCS 11065, pp. 670–679, 2018.
https://doi.org/10.1007/978-3-030-00012-7_61

In general, RDH-EI algorithms realizes data embedding by exploiting the local correlations within the encrypted image content, where the local correlation is relative low compared to the non-encrypted image [2,4–6]. Therefore, most of RDH-EI methods provide full recoverability only when the payload is relatively low. However, when payload gets high, most of them fail in lossless data extraction and/or image recovery. As a result, improving the effective embedding capacity becomes a challenging task for RDH-EI methods.

In fact, among the existing RDH-EI works, there exists a general assumption that the content owner requires full-encryption to all image content before uploading an image into the cloud [1–3]. However, what the content owner really want to protect is only those image content with critical information, e.g. the body areas in medical images is considered to be of privacy while the background areas contains little privacy information and thus requires few protection. Therefore, partial-encryption is enough to meet the requirements in some of the real-world applications.

To handle the above mentioned problems in RDH-EI, this paper proposes a novel RDH method with partial image encryption, and terms it as RDH-PEI for short. Specifically, encryption is performed to only the privacy image areas while data are embedded in the remaining areas. Firstly, a gray-scale threshold is derived to segment the cover image into two layers: the foreground layer where privacy protection is required, and the background layer where little privacy exists. Secondly, a parameter, termed as shadowing factor, for the image foreground is proposed to balance between privacy protection and embedding capacity. With the shadowing factor, the image is split into two areas including the privacy area and the embedding area. The privacy area consists of the image foreground and also some of its neighboring pixels (the shadowing pixels), and the remaining image content is termed as the embedding area. As a result, the proposed work is made content adaptive to the payload. At last, the privacy area is encrypted via location scrambling, and the embedding area is exploited for data embedding. In fact, most of the existing RDH techniques, e.g. prediction-error expansion (PEE) [7], histogram modification (HM) [8], and pixel value ordering (PVO) [9] etc. are suitable for data embedding in the embedding area. In this paper, PEE with the simple-yet-effective median-edge-detection (MED) technique is employed as the embedding technique. In short, the proposed RDH-PEI method works well in providing privacy protection, high embedding capacity and full recoverability.

2 The Proposed Work

This section presents the implementation details of RDH-PEI with the overall procedures as illustrated in Fig. 1. For convenience, the cover image, the pre-processed image, and the marked image are denoted by $\hat{I}$, I, and I', respectively. In the embedding procedure, the cover image $\hat{I}$ is first segmented with a gray-scale threshold so as to differ the foreground from the background; then the cover gray-scale histogram is pre-processed to make room for PEE based data

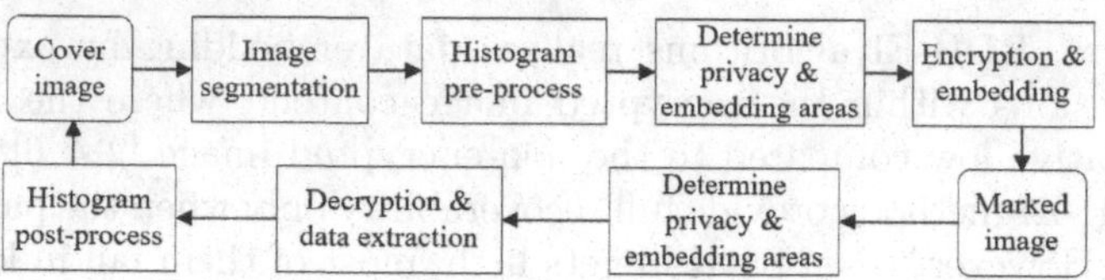

Fig. 1. Procedures of RDH-PEI.

embedding; next, the privacy area is obtained by dilating the foreground and adapting to the size of payload, and the embedding area is identified as the rest of image contents, as illustrated in Fig. 2, where the shadowing area is induced by dilation to the foreground; finally, the privacy area is encrypted via location scrambling and data are embedded in the embedding area with PEE. Since location scrambling is employed as the encryption algorithm, the gray-scale distribution of the privacy area is reserved, and thus it can be easily distinguished from the embedding area at the receiver side.

In the procedure of data extraction and image recovery, the privacy area and the embedding area are firstly obtained with the side information of the gray-scale threshold and shadowing factor. Then decryption is executed to recover the privacy area, and data extraction and image recovery are performed on the embedding area. Finally, after histogram post-processing on I, the cover image $\hat{I}$ is restored.

2.1 Image Segmentation

In the proposed work, data embedding is performed on the embedding area, while encryption is applied to the privacy area where privacy protection is required. Let x be the gray-scale value, and $h(x)$ be the gray-scale histogram. A cover image is segmented using the Otsu algorithm [10], which tries to find a gray-scale threshold, denoted by T_x, so as to split the image into two layers including the background layer and the foreground layer. Otsu is based on the principle of maximum intra-layer variance, and thus the single threshold T_x is optimized in separating the histogram into two consecutive segments. For eight-bit-depth gray-scale images, the gray-scales for the two segments are denoted by $[0, T_x)$ and $[T_x, 255]$, corresponding to the background layer and the foreground layer, respectively.

2.2 Image Pre-processing

In this paper, the well-known high performance technique PEE is employed for data hiding into the embedding area. Since PEE embeds data by adding 1 or -1 to the pixel values, the cover image has to be pre-processed to avoid overflow and overflow before data embedding. In this paper, the process of image pre-processing is designed to minimize the number of modified pixels, with detailed steps as illustrated below:

(1) Identify a pair of consecutive histogram bins with the minimum sum of occurrence rates. We denote the smaller bin as T_s.
(2) Shift the gray-scale histogram to make room for PEE-based data embedding on pixels with $x \in [0, T_x)$. The shifted pixels are registered in a location map, which is compressed and later embedded along with payload.
(3) Determine the privacy area I_p with respect to the size of payload, as specified by the following Sect. 2.3.

Note that, after image pre-processing, the gray-scale threshold T_x is still effective in segmenting the image background and the foreground.

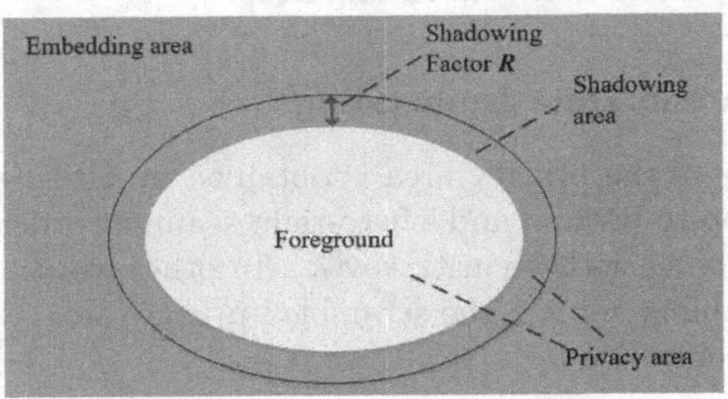

Fig. 2. Illustration of privacy and embedding areas.

2.3 Privacy Area and Embedding Area

With the gray-scale threshold T_x, the cover image is split into two layers. Even though the obtained foreground layer is deems as privacy area, its neighboring pixels may also contain some privacy information. Therefore, we treat both the image foreground and some of its neighboring pixels as the privacy area, as illustrated in Fig. 2. The image area of the neighboring pixels is termed as the shadowing area to the foreground layer. Note that the shadowing area falls in the background layer but is classified as part of the privacy area since it may possibly contain some privacy information.

Let I_f, I_p and I_e denote the image foreground, the privacy area and the embedding area, respectively, L_f, L_p and L_e represent their corresponding location maps. In this paper, the shadowing area is derived with morphological image dilation onto the location map of the image foreground. The employed morphological operation is performed with a disk-shaped structuring element, denoted by S_R where R is the radius. For convenience, R is termed as the shadowing factor for the foreground. With S_R, the location map for the privacy area I_p can be obtained with morphological dilation to the location map of the image foreground, as specified by

$$L_p = L_f \oplus S_R, \tag{1}$$

where $\oplus$ denotes morphological dilation. With the privacy area I_p, the data embedding area I_e is derived by $I_e = I - I_p$.

It's obvious that, the bigger the shadowing factor R, the better the protected privacy, and the smaller the embedding capacity (denoted by EC). To balance between the requirements of privacy protection and EC, R can be optimized for the given size of payload (denoted by PS), as specified by

$$\begin{aligned} &max(R), \text{ with respect to} \\ &EC \geq PS. \end{aligned} \tag{2}$$

Note that, since EC for the embedding area I_e correlates closely to the embedding method, a better embedding technique is able to increase the EC, which in turn can also improve the level of privacy protection. In this paper, the PEE technique is employed for data embedding in I_e.

2.4 Encryption and Data Embedding

The pixel sequence of the privacy area is obtained by visiting the pixels in the privacy area in a top-to-bottom and left-to-right scanning order, and is encrypted via location scrambling with security key κ_p. In other words, with the location map L_p and scrambling key κ_p, the scrambled privacy area, denoted by I_p', can be obtained as specified by

$$I_p' = Scramble(I_p, L_p, \kappa_p). \tag{3}$$

Data embedding is performed in the embedding area I_e using PEE with MED. Let (i, j) denote the pixel coordinates, $I_e(i, j)$ be a pixel in I_e, $\bar{I}_e(i, j)$ be the prediction of $I_e(i, j)$, $N = I(i-1, j)$, $W = I(i, j-1)$, $NW = I(i-1, j-1)$ represent the neighboring pixels in the north, west and northwest directions, respectively. The pixels in the embedding area are firstly visited in a top-to-bottom and left-to-right order, and then predicted using MED, as specified by the equation

$$\bar{I}_e(i,j) = \begin{cases} \max(N, W) & NW \leq \min(N, W), \\ \min(N, W) & NW \geq \max(N, W), \\ N + W - NW & \text{otherwise}. \end{cases} \tag{4}$$

Note that, the three neighbors of $I_e(i, j)$, including N, W and NW, must NOT fall in the privacy area for the sake of reversibility. Therefore, only part of the pixels, denoted by X_e, where N, W and NW all reside in the embedding area, can be employed for data embedding. Due to the existence of side information T_x, the set of suitable pixels can be easily identified during data embedding and also data extraction.

With prediction $\bar{I}_e(i, j)$, the prediction-error (PE) is obtained using the equation

$$e = I_e(i, j) - \bar{I}_e(i, j). \tag{5}$$

Since the histogram of PE, denoted by $h(e)$, generally follows a Gaussian-like distribution with sharp peak bins close to $e = 0$, data embedding is performed by expanding $e = -1$ and $e = 0$, as specified by

$$e' = \begin{cases} e-1 & e<-1, \\ e-m & e=-1, \\ e+m & e=0, \\ e+1 & e>0, \end{cases} \tag{6}$$

where e' is the PE after data embedding, and $m \in \{0,1\}$ is a to-be-embedded message bit. Note that, the payload must be encrypted before data embedding. With e', the marked pixel $I'_e(i,j)$ can be obtained using the equation

$$I'_e(i,j) = \bar{I}_e(i,j) + e'. \tag{7}$$

To make the data embedding procedure reversible, the side information including T_x, T_s and R, are first encrypted in the same way of the payload, and then stored as the LSBs of a preserved region in the cover image. Since either T_x, T_s or R requires only eight LSBs for storage, the first $N_s = 24$ pixels in the first row of cover image is kept as the preserved region, and their LSBs are embedded along the secret message.

2.5 Implementation Details

Since the overall implementation procedures have been presented in Fig. 1, this subsection focus on providing the implementation detail. The steps of encryption and embedding procedure are listed as below:

(1) Using the Otsu [10] algorithm, calculate the segmentation threshold T_x for cover image $\hat{I}$. The gray-scale values of the foreground falls in the scope of $[T_x, 255]$.
(2) Find two consecutive histogram bins T_s and $T_s + 1$ by minimizing the sum of their occurrence rates, and then pre-process the cover image. The pre-processed pixels are registered in a location map.
(3) Given the payload size PS, determine the maximum shadowing factor R at the restriction of $EC \leq PS$. With R, obtain the location maps for privacy area L_p (see Eq. (1)) and the embedding area L_e. By far, the privacy area I_p and embedding area I_e are derived.
(4) With privacy encryption key κ_p, scramble the locations for privacy area as specified by Eq. (3).
(5) With data encryption key, denoted by κ_e, encrypt the bit sequence of the message.
(6) Select the set of suitable pixels X_e for MED based prediction according to the criteria that the neighboring pixels N, W and NW all falls in the embedding area.
(7) Perform MED prediction and obtain the sequence of PE (see Eq. (5)) for pixels in X_e.
(8) Using Eq. (6), perform PEE based data embedding. The embedded data includes the compressed location map, the secret payload and the N_s LSBs of the preserved region.

(9) Encrypt side information including T_x, T_s and R with the third encryption key κ_t, and store their encryption results in the LSBs of the preserved region. By far, the marked and encrypted image I' is derived.

The steps of decryption, data extraction and image recovery are provided as below:

(1) From the LSBs of preserved image area, derive the side information including T_x, T_s and R.
(2) With T_x and R, identify the foreground layer, and then obtain the privacy area and the embedding area.
(3) Decrypt the privacy area with scrambling key κ_p.
(4) Identify the suitable pixels for MED prediction from the embedding area, and then perform PEE-based data extraction and image recovery. The extracted data includes the compressed location map, the secret payload and the N_s LSBs of the preserved region. By far, the pre-processed image I is restored.
(5) Post-precess the histogram with the de-compressed location map and T_s, and restores the LSBs of the preserved region. By far, the cover image $\hat{I}$ is recovered.

Note that, after encryption and data embedding, the privacy area can be fully recovered without data extraction. Furthermore, little modification is induced to the visual effect of the embedding area, which makes it possible to understand some of the image content (e.g. the class of image) even without decryption. Therefore, the data embedder is able to extract data bits without knowing the privacy content, and the content reader can know the class of image without decryption and also can read the privacy area without data extraction.

3 Performance Evaluation

The embedding performance is evaluated on eight medical images obtained from National Biomedical Imaging Archive (NBIA) [11], including Chest, Shoulder, Sternum, Wrist and four other medical images (named as M1, M2, M3 and M4 for convenience), illustrated in Fig. 3. Before data embedding, these images are converted to gray-scale images sized of 512 × 512. The secret message is a bit sequence, where the data bits including 0s and 1s, are randomly generated and then encrypted. During the experiments, the visual effect is first illustrated and then the pure embedding capacity (EC) is employed for performance comparison.

Figure 4 presents the marked counterparts of cover image Chest (see Fig. 3(a)) with different sizes of payload. Note that, the privacy area and the image background can be correctly identified from the marked image. Besides, as the increment of the payload, the value of shadowing factor R decreases, and more details of the image foreground shows up. As illustrated in Fig. 4(c) and (d), even though the privacy part is encrypted, we can still speculate that they are images related

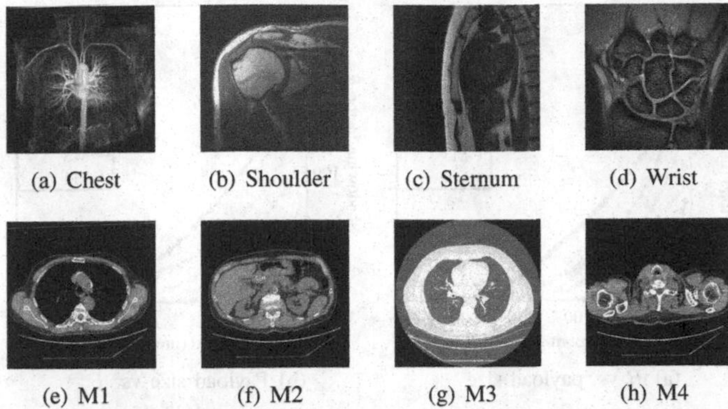

Fig. 3. The eight test medical images.

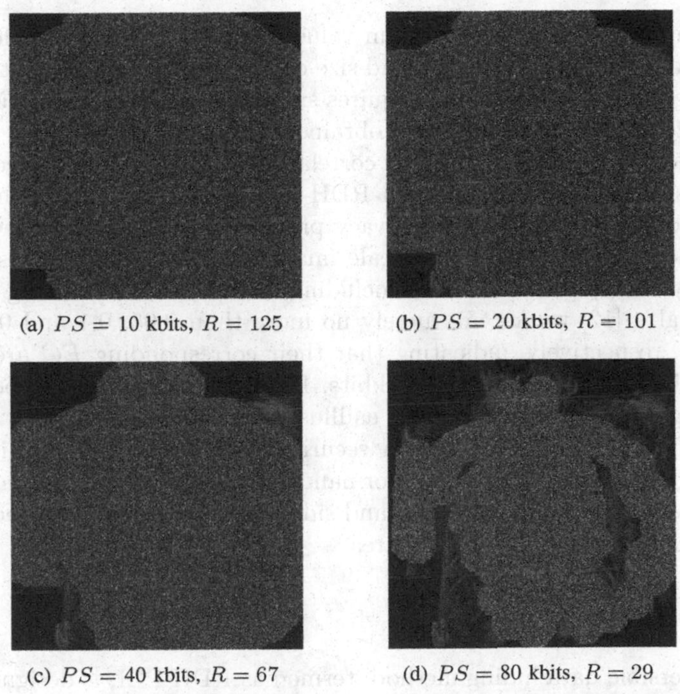

(a) PS = 10 kbits, R = 125
(b) PS = 20 kbits, R = 101
(c) PS = 40 kbits, R = 67
(d) PS = 80 kbits, R = 29

Fig. 4. The encrypted and marked images for chest.

to Chest. Therefore, the shadowing factor R can be seen as the balancing parameter between embedding capacity and the level of privacy protection employed in the proposed work.

In addition to illustrating the visual effects, we further check the embedding capacity, and the relationship between the payload size and the shadowing factor R. Figure 5(a) presents the performance of the payload size for given values of

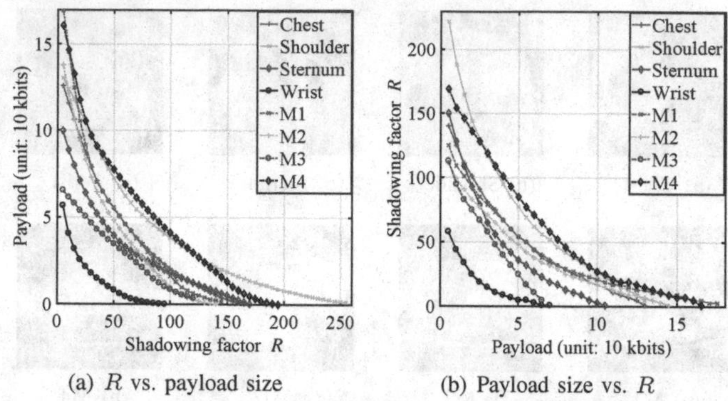

(a) R vs. payload size

(b) Payload size vs. R

Fig. 5. The relationship between EC and R.

R, while Fig. 5(b) gives the maximum value of shadowing factor R for a given size of payload. Note that, the payload size decreases as the increment of R, and the increment of the payload size requires smaller shadowing factor R. When R is reduced to 0, the maximum EC is obtained. Compared to the fully the RDH-EI methods [4,5,12] where the local correlation within the encrypted image is tremendously reduced, the proposed RDH-PEI significantly improves the EC while providing the capability of privacy protection and complete reversibility. For example, with 512 × 512 gray-scale images, the embedding rates for three related fully-encrypted RDH works including Hong et al.'s [4], Zhang et al.'s [5] and Xu et al.'s [12] works, are merely no more than 0.05, 0.1 and 0.2 bit per pixel (bpp), respectively, indicating that their corresponding EC are no more than 13.2 kbits, 26.3 kbits, and 52.5 kbits. Its obvious that the proposed work produces significantly improved EC, as illustrated in Fig. 5(b).

In this paper, the evaluation on security performance is not highlighted. The reason is that the security performance is dependent on the technique of bit sequence encryption for payload and side information, and the technique of location scrambling for the privacy area.

4 Conclusion

A novel reversible data hiding method, termed as RDH-PEI, is designed to partially encrypt cover images so as to improve the embedding capacity while providing full recoverability. Firstly, a medical image is divided into a privacy area and an embedding area. Then, encryption is applied to the privacy area. Finally, data are embedded into the embedding area. In addition to providing full recoverability, the proposed work is also proved to be effective in providing high embedding capacity while protecting the image privacy contents.

Acknowledgment. This work was supported in part by the National Natural Science Foundation of China under grants 61379156 and 61772573, and in part by the Science and Technology Program of Guangzhou, China under grant 201707010029.

References

1. Shi, Y.-Q., Li, X., Zhang, X., Wu, H.T., Ma, B.: Reversible data hiding: advances in the past two decades. IEEE Access **4**, 3210–3237 (2016)
2. Zhang, X.: Reversible data hiding in encrypted images. IEEE Signal Process. Lett. **18**(4), 255–258 (2011)
3. Huang, F., Huang, J., Shi, Y.-Q.: New framework for reversible data hiding in encrypted domain. IEEE Trans. Inf. Forensics Secur. **11**, 2777–2789 (2016)
4. Hong, W., Chen, T.S., Wu, H.Y.: An improved reversible data hiding in encrypted images using side match. IEEE Signal Process. Lett. **19**(4), 199–202 (2012)
5. Zhang, W., Ma, K., Yu, N.: Reversibility improved data hiding in encrypted images. Signal Process. **94**, 118–127 (2014)
6. Ma, K., Zhang, W., Zhao, X., Yu, N., Li, F.: Reversible data hiding in encrypted images by reserving room before encryption. IEEE Trans. Inf. Forensics Secur. **8**(3), 553–562 (2013)
7. Li, X., Zhang, W., Gui, X., Yang, B.: Efficient reversible data hiding based on multiple histograms modification. IEEE Trans. Inf. Forensics Secur. **10**(9), 2016–2027 (2015)
8. Li, X., Li, B., Yang, B., Zeng, T.: General framework to histogram-shifting-based reversible data hiding. IEEE Trans. Image Process. **22**(6), 2181–2191 (2013)
9. Li, X., Li, J., Li, B., Yang, B.: High-fidelity reversible data hiding scheme based on pixel-value-ordering and prediction-error expansion. Signal Process. **93**(1), 198–205 (2013)
10. Otsu, N.: A threshold selection method from gray-level histograms. IEEE Trans. Syst. Man Cybern. **9**(1), 62–66 (1979)
11. National Biomedical Imaging Archive (NBIA) [Online]. https://imaging.nci.nih.gov/ncia/login.jsf#
12. Xu, D., Wang, R.: Separable and error-free reversible data hiding in encrypted images. Signal Process. **123**, 9–21 (2016)

Secure Multiparty Quantum Summation Based on d-Level Single Particles

Xin Tang[1], Gang Xu[1(✉)], Kun-Chang Li[1], Xiu-Bo Chen[1,2], and Yi-Xian Yang[1,2]

[1] Information Security Center, State Key Laboratory of Networking and Switching Technology, Beijing University of Posts and Telecommunications, Beijing 100876, China
gangxu_bupt@163.com
[2] Guizhou Provincial Key Laboratory of Public Big Data, Guizhou University, Guiyang 550025, Guizhou, China

Abstract. In this paper, we propose a multiparty quantum summation module d protocol based on d-level single particles (where d is a prime number). A semi-trusted additional party is introduced to help multiple participants achieve this summation task. Our protocol is more practical and efficient, because it uses only single particles rather than entangled states. After that, the Chinese remainder theorem is utilized to get the summation without module d. Furthermore, the security of our protocols is analyzed, it shows that our protocols could resist some well-known attacks.

Keywords: Secure multiparty quantum summation · d-Level single particles
The Chinese remainder theorem

1 Introduction

Secure Multiparty Computation (SMC) is an important field in modern cryptography. It includes many subfields, such as Yao's millionaire problem [1], secret sharing [2] and secure multiparty summation [3]. Secure multiparty summation is a fundamental primitive of SMC. Based on secure multiparty summation, we could solve other SMC problems, such as numerical computations. In secure multiparty summation, n $(n \geq 3)$ participants want to jointly compute the summation of their private data without revealing any private data.

There exist some classical protocols for secure multiparty summation based on classical cryptography [3–5]. However, the security of these protocols is based on the computational complexity assumption, which cannot provide the unconditional security. Especially, these protocols cannot resist the attack of the quantum computer [6]. As we all know, quantum cryptography can provide the unconditional security and resist the attack of quantum computer. The combination of quantum cryptography and secure multiparty summation is proposed, which is called secure multiparty quantum summation.

In 2007, Du et al. [7] presented a secure n-party quantum addition module $n + 1$ protocol based on non-orthogonal states. Later, a quantum addition module 2 protocol

X. Sun et al. (Eds.): ICCCS 2018, LNCS 11065, pp. 680–690, 2018.
https://doi.org/10.1007/978-3-030-00012-7_62

based on multi-particle entangled states with a semi-honest third party was proposed by Chen et al. [8]. In 2013, Zhang et al. [9] put forward a quantum summation protocol with single photons in both polarization and spatial-mode degrees of freedom. After that, they put forward another three-party quantum summation protocol without a trusted third party based on the genuinely maximally entangled six-qubit states [10]. In 2016, Shi et al. [6] presented a quantum approach to compute the summation and multiplication of multiparty private inputs, respectively. After that, a multi-party quantum summation protocol using single particles to construct entangled states by controlled-not operations without a trusted third party was proposed by Zhang et al. [11]. Later, Liu et al. [12] put forward a quantum secure multi-party summation based on Bell states.

Most of existing protocols are based on entangled states, which are difficult to prepare. With the number of involved particles increasing, the difficulty of obtaining the required quantum correlations grows rapidly. Zhang et al.'s [11] protocol is based on single particles. However, the module of their protocol is 2 which is too small to extend applications. Inspired by the works of Tavakoli et al. [13] and Lin et al. [14], we propose a secure multiparty quantum summation protocol based on d-level single particles (where d is a prime number). The module of our protocol is d. In addition, if n participants want to compute the summation without module d, the Chinese remainder theorem is utilized to achieve this task.

The rest of this paper is organized as follows. In Sect. 2, we briefly introduce the essential preliminaries. In Sect. 3, we propose our protocols. The security of our protocols is analyzed in Sect. 4. Finally, we give our conclusion in Sect. 5.

2 Preliminaries

For any prime number d, there are $d+1$ mutually unbiased bases (MUBs) [15]. The unit vectors belonging to the full set of d + 1 MUBs will be denoted as $G_{l,j} = \left|g_l^{(j)}\right\rangle$, where $j = 0, \ldots, d$ and $l = 0, \ldots, d-1$. We denote the computational basis $|l\rangle$ as $G_{l,d}$, the remaining d MUBs are denoted as

$$G_{l,j} = \left|g_l^{(j)}\right\rangle = \frac{1}{\sqrt{d}}\sum_{k=0}^{d-1} \omega^{k(l+jk)}|k\rangle, \tag{1}$$

where $\omega = e^{2\pi i/d}$. The d MUBs, $G_{l,0}, \ldots, G_{l,d-1}$, are used in our protocols. The encoding operation consists of two unitary operators, V_d and W_d, which are depicted as follows:

$$\begin{aligned} V_d &= \sum_{n=0}^{d-1} \omega^n |n\rangle\langle n|, \\ W_d &= \sum_{n=0}^{d-1} \omega^{n^2} |n\rangle\langle n|. \end{aligned} \tag{2}$$

When applying the operator V_d to $G_{l,j}$, $G_{l,j}$ will be transformed into $G_{l+1,j}$ as

$$\begin{aligned} V_d G_{l,j} = V_d\left|g_l^{(j)}\right\rangle &= \frac{1}{\sqrt{d}}\sum_{n=0}^{d-1}\omega^n|n\rangle\langle n|\sum_{k=0}^{d-1}\omega^{k(l+jk)}|k\rangle \\ &= \frac{1}{\sqrt{d}}\sum_{k=0}^{d-1}\omega^{k((l+1)+jk)}|k\rangle = \left|g_{l+1}^{(j)}\right\rangle = G_{l+1,j}. \end{aligned} \tag{3}$$

In addition, any $G_{l,j}$ can be transformed into $G_{l,j+1}$ by W_d as

$$\begin{aligned} W_d G_{l,j} = W_d\left|g_l^{(j)}\right\rangle &= \frac{1}{\sqrt{d}}\sum_{n=0}^{d-1}\omega^{n^2}|n\rangle\langle n|\sum_{k=0}^{d-1}\omega^{k(l+jk)}|k\rangle \\ &= \frac{1}{\sqrt{d}}\sum_{k=0}^{d-1}\omega^{k(l+(j+1)k)}|k\rangle = \left|g_l^{(j+1)}\right\rangle = G_{l,j+1}. \end{aligned} \tag{4}$$

Therefore, any $G_{l,j}$ can be mapped into $G_{l+l',j+j'}$ by $V_d^{l'}W_d^{j'}$.

The Chinese remainder theorem [16] was first proposed by the Chinese mathematician Sun Tzu. It can be stated like that if one knows the remainders of the Euclidean division of an integer n by several integers, then one can determine uniquely the remainder of the division of n by the product of these integers, under the condition that the divisors are pairwise coprime. For example, there are q positive integers, $d_1, \ldots, d_q$, which are pairwise coprime. Assuming we have the equations:

$$\begin{aligned} x \bmod d_1 &= c_1, \\ x \bmod d_2 &= c_2, \\ &\ldots, \\ x \bmod d_q &= c_q. \end{aligned} \tag{5}$$

According to the Chinese remainder theorem, the x satisfies that

$$x = \sum_{k=1}^{q} D_k \times e_k \times c_k \bmod D, \tag{6}$$

where $D = \prod_{k=1}^{q} d_k$, $D_k = \frac{D}{d_k}$, and $e_k \times D_k \bmod d_k = 1$.

3 Secure Multiparty Quantum Summation

There are n participants, Alice$_1$, …, and Alice$_n$, who possess N private data sets, M_1, …, and M_n, respectively. Here, $M_z = \{m_z^j | m_z^j \in Z_d, j = 1, \ldots, N\}$. All of the n participants want to compute the summation without revealing their private data sets. An additional party (denoted as Server) is introduced to help all of the participants achieve this summation task. The Server in our protocols is permitted to execute attack by himself, but conspire with none of the participants.

3.1 Secure Multiparty Quantum Summation Module d

In the first protocol, all of the n participants want to compute the summation module d ($S = \{s_j | s_j = \sum_{k=1}^{n} m_k^j \mod d,\ j = 1,\ldots,N\}$) without revealing their private data. The first protocol runs as follow:

Protocol 1

Step 1. Server generates two random sequences with the length of $N + (n+1) \times \xi + n \times \delta$, $X_0 = \{x_0^j | x_0^j \in Z_d, j = 1,\ldots,N + (n+1) \times \xi + n \times \delta\}$ and $Y_0 = \{y_0^j | y_0^j \in Z_d, j = 1,\ldots,N + (n+1) \times \xi + n \times \delta\}$. Then, Server generates $N + (n+1) \times \xi + n \times \delta$ d-level single particles $\left|g_0^{(0)}\right\rangle = \frac{1}{\sqrt{d}} \sum_{j=0}^{d-1} |j\rangle$ called sequence Q_0'. He performs $V_d^{x_0^j} W_d^{y_0^j}$ on the jth particle of sequence Q_0' to get the sequence Q_0. Finally, Server sends sequence Q_0 to Alice$_1$.

Step 2. After receiving the particle sequence Q_0, Alice$_1$ randomly selects ξ particles as a sample and keeps them. The remaining particles compose a new sequence Q_0^*. Alice$_1$ generates two secret random numerical strings $X_1 = \{x_1^j | x_1^j \in Z_d, j = 1,\ldots,N + n \times \xi + n \times \delta\}$ and $Y_1 = \{y_1^j | y_1^j \in Z_d, j = 1,\ldots,N + n \times \xi + n \times \delta\}$. Then, he performs $V_d^{x_1^j} W_d^{y_1^j}$ on the jth particle of sequence Q_0^* to get the new sequence Q_1. Finally, Alice$_1$ transmits sequence Q_1 to Alice$_2$.

Step 3. Alice$_2$, …, and Alice$_n$ execute a process similar to Alice$_1$, respectively. Especially, Alice$_i$ ($i = 2,\ldots,n$) randomly selects ξ sample particles from the received particle sequence Q_{i-1} and keeps them. Then, he encodes his secret strings $X_i = \{x_i^j | x_i^j \in Z_d, j = 1,\ldots,N + (n - i + 1) \times \xi + n \times \delta\}$ and $Y_i = \{y_i^j | y_i^j \in Z_d, j = 1,\ldots,N + (n - i + 1) \times \xi + n \times \delta\}$ into the remaining particles through the operation $V_d^{x_i^j} W_d^{y_i^j}$. After that, Alice$_i$ obtains a new particle sequence Q_i. Finally, he sends Q_i to Alice$_{i+1}$, while the last participant Alice$_n$ sends sequence Q_n back to Server.

Step 4. Alice$_1$, …, Alice$_n$ execute their eavesdropping check in order. For example, Alice$_i$ announces the positions of his sample particles. For these sample particles, Server and Alice$_1$, …, Alice$_{i-1}$ have encoded their corresponding x and y on them. According to the encoding operations Eqs. (3) and (4), the initial particle $\left|g_0^{(0)}\right\rangle = \frac{1}{\sqrt{d}} \sum_{j=0}^{d-1} |j\rangle$ have been changed to

$$V_d^{x_{i-1}^j} W_d^{y_{i-1}^j} \cdots V_d^{x_0^j} W_d^{y_0^j} \left|g_0^{(0)}\right\rangle = \left|g_{\sum_{k=0}^{i-1} x_k^j \bmod d}^{\left(\sum_{k=0}^{i-1} y_k^j \bmod d\right)}\right\rangle. \tag{7}$$

First, Alice$_i$ asks Alice$_{i-1}$, …, Alice$_1$ and Server to declare the corresponding x in order. Then, he asks Server and Alice$_1$, …, Alice$_{i-1}$ to declare the corresponding y in order. After that, Alice$_i$ measures each sample particles with corresponding measurement base $(\sum_{k=0}^{i-1} y_k^j \bmod d)$. The measurement results are denoted as $R_i = \left\{r_i^1, \ldots, r_i^{\xi}\right\}$. If R_i satisfies

$$r_i^j = \sum_{k=0}^{i-1} x_k^j \bmod d, \tag{8}$$

Alice$_i$ declares that there does not exist eavesdropping. Otherwise, Alice$_i$ terminates the protocol and asks Server to restart the protocol.

Step 5. Similarly, Server executes eavesdropping check. Server randomly selects ξ sample particles from the received particles sequence Q_n. For these sample particles, Server and Alice$_1$, …, Alice$_n$ have encoded their corresponding x and y on them. According to the encoding operations Eqs. (3) and (4), the initial particle $\left|g_0^{(0)}\right\rangle = \frac{1}{\sqrt{d}}\sum_{j=0}^{d-1}|j\rangle$ have been changed to

$$V_d^{x_n^j} W_d^{y_n^j} \cdots V_d^{x_0^j} W_d^{y_0^j} \left|g_0^{(0)}\right\rangle = \left|g_{\sum_{k=0}^{n} x_k^j \bmod d}^{(\sum_{k=0}^{n} y_k^j \bmod d)}\right\rangle. \tag{9}$$

Server asks Alice$_1$, …, Alice$_n$ to declare the corresponding x in a random order. Then, he asks Alice$_1$, …, Alice$_n$ to declare the corresponding y in the reverse order. Server measures each sample particles with corresponding measurement base $(\sum_{k=1}^{n} y_k^j \bmod d)$. The measurement results are denoted as $R_0 = \left\{r_0^1, \ldots, r_0^{\xi}\right\}$. If R_0 satisfies

$$r_0^j = \sum_{k=0}^{n} x_k^j \bmod d, \tag{10}$$

Server declares that there does not exist eavesdropping. Otherwise, Server restarts the protocol.

Step 6. Server asks all participants to announce their Y of remanding particles. According to these messages, Server measures Q_n with corresponding measurement base $(\sum_{k=0}^{n} y_k^j \bmod d)$. The measurement results are denoted as $R = \{r_1, \ldots, r_{N+n\times\delta}\}$. According to Eq. (9), r_j satisfies

$$r_j = \sum_{k=0}^{n} x_k^j \bmod d. \tag{11}$$

Then, Server calculates

$$P_0 = \{p_0^j | p_0^j = (x_0^j - r_j) \bmod d,\ j = 1,\ldots,N + n \times \delta\} \tag{12}$$

and publishes P_0.

Step 7. The n participants choose δ particles from the remaining $N + n \times \delta$ particles as a sample and execute the eavesdropping check, respectively. For example, Alice$_i$ randomly chooses δ particles and publishes the positions of the chosen particles. He asks other participants to declare the corresponding x in a random order. If these sample particles satisfy

$$(p_0^j + \sum_{k=1}^{n} x_k^j) \bmod d = 0, \tag{13}$$

it shows that Server publishes the true P_0. Otherwise, Server may publish the fake message. Then, all participants ask Server to restarts the protocol.

Step 8. The remaining N particles are composed a new sequence. Alice$_1$, …, Alice$_n$ respectively calculate equation

$$P_i = \{p_i^j | p_i^j = (x_i^j + m_i^j) \bmod d,\ j = 1,\ldots,N\}, \tag{14}$$

then they publish P_i. Server calculates

$$S = \{s_j | s_j = \sum_{k=0}^{n} p_k^j \bmod\ d,\ j = 1,\ldots,N\} \tag{15}$$

For s_j, we have

$$\begin{aligned} s_j &= \sum_{k=0}^{n} p_k^j \bmod\ d \\ &= ((x_0^j - r_j) + \sum_{k=1}^{n} (x_k^j + m_k^j)) \bmod d \\ &= (\sum_{k=0}^{n} x_k^j - r_j + \sum_{k=1}^{n} m_k^j) \bmod d \\ &= \sum_{k=1}^{n} m_k^j \bmod d, \end{aligned} \tag{16}$$

which is the summation of Alice$_1$, …, and Alice$_n$'s private data. Actually, everyone could calculate S correctly since all P_i has been published. We assign Server to calculate S just for the convenience of expression.

Step 9. Server publishes S.

3.2 Secure Multiparty Quantum Summation Without Module d

If n participants want to jointly compute the summation without module d, i.e. $F = \{f_j | f_j = \sum_{k=1}^{n} m_k^j, j = 1, \ldots, N\}$, the Chinese remainder theorem is a useful method to achieve this summation task. Protocol 2 is the application of the Chinese remainder theorem.

Without the Chinese remainder theorem, if n participants want to jointly compute the summation without module d, Server has to choose a great prime number d_f which satisfies $d_f > n \times m_{\max}$ and generates d_f-level single particles. However, it is very hard to generate d_f-level quantum particles when d_f is a large number. In this case, we could use the Chinese remainder theorem to reduce the level of single particles, by which we only need generate some different small d-level single particles rather than d_f-level quantum particles. Therefore, Protocol 2 is very practical.

Protocol 2 is detailedly described as follows.

Protocol 2

Step i. Server chooses q different prime numbers $d_1, \ldots, d_q$, which satisfy the equation

$$D = \prod_{k=1}^{q} d_k > n \times m_{\max}, \tag{17}$$

where m_{max} represents the maximal value of data sets.

Step ii. Server begins from $k = 1$ and repeatedly executes Protocol 1 based on d_k-level single particles. Then, Server gets q calculation results $S_1, \ldots, S_q$, where $S_k = \{s_k^j | s_k^j \in Z_{d_k}, j = 1, \ldots, N\}, k = 1, \ldots, q$.

Step iii. According to $S_1, \ldots, S_q$ and $d_1, \ldots, d_q$, Server can calculate the final summation $F = \{f_j, j = 1, \ldots, N\}$ using the Chinese remainder theorem. In detail, these data satisfy the following equations:

$$\begin{aligned} f_j \bmod d_1 &= s_1^j, \\ f_j \bmod d_2 &= s_2^j, \\ &\ldots, \\ f_j \bmod d_q &= s_q^j. \end{aligned} \tag{18}$$

Server holds $S_1, \ldots, S_q$ and $d_1, \ldots, d_q$. Using the Eq. (6), Server gets the summation without module d as Eq. (19). Actually, everyone could calculate F correctly since $S_1, \ldots, S_q$ and $d_1, \ldots, d_q$ has been published. We ask Server to calculate F just for the convenience of expression.

Step iv. Server publishes F.

$$
\begin{aligned}
f_j &= \sum_{k=1}^{q} (D_k \times e_k \times s_k^j) \bmod D, \\
D &= \prod_{k=1}^{q} d_k, \\
D_k &= \frac{D}{d_k}, \\
e_k &\times D_k \bmod d_k = 1, \\
k &= 1, \ldots, q.
\end{aligned} \tag{19}
$$

4 Security Analysis

In this section, we analyze the security of the multiparty quantum summation protocols proposed in Sect. 3. Except for step ii in Protocol 2, Server executes only simple classical calculations which have no effect on the security of the protocol. Furthermore, the security of step ii is based on Protocol 1. Hence, the security of Protocol 2 is the same as Protocol 1's. Therefore, we mainly analyze the security of Protocol 1 in this section.

In Protocol 1, after receiving the particles sequence, Server and participants could use the photon number splitter and the wavelength filter to detect the Trojan horse attacks [17]. Hence, this attack is invalid to our protocol.

According to the attacks from different roles, we divide the possible attacks into three cases. The first one is the attack from an external eavesdropper (Eve). The second case is that one or more dishonest participants try to obtain the private data of other honest participants. In the third case, the attack from Server is discussed.

4.1 Outside Attack

In general, we assume that Eve wants to steal the key of Alice$_i$. When single particles sequence Q_{i-1} is transmitted between Alice$_{i-1}$ and Alice$_i$, Eve intercepts Q_{i-1}. Because Eve does not know the value of sequence $X_0 = \{x_0^j | x_0^j \in Z_d, j = 1, \ldots, N + (n+1) \times \xi + n \times \delta\}$, he has to measure Q_{i-1} with random measurement bases. Therefore, Eve chooses the correctly measurement bases with the probability $1/d$ for every single particle. Then, Eve prepares some fake single particles according to his measurement bases and the measurement results. After that, he transmits the fake single particles to Alice$_i$.

When Alice$_i$ receives the fake single particles from Eve, he selects ξ sample particles randomly and keeps them. In step 4 of Protocol 1, Alice$_i$ executes eavesdropping checks. For every sample single particle, Alice$_i$ measures it with corresponding measurement bases. If Eve measures the single particle with correctly measurement bases, Eve can escape the eavesdropping check. If Eve measures it with wrong measurement bases, the measurement result of Alice$_i$ is a random number, Eve can escape the eavesdropping check with probability $1/d$. Therefore, for every sample single particle,

Eve can escape the eavesdropping check with probability $\frac{1}{d} \times 1 + \frac{d-1}{d} \times \frac{1}{d} = \frac{2d-1}{d^2}$. There are ξ sample particles, so Alice$_i$ can detect the existence of Eve with probability $1 - \left(\frac{2d-1}{d^2}\right)^{\xi}$. When ξ is enough larger number, it is close to 1. Hence, this attack is invalid to our protocol.

4.2 Participant Attack

In this kind of attack, several dishonest participants collaborate to eavesdrop on the key of one honest participant (called Alice$_i$). In secure n-party quantum summation, there are at most $n-2$ dishonest participants. If there are $n-1$ dishonest participants, they could easily compute the only one honest participant's private data by the summation results and their private data. The attack from the dishonest participants is analyzed in detail as follow.

This attack succeeds only when it cannot be detected in Alice$_i$'s eavesdropping check. In step 4, Alice$_i$ executes the eavesdropping check with the help of Server and the participants ahead of him. The participants behind of him have nothing to do with Alice$_i$'s eavesdropping check. In step 4, Alice$_i$ asks the participants ahead of him to publish their x before Server and their y after Server. Therefore, we can treat the participants ahead of Alice$_i$ as a unit (called Alice$_1^*$).

In step 2 and step 3 of our protocol, Alice$_1^*$ receives the sequence Q_0 from Server and transmits the sequence Q_{i-1} to Alice$_i$. If Alice$_1^*$ could measure the sequence Q_0 with the corresponding measurement bases, then he could generate a correct fake sequence and transmit it to Alice$_i$ without being detected. However, Alice$_1^*$ does not know the measurement bases of sequence Q_0 since he does not know y_0. Alice$_1^*$ has to store Q_0 and transmits a random fake sequence to Alice$_i$.

In step 4 of our protocol, if Alice$_1^*$ publishes x and y both after Server, he could publish fake information to escape the eavesdropping check. For the convenience of expression, we analyze every single particle in detail, respectively. We assume that the fake single particle which Alice$_1^*$ transmits to Alice$_i$ is $G_{x',y'} = \left|g_{x'}^{(y')}\right\rangle = \frac{1}{\sqrt{d}} \sum_{k=0}^{d-1} \omega^{k(x'+y'k)}|k\rangle$. In the eavesdropping check, if Server publishes x_0 and y_0 both before Alice$_1^*$, Alice$_1^*$ could publish fake $x'' = (x' - x_0) \bmod d$ and $y'' = (y' - y_0) \bmod d$. Then, Alice$_i$ measure the fake single particle $G_{x',y'} = \left|g_{x'}^{(y')}\right\rangle$ with the corresponding MUB $y' = (y'' + y_0) \bmod d$ to get result $x' = (x'' + x_0) \bmod d$ which satisfies the Eq. (8). Therefore, Alice$_1^*$ escapes the eavesdropping check. However, Alice$_i$ asks Alice$_1^*$ to publish x before Server. Because Alice$_1^*$ still does not know the corresponding measurement bases of Q_0, he could not get x_0. Hence, Alice$_1^*$ could not publish a corresponding fake number according to x_0. Therefore, Alice$_i$ could detect the existence of attacker.

In conclusion, participant attack is invalid to our protocol.

4.3 Server's Attack

In this part, we will discuss the attack from Server. In our protocol, Server generates and measures the quantum single particles. Hence, it is more possible for him to escape the eavesdropping check. Since Server only holds x_0 and measurement results, he cannot infer participants' key through these information. If Server wants to steal the data of participants, he has to execute active attack. In our protocol, Server is permitted to execute attack by himself, but conspire with none of the participants. There are two attack strategies that Server may adopt. The details are descripted as follows.

The First Attack Strategy. At first, we assume that Server wants to steal the data of Alice$_1$. In Protocol 1, Server prepares the sequence Q_0 and sends it to Alice$_1$. When Alice$_1$ transmits sequence Q_1 to Alice$_2$ in step 2, Server intercepts this sequence. Then, Server generates a fake particle sequence Q_1^f with the length of $N + n \times \xi + n \times \delta$, and sends this sequence to Alice$_2$. Because the measurement bases of sequence Q_1 are decided by y_0 and y_1 and Server does not know y_1, Server has to store the sequence Q_1 until the Y is declared in step 6. However, Alice$_2$ executes the eavesdropping check in step 4. Alice$_2$ firstly asks Alice$_1$ and Server to publish their corresponding x in order. Because Server still does not know y_1, he cannot measure sequence Q_1 with correct measurement bases. He has to publish the correct x_0 of sample particles. Since Alice$_2$ receives the fake particle sequence Q_1^f instead of Q_1, Eq. (8) does not hold. Therefore, Alice$_2$ terminates the protocol. Server gets no information of Alice$_1$'s data.

In general, we assume that Server wants to steal the data of Alice$_i$. In this case, we could treat Alice$_1$, …, Alice$_{i-1}$ as a unit. Just like Alice$_2$, Alice$_i$ could detect the eavesdropping. Hence, Server cannot get any information of participants' data.

The Second Attack Strategy. In order to mislead participants, Server may publish a fake P_0 in step 6 of Protocol 1. After that, he could be the only one who obtains the correct summation. In step 7 of Protocol 1, all participants randomly choose δ particles to verify the correctness of P_0, respectively. If Server publishes a fake P_0 in step 6 of Protocol 1, the Eq. (13) will not be satisfied. Then, all participants could discover the fake P_0. Therefore, this attack is invalid to our protocol.

5 Conclusion

In this paper, we first present an efficient multiparty quantum summation module d protocol with d-level single particles rather than entangled states which is more difficult to generate. In this protocol, a semi-trusted additional party is introduced to help multiple participants achieve summation task. In order to compute the summation without module d, the Chinese remainder theorem is used in our second protocol. Finally, we analyze the security of our protocols and prove that they can resist some well-known attacks.

Acknowledgments. This work is supported by NSFC (Grant Nos. 61671087, 61272514, 61170272, 61003287), the Major Science and Technology Support Program of Guizhou Province (Grant Nos. 20183001), the Fok Ying Tong Education Foundation (Grant No. 131067), and Open Foundation of Guizhou Provincial Key Laboratory of Public Big Data (2017BDKFJJ007).

References

1. Yao, A.C.: Protocols for secure computations. In: Proceedings of the 23rd Annual IEEE Symposium on Foundations of Computer Science, pp. 160–164. IEEE, Chicago (1982)
2. Shamir, A.: How to share a secret. Commun. ACM **22**(11), 612–613 (1979)
3. Clifton, C., Kantarcioglu, M., Vaidya, J., et al.: Tools for privacy preserving distributed data mining. ACM SIGKDD Explor. Newsl. **4**(2), 28–34 (2002)
4. Sanil, A.P., Karr, A.F., Lin X., et al.: Privacy preserving regression modelling via distributed computation. In: Proceedings of the Tenth ACM SIGKDD International Conference on Knowledge Discovery and Data Mining, pp. 677–682. ACM, Seattle (2004)
5. Atallah, M., Bykova, M., Li, J., et al.: Private collaborative forecasting and benchmarking. In: Proceedings of the 2004 ACM Workshop on Privacy in the Electronic Society, pp. 103–114. ACM, Washington (2004)
6. Shi, R.H., Mu, Y., Zhong, H., Cui, J., et al.: Secure multiparty quantum computation for summation and multiplication. Sci. Rep. **6**, 19655 (2016)
7. Du, J.Z., Chen, X.B., Wen, Q.Y., et al.: Secure multiparty quantum summation. Acta Physica Sinica **56**, 6214 (2007)
8. Chen, X.B., Xu, G., Yang, Y.X., et al.: An efficient protocol for the secure multi-party quantum summation. Int. J. Theor. Phys. **49**(11), 2793–2804 (2010)
9. Zhang, C., Sun, Z., Huang, Y., et al.: High-capacity quantum summation with single photons in both polarization and spatial-mode degrees of freedom. Int. J. Theor. Phys. **53**(3), 933–941 (2014)
10. Zhang, C., Sun, Z.W., Huang, X., et al.: Three-party quantum summation without a trusted third party. Int. J. Quant. Inf. **13**(02), 1550011 (2015)
11. Zhang, C., Situ, H.Z., Huang, Q., et al.: Multi-party quantum summation without a trusted third party based on single particles. Int. J. Quant. Inf. **15**(02), 1750010 (2017)
12. Liu, W., Wang, Y.B., Fan, W.Q.: An novel protocol for the quantum secure multi-party summation based on two-particle Bell states. Int. J. Theor. Phys. **56**(9), 2783–2791 (2017)
13. Tavakoli, A., Herbauts, I., Żukowski, M., et al.: Secret sharing with a single d-level quantum system. Phys. Rev. A **92**(3), 030302 (2015)
14. Lin, S., Guo, G.D., Huang, F., et al.: Quantum anonymous ranking based on the Chinese remainder theorem. Phys. Rev. A **93**(1), 012318 (2016)
15. Wootters, W.K., Fields, B.D.: Optimal state-determination by mutually unbiased measurements. Ann. Phys. **191**(2), 363–381 (1989)
16. Ding, C., Pei, D., Salomaa, A.: Chinese Remainder Theorem: Applications in Computing, Coding, Cryptography. World Scientific, Singapore (1996)
17. Deng, F.G., Li, X.H., Zhou, H.Y., et al.: Improving the security of multiparty quantum secret sharing against Trojan horse attack. Phys. Rev. A **72**(4), 044302 (2005)

Survey and Analysis of Cryptographic Techniques for Privacy Protection in Recommender Systems

Taiwo Blessing Ogunseyi(✉) and Cheng Yang

College of Information Engineering, Communication University of China, Beijing, China
ogunseyitaiwo@outlook.com, cafeeyang@163.com

Abstract. In recent years, internet is packed with a lot of information, which has prevented timely retrieval of useful information. Recommender systems have helped to solve this information surplus and also provide personalized information retrieval. However, for an efficient recommendation, the recommender systems require users' personal information which is a serious privacy concern for many. Some Cryptographic techniques are used for protecting users' privacy in recommender systems while still allowing the system to generate a useful and accurate recommendation to the users. In this paper, we have surveyed recent studies, observed the current trends and proposed future insight in the use of cryptographic techniques e.g. homomorphic encryption for users' privacy protection in recommender systems. We have also highlighted the protocol used in terms of whether it is centralized or decentralized and some of their limitations e.g. heavy reliance on trusted/semi-trusted third party etc. In addition, we considered the adversary each protocol is protected against with the purpose of guiding researchers interested in the use of cryptographic techniques for privacy protection in recommender systems.

Keywords: Cryptographic techniques · Privacy protection
Recommender systems · Homomorphic encryption

1 Introduction

Currently, the quantity of information available on the internet nowadays has created information overload for internet users [1] which hampers timely retrieval of useful information. This problem has been somewhat solved by search engines but it lacks personalization [2]. Recommender systems have become a system known for suggesting personalized recommendations to users of online services.

The accuracy and effectiveness of the recommendations generated for users depends on the amount of users' private information known to the system. Some of the users' information needed for generating recommendations which are explicitly or implicitly generated from the users include users' ratings, consumption histories, preference and personal profiles [3]. Figure 1 shows a simple recommendation generation procedure from the data collection stage to the final output stage i.e. recommendations to users.

X. Sun et al. (Eds.): ICCCS 2018, LNCS 11065, pp. 691–706, 2018.
https://doi.org/10.1007/978-3-030-00012-7_63

This information (users' preferences) enables the recommender systems to make recommendations to users about other items that might be of interest [4]. Some of the most prevalent kinds of recommender systems are Collaborative filtering (CF), Content-based (CB) and the Hybrid approach. Others include Knowledge-based (KB), Context-aware (CA) and Demographic-based (DB) [3, 5–8]. Each method has its unique strengths and weakness [9].

With mass aggregate of data being generated every day from various sources e.g. social media, online shopping, etc., [45] big data has brought about an opportunity to draw insight from this immense dataset for better decision making. However, this era of big data has come with its own problem of privacy protection, which is associated with all of its phases, namely data collection, data storage and data processing. Therefore, it is expected that the privacy of big data should be ensured across these stages. Figure 1 shows an example of the stages involved in the big data lifecycle using a recommender systems framework.

The advancement in technology has made the collection of big data, its storage and processing much easier and affordable [42]. Data can now be collected through users' interaction with websites and apps. Data storage technology such as cloud computing is now being used for big data storage, technologies such as machine learning, artificial intelligence, etc. are now used for data processing. In addition, recommender systems as a data mining tool have helped to make sense of the data and then generate recommendations to users based on the extracted useful information. However, the common problem in big data, data mining and even recommender systems, remains the issue of the privacy of users' information [1] which is mostly underestimated by service providers. This privacy challenge could be in the form of unsolicited access to users' information either by service providers or their employees, unlawful data disclosure, selling of users' information to third party, or hacking, which could wreak havoc and damage users' privacy [43]..

Cryptography has been proven to be a very useful technique in addressing privacy and security challenges, particularly in recommender systems [4]. Cryptographic techniques have helped to protect user privacy, hence ensuring equilibrium between user privacy, data utility and the accuracy of recommender systems. This paper surveys data privacy protection in recommender systems and analyzes the various cryptographic approaches used for privacy protection in recommender systems under different protocols (centralized and decentralized protocol) with the intention of showing the current research trends, and highlighting the applications and challenges of cryptographic techniques for privacy protection in recommender systems.

In Sect. 2, the authors introduce data privacy in recommender systems under two different adversaries. Section 3 discusses the various cryptographic techniques for privacy protection in recommender systems for both centralized and decentralized protocols. Section 4 focuses on the limitations for some of the existing solutions while Sects. 5 and 6 covers the current trends, proposed future insights and conclusion respectively.

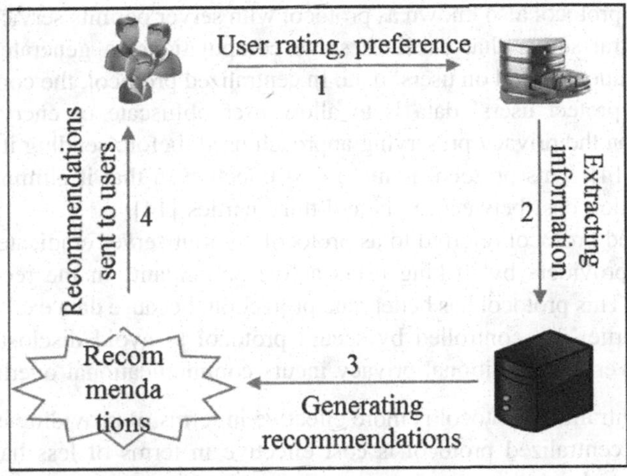

Fig. 1. Simple recommender systems

2 Data Privacy in Recommender Systems

Recommender systems poses a threat to users' privacy as users' personal information can be hacked, leaked or misused. Cryptography supports the design of privacy-preserving protocols that protect users' information even in the presence of malicious adversaries [10], hence helps to preserve confidentiality. The two kinds of adversaries considered in cryptography are semi-honest (honest but curious) and malicious adversary.

- A semi-honest (honest but curious) adversary correctly carries out all computation and follows all protocol, but the adversary attempts to learn additional information about the computation and protocol executed.
- A malicious adversary may stray from the specified protocol by colluding with other malicious parties or acting alone in order to infringe on the integrity of the computation and protocol [10, 11]. Privacy protection protocols should be designed in the event that both adversaries exist so as to ensure system security against any of these adversaries.

3 Cryptographic Techniques

Cryptographic techniques are generally used for privacy protection in recommender systems and to preserve confidential data [12]. The amount of privacy protection provided for users' information is partly determined by the protocol used in the design of the privacy- preserving recommender systems. The protocols used can either be centralized or decentralized protocols.

- Centralized protocol also known as protocol with server permits service providers to have a central server that executes some computations to generate user-specific recommendations based on users' data. In centralized protocol, the common method adopted to protect users' data is to allow user obfuscate or encrypt their data, depending on the privacy preserving approach used, before sending it to the central server [13, 14]. This protocol is more cost effective in that it eliminates the extra communication cost between users and third parties [14].
- Decentralized protocol referred to as protocol without server eradicates the reliance on service providers by making users active participants in the recommendation process [3]. This protocol has better data protection, because data exchange between involved parties are controlled by secure protocol to avoid disclosure of private data. However, that additional privacy incurs communicational overhead [14].

While the decentralized protocol is more effective in terms of providing enhanced data protection, the centralized protocol is cost effective in terms of less bandwidth, less execution time and storage.

Some of the cryptographic techniques used in privacy preserving recommender systems include; homomorphic encryption (HE), secure multi-party computation (SMC), secret sharing (SS) and zero-knowledge proofs (ZKP) [3, 13, 15]. HE [16] and SMC supports both centralized and decentralized protocol and also safeguards against semi-honest and malicious adversaries, depending on their implementation. SS mostly supports centralized protocol and safeguards against malicious adversary, whereas ZKP supports decentralized protocol and it's safe against semi-honest adversary. The authors provide an outline of the techniques used in some of the state-of-the-art literature, classifying them under the protocol used and the adversary protected against as presented in Table 1.

3.1 Homomorphic Encryption

Homomorphic encryption (HE) is a cryptosystem that permits computation on ciphertext without the knowledge of the actual value, thus generating a ciphertext that equals to the actual value when decrypted. It is the most common cryptographic technique used for privacy protection in recommender systems [12, 17] and it is also used together with other cryptographic techniques including secure multi-party computation, secret sharing, among others.

Figure 2 shows an architecture of a privacy preserving recommender system using homomorphic encryption for a decentralized protocol. For an arbitrary user who wants to generate recommendations, his/her preferences are being encrypted by the trusted third party and sent to the service providers for recommendation generation. The service provider performs computation on the encrypted data, and sends recommendations back to the trusted third party, who in turn decrypts the recommendation and now sends it to the user. For a centralized protocol, the same protocol is being followed, except that users do the encryption and decryption process on their own, hence eradicating the need for a trusted third party.

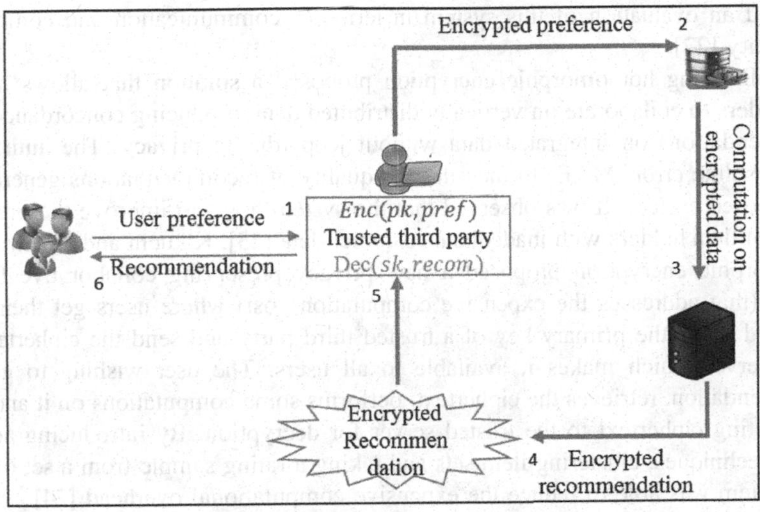

Fig. 2. Decentralized privacy preserving recommender systems using homomorphic encryption

Hsieh et al. adapted homomorphic encryption to preserve privacy in merging recommender system databases, in order to maximize precision of target marketing with 100% accuracy [18]. Zhan et al. employed homomorphic encryption and the scalar product approach to combine recommender systems databases between companies, which is similar to what Hsieh et al. asserted except with the use of the scalar product approach. This eliminated the need for a neutral/trusted third party in their system and thus made the system require less time and cost [19].

Tada et al. utilized Paillier additive homomorphic encryption for privacy protection of users' rating using item to item similarities for providing a prediction of arbitrary values of rating. These scholars argued that their item-base algorithm provides more accurate prediction of rating with 90% accuracy of the optimal solution and reduces both communication and computational overhead in the conventional user-based algorithm than the conventional algorithms [20]. Using a novel homomorphic encryption scheme that processes real value data instead of the usual integer, Armknecht and Strufe proposed a distributed privacy preserving recommender systems for spot in location-based online social network. They divide the system users into two groups: the plain users and the premium users. The plain users send their information to the server without encrypting it, while the premium users can encrypt their data before sending it to the server for recommendation. Their proposed system was able to overcome some of the challenges related to the encryption of integers such as; exponential expansion of ciphertext size, complex computation etc. [21]. The paper by Basu et al. presented a privacy preserving item-based collaborative filtering scheme using additive homomorphic cryptosystem on weighted slope one predictor. Exploiting some of the advantages of the weighted slope one predictor which has shown to be accurate on large datasets, efficient to compute and able to work with sparse input [44], their proposed system was tested on vertical and horizontal partition datasets. They presented an evaluation of this system in terms of communication and computation complexity [22].

Kaleli, using homomorphic encryption proposed a solution that allows multiple data holders to collaborate on vertically distributed data, producing concordance-based recommendations on integrated data without jeopardizing privacy. The author used mean absolute error (MAE) to measure the quality of recommendations generated by the proposed system. It was observed that the system helps to improve the prediction quality of data holders with inadequate customer data [23]. Kikuchi and Kizawa, using homomorphic encryption proposed a new privacy preserving collaborative filtering scheme (that addresses the expensive computation cost) where users get their rating encrypted using the primary key of a trusted third party and send the ciphertext to a public server which makes it available to all users. The user wishing to generate recommendation, retrieves the ciphertext, performs some computations on it and sends the resulting ciphertext to the trusted server for decryption. By introducing approximation techniques, clustering item sets and taking a rating sample from a set of users, their system was able to reduce the expensive computational overhead [24].

Jeckmans et al. in their paper designed a collaborative algorithm that allows two companies to merge their customers' dataset to generate recommendations. Their neighborhood-based approach permits company A to encrypt its customers' data and send the ciphertext to company B which computes its contribution to the ciphertext in the encrypted domain. This allows company A to obtain aggregated and anonymized data which it uses to generate the top X recommendations for its customers [25]. In a paper by Erkin et al., they designed a privacy preserving content-based recommender system, using Paillier homomorphic encryption scheme. They introduced the look-up table and data packing, such that a user (Alice) who wants a recommendation encrypts her rating and sends it to the service provider (Bob) who computes the item-item similarity in the encrypted domain and sends the resulting ciphertext to Alice to decrypt and generate recommendations on her own. The introduction of the look-up table and data packing were advantageous as these help to drastically reduce the computational and communication overhead [26].

Badsha et al. proposed a privacy preserving recommender system which allows all computation to be done in a privately distributed manner using ElGamal homomorphic encryption, without compromising recommendation accuracy and efficiency. This is semantically secure and permits certain types of computations on the ciphertext. The system involves users' active participation in the recommendation process [4]. The authors later proposed another user-based approach that protect users' data using BGN homomorphic cryptosystem and the weighted sum approach to predict item score. The authors adopt the use of BGN and the weighted sum approach because they support secure multiplying of two different cipher texts and also a more efficient method to generate recommendations [17]. Tang and Wang analyzed an earlier JPH solution, highlighting some of its shortcomings and proposed a better protocol which generates recommendations when friends are offline using a somewhat homomorphic encryption [27].

Having considered the various forms in which HE has been applied and the various approaches used, it is therefore, evident that HE is one of the cryptographic techniques that provides vigorous privacy for users' information in recommender systems.

Table 1. Analyzes of cryptographic technique used by recent studies

Cryptographic techniques	Year of publication	Reference no	Protocol used		Adversary guard against	
			Centralized	Decentralized	Semi-honest	Malicious
Homomorphic encryption	2008	18		✓	✓	
	2008	19		✓	✓	
	2010	20	✓		✓	
	2011	21		✓	✓	
	2011	22		✓	✓	
	2012	23		✓	✓	
	2012	24		✓	✓	
	2012	25		✓	✓	
	2012	26	✓		✓	
	2015	28	✓		✓	
	2016 & 2017	27 & 17		✓	✓	
Secure Multi-party computation (only or with homomorphic encryption)	2007	31		✓		✓
	2008	7		✓		✓
	2010	32		✓	✓	
	2011 & 2012	33 & 34	✓		✓	
	2014	35	✓			✓
	2015	36		✓	✓	
	2015	30		✓		✓
Secret sharing	2015	38	✓			✓
	2015	39	✓			✓
ZKP	2012	41		✓	✓	

3.2 Secure Multi-party Computation

This is an aspect of cryptography that allows different parties to perform joint computation on their inputs, without revealing the input [28].

Figure 3 shows a generic framework for a centralized (protocol) secure multi-party computation recommender systems. For an arbitrary number of users/companies that intend to have a joint computation on their data (input), for the purpose of generating recommendations without jeopardizing privacy, encrypt their data and send it to a central server that computes the recommendation and then send the resulting ciphertext to user for decryption. In theory, secure multi-party computation techniques allows users to securely and jointly compute the recommendations themselves, however, for a large number of users, that approach is impractical [29].

Ahmad and Khokhar proposed a framework based on the biclustering algorithm which eliminates the need for a trusted server. They ensured privacy by using secure

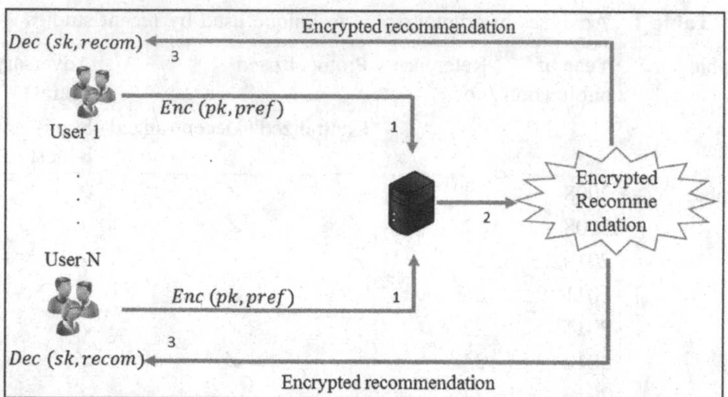

Fig. 3. Privacy preserving recommender systems with secure multi-party computation

multi-party computation carried out by additive homomorphic cryptosystem. An analysis of their system shows that the system is scalable [30]. Aimeur et al. in their approach to privacy preservation developed a hybrid recommender system that supports demographic filtering, content-based and collaborative filtering recommender systems together using secure two-party computation. Their system called ALAMBIC shared users' data between Merchant (service provider) and Still Maker (a semi-trusted third party) such that none of these two parties can solely derive sensitive information from the user data except they collude [7]. Hoens et al. proposed a system that enables users to query a neighborhood of their social network to learn recommendations about a product. They integrated their system with Facebook's social network using secure multi-party computation and homomorphic encryption to preserve the privacy of individual user ratings [31]. Erkin et al. used homomorphic encryption and secure multi-party computation to preserve the privacy of users in a centralized protocol. They used data packing to reduce the overhead caused by the use of these cryptographic techniques [32]. The authors further improved the system and introduced a semi-trusted third party who is trusted to perform the assigned task correctly, but not allowed to observe the private data, however the same cryptographic techniques were used [33]. Li et al. proposed an efficient privacy preserving item based collaborative filtering recommender system using secure multi-party computation. In their system item similarities are calculated incrementally using an unsynchronized approach (which achieves joint computation even when users are not simultaneously online at the same time) [34]. Samanthula et al. proposed two methods to privacy preserving friend recommender system, one of their approaches uses secure multi-party computation and additive homomorphic encryption in protecting users' privacy. In this method, a target user A can get friend recommendations from his/her list of friends by using the common neighbor method [35]. Veugen et al. using secure multi-party computation, proposed a two-server recommender system where one of the servers act as the service provider and the other server as a privacy service provider. With the help of a preprocessing phase, independent of users' input, and suitable for dealing with a large number of users, they provide a generic framework for outsourcing ongoing computation. Their approach allows an arbitrary number of users to securely outsource a computation to the two-non-colluding servers [29].

Secure multi-party computation, as one of the cryptographic techniques, is mostly used when individual (users) or companies have to merge their dataset together to make recommendations, and can be used with homomorphic encryption.

3.3 Secret Sharing

Secret sharing is a scheme in which different shares are distributed to parties such that only fixed subsets of parties can reconstruct the secret. Secret sharing is an important tool in cryptography and can be used as a building block in many secure protocols [36].

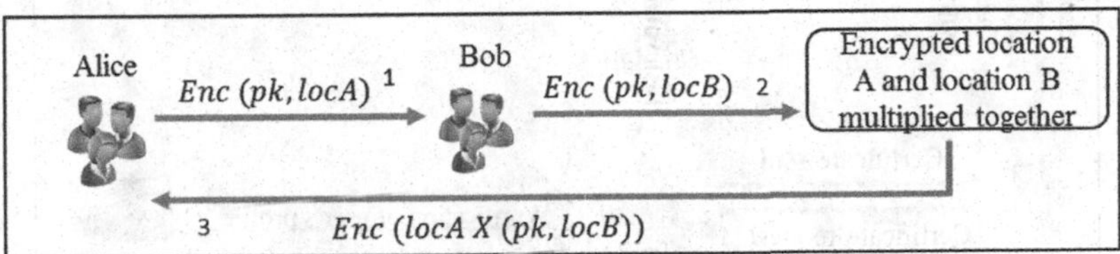

Fig. 4. Privacy preserving recommender systems with secret sharing (adapted from [37])

Figure 4 shows a simple secret sharing framework, where Alice encrypts her location A, and sends it to Bob. Bob encrypts his location B, with his public key, and also multiplies his location B with Alice's location A, in the encrypted domain, which results in a new ciphertext. Bob now sends the resulting ciphertext to Alice. For Alice to decrypt the shared secret, she applies the combined decryption key (contributed by her and Bob), since the resulting ciphertext are encrypted with both of their encryption keys and multiplied together.

Shieh proposed an end to end encrypted domain proximity recommender system, using secret sharing homomorphic cryptography. The system which allows all users to generate their private and public key, uses a 3D geometric location privacy for alerting people of nearby friends. The system permits users to protect their exact location but still receives an alert if there's a nearby friend or to know when their friends are getting closer [37]. In their work, Asny et al. proposed privacy preserving collaborative filtering recommender systems, their framework allows an arbitrary number of users to securely outsource a computation to two non-colluding external servers. They used a secret sharing scheme to share a set of values between the two external servers, that can't individually determine the values except when they come together [38].

Secret sharing permits individuals to hold a subset of the secret, which one individual alone cannot make sense of.

3.4 Zero Knowledge Proof

In cryptography, ZKPs are used as a method for entity authentication [39]. This protocol is a proof of some statements which does not disclose anything other than the accuracy of the statements [39]. It involves two entities, a prover who intends to prove a statement and a verifier who wants to authenticate, in a certain way if the statement is correct.

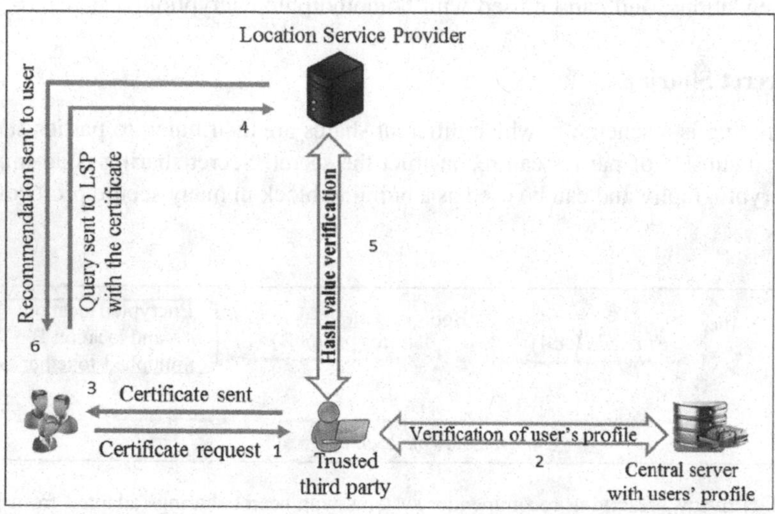

Fig. 5. Privacy preserving recommender systems with zero knowledge proof

Figure 5 shows a framework for a basic zero knowledge proof recommender system. Here the central server, which is managed by the trusted third party, contains all users' information. The user (Prover) is able to prove to the location service provider (LSP) (Verifier) that he/she is authorized to generate spot recommendation without the user revealing his/her present location to the LSP. For an arbitrary user who wants to generate recommendations, the trusted third party, having verified the user's identity, generates an encrypted certificate for the user, and also calculates the hash value of the encrypted certificate and stores it. The user sends the encrypted certificate to the LSP (verifier) along with the recommendation query. The LSP in turn calculates the hash value of the certificate and compares this with the hash value stored by the trusted third party. If the hash values are the same, the LSP responds and sends a recommendation back to the user, otherwise the user cannot get the recommendation.

Jagwani and Kaushik employed zero knowledge proof for protecting users' location in location-based recommender systems. In their design, middleware (trusted third party) generates certificates for users (Prover) in an encrypted form, the user sends this certificate to the location service provider (Verifier) when it need to generate a recommendation. The location service provider can then be assured of users' authenticity by this certificate without knowing any information about users' location; this helps the users to get the needed recommendation without disclosing their location to the service provider [40].

4 Limitations of Some Existing Solutions

The main limitations with most cryptographic techniques are the computational and communication overhead [20, 24, 41] which has made it difficult for practical implementation. Some of the observed limitations in the study surveyed are classified into several categories and presented in Table 2.

i. For some studies, the limitation was the heavy reliance on trusted/semi-trusted third parties which could be in the form of an external server or a privacy service provider. This reliance incurs more communication cost which makes the system impractical to implement, though this is done to ensure more privacy. Instances of such studies include [4, 17, 32, 33].
ii. Another limitation is the users' active involvement in the recommendation generation process, which hampers recommendation accuracy, as most systems with this limitation requires at least t user to be online most times in order to generate recommendations. Examples of these studies are [31–33].
iii. Studies with other limitations observed are as follows. The researchers in [19] built their merger recommender system on homomorphic encryption and the scalar product approach but the need for a commodity server for generating random numbers will incur more computational costs. The inability of a weighted slope one predictor in [22] to support binary ratings is seen as a limitation in the study. Paper [7] developed a hybrid recommender system on the assumption that the service provider and the semi-trusted third party will not collude (which cannot be guaranteed) without an indicator to detect if they collude. Paper [35], in one of its approaches used universal hash function for improving efficiency, but that comes at the expense of system accuracy.

Table 2. Summary of the observed limitations in the literature

S/N	Observed limitations	Reference no
1	Reliance on trusted/semi-trusted third party	[4, 17, 32, 33]
2	Users' active involvement in recommendation generation	[31–33]
3	Other limitations	[7, 19, 22, 35]

5 Current Trends and Future Directions in Privacy Preserving Recommender Systems

5.1 Current Trends

Since the emphasis of this research is on the use of cryptographic techniques (HE, SMC, SS, and ZKP) for privacy protection in recommender systems, every study surveyed used at least one cryptographic technique for privacy protection in their proposed recommender systems. We consider that as a generic trend, hence, in this section we focus on current (specific) trends in the provision of privacy for recommender systems using any of the cryptographic techniques discussed earlier.

Various researches take different approaches to privacy protection in recommender systems hence there are different trends in the provision of privacy for recommender systems. By examining the recent state-of-the-art literature, we identified the following trends.

i. Some researches focus on providing more robust privacy in recommender systems, such studies use one or more cryptographic techniques to ensure the privacy of users' data. Examples of such studies include [30–33, 35].
ii. Some studies focus on improving the performance of the existing schemes (cryptographic techniques) used for privacy protection in recommender systems, so as to reduce the computational and communication overhead. Such studies include those that utilize data packing, a look-up table, encryption of real numbers instead of integers. Instances of such state-of-the-art are [21, 26].
iii. And some other studies focus on improving the recommender systems performance and accuracy while preserving privacy, some of these studies combined two or more recommendation algorithms. Examples of such studies include [7, 20, 22, 30–32].

In future studies, the researcher intend to follow the trend of improving the performance of cryptographic techniques used in privacy protection for recommendation generation by researching on the use of ElGamal homomorphic cryptosystem and data packing for privacy protection in recommender systems.

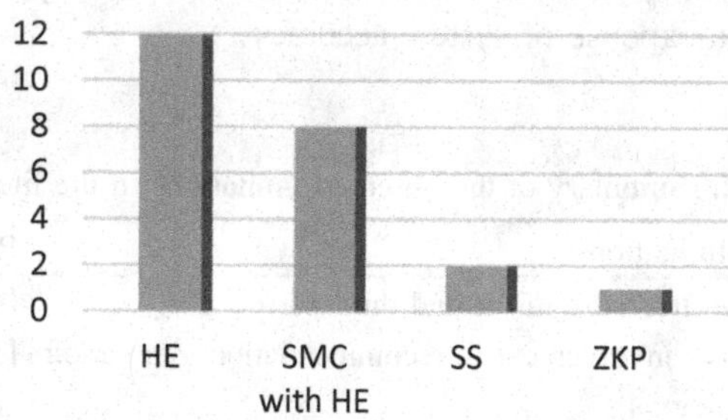

Fig. 6. Cryptographic techniques used for privacy protection in existing solutions

5.2 Solutions and Directions for Future Study

Based on the literature reviewed, the authors have highlighted some of the limitations of privacy protection in recommender systems, while pointing out the current trends. As a result the authors present directions for future study which will provide solutions to the problems identified above. Some of the solutions are;

i. Blockchain: Blockchain can be used for a decentralized personal data management system that ensures users own and control their data [46]. It can offer an enhanced security for privacy of sensitive data. Various decentralized privacy preserving systems have been proposed based on blockchain technology [47].

ii. Quantum computing: The practical use of quantum computing for absolute privacy protection is becoming eminent. Quantum computing can offer fantastic solutions for security and privacy protection, while providing blind computing such that through this method, a quantum server can compute a task for a user without knowing the input, output or the identity of the user [48].

iii. Game theory: Game theory is used in recommender systems to deal with conflict and cooperation between intelligent and rationale decision-makers [48] e.g. users, service providers etc. It has been widely used in various security and privacy studies. Studies such as [49] have employed game theory to address the trade-off between privacy preservation and high-quality recommendations.

iv. Machine learning: Machine learning can also be applied in the security domain to provide security and privacy [50]. A comprehensive study was done by [50] to examine various researches on machine learning for security and privacy. Similarly, studies such as [51–53] have deployed machine learning for security and privacy protection in various systems like recommender systems, cloud computing etc.

6 Conclusion

In this paper, the authors have reviewed the various cryptographic techniques used for privacy protection in recommender systems in most recent studies, classifying them under the protocol used (as either centralized or decentralized), and the adversary protected against (semi-honest or malicious adversaries). In addition, we have highlighted the limitations in some of the studies, showed the current trends and provided future insight for privacy protection of recommender systems. In order to guide researchers interested in the use of cryptographic techniques for privacy protection, and also to show some of the applications and challenges of cryptographic techniques for privacy protection in recommender systems. The researchers also call for more research in the use of other cryptographic techniques for privacy protection in recommender systems as Fig. 6 shows that little or no research has been done in the use of secret sharing and zero knowledge proof for privacy protection in recommender systems. This will help to take advantage of these techniques to further provide a more robust privacy for users' data in location-based recommender systems.

References

1. Ozturk, A., Polat. H.: From existing trends to future trends in privacy-preserving collaborative filtering. Wiley Interdiscip. Rev. Data Min. Knowl. Discov. **5**(6), 276–291 (2015)
2. Isinkaye, F.O., Folajimi, Y.O., Ojokoh, B.A.: Recommendation systems: principles, methods and evaluation. Egypt. Inform. J. **16**(3), 261–273 (2015)

3. Jeckmans, A.J.P., Beye, M., Erkin, Z., Hartel, P., Lagendijk, R.L., Tang, Q.: Privacy in recommender systems. In: Ramzan, N., van Zwol, R., Lee, J.S., Clüver, K., Hua, X.S. (eds.) Computer Communications and Networks, pp. 263–281. Springer, London (2013). https://doi.org/10.1007/978-1-4471-4555-4_12
4. Badsha, S., Yi, X., Khalil, I.: A practical privacy-preserving recommender system. Data Sci. Eng. **1**(3), 161–177 (2016)
5. Itmazi, J., Gea, M.: The recommendation systems, types, domains and the ability usage in learning management system. In: 2006 International Arab Conference on Information Technology (ACIT 2006), December 2006
6. Daniar, A.: Algorithms and methods in recommender systems. In: Other Conferences, vol. 1, no. 2, pp. 417–444 (2015). https://www.snet.tu-berlin.de/fileadmin/fg220/courses/SS11/snet-project/recommender-systems_asanov.pdf
7. Aımeur, E., Brassard, G., Fernandez, J.M., Onana, F.S.M.: Alambic: a privacy-preserving recommender system for electronic commerce. Int. J. Inf. Secur. **7**(5), 307–334 (2008)
8. Wu, Z., Li, G., Liu, Q., Xu, G., Chen, E.: Covering the sensitive subjects to protect personal privacy in personalized recommendation. IEEE Trans. Serv. Comput. **11**(3), 493–506 (2016)
9. Adomavicius, G., Tuzhilin, A.: Toward the next generation of recommender systems: a survey of the state of the art and possible extensions. IEEE Trans. Knowl. Data Eng. **17**(6), 734–749 (2005)
10. Sharma, A., Ojha, V.: implementation of cryptography for privacy preservation data mining. J. Database Manag. **2**(3), 57–65 (2010)
11. Yakoubov, S., Gadepally, V., Schear, N., Shen, E., Yerukhimovich, A.: A survey of cryptographic approaches to securing big-data analytics in the cloud. In: 2014 IEEE High Performance Extreme Computing Conference, HPEC 2014 (2014)
12. Batmaz, Z., Kaleli, C.: Methods of privacy preserving in collaborative filtering. In: 2nd International Conference on Computer Science and Engineering, pp. 261–266 (2017)
13. Zhao, Y., Chow, S.S.M.: Privacy preserving collaborative filtering from asymmetric randomized encoding. In: Böhme, R., Okamoto, T. (eds.) FC 2015. LNCS, vol. 8975, pp. 459–477. Springer, Heidelberg (2015). https://doi.org/10.1007/978-3-662-47854-7_28
14. Casino, F., Patsakis, C., Puig, D., Solanas, A.: On privacy preserving collaborative filtering: current trends, open problems, and new issues. In: 2013 IEEE 10th International Conference on E-bus. Eng. (ICEBE), pp. 244–249 (2013)
15. Goldreich, O.: Foundations of cryptography: a primer. Found. Trend Theor. Comput. Sci. **1**, 11–116 (2005)
16. Bilge, A., Kaleli, C., Yakut, I., Gunes, I., Polat, H.: A survey of privacy-preserving collaborative filtering schemes. Int. J. Soft. Eng Knowl. Eng. **23**(8), 1085–1108 (2013)
17. Badsha, S., Yi, X., Khalil, I., Bertino, E.: Privacy preserving user-based recommender system. In: Proceedings - International Conference on Distributed Computer Systems, pp. 1074–1083 (2017)
18. Hsieh, C.-L.A., Zhan, J., Zeng, D., Wang, F.: Preserving privacy in joining recommender systems. In: International Conference on Information Security and Assurance, Busan, Korea, pp. 561–566 (2008)
19. Zhan, J., Wang, I.-C., Hsieh, C.-L., Hsu, T.-S., Liau, C.-J., Wang, D.-W.: Towards efficient privacy-preserving collaborative recommender systems. In: IEEE International Conference on Granular Computing, Hangzhou, China, pp. 778–783 (2008)
20. Tada, M., Kikuchi, H., Puntheeranurak, S.: Privacy preserving collaborative filtering protocol based on similarity between items. In: Twenty-Fourth IEEE International Conference on Advanced Networking and Applications, Perth, Australia (2010)

21. Armknecht, F., Strufe, T.: An efficient distributed privacy preserving recommendation system. In: Tenth IEEE IFIP Annual Mediterranean Ad Hoc Networking Workshop, Favignana Island, Sicily, Italy, pp. 65–70 (2011)
22. Basu, A., Kikuchi, H., Vaidya, J.: Privacy-preserving weighted slope one predictor for item-based Collaborative filtering. In: Proceedings of the International Workshop on Trust and Privacy in Distributed Information Processing, Copenhagen, Denmark (2011)
23. Kaleli, C.: Privacy-preserving concordance-based recommendations on vertically distributed data. In: Tenth International Conference on ICT and Knowledge Engineering, Bangkok, Thailand, pp. 19–24 (2012)
24. Kikuchi, H., Kizawa, H.: Privacy-preserving collaborative filtering schemes with sampling users. J. Jpn. Soc. Fuzzy Theory Intell. Inform. **24**(3), 753–762 (2012)
25. Jeckmans, A., Tang, Q., Hartel, P.: Privacy-preserving collaborative filtering based on horizontally partitioned dataset. In: International Conference on Collaboration Technologies and Systems, Denver, CO, USA, pp. 439–446 (2012)
26. Erkin, Z., Beye, M., Veugen, T., Lagendijk, R.L.: Privacy preserving content-based recommender system. In: Proceedings of the Fourteenth ACM Workshop on Multimedia and Security, Coventry, United Kingdom (2012)
27. Tang, Q., Wang, J.: Privacy-preserving context-aware recommender systems: analysis and new solutions. In: Pernul, G., Ryan, P.Y.A., Weippl, E. (eds.) ESORICS 2015. LNCS, vol. 9327, pp. 101–119. Springer, Cham (2015). https://doi.org/10.1007/978-3-319-24177-7_6
28. http://everything.explained.today/Secure_multi-party_computation/. Accessed 17 Jan 2018
29. Veugen, T., De Haan, R., Cramer, R., Muller, F.: A framework for secure computations with two non-colluding servers and multiple clients, applied to recommendations. IEEE Trans. Inf. Forensics Secur. **10**(3), 445–457 (2015)
30. Ahmad, W., Khokhar, A.: Privacy preserving collaborative filtering using biclustering in ubiquitous computing environments. In: Proceedings of Fifth International Workshop on Databases, Information Systems and Peer-to-Peer Computing, Vienna, Austria (2007)
31. Hoens, T.R., Blanton, M., Chawla, N.V.: A private and reliable recommendation system for social networks. In: International Conference on Privacy, Security, Risk and Trust, Minneapolis, USA (2010)
32. Erkin, Z., Beye, M., Veugen, T., Lagendijk, R.L.: Efficiently computing private recommendations. In: IEEE International Conference on Acoustics, Speech and Signal Processing, Prague, Czech Republic, pp. 5864–5867 (2011)
33. Erkin, Z., Veugen, T., Toft, T., Lagendijk, R.L.: Generating private recommendations efficiently using homomorphic encryption and data packing. IEEE Trans. Inf. Forensics Secur. **7**(3), 1053–1066 (2012)
34. Li, D., et al.: An algorithm for efficient privacy-preserving item-based collaborative filtering. Future Gener. Comput. Syst. **55**, 311–320 (2016)
35. Samanthula, B.K., Cen, L., Jiang, W., Si, L.: Privacy-preserving and efficient friend recommendation in online social networks. Trans. Data Priv. **8**(2), 141–171 (2015)
36. Beimel, A.: Secret-sharing schemes: a survey. In: Third International Workshop on Coding and Cryptology, IWCC, Qingdao, China, vol. 1, pp. 1–36 (2011)
37. Shieh, J.: An end-to-end encrypted domain proximity recommendation system using secret sharing homomorphic cryptography. In: The Forty-Ninth IEEE International Carnahan Conference on Security Technology (ICCST 2015), Taipei, Taiwan (2015)
38. Asny, P.A., Santhosh, S.M.: A Secure schema for recommendation systems. Int. J. Cybern. Inform. **5**(2), 99–107 (2016)
39. Mohr, A.: A Survey of Zero-Knowledge Proofs with Applications to Cryptography, pp. 1–12. Southern Illinois University, Carbondale (2008)

40. Jagwani, P., Kaushik, S.: Defending location privacy using zero knowledge proof concept in location based services. In: Proceedings of 2012 IEEE 13th International Conference on Mobile Data Management MDM 2012, pp. 368–371 (2012)
41. Damgård, I., Ishai, Y., Krøigaard, M.: Perfectly secure multiparty computation and the computational overhead of cryptography. In: Gilbert, H. (ed.) EUROCRYPT 2010. LNCS, vol. 6110, pp. 445–465. Springer, Heidelberg (2010). https://doi.org/10.1007/978-3-642-13190-5_23
42. Mehmood, A., Natgunanathan, I., Xiang, Y., Hua, G., Guo, S.: Protection of big data privacy. IEEE Access **4**, 1821–1834 (2016)
43. Tang, Q., Wang, J.: Privacy-preserving friendship-based recommender systems. IEEE Trans. Dependable Secur. Comput. **5971**(c), 1 (2016)
44. Lemire, D., Maclachlan, A.: Slope One Predictors for Online Rating-Based Collaborative Filtering. Society for Industrial Mathematics, Philadelphia (2007)
45. Wu, X., Wu, T., Khan, M., Ni, Q., Dou, W.: Game theory based correlated privacy preserving analysis in big data. IEEE Trans. Big Data **7790**(c), 1 (2017)
46. Zyskind, G., Nathan, O., Pentland, A.: Decentralizing privacy: using blockchain to protect personal data, pp. 180–184 (2015)
47. Zheng, Z., Xie, S., Dai, H.-N., Wang, H.: Blockchain challenges and opportunities: a survey. Int. J. Web Grid Serv. (January), 1–24 (2017)
48. Yu, S.: Big privacy: challenges and opportunities of privacy study in the age of big data. IEEE Access **4**, 2751–2763 (2016)
49. Halkidi, M., Koutsopoulos, I.: A game theoretic framework for data privacy preservation in recommender systems. In: Gunopulos, D., Hofmann, T., Malerba, D., Vazirgiannis, M. (eds.) ECML PKDD 2011. LNCS (LNAI), vol. 6911, pp. 629–644. Springer, Heidelberg (2011). https://doi.org/10.1007/978-3-642-23780-5_50
50. Jiang, H., Nagra, J., Ahammad, P.: SoK: applying machine learning in security - a survey (2016). http://arxiv.org/abs/1611.03186
51. Hesamifard, E., Takabi, H., Ghasemi, M., Jones, C.: Privacy-preserving machine learning in cloud. In: Proceedings of the 2017 on Cloud Computing Security Workshop - CCSW 2017, pp. 39–43 (2017)
52. Abadi, M., et al.: Deep learning with differential privacy. In: 23rd ACM Conference on Computer and Communication Security (CCS 2016) (2016)
53. Shokri, R., Shmatikov, V.: Privacy-preserving deep learning. In: ACM Conference on Computer and Communication Security, CCS 2015 (2015)

The CP-ABE with Full Verifiability Outsourced Decryption and White-Box Traceability

Li Cong(✉), Yang Xiaoyuan, Liu Yazhou, and Wang Xu'an

Key Laboratory of Network and Information Security of the Chinese Armed Police Force, Xi'an 710086, Shaanxi, China
wugongcong@163.com

Abstract. In the CP-ABE scheme, the private key is defined on attributes shared by multiple users. For any private key that can not be traced back to the owner of the original key, the malicious users may sell their decryption privileges to third parties for economic benefit and will not be discoverable. In addition, most of the existing ABE schemes have a linear increase in decryption cost and ciphertext size with the complexity of access structure. These problems severely limit the application of CP-ABE. By defining the traceable table to trace the user who intentionally disclosed the key, the cost of the decryption operation is reduced through the outsourcing operation, in this paper, a CP-ABE scheme was proposed that is traceable and fully verifiability for outsourced decryption. The scheme can simultaneously check the correctness for transformed ciphertext of the authorized user and unauthorized user. And this scheme supports any monotonous access structure, increasing traceability in the existing CP-ABE scheme will not have any impact on its security. This paper is proved to be selective CPA-secure in the standard model.

Keywords: Attribute-Based Encryption · Full verifiability
Outsourced decryption · Traceability · CPA-security

1 Introduction

In recent years, with the development of cloud computing, how to implement secure storage of sensitive data is a problem that needs to be solved. Sahai et al. [1]. firstly proposed the concept of Attribute-Based Encryption (ABE) to implement the confidentiality and flexible access control of user encrypted data. In ABE, identities are described by a set of attributes. ABE schemes are usually divided into two types [2]: one is a Key-Policy Attribute-Based Encryption (KP-ABE) and the other is a Ciphertext-Policy Attribute- Based Encryption(CP-ABE).

In many existing CP-ABE schemes, the bilinear pairing operation and decryption time increase with the complexity of the access policy. Users with limited resources will not be able to handle such complex bilinear pairings or take a long time to decrypt them. In order to reduce the user's computational cost and decryption time, Green et al. [3]. proposed an outsourced decryption of ABE scheme, in this scheme, the user reduce the computational complexity by performing partial decryption calculations with the

X. Sun et al. (Eds.): ICCCS 2018, LNCS 11065, pp. 707–719, 2018.
https://doi.org/10.1007/978-3-030-00012-7_64

cloud serveroutsources. In order to solve the above problems, researchers have proposed some ABE schemes with verifiable outsourced decryption [4–7].

In addition, the traditional CP-ABE solution has another problem of private key leakage that needs to solute. The decryption key is defined on attributes shared by multiple users and is not uniquely associated with personal identification information. Although it allows the CP-ABE to implement efficient one-to-many encryption and access control, however, since there are always many users sharing their attributes, so the decryption key is not traceable after being maliciously sold. In order to solve the problem of the decryption key's traceability in the ABE systems, the researchers has proposed the traceable ABE systems [8]. The traceable ABE is divided into white box traceable ABE [9, 10] and black box traceable ABE. Liu et al. [9] proposed the white-box-traceable CP-ABE systems that supported arbitrary monotonic access structure for the first time based on the composite medium group, and proved that the scheme is adaptive secure. Li et al. [11] proposed for the first time a multi-authority traceable CP-ABE scheme, but it only supports the access structure of the "AND". Zhou et al. [12] proposed a multi-authority traceable CP-ABE scheme that supported a monotonic access structure, but the calculation and storage overhead of this scheme is too large. And at present, the most scheme cannot support key trace and outsourced computing at the same time.

Our Motivation and Contribution. In this paper, we proposed a traceable and fully verifiable outsourced decryption CP-ABE scheme, it focuses on achieving white-box traceable with high expressiveness, and it support any monotonic access structure and adaptive security, and each decryption key can be traced to its owner. At the same time, local users use cloud computing's powerful computing capabilities to reduce decryption computational complexity through outsourced decryption methods. And it can check the correctness of outsourced transformation ciphertext of authorized users and unauthorized users. In this scheme, We design two different access policies for authorized users and non-authorized users, respectively. Then, we add a message authentication code (MAC) in each ciphertext to ensure that users can verify the correctness of the converted ciphertext. In addition, the structure of this paper has the characteristics of "verify-decrypt" rather than "decrypt-verify", that is, after the user receives the transformation ciphertext from the cloud service providers (CSP), the user first verifies the correctness of the transformation ciphertext with his own private key, if the transformation ciphertext is right, the user decrypts the ciphertext and obtains a plaintext or random message; otherwise, it is wrong. This scheme has proved to be selective CPA security in the standard model.

2 Preliminaries

2.1 Message Authentication

The message authentication code (**Mac**,**Vrfy**) is a probabilistic polynomial time (PPT) [13]. The authentication algorithm enters a message $M \in \mathcal{M}$ and a key $\eta \in \mathcal{K}$, and outputs a series of labels $tag \in \mathcal{T}$, where $\mathcal{M}$ is the message space, $\mathcal{K}$ is the key space, and $\mathcal{T}$ is the label space. The verification algorithm enters the message M, key η, and tag *tag*, and finally it outputs 1 for acceptance and 0 for rejection. If for all M and η, $Vrfy_\eta(M, \mathrm{Mac}_\eta(M)) = 1$, the message M is authenticated.

2.2 Assumptions

Definition 1 (***l-SDH*** **Assumption) [9]:** Let $\mathbb{G}$ be a bilinear group, where p is the prime order of group $\mathbb{G}$ and g is the generator of $\mathbb{G}$. The l-Strong Diffie-Hellman (l-*SDH*) assumption can be described as follows:
It inputs $(g, g^x, g^{x^2}, \cdots, g^{x^l})$, it calculates and outputs a pair $(c, g^{1/(x+c)}) \in \mathbf{Z}_p \times \mathbb{G}$, where $x \in \mathbf{Z}_p^*$, $c \in \mathbf{Z}_p^*$. If $\Pr\left[\mathcal{A}(g, g^x, g^{x^2}, \cdots, g^{x^l}) = (c, g^{1/(x+c)})\right] \geq \epsilon$, then the advantage of algorithm $\mathcal{A}$ in solving the l-*SDH* problem is ϵ

If the advantageϵ of the probabilistic polynomial time (PPT) algorithm in solving the l-*SDH* assumption is negligible, then the l-*SDH* assumption holds in the group $\mathbb{G}$.

3 Our System Model and Security Definition

The CP-ABE scheme consists of the following eight algorithms: Setup, KeyGen, Encrypt, Decrypt, KeyGen, Transform, Decrypt, Trace.

3.1 Security Definition

This section proposes a selective CPA security model that supports the traceable and full verifiability of outsourced decryption CP-ABE schemes. It can be described by the following game between the attacker $\mathcal{A}$ and the challenger $\mathcal{C}$.

Init: The attacker $\mathcal{A}$ sets a challenge access policy $\mathbb{A}^*$ that it wishes to challenge.

Setup: The challenger $\mathcal{C}$ executes the initialization algorithm Setup$(1^\lambda, U)$ and transmits *PK* to the attacker $\mathcal{A}$, and keeps *MSK* for itself.

Phase 1: Firstly it sets the set D and the table F are initialized to empty, and the attacker $\mathcal{A}$ initiates the following query to the challenger $\mathcal{C}$:

(1) Private key query: The attacker $\mathcal{A}$ performs key query on the attribute S, The challenger $\mathcal{C}$ runs a key generation algorithm to generate the private key SK_S, and sets $D = D \cup \{S\}$, Then private key SK_S is returned to the attacker's $\mathcal{A}$, but the restriction is that the private key cannot satisfy the access policy $\mathbb{A}^*$.
(2) Transformation key query: The attacker $\mathcal{A}$ makes the transformation key query on the attribute S, and the challenger $\mathcal{C}$ the tuple (S, SK_S, TK_S, RK_S). If this tuple exists, TK_S is returned to $\mathcal{A}$. Otherwise, it runs the transformation key generation algorithm is to obtain (TK_S, RK_S), and stores the tuple (S, SK_S, TK_S, RK_S) in table F, and it returns TK_S to $\mathcal{A}$.

We assume that if a user has issued a private key query for a set of attributes S, $\mathcal{A}$ will not perform the transformation key query for this same attribute S. Otherwise, $\mathcal{A}$ can directly ultilize the transformation key generation algorithm to obtain the transformation key.

Challenge: The attacker $\mathcal{A}$ submits two plain text M_0, M_1 with the same string. Then the challenger $\mathcal{C}$ random selects a bit $\beta \in \{0, 1\}$ and a message R with the same character length as the plaintext M_0, M_1. It encrypts M_β and R to generate ciphertext $(CT^*_{M_\beta}, CT^*_R)$. The challenger calculates $\text{Mac}_{\eta*}(CT^*_{M_\beta}) \rightarrow \sigma^*_{M_\beta}$ and $\text{Mac}_{\eta_2}(CT^*_R) \rightarrow \sigma^*_R$. Finally, the challenger ciphertext $(CT^*_{M_\beta}, CT^*_R, \sigma^*_{M_\beta}, \sigma^*_R, \mathbb{A}^*)$ is sent to the attacker $\mathcal{A}$.

Phase 2: In this phase, the attacker $\mathcal{A}$ continues the same private key queries with ***Phase 1***. But the only restriction is that the private key attribute cannot satisfy access policy $\mathbb{A}^*$.

Guess: The attacker $\mathcal{A}$ outputs its guess $\beta' \in \{0, 1\}$ for β, if $\beta' = \beta$, the attacker wins the game.

The advantage of the attacker $\mathcal{A}$ in the game can be defined to be $|\Pr[\beta = \beta'] - 1/2|$.

Definition 2: If all polynomial-time adversaries have negligible advantages in the above security model, an outsourced decryption CP-ABE schemes with traceable and full verification is selective CPA-secure.

4 Our Traceable and Full Verifiability CP-ABE System

In this section, we propose a Traceable and Full Verifiability for Outsourced Decryption in CP-ABE (T-FVO-CP-ABE). In this system, a tracking mechanism can be used to determine if a legitimate user has sold a private key. Meanwhile, by studying the outsourcing decryption of Green [3], we set up two access structures, which can also verify the transform ciphertext of authorized users and unauthorized users.

Setup$(1^\lambda, U)$: This algorithm takes attribute sets $U = \{1, 2, \cdots, l\}$ and security parameters 1^λ as input. It runs $\mathcal{G}(1^\lambda)$ to obtain a bilinear group $(p, \mathbb{G}, \mathbb{G}_T, e)$, where $\mathbb{G}$ and $\mathbb{G}_T$ are multiplicative cyclic groups with prime order p. It selects a random generator $g \in \mathbb{G}$, random values $\alpha, a \in \mathbf{Z}^*_p$ and $h_1, h_2, \cdots, h_{|U|} \in \mathbb{G}$, and calculates $y = g^a$. And then it selects three collision-resistance hash functions $H_1 : \mathbb{G}_T \rightarrow \mathbf{Z}_p$, $H_2 : \{0, 1\}^* \rightarrow \mathbb{G}, H_3 : \mathbb{G}_T \rightarrow \{0.1\}^m$. Finally, it outputs the master secret key $MSK = \alpha$ and the public parameters $PK = (\mathbb{G}, \mathbb{G}_T, e, g, y, e(g, g)^\alpha, \{T_i = g^{h_i}\}_{i \in U}, H_1, H_2, H_3)$.

KeyGen(PK, MSK, S): The algorithm inputs the public parameters PK and the master secret key MSK generate two types of private keys for authorized users and non-authoritative users. It randomly selects a value $c \in \mathbf{Z}^*_p$. If S is the authorized user's attribute set, it selects a random value $t_1 \in \mathbf{Z}^*_p$ to generate the authorized user's private key: $SK_{DS} = (DS, K = g^{\alpha/(a+c)} y^{t_1}, K' = c, L = g^{t_1},\ L' = g^{at_1}, \{K_i = T_i^{(a+c)t_1}\}_{i \in DS})$. If S is the non-authorized user's attribute set, it selects a random value $t_2 \in \mathbf{Z}^*_p$ to generate the non- authorized user's private key:

$$SK_{VS} = (VS, KP = g^{\alpha/(a+c)} y^{t_2}, KP' = c, LP = g^{t_2},\ LP' = g^{at_2}, \{KP_i = T_i^{(a+c)t_2}\}_{i \in VS})$$

Encrypt$(PK, M, \mathbb{A}_1, \mathbb{A}_2)$: The algorithm inputs a plaintext message $M \in \{0.1\}^m$ and two LSSS [14] access structures $\mathbb{A}_1 = (\boldsymbol{A}_1, \rho_1), \mathbb{A}_2 = (\boldsymbol{A}_2, \rho_2)$. Where $\boldsymbol{A}_1$ and $\boldsymbol{A}_2$ are both $l \times n$ matrices, ρ_1 is a mapping from the first row $\boldsymbol{A}_{1,i}$ in matrix $\boldsymbol{A}_1$ to a attribute $\rho_1(i)$. ρ_2 is a mapping from the first row $\boldsymbol{A}_{2,i}$ in the matrix $\boldsymbol{A}_2$ to a attribute $\rho_2(i)$. Firstly it selects a random string $R \in \{0.1\}^m$ and two random vectors $\boldsymbol{v}_1 = (s_1, v_{12}, \cdots, v_{1n}) \in Z_p^{*n}$ and $\boldsymbol{v}_2 = (s_2, v_{22}, \cdots, v_{2n}) \in Z_p^{*n}$. For each row $\boldsymbol{A}_{1,i}$ and $\boldsymbol{A}_{2,i}$ in the matrix $\boldsymbol{A}_1$ and $\boldsymbol{A}_2$, it computes $\lambda_{1,i} = \boldsymbol{A}_{1,i} \cdot \boldsymbol{v}_1$ and $\lambda_{2,i} = \boldsymbol{A}_{2,i} \cdot \boldsymbol{v}_2$ respectively, and randomly picks $r_{1,i}, r_{2,i} \in \boldsymbol{Z}_p^*$. Then it calculates the ciphertext:

$$C_M = M \oplus H_3(e(g,g)^{\alpha s_1}), \quad \eta_1 = H_1(e(g,g)^{\alpha s_1}), \quad C_1 = g^{s_1}, \quad C_1' = g^{a s_1},$$
$$C_{1,i} = y^{\lambda_{1,i}} T_{\rho_1(i)}^{-r_{1,i}}, \quad D_{1,i} = g^{r_{1,i}}, \quad \forall i \in \{1,2,\cdots,l\}, \quad C_{TM} = (C_M, C_1, C_1', \{C_{1,i}, D_{1,i}\}_{i\in[l]})$$

and

$$C_R = M \oplus H_3(e(g,g)^{\alpha s_2}), \quad \eta_2 = H_1(e(g,g)^{\alpha s_2}), \quad C_2 = g^{s_2}, \quad C_2' = g^{a s_2}$$
$$C_{2,i} = y^{\lambda_{2,i}} T_{\rho_2(i)}^{-r_{2,i}}, \quad D_{2,i} = g^{r_{2,i}}, \quad \forall i \in \{1,2,\cdots,l\}, \quad C_{TR} = (C_R, C_2, C_2', \{C_{2,i}, D_{2,i}\}_{i\in[l]})$$

Set:

$$\sigma_1 = H_2(C_M \| C_R)^{\eta_1}, \quad \sigma_M = \{\sigma_1, H_2(C_M \| C_R)\}$$
$$\sigma_2 = H_2(C_M \| C_R)^{\eta_2}, \quad \sigma_R = \{\sigma_2, H_2(C_M \| C_R)\}$$

Finally it outputs the ciphertext: $CT = (\mathbb{A}_1, \mathbb{A}_2, C_{TM}, \sigma_M, C_{TR}, \sigma_R)$.

Decrypt(SK, CT, S): The algorithm inputs the private key SK, attribute set S, and ciphertext CT.

(1) If the attribute set S satisfies access policy $\mathbb{A}_1$, and $SK = SK_{DS}$. It can calculate a fixed value $\omega_{2,i} \in \boldsymbol{Z}_p^*, i \in I$ such that $\sum_{i\in I} \omega_{1,i} \boldsymbol{A}_{1,i} = (1,0,\cdots,0)$ and then calculate:

$$D_M = \prod_{\rho_1(i)\in S} \left(e(L^{K'}L', C_{1,i}) \cdot e(K_{\rho_1(i)}, D_{1,i})\right)^{\omega_{1,i}} = \prod_{\rho_1(i)\in S} \left(e(g^{ct_1} g^{at_1}, y^{\lambda_{1,i}} T_{\rho_1(i)}^{-r_{1,i}}) \cdot e(T_{\rho_1(i)}^{(a+c)t_1}, g^{r_{1,i}})\right)^{\omega_{1,i}}$$
$$= \prod_{\rho_1(i)\in S} e(g,y)^{(a+c)t_1\omega_{1,i}\lambda_{1,i}} = e(g,y)^{(a+c)t_1 s_1}$$

$$E_M = e\left(K, C_1^{K'} C_1'\right) = e\left(g^{\alpha/(a+c)} y^{t_1}, g^{cs_1} g^{as_1}\right) = e(g,g)^{\alpha s_1} \cdot e(g,y)^{(a+c)t_1 s_1}$$

$\eta_1 = H_1(E_M/D_M)$. Whether $e(\sigma_1, g) = e(H_2(C_M \| C_R), g^{\eta_1})$ is true. If it is true, then we can calculate the plaintext $M = C_M \oplus H_3(E_M/D_M)$. Otherwise it outputs $\perp$.

(2) If the attribute set S satisfies access policy $\mathbb{A}_2$, and $SK = SK_{VS}$. It can calculate a fixed value $\omega_{2,i} \in \boldsymbol{Z}_p^*, i \in I$ such that $\sum_{i\in I} \omega_{2,i} \boldsymbol{A}_{2,i} = (1,0,\cdots,0)$ and then calculate:

$$D_R = \prod_{\rho_2(i)\in S}\left(e(LP^{KP'}LP', C_{2,i})\cdot e(KP_{\rho_2(i)}, D_{2,i})\right)^{\omega_{2,i}} = \prod_{\rho_2(i)\in S}\left(e(g^{ct_2}g^{at_2}, y^{\lambda_{2,i}}T_{\rho_2(i)}^{-r_{2,i}})\cdot e(T_{\rho_2(i)}^{(a+c)t_2}, g^{r_{2,i}})\right)^{\omega_{2,i}}$$
$$= \prod_{\rho_2(i)\in S} e(g,y)^{(a+c)t_2\omega_{2,i}\lambda_{2,i}} = e(g,y)^{(a+c)t_2 s_2}$$

$$E_R = e\left(KP, C_2^{KP'}C_2'\right) = e\left(g^{\alpha/(a+c)}y^{t_2}, g^{cs_2}g^{as_2}\right) = e(g,g)^{\alpha s_2}\cdot e(g,y)^{(a+c)t_2 s_2}$$

$\eta_2 = H_1(E_R/D_R)$, Whether $e(\sigma_2, g) = e(H_2(C_M||C_R), g^{\eta_2})$ is true. If it is true, then we can calculate the plaintext $R = C_R \oplus H_3(E_M/D_M)$. Otherwise it outputs $\perp$.

KeyGen$_{out}$ (SK, PK): The outsource key generation algorithm inputs the master key PK and the private key SK. It selects two random values $z_1, z_2 \in Z_p^*$. If the user is an authorized user, it generates the transformation public key TK_{DS} of the authorized user. $TK_{DS} = (DS, K_1 = K^{1/z_1}, K_1' = K', L_1 = L^{1/z_1},\ L_1' = (L')^{1/z_1}, \{K_{1,i} = K_i^{1/z_1}\}_{i\in DS})$

If the user is an non- authorized user, it generates the transformation public key TK_{VS} of the non- authorized user.

$$TK_{VS} = (VS, KP_2 = KP^{1/z_2}, KP_2' = KP', LP_2 = LP^{1/z_2},\ LP_2' = (LP')^{1/z_2},\ \{KP_{2,i} = K_i^{1/z_2}\}_{i\in VS})$$

The corresponding transformation private key is $RK_{DS} = z_1$ and $RK_{VS} = z_2$.

Transform(TK, CT): The outsource decryption algorithm inputs ciphertext CT and transformation public key TK. If it is an authorized user, the transformation public key $TK = TK_{DS}$, and if it is an unauthorized user, the transformation public key $TK = TK_{VS}$. Then part of the decryption process is as follows:

$$D_M' = \prod_{\rho_1(i)\in S}\left(e(L_1^{K_1'}L_1', C_{1,i})\cdot e(K_{1,\rho_1(i)}, D_{1,i})\right)^{\omega_{1,i}} = \prod_{\rho_1(i)\in S}\begin{pmatrix} e(g^{ct_1/z_1}g^{at_1/z_1}, y^{\lambda_{1,i}}T_{\rho_1(i)}^{-r_{1,i}})\cdot \\ e(T_{\rho_1(i)}^{(a+c)t_1/z_1}, g^{r_{1,i}})\end{pmatrix}^{\omega_{1,i}}$$
$$= \prod_{\rho_1(i)\in S} e(g,y)^{(a+c)t_1\omega_{1,i}\lambda_{1,i}/z_1} = e(g,y)^{(a+c)t_1 s_1/z_1}$$

$$E_M' = e\left(K_1, C_1^{K_1'}C_1'\right) = e\left(g^{\alpha/(a+c)z_1}y^{t_1/z_1}, g^{cs_1}g^{as_1}\right) = e(g,g)^{\alpha s_1/z_1}\cdot e(g,y)^{(a+c)t_1 s_1/z_1}$$

unauthorized user:

$$D_R' = \prod_{\rho_2(i)\in S}\left(e(LP_2^{KP_2'}LP_2', C_{2,i})\cdot e(KP_{2,\rho_2(i)}, D_{2,i})\right)^{\omega_{2,i}} = \prod_{\rho_2(i)\in S}\left(e(g^{ct_2/z_2}g^{at_2/z_2}, y^{\lambda_{2,i}}T_{\rho_2(i)}^{-r_{2,i}})\cdot e(T_{\rho_2(i)}^{(a+c)t_2/z_2}, g^{r_{2,i}})\right)^{\omega_{2,i}}$$
$$= \prod_{\rho_2(i)\in S} e(g,y)^{(a+c)t_2\omega_{2,i}\lambda_{2,i}/z_2} = e(g,y)^{(a+c)t_2 s_2/z_2}$$

$$E_R' = e\left(KP_2, C_2^{KP_2'}C_2'\right) = e\left(g^{\alpha/(a+c)z_2}y^{t_2/z_2}, g^{cs_2}g^{as_2}\right) = e(g,g)^{\alpha s_2/z_2}\cdot e(g,y)^{(a+c)t_2 s_2/z_2}$$

If the attribute set S satisfies the access policy $\mathbb{A}_1$, the part of the decryption ciphertext $CT' = (C_M, D'_M, E'_M, \sigma_M)$ is output. If the attribute set S satisfies the access policy $\mathbb{A}_2$, the part of the decryption ciphertext $CT' = (C_R, D'_R, E'_R, \sigma_R)$ is output.

Decrypt$_{out}(CT, CT', RK)$: The decryption algorithm inputs the original ciphertext CT, part of the decryption ciphertext CT', and transformation private key RK. The authorized user transformation private key is $RK = RK_{DS}$ and the non- authorized user transformation private key is $RK = RK_{VS}$.

(1) If the attribute set S satisfies access policy $\mathbb{A}_1$, the user checks if $e(\sigma_1, g) = e(H_2(C_M||C_R), g^{H_1((E'_M/D'_M)^{z_1})})$ is true. If it is true, it outputs the plaintext $M = C_M \oplus H_3((E'_M/D'_M)^{z_1})$.
(2) If the attribute set S satisfies access policy $\mathbb{A}_2$, the user checks if $e(\sigma_2, g) = e(H_2(C_M||C_R), g^{H_1((E'_R/D'_R)^{z_2})})$ is true. If it is true, it outputs the plaintext $R = C_R \oplus H_3((E'_R/D'_R)^{z_2})$.

Trace(PK, T, SK): The algorithm inputs the public key PK, the traceable table T and the private key SK. If SK is the form of $SK = (K, K', L, L', \{K_i\}_{i \in S})$ and meets all of the following four checks, then it is a well-formed private key, whose decryption authority is described by the attribute set $S_\omega = \{i | i \in S \wedge e(T_i, L^{K'}L') = e(g, K_i) \neq 1\}$. Otherwise, it will output $\top$ to indicate that it is not a well-formed private key. If the key SK is well-formed, it will search if K' is in the T, if K' is in the traceable table T, the algorithm outputs the corresponding identity id, otherwise it outputs a special identity id_ϕ.

The key sanity check:

$$K' \in \mathbb{Z}_p^*,\ K,\ L,\ L',\ K_i \in \mathbb{G} \tag{1}$$

$$e(g, L') = e(g^a, L) \neq 1 \tag{2}$$

$$e(g^a g^{K'}, K) = e(g, g)^\alpha \cdot e(L^{K'} L', y) \neq 1 \tag{3}$$

$$\exists i \in S, s.t.\ e(T_i, L^{K'} L') = e(g, K_i) \neq 1 \tag{4}$$

5 Security Proof

5.1 IND-CPA Security

In this section, we will prove that the above scheme is to selectively CPA-secure. Since access policies $\mathbb{A}_1$ and $\mathbb{A}_2$ have the same proof method, this paper only considers the proof of access policy $\mathbb{A}_1$.

Theorem 1. If the outsourced decryption scheme of ABE [3] is selectively CPA-secure, and the message authentication code [15] is a one-time signature, then the scheme of this paper is selectively CPA-secure.

Proof: In order to prove the correctness of this theorem, we established three security games.

Game_0: The attacker $\mathcal{A}$ sends two equal-length challenge ciphertexts M_0, M_1 and challenges the access strategy $\mathbb{A}^*$, the challenger chooses a random bit $b \in \{0, 1\}$, The challenge ciphertext components $ct^{*'}$ and σ^* are calculated by algorithms $\text{Encrypt}'(PK, M_b, \mathbb{A}^*) \rightarrow ct^{*'}$ and $\text{Mac}_\eta(ct^{*'}) \rightarrow \sigma^*$, respectively, where η is calculated from the secret shared value. Finally it outputs the challenge ciphertext $(\mathbb{A}^*, ct^{*'}, \sigma^*)$.

Game_1: In addition to the attacker selecting two equal-length challenge messages, Game_1 and Game_0 are basically the same. The challenger $\mathcal{C}$ computes the component $ct^{*''}$ for the challenge ciphertext by the algorithm $\text{Encrypt}'(0^{l_1}, \mathbb{A}^*) \rightarrow ct^{*'}$, where 0^{l_1} is a random value of the same length as the message M_b. Finally it outputs the challenge ciphertext $(\mathbb{A}^*, ct^{*'}, \sigma^*)$.

Game_2: Game_2 is basically the same as Game_1, except that the challenge ciphertext returned to the attacker is different. The challenge ciphertext is calculated as follows: $\text{Encrypt}'(0^{l_1}, \mathbb{A}^*) \rightarrow ct^{*'}$, $\text{Mac}_\eta(0^{l_2}) \rightarrow \sigma^*$, where 0^{l_2} is a random value. Finally it outputs the challenge ciphertext $(\mathbb{A}^*, ct^{*'}, \sigma^*)$.

Lemma 1. If the attribute-based encryption scheme [3] is selectively CPA-secure, then Game_1 and Game_0 are computationally indistinguishable.

Proof: We assume that there is a PPT adversary with non-negligible advantages to distinguish Game_1 and Game_0, then we can find a simulator $\mathcal{B}$ to break the CPA security for ABE scheme [3] with a non-negligible advantage. If $\mathcal{C}$ is a challenger, $\mathcal{B}$ asks $\mathcal{A}$ to run the following steps:

Init: The adversary $\mathcal{A}$ sets a challenge access policy $\mathbb{A}^*$ that it wishes to challenge.

Setup$(1^\lambda, U)$: The challenger $\mathcal{C}$ executes the initialization algorithm $\text{Setup}'(1^\lambda, U)$ to obtain the master key pair, and the simulator $\mathcal{B}$ transmits the public parameter PK to the adversary $\mathcal{A}$.

Phase 1: The adversary $\mathcal{A}$ can obtain the results of the private key query and the transformation key query on the attribute S because $\mathcal{B}$ can run the same key query through challenger $\mathcal{C}$ to get the same result.

Challenge: The adversary $\mathcal{A}$ submits two plain text M_0, M_1 with the same string. Then the simulator $\mathcal{B}$ random selects a bit $b \in \{0, 1\}$ to calculate $\text{Mac}_\eta(\text{Encrypt}'(M_b, \mathbb{A}^*))$ for σ^*, it returns $(m_0, m_1) = (M_b, 0^{l_1})$ to the challenger $\mathcal{C}$. The challenger $\mathcal{C}$ random selects a bit $\beta \in \{0, 1\}$ and runs encryption algorithm $\text{Encrypt}'(m_\beta, \mathbb{A}^*)$ to generate ciphertext C^*. Finally, the simulator returns the challenge ciphertext $(\mathbb{A}^*, C^*, \sigma^*)$ to the adversary.

Phase 2: In this phase, the adversary $\mathcal{A}$ continues the same private key queries with ***Phase 1***. But the only restriction is that the private key attribute cannot satisfy access policy $\mathbb{A}^*$.

Guess: The adversary $\mathcal{A}$ outputs its guess $b' \in \{0, 1\}$ for b, if $b' = b$, the attacker wins the game.

When the ciphertext is generated by message M_b, we regard that $\mathcal{A}$'s view is exactly the same as Game$_0$. When $\mathcal{B}$'s encryption query responds with a random value 0^{l_1}, $\mathcal{A}$'s view is exactly the same as Game$_1$. According to the security of ABE scheme [3], we can determine that the advantages of distinguishing Game$_1$ and Game$_0$ are negligible.

Lemma 2. If the message authentication code used in this paper is strong one-time message authentication code, then there is no PPT adversary that distinguishes Game$_1$ and Game$_2$ with a non-negligible advantage.

Proof: We assume that there is a PPT adversary could distinguish Game$_1$ and Game$_2$ with a non-negligible advantage, then we can find a simulator $\mathcal{B}$ that breaks the strong one-time message authentication code with a non-negligible advantage. If $\mathcal{C}$ is a challenger, the simulator $\mathcal{B}$ asks the adversary $\mathcal{A}$ to perform the following steps:

Init: The attacker $\mathcal{A}$ sets a challenge access policy $\mathbb{A}^*$ that it wishes to challenge.

Setup$(1^\lambda, U)$: The challenger $\mathcal{C}$ executes the initialization algorithm Setup$'(1^\lambda, U)$ to obtain the master key pair (PK, MSK), and the simulator $\mathcal{B}$ transmits the public parameter PK to the adversary $\mathcal{A}$.

Phase 1: Since $\mathcal{B}$ owns the master key (PK, MSK), it can generate the transformation public key TK, and answer the relevant key inquiry and transformation n key inquiry.

Challenge: The adversary $\mathcal{A}$ submits two plain text M_0, M_1 with the same string. Then the simulator $\mathcal{B}$ random selects a bit $b \in \{0,1\}$ to calculate Encrypt$'(M_b, \mathbb{A}^*) \rightarrow C^{*'}$ and Encrypt$'(0^{l_1}, \mathbb{A}^*) \rightarrow C^*$, the simulator $\mathcal{B}$ retruns $(C_0^*, C_1^*) = (C^{*'}, 0^{l_2})$ to the challenger $\mathcal{C}$. The challenger $\mathcal{C}$ random selects a bit $\beta \in \{0,1\}$ and runs encryption algorithm $\text{Mac}_\eta(C_\beta^*) \rightarrow \sigma^*$ and transmits σ^* to $\mathcal{A}$. Finally, the simulator $\mathcal{B}$ returns the challenge ciphertext $(\mathbb{A}^*, C^*, \sigma^*)$ to the adversary $\mathcal{A}$.

Phase 2: In this phase, the adversary $\mathcal{A}$ continues the same private key queries with ***Phase 1***. But the only restriction is that the private key attribute cannot satisfy access policy $\mathbb{A}^*$.

Guess: The adversary $\mathcal{A}$ outputs its guess $b' \in \{0,1\}$ for b, if $b' = b$, the attacker wins the game.

Obviously, if σ^* is generated by $\text{Mac}_\eta(C_0^*)$, then $\mathcal{A}$'s view is exactly the same as Game1. If σ^* is generated by $\text{Mac}_\eta(C_1^*)$, $\mathcal{A}$'s view is exactly the same as Game$_2$. According to the strong one-time message authentication code scheme, it can be seen that the advantages of distinguishing Game$_1$ and Game$_2$ are negligible.

5.2 Full Verifiability

The following proves that our CP-ABE scheme is fully verifiable.

Theorem 2. If the hash function is collision-resistant, the outsourced decryption CP-ABE scheme constructed in this paper is fully verifiable.

Proof: We assume that there is a non-negligible advantage of a PPT attacker $\mathcal{A}$ can attack the verifiability of the outsourced decryption CP-ABE scheme. Then we can build an algorithm $\mathcal{B}$ attack message authentication with non-negligible advantage. The simulator $\mathcal{B}$ takes advantage of $(p, \mathbb{G}, \mathbb{G}_T, e)$ and runs the attacker $\mathcal{A}$ to perform the following steps:

Setup: The simulator $\mathcal{B}$ selects the random values $h_1, h_2, \cdots, h_{|U|} \in \mathbb{G}$ and $\alpha, a \in \mathbf{Z}_p^*$. At the same time it selects three collision-resistant hash functions $H_1 : \mathbb{G}_T \rightarrow \mathbb{Z}_p, H_2 : \{0,1\}^* \rightarrow \mathbb{G}, H_3 : \mathbb{G}_T \rightarrow \{0.1\}^m$, The simulator $\mathcal{B}$ sets the public parameter $PK = (\mathbb{G}, \mathbb{G}_T, e, g, y, e(g,g)^\alpha, \{T_i = g^{h_i}\}_{i \in U}, H_1, H_2, H_3)$ and master private key $MSK = \alpha$. Then, it sends the common parameter PK to the opponent $\mathcal{A}$.

Phase 1: Because $\mathcal{B}$ has a master key pair (PK, MSK), the adversary $\mathcal{A}$ can perform private key inquiry and transformation key inquiry.

Challenge: $\mathcal{A}$ submits a plaintext M^* and an access policy $\mathbb{A}^*$. Then $\mathcal{B}$ outputs ciphertext: $C_{TM}^* = (C_{M^{*\prime}}, C_1, C_1^{\prime}, \{C_{1,i}, D_{1,i}\}_{i \in [l]})$ and $\eta_1 = H_1(e(g,g)^{\alpha s_1})$, $\sigma_1 = H_2(C_{M^*} || C_R)^{\eta_1}$, $\sigma_{M^*} = \{\sigma_1, H_2(C_{M^*} || C_R)\}$. Where R is a randomly selected message of the same length as the plaintext M^*.

Phase 2: In this phase, the adversary $\mathcal{A}$ continues the same private key queries with ***Phase 1***.

Output: The adversary $\mathcal{A}$ outputs a set of attributes S^* and converted ciphertext $CT^{*\prime} = (C_{TM}^*, D_M^{\prime *}, E_M^{\prime *}, \sigma_{M^*})$. $\mathcal{B}$ calculates $\boldsymbol{Decrypt_{out}}(C_{TM}^*, CT^{*\prime}, RK^*)$ through the transformation private key RK^* that has obtained the plaintext M'. If the adversary $\mathcal{A}$ wins the game, simulator $\mathcal{B}$ can get $H_2(C_{M^*} || C_R)^{\eta_1} = H_2(C_{M'} || C_R)^{\eta_1}$, where $M' \neq M^*$, $C_{M^*} || C_R \neq C_{M'} || C_R$. However, because H_2 is a collision-resistant hash function, and $H_2(C_{M^*} || C_R)^{\eta_1} \neq H_2(C_{M'} || C_R)^{\eta_1}$. Therefore, the adversary cannot win the game with a non-negligible advantage.

5.3 Traceability

Lemma 3. Assume that the BB2 signature scheme [16] is not unforgeable in the presence of weak CPA, and the traceable and fully verifiable outsourced decryption CP-ABE scheme in this paper is traceablility.

Proof: Suppose there is a PT attacker that has a non-negligible advantage ϵ to win this traceable game, we can construct a simulation algorithm $\mathcal{B}$ to forge a BB2 signature with the same advantage ϵ under weak selective CPA attacks. Let $\mathcal{C}$ be the challenger who interacts with $\mathcal{B}$.

Setup: The Challenger $\mathcal{C}$ runs the signature algorithm to pass the public key $PK = (p, \mathbb{G}, g, g^a)$ in the BB2 signature scheme to the simulator $\mathcal{B}$, $\mathcal{B}$ selects random values $h_1, h_2, \cdots, h_{|U|} \in \mathbb{G}$ and $\alpha, a \in \mathbf{Z}_p^*$, and calculates $y = g^a$. It outputs the public parameter $PK = (\mathbb{G}, \mathbb{G}_T, e, g, y, e(g,g)^\alpha, \{T_i = g^{h_i}\}_{i \in U}, H_1, H_2, H_3)$ to the attacker $\mathcal{A}$ and sets up an empty table $T = \phi$ as the responsibility list.

KeyQuery: At this stage, the attacker $\mathcal{A}$ makes l private key queries and the simulator $\mathcal{B}$ answers the attacker's private key query. When the attacker performs the $j < l$ th private key query, the attacker sends (id_j, S_j) to the simulator, where $S_j = \{a_1, a_2, \cdots, a_k\} \subseteq \mathbf{Z}_p$, and it makes the corresponding private key query in this scheme. $\mathcal{B}$ randomly selects $c_j \in \mathbf{Z}_p^*$, if c_j is already in table T, then reselects $c_j \in \mathbf{Z}_p^*$, and then query B for c_j's BB2 signature. The challenger returns the simulator signature $(c_j, \sigma_j = g^{1/(a+c_j)})$. The simulator randomly selects $t \in \mathbf{Z}_p^*$ and then calculates:

$$K_j = g^{\alpha/(a+c_j)} y^t, \quad K_j' = c_j, \quad L_j = g^t, \quad L_j' = g^{at}, \quad K_{i,j} = T_{i,j}^{(a+c_j)t} = (g^{h_i})^{(a+c_j)t} \tag{5}$$

For the case of $c_j = -a$, the signature returned by the challenger $\mathcal{C}$ to the simulator is $(c_j, 1)$. At this time, the simulator $\mathcal{B}$ needs to select $c_j \in \mathbf{Z}_p^*$ again and repeat the above process. Finally, the private key $SK_{id_j,S_j} = (S_j, K_j, K_j', L_j, L_j', \{K_{i,j}\})$ is sent to the attacker $\mathcal{A}$ and the array (DMD) is added to the traceable table T.

KeyForgery: The attacker $\mathcal{A}$ outputs a private key SK^* to the simulator.

Assume that the adversary $\mathcal{A}$ wins the above game:

$$\Pr[\mathrm{Trace}(PK, T, SK^*) \notin \{\top, id_1, id_2, \cdots, id_l\}] \tag{6}$$

So $SK^* = (S, K, K', L, L', \{K_i\})$ passes the private key plausibility check, and

$$K' \notin \{c_1, c_2, \cdots, c_l\} \tag{7}$$

So we have:

$$S = \{a_1, a_2, \cdots, a_k\}, \; K' \in \mathbb{Z}_p^*, \; K, L, L', \{K_i\} \in \mathbb{G} \tag{8}$$

$$e(g, L') = e(g^a, L) \neq 1 \tag{9}$$

$$e(g^a g^{K'}, K) = e(g, g)^\alpha \cdot e(L^{K'} L', y) \neq 1 \tag{10}$$

Assume that $L = g^r$, where r is an unknown element in $\mathbf{Z}_p$, we can get $L' = L^a = g^{ar}$ from Eq. (9).

From formula (10) available:

$$e(g^{a+K'}, K) = e(g, g)^\alpha \cdot e(L^{K'} L', y) = e(g, g)^\alpha \cdot e(g^{(a+K')r}, y) = e(g^{(a+K')}, g^{\alpha/(a+K')} y^r) \tag{11}$$

So $K = g^{\alpha/(a+K')} y^r$, the simulator calculations:

$$\left(\frac{K}{g^{ar}}\right)^{\alpha^{-1}} = \left(\frac{K}{y^a}\right)^{\alpha^{-1}} = \left(g^{\frac{\alpha}{a+K'}}\right)^{\alpha^{-1}} = g^{\frac{1}{a+K'}} \tag{12}$$

Since $K' \in \mathbf{Z}_p^*$, $(K', g^{1/(a+K')})$ is a valid BB2 signature, and $K' \notin \{c_1, c_2, \cdots, c_l\}$, Therefore, the simulant forges the BB2 signature scheme with advantage ϵ under weak selective message attack.

Lemma 4 [16]. If l-SDH assumptions hold and the number of private key queries $l^s \le l$, the BB2 signature scheme is not unforgeable under weak selective CPA attacks.

Theorem 3. If l-SDH assumptions hold and the number of private key queries $l^s \le l$, then this scheme is traceable.

6 Conclusion

In order to solve the problem of users' private key leakage and slow operation in the CP-ABE scheme, this paper proposes an outsourced decrypt CP-ABE scheme that can be traced and fully verified. Compared with the traditional scheme, this paper has realized the traceable of key, and it has achieved both authorized and non-authorized users can verify the correctness of outsourced ciphertexts. One is that the authorized user can verify the correctness of the outsourced ciphertext and decrypt the ciphertext to obtain the original information. The other is that an unauthorized user can also verify the correctness of the outsourced ciphertext, but he cannot decrypt the ciphertext. In addition, this paper proved that this scheme is selective CPA security in the standard model, and also proved that it could trace the key leaker. The increased computational complexity of this scheme compared to existing verifiable schemes is negligible.

References

1. Sahai, A., Waters, B.: Fuzzy identity-based encryption. In: Cramer, R. (ed.) EUROCRYPT 2005. LNCS, vol. 3494, pp. 457–473. Springer, Heidelberg (2005). https://doi.org/10.1007/11426639_27
2. Goyal, V., Pandey, O., Sahai, A., et al.: Attribute-based encryption for fine-grained access control of encrypted data. In: ACM Conference on Computer and Communications Security, pp. 89–98. ACM (2006)
3. Green, M., Hohenberger, S., Waters, B.: Outsourcing the decryption of ABE ciphertexts. In: USENIX Conference on Security, pp. 34–34. USENIX Association (2011)
4. Lai, J., Deng, R.H., Guan, C., et al.: Attribute-based encryption with verifiable outsourced decryption. IEEE Trans. Inf. Forensics Secur. **8**(8), 1343–1354 (2013)
5. Qin, B., Deng, R.H., Liu, S., et al.: Attribute-based encryption with efficient verifiable outsourced decryption. IEEE Trans. Inf. Forensics Secur. **10**(7), 1384–1393 (2015)
6. Mao, X., Lai, J., Mei, Q., et al.: Generic and efficient constructions of attribute-based encryption with verifiable outsourced decryption. IEEE Trans. Dependable Secur. Comput. **13**(5), 533–546 (2016)
7. Li, J., Wang, Y., Zhang, Y., et al.: Full verifiability for outsourced decryption in attribute based encryption. IEEE Trans. Serv. Comput. **19**(99), 1–12 (2017)
8. Zhang, K.: The design and analysis of attribute-based encryption algorithms. Xidian University, Xian (2017)

9. Liu, Z., Cao, Z., Wong, D.S.: White-box traceable ciphertext-policy attribute-based encryption supporting any monotone access structures. IEEE Trans. Inf. Forensics Secur. **8** (1), 76–88 (2013)
10. Ning, J., Dong, X., Cao, Z., et al.: White-box traceable ciphertext-policy attribute-based encryption supporting flexible attributes. IEEE Trans. Inf. Forensics Secur. **10**(6), 1274–1288 (2015)
11. Li, J., Huang, Q., Chen, X., et al.: Multi-authority ciphertext-policy attribute-based encryption with accountability. In: ACM Symposium on Information, Computer and Communications Security, ASIACCS 2011, Hong Kong, China, pp. 386–390. DBLP (2011)
12. Zhou, J., Cao, Z., Dong, X., et al.: TR-MABE: white-box traceable and revocable multi-authority attribute-based encryption and its applications to multi-level privacy-preserving e-healthcare cloud computing systems. In: IEEE Computer Communications, pp. 2398–2406 (2015)
13. Boneh, D., Katz, J.: Improved efficiency for CCA-secure cryptosystems built using identity-based encryption. In: Menezes, A. (ed.) CT-RSA 2005. LNCS, vol. 3376, pp. 87–103. Springer, Heidelberg (2005). https://doi.org/10.1007/978-3-540-30574-3_8
14. Waters, B.: Ciphertext-policy attribute-based encryption: an expressive, efficient, and provably secure realization. In: Catalano, D., Fazio, N., Gennaro, R., Nicolosi, A. (eds.) PKC 2011. LNCS, vol. 6571, pp. 53–70. Springer, Heidelberg (2011). https://doi.org/10.1007/978-3-642-19379-8_4
15. Ibraimi, L., Tang, Q., Hartel, P., Jonker, W.: Efficient and provable secure ciphertext-policy attribute-based encryption schemes. In: Bao, F., Li, H., Wang, G. (eds.) ISPEC 2009. LNCS, vol. 5451, pp. 1–12. Springer, Heidelberg (2009). https://doi.org/10.1007/978-3-642-00843-6_1
16. Dan, B., Boyen, X.: Short signatures without random oracles and the SDH assumption in bilinear groups. J. Cryptol. **21**(2), 149–177 (2008)

Printed in the United States
Bookmasters